Dedication

To

Jon, Leigh, Alex, Miles, Josh, Julie,
Sarah, and Kathy

About the Author

ROBERT S. FELDMAN is Professor of Psychological and Brain Sciences and Deputy Chancellor of the University of Massachusetts Amherst. A recipient of the College Distinguished Teacher Award, he teaches psychology classes ranging in size from 15 to nearly 500 students. During the course of more than two decades as a college instructor, he has taught undergraduate and graduate courses at Mount Holyoke College, Wesleyan University, and Virginia Commonwealth University in addition to the University of Massachusetts.

Professor Feldman, who initiated the Minority Mentoring Program at the University of Massachusetts, also has served as a Hewlett Teaching Fellow and Senior Online Teaching Fellow. He initiated distance-learning courses in psychology at the University of Massachusetts.

A Fellow of the American Psychological Association and the Association for Psychological Science, Professor Feldman received a BA with High Honors from Wesleyan University and an MS and PhD from the University of Wisconsin-Madison. He is a winner of a Fulbright Senior Research Scholar and Lecturer Award and the Distinguished Alumnus Award from Wesleyan. He is on the Board of the Federation of Associations in Behavioral and Brain Sciences (FABBS) and the president-elect of the FABBS Foundation, which advocates for the field of psychology.

He has written and edited more than 200 books, book chapters, and scientific articles. He has edited *Development of Nonverbal Behavior in Children, Applications of Nonverbal Behavioral Theory and Research, Improving the First Year of College: Research and Practice,* and co-edited *Fundamentals of Nonverbal Behavior.* He is also author of *P.O.W.E.R. Learning: Strategies for Success in College and Life.* His textbooks, which have been used by more than 2 million students around the world, have been translated into Spanish, French, Portuguese, Dutch, German, Italian, Chinese, Korean, and Japanese. His research interests include deception and honesty in everyday life, work that he described in *The Liar in Your Life,* a trade book published in 2009. His research has been supported by grants from the National Institute of Mental Health and the National Institute on Disabilities and Rehabilitation Research.

Professor Feldman loves music, is an enthusiastic pianist, and enjoys cooking and traveling. He has three children and two young grandsons. He and his wife, a psychologist, live in western Massachusetts in a home overlooking the Holyoke mountain range.

Brief Contents

Contents

Preface

Students First

If I were to use only two words to summarize my goal across the eleven editions of this introduction to psychology, as well as my teaching philosophy, that's what I would say: Students first.

I believe that an effective introduction to a discipline must be oriented to students–informing them, engaging them, and exciting them about the field and helping them connect it to their worlds.

The difference between this and earlier editions, though, is that now we have an array of digital tools available that allow students to study more effectively, and learn the material more deeply, than was ever before possible.

BETTER DATA, SMARTER REVISION, IMPROVED RESULTS

SMARTBOOK™

Students study more effectively with Smartbook.

- **Make It Effective.** Powered by Learnsmart, SmartBook™ creates a personalized reading experience by highlighting the most impactful concepts a student needs to learn at that moment in time. This ensures that every minute spent with SmartBook™ is returned to the student as the most value-added minute possible.
- **Make It Informed.** Real-time reports quickly identify the concepts that require more attention from individual students–or the entire class. SmartBook™ detects the content a student is most likely to forget and brings it back to improve long-term knowledge retention.

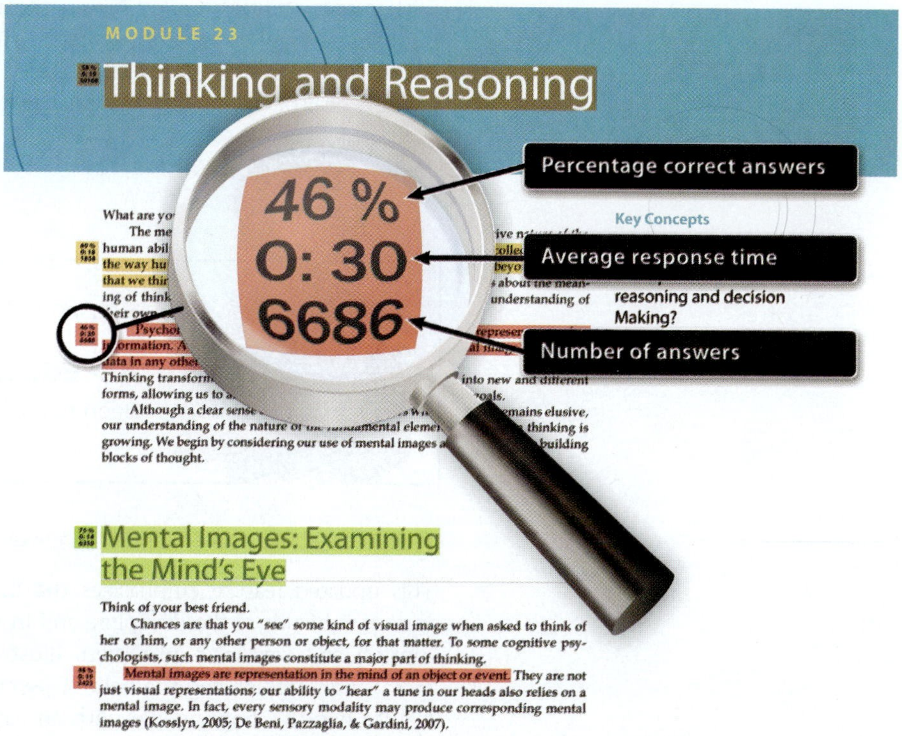

Students help inform the revision strategy.

- **Make It Precise.** Systematic and precise, a heat map tool collates data anonymously collected from thousands of students who used Connect Psychology's Learnsmart.
- **Make It Accessible.** The data is graphically represented in a heat map as "hot spots" showing specific concepts with which students had the most difficulty. Revising these concepts, then, can make them more accessible for students.

PERSONALIZED GRADING, ON THE GO, MADE EASIER

The first and only analytics tool of its kind, Connect Insight™ is a series of visual data displays–each framed by an intuitive question–to provide at-a-glance information regarding how your class is doing.

- **Make It Intuitive.** You receive instant, at-a-glance views of student performance matched with student activity.
- **Make It Dynamic.** Connect Insight™ puts real-time analytics in your hands so you can take action early and keep struggling students from falling behind.
- **Make It Mobile.** Connect Insight™ travels from office to classroom, available on demand wherever and whenever it's needed.

Student Tools: Mastering the Material

Student success in psychology means mastering the material at a deep level. These are some of the tools that help students maximize their performance:

STUDY ALERTS

Throughout, marginal notes point out important and difficult concepts and topics. These Study Alerts offer suggestions for learning the material effectively and for studying for tests. In Module 14, for example, a Study Alert emphasizes the importance of differentiating the five stages of sleep; the feature in Module 15 makes clear the key issue about hypnosis–whether it represents a different state of consciousness or is similar to normal waking consciousness; and in Module 16 it highlights Figure 2 for its clear view of the different ways that drugs produce their effects at a neurological level.

Study Alert

Differentiate the five stages of sleep (stage 1, stage 2, stage 3, stage 4, and REM sleep), which produce different brain-wave patterns.

FROM THE PERSPECTIVE OF . . .

Every chapter includes questions to help students connect psychological concepts with career realities. Called "From the Perspective of . . .," this feature helps students understand how psychology impacts their chosen program of study and answers the "why does psychology matter to me?" question. Examples of the some career fields include health, technology, criminal justice, and marketing.

From the perspective of . . .

An Educator How might you use the findings in sleep research to maximize student learning?

NEUROSCIENCE IN YOUR LIFE

This updated feature emphasizes the importance of neuroscientific research within the various subfields of the discipline and in students' lives. Compelling brain scans, with both caption and textual explanation, illustrate significant neuroscientific findings that are increasingly influencing the field of psychology. For example, one *Neuroscience in Your Life* feature explains how people with an eating disorder process information differently.

Neuroscience in Your Life: When Regulation of Eating Behavior Goes Wrong

Research suggests that individuals with eating disorders process information differently. This difference in processing may lead to eating disorders or may be a result of such disordered eating. For example, as seen in these images, those with bulimia show greater connectivity in areas of the brain associated with eating behavior, such as the cerebellum (in red), whereas those who do not have bulimia show greater connectivity in other areas of the brain (in blue) (Amianto et al., 2013).

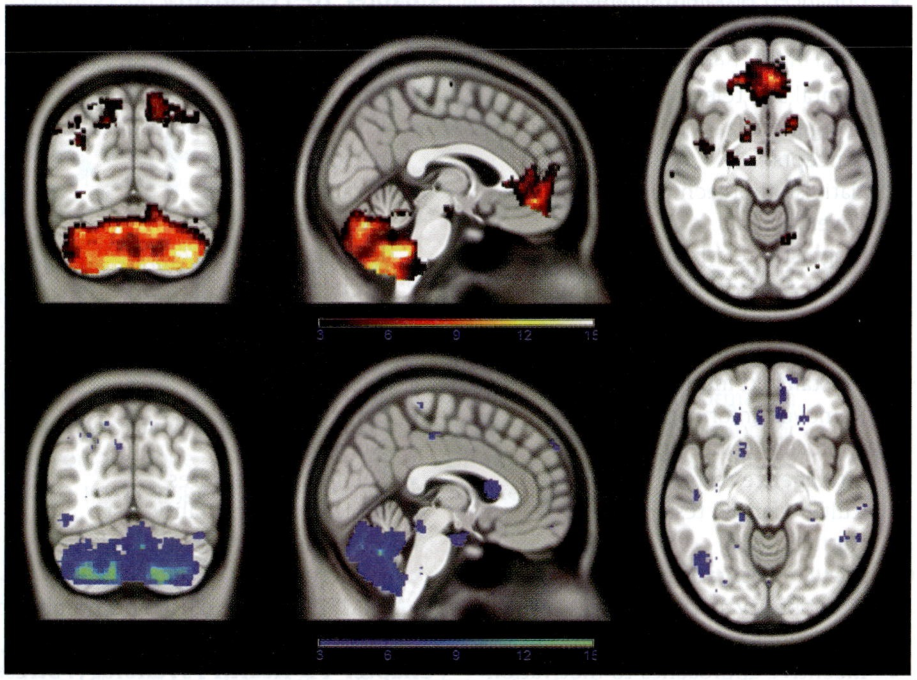

Student Learning: Content and Concepts

The following sample of new and revised topics and textual changes, including new definitions based on heat map data, provides a good indication of the content's currency and clarification for students.

Chapter 1–Introduction to Psychology

- Psychological explanations of Boston Marathon bomber and about autism spectrum disorder
- Psychology's reputation will grow with increase in evidence-based practices
- Increase in program evaluation psychologists
- Stream of consciousness
- Neuroscience, behavioral perspective, observable behavior, and universal principles
- Biological foundations of behavior and information about William James
- Lack of bystander intervention
- Dispositional factors in helping
- Definitions of confederate, dependent variable
- Participant expectations
- Deficiencies in web surveys

Chapter 2–Neuroscience and Behavior

- Single-channel scanning to translate brain waves to communication
- Deleted information on location effects of neurotransmitters and the term *interneuron*

Making the Grade: A Practical Guide

No matter why you are taking introductory psychology, it's a safe bet you're interested in maximizing your understanding of the material and getting a good grade. And you want to accomplish these goals as quickly and efficiently as possible.

Good news: Several subfields of psychology have identified different ways to help you learn and remember material you will study throughout college. Here's my guarantee to you: If you learn and follow the guidelines in each of these areas, you'll become a better student and get better grades. Always remember that *good students are made, not born*.

Adopt a General Study Strategy

Psychologists have devised several proven techniques to improve study skills, two of which are described here: "P.O.W.E.R," or *P*repare, *O*rganize, *W*ork, *E*valuate, and *R*ethink; and "SQ3R," or *S*urvey, *Q*uestion, *R*ead, *R*ecite, and *R*eview.

P.O.W.E.R. This learning system entails the following steps:

- **Prepare.** In *Essentials of Understanding Psychology,* Eleventh Edition, read the broad questions called *Learning Outcomes* to *Prepare* yourself for the material that follows. *Learning Outcomes* are at the start of each chapter and of each module.
- **Organize.** The *Organize* stage involves developing a mental roadmap of where you are headed. *Essentials of Understanding Psychology* includes the outline at the beginning of each chapter. Read it to get an idea of what topics are covered and how they are organized.
- **Work.** Because of your effort in the *Power* and *Organize* stages, the *Work* stage will be easier. You know what questions the material will answer based on the *Learning Outcomes* and you know how it is organized based on the outline. Read everything in the content including the material in boxes and the margins to fully understand the material.
- **Evaluate.** *Evaluate* provides the opportunity to determine how effectively you have mastered the material. In *Essentials of Understanding Psychology,* questions at the end of each module offer a rapid check of your understanding of the material. *Evaluate* your progress to assess your degree of mastery.
- **Rethink.** This final stage, *Rethink,* entails re-analyzing, reviewing, questioning, and challenging assumptions. Rethinking allows you to consider how the material fits with other information you have already learned. Every major section of *Essentials of Understanding Psychology* ends with a *Rethink* section. Answering its thought-provoking questions will help you think about the material at a deeper level.

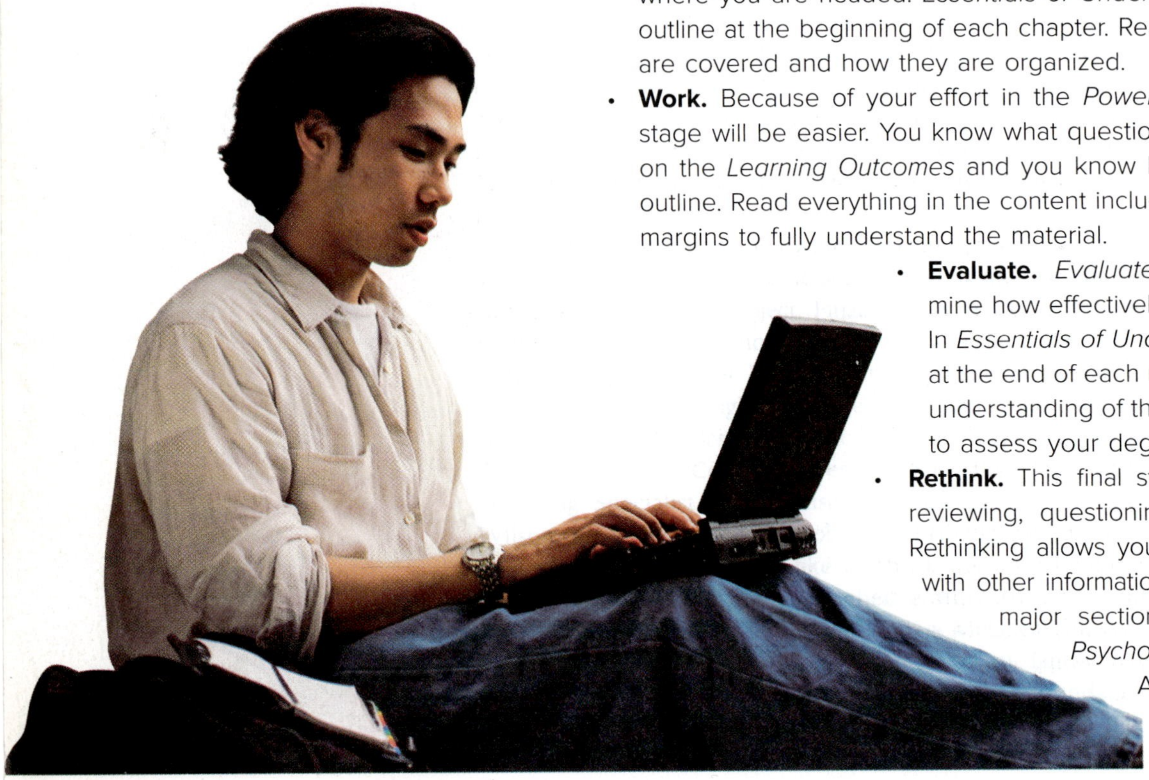

to Smarter Studying

SQ3R. The SQ3R learning system entails these specific steps:

- **Survey.** *Survey* the material by reading the outlines that open each module, the headings, figure captions, recaps, and Looking Ahead and Looking Back sections, providing yourself with an overview of the major points of the chapter.
- **Question.** In the *Q* step, formulate *questions* about the material, either aloud or in writing, prior to reading a section of text. The *Learning Outcomes,* written as questions at the beginning of each module and the *Evaluate* and *Rethink* questions that end each module are examples.
- **Read.** Read actively and critically. While you are reading, answer the questions you have asked yourself. Consider the implications of what you are reading, thinking about possible exceptions and contradictions, and examining underlying assumptions.
- **Recite.** Describe and explain to yourself or a study partner the material that you have just read. Answer questions you have posed. *Recite* aloud to help you know how well you understand what you have just read.
- **Review.** In this final step, review the material: read the Epilogue and answer those questions, review the Visual Summary, and answer any review questions at the end of each module.

Manage Your Time

Managing your time as you study is a central aspect of academic success. But remember: The goal of time management is to permit us to make informed choices about how we use our time. Use these time management procedures to harness time for your own advantage.

SET YOUR PRIORITIES. First, determine your priorities. *Priorities* are the tasks and activities you need and want to do, rank-ordered from most important to least important.

The best procedure is to start off by identifying priorities for an entire term. What do you need to accomplish? Rather than making these goals too general, make them specific, such as "studying 10 hours before each chemistry exam."

IDENTIFY YOUR PRIME TIME. Are you a morning person or do you prefer studying later at night? Being aware of the time or times of day when you can do your best work will help you plan and schedule your time most effectively.

MASTER THE MOMENT. Here's what you'll need to organize your time:

- *A master calendar* that shows all the weeks of the term on one page. It should include every week of the term and seven days per week. On the master calendar note the due date of every assignment and test you will have. Also include important activities from your personal life, drawn from your list of priorities. Add some free time for yourself.

- *A weekly timetable* that shows the days of the week across the top and the hours, from 6:00 a.m. to midnight, along the side. Fill in the times of all your fixed, prescheduled activities—the times that your classes meet, when you have to be at work, the times you have to pick up your child at day care, and any other recurring appointments. Add assignment due dates, tests, and any other activities on the appropriate days of the week. Then add blocks of time necessary to prepare for those events.
- *A daily to-do list* using a small calendar or your smartphone. List all the things that you intend to do during the day and their priority. Start with the things you *must* do and that have fixed times, such as classes and work schedules. Then add in the other things that you *should* accomplish, such as researching an upcoming paper or finishing a lab report. Finally, list things that are a low priority like taking in a new movie.

CONTROL YOUR TIME. If you follow the schedules that you've prepared, you've taken the most important steps in time management. Things, however, always seem to take longer than planned.

When inevitable surprises occur, there are several ways to take control of your days to follow your intended schedule:

- **Say no.** You don't have to agree to every favor that others ask of you.
- **Get away from it all.** Adopt a specific spot to call your own, such as a corner desk in a secluded nook in the library. If you use it enough, your body and mind will automatically get into study mode as soon as you get there.
- **Enjoy the sounds of silence.** Studies suggest that we are able to concentrate most when our environment is silent. Experiment and work in silence for a few days. You may find that you get more done in less time than you would in a more distracting environment.
- **Take an e-break.** Take an e-break and shut down your communication sources for some period of time. Phone calls, text messages, IMs, and e-mail can be saved on a phone or computer. They'll wait.
- **Expect the unexpected.** You'll never be able to escape from unexpected interruptions and surprises that require your attention. But by trying to anticipate them and thinking about how you'll react to them, you can position yourself to react effectively when they do occur.

Take Good Notes in Class

Let's consider some of the basic principles of notetaking:

- **Identify the instructor's—and your—goals for the course.** The information you get during the first day of class and through the syllabus is critical. In addition to the instructor's goals, you should have your own. How will the information from the course help you to enhance your knowledge, improve yourself as a person, achieve your goals?

- **Complete assignments before coming to class.**
- **Choose a notebook that assists in notetaking.**
- **Listen for the key ideas.** Listen for phrases like "you need to know . . . ," "the most important thing to consider . . . ," "there are four problems with this approach . . . ," and—a big one—"this will be on the test . . . " should cause you to sit up and take notice. Also, if an instructor says the same thing in several ways, the material being discussed is important.

- **Use short, abbreviated phrases—not full sentences when taking notes.**
- **Pay attention to what is written on the board or projected from PowerPoint slides. Remember these tips:**
  - Listening is more important than seeing.
  - Don't copy everything that is on every slide.
  - Remember that key points on slides are . . . key points.
  - Check to see if the presentation slides are available online.
  - Remember that presentation slides are not the same as good notes for a class.

Memorize Efficiently

Here's a key principle of effective memorization: Memorize what you need to memorize. *Forget about the rest.*

You have your choice of dozens of techniques of memorization. Also, feel free to devise your own strategies or add those that have worked for you in the past.

REHEARSAL. Say it aloud: rehearsal. Think of this word in terms of its three syllables: re—hear—sal. If you're scratching your head about why you should do this, it's to illustrate the point of *rehearsal:* to transfer material that you encounter into long-term memory.

MNEMONICS. This odd word (pronounced with the "m" silent—"neh MON ix") describes formal techniques used to make material more readily remembered.

Among the most common mnemonics are the following:

- **Acronyms.** *Acronyms* are words or phrases formed by the first letters of a series of terms.

  For example, Roy G. Biv helps people to remember the colors of the spectrum (red, orange, yellow, green, blue, indigo, and violet).
- **Acrostics.** *Acrostics* are sentences in which the first letters spell out something that needs to be recalled. The benefits of acrostics are similar to those of acronyms.

- **Rhymes and jingles.** "Thirty days hath September, April, June, and November." If you know the rest of the rhyme, you're familiar with one of the most commonly used mnemonic jingles in the English language.

USE OF MULTIPLE SENSES. Every time we encounter new information, all of our senses are potentially at work. Each piece of sensory information is stored in a separate location in the brain, and yet all the pieces are linked together in extraordinarily intricate ways.

- **When you learn something, use your body.** Move around. Stand up; sit down. Touch the page. Trace figures with your fingers. Talk to yourself. Think out loud. By involving every part of your body, you've increased the number of potential ways to trigger a relevant memory later, when you need to recall it.
- **Draw and diagram the material.** Structuring written material by graphically grouping and connecting key ideas and themes is a powerful technique. Creating drawings, sketches, and even cartoons can help us remember better.
- **Visualize.** Visualization is effective because it helps make abstract ideas concrete; it engages multiple senses; it permits us to link different bits of information together; and it provides us with a context for storing information.
- **Overlearning.** *Overlearning* consists of studying and rehearsing material past the point of initial mastery. Through overlearning, you can recall the information without even thinking about it.

Study for Tests Strategically

Here are some guidelines that can help you do your best on tests:

KNOW WHAT YOU ARE PREPARING FOR. To find out about an upcoming test, ask if it is a "test," an "exam," a "quiz," or something else. These names imply different things. In addition, each kind of test question requires a somewhat different style of preparation.

- **Essay questions.** The best approach to studying for an essay test involves four steps:

  1. Reread your class notes and any notes you've made on assigned readings that will be covered on the upcoming exam. Also go through the readings themselves, reviewing underlined or highlighted material and marginal notes.
  2. Think of likely exam questions. Some instructors give lists of possible essay topics; if yours does, focus on this list, and think of other possibilities.

3. Answer each potential essay question—aloud. You can also write down the main points that any answer should cover.
4. After you've answered the questions, look at the notes and readings once again. If you feel confident that you've answered specific questions adequately, check them off. If you had trouble with some questions, review that material immediately. Then repeat the third step 3, answering the questions again.

- **Multiple-choice, true–false, and matching questions.** Studying for multiple-choice, true–false, and matching questions requires attention to the details. Write down important facts on index cards: They're portable and available all the time, and the act of creating them helps drive the material into your memory.
- **Short-answer and fill-in questions.** Short-answer and fill-in questions are similar to essays in that they require you to recall key pieces of information but they don't demand that you integrate or compare different types of information. Consequently, the focus of your study should be on the recall of specific, detailed information.

TEST YOURSELF. When you believe you've mastered the material, test yourself on it. You can create a test for yourself, in writing, making its form as close as possible to what you expect the actual test to be.

DEAL WITH TEST ANXIETY. What does the anticipation of a test do to you? *Test anxiety* is a temporary condition characterized by fears and concerns about test-taking. You'll never eliminate test anxiety completely, nor do you want to. A little bit of nervousness can energize us, making us more attentive and vigilant.

On the other hand, for some students, anxiety can spiral into the kind of paralyzing fear that makes their minds go blank. There are several ways to keep this from happening to you:

- *Prepare thoroughly.*
- *Take a realistic view of the test.*
- *Learn relaxation techniques.*
- *Visualize success.*

FORM A STUDY GROUP. *Study groups* can be extremely powerful tools because they help accomplish several things:

- They help members organize and structure the material to approach their studying in a systematic and logical way.
- They allow students to share different perspectives on the material.
- They make it more likely that students will not overlook any potentially important information.

- They force members to rethink the course material, explaining it in words that other group members will understand. This helps both understanding and recall of the information when it is needed on the test.
- Finally, they help motivate members to do their best. When you're part of a study group, you're no longer working just for yourself; your studying also benefits the other study group members. Not wanting to let down your classmates in a study group may encourage you to put in your best effort.

Essentials of Understanding Psychology

1 Introduction to Psychology

Learning Outcomes for Chapter 1

MODULE 1

LO 1-1 What is the science of psychology?

LO 1-2 What are the major specialties in the field of psychology?

LO 1-3 Where do psychologists work?

Psychologists at Work

The Subfields of Psychology: Psychology's Family Tree

Working at Psychology

MODULE 2

LO 2-1 What are the origins of psychology?

LO 2-2 What are the major approaches in contemporary psychology?

LO 2-3 What are psychology's key issues and controversies?

LO 2-4 What is the future of psychology likely to hold?

A Science Evolves: The Past, the Present, and the Future

The Roots of Psychology

Today's Perspectives

Psychology's Key Issues and Controversies

Applying Psychology in the 21st Century: Psychology Matters

Psychology's Future

Neuroscience in Your Life: Reading the Movies in Your Mind

MODULE 3

LO 3-1 What is the scientific method?

LO 3-2 What role do theories and hypotheses play in psychological research?

LO 3-3 What research methods do psychologists use?

LO 3-4 How do psychologists establish cause-and-effect relationships in research studies?

Research in Psychology

The Scientific Method

Psychological Research

Descriptive Research

Experimental Research

MODULE 4

LO 4-1 What major issues confront psychologists conducting research?

Critical Research Issues

The Ethics of Research

Exploring Diversity: Choosing Participants Who Represent the Scope of Human Behavior

Neuroscience in Your Life: The Importance of Using Representative Participants

Should Animals Be Used in Research?

Threats to Experimental Validity: Avoiding Experimental Bias

Becoming an Informed Consumer of Psychology: Thinking Critically About Research

The Subfields of Psychology: Psychology's Family Tree

As the study of psychology has grown, it has given rise to a number of subfields (described in Figure 2). The subfields of psychology can be likened to an extended family, with assorted nieces and nephews, aunts and uncles, and cousins who, although they may not interact on a day-to-day basis, are related to one another, because they share a common goal: understanding behavior. One way to identify the key subfields is to look at some of the basic questions about behavior that they address.

Study Alert
The different subfields of psychology allow psychologists to explain the same behavior in multiple ways. Review Figure 2 for a summary of the subfields.

WHAT ARE THE BIOLOGICAL FOUNDATIONS OF BEHAVIOR?

In the most fundamental sense, people are biological organisms. *Behavioral neuroscience* is the subfield of psychology that focuses on how the brain and the nervous system, as well as other biological aspects of the body, determine behavior.

Thus, neuroscientists consider how our bodies influence our behavior. For example, they may examine the link between specific sites in the brain and the muscular tremors of people affected by Parkinson's disease or attempt to determine how our emotions are related to physical sensations.

PsychTech
How well can you text and drive at the same time? Cognitive psychologists have demonstrated that it is impossible to do both without a serious and potentially deadly decline in driving ability.

HOW DO PEOPLE SENSE, PERCEIVE, LEARN, AND THINK ABOUT THE WORLD?

If you have ever wondered why you are susceptible to optical illusions, how your body registers pain, or how to make the most of your study time, an experimental psychologist can answer your questions. *Experimental psychology* is the branch of psychology that studies the processes of sensing, perceiving, learning, and thinking about the world. (The term *experimental psychologist* is somewhat misleading: Psychologists in every specialty area use experimental techniques.)

Several subspecialties of experimental psychology have become specialties in their own right. One is *cognitive psychology*, which focuses on higher mental processes, including thinking, memory, reasoning, problem solving, judging, decision making, and language.

WHAT ARE THE SOURCES OF CHANGE AND STABILITY IN BEHAVIOR ACROSS THE LIFE SPAN?

A baby producing her first smile . . . taking his first step . . . saying her first word. These universal milestones in development are also singularly special and unique for each person. *Developmental psychology* studies how people grow and change from the moment of conception through death. *Personality psychology* focuses on the consistency in people's behavior over time and the traits that differentiate one person from another.

HOW DO PSYCHOLOGICAL FACTORS AFFECT PHYSICAL AND MENTAL HEALTH?

Frequent depression, stress, and fears that prevent people from carrying out their normal activities are topics that interest a health psychologist, a clinical psychologist, and a counseling psychologist. *Health psychology* explores the relationship between psychological factors and physical ailments or disease. For example, health psychologists are interested in assessing how long-term stress (a psychological factor) can affect physical health and in identifying ways to promote behavior that brings about good health (Belar, 2008; Yardley & Moss-Morris, 2009; Proyer et al., 2013).

Subfield	Description
Behavioral genetics	*Behavioral genetics* studies the inheritance of traits related to behavior.
Behavioral neuroscience	*Behavioral neuroscience* examines the biological basis of behavior.
Clinical psychology	*Clinical psychology* deals with the study, diagnosis, and treatment of psychological disorders.
Clinical neuropsychology	*Clinical neuropsychology* unites the areas of biopsychology and clinical psychology, focusing on the relationship between biological factors and psychological disorders.
Cognitive psychology	*Cognitive psychology* focuses on the study of higher mental processes.
Counseling psychology	*Counseling psychology* focuses primarily on educational, social, and career adjustment problems.
Cross-cultural psychology	*Cross-cultural psychology* investigates the similarities and differences in psychological functioning in and across various cultures and ethnic groups.
Developmental psychology	*Developmental psychology* examines how people grow and change from the moment of conception through death.
Educational psychology	*Educational psychology* is concerned with teaching and learning processes, such as the relationship between motivation and school performance.
Environmental psychology	*Environmental psychology* considers the relationship between people and their physical environment.
Evolutionary psychology	*Evolutionary psychology* considers how behavior is influenced by our genetic inheritance from our ancestors.
Experimental psychology	*Experimental psychology* studies the processes of sensing, perceiving, learning, and thinking about the world.
Forensic psychology	*Forensic psychology* focuses on legal issues, such as determining the accuracy of witness memories.
Health psychology	*Health psychology* explores the relationship between psychological factors and physical ailments or disease.
Industrial/organizational psychology	*Industrial/organizational psychology* is concerned with the psychology of the workplace.
Personality psychology	*Personality psychology* focuses on the consistency in people's behavior over time and the traits that differentiate one person from another.
Program evaluation	*Program evaluation* focuses on assessing large-scale programs, such as the Head Start preschool program, to determine whether they are effective in meeting their goals.
Psychology of women	*Psychology of women* focuses on issues such as discrimination against women and the causes of violence against women.
School psychology	*School psychology* is devoted to counseling children in elementary and secondary schools who have academic or emotional problems.
Social psychology	*Social psychology* is the study of how people's thoughts, feelings, and actions are affected by others.
Sport psychology	*Sport psychology* applies psychology to athletic activity and exercise.

FIGURE 2 The major subfields of psychology.

Clinical psychology deals with the study, diagnosis, and treatment of psychological disorders. Clinical psychologists are trained to diagnose and treat problems that range from the crises of everyday life, such as unhappiness over the breakup of a relationship, to more extreme conditions, such as profound, lingering depression. Some clinical psychologists also research and investigate issues that vary from identifying the early signs of psychological disturbance to studying the relationship between family communication patterns and psychological disorders.

Like clinical psychologists, counseling psychologists deal with people's psychological problems, but the problems they deal with are more specific. *Counseling psychology* focuses primarily on educational, social, and career adjustment problems. Almost every college has a center staffed with counseling psychologists. This is where students can get advice on the kinds of jobs they might be best suited for, on methods of studying effectively, and on strategies for resolving everyday difficulties, such as problems with roommates and concerns about a specific professor's grading practices. Many large business organizations also employ counseling psychologists to help employees with work-related problems.

HOW DO OUR SOCIAL NETWORKS AFFECT BEHAVIOR?

Our complex networks of social interrelationships are the focus for many subfields of psychology. For example, *social psychology* is the study of how people's thoughts, feelings, and actions are affected by others. Social psychologists concentrate on such diverse topics as human aggression, liking and loving, persuasion, and conformity.

Cross-cultural psychology investigates the similarities and differences in psychological functioning in and across various cultures and ethnic groups. For example, cross-cultural psychologists examine how cultures differ in their use of punishment during child rearing.

EXPANDING PSYCHOLOGY'S FRONTIERS

The boundaries of the science of psychology are constantly growing. Three newer members of the field's family tree–evolutionary psychology, behavioral genetics, and clinical neuropsychology–have sparked particular excitement, and debate, within psychology.

Evolutionary Psychology. *Evolutionary psychology* considers how behavior is influenced by our genetic inheritance from our ancestors. The evolutionary approach suggests that the chemical coding of information in our cells not only determines traits such as hair color and race but also holds the key to understanding a broad variety of behaviors that helped our ancestors survive and reproduce.

Evolutionary psychology stems from Charles Darwin's arguments in his groundbreaking 1859 book, *On the Origin of Species*. Darwin suggested that a process of natural selection leads to the survival of the fittest and the development of traits that enable a species to adapt to its environment.

Evolutionary psychologists take Darwin's arguments a step further. They argue that our genetic inheritance determines not only physical traits such as skin and eye color but certain personality traits and social behaviors as well. For example, evolutionary psychologists suggest that behavior such as shyness, jealousy, and cross-cultural similarities in qualities desired in potential mates are at least partially determined by genetics, presumably because such behavior helped increase the survival rate of humans' ancient relatives (Buss, 2003; Sefcek, Brumbach, & Vasquez, 2007; Ward, Kogan, & Pankove, 2007).

Although they are increasingly popular, evolutionary explanations of behavior have stirred controversy. By suggesting that many significant behaviors unfold automatically, because they are wired into the human species, evolutionary approaches minimize the role of environmental and social forces. Still, the evolutionary approach has stimulated a significant amount of research on how our biological inheritance influences our traits and behaviors (Buss, 2004; Neher, 2006; Mesoudi, 2011).

Behavioral Genetics. Another rapidly growing area in psychology focuses on the biological mechanisms, such as genes and chromosomes, that enable inherited behavior to unfold. *Behavioral genetics* seeks to understand how we might inherit certain behavioral traits and how the environment influences whether we actually display such traits (Moffitt & Caspi, 2007; Rende, 2007; Maxson, 2013).

Clinical Neuropsychology. *Clinical neuropsychology* unites the areas of neuroscience and clinical psychology: It focuses on the origin of psychological disorders in biological factors. Building on advances in our understanding of the structure and chemistry of the brain, this specialty has already led to promising new treatments for psychological disorders as well as debates over the use of medication to control behavior (Boake, 2008; Holtz, 2011).

Working at Psychology

Help Wanted: Assistant professor at a small liberal arts college. Teach undergraduate courses in introductory psychology and courses in specialty areas of cognitive psychology, perception, and learning. Strong commitment to quality teaching, as well as evidence of scholarship and research productivity, necessary.

Help Wanted: Industrial-organizational consulting psychologist. International firm seeks psychologists for full-time career positions as consultants to management. Candidates must have the ability to establish a rapport with senior business executives and help them find innovative and practical solutions to problems concerning people and organizations.

Help Wanted: Clinical psychologist. PhD, internship experience, and license required. Comprehensive clinic seeks psychologist to work with children and adults providing individual and group therapy, psychological evaluations, crisis intervention, and development of behavior treatment plans on multidisciplinary team.

As these job ads suggest, psychologists are employed in a variety of settings. Many doctoral-level psychologists are employed by institutions of higher learning (universities and colleges) or are self-employed, usually working as private practitioners treating clients (see Figure 3). Other work sites include hospitals, clinics, mental health centers, counseling centers, government human-services organizations, businesses, schools, and even prisons. Psychologists are employed in the military, working with soldiers, veterans, and their families, and they work for the federal government Department of

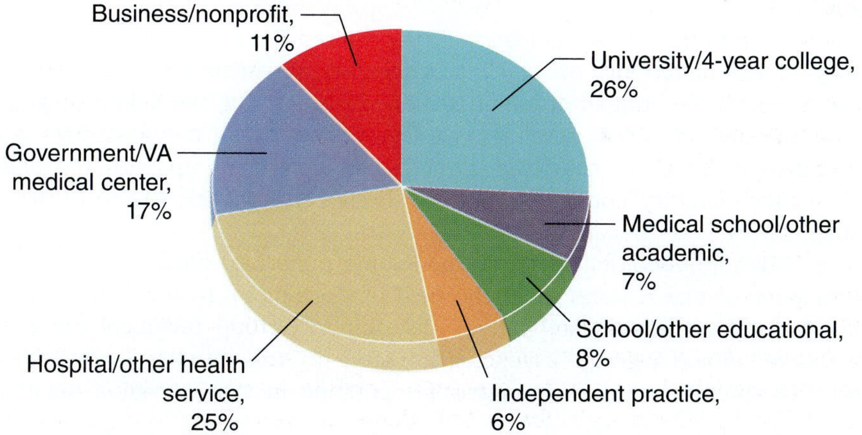

FIGURE 3 The breakdown of where U.S. psychologists (who have a PhD or PsyD degree) work. (Source: Adapted from Michaels, 2011.)

Homeland Security, fighting terrorism. Psychologists who specialize in program evaluation are increasingly employed by foundations who want to assess the value of programs they fund (American Psychological Association, 2007; DeAngelis & Monahan, 2008; Moscoso et al., 2013).

Most psychologists, though, work in academic settings, allowing them to combine the three major roles played by psychologists in society: teacher, scientist, and clinical practitioner. Many psychology professors are also actively involved in research or in serving clients. Whatever the particular job site, however, psychologists share a commitment to improving individual lives as well as society in general.

Keep in mind that professionals from a variety of occupations use the findings of psychologists. To understand how nonpsychologists use psychology, see the feature titled "From the Perspective of . . ." throughout the text.

From the perspective of . . .

An Educator Imagine that a classroom teacher wants to improve the performance of a 10-year-old boy who is not doing well in math. What branches of psychology might she draw on to get ideas about how to help him?

PSYCHOLOGISTS: A PORTRAIT

Although there is no "average" psychologist in terms of personal characteristics, we can draw a statistical portrait of the field. There are close to 300,000 psychologists working today in the United States, but they are outnumbered by psychologists in other countries. Europe has more than 290,000 psychologists, and in Brazil alone there are 140,000 licensed psychologists. Although most research is conducted in the United States, psychologists in other countries are increasingly influential in adding to the knowledge base and practices of psychology (Peiro & Lunt, 2002; Stevens & Gielen, 2007; Rees & Seaton, 2011).

In the United States, women outnumber men in the field, a big change from earlier years when women faced bias and were actively discouraged from becoming psychologists. Today, women earn around three-fourths of new psychology doctorate degrees. There is an active debate about whether, and how, to seek balance in the percentage of men and women in the field (Frincke & Pate, 2004; Cynkar, 2007; Willyard, 2011).

The vast majority of psychologists in the United States are white, limiting the diversity of the field. Only 6% of all psychologists are members of racial minority groups. Although the number of minority individuals entering the field is greater than a decade ago–around 20% of new master's degrees and 16% of new doctorate degrees are awarded to people of color–the numbers have not kept up with the dramatic growth of the minority population at large (Hoffer et al., 2005; Maton et al., 2006; Chandler, 2011).

The underrepresentation of racial and ethnic minorities among psychologists is significant for several reasons. First, the field of psychology is diminished by a lack of the diverse perspectives and talents that minority-group members can provide. Furthermore, minority-group psychologists serve as role models for members of minority communities, and their underrepresentation in the profession might deter other minority-group members from entering the field. Finally, because members of minority groups often prefer to receive psychological therapy from treatment providers of their own race or ethnic group, the rarity of minority psychologists can discourage some members of minority groups from seeking treatment (Bernal et al., 2002; Jenkins et al., 2003; Bryant et al., 2005).

THE EDUCATION OF A PSYCHOLOGIST

How do people become psychologists? The most common route is a long one. Most psychologists have a doctorate, either a *PhD* (doctor of philosophy) or, less frequently, a *PsyD* (doctor of psychology). The PhD is a research degree that requires a dissertation based on an original investigation. The PsyD is obtained by psychologists who want to focus on the treatment of psychological disorders. (Psychologists are distinct from psychiatrists, who have a medical degree and specialize in the diagnosis and treatment of psychological disorders, often using treatments that involve the prescription of drugs.)

Both the PhD and the PsyD typically take four or five years of work past the bachelor's level. Some fields of psychology involve education beyond the doctorate. For instance, doctoral-level clinical psychologists, who deal with people with psychological disorders, typically spend an additional year doing an internship.

Study Alert
Be sure you can differentiate between a PhD (doctor of philosophy) and a PsyD (doctor of psychology), as well as between psychologists and psychiatrists.

Positions Obtained by Psychology Majors

Business Field	Education/ Academic Field	Social Field
Administrative assistant	Administration	Activities coordinator
Advertising trainee	Child-care provider	Behavioral specialist
Affirmative action officer	Child-care worker/ supervisor	Career counselor
Benefits manager	Data management	Case worker
Claims specialist	Laboratory assistant	Child protection worker
Community relations officer	Parent/family education	Clinical coordinator
Customer relations	Preschool teacher	Community outreach worker
Data management	Public opinion surveyor	Corrections officer
Employee counselor	Research assistant	Counselor assistant
Employee recruitment	Teaching assistant	Crisis intervention counselor
Human resources coordinator/ manager/specialist	Youth counselor	Employment counselor
Labor relations manager/ specialist		Group home attendant
Loan officer		Mental health assistant
Management trainee		Occupational therapist
Marketing		Probation officer
Personnel manager/officer		Program manager
Product and services research		Rehabilitation counselor
Programs/events coordination		Residence counselor
Public relations		Social service assistant
Retail sales management		Social worker
Sales representative		Substance abuse counselor
Special features writing/ reporting		
Staff training and development		
Trainer/training office		

FIGURE 4 Although many psychology majors pursue employment in social services, a background in psychology can prepare one for many professions outside the social services field. What is it about the science and art of psychology that makes it such a versatile field? (Source: Adapted from Kuther, 2003.)

About a third of people working in the field of psychology have a master's degree as their highest degree, which they earn after two or three years of graduate work. These psychologists teach, provide therapy, conduct research, or work in specialized programs dealing with drug abuse or crisis intervention. Some work in universities, government, and business, collecting and analyzing data.

CAREERS FOR PSYCHOLOGY MAJORS

Although some psychology majors head for graduate school in psychology or an unrelated field, the majority join the workforce immediately after graduation. Most report that the jobs they take after graduation are related to their psychology background.

An undergraduate major in psychology provides excellent preparation for a variety of occupations. Because undergraduates who specialize in psychology develop good analytical skills, are trained to think critically, and are able to synthesize and evaluate information well, employers in business, industry, and the government value their preparation (Kuther, 2003).

The most common areas of employment for psychology majors are in the social services, including working as an administrator, serving as a counselor, and providing direct care. Some 20% of recipients of bachelor's degrees in psychology work in the social services or in some other form of public affairs. In addition, psychology majors often enter the fields of education or business or work for federal, state, and local governments (see Figure 4; American Psychological Association, 2000; Murray, 2002; Rajecki & Borden, 2011).

RECAP/EVALUATE/RETHINK

RECAP

LO 1-1 What is the science of psychology?

- Psychology is the scientific study of behavior and mental processes, encompassing not just what people do but also their biological activities, feelings, perceptions, memory, reasoning, and thoughts.

LO 1-2 What are the major specialties in the field of psychology?

- Behavioral neuroscientists focus on the biological basis of behavior, and experimental psychologists study the processes of sensing, perceiving, learning, and thinking about the world.
- Cognitive psychology, an outgrowth of experimental psychology, studies higher mental processes, including memory, knowing, thinking, reasoning, problem solving, judging, decision making, and language.
- Developmental psychologists study how people grow and change throughout the life span.
- Personality psychologists consider the consistency and change in an individual's behavior, as well as the individual differences that distinguish one person's behavior from another's.
- Health psychologists study psychological factors that affect physical disease, whereas clinical psychologists consider the study, diagnosis, and treatment of abnormal behavior. Counseling psychologists focus on educational, social, and career adjustment problems.
- Social psychology is the study of how people's thoughts, feelings, and actions are affected by others.
- Cross-cultural psychology examines the similarities and differences in psychological functioning among various cultures.
- Other increasingly important fields are evolutionary psychology, behavioral genetics, and clinical neuropsychology.

LO 1-3 Where do psychologists work?

- Psychologists are employed in a variety of settings. Although the primary sites of employment are private practice and colleges, many psychologists are found in hospitals, clinics, community mental health centers, and counseling centers.

EVALUATE

Match each subfield of psychology with the issues or questions posed below.

a. behavioral neuroscience
b. experimental psychology
c. cognitive psychology
d. developmental psychology
e. personality psychology
f. health psychology
g. clinical psychology
h. counseling psychology
i. educational psychology
j. school psychology
k. social psychology
l. industrial psychology

1. Joan, a college freshman, is worried about her grades. She needs to learn better organizational skills and study habits to cope with the demands of college.
2. At what age do children generally begin to acquire an emotional attachment to their fathers?
3. It is thought that pornographic films that depict violence against women may prompt aggressive behavior in some men.
4. What chemicals are released in the human body as a result of a stressful event? What are their effects on behavior?
5. Luis is unique in his manner of responding to crisis situations, with an even temperament and a positive outlook.
6. The teachers of 8-year-old Jack are concerned that he has recently begun to withdraw socially and to show little interest in schoolwork.
7. Janetta's job is demanding and stressful. She wonders if her lifestyle is making her more prone to certain illnesses, such as cancer and heart disease.
8. A psychologist is intrigued by the fact that some people are much more sensitive to painful stimuli than others are.
9. A strong fear of crowds leads a young man to seek treatment for his problem.
10. What mental strategies are involved in solving complex word problems?
11. What teaching methods most effectively motivate elementary school students to successfully accomplish academic tasks?
12. Jessica is asked to develop a management strategy that will encourage safer work practices in an assembly plant.

RETHINK

Do you think intuition and common sense are sufficient for understanding why people act the way they do? In what ways is a scientific approach appropriate for studying human behavior?

Answers to Evaluate Questions

a-4; b-8; c-10; d-2; e-5; f-7; g-9; h-1; i-11; j-6; k-3; l-12

KEY TERM

psychology

MODULE 2

A Science Evolves: The Past, the Present, and the Future

Learning Outcomes

LO 2-1 What are the origins of psychology?

LO 2-2 What are the major approaches in contemporary psychology?

LO 2-3 What are psychology's key issues and controversies?

LO 2-4 What is the future of psychology likely to hold?

Seven thousand years ago, people assumed that psychological problems were caused by evil spirits. To allow those spirits to escape from a person's body, ancient healers chipped a hole in a patient's skull with crude instruments—a procedure called *trephining*.

According to the 17th-century philosopher Descartes, nerves were hollow tubes through which "animal spirits" conducted impulses in the same way that water is transmitted through a pipe. When a person put a finger too close to a fire, heat was transmitted to the brain through the tubes.

Franz Josef Gall, an 18th-century physician, argued that a trained observer could discern intelligence, moral character, and other basic personality characteristics from the shape and number of bumps on a person's skull. His theory gave rise to the field of phrenology, employed by hundreds of practitioners in the 19th century.

Although these explanations might sound far-fetched, in their own times they represented the most advanced thinking about what might be called the psychology of the era. Our understanding of behavior has progressed tremendously since the 18th century, but most of the advances have been recent. As sciences go, psychology is one of the new kids on the block. (For highlights in the development of the field, see Figure 1.)

Wilhelm Wundt

structuralism Wundt's approach, which focuses on uncovering the fundamental mental components of consciousness, thinking, and other kinds of mental states and activities.

introspection A procedure used to study the structure of the mind in which subjects are asked to describe in detail what they are experiencing when they are exposed to a stimulus.

The Roots of Psychology

We can trace psychology's roots back to the ancient Greeks, who considered the mind to be a suitable topic for scholarly contemplation. Later philosophers argued for hundreds of years about some of the questions psychologists grapple with today. For example, the 17th-century British philosopher John Locke believed that children were born into the world with minds like "blank slates" (*tabula rasa* in Latin) and that their experiences determined what kind of adults they would become. His views contrasted with those of Plato and the 17th-century French philosopher René Descartes, who argued that some knowledge was inborn in humans.

However, the formal beginning of psychology as a scientific discipline is generally considered to be in the late 19th century, when Wilhelm Wundt established the first experimental laboratory devoted to psychological phenomena in Leipzig, Germany. At about the same time, William James was setting up his laboratory in Cambridge, Massachusetts.

When Wundt set up his laboratory in 1879, his aim was to study the building blocks of the mind. He considered psychology to be the study of conscious experience. His perspective, which came to be known as **structuralism**, focused on uncovering the fundamental mental components of perception, consciousness, thinking, emotions, and other kinds of mental states and activities.

To determine how basic sensory processes shape our understanding of the world, Wundt and other structuralists used a procedure called **introspection**, in which they presented people with a stimulus—such as a bright green object or a sentence printed on a card–and asked them to describe, in their own words and in as much detail as they could, what they were experiencing. Wundt argued that by analyzing people's reports, psychologists could come to a better understanding of the structure of the mind.

Over time, psychologists challenged Wundt's approach. They became increasingly dissatisfied with the assumption that introspection could reveal the structure of the mind. Introspection was not a truly scientific technique, because there were few ways an outside observer could confirm the accuracy of others' introspections. Moreover, people had difficulty describing some kinds of inner experiences, such as emotional responses. Those drawbacks led to the development of new approaches, which largely replaced structuralism.

The perspective that replaced structuralism is known as functionalism. Rather than focusing on the mind's structure, **functionalism** concentrated on what the mind *does* and how behavior *functions*. Functionalists, whose perspective became prominent in the early 1900s, asked what role behavior plays in allowing people to adapt to their environments. For example, a functionalist might examine the function of the emotion of fear in preparing us to deal with emergency situations.

William James, an American psychologist, led the functionalist movement. Functionalists examined how people satisfy their needs through their behavior. The functionalists also discussed how our stream of consciousness–the flow of thoughts in our conscious minds–permits us to adapt to our environment. The American educator John Dewey drew on functionalism to develop the field of school psychology, proposing ways to best meet students' educational needs.

William James

Another important reaction to structuralism was the development of gestalt psychology in the early 1900s. **Gestalt psychology** emphasizes how perception is organized. Instead of considering the individual parts that make up thinking, gestalt psychologists took the opposite tack, studying how people consider individual elements together as units or wholes. Led by German scientists such as Hermann Ebbinghaus and Max Wertheimer, gestalt psychologists proposed that "The whole is different from the sum of its parts," meaning that our perception, or understanding, of objects is greater and more meaningful than the individual elements that make up our perceptions. Gestalt psychologists have made substantial contributions to our understanding of perception.

functionalism An early approach to psychology, led by William James, that concentrated on what the mind does–the functions of mental activity–and the role of behavior in allowing people to adapt to their environments.

gestalt (geh-SHTALLT) psychology An approach to psychology that focuses on the organization of perception and thinking in a "whole" sense rather than on the individual elements of perception.

WOMEN IN PSYCHOLOGY: FOUNDING MOTHERS

As in many scientific fields, social prejudices hindered women's participation in the early development of psychology. For example, many universities would not admit women to their graduate psychology programs in the early 1900s.

Despite the hurdles they faced, women made notable contributions to psychology, although their impact on the field was largely overlooked until recently. For example, Margaret Floy Washburn (1871–1939) was the first woman to receive a doctorate in psychology, and she did important work on animal behavior. Leta Stetter Hollingworth (1886–1939) was one of the first psychologists to focus on child development and on women's issues. She collected data to refute the view, popular in the early 1900s, that women's abilities periodically declined during parts of the menstrual cycle (Hollingworth, 1943/1990; Denmark & Fernandez, 1993; Furumoto & Scarborough, 2002).

Mary Calkins (1863–1930), who studied memory in the early part of the 20th century, became the first female president of the American Psychological Association. Karen Horney (pronounced "HORN-eye") (1885–1952) focused on the social and cultural factors behind personality, and June Etta Downey (1875–1932) spearheaded the study of personality traits and became the first woman to head a psychology department at a state university. Anna Freud (1895–1982), the daughter of Sigmund Freud, also made notable contributions to the treatment of abnormal behavior, and Mamie Phipps Clark (1917–1983) carried out pioneering work on how children of color grew to recognize racial differences (Horney, 1937; Stevens & Gardner, 1982; Lal, 2002).

Study Alert

Knowing the basic outlines of the history of the field will help you understand how today's major perspectives have evolved.

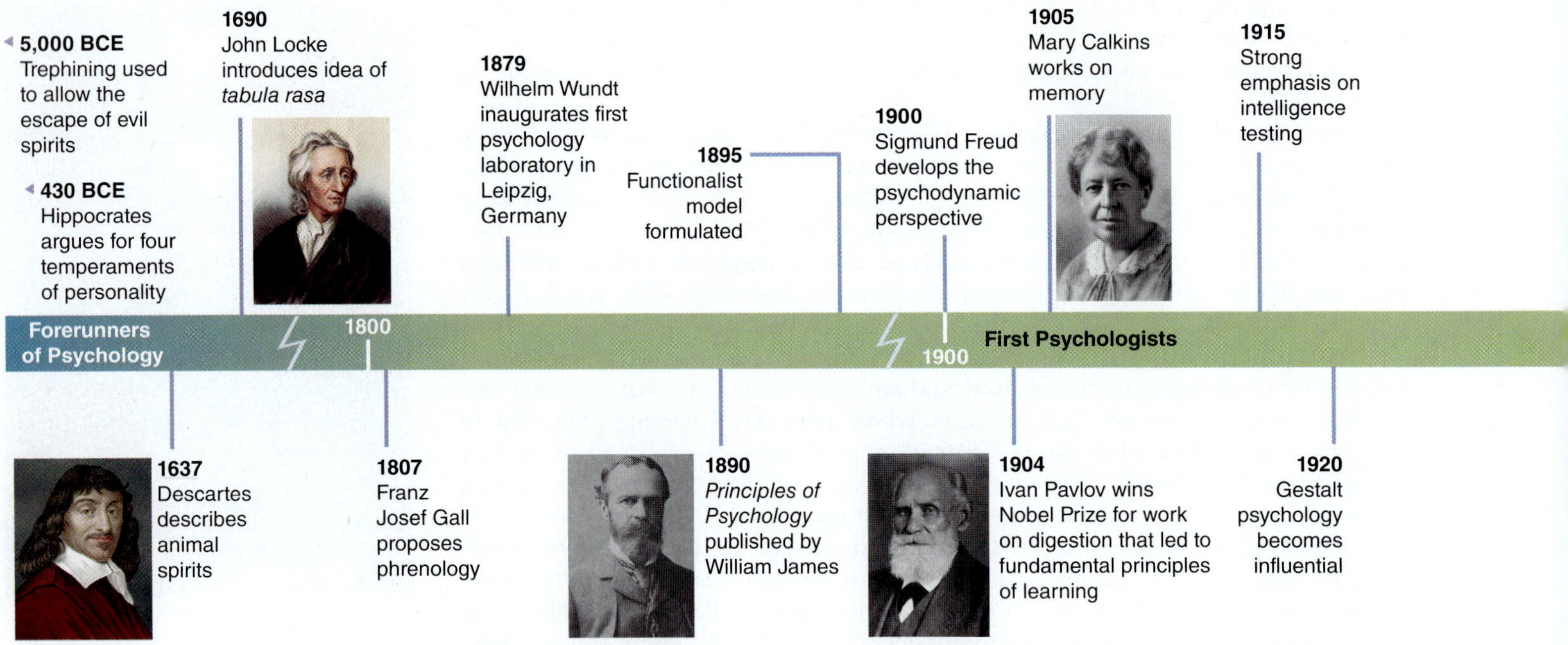

FIGURE 1 This time line illustrates major milestones in the development of psychology.

Today's Perspectives

Study Alert
Use Figure 2 to differentiate the five perspectives, which are important because they provide a foundation for every topic covered throughout the text.

The men and women who laid the foundations of psychology shared a common goal: to explain and understand behavior using scientific methods. Seeking to achieve the same goal, the tens of thousands of psychologists who followed those early pioneers embraced–and often rejected–a variety of broad perspectives.

The perspectives of psychology offer distinct outlooks and emphasize different factors. Just as we can use more than one map to find our way around a particular region–for instance, a map that shows roads and highways and another map that shows major landmarks–psychologists developed a variety of approaches to understanding behavior. When considered jointly, the different perspectives provide the means to explain behavior in its amazing variety.

Today, the field of psychology includes five major perspectives (summarized in Figure 2). These broad perspectives emphasize different aspects of behavior and mental processes, and each takes our understanding of behavior in a somewhat different direction.

THE NEUROSCIENCE PERSPECTIVE: BLOOD, SWEAT, AND FEARS

neuroscience perspective The approach that views behavior from the perspective of the brain, the nervous system, and other biological functions.

When we get down to the basics, humans are animals made of skin and bones. The **neuroscience perspective** considers how people and nonhumans function biologically: how individual nerve cells are joined together, how the inheritance of certain characteristics from parents and other ancestors influences behavior, how the functioning of the body affects hopes and fears, which behaviors are instinctual, and so forth. Even more complex kinds of behaviors, such as a baby's response to strangers, are viewed as having critical biological components by psychologists who embrace the neuroscience perspective. This perspective includes the study of heredity and evolution, which considers how heredity may influence behavior; and behavioral neuroscience, which examines how the brain and the nervous system affect behavior.

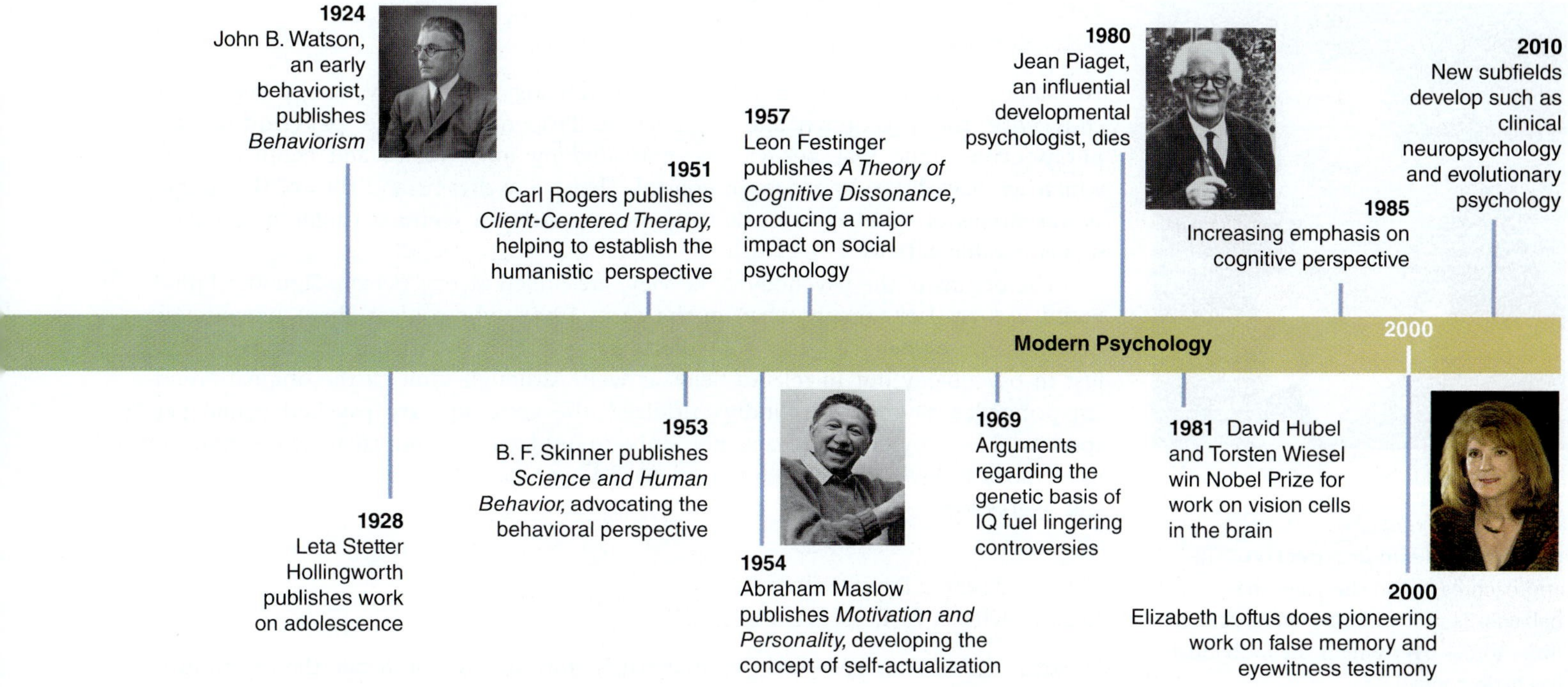

Because every behavior ultimately can be broken down into its biological components, the neuroscience perspective has broad appeal. Psychologists who subscribe to this perspective have made major contributions to the understanding and betterment of human life, ranging from cures for certain types of deafness to drug treatments for people with severe mental disorders. Furthermore, advances in methods for examining the anatomy and functioning of the brain have permitted the neuroscientific perspective to extend its influence across a broad range of subfields in psychology. (We'll see examples of these methods throughout this book in *Neuroscience in Your Life.*)

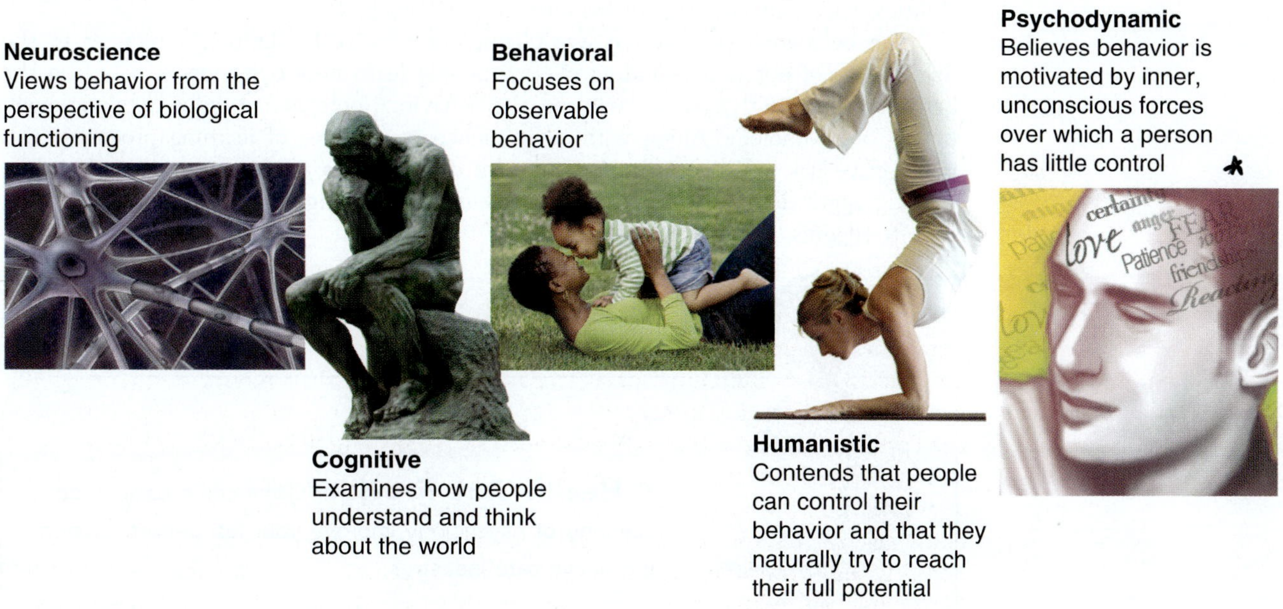

FIGURE 2 The major perspectives of psychology.

Sigmund Freud

psychodynamic perspective The approach based on the view that behavior is motivated by unconscious inner forces over which the individual has little control.

behavioral perspective The approach that suggests that observable, measurable behavior should be the focus of study.

THE PSYCHODYNAMIC PERSPECTIVE: UNDERSTANDING THE INNER PERSON

To many people who have never taken a psychology course, psychology begins and ends with the psychodynamic perspective. Proponents of the **psychodynamic perspective** argue that behavior is motivated by inner forces and conflicts about which we have little awareness or control. They view dreams and slips of the tongue as indications of what a person is truly feeling within a seething cauldron of unconscious psychic activity.

The origins of the psychodynamic view are linked to one person: Sigmund Freud. Freud was an Austrian physician in the early 1900s whose ideas about unconscious determinants of behavior had a revolutionary effect on 20th-century thinking, not just in psychology but in related fields as well. Although some of the original Freudian principles have been roundly criticized, the contemporary psychodynamic perspective has provided a means not only to understand and treat some kinds of psychological disorders but also to understand everyday phenomena such as prejudice and aggression.

THE BEHAVIORAL PERSPECTIVE: OBSERVING THE OUTER PERSON

Whereas the neuroscience and psychodynamic approaches look inside the organism to determine the causes of its behavior, the behavioral perspective takes a different approach. Proponents of the behavioral perspective rejected psychology's early emphasis on the inner workings of the mind. Instead, the **behavioral perspective** suggests that the focus should be on observable behavior that can be measured objectively.

John B. Watson was the first major American psychologist to advocate a behavioral approach. Working in the 1920s, Watson was adamant in his view that one could gain a complete understanding of behavior by studying and modifying the environment in which people operate.

In fact, Watson believed rather optimistically that it was possible to elicit any desired type of behavior by controlling a person's environment. This philosophy is clear in his own words: "Give me a dozen healthy infants, well-formed, and my own specified world to bring them up in and I'll guarantee to take any one at random and train him to become any type of specialist I might select—doctor, lawyer, artist, merchant-chief, and yes, even beggar-man and thief, regardless of his talents, penchants, tendencies, abilities, vocations and race of his ancestors" (Watson, 1924).

The behavioral perspective was championed by B. F. Skinner, a pioneer in the field. Much of our understanding of how people learn new behaviors is based on the behavioral perspective. As we will see, the behavioral perspective crops up along every byway of psychology. Along with its influence in the area of learning processes, this perspective has made contributions in such diverse areas as treating mental disorders, curbing aggression, resolving sexual problems, and ending drug addiction (Silverman, Roll, & Higgins, 2008; Schlinger, 2011).

From the perspective of . . .

A Health-Care Provider How can a basic understanding of psychology improve your job performance in the health-care industry?

THE COGNITIVE PERSPECTIVE: IDENTIFYING THE ROOTS OF UNDERSTANDING

Efforts to understand behavior lead some psychologists straight into the mind. Evolving in part from structuralism and in part as a reaction to behaviorism, which focused so heavily on observable behavior and the environment, the **cognitive perspective** focuses on how people think, understand, and know about the world. The emphasis is on learning how people comprehend and represent the outside world within themselves and how our ways of thinking about the world influence our behavior.

cognitive perspective The approach that focuses on how people think, understand, and know about the world.

Many psychologists who adhere to the cognitive perspective compare human thinking to the workings of a computer, which takes in information and transforms, stores, and retrieves it. In their view, thinking is *information processing.*

Psychologists who rely on the cognitive perspective ask questions on subjects ranging from how people make decisions to whether a person can watch television and study at the same time. The common elements that link cognitive approaches are an emphasis on how people understand and think about the world and an interest in describing the patterns and irregularities in the operation of our minds.

THE HUMANISTIC PERSPECTIVE: THE UNIQUE QUALITIES OF THE HUMAN SPECIES

Rejecting the view that behavior is determined largely by automatically unfolding biological forces, unconscious processes, or the environment, the **humanistic perspective** instead suggests that all individuals naturally strive to grow, develop, and be in control of their lives and behavior. Humanistic psychologists maintain that each of us has the capacity to seek and reach fulfillment.

humanistic perspective The approach that suggests that all individuals naturally strive to grow, develop, and be in control of their lives and behavior.

According to Carl Rogers and Abraham Maslow, who were central figures in the development of the humanistic perspective, people strive to reach their full potential if they are given the opportunity. The emphasis of the humanistic perspective is on *free will,* the ability to freely make decisions about one's own behavior and life. The notion of free will stands in contrast to *determinism,* which sees behavior as caused, or determined, by things beyond a person's control.

The humanistic perspective assumes that people have the ability to make their own choices about their behavior rather than relying on societal standards. More than any other approach, it stresses the role of psychology in enriching people's lives and helping them achieve self-fulfillment. By reminding psychologists of their commitment to the individual person in society, the humanistic perspective has been an important influence (Robbins, 2008; Nichols, 2011; Linley, 2013).

Don't let the abstract qualities of the broad approaches we have discussed lull you into thinking that they are purely theoretical: These perspectives underlie ongoing work of a practical nature, as we discuss throughout this book. To start seeing how psychology can improve everyday life, read *Applying Psychology in the 21st Century.*

Psychology's Key Issues and Controversies

As you consider the many topics and perspectives that make up psychology, ranging from a narrow focus on minute biochemical influences on behavior to a broad focus on social behaviors, you might find yourself thinking that the discipline lacks cohesion. However, the field is more unified than a first glimpse might suggest. For one thing, no matter what topical area a psychologist specializes in, he or she relies primarily on one of the five major perspectives. For example, a developmental psychologist who specializes in the study of children could make use of the cognitive perspective or the psychodynamic perspective or any of the other major perspectives.

Applying Psychology in the 21st Century

Psychology Matters

"Investigators search for clues at site of suicide bombing."

"Unemployment for college graduates remains at historically high levels following the deepest recession since the Great Depression."

"Eyewitness to killing proves unable to provide reliable clues."

"Social media like Facebook, Twitter, and Instagram change how teenagers interact with their friends."

"Childhood obesity rates surge."

A quick review of any day's news headlines reminds us that the world is beset by a variety of stubborn problems that resist easy solutions. At the same time, a considerable number of psychologists are devoting their energies and expertise to addressing these problems and improving the human condition. Let's consider some of the ways in which psychology has addressed and helped work toward solutions of major societal problems:

- What are the causes of terrorism? What motivates suicide bombers? Are they psychologically disordered, or can their behavior be seen as a rational response to a particular system of beliefs? As we'll see when we discuss psychological disorders, psychologists are gaining an understanding of the factors that lead people to embrace suicide and to engage in terrorism to further a cause in which they deeply believe (Locicero & Sinclair, 2008; Mintz & Brule, 2009; Post et al., 2009).
- How are social media changing the way we live? Social networking media such as Facebook and Twitter have changed the way people communicate and the way news spreads around the world. How do social media affect the way people relate to each other? How do they affect our perceptions of world events? Psychologists are examining the motivations behind social networking, its influence on individuals and social institutions, and possible beneficial applications of the technology (Bergman et al., 2011; Powell, Richmond, & Williams, 2011; Rice, Milburn, & Monro, 2011).
- What are the roots of autism spectrum disorder, and why is it on the rise? Autism spectrum disorder is a severe developmental disability that impairs one's ability to communicate and relate to others. It exists on a continuum from mild symptoms, such as social awkwardness, to profound dysfunction, such as a complete inability to communicate or care for oneself. Psychologists are rapidly gaining insights into the hereditary and environmental factors that influence autism; the need for this understanding is urgent because the incidence of autism has been growing sharply in recent years and it's unclear why (Silverman, 2012; Pelphrey & Shultz, 2013).
- Why do eyewitnesses to crimes often remember the events inaccurately, and how can we increase the precision of eyewitness accounts? Psychologists' research has come to an important conclusion: Eyewitness testimony in criminal cases is often inaccurate and biased. Memories of crimes are often clouded by emotion, and the questions asked by police investigators often elicit inaccurate responses. Work by psychologists has been used to provide national guidelines for obtaining more accurate memories during criminal investigations (Kassin, 2005; Loftus & Bernstein, 2005; Busey & Loftus, 2007).
- What are the roots of obesity, and how can healthier eating and better physical fitness be encouraged? Why are some people more predisposed to obesity than others are? What social factors might be at play in the rising rate of obesity in childhood? As is becoming increasingly clear, obesity is a complex problem with biological, psychological, and social underpinnings. Therefore, to be successful, approaches to treating obesity must take many factors into account. There is no magic bullet providing a quick fix, but psychologists recommend a number of strategies that help make weight-loss goals more achievable (Puhl & Latner, 2007; MacLean et al., 2009; Neumark-Sztainer, 2009).
- What gives people satisfaction with life and a sense of well being? Research has found that during difficult economic times, it's important to understand that wealth and possessions don't make people happy. Instead, happiness comes from enjoying life's little moments and finding purpose and meaning in what you do (Seligman, 2011; Pavot & Diener, 2013).

These topics represent just a few of the issues that psychologists address daily. To further explore the many ways that psychology has an impact on everyday life, check out the American Psychological Association (APA) website, at www.apa.org, which features psychological applications in everyday life.

RETHINK

- What do *you* think are the major problems affecting society today?
- What are the psychological issues involved in these problems, and how might psychologists help find solutions to them?

Psychologists also agree on what the key issues of the field are (see Figure 3). Although there are major arguments regarding how best to address and resolve the key issues, psychology is a unified science, because psychologists of all perspectives agree that the issues must be addressed if the field is going to advance. As you contemplate these key issues, try not to think of them in "either/or" terms. Instead, consider the opposing viewpoints on each issue as the opposite ends of a continuum, with the positions of individual psychologists typically falling somewhere between the two ends.

Study Alert

Use Figure 3 to learn the key issues that underlie every subfield of psychology.

Nature (heredity) versus nurture (environment) is one of the major issues that psychologists address. How much of people's behavior is due to their genetically determined nature (heredity), and how much is due to nurture, the influences of the physical and social environment in which a child is raised? Furthermore, what is the interplay between heredity and environment? These questions have deep philosophical and historical roots, and they are involved in many topics in psychology.

A psychologist's take on this issue depends partly on which major perspective he or she subscribes to. For example, developmental psychologists whose focus is on how people grow and change throughout the course of their lives may be most interested in learning more about hereditary influences if they follow a neuroscience perspective. In contrast, developmental psychologists who are proponents of the behavioral perspective are more likely to focus on environment (Rutter, 2002, 2006; Barrett, 2011).

However, every psychologist would agree that neither nature nor nurture alone is the sole determinant of behavior; rather, it is a combination of the two. In a sense, then, the real controversy involves how much of our behavior is caused by heredity and how much is caused by environmental influences.

A second major question addressed by psychologists concerns *conscious versus unconscious causes of behavior*. How much of our behavior is produced by forces of which we are fully aware, and how much is due to unconscious activity–mental processes that are not accessible to the conscious mind? This question represents one of the great controversies in the field of psychology. For example, clinical psychologists adopting a psychodynamic perspective argue that psychological disorders

Issue	Neuroscience	Cognitive	Behavioral	Humanistic	Psychodynamic
Nature (heredity) vs. nurture (environment)	Nature (heredity)	Both	Nurture (environment)	Nurture (environment)	Nature (heredity)
Conscious vs. unconscious determinants of behavior	Unconscious	Both	Conscious	Conscious	Unconscious
Observable behavior vs. internal mental processes	Internal emphasis	Internal emphasis	Observable emphasis	Internal emphasis	Internal emphasis
Free will vs. determinism	Determinism	Free will	Determinism	Free will	Determinism
Individual differences vs. universal principles	Universal emphasis	Individual emphasis	Both	Individual emphasis	Universal emphasis

FIGURE 3 Key issues in psychology and the positions taken by psychologists subscribing to the five major perspectives of psychology.

are brought about by unconscious factors, whereas psychologists employing the cognitive perspective suggest that psychological disorders largely are the result of faulty thinking processes.

The next issue is *observable behavior versus internal mental processes*. Should psychology concentrate solely on behavior that can be seen by outside observers, or should it focus on unseen thinking processes? Some psychologists, particularly those relying on the behavioral perspective, contend that the only legitimate source of information for psychologists is behavior that can be observed directly. Other psychologists, building on the cognitive perspective, argue that what goes on inside a person's mind is critical to understanding behavior, and so we must concern ourselves with mental processes.

free will The idea that behavior is caused primarily by choices that are made freely by the individual.

determinism The idea that people's behavior is produced primarily by factors outside of their willful control.

Free will versus determinism is another key issue. How much of our behavior is a matter of **free will** (choices made freely by an individual), and how much is subject to **determinism,** the notion that behavior is largely produced by factors beyond people's willful control? An issue long debated by philosophers, the free-will/determinism argument is also central to the field of psychology (Cary, 2007; Nichols, 2011; Vonasch & Baumeister, 2013).

For example, some psychologists who specialize in psychological disorders argue that people make intentional choices and that those who display so-called abnormal behavior should be considered responsible for their actions. Other psychologists disagree and contend that such individuals are the victims of forces beyond their control. The position psychologists take on this issue has important implications for the way they treat psychological disorders, especially in deciding whether treatment should be forced on people who don't want it.

The last of the key issues concerns *individual differences versus universal principles*. Specifically, how much of our behavior is a consequence of our unique and special qualities, the individual differences that differentiate us from other people? Conversely, how much reflects the culture and society in which we live, stemming from universal principles that underlie the behavior of all humans? Psychologists who rely on the neuroscience perspective tend to look for universal principles of behavior, such as how the nervous system operates or the way certain hormones automatically prime us for sexual activity. Such psychologists concentrate on the similarities in our behavioral destinies despite vast differences in our upbringing. In contrast, psychologists who employ the humanistic perspective focus more on the uniqueness of every individual. They consider every person's behavior a reflection of distinct and special individual qualities.

The question of the degree to which psychologists can identify universal principles that apply to all people has taken on new significance in light of the tremendous demographic changes now occurring in the United States and around the world. As we discuss next, these changes raise new and critical issues for the discipline of psychology in the 21st century.

Psychology's Future

We have examined psychology's foundations, but what does the future hold for the discipline? Although the course of scientific development is notoriously difficult to predict, several trends seem likely:

- As its knowledge base grows, psychology will become increasingly specialized and new perspectives will evolve. For example, our growing understanding of the brain and the nervous system, combined with scientific advances in genetics and gene therapy, will allow psychologists to focus on *prevention* of psychological disorders rather than only on their treatment (Cuijpers et al., 2008).

Neuroscience in Your Life: Reading the Movies in Your Mind

Technology is changing at an ever-increasing rate. Whereas previously the idea of seeing one's thoughts was found only in the realm of science fiction, today it is becoming a reality—almost. Though researchers expect it will be decades before they can have a good representation of our thoughts, they are starting to see ways in which it might happen. In a recent study researchers asked participants to watch movies while technicians measured the activity of their brain using fMRI (functional Magnetic Resonance Imaging). The researchers used that activity to develop models of how each person's brain activity related to what they were watching. They then were able to create an image that approximated what the participants were watching based on the brain activity. Although the images admittedly are ill-defined, the results do show the possibilities of creating higher-definition images in the future. (Source: Nishimoto et al., 2011.)

- The evolving sophistication of neuroscientific approaches is likely to have an increasing influence over other branches of psychology. For instance, social psychologists already are increasing their understanding of social behaviors such as persuasion by using brain scans as part of an evolving field known as *social neuroscience*. Furthermore, as neuroscientific techniques become more sophisticated, there will be new ways of applying that knowledge, as we discuss in *Neuroscience in Your Life* (Bunge & Wallis, 2008; Cacioppo & Decety, 2009).
- Psychology's influence on issues of public interest also will grow. The major problems of our time–such as violence, terrorism, racial and ethnic prejudice, poverty, and environmental and technological disasters–have important psychological components (Zimbardo, 2004; Hobfoll, Hall, & Canetti-Nisim, 2007; Marshall, Bryant, & Amsel, 2007).
- The public's view of psychology will become more informed. Surveys show that the public at large does not fully understand the scientific underpinnings of the field. However, as the field itself embraces such practices as using scientific evidence to choose the best treatments for psychological disorders, psychology's reputation will grow (Lilienfeld, 2012).
- Finally, as the population becomes more diverse, issues of diversity–embodied in the study of racial, ethnic, linguistic, and cultural factors–will become more important to psychologists providing services and doing research. The result will be a field that can provide an understanding of *human* behavior in its broadest sense (Leong & Blustein, 2000; Chang & Sue, 2005; Quintana et al., 2006).

From the perspective of . . .

A Social Worker Imagine that you have a caseload of clients who come from diverse cultures, ethnicities, and races. How might you consider their diverse backgrounds when assisting them?

RECAP/EVALUATE/RETHINK

RECAP

LO 2-1 What are the origins of psychology?

- Wilhelm Wundt laid the foundation of psychology in 1879, when he opened his laboratory in Germany.
- Early perspectives that guided the work of psychologists were structuralism, functionalism, and gestalt theory.

LO 2-2 What are the major approaches in contemporary psychology?

- The neuroscience approach focuses on the biological components of the behavior of people and animals.
- The psychodynamic perspective suggests that powerful, unconscious inner forces and conflicts about which people have little or no awareness are the primary determinants of behavior.
- The behavioral perspective deemphasizes internal processes and concentrates instead on observable, measurable behavior, suggesting that understanding and control of a person's environment are sufficient to fully explain and modify behavior.
- Cognitive approaches to behavior consider how people know, understand, and think about the world.
- The humanistic perspective emphasizes that people are uniquely inclined toward psychological growth and higher levels of functioning and that they will strive to reach their full potential.

LO 2-3 What are psychology's key issues and controversies?

- Psychology's key issues and controversies center on how much of human behavior is a product of nature or nurture, conscious or unconscious thoughts, observable actions or internal mental processes, free will or determinism, and individual differences or universal principles.

LO 2-4 What is the future of psychology likely to hold?

- Psychology will become increasingly specialized, will pay greater attention to prevention instead of just treatment, will become more and more concerned with the public interest, and will take the growing diversity of the country's population into account more fully.

EVALUATE

1. Wundt described psychology as the study of conscious experience, a perspective he called __________.
2. Early psychologists studied the mind by asking people to describe what they were experiencing when exposed to various stimuli. This procedure was known as __________.
3. The statement "In order to study human behavior, we must consider the whole of perception rather than its component parts" might be made by a person subscribing to which perspective of psychology?
4. Jeanne's therapist asks her to recount a violent dream she recently experienced in order to gain insight into the unconscious forces affecting her behavior. Jeanne's therapist is working from a __________ perspective.
5. "It is behavior that can be observed that should be studied, not the suspected inner workings of the mind." This statement was most likely made by someone with which perspective?
   a. Cognitive perspective
   b. Neuroscience perspective
   c. Humanistic perspective
   d. Behavioral perspective
6. "My therapist is wonderful! He always points out my positive traits. He dwells on my uniqueness and strength as an individual. I feel much more confident about myself–as if I'm really growing and reaching my potential." The therapist being described most likely follows a __________ perspective.
7. In the nature-nurture issue, nature refers to heredity, and nurture refers to the __________.
8. Race is a biological concept, not a psychological one. True or false?

RETHINK

Focusing on one of the five major perspectives in use today (that is, neuroscience, psychodynamic, behavioral, cognitive, and humanistic), can you describe the kinds of research questions and studies that researchers using that perspective might pursue?

Answers to Evaluate Questions

1. structuralism; **2.** introspection; **3.** gestalt; **4.** psychodynamic; **5.** d; **6.** humanistic; **7.** environment; **8.** true

KEY TERMS

structuralism
introspection
functionalism
gestalt (geh-SHTALLT) psychology
neuroscience perspective
psychodynamic perspective
behavioral perspective
cognitive perspective
humanistic perspective
free will
determinism

MODULE 3

Research in Psychology

Learning Outcomes

LO 3-1 What is the scientific method?

LO 3-2 What role do theories and hypotheses play in psychological research?

LO 3-3 What research methods do psychologists use?

LO 3-4 How do psychologists establish cause-and-effect relationships in research studies?

The Scientific Method

"Birds of a feather flock together". . . or "Opposites attract"? "Two heads are better than one". . . or "If you want a thing done well, do it yourself"? "The more the merrier". . . or "Two's company, three's a crowd"?

If we were to rely on common sense to understand behavior, we'd have considerable difficulty–especially because commonsense views are often contradictory. In fact, one of the major undertakings for the field of psychology is to develop suppositions about behavior and to determine which of those suppositions are accurate.

Psychologists–as well as scientists in other disciplines–meet the challenge of posing appropriate questions and properly answering them by relying on the scientific method. The **scientific method** is the approach used by psychologists to systematically acquire knowledge and understanding about behavior and other phenomena of interest. As illustrated in Figure 1, it consists of four main steps: (1) identifying questions of interest, (2) formulating an explanation, (3) carrying out research designed to support or refute the explanation, and (4) communicating the findings.

scientific method The approach through which psychologists systematically acquire knowledge and understanding about behavior and other phenomena of interest.

Study Alert
Use Figure 1 to remember the four steps of the scientific method (identifying questions, formulating an explanation, carrying out research, and communicating the findings).

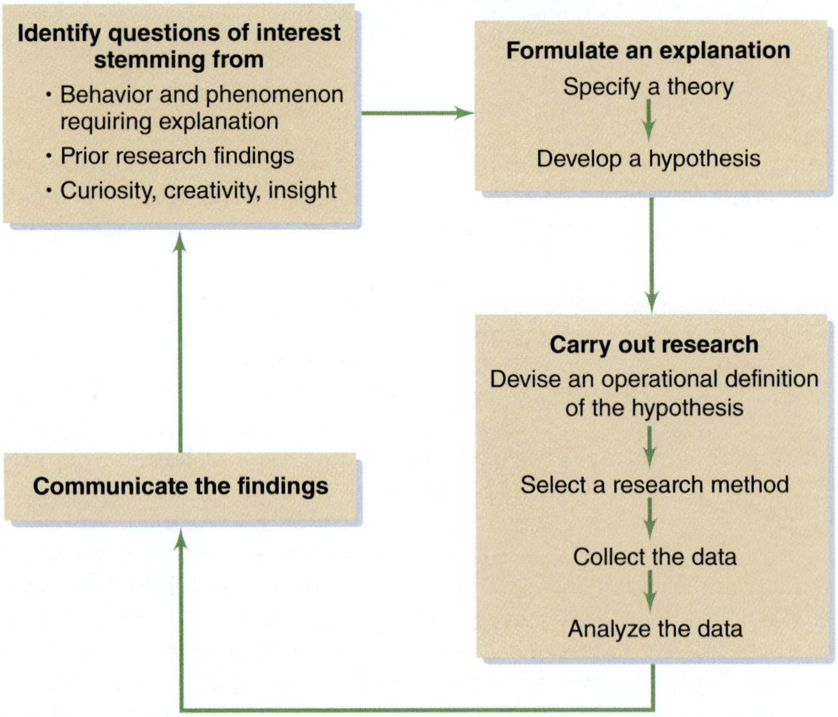

FIGURE 1 The scientific method, which encompasses the process of identifying, asking, and answering questions, is used by psychologists, and by researchers from every other scientific discipline, to come to an understanding about the world. What do you think are the advantages of this method?

THEORIES: SPECIFYING BROAD EXPLANATIONS

In using the scientific method, psychologists start by identifying questions of interest. We have all been curious at some time about our observations of everyday behavior. If you have ever asked yourself why a particular teacher is so easily annoyed, why a friend is always late for appointments, or how your dog understands your commands, you have been formulating questions about behavior.

Psychologists, too, ask questions about the nature and causes of behavior. They may want to explore explanations for everyday behaviors or for various phenomena. They may also pose questions that build on findings from their previous research or from research carried out by other psychologists. Or they may produce new questions that are based on curiosity, creativity, or insight.

After a question has been identified, the next step in the scientific method is to develop a theory to explain the observed phenomenon. **Theories** are broad explanations and predictions concerning phenomena of interest. They provide a framework for understanding the relationships among a set of otherwise unorganized facts or principles.

theories Broad explanations and predictions concerning phenomena of interest.

All of us have developed our own informal theories of human behavior, such as "People are basically good" or "People's behavior is usually motivated by self-interest." However, psychologists' theories are more formal and focused. They are established on the basis of a careful study of the psychological literature to identify earlier relevant research and previously formulated theories, as well as psychologists' general knowledge of the field.

Growing out of the diverse approaches employed by psychologists, theories vary both in their breadth and in their level of detail. For example, one theory might seek to explain and predict a phenomenon as broad as emotional experience. A narrower theory might attempt to explain why people display the emotion of fear nonverbally after receiving a threat (Guerrero, La Valley, & Farinelli, 2008; Waller, Cray, & Burrows, 2008; Anker & Feeley, 2011).

Psychologists Bibb Latané and John Darley, responding to the failure of bystanders to intervene when Kitty Genovese was murdered in New York, developed what they called a theory of *diffusion of responsibility* (Latané & Darley, 1970). According to their theory, the greater the number of bystanders or witnesses to an event that calls for helping behavior, the more the responsibility for helping is perceived to be shared by all the bystanders. Thus, the greater the number of bystanders in an emergency situation, the smaller the share of the responsibility each person feels–and the less likely that any single person will come forward to help.

HYPOTHESES: CRAFTING TESTABLE PREDICTIONS

Although the diffusion of responsibility theory seems to make sense, it represented only the beginning phase of Latané and Darley's investigative process. Their next step was to devise a way to test their theory. To do this, they needed to create a hypothesis. A **hypothesis** is a prediction stated in a way that allows it to be tested. Hypotheses stem from theories; they help test the underlying soundness of theories.

hypothesis A prediction, stemming from a theory, stated in a way that allows it to be tested.

In the same way that we develop our own broad theories about the world, we also construct hypotheses about events and behavior. Those hypotheses can range from trivialities (such as why our English instructor wears those weird shirts) to more meaningful matters (such as what is the best way to study for a test). Although we rarely test these hypotheses systematically, we do try to determine whether they are right. Perhaps we try comparing two strategies: cramming the night before an exam versus spreading out our study over several nights. By assessing which approach yields better test performance, we have created a way to compare the two strategies.

A hypothesis must be restated in a way that will allow it to be tested, which involves creating an operational definition. An **operational definition** is the translation of a hypothesis into specific, testable procedures that can be measured and observed.

operational definition The translation of a hypothesis into specific, testable procedures that can be measured and observed.

There is no single way to go about devising an operational definition for a hypothesis; it depends on logic, the equipment and facilities available, the psychological perspective being employed, and ultimately the creativity of the researcher. For example, one researcher might develop a hypothesis that uses as an operational definition of "fear" an increase in heart rate. In contrast, another psychologist might use as an operational definition of "fear" a written response to the question "How much fear are you experiencing at this moment?"

Latané and Darley's hypothesis was a straightforward prediction from their more general theory of diffusion of responsibility: The more people who witness an emergency situation, the less likely it is that help will be given to a victim. They could, of course, have chosen another hypothesis (try to think of one!), but their initial formulation seemed to offer the most direct test of the theory.

Psychologists rely on formal theories and hypotheses for many reasons. For one thing, theories and hypotheses allow them to make sense of unorganized, separate observations and bits of information by permitting them to place the pieces within a coherent framework. In addition, theories and hypotheses offer psychologists the opportunity to move beyond known facts and make deductions about unexplained phenomena and develop ideas for future investigation (Cohen, 2003; Gurin, 2006; van Wesel, Boeije, & Hoijtink, 2013).

Study Alert
Remember that a theory is a broad explanation, while a hypothesis is a more narrow prediction.

In short, the scientific method, with its emphasis on theories and hypotheses, helps psychologists pose appropriate questions. With properly stated questions in hand, psychologists then can choose from a variety of research methods to find answers.

Psychological Research

Research—systematic inquiry aimed at the discovery of new knowledge—is a central ingredient of the scientific method in psychology. It provides the key to understanding the degree to which hypotheses (and the theories behind them) are accurate.

Just as we can apply different theories and hypotheses to explain the same phenomena, we can use a number of alternative methods to conduct research. As we consider the major tools that psychologists use to conduct research, keep in mind that their relevance extends beyond testing and evaluating hypotheses in psychology. All of us carry out elementary forms of research on our own. For instance, a supervisor might evaluate an employee's performance; a physician might systematically test the effects of different doses of a drug on a patient; a salesperson might compare different persuasive strategies. Each of these situations draws on the research practices we are about to discuss.

Descriptive Research

Let's begin by considering several types of *descriptive research* designed to systematically investigate a person, group, or patterns of behavior. These methods include archival research, naturalistic observation, survey research, and case studies.

ARCHIVAL RESEARCH

Suppose that, like the psychologists Latané and Darley (1970), you were interested in finding out more about emergency situations in which bystanders did not provide help. One of the first places you might turn to would be historical accounts. By searching newspaper records, for example, you might find support for the notion that a decrease in helping behavior historically has accompanied an increase in the number of bystanders.

archival research Research in which existing data, such as census documents, college records, online databases, and newspaper clippings, are examined to test a hypothesis.

Using newspaper articles is an example of archival research. In **archival research,** existing data, such as census documents, college records, online databases, and newspaper clippings, are examined to test a hypothesis. For example, college transcripts may be used to determine if gender differences exist in academic performance (Sullivan, Riccio, & Reynolds, 2008; Fisher & Barnes-Farrell, 2013).

Archival research is a relatively inexpensive means of testing a hypothesis because someone else has already collected the basic data. Of course, the use of existing data has several drawbacks. For one thing, the data may not be in a form that allows the researcher to test a hypothesis fully. The information could be incomplete, or it could have been collected haphazardly (Simonton, 2000; Riniolo et al., 2003; Vega, 2006).

Most attempts at archival research are hampered by the simple fact that records with the necessary information often do not exist. In these instances, researchers often turn to another research method: naturalistic observation.

Dian Fossey, a pioneer in the study of endangered mountain gorillas in their native habitat, relied on naturalistic observation for her research. What are the advantages of this approach?

NATURALISTIC OBSERVATION

In **naturalistic observation,** the investigator observes some naturally occurring behavior and does not make a change in the situation. For example, a researcher investigating helping behavior might observe the kind of help given to victims in a high-crime area of a city. The important point to remember about naturalistic observation is that the researcher simply records what occurs, making no modification in the situation that is being observed (Moore, 2002; Rustin, 2006; Kennison & Bowers, 2011).

Although the advantage of naturalistic observation is obvious—we get a sample of what people do in their "natural habitat"—there is also an important drawback: the inability to control any of the factors of interest. For example, we might find so few naturally occurring instances of helping behavior that we would be unable to draw any conclusions. Because naturalistic observation prevents researchers from making changes in a situation, they must wait until the appropriate conditions occur. Furthermore, if people know they are being watched, they may alter their reactions and produce behavior that is not truly representative.

naturalistic observation Research in which an investigator observes some naturally occurring behavior and does not make a change in the situation.

SURVEY RESEARCH

There is no more straightforward way of finding out what people think, feel, and do than asking them directly. For this reason, surveys are an important research method. In **survey research,** a *sample* of people chosen to represent a larger group of interest (a *population*) is asked a series of questions about their behavior, thoughts, or attitudes. Survey methods have become so sophisticated that even with a very small sample researchers are able to infer with great accuracy how a larger group would respond. For instance, a sample of just a few thousand voters is sufficient to predict within one or two percentage points who will win a presidential election—if the representative sample is chosen with care (Sommer & Sommer, 2001; Groves et al., 2004; Igo, 2006).

survey research Research in which people chosen to represent a larger population are asked a series of questions about their behavior, thoughts, or attitudes.

Researchers investigating helping behavior might conduct a survey by asking people to complete a questionnaire in which they indicate their reluctance for giving aid to someone. Similarly, researchers interested in learning about sexual practices have carried out surveys to learn which practices are common and which are not and to chart changing notions of sexual morality over the last several decades (Reece et al., 2009; Santelli et al., 2009).

However, survey research has several potential pitfalls. For one thing, if the sample of people who are surveyed is not representative of the broader population of interest, the results of the survey will have little meaning. For instance, if a sample of voters in a town includes only Republicans, it would hardly be useful for predicting the results of an election in which both Republicans and Democrats are voting. Consequently, researchers using surveys strive to obtain a *random sample* of the population in question, in which every voter in the town has an equal chance of being included in the sample receiving the survey (Dale, 2006; Vitak et al., 2011; Davern, 2013).

In addition, survey respondents may not want to admit to holding socially undesirable attitudes. (Most racists know they are racists and might not want to admit it.)

PsychTech
One of the most efficient ways to conduct surveys is via the web. But web surveys may have sampling problems, given that not everyone has easy access to the web, such as people living in poverty. Consequently, web surveys may not be representative of the broader population.

Furthermore, people may not want to admit they engage in behaviors that they feel are somehow abnormal–a problem that plagues surveys of sexual behavior because people are often reluctant to admit what they really do in private. Finally, in some cases, people may not even be consciously aware of what their true attitudes are or why they hold them.

From the perspective of . . .

A Marketing Manager How would you design a survey that targets the customers in which you are most interested?

THE CASE STUDY

case study An in-depth, intensive investigation of an individual or small group of people.

When they read of a suicide bomber in the Middle East, many people wonder what it is about the terrorist's personality or background that leads to such behavior. To answer this question, psychologists might conduct a case study. In contrast to a survey, in which many people are studied, a **case study** is an in-depth, intensive investigation of a single individual or a small group. Case studies often include *psychological testing*, a procedure in which a carefully designed set of questions is used to gain some insight into the personality of the individual or group (Gass et al., 2000; Addus, Chen, & Khan, 2007).

When case studies are used as a research technique, the goal is often not only to learn about the few individuals being examined but also to use the insights gained from the study to improve our understanding of people in general. Sigmund Freud developed his theories through case studies of individual patients. Similarly, case studies of terrorists might help identify others who are prone to violence.

The drawback to case studies? If the individuals examined are unique in certain ways, it is impossible to make valid generalizations to a larger population. Still, they sometimes lead the way to new theories and treatments for psychological disorders.

CORRELATIONAL RESEARCH

variables Behaviors, events, or other characteristics that can change, or vary, in some way.

correlational research Research in which the relationship between two sets of variables is examined to determine whether they are associated, or "correlated."

In using the descriptive research methods we have discussed, researchers often wish to determine the relationship between two variables. **Variables** are behaviors, events, or other characteristics that can change, or vary, in some way. For example, in a study to determine whether the amount of studying makes a difference in test scores, the variables would be study time and test scores.

In **correlational research,** two sets of variables are examined to determine whether they are associated, or "correlated." The strength and direction of the relationship between the two variables are represented by a mathematical statistic known as a *correlation* (or, more formally, a *correlation coefficient*), which can range from +1.0 to −1.0.

A *positive correlation* indicates that as the value of one variable increases, we can predict that the value of the other variable will also increase. For example, if we predict that the more time students spend studying for a test, the higher their grades on the test will be, and that the less they study, the lower their test scores will be, we are expecting to find a positive correlation. (Higher values of the variable "amount of study time" would be associated with higher values of the variable "test score," and lower values of "amount of study time" would be associated with lower values of "test score.") The correlation, then, would be indicated by a positive number, and the stronger the association was between studying and test scores, the closer the number would be to +1.0. For example, we might find a correlation of +.85 between test scores and amount of study time, indicating a strong positive association.

In contrast, a *negative correlation* tells us that as the value of one variable increases, the value of the other decreases. For instance, we might predict that as the number of hours spent studying increases, the number of hours spent partying decreases. Here we are expecting a negative correlation, ranging between 0 and −1.0. More studying is associated with less partying, and less studying is associated with more partying. The stronger the association between studying and partying is, the closer the correlation will be to −1.0. For instance, a correlation of −.85 would indicate a strong negative association between partying and studying.

Of course, it's quite possible that little or no relationship exists between two variables. For instance, we would probably not expect to find a relationship between number of study hours and height. Lack of a relationship would be indicated by a correlation close to 0. For example, if we found a correlation of −.02 or +.03, it would indicate that there is virtually no association between the two variables; knowing how much someone studies does not tell us anything about how tall he or she is.

When two variables are strongly correlated with each other, we are tempted to assume that one variable causes the other. For example, if we find that more study time is associated with higher grades, we might guess that more studying *causes* higher grades. Although this is not a bad guess, it remains just a guess—because finding that two variables are correlated does not mean that there is a causal relationship between them. The strong correlation suggests that knowing how much a person studies can help us predict how that person will do on a test, but it does not mean that the studying *causes* the test performance. Instead, for instance, people who are more interested in the subject matter might study more than do those who are less interested, and so the amount of interest, not the number of hours spent studying, would predict test performance. The mere fact that two variables occur together does not mean that one causes the other.

Similarly, suppose you learned that the number of houses of worship in a large sample of cities was positively correlated with the number of people arrested, meaning that the more houses of worship, the more arrests there were in a city. Does this mean that the presence of more houses of worship caused the greater number of arrests? Almost surely not, of course. In this case, the underlying cause is probably the size of the city: In bigger cities, there are both more houses of worship *and* more arrests.

Study Alert

The concept that "correlation does not imply causation" is a key principle.

One more example illustrates the critical point that correlations tell us nothing about cause and effect but merely provide a measure of the strength of a relationship between two variables. We might find that children who watch a lot of television programs featuring high levels of aggression are likely to demonstrate a relatively high degree of aggressive behavior and that those who watch few television shows that portray aggression are apt to exhibit a relatively low degree of such behavior (see Figure 2). But we cannot say that the aggression is *caused* by the TV viewing, because many other explanations are possible.

For instance, it could be that children who have an unusually high level of energy seek out programs with aggressive content *and* are more aggressive. The children's energy level, then, could be the true cause of the children's higher incidence of aggression. Also, people who are already highly aggressive might choose to watch shows with a high aggressive content *because* they are aggressive. Clearly, then, any number of causal sequences are possible—none of which can be ruled out by correlational research (Feshbach & Tangney, 2008; Grimes & Bergen, 2008).

The inability of correlational research to demonstrate cause-and-effect relationships is a crucial drawback to its use. There is, however, an alternative technique that does establish causality: the experiment.

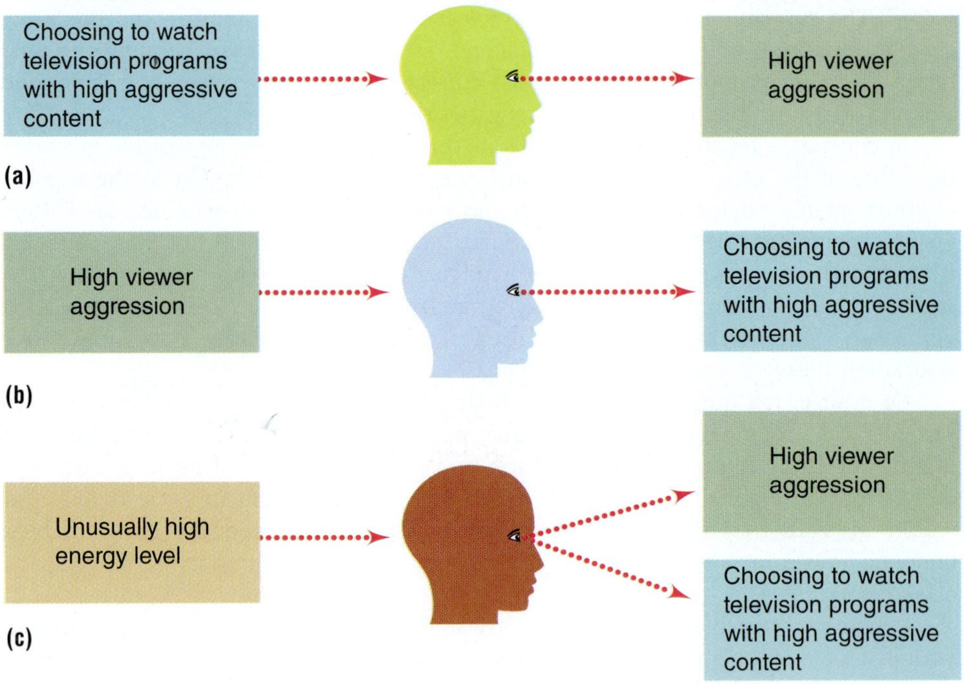

FIGURE 2 If we find that frequent viewing of television programs with aggressive content is associated with high levels of aggressive behavior, we might cite several plausible causes, as suggested in this figure. For example, (a) choosing to watch shows with aggressive content could produce aggression; or (b) being a highly aggressive person might cause one to choose to watch televised aggression; or (c) having a high energy level might cause a person to both choose to watch aggressive shows and to act aggressively. Correlational findings, then, do not permit us to determine causality. Can you think of a way to study the effects of televised aggression on aggressive behavior that is not correlational?

Experimental Research

experiment The investigation of the relationship between two (or more) variables by deliberately producing a change in one variable in a situation and observing the effects of that change on other aspects of the situation.

experimental manipulation The change that an experimenter deliberately produces in a situation.

Many studies show that the observation of violence in the media is associated with aggression in viewers. Can we conclude that the observations of violence cause aggression?

The *only* way psychologists can establish cause-and-effect relationships through research is by carrying out an experiment. In a formal **experiment,** the researcher investigates the relationship between two (or more) variables by deliberately changing one variable in a controlled situation and observing the effects of that change on other aspects of the situation. In an experiment, then, the conditions are created and controlled by the researcher, who deliberately makes a change in those conditions in order to observe the effects of that change.

The change that the researcher deliberately makes in an experiment is called the **experimental manipulation.** Experimental manipulations are used to detect relationships between different variables (Staub, 2011).

Several steps are involved in carrying out an experiment, but the process typically begins with the development of one or more hypotheses for the experiment to test. For example, Latané and Darley, in testing their theory of the diffusion of responsibility in bystander behavior, developed this hypothesis: The higher the number of people who witness an emergency situation is, the less likely it is that any of them will help the victim. They then designed an experiment to test this hypothesis.

Their first step was to formulate an operational definition of the hypothesis by conceptualizing it in a way that could be tested. Latané and Darley had to take into account the fundamental principle of experimental research mentioned earlier: Experimenters must manipulate at least one variable in order to observe the effects of the manipulation on another variable while keeping other factors in the situation constant. However, the manipulation cannot be viewed by itself, in isolation; if a cause-and-effect relationship is to be established, the effects of the manipulation must be compared with the effects of no manipulation or a different kind of manipulation.

EXPERIMENTAL GROUPS AND CONTROL GROUPS

Experimental research requires, then, that the responses of at least two groups be compared. One group will receive some special **treatment**–the manipulation implemented by the experimenter–and another group will receive either no treatment or a different treatment. Any group that receives a treatment is called an **experimental group;** a group that receives no treatment is called a **control group.** (In some experiments there are multiple experimental and control groups, each of which is compared with another group.)

treatment The manipulation implemented by the experimenter.

experimental group Any group participating in an experiment that receives a treatment.

control group A group participating in an experiment that receives no treatment.

By employing both experimental and control groups in an experiment, researchers are able to rule out the possibility that something other than the experimental manipulation produced the results observed in the experiment. Without a control group, we couldn't be sure that some other variable, such as the temperature at the time we were running the experiment, the color of the experimenter's hair, or even the mere passage of time, wasn't causing the changes observed.

For example, consider a medical researcher who thinks he has invented a medicine that cures the common cold. To test his claim, he gives the medicine one day to a group of 20 people who have colds and finds that 10 days later all of them are cured.

Eureka? Not so fast. An observer viewing this flawed study might reasonably argue that the people would have gotten better even without the medicine. What the researcher obviously needed was a control group consisting of people with colds who *don't* get the medicine and whose health is also checked 10 days later. Only if there is a significant difference between experimental and control groups can the effectiveness of the medicine be assessed. Through the use of control groups, then, researchers can isolate specific causes for their findings–and draw cause-and-effect inferences.

Returning to Latané and Darley's experiment, we see that the researchers needed to translate their hypothesis into something testable. To do this, they decided to create a false emergency situation that would appear to require the aid of a bystander. As their experimental manipulation, they decided to vary the number of bystanders present. They could have had just one experimental group with, say, two people present, and a control group for comparison purposes with just one person present. Instead, they settled on a more complex procedure involving the creation of groups of three sizes–consisting of two, three, and six people–that could be compared with one another.

independent variable The variable that is manipulated by an experimenter.

dependent variable The variable that is measured in an experiment. It is expected to change as a result of the experimenter's manipulation of the independent variable.

INDEPENDENT AND DEPENDENT VARIABLES

Latané and Darley's experimental design now included an operational definition of what is called the **independent variable.** The independent variable is the condition that is manipulated by an experimenter. (You can think of the independent variable as being independent of the actions of those taking part in an experiment; it is controlled by the experimenter.) In the case of the Latané and Darley experiment, the independent variable was the number of people present, which was manipulated by the experimenters.

The next step was to decide how they were going to determine the effect that varying the number of bystanders had on behavior of those in the experiment. Crucial to every experiment is the **dependent variable**. The dependent variable is the variable that is measured in a study. The dependent variable is expected to change as a result of the experimenter's manipulation of the independent variable. The dependent variable is dependent on the actions of the *participants* or *subjects*–the people taking part in the experiment.

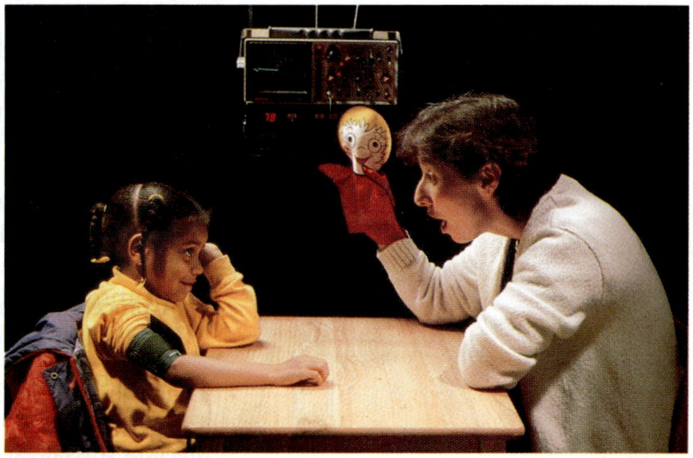

In this experiment, preschoolers' reactions to the puppet are monitored. Can you think of a hypothesis that might be tested in this way?

Latané and Darley had several possible choices for their dependent measure. One might have been a simple yes/no

RECAP/EVALUATE/RETHINK

RECAP

LO 3-1 What is the scientific method?

- The scientific method is the approach psychologists use to understand behavior. It consists of four steps: identifying questions of interest, formulating an explanation, carrying out research that is designed to support or refute the explanation, and communicating the findings.
- To test a hypothesis, researchers must formulate an operational definition, which translates the abstract concepts of the hypothesis into the actual procedures used in the study.

LO 3-2 What role do theories and hypotheses play in psychological research?

- Research in psychology is guided by theories (broad explanations and predictions regarding phenomena of interest) and hypotheses (theory-based predictions stated in a way that allows them to be tested).

LO 3-3 What research methods do psychologists use?

- Archival research uses existing records, such as old newspapers, online databases, or other documents, to test a hypothesis. In naturalistic observation, the investigator acts mainly as an observer, making no change in a naturally occurring situation. In survey research, people are asked a series of questions about their behavior, thoughts, or attitudes. The case study is an in-depth interview and examination of one person or group.
- These descriptive research methods rely on correlational techniques, which describe associations between variables but cannot determine cause-and-effect relationships.

LO 3-4 How do psychologists establish cause-and-effect relationships in research studies?

- In a formal experiment, the relationship between variables is investigated by deliberately producing a change–called the experimental manipulation–in one variable and observing changes in the other variable.
- In an experiment, at least two groups must be compared to assess cause-and-effect relationships. The group receiving the treatment (the special procedure devised by the experimenter) is the experimental group; the second group (which receives no treatment) is the control group. There also may be multiple experimental groups, each of which is subjected to a different procedure and then compared with the others.
- The variable that experimenters manipulate is the independent variable. The variable that they measure and expect to change as a result of manipulation of the independent variable is called the dependent variable.
- In a formal experiment, participants must be assigned randomly to treatment conditions, so that participant characteristics are distributed evenly across the different conditions.
- Psychologists use statistical tests to determine whether research findings are significant.

EVALUATE

1. An explanation for a phenomenon of interest is known as a ________.
2. To test this explanation, a researcher must state it in terms of a testable question known as a ________.
3. An experimenter is interested in studying the relationship between hunger and aggression. She decides that she will measure aggression by counting the number of times a participant will hit a punching bag. In this case, her ________ definition of aggression is the number of times the participant hits the bag.
4. Match the following forms of research to their definitions:

1. archival research	**a.** directly asking a sample of people questions about their behavior
2. naturalistic observation	**b.** examining existing records to test a hypothesis
3. survey research	**c.** looking at behavior in its true setting without intervening in the setting
4. case study	**d.** doing an in-depth investigation of a person or small group

5. Match each of the following research methods with its primary disadvantage:

1. archival research	**a.** The researcher may not be able to generalize to the population at large.
2. naturalistic observation	**b.** People's behavior can change if they know they are being watched.
3. survey research	**c.** The data may not exist or may be unusable.
4. case study	**d.** People may lie in order to present a good image.

6. A psychologist wants to study the effect of attractiveness on willingness to help a person with a math problem. Attractiveness would be the ________ variable, and the amount of helping would be the ________ variable.
7. The group in an experiment that receives no treatment is called the ________ group.

RETHINK

Starting with the theory that diffusion of responsibility causes responsibility for helping to be shared among bystanders, Latané and Darley derived the hypothesis that the more people who witness an emergency situation, the less likely it is that help will be given to a victim. Can you think of other hypotheses that are based on the same theory of diffusion of responsibility?

Answers to Evaluate Questions

1. theory; **2.** hypothesis; **3.** operational; **4.** 1-b, 2-c, 3-a, 4-d; **5.** 1-c, 2-b, 3-d, 4-a; **6.** independent, dependent; **7.** control

KEY TERMS

scientific method
theories
hypothesis
operational definition
archival research
naturalistic observation
survey research
case study
variables
correlational research
experiment
experimental manipulation
treatment
experimental group
control group
independent variable
dependent variable
random assignment to condition
significant outcome
replicated research

MODULE 4

Critical Research Issues

Learning Outcome

LO 4-1 What major issues confront psychologists conducting research?

Study Alert

Because the protection of experiment participants is essential, remember the key ethical guideline of informed consent.

You probably realize by now that there are few simple formulas for psychological research. Psychologists must make choices about the type of study to conduct, the measures to take, and the most effective way to analyze the results. Even after they have made these essential decisions, they must still consider several critical issues. We turn first to the most fundamental of these issues: ethics.

The Ethics of Research

Put yourself in the place of one of the participants in the experiment conducted by Latané and Darley to examine the helping behavior of bystanders, in which another "bystander" simulating a seizure turned out to be a confederate of the experimenters (Latané & Darley, 1970). How would you feel when you learned that the supposed victim was in reality a paid accomplice?

Although you might at first experience relief that there had been no real emergency, you might also feel some resentment that you had been deceived by the experimenter. You might also experience concern that you had been placed in an embarrassing or compromising situation–one that might have dealt a blow to your self-esteem, depending on how you had behaved.

Most psychologists argue that deception is sometimes necessary to prevent participants from being influenced by what they think a study's true purpose is. (If you knew that Latané and Darley were actually studying your helping behavior, wouldn't you automatically have been tempted to intervene in the emergency?) To avoid such outcomes, a small proportion of research involves deception.

Nonetheless, because research has the potential to violate the rights of participants, psychologists are expected to adhere to a strict set of ethical guidelines aimed at protecting participants (American Psychological Association, 2002). Those guidelines involve the following safeguards:

- Protection of participants from physical and mental harm.
- The right of participants to privacy regarding their behavior.
- The assurance that participation in research is completely voluntary.
- The necessity of informing participants about the nature of procedures before their participation in the experiment.
- All experiments must be reviewed by an independent panel before being conducted (Fisher et al., 2002; Fisher, 2003; Smith, 2003).

informed consent A document signed by participants affirming that they have been told the basic outlines of the study and are aware of what their participation will involve.

One of psychologists' key ethical principles is **informed consent.** Before participating in an experiment, the participants must sign a document affirming that they have been told the basic outlines of the study and are aware of what their participation will involve, what risks the experiment may hold, and the fact that their participation is purely voluntary and they may terminate it at any time. Furthermore, after participation in a study, they must be given a debriefing in which they receive an explanation of the study and the procedures that were involved. The only time informed consent and a debriefing can be eliminated is in experiments in which the

Although readily available and widely used as research subjects, college students may not represent the population at large. What are some advantages and drawbacks of using college students as subjects?

risks are minimal, as in a purely observational study in a public place (Koocher, Norcross, & Hill, 2005; Fallon, 2006; Barnett, Wise, & Johnson-Greene, 2007; Nagy, 2011).

Exploring DIVERSITY

Choosing Participants Who Represent the Scope of Human Behavior

When Latané and Darley, both college professors, decided who would participate in their experiment, they turned to the people at hand: college students. Using college students as participants has both advantages and drawbacks. The big benefit is that because most research occurs in university settings, college students are readily available. Typically, they cost the researcher very little: They participate for either extra course credit or a relatively small payment.

The problem is that college students may not represent the general population adequately. In fact, undergraduate research participants are typically a special group of people: Relative to the general population, college students tend to be from **W**estern, **e**ducated, **i**ndustrialized, **r**ich, and **d**emocratic cultures. That description forms the acronym WEIRD, which led one researcher to apply the nickname to research participants (Jones, 2010).

It's not that there's anything particularly wrong with WEIRD participants. It's just that they may be different from most other people—those who don't go to college or who didn't grow up in a democratic Western culture, who are less affluent, and so forth. All these characteristics could be psychologically relevant. Yet one review found that most research participants do come from the United States, and about the same proportion of those are psychology majors (Arnett, 2008; Henrich, Heine, & Norenzayan, 2010).

Because psychology is a science whose goal is to explain *all* human behavior generally, its studies must use participants who are fully representative of the general population in terms of gender, age, race, ethnicity, socioeconomic status, and educational level (see *Neuroscience in Your Life*). To encourage a wider range of participants, the National Institute of Mental Health and the National Science Foundation—the primary U.S. funding sources for psychological research—now require that experiments address issues of diverse populations (Carpenter, 2002; Lindley, 2006).

Neuroscience in Your Life: The Importance of Using Representative Participants

We often think of the brain working the same way for everyone, regardless of cultural background or the society in which people live. However, our culture, our experiences, and our individual circumstances shape how our brains function and react to the world. For example, in the fMRI images we see how Japanese as compared to Caucasian individuals process social interactions (in this case by watching videos of small geometric shapes "interacting" in ways that suggest they are reading each other's minds). While Japanese and Caucasian participants used the same kinds of vocabulary to describe the shapes and what was happening in the videos, their brains showed different activity, with Japanese individuals showing less activity in the prefrontal cortex than Caucasians show (activity here is seen in yellow). The findings of the study vividly remind us that fundamental biological processes—such as the basic functioning of the brain—may differ across cultures and that we need to be sure we have a representative sample of participants when drawing conclusions meant to apply to all people (Koelkebeck et al., 2011).

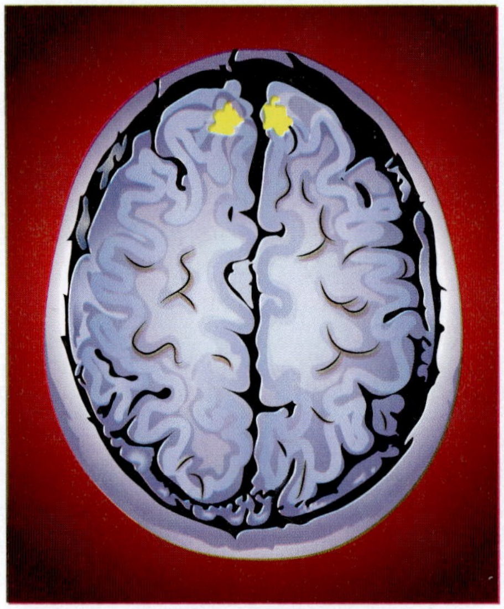

Caucasian Participants

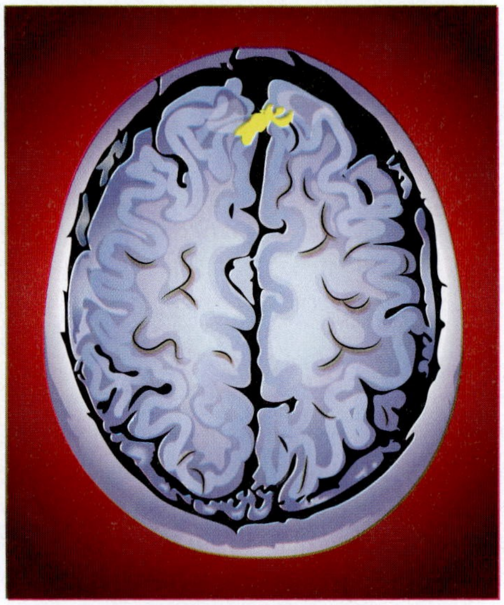

Japanese Participants

Should Animals Be Used in Research?

Like those who work with humans, researchers who use nonhuman animals in experiments have their own set of exacting guidelines to ensure that the animals do not suffer. Specifically, researchers must make every effort to minimize discomfort, illness, and pain. Procedures that subject animals to distress are permitted only when an alternative procedure is unavailable and when the research is justified by its prospective value. Moreover, researchers strive to avoid causing physical discomfort, but they are also required to promote the *psychological* well-being of some species of research animals, such as primates (Rusche, 2003; Lutz & Novak, 2005; Miller & Williams, 2011).

But why should animals be used for research in the first place? Is it really possible to learn about human behavior from the results of research employing rats, gerbils, and pigeons?

Research involving animals is controversial but when conducted within ethical guidelines yields significant benefits for humans.

The answer is that psychological research that does employ nonhumans is designed to answer questions different from those posed in research with humans. For example, the shorter life span of animals (rats live an average of 2 years) allows researchers to learn about the effects of aging in a relatively short time frame. It is also possible to provide greater experimental control over nonhumans and to carry out procedures that might not be possible with people. For example, some studies require large numbers of participants that share similar backgrounds or have been exposed to particular environments–conditions that could not practically be met with human beings.

Research with animals has provided psychologists with information that has profoundly benefited humans. For instance, it furnished the keys to detecting eye disorders in children early enough to prevent permanent damage, to communicating more effectively with severely retarded children, and to reducing chronic pain in people. Still, the use of research using nonhumans is controversial, involving complex moral and philosophical concerns. Consequently, all research involving non-humans must be carefully reviewed beforehand to ensure that it is conducted ethically (Hackam, 2007; Shankar & Simmons, 2009; Baker & Serdikoff, 2013).

Threats to Experimental Validity: Avoiding Experimental Bias

Even the best-laid experimental plans are susceptible to **experimental bias**–factors that distort the way the independent variable affects the dependent variable in an experiment. One of the most common forms of experimental bias is *experimenter expectations:* An experimenter unintentionally transmits cues to participants about the way they are expected to behave in a given experimental condition. The danger is that those expectations will bring about an "appropriate" behavior–one that otherwise might not have occurred (Rosenthal, 2002, 2003).

experimental bias Factors that distort how the independent variable affects the dependent variable in an experiment.

A related problem is *participant expectations* about appropriate behavior. If you have ever been a participant in an experiment, you probably developed guesses about what was expected of you. In fact, participants often develop their own hypotheses about what the experimenter hopes to learn from the study. If participants form their own hypotheses, and then act on their hunches, it may be their expectations, rather than the experimental manipulation, that produce the results (Rutherford et al., 2009).

Study Alert

Learn the main types of potential bias in experiments: experimenter expectations, participant expectations, and placebo effects.

Looking Back

Epilogue

In light of what you've already learned about the field of psychology, reconsider the Boston Marathon massacre described at the start of the chapter and answer the following questions:

1. Why do you think people find it surprising when someone who commits a terrible crime turns out to look like an ordinary person?
2. Tsarnaev's story illustrates how the complexity of human behavior cannot be easily addressed. What aspects might psychologists from each of the five major perspectives focus on?
3. How might a psychologist's position on the free will versus determinism issue influence his or her perception of Tsarnaev's crime?
4. What might be some ways in which both nature and nurture could have given rise to Tsarnaev's actions?
5. What aspects of the Boston Marathon bombing would most likely interest a clinical psychologist? A forensic psychologist? A social psychologist?

VISUAL SUMMARY 1 Introduction to Psychology

MODULE 1 Psychologists at Work

Subfields of Psychology

- Biological foundations
  - Behavioral neuroscience
- Sensing, perceiving, learning, and thinking
  - Experimental and cognitive psychology
- Sources of change and stability
  - Development and personality psychology
- Physical and mental health
  - Health, clinical, and counseling psychology
- Social networks
  - Social and cross-cultural psychology
- Expanding frontiers
  - Evolutionary psychology
  - Behavioral genetics
  - Clinical neuropsychology

Working at Psychology

Where U.S. psychologists work

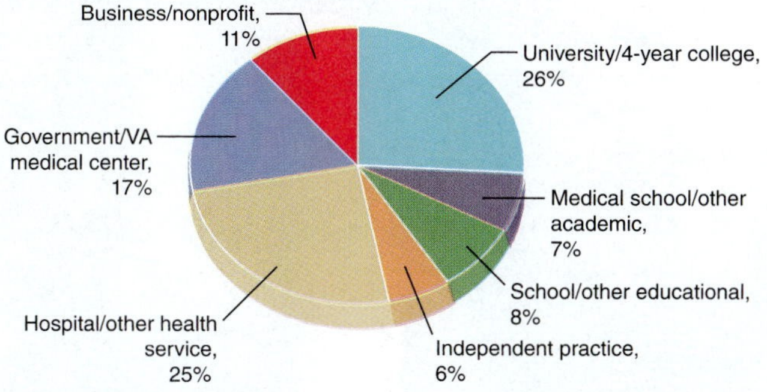

MODULE 2 A Science Evolves

Roots

- Structuralism
- Functionalism

Today's Perspectives: Five major perspectives

Neuroscience
Views behavior from the perspective of biological functioning

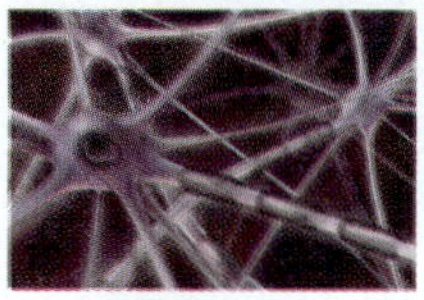

Behavioral
Focuses on observable behavior

Psychodynamic
Believes behavior is motivated by inner, unconscious forces over which a person has little control

Cognitive
Examines how people understand and think about the world

Humanistic
Contends that people can control their behavior and that they naturally try to reach their full potential

MODULE 3 Research in Psychology

Scientific Method

- Theories: Broad explanations
- Hypotheses: Testable predictions

Descriptive Research: Describes variables and does not explain causality

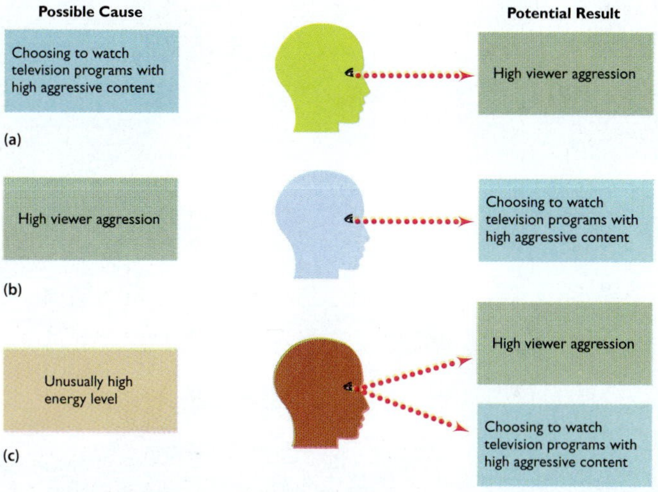

Experimental Research: Assesses cause-and-effect relationships between variables

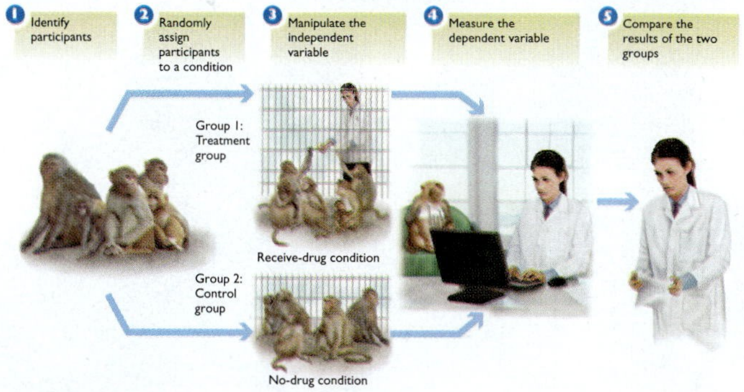

MODULE 4 Critical Research Issues

Ethics of Research

Informed consent

Animal Research

Has significantly benefited humans

Threats to Validity

- Experimental bias
- Participant and experimenter expectations

2 Neuroscience and Behavior

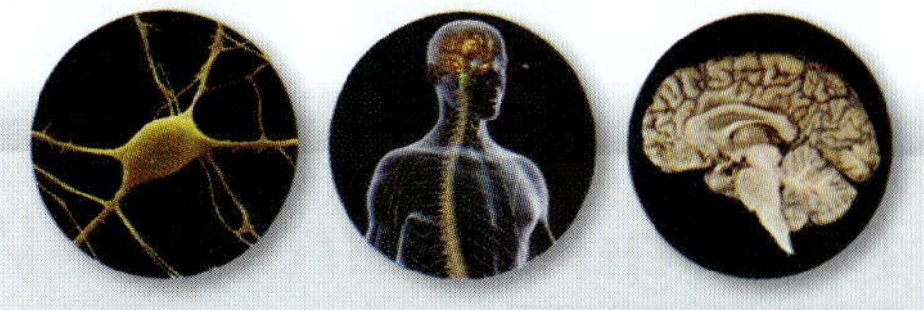

Learning Outcomes for Chapter 2

MODULE 5

LO 5-1 Why do psychologists study the brain and the nervous system?

LO 5-2 What are the basic elements of the nervous system?

LO 5-3 How does the nervous system communicate electrical and chemical messages from one part to another?

MODULE 6

LO 6-1 How are the structures of the nervous system linked?

LO 6-2 How does the endocrine system affect behavior?

MODULE 7

LO 7-1 How do researchers identify the major parts and functions of the brain?

LO 7-2 What are the major parts of the brain, and for what behaviors is each part responsible?

LO 7-3 How do the halves of the brain operate interdependently?

LO 7-4 How can an understanding of the nervous system help us find ways to alleviate disease and pain?

neurons where the axon of a sending neuron communicates with the dendrites of a receiving neuron by using chemical messages (Fanselow & Poulos, 2005; Dean & Dresbach, 2006).

When a nerve impulse comes to the end of the axon and reaches a terminal button, the terminal button releases a chemical courier called a neurotransmitter. **Neurotransmitters** are chemicals that carry messages across the synapse to a dendrite (and sometimes the cell body) of a receiving neuron. Like a boat that ferries passengers across a river, these chemical messengers move toward the shorelines of other neurons. The chemical mode of message transmission that occurs between neurons is strikingly different from the means by which communication occurs inside neurons: Although messages travel in electrical form *within* a neuron, they move *between* neurons through a chemical transmission system.

neurotransmitters Chemicals that carry messages across the synapse to the dendrite (and sometimes the cell body) of a receiver neuron.

Study Alert

Remember this key fact: Messages inside neurons are transmitted in electrical form, whereas messages traveling between neurons travel via chemical means.

There are several types of neurotransmitters, and not all neurons are capable of receiving the chemical message carried by a particular neurotransmitter. In the same way that a jigsaw puzzle piece can fit in only one specific location in a puzzle, each kind of neurotransmitter has a distinctive configuration that allows it to fit into a specific type of receptor site on the receiving neuron (see Figure 4b). It is only when a neurotransmitter fits precisely into a receptor site that successful chemical communication is possible.

If a neurotransmitter does fit into a site on the receiving neuron, the chemical message it delivers is basically one of two types: excitatory or inhibitory. **Excitatory messages** make it more likely that a receiving neuron will fire and an action potential will travel down its axon. **Inhibitory messages,** in contrast, do just the opposite; they provide chemical information that prevents or decreases the likelihood that the receiving neuron will fire.

excitatory message A chemical message that makes it more likely that a receiving neuron will fire and an action potential will travel down its axon.

inhibitory message A chemical message that prevents or decreases the likelihood that a receiving neuron will fire.

Because the dendrites of a neuron receive both excitatory and inhibitory messages simultaneously, the neuron must integrate the messages by using a kind of chemical calculator. Put simply, if the excitatory messages ("Fire!") outnumber the inhibitory ones ("Don't fire!"), the neuron fires. In contrast, if the inhibitory messages outnumber the excitatory ones, nothing happens, and the neuron remains in its resting state (Mel, 2002; Rapport, 2005; Flavell et al., 2006).

If neurotransmitters remained at the site of the synapse, receiving neurons would be awash in a continual chemical bath, producing constant stimulation or constant inhibition of the receiving neurons–and effective communication across the synapse would no longer be possible. To avoid this problem, neurotransmitters are either deactivated by enzymes or–more commonly–reabsorbed by the terminal button in an example of chemical recycling called **reuptake.** Like a vacuum cleaner sucking up dust, neurons reabsorb the neurotransmitters that are now clogging the synapse. All this activity occurs at lightning speed, with the process taking just several milliseconds (Helmuth, 2000; Holt & Jahn, 2004).

reuptake The reabsorption of neurotransmitters by a terminal button.

Our understanding of the process of reuptake has permitted the development of a number of drugs used in the treatment of psychological disorders. Some antidepressant drugs, called *SSRIs,* or *selective serotonin reuptake inhibitors,* permit certain neurotransmitters to remain active for a longer period at certain synapses in the brain, thereby reducing the symptoms of depression (Ramos, 2006; Guiard et al., 2011; Hilton et al., 2013).

Neurotransmitters: Multitalented Chemical Couriers

Neurotransmitters are a particularly important link between the nervous system and behavior. Not only are they important for maintaining vital brain and body functions, a deficiency or an excess of a neurotransmitter can produce severe behavior disorders. More than a hundred chemicals have been found to act as neurotransmitters, and neuroscientists believe that more may ultimately be identified. The major neurotransmitters and their effects are described in Figure 5 (Penney, 2000; Schmidt, 2006).

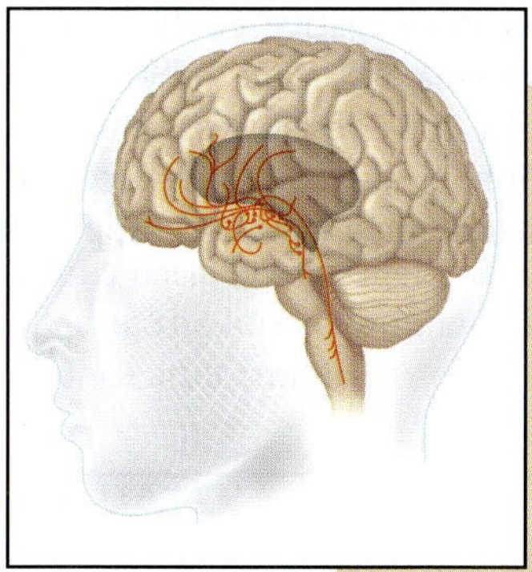

Dopamine pathways

Serotonin pathways

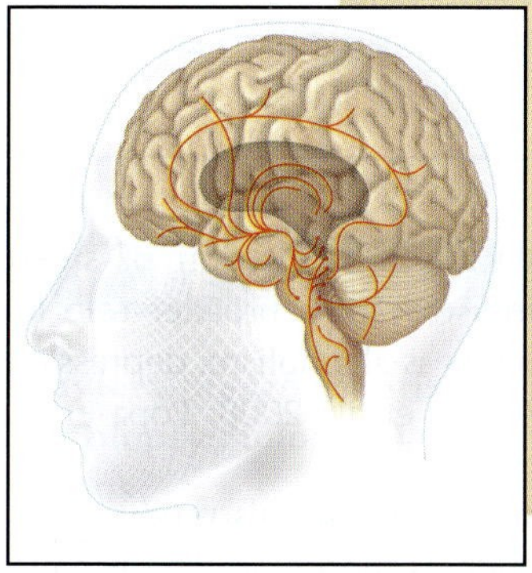

Neurotransmitter Name	Location	Effect	Function
Acetylcholine (ACh)	Brain, spinal cord, peripheral nervous system, especially some organs of the parasympathetic nervous system	Excitatory in brain and autonomic nervous system; inhibitory elsewhere	Muscle movement, cognitive functioning
Glutamate	Brain, spinal cord	Excitatory	Memory
Gamma-amino butyric acid (GABA)	Brain, spinal cord	Main inhibitory neurotransmitter	Eating, aggression, sleeping
Dopamine (DA)	Brain	Inhibitory or excitatory	Movement control, pleasure and reward, attention
Serotonin	Brain, spinal cord	Inhibitory	Sleeping, eating, mood, pain, depression
Endorphins	Brain, spinal cord	Primarily inhibitory, except in hippocampus	Pain suppression, pleasurable feelings, appetites, placebos

FIGURE 5 Major neurotransmitters.

One of the most common neurotransmitters is *acetylcholine* (or *ACh,* its chemical symbol), which is found throughout the nervous system. ACh is involved in our every move, because–among other things–it transmits messages relating to our skeletal muscles. ACh is also involved in memory capabilities, and diminished production of ACh may be related to Alzheimer's disease (Mohapel et al., 2005; Bazalakova et al., 2007; Van der Zee, Platt, & Riedel, 2011).

Another common excitatory neurotransmitter, *glutamate,* plays a role in memory. Memories appear to be produced by specific biochemical changes at particular synapses, and glutamate, along with other neurotransmitters, plays an important role in this process (Riedel, Platt, & Micheau, 2003; Winters & Bussey, 2005; Micheau & Marighetto, 2011).

Gamma-amino butyric acid (GABA), which is found in both the brain and the spinal cord, appears to be the nervous system's primary inhibitory neurotransmitter. It moderates a variety of behaviors, ranging from eating to aggression. Several common substances, such as the tranquilizer Valium and alcohol, are effective because they permit GABA to operate more efficiently (Ball, 2004; Criswell et al., 2008; Lobo & Harris, 2008).

Another major neurotransmitter is *dopamine (DA),* which is involved in movement, attention, and learning. The discovery that certain drugs can have a significant effect on dopamine release has led to the development of effective treatments for a wide variety of physical and mental ailments. For instance, Parkinson's disease, from which actor Michael J. Fox suffers among others, is caused by a deficiency of dopamine in the brain. Techniques for increasing the production of dopamine in Parkinson's patients are proving effective (Willis, 2005; Iversen & Iversen, 2007; Antonini & Barone, 2008).

Michael J. Fox suffers from Parkinson's disease, and he has become a strong advocate for research into the disorder.

Over millions of years, the spinal cord became more specialized, and organisms became capable of distinguishing between different kinds of stimuli and responding appropriately to them. Ultimately, a portion of the spinal cord evolved into what we would consider a primitive brain.

Today, the nervous system is *hierarchically organized,* meaning that relatively newer (from an evolutionary point of view) and more sophisticated regions of the brain regulate the older, and more primitive, parts of the nervous system. As we move up along the spinal cord and continue upward into the brain, then, the functions controlled by the various regions become progressively more advanced.

Why should we care about the evolutionary background of the human nervous system? The answer comes from researchers working in the area of **evolutionary psychology,** the branch of psychology that seeks to identify how behavior is influenced and produced by our genetic inheritance from our ancestors.

evolutionary psychology The branch of psychology that seeks to identify behavior patterns that are a result of our genetic inheritance from our ancestors.

Evolutionary psychologists argue that the course of evolution is reflected in the structure and functioning of the nervous system and that evolutionary factors consequently have a significant influence on our everyday behavior. Their work, in conjunction with the research of scientists studying genetics, biochemistry, and medicine, has led to an understanding of how our behavior is affected by heredity, our genetically determined heritage.

Evolutionary psychologists have spawned a new and increasingly influential field: behavioral genetics. As we will discuss further in the chapter on development, **behavioral genetics** is the study of the effects of heredity on behavior. Consistent with the evolutionary perspective, behavioral genetics researchers are finding increasing evidence that cognitive abilities, personality traits, sexual orientation, and psychological disorders are determined to some extent by genetic factors (Livesley & Jang, 2008; Vernon et al., 2008; Schermer et al., 2011; Maxson, 2013).

behavioral genetics The study of the effects of heredity on behavior.

The Endocrine System: Of Chemicals and Glands

Another of the body's communication systems, the **endocrine system** is a chemical communication network that sends messages throughout the body via the bloodstream. Its job is to secrete **hormones,** chemicals that circulate through the blood and regulate the functioning or growth of the body. It also influences—and is influenced by—the functioning of the nervous system. Although the endocrine system is not part of the brain, it is closely linked to the hypothalamus.

endocrine system A chemical communication network that sends messages throughout the body via the bloodstream.

hormones Chemicals that circulate through the blood and regulate the functioning or growth of the body.

As chemical messengers, hormones are like neurotransmitters, although their speed and mode of transmission are quite different. Whereas neural messages are measured in thousandths of a second, hormonal communications may take minutes to reach their destination. Furthermore, neural messages move through neurons in specific lines (like a signal carried by wires strung along telephone poles), whereas hormones travel throughout the body, similar to the way radio waves are transmitted across the entire landscape. Just as radio waves evoke a response only when a radio is tuned to the correct station, hormones flowing through the bloodstream activate only those cells that are receptive and "tuned" to the appropriate hormonal message.

A key component of the endocrine system is the tiny **pituitary gland,** which is found near—and regulated by—the hypothalamus in the brain. The pituitary gland has sometimes been called the "master gland" because it controls the functioning of the rest of the endocrine system. But the pituitary gland is more than just the taskmaster of other glands; it has important functions in its own right. For instance, hormones secreted by the pituitary gland control growth. Extremely short people and unusually tall ones usually have pituitary gland abnormalities. Other endocrine glands, shown in Figure 4, affect emotional reactions, sexual urges, and energy levels.

pituitary gland The major component of the endocrine system, or "master gland," which secretes hormones that control growth and other parts of the endocrine system.

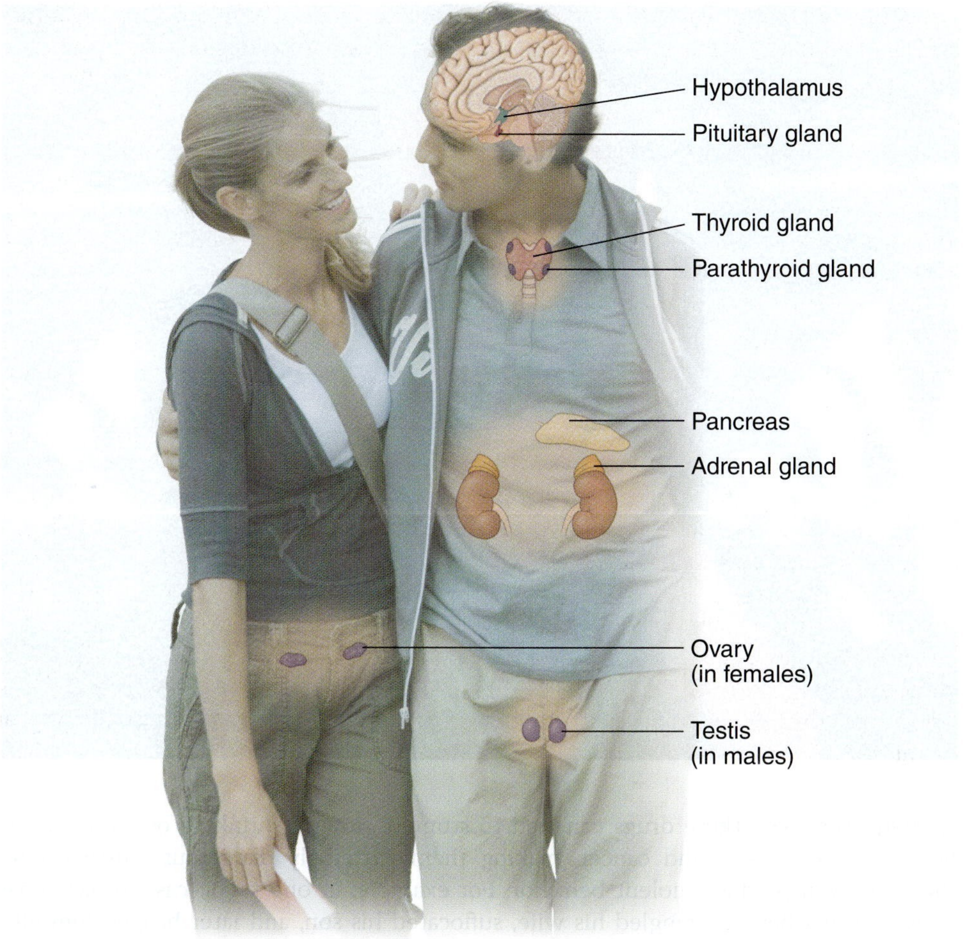

FIGURE 4 Location and function of the major endocrine glands. The pituitary gland controls the functioning of the other endocrine glands and, in turn, is regulated by the hypothalamus.

Despite its designation as the "master gland," the pituitary is actually a servant of the brain, because the brain is ultimately responsible for the endocrine system's functioning. The brain maintains the internal balance of the body through the hypothalamus.

Individual hormones can wear many hats, depending on circumstances. For example, the hormone oxytocin is at the root of many of life's satisfactions and pleasures. In new mothers, oxytocin produces an urge to nurse newborn offspring. The same hormone also seems to stimulate cuddling between species members. And–at least in rats–it encourages sexually active males to seek out females more passionately, and females to be more receptive to males' sexual advances. There's even evidence that oxytocin is related to the development of trust in others, helping to grease the wheels of effective social interaction (Meinlschmidt & Heim, 2007; Guastella, Mitchell, & Dadds, 2008; De Dreu et al., 2011).

Although hormones are produced naturally by the endocrine system, the ingestion of artificial hormones has proved to be both beneficial and potentially dangerous. For example, before the early 2000s, physicians frequently prescribed hormone replacement therapy (HRT) to treat symptoms of menopause in older women. However, because recent research suggests that the treatment has potentially dangerous side effects, health experts now warn that in many cases the dangers outweigh the benefits (Alexandersen, Karsdal, & Christiansen, 2009; Jacobs et al., 2013).

The use of testosterone, a male hormone, and drugs known as *steroids*, which act like testosterone, is increasingly common. For athletes and others who want to bulk up their appearance, steroids provide a way to add muscle weight and increase

Study Alert

The endocrine system produces hormones, chemicals that circulate through the body via the bloodstream.

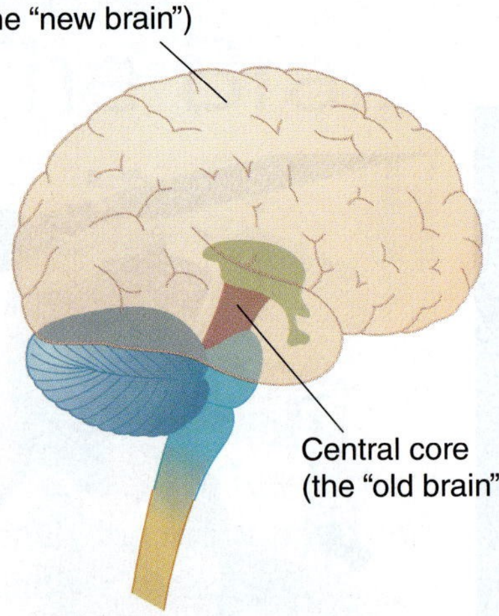

FIGURE 2 The major divisions of the brain: the cerebral cortex and the central core.

interruption on normal brain functioning. The procedure is sometimes called a "virtual lesion," because it produces effects analogous to what would occur if areas of the brain were physically cut. The enormous advantage of TMS, of course, is that the virtual cut is only temporary. In addition to identifying areas of the brain that are responsible for particular functions, TMS has the potential to treat certain kinds of psychological disorders, such as depression and schizophrenia, by shooting brief magnetic pulses through the brain (Fitzgerald & Daskalakis, 2008; Rado, Dowd, & Janicak, 2008; Pallanti & Bernardi, 2009).

Future discoveries may yield even more sophisticated methods of examining the brain. For example, the emerging field of *optogenetics* involves genetic engineering and the use of special types of light to view individual circuits of neurons (Miesenbock, 2008; Gradinaru et al., 2009; Iwai et al., 2011).

Advances in our understanding of the brain also are paving the way for the development of new methods for harnessing the brain's neural signals. We consider some of these intriguing findings in *Applying Psychology in the 21st Century*.

The Central Core: Our "Old Brain"

central core The "old brain," which controls basic functions such as eating and sleeping and is common to all vertebrates.

Although the capabilities of the human brain far exceed those of the brain of any other species, humans share some basic functions, such as breathing, eating, and sleeping, with more primitive animals. Not surprisingly, those activities are directed by a relatively primitive part of the brain. A portion of the brain known as the **central core** (see Figure 2) is quite similar in all vertebrates (species with backbones). The central core is sometimes referred to as the "old brain," because its evolution can be traced back some 500 million years to primitive structures found in nonhuman species.

If we were to move up the spinal cord from the base of the skull to locate the structures of the central core of the brain, the first part we would come to would be the *hindbrain,* which contains the medulla, pons, and cerebellum (see Figure 3). The *medulla* controls a number of critical body functions, the most important of which are breathing and heartbeat. The *pons* is a bridge in the hindbrain. Containing large bundles of nerves, the pons acts as a transmitter of motor information, coordinating muscles and integrating movement between the right and left halves of the body. It is also involved in regulating sleep.

cerebellum (ser-uh-BELL-um) The part of the brain that controls bodily balance.

The **cerebellum** extends from the rear of the hindbrain. Without the help of the cerebellum we would be unable to walk a straight line without staggering and lurching forward, for it is the job of the cerebellum to control bodily balance. It constantly monitors feedback from the muscles to coordinate their placement, movement, and tension. In fact, drinking too much alcohol seems to depress the activity of the cerebellum, leading to the unsteady gait and movement characteristic of drunkenness. The cerebellum is also involved in several intellectual functions, ranging from the analysis and coordination of sensory information to problem solving (Paquier & Mariën, 2005; Vandervert, Schimpf, & Liu, 2007; Swain, Kerr, & Thompson, 2011).

reticular formation The part of the brain extending from the medulla through the pons; it is related to changes in the level of arousal of the body.

The **reticular formation** extends from the medulla through the pons, passing through the middle section of the brain—or *midbrain*—and into the front-most part of the brain, called the *forebrain.* Like an ever-vigilant guard, the reticular formation produces general arousal of our body. If, for example, we are startled by a loud noise, the reticular formation can prompt a heightened state of awareness to determine whether a response is necessary. The reticular formation also helps regulate our sleep-wake cycle by filtering out background stimuli to allow us to sleep undisturbed.

thalamus The part of the brain located in the middle of the central core that acts primarily to relay information about the senses.

Hidden within the forebrain, the **thalamus** acts primarily as a relay station for information about the senses. Messages from the eyes, ears, and skin travel to the thalamus to be communicated upward to higher parts of the brain. The thalamus also integrates information from higher parts of the brain, sorting it out so that it can be sent to the cerebellum and medulla.

Applying Psychology in the 21st Century

Mind Over Cursor: Harnessing Brainpower to Improve Lives

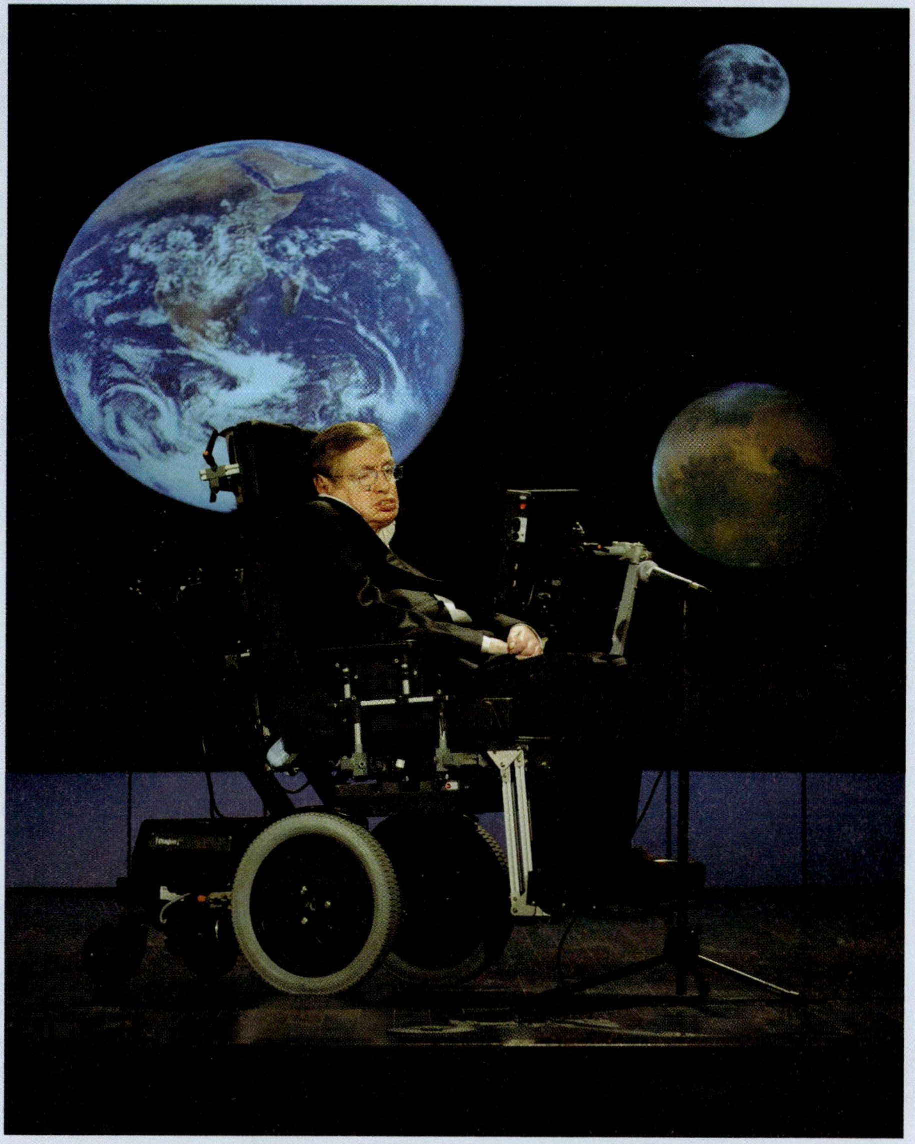

For Stephen Hawking, world-renowned physicist, time is running out. Now in his 70s, Hawking suffers from amyotrophic lateral sclerosis, or Lou Gehrig's disease. The illness has paralyzed his body and has left him unable to move, eat, or speak on his own. Although his mind still functions normally, his ability to communicate is extremely limited.

That may change, however, as neuroscientists develop increasingly sophisticated devices to facilitate communication. Hawking has been testing the iBrain, a brain-scanning device that employs a headband and an extremely lightweight sensor the size of a small matchbox. The iBrain uses a single channel to detect waves of electrical brain activity.

To test the device, Hawking was asked to wear the headband and to imagine that he was making a fist. Although he was physically unable to carry out the command, the neurons in his brain reacted and triggered a series of brain waves that the iBrain could sense. The iBrain could "read" those commands and produced a series of spikes on a graph. This is just a first step in moving toward real communication, but it holds great promise for people with spinal cord injuries and diseases that have left them paralyzed (Duncan, 2012; Genzlinger, 2013).

Other advances are showing how the innermost workings of the brain can be harnessed. Consider, for example, a man in his 20s who had a severe form of epilepsy. As part of his treatment, surgeons inserted a group of electrodes, called an *electrocorticographic* (ECoG) *implant*, on top of his brain's cortex to help control the severe seizures he was experiencing. But the ECoG implant did more than alleviate the seizures: Research scientists were able to teach him to control activities on a computer via the implant in his brain. Remarkably, he was able to use only his thoughts to play the video game "Galaga," moving a spaceship back and forth and shooting at menacing creatures on the screen (Kennedy, 2011; Leuthardt et al., 2011; Leuthardt et al., 2013).

Although the ability to play video games mentally may seem like a trivial advance, the accomplishment holds serious implications for future advances. It ultimately may permit people to "speak" using only their neurons. For example, we might think of a dog and immediately see the word *dog* appear on a video screen (Kennedy, 2011).

Neuroscience researchers are making significant progress at developing the technology of thought-based interfaces. Though many hurdles remain before paralyzed people will be using thought-controlled devices routinely, researchers are making inroads into this technology (Genzlinger, 2013).

RETHINK

- What would be required to make brain wave communication two-way instead of only one-way?
- What implications would there be if people gained the ability to communicate with each other in this way?

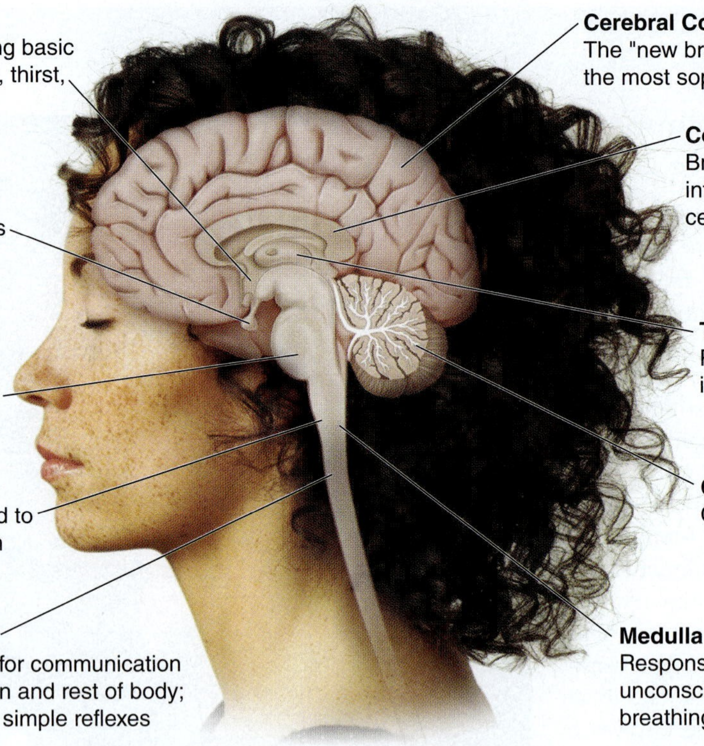

FIGURE 3 The major structures in the brain. (Source: Adapted from Bloom, 1975.)

hypothalamus A tiny part of the brain, located below the thalamus, that maintains homeostasis and produces and regulates vital behavior, such as eating, drinking, and sexual behavior.

The **hypothalamus** is located just below the thalamus. Although tiny–about the size of a fingertip–the hypothalamus plays an extremely important role. One of its major functions is to maintain *homeostasis,* a steady internal environment for the body. The hypothalamus helps provide a constant body temperature and monitors the amount of nutrients stored in the cells. A second major function is equally important: the hypothalamus produces and regulates behavior that is critical to the basic survival of the species, such as eating, self-protection, and sex.

The Limbic System: Beyond the Central Core

In an eerie view of the future, science fiction writers have suggested that people someday will routinely have electrodes implanted in their brains. Those electrodes will permit them to receive tiny shocks that will produce the sensation of pleasure by stimulating certain centers of the brain. When they feel upset, people will simply activate their electrodes to achieve an immediate high.

Although far-fetched–and ultimately improbable–such a futuristic fantasy is based on fact. The brain does have pleasure centers in several areas, including some in the **limbic system.** Consisting of a series of doughnut-shaped structures that include the *amygdala* and *hippocampus,* the limbic system borders the top of the central core and has connections with the cerebral cortex (see Figure 4).

limbic system The part of the brain that controls eating, aggression, and reproduction.

The structures of the limbic system jointly control a variety of basic functions relating to emotions and self-preservation, such as eating, aggression, and reproduction. Injury to the limbic system can produce striking changes in behavior. For example, injury to the amygdala, which is involved in fear and aggression, can turn animals that are usually docile and tame into belligerent savages. Conversely, animals that are usually wild and uncontrollable may become meek and obedient following injury to the amygdala (Bedard & Persinger, 1995; Gontkovsky, 2005; Smith et al., 2013).

Research examining the effects of mild electric shocks to parts of the limbic system and other parts of the brain has produced some thought-provoking findings. In one experiment, rats that pressed a bar received mild electric stimulation through an electrode implanted in their brains, which produced pleasurable feelings. Even starving rats on their way to food would stop to press the bar as many times as they could. Some rats would actually stimulate themselves literally thousands of times an hour–until they collapsed with fatigue (Routtenberg & Lindy, 1965; Olds & Fobes, 1981; Fountas & Smith, 2007).

Some humans have also experienced the extraordinarily pleasurable quality of certain kinds of stimulation: As part of the treatment for certain kinds of brain disorders, some people have received electrical stimulation to certain areas of the limbic system. Although at a loss to describe just what it feels like, these people report the experience to be intensely pleasurable, similar in some respects to sexual orgasm.

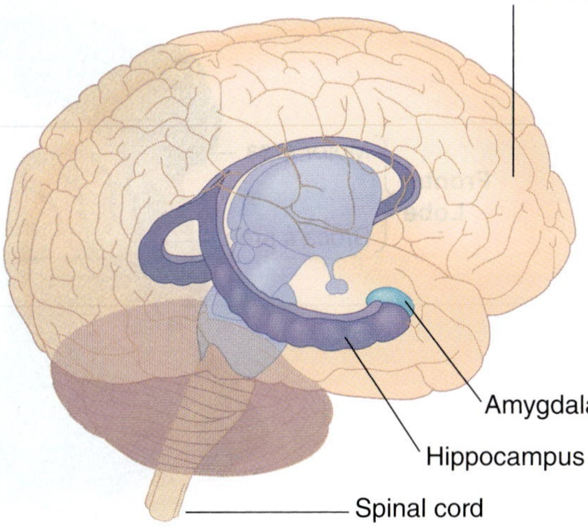

FIGURE 4 The limbic system is involved in self-preservation, learning, memory, and the experience of pleasure.

The limbic system and hippocampus, in particular, play an important role in learning and memory. Their importance is demonstrated in certain patients with epilepsy, who, in an effort to stop their seizures, have had portions of the limbic system removed. One unintended consequence of the surgery is that individuals sometimes have difficulty learning and remembering new information. In one case, a patient who had undergone surgery was unable to remember where he lived, although he had resided at the same address for 8 years. Further, even though the patient was able to carry on animated conversations, he was unable, a few minutes later, to recall what had been discussed (Milner, 1966; Rich & Shapiro, 2007; Grimm, 2011).

The limbic system, then, is involved in several important functions, including self-preservation, learning, memory, and the experience of pleasure. These functions are hardly unique to humans; in fact, the limbic system is sometimes referred to as the "animal brain," because its structures and functions are so similar to those of other mammals. To identify the part of the brain that provides the complex and subtle capabilities that are uniquely human, we need to turn to another structure–the cerebral cortex.

The Cerebral Cortex: Our "New Brain"

As we have proceeded up the spinal cord and into the brain, our discussion has centered on areas of the brain that control functions similar to those found in less sophisticated organisms. But where, you may be asking, are the portions of the brain that enable humans to do what they do best and that distinguish humans from all other animals? Those unique features of the human brain–indeed, the very capabilities that allow you to come up with such a question in the first place–are embodied in the ability to think, evaluate, and make complex judgments. The principal location of these abilities, along with many others, is the **cerebral cortex.**

cerebral cortex The "new brain," responsible for the most sophisticated information processing in the brain; contains four lobes.

The cerebral cortex is referred to as the "new brain" because of its relatively recent evolution. It consists of a mass of deeply folded, rippled, convoluted tissue. Although only about 1⁄12 of an inch thick, it would, if flattened out, cover an area more than 2 feet square. This configuration allows the surface area of the cortex to be considerably greater than it would be if it were smoother and more uniformly packed into the skull. The uneven shape also permits a high level of integration of neurons, allowing sophisticated information processing.

3 Sensation and Perception

Learning Outcomes for Chapter 3

MODULE 8

LO 8-1 What is sensation, and how do psychologists study it?

LO 8-2 What is the relationship between a physical stimulus and the kinds of sensory responses that result from it?

Sensing the World Around Us

Absolute Thresholds: Detecting What's Out There

Difference Thresholds: Noticing Distinctions Between Stimuli

Sensory Adaptation: Turning Down Our Responses

MODULE 9

LO 9-1 What basic processes underlie the sense of vision?

LO 9-2 How do we see colors?

Vision: Shedding Light on the Eye

Illuminating the Structure of the Eye

Color Vision and Color Blindness: The 7-Million-Color Spectrum

MODULE 10

LO 10-1 What role does the ear play in the senses of sound, motion, and balance?

LO 10-2 How do smell and taste function?

LO 10-3 What are the skin senses, and how do they relate to the experience of pain?

Hearing and the Other Senses

Sensing Sound

Smell and Taste

The Skin Senses: Touch, Pressure, Temperature, and Pain

Becoming an Informed Consumer of Psychology: Managing Pain

How Our Senses Interact

Neuroscience in Your Life: Synesthesia and the Overconnected Brain

MODULE 11

LO 11-1 What principles underlie our organization of the visual world and allow us to make sense of our environment?

LO 11-2 How are we able to perceive the world in three dimensions when our retinas are capable of sensing only two-dimensional images?

LO 11-3 What clues do visual illusions give us about our understanding of general perceptual mechanisms?

Perceptual Organization: Constructing Our View of the World

The Gestalt Laws of Organization

Top-Down and Bottom-Up Processing

Depth Perception: Translating 2-D to 3-D

Perceptual Constancy

Motion Perception: As the World Turns

Applying Psychology in the 21st Century: Study-Break Soundtrack

Perceptual Illusions: The Deceptions of Perceptions

Exploring Diversity: Culture and Perception

Prologue *Never Forgetting a Face*

She never forgets a face. Literally. For a woman known as C.S., remembering people is not a problem. In fact, she—like a very few other individuals—can remember faces of people she met years ago, sometimes only in passing. These *super-recognizers,* as they are called, excel at recalling faces. One super-recognizer said she had identified a woman on the street who had been her waitress five years earlier in a different city. Often, super-recognizers are able to recognize another person despite significant changes in that person's appearance, such as aging or a different hair color.

But being a super-recognizer is a mixed blessing. As one woman with this ability says, "It doesn't matter how many years pass, if I've seen your face before I will be able to recall it." In fact, she sometimes pretends she doesn't remember a person, "because it seems like I stalk them, or that they mean more to me than they do when I recall that we saw each other once walking on campus four years ago in front of the quad!" (Munger, 2009; Russell, Duchaine, & Nakayma, 2009).

Looking Ahead

Most of us are reasonably good at recognizing people's faces, thanks in part to regions of the brain that specialize in detecting facial patterns. Super-recognizers represent a small minority of people who happen to be exceptionally good at facial recognition. At the other extreme are people with *faceblindness,* a rare disorder that makes it extremely difficult for them to recognize faces at all—even those of friends and family.

Disorders such as super-recognition and faceblindness illustrate how much we depend on our senses to function normally. Our senses offer a window to the world, not only providing us with an awareness, understanding, and appreciation of the world's beauty, but alerting us to its dangers. Our senses enable us to feel the gentlest of breezes, see flickering lights miles away, and hear the soft murmuring of distant songbirds.

In the upcoming modules, we focus on the field of psychology that is concerned with the ways our bodies take in information through the senses and the ways we interpret that information. We explore both sensation and perception. *Sensation* encompasses the processes by which our sense organs receive information from the environment. *Perception* is the brain's and the sense organs' sorting out, interpretation, analysis, and integration of stimuli.

Although perception clearly represents a step beyond sensation, in practice it is sometimes difficult to find the precise boundary between the two. Indeed, psychologists—and philosophers as well—have argued for years over the distinction. The primary difference is that sensation can be thought of as an organism's first encounter with a raw sensory stimulus, whereas perception is the process by which it interprets, analyzes, and integrates that stimulus with other sensory information.

For example, if we were considering sensation, we might ask about the loudness of a ringing fire alarm. If we were considering perception, we might ask whether someone recognizes the ringing sound as an alarm and identifies its meaning.

To a psychologist interested in understanding the causes of behavior, sensation and perception are fundamental topics, because so much of our behavior is a reflection of how we react to and interpret stimuli from the world around us. The areas of sensation and perception deal with a wide range of questions—among them, how we respond to the characteristics of physical stimuli; what processes enable us to see, hear, and experience pain; why visual illusions fool us; and how we distinguish one person from another. As we explore these issues, we'll see how the senses work together to provide us with an integrated view and understanding of the world.

MODULE 8

Sensing the World Around Us

Learning Outcomes

LO 8-1 What is sensation, and how do psychologists study it?

LO 8-2 What is the relationship between a physical stimulus and the kinds of sensory responses that result from it?

As Isabel sat down to Thanksgiving dinner, her father carried the turkey in on a tray and placed it squarely in the center of the table. The noise level, already high from the talking and laughter of family members, grew louder still. As Isabel picked up her fork, the smell of the turkey reached her and she felt her stomach growl hungrily. The sight and sound of her family around the table, along with the smells and tastes of the holiday meal, made Isabel feel more relaxed than she had since starting school in the fall.

Put yourself in this setting and consider how different it might be if any one of your senses were not functioning. What if you were blind and unable to see the faces of your family members or the welcome shape of the golden-brown turkey? What if you had no sense of hearing and could not listen to the conversations of family members or were unable to feel your stomach growl, smell the dinner, or taste the food? Clearly, you would experience the dinner very differently from someone whose sensory apparatus was intact.

Moreover, the sensations mentioned above barely scratch the surface of sensory experience. Although perhaps you were taught, as I was, that there are just five senses—sight, sound, taste, smell, and touch—that enumeration is too modest. Human sensory capabilities go well beyond the basic five senses. For example, we are sensitive not merely to touch but to a considerably wider set of stimuli—pain, pressure, temperature, and vibration, to name a few. In addition, vision has two subsystems—relating to day and night vision—and the ear is responsive to information that allows us not only to hear but also to keep our balance.

Study Alert

Remember that *sensation* refers to the activation of the sense organs (a physical response), whereas *perception* refers to how stimuli are interpreted (a psychological response).

To consider how psychologists understand the senses and, more broadly, sensation and perception, we first need a basic working vocabulary. In formal terms, **sensation** is the activation of the sense organs by a source of physical energy. **Perception** is the sorting out, interpretation, analysis, and integration of stimuli carried out by the sense organs and brain. A **stimulus** is any passing source of physical energy that produces a response in a sense organ.

sensation The activation of the sense organs by a source of physical energy.

perception The sorting out, interpretation, analysis, and integration of stimuli by the sense organs and brain.

stimulus Energy that produces a response in a sense organ.

Stimuli vary in both type and intensity. Different types of stimuli activate different sense organs. For instance, we can differentiate light stimuli (which activate the sense of sight and allow us to see the colors of a tree in autumn) from sound stimuli (which, through the sense of hearing, permit us to hear the sounds of an orchestra). In addition, stimuli differ in intensity, relating to how strong a stimulus needs to be before it can be detected.

Questions of stimulus type and intensity are considered in a branch of psychology known as psychophysics. **Psychophysics** is the study of the relationship between the physical aspects of stimuli and our psychological experience of them. Psychophysics played a central role in the development of the field of psychology. Many of the first psychologists studied issues related to psychophysics, and there is still an active group of psychophysics researchers (Gardner, 2005; Hock & Ploeger, 2006; Bonezzi, Brendl, & De Angelis, 2011).

psychophysics The study of the relationship between the physical aspects of stimuli and our psychological experience of them.

Absolute Thresholds: Detecting What's Out There

absolute threshold The smallest intensity of a stimulus that must be present for the stimulus to be detected.

Just when does a stimulus become strong enough to be detected by our sense organs? The answer to this question requires an understanding of the concept of absolute threshold. An **absolute threshold** is the smallest intensity of a stimulus that must be present for it to be detected (Aazh & Moore, 2007).

Despite the "absolute" in absolute threshold, things are not so cut-and-dried. As the strength of a stimulus increases, the likelihood that it will be detected increases gradually. Technically, then, an absolute threshold is the stimulus intensity that is detected 50% of the time.

It often takes a very small stimulus to produce a response in our senses. For example, the sense of touch is so sensitive that we can feel a bee's wing falling on our cheeks when it is dropped from a distance of 1 centimeter. Test your knowledge of the absolute thresholds of other senses by completing the questionnaire in Figure 1.

In fact, our senses are so fine-tuned that we might have problems if they were any more sensitive. For instance, if our ears were slightly more acute, we would be able to hear the sound of air molecules in our ears knocking into the eardrum—a phenomenon that would surely prove distracting and might even prevent us from hearing sounds outside our bodies.

Of course, the absolute thresholds we have been discussing are measured under ideal conditions. Normally our senses cannot detect stimulation quite as well because of the presence of noise. *Noise,* as defined by psychophysicists, is background stimulation that interferes with the perception of other stimuli. Hence, noise refers not just to auditory stimuli, as the word suggests, but also to unwanted stimuli that interfere with other senses.

For example, picture a talkative group of people crammed into a small, crowded room at a party. The din of the crowd makes it hard to hear individual voices. In this

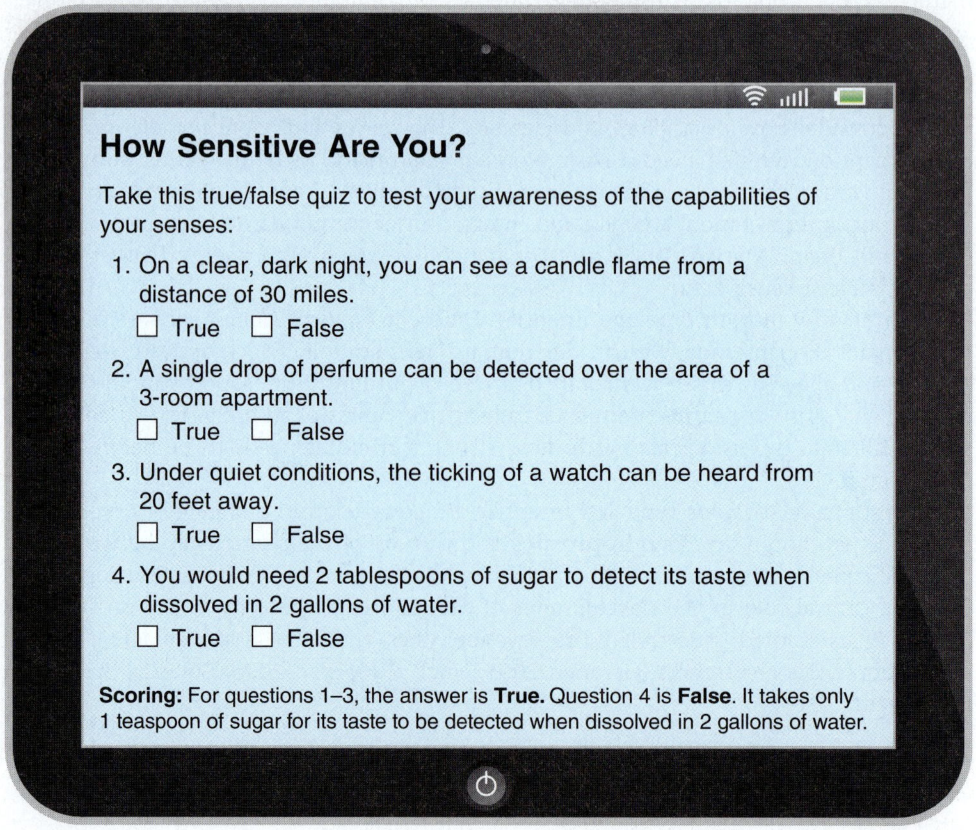

FIGURE 1 This test can shed some light on how sensitive the human senses are. (Source: Galanter, 1962.)

Crowded conditions, sounds, and sights can all be considered as noise that interferes with sensation. Can you think of other examples of noise that is not auditory in nature?

case, the crowded conditions would be considered "noise," because it is preventing sensation at more discriminating levels. Similarly, we have limited ability to concentrate on several stimuli simultaneously.

PsychTech

Our inability to focus on multiple stimuli simultaneously is the reason why texting while driving is so dangerous. One study mounted video cameras inside trucks and found that truckers were 23 times more likely to be in a collision while texting than while not texting.

Difference Thresholds: Noticing Distinctions Between Stimuli

Suppose you wanted to choose the six best apples from a supermarket display–the biggest, reddest, and sweetest apples. One approach would be to compare one apple with another systematically until you were left with a few so similar that you could not tell the difference between them. At that point, it wouldn't matter which ones you chose.

Psychologists have discussed this comparison problem in terms of the **difference threshold,** the smallest level of added (or reduced) stimulation required to sense that a *change* in stimulation has occurred. Thus, the difference threshold is the minimum change in stimulation required to detect the difference between two stimuli, and so it also is called a **just noticeable difference** (Nittrouer & Lowenstein, 2007).

difference threshold (just noticeable difference) The smallest level of added or reduced stimulation required to sense that a change in stimulation has occurred.

The size of a stimulus that constitutes a just noticeable difference depends on the initial intensity of the stimulus. The relationship between changes in the original size of a stimulus and the degree to which a change will be noticed forms one of the basic laws of psychophysics: Weber's law. **Weber's law** (*Weber* is pronounced "VAY-ber") states that a just noticeable difference is a *constant proportion* of the intensity of an initial stimulus (rather than a constant amount).

Weber's law A basic law of psychophysics stating that a just noticeable difference is a constant proportion to the intensity of an initial stimulus (rather than a constant amount).

For example, Weber found that the just noticeable difference for weight is 1:50. Consequently, it takes a 1-ounce increase in a 50-ounce weight to produce a noticeable difference, and it would take a 10-ounce increase to produce a noticeable difference if the initial weight were 500 ounces. In both cases, the same proportional increase is necessary to produce a just noticeable difference–1:50 = 10:500. Similarly, the just noticeable difference distinguishing changes in loudness between sounds is larger for sounds that are initially loud than it is for sounds that are initially soft, but the *proportional* increase remains the same.

Study Alert

Remember that Weber's law holds for every type of sensory stimuli: vision, sound, taste, and so on.

Why shouldn't the pupil be open completely all the time, allowing the greatest amount of light into the eye? The answer relates to the basic physics of light. A small pupil greatly increases the range of distances at which objects are in focus. With a wide-open pupil, the range is relatively small, and details are harder to discern. The eye takes advantage of bright light by decreasing the size of the pupil and thereby becoming more discriminating. In dim light the pupil expands to enable us to view the situation better–but at the expense of visual detail. (Perhaps one reason candlelight dinners are thought of as romantic is that the dim light prevents one from seeing a partner's physical flaws.)

Once light passes through the pupil, it enters the *lens,* which is directly behind the pupil. The lens acts to bend the rays of light so that they are properly focused on the rear of the eye. The lens focuses light by changing its own thickness, a process called *accommodation:* It becomes flatter when viewing distant objects and rounder when looking at closer objects.

REACHING THE RETINA

retina The part of the eye that converts the electromagnetic energy of light to electrical impulses for transmission to the brain.

Having traveled through the pupil and lens, the image of the tree finally reaches its ultimate destination in the eye–the **retina.** It is within the retina that the electromagnetic energy of light is converted to electrical impulses for transmission to the brain. Note that, because of the physical properties of light, the image has reversed itself in traveling through the lens, and it reaches the retina upside down (relative to its original position). Although it might seem that this reversal would cause difficulties in understanding and moving about the world, this is not the case. The brain interprets the image in terms of its original position.

rods Thin, cylindrical receptor cells in the retina that are highly sensitive to light.

cones Cone-shaped, light-sensitive receptor cells in the retina that are responsible for sharp focus and color perception, particularly in bright light.

The retina consists of a thin layer of nerve cells at the back of the eyeball (see Figure 3). There are two kinds of light-sensitive receptor cells in the retina. The names they have been given describe their shapes: rods and cones. **Rods** are thin, cylindrical receptor cells that are highly sensitive to light. **Cones** are typically cone-shaped, light-sensitive receptor cells that are responsible for sharp focus and color perception, particularly in bright light. The rods and cones are distributed unevenly throughout the retina. Cones are concentrated on the part of the retina called the *fovea.* The fovea is a particularly sensitive region of the retina. If you want to focus on something of particular interest, you will automatically try to center the image on the fovea to see it more sharply.

Study Alert

Remember that cones relate to color vision.

The rods and cones not only are structurally dissimilar but they also play distinctly different roles in vision. Cones are primarily responsible for the sharply focused perception of color, particularly in brightly lit situations; rods are related to vision in dimly lit situations and are largely insensitive to color and to details as sharp as those the cones are capable of recognizing. The rods play a key role in *peripheral vision*–seeing objects that are outside the main center of focus–and in night vision.

Rods and cones also are involved in *dark adaptation,* the phenomenon of adjusting to dim light after being in brighter light. (Think of the experience of walking into a dark movie theater and groping your way to a seat but a few minutes later seeing the seats quite clearly.) The speed at which dark adaptation occurs is a result of the rate of change in the chemical composition of the rods and cones. Although the cones reach their greatest level of adaptation in just a few minutes, the rods take 20 to 30 minutes to reach the maximum level. The opposite phenomenon–*light adaptation,* or the process of adjusting to bright light after exposure to dim light–occurs much faster, taking only a minute or so.

SENDING THE MESSAGE FROM THE EYE TO THE BRAIN

When light energy strikes the rods and cones, it starts a chain of events that transforms light into neural impulses that can be communicated to the brain. Even before the neural message reaches the brain, however, some initial coding of the visual information takes place.

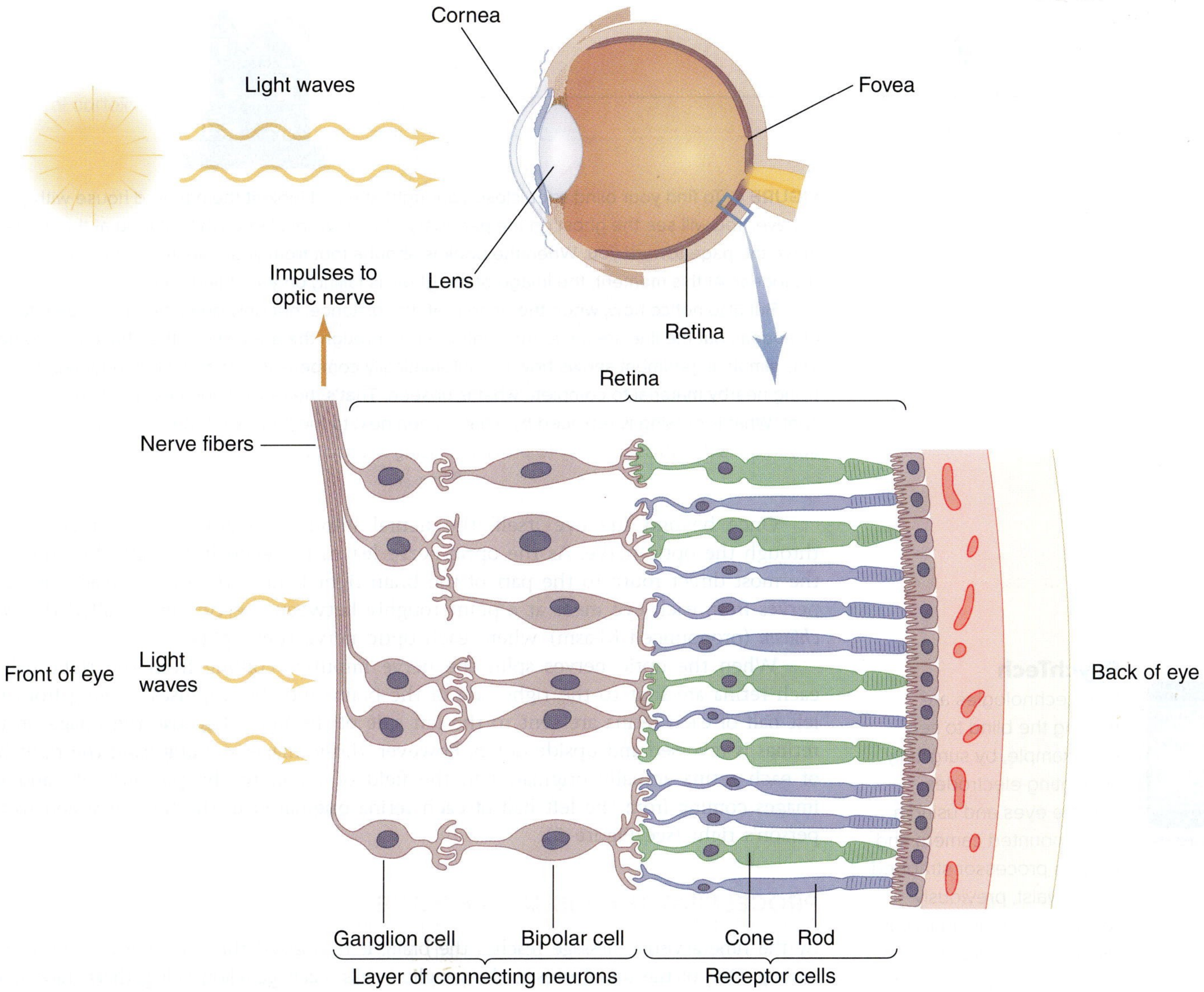

FIGURE 3 The basic cells of the eye. Light entering the eye travels through the ganglion and bipolar cells and strikes the light-sensitive rods and cones located at the back of the eye. The rods and cones then transmit nerve impulses to the brain via the bipolar and ganglion cells.

What happens when light energy strikes the retina depends in part on whether it encounters a rod or a cone. Rods contain *rhodopsin,* a complex reddish-purple protein whose composition changes chemically when energized by light. The substance in cone receptors is different, but the principles are similar. Stimulation of the nerve cells in the eye triggers a neural response that is transmitted to other nerve cells in the retina called *bipolar cells* and *ganglion cells.*

Bipolar cells receive information directly from the rods and cones and communicate that information to the ganglion cells. The ganglion cells collect and summarize visual information, which is then moved out the back of the eyeball and sent to the brain through a bundle of ganglion axons called the **optic nerve.**

Because the opening for the optic nerve passes through the retina, there are no rods or cones in the area, and that creates a blind spot. Normally, however, this absence of nerve cells does not interfere with vision because you automatically compensate for the missing part of your field of vision. (To find your blind spot, see Figure 4.)

optic nerve A bundle of ganglion axons that carry visual information to the brain.

FIGURE 6 Those with color blindness see a very different view of the world (left) compared to those who have normal vision (right).

Although the variety of colors that people are generally able to distinguish is vast, there are certain individuals whose ability to perceive color is quite limited–the color blind. Interestingly, the condition of these individuals has provided some of the most important clues to understanding how color vision operates (Neitz, Neitz, & Kainz, 1996; Bonnardel, 2006; Nijboer, te Pas, & van der Smagt, 2011).

Approximately 7% of men and 0.4% of women are color blind. For most people with color-blindness, the world looks quite dull (see Figure 6). Red fire engines appear yellow, green grass seems yellow, and the three colors of a traffic light all look yellow. In fact, in the most common form of color-blindness, all red and green objects are seen as yellow. In other forms of color-blindness, people are unable to tell the difference between yellow and blue. In the most extreme cases of color-blindness, which are quite rare, people perceive no color at all. To such individuals, the world looks something like the picture on an old black-and-white TV.

From the perspective of . . .

A Graphic Designer How might you market your products similarly or differently to those who are color blind versus those who have normal color vision?

EXPLAINING COLOR VISION

trichromatic theory of color vision The theory that there are three kinds of cones in the retina, each of which responds primarily to a specific range of wavelengths.

To understand why some people are color blind, we need to consider the basics of color vision. Two processes are involved. The first process is explained by the **trichromatic theory of color vision,** which was first proposed by Thomas Young and extended by Hermann von Helmholtz in the first half of the 1800s. This theory suggests that there are three kinds of cones in the retina, each of which responds primarily to a specific range of wavelengths. One is most responsive to blue-violet colors, one to green, and the third to yellow-red (Brown & Wald, 1964). According to trichromatic theory,

FIGURE 7 Stare at the dot in this flag for about a minute and then look at a piece of plain white paper. What do you see? Most people see an afterimage that converts the colors in the figure into the traditional red, white, and blue U.S. flag. If you have trouble seeing it the first time, blink once and try again.

perception of color is influenced by the relative strength with which each of the three kinds of cones is activated. If we see a blue sky, the blue-violet cones are primarily triggered, and the others show less activity.

However, there are aspects of color vision that the trichromatic theory is less successful at explaining. For example, the theory does not explain what happens after you stare at something like the flag shown in Figure 7 for about a minute. Try this yourself and then look at a blank white page: You'll see an image of the traditional red, white, and blue U.S. flag. Where there was yellow, you'll see blue, and where there were green and black, you'll see red and white.

The phenomenon you have just experienced is called an *afterimage*. It occurs because activity in the retina continues even when you are no longer staring at the original picture. However, it also demonstrates that the trichromatic theory does not explain color vision completely. Why should the colors in the afterimage be different from those in the original?

Because trichromatic processes do not provide a full explanation of color vision, alternative explanations have been proposed. According to the **opponent-process theory of color vision,** first proposed by German physiologist Ewald Hering in the 19th century, receptor cells are linked in pairs, working in opposition to each other. Specifically, there are a blue-yellow pairing, a red-green pairing, and a black-white pairing. If an object reflects light that contains more blue than yellow, it will stimulate the firing of the cells sensitive to blue, simultaneously discouraging or inhibiting the firing of receptor cells sensitive to yellow–and the object will appear blue. If, in contrast, a light contains more yellow than blue, the cells that respond to yellow will be stimulated to fire while the blue ones are inhibited, and the object will appear yellow (D. N. Robinson, 2007).

opponent-process theory of color vision The theory that receptor cells for color are linked in pairs, working in opposition to each other.

The opponent-process theory provides a good explanation for afterimages. When we stare at the yellow in the figure, for instance, our receptor cells for the yellow component of the yellow-blue pairing become fatigued and are less able to respond to yellow stimuli. In contrast, the receptor cells for the blue part of the pair are not tired, because they are not being stimulated. When we look at a white surface, the light reflected off it would normally stimulate both the yellow and the blue receptors equally. But the fatigue of the yellow receptors prevents this from happening. They temporarily do not respond to the yellow, which makes the white light appear to be blue. Because the other colors in the figure do the same thing relative to their specific opponents, the afterimage produces the opponent

Study Alert

Keep in mind that there are two explanations for color vision: trichromatic and opponent-process theories.

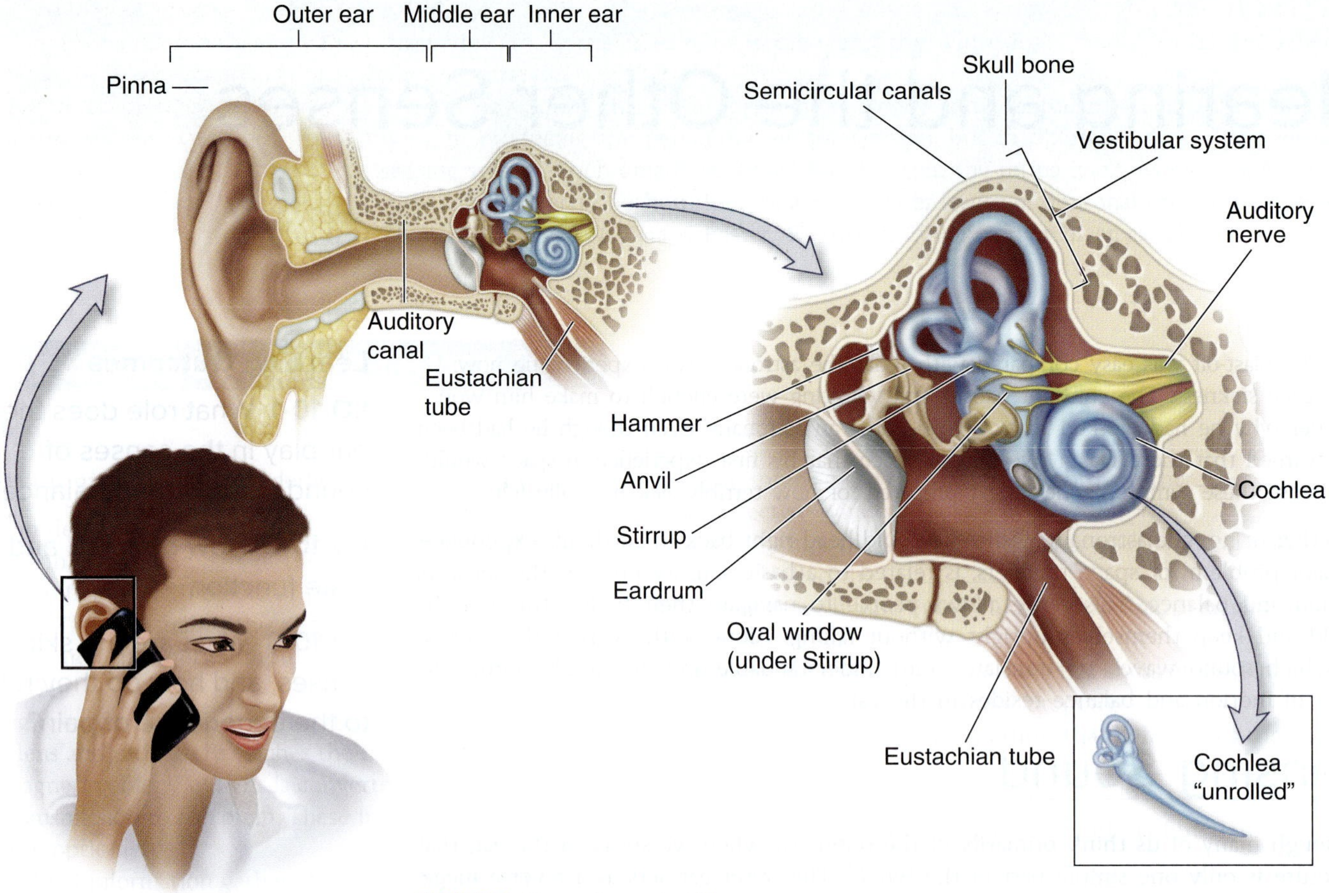

FIGURE 1 The major parts of the ear.

hair cells Tiny cells covering the basilar membrane that, when bent by vibrations entering the cochlea, transmit neural messages to the brain.

chamber and a lower chamber. The basilar membrane is covered with **hair cells.** When the hair cells are bent by the vibrations entering the cochlea, the cells send a neural message to the brain (Cho, 2000; Zhou, Liu, & Davis, 2005; Møller, 2011).

THE PHYSICAL ASPECTS OF SOUND

As we mentioned earlier, what we refer to as sound is actually the physical movement of air molecules in regular, wavelike patterns caused by a vibrating source. Sometimes it is even possible to see these vibrations: If you have ever seen an audio speaker that has no enclosure, you know that, at least when the lowest notes are playing, you can see the speaker moving in and out. Less obvious is what happens next: The speaker pushes air molecules into waves with the same pattern as its movement. Those wave patterns soon reach your ear, although their strength has been weakened considerably during their travels. All other sources that produce sound work in essentially the same fashion, setting off wave patterns that move through the air to the ear. Air—or some other medium, such as water—is necessary to make the vibrations of objects reach us. This explains why there can be no sound in a vacuum.

We are able to see the audio speaker moving when low notes are played because of a primary characteristic of sound called frequency. *Frequency* is the number of wave cycles that occur in a second. At very low frequencies there are relatively few wave cycles per second (see Figure 2). These cycles are visible to the naked eye as vibrations in the speaker. Low frequencies are translated into a sound that is very low in pitch. (*Pitch* is the characteristic that makes sound seem "high" or "low.") For example, the lowest frequency that humans are capable of hearing is 20 cycles per second. Higher frequencies are heard as sounds of higher pitch. At the upper end of the sound spectrum, people can detect sounds with frequencies as high as 20,000 cycles per second.

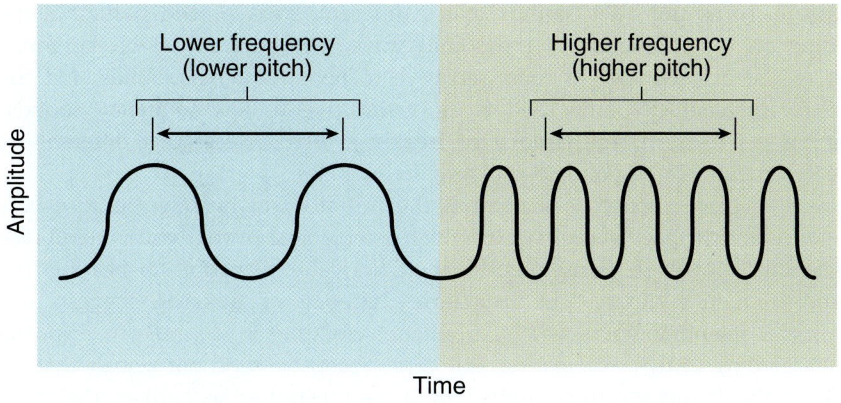

FIGURE 2 The sound waves produced by different stimuli are transmitted—usually through the air—in different patterns, with lower frequencies indicated by fewer peaks and valleys per second.

Amplitude is a feature of wave patterns that allows us to distinguish between loud and soft sounds. Amplitude is the spread between the up-and-down peaks and valleys of air pressure in a sound wave as it travels through the air. Waves with small peaks and valleys produce soft sounds; those with relatively large peaks and valleys produce loud sounds.

We are sensitive to broad variations in sound amplitudes. The strongest sounds we are capable of hearing are over a trillion times as intense as the very weakest sound we can hear. This range is measured in *decibels*. When sounds get higher than 120 decibels, they become painful to the human ear.

Our sensitivity to different frequencies changes as we age. For instance, as we get older, the range of frequencies we can detect declines, particularly for high-pitched sounds. This is why high school students sometimes choose high-pitched ring tones for their cell phones in settings where cell phone use is forbidden: the ringing sound goes undetected by their aging teachers (Vitello, 2006) (see Figure 3).

Sorting Out Theories of Sound. How are our brains able to sort out wavelengths of different frequencies and intensities? One clue comes from studies of the basilar membrane, the area in the cochlea that translates physical vibrations into neural

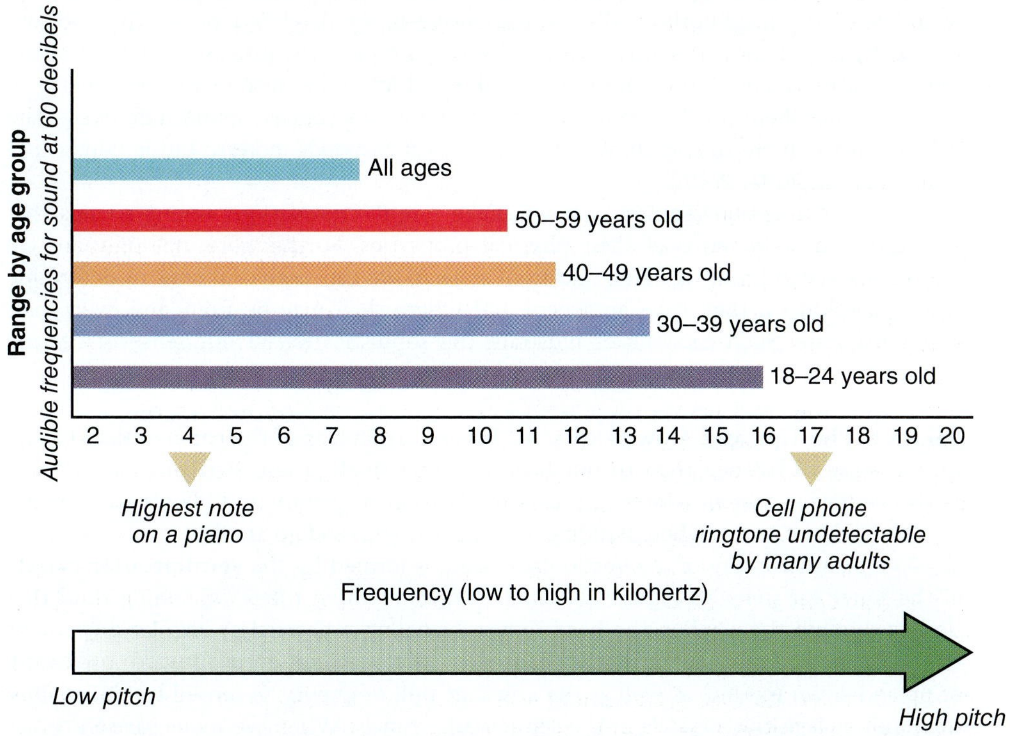

FIGURE 3 Some teenagers set their text-message ring tone to a frequency too high for most adults to hear, allowing them to use cell phones where they are prohibited. (Source: Adapted from Vitello, 2006.)

impulses. It turns out that sounds affect different areas of the basilar membrane, depending on the frequency of the sound wave. The part of the basilar membrane nearest to the oval window is most sensitive to high-frequency sounds, and the part nearest to the cochlea's inner end is most sensitive to low-frequency sounds. This finding has led to the **place theory of hearing,** which states that different areas of the basilar membrane respond to different frequencies.

place theory of hearing The theory that different areas of the basilar membrane respond to different frequencies.

However, place theory does not tell the full story of hearing, because very low frequency sounds trigger neurons across such a wide area of the basilar membrane that no single site is involved. Consequently, an additional explanation for hearing has been proposed: frequency theory. The **frequency theory of hearing** suggests that the entire basilar membrane acts as a microphone, vibrating as a whole in response to a sound. According to this explanation, the nerve receptors send out signals that are tied directly to the frequency (the number of wave crests per second) of the sounds to which we are exposed, with the number of nerve impulses being a direct function of a sound's frequency. Thus, the higher the pitch of a sound (and therefore the greater the frequency of its wave crests), the greater the number of nerve impulses that are transmitted up the auditory nerve to the brain.

frequency theory of hearing The theory that the entire basilar membrane acts like a microphone, vibrating as a whole in response to a sound.

Neither place theory nor frequency theory provides the full explanation for hearing. Place theory provides a better explanation for the sensing of high-frequency sounds, whereas frequency theory explains what happens when low-frequency sounds are encountered. Medium-frequency sounds incorporate both processes (Hirsh & Watson, 1996; Hudspeth, 2000).

Study Alert

Be sure to understand the differences between the place and frequency theories of hearing.

After an auditory message leaves the ear, it is transmitted to the auditory cortex of the brain through a complex series of neural interconnections. As the message is transmitted, it is communicated through neurons that respond to specific types of sounds. Within the auditory cortex itself, there are neurons that respond selectively to very specific sorts of sound features, such as clicks and whistles. Some neurons respond only to a specific pattern of sounds, such as a steady tone but not an intermittent one. Furthermore, specific neurons transfer information about a sound's location through their particular pattern of firing (Middlebrooks et al., 2005; Wang et al., 2005; Alho et al., 2006).

If we were to analyze the configuration of the cells in the auditory cortex, we would find that neighboring cells are responsive to similar frequencies. The auditory cortex, then, provides us with a "map" of sound frequencies, just as the visual cortex furnishes a representation of the visual field. In addition, because of the asymmetry in the two hemispheres of the brain, the left and right ears process sound differently. The right ear reacts more to speech, whereas the left ear responds more to music (Sininger & Cone-Wesson, 2004, 2006).

Speech perception requires that we make fine discriminations among sounds that are quite similar in terms of their physical properties. Furthermore, not only are we able to understand *what* is being said from speech, we can use vocal cues to determine who is speaking, if they have an accent and where they may be from, and even their emotional state. Such capabilities illustrate the sophistication of our sense of hearing (Pell et al., 2009; Ross et al., 2011; Mattys et al., 2013).

Balance: The Ups and Downs of Life. Several structures of the ear are related more to our sense of balance than to our hearing. Collectively, these structures are known as the *vestibular system,* which responds to the pull of gravity and allows us to maintain our balance, even when standing in a bus in stop-and-go traffic.

The main structure of the vestibular system is formed by the **semicircular canals** of the inner ear (refer to Figure 1), which consist of three tubes containing fluid that sloshes through them when the head moves, signaling rotational or angular movement to the brain. The pull on our bodies caused by the acceleration of forward, backward, or up-and-down motion, as well as the constant pull of gravity, is sensed by the *otoliths,* tiny, motion-sensitive crystals in the semicircular canals. When we move, these crystals shift as sands do on a windy beach, contacting the specialized receptor *hair cells* in

semicircular canals Three tube-like structures of the inner ear containing fluid that sloshes through them when the head moves, signaling rotational or angular movement to the brain.

Zero gravity presents numerous challenges, some of which were depicted in the film *Gravity* with Sandra Bullock. For example, the weightlessness of the ear's ototliths produces space sickness in most astronauts.

the semicircular canals. The brain's inexperience in interpreting messages from the weightless otoliths is the cause of the space sickness commonly experienced by two-thirds of all space travelers, mentioned at the start of this module (Flam, 1991; Stern & Koch, 1996).

Smell and Taste

> Until he bit into a piece of raw cabbage on that February evening . . . , Raymond Fowler had not thought much about the sense of taste. The cabbage, part of a pasta dish he was preparing for his family's dinner, had an odd, burning taste, but he did not pay it much attention. Then a few minutes later, his daughter handed him a glass of cola, and he took a swallow. "It was like sulfuric acid," he said. "It was like the hottest thing you could imagine boring into your mouth." (Goode, 1999, pp. D1-D2)

It was evident that something was very wrong with Fowler's sense of taste. After extensive testing, it became clear that he had damaged the nerves involved in his sense of taste, probably because of a viral infection or a medicine he was taking. (Luckily for him, a few months later his sense of taste returned to normal.)

Even without disruptions in our ability to perceive the world such as those experienced by Fowler, we all know the important roles that taste and smell play. We'll consider these two senses next.

SMELL

Although many animals have keener abilities to detect odors than we do, the human sense of smell (*olfaction*) permits us to detect more than 10,000 separate smells. We also have a good memory for smells, and long-forgotten events and memories—good and bad—can be brought back with the mere whiff of an odor associated with a memory (Willander & Larsson, 2006; Schroers, Prigot, & Fagen, 2007; Arshamian et al., 2013).

Results of "sniff tests" have shown that women generally have a better sense of smell than men do (Engen, 1987). People also have the ability to distinguish males from females on the basis of smell alone. In one experiment, blindfolded students who were asked to sniff the breath of a female or male volunteer who was hidden from view were able to distinguish the sex of the donor at better than chance levels. People can also distinguish happy from sad emotions by sniffing underarm smells, and women are able to identify their babies solely on the basis of smell just a few hours after birth (Doty et al., 1982; Haviland-Jones & Chen, 1999; Fusari & Ballesteros, 2008; Silva, 2011).

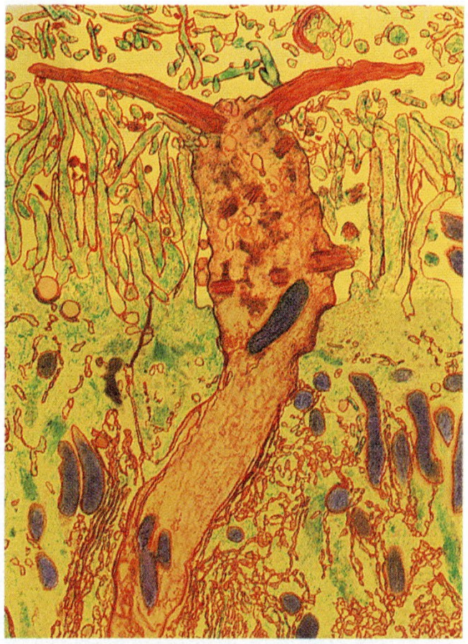

More than 1,000 receptor cells, known as olfactory cells, are spread across the nasal cavity. The cells are specialized to react to particular odors. Do you think it is possible to "train" the nose to pick up a greater number of odors?

Applying Psychology in the 21st Century

Study-Break Soundtrack

Headphones and earbuds are as common on a college campus as flip-flops and no. 2 pencils. In residence halls, classrooms, and the library, students can be found studying textbooks or writing papers while engrossed in their favorite music. And if you ask them why, the answer is often that the music helps them to concentrate. But is that true?

There is some research showing that background music can improve performance on certain cognitive tasks. These tasks, however, tend to be unrelated to studying. For example, background music may help someone who is mentally rotating a three-dimensional image. The boost to a person's performance seems to be the result of the music both improving mood and increasing overall physical arousal. Furthermore, in loud and chaotic environments, music without lyrics can help block out the more distracting stimuli (Angel, Polzella, & Elvers, 2010).

On the other hand, when it comes to academic and work-related tasks, research generally doesn't support the notion that listening to music improves studying or writing. For example, the results of one study of students who were listening to music with lyrics showed a decline in their performance on a test of concentration. The results in another study of participants who listened to hip-hop music showed a decline in tests of their reading comprehension. And in yet another study, workers who either strongly liked or strongly disliked the background music in their work environment scored lower on tests of attention than their co-workers who had no strong feeling about the music or who worked in areas where they couldn't hear it. Taken together, these studies suggest, then, that background music is usually more of a distractor than a help—and this seems to be especially true when the music has lyrics (Perham & Sykora, 2012; Shellenbarger, 2012).

Do headphones and earbuds do anything useful to help studying? Yes, they do. They ward off distracting social interaction, much like a sign that says, "I'm busy—don't interrupt." That might be the devices' biggest benefit of all—and for that, they don't even have to be plugged in (Shellenbarger, 2012).

RETHINK

- Why do you think music with lyrics is more distracting than music without lyrics?
- Are there other ways that help you to tune out the external environment without listening to music?

object is moving. It occurs when different areas of the retina are quickly stimulated, leading us to interpret motion (Ekroll & Scherzer, 2009; Lindemann & Bekkering, 2009; Brandon & Saffran, 2011).

Perceptual Illusions: The Deceptions of Perceptions

If you look carefully at the Parthenon, one of the most famous buildings of ancient Greece, still standing at the top of an Athens hill, you'll see that it was built with a bulge on one side. If it didn't have that bulge—and quite a few other architectural "tricks" like it, such as columns that incline inward—it would look as if it were crooked and about to fall down. Instead, it appears to stand completely straight, at right angles to the ground.

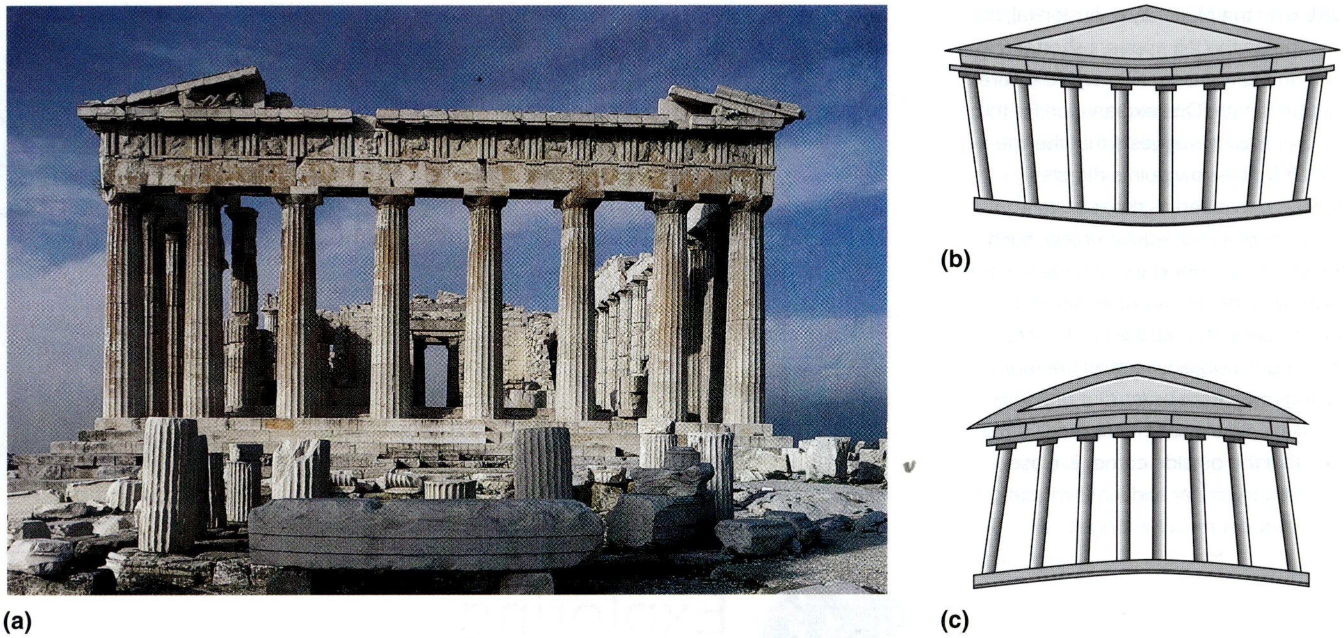

FIGURE 5 (a) In building the Parthenon, the Greeks constructed an architectural wonder that looks perfectly straight, with right angles at every corner. (b) However, if it had been built with completely true right angles, it would have looked as it does here. (c) To compensate for this illusion, the Parthenon was designed to have a slight upward curvature, as shown here.
(Source: Adapted from Lukeish, 1921.)

The fact that the Parthenon appears to be completely upright is the result of a series of visual illusions. **Visual illusions** are physical stimuli that consistently produce errors in perception. In the case of the Parthenon, the building appears to be completely square, as illustrated in Figure 5a. However, if it had been built that way, it would look to us as it does in Figure 5b. The reason for this is an illusion that makes right angles placed above a line appear as if they were bent. To offset the illusion, the Parthenon was constructed as in Figure 5c, with a slight upward curvature.

visual illusions Physical stimuli that consistently produce errors in perception.

The *Müller-Lyer illusion* (illustrated in Figure 6) has fascinated psychologists for decades. Although the two lines are the same length, the one with the arrow tips pointing outward, away from the vertical line (Figure 6a, left) appears to be shorter than the one with the arrow tips pointing inward (Figure 6a, right).

Study Alert
The explanation for the Müller-Lyer illusion is complicated. Figure 6 will help you master it.

Although all kinds of explanations for visual illusions have been suggested, most concentrate either on the physical operation of the eye or on our misinterpretation of the visual stimulus. For example, one explanation for the Müller-Lyer illusion is that eye movements are greater when the arrow tips point inward, making us perceive the line as longer than it is when the arrow tips face outward. In contrast, a different explanation for the illusion suggests that we unconsciously attribute particular significance to each of the lines (Gregory, 1978; Redding & Hawley, 1993). When we see the left line in Figure 6a, we tend to perceive it as if it were the relatively close outside corner of a rectangular object, such as the outside corner of the room illustrated in Figure 6b. In contrast, when we view the line on the right in Figure 6a, we perceive it as the relatively more distant inside corner of a rectangular object, such as the inside room corner in Figure 6c. Because previous experience leads us to assume that the outside corner is closer than the inside corner, we make the further assumption that the inside corner must therefore be longer.

Despite the complexity of the latter explanation, a good deal of evidence supports it. For instance, cross-cultural studies show that people raised in areas where there are few right angles–such as the Zulu in Africa–are much less susceptible to the illusion than are people who grow up where most structures are built using right angles and rectangles (Segall, Campbell, & Herskovits, 1966).

However, a debate in one of the most prestigious psychology journals, *Psychological Bulletin,* heightened interest in ESP. According to proponents of ESP, reliable evidence exists for an "anomalous process of information transfer," or *psi.* These researchers, who painstakingly reviewed considerable evidence, argue that a cumulative body of research shows reliable support for the existence of psi (Bem & Honorton, 1994; Storm & Ertel, 2001; Parra & Argibay, 2007).

Their conclusion has been challenged on several counts. For example, critics suggest that the research methodology was inadequate and that the experiments supporting psi are flawed (Milton & Wiseman, 1999; Kennedy, 2004; Rouder, Morey, & Province, 2013).

Because of questions about the quality of the research, as well as a lack of any credible theoretical explanation for how extrasensory perception might take place, the vast majority of psychologists continue to believe that there is no reliable scientific support for ESP (Rose & Blackmore, 2002; Wiseman & Greening, 2002). Still, the exchanges in *Psychological Bulletin* are likely to heighten the debate. More important, the renewed interest in ESP among psychologists is likely to inspire more research, which is the only way the issue can be resolved.

RECAP/EVALUATE/RETHINK

RECAP

LO 11-1 What principles underlie our organization of the visual world and allow us to make sense of our environment?

- Perception is a constructive process in which people go beyond the stimuli that are physically present and try to construct a meaningful interpretation.
- The gestalt laws of organization are used to describe the way in which we organize bits and pieces of information into meaningful wholes, known as gestalts, through closure, proximity, similarity, and simplicity.
- In top-down processing, perception is guided by higher-level knowledge, experience, expectations, and motivations. In bottom-up processing, perception consists of the progression of recognizing and processing information from individual components of a stimuli and moving to the perception of the whole.

LO 11-2 How are we able to perceive the world in three dimensions when our retinas are capable of sensing only two-dimensional images?

- Depth perception is the ability to perceive distance and view the world in three dimensions even though the images projected on our retinas are two-dimensional. We are able to judge depth and distance as a result of binocular disparity and monocular cues, such as motion parallax, the relative size of images on the retina, and linear perspective.
- Perceptual constancy permits us to perceive stimuli as unvarying in size, shape, and color despite changes in the environment or the appearance of the objects being perceived.
- Motion perception depends on cues such as the perceived movement of an object across the retina and information about how the head and eyes are moving.

LO 11-3 What clues do visual illusions give us about our understanding of general perceptual mechanisms?

- Visual illusions are physical stimuli that consistently produce errors in perception, causing judgments that do not reflect the physical reality of a stimulus accurately. One of the best-known illusions is the Müller-Lyer illusion.
- Visual illusions are usually the result of errors in the brain's interpretation of visual stimuli. Furthermore, culture clearly affects how we perceive the world.
- Subliminal perception refers to the perception of messages about which we have no awareness. The reality of the phenomenon, as well as of ESP, is open to question and debate.

EVALUATE

1. Match each of the following organizational laws with its meaning:

a. closure	**1.** Elements close together are grouped together.
b. proximity	**2.** Patterns are perceived in the most basic, direct manner possible.
c. similarity	**3.** Groupings are made in terms of complete figures.
d. simplicity	**4.** Elements similar in appearance are grouped together.

2. __________ analysis deals with the way in which we break an object down into its component pieces in order to understand it.
3. Processing that involves higher functions such as expectations and motivations is known as __________, whereas processing that recognizes the individual components of a stimulus is known as __________.
4. When a car passes you on the road and appears to shrink as it gets farther away, the phenomenon of __________ permits you to realize that the car is not in fact getting smaller.
5. __________ __________ is the ability to view the world in three dimensions instead of two.
6. The brain makes use of a phenomenon known as __________ __________, or the difference in the images the two eyes see, to give three dimensions to sight.

RETHINK

1. In what ways do painters represent three-dimensional scenes in two dimensions on a canvas? Do you think artists in non-Western cultures use the same or different principles to represent three-dimensionality? Why?
2. Can you think of examples of the combined use of top-down and bottom-up processing in everyday life? Is one type of processing superior to the other?

Answers to Evaluate Questions

1. a-3, b-1, c-4, d-2; **2.** Feature; **3.** top-down, bottom-up; **4.** perceptual constancy; **5.** Depth perception; **6.** binocular disparity

KEY TERMS

gestalt laws of organization

top-down processing

bottom-up processing

depth perception

perceptual constancy

visual illusions

Looking Back

Epilogue

We have noted the important distinction between sensation and perception, and we have examined the processes that underlie both of them. We've seen how external stimuli evoke sensory responses and how our different senses process the information contained in those responses. We also have focused on the physical structure and internal workings of the individual senses, including vision, hearing, balance, smell, taste, and the skin senses, and we've explored how our brains organize and process sensory information to construct a consistent, integrated picture of the world around us.

To end our investigation of sensation and perception, let's reconsider super-recognizers like C.S., who are able to recognize faces years after they have met people, often only in passing. Using your knowledge of sensation and perception, answer the following questions:

1. Why might some people be extremely capable at recognizing faces?

2. Is having extremely sensitive perception always a good thing? What might be some drawbacks to being a super-recognizer?

3. Does the ability of super-recognizers seem to be a matter of sensation or of perception? Why do you think so?

VISUAL SUMMARY 3 Sensation and Perception

MODULE 8 Sensing the World

Absolute thresholds

Difference thresholds

- Just noticeable difference
- Weber's law

Sensory Adaptation

MODULE 9 Vision

Eye Structure

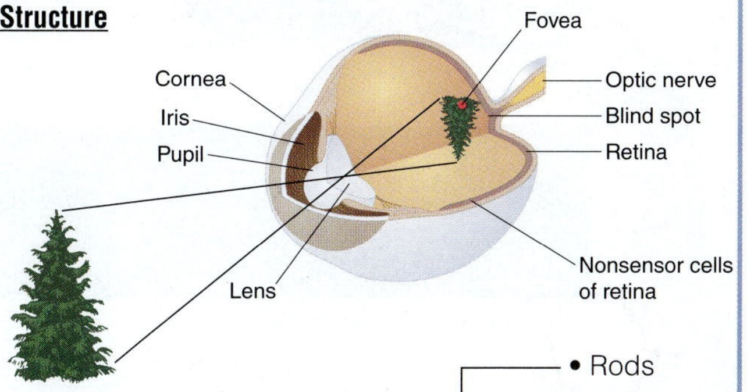

Retina
- Rods
- Cones

Visual Processing

- Color vision
  - Trichromatic theory
  - Opponent process theory
- Feature detection

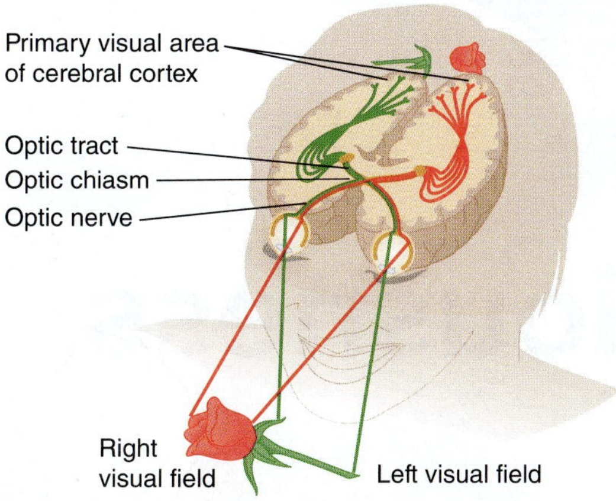

MODULE 10 Hearing and Other Senses

Ear Structure

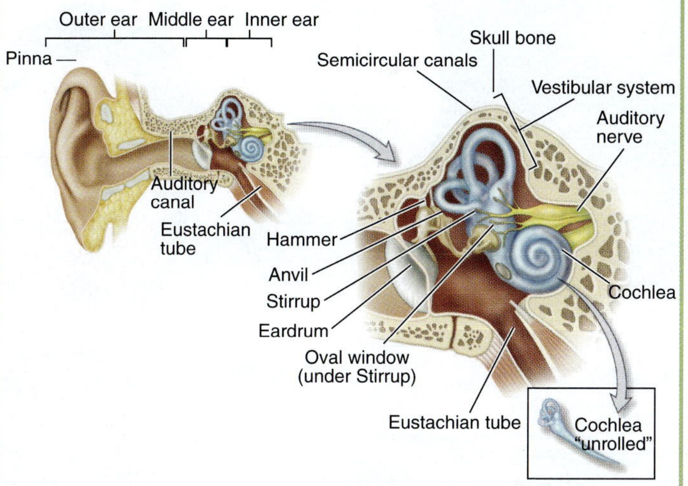

Other Senses

- Smell
- Taste
- Skin senses

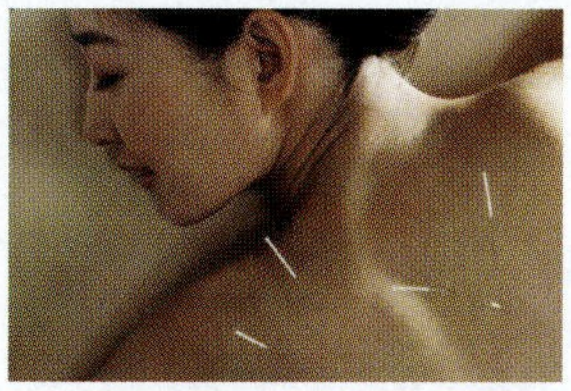

MODULE 11 Perception

Gestalt Laws of Organization

(a) Closure **(b)** Proximity **(c)** Similarity **(d)** Simplicity

Top-down and Bottom-up Processing

Perceptual Constancy

Depth Perception

Motion Perception

Perceptual Illusions

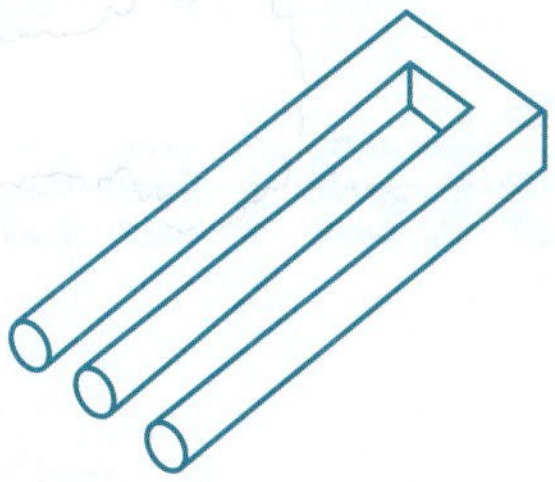

4 States of Consciousness

Learning Outcomes for Chapter 4

MODULE 12

LO 12-1 What are the different states of consciousness?

LO 12-2 What happens when we sleep, and what are the meaning and function of dreams?

LO 12-3 What are the major sleep disorders, and how can they be treated?

LO 12-4 How much do we daydream?

MODULE 13

LO 13-1 What is hypnosis, and are hypnotized people in a different state of consciousness?

LO 13-2 What are the effects of meditation?

MODULE 14

LO 14-1 What are the major classifications of drugs, and what are their effects?

The Stages of Sleep

Most of us consider sleep a time of tranquility when we set aside the tensions of the day and spend the night in uneventful slumber. However, a closer look at sleep shows that a good deal of activity occurs throughout the night.

Measures of electrical activity in the brain show that the brain is quite active during the night. It produces electrical discharges with systematic, wavelike patterns that change in height (or amplitude) and speed (or frequency) in regular sequences. There is also significant physical activity in muscle and eye movements.

People progress through a series of distinct stages of sleep during a night's rest—known as *stage 1* through *stage 4* and *REM sleep*—moving through the stages in cycles lasting about 90 minutes. Each of these sleep stages is associated with a unique pattern of brain waves, which you can see in Figure 2.

When people first go to sleep, they move from a waking state in which they are relaxed with their eyes closed into **stage 1 sleep,** which is characterized by relatively rapid, low-amplitude brain waves. This is actually a stage of transition between wakefulness and sleep and lasts only a few minutes. During stage 1, images sometimes appear, as if we were viewing still photos, although this is not true dreaming, which occurs later in the night.

stage 1 sleep The state of transition between wakefulness and sleep, characterized by relatively rapid, low-amplitude brain waves.

As sleep becomes deeper, people enter **stage 2 sleep,** which makes up about half of the total sleep of those in their early 20s and is characterized by a slower, more regular wave pattern. However, there are also momentary interruptions of sharply pointed, spiky waves that are called, because of their configuration, *sleep spindles.* It becomes increasingly difficult to awaken a person from sleep as stage 2 progresses.

stage 2 sleep A sleep deeper than that of stage 1, characterized by a slower, more regular wave pattern, along with momentary interruptions of "sleep spindles."

As people drift into **stage 3 sleep,** the brain waves become slower, with higher peaks and lower valleys in the wave pattern. By the time sleepers arrive at **stage 4 sleep,** the pattern is even slower and more regular, and people are least responsive to outside stimulation.

stage 3 sleep A sleep characterized by slow brain waves, with greater peaks and valleys in the wave pattern than in stage 2 sleep.

stage 4 sleep The deepest stage of sleep, during which we are least responsive to outside stimulation.

As you can see in Figure 3, stage 4 sleep is most likely to occur during the early part of the night. In the first half of the night, sleep is dominated by stages 3 and 4. The second half is characterized by stages 1 and 2—as well as a fifth stage during which dreams occur.

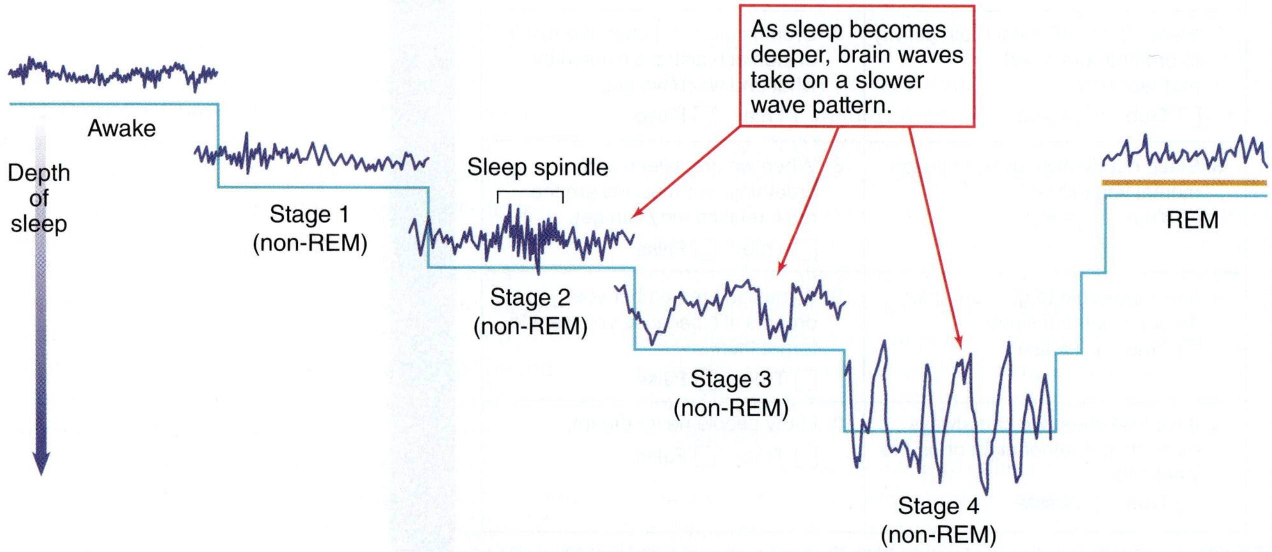

FIGURE 2 Brain-wave patterns (measured by an EEG apparatus) vary significantly during the different stages of sleep (adapted from Hobson, 1989). As sleep moves from stage 1 through stage 4, brain waves become slower. During REM sleep, however, the fast wave patterns are similar to relaxed wakefulness.

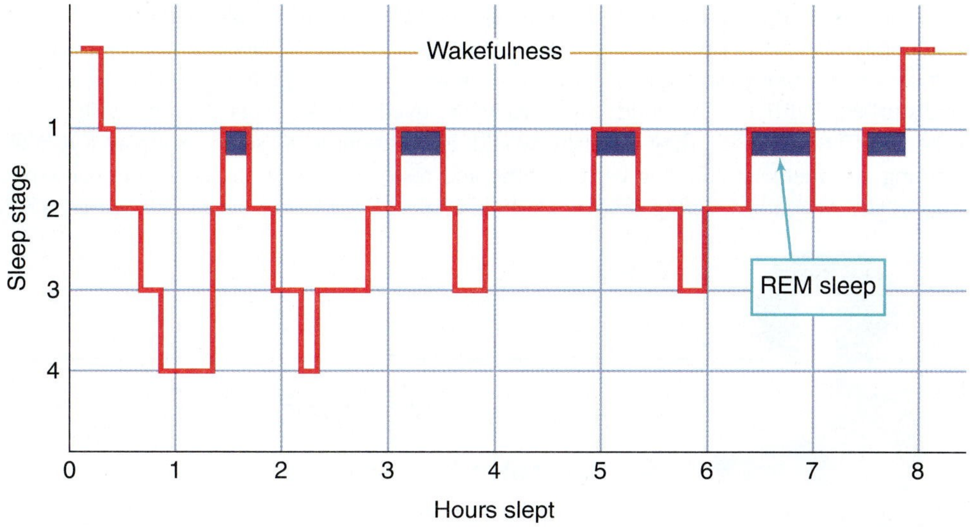

FIGURE 3 During the night, the typical sleeper passes through all four stages of sleep and several REM periods. (Source: Adapted from Hartmann, 1967.)

REM Sleep: The Paradox of Sleep

Several times a night, when sleepers have cycled back to a shallower state of sleep, something curious happens. Their heart rate increases and becomes irregular, their blood pressure rises, and their breathing rate increases. Most characteristic of this period is the back-and-forth movement of their eyes, as if they were watching an action-filled movie. This period of sleep is called **rapid eye movement,** or **REM sleep,** and it contrasts with stages 1 through 4, which are collectively labeled *non-REM* (or *NREM*) sleep. REM sleep occupies a little more than 20% of adults' total sleeping time.

rapid eye movement (REM) sleep Sleep occupying 20% of an adult's sleeping time, characterized by increased heart rate, blood pressure, and breathing rate; erections; eye movements; and the experience of dreaming.

Paradoxically, while all this activity is occurring, the major muscles of the body appear to be paralyzed. In addition, and most important, REM sleep is usually accompanied by dreams, which—whether or not people remember them—are experienced by *everyone* during some part of their night's sleep. Although some dreaming occurs in non-REM stages of sleep, dreams are most likely to occur in the REM period, where they are the most vivid and easily remembered (Conduit, Crewther, & Coleman, 2004; Lu et al., 2006; Leclair-Visonneau et al., 2011; Manni, Raffaele, & Terzaghi, 2013).

People progress through four distinct stages of sleep during a night's rest spread over cycles lasting about 90 minutes. REM sleep, which occupies only 20% of adults' sleeping time, occurs in stage 1 sleep. These photos, taken at different times of night, show the synchronized patterns of a couple accustomed to sleeping in the same bed.

Study Alert
Differentiate the five stages of sleep (stage 1, stage 2, stage 3, stage 4, and REM sleep), which produce different brain-wave patterns.

There is good reason to believe that REM sleep plays a critical role in everyday human functioning. People deprived of REM sleep–by being awakened every time they begin to display the physiological signs of that stage–show a *rebound effect* when allowed to rest undisturbed. With this rebound effect, REM-deprived sleepers spend significantly more time in REM sleep than they normally would. In addition, REM sleep may play a role in learning and memory, allowing us to rethink and restore information and emotional experiences that we've had during the day (Nishida et al., 2009; Walker & van der Helm, 2009).

From the perspective of . . .

An Educator How might you use the findings in sleep research to maximize student learning?

Why Do We Sleep, and How Much Sleep Is Necessary?

Sleep is a requirement for normal human functioning, although, surprisingly, we don't know exactly why. It is reasonable to expect that our bodies would require a tranquil "rest and relaxation" period to revitalize themselves, and experiments with rats show that total sleep deprivation results in death. But why?

One explanation, based on an evolutionary perspective, suggests that sleep permitted our ancestors to conserve energy at night, a time when food was relatively hard to come by. Consequently, they were better able to forage for food when the sun was up.

A second explanation for why we sleep is that sleep restores and replenishes our brains and bodies. For instance, the reduced activity of the brain during non-REM sleep may give neurons in the brain a chance to repair themselves. Furthermore, the onset of REM sleep stops the release of neurotransmitters called *monoamines* and so permits receptor cells to get some necessary rest and to increase their sensitivity during periods of wakefulness (McNamara, 2004; Steiger, 2007; Bub, Buckhalt, & El-Sheikh, 2011).

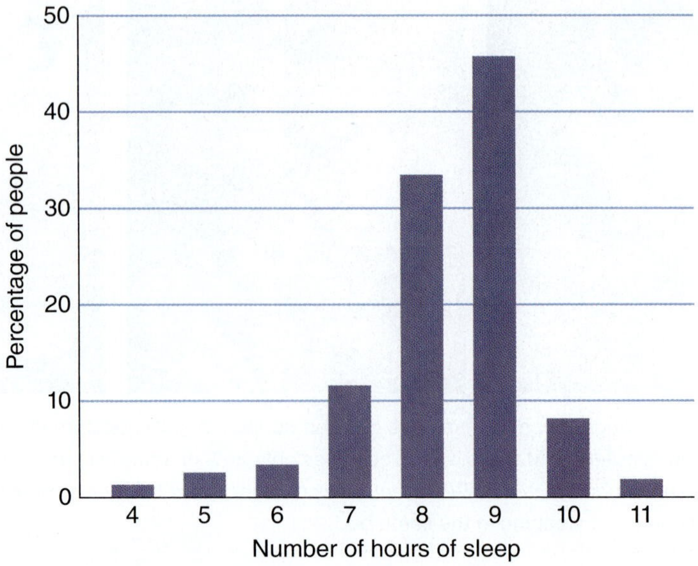

FIGURE 4 Although most people report sleeping between 8 and 9 hours per night, the amount that individuals need varies a great deal (Borbely, 1986). Where would you place yourself on this graph, and why do you think you need more or less sleep than others? (Source: Adapted from Borbely, 1986.)

Finally, sleep may be essential because it assists physical growth and brain development in children. For example, the release of growth hormones is associated with deep sleep (Peterfi et al., 2010).

Still, these explanations remain speculative, and there is no definitive answer as to why sleep is essential. Furthermore, scientists have been unable to establish just how much sleep is absolutely required. Most people today sleep between 7 and 8 hours each night, which is 3 hours a night *less* than people slept a hundred years ago. In addition, there is wide variability among individuals, with some people needing as little as 3 hours of sleep (see Figure 4).

Men and women sleep differently. Women typically fall asleep more quickly, sleep for longer periods and more deeply than men, and they get up fewer times in the night. On the other hand, men have fewer concerns about the amount of sleep they get than women do, even though they get less sleep. Furthermore, sleep requirements vary over the course of a lifetime: As they age, people generally need less and less sleep (Monk et al., 2011; Petersen, 2011).

People who participate in sleep deprivation experiments, in which they are kept awake for stretches as long as 200 hours, show no lasting effects. It's no fun–they feel weary and irritable, can't concentrate, and show a loss of creativity, even after only minor deprivation. They also show a decline in logical reasoning ability. However, after being allowed to sleep normally, they bounce back quickly and are able to perform at predeprivation levels after just a few days (Babson et al., 2009; Mograss et al., 2009; Jackson et al., 2013).

Neuroscience in Your Life: Why Are You So Irritable When You Don't Get Enough Sleep?

Although we're always hearing about the importance of getting enough sleep, we often don't. And we all know the consequences: we can be irritable and easily annoyed throughout the following day. But why? Recent studies provide at least one explanation. It seems that the parts of our brain that process emotion, such as the amygdala, become more sensitive and overreact when we do not get sufficient sleep. For example, these fMRI images show the amygdala reacting more strongly (illustrated in yellow areas) to images of fearful faces when participants had been deprived of sleep across the course of 5 days. In short, blame the jumpiness of your amygdala for your crankiness when you've slept badly (Motomura et al., 2013).

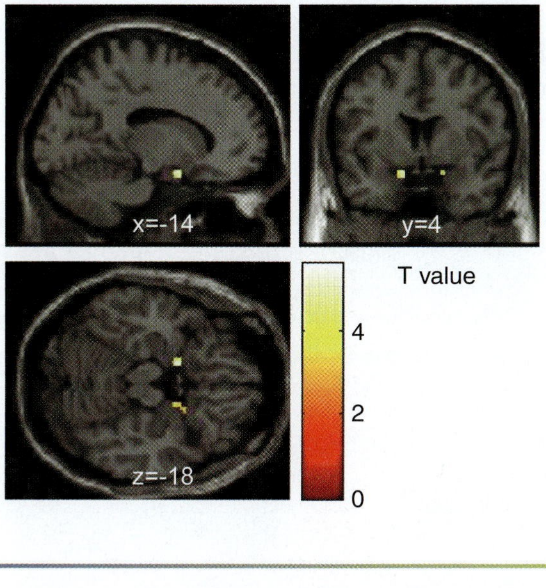

In short, as far as we know, most people suffer no permanent consequences of such temporary sleep deprivation. But–and this is an important but–a lack of sleep can make us feel edgy, slow our reaction time, and lower our performance on academic and physical tasks. In addition, we put ourselves, and others, at risk when we carry out routine activities, such as driving, when we're very sleepy (Philip et al., 2005; Anderson & Home, 2006; Morad et al., 2009). (Also see *Neuroscience in Your Life.*)

The Function and Meaning of Dreaming

> I was being chased, and I couldn't get away. My attacker, wearing a mask, was carrying a long knife. He was gaining ground on me. I felt it was hopeless; I knew I was about to be killed.

If you have had a similar dream, you know how utterly convincing are the panic and fear that the events in the dream can bring about. *Nightmares*, unusually frightening dreams, occur fairly often. In one survey, almost half of a group of college students who kept records of their dreams over a 2-week period reported having at least one nightmare. This works out to some 24 nightmares per person each year, on average (Levin & Nielsen, 2009; Schredl et al., 2009; Schredl & Reinhard, 2011).

However, most of the 150,000 dreams the average person experiences by the age of 70 are much less dramatic. They typically encompass everyday events such as going to the supermarket, working at the office, and preparing a meal. Students dream about going to class; professors dream about lecturing. Dental patients dream of getting their teeth drilled; dentists dream of drilling the wrong tooth. The English have tea with the queen in their dreams; in the United States, people go to a bar with the president (Domhoff, 1996; Schredl & Piel, 2005; Taylor & Bryant, 2007). Figure 5 shows the most common themes found in people's dreams.

Study Alert
Use Figure 6 to learn the differences between the three main explanations of dreaming.

But what, if anything, do all these dreams mean? Whether dreams have a specific significance and function is a question that scientists have considered for many years, and they have developed the three alternative theories we discuss below (and summarized in Figure 6).

PSYCHOANALYTIC EXPLANATIONS OF DREAMS: DO DREAMS REPRESENT UNCONSCIOUS WISH FULFILLMENT?

unconscious wish fulfillment theory Sigmund Freud's theory that dreams represent unconscious wishes that dreamers desire to see fulfilled.

Using psychoanalytic theory, Sigmund Freud viewed dreams as a guide to the unconscious (Freud, 1900). In his **unconscious wish fulfillment theory,** he proposed that dreams represent unconscious wishes that dreamers desire to see fulfilled. To Freud, the *manifest content* of the dream is what we remember and report about the dream–its storyline. The manifest content, however, disguises the *latent content*, which includes

	Percentage of Dreams Reporting at Least One Event	
Thematic Event	**Males**	**Females**
Aggression	47%	44%
Friendliness	38	42
Sexuality	12	4
Misfortune	36	33
Success	15	8
Failure	15	10

FIGURE 5 Although dreams tend to be subjective to the person having them, common elements frequently occur in everyone's dreams. Why do you think so many common dreams are unpleasant and so few are pleasant? Do you think this tells us anything about the function of dreams? (Source: Adapted from Schneider & Domhoff, 2002.)

Theory	Basic Explanation	Meaning of Dreams	Is Meaning of Dream Disguised?
Unconscious wish fulfillment theory (Freud)	Psychoanalytical explanation where dreams represent unconscious wishes the dreamer wants to fulfill	Latent content reveals unconscious wishes	Yes, by manifest content of dreams
Dreams-for-survival theory	Evolutionary explanation where information relevant to daily survival is reconsidered and reprocessed	Clues to everyday concerns about survival	Not necessarily
Activation-synthesis theory	Neuroscience explanation where dreams are the result of random activation of various memories, which are tied together in a logical story line	Dream scenario that is constructed is related to dreamer's concerns	Not necessarily

FIGURE 6 Three theories of dreams. As researchers have yet to agree on the fundamental meaning of dreams, several theories about dreaming have emerged.

the actual, underlying wishes that the dream represents. Because the underlying wishes (the latent content) are threatening to the dreamer, they are hidden in the dream's storyline (the manifest content).

To Freud, it was important to pierce the armor of a dream's manifest content to understand its true meaning. To do this, Freud tried to get people to discuss their dreams, associating symbols in the dreams with events in the past. He also suggested that certain common symbols with universal meanings appear in dreams. For example, to Freud, dreams in which a person is flying symbolize a wish for sexual intercourse. (See Figure 7 for other common symbols.)

Many psychologists reject Freud's view that dreams typically represent unconscious wishes and that particular objects and events in a dream are symbolic. Rather, they believe that the direct, overt action of a dream is the focal point of its meaning. For example, a dream in which we are walking down a long hallway to take an exam for which we haven't studied does not relate to unconscious, unacceptable wishes. Instead, it simply may mean that we are concerned about an impending test. Even more complex dreams can often be interpreted in terms of everyday concerns and stress (Picchioni et al., 2002; Cartwright, Agargum, & Kirkby, 2006).

Moreover, some dreams reflect events occurring in the dreamer's environment as he or she is sleeping. For example, sleeping participants in one experiment were sprayed with water while they were dreaming. Those unlucky volunteers reported more dreams involving water than did a comparison group of participants who were

Symbol (Manifest Content of Dream)	Interpretation (Latent Content)
Climbing up a stairway, crossing a bridge, riding an elevator, flying in an airplane, walking down a long hallway, entering a room, train traveling through a tunnel	Sexual intercourse
Apples, peaches, grapefruits	Breasts
Bullets, fire, snakes, sticks, umbrellas, guns, hoses, knives	Male sex organs
Ovens, boxes, tunnels, closets, caves, bottles, ship	Female sex organs

FIGURE 7 According to Freud, dreams contain common symbols with universal meanings.

MODULE 13

Hypnosis and Meditation

Learning Outcomes

LO 13-1 What is hypnosis, and are hypnotized people in a different state of consciousness?

LO 13-2 What are the effects of meditation?

> You are feeling relaxed and drowsy. You are getting sleepier. Your body is becoming limp. Your eyelids are feeling heavier. Your eyes are closing; you can't keep them open anymore. You are totally relaxed. Now, place your hands above your head. But you will find they are getting heavier and heavier—so heavy you can barely keep them up. In fact, although you are straining as hard as you can, you will be unable to hold them up any longer.

An observer watching this scene would notice a curious phenomenon. Many of the people listening to the voice are dropping their arms to their sides. The reason for this strange behavior? Those people have been hypnotized.

Hypnosis: A Trance-Forming Experience?

hypnosis A trancelike state of heightened susceptibility to the suggestions of others.

People under **hypnosis** are in a trancelike state of heightened susceptibility to the suggestions of others. In some respects, it appears that they are asleep. Yet other aspects of their behavior contradict this notion, for people are attentive to the hypnotist's suggestions and may carry out bizarre or silly suggestions.

How is someone hypnotized? Typically, the process follows a series of four steps. First, a person is made comfortable in a quiet environment. Second, the hypnotist explains what is going to happen, such as telling the person that he or she will experience a pleasant, relaxed state. Third, the hypnotist tells the person to concentrate on a specific object or image, such as the hypnotist's moving finger or an image of a calm lake. The hypnotist may have the person concentrate on relaxing different parts of the body, such as the arms, legs, and chest. Fourth, once the subject is in a highly relaxed state, the hypnotist may make suggestions that the person interprets as being produced by hypnosis, such as "Your arms are getting heavy" and "Your eyelids are more difficult to open." Because the person begins to experience these sensations, he or she believes they are caused by the hypnotist and becomes susceptible to the suggestions of the hypnotist.

Despite their compliance when hypnotized, people do not lose all will of their own. They will not perform antisocial behaviors, and they will not carry out self-destructive acts. People will not reveal hidden truths about themselves, and they are capable of lying. Moreover, people cannot be hypnotized against their will—despite popular misconceptions (Gwynn & Spanos, 1996; Raz, 2007).

There are wide variations in people's susceptibility to hypnosis. About 5% to 20% of the population cannot be hypnotized at all, and some 15% are very easily hypnotized. Most people fall somewhere in between. Moreover, the ease with which a person is hypnotized is related to a number of other characteristics. People who are readily hypnotized are also easily absorbed while reading books or listening to music, becoming unaware of what is happening around them, and they often spend an unusual

Despite common misconceptions, people cannot be hypnotized against their will, nor do they lose all will of their own when they are hypnotized. Why, then, do people sometimes behave so unusually when asked to by a hypnotist?

amount of time daydreaming. In sum, then, they show a high ability to concentrate and to become completely absorbed in what they are doing (Kirsch & Braffman, 2001; Rubichi et al., 2005; Benham, Woody, & Wilson, 2006).

A DIFFERENT STATE OF CONSCIOUSNESS?

The question of whether hypnosis is a state of consciousness that is qualitatively different from normal waking consciousness is controversial. Some psychologists believe that hypnosis represents a state of consciousness that differs significantly from other states. In this view, high suggestibility, increased ability to recall and construct images, and acceptance of suggestions that clearly contradict reality suggest it is a different state. Moreover, changes in electrical activity in the brain are associated with hypnosis, supporting the position that hypnosis is a state of consciousness different from normal waking (Hilgard, 1992; Fingelkurts, Fingelkurts, & Kallio, 2007; Hinterberger, Schöner, & Halsband, 2011).

In this view, hypnosis represents a state of *divided consciousness*. According to famed hypnosis researcher Ernest Hilgard, hypnosis brings about a *dissociation*, or division, of consciousness into two simultaneous components. In one stream of consciousness, hypnotized people are following the commands of the hypnotist. Yet on another level of consciousness, they are acting as "hidden observers," aware of what is happening to them. For instance, hypnotic subjects may appear to be following the hypnotist's suggestion about feeling no pain, yet in another stream of consciousness they may be actually aware of the pain.

Study Alert
The question of whether hypnosis represents a different state of consciousness or is similar to normal waking consciousness is a key issue.

On the other side of the controversy are psychologists who reject the notion that hypnosis is a state significantly different from normal waking consciousness. They argue that altered brain-wave patterns are not sufficient to demonstrate a qualitative difference, because no other specific physiological changes occur when people are in trances. Furthermore, little support exists for the contention that adults can recall memories of childhood events accurately while hypnotized. That lack of evidence suggests that there is nothing qualitatively special about the hypnotic trance (Hongchun & Ming, 2006; Wagstaff, 2009; Wagstaff, Wheatcroft, & Jones, 2011).

There is increasing agreement that the controversy over the nature of hypnosis has led to extreme positions on both sides of the issue. More recent approaches suggest that the hypnotic state may best be viewed as lying along a continuum in

Applying Psychology in the 21st Century

Will the Person on the Cell Phone Please Pipe Down!

You're relaxing at your favorite coffee shop, engrossed in a good book. You're easily able to tune out the distractions happening around you–people coming and going, animated conversations, traffic noises outside–and remain ensconced in your own little meditative world. That is, until another patron starts having a conversation on her cell phone. You can't tune her out. You now find that you have to read each sentence three times. Why does she have to talk so loud? With every passing minute you get increasingly annoyed, until finally the call ends and you can resume tuning out the world around you.

We've all had this experience of finding cell phone conversations to be particularly distracting and annoying, even in contexts that are already filled with other kinds of distractors. Is there something special about cell phone conversations that make them particularly difficult to ignore?

Yes there is, research finds. In one study, college students were to complete anagrams while a bystander talked on a cell phone. They reported feeling more irritated and more distracted than did students who completed the same task while two bystanders engaged in a conversation with each other. It's not the talking itself that's bothersome–it's the one-sided nature of a cell-phone conversation. The normal back and forth of a conversation that is occurring nearby is a familiar stimulus that we can readily tune out. But a one-sided conversation is practically tailor-made to grab our attention. The long pauses between utterances make it difficult to anticipate when the next one is coming. When we hear the talker again, it comes as a surprise–and unexpected stimuli tend to grab our attention (Galván, Vessal, & Golley, 2013).

Why is it so hard to tune out the conversation of someone talking on a cell phone?

The inability to tune out a nearby cell phone conversation is what makes us feel that the talker is unusually loud. In one study, participants were exposed to a conversation that was either face-to-face or on a cell phone. The researchers varied the volume levels of the speaker in both types of conversation. Participants judged the cell phone conversations, but not the face-to-face conversations, to be louder than they actually were. As one of the researchers explains, it's much like how a light seems brighter when you stare at it–a noise that keeps grabbing your attention, forcing you to listen to it, similarly seems louder (Emberson et al., 2010).

So it's not just your imagination; cell phone conversations really are particularly grating to those forced to listen in. Remember that the next time your phone rings in a public place!

RETHINK

- Why might incomplete stimuli, such as a one-sided phone conversation, be particularly likely to break our focus?
- Rapidly advancing technology is making the one-sided phone conversation a more ubiquitous phenomenon. Do you think humanity will adapt to this relatively new sensory feature of our environment?

Meditation is a means of altering consciousness that is practiced in many cultures, though it can take different forms and serve different purposes across cultures. In fact, one impetus for the study of consciousness is the realization that people in different cultures routinely seek ways to alter their states of consciousness (Walsh & Shapiro, 2006).

Exploring DIVERSITY

Cross-Cultural Routes to Altered States of Consciousness

> A group of Native-American Sioux men sit naked in a steaming sweat lodge as a medicine man throws water on sizzling rocks to send billows of scalding steam into the air.
>
> Aztec priests smear themselves with a mixture of crushed poisonous herbs, hairy black worms, scorpions, and lizards. Sometimes they drink the potion.
>
> During the 16th century, a devout Hasidic Jew lies across the tombstone of a celebrated scholar. As he murmurs the name of God repeatedly, he seeks to be possessed by the soul of the dead wise man's spirit. If successful, he will attain a mystical state, and the deceased's words will flow out of his mouth.

Each of these rituals has a common goal: suspension from the bonds of everyday awareness and access to an altered state of consciousness. Although they may seem exotic from the vantage point of many Western cultures, these rituals represent an apparently universal effort to alter consciousness (Bartocci, 2004; Irwin, 2006).

Some scholars suggest that the quest to alter consciousness represents a basic human desire (Siegel, 1989). Whether or not we accept such an extreme view, variations in states of consciousness clearly share some basic characteristics across a variety of cultures. One is an alteration in thinking, which may become shallow, illogical, or otherwise different from normal. In addition, people's sense of time can become disturbed, and their perceptions of the physical world and of themselves may change. They may lose self-control, doing things that they would never otherwise do. Finally, they may feel a sense of *ineffability*—the inability to understand an experience rationally or describe it in words (Finkler, 2004; Travis, 2006).

Study Alert
Remember that although there are alternate techniques used in meditation, they are all designed to bring about an altered state of consciousness in which attention is refocused.

Of course, realizing that efforts to produce altered states of consciousness are widespread throughout the world's societies does not answer a fundamental question: Is the experience of unaltered states of consciousness similar across different cultures?

Because humans share basic biological commonalities in the ways their brains and bodies are wired, we might assume that the fundamental experience of consciousness is similar across cultures. As a result, we could suppose that consciousness shows some basic similarities across cultures. However, the ways in which certain aspects of consciousness are interpreted and viewed show substantial differences from culture to culture. For example, people in disparate cultures view the experience of the passage of time in varying ways. For instance, Arabs appear to perceive the passage of time more slowly than North Americans (Alon & Brett, 2007; Haynes, Nixon, & West, 2007).

RECAP/EVALUATE/RETHINK

RECAP

LO 13-1 What is hypnosis, and are hypnotized people in a different state of consciousness?

- Hypnosis produces a state of heightened susceptibility to the suggestions of the hypnotist. Under hypnosis, significant behavioral changes occur, including increased concentration and suggestibility, heightened ability to recall and construct images, lack of initiative, and acceptance of suggestions that clearly contradict reality.

LO 13-2 What are the effects of meditation?

- Meditation is a learned technique for refocusing attention that brings about an altered state of consciousness.
- Different cultures have developed their own unique ways to alter states of consciousness.

EVALUATE

1. __________ is a state of heightened susceptibility to the suggestions of others.

2. A friend tells you, "I once heard of a person who was murdered by being hypnotized and then told to jump from the Golden Gate Bridge!" Could such a thing have happened? Why or why not?

3. __________ is a learned technique for refocusing attention to bring about an altered state of consciousness.

4. Leslie repeats a unique sound, known as a __________ when she engages in meditation.

RETHINK

1. Why do you think people in almost every culture seek ways of altering their states of consciousness?

2. Meditation produces several physical and psychological benefits. Does this suggest that we are physically and mentally burdened in our normal state of waking consciousness? Why?

Answers to Evaluate Questions

1. Hypnosis; **2.** no; people who are hypnotized cannot be made to perform self-destructive acts; **3.** Meditation; **4.** mantra

KEY TERMS

hypnosis
meditation

MODULE 14

Drug Use: The Highs and Lows of Consciousness

John Brodhead's bio reads like a script for an episode of VH1's *Behind the Music*. A young rebel from the New Jersey suburbs falls in with a fast crowd, gets hooked on parties and booze, and, with intensive counseling and a bit of tough love, manages to get his life back together. What makes his story different? Just one thing: his age. John is 13 (Rogers, 2002).

Learning Outcome

LO 14-1 What are the major classifications of drugs, and what are their effects?

John Brodhead was lucky. Now in recovery, John had begun to drink when he was in the 6th grade. He is not alone: The number of teens who start drinking by the 8th grade has increased by almost a third since the 1970s, even though alcohol consumption overall has stayed fairly steady among the general population.

Drugs of one sort or another are a part of almost everyone's life. From infancy on, most people take vitamins, aspirin, cold-relief medicine, and the like, and surveys find that 80% of adults in the United States have taken an over-the-counter pain reliever in the last 6 months. However, these drugs rarely produce an altered state of consciousness (Dortch, 1996).

In contrast, some substances, known as psychoactive drugs, lead to an altered state of consciousness. **Psychoactive drugs** influence a person's emotions, perceptions, and behavior. Yet even this category of drugs is common in most of our lives. If you have ever had a cup of coffee or sipped a beer, you have taken a psychoactive drug. A large number of individuals have used more potent–and more dangerous–psychoactive drugs than coffee and beer (see Figure 1); for instance, surveys find that 41% of high school seniors have used an illegal drug in the last year. In addition, 30% report having been drunk on alcohol. The figures for the adult population are even higher (Johnston et al., 2012).

John Brodhead began to drink heavily when he was in 6th grade.

psychoactive drugs Drugs that influence a person's emotions, perceptions, and behavior.

addictive drugs Drugs that produce a biological or psychological dependence in the user so that withdrawal from them leads to a craving for the drug that, in some cases, may be nearly irresistible.

Of course, drugs vary widely in the effects they have on users, in part because they affect the nervous system in very different ways. Some drugs alter the limbic system, and others affect the operation of specific neurotransmitters across the synapses of neurons. For example, some drugs block or enhance the release of neurotransmitters, others block the receipt or the removal of a neurotransmitter, and still others mimic the effects of a particular neurotransmitter (see Figure 2).

Addictive drugs produce a physiological or psychological dependence (or both) in the user, and withdrawal from the drugs leads to a craving for the drug that may be overpowering and nearly irresistible. In physiological dependence, the body becomes so accustomed to functioning in the presence of a drug that it cannot function without it. In psychological dependence, people believe that they need the drug to respond to the stresses of daily living. Although we generally associate addiction with drugs such as heroin, everyday sorts of drugs, such as caffeine (found in coffee) and nicotine (found in cigarettes), have addictive aspects as well (Li, Volkow, & Balu, 2007).

We know surprisingly little about the underlying causes of addiction. One of the problems in identifying those causes is that different drugs (such as alcohol and cocaine) affect the brain in very different ways–yet they may be equally addicting. Furthermore, it takes longer to become addicted to some drugs than to others, even though the ultimate consequences of addiction may be equally grave (Crombag & Robinson, 2004; Nestler & Malenka, 2004; Smart, 2007).

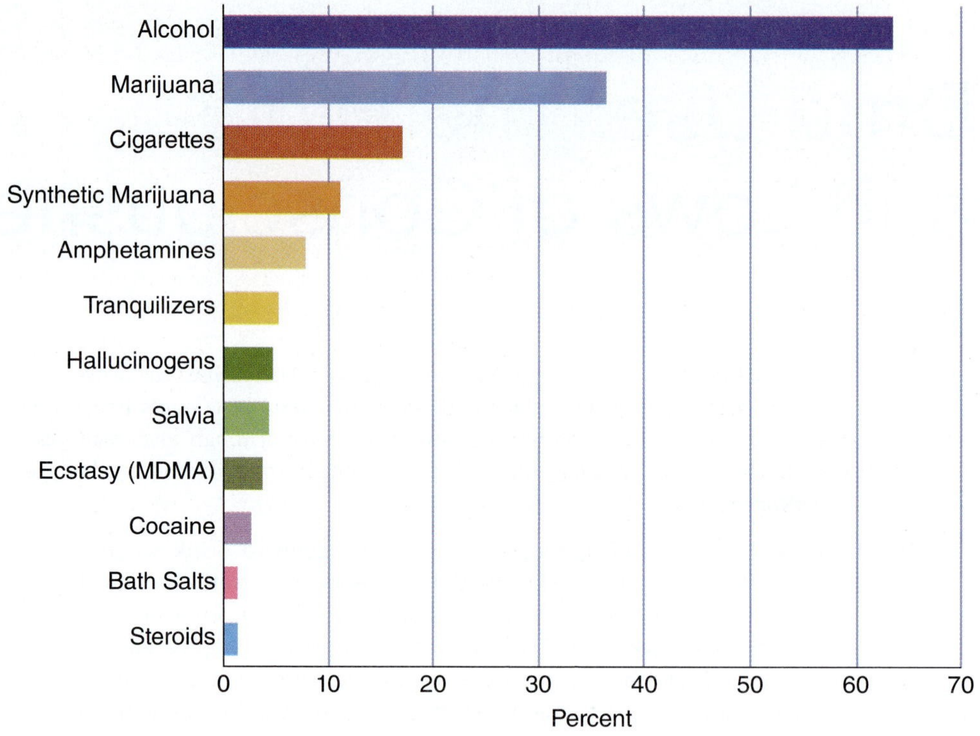

FIGURE 1 How many teenagers use drugs? The results of the most recent comprehensive survey of 14,000 high school seniors across the United States show the percentage of respondents who have used various substances for nonmedical purposes at least once. Can you think of any reasons why teenagers—as opposed to older people—might be particularly likely to use drugs? (Source: Adapted from Johnston et al., 2012.)

PsychTech

Drugs are not the only source of addiction. Increasing evidence suggests that people can develop psychological dependence to the use of technologies, such as social networking sites like Facebook or e-mail.

Why do people take drugs in the first place? There are many reasons, ranging from the perceived pleasure of the experience itself, to the escape that a drug-induced high affords from the everyday pressures of life, to an attempt to achieve a religious or spiritual state. However, other factors having little to do with the nature of the experience itself also lead people to try drugs (McDowell & Spitz, 1999; Korcha et al., 2011).

For instance, the highly publicized drug use of role models such as movie stars and professional athletes, the easy availability of some illegal drugs, and peer pressure all play a role in the decision to use drugs. In some cases, the motive is simply the thrill of trying something new. Finally, genetic factors may predispose some people to be more susceptible to drugs and to become addicted to them. Regardless of the forces

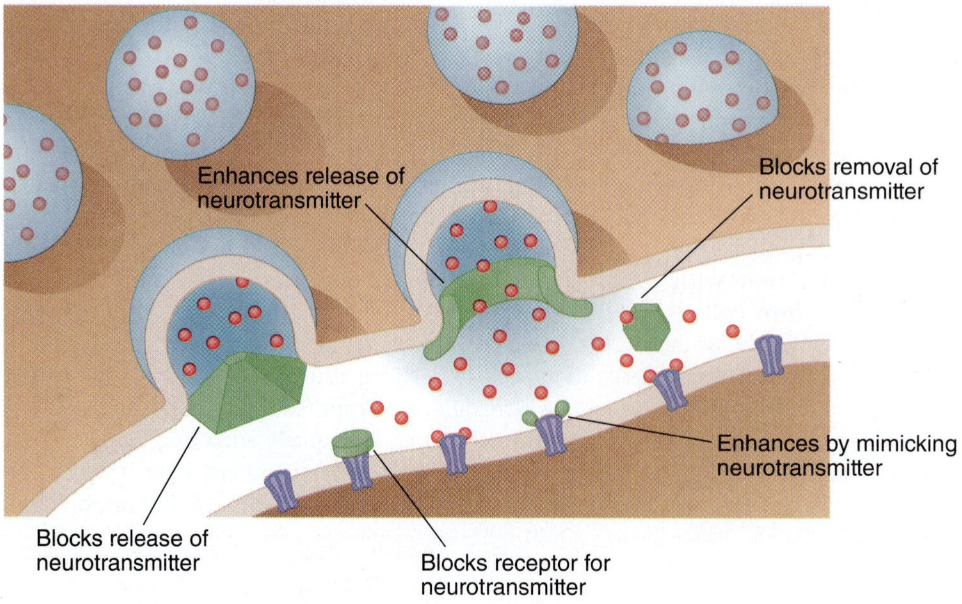

FIGURE 2 Different drugs affect different parts of the nervous system and brain, and each drug functions in one of these specific ways.

Study Alert

Use Figure 2 to learn the different ways that drugs produce their effects on a neurological level.

that lead a person to begin using drugs, drug addiction is among the most difficult of all behaviors to modify, even with extensive treatment (Mosher & Akins, 2007; Ray & Hutchison, 2007; Vrieze et al., 2013).

Because of the difficulty in treating drug problems, there is little disagreement that the best hope for dealing with the overall societal problem of substance abuse is to prevent people from becoming involved with drugs in the first place. However, there is little accord on how to accomplish this goal.

Even drug reduction programs widely publicized for their effectiveness–such as D.A.R.E. (Drug Abuse Resistance Education)–are of questionable effectiveness. Used in more than 80% of school districts in the United States, D.A.R.E. consists of a series of 17 lessons on the dangers of drugs, alcohol, and gangs taught to 5th- and 6th-graders by a police officer. The program is highly popular with school officials, parents, and politicians. The problem? Repeated careful evaluations have been unable to demonstrate that the D.A.R.E. program is effective in reducing drug use over the long term. In fact, one study even showed that D.A.R.E. graduates were more likely to use marijuana than was a comparison group of nongraduates (West & O'Neal, 2004; Des Jarlais et al., 2006; Lucas, 2008; Vincus et al., 2010).

Stimulants: Drug Highs

It's 1:00 a.m., and you still haven't finished reading the last chapter of the text on which you will be tested later in the morning. Feeling exhausted, you turn to the one thing that may help you stay awake for the next 2 hours: a cup of strong black coffee.

If you have ever found yourself in such a position, you have resorted to a major *stimulant*, caffeine, to stay awake. *Caffeine* is one of a number of **stimulants,** drugs whose effect on the central nervous system causes a rise in heart rate, blood pressure, and muscular tension. Caffeine is present not only in coffee; it is an important ingredient in tea, soft drinks, and chocolate as well (see Figure 3).

stimulants Drugs that have an arousal effect on the central nervous system, causing a rise in heart rate, blood pressure, and muscular tension.

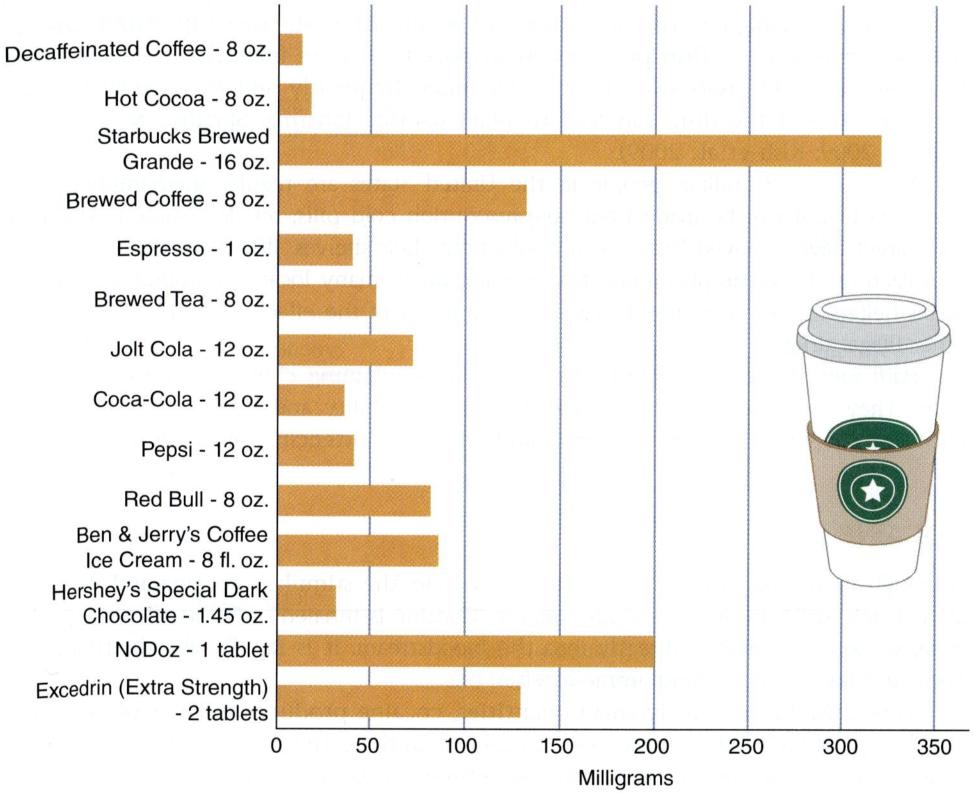

FIGURE 3 How much caffeine do you consume? This chart shows the range of caffeine found in common foods, drinks, and legal drugs. (Source: Adapted from Center for Science in the Public Interest, 2007.)

Prologue *Learning to Love Facebook*

"Facebook is my arch-nemesis!" complained Jean Davis, a college sophomore majoring in accounting. "I tell myself that I'm going to be productive today and get a bunch of studying done, but I can't resist just checking my Facebook news feed first. I tell myself it'll be just a quick peek, and then bam! Half the day is shot!

"The most frustrating thing is, no matter how mad I get at myself or how guilty I feel, the next day I turn around and do the same thing again."

Looking Ahead

Do you eagerly check for texts, tweets, and Facebook updates at every opportunity? Do you wonder why you find yourself so drawn to the possibility that some intriguing communication is about to come your way?

The same processes that make social media so reinforcing allow us to learn to read a book, drive a car, play poker, study for a test, or perform any of the numerous activities that make up our daily routine. Each of us must acquire and then refine our skills and abilities through learning.

Learning is a fundamental topic for psychologists and plays a central role in almost every specialty area of psychology. For example, a psychologist studying perception might ask, "How do we learn that people who look small from a distance are far away and not simply tiny?" A developmental psychologist might inquire, "How do babies learn to distinguish their mothers from other people?" A clinical psychologist might wonder, "Why do some people learn to be afraid when they see a spider?" A social psychologist might ask, "How do we learn to believe that we've fallen in love?"

Each of these questions, although drawn from very different branches of psychology, can be answered only through an understanding of basic learning processes. In each case, a skill or a behavior is acquired, altered, or refined through experience.

Psychologists have approached the study of learning from several angles. Among the most fundamental are studies of the type of learning that is illustrated in responses ranging from a dog salivating when it hears its owner opening a can of dog food to the emotions we feel when our national anthem is played. Other theories consider how learning is a consequence of rewarding circumstances. Finally, several other approaches focus on the cognitive aspects of learning, or the thought processes that underlie learning.

MODULE 15

Classical Conditioning

Learning Outcomes

LO 15-1 What is learning?

LO 15-2 How do we learn to form associations between stimuli and responses?

Does the mere sight of the golden arches in front of McDonald's make you feel pangs of hunger and think about hamburgers? If it does, you are displaying an elementary form of learning called classical conditioning. *Classical conditioning* helps explain such diverse phenomena as crying at the sight of a bride walking down the aisle, fearing the dark, and falling in love.

Classical conditioning is one of a number of different types of learning that psychologists have identified, but a general definition encompasses them all: **Learning** is a relatively permanent change in behavior that is brought about by experience.

learning A relatively permanent change in behavior brought about by experience.

How do we know when a behavior has been influenced by learning—or even is a result of learning? Part of the answer relates to the nature-nurture question, one of the fundamental issues underlying the field of psychology. In the acquisition of behaviors, experience—which is essential to the definition of learning—is the "nurture" part of the nature-nurture question.

However, it's not always easy to identify whether a change in behavior is due to nature or nurture, because some changes in behavior or performance come about through maturation alone and don't involve experience. For instance, children become better tennis players as they grow older partly because their strength increases with their size—a maturational phenomenon. To understand when learning has occurred, we must differentiate maturational changes from improvements resulting from practice, which indicate that learning actually has occurred.

Similarly, short-term changes in behavior that are due to factors other than learning, such as declines in performance resulting from fatigue or lack of effort, are different from performance changes that are due to actual learning. If Serena Williams has a bad day on the tennis court because of tension or fatigue, this does not mean that she has not learned to play correctly or has "unlearned" how to play well. Because there is not always a one-to-one correspondence between learning and performance, understanding when true learning has occurred is difficult.

It is clear that we are primed for learning from the beginning of life. Infants exhibit a simple type of learning called habituation. *Habituation* is the decrease in response to a stimulus that occurs after repeated presentations of the same stimulus. For example, young infants may initially show interest in a novel stimulus, such as a brightly colored toy, but they will soon lose interest if they see the same toy over and over. (Adults exhibit habituation, too: Newlyweds soon stop noticing that they are wearing a wedding ring.) Habituation permits us to ignore things that have stopped providing new information.

Most learning is considerably more complex than habituation, and the study of learning has been at the core of the field of psychology. Although philosophers since the time of Aristotle have speculated on the foundations of learning, the first systematic research on learning was done at the beginning of the 20th century, when Ivan Pavlov (does the name ring a bell?) developed the framework for learning called classical conditioning.

Ivan Pavlov (center) developed the principles of classical conditioning.

The Basics of Classical Conditioning

Ivan Pavlov, a Russian physiologist, never intended to do psychological research. In 1904 he won the Nobel Prize for his work on digestion, testimony to his contribution to that field. Yet Pavlov is remembered not for his physiological research but for his experiments on basic learning processes–work that he began quite accidentally (Marks, 2004; Samoilov & Zayas, 2007; Grant & Wingate, 2011).

Pavlov had been studying the secretion of stomach acids and salivation in dogs in response to the ingestion of varying amounts and kinds of food. While doing that, he observed a curious phenomenon: Sometimes stomach secretions and salivation would begin in the dogs when they had not yet eaten any food. The mere sight of the experimenter who normally brought the food, or even the sound of the experimenter's footsteps, was enough to produce salivation in the dogs. Pavlov's genius lay in his ability to recognize the implications of this discovery. He saw that the dogs were responding not only on the basis of a biological need (hunger) but also as a result of learning–or, as it came to be called, classical conditioning. **Classical conditioning** is a type of learning in which a neutral stimulus (such as the experimenter's footsteps) comes to elicit a response after being paired with a stimulus (such as food) that naturally brings about that response.

classical conditioning A type of learning in which a neutral stimulus comes to bring about a response after it is paired with a stimulus that naturally brings about that response.

To demonstrate classical conditioning, Pavlov (1927) attached a tube to the salivary gland of a dog, allowing him to measure precisely the dog's salivation. He then rang a bell and, just a few seconds later, presented the dog with meat. This pairing occurred repeatedly and was carefully planned so that, each time, exactly the same amount of time elapsed between the presentation of the bell and the meat. At first the dog would salivate only when the meat was presented, but soon it began to salivate at the sound of the bell. In fact, even when Pavlov stopped presenting the meat, the dog still salivated after hearing the sound. The dog had been classically conditioned to salivate to the bell.

As you can see in Figure 1, the basic processes of classical conditioning that underlie Pavlov's discovery are straightforward, although the terminology he chose is not simple. First, consider the diagram in Figure 1a. Before conditioning, there are two unrelated stimuli: the ringing of a bell and meat. We know that normally the ringing of a bell does not lead to salivation but to some irrelevant response, such as pricking up the ears or perhaps a startle reaction. The bell is therefore called the **neutral stimulus,** because it is a stimulus that, before conditioning, does not naturally bring about the response in which we are interested. We also have meat, which naturally causes a dog to salivate–the response we are interested in conditioning. The meat is called an **unconditioned stimulus (UCS)** because food placed in a dog's mouth automatically causes salivation to occur. The response that the meat elicits (salivation) is called an **unconditioned response (UCR)**–a natural, innate response that occurs automatically and needs no training. Unconditioned responses are always brought about by the presence of unconditioned stimuli.

neutral stimulus A stimulus that, before conditioning, does not naturally bring about the response of interest.

unconditioned stimulus (UCS) A stimulus that naturally brings about a particular response without having been learned.

unconditioned response (UCR) A response that is natural and needs no training (e.g., salivation at the smell of food).

Figure 1b illustrates what happens during conditioning. The bell is rung just before each presentation of the meat. The goal of conditioning is for the dog to associate the bell with the unconditioned stimulus (meat) and therefore to bring about the same sort of response as the unconditioned stimulus.

After a number of pairings of the bell and meat, the bell alone causes the dog to salivate (as in Figure 1c). When conditioning is complete, the bell has changed from a neutral stimulus to a **conditioned stimulus (CS).** At this time, salivation that occurs as a response to the conditioned stimulus (bell) is considered a **conditioned response (CR).** After conditioning, then, the conditioned stimulus brings about the conditioned response.

conditioned stimulus (CS) A once-neutral stimulus that has been paired with an unconditioned stimulus to bring about a response formerly caused only by the unconditioned stimulus.

conditioned response (CR) A response that, after conditioning, follows a previously neutral stimulus (e.g., salivation at the ringing of a bell).

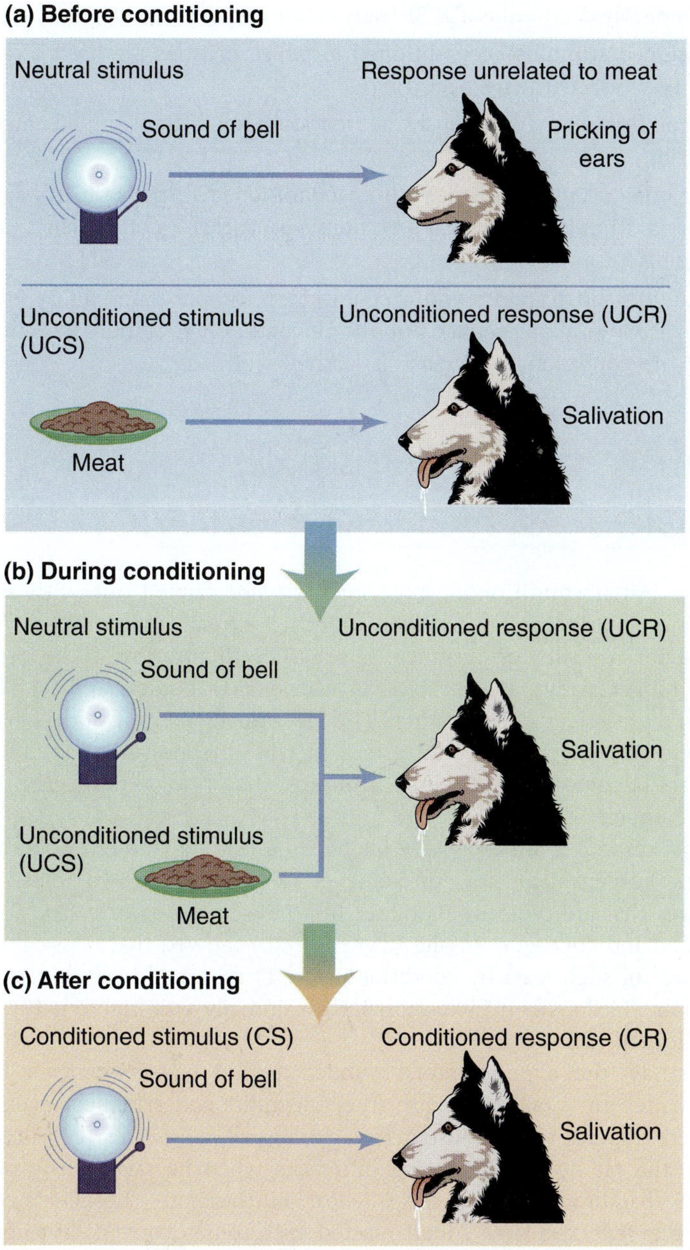

FIGURE 1 The basic process of classical conditioning. (a) Before conditioning, the ringing of a bell does not bring about salivation—making the bell a neutral stimulus. In contrast, meat naturally brings about salivation, making the meat an unconditioned stimulus (UCS) and salivation an unconditioned response (UCR). (b) During conditioning, the bell is rung just before the presentation of the meat. (c) Eventually, the ringing of the bell alone brings about salivation. We now can say that conditioning has been accomplished: The previously neutral stimulus of the bell is now considered a conditioned stimulus (CS) that brings about the conditioned response of salivation (CR).

Study Alert
Figure 1 can help you to learn and understand the process (and terminology) of classical conditioning, which can be confusing.

The sequence and timing of the presentation of the unconditioned stimulus and the conditioned stimulus are particularly important. Like a malfunctioning warning light at a railroad crossing that goes on after the train has passed by, a neutral stimulus that *follows* an unconditioned stimulus has little chance of becoming a conditioned stimulus. However, just as a warning light works best if it goes on right before a train passes, a neutral stimulus that is presented *just before* the unconditioned stimulus is most apt to result in successful conditioning. More specifically, conditioning is most effective if the neutral stimulus (which will become a conditioned stimulus) precedes the unconditioned stimulus by between a half second and several seconds, depending on what kind of response is being conditioned (Wasserman & Miller, 1997; Bitterman, 2006; Jennings et al., 2013).

Although the terminology Pavlov used to describe classical conditioning may seem confusing, the following summary can help make the relationships between stimuli and responses easier to understand and remember:

- Conditioned = learned.
- Unconditioned = not learned.

- An *un*conditioned stimulus (UCS) leads to an *un*conditioned response (UCR).
- *Un*conditioned stimulus-*un*conditioned response pairings are *not* learned and *not* trained: They are naturally occurring.
- During conditioning, a previously neutral stimulus is transformed into the conditioned stimulus.
- A conditioned stimulus (CS) leads to a conditioned response (CR), and a conditioned stimulus-conditioned response pairing is a consequence of learning and training.
- An unconditioned response and a conditioned response are similar (such as salivation in Pavlov's experiment), but the unconditioned response occurs naturally, whereas the conditioned response is learned.

Applying Conditioning Principles to Human Behavior

Although the initial conditioning experiments were carried out with animals, classical conditioning principles were soon found to explain many aspects of everyday human behavior. Recall, for instance, the earlier illustration of how people may experience hunger pangs at the sight of McDonald's golden arches. The cause of this reaction is classical conditioning: The previously neutral arches have become associated with the food inside the restaurant (the unconditioned stimulus), causing the arches to become a conditioned stimulus that brings about the conditioned response of hunger.

Emotional responses are especially likely to be learned through classical conditioning processes. For instance, how do some of us develop fears of mice, spiders, and other creatures that are typically harmless? In a now infamous case study, psychologist John B. Watson and colleague Rosalie Rayner (1920) showed that classical conditioning was at the root of such fears by conditioning an 11-month-old infant named Albert to be afraid of rats. "Little Albert," like most infants, initially was frightened by loud noises but had no fear of rats.

In the study, the experimenters sounded a loud noise whenever Little Albert touched a white, furry rat. The noise (the unconditioned stimulus) evoked fear (the unconditioned response). After just a few pairings of noise and rat, Albert began to show fear of the rat by itself, bursting into tears when he saw it. The rat, then, had become a CS that brought about the CR, fear. Furthermore, the effects of the conditioning lingered: five days later, Albert reacted with some degree of fear not only when shown a rat, but when shown objects that looked similar to the white, furry rat, including a white rabbit, a white seal-skin coat, and even a white Santa Claus mask. (By the way, although we don't know for certain what happened to the unfortunate Little Albert, it appears he was a sickly child who died at the age of 5. In any case, Watson, the experimenter, has been condemned for using ethically questionable procedures that could never be conducted today; Beck, Levinson, & Irons, 2009; Powell, 2011.)

Learning by means of classical conditioning also occurs during adulthood. For example, you may not go to a dentist as often as you should because of previous associations of dentists with pain. In more extreme cases, classical conditioning can lead to the development of *phobias,* which are intense, irrational fears. For example, an insect phobia might develop in someone who is stung by a bee. The insect phobia might be so severe that the person refrains from leaving home.

Posttraumatic stress disorder (PTSD), suffered by some war veterans and others who have had traumatic experiences, can also be produced by classical conditioning. Even years after their battlefield experiences, veterans may feel a rush of fear and anxiety at a stimulus such as a loud noise (Kaštelan et al., 2007; Roberts, Moore, & Beckham, 2007; Schreurs, Smith-Bell, & Burhans, 2011).

On the other hand, classical conditioning also relates to pleasant experiences. For instance, you may have a particular fondness for the smell of a certain perfume or aftershave lotion because thoughts of an early love come rushing back whenever you encounter it. Or hearing a certain song can bring back happy or bittersweet emotions due to associations that you have developed in the past.

Classical conditioning also explains why drug addictions are so difficult to treat. Drug addicts learn to associate certain stimuli–such as drug paraphernalia like a syringe or a room where they use drugs–with the pleasant feelings produced by the drugs. So simply seeing a syringe or entering a room can produce reactions associated with the drug and continued cravings for it (James et al., 2011; Saunders, Yager, & Robinson, 2013).

From the perspective of . . .

An Advertising Executive How might knowledge of classical conditioning be useful in creating an advertising campaign? What, if any, ethical issues arise from this use?

Extinction

What do you think would happen if a dog that had become classically conditioned to salivate at the ringing of a bell never again received food when the bell was rung? The answer lies in one of the basic phenomena of learning: extinction. **Extinction** occurs when a previously conditioned response decreases in frequency and eventually disappears.

extinction A basic phenomenon of learning that occurs when a previously conditioned response decreases in frequency and eventually disappears.

To produce extinction, one needs to end the association between conditioned stimuli and unconditioned stimuli. For instance, if we had trained a dog to salivate (the conditioned response) at the ringing of a bell (the conditioned stimulus), we could produce extinction by repeatedly ringing the bell but *not* providing meat (the unconditioned stimulus; see Figure 2). At first the dog would continue to salivate when it heard

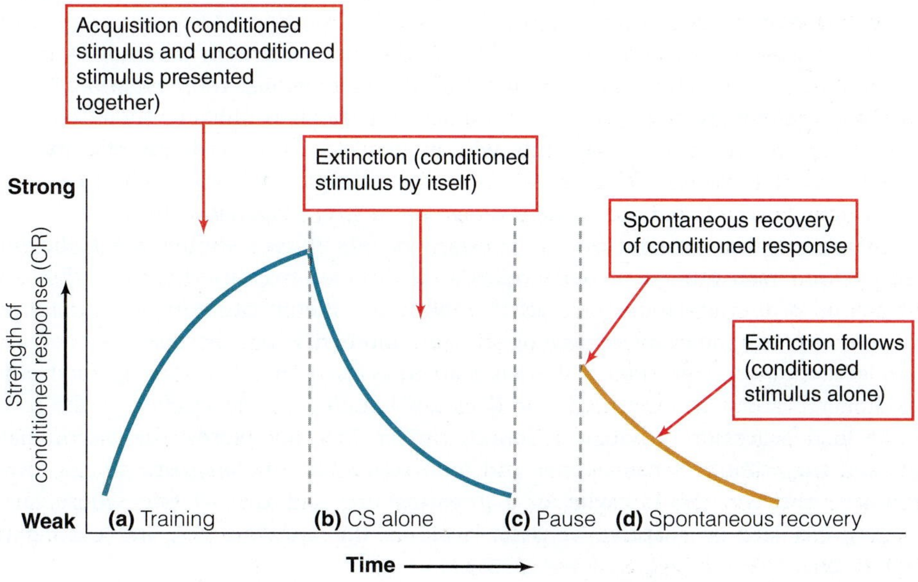

FIGURE 2 Acquisition, extinction, and spontaneous recovery of a classically conditioned response. (a) A conditioned response (CR) gradually increases in strength during training. (b) However, if the conditioned stimulus (CS) is presented by itself enough times, the conditioned response gradually fades, and extinction occurs. (c) After a pause (d) in which the conditioned stimulus is not presented, spontaneous recovery can occur. However, extinction typically reoccurs soon after.

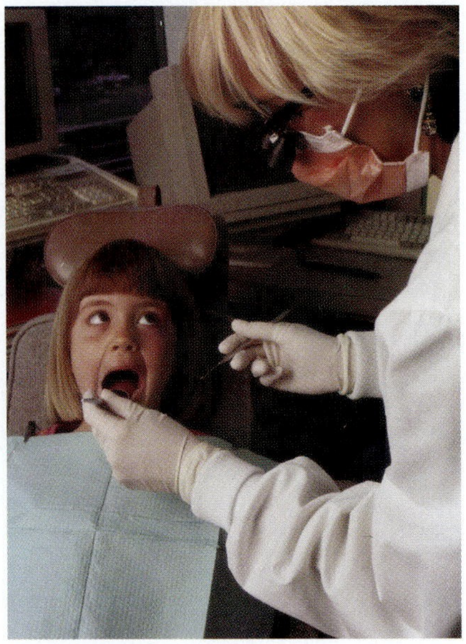

Because of a previous unpleasant experience, a person may expect a similar occurrence when faced with a comparable situation in the future, a process known as stimulus generalization. Can you think of ways that this process occurs in everyday life?

Study Alert
Remember that stimulus generalization relates to stimuli that are similar to one another, while stimulus discrimination relates to stimuli that are different from one another.

spontaneous recovery The reemergence of an extinguished conditioned response after a period of rest and with no further conditioning.

stimulus generalization A process in which, after a stimulus has been conditioned to produce a particular response, stimuli that are similar to the original stimulus produce the same response.

stimulus discrimination The process that occurs if two stimuli are sufficiently distinct from one another that one evokes a conditioned response but the other does not; the ability to differentiate between stimuli.

the bell, but after a few such instances, the amount of salivation would probably decline, and the dog would eventually stop responding to the bell altogether. At that point, we could say that the response had been extinguished. In sum, extinction occurs when the conditioned stimulus is presented repeatedly without the unconditioned stimulus.

We should keep in mind that extinction can be a helpful phenomenon. Consider, for instance, what it would be like if the fear you experienced while watching the shower murder scene in the classic movie *Psycho* never was extinguished. You might well tremble with fright every time you took a shower.

Once a conditioned response has been extinguished, has it vanished forever? Not necessarily. Pavlov discovered this phenomenon when he returned to his dog a few days after the conditioned behavior had seemingly been extinguished. If he rang a bell, the dog once again salivated—an effect known as **spontaneous recovery,** or the reemergence of an extinguished conditioned response after a period of time and with no further conditioning.

Spontaneous recovery also helps explain why it is so hard to overcome drug addictions. For example, cocaine addicts who are thought to be "cured" can experience an irresistible impulse to use the drug again if they are subsequently confronted by a stimulus with strong connections to the drug, such as a white powder (Diaz & De la Casa, 2011; Tunstall, Verendeev, & Kearns, 2013).

Generalization and Discrimination

Despite differences in color and shape, to most of us a rose is a rose is a rose. The pleasure we experience at the beauty, smell, and grace of the flower is similar for different types of roses. Pavlov noticed a similar phenomenon. His dogs often salivated not only at the ringing of the bell that was used during their original conditioning but at the sound of a buzzer as well.

Such behavior is the result of stimulus generalization. **Stimulus generalization** is a process in which, after a stimulus has been conditioned to produce a particular response, stimuli that are similar to the original stimulus produce the same response. The greater the similarity between two stimuli, the greater the likelihood of stimulus generalization. Little Albert, who, as we mentioned earlier, was conditioned to be fearful of white rats, grew afraid of other furry white things as well. However, according to the principle of stimulus generalization, it is unlikely that he would have been afraid of a black dog, because its color would have differentiated it sufficiently from the original fear-evoking stimulus.

The conditioned response elicited by the new stimulus is usually not as intense as the original conditioned response, although the more similar the new stimulus is to the old one, the more similar the new response will be. It is unlikely, then, that Little Albert's fear of the Santa Claus mask was as great as his learned fear of a rat. Still, stimulus generalization permits us to know, for example, that we ought to brake at all red lights, even if there are minor variations in size, shape, and shade.

Stimulus discrimination, in contrast, occurs if two stimuli are sufficiently distinct from each other that one evokes a conditioned response but the other does not. Stimulus discrimination provides the ability to differentiate between stimuli. For example, my dog Cleo comes running into the kitchen when she hears the sound of the electric can opener, which she has learned is used to open her dog food when her dinner is about to be served. She does not bound into the kitchen at the sound of the food processor, although it sounds similar. In other words, she discriminates between the stimuli of can opener and food processor. Similarly, our ability to discriminate between the behavior of a growling dog and that of one whose tail is wagging can lead to adaptive behavior—avoiding the growling dog and petting the friendly one.

Beyond Traditional Classical Conditioning: Challenging Basic Assumptions

Although Pavlov hypothesized that all learning is nothing more than long strings of conditioned responses, this notion has not been supported by subsequent research. It turns out that classical conditioning provides us with only a partial explanation of how people and animals learn; indeed, Pavlov was wrong in some of his basic assumptions (Hollis, 1997).

For example, according to Pavlov, the process of linking stimuli and responses occurs in a mechanistic, unthinking way. In contrast to this perspective, learning theorists influenced by cognitive psychology have argued that learners actively develop an understanding and expectancy about which particular unconditioned stimuli are matched with specific conditioned stimuli. A ringing bell, for instance, gives a dog something to think about: the impending arrival of food (Rescorla, 1988; Kirsch et al., 2004).

Traditional explanations of how classical conditioning operates have also been challenged by John Garcia, a learning psychologist. He found that some organisms—including humans—were *biologically prepared* to quickly learn to avoid foods that smelled or tasted like something that made them sick. For instance, a dog quickly learns to avoid rotting food that in the past made it sick. Similarly, if every time you ate peanuts you had an upset stomach several hours later, eventually you would learn to avoid peanuts. In fact, you might develop a learned *taste aversion,* when the taste of a particular food is associated with unpleasant symptoms such as nausea or vomiting. If you developed a taste aversion to peanuts, merely tasting (or even smelling or in more extreme cases seeing a peanut) could produce such disagreeable symptoms (Garcia, 1990, 2003; Masi et al., 2013).

The surprising part of Garcia's discovery was his demonstration that conditioning could occur even when the interval between exposure to the conditioned stimulus of tainted food and the response of sickness was as long as eight hours. Furthermore, the conditioning persisted over very long periods and sometimes occurred after just one exposure.

These findings have had important practical implications. For example, to keep crows from stealing eggs, dairy farmers may lace an egg with a chemical and leave it in a place where crows will find it. The drug temporarily makes the crows ill, but it does not harm them permanently. After exposure to a chemical-laden egg, crows no longer find them appetizing (Cox et al., 2004; Baker, Johnson, & Slater, 2007; Bouton et al., 2011).

RECAP/EVALUATE/RETHINK

RECAP

LO 15-1 What is learning?

- Learning is a relatively permanent change in behavior resulting from experience.

LO 15-2 How do we learn to form associations between stimuli and responses?

- One major form of learning is classical conditioning, which occurs when a neutral stimulus—one that normally brings about no relevant response—is repeatedly paired with a stimulus (called an unconditioned stimulus) that brings about a natural, untrained response.
- Conditioning occurs when the neutral stimulus is repeatedly presented just before the unconditioned stimulus. After repeated pairings, the neutral stimulus elicits the same response that the unconditioned stimulus brings about. When this occurs, the neutral stimulus has become a conditioned stimulus, and the response a conditioned response.
- Learning is not always permanent. Extinction occurs when a previously learned response decreases in frequency and eventually disappears.
- Stimulus generalization is the tendency for a conditioned response to follow a stimulus that is similar to, but not the same as, the original conditioned stimulus. The converse phenomenon, stimulus discrimination, occurs when an organism learns to distinguish between stimuli.

EVALUATE

1. __________ involves changes brought about by experience, whereas maturation describes changes resulting from biological development.
2. __________ is the name of the scientist responsible for discovering the learning phenomenon known as __________ conditioning, whereby an organism learns a response to a stimulus to which it normally would not respond.

Refer to the passage below to answer questions 3 through 5:

The last three times little Theresa visited Dr. Lopez for checkups, he administered a painful preventive immunization shot that left her in tears. Today, when her mother takes her for another checkup, Theresa begins to sob as soon as she comes face to face with Dr. Lopez, even before he has had a chance to say hello.

3. The painful shot that Theresa received during each visit was a(n) __________ __________ that elicited the __________ __________, her tears.
4. Dr. Lopez is upset because his presence has become a __________ __________ for Theresa's crying.
5. Fortunately, Dr. Lopez gave Theresa no more shots for quite some time. Over that period she gradually stopped crying and even came to like him. __________ had occurred.

RETHINK

1. How likely is it that Little Albert, Watson's experimental subject, might have gone through life afraid of Santa Claus? Describe what could have happened to prevent his continual dread of Santa.
2. Can you think of ways that classical conditioning is used by politicians? advertisers? moviemakers? Do ethical issues arise from any of these uses?

Answers to Evaluate Questions

1. Learning; **2.** Pavlov, classical; **3.** unconditioned stimulus, unconditioned response; **4.** conditioned stimulus; **5.** Extinction

KEY TERMS

learning
classical conditioning
neutral stimulus
unconditioned stimulus (UCS)
unconditioned response (UCR)
conditioned stimulus (CS)
conditioned response (CR)
extinction
spontaneous recovery
stimulus generalization
stimulus discrimination

MODULE 16

Operant Conditioning

Learning Outcomes

LO 16-1 What is the role of reward and punishment in learning?

LO 16-2 What are some practical methods for bringing about behavior change, both in ourselves and in others?

Very good . . . What a clever idea . . . Fantastic . . . I agree . . . Thank you . . . Excellent . . . Super . . . Right on . . . This is the best paper you've ever written; you get an A . . . You are really getting the hang of it . . . I'm impressed . . . You're getting a raise . . . Have a cookie . . . You look great . . . I love you . . .

Few of us mind being the recipient of any of these comments. But what is especially noteworthy about them is that each of these simple statements can be used, through a process known as operant conditioning, to bring about powerful changes in behavior and to teach the most complex tasks. Operant conditioning is the basis for many of the most important kinds of human, and animal, learning.

Operant conditioning is learning in which a voluntary response is strengthened or weakened, depending on its favorable or unfavorable consequences. When we say that a response has been strengthened or weakened, we mean that it has been made more or less likely to recur regularly.

operant conditioning Learning in which a voluntary response is strengthened or weakened, depending on its favorable or unfavorable consequences.

Unlike classical conditioning, in which the original behaviors are the natural, biological responses to the presence of a stimulus such as food, water, or pain, operant conditioning applies to voluntary responses, which an organism performs deliberately to produce a desirable outcome. The term *operant* emphasizes this point: The organism *operates* on its environment to produce a desirable result. Operant conditioning is at work when we learn that toiling industriously can bring about a raise or that studying hard results in good grades.

As with classical conditioning, the basis for understanding operant conditioning was laid by work with animals. We turn now to some of that early research, which began with a simple inquiry into the behavior of cats.

Thorndike's Law of Effect

If you placed a hungry cat in a cage and then put a small piece of food outside the cage, just beyond the cat's reach, chances are that the cat would eagerly search for a way out of the cage. The cat might first claw at the sides or push against an opening. Suppose, though, you had rigged things so that the cat could escape by stepping on a small paddle that released the latch to the door of the cage (see Figure 1). Eventually, as it moved around the cage, the cat would happen to step on the paddle, the door would open, and the cat would eat the food.

What would happen if you then returned the cat to the box? The next time, it would probably take a little less time for the cat to step on the paddle and escape. After a few trials, the cat would deliberately step on the paddle as soon as it was placed in the cage. What would have occurred, according to Edward L. Thorndike (1932), who studied this situation extensively, was that the cat would have learned that pressing the paddle was associated with the desirable consequence of getting food. Thorndike summarized that relationship by formulating the *law of effect:* Responses that lead to satisfying consequences are more likely to be repeated.

Thorndike believed that the law of effect operates as automatically as leaves fall off a tree in autumn. It was not necessary for an organism to understand that there was a link between a response and a reward. Instead, Thorndike believed, over time

positive reinforcer A stimulus added to the environment that brings about an increase in a preceding response.

A **positive reinforcer** is a stimulus *added* to the environment that brings about an increase in a preceding response. If food, water, money, or praise is provided after a response, it is more likely that that response will occur again in the future. The paychecks that workers get at the end of the week, for example, increase the likelihood that they will return to their jobs the following week.

negative reinforcer An unpleasant stimulus whose removal leads to an increase in the probability that a preceding response will be repeated in the future.

In contrast, a **negative reinforcer** refers to an unpleasant stimulus whose removal leads to an increase in the probability that a preceding response will be repeated in the future. For example, if you have an itchy rash (an unpleasant stimulus) that is relieved when you apply a certain brand of ointment, you are more likely to use that ointment the next time you have an itchy rash. Using the ointment, then, is negatively reinforcing, because it removes the unpleasant itch. Similarly, if your iPod volume is so loud that it hurts your ears when you first turn it on, you are likely to reduce the volume level. Lowering the volume is negatively reinforcing, and you are more apt to repeat the action in the future when you first turn it on. Negative reinforcement, then, teaches the individual that taking an action removes a negative condition that exists in the environment. Like positive reinforcers, negative reinforcers increase the likelihood that preceding behaviors will be repeated (Magoon & Critchfield, 2008).

punishment A stimulus that decreases the probability that a previous behavior will occur again.

Note that negative reinforcement is not the same as punishment. **Punishment** refers to a stimulus that *decreases* the probability that a prior behavior will occur again. Unlike negative reinforcement, which produces an *increase* in behavior, punishment reduces the likelihood of a prior response. If we receive a shock that is meant to decrease a certain behavior, then we are receiving punishment, but if we are already receiving a shock and do something to stop that shock, the behavior that stops the shock is considered to be negatively reinforced. In the first case, the specific behavior is apt to decrease because of the punishment; in the second, it is likely to increase because of the negative reinforcement.

There are two types of punishment: positive punishment and negative punishment, just as there are positive reinforcement and negative reinforcement. (In both cases, "positive" means adding something, and "negative" means removing something.) *Positive punishment* weakens a response through the application of an unpleasant stimulus. For instance, spanking a child for misbehaving or spending 10 years in jail for committing a crime is positive punishment. In contrast, *negative punishment* consists of the removal of something pleasant. For instance, when a teenager is told she is "grounded" and will no longer be able to use the family car because of her poor grades, or when an employee is informed that he has been demoted with a cut in pay because of a poor job evaluation, negative punishment is being administered. Both positive and negative punishment result in a decrease in the likelihood that a prior behavior will be repeated.

The following rules (and the summary in Figure 3) can help you distinguish these concepts from one another:

- Reinforcement *increases* the frequency of the behavior preceding it; punishment *decreases* the frequency of the behavior preceding it.
- The *application* of a *positive* stimulus brings about an increase in the frequency of behavior and is referred to as positive reinforcement; the *application* of a *negative* stimulus decreases or reduces the frequency of behavior and is called punishment.
- The *removal* of a *negative* stimulus that results in an increase in the frequency of behavior is negative reinforcement; the *removal* of a *positive* stimulus that decreases the frequency of behavior is negative punishment.

Study Alert
The differences between positive reinforcement, negative reinforcement, positive punishment, and negative punishment are tricky, so pay special attention to Figure 3 and the definitions in the text.

THE PROS AND CONS OF PUNISHMENT: WHY REINFORCEMENT BEATS PUNISHMENT

Is punishment an effective way to modify behavior? Punishment often presents the quickest route to changing behavior that, if allowed to continue, might be dangerous to an individual. For instance, a parent may not have a second chance to warn a child not to

Intended Result	When stimulus is added, the result is . . .	When stimulus is removed or terminated, the result is . . .
Increase in behavior (reinforcement)	**Positive reinforcement** Example: Giving a raise for good performance Result: *Increase* in response of good performance 	**Negative reinforcement** Example: Applying ointment to relieve an itchy rash leads to a higher future likelihood of applying the ointment Result: *Increase* in response of using ointment 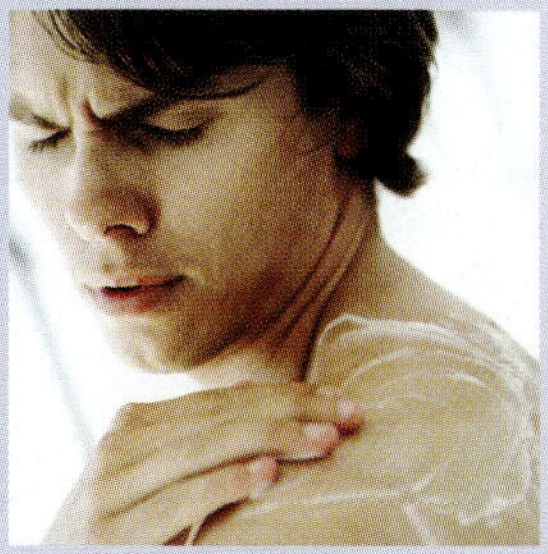
Decrease in behavior (punishment)	**Positive punishment** Example: Yelling at a teenager when she steals a bracelet Result: *Decrease* in frequency of response of stealing 	**Negative punishment** Example: Restricting teenager's access to car due to breaking curfew Result: *Decrease* in response of breaking curfew 

FIGURE 3 Types of reinforcement and punishment.

run into a busy street, and so punishing the first incidence of this behavior may prove to be wise. Moreover, the use of punishment to suppress behavior, even temporarily, provides an opportunity to reinforce a person for subsequently behaving in a more desirable way.

There are some rare instances in which punishment can be the most humane approach to treating certain severe disorders. For example, some children suffer from *autism*, a psychological disorder that can lead them to abuse themselves by tearing at their skin or banging their heads against the wall, injuring themselves severely in the process. In such cases–and when all other treatments have failed–punishment in the form of a quick but intense electric shock has been used to prevent self-injurious behavior. Such punishment, however, is used only to keep the child safe and to buy time until positive reinforcement procedures can be initiated (Humphreys & Lee, 2011; Madden et al., 2013).

Punishment has several disadvantages that make its routine use questionable. For one thing, punishment is frequently ineffective, particularly if it is not delivered shortly after the undesired behavior or if the individual is able to leave the setting in which the punishment is being given. An employee who is reprimanded by the boss may quit; a teenager who loses the use of the family car may borrow a friend's car instead. In such instances, the initial behavior that is being punished may be replaced by one that is even less desirable.

Even worse, physical punishment can convey to the recipient the idea that physical aggression is permissible and perhaps even desirable. A father who yells at and hits his son for misbehaving teaches the son that aggression is an appropriate, adult response. The son soon may copy his father's behavior by acting aggressively toward others. In addition, physical punishment is often administered by people who are themselves angry or enraged. It is unlikely that individuals in such an emotional state will be able to think through what they are doing or control carefully the degree of punishment they are inflicting. Ultimately, those who resort to physical punishment run the risk that they will grow to be feared. Punishment can also reduce the self-esteem of recipients unless they can understand the reasons for it (Leary et al., 2008; Zolotor et al., 2008; Miller-Perrin, Perrin, & Kocur, 2009; Smith, Springer, & Barrett, 2011).

Finally, punishment does not convey any information about what an alternative, more appropriate behavior might be. To be useful in bringing about more desirable behavior in the future, punishment must be accompanied by specific information about the behavior that is being punished, along with specific suggestions concerning a more desirable behavior. Punishing a child for staring out the window in school could merely lead her to stare at the floor instead. Unless we teach her appropriate ways to respond, we have merely managed to substitute one undesirable behavior for another. If punishment is not followed up with reinforcement for subsequent behavior that is more appropriate, little will be accomplished. That's why the scientific research is clear: spanking is both ineffective and ultimately harmful to children. Even punishment in the form of yelling is damaging (Gershoff, 2013; Wang & Kenny, 2013).

In short, reinforcing desired behavior is a more appropriate technique for modifying behavior than using punishment. Both in and out of the scientific arena, then, reinforcement usually beats punishment (Pogarsky & Piquero, 2003; Hiby, Rooney, & Bradshaw, 2004; Sidman, 2006; Hall et al., 2011).

SCHEDULES OF REINFORCEMENT: TIMING LIFE'S REWARDS

The world would be a different place if poker players never played cards again after the first losing hand, fishermen returned to shore as soon as they missed a catch, or telemarketers never made another phone call after their first hang-up. The fact that such unreinforced behaviors continue, often with great frequency and persistence, illustrates that reinforcement need not be received continually for behavior to be learned and maintained. In fact, behavior that is reinforced only occasionally can ultimately be learned better than can behavior that is always reinforced.

When we refer to the frequency and timing of reinforcement that follows desired behavior, we are talking about **schedules of reinforcement.** Behavior that is reinforced every time it occurs is said to be on a **continuous reinforcement schedule;** if it is reinforced some but not all of the time, it is on a **partial** (or **intermittent) reinforcement schedule.** Although learning occurs more rapidly under a continuous reinforcement schedule, behavior lasts longer after reinforcement stops when it is learned under a partial reinforcement schedule (Casey, Cooper-Brown, & Wacher, 2006; Reed, 2007; Holtyn & Lattal, 2013).

schedules of reinforcement Different patterns of frequency and timing of reinforcement following desired behavior.

continuous reinforcement schedule A schedule in which behavior is reinforced every time the behavior occurs.

partial (or intermittent) reinforcement schedule A schedule in which behavior is reinforced some but not all of the time.

Why should intermittent reinforcement result in stronger, longer-lasting learning than continuous reinforcement? We can answer the question by examining how we might behave when using a candy vending machine compared with a Las Vegas slot machine. When we use a vending machine, previous experience has taught us that every time we put in the appropriate amount of money, the reinforcement, a candy bar, ought to be delivered. In other words, the schedule of reinforcement is continuous. In comparison, a slot machine offers intermittent reinforcement. We have learned that after putting in our cash, most of the time we will not receive anything in return. At the same time, though, we know that we will occasionally win something.

Now suppose that, unknown to us, both the candy vending machine and the slot machine are broken, and so neither one is able to dispense anything. It would not be very long before we stopped depositing coins into the broken candy machine. Probably at most we would try only two or three times before leaving the machine in disgust. But the story would be quite different with the broken slot machine. Here, we would drop in money for a considerably longer time, even though there would be no payoff.

In formal terms, we can see the difference between the two reinforcement schedules: Partial reinforcement schedules (such as those provided by slot machines) maintain performance longer than do continuous reinforcement schedules (such as those established in candy vending machines) before *extinction*—the disappearance of the conditioned response—occurs.

Certain kinds of partial reinforcement schedules produce stronger and lengthier responding before extinction than do others. Although many different partial reinforcement schedules have been examined, they can most readily be put into two categories: schedules that consider the *number of responses* made before reinforcement is given, called fixed-ratio and variable-ratio schedules, and those that consider the *amount of time* that elapses before reinforcement is provided, called fixed-interval and variable-interval schedules (Gottlieb, 2006; Reed & Morgan, 2008; Miguez, Witnauer, & Miller, 2011).

Fixed- and Variable-Ratio Schedules. In a **fixed-ratio schedule,** reinforcement is given only after a specific number of responses. For instance, a rat might receive a food pellet every 10th time it pressed a lever; here, the ratio would be 1:10. Similarly, garment workers are generally paid on fixed-ratio schedules: They receive a specific number of dollars for every blouse they sew. Because a greater rate of production means more reinforcement, people on fixed-ratio schedules are apt to work as quickly as possible (see Figure 4).

fixed-ratio schedule A schedule in which reinforcement is given only after a specific number of responses are made.

variable-ratio schedule A schedule by which reinforcement occurs after a varying number of responses rather than after a fixed number.

In a **variable-ratio schedule,** reinforcement occurs after a varying number of responses rather than after a fixed number. Although the specific number of responses necessary to receive reinforcement varies, the number of responses usually hovers around a specific average. A good example of a variable-ratio schedule is a telephone salesperson's job. He might make a sale during the 3rd, 8th, 9th, and 20th calls without being successful during any call in between. Although the number of responses he must make before making a sale varies, it averages out to a 20% success rate. Under these circumstances, you might expect that the salesperson would try to make as many calls as possible in as short a time as possible. This is the case with all variable-ratio schedules, which lead to a high rate of response and resistance to extinction.

Study Alert
Remember that the different schedules of reinforcement affect the rapidity with which a response is learned and how long it lasts after reinforcement is no longer provided.

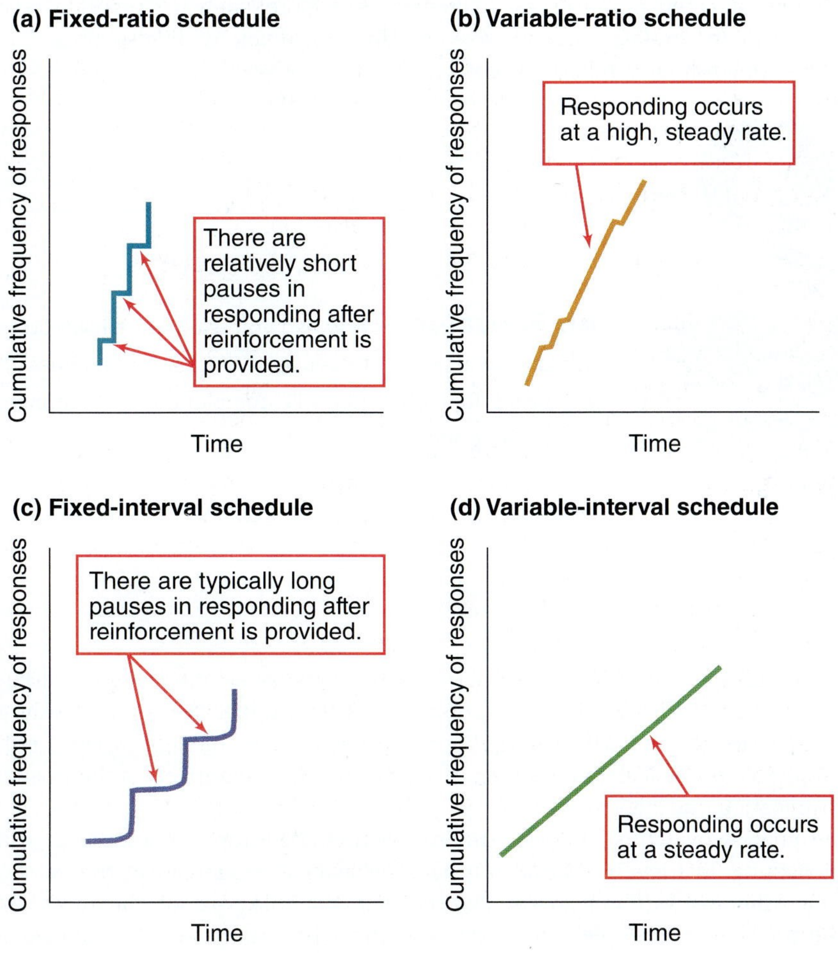

FIGURE 4 Typical outcomes of different reinforcement schedules. (a) In a fixed-ratio schedule, reinforcement is provided after a specific number of responses are made. Because the more responses, the more reinforcement, fixed-ratio schedules produce a high rate of responding. (b) In a variable-ratio schedule, responding also occurs at a high rate. (c) A fixed-interval schedule produces lower rates of responding, especially just after reinforcement has been presented, because the organism learns that a specified time period must elapse between reinforcements. (d) A variable-interval schedule produces a fairly steady stream of responses.

Fixed- and Variable-Interval Schedules: The Passage of Time. In contrast to fixed and variable-ratio schedules, in which the crucial factor is the number of responses, fixed-*interval* and variable-*interval* schedules focus on the amount of time that has elapsed since a person or animal was rewarded. One example of a fixed-interval schedule is a weekly paycheck. For people who receive regular, weekly paychecks, it typically makes relatively little difference exactly how much they produce in a given week.

fixed-interval schedule A schedule in which reinforcement is provided for a response only after a fixed time period has elapsed.

Because a **fixed-interval schedule** provides reinforcement for a response only if a fixed time period has elapsed, overall rates of response are relatively low. This is especially true in the period just after reinforcement, when the time before another reinforcement is relatively great. Students' study habits often exemplify this reality. If the periods between exams are relatively long (meaning that the opportunity for reinforcement for good performance is given fairly infrequently), students often study minimally or not at all until the day of the exam draws near. Just before the exam, however, students begin to cram for it, signaling a rapid increase in the rate of their studying response. As you might expect, immediately after the exam there is a rapid decline in the rate of responding, with few people opening a book the day after a test. Fixed-interval schedules produce the kind of "scalloping effect" shown in Figure 4 (Saville, 2009).

variable-interval schedule A schedule by which the time between reinforcements varies around some average rather than being fixed.

One way to decrease the delay in responding that occurs just after reinforcement, and to maintain the desired behavior more consistently throughout an interval, is to use a variable-interval schedule. In a **variable-interval schedule,** the time between reinforcements varies around some average rather than being fixed. For example, a professor who gives surprise quizzes that vary from one every 3 days to one every 3 weeks, averaging one every 2 weeks, is using a variable-interval schedule. Compared to the study habits we observed with a fixed-interval schedule, students' study habits under such a variable-interval schedule would most likely be very different. Students would be apt to study more regularly because they would never know when the next surprise quiz was coming. Variable-interval schedules, in general, are more likely to produce relatively steady rates of responding than are fixed-interval schedules, with responses that take longer to extinguish after reinforcement ends.

From the perspective of . . .

An Educator How would you use your knowledge of operant conditioning to set up a program to increase the likelihood that students will complete their homework more frequently?

DISCRIMINATION AND GENERALIZATION IN OPERANT CONDITIONING

It does not take a child long to learn that a red light at an intersection means stop and a green light indicates that it is permissible to continue, in the same way that a pigeon can learn to peck a key when a green light goes on but not when a red light appears. Just as in classical conditioning, then, operant learning involves the phenomena of discrimination and generalization.

The process by which people learn to discriminate stimuli is known as stimulus control training. In *stimulus control training,* a behavior is reinforced in the presence of a specific stimulus, but not in its absence. For example, one of the most difficult discriminations many people face is determining when someone's friendliness is not mere friendliness, but a signal of romantic interest. People learn to make the discrimination by observing the presence of certain nonverbal cues–such as increased eye contact and touching–that indicate romantic interest. When such cues are absent, people learn that no romantic interest is indicated. In this case, the nonverbal cue acts as a discriminative stimulus, one to which an organism learns to respond during stimulus control training. A *discriminative stimulus* signals the likelihood that reinforcement will follow a response. For example, if you wait until your roommate is in a good mood before you ask to borrow her favorite CD, your behavior can be said to be under stimulus control because you can discriminate between her moods.

Just as in classical conditioning, the phenomenon of stimulus generalization, in which an organism learns a response to one stimulus and then exhibits the same response to slightly different stimuli, occurs in operant conditioning. If you have learned that being polite helps you to get your way in a certain situation (reinforcing your politeness), you are likely to generalize your response to other situations. Sometimes, though, generalization can have unfortunate consequences, as when people behave negatively toward all members of a racial group because they have had an unpleasant experience with one member of that group.

PsychTech

Computer-based *adaptive learning* techniques—based on the principles of shaping—present students with new material and then quiz them on it online. Presentation of subsequent material is based on students' previous performance on the quiz, so that the level and difficulty of new material is personalized, leading to great student success.

SHAPING: REINFORCING WHAT DOESN'T COME NATURALLY

Consider the difficulty of using operant conditioning to teach people to repair an automobile transmission. If you had to wait until they chanced to fix a transmission perfectly before you provided them with reinforcement, the Model T Ford might be back in style long before they mastered the repair process.

There are many complex behaviors, ranging from auto repair to zoo management, that we would not expect to occur naturally as part of anyone's spontaneous behavior. For such behaviors, for which there might otherwise be no opportunity to provide reinforcement (because the behavior would never occur in the first place), a procedure known as shaping is used. **Shaping** is the process of teaching a complex behavior by rewarding closer and closer approximations of the desired behavior. In shaping, you start by reinforcing any behavior that is at all similar to the behavior you want the person to learn. Later, you reinforce only responses that are closer to the behavior you ultimately want to teach. Finally, you reinforce only the desired response. Each step in shaping, then, moves only slightly beyond the previously learned behavior, permitting the person to link the new step to the behavior learned earlier (Krueger & Dayan, 2009).

shaping The process of teaching a complex behavior by rewarding closer and closer approximations of the desired behavior.

Shaping allows even lower animals to learn complex responses that would never occur naturally, ranging from lions jumping through hoops, dolphins rescuing divers lost at sea, or rodents finding hidden land mines. Shaping also underlies the learning of many complex human skills. For instance, the organization of most textbooks is based on the principles of shaping. Typically, information is presented so that new material builds on previously learned concepts or skills. Thus, the concept of shaping could not be presented until we had discussed the more basic principles of operant learning (Meyer & Ladewig, 2008).

BIOLOGICAL CONSTRAINTS ON LEARNING: YOU CAN'T TEACH AN OLD DOG JUST ANY TRICK

Not all behaviors can be trained in all species equally well. Instead, there are *biological constraints*, built-in limitations in the ability of animals to learn particular behaviors. In some cases, an organism has a special predisposition that will aid in its learning a behavior (such as pecking behaviors in pigeons). In other cases, biological constraints act to prevent or inhibit an organism from learning a behavior. For example, it's impossible to train pigs to pick up a disk, because they are biologically programmed to push objects like it along the ground. Similarly, although a raccoon can be conditioned to drop a single coin into a piggy bank, it will do so only after rubbing the coin against the outside of the bank. The reason? After catching a fish, raccoons instinctually rub them against the ground to remove their outer covering (Breland & Breland, 1966; Stevens & Pashler, 2002; Thurman & Lu, 2013).

Biological constraints make it nearly impossible for animals to learn certain behaviors. Here, psychologist Marian Breland attempts to overcome the natural limitations that inhibit the success of conditioning this rooster.

The existence of biological constraints is consistent with evolutionary explanations of behavior. Clearly, there are adaptive benefits that promote survival for organisms that quickly learn—or avoid—certain behaviors. For example, our ability to rapidly learn to avoid touching hot surfaces increases our chances of survival. Additional support for the evolutionary interpretation of biological constraints lies in the fact the associations that animals learn most readily involve stimuli that are most relevant to the specific environment in which they live (Cosmides & Tooby, 2004; Davis, 2007; Behrendt, 2011).

Furthermore, psychologists taking an evolutionary perspective have suggested that we may be genetically predisposed to be fearful of certain stimuli, such as snakes or even threatening faces. For example, people in experiments learn associations relatively quickly between photos of faces with threatening expressions and neutral stimuli (such as an umbrella). In contrast, they are slower to learn associations between faces that have pleasant expressions and neutral stimuli. Stimuli that pose potential threats, like snakes or people with hostile facial expressions, posed a potential danger to early humans, and there may be an evolved "fear module" in the brain that is sensitized to such threats (Endres & Fendt, 2007; DeLoache & LoBue, 2009; Gerdes, Uhl, & Alpers, 2009).

COMPARING CLASSICAL AND OPERANT CONDITIONING

We've considered classical conditioning and operant conditioning as two completely different processes. And, as summarized in Figure 5, there are a number of key distinctions between the two forms of learning. For example, the key concept in classical

Concept	Classical Conditioning	Operant Conditioning
Basic principle	Building associations between a conditioned stimulus and conditioned response.	Reinforcement *increases* the frequency of the behavior preceding it; punishment *decreases* the frequency of the behavior preceding it.
Nature of behavior	Based on involuntary, natural, innate behavior. Behavior is elicited by the unconditioned or conditioned stimulus.	Organism voluntarily operates on its environment to produce a desirable result. After behavior occurs, the likelihood of the behavior occurring again is increased or decreased by the behavior's consequences.
Order of events	Before conditioning, an unconditioned stimulus leads to an unconditioned response. After conditioning, a conditioned stimulus leads to a conditioned response.	Reinforcement leads to an increase in behavior; punishment leads to a decrease in behavior.
Example	After a physician gives a child a series of painful injections (an unconditioned stimulus) that produce an emotional reaction (an unconditioned response), the child develops an emotional reaction (a conditioned response) whenever he sees the physician (the conditioned stimulus).	A student who, after studying hard for a test, earns an A (the positive reinforcer), is more likely to study hard in the future. A student who, after going out drinking the night before a test, fails the test (punishment) is less likely to go out drinking the night before the next test.

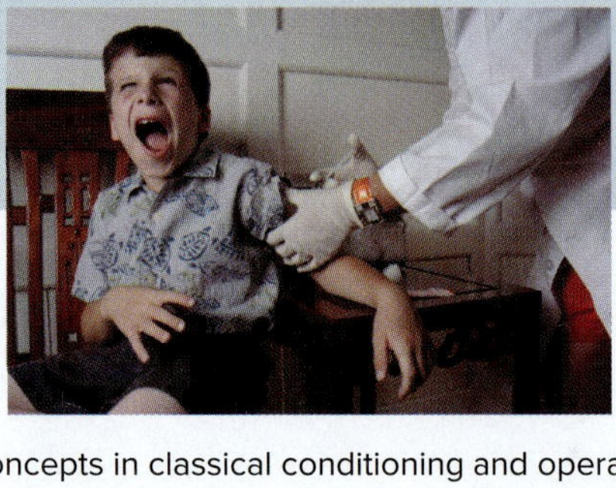

FIGURE 5 Comparing key concepts in classical conditioning and operant conditioning.

conditioning is the association between stimuli, whereas in operant conditioning it is reinforcement. Furthermore, classical conditioning involves an involuntary, natural, innate behavior, but operant conditioning is based on voluntary responses made by an organism.

Some researchers are asking if, in fact, the two types of learning are so different after all. Some learning psychologists have suggested that classical and operant conditioning might share some underlying processes. Arguing from an evolutionary viewpoint, they contend that it is unlikely that two completely separate basic processes would evolve. Instead, one process–albeit with considerable complexity in the way it operates–might better explain behavior. Although it's too early to know if this point of view will be supported, it is clear that there are a number of processes that operate both in classical and operant conditioning, including extinction, stimulus generalization, and stimulus discrimination (Donahoe, 2003; Donahoe & Vegas, 2004; Silva, Gonçalves, & Garcia-Mijares, 2007).

BECOMING AN INFORMED CONSUMER of Psychology

Using Behavior Analysis and Behavior Modification

A couple who had been living together for 3 years began to fight frequently. The issues of disagreement ranged from who was going to do the dishes to the quality of their love life.

Disturbed, the couple went to a *behavior analyst,* a psychologist who specialized in behavior-modification techniques. He asked them to keep a detailed written record of their interactions over the next 2 weeks.

When they returned with the data, he carefully reviewed the records with them. In doing so, he noticed a pattern: Each of their arguments had occurred just after one or the other had left a household chore undone, such as leaving dirty dishes in the sink or draping clothes on the only chair in the bedroom.

Using the data the couple had collected, the behavior analyst asked them to list all the chores that could possibly arise and assign each one a point value depending on how long it took to complete. Then he had them divide the chores equally and agree in a written contract to fulfill the ones assigned to them. If either failed to carry out one of the assigned chores, he or she would have to place $1 per point in a fund for the other to spend. They also agreed to a program of verbal praise, promising to reward each other verbally for completing a chore.

The couple agreed to try it for a month and to keep careful records of the number of arguments they had during that period. To their surprise, the number declined rapidly.

The case just presented provides an illustration of **behavior modification,** a formalized technique for promoting the frequency of desirable behaviors and decreasing the incidence of unwanted ones. Using the basic principles of learning theory, behavior-modification techniques have proved to be helpful in a variety of situations. People with severe mental retardation have, for the first time in their lives, started dressing and feeding themselves. Behavior modification has also helped people lose weight, give up smoking, and behave more safely (Carels et al., 2011; Geller, 2011; Etienne, 2013).

behavior modification A formalized technique for promoting the frequency of desirable behaviors and decreasing the incidence of unwanted ones.

The techniques used by behavior analysts are as varied as the list of processes that modify behavior. They include reinforcement scheduling, shaping, generalization training, discrimination training, and extinction. Participants in a behavior-change program do, however, typically follow a series of similar basic steps that include the following:

- *Identifying goals and target behaviors*. The first step is to define desired behavior. Is it an increase in time spent studying? A decrease in weight? An increase in the use of language? A reduction in the amount of aggression displayed by a child? The goals must be stated in observable terms and must lead to specific targets. For instance, a goal might be "to increase study time," whereas the target behavior would be "to study at least 2 hours per day on weekdays and an hour on Saturdays."

- *Designing a data-recording system and recording preliminary data.* To determine whether behavior has changed, it is necessary to collect data before any changes are made in the situation. This information provides a baseline against which future changes can be measured.
- *Selecting a behavior-change strategy.* The crucial step is to select an appropriate strategy. Because all the principles of learning can be employed to bring about behavior change, a "package" of treatments is normally used. This might include the systematic use of positive reinforcement for desired behavior (verbal praise or something more tangible, such as food), as well as a program of extinction for undesirable behavior (ignoring a child who throws a tantrum). Selecting the right reinforcers is critical, and it may be necessary to experiment a bit to find out what is important to a particular individual.
- *Implementing the program.* Probably the most important aspect of program implementation is consistency. It is also important to reinforce the intended behavior. For example, suppose a mother wants her son to spend more time on his homework, but as soon as he sits down to study, he asks for a snack. If the mother gets a snack for him, she is likely to be reinforcing her son's delaying tactic, not his studying.
- *Keeping careful records after the program is implemented.* Another crucial task is record keeping. If the target behaviors are not monitored, there is no way of knowing whether the program has actually been successful.
- *Evaluating and altering the ongoing program.* Finally, the results of the program should be compared with baseline, pre-implementation data to determine its effectiveness. If the program has been successful, the procedures employed can be phased out gradually. For instance, if the program called for reinforcing every instance of picking up one's clothes from the bedroom floor, the reinforcement schedule could be modified to a fixed-ratio schedule in which every third instance was reinforced. However, if the program has not been successful in bringing about the desired behavior change, consideration of other approaches might be advisable.

Behavior-change techniques based on these general principles have enjoyed wide success and have proved to be one of the most powerful means of modifying behavior. Clearly, it is possible to employ the basic notions of learning theory to improve our lives.

RECAP/EVALUATE/RETHINK

RECAP

LO 16-1 What is the role of reward and punishment in learning?

- Operant conditioning is a form of learning in which a voluntary behavior is strengthened or weakened. According to B. F. Skinner, the major mechanism underlying learning is reinforcement, the process by which a stimulus increases the probability that a preceding behavior will be repeated.
- Primary reinforcers are rewards that are naturally effective without previous experience, because they satisfy a biological need. Secondary reinforcers begin to act as if they were primary reinforcers through association with a primary reinforcer.
- Positive reinforcers are stimuli that are added to the environment and lead to an increase in a preceding response. Negative reinforcers are stimuli that remove something unpleasant from the environment, also leading to an increase in the preceding response.
- Punishment decreases the probability that a prior behavior will occur. Positive punishment weakens a response through the application of an unpleasant stimulus, whereas negative punishment weakens a response by the removal of something positive. In contrast to reinforcement, in which the goal is to increase the incidence of behavior, punishment is meant to decrease or suppress behavior.
- Schedules and patterns of reinforcement affect the strength and duration of learning. Generally, partial reinforcement schedules–in which reinforcers are not delivered on every trial–produce stronger and longer-lasting learning than do continuous reinforcement schedules.
- Among the major categories of reinforcement schedules are fixed- and variable-ratio schedules, which are based on the number of responses made, and fixed- and variable-interval schedules, which are based on the time interval that elapses before reinforcement is provided.

- Stimulus control training (similar to stimulus discrimination in classical conditioning) is reinforcement of a behavior in the presence of a specific stimulus but not in its absence. In stimulus generalization, an organism learns a response to one stimulus and then exhibits the same response to slightly different stimuli.
- Shaping is a process for teaching complex behaviors by rewarding closer and closer approximations of the desired final behavior.
- There are biological constraints, or built-in limitations, on the ability of an organism to learn: Certain behaviors will be relatively easy for individuals of a species to learn, whereas other behaviors will be either difficult or impossible for them to learn.

LO 16-2 What are some practical methods for bringing about behavior change, both in ourselves and in others?

- Behavior modification is a method for formally using the principles of learning theory to promote the frequency of desired behaviors and to decrease or eliminate unwanted ones.

EVALUATE

1. __________ conditioning describes learning that occurs as a result of reinforcement.
2. Match the type of operant learning with its definition:
   1. An unpleasant stimulus is presented to decrease behavior.
   2. An unpleasant stimulus is removed to increase behavior.
   3. A pleasant stimulus is presented to increase behavior.
   4. A pleasant stimulus is removed to decrease behavior.

   a. positive reinforcement
   b. negative reinforcement
   c. positive punishment
   d. negative punishment
3. Sandy had had a rough day, and his son's noisemaking was not helping him relax. Not wanting to resort to scolding, Sandy told his son in a serious manner that he was very tired and would like the boy to play quietly for an hour. This approach worked. For Sandy, the change in his son's behavior was
   a. positively reinforcing.
   b. negatively reinforcing.
4. In a __________ reinforcement schedule, behavior is reinforced some of the time, whereas in a __________ reinforcement schedule, behavior is reinforced all the time.
5. Match the type of reinforcement schedule with its definition.
   1. Reinforcement occurs after a set time period.
   2. Reinforcement occurs after a set number of responses.
   3. Reinforcement occurs after a varying time period.
   4. Reinforcement occurs after a varying number of responses.

   a. fixed-ratio
   b. variable-interval
   c. fixed-interval
   d. variable-ratio

RETHINK

1. Using the scientific literature as a guide, what would you tell parents who want to know if the routine use of physical punishment is a necessary and acceptable form of child rearing?
2. How might operant conditioning be used to address serious personal concerns, such as smoking and unhealthy eating?

Answers to Evaluate Questions

1. Operant; **2.** 1-c, 2-b, 3-a, 4-d; **3.** b; **4.** partial (or intermittent), continuous; **5.** 1-c, 2-a, 3-b, 4-d

KEY TERMS

operant conditioning
reinforcement
reinforcer
positive reinforcer
negative reinforcer
punishment
schedules of reinforcement
continuous reinforcement schedule
partial (or intermittent) reinforcement schedule
fixed-ratio schedule
variable-ratio schedule
fixed-interval schedule
variable-interval schedule
shaping
behavior modification

MODULE 17

Cognitive Approaches to Learning

Learning Outcome

LO 17-1 What is the role of cognition and thought in learning?

Consider what happens when people learn to drive a car. They don't just get behind the wheel and stumble around until they randomly put the key into the ignition and, later, after many false starts, accidentally manage to get the car to move forward, thereby receiving positive reinforcement. Rather, they already know the basic elements of driving from previous experience as passengers, when they more than likely noticed how the key was inserted into the ignition, the car was put in drive, and the gas pedal was pressed to make the car go forward.

Clearly, not all learning is due to operant and classical conditioning. In fact, such activities as learning to drive a car imply that some kinds of learning must involve higher-order processes in which people's thoughts and memories and the way they process information account for their responses. Such situations argue against regarding learning as the unthinking, mechanical, and automatic acquisition of associations between stimuli and responses, as in classical conditioning, or the presentation of reinforcement, as in operant conditioning.

cognitive learning theory An approach to the study of learning that focuses on the thought processes that underlie learning.

Some psychologists view learning in terms of the thought processes, or cognitions, that underlie it—an approach known as **cognitive learning theory.** Although psychologists working from the cognitive learning perspective do not deny the importance of classical and operant conditioning, they have developed approaches that focus on the unseen mental processes that occur during learning, rather than concentrating solely on external stimuli, responses, and reinforcements.

Study Alert

Remember that the cognitive learning approach focuses on the *internal* thoughts and expectations of learners, whereas classical and operant conditioning approaches focus on *external* stimuli, responses, and reinforcement.

In its most basic formulation, cognitive learning theory suggests that it is not enough to say that people make responses because there is an assumed link between a stimulus and a response—a link that is the result of a past history of reinforcement for a response. Instead, according to this point of view, people, and even lower animals, develop an *expectation* that they will receive a reinforcer after making a response. Two types of learning in which no obvious prior reinforcement is present are latent learning and observational learning.

Latent Learning

Evidence for the importance of cognitive processes comes from a series of animal experiments that revealed a type of cognitive learning called latent learning. In **latent learning,** a new behavior is learned but not demonstrated until some incentive is provided for displaying it (Tolman & Honzik, 1930). In short, latent learning occurs without reinforcement.

latent learning Learning in which a new behavior is acquired but is not demonstrated until some incentive is provided for displaying it.

In the studies demonstrating latent learning, psychologists examined the behavior of rats in a maze such as the one shown in Figure 1a. In one experiment, a group of rats was allowed to wander around the maze once a day for 17 days without ever receiving a reward (called the unrewarded group). Understandably, those rats made many errors and spent a relatively long time reaching the end of the maze. A second group, however, was always given food at the end of the maze (the rewarded group). Not surprisingly, those rats learned to run quickly and directly to the food box, making few errors.

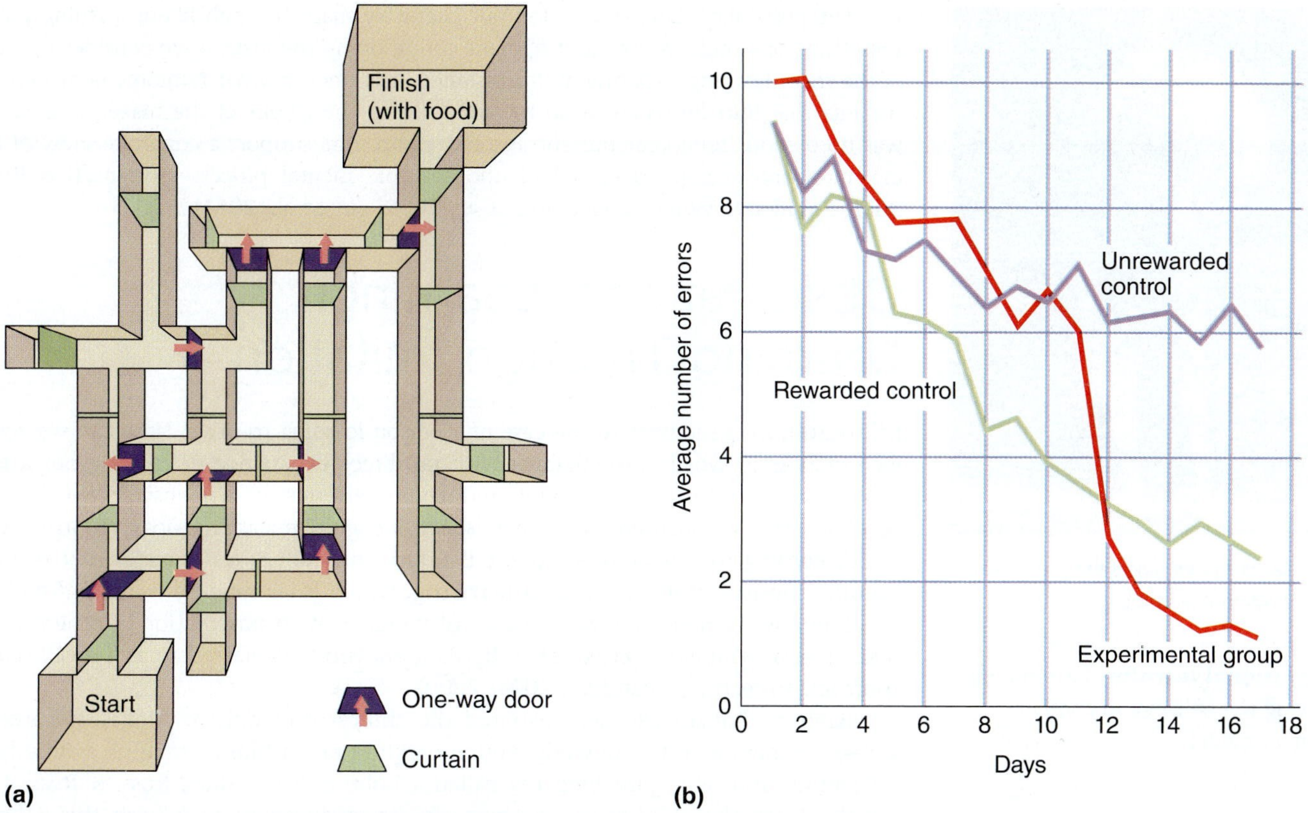

FIGURE 1 Latent learning. (a) Rats were allowed to roam through a maze of this sort once a day for 17 days. (b) The rats that were never rewarded (the unrewarded control condition) consistently made the most errors, whereas those that received food at the finish every day (the rewarded control condition) consistently made far fewer errors. But the results also showed latent learning: Rats that were rewarded only after the 10th day (the experimental group) showed an immediate reduction in errors and soon became similar in error rate to the rats that had been rewarded consistently. According to cognitive learning theorists, the reduction in errors indicates that the rats had developed a cognitive map—a mental representation—of the maze. Can you think of other examples of latent learning? (Source: Adapted from Tolman & Honzik, 1930.)

A third group of rats (the experimental group) started out in the same situation as the unrewarded rats, but only for the first 10 days. On the 11th day, a critical experimental manipulation was introduced: From that point on, the rats in this group were given food for completing the maze. The results of this manipulation were dramatic, as you can see from the graph in Figure 1b. The previously unrewarded rats, which had earlier seemed to wander about aimlessly, showed such reductions in running time and declines in error rates that their performance almost immediately matched that of the group that had received rewards from the start.

To cognitive theorists, it seemed clear that the unrewarded rats had learned the layout of the maze early in their explorations; they just never displayed their latent learning until the reinforcement was offered. Instead, those rats seemed to develop a *cognitive map* of the maze–a mental representation of spatial locations and directions.

People, too, develop cognitive maps of their surroundings. For example, latent learning may permit you to know the location of a kitchenware store at a local mall you've frequently visited, even though you've never entered the store and don't even like to cook.

The possibility that we develop our cognitive maps through latent learning presents something of a problem for strict operant conditioning theorists. If we consider the results of the maze-learning experiment, for instance, it is unclear what reinforcement permitted the rats that initially received no reward to learn the layout of the maze, because there was no obvious reinforcer present. Instead, the results support a cognitive view of learning, in which changes occurred in unobservable mental processes (Frensch & Rünger, 2003; Stouffer & White, 2006; Iaria et al., 2009; Lin et al., 2011).

Albert Bandura examined the principles of observational learning.

observational learning Learning by observing the behavior of another person, or model.

Observational Learning: Learning Through Imitation

Let's return for a moment to the case of a person learning to drive. How can we account for instances in which an individual with no direct experience in carrying out a particular behavior learns the behavior and then performs it? To answer this question, psychologists have focused on another aspect of cognitive learning: observational learning.

According to psychologist Albert Bandura and colleagues, a major part of human learning consists of **observational learning,** which is learning by watching the behavior of another person, or *model.* Because of its reliance on observation of others–a social phenomenon–the perspective taken by Bandura is often referred to as a *social cognitive* approach to learning (Bandura, 2004, 2009).

Bandura dramatically demonstrated the ability of models to stimulate learning in a classic experiment. In the study, young children saw a film of an adult wildly hitting a 5-feet-tall inflatable punching toy called a Bobo doll (Bandura, Ross, & Ross, 1963a, 1963b). Later the children were given the opportunity to play with the Bobo doll themselves, and, sure enough, most displayed the same kind of behavior, in some cases mimicking the aggressive behavior almost identically.

Study Alert
A key point of observational learning approaches: Behavior of models who are rewarded for a given behavior is more likely to be imitated than that of models who are punished for the behavior.

Not only negative behaviors are acquired through observational learning. In one experiment, for example, children who were afraid of dogs were exposed to a model–dubbed the Fearless Peer–playing with a dog (Bandura, Grusec, & Menlove, 1967). After exposure, observers were considerably more likely to approach a strange dog than were children who had not viewed the Fearless Peer.

Observational learning is particularly important in acquiring skills in which the operant conditioning technique of shaping is inappropriate. Piloting an airplane and performing brain surgery, for example, are behaviors that could hardly be learned by using trial-and-error methods without grave cost–literally–to those involved in the learning process.

Observational learning may have a genetic basis. For example, we find observational learning at work with mother animals teaching their young such activities as hunting. In addition, the discovery of *mirror neurons* that fire when we observe another person carrying out a behavior suggests that the capacity to imitate others may be innate (Lepage & Theoret, 2007; Huesmann, Dubow, & Boxer, 2011; McElreath, Wallin, & Fasolo, 2013) (see *Neuroscience in Your Life*).

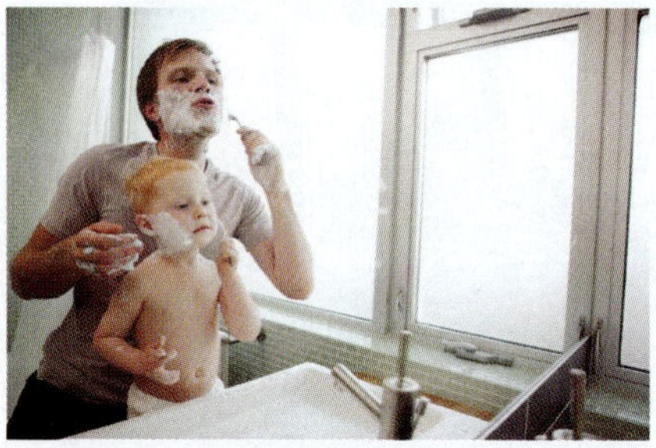

This boy is displaying observational learning based on previous observation of his father. How does observational learning contribute to learning gender roles?

Not all behavior that we witness is learned or carried out, of course. One crucial factor that determines whether we later imitate a model is whether the model is rewarded for his or her behavior. If we observe a friend being rewarded for putting more time into his studies by receiving higher grades, we are more likely to imitate his behavior than we would if his behavior resulted only in being stressed and tired. Models who are rewarded for behaving in a particular way are more apt to be mimicked than are models who receive punishment. Observing the punishment of a model, however, does not necessarily stop observers from learning the behavior. Observers can still describe the model's behavior–they are just less apt to perform it (Bandura, 1977, 1986, 1994).

Observational learning is central to a number of important issues relating to the extent to which people learn simply by watching the behavior of others. For instance,

Neuroscience in Your Life: Learning Through Imitation

As any parent will tell you, children learn in part through imitation of others. Researchers are beginning to understand how this learning occurs in the brain. This graph shows brain activity in 14- to 15-month-old children as they observe a sequence of objects. Evidence that they remember those objects in a sequence can be seen when they show more activity when learned associations are violated, as represented by the yellow line (adapted from Heimann et al., 2013).

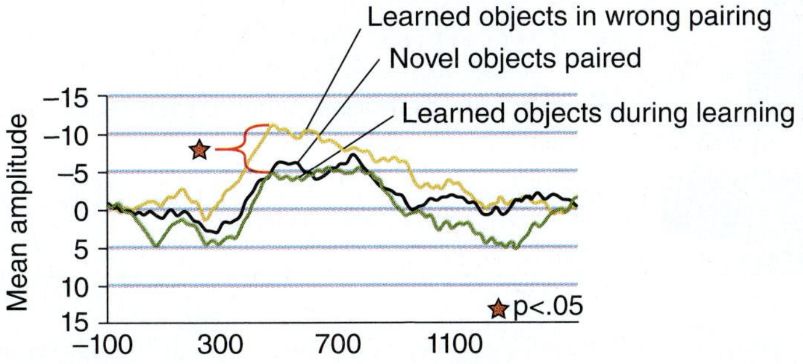

the degree to which observation of media aggression produces subsequent aggression on the part of viewers is a crucial–and controversial–question, as we discuss next.

VIOLENCE IN TELEVISION AND VIDEO GAMES: DOES THE MEDIA'S MESSAGE MATTER?

In an episode of *The Sopranos*, a former television series, fictional mobster Tony Soprano murdered one of his associates. To make identification of the victim's body difficult, Soprano and one of his henchmen dismembered the body and dumped the body parts.

A few months later, in real life, two half brothers in Riverside, California, strangled their mother and then cut her head and hands from her body. Victor Bautista, 20, and Matthew Montejo, 15, were caught by police after a security guard noticed that the bundle they were attempting to throw in a Dumpster had a foot sticking out of it. They told police that the plan to dismember their mother was inspired by the *Sopranos* episode (Martelle, Hanley, & Yoshino, 2003).

Like other "media copycat" killings, the brothers' cold-blooded brutality raises a critical issue: Does observing violent, antisocial acts in the media lead viewers to behave in similar ways? Because research on modeling shows that people frequently learn and imitate the aggression that they observe, this question is among the most important issues being addressed by psychologists.

Certainly, the amount of violence in the mass media is enormous. By the time of elementary school graduation, the average child in the United States will have viewed more than 8,000 murders and more than 800,000 violent acts on network television (Huston et al., 1992; Mifflin, 1998).

Most psychologists agree that watching high levels of media violence makes viewers more susceptible to acting aggressively. For example, one survey showed that one-fourth of violent young male offenders incarcerated in Florida had attempted to commit a media-inspired copycat crime. A significant proportion of those teenage offenders noted that they paid close attention to the media (Surette, 2002; Savage & Yancey, 2008; Boxer et al., 2009).

Violent video games have also been linked with actual aggression. In one of a series of studies by psychologist Craig Anderson and his colleagues, college students

PsychTech
Video gaming can also have positive consequences: Playing video games with positive, prosocial themes increases empathy and thoughts about helping others.

who frequently played violent video games, such as *Postal* or *Doom,* were more likely to have been involved in delinquent behavior and aggression. Frequent players also had lower academic achievement. Some researchers believe that violent video games may produce certain positive results–such as a rise in social networking (Ferguson, 2010, 2011). But most agree the preponderance of evidence suggests that they produce negative outcomes (Anderson & Carnagey, 2009; Anderson et al., 2010; Bailey, West, & Anderson, 2011).

From the perspective of . . .

A Social Worker What advice would you give to families about children's exposure to violent media and video games?

Several aspects of media violence may contribute to real-life aggressive behavior. For one thing, experiencing violent media content seems to lower inhibitions against carrying out aggression–watching television portrayals of violence or using violence to win a video game makes aggression seem a legitimate response to particular situations. Exposure to media violence also may distort our understanding of the meaning of others' behavior, predisposing us to view even nonaggressive acts by others as aggressive. Finally, a continuous diet of aggression may leave us desensitized to violence, and what previously would have repelled us now produces little emotional response. Our sense of the pain and suffering brought about by aggression may be diminished (Bartholow, Bushman, & Sestir, 2006; Carnagey, Anderson, & Bushman, 2007; Ramos et al., 2013).

What about real-life exposure to *actual* violence? Does it also lead to increases in aggression? The answer is yes. Exposure to actual firearm violence (being shot or being shot at) doubles the probability that an adolescent will commit serious violence over the next 2 years. Whether the violence is real or fictionalized, then, observing violent behavior leads to increases in aggressive behavior (Bingenheimer, Brennan, & Earls, 2005; Allwood, 2007). (For other consequences of observational learning, see *Applying Psychology in the 21st Century.*)

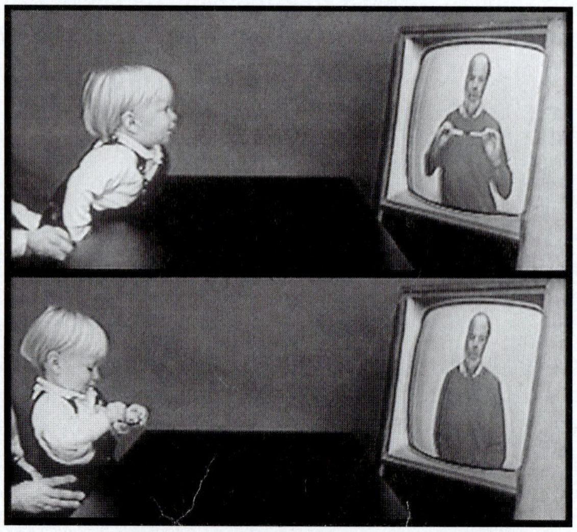

Illustrating observational learning, this infant observes an adult on television and then is able to imitate his behavior. Learning has obviously occurred through the mere observation of the television model.

Applying Psychology in the 21st Century

What Do We Learn About Gender from the Media?

Fathers are often portrayed as bungling and foolish in the media.

It probably comes as no surprise to you that young people like to watch television and play video games–but you might be surprised just how much. According to the Kaiser Family Foundation (2010), children 8 to 18 years old watch about 4.5 hours of television a day–about 40 minutes more than a decade ago–and they spend almost 75 minutes on video games, a nearly threefold increase over 10 years. And what these viewers are learning from all this media exposure concerns some psychologists.

One issue is that these media present a distorted view of gender. For example, video games overwhelmingly favor male characters over females, by a ratio of 5 to 1. When female characters are present, they are often highly sexualized or represented as passive and weak and in need of rescue. Women are a minority of characters on television, too, particularly during children's programming. They are also more likely than men to be thin, scantily dressed, and to be judged for their appearance (Ross, 2010; Scharrer, 2013).

Perhaps even more troubling is what television seems to be teaching young people about gender roles. When characters are shown doing household chores, they are more likely to be women–and when they are men, half the time they are shown to be incompetent at it for humorous effect. Male characters on crime dramas are consistently portrayed as hypermasculine, violent, unemotional, and likely to engage in risky behaviors. On the other hand, nurturing males, such as fathers on domestic sitcoms, are increasingly portrayed as slow and foolish (think Homer Simpson) (Dill, 2013; Scharrer, 2013; Shafer, Bobkowski, & Brown, 2013).

These data show a pattern of linking the masculine role with dominance and physical aggression and linking the feminine role with passivity and objectification. Psychologists are concerned that frequent and prolonged exposure to these distorted images is giving young people a similarly distorted worldview in terms of appropriate gender roles. What can be done about this? Apart from putting pressure on media suppliers to present more realistic depictions of men and women, consumers can minimize the effect on children by being aware of the issue, monitoring children's media consumption, and teaching more gender-egalitarian values (Green & Dill, 2013; Scharrer, 2013).

RETHINK

- Why do you think women and men are represented in these ways in video games and on television?
- In what other ways do entertainment media present a distorted picture of the world to young people?

Exploring DIVERSITY

Does Culture Influence How We Learn?

When a member of the Chilcotin Indian tribe teaches her daughter to prepare salmon, at first she allows the daughter only to observe the entire process. A little later, she permits her child to try out some basic parts of the task. Her response to questions is noteworthy. For example, when the daughter asks about how to do "the backbone part," the mother's response is to repeat the entire process with another salmon. The reason? The mother feels that one cannot learn the individual parts of the task apart from the context of preparing the whole fish (Tharp, 1989).

It should not be surprising that children raised in the Chilcotin tradition, which stresses instruction that starts by communicating the entire task, may have difficulty with traditional Western schooling. In the approach to teaching most characteristic of Western culture, tasks are broken down into their component parts. Only after each small step is learned is it thought possible to master the complete task.

Do the differences in teaching approaches between cultures affect how people learn? Some psychologists, taking a cognitive perspective on learning, suggest that people develop particular *learning styles,* characteristic ways of approaching material, based on their cultural background and unique pattern of abilities (Barmeyer, 2004; Wilkinson & Olliver-Gray, 2006; Sternberg, 2011).

Learning styles differ along several dimensions. For example, one central dimension is relational versus analytical approaches to learning. As illustrated in Figure 2, people with a *relational learning style* master material best through exposure to a complete unit or phenomenon. Parts of the unit are comprehended only when their relationship to the whole is understood. For example, students with a relational learning style might learn about the brain by first focusing on the brain as a whole and how it functions. Only after doing that would they then focus on the specific functions of separate areas of the brain.

In contrast, those with an *analytical learning style* do best when they first analyze the principles or components underlying an object, phenomenon, or situation. By developing an understanding of the fundamental principles and components, they are best able to grasp the full picture. So students with an analytic learning style might learn about the brain most easily by first considering its component parts (neurons, specific areas, lobes) and then by focusing on how they fit together to form the brain.

According to educators James Anderson and Maurianne Adams, particular minority groups in Western societies display characteristic learning styles. For instance, they argue that Caucasian females and African-American, Native-American, and Hispanic-American males and females are more apt to use a relational style of learning than are Caucasian and Asian-American males, who are more likely to employ an analytical style (Anderson & Adams, 1992; Adams, Bell, & Griffin, 2007; Chin, 2013).

Relational Style	Analytical Style
• Perceive information as part of total picture	• Focus on detail
• Show intuitive thinking	• Show sequential and structured thinking
• More easily learn materials that have a human, social content	• More easily learn materials that are impersonal
• Have a good memory for verbally presented ideas and information	• Have a good memory for abstract ideas
• Are influenced by others' opinion	• Are not greatly affected by the opinions of others
• Style conflicts with the traditional school environment	• Style matches traditional school environments

FIGURE 2 A comparison of relational versus analytical approaches to learning offers one example of how learning styles differ along several dimensions. (Source: Anderson & Adams, 1992.)

The conclusion that members of particular ethnic and gender groups have similar learning styles is controversial. Because there is so much diversity within each particular racial and ethnic group, critics argue that generalizations about learning styles cannot be used to predict the style of any single individual, regardless of group membership.

Still, it is clear that values about learning, which are communicated through a person's family and cultural background, have an impact on how successful students are in school. One theory suggests that members of minority groups who were voluntary immigrants are more apt to be successful in school than those who were brought into a majority culture against their will. For example, Korean children in the United States—the sons and daughters of voluntary immigrants—perform quite well, as a group, in school. In contrast, Korean children in Japan, who were often the sons and daughters of people who were forced to immigrate during World War II, essentially as forced laborers, do less well in school. The theory suggests that the motivation to succeed is lower for children in forced immigration groups (Ogbu, 1992, 2003; Foster, 2005).

RECAP/EVALUATE/RETHINK

RECAP

LO 17-1 What is the role of cognition and thought in learning?

- Cognitive approaches to learning consider learning in terms of thought processes, or cognition. Phenomena such as latent learning–in which a new behavior is learned but not performed until some incentive is provided for its performance–and the apparent development of cognitive maps support cognitive approaches.
- Learning also occurs from observing the behavior of others. The major factor that determines whether an observed behavior will actually be performed is the nature of the reinforcement or punishment a model receives.
- Observation of violence is linked to a greater likelihood of subsequently acting aggressively.
- Learning styles are characteristic ways of approaching learning, based on a person's cultural background and unique pattern of abilities. Whether an individual has an analytical or a relational style of learning, for example, may reflect family background or culture.

EVALUATE

1. Cognitive learning theorists are concerned only with overt behavior, not with its internal causes. True or false?
2. In cognitive learning theory, it is assumed that people develop a(n) __________ about receiving a reinforcer when they behave a certain way.
3. In __________ learning, a new behavior is learned but is not shown until appropriate reinforcement is presented.
4. Bandura's __________ theory of learning states that people learn through watching a(n) __________ (another person displaying the behavior of interest).

RETHINK

1. The relational style of learning sometimes conflicts with the traditional school environment. Could a school be created that takes advantage of the characteristics of the relational style? How? Are there types of learning for which the analytical style is clearly superior?
2. What is the relationship between a model (in Bandura's sense) and a role model (as the term is used popularly)? Celebrities often complain that their actions should not be scrutinized closely because they do not want to be role models. How would you respond?

Answers to Evaluate Questions

1. False; cognitive learning theorists are primarily concerned with mental processes; **2.** expectation; **3.** latent; **4.** observational, model

KEY TERMS

cognitive learning theory
latent learning
observational learning

Looking Back

Epilogue

Here we have discussed several kinds of learning, ranging from classical conditioning, which depends on the existence of natural stimulus–response pairings, to operant conditioning, in which reinforcement is used to increase desired behavior. These approaches to learning focus on outward, behavioral learning processes. Cognitive approaches to learning focus on mental processes that enable learning.

We have also noted that learning is affected by culture and individual differences, with individual learning styles potentially affecting the ways in which people learn most effectively. And we saw some ways in which our learning about learning can be put to practical use, through such means as behavior-modification programs designed to decrease negative behaviors and increase positive ones.

Return to the prologue for this set of modules and consider the following questions about Jean Davis's addiction to Facebook:

1. Why is it so hard for Jean Davis to resist checking her Facebook news feed?
2. What is the most likely reinforcement schedule for Jean's Facebook-checking behavior?
3. Is Jean's Facebook habit most likely positively reinforced, negatively reinforced, or both? Why do you think so?
4. What could Jean do to break the Facebook habit?

VISUAL SUMMARY 5 Learning

MODULE 15 Classical Conditioning

Ivan Pavlov: Basic principles of classical conditioning

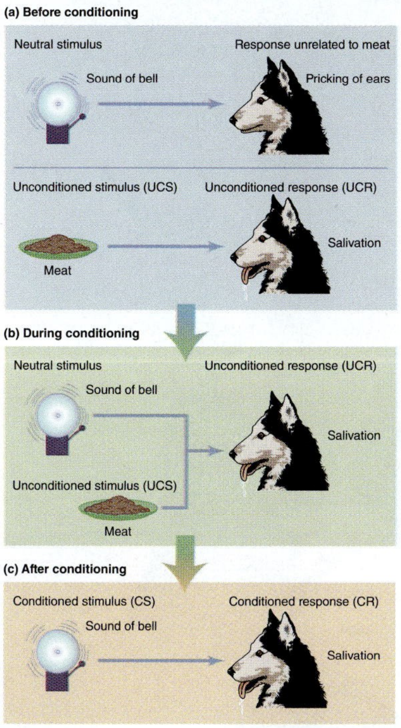

- Extinction: Conditioned response disappears over time
- Stimulus generalization: Stimuli that are similar to the conditioned stimulus also elicit the conditioned response
- Stimulus discrimination: Stimuli that are different from the conditioned stimulus do not elicit the conditioned response

MODULE 16 Operant Conditioning

Basic Principle: Behavior changes in frequency according to its consequences

- Reinforcement: A stimulus that increases the probability that a preceding behavior will be repeated
  - Positive reinforcement: A pleasant stimulus is presented

  - Negative reinforcement: An unpleasant stimulus is withdrawn

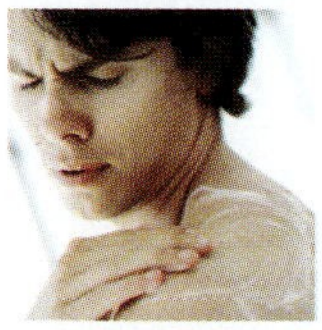

Basic Principle: Behavior changes in frequency according to its consequences *(continued)*

- Punishment : A stimulus that decreases the probability that a preceding behavior will be repeated
  - Positive punishment: An unpleasant stimulus is presented

  - Negative punishment: A pleasant stimulus is withdrawn

- Schedules of reinforcement

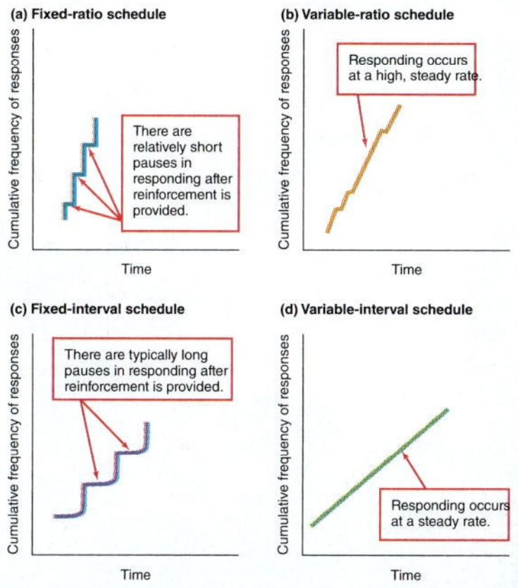

- Shaping: Reinforcing successive approximations of behavior

MODULE 17 Cognitive Approaches to Learning

Cognitive Learning Theory: Focuses on the internal thoughts and expectations

- Latent learning: A new behavior is learned but is not demonstrated until it is reinforced

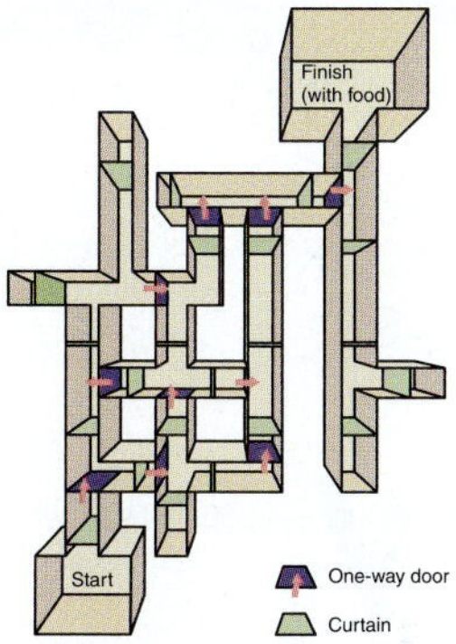

- Observational learning: We learn by watching the behavior of others

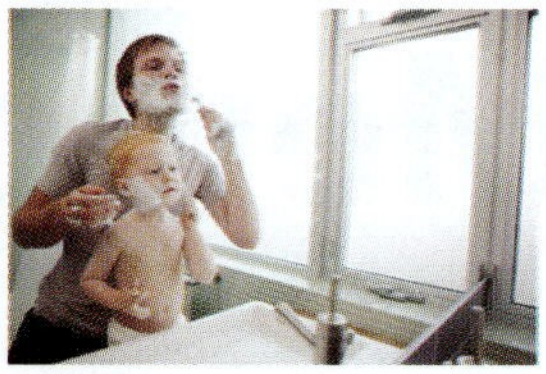

6 Memory

Learning Outcomes for Chapter 6

MODULE 18

LO 18-1 What is memory?

LO 18-2 Are there different kinds of memory?

LO 18-3 What are the biological bases of memory?

The Foundations of Memory

Sensory Memory

Short-Term Memory

Working Memory

Long-Term Memory

Neuroscience in Your Life: The Building Blocks of Memory: Do You Have a Jennifer Aniston Neuron?

MODULE 19

LO 19-1 What causes difficulties and failures in remembering?

Recalling Long-Term Memories

Retrieval Cues

Levels of Processing

Explicit and Implicit Memory

Flashbulb Memories

Constructive Processes in Memory: Rebuilding the Past

Applying Psychology in the 21st Century: Mind Pops

Exploring Diversity: Are There Cross-Cultural Differences in Memory?

MODULE 20

LO 20-1 Why do we forget information?

LO 20-2 What are the major memory impairments?

Forgetting: When Memory Fails

Why We Forget

Proactive and Retroactive Interference: The Before and After of Forgetting

Memory Dysfunctions: Afflictions of Forgetting

Becoming an Informed Consumer of Psychology: Improving Your Memory

FIGURE 3 Examine the chessboard on the left for about 5 seconds. Then cover up the board and draw the position of the pieces on the blank chessboard. (You could also use your own chessboard and place the pieces in the same positions.) Unless you are an experienced chess player, you are likely to have great difficulty carrying out such a task. Yet chess masters—those who win tournaments—do this quite well (deGroot, 1966). They are able to reproduce correctly 90% of the pieces on the board. In comparison, inexperienced chess players are typically able to reproduce only 40% of the board properly. The chess masters do not have superior memories in other respects; they generally test normally on other measures of memory. What they can do better than others is see the board in terms of chunks or meaningful units and reproduce the position of the chess pieces by using those units.

chunk A grouping of information that can be stored in short-term memory.

In fact, the specific amount of information that can be held in short-term memory has been identified as seven items, or "chunks," of information, with variations up to plus or minus two chunks. A **chunk** is a grouping of information that can be stored in short-term memory. For example, a chunk can be a group of seven individual letters or numbers, permitting us to hold a seven-digit phone number (such as 226-4610) in short-term memory.

But a chunk also may consist of larger categories, such as words or other meaningful units. For example, consider the following list of 21 letters:

P B S F O X C N N A B C C B S M T V N B C

Because the list of individual letters exceeds seven items, it is difficult to recall the letters after one exposure. But suppose they were presented as follows:

PBS FOX CNN ABC CBS MTV NBC

In this case, even though there are still 21 letters, you'd be able to store them in short-term memory since they represent only seven chunks.

Chunks can vary in size from single letters or numbers to categories that are far more complicated. The specific nature of what constitutes a chunk varies according to one's past experience. You can see this for yourself by trying an experiment that was first carried out as a comparison between expert and inexperienced chess players and is illustrated in Figure 3 (deGroot, 1978; Gilchrist, Cowan, & Naveh-Benjamin, 2009; Grossberg, 2013).

Although it is possible to remember seven or so relatively complicated sets of information entering short-term memory, the information cannot be held there very long. Just how brief is short-term memory? If you've ever looked up a telephone number in a phone directory, repeated the number to yourself, put away the directory, and then forgotten the number after you've tapped the first three numbers into your phone, you know that information does not remain in short-term memory very long. Most psychologists believe that information in short-term memory is lost after 15 to 25 seconds—unless it is transferred to long-term memory.

REHEARSAL

The transfer of material from short- to long-term memory proceeds largely on the basis of **rehearsal,** the repetition of information that has entered short-term memory. Rehearsal accomplishes two things. First, as long as the information is repeated, it is maintained in short-term memory. More important, however, rehearsal allows us to transfer the information into long-term memory (Jarrold & Tam, 2011; Grenfell-Essam, Ward, & Tan, 2013).

Whether the transfer is made from short- to long-term memory seems to depend largely on the kind of rehearsal that is carried out. If the information is simply repeated over and over again—as we might do with a telephone number someone tells us as we rush to store it in our phone—it is kept current in short-term memory, but it will not necessarily be placed in long-term memory. Instead, as soon as we stop punching in the phone numbers, the number is likely to be replaced by other information and will be completely forgotten.

rehearsal The repetition of information that has entered short-term memory.

In contrast, if the information in short-term memory is rehearsed using a process called elaborative rehearsal, it is much more likely to be transferred into long-term memory. *Elaborative rehearsal* occurs when the information is considered and organized in some fashion. The organization might include expanding the information to make it fit into a logical framework, linking it to another memory, turning it into an image, or transforming it in some other way. For example, a list of vegetables to be purchased at a store could be woven together in memory as items being used to prepare an elaborate salad, could be linked to the items bought on an earlier shopping trip, or could be thought of in terms of the image of a farm with rows of each item.

By using organizational strategies such as these—called *mnemonics*—we can vastly improve our retention of information. Mnemonics (pronounced "neh MON ix") are formal techniques for organizing information in a way that makes it more likely to be remembered. For instance, when a beginning musician learns that the spaces on the music staff spell the word *FACE*, or when we learn the rhyme "Thirty days hath September, April, June, and November . . . ," we are using mnemonics (Carney & Levin, 2003; Sprenger, 2007; Worthen & Hunt, 2011).

Working Memory

Rather than seeing short-term memory as an independent way station into which memories arrive, either to fade or to be passed on to long-term memory, most contemporary memory theorists conceive of short-term memory as far more active. In this view, short-term memory is like an information-processing system that manages

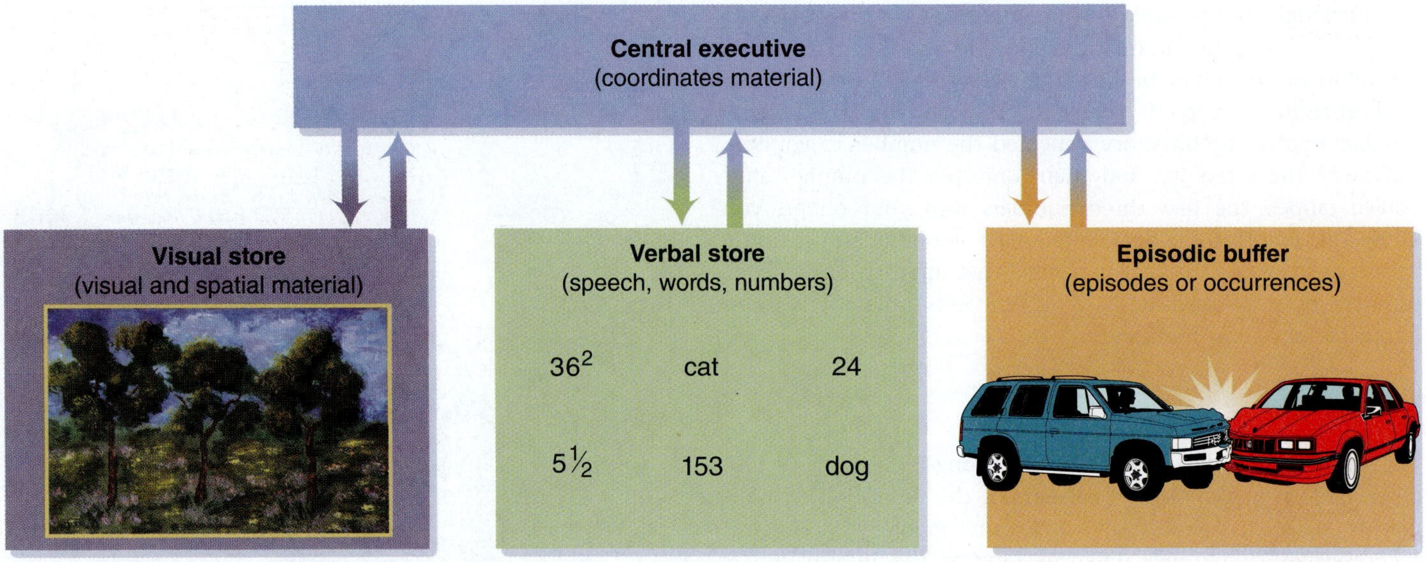

FIGURE 4 Working memory is an active "workspace" in which information is retrieved and manipulated and in which information is held through rehearsal. (Source: Adapted from Baddeley, Chincotta, & Adlam, 2001.)

working memory A memory system that holds information temporarily while actively manipulating and rehearsing that information.

both new material gathered from sensory memory and older material that has been pulled from long-term storage. In this increasingly influential view, short-term memory is referred to as working memory. **Working memory** is the memory system that holds information temporarily while actively manipulating and rehearsing that information. If you use the analogy of a computer, working memory is the processing that occurs in an open window on your desktop, as compared with the long-term storage of information in the computer's hard drive (Unsworth & Engle, 2005; Vandierendonck & Szmalec, 2011).

Working memory contains a *central executive* processor that is involved in reasoning and decision making. The central executive coordinates three distinct storage-and-rehearsal systems: the *visual store*, the *verbal store*, and the *episodic buffer*. The visual store specializes in visual and spatial information, whereas the verbal store holds and manipulates material relating to speech, words, and numbers. The episodic buffer contains information that represents episodes or events (Rudner & Rönnberg, 2008; Baddeley, Allen, & Hitch, 2011; Kuncel & Beatty, 2013; see Figure 4).

Working memory permits us to keep information in an active state briefly so that we can do something with the information. For instance, we use working memory when we're doing a multistep arithmetic problem in our heads, storing the result of one calculation while getting ready to move to the next stage. (I make use of my working memory when I figure a 20% tip in a restaurant by first calculating 10% of the total bill and then doubling it.)

Although working memory aids in the recall of information, it uses a significant amount of cognitive resources during its operation. In turn, this can make us less aware of our surroundings–something that has implications for why it's unsafe to use cell phones while driving. If a phone conversation requires thinking, it will burden working memory and leave drivers less aware of their surroundings, an obviously dangerous state of affairs (Sifrit, 2006; Strayer & Drews, 2007).

Furthermore, stress can reduce the effectiveness of working memory by reducing its capacity. In fact, one study found that students with the highest working memory capacity and greatest math ability were the ones who were most vulnerable to pressure to perform well. Those who should have performed best, then, were the ones most apt to choke on the test because their working memory capacities were reduced by the stress (Schweizer & Dalgleish, 2011; Schoofs et al., 2013).

Long-Term Memory

Material that makes its way from short-term memory to long-term memory enters a storehouse of almost unlimited capacity. Like a new file we save on a hard drive, the information in long-term memory is filed and coded so that we can retrieve it when we need it.

Evidence of the existence of long-term memory, as distinct from short-term memory, comes from a number of sources. For example, people with certain kinds of brain damage have no lasting recall of new information received after the damage occurred, although people and events stored in memory before the injury remain intact (Milner, 1966). Because information that was encoded and stored before the injury can be recalled and because short-term memory after the injury appears to be operational–new material can be recalled for a very brief period–we can infer that there are two distinct types of memory: one for short-term and one for long-term storage.

Results from laboratory experiments are also consistent with the notion of separate short-term and long-term memory. For example, in one set of studies, people were asked to recall a relatively small amount of information (such as a set of three letters). Then, to prevent practice of the initial information, participants were required to recite some extraneous material aloud, such as counting backward by threes (Brown, 1958; Peterson & Peterson, 1959). By varying the amount of time between the presentation of the initial material and the need for its recall, investigators found that recall was quite good when the interval was very short but declined rapidly thereafter. After 15 seconds had gone by, recall hovered at around 10% of the material initially presented.

Apparently, the distraction of counting backward prevented almost all the initial material from reaching long-term memory. Initial recall was good because it was coming from short-term memory, but those memories were lost at a rapid rate. Eventually, all that could be recalled was the small amount of material that had made its way into long-term storage despite the distraction of counting backward.

The distinction between short- and long-term memory is also supported by the *serial position effect,* in which the ability to recall information in a list depends on where in the list an item appears. For instance, often a *primacy effect* occurs, in which items presented early in a list are remembered better. There is also a *recency effect,* in which items presented late in a list are remembered best (Tan & Ward, 2008; Tydgat & Grainger, 2009; Jacoby & Wahlheim, 2013).

PsychTech

Research shows that when we are faced with complicated questions and material, we are primed to think of computers and search engines like Google. In what is called the *Google effect,* we are then less likely to store the information in short-term memory and be less likely to recall it—but have a better memory for where we can find it on the web (Sparrow, Liu, & Wegner, 2011).

LONG-TERM MEMORY MODULES

Just as short-term memory is often conceptualized in terms of working memory, many contemporary researchers now regard long-term memory as having several different components, or *memory modules.* Each of these modules represents a separate memory system in the brain.

One major distinction within long-term memory is that between declarative memory and procedural memory. **Declarative memory** is memory for factual information: names, faces, dates, and facts, such as "a bike has two wheels." In contrast, **procedural memory** (or *nondeclarative memory*) refers to memory for skills and habits, such as how to ride a bike or hit a baseball. Information about *things* is stored in declarative memory; information about *how to do things* is stored in procedural memory (Brown & Robertson, 2007; Bauer, 2008; Freedberg, 2011).

Declarative memory can be subdivided into semantic memory and episodic memory. **Semantic memory** is memory for general knowledge and facts about the world, as well as memory for the rules of logic that are used to deduce other facts. Because of semantic memory, we remember that the ZIP code for Beverly Hills is 90210, that Mumbai is on the Arabian Sea, and that *memoree* is the incorrect spelling of *memory.* Thus, semantic memory is somewhat like a mental almanac of facts (Nyberg & Tulving, 1996; Tulving, 2002; McNamara, 2013).

declarative memory Memory for factual information: names, faces, dates, and the like.

procedural memory Memory for skills and habits, such as riding a bike or hitting a baseball; sometimes referred to as *nondeclarative memory.*

semantic memory Memory for general knowledge and facts about the world, as well as memory for the rules of logic that are used to deduce other facts.

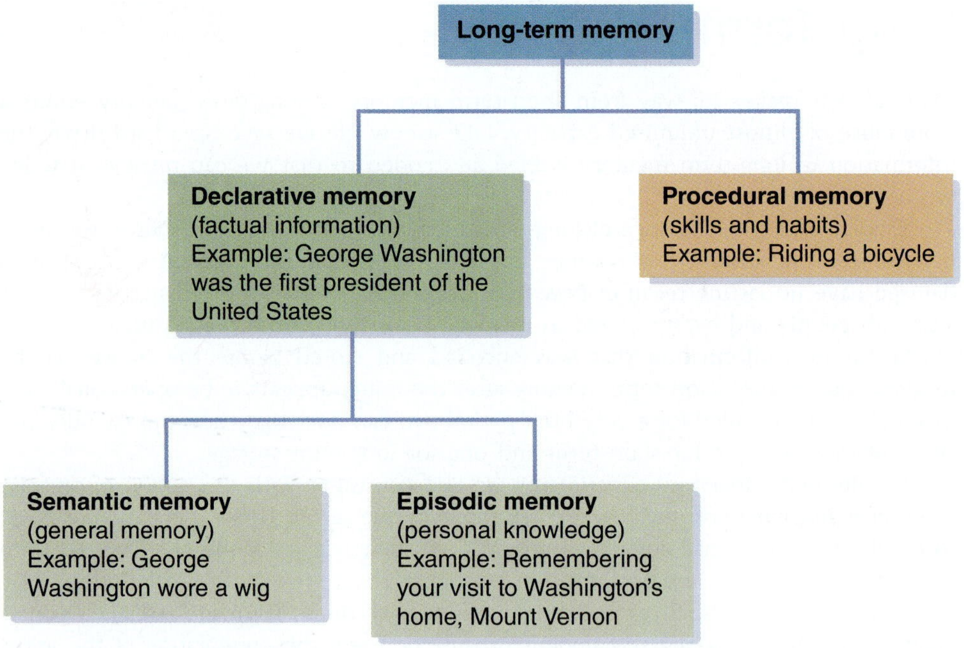

FIGURE 5 Long-term memory can be subdivided into several different types. What type of long-term memory is involved in your recollection of the moment you first arrived on your campus at the start of college? What type of long-term memory is involved in remembering the lyrics to a song, compared with the tune of a song?

Study Alert
Use Figure 5 to help clarify the distinctions between the different types of long-term memory.

episodic memory Memory for events that occur in a particular time, place, or context.

In contrast, **episodic memory** is memory for events that occur in a particular time, place, or context. For example, recall of learning to hit a baseball, our first kiss, or arranging a surprise 21st birthday party for our brother is based on episodic memories. Episodic memories relate to particular contexts. For example, remembering *when* and *how* we learned that $2 \times 2 = 4$ would be an episodic memory; the fact itself (that $2 \times 2 = 4$) is a semantic memory. (Also see Figure 5.)

Episodic memories can be surprisingly detailed. Consider, for instance, how you'd respond if you were asked to identify what you were doing on a specific day 2 years ago. Impossible? You may think otherwise as you read the following exchange between a researcher and a participant in a study who was asked, in a memory experiment, what he was doing "on Monday afternoon in the third week of September two years ago."

PARTICIPANT: Come on. How should I know?

EXPERIMENTER: Just try it anyhow.

PARTICIPANT: OK. Let's see: Two years ago . . . I would be in high school in Pittsburgh. . . . That would be my senior year. Third week in September–that's just after summer–that would be the fall term. . . . Let me see. I think I had chemistry lab on Mondays. I don't know. I was probably in chemistry lab. Wait a minute–that would be the second week of school. I remember he started off with the atomic table–a big fancy chart. I thought he was crazy trying to make us memorize that thing. You know, I think I can remember sitting . . . (Lindsay & Norman, 1977).

Episodic memory, then, can provide information about events that happened long in the past. But semantic memory is no less impressive, permitting us to dredge up tens of thousands of facts ranging from the date of our birthday to the knowledge that $1 is less than $5.

SEMANTIC NETWORKS

Try to recall, for a moment, as many things as you can think of that are the color red. Now pull from your memory the names of as many fruits as you can recall.

Did the same item appear when you did both tasks? For many people, an apple comes to mind in both cases since it fits equally well in each category. And the fact that you might have thought of an apple when doing the first task makes it even more likely that you'll think of it when doing the second task.

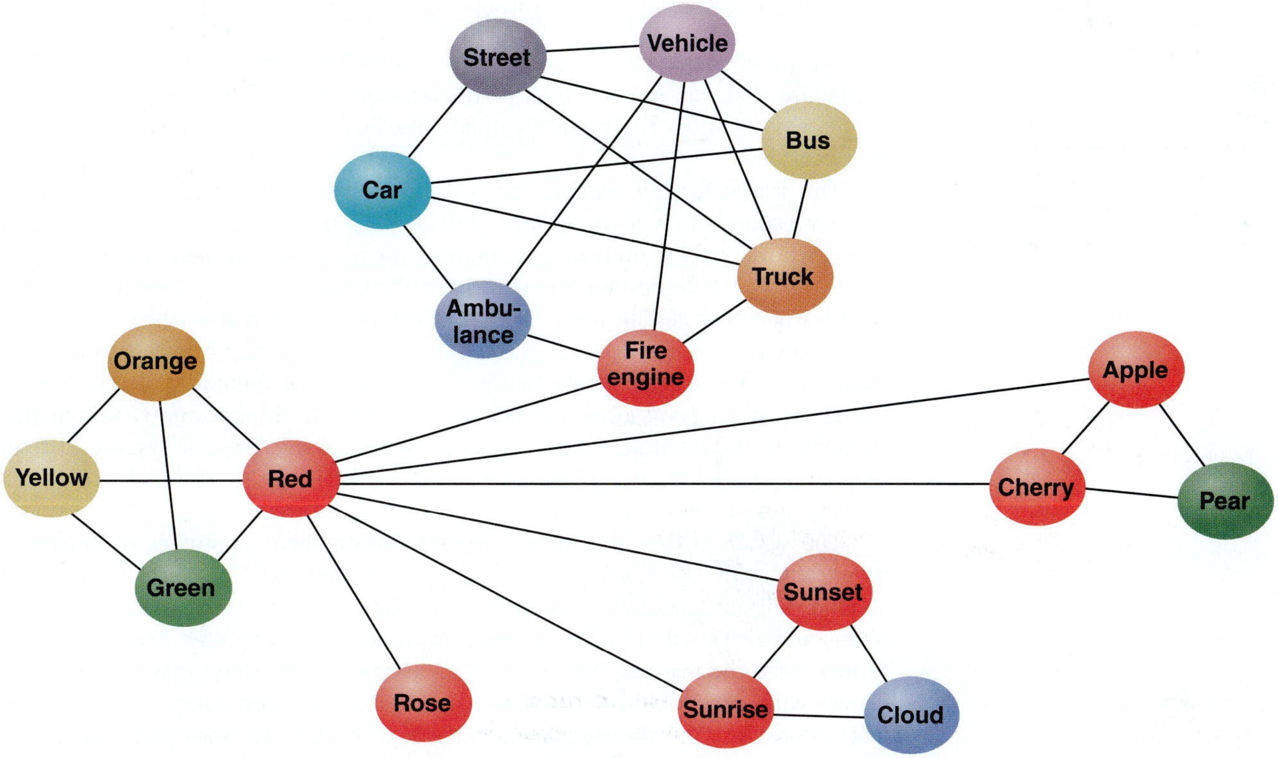

FIGURE 6 Semantic networks in memory consist of relationships between pieces of information, such as those relating to the concept of a fire engine. The lines suggest the connections that indicate how the information is organized within memory. The closer together two concepts are, the greater the strength of the association. (Source: Adapted from Collins & Loftus, 1975.)

It's actually quite amazing that we're able to retrieve specific material from the vast store of information in our long-term memories. According to some memory researchers, one key organizational tool that allows us to recall detailed information from long-term memory is the associations that we build between different pieces of information. In this view, knowledge is stored in **semantic networks,** mental representations of clusters of interconnected information (Collins & Quillian, 1969; Collins & Loftus, 1975; Cummings, Ceponiene, & Koyama, 2006).

semantic networks Mental representations of clusters of interconnected information.

Consider, for example, Figure 6, which shows some of the relationships in memory relating to fire engines, the color red, and a variety of other semantic concepts. Thinking about a particular concept leads to recall of related concepts. For example, seeing a fire engine may activate our recollections of other kinds of emergency vehicles, such as an ambulance, which in turn may activate recall of the related concept of a vehicle. And thinking of a vehicle may lead us to think about a bus that we've seen in the past. Activating one memory triggers the activation of related memories in a process known as *spreading activation* (Kreher et al., 2008; Nelson et al., 2013).

From the perspective of . . .

A Marketing Specialist How might advertisers use ways of enhancing memory to promote their products? What ethical principles are involved?

THE NEUROSCIENCE OF MEMORY

Can we pinpoint a location in the brain where long-term memories reside? Is there a single site that corresponds to a particular memory, or is memory distributed in different regions across the brain? Do memories leave an actual physical trace that scientists can view?

The search for the *engram,* the term for the physical memory trace in the brain that corresponds to a memory, has proved to be a major puzzle to psychologists and other neuroscientists interested in memory. Using advanced brain scanning procedures in their efforts to determine the neuroscientific basis of memory formation, investigators have learned that certain areas and structures of the brain specialize in different types of memory-related activities. The *hippocampus,* a part of the brain's limbic system (see Figure 7), plays a central role in the consolidation of memories. Located within the brain's *medial temporal lobes* just behind the eyes, the hippocampus aids in the initial encoding of information, acting as a kind of neurological e-mail system. That information is subsequently passed along to the cerebral cortex of the brain, where it is actually stored (J. Peters et al., 2007; Lavenex & Lavenex, 2009; Dudai, 2011).

The significance of the hippocampus is exemplified by studies of individuals who have particularly good, yet specialized, types of memories. For instance, taxi drivers in London, England, must have accurate, complete recall of the location of the maze of streets and alleys within a 6-mile radius of the center of the city. It takes years of study to memorize the material. MRI brain scans of taxi drivers show that, relative to non-taxi drivers with fewer navigational skills, the back of the hippocampus is larger while the front is smaller. The findings are consistent with the idea that particular areas of the hippocampus are involved in the consolidation of spatial memories (Maguire, Woollett, & Spiers, 2006; Spiers & Maguire, 2007; Woollett & Maguire, 2009).

The *amygdala,* another part of the limbic system, also plays an important role in memory. The amygdala is especially involved with memories involving emotion. For example, if you are frightened by a large Doberman, you're likely to remember the event vividly–an outcome related to the functioning of the amygdala. Encountering the Doberman or any large dog in the future is likely to reactivate the amygdala and bring back the unpleasant memory (Buchanan & Adolphs, 2004; Talmi et al., 2008; Pendyam et al., 2013).

Memory at the Level of Neurons. Although it is clear that the hippocampus and amygdala play a central role in memory formation, how is the transformation of information into a memory reflected at the level of neurons?

One answer is *long-term potentiation,* which shows that certain neural pathways become easily excited while a new response is being learned. At the same time, the number of synapses between neurons increase as the dendrites branch out to receive messages. These changes reflect a process called *consolidation,* in which memories become fixed and stable in long-term memory. Long-term memories take some time to stabilize; this explains why events and other stimuli are not suddenly fixed in memory. Instead, consolidation may continue for days and even years (McGaugh, 2003; Meeter & Murre, 2004; Kawashima, Izaki, & Grace, 2006).

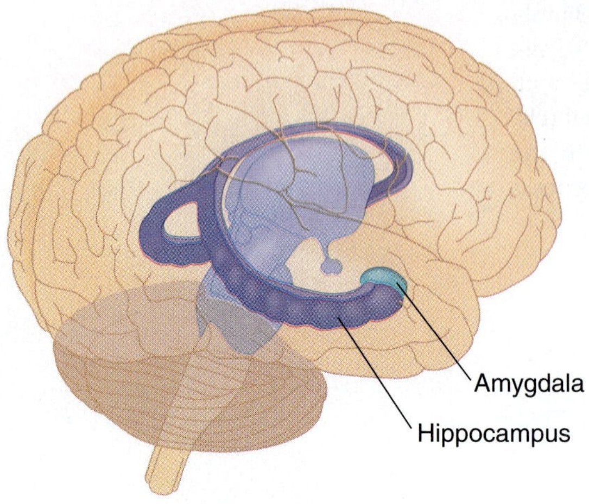

FIGURE 7 The hippocampus and amygdala, parts of the brain's limbic system, play a central role in the consolidation of memories. (Source: Adapted from Van De Graaff, 2000.)

Because a stimulus may contain different sensory aspects, visual, auditory, and other areas of the brain may be simultaneously processing information about that stimulus. Information storage appears to be linked to the sites where this processing occurs, and it is therefore located in the particular areas that initially processed the information in terms of its visual, auditory, and other sensory stimuli. For this reason, memory traces are distributed throughout the brain. For example, when you recall a beautiful beach sunset, your recollection draws on memory stores located in visual areas of the brain (the view of the sunset), auditory areas (the sounds of the ocean), and tactile areas (the feel of the wind) (Squire, Clark, & Bayley, 2004; Murayama & Kitagami, 2013).

In short, the physical stuff of memory–the engram–is produced by a complex of biochemical and neural processes. Scientists are just beginning to understand how the brain compiles the individual neural components into a single, coherent memory. It may be that the same neurons that fire when we are initially exposed to material are reactivated during efforts to recall that information. Still, although memory researchers have made considerable strides in understanding the neuroscience behind memory, more remains to be learned–and remembered (Gelbard-Sagiv et al., 2008). (For more on the biological basis of memory, see *Neuroscience in Your Life.*)

Neuroscience in Your Life: The Building Blocks of Memory: Do You Have a Jennifer Aniston Neuron?

Can you bring to mind an image of your grandmother's face from memory? How about the sound of Maroon 5 lead singer Adam Levine's voice or the name of the short green-skinned Jedi master who trained Luke Skywalker?

If these images can come to mind, they are clearly stored in the neurons of your brain. But where, exactly? Is there a relatively small cluster of specific neurons that holds the "grandmother" memory, or does it take many millions of cells distributed all over your brain?

To help answer this question, neuroscientists presented patients with a wide array of various stimuli to see what would provoke a response in individually monitored neurons. They discovered a surprising degree of specificity. For example, in one case, an individual neuron responded specifically to photographs of actor Jennifer Aniston, and no other person. In another case, one neuron responded to pictures of the Star Wars character Luke Skywalker and to his written or spoken name (Viskontas, Quiroga, & Fried, 2009; Quiroga, Fried, & Koch, 2013; see the figure below showing neuronal responses to different photos).

Further investigation revealed that these individual neurons were responding to concepts rather than to any specific kind of stimulus. Specifically, the "Jennifer Aniston neuron" didn't just fire when Aniston's face was seen, but also when her name was mentioned, or her voice was heard, or the television show that made her famous was recalled. In short, there appear to be concept cells that respond to a general concept rather than specific features of a stimulus.

The existence of small clusters of concept cells suggests how high-level memory works. By activating a given concept, we can then quickly activate other related concepts. We think of Starbucks, and the concept of our friend is also activated, as well as the topics we talked about. Concept cells therefore act like building blocks of memory, which can be assembled together in a variety of ways to store memories for complex concepts and events—memories that leave out unimportant trivial details (Quiroga, 2012).

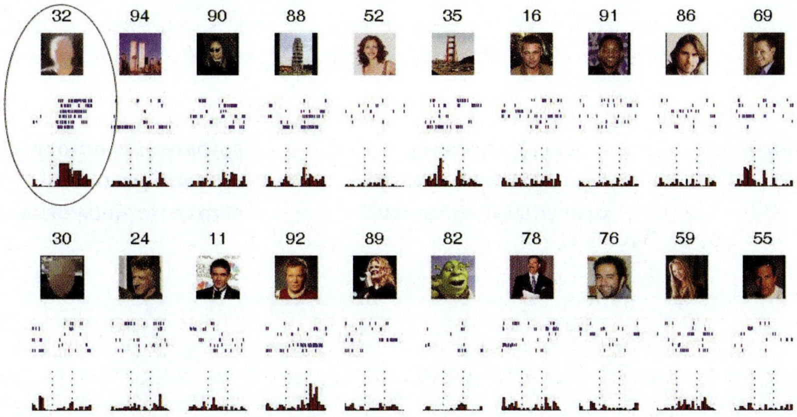

RECAP/EVALUATE/RETHINK

RECAP

LO 18-1 What is memory?

- Memory is the process by which we encode, store, and retrieve information.

LO 18-2 Are there different kinds of memory?

- Sensory memory, corresponding to each of the sensory systems, is the first place where information is saved. Sensory memories are very brief, but they are precise, storing a nearly exact replica of a stimulus.
- Roughly seven (plus or minus two) chunks of information can be transferred and held in short-term memory. Information in short-term memory is held from 15 to 25 seconds and, if not transferred to long-term memory, is lost.
- Memories are transferred into long-term storage through rehearsal. If memories are transferred into long-term memory, they become relatively permanent.
- Some theorists view short-term memory as a working memory in which information is retrieved and manipulated and held through rehearsal. In this view, it is a central executive processor involved in reasoning and decision making; it coordinates a visual store, a verbal store, and an episodic buffer.
- Long-term memory can be viewed in terms of memory modules, each of which is related to separate memory systems in the brain. For instance, we can distinguish between declarative memory and procedural memory. Declarative memory is further divided into episodic memory and semantic memory.
- Semantic networks suggest that knowledge is stored in long-term memory as mental representations of clusters of interconnected information.

LO 18-3 What are the biological bases of memory?

- The hippocampus and amygdala are especially important in the establishment of memory.
- Memories are distributed across the brain, relating to the different sensory information-processing systems involved during the initial exposure to a stimulus.

EVALUATE

1. Match the type of memory with its definition:

1. long-term memory	**a.** holds information 15 to 25 seconds
2. short-term memory	**b.** stores information on a relatively permanent basis
3. sensory memory	**c.** direct representation of a stimulus

2. A(n) ________ is a meaningful group of stimuli that can be stored together in short-term memory.

3. There appear to be two types of declarative memory: ________ memory for knowledge and facts and ________ memory for personal experiences.

4. Some memory researchers believe that long-term memory is stored as associations between pieces of information in ________ networks.

RETHINK

1. It is a truism that "you never forget how to ride a bicycle." Why might this be so? In what type of memory is information about bicycle riding stored?

2. The ability to remember specific skills and the order in which they are used is known as procedural memory. Because driving involves procedural memory, why is it so unsafe to use a cell phone while driving?

Answers to Evaluate Questions

1. 1-b, 2-a, 3-c; **2.** chunk; **3.** semantic, episodic; **4.** semantic

KEY TERMS

memory
sensory memory
short-term memory
long-term memory
chunk
rehearsal
working memory
declarative memory
procedural memory
semantic memory
episodic memory
semantic networks

MODULE 19

Recalling Long-Term Memories

Learning Outcome

LO 19-1 What causes difficulties and failures in remembering?

An hour after his job interview, Ricardo was sitting in a coffee shop, telling his friend Laura how well it had gone, when the woman who had interviewed him walked in. "Well, hello, Ricardo. How are you doing?" Trying to make a good impression, Ricardo began to make introductions, but suddenly realized he could not remember the interviewer's name. Stammering, he desperately searched his memory but to no avail. "I *know* her name," he thought to himself, "but here I am, looking like a fool. I can kiss this job good-bye."

Have you ever tried to remember someone's name, convinced that you knew it but unable to recall it no matter how hard you tried? This common occurrence–known as the **tip-of-the-tongue phenomenon**–exemplifies how difficult it can be to retrieve information stored in long-term memory (Brennen, Vikan, & Dybdahl, 2007; Schwartz, 2002, 2008; Schwartz & Metcalfe, 2011).

tip-of-the-tongue phenomenon The inability to recall information that one realizes one knows–a result of the difficulty of retrieving information from long-term memory.

Retrieval Cues

Perhaps recall of names and other memories is not perfect because there is so much information stored in long-term memory. Because the material that makes its way to long-term memory is relatively permanent, the capacity of long-term memory is vast. For instance, if you are like the average college student, your vocabulary includes some 50,000 words, you know hundreds of mathematical "facts," and you are able to conjure up images–such as the way your childhood home looked–with no trouble at all. In fact, simply cataloging all your memories would probably take years of work.

recall Memory task in which specific information must be retrieved.

recognition Memory task in which individuals are presented with a stimulus and asked whether they have been exposed to it in the past or to identify it from a list of alternatives.

How do we sort through this vast array of material and retrieve specific information at the appropriate time? One way is through retrieval cues. A *retrieval cue* is a stimulus that allows us to recall more easily information that is in long-term memory. It may be a word, an emotion, or a sound; whatever the specific cue, a memory will suddenly come to mind when the retrieval cue is present. For example, the smell of roasting turkey may evoke memories of Thanksgiving or family gatherings.

Retrieval cues guide people through the information stored in long-term memory in much the same way that a search engine such as Google guides people through the Internet. They are particularly important when we are making an effort to *recall* information, as opposed to being asked to *recognize* material stored in memory. In **recall,** a specific piece of information must be retrieved–such as that needed to answer a fill-in-the-blank question or to write an essay on a test. In contrast, **recognition** occurs when people are presented with a stimulus and asked whether they have been exposed to it previously or are asked to identify it from a list of alternatives.

FIGURE 1 Try to recall the names of these characters. Because this is a recall task, it is relatively difficult.

As you might guess, recognition is generally a much easier task than recall (see Figures 1 and 2). Recall is more difficult because it consists of a series of processes: a search through memory, retrieval of potentially relevant information, and then a decision regarding whether

FIGURE 2 Naming the characters in Figure 1 (a recall task) is more difficult than solving the recognition problem posed in this list.

Answer this recognition question:
Which of the following are the names of the seven dwarfs in the Disney movie *Snow White and the Seven Dwarfs?*

Goofy	Bashful
Sleepy	Meanie
Smarty	Doc
Scaredy	Happy
Dopey	Angry
Grumpy	Sneezy
Wheezy	Crazy

(The correct answers are Bashful, Doc, Dopey, Grumpy, Happy, Sleepy, and Sneezy.)

Study Alert
Remember the distinction between recall (in which specific information must be retrieved) and recognition (in which information is presented and must be identified or distinguished from other material).

levels-of-processing theory The theory of memory that emphasizes the degree to which new material is mentally analyzed.

the information you have found is accurate. If the information appears to be correct, the search is over, but if it is not, the search must continue. In contrast, recognition is simpler because it involves fewer steps (Miserando, 1991; Leigh, Zinkhan, & Swaminathan, 2006).

Levels of Processing

One determinant of how well memories are recalled is the way in which material is first perceived, processed, and understood. The **levels-of-processing theory** emphasizes the degree to which new material is mentally analyzed. It suggests that the amount of information processing that occurs when material is initially encountered is central in determining how much of the information is ultimately remembered. According to this approach, the depth of information processing during exposure to material–meaning the degree to which it is analyzed and considered–is critical; the greater the intensity of its initial processing, the more likely we are to remember it (Craik & Lockhart, 2008; Mungan, Peynircioğlu, & Halpern, 2011).

Because we do not pay close attention to much of the information to which we are exposed, very little mental processing typically takes place, and we forget new material almost immediately. However, information to which we pay greater attention is processed more thoroughly. Therefore, it enters memory at a deeper level–and is less apt to be forgotten than is information processed at shallower levels.

The theory goes on to suggest that there are considerable differences in the ways in which information is processed at various levels of memory. At shallow levels, information is processed merely in terms of its physical and sensory aspects. For example, we may pay attention only to the shapes that make up the letters in the word *dog*. At an intermediate level of processing, the shapes are translated into meaningful units–in this case, letters of the alphabet. Those letters are considered in the context of words, and specific phonetic sounds may be attached to the letters.

At the deepest level of processing, information is analyzed in terms of its meaning. We may see it in a wider context and draw associations between the meaning of the information and broader networks of knowledge. For instance, we may think of dogs not merely as animals with four legs and a tail, but also in terms of their relationship to cats and other mammals. We may form an image of our own dog, thereby relating the concept to our own lives. According to the levels-of-processing approach, the deeper the initial level of processing of specific information, the longer the information will be retained.

There are considerable practical implications to the notion that recall depends on the degree to which information is initially processed. For example, the depth of information processing is critical when learning and studying course material. Rote memorization of a list of key terms for a test is unlikely to produce long-term recollection of information because processing occurs at a shallow level. In contrast, thinking about the meaning of the terms and reflecting on how they relate to information that one currently knows results in far more effective long-term retention (Conway, 2002; Wenzel, Zetocha, & Ferraro, 2007).

Explicit and Implicit Memory

If you've ever had surgery, you probably hoped that the surgeons were focused completely on the surgery and gave you their undivided attention while slicing into your body. The reality in most operating rooms is quite different, though. Surgeons may be chatting with nurses about a new restaurant as soon as they sew you up.

If you are like most patients, you are left with no recollection of the conversation that occurred while you were under anesthesia. However, it is very possible that although you had no conscious memories of the discussions on the merits of the restaurant, on some level you probably did recall at least some information. In fact, careful studies have found that people who are anesthetized during surgery can sometimes recall snippets of conversations they heard during surgery—even though they have no conscious recollection of the information (Kihlstrom et al., 1990; Sebel, Bonke, & Winograd, 1993).

The discovery that people have memories about which they are unaware has been an important one. It has led to speculation that two forms of memory, explicit and implicit, may exist side by side. **Explicit memory** refers to intentional or conscious recollection of information. When we try to remember a name or date we have encountered or learned about previously, we are searching our explicit memory.

explicit memory Intentional or conscious recollection of information.

In contrast, **implicit memory** refers to memories of which people are not consciously aware but that can affect subsequent performance and behavior. Skills that operate automatically and without thinking, such as jumping out of the path of an automobile coming toward us as we walk down the side of a road, are stored in implicit memory. Similarly, a feeling of vague dislike for an acquaintance, without knowing why we have that feeling, may be a reflection of implicit memories. Perhaps the person reminds us of someone else in our past that we didn't like, even though we are not aware of the memory of that other individual (Voss & Paller, 2008; Gopie, Craik, & Hasher, 2011; Wu, Y., 2013).

implicit memory Memories of which people are not consciously aware but that can affect subsequent performance and behavior.

Implicit memory is closely related to the prejudice and discrimination people exhibit toward members of minority groups. Although people may say and even believe they harbor no prejudice, assessment of their implicit memories may reveal that they have negative associations about members of minority groups. Such associations can influence people's behavior without their being aware of their underlying beliefs (Greenwald, Nosek, & Banaji, 2003; Greenwald, Nosek, & Sriram, 2006; Hofmann et al., 2008).

One way that memory specialists study implicit memory is through experiments that use priming. **Priming** occurs when exposure to a word or concept (called a *prime*) later makes it easier to recall related information. Priming allows us to remember new information better and faster because of material we already have stored in memory. Priming effects occur even when people have no conscious memory of the original word or concept (Toth & Daniels, 2002; Schacter, Dobbins, & Schnyer, 2004; Geyer, Gokce, & Müller, 2011).

priming A phenomenon that occurs when exposure to a word or concept (called a *prime*) later makes it easier to recall related information.

The typical experiment designed to illustrate priming helps clarify the phenomenon. In priming experiments, participants are rapidly exposed to a stimulus such as a word, an object, or perhaps a drawing of a face. The second phase of the experiment is done after an interval ranging from several seconds to several months. At that point, participants are exposed to incomplete perceptual information that is related to the first stimulus, and they are asked whether they recognize it. For example, the new material may consist of the first letter of a word that had been presented earlier or a part of a face that had been shown earlier. If participants are able to identify the stimulus more readily than they identify stimuli that have not been presented earlier, priming has taken place. Clearly, the earlier stimulus has been remembered—although the material resides in implicit memory, not explicit memory.

The same thing happens to us in our everyday lives. Suppose several months ago you watched a documentary on the planets, and the narrator described the moons of Mars, focusing on its moon named Phobos. You promptly forget the name of the moon, at least consciously. Then, several months later, you're completing a crossword puzzle that you have partially filled in, and it includes the letters *obos*. As soon as you look at the set of letters, you think of Phobos, and suddenly you recall for the first time since your initial exposure to the information that it is one of the moons of Mars. The sudden recollection occurred because your memory was primed by the letters *obos*.

In short, when information that we are unable to consciously recall affects our behavior, implicit memory is at work. Our behavior may be influenced by experiences of which we are unaware–an example of what has been called "retention without remembering" (Horton et al., 2005; White, 2013).

Flashbulb Memories

Do you remember where you were on September 11, 2001?

You may recall your location and a variety of other details that occurred when you heard about the terrorist attacks on the United States, even though the incident happened more than a dozen years ago. Your ability to remember details about this fatal event illustrates a phenomenon known as flashbulb memory. **Flashbulb memories** are memories related to a specific, important, or surprising event that are recalled easily and with vivid imagery.

flashbulb memories Memories of a specific, important, or surprising emotionally significant event that are recalled easily and with vivid imagery.

Several types of flashbulb memories are common among college students. For example, involvement in a car accident, meeting one's roommate for the first time, and the night of high school graduation are all typical flashbulb memories (Bohn & Berntsen, 2007; Talarico, 2009; Lanciano et al., 2013; see Figure 3).

Of course, flashbulb memories do not contain every detail of an original scene. I remember vividly that more than five decades ago I was sitting in Mr. Sharp's 10th-grade geometry class when I heard that President John Kennedy had been shot. However,

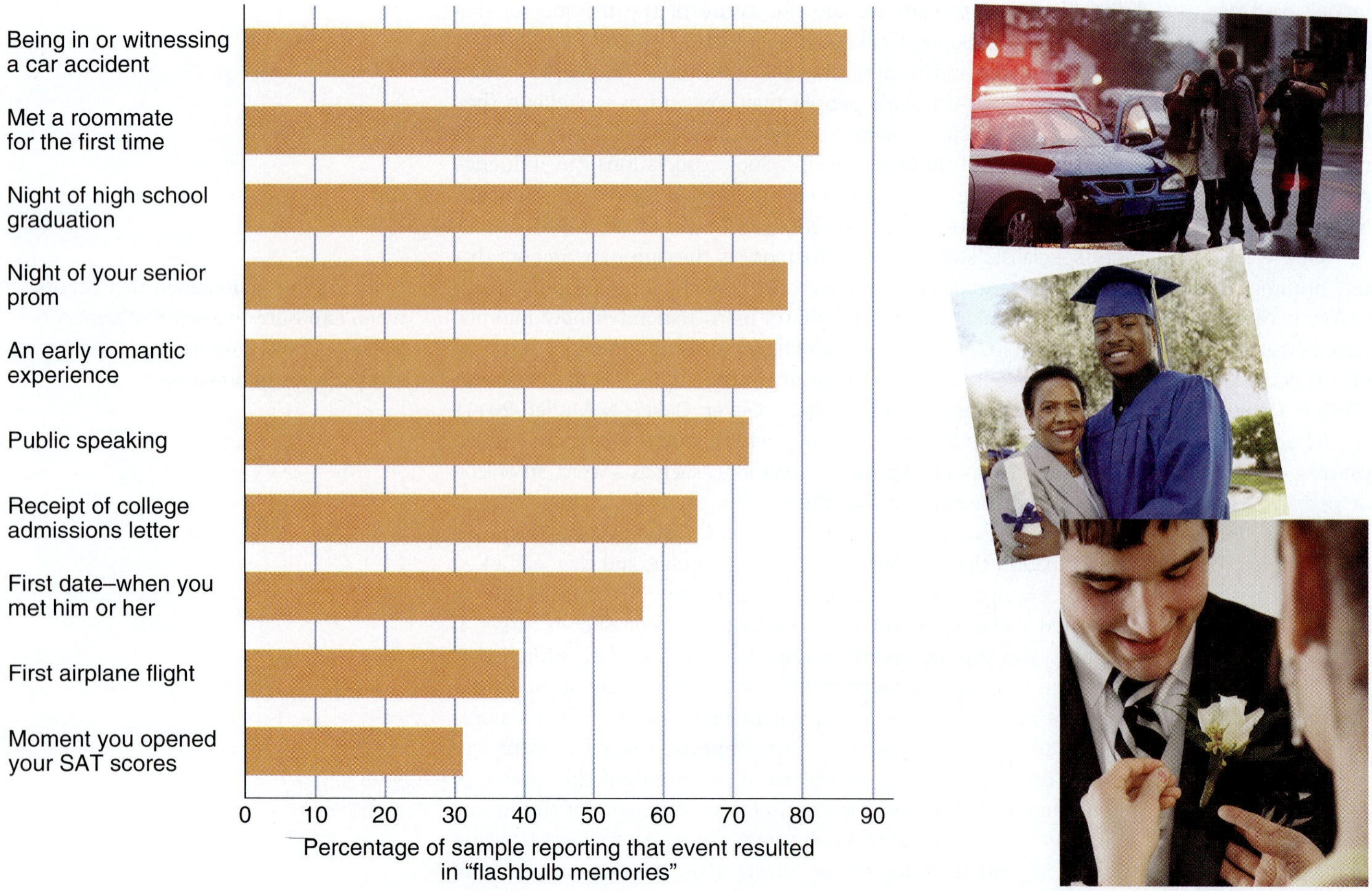

FIGURE 3 These are the most common flashbulb memory events, based on a survey of college students. What are some of your flashbulb memories? (Source: Adapted from Rubin, 1985.)

although I recall where I was sitting and how my classmates reacted to the news, I do not recollect what I was wearing or what I had for lunch that day.

Furthermore, the details recalled in flashbulb memories are often inaccurate, particularly when they involve highly emotional events. For example, those old enough to remember the day when the World Trade Center in New York was attacked by terrorists typically remember watching television that morning and seeing images of the first plane, and then the second plane, striking the towers. However, that recollection is wrong: In fact, television broadcasts showed images only of the second plane on September 11. No video of the first plane was available until early the following morning, September 12, when it was shown on television (Begley, 2002; Schaefer, Halldorson, & Dizon-Reynante, 2011).

Flashbulb memories illustrate a more general phenomenon about memory: Memories that are exceptional are more easily retrieved (although not necessarily accurately) than are those relating to events that are commonplace. The more distinctive a stimulus is, and the more personal relevance the event has, the more likely we are to recall it later (Shapiro, 2006; Talarico & Rubin, 2007; Schaefer et al., 2011).

Even with a distinctive stimulus, however, we may not remember where the information came from. *Source amnesia* occurs when an individual has a memory for some material but cannot recall where he or she encountered it. For example, source amnesia can explain situations in which you meet someone you know but can't remember where you'd met that person initially.

Similarly, our motivation to remember material when we are exposed to it initially affects how well we can later recall it. If we know we are going to need to recall material later, we are going to be more attentive to it. In contrast, if we don't expect to need to recall material later, then we are less likely to remember it (Naveh-Benjamin et al., 2000; Kassam et al., 2009). (Also see *Applying Psychology in the 21st Century*.)

Constructive Processes in Memory: Rebuilding the Past

As we have seen, although it is clear that we can have detailed recollections of significant and distinctive events, it is difficult to gauge the accuracy of such memories. In fact, it is apparent that our memories reflect, at least in part, **constructive processes,** processes in which memories are influenced by the meaning we give to events. When we retrieve information, then, the memory that is produced is affected not just by the direct prior experience we have had with the stimulus, but also by our guesses and inferences about its meaning.

constructive processes Processes in which memories are influenced by the meaning we give to events.

The notion that memory is based on constructive processes was first put forward by Frederic Bartlett, a British psychologist. He suggested that people tend to remember information in terms of **schemas,** organized bodies of information stored in memory that bias the way new information is interpreted, stored, and recalled (Bartlett, 1932). Because we use schemas to organize information, our memories often consist of a reconstruction of previous experience. Consequently, our schemas are based not only on the actual material to which people are exposed, but also on their understanding of the situation, their expectations about the situation, and their awareness of the motivations underlying the behavior of others.

schemas Organized bodies of information stored in memory that bias the way new information is interpreted, stored, and recalled.

One of the earliest demonstrations of schemas came from a classic study that involved a procedure similar to the children's game of "telephone," in which information from memory is passed sequentially from one person to another. In the study, a participant viewed a drawing in which there were a variety of people of differing racial and ethnic backgrounds on a subway car, one of whom—a white person—was shown with a razor in his hand (Allport & Postman, 1958). The first participant was asked to describe the drawing to someone else without looking back at it. Then that person was asked to describe it to another person (without looking at the drawing), and then the process was repeated with still one more participant.

Study Alert

A key fact about memory is that it is a constructive process in which memories are influenced by the meaning given to what is being recalled.

Applying Psychology in the 21st Century

Mind Pops

Most of the time, our memory works the way we expect it to. Sometimes we use it to mentally replay events from the past, such as reminiscing about the first day of summer vacation. Other times we use it to conjure up facts and information, such as the name of the president of France or where we parked our car at the mall. In these cases, memory operates under our control—we deliberately retrieve information that we specifically want. But sometimes memory acts as if it has a mind of its own, delivering seemingly random information to us at surprising times. Researchers call these spontaneous bursts of memory "mind pops."

Mind pops are bits of knowledge, such as words or images, that spontaneously pop into mind suddenly and without warning. Mind pops differ from a triggered memory—information that spontaneously comes to mind because something in our surroundings cued it, such as when the scent of baking bread brings back memories of childhood trips to Grandma's house. Instead, mind pops lack any obvious trigger. They are typically words or phrases rather than visual or auditory memories, and they usually happen when we are doing something routine and mindless, such as taking a shower (Mandler, 2007).

Researchers are interested in what mind pops can tell us about the way memory works. For one thing, we know that they are a common phenomenon. And we know that they aren't actually as random as they seem—they are connected to our experiences, but in a deep and non-obvious way. Normally as we go about our day, we encounter stimuli in the environment that trigger related memory concepts. If a fire engine passes by, for example, it activates our concept for fire engines and other related concepts as well, such as fire, fire fighters, other emergency responders, and more. Such memories may also include certain concepts that we might have connected with fire engines, such as birthdays if every birthday throughout childhood our aunt gave us a toy fire engine as a gift. These concepts are normally activated for a short duration, but they may remain primed—readily accessible in memory—for hours or even days thereafter. They are, in a sense, waiting to pop into view. And later on, that's exactly what happens when a distantly related environmental cue that wouldn't typically trigger that particular concept does trigger it, simply because it was so accessible (Bradley, Moulin, & Kvavilashvili, 2013).

What might mind pops do for us? For one thing, they might help us be more creative if they allow us to see new links between concepts. Some evidence, however, suggests that they might also be associated with mental illness. Research on mind pops is still in its infancy, so it's too early to say whether they are helpful or harmful or both. But they do reflect our mind's ability to make connections between events, even without our specific awareness (Elua, Laws, & Kvavilashvili, 2012).

RETHINK

- What might happen if involuntary memories such as mind pops become intrusive and disturbing?
- What would be some particularly difficult challenges in trying to study the phenomenon of mind pops?

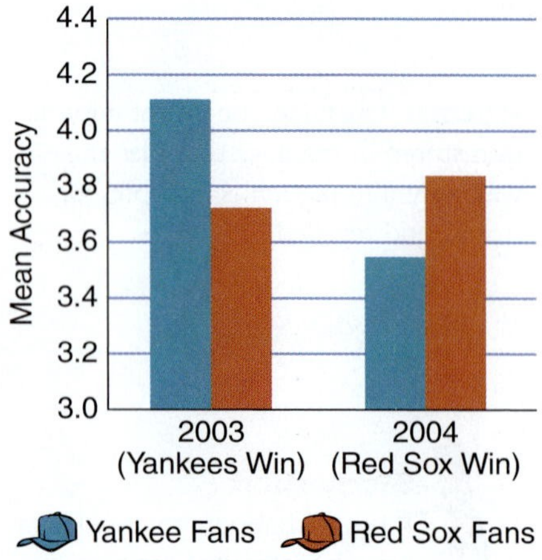

FIGURE 4 Yankee and Red Sox fans were more accurate recalling details of a championship game their team won than they were of a championship game that their team lost. (Source: Adapted from Breslin & Safer, 2011.)

The report of the last person differed in significant, yet systematic, ways from the initial drawing. Specifically, many people described the drawing as depicting an African American with a knife—an incorrect recollection, given that the drawing showed a razor in the hand of a Caucasian person. The transformation of the Caucasian's razor into an African American's knife clearly indicates that the participants held a schema that included the unwarranted prejudice that African Americans are more violent than Caucasians and thus more apt to be holding a knife. In short, our expectations and knowledge—and prejudices—affect the reliability of our memories (McDonald & Hirt, 1997; Newby-Clark & Ross, 2003).

Although the constructive nature of memory can result in memories that are partially or completely false, they also may be beneficial in some ways. For example, false memories may allow us to keep hold of positive self-images. In addition, they may help us maintain positive relationships with others as we construct overly positive views of others (Howe, 2011).

Similarly, memory is affected by the emotional meaning of experiences. For example, in one experiment, researchers asked devoted Yankee or Red Sox fans about details of two decisive baseball championship games between the teams, one won by the Yankees and the other won by the Red Sox. Fans recalled details of the game their team won significantly more accurately than the game their team lost (see Figure 4; Breslin & Safer, 2011; Guida et al., 2013).

MEMORY IN THE COURTROOM: THE EYEWITNESS ON TRIAL

For Calvin Willis, the inadequate memories of two people cost him more than two decades of his life. Willis was the victim of mistaken identity when a young rape victim picked out his photo as the perpetrator of the rape. On that basis, he was tried, convicted, and sentenced to life in prison. Twenty-one years later, DNA testing showed that Willis was innocent, and the victim's identification wrong (Corsello, 2005).

Unfortunately, Willis is not the only victim to whom apologies have had to be made; many cases of mistaken identity have led to unjustified legal actions. Research on eyewitness identification of suspects, as well as on memory for other details of crimes, has shown that eyewitnesses are apt to make significant errors when they try to recall details of criminal activity–even if they are highly confident about their recollections. Because more than 75,000 prosecutions a year are totally based on eyewitness recollections, the problem is significant (Zaragoza, Belli, & Payment, 2007; Paterson, Kemp, & Ng, 2011; Lehrer, 2012).

One reason is the impact of the weapons used in crimes. When a criminal perpetrator displays a gun or knife, it acts like a perceptual magnet, attracting the eyes of the witnesses. As a consequence, witnesses pay less attention to other details of the crime and are less able to recall what actually occurred (Steblay et al., 2003; Zaitsu, 2007; Pickel, 2009).

One reason eyewitnesses are prone to memory-related errors is that the specific wording of questions posed to them by police officers or attorneys can affect the way they recall information, as a number of experiments illustrate. For example, in one experiment the participants were shown a film of two cars crashing into each other. Some were then asked the question, "About how fast were the cars going when they *smashed* into each other?" On average, they estimated the speed to be 40.8 miles per hour. In contrast, when another group of participants was asked, "About how fast were the cars going when they *contacted* each other?" the average estimated speed was only 31.8 miles per hour (Loftus & Palmer, 1974; see Figure 5).

Children's Reliability. The problem of memory reliability becomes even more acute when children are witnesses because increasing evidence suggests that children's memories are highly vulnerable to the influence of others (Loftus, 1993; Douglas, Goldstein, & Bjorklund, 2000). For instance, in one experiment, 5- to 7-year-old girls who had just had a routine physical examination were shown an anatomically explicit doll. The girls were shown the doll's genital area and asked, "Did the doctor touch you here?" Three of the girls who did not have a vaginal or anal exam said that the doctor had in fact touched them in the genital area, and one of those three made up the detail "The doctor did it with a stick" (Saywitz & Goodman, 1990).

Children's memories are especially susceptible to influence when the situation is highly emotional or stressful. For example, in trials in which there is significant pretrial publicity

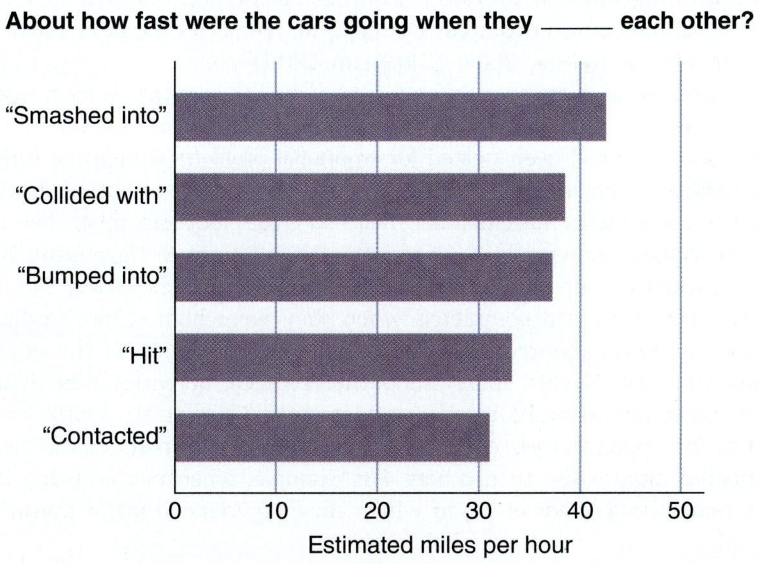

FIGURE 5 After viewing an accident involving two cars, the participants in a study were asked to estimate the speed of the two cars involved in the collision. Estimates varied substantially, depending on the way the question was worded. (Source: Adapted from Loftus & Palmer, 1974.)

Paul Shanley, a Catholic priest, was convicted of sexual abuse on the basis of memories of a man who claimed to have been abused for a six-year period during childhood, but who only recalled the abuse years later when he was an adult.

or in which alleged victims are questioned repeatedly, often by untrained interviewers, the memories of the alleged victims may be influenced by the types of questions they are asked (Lamb & Garretson, 2003; Quas, Malloy, & Melinder, 2007; Goodman & Quas, 2008).

Repressed and False Memories: Separating Truth from Fiction. Consider the case of Paul Shanley, a Catholic priest. He was convicted of sexual abuse of a man who claimed he had no memory until adulthood of being abused as a child over a six-year period, when his repressed memories gradually moved into consciousness. At that point, he recalled his years of abuse, and on the basis of those previously repressed memories, the priest was convicted (Wolf & Guyer, 2010).

There is good reason to question the validity of *repressed memories*, recollections of events that are initially so shocking that the mind responds by pushing them into the unconscious. Supporters of the notion of repressed memory (based on Freud's psychoanalytic theory) suggest that such memories may remain hidden, possibly throughout a person's lifetime, unless they are triggered by some current circumstance, such as the probing that occurs during psychological therapy.

However, memory researcher Elizabeth Loftus maintains that so-called repressed memories may well be inaccurate or even wholly false–representing *false memory*. For example, false memories develop when people are unable to recall the source of a memory of a particular event about which they have only vague recollections. When the source of the memory becomes unclear or ambiguous, people may become confused about whether they actually experienced the event or whether it was imagined. Ultimately, people come to believe that the event actually occurred (Wade, Sharman, & Garry, 2007; Bernstein & Loftus, 2009a; Choi, Kensinger, & Rajaram, 2013).

There is great controversy regarding the legitimacy of repressed memories. Many therapists give great weight to authenticity of repressed memories, and their views are supported by research showing that there are specific regions of the brain that help keep unwanted memories out of awareness. On the other side of the issue are researchers who maintain that there is insufficient scientific support for the existence of such memories. There is also a middle ground: memory researchers who suggest that false memories are a result of normal information processing. The challenge for those on all sides of the issue is to distinguish truth from fiction (Brown & Pope, 1996; Strange, Clifasefi, & Garry, 2007; Bernstein & Loftus, 2009b).

autobiographical memory Our recollections of our own life experiences.

AUTOBIOGRAPHICAL MEMORY: WHERE PAST MEETS PRESENT

Your memory of experiences in your own past may well be a fiction–or at least a distortion of what actually occurred. The same constructive processes that make us inaccurately recall the behavior of others also reduce the accuracy of autobiographical memories. **Autobiographical memory** is our recollections of our own life experiences. Autobiographical memories encompass the episodic memories we hold about ourselves (Rubin, 1999; Sutin & Robins, 2007; Nalbantian, 2011).

For example, we tend to forget information about our past that is incompatible with the way in which we currently see ourselves. One study found that adults who were well adjusted but who had been treated for emotional problems during the early years of their lives tended to forget important but troubling childhood events, such as being in foster care. College students misremember their bad grades–but remember their good ones (see Figure 6; Walker, Skowronski, & Thompson, 2003; Kemps & Tiggemann, 2007).

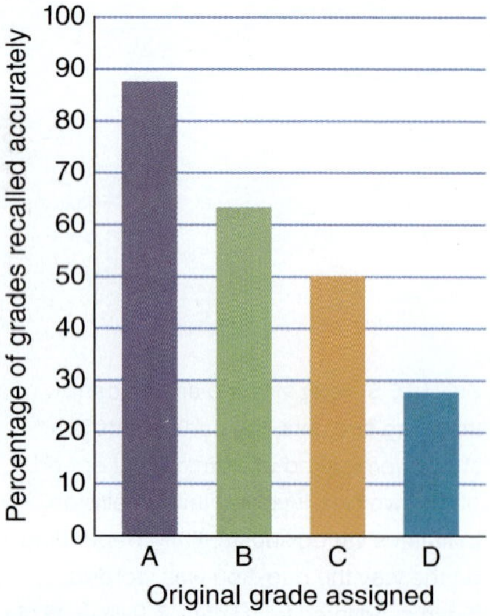

FIGURE 6 We tend to distort memories of unpleasant events. For example, college students are much more likely to accurately recall their good grades while inaccurately recalling their poor ones (Bahrick, Hall, & Berger, 1996). Now that you know this, how well do you think you can recall your high school grades? (Source: Adapted from Barick, Hall, and Berger, 1996.)

Similarly, when a group of 48-year-olds were asked to recall how they had responded on a questionnaire they had completed when they were high school freshman, their accuracy was no better than chance. For example, although 61% of the questionnaire respondents said that playing sports and other physical activities was their favorite pastime, only 23% of the adults recalled it accurately (Offer et al., 2000).

It is not just certain kinds of events that are distorted; particular periods of life are remembered more easily than others. For example, when people reach late adulthood, they remember periods of life in which they experienced major transitions, such as attending college and working at their first job, better than they remember their middle-age years. Similarly, although most adults' earliest memories of their own lives are of events that occurred when they were toddlers, toddlers show evidence of recall of events that occurred when they were as young as 6 months old (Simcock & Hayne, 2002; Wang, 2003; Cordnoldi, De Beni, & Helstrup, 2007).

Exploring DIVERSITY

Are There Cross-Cultural Differences in Memory?

Travelers who have visited areas of the world in which there is no written language often have returned with tales of people with phenomenal memories. For instance, storytellers in some preliterate cultures can recount long chronicles that recall the names and activities of people over many generations. Those feats led experts to argue initially that people in preliterate societies develop a different, and perhaps better, type of memory than do those in cultures that employ a written language. They suggested that in a society that lacks writing, people are motivated to recall information with accuracy, especially information

Storytellers in many cultures can recount hundreds of years of history in vivid detail. Research has found that this amazing ability is due less to basic memory processes than to the ways in which they acquire and retain information.

relating to tribal histories and traditions that would be lost if they were not passed down orally from one generation to another (Daftary & Meri, 2002; Berntsen & Rubin, 2004).

Today, memory researchers dismiss that view. For one thing, preliterate peoples don't have an exclusive claim to amazing memory feats. Some Hebrew scholars memorize thousands of pages of text and can recall the locations of particular words on the page. Similarly, poetry singers in the Balkans can recall thousands of lines of poetry. Even in cultures in which written language exists, then, astounding feats of memory are possible (Strathern & Stewart, 2003; Rubin et al., 2007).

Memory researchers now suggest that there are both similarities and differences in memory across cultures. Basic memory processes such as short-term memory capacity and the structure of long-term memory—the "hardware" of memory—are universal and operate similarly in people in all cultures. In contrast, the way information is acquired and the degree to which it is rehearsed—the "software" of memory—show differences between cultures. Culture determines how people frame information initially, how much they practice learning and recalling it, and the strategies they use to try to recall it (Mack, 2003; Wang & Conway, 2006; Rubin et al., 2007).

RECAP/EVALUATE/RETHINK

RECAP

LO 19-1 What causes difficulties and failures in remembering?

- The tip-of-the-tongue phenomenon is the temporary inability to remember information that one is certain one knows. Retrieval cues are a major strategy for recalling information successfully.
- The levels-of-processing approach to memory suggests that the way in which information is initially perceived and analyzed determines the success with which it is recalled. The deeper the initial processing, the greater the recall.
- Explicit memory refers to intentional or conscious recollection of information. In contrast, implicit memory refers to memories of which people are not consciously aware but that can affect subsequent performance and behavior.
- Flashbulb memories are memories centered on a specific, emotionally significant event. The more distinctive a memory is, the more easily it can be retrieved.
- Memory is a constructive process: We relate memories to the meaning, guesses, and expectations we give to events. Specific information is recalled in terms of schemas, organized bodies of information stored in memory that bias the way new information is interpreted, stored, and recalled.
- Eyewitnesses are apt to make substantial errors when they try to recall the details of crimes. The problem of memory reliability becomes even more acute when the witnesses are children.
- Autobiographical memory is influenced by constructive processes.

EVALUATE

1. While with a group of friends at a dance, Eva bumps into a man she dated last month. But when she tries to introduce him to her friends, she cannot remember his name. What is the term for this occurrence?
2. __________ is the process of retrieving a specific item from memory.
3. A friend tells you, "I know exactly where I was and what I was doing when I heard that Michael Jackson died." What is this type of memory phenomenon called?
4. __________ __________ __________ theory states that the more a person analyzes a statement, the more likely he or she is to remember it later.

RETHINK

1. Research shows that an eyewitness's memory for details of crimes can contain significant errors. How might a lawyer use this information when evaluating an eyewitness's testimony? Should eyewitness accounts be permissible in a court of law?
2. How do schemas help people process information during encoding, storage, and retrieval? In what ways are they helpful? How can they contribute to inaccurate autobiographical memories?

Answers to Evaluate Questions

1. tip-of-the-tongue phenomenon; **2.** Recall; **3.** flashbulb memory; **4.** Levels-of-processing

KEY TERMS

tip-of-the-tongue phenomenon
recall
recognition
levels-of-processing theory
explicit memory
implicit memory
priming
flashbulb memories
constructive processes
schemas
autobiographical memory

MODULE 20

Forgetting: When Memory Fails

He could not remember his childhood friends, the house he grew up in, or what he had eaten for breakfast that morning. H.M., as he is referred to in the scientific literature, had lost his ability to remember anything beyond a few minutes, the result of experimental surgery intended to minimize his epileptic seizures. But the removal of his brain's hippocampus and the loss of his temporal lobes quite literally erased H.M.'s past. He had enjoyed a normal memory until he underwent the operation at age 27. After that, H.M. said, every moment felt like waking from a dream. He never knew where he was or the identities of the people around him (Milner, 2005).

As the case of H.M. illustrates, a person without a normal memory faces severe difficulties. All of us who have experienced even routine instances of forgetting–such as not remembering an acquaintance's name or a fact on a test–understand the very real consequences of memory failure.

Of course, memory failure is also essential to remembering important information. The ability to forget inconsequential details about experiences, people, and objects helps us avoid being burdened and distracted by trivial stores of meaningless data. Forgetting helps keep unwanted and unnecessary information from interfering with retrieving information that is wanted and necessary (Schooler & Hertwig, 2011).

Forgetting also permits us to form general impressions and recollections. For example, the reason our friends consistently look familiar to us is because we're able to forget their clothing, facial blemishes, and other transient features that change from one occasion to the next. Instead, our memories are based on a summary of various critical features–a far more economical use of our memory capabilities.

The first attempts to study forgetting were made by German psychologist Hermann Ebbinghaus about 100 years ago. Using himself as the only participant in his study, Ebbinghaus memorized lists of three-letter nonsense syllables–meaningless sets of two consonants with a vowel in between, such as FIW and BOZ. By measuring how easy it was to relearn a given list of words after varying periods of time had passed since the initial learning, he found that forgetting occurred systematically, as shown in Figure 1. As the figure indicates, the most rapid forgetting occurs in the first 9 hours, particularly in the first hour. After 9 hours, the rate of forgetting slows and declines little, even after the passage of many days.

Despite his primitive methods, Ebbinghaus's study had an important influence on subsequent research, and his basic conclusions have been upheld. There is almost always a strong initial decline in memory, followed by a more gradual drop over time. Furthermore, relearning of previously mastered material is almost always faster than starting from scratch, whether the material is academic information or a motor skill such as serving a tennis ball (Wixted & Carpenter, 2007).

Learning Outcomes

LO 20-1 Why do we forget information?

LO 20-2 What are the major memory impairments?

7 Thinking, Language, and Intelligence

Learning Outcomes for Chapter 7

MODULE 21

LO 21-1 What is thinking?

LO 21-2 What processes underlie reasoning and decision making?

LO 21-3 How do people approach and solve problems?

LO 21-4 What are the major obstacles to problem solving?

Thinking and Reasoning

Mental Images: Examining the Mind's Eye

Concepts: Categorizing the World

Neuroscience in Your Life: How Culture Influences How We Categorize the World

Algorithms and Heuristics

Solving Problems

Applying Psychology in the 21st Century: Sleep On It

Creativity and Problem Solving

Becoming an Informed Consumer of Psychology: Thinking Critically and Creatively

MODULE 22

LO 22-1 How do people use language?

LO 22-2 How does language develop?

Language

Grammar: Language's Language

Language Development: Developing a Way with Words

Understanding Language Acquisition: Identifying the Roots of Language

The Influence of Language on Thinking: Do Eskimos Have More Words for Snow Than Texans Do?

Do Animals Use Language?

Exploring Diversity: Teaching with Linguistic Variety: Bilingual Education

MODULE 23

LO 23-1 What are the different definitions and conceptions of intelligence?

LO 23-2 What are the major approaches to measuring intelligence, and what do intelligence tests measure?

LO 23-3 How can the extremes of intelligence be characterized?

LO 23-4 Are traditional IQ tests culturally biased?

LO 23-5 To what degree is intelligence influenced by the environment and to what degree by heredity?

Intelligence

Theories of Intelligence: Are There Different Kinds of Intelligence?

Assessing Intelligence

Variations in Intellectual Ability

Group Differences in Intelligence: Genetic and Environmental Determinants

Exploring Diversity: The Relative Influence of Genetics and Environment: Nature, Nurture, and IQ

Prologue *I'll take "Artificial Intelligence" for $1,000, Alex*

"This facial wear made Israel's Moshe Dayan instantly recognizable worldwide."

Such was the $1,600 clue in the category "The eyes have it" of a mock round of the popular television game show, *Jeopardy*.

The contestants had mere moments to think about the question that appeared in writing in front of them—as long as it took the host to read the words aloud. As soon as he was done, it was time for the contestants to compete to be the first to buzz in and give an answer.

The three contestants quickly performed these mental gymnastics to come up with the correct answer, but only one hit the buzzer first. "What is an eye patch?" he correctly replied, adding $1,600 to his pot and handily beating his opponents—opponents who happened to be former *Jeopardy* champions. But this competitor was special in his own right: he wasn't even human. He was a computer named Watson, and he was winning (Baker, 2011; Rachlin, 2012).

Looking Ahead

Watson has gone on to do a lot more than win *Jeopardy* (which it did easily, beating a team of human *Jeopardy* champions). Watson is now better at diagnosing cancer than humans, is partnering with banks to help make investment decisions, and is helping workers who answer the phone at corporate call centers personalize their responses (IBM, 2012, 2013; Love, 2013).

Despite its capabilities, though, Watson is still no match for the amazing human computer that resides within our bodies: the brain. Our brains can recognize emotions displayed through subtle nonverbal behavior, can comprehend complicated grammatical linguistic constructions, and can tell and understand jokes. It can accomplish all this in the course of our daily lives, even though we may have little or no idea how it does so. The mystery of how the brain processes language and all its nuances—as well as how it uses information to solve problems and make decisions—is the subject to which we now turn.

Answers to these questions come from **cognitive psychology,** the branch of psychology that focuses on the study of higher mental processes, including thinking, language, memory, problem solving, knowing, reasoning, judging, and decision making. Clearly, the realm of cognitive psychology is broad.

We begin by considering concepts, the building blocks of thinking. We examine different strategies for approaching problems, means of generating solutions, and ways of making judgments about the usefulness and accuracy of solutions.

Next we turn to the way we communicate with others: Language. We consider how language is developed and acquired, its basic characteristics, and the relationship between language and thought.

Finally, we examine intelligence. We consider the challenges involved in defining and measuring intelligence, and then examine the two groups displaying extremes of intelligence: people with mental retardation and the gifted. We explore what are probably the two most controversial issues surrounding intelligence: the degree to which intelligence is influenced by heredity and by the environment and whether traditional tests of intelligence are biased toward the dominant cultural groups in society—a difficult issue that has both psychological and social significance.

cognitive psychology The branch of psychology that focuses on the study of higher mental processes, including thinking, language, memory, problem solving, knowing, reasoning, and judging.

MODULE 21

Thinking and Reasoning

Learning Outcomes

LO 21-1 What is thinking?

LO 21-2 What processes underlie reasoning and decision making?

LO 21-3 How do people approach and solve problems?

LO 21-4 What are the major obstacles to problem solving?

What are you thinking about at this moment?

The mere ability to pose such a question underscores the distinctive nature of the human ability to think. No other species contemplates, analyzes, recollects, or plans the way humans do. Understanding what thinking is, however, goes beyond knowing that we think. Philosophers, for example, have argued for generations about the meaning of thinking, with some placing it at the core of human beings' understanding of their own existence.

Psychologists define **thinking** as brain activity in which we mentally manipulate information, including words, visual images, sounds, or other data. Thinking transforms information into new and different forms, allowing us to answer questions, make decisions, solve problems, or make plans.

Although a clear sense of what specifically occurs when we think remains elusive, our understanding of the nature of the fundamental elements involved in thinking is growing. We begin by considering our use of mental images and concepts, the building blocks of thought.

thinking Brain activity in which people mentally manipulate information, including words, visual images, sounds, or other data.

Mental Images: Examining the Mind's Eye

Think of your best friend.

Chances are that you "see" some kind of visual image when asked to think of her or him, or any other person or object for that matter. To some cognitive psychologists, such mental images constitute a major part of thinking.

Mental images are representations in the mind of an object or event. They are not just visual representations; our ability to "hear" a tune in our heads also relies on a mental image. In fact, every sensory modality may produce corresponding mental images (De Beni, Pazzaglia, & Gardini, 2007; Gardini et al., 2009; Koçak et al., 2011).

mental images Representations in the mind of an object or event.

Research has found that our mental images have many of the properties of the actual stimuli they represent. For example, it takes the mind longer to scan mental images of large objects than small ones, just as the eye takes longer to scan an actual large object than an actual small one. Similarly, we are able to manipulate and rotate mental images of objects, just as we are able to manipulate and rotate them in the real world (Mast & Kosslyn, 2002; Zacks, 2008; Reisberg, 2013; see Figure 1).

Some experts see the production of mental images as a way to improve various skills. For instance, many athletes use mental imagery in their training. Basketball players may try to produce vivid and detailed images of the court, the basket, the ball, and the noisy crowd. They may visualize themselves taking a foul shot, watching the ball, and hearing the swish as it goes through the net. And it works: The use of mental imagery can lead to improved performance in sports (Fournier, Deremaux, & Bernier, 2008; Moran, 2009; Velentzas, Heinen, & Schack, 2011).

PsychTech
Researcher Adam Wilson has developed a method of tweeting by thinking. The process involves being outfitted with electrodes that react to changes in brain activity. It's slow going, though: the fastest tweeters are able to create tweets at only 8 characters per minute.

FIGURE 1 Try to mentally rotate one of each pair of patterns to see if it is the same as the other member of that pair. It's likely that the more you have to mentally rotate a pattern, the longer it will take to decide if the patterns match one another. Does this mean that it will take you longer to visualize a map of the world than a map of the United States? Why or why not? (Source: Adapted from Shepard & Metzler, 1971.)

Athletes use mental imagery to focus on a task, a process they call "getting in the zone." What other occupations might require the use of strong mental imagery?

From the perspective of . . .

A Human Resources Specialist How might you use the research on mental imagery to improve employees' performance?

Concepts: Categorizing the World

concept A mental grouping of similar objects, events, or people.

If someone asks you what is in your kitchen cabinet, you might answer with a detailed list of items (a jar of peanut butter, three boxes of macaroni and cheese, six unmatched dinner plates, and so forth). More likely, though, you would respond by naming some broader categories, such as "food" and "dishes."

Using such categories reflects the operation of concepts. **Concepts** are mental groupings of similar objects, events, or people. Concepts enable us to organize complex phenomena into cognitive categories that are easier to understand and remember (Murphy, 2005; Connolly, 2007; Kreppner et al., 2011).

Concepts help us classify newly encountered objects on the basis of our past experience. For example, we can surmise that someone tapping a handheld screen is probably using some kind of computer or PDA, even if we have never encountered that specific model before. Ultimately, concepts influence behavior. We would assume, for instance, that it might be appropriate to pet an animal after determining that it is a dog, whereas we would behave differently after classifying the animal as a wolf. (Also see *Neuroscience in Your Life*.)

When cognitive psychologists first studied concepts, they focused on those that were clearly defined by a unique set of properties or features. For example, an equilateral

Neuroscience in Your Life: How Culture Influences How We Categorize the World

The way we categorize our world is heavily influenced by the culture in which we develop. For example, when English-speaking and Mandarin Chinese-speaking individuals are asked if certain things belong in a category, they will place them in the same one. For example, if they are asked if ducks and penguins are both birds, they will process the information similarly as seen in the fMRI images (A). However, when they are asked if those same items are typical or atypical of that category, different patterns of brain activity are seen in images (B). Only English speakers, however, show different processing between typical and atypical images within categories, suggesting that while overall we use similar areas for categorization across cultures, the way we distinguish between those in a category may be different (Liu et al., 2013).

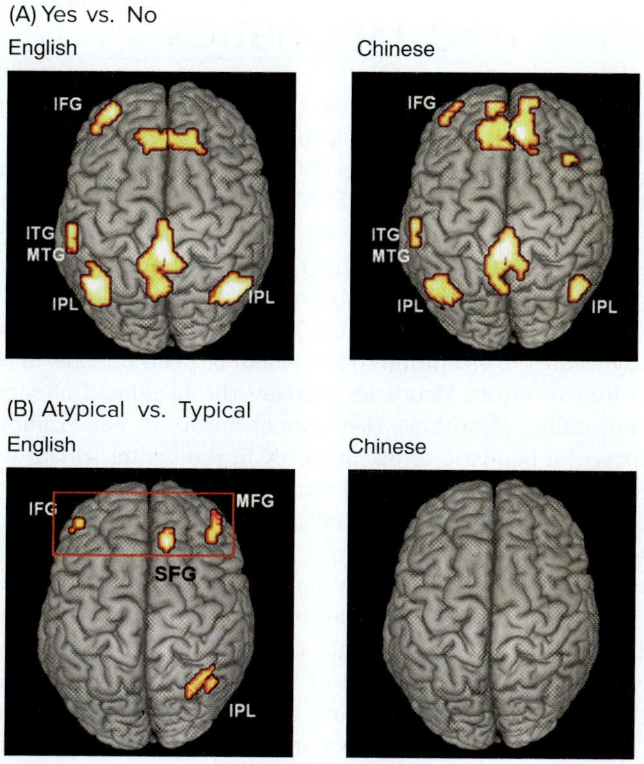

triangle is a closed shape that has three sides of equal length. If an object has these characteristics, it is an equilateral triangle; if it does not, it is not an equilateral triangle.

Other concepts—often those with the most relevance to our everyday lives—are more ambiguous and difficult to define. For instance, broader concepts such as "table" and "bird" have a set of general, relatively loose characteristic features, rather than unique, clearly defined properties that distinguish an example of the concept from a nonexample. When we consider these more ambiguous concepts, we usually think in terms of examples called **prototypes.** Prototypes are typical, highly representative examples of a concept that correspond to our mental image or best example of the concept. For instance, although a robin and an ostrich are both examples of birds, the robin is an example that comes to most people's minds far more readily. Consequently, robin is a prototype of the concept "bird." Similarly, when we think of the concept of a table, we're likely to think of a coffee table before we think of a drafting table, making a coffee table closer to our prototype of a table.

prototypes Typical, highly representative examples of a concept.

Relatively high agreement exists among people in a particular culture about which examples of a concept are prototypes as well as which examples are not. For instance, most people in Western cultures consider cars and trucks good examples of vehicles, whereas elevators and wheelbarrows are not considered very good examples. Consequently, cars and trucks are prototypes of the concept of a vehicle.

Concepts enable us to think about and understand more readily the complex world in which we live. For example, the suppositions we make about the reasons for other people's behavior are based on the ways in which we classify behavior. Hence, our conclusion about a person who washes her hands 20 times a day could vary, depending on whether we place her behavior within the conceptual framework of a health-care worker or a mental patient. Similarly, physicians make diagnoses by drawing on concepts and prototypes of symptoms that they learned about in medical school. Finally, concepts and prototypes facilitate our efforts to draw suitable conclusions through the cognitive process we turn to next: reasoning.

Algorithms and Heuristics

algorithm A rule that, if applied appropriately, guarantees a solution to a problem.

When faced with making a decision, we often turn to various kinds of cognitive shortcuts, known as algorithms and heuristics, to help us. An **algorithm** is a rule that, if applied appropriately, guarantees a solution to a problem. We can use an algorithm even if we cannot understand why it works. For example, you may know that you can find the length of the third side of a right triangle by using the formula $a^2 + b^2 = c^2$, although you may not have the foggiest notion of the mathematical principles behind the formula.

heuristic A thinking strategy that may lead us to a solution to a problem or decision, but–unlike algorithms–may sometimes lead to errors.

For many problems and decisions, however, no algorithm is available. In those instances, we may be able to use heuristics to help us. A **heuristic** is a thinking strategy that may lead us to a solution to a problem or decision, but–unlike algorithms–may sometimes lead to errors. Heuristics increase the likelihood of success in coming to a solution, but, unlike algorithms, they cannot ensure it. For example, when I play tic-tac-toe, I follow the heuristic of placing an X in the center square when I start the game. This tactic doesn't guarantee that I will win, but experience has taught me that it will increase my chances of success. Similarly, some students follow the heuristic of preparing for a test by ignoring the assigned textbook reading and only studying their lecture notes–a strategy that may or may not pay off.

Study Alert

Remember that algorithms are rules that *always* provide a solution, whereas heuristics are shortcuts that *may* provide a solution.

Although heuristics often help people solve problems and make decisions, certain kinds of heuristics may lead to inaccurate conclusions. For example, the *availability heuristic* involves judging the likelihood of an event occurring on the basis of how easy it is to think of examples. According to this heuristic, we assume that events we remember easily are likely to have occurred more frequently in the past–and are more likely to occur in the future–than events that are harder to remember.

For instance, the availability heuristic makes us more afraid of dying in a plane crash than in an auto accident, despite statistics clearly showing that airplane travel is much safer than auto travel. Similarly, although 10 times as many people die from falling out of bed than from lightning strikes, we're more afraid of being hit by lightning. The reason is that plane crashes and lightning strikes receive far more publicity, and they are therefore more easily remembered (Oppenheimer, 2004; Fox, 2006; Kluger, 2006; Caruso, 2008).

We also make use of a *familiarity heuristic*, in which familiar items are seen as superior to those that are unfamiliar. For example, suppose each time you went to a supermarket you had to ponder every type of yogurt to decide which you wanted–as well as every other item on your grocery list. Instead, you see the brand of yogurt you usually buy and settle for it. Usually it's a good rule of thumb because it saves a lot of time.

On the other hand, it's not so good if you are an emergency room physician susceptible to the familiarity heuristic. If you simply settle on the first, most obvious diagnosis for a patient presenting particular symptoms (the ones that are most familiar to you), you may miss making a more accurate diagnosis (Herbert, 2011).

Algorithms and heuristics may be characteristic of human thinking, but scientists are now programming computers to mimic human thinking and problem solving. In fact, they are making significant inroads with computers in terms of the ability to solve problems and carry out some forms of intellectual activities. According to experts who study *artificial intelligence,* the field that examines how to use technology to imitate the outcome of human thinking, problem solving, and creative activities, computers can show rudiments of humanlike thinking because of their knowledge of where to look–and where not to look–for an answer to a problem. They suggest that the capacity of computer programs (such as those that play chess) to evaluate potential moves and to ignore unimportant possibilities gives them thinking ability (Prasad, 2006; Copeland & Proudfoot, 2007; Megill, 2013).

Solving Problems

According to an old legend, a group of Vietnamese monks guard three towers on which sit 64 golden rings. The monks believe that if they succeed in moving the rings from the first tower to the third according to a series of rigid rules, the world as we know it will come to an end. (Should you prefer that the world remain in its present state, there's no need for immediate concern: The puzzle is so complex that it will take the monks about a trillion years to solve it.)

In the Tower of Hanoi puzzle, a simpler version of the task facing the monks, three disks are placed on three posts in the order shown in Figure 2. The goal of the puzzle is to move all three disks to the third post, arranged in the same order, by using as few moves as possible. There are two restrictions: Only one disk can be moved at a time, and no disk can ever cover a smaller one during a move.

Why are cognitive psychologists interested in the Tower of Hanoi problem? Because the way people go about solving such puzzles helps illuminate how people solve complex, real-life problems. Psychologists have found that problem solving typically involves the three steps illustrated in Figure 3: preparing to create solutions, producing solutions, and evaluating the solutions that have been generated.

Study Alert
Use the three steps of problem solving to organize your studying: Preparation, Production, and Judgment (PPJ).

PREPARATION: UNDERSTANDING AND DIAGNOSING PROBLEMS

When approaching a problem like the Tower of Hanoi, most people begin by trying to understand the problem thoroughly. If the problem is a novel one, they probably will pay particular attention to any restrictions placed on coming up with a solution–such as the rule for moving only one disk at a time in the Tower of Hanoi problem. If, by contrast, the problem is a familiar one, they are apt to spend considerably less time in this preparation stage.

Problems vary from well defined to ill defined. In a *well-defined problem*–such as a mathematical equation or the solution to a jigsaw puzzle–both the nature of the problem itself and the information needed to solve it are available and clear. Thus, we can

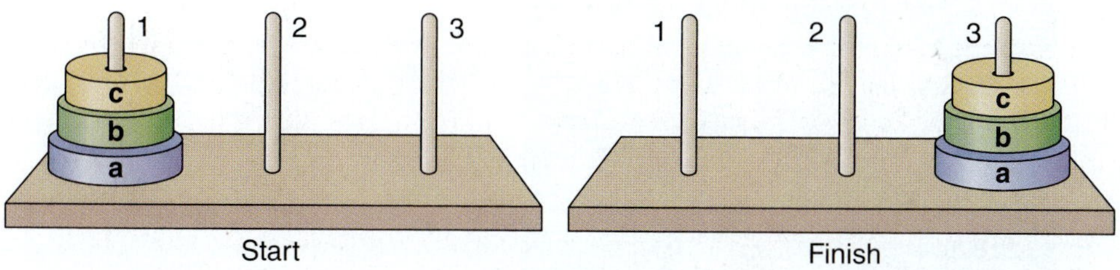

FIGURE 2 The goal of the Tower of Hanoi puzzle is to move all three disks from the first post to the third and still preserve the original order of the disks, using the fewest number of moves possible while following the rules that only one disk at a time can be moved and no disk can cover a smaller one during a move. Try it yourself before you look at the solution, which is listed according to the sequence of moves.

(Solution: Move C to 3, B to 2, C to 2, A to 3, C to 1, B to 3, and C to 3.)

FIGURE 3 Steps in problem solving.

FIGURE 4 The three major categories of problems: (a) arrangement, (b) inducing structure, and (c) transformation. Solutions appear in Figure 5. (Source: Adapted from Bourne et al., 1986.)

a. Arrangement problems

1. Anagrams: Rearrange the letters in each set to make an English word:

2. Two strings hang from a ceiling but are too far apart to allow a person to hold one and walk to the other. On the floor are a book of matches, a screwdriver, and a few pieces of cotton. How could the strings be tied together?

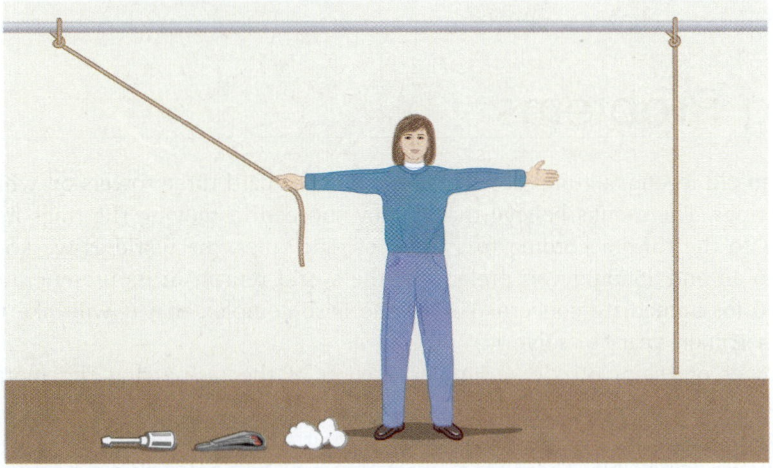

b. Problems of inducing structure

1. What number comes next in the series?

   1 4 2 4 3 4 4 4 5 4 6 4

2. Complete these analogies:

   baseball is to bat as tennis is to __________

   merchant is to sell as customer is to __________

c. Transformation problems

1. Water jars: A person has three jars with the following capacities:

Jar A: 28 ounces

Jar B: 7 ounces

Jar C: 5 ounces

How can the person measure exactly 11 ounces of water?

2. Ten coins are arranged in the following way. By moving only *two* of the coins, make two rows that each contains six coins.

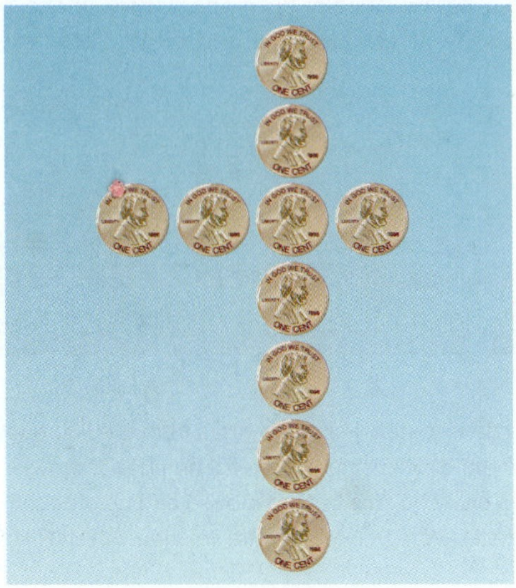

a. Arrangement problems

1. FACET, DOUBT, THICK, NAIVE, ANVIL

2. The screwdriver is tied to one of the strings. This makes a pendulum that can be swung to reach the other string.

b. Problems of inducing structure

1. 7

2. racket; buy

c. Transformation problems

1. Fill jar A; empty into jar B once and into jar C twice. What remains in jar A is 11 ounces.

2.

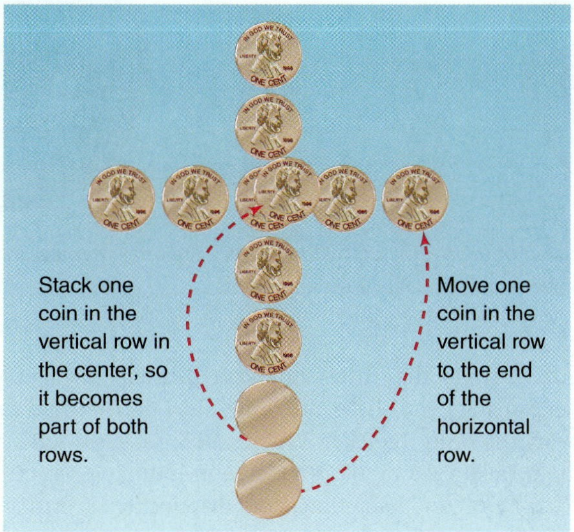

FIGURE 5 Solutions to the problems in Figure 4. (Source: Adapted from Bourne et al., 1986.)

make straightforward judgments about whether a potential solution is appropriate. With an *ill-defined problem,* such as how to increase morale on an assembly line or to bring peace to the Middle East, not only may the specific nature of the problem be unclear, the information required to solve the problem may be even less obvious (Newman, Willoughby, & Pruce, 2011; Mayer, 2013).

Kinds of Problems. Typically, a problem falls into one of the three categories shown in Figure 4: arrangement, inducing structure, and transformation. Solving each type requires somewhat different kinds of psychological skills and knowledge.

Arrangement problems require the problem solver to rearrange or recombine elements in a way that will satisfy a certain criterion. Usually, several different arrangements can be made, but only one or a few of the arrangements will produce a solution. Anagram problems and jigsaw puzzles are examples of arrangement problems (Coventry et al., 2003).

In *problems of inducing structure,* a person must identify the existing relationships among the elements presented and then construct a new relationship among them. In such a problem, the problem solver must determine not only the relationships among the elements but also the structure and size of the elements involved. In the example shown in Figure 4b, a person must first determine that the solution requires the numbers to be considered in pairs (14-24-34-44-54-64). Only after identifying that part of the problem can a person determine the solution rule (the first number of each pair increases by one, whereas the second number remains the same).

The Tower of Hanoi puzzle represents the third kind of problem—*transformation problems*—that consist of an initial state, a goal state, and a method for changing the initial

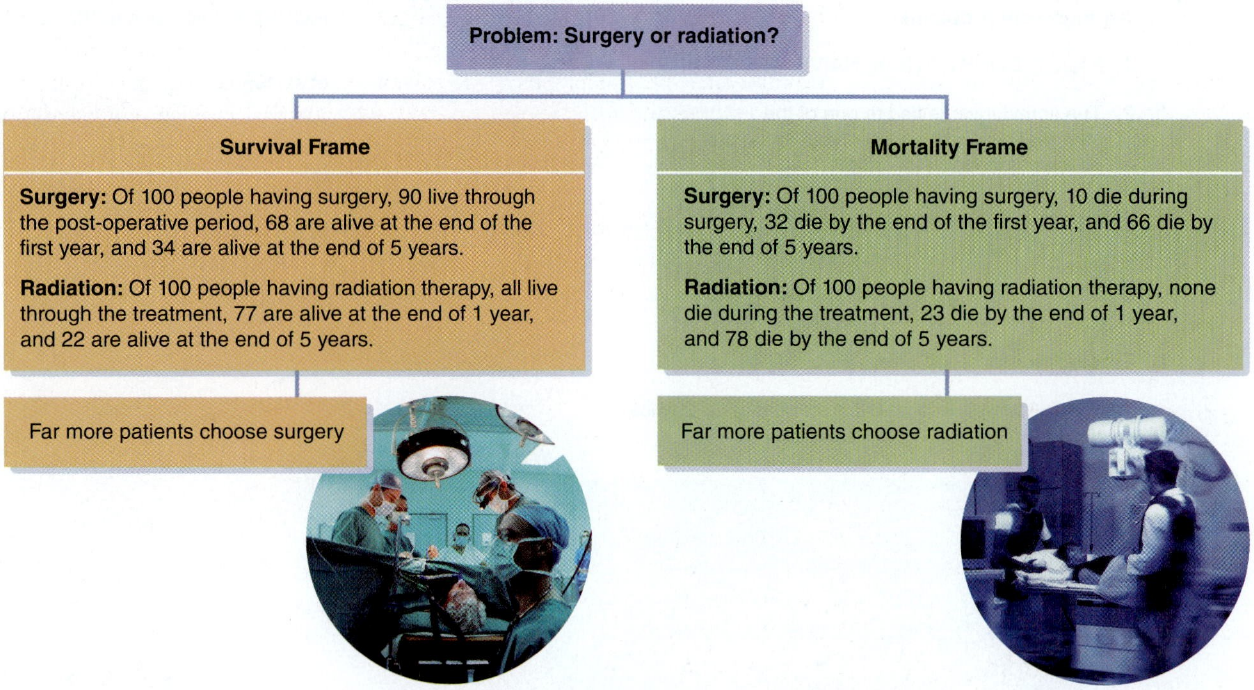

FIGURE 6 A decision often is affected by the way a problem is framed. In this case, most would choose radiation over surgery, despite similar results.

state into the goal state. In the Tower of Hanoi problem, the initial state is the original configuration, the goal state is to have the three disks on the third peg, and the method is the rules for moving the disks (Emick & Welsh, 2005; Majeres, 2007; Van Belle et al., 2011).

Whether the problem is one of arrangement, inducing structure, or transformation, the preparation stage of understanding and diagnosing is critical in problem solving because it allows us to develop our own cognitive representation of the problem and to place it within a personal framework. We may divide the problem into subparts or ignore some information as we try to simplify the task. Winnowing out nonessential information is often a critical step in the preparation stage of problem solving. Our ability to represent a problem—and the solution we eventually come to—depends on the way a problem is framed. Imagine that you were a cancer patient having to choose between either the option of surgery or of radiation, as shown in Figure 6. When the options are framed in terms of *survival,* only 18% of participants in a study chose radiation over surgery. However, when the choice was framed in terms of *dying,* 44% chose radiation over surgery—even though the outcomes are similar with either treatment option (Tversky & Kahneman, 1987; Chandran & Menon, 2004).

PRODUCTION: GENERATING SOLUTIONS

After preparation, the next stage in problem solving is the production of possible solutions. If a problem is relatively simple, we may already have a direct solution stored in long-term memory, and all we need to do is retrieve the appropriate information. If we cannot retrieve or do not know the solution, we must generate possible solutions and compare them with information in long- and short-term memory.

At the most basic level, we can solve problems through trial and error. Thomas Edison invented the lightbulb only because he tried thousands of different kinds of materials for a filament before he found one that worked (carbon). The difficulty with trial and error, of course, is that some problems are so complicated that it would take a lifetime to try out every possibility. For example, according to some estimates, there are some 10^{120} possible sequences of chess moves (Fine & Fine, 2003).

In place of trial and error, complex problem solving often involves the use of heuristics, cognitive shortcuts that can generate solutions. Probably the most frequently applied heuristic in problem solving is a **means-ends analysis,** which involves repeated tests for differences between the desired outcome and what currently exists. Consider this simple example (Huber, Beckmann, & Herrmann, 2004; Chrysikou, 2006; Bosse, Gerritsen, & Treur, 2011):

means-ends analysis Involves repeated tests for differences between the desired outcome and what currently exists.

> I want to take my son to preschool. What's the difference between what I have and what I want? One of distance. What changes distance? My automobile. My automobile won't work. What is needed to make it work? A new battery. What has new batteries? An auto repair shop. . . .

In a means-end analysis, each step brings the problem solver closer to a resolution. Although this approach is often effective, if the problem requires indirect steps that temporarily *increase* the discrepancy between a current state and the solution, means-ends analysis can be counterproductive. For example, sometimes the fastest route to the summit of a mountain requires a mountain climber to backtrack temporarily; a means-end approach–that implies that the mountain climber should always forge ahead and upward–will be ineffective in such instances.

For other problems, the best approach is to work backward by focusing on the goal, rather than the starting point, of the problem. Consider, for example, the water lily problem:

> Water lilies are growing on Blue Lake. The water lilies grow rapidly, so that the amount of water surface covered by lilies doubles every 24 hours. On the first day of summer, there was just one water lily. On the 90th day of the summer, the lake was entirely covered. On what day was the lake half covered? (Reisberg, 1997)

If you start searching for a solution to the problem by thinking about the initial state on day 1 (one water lily) and move forward from there, you're facing a daunting task of trial-and-error estimation. But try taking a different approach: Start with day 90, when the entire lake was covered with lilies. Given that the lilies double their coverage daily, on the prior day only half the lake was covered. The answer, then, is day 89, a solution found by working backward (Bourne et al., 1986; Hunt, 1994).

Forming Subgoals: Dividing Problems into Their Parts. Another heuristic commonly used to generate solutions is to divide a problem into intermediate steps, or *subgoals,* and solve each of those steps. For instance, in our modified Tower of Hanoi problem, we could choose several obvious subgoals, such as moving the largest disk to the third post.

If solving a subgoal is a step toward the ultimate solution to a problem, identifying subgoals is an appropriate strategy. In some cases, however, forming subgoals is not all that helpful and may actually increase the time needed to find a solution. For example, some problems cannot be subdivided. Others–like some complicated mathematical problems–are so complex that it takes longer to identify the appropriate subdivisions than to solve the problem by other means (Reed, 1996; Kaller et al., 2004; Fishbach, Dhar, & Zhang, 2006).

Insight: Sudden Awareness. Some approaches to generating possible solutions focus less on step-by-step heuristics than on the sudden bursts of comprehension that one may experience during efforts to solve a problem. In a classic study the German psychologist Wolfgang Köhler examined learning and problem-solving processes in chimpanzees (Köhler, 1927). In his studies, Köhler exposed chimps to challenging situations in which the elements of the solution were all present; all the chimps needed to do was put them together.

In one of Köhler's studies, chimps were kept in a cage in which boxes and sticks were strewn about, and a bunch of tantalizing bananas hung from the ceiling, out of reach. Initially, the chimps made trial-and-error attempts to get to the bananas: They would throw the sticks at the bananas, jump from one of the boxes, or leap wildly from

PsychTech

Research comparing people working together to solve problems face-to-face versus communicating via e-mail finds that those using e-mail are more satisfied with the process and believe they find better solutions.

(a) (b) (c)

FIGURE 7 (a) In an impressive display of insight, Sultan, one of the chimpanzees in Köhler's experiments in problem solving, sees a bunch of bananas that is out of reach. (b) He then carries over several crates, stacks them, and (c) stands on them to reach the bananas.

the ground. Frequently, they would seem to give up in frustration, leaving the bananas dangling temptingly overhead. But then, in what seemed like a sudden revelation, they would stop whatever they were doing and stand on a box to reach the bananas with a stick (Figure 7). Köhler called the cognitive process underlying the chimps' new behavior **insight,** a sudden awareness of the relationships among various elements that had previously appeared to be unrelated.

insight A sudden awareness of the relationships among various elements that had previously appeared to be independent of one another.

Although Köhler emphasized the apparent suddenness of insightful solutions, subsequent research has shown that prior experience and trial-and-error practice in problem solving must precede "insight." Consequently, the chimps' behavior may simply represent the chaining together of previously learned responses, no different from the way a pigeon learns, by trial and error, to peck a key (Fields, 2011; Wen, Butler, & Koutstaal, 2013; also see *Applying Psychology in the 21st Century*).

JUDGMENT: EVALUATING SOLUTIONS

The final stage in problem solving is judging the adequacy of a solution. Often this is a simple matter: If the solution is clear–as in the Tower of Hanoi problem–we will know immediately whether we have been successful (Varma, 2007).

If the solution is less concrete or if there is no single correct solution, evaluating solutions becomes more difficult. In such instances, we must decide which alternative solution is best. Unfortunately, we often quite inaccurately estimate the quality of our own ideas. For instance, a team of drug researchers working for a particular company may consider their remedy for an illness to be superior to all others, overestimating the likelihood of their success and downplaying the approaches of competing drug companies (Eizenberg & Zaslavsky, 2004).

Theoretically, if we rely on appropriate heuristics and valid information to make decisions, we can make accurate choices among alternative solutions. However, as we see next, several kinds of obstacles to and biases in problem solving affect the quality of the decisions and judgments we make.

Applying Psychology in the 21st Century

Sleep On It

Have you ever had the experience of trying desperately to recall the name of a song or the title of a movie, and try as you might, you just can't–so you forget about it for a while, and then hours later, the answer just pops into your head, seemingly out of nowhere?

Most of us can relate to this kind of "aha!" phenomenon, just as many of us have had the experience of struggling for a long time with a problem and then having the answer emerge in a dream or after a good night's sleep. It's as if our brains are continuing to work on the problem "in the background," even as we turn our conscious attention elsewhere. And that is, in fact, what cognitive scientists say is going on.

It's rather like running a task in a computer program that takes a long time to complete; you can minimize the program on your screen to work on something else, but your computer continues to work on the task outside of your awareness. It turns out this nonconscious problem-solving ability of the brain may be improved during sleep. The prefrontal cortex, which keeps the brain on task during wakeful consciousness, eases off during sleep, allowing thoughts to wander, and when your thoughts take new direction, you're more likely to find creative solutions to problems (Barrett, 2001; Sio, Monaghan, & Ormerod, 2013).

To demonstrate this phenomenon, participants in a study were given a set of word-association puzzles to solve. In these puzzles, three words were provided and the participants were asked to find a fourth word that linked them. (For example, for the words *water, shot,* and *eye*, the answer would be *glass.*) Participants took the test twice; some merely rested between sessions, some had a light nap, and others were induced into sleep that included a period of dreaming. Those who dreamed between sessions showed a 40% improvement afterward, whereas the others actually did a bit worse (Cai et al., 2009).

Is this person really problem solving, despite outward appearances?

In another study, participants were given a set of tedious math problems to solve. What they weren't told, though, was that there was a simple shortcut to finding the solutions. About a quarter of the participants discovered this shortcut on their own during a single session. But when participants were allowed a full night's sleep, nearly 60% discovered the shortcut the next day (Wagner et al., 2004).

In short, an increasing number of studies demonstrate that the brain continues to think during sleep, particularly when considering difficult problems. In fact, even creativity may increase while we are asleep (Ritter et al., 2012; Sio, Monaghan, & Ormerod, 2013).

RETHINK

- Why would insight be facilitated by the kind of nonlinear thinking that occurs during sleep?
- How might you make use of the brain's ability to continue thinking about a problem nonconsciously?

IMPEDIMENTS TO SOLUTIONS: WHY IS PROBLEM SOLVING SUCH A PROBLEM?

Consider the following problem-solving test illustrated in Figure 8 (Duncker, 1945):

> You are given a set of tacks, candles, and matches, each in a small box, and told your goal is to place three candles at eye level on a nearby door so that wax will not drip on the floor as the candles burn. How would you approach this challenge?

If you have difficulty solving the problem, you are not alone. Most people cannot solve it when it is presented in the manner illustrated in the figure, in which the objects are *inside* the boxes. However, if the objects were presented *beside* the boxes, just resting on the table, chances are that you would solve the problem much more readily–which, in case you are wondering, requires tacking the boxes to the door and then placing the candles inside them (see Figure 10).

and berries and whipped cream in it for a fancy dessert. You can keep your loose change in a jar or use it as a cocktail shaker. You can keep your goldfish in it while you clean the tank. You can organize shelves in the garage or basement by putting small things like nails and screws and bolts with others of the same size, each in their own jar. You can organize your pantry, too: a jar for white rice, one for wild rice, another for black beans, and so on. You can measure rainfall for a month with a jar. Or place it beneath a leaky sink pipe.

This list shows extraordinary creativity. Unfortunately, it is much easier to identify *examples* of creativity than to determine its causes. Similarly, it's not clear that the kind of creativity shown by highly creative people in the arts, such as Pablo Picasso, is the same kind of creativity shown by highly creative people in the sciences, such as Albert Einstein (Simonton, 2009; Lavazza & Manzotti, 2013).

From the perspective of . . .

A Manufacturer How might you encourage your employees to develop creative ways to improve the products that you produce?

divergent thinking Thinking that generates unusual, yet nonetheless apropriate, responses to problems or questions.

convergent thinking Thinking in which a problem is viewed as having a single answer and which produces responses that are based primarily on knowledge and logic.

However, we do know that several characteristics are associated with creativity. For one thing, highly creative individuals show **divergent thinking,** thinking that generates unusual, yet appropriate, responses to problems or questions. This type of thinking contrasts with **convergent thinking,** which is thinking in which a problem is viewed as having a single answer and which produces responses that are based primarily on knowledge and logic. For instance, someone relying on convergent thinking would answer "You can store food in it" to the query "What can you do with a jar?" In contrast, "You can use it as a vase" is a more divergent–and creative–response (Cropley, 2006; Schepers & van den Berg, 2007; Zeng, Proctor, & Salvendy, 2011).

Pablo Picasso is considered one of the greatest artists of the 20th century. Do you think he relied more on convergent or divergent thinking in his art?

Another aspect of creativity is its *cognitive complexity,* or preference for elaborate, intricate, and complex stimuli and thinking patterns. For instance, creative people often have a wider range of interests and are more independent and more interested in philosophical or abstract problems than are less creative individuals (Barron, 1990; Richards, 2006; Kaufman & Plucker, 2011).

One factor that is *not* closely related to creativity is intelligence. Traditional intelligence tests, which ask focused questions that have only one acceptable answer, tap convergent thinking skills. Highly creative people may therefore find that such tests penalize their divergent thinking. This may explain why researchers consistently find that creativity is only slightly related to school grades and intelligence when intelligence is measured using traditional intelligence tests (Sternberg & O'Hara, 2000; Heilman, 2005; Norton, Heath, & Ventura, 2013).

Study Alert

Remember *d*ivergent thinking produces *d*ifferent and *d*iverse kinds of responses, whereas *c*onvergent thinking produces more *c*ommonsense kinds of responses.

BECOMING AN INFORMED CONSUMER of Psychology

Thinking Critically and Creatively

Can we learn to be better and more creative thinkers?

Cognitive researchers have found that people can learn the abstract rules of logic and reasoning and that such knowledge can improve our reasoning about the underlying causes of everyday events in our lives. Research suggests that critical and creative thinkers are made, not born. Consider, for instance, the following suggestions for increasing critical thinking and creativity (Burbach, Matkin, & Fritz, 2004; Kaufman & Baer, 2006).

- *Redefine problems.* We can modify boundaries and assumptions by rephrasing a problem at either a more abstract or a more concrete level.
- *Use subgoals.* By developing subgoals, we can divide a problem into intermediate steps. This process, known as *fractionation,* allows us to examine each part for new possibilities and approaches, leading to a novel solution for the problem as a whole.
- *Adopt a critical perspective.* Rather than passively accepting assumptions or arguments, we can evaluate material critically, consider its implications, and think about possible exceptions and contradictions.
- *Consider the opposite.* By considering the opposite of a concept we're seeking to understand, we can sometimes make progress. For example, to define "good mental health," it may be useful to consider what "bad mental health" means.
- *Use analogies.* Analogies provide alternative frameworks for the interpretation of facts and help us uncover new understanding. One particularly effective means of coming up with analogies is to look for examples in the animal world. For instance, architects discovered how to construct the earliest skyscrapers by noting how lily pads on a pond could support the weight of a person (Getner & Holyoak, 1997; Bearman, Ball, & Ormerod, 2007; Cho, Holyoak, & Cannon, 2007).
- *Think divergently.* Instead of the most logical or common use for an object, consider how you might use the object if you were forbidden to use it in the usual way.
- *Think convergently.* Although it sounds counter-intuitive, researchers have found that a combination of divergent *and* convergent thinking can lead to greater creativity. Programs that attempt to teach children to be more creative train participants to alternate periods of divergent thinking with intense convergent thinking (Beghetto & Kaufman, 2010).
- *Use heuristics.* Heuristics are cognitive shortcuts that can help bring about a solution to a problem. If the problem has a single correct answer and you can use or construct a heuristic, you can often find the solution more rapidly and effectively.
- *Experiment with various solutions.* Don't be afraid to use different routes to find solutions for problems (verbal, mathematical, graphic, even dramatic). For instance, try to come up with every conceivable idea you can, no matter how wild or bizarre it may seem at first. After you've come up with a list of solutions, review each one and try to think of ways to make what at first appeared impractical seem more feasible.

RECAP/EVALUATE/RETHINK

RECAP

LO 21-1 What is thinking?

- Cognitive psychology encompasses the higher mental processes, including the way people know and understand the world, process information, make decisions and judgments, and describe their knowledge and understanding to others.
- Thinking is the manipulation of mental representations of information. Thinking transforms such representations into novel and different forms, permitting people to answer questions, solve problems, and reach goals.
- Mental images are representations in the mind of an object or event.
- Concepts are categorizations of objects, events, or people that share common properties.

LO 21-2 What processes underlie reasoning and decision making?

- Decisions sometimes (but not always) may be improved through the use of algorithms and heuristics. An algorithm is a rule that, if applied appropriately, guarantees a solution; a heuristic is a cognitive shortcut that may lead to a solution but is not guaranteed to do so.

LO 21-3 How do people approach and solve problems?

- Problem solving typically involves three major stages: preparation, production of solutions, and evaluation of solutions that have been generated.
- Preparation involves placing the problem in one of three categories. In arrangement problems, a group of elements must be rearranged or recombined in a way that will satisfy a certain criterion. In problems of inducing structure, a person first must identify the existing relationships among the elements presented and then construct a new relationship among them. Finally, transformation problems consist of an initial state, a goal state, and a method for changing the initial state into the goal state.
- In the production stage, people try to generate solutions. They may find solutions to some problems in long-term memory. Alternatively, they may solve some problems through simple trial and error and use algorithms and heuristics to solve more complex problems.
- Using the heuristic of a means-ends analysis, a person will repeatedly test for differences between the desired outcome and what currently exists, trying each time to come closer to the goal.
- Köhler's research with chimpanzees illustrates insight, a sudden awareness of the relationships among elements that had previously seemed unrelated.

LO 21-4 What are the major obstacles to problem solving?

- Several factors hinder effective problem solving. Mental set, of which functional fixedness is an example, is the tendency for old patterns of problem solving to persist. Inappropriate use of algorithms and heuristics can also act as an obstacle to the production of solutions. Confirmation bias, in which initial hypotheses are favored, can hinder the accurate evaluation of solutions to problems.
- Creativity is the ability to combine responses or ideas in novel ways. Creativity is related to divergent thinking (the ability to generate unusual, but still appropriate, responses to problems or questions) and cognitive complexity.

EVALUATE

1. __________ are representations in the mind of an object or event.
2. __________ are categorizations of objects that share common properties.
3. Solving a problem by trying to reduce the difference between the current state and the goal state is known as a __________.
4. __________ is the term used to describe the sudden "flash" of revelation that often accompanies the solution to a problem.
5. Thinking of an object only in terms of its typical use is known as __________ __________. A broader, related tendency to approach a problem in a certain way because that method worked previously is known as a __________ __________.
6. Generating unusual but appropriate approaches to a question is known as __________.

RETHINK

1. How might the availability heuristic contribute to prejudices based on race, age, and gender? Can awareness of this heuristic prevent this from happening?
2. Why do you think people use algorithms and heuristics? How can we avoid coming to poor solutions based on their use?

Answers to Evaluate Questions

1. Mental images; **2.** Concepts; **3.** means-end analysis; **4.** Insight; **5.** functional fixedness, mental set; **6.** divergent thinking

KEY TERMS

cognitive psychology
thinking
mental images
concepts
prototypes
algorithm
heuristic
means-ends analysis
insight
functional fixedness
mental set
confirmation bias
creativity
divergent thinking
convergent thinking

MODULE 22

Language

'Twas brillig, and the slithy toves
Did gyre and gimble in the wabe:
All mimsy were the borogoves,
And the mome raths outgrabe.

Although few of us have ever come face to face with a tove, we have little difficulty in discerning that in Lewis Carroll's (1872) poem "Jabberwocky," the expression *slithy toves* contains an adjective, *slithy,* and the noun it modifies, *toves.*

Our ability to make sense out of nonsense, if the nonsense follows typical rules of language, illustrates the complexity of both human language and the cognitive processes that underlie its development and use. The use of **language**—the communication of information through symbols arranged according to systematic rules—is a central cognitive ability, one that is indispensable for us to communicate with one another. Not only is language central to communication, it is also closely tied to the very way in which we think about and understand the world. Without language, our ability to transmit information, acquire knowledge, and cooperate with others would be tremendously hindered. No wonder psychologists have devoted considerable attention to studying language (Stapel & Semin, 2007; Hoff, 2008; Reisberg, 2009; LaPointe, 2013).

Learning Outcomes

LO 22-1 How do people use language?

LO 22-2 How does language develop?

language The communication of information through symbols arranged according to systematic rules.

Grammar: Language's Language

To understand how language develops and relates to thought, we first need to review some of the formal elements of language. The basic structure of language rests on **grammar,** the system of rules that determine how our thoughts can be expressed.

Grammar deals with three major components of language: phonology, syntax, and semantics. **Phonology** is the study of **phonemes,** the smallest basic units of speech that affect meaning, and of the way we use those sounds to form words and produce meaning. For instance, the *a* sound in *fat* and the *a* sound in *fate* represent two different phonemes in English (Hardison, 2006; Creel & Bregman, 2011).

Linguists have identified more than 800 different phonemes among all the world's languages. Although English speakers use just 52 phonemes to produce words, other languages use as few as 15 to as many as 141. Differences in phonemes are one reason people have difficulty learning other languages. For example, to a Japanese speaker, whose native language does not have an *r* phoneme, pronouncing such English words as *roar* presents some difficulty (Gibbs, 2002; Iverson et al., 2003).

Syntax refers to the rules that indicate how words and phrases can be combined to form sentences. Every language has intricate rules that guide the order in which words may be strung together to communicate meaning. English speakers have no difficulty recognizing that "TV down the turn" is not a meaningful sequence, whereas "Turn down the TV" is. To understand the effect of syntax in English, consider the changes in meaning caused by the different word orders in the following three utterances: "John kidnapped the boy," "John, the kidnapped boy," and "The boy kidnapped John" (Robert, 2006; Frank, Goldwater, & Keller, 2013).

grammar The system of rules that determine how our thoughts can be expressed.

phonology The study of the smallest units of speech, called phonemes.

phonemes The smallest units of speech.

syntax Ways in which words and phrases can be combined to form sentences.

semantics The meanings of words and sentences.

The third major component of language is **semantics,** the meanings of words and sentences. Every word has particular semantic features. For example, *boy* and *man* share certain semantic features (both refer to males), but they also differ semantically (in terms of age). Semantic rules allow us to use words to convey the subtle nuances in meaning. For instance, we can use slightly different wording–semantics–about an event to convey subtle differences in meaning. If we had just seen a girl named Laura get hit by a truck, we might say, "A truck hit Laura." But if we were answering a question about why Laura was not at a party the night before, we might say, "Laura was hit by a truck" (Richgels, 2004; Pietarinen, 2006).

Despite the complexities of language, most of us acquire the basics of grammar without even being aware that we have learned its rules. Moreover, even though we may have difficulty explicitly stating the rules of grammar, our linguistic abilities are so sophisticated that we can utter an infinite number of different statements. How do we acquire such abilities?

Language Development: Developing a Way with Words

To parents, the sounds of their infant babbling and cooing are music to their ears (except, perhaps, at three o'clock in the morning). These sounds also serve an important function. They mark the first step on the road to the development of language.

BABBLING

babble Meaningless speech-like sounds made by children from around the age of 3 months through 1 year.

Children **babble**–make speech-like but meaningless sounds–from around the age of 3 months through 1 year. While babbling, they may produce, at one time or another, any of the sounds found in all languages, not just the one to which they are exposed. Even deaf children display their own form of babbling, for infants who are unable to hear yet who are exposed to sign language from birth "babble" with their hands (Petitto, 1993; Majorano & D'Odorico, 2011; Shehata-Dieler et al., 2013).

An infant's babbling increasingly reflects the specific language being spoken in the infant's environment, initially in terms of pitch and tone and eventually in terms of specific sounds. Young infants can distinguish among all 869 phonemes that have been identified across the world's languages. However, after the age of 6 to 8 months, that ability begins to decline. Infants begin to "specialize" in the language to which they are exposed as neurons in their brains reorganize to respond to the particular phonemes infants routinely hear.

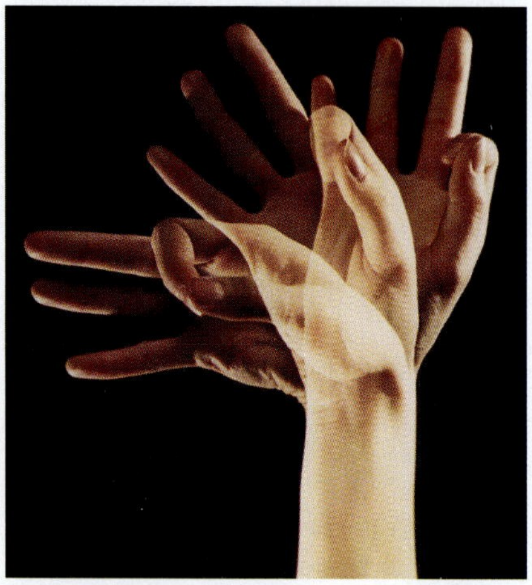

A syllable in signed language, similar to the ones seen in the manual babbling of deaf infants and in the spoken babbling of hearing infants. The similarities in language structure suggest that language has biological roots.

Some theorists argue that a *critical period* exists for language development early in life in which a child is particularly sensitive to language cues and most easily acquires language. In fact, if children are not exposed to language during this critical period, later they will have great difficulty overcoming this deficit (Bates, 2005; Shafer & Garrido-Nag, 2007).

Cases in which abused children have been isolated from contact with others support the theory of such critical periods. In one case, for example, a girl named Genie was exposed to virtually no language from the age of 20 months until she was rescued at age 13. She was unable to speak at all. Despite intensive instruction, she learned only some words and was never able to master the complexities of language (Rymer, 1994; Veltman & Browne, 2001).

PRODUCTION OF LANGUAGE

By the time children are approximately 1 year old, they stop producing sounds that are not in the language to which they have been exposed. It is then a short step to the production of actual words. In English, these are typically short words that start with a consonant sound such as *b, d, m, p,* and *t*—this helps explain why *mama* and *dada* are so often among babies' first words. Of course, even before they produce their first words, children can understand a fair amount of the language they hear. Language comprehension precedes language production.

After the age of 1 year, children begin to learn more complicated forms of language. They produce two-word combinations, the building blocks of sentences, and sharply increase the number of different words they are able to use. By age 2, the average child has a vocabulary of more than 50 words. Just 6 months later, that vocabulary has grown to several hundred words. At that time, children can produce short sentences, although they use **telegraphic speech**—sentences in which only essential words are used. Rather than saying, "I showed you the book," a child using telegraphic speech may say, "I show book," and "I am drawing a dog" may become "Drawing dog." As children get older, of course, they use less telegraphic speech and produce increasingly complex sentences (Volterra et al., 2003; Pérez-Leroux, Pirvulescu, & Roberge, 2011).

telegraphic speech Sentences in which only essential words are used.

By age 3, children learn to make plurals by adding *s* to nouns and to form the past tense by adding *-ed* to verbs. This skill also leads to errors, since children tend to apply rules inflexibly. In such **overgeneralization,** children employ rules even when doing so results in an error. Thus, although it is correct to say "he walked" for the past tense of *walk*, the *-ed* rule doesn't work quite so well when children say "he runned" for the past tense of *run* (Howe, 2002; Rice et al., 2004; Gershkoff-Stowe, Connell, & Smith, 2006; Kidd & Lum, 2008).

overgeneralization The phenomenon by which children over-apply a language rule, thereby making a linguistic error.

By age 5, children have acquired the basic rules of language. However, they do not attain a full vocabulary and the ability to comprehend and use subtle grammatical rules until later. For example, a 5-year-old boy who sees a blindfolded doll and is asked, "Is the doll easy or hard to see?" would have great trouble answering the question. In fact, if he were asked to make the doll easier to see, he would probably try to remove the doll's blindfold. By the time they are 8 years old, however, children have little difficulty understanding this question because they realize that the doll's blindfold has nothing to do with an observer's ability to see the doll (Chomsky, 1968; Hoff, 2003).

Understanding Language Acquisition: Identifying the Roots of Language

Anyone who spends even a little time with children will notice the enormous strides that they make in language development throughout childhood. However, the reasons for this rapid growth are far from obvious. Psychologists have offered three major explanations: one based on learning theory, one based on innate processes, and one that involves something of a combination of the two.

Learning-Theory Approaches: Language as a Learned Skill. The **learning-theory approach** suggests that language acquisition follows the principles of reinforcement and conditioning discovered by psychologists who study learning. For example, a child who says "mama" receives hugs and praise from her mother, which reinforce the behavior of saying "mama" and make its repetition more likely. This view suggests that children first learn to speak by being rewarded for making sounds that approximate speech. Ultimately, through a process of shaping, language becomes more and more like adult speech (Skinner, 1957; Ornat & Gallo, 2004).

learning-theory approach (to language development) The theory that language acquisition follows the principles of reinforcement and conditioning.

In support of the learning-theory approach to language acquisition, the more that parents speak to their young children, the more proficient the children become in language use. In addition, by the time they are 3 years old, children who hear higher levels of linguistic sophistication in their parents' speech show a greater rate of vocabulary growth, vocabulary use, and even general intellectual achievement than do children whose parents' speech is more simple (Hart & Risley, 1997).

The learning-theory approach is less successful in explaining how children acquire language rules. Children are reinforced not only when they use language correctly, but also when they use it incorrectly. For example, parents answer a child's query of "Why the dog won't eat?" as readily as they do the correctly phrased question, "Why won't the dog eat?" Listeners understand both sentences equally well. Learning theory, then, has difficulty fully explaining language acquisition.

NATIVIST APPROACHES: LANGUAGE AS AN INNATE SKILL

nativist approach (to language development) The theory that humans are biologically pre-wired to learn language at certain times and in particular ways.

Pointing to such problems with learning-theory approaches to language acquisition, linguist Noam Chomsky (1968, 1978, 1991) provided a groundbreaking alternative. Chomsky argued that humans are born with an innate linguistic capability that emerges primarily as a function of maturation. According to his **nativist approach** to language, humans are biologically pre-wired to learn language at certain times and in a particular way. Furthermore, he suggests that all the world's languages share a common underlying structure that is pre-wired, biologically determined, and universal. The nativist approach argues that the human brain has an inherited neural system that lets us understand the structure language provides—a kind of universal grammar. These inborn capabilities give us strategies and techniques for learning the unique characteristics of our own native language (Lidz & Gleitman, 2004; McGilvray, 2004; White, 2007).

Supporting Chomsky's view is evidence collected by neuroscientists that suggests that the ability to use language, which was a significant evolutionary advance in human beings, is tied to specific neurological developments. For example, scientists have discovered a gene related to the development of language abilities that may have emerged as recently—in evolutionary terms—as 100,000 years ago. Furthermore, it is clear that there are specific sites within the brain that are closely tied to language and that the shape of the human mouth and throat are tailored to the production of speech. And there is evidence that features of specific types of languages are tied to particular genes, such as in "tonal" languages in which pitch is used to convey meaning (Sahin, Pinker, & Halgren, 2006; Gontier, 2008; Grigorenko, 2009; Perovic & Radenovic, 2011).

Still, Chomsky's view has its critics. For instance, learning theorists contend that the apparent ability of certain animals, such as chimpanzees, to learn the fundamentals of human language (as we discuss later in this module) contradicts the innate linguistic capability view.

Noam Chomsky argues that all languages share a universal grammar.

INTERACTIONIST APPROACHES

To reconcile the differing views, many theorists take an **interactionist approach** to language development. The interactionist approach suggests that language development is produced through a combination of genetically determined predispositions and environmental circumstances that help teach language.

interactionist approach (to language development) The view that language development is produced through a combination of genetically determined predispositions and environmental circumstances that help teach language.

Specifically, proponents of the interactionist approach suggest that the brain is hardwired for our acquisition of language, in essence providing the "hardware" that allows us to develop language. However, it is the exposure to language in our environment that allows us to develop the appropriate "software" to understand and produce language.

The interactionist approach has many proponents. Still, the issue of how language is acquired remains hotly contested (Pinker & Jackendoff, 2005; Hoff, 2008; Waxman, 2009).

Study Alert

It's important to be able to compare and contrast the major approaches to language development: learning-theory, nativist, and interactionist approaches.

From the perspective of . . .

A Child-Care Provider How would you encourage children's language abilities at the different stages of development?

The Influence of Language on Thinking: Do Eskimos Have More Words for Snow Than Texans Do?

Do Eskimos living in the frigid Arctic have a more expansive vocabulary for discussing snow than people living in warmer climates?

It makes sense, and arguments that the Eskimo language has many more words than English for snow have been made since the early 1900s. At that time, linguist Benjamin Lee Whorf contended that because snow is so relevant to Eskimos' lives, their language provides a particularly rich vocabulary to describe it—considerably larger than what we find in other languages, such as English (Martin & Pullum, 1991; Pinker, 1994).

The contention that the Eskimo language is especially abundant in snow-related terms led to the **linguistic-relativity hypothesis,** the hypothesis that language shapes and may determine the way people perceive and understand the world. According to this view, language provides us with categories that we use to construct our view of others and events in the world around us. Consequently, language shapes and produces thought (Whorf, 1956; Casasanto, 2008; Tan et al., 2008).

linguistic-relativity hypothesis The hypothesis that language shapes and may determine the way people perceive and understand the world.

Let's consider another possibility, however. Suppose that instead of language being the *cause* of certain ways of thinking, thought *produces* language. The only reason to expect that Eskimo language might have more words for snow than English does is that snow is considerably more relevant to Eskimos than it is to people in other cultures.

Which view is correct? Most recent research refutes the linguistic-relativity hypothesis and suggests, instead, that thinking produces language. In fact, new analyses of the Eskimo language suggest that Eskimos have no more words for snow than English speakers. If one examines the English language closely, one sees that it is hardly impoverished when it comes to describing snow (consider, for example, *sleet, slush, blizzard, dusting,* and *avalanche*).

Study Alert

The linguistic-relativity hypothesis suggests *l*anguage *l*eads to thought.

Still, the linguistic-relativity hypothesis has not been entirely discarded. A newer version of the hypothesis suggests that speech patterns may influence certain aspects of thinking. For example, in some languages, such as English, speakers distinguish between nouns that can be counted (such as "five chairs") and nouns that require a measurement unit to be quantified (such as "a liter of water"). In some other languages, such as the Mayan language called Yucatec, however, all nouns require a measurement unit. In such cultures, people appear to think more closely about what things are made of than do people in cultures in which languages such as English are spoken (Gentner, Goldin, & Goldin-Meadow, 2003; Tsukasaki & Ishii, 2004).

Similarly, Russian speakers have more words for light and dark blues and are better able to discriminate shades of blue visually. The Icelandic language contains 24 words for different types of waves. Furthermore, some tribes say north, south, east, and west instead of left and right, and they have better spatial orientation. Finally, the Piraha language uses terms like *few* and *many* rather than specific numbers, and speakers are unable to keep track of exact quantities (Boroditsky, 2010; Fuhrman et al., 2011).

In short, although research does not support the linguistic-relativity hypothesis that language *causes* thought, it is clear that language influences how we think. And, of course, it certainly is the case that thought influences language, suggesting that language and thinking interact in complex ways (Ross, 2004; Thorkildsen, 2006; Proudfoot, 2009).

Do Animals Use Language?

One question that has long puzzled psychologists is whether language is uniquely human or if other animals are able to acquire it as well. Many animals communicate with one another in rudimentary forms. For instance, fiddler crabs wave their claws to signal, bees dance to indicate the direction in which food will be found, and certain birds call "*zick, zick*" during courtship and "*kia*" when they are about to fly away. However, researchers have yet to demonstrate conclusively that these animals use true language, which is characterized in part by the ability to produce and communicate new and unique meanings by following a formal grammar.

Sue Savage-Rumbaugh with a primate friend, Panbanisha. Does the use of sign language by primates indicate true mastery of language?

Psychologists, however, have been able to teach chimps to communicate at surprisingly high levels. For instance, after 4 years of training, a chimp named Washoe learned to make signs for 132 words and combine those signs into simple sentences. Even more impressively, Kanzi, a pygmy chimpanzee, has linguistic skills that some psychologists claim are close to those of a 2-year-old human being. Kanzi's trainers suggest that he can create grammatically sophisticated sentences and can even invent new rules of syntax (Savage-Rumbaugh, Toth, & Schick, 2007; Slocombe, Waller, & Liebal, 2011).

Despite the skills primates such as Kanzi display, critics contend that the language such animals use still lacks the grammar and the complex and novel constructions of human language. Instead, they maintain that the chimps are displaying a skill no different from that of a dog that learns to lie down on command to get a reward. Furthermore, we lack firm evidence that animals can recognize and respond to the mental states of others of their species, an important aspect of human communication. Consequently, the issue of whether other animals can use language in a way that humans do remains controversial (Hillix, 2007; Liszkowski et al., 2009; Beran, Smith, & Perdue, 2013).

Exploring DIVERSITY

Teaching with Linguistic Variety: Bilingual Education

In New York City, 1 in 6 of the city's 1.1 million students is enrolled in some form of bilingual or English as a Second Language instruction. And New York City is far from the only school district with a significant population of nonnative English speakers. From the biggest cities to the most rural areas, the face—and voice—of education in the United States is changing. More and more schoolchildren today have last names like Kim, Valdez, and Karachnicoff. In seven states, including Texas and Colorado, more than one-quarter of the students are not native English speakers. For some 55 million Americans, English is their second language (Holloway, 2000; Shin & Kominski, 2010; see Figure 1).

How to appropriately and effectively teach the increasing number of children who do not speak English is not always clear. Many educators maintain that *bilingual education* is best. With a bilingual approach, students learn some subjects in their native language while simultaneously learning English. Proponents of bilingualism believe that students must develop a sound footing in basic subject areas and that, initially at least, teaching those subjects in their native language is the only way to provide them with that foundation. During the same period, they learn English, with the eventual goal of shifting all instruction into English.

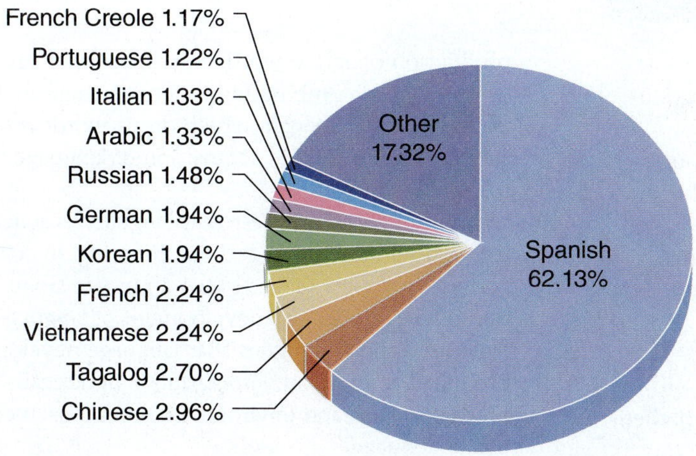

FIGURE 1 The language of diversity. One-fifth of the people in the United States speak a language other than English at home. Spanish is most prevalent; the rest of non-English speakers use an astounding variety of different languages. (Source: Adapted from MLA, 2010.)

In contrast, other educators insist that all instruction ought to be in English from the moment students, including those who speak no English at all, enroll in school. In *immersion programs,* students are immediately plunged into English instruction in all subjects. The reasoning—endorsed by voters in California in a referendum designed to end bilingual education—is that teaching students in a language other than English simply hinders nonnative English speakers' integration into society and ultimately does them a disservice. Proponents of English immersion programs point as evidence to improvements in standardized test scores that followed the end of bilingual education programs (Wildavsky, 2000).

Although the controversial issue of bilingual education versus immersion has strong political undercurrents, evidence shows that the ability to speak two languages provides significant cognitive benefits over speaking only one language. For example, bilingual speakers show more cognitive flexibility and may understand concepts more easily than those who speak only one language. They have more linguistic tools for thinking because of their multiple-language abilities. In turn, this makes them more creative and flexible in solving problems (Bialystok & Martin, 2004; Kuo, 2007; Yim & Rudoy, 2013).

In addition, the advantages of bilingualism start early: by the time bilingual children are 3 or 4 years old, their cognitive development is superior to that of children who speak only one language. It's an advantage that lasts into old age. In fact, bilingualism provides protection from the cognitive declines that are typical in late adulthood (Bialystok & Craik, 2010; Bialystok et al., 2010; Bialystok, 2011).

Furthermore, speaking several languages changes the organization of the brain. For example, bilingual speakers who learn their second language as adults show different areas of brain activation compared with those who learn their second language in childhood. And those who are immersed in intensive language instruction show growth in the hippocampus. In addition, brain scans show that people who speak multiple languages have distinct patterns of brain activity according to the language that they are using, and bilingualism produces more efficient processing on some cognitive tasks (Kovelman, Baker, & Petitto, 2008; Kovacs & Mehler, 2009; Bialystok et al., 2010; Kluger, 2013).

Related to questions about bilingual education is the matter of *biculturalism*—that is, being a member of two cultures and its psychological impact. Some psychologists argue that society should promote an *alternation model* of bicultural competence. Such a model supports members of a culture in their efforts to maintain their original cultural identity as well as in their integration into the adopted culture. In this view, a person can belong to two cultures and have two cultural identities without having to choose between them. Whether society will adopt the alternation model remains to be seen (Carter, 2003; Benet-Martínez, Lee, & Leu, 2006; Tadmor, 2007).

RECAP/EVALUATE/RETHINK

RECAP

LO 22-1 How do people use language?

- Language is the communication of information through symbols arranged according to systematic rules. All languages have a grammar–a system of rules that determines how thoughts can be expressed–that encompasses the three major components of language: phonology, syntax, and semantics.

LO 22-2 How does language develop?

- Language production, which follows language comprehension, develops out of babbling, which then leads to the production of actual words. After 1 year of age, children use two-word combinations, increase their vocabulary, and use telegraphic speech, which drops words not critical to the message. By age 5, acquisition of language rules is relatively complete.
- Learning theorists suggest that language is acquired through reinforcement and conditioning. In contrast, the nativist approach suggests that an innate language-acquisition device guides the development of language. The interactionist approach argues that language development is produced through a combination of genetically determined predispositions and environmental circumstances that help teach language.

- The linguistic-relativity hypothesis suggests that language shapes and may determine the way people think about the world. Most evidence suggests that although language does not determine thought, it does affect the way people store information in memory and how well they can retrieve it.
- The degree to which language is a uniquely human skill remains an open question. Some psychologists contend that even though certain primates communicate at a high level, those animals do not use language. Other psychologists suggest that those primates truly understand and produce language in much the same way as humans.
- People who speak more than one language may have a cognitive advantage over those who speak only one.

EVALUATE

1. Match the component of grammar with its definition:

1. Syntax	**a.** Rules showing how words can be combined into sentences.
2. Phonology	**b.** Rules governing the meaning of words and sentences.
3. Semantics	**c.** The study of the sound units that affect speech.

2. Language production and language comprehension develop in infants about the same time. True or false?

3. __________ __________ refers to the phenomenon in which young children omit nonessential portions of sentences.

4. A child knows that adding *-ed* to certain words puts them in the past tense. As a result, instead of saying "He came," the child says "He comed." This is an example of __________.

5. __________ theory assumes that language acquisition is based on principles of operant conditioning and shaping.

6. In his theory of language acquisition, Chomsky argues that language acquisition is an innate ability tied to the structure of the brain. True or false?

RETHINK

1. Do people who use two languages, one at home and one at school, automatically have two cultures? Why might people who speak two languages have cognitive advantages over those who speak only one?

2. Why is overgeneralization seen as an argument against a strict learning-theory approach to explaining language acquisition?

Answers to Evaluate Questions

1. 1-a, 2-c, 3-b; **2.** false; language comprehension precedes language; **3.** Telegraphic speech; **4.** overgeneralization; **5.** Learning; **6.** true

KEY TERMS

language
grammar
phonology
phonemes
syntax
semantics
babble
telegraphic speech
overgeneralization
learning-theory approach (to language development)
nativist approach (to language development)
interactionist approach (to language development)
linguistic-relativity hypothesis

MODULE 23

Intelligence

Learning Outcomes

LO 23-1 What are the different definitions and conceptions of intelligence?

LO 23-2 What are the major approaches to measuring intelligence, and what do intelligence tests measure?

LO 23-3 How can the extremes of intelligence be characterized?

LO 23-4 Are traditional IQ tests culturally biased?

LO 23-5 To what degree is intelligence influenced by the environment and to what degree by heredity?

Members of the Trukese tribe in the South Pacific often sail a hundred miles in open ocean waters. Although their destination may be just a small dot of land less than a mile wide, the Trukese are able to navigate precisely toward it without the aid of a compass, chronometer, sextant, or any of the other sailing tools that are used by Western navigators. They are able to sail accurately even when the winds do not allow a direct approach to the island and they must take a zigzag course (Gladwin, 1964; Mytinger, 2001).

How are the Trukese able to navigate so effectively? If you asked them, they could not explain it. They might tell you that they use a process that takes into account the rising and setting of the stars and the appearance, sound, and feel of the waves against the side of the boat. But at any given moment as they are sailing along, they could not identify their position or say why they are doing what they are doing. Nor could they explain the navigational theory underlying their sailing technique.

Some people might say that the inability of the Trukese to explain in Western terms how their sailing technique works is a sign of primitive or even unintelligent behavior. In fact, if we gave Trukese sailors a Western standardized test of navigational knowledge and theory or, for that matter, a traditional test of intelligence, they might do poorly on it. Yet, as a practical matter, it is not possible to accuse the Trukese of being unintelligent: Despite their inability to explain how they do it, they are able to navigate successfully through the open ocean waters.

Trukese navigation points out the difficulty in coming to grips with what is meant by intelligence. To a Westerner, traveling in a straight line along the most direct and quickest route by using a sextant and other navigational tools is likely to represent the most "intelligent" kind of behavior; in contrast, a zigzag course, based on the "feel" of the waves, would not seem very reasonable. To the Trukese, who are used to their own system of navigation, however, the use of complicated navigational tools might seem so overly complex and unnecessary that they might think of Western navigators as lacking in intelligence.

What does the Trukese people's method of navigation—which is done without maps or instruments—tell us about the nature of intelligence?

It is clear from this example that the term *intelligence* can take on many different meanings. If, for instance, you lived in a remote part of the Australian outback, the way you would differentiate between more intelligent and less intelligent people might have to do with successfully mastering hunting skills, whereas to someone living in the heart of urban Miami, intelligence might be exemplified by being "streetwise" or by achieving success in business.

Each of these conceptions of intelligence is reasonable. Each represents an instance in which more intelligent people are better able to use the resources of their environment than are less intelligent people, a distinction that is presumably basic to any definition of intelligence. Yet it is also clear that these conceptions represent very different views of intelligence.

That two such different sets of behavior can exemplify the same psychological concept has long posed a challenge to psychologists. For years they have grappled with the issue of devising a general definition of intelligence. Ironically, laypersons have fairly clear ideas of what intelligence is, although the nature of their ideas is related to their culture. Westerners view intelligence as the ability to establish categories and debate rationally. In contrast, people in Eastern cultures and some African communities view intelligence more in terms of understanding and relating to one another (Nisbett, 2003; Sternberg, 2005, 2007; Niu & Brass, 2011; Crowne, 2013).

The definition of intelligence that psychologists employ contains some of the same elements found in the layperson's conception. To psychologists, **intelligence** is the capacity to understand the world, think rationally, and use resources effectively when faced with challenges.

intelligence The capacity to understand the world, think rationally, and use resources effectively when faced with challenges.

This definition does not lay to rest a key question asked by psychologists: Is intelligence a unitary attribute, or are there different kinds of intelligence? We turn now to various theories of intelligence that address the issue.

Theories of Intelligence: Are There Different Kinds of Intelligence?

Perhaps you see yourself as a good writer but as someone who lacks ability in math. Or maybe you view yourself as a "science" person who easily masters physics but has few strengths in interpreting literature. Perhaps you view yourself as generally fairly smart with intelligence that permits you to excel across domains.

The different ways in which people view their own talents mirror a question that psychologists have grappled with. Is intelligence a single, general ability, or is it multifaceted and related to specific abilities? Early psychologists interested in intelligence assumed that there was a single, general factor for mental ability, which they called ***g*,** or the ***g*-factor.** This assumption was based on the fact that different types of measures of intelligence, whether they focused on, say, mathematical expertise, verbal competency, or spatial visualization skills, all ranked test-takers in roughly the same order. People who were good on one test generally were good on others; those who did poorly on one test tended to do poorly on others.

***g* or *g*-factor** The single, general factor for mental ability assumed to underlie intelligence in some early theories of intelligence.

Given that there was a correlation between performance on the different types of tests, the assumption was that there was a general, global intellectual ability underlying performance on the various measures—the *g-factor*. This general intelligence factor was thought to underlie performance in every aspect of intelligence, and it was the *g*-factor that was presumably being measured on tests of intelligence (Spearman, 1927; Colom, Jung, & Haier, 2006; Haier et al., 2009; Major, Johnson, & Bouchard, 2011).

More recent theories explain intelligence in a different light. Rather than viewing intelligence as a unitary entity, some psychologists consider it to be a multidimensional concept that includes different types of intelligence (Stankov, 2003; Sternberg & Pretz, 2005; Tutwiler, Lin, & Chang, 2013).

Piloting a helicopter requires the use of both fluid intelligence and crystallized intelligence. Which of the two kinds of intelligence do you believe is more important for such a task?

FLUID AND CRYSTALLIZED INTELLIGENCE

Some psychologists suggest that there are two different kinds of intelligence: fluid intelligence and crystallized intelligence. **Fluid intelligence** is the ability to reason abstractly. It reflects our ability to reason effectively, identify patterns, and recognize relationships between concepts. If we were asked to solve an analogy or group a series of letters according to some principle, we would be using fluid intelligence (Kane & Engle, 2002; Saggino, Perfetti, & Spitoni, 2006; Di Fabio & Palazzeschi, 2009).

In contrast, **crystallized intelligence** is the accumulation of information, knowledge, and skills that people have learned through experience and education. It reflects our ability to call up information from long-term memory. We would be likely to rely on crystallized intelligence, for instance, if we were asked to participate in a discussion about the solution to the causes of poverty, a task that allows us to draw on our own past experiences, education, and knowledge of the world. In contrast to fluid intelligence, which reflects a more general kind of intelligence, crystallized intelligence is more a reflection of the culture in which a person is raised. The differences between fluid intelligence and crystallized intelligence become especially evident in late adulthood, when people show declines in fluid, but not crystallized, intelligence (Buehner, Krumm, & Ziegler, 2006; Tranter & Koutstaal, 2008; Ackerman, 2011).

fluid intelligence Intelligence that reflects the ability to reason abstractly.

crystallized intelligence The accumulation of information, knowledge, and skills that people have learned through experience and education.

GARDNER'S MULTIPLE INTELLIGENCES: THE MANY WAYS OF SHOWING INTELLIGENCE

Psychologist Howard Gardner has taken an approach very different from traditional thinking about intelligence. Gardner argues that rather than asking "How smart are you?" we should be asking a different question: "How are you smart?" In answering the latter question, Gardner has developed a **theory of multiple intelligences** that has become quite influential (Gardner, 2000; Kaufman, Kaufman, & Plucker, 2013).

theory of multiple intelligences Gardner's intelligence theory that proposes that there are eight distinct spheres of intelligence.

Gardner argues that we have a minimum eight different forms of intelligence, each relatively independent of the others: musical, bodily kinesthetic, logical-mathematical, linguistic, spatial, interpersonal, intrapersonal, and naturalist. (Figure 1 describes the eight types of intelligence, with some of Gardner's examples of people who excel in each type.) In Gardner's view, each of the multiple intelligences is linked to an independent system in the brain. Furthermore, he suggests that there may be even more types of intelligence, such as *existential intelligence,* which involves identifying and thinking about the fundamental questions of human existence. For example, the Dalai Lama might exemplify this type of intelligence (Gardner, 1999, 2000).

Although Gardner illustrates his conception of the specific types of intelligence with descriptions of well-known people, each person has the same eight kinds of intelligence–in different degrees. Moreover, although the eight basic types of intelligence are presented individually, Gardner suggests that these separate intelligences do not operate in isolation. Normally, any activity encompasses several kinds of intelligence working together.

Study Alert
Remember, Gardner's theory suggests that each individual has every kind of intelligence but in different degrees.

The concept of multiple intelligences has led to the development of intelligence tests that include questions in which more than one answer can be correct; these provide an opportunity for test-takers to demonstrate creative thinking. In addition, many educators, embracing the concept of multiple intelligences, have designed classroom curricula that are meant to draw on different aspects of intelligence (Douglas, Burton, & Reese-Durham, 2008; Tirri & Nokelainen, 2008; Davis et al., 2011).

1. Musical intelligence (skills in tasks involving music). Case example:

When he was 3, Yehudi Menuhin was smuggled into San Francisco Orchestra concerts by his parents. By the time he was 10 years old, Menuhin was an international performer.

2. Bodily kinesthetic intelligence (skills in using the whole body or various portions of it in the solution of problems or in the construction of products or displays, exemplified by dancers, athletes, actors, and surgeons). Case example:

Fifteen-year-old Babe Ruth played third base. During one game, his team's pitcher was doing very poorly and Babe loudly criticized him from third base. Brother Matthias, the coach, called out, "Ruth, if you know so much about it, *you* pitch!" Ruth said later that at the very moment he took the pitcher's mound, he *knew* he was supposed to be a pitcher.

3. Logical-mathematical intelligence (skills in problem solving and scientific thinking). Case example:

Barbara McClintock, who won the Nobel Prize in medicine, describes one of her breakthroughs, which came after thinking about a problem for half an hour . . . : "Suddenly I jumped and ran back to the (corn) field. At the top of the field (the others were still at the bottom) I shouted, 'Eureka, I have it!'"

4. Linguistic intelligence (skills involved in the production and use of language). Case example:

At the age of 10, T. S. Eliot created a magazine called *Fireside,* to which he was the sole contributor.

5. Spatial intelligence (skills involving spatial configurations, such as those used by artists and architects). Case example:

Natives of the Truk Islands navigate at sea without instruments. During the actual trip, the navigator must envision mentally a reference island as it passes under a particular star and from that he computes the number of segments completed, the proportion of the trip remaining, and any corrections in heading.

6. Interpersonal intelligence (skills in interacting with others, such as sensitivity to the moods, temperaments, motivations, and intentions of others). Case example:

When Anne Sullivan began instructing the deaf and blind Helen Keller, her task was one that had eluded others for years. Yet, just 2 weeks after beginning her work with Keller, Sullivan achieved great success.

7. Intrapersonal intelligence (knowledge of the internal aspects of oneself; access to one's own feelings and emotions). Case example:

In her essay "A Sketch of the Past," Virginia Woolf displays deep insight into her own inner life through these lines, describing her reaction to several specific memories from her childhood that still, in adulthood, shock her: "Though I still have the peculiarity that I receive these sudden shocks, they are now always welcome; after the first surprise, I always feel instantly that they are particularly valuable. And so I go on to suppose that the shock-receiving capacity is what makes me a writer."

8. Naturalist intelligence (ability to identify and classify patterns in nature). Case example:

During prehistoric times, hunter/gatherers would rely on naturalist intelligence to identify what flora and fauna were edible. People who are adept at distinguishing nuances between large numbers of similar objects may be expressing naturalist intelligence abilities.

FIGURE 1 Howard Gardner believes that there are eight major kinds of intelligences, corresponding to abilities in different domains. In what area does your greatest intelligence reside, and why do you think you have particular strengths in that area? (Source: Adapted from Gardner, 2000.)

PRACTICAL AND EMOTIONAL INTELLIGENCE: TOWARD A MORE INTELLIGENT VIEW OF INTELLIGENCE

Consider the following situation:

> An employee who reports to one of your subordinates has asked to talk with you about waste, poor management practices, and possible violations of both company policy and the law on the part of your subordinate. You have been in your present position only a year, but in that time you have had no indications of trouble about the subordinate in question. Neither you nor your company has an "open door" policy, so it is expected that employees should take their concerns to their immediate supervisors before bringing a matter to the attention of anyone else. The employee who wishes to meet with you has not discussed this matter with her supervisors because of its delicate nature. (Sternberg, 1998, p. 17)

Your response to this situation has a lot to do with your future success in a business career, according to psychologist Robert Sternberg. The question is one of a series designed to help give an indication of your intelligence. However, it is not traditional intelligence that the question is designed to tap but rather intelligence of a specific kind: practical intelligence. **Practical intelligence** is intelligence related to overall success in living (Sternberg, 2000, 2002; Muammar, 2007; Wagner, 2002, 2011).

practical intelligence According to Sternberg, intelligence related to overall success in living.

Noting that traditional tests were designed to relate to academic success, Sternberg points to evidence showing that most traditional measures of intelligence do not relate especially well to *career* success (McClelland, 1993). Specifically, although successful business executives usually score at least moderately well on intelligence tests, the rate at which they advance and their ultimate business achievements are only minimally associated with traditional measures of their intelligence.

Sternberg argues that career success requires a very different type of intelligence from that required for academic success. Whereas academic success is based on knowledge of a specific information base obtained from reading and listening, practical intelligence is learned mainly through observation of others' behavior. People who are high in practical intelligence are able to learn general norms and principles and apply them appropriately. Consequently, practical intelligence tests, like the one shown in Figure 2, measure the ability to employ broad principles in solving everyday problems (Stemler & Sternberg, 2006; Stemler et al., 2009; Sternberg, 2013).

In addition to practical intelligence, Sternberg argues there are two other basic, interrelated types of intelligence related to life success: analytical and creative. Analytical intelligence focuses on abstract but traditional types of problems measured on IQ tests, whereas creative intelligence involves the generation of novel ideas and products (Benderly, 2004; Sternberg, Kaufman, & Pretz, 2004; Sternberg, Grigorenko, & Kidd, 2005).

Some psychologists broaden the concept of intelligence even further beyond the intellectual realm to include emotions. **Emotional intelligence** is the set of skills that underlie the accurate assessment, evaluation, expression, and regulation of emotions (Mayer, Salovey, & Caruso, 2004; Humphrey, Curran, & Morris, 2007; Mayer, Salovey, & Caruso, 2008).

emotional intelligence The set of skills that underlie the accurate assessment, evaluation, expression, and regulation of emotions.

Emotional intelligence is the basis of empathy for others, self-awareness, and social skills. It encompasses the ability to get along well with others. It provides us with an understanding of what other people are feeling and experiencing, which permits us to respond appropriately to others' needs. These abilities may help explain why people with only modest scores on traditional intelligence tests can be quite successful: the basis of their success may be a high emotional intelligence, which allows them to respond appropriately and quickly to others' feelings.

Study Alert
Traditional intelligence relates to academic performance; practical intelligence relates to success in life; emotional intelligence relates to emotional skills.

Although the notion of emotional intelligence makes sense, it has yet to be quantified in a rigorous manner. Furthermore, the view that emotional intelligence is so important that skills related to it should be taught in school has raised concerns

FIGURE 2 Most standard tests of intelligence primarily measure analytical skills; more comprehensive tests measure creative and practical abilities as well. (Source: Adapted from Sternberg, 2000.)

among some educators. They suggest that the nurturance of emotional intelligence is best left to students' families, especially because there is no well-specified set of criteria for what constitutes emotional intelligence (Becker, 2003; Vesely, Saklofske, & Leschied, 2013).

Still, the notion of emotional intelligence reminds us that there are many ways to demonstrate intelligent behavior—just as there are multiple views of the nature of intelligence (Fox & Spector, 2000; Barrett & Salovey, 2002). Figure 3 presents a summary of the different approaches used by psychologists.

Major Approaches to Intelligence

Approach	Characteristics
Fluid and crystallized intelligence	Fluid intelligence relates to reasoning, memory, and information-processing capabilities; crystallized intelligence relates to information, skills, and strategies learned through experience
Gardner's multiple intelligences	Eight independent forms of intelligence
Practical intelligence	Intelligence in terms of nonacademic, career, and personal success
Emotional intelligence	Intelligence that provides an understanding of what other people are feeling and experiencing and permits us to respond appropriately to others' needs

FIGURE 3 Just as there are many views of the nature of intelligence, there are also numerous ways to demonstrate intelligent behavior. This summary provides an overview of the various approaches used by psychologists.

Assessing Intelligence

intelligence tests Tests devised to quantify a person's level of intelligence.

Given the variety of approaches to the components of intelligence, it is not surprising that measuring intelligence has proved challenging. Psychologists who study intelligence have focused much of their attention on the development of **intelligence tests** that quantify a person's level of intelligence. These tests have proved to be of great benefit in identifying students in need of special attention in school, diagnosing specific learning difficulties, and helping people make the best educational and vocational choices. At the same time, their use has proved controversial, raising important social and educational issues.

Historically, the first effort at intelligence testing was based on an uncomplicated but completely wrong assumption: that the size and shape of a person's head could be used as an objective measure of intelligence. The idea was put forward by Sir Francis Galton (1822–1911), an eminent English scientist whose ideas in other domains proved to be considerably better than his notions about intelligence.

Galton's motivation to identify people of high intelligence stemmed from personal prejudices. He sought to demonstrate the natural superiority of people of high social class (including himself) by showing that intelligence is inherited. He hypothesized that head configuration, which is genetically determined, is related to brain size and therefore is related to intelligence.

Galton's theories were proved wrong on virtually every count. Head size and shape are not related to intellectual performance, and subsequent research has found little relationship between brain size and intelligence. However, Galton's work did have at least one desirable result: He was the first person to suggest that intelligence could be quantified and measured in an objective manner (Jensen, 2002).

BINET AND THE DEVELOPMENT OF IQ TESTS

The first real intelligence tests were developed by the French psychologist Alfred Binet (1857–1911). His tests followed from a simple premise: If performance on certain tasks or test items improved with *chronological*, or physical, age, performance could be used to distinguish more intelligent people from less intelligent ones within a particular age group. On the basis of this principle, Binet devised the first formal intelligence test, which was designed to identify the "dullest" students in the Paris school system in order to provide them with remedial aid.

mental age The age for which a given level of performance is average or typical.

Alfred Binet.

Binet began by presenting tasks to same-age students who had been labeled "bright" or "dull" by their teachers. If a task could be completed by the bright students but not by the dull ones, he retained that task as a proper test item; otherwise it was discarded. In the end he came up with a test that distinguished between the bright and dull groups, and—with further work—one that distinguished among children in different age groups (Binet & Simon, 1916; Sternberg & Jarvin, 2003).

On the basis of the Binet test, children were assigned a score relating to their **mental age,** the age for which a given level of performance is average or typical. For example, if the average 8-year-old answered, say, 45 items correctly on a test, anyone who answered 45 items correctly would be assigned a mental age of 8 years. Consequently, whether the person taking the test was 20 years old or 5 years old, he or she would have the same mental age of 8 years (Cornell, 2006).

Assigning a mental age to students provided an indication of their general level of performance. However, it did not allow for adequate comparisons among people of different chronological ages. By using mental age alone, for instance, we might assume that an 18-year-old responding at a 20-year-old's level would be demonstrating the same degree of intelligence as a 5-year-old answering at a 7-year-old's level, when actually the 5-year-old would be displaying a much greater *relative* degree of intelligence.

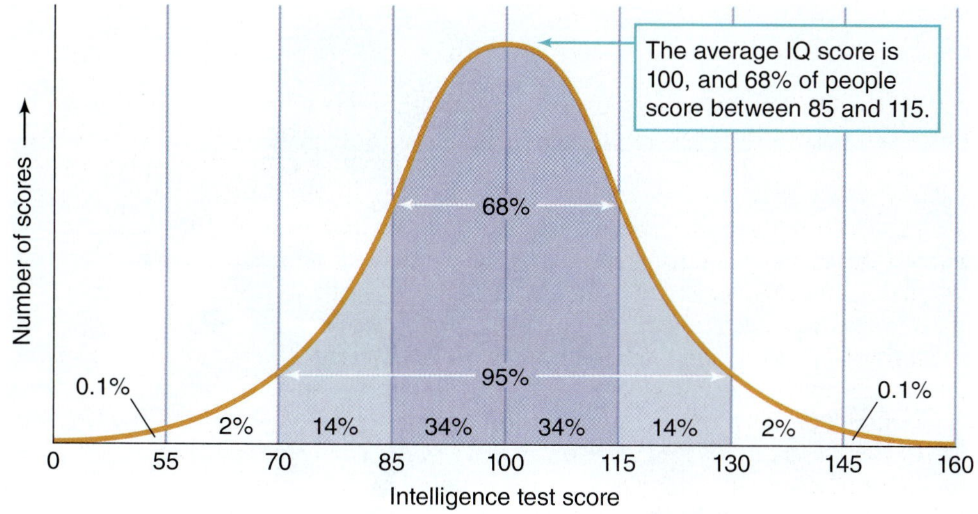

FIGURE 4 The average and most common IQ score is 100, and 68% of all people are within a 30-point range centered on 100. Some 95% of the population have scores that are within 30 points above or below 100, and 99.8% have scores that are between 55 and 145.

A solution to the problem came in the form of the **intelligence quotient (IQ),** a measure of intelligence that takes into account an individual's mental *and* chronological (physical) age. Historically, the first IQ scores employed the following formula in which *MA* stands for mental age and *CA* for chronological age:

intelligence quotient (IQ) A measure of intelligence that takes into account an individual's mental and chronological ages.

$$\text{IQ score} = \frac{\text{MA}}{\text{CA}} \times 100$$

Using this formula, we can return to the earlier example of an 18-year-old performing at a mental age of 20 and calculate an IQ score of (20/18) × 100 = 111. In contrast, the 5-year-old performing at a mental age of 7 comes out with a considerably higher IQ score: (7/5) × 100 = 140.

As a bit of trial and error with the formula will show you, anyone who has a mental age equal to his or her chronological age will have an IQ equal to 100. Moreover, people with a mental age that is lower than their chronological age will have IQs that are lower than 100.

Study Alert

It's important to know the traditional formula for IQ scores in which IQ is the ratio of mental age divided by chronological age, multiplied by 100. Remember, though, that today, the actual calculator of IQ scores is done in a more sophisticated manner.

Although the basic principles behind the calculation of an IQ score still hold, today IQ scores are determined in a different manner and are known as *deviation IQ scores.* First, the average test score for everyone of the same age who takes the test is determined, and that average score is assigned an IQ of 100. Then, with the aid of statistical techniques that calculate the differences (or "deviations") between each score and the average, IQ scores are assigned.

As you can see in Figure 4, when IQ scores from large numbers of people are plotted on a graph, they form a *bell-shaped distribution* (called "bell-shaped" because it looks like a bell when plotted). Approximately two-thirds of all individuals fall within 15 IQ points of the average score of 100. As scores increase or fall beyond that range, the percentage of people in a category falls considerably.

CONTEMPORARY IQ TESTS: GAUGING INTELLIGENCE

Remnants of Binet's original intelligence test are still with us, although the test has been revised in significant ways. Now in its fifth edition and called the *Stanford-Binet Intelligence Scale,* the test consists of a series of items that vary according to the age of the person being tested (Roid, Nellis, & McClellan, 2003). For example, young children are asked to copy figures or answer questions about everyday activities. Older people are asked to solve analogies, explain proverbs, and describe similarities that underlie sets of words.

The test is administered orally and includes both verbal and nonverbal assessments. An examiner begins by finding a mental age level at which a person is able to answer

Now in its fifth edition, the Stanford-Binet test consists of a series of items that vary in nature according to the age of the person being tested. What can we learn about a person from a test of this type?

all the questions correctly and then moves on to successively more difficult problems. When a mental age level is reached at which no items can be answered, the test is over. By studying the pattern of correct and incorrect responses, the examiner is able to compute an IQ score for the person being tested. In addition, the Stanford-Binet test yields separate subscores that provide clues to a test-taker's particular strengths and weaknesses.

The IQ tests most frequently used in the United States were devised by psychologist David Wechsler and are known as the *Wechsler Adult Intelligence Scale–IV*, or, more commonly, the *WAIS-IV* (for adults) and a children's version, the *Wechsler Intelligence Scale for Children–IV*, or *WISC-IV*. Both the WAIS-IV and the WISC-IV measure verbal comprehension, perceptual reasoning, working memory, and processing speed (see sample WAIS-IV items in Figure 5).

Because the Stanford-Binet, WAIS-IV, and WISC-IV all require individualized, one-on-one administration, they are relatively difficult to administer and score on a large-scale basis. Consequently, there are now a number of IQ tests that allow group administration. Rather than having one examiner ask one person at a time to respond to individual items, group IQ tests are strictly paper-and-pencil tests. The primary advantage of group tests is their ease of administration (Anastasi & Urbina, 1997; Danner et al., 2011).

However, sacrifices are made in group testing that, in some cases, may outweigh the benefits. For instance, group tests generally offer fewer kinds of questions than do tests administered individually. Furthermore, people may be more motivated to perform at their highest ability level when working on a one-to-one basis with a test administrator than they are in a group. Finally, in some cases, it is simply impossible to employ group tests, particularly with young children or people with unusually low IQs (Aiken, 1996).

RELIABILITY AND VALIDITY: TAKING THE MEASURE OF TESTS

When we use a ruler, we expect to find that it measures an inch in the same way it did the last time we used it. When we weigh ourselves on the bathroom scale, we hope that the variations we see on the scale are due to changes in our weight and not to errors on the part of the scale (unless the change in weight is in an unwanted direction!).

Types of Items on WAIS-IV		
Name	**Goal of Item**	**Example**
Information	Assess general information	Who wrote *Tom Sawyer?*
Comprehension	Assess understanding and evaluation of social norms and past experience	Why is copper often used for electrical wires?
Arithmetic	Assess math reasoning through verbal problems	Three women divided 18 golf balls equally among themselves. How many golf balls did each person receive?
Similarities	Test understanding of how objects or concepts are alike, tapping abstract reasoning	In what way are a circle and a triangle alike?
Figure weights	Test perceptual reasoning	Problems require test-taker to determine which possibility balances the final scale. 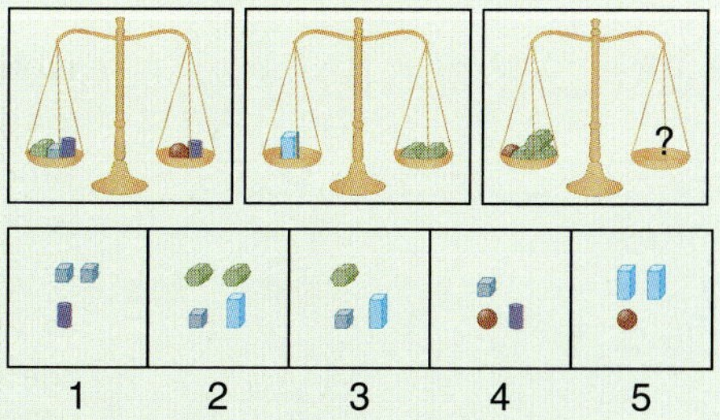
Matrix reasoning	Test spatial reasoning	Test-taker must decide which of the five possibilities replaces the question mark and completes the sequence. 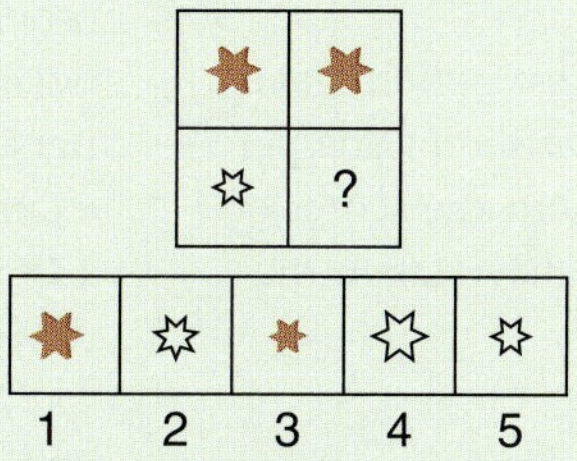
Block design item	Test understanding of relationship of parts to whole	Problems require test-takers to reproduce a design in fixed amount of time. 

FIGURE 5 Typical kinds of items found on the Wechsler Adult Intelligence Scales (WAIS-IV). (Simulated items similar to those in the *Wechsler Adult Intelligence Scale, Fourth Edition (WAIS-IV)*. Source: Adapted from Wechsler Adult Intelligence Scale, 2008.)

In the same way, we hope that psychological tests have **reliability**—that they measure consistently what they are trying to measure. We need to be sure that each time we administer the test, a test-taker will achieve the same results—assuming that nothing about the person has changed relevant to what is being measured.

reliability The property by which tests measure consistently what they are trying to measure.

Suppose, for instance, that when you first took the SAT exams, you scored 400 on the verbal section of the test. Then, after taking the test again a few months later, you scored 700. Upon receiving your new score, you might well stop celebrating for a moment to question whether the test is reliable, because it is unlikely that your abilities could have changed enough to raise your score by 300 points (T. R. Coyle, 2006).

But suppose your score changed hardly at all, and both times you received a score of about 400. You couldn't complain about a lack of reliability. However, if you knew your verbal skills were above average, you might be concerned that the test did not adequately measure what it was supposed to measure. In sum, the question has now become one of validity rather than reliability. A test has **validity** when it actually measures what it is supposed to measure.

validity The property by which tests actually measure what they are supposed to measure.

Knowing that a test is reliable is no guarantee that it is also valid. For instance, Sir Francis Galton assumed that skull size is related to intelligence, and he was able to measure skull size with great reliability. However, the measure of skull size was not valid–it had nothing to do with intelligence. In this case, then, we have reliability without validity.

However, if a test is unreliable, it cannot be valid. Assuming that all other factors–motivation to score well, knowledge of the material, health, and so forth–are similar, if a person scores high the first time he or she takes a specific test and low the second time, the test cannot be measuring what it is supposed to measure. Therefore, the test is both unreliable and not valid.

Test validity and reliability are prerequisites for accurate assessment of intelligence–as well as for any other measurement task carried out by psychologists. Consequently, the measures of personality carried out by personality psychologists, clinical psychologists' assessments of psychological disorders, and social psychologists' measures of attitudes must meet the tests of validity and reliability for the results to be meaningful (Phelps, 2005; Yao, Zhour, & Jiang, 2006; Markus & Borsboom, 2013).

Assuming that a test is both valid and reliable, one further step is necessary in order to interpret the meaning of a particular test-taker's score: the establishment of norms. **Norms** are standards of test performance that permit the comparison of one person's score on a test to the scores of others who have taken the same test. For example, a norm permits test-takers to know that they have scored, say, in the top 15% of those who have taken the test previously. Tests for which norms have been developed are known as *standardized tests.*

norms Standards of test performance that permit the comparison of one person's score on a test with the scores of other individuals who have taken the same test.

Test designers develop norms by calculating the average score achieved by a specific group of people for whom the test has been designed. Then the test designers can determine the extent to which each person's score differs from the scores of the other individuals who have taken the test in the past and provide future test-takers with a qualitative sense of their performance.

Obviously, the samples of test-takers who are employed in the establishment of norms are critical to the norming process. The people used to determine norms must be representative of the individuals to whom the test is directed.

From the perspective of . . .

A Human Resource Specialist Job interviews are really a kind of test, but they rely on interviewers' judgments and have no formal validity or reliability. Do you think job interviews can be made to have greater validity and reliability?

ADAPTIVE TESTING: USING COMPUTERS TO ASSESS PERFORMANCE

Ensuring that tests are reliable, valid, and based on appropriate norms has become more critical with computer-administered testing. In computerized versions of tests such as the Graduate Record Exam, a test used to determine entrance to graduate school, not only are test questions viewed and answered on a computer, but the test itself is individualized. With *adaptive testing*, every test-taker does not receive identical sets of test questions. Instead, the computer first presents a randomly selected question of moderate difficulty. If the test-taker answers it correctly, the computer then presents a randomly chosen item of slightly greater difficulty. If the test-taker answers it incorrectly, the computer presents a slightly easier item. Each question becomes slightly harder or easier than the question preceding it, depending on whether the previous response is correct. Ultimately, the greater the number of difficult questions answered correctly, the higher the score (Marszalek, 2007; Belov & Armstrong, 2009; Barrada, Abad, & Olea, 2011).

Variations in Intellectual Ability

More than 7 million people in the United States, including around 11 per 1,000 children, have been identified as far enough below average in intelligence that they can be regarded as having a serious deficit. Individuals with low IQs (people with intellectual disabilities) as well as those with unusually high IQs (the intellectually gifted) require special attention if they are to reach their full potential.

INTELLECTUAL DISABILITIES (MENTAL RETARDATION)

Although sometimes thought of as a rare phenomenon, intellectual disability (or mental retardation as it was more traditionally called) occurs in 1%–3% of the population. There is wide variation among those labeled intellectually disabled, in large part because of the inclusiveness of the definition developed by the American Association on Intellectual and Developmental Disabilities. The association suggests that **intellectual disability** (or **mental retardation**) is a disability characterized by significant limitations both in intellectual functioning and in conceptual, social, and practical adaptive skills (American Association of Mental Retardation, 2002).

intellectual disability (or mental retardation) A condition characterized by significant limitations both in intellectual functioning and in conceptual, social, and practical adaptive skills.

Although below-average intellectual functioning can be measured in a relatively straightforward manner—using standard IQ tests—it is more difficult to determine how to gauge limitations in adaptive behavior. Consequently, there is a lack of uniformity in how experts apply the labels *intellectual disabilities* and *mental retardation*. People labeled intellectually disabled vary from those who can be taught to work and function with little special attention to those who cannot be trained and are institutionalized throughout their lives (Detterman, Gabriel, & Ruthsatz, 2000; Greenspan, 2006).

Study Alert

Remember that in most cases of intellectual disability, there is no apparent biological deficiency, but a history of mental retardation exists in the family.

Most people with intellectual disabilities have relatively minor deficits and are classified as having *mild retardation*. These individuals, who have IQ scores ranging from 55 to 69, constitute some 90% of all people with intellectual disabilities. Although their development is typically slower than that of their peers, they can function quite independently by adulthood and are able to hold jobs and have families of their own (Bates et al., 2001; Smith, 2006; van Nieuwenhuijzen et al., 2011).

With greater degrees of intellectual deficit—*moderate retardation* (IQs of 40 to 54), *severe retardation* (IQs of 25 to 39), and *profound retardation* (IQs below 25)—the difficulties are more pronounced. For people with moderate retardation, deficits are obvious early, with language and motor skills lagging behind those of peers. Although these individuals can hold simple jobs, they need to have a moderate degree of supervision throughout their lives. Individuals with severe and profound mental retardation are generally unable to function independently and typically require care for their entire lives (Garwick, 2007).

From the perspective of . . .

A College Admissions Officer Imagine you notice that students who are members of minority groups systematically receive lower scores on standardized college entrance exams. What suggestions do you have for helping these students improve their scores?

RECAP/EVALUATE/RETHINK

RECAP

LO 23-1 What are the different definitions and conceptions of intelligence?

- Because intelligence can take many forms, defining it is challenging. One commonly accepted view is that intelligence is the capacity to understand the world, think rationally, and use resources effectively when faced with challenges.
- The earliest psychologists assumed that there is a general factor for mental ability called *g*. However, later psychologists disputed the view that intelligence is uni-dimensional.
- Some researchers suggest that intelligence can be broken down into fluid intelligence and crystallized intelligence. Gardner's theory of multiple intelligences proposes that there are eight spheres of intelligence.
- Information-processing approaches examine the processes underlying intelligent behavior rather than focusing on the structure of intelligence.
- Practical intelligence is intelligence related to overall success in living; emotional intelligence is the set of skills that underlie the accurate assessment, evaluation, expression, and regulation of emotions.

LO 23-2 What are the major approaches to measuring intelligence, and what do intelligence tests measure?

- Intelligence tests have traditionally compared a person's mental age and chronological age to yield an IQ, or intelligence quotient, score.
- Specific tests of intelligence include the Stanford-Binet test, the Wechsler Adult Intelligence Scale–IV (WAIS-IV), and the Wechsler Intelligence Scale for Children–IV (WISC-IV).
- Tests are expected to be both reliable and valid. Reliability refers to the consistency with which a test measures what it is trying to measure. A test has validity when it actually measures what it is supposed to measure.

LO 23-3 How can the extremes of intelligence be characterized?

- The levels of intellectual disability (or mental retardation) include mild, moderate, severe, and profound intellectual disability.
- About one-third of the cases of intellectual disability have a known biological cause; fetal alcohol syndrome is the most common. Most cases, however, are classified as familial retardation, for which there is no known biological cause.
- The intellectually gifted are people with IQ scores greater than 130. Intellectually gifted people tend to be healthier and more successful than the nongifted.

LO 23-4 Are traditional IQ tests culturally biased?

- Traditional intelligence tests have frequently been criticized for being biased in favor of the white middle-class population. This controversy has led to attempts to devise culture-fair tests, IQ measures that avoid questions that depend on a particular cultural background.

LO 23-5 To what degree is intelligence influenced by the environment and to what degree by heredity?

- Attempting to distinguish environmental from hereditary factors in intelligence is probably futile and certainly misguided. Because individual IQ scores vary far more than group IQ scores, it is more critical to ask what can be done to maximize the intellectual development of each individual.

EVALUATE

1. ________ is a measure of intelligence that takes into account a person's chronological and mental ages.
2. Some psychologists make the distinction between ________ intelligence, which reflects reasoning, memory, and information-processing capabilities, and ________ intelligence, which is the accumulation of information, knowledge, and skills that people have learned through experience and education.

3. __________________ is the most common biological cause of mental retardation.
4. People with high intelligence are generally shy and socially withdrawn. True or false?
5. A(n) __________ test tries to use only questions appropriate to all the people taking the test.

RETHINK

1. What is the role of emotional intelligence in the classroom? How might emotional intelligence be tested? Should emotional intelligence be a factor in determining academic promotion to the next grade?
2. Why might a test that identifies a disproportionate number of minority group members for special educational services and remedial assistance be considered potentially biased? Isn't the purpose of the test to help persons at risk of falling behind academically? How can a test created for a good purpose be biased?

Answers to Evaluate Questions

1. IQ; 2. fluid, crystallized; 3. Fetal alcohol syndrome; 4. false; the gifted are generally more socially adept than those with lower IQs; 5. culture-fair

KEY TERMS

intelligence
***g* or *g*-factor**
fluid intelligence
crystallized intelligence
theory of multiple intelligences
practical intelligence
emotional intelligence
intelligence tests
mental age
intelligence quotient (IQ)
reliability
validity
norms
intellectual disability (or mental retardation)
fetal alcohol syndrome
familial retardation
intellectually gifted
culture-fair IQ test
heritability

8
Motivation and Emotion

Learning Outcomes for Chapter 8

MODULE 24

LO 24-1 How does motivation direct and energize behavior?

Explaining Motivation

Instinct Approaches: Born to Be Motivated

Drive-Reduction Approaches: Satisfying Our Needs

Arousal Approaches: Beyond Drive Reduction

Incentive Approaches: Motivation's Pull

Cognitive Approaches: The Thoughts Behind Motivation

Maslow's Hierarchy: Ordering Motivational Needs

Applying the Different Approaches to Motivation

MODULE 25

LO 25-1 What biological and social factors underlie hunger?

LO 25-2 What are the varieties of sexual behavior?

LO 25-3 How are needs relating to achievement, affiliation, and power motivation exhibited?

Human Needs and Motivation: Eat, Drink, and Be Daring

The Motivation Behind Hunger and Eating

Applying Psychology in the 21st Century: Finding the Motivation to Get Unstuck

Neuroscience in Your Life: When Regulation of Eating Behavior Goes Wrong

Becoming an Informed Consumer of Psychology: Dieting and Losing Weight Successfully

Sexual Motivation

The Needs for Achievement, Affiliation, and Power

MODULE 26

LO 26-1 What are emotions, and how do we experience them?

LO 26-2 What are the functions of emotions?

LO 26-3 What are the explanations for emotions?

LO 26-4 How does nonverbal behavior relate to the expression of emotions?

Understanding Emotional Experiences

The Functions of Emotions

Determining the Range of Emotions: Labeling Our Feelings

The Roots of Emotions

Exploring Diversity: Do People in All Cultures Express Emotion Similarly?

Prologue *Disabled No More*

A YouTube video that went viral tells the story of Arthur Boorman, a disabled veteran of the Persian Gulf War. The video opens with a scene of Boorman, extremely overweight, slowly moving in his home with a pair of crutches. Doctors had told him that he would never again be able to walk on his own without assistance, and for 15 years he had accepted that fact. As his weight ballooned to almost 300 pounds, he had given up hope.

But one dedicated yoga instructor refused to give up on Boorman, pushing him to stretch and train and exercise his body. Boorman struggled a lot—he couldn't keep his balance, and he fell repeatedly. But he kept trying, at one point turning to the camera to declare, "Just because I can't do it today, that doesn't mean I'm not going to be able to do it someday."

By the end of the video, Boorman, 140 pounds lighter, easily sprints down a road (Kelly, 2012).

Looking Ahead

What explains Arthur Boorman's transformation? Was it some inner motivational strength that drove him beyond what his doctors said was possible? Was it having someone else believe in him and push him beyond what he thought he could accomplish? Where did he find the motivation to overcome his lack of hope?

These questions and many others are addressed by psychologists who study the topics of motivation and emotion. Psychologists who study motivation seek to discover the particular desired goals—the motives—that underlie behavior. Behaviors as basic as drinking to satisfy thirst and as inconsequential as taking a stroll to get exercise exemplify motives. Psychologists specializing in the study of motivation assume that such underlying motives steer our choices of activities.

While motivation concerns the forces that direct future behavior, emotion pertains to the feelings we experience throughout our lives. The study of emotions focuses on our internal experiences at any given moment. All of us feel a variety of emotions: happiness at succeeding at a difficult task, sadness over the death of a loved one, anger at being treated unfairly. Because emotions not only play a role in motivating our behavior but also act as a reflection of our underlying motivation, they play an important role in our lives.

We begin this set of modules by focusing on the major conceptions of motivation, discussing how different motives and needs jointly affect behavior. We consider motives that are biologically based and universal in the animal kingdom, such as hunger, as well as motives that are unique to humans, such as the need for achievement.

We then turn to emotions. We consider the roles and functions that emotions play in people's lives and discuss several approaches that explain how people understand their emotions. Finally, we look at how nonverbal behavior communicates emotions.

MODULE 24

Explaining Motivation

Learning Outcome

LO 24-1 How does motivation direct and energize behavior?

In just a moment, 27-year-old Aron Ralston's life changed. An 800-pound boulder dislodged in a narrow canyon where Ralston was hiking in an isolated Utah canyon, pinning his lower arm to the ground.

For the next five days, Ralston lay in the dense, lonely forest, unable to escape. An experienced climber who had search-and-rescue training, he had ample time to consider his options. He tried unsuccessfully to chip away at the rock, and he rigged up ropes and pulleys around the boulder in a vain effort to move it.

Finally, out of water and nearly dehydrated, Ralston reasoned there was only one option left short of dying. In acts of incredible bravery, Ralston broke two bones in his wrist, applied a tourniquet, and used a dull pen knife to amputate his arm beneath the elbow.

Freed from his entrapment, Ralston climbed down from where he had been pinned and then hiked five miles to safety (Cox, 2003; Lofholm, 2003).

What motivation lay behind Ralston's resolve?

To answer this question, psychologists employ the concept of **motivation,** the factors that direct and energize the behavior of humans and other organisms. Motivation has biological, cognitive, and social aspects, and the complexity of the concept has led psychologists to develop a variety of approaches. All seek to explain the energy that guides people's behavior in specific directions.

Aron Ralston today.

motivation The factors that direct and energize the behavior of humans and other organisms.

instincts Inborn patterns of behavior that are biologically determined rather than learned.

Instinct Approaches: Born to Be Motivated

When psychologists first tried to explain motivation, they turned to **instincts,** inborn patterns of behavior that are biologically determined rather than learned. According to instinct approaches to motivation, people and animals are born preprogrammed with sets of behaviors essential to their survival. Those instincts provide the energy that channels behavior in appropriate directions. Hence, sexual behavior may be a response to an instinct to reproduce, and exploratory behavior may be motivated by an instinct to examine one's territory.

This instinct approach presents several difficulties, however. For one thing, psychologists do not agree on what, or even how many, primary instincts exist. One early psychologist, William McDougall (1908), suggested that there are 18 instincts. Other theorists came up with even more—with one sociologist (Bernard, 1924) claiming that there are exactly 5,759 distinct instincts!

Furthermore, explanations based on the approach of instincts do not go very far toward explaining why certain specific patterns of behavior have evolved in a given species while other patterns have not evolved. In addition, although it is clear that much animal behavior is based on instincts, much of the variety and complexity of human behavior is learned and thus cannot be seen as instinctual.

As a result of these shortcomings, newer explanations have replaced conceptions of motivation based on instincts. However, instinct approaches still play a role in certain theories, especially those based on evolutionary approaches that focus on our genetic inheritance. Furthermore, Freud's work suggests that instinctual drives of sex and aggression motivate behavior (Katz, 2001).

Drive-Reduction Approaches: Satisfying Our Needs

drive-reduction approaches to motivation Theories suggesting that a lack of some basic biological need produces a drive to push an organism to satisfy that need.

drive Motivational tension, or arousal, that energizes behavior to fulfill a need.

After rejecting instinct theory, psychologists first proposed simple drive-reduction theories of motivation to take its place (Hull, 1943). **Drive-reduction approaches to motivation** suggest that a lack of some basic biological need (such as a lack of water) produces a drive to push an organism to satisfy that need (in this case, seeking water).

To understand this approach, we begin with the concept of drive. A **drive** is motivational tension, or arousal, that energizes behavior to fulfill a need. Many basic drives, such as hunger, thirst, sleep, and sex, are related to biological needs of the body or of the species as a whole. These are called *primary drives*. Primary drives contrast with secondary drives in which behavior fulfills no obvious biological need. In *secondary drives*, prior experience and learning bring about needs. For instance, some people have strong needs to achieve academically and professionally. We can say that their achievement need is reflected in a secondary drive that motivates their behavior (McKinley et al., 2004; Seli, 2007).

We usually try to satisfy a primary drive by reducing the need underlying it. For example, we become hungry after not eating for a few hours and may raid the refrigerator, especially if the next scheduled meal is not imminent. If the weather turns cold, we put on extra clothing or raise the setting on the thermostat to keep warm. If our bodies need liquids to function properly, we experience thirst and seek out water.

HOMEOSTASIS

homeostasis The body's tendency to maintain a steady internal state.

Homeostasis, the body's tendency to maintain a steady internal state, underlies primary drives. Using feedback loops, homeostasis brings deviations in body functioning back to an optimal state, similar to the way a thermostat and a furnace work in a home heating system to maintain a steady temperature. Receptor cells throughout the body constantly monitor factors such as temperature and nutrient levels. When deviations from the ideal state occur, the body adjusts in an effort to return to an optimal state. Many fundamental needs, including the needs for food, water, stable body temperature, and sleep, operate via homeostasis (Vassalli & Dijk, 2009; Porkka-Heiskanen & Kalinchuk, 2011; Porkka-Heiskanen, 2013).

Although drive-reduction theories provide a good explanation of how primary drives motivate behavior, they cannot fully explain a behavior in which the goal is not to reduce a drive but rather to maintain or even increase the level of excitement or arousal. For instance, some behaviors seem to be motivated by nothing more than curiosity, such as rushing to check e-mail messages. Similarly, many people pursue thrilling activities such as riding a roller coaster or steering a raft down the rapids of a river. Such behaviors certainly don't suggest that people seek to reduce all drives as drive-reduction approaches would indicate (Begg & Langley, 2001; Rosenbloom & Wolf, 2002).

Study Alert
To remember the concept of homeostasis, keep in mind the analogy of a thermostat that regulates the temperature in a house.

Both curiosity and thrill-seeking behavior, then, shed doubt on drive-reduction approaches as a complete explanation for motivation. In both cases, rather than seeking to reduce an underlying drive, people and animals appear to be motivated to increase their overall level of stimulation and activity. To explain this phenomenon, psychologists have devised an alternative: arousal approaches to motivation.

Arousal Approaches: Beyond Drive Reduction

Arousal approaches seek to explain behavior in which the goal is to maintain or increase excitement. According to **arousal approaches to motivation,** each person tries to maintain a certain level of stimulation and activity. As with the drive-reduction model, this approach suggests that if our stimulation and activity levels become too high, we try to reduce them. But, in contrast to the drive-reduction perspective, the arousal approach also suggests that if levels of stimulation and activity are too low, we will try to increase them by seeking stimulation.

arousal approaches to motivation The belief that we try to maintain certain levels of stimulation and activity.

People vary widely in the optimal level of arousal they seek out, with some people looking for especially high levels of arousal. For example, people who participate in daredevil sports, high-stakes gamblers, and criminals who pull off high-risk robberies may be exhibiting a particularly high need for arousal (see Figure 1; Cavenett & Nixon, 2006; Roets & Van Hiel, 2011; Lang & Bradley, 2013).

Incentive Approaches: Motivation's Pull

When a luscious dessert appears on the table after a filling meal, its appeal has little or nothing to do with internal drives or the maintenance of arousal. Rather, if we choose to eat the dessert, such behavior is motivated by the external stimulus of the dessert itself, which acts as an anticipated reward. This reward, in motivational terms, is an *incentive*.

Incentive approaches to motivation suggest that motivation stems from the desire to attain external rewards, known as incentives. In this view, the desirable properties of external stimuli–whether grades, money, affection, food, or sex–account for a person's motivation (Festinger et al., 2009).

incentive approaches to motivation Theories suggesting that motivation stems from the desire to attain external rewards, known as incentives.

Although the theory explains why we may succumb to an incentive (such as a mouth-watering dessert) even though we lack internal cues (such as hunger), it does not provide a complete explanation of motivation because organisms sometimes seek to fulfill needs even when incentives are not apparent. Consequently, many psychologists believe that the internal drives proposed by drive-reduction theory work in tandem with the external incentives of incentive theory to "push" and "pull" behavior, respectively. Thus, at the same time that we seek to satisfy our underlying hunger needs (the push of drive-reduction theory), we are drawn to food that appears very appetizing (the pull of incentive theory). Rather than contradicting each other, then, drives and incentives may work together in motivating behavior (Lowery, Fillingim, & Wright, 2003; Berridge, 2004; Belasen & Fortunato, 2013).

Cognitive Approaches: The Thoughts Behind Motivation

Cognitive approaches to motivation suggest that motivation is a result of people's thoughts, beliefs, expectations, and goals. For instance, the degree to which people are motivated to study for a test is based on their expectation of how well studying will pay off in terms of a good grade.

cognitive approaches to motivation Theories suggesting that motivation is a result of people's thoughts, beliefs, expectations, and goals.

Cognitive theories of motivation draw a key distinction between intrinsic and extrinsic motivation. *Intrinsic motivation* causes us to participate in an activity for our

FIGURE 1 Some people seek high levels of arousal, while others are more easygoing. You can get a sense of your own preferred level of stimulation by completing this questionnaire. (Source: Adapted from Zuckerman, 1978.)

Are You a Sensation Seeker?

How much do you crave stimulation in your everyday life? Complete the following questionnaire to find out. Circle either A or B in each pair or statements.

1. A My definition of the good life is to be at peace and comfortable in your skin.
   B My definition of the good life is to grab every experience possible.
2. A When I see an unfamiliar ride at an amusement park, I get right in line.
   B When I see a new ride I need to watch how it works a few times before trying it.
3. A My ideal job would involve travel and a wealth of new experiences.
   B My ideal job would be to do something I like and keep getting better at it.
4. A I am a big fan of a lazy summer day, a beach or backyard, and a good book.
   B I love winter with its brisk days and outdoor activities like skiing and snowboarding.
5. A I look forward to meeting new people and trying new things.
   B I like hanging out with my friends and doing things we know we enjoy.
6. A I think it's foolish to take unnecessary risks just for a sense of adventure.
   B I am attracted to challenges, even if they're a bit dangerous.
7. A I like movies that are funny or where I know the good guys are going to win.
   B I like edgy movies that are unpredictable or explore new ideas.
8. A The best art makes you think or shakes up your old ideas and preconceptions.
   B Good art is beautiful and makes you feel serene.
9. A For vacations I prefer to go places I like and eat at restaurants I know.
   B My ideal vacation is to go somewhere new where I can try different things.
10. A If I lived in frontier days, I would head West to pursue potential opportunities.
    B If I lived in frontier days, I would stay in the East and make a good life there.
11. A The people I'm drawn to are unusual and have kind of wild ideas.
    B I like people who are like me and know who they are.
12. A I would never allow myself to be hypnotized, especially in public.
    B I would probably volunteer to be hypnotized, just to give it a try.
13. A I would love to try things like parachuting, bungee jumping, and hang gliding.
    B It makes no sense to jump out of a perfectly good airplane or off a bridge.

Scoring: Give yourself a point for each of these responses: 1B, 2A, 3A, 4B, 5A, 6B, 7B, 8A, 9B, 10A, 11A, 12B, 13A. Add up the points, and then use the following key to find your sensation-seeking score.

12–13 Very high sensation seeking
10–11 High sensation seeking
6–9 Average sensation seeking
4–5 Low sensation seeking
1–3 Very low sensation seeking

Your results can give you a rough idea of your sensation-seeking tendencies. Understand that this is a short questionnaire based on the responses of a small sample of college students, giving at best an imprecise picture. Understand, too, that as people age, their sensation scores tend to become lower.

own enjoyment rather than for any actual or concrete reward that it will bring us. In contrast, *extrinsic motivation* causes us to do something for money, a grade, or some other actual, concrete reward (Lepper, Corpus, & Iyengar, 2005; Shaikholeslami & Khayyer, 2006; Finkelstein, 2009).

For example, when a physician works long hours because she loves medicine, intrinsic motivation is prompting her; if she works hard to make a lot of money, extrinsic motivation underlies her efforts. Similarly, if we study a lot because we love the subject matter, we are being guided by intrinsic motivation. On the other hand, if all we care about is the grade we get in the course, that studying is due to extrinsic motivation (Emmett & McGee, 2013).

We are more apt to persevere, work harder, and produce work of higher quality when motivation for a task is intrinsic rather than extrinsic. In fact, in some cases providing rewards for desirable behavior (thereby increasing extrinsic motivation) actually may decrease intrinsic motivation (James, 2005; Grant, 2008; Nishimura, Kawamura, & Sakurai, 2011).

From the perspective of . . .

An Educator Do you think that giving students grades serves as an external reward that may decrease intrinsic motivation for learning about the subject matter? Why or why not?

Maslow's Hierarchy: Ordering Motivational Needs

What do Eleanor Roosevelt, Abraham Lincoln, and Albert Einstein have in common? The common thread, according to a model of motivation devised by psychologist Abraham Maslow, is that each of them fulfilled the highest levels of motivational needs underlying human behavior.

Maslow's model places motivational needs in a hierarchy and suggests that before more sophisticated, higher-order needs can be met, certain primary needs must be satisfied (Maslow, 1970, 1987). A pyramid can represent the model with the more basic needs at the bottom and the higher-level needs at the top (see Figure 2). To activate a specific higher-order need, thereby guiding behavior, a person must first fulfill the more basic needs in the hierarchy.

The basic needs are primary drives: needs for water, food, sleep, sex, and the like. To move up the hierarchy, a person must first meet these basic physiological needs. Safety needs come next in the hierarchy; Maslow suggests that people need a safe, secure environment in order to function effectively. Physiological and safety needs compose the lower-order needs.

Only after meeting the basic lower-order needs can a person consider fulfilling

FIGURE 2 Maslow's hierarchy shows how our motivation progresses up the pyramid from the broadest, most fundamental biological needs to higher-order ones. Do you agree that lower-order needs must be satisfied before higher-order needs? Do hermits and monks who attempt to fulfill spiritual needs while denying basic physical needs contradict Maslow's hierarchy? (Maslow, 1970.)

higher-order needs, such as the needs for love and a sense of belonging, esteem, and self-actualization. Love and belongingness needs include the needs to obtain and give affection and to be a contributing member of some group or society. After fulfilling these needs, a person strives for esteem. In Maslow's thinking, esteem relates to the need to develop a sense of self-worth by recognizing that others know and value one's competence.

self-actualization A state of self-fulfillment in which people realize their highest potential in their own unique way.

After these four sets of needs are fulfilled–no easy task–a person is able to strive for the highest-level need, self-actualization. **Self-actualization** is a state of self-fulfillment in which people realize their highest potentials in their own unique way. Although Maslow first suggested that self-actualization occurred in only a few famous individuals, he later expanded the concept to encompass everyday people. For example, a parent with excellent nurturing skills who raises a family, a teacher who year after year creates an environment that maximizes students' opportunities for success, and an artist who realizes his creative potential all may be self-actualized. The important thing is that people feel at ease with themselves and satisfied that they are using their talents to the fullest. In a sense, achieving self-actualization reduces the striving and yearning for greater fulfillment that mark most people's lives and instead provides a sense of satisfaction with the current state of affairs (Laas, 2006; Bauer, Schwab, & McAdams, 2011; Ivtzan et al., 2013).

Although research has been unable to validate the specific ordering of Maslow's stages, and it is difficult to measure self-actualization objectively, Maslow's hierarchy of needs is important for two reasons: It highlights the complexity of human needs, and it emphasizes the idea that until more basic biological needs are met, people will be relatively unconcerned with higher-order needs. For example, if people are hungry, their first interest will be in obtaining food; they will not be concerned with needs such as love and self-esteem (Samantaray, Srivastava, & Mishra, 2002; Ojha & Pramanick, 2009; LaLumiere & Kalivas, 2013).

Maslow's hierarchy of needs has also spawned other approaches to motivation. For example, Edward Deci and Richard Ryan (2011) have considered human needs in terms of psychological well-being. They suggest in their *self-determination theory* that people have the three basic needs of competence, autonomy, and relatedness. Competence is the need to produce desired outcomes, while autonomy is the perception that we have control over our own lives. Finally, relatedness is the need to be involved in close, warm relationships with others. In the view of self-determination theory, these three psychological needs are innate and universal across cultures, and they are essential as basic biological needs (Jang et al., 2009; Ryan & Deci, 2011).

Applying the Different Approaches to Motivation

The various theories of motivation (summarized in Figure 3) give several perspectives on it. Which provides the fullest account of motivation? Actually, many of the approaches are complementary rather than contradictory. In fact, employing more than one approach can help us understand motivation in a particular instance.

Study Alert

Review the distinctions among the different explanations for motivation (instinct, drive reduction, arousal, incentive, cognitive, and Maslow's hierarchy of needs).

Consider, for example, Aron Ralston's accident while hiking (described earlier). His interest in climbing in an isolated and potentially dangerous area may be explained by arousal approaches to motivation. From the perspective of instinct approaches, we realize that Aron had an overwhelming instinct to preserve his life at all costs. From a cognitive perspective, we see his careful consideration of various strategies to extricate himself from the boulder.

In short, applying multiple approaches to motivation in a given situation provides a broader understanding than we might obtain by employing only a single approach. We'll see this again when we consider specific motives–such as the needs for food, achievement, affiliation, and power–and draw on several of the theories for the fullest account of what motivates our behavior.

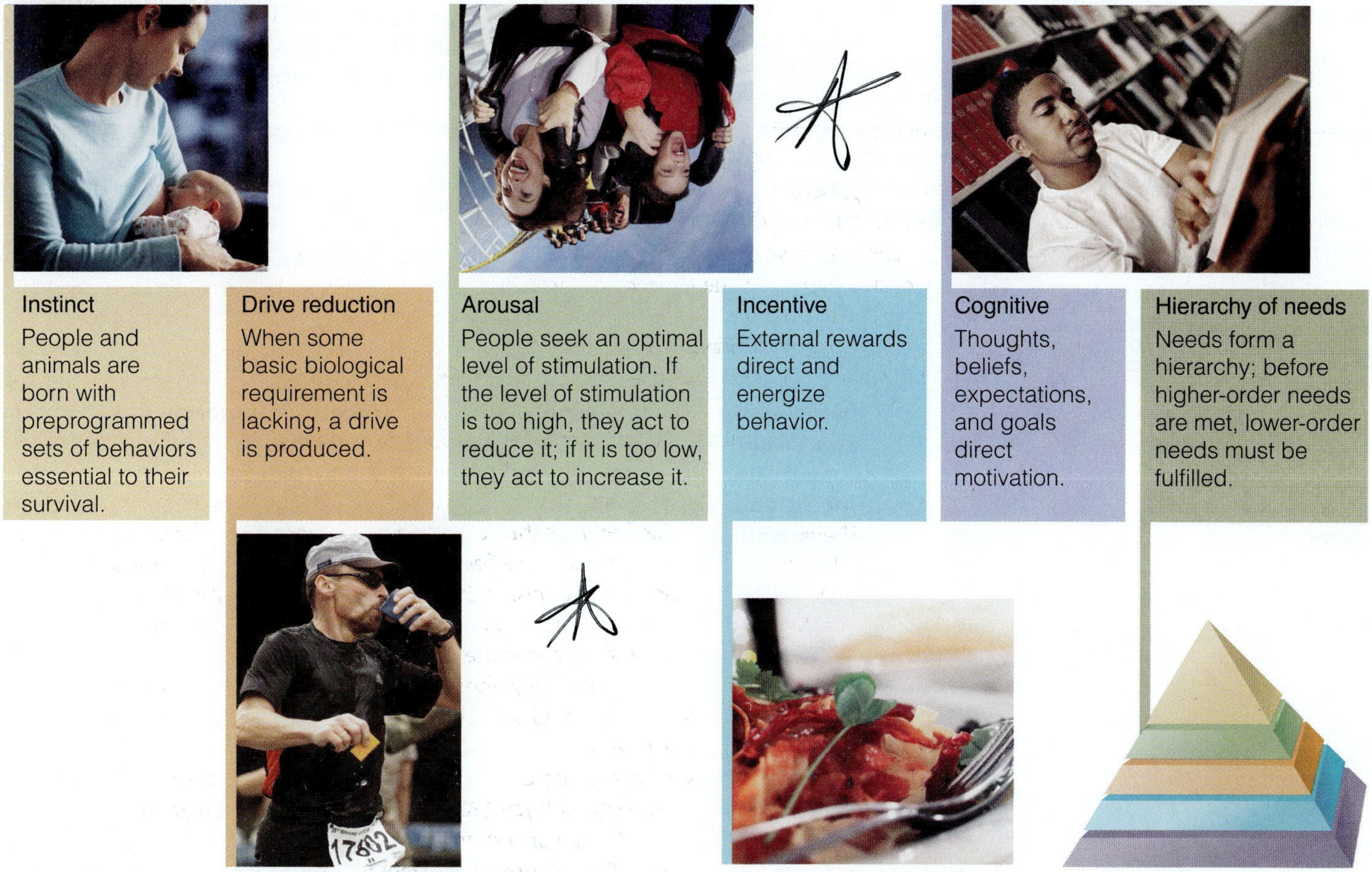

FIGURE 3 The major approaches to motivation.

RECAP/EVALUATE/RETHINK

RECAP

LO 24-1 How does motivation direct and energize behavior?

- Motivation relates to the factors that direct and energize behavior.
- Drive is the motivational tension that energizes behavior to fulfill a need.
- Homeostasis, the maintenance of a steady internal state, often underlies motivational drives.
- Arousal approaches suggest that we try to maintain a particular level of stimulation and activity.
- Incentive approaches focus on the positive aspects of the environment that direct and energize behavior.
- Cognitive approaches focus on the role of thoughts, expectations, and understanding of the world in producing motivation.
- Maslow's hierarchy suggests that there are five basic needs: physiological, safety, love and belongingness, esteem, and self-actualization. Only after the more basic needs are fulfilled can a person move toward meeting higher-order needs.

EVALUATE

1. __________ are forces that guide a person's behavior in a certain direction.
2. Biologically determined, inborn patterns of behavior are known as __________.
3. Your psychology professor tells you, "Explaining behavior is easy! When we lack something, we are motivated to get it." Which approach to motivation does your professor subscribe to?
4. By drinking water after running a marathon, a runner tries to keep his or her body at an optimal level of functioning. This process is called __________.
5. I help an elderly person cross the street because doing a good deed makes me feel good. What type of motivation is at work here? What type of motivation would be at work if I were to help an elderly man across the street because he paid me $20?
6. According to Maslow, a person with no job, no home, and no friends can become self-actualized. True or false?

RETHINK

1. Which approaches to motivation are more commonly used in the workplace? How might each approach be used to design employment policies that can sustain or increase motivation?
2. A writer who works all day composing copy for an advertising firm has a hard time keeping her mind on her work and continually watches the clock. After work she turns to a collection of stories she is creating and writes long into the night, completely forgetful of the clock. What ideas from your reading on motivation help to explain this phenomenon?

Answers to Evaluate Questions

1. Motives; **2.** instincts; **3.** drive reduction; **4.** homeostasis; **5.** intrinsic, extrinsic; **6.** false; lower-order needs must be fulfilled before self-actualization can occur

KEY TERMS

motivation
instincts
drive-reduction approaches to motivation
drive
homeostasis
arousal approaches to motivation
incentive approaches to motivation
cognitive approaches to motivation
self-actualization

MODULE 25

Human Needs and Motivation: Eat, Drink, and Be Daring

> As a sophomore at the University of California, Santa Cruz, Lisa Arndt followed a menu of her own making: For breakfast she ate cereal or fruit with 10 diet pills and 50 chocolate-flavored laxatives. Lunch was a salad or sandwich; dinner: chicken and rice. But it was the feast that followed that Arndt relished most. Almost every night at about 9 p.m., she would retreat to her room and eat an entire small pizza and a whole batch of cookies. Then she'd wait for the day's laxatives to take effect. "It was extremely painful," says Arndt of those days. . . . "But I was that desperate to make up for my binging. I was terrified of fat the way other people are afraid of lions or guns." (Hubbard, O'Neill, & Cheakalos, 1999)

Lisa was one of the 10 million women (and 1 million men) who are estimated to suffer from an eating disorder. These disorders, which usually appear during adolescence, can bring about extraordinary weight loss and other forms of physical deterioration. Extremely dangerous, they sometimes result in death.

Why are Lisa and others like her subject to such disordered eating, which revolves around the motivation to avoid weight gain at all costs? And why do so many other people engage in overeating, which leads to obesity?

To answer these questions, we must consider some of the specific needs that underlie behavior. In this module, we examine several of the most important human needs. We begin with hunger, the primary drive that has received the most attention from researchers, and then we turn to secondary drives—those uniquely human endeavors based on learned needs and past experience that help explain why people strive to achieve, to affiliate with others, and to seek power over others.

Learning Outcomes

LO 25-1 What biological and social factors underlie hunger?

LO 25-2 What are the varieties of sexual behavior?

LO 25-3 How are needs relating to achievement, affiliation, and power motivation exhibited?

The Motivation Behind Hunger and Eating

Two hundred million people in the United States—some two-thirds of the population—are overweight. More than a quarter are so heavy that they have **obesity,** body weight that is more than 20% above the average weight for a person of a particular height. And the rest of the world is not far behind: A billion people around the globe are overweight or obese. The World Health Organization has said that worldwide obesity has reached epidemic proportions, producing increases in heart disease, diabetes, cancer, and premature deaths. Projections are that by 2018, 40% of U.S. residents may be obese (Thorpe, 2009; Shugart, 2011; Sharpe, 2013).

obesity Body weight that is more than 20% above the average weight for a person of a particular height.

The most widely used measure of obesity is *body mass index (BMI),* which is based on a ratio of weight to height. People with a BMI greater than 30 are considered obese, whereas those with a BMI between 25 and 30 are overweight. (Use the formulas in Figure 1 to determine your own BMI.)

Although the definition of obesity is clear from a scientific point of view, people's perceptions of what an ideal body looks like vary significantly across different cultures and, within Western cultures, from one time period to another. For instance, many contemporary Western cultures stress the importance of slimness in women—a relatively

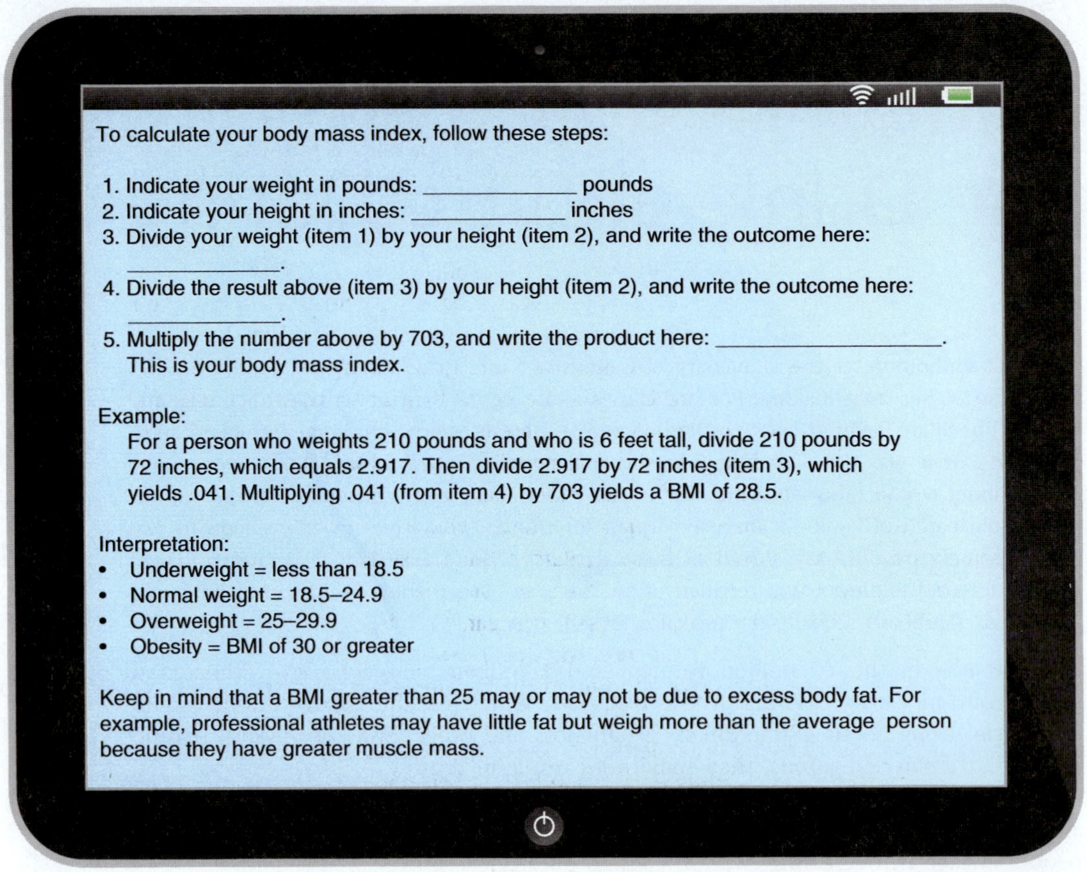

FIGURE 1 Use this procedure to find your body mass index.

recent view. In 19th-century Hawaii, the most attractive women were those who were the heaviest. Furthermore, for most of the 20th century–except for periods in the 1920s and the most recent decades–the ideal female figure was relatively full. Even today, weight standards differ among different cultural groups. For instance, in some traditional Arab cultures, obese women are so prized as wives that parents force-feed their female children to make them more desirable (Blixen, Singh, & Xu, 2006; Marsh, Hau, & Sung, 2007; Franko & Roehrig, 2011).

Regardless of cultural standards for appearance and weight, no one doubts that being overweight represents a major health risk. However, controlling weight is complicated because eating behavior involves a variety of mechanisms. In our discussion of what motivates people to eat, we'll start with the biological aspects of eating.

"Gee, I had no idea you were married to a supermodel."

BIOLOGICAL FACTORS IN THE REGULATION OF HUNGER

In contrast to human beings, other species are unlikely to become obese. Internal mechanisms regulate not only the quantity of food they take in, but also the kind of food they desire. For example, rats that have been deprived of particular foods seek out alternatives that contain the specific nutrients their diet is lacking, and many species, given the choice of a wide variety of foods, select a well-balanced diet (Woods et al., 2000; Jones & Corp, 2003; Adler, 2013).

Complex biological mechanisms tell organisms whether they require food or should stop eating. It's not just a matter of an empty stomach causing hunger pangs and a full one alleviating those pangs. (Even individuals who have had their stomachs removed still experience the sensation of hunger.) One important factor is changes in the chemical composition of the blood. For instance, changes in levels of glucose, a kind of sugar, regulate feelings of hunger. In addition, the hormone *insulin* leads the body to store excess sugar in the blood as fats and carbohydrates. Finally, the hormone *ghrelin* communicates to the brain feelings of hunger. The production of ghrelin increases according to meal schedules as well as the sight or smell of food, producing the feeling that tells us we're hungry and should eat (Wren & Bloom, 2007; Kojima & Kangawa, 2008; Langlois et al., 2011).

The brain's *hypothalamus* monitors glucose levels. Increasing evidence suggests that the hypothalamus carries the primary responsibility for monitoring food intake. Injury to the hypothalamus has radical consequences for eating behavior, depending on the site of the injury. For example, rats whose *lateral hypothalamus* is damaged may literally starve to death. They refuse food when it is offered; unless they are force-fed, they eventually die. Rats with an injury to the *ventromedial hypothalamus* display the opposite problem: extreme overeating. Rats with this injury can increase in weight by as much as 400%. Similar phenomena occur in humans who have tumors of the hypothalamus (Seymour, 2006; Fedeli et al., 2009; Barson, Morganstern, & Leibowitz, 2011).

Although the important role the hypothalamus plays in regulating food intake is clear, the exact way this organ operates is still unclear. One hypothesis suggests that injury to the hypothalamus affects the **weight set point,** or the particular level of weight that the body strives to maintain, which in turn regulates food intake. Acting as a kind of internal weight thermostat, the hypothalamus calls for either greater or less food intake (Woods et al., 2000; Berthoud, 2002; Cornier, 2011).

weight set point The particular level of weight that the body strives to maintain.

In most cases, the hypothalamus does a good job. Even people who are not deliberately monitoring their weight show only minor weight fluctuations in spite of substantial day-to-day variations in how much they eat and exercise. However, injury to the hypothalamus can alter the weight set point, and a person then struggles to meet the internal goal by increasing or decreasing food consumption. Even temporary exposure to certain drugs can alter the weight set point (Hallschmid et al., 2004; Khazaal et al., 2008; Sternson, Betley, & Cao, 2013).

Genetic factors determine the weight set point, at least in part. People seem destined, through heredity, to have a particular **metabolism,** the rate at which food is converted to energy and expended by the body. People with a high metabolic rate can eat virtually as much as they want without gaining weight, whereas others with low metabolism may eat literally half as much yet gain weight readily (Jequier, 2002; Westerterp, 2006).

metabolism The rate at which food is converted to energy and expended by the body.

SOCIAL FACTORS IN EATING

You've just finished a full meal and feel completely stuffed. Suddenly your host announces with great fanfare that he will be serving his "house specialty" dessert, bananas flambé, and that he has spent the better part of the afternoon preparing it. Even though you are full and don't even like bananas, you accept a serving of his dessert and eat it all.

Study Alert
A key point: Eating and hunger are influenced both by biological and social factors.

Clearly, internal biological factors do not fully explain our eating behavior. External social factors, based on societal rules and on what we have learned about appropriate eating behavior, also play an important role. Take, for example, the simple fact that people customarily eat breakfast, lunch, and dinner at approximately the same times every day. Because we tend to eat on schedule every day, we feel hungry as the usual hour approaches, sometimes quite independently of what our internal cues are telling us.

Similarly, we put roughly the same amount of food on our plates every day, even though the amount of exercise we may have had (and consequently our need for energy replenishment) varies from day to day. We also tend to prefer particular foods over others. Rats and dogs may be a delicacy in certain Asian cultures, but few people in Western cultures find them appealing despite their potentially high nutritional value.

Even the amount of food we eat varies according to cultural norms. For instance, people in the United States eat bigger portions than people in France. In sum, cultural influences and our individual habits play important roles in determining when, what, and how much we eat (Miller & Pumariega, 2001; Rozin et al., 2003; Leeman, Fischler, & Rozin, 2011).

Other social factors relate to our eating behavior as well. Some of us head toward the refrigerator after a difficult day seeking solace in a pint of Heath Bar Crunch ice cream. Why? Perhaps when we were children, our parents gave us food when we were upset. Eventually, we may have learned through the basic mechanisms of classical and operant conditioning to associate food with comfort and consolation. Similarly, we may learn that eating, which focuses our attention on immediate pleasures, provides an escape from unpleasant thoughts. Consequently, we may eat when we feel distressed (Elfhag, Tynelius, & Rasmussen, 2007; Tsenkova, Boylan, & Ryff, 2013).

THE ROOTS OF OBESITY

Given that both biological and social factors influence eating behavior, determining the causes of obesity has proved to be a challenging task. Researchers have followed several paths.

Some psychologists suggest that oversensitivity to external eating cues based on social factors, coupled with insensitivity to internal hunger cues, produce obesity. Others argue that overweight people have higher weight set points than other people do. Because their set points are unusually high, their attempts to lose weight by eating less may make them especially sensitive to external, food-related cues and therefore more apt to overeat and perpetuate their obesity (West, Harvey-Berino, & Raczynski, 2004; Tremblay, 2004; Kanoski et al., 2011).

But why may some people's weight set points be higher than those of others? One biological explanation is that obese individuals have a higher level of the hormone *leptin,* which appears to be designed, from an evolutionary standpoint, to "protect" the body against weight loss. The body's weight-regulation system thus appears to be designed more to protect against losing weight than to protect against gaining it. Therefore, it's easier to gain weight than to lose it (Zhang et al., 2005; Levin, 2006; Thanos et al., 2013).

Although obesity is reaching epidemic proportions in the United States, its exact causes remain unclear.

Applying Psychology in the 21st Century

Finding the Motivation to Get Unstuck

"I know I should do something about this. I will. I promise. I just don't want to face it right now."

You've probably heard someone say words to this effect. In fact, you may have even said them yourself at some point. Perhaps you were talking about losing weight, quitting smoking, or writing your resume. We often know what we need to do, but it can be easy to get stuck and just not have the motivation to take action.

A growing body of research, though, suggests that getting other people involved may be the key to reach your own goal. One reason that other people can be helpful is that they provide accountability. It's easy to put a challenging or anxiety-provoking goal on hold when you don't have to answer to others. It's harder, though, when you have made a public commitment to a goal. In effect, you're not just letting yourself down, but you're letting other people down, too.

For example, one study explored accountability in terms of compliance with medical instructions. Patients who were taking a regimen of medications to control their blood pressure were given workbooks and advice on staying on track with their medications. Some were given counseling and periodic follow-ups. Those who expected to have to answer to their counselor for their behavior were significantly more likely to remain compliant with their drug regimen than were those who were not expecting to answer to anyone (Johnson et al., 2006; Mohr, Cuijpers, & Lehman, 2011).

Another way that others can help people achieve their goals is by providing inspiration. This influence can be seen in the results of a large study that examined the success rates of thousands of people who had committed themselves to a 12-week weight-loss challenge. The participants divided themselves into weight-loss teams of 5 to 11 people, each who stayed in contact with the others and shared their progress. The researchers found that when a team had at least one highly motivated and successful member, other members pushed themselves harder and enjoyed greater success, too (Leahey, Kumar, Weinberg, & Wing, 2012; Gorin et al., 2013).

Finally, one of the hardest obstacles in taking action is simply getting started. Getting other people involved can make the difference between saying, "I should do this" and actually doing it (Oz, 2012; Jones et al., 2013).

RETHINK

- Why do you think people tend to get stuck between knowing that something needs to be done and actually doing it?
- What other strategies might work for translating intentions into actions?

Another biologically based explanation for obesity relates to fat cells in the body. Starting at birth, the body stores fat either by increasing the number of fat cells or by increasing the size of existing fat cells. Furthermore, any loss of weight past infancy does not decrease the number of fat cells; it only affects their size. Consequently, people are stuck with the number of fat cells they inherit from an early age, and the rate of weight gain during the first 4 months of life is related to being overweight during later childhood (Stettler et al., 2005).

According to the weight-set-point hypothesis, the presence of too many fat cells from earlier weight gain may result in the set point's becoming "stuck" at a higher level than desirable. In such circumstances, losing weight becomes a difficult proposition because one is constantly at odds with one's own internal set point when dieting (Freedman, 1995; Leibel, Rosenbaum, & Hirsch, 1995).

Not everyone agrees with the set-point explanation for obesity. For example, it's hard to see how the set-point explanation alone could explain the rapid rise in obesity over the last several decades in the United States. How could so many people's weight set points simultaneously increase?

Consequently, some researchers argue that the body does not try to maintain a fixed weight set point. Instead, they suggest, the body has a *settling point*, determined by a combination of our genetic heritage and the nature of the environment in which we live. If high-fat foods are prevalent in our environment and we are genetically predisposed to obesity, we settle into an equilibrium that maintains relatively high weight. In contrast, if our environment is nutritionally healthier, a genetic predisposition to obesity will not be triggered, and we will settle into an equilibrium in which our weight is lower (also see *Applying Psychology in the 21st Century;* Pi-Sunyer, 2003; Sullivan, Smith, & Grove, 2011).

EATING DISORDERS

anorexia nervosa A severe eating disorder in which people may refuse to eat while denying that their behavior and appearance—which can become skeleton-like—are unusual.

Eating disorders are among the 10 most frequent causes of disability in young women. One devastating weight-related disorder is **anorexia nervosa.** In this severe eating disorder, people may refuse to eat while denying that their behavior and appearance—which can become skeleton-like—are unusual. Some 10% of people with anorexia literally starve themselves to death (Striegel-Moore & Bulik, 2007; Arcelus et al., 2011).

Anorexia nervosa mainly afflicts females between the ages of 12 and 40, although both men and women of any age may develop it. People with the disorder are often successful, attractive, and relatively affluent. The disorder often begins after serious dieting, which somehow gets out of control. Life begins to revolve around food: Although people with the disorder eat little, they may cook for others, go shopping for food frequently, or collect cookbooks (Polivy, Herman, & Boivin, 2005; Myers, 2007; Jacobs et al., 2009).

bulimia A disorder in which a person binges on large quantities of food, followed by efforts to purge the food through vomiting or other means.

A related problem, **bulimia,** from which Lisa Arndt (described earlier) suffered, is a disorder in which people binge on large quantities of food. For instance, they may consume an entire gallon of ice cream and a whole pie in a single sitting. After such a binge, sufferers feel guilt and depression and often induce vomiting or take laxatives to rid themselves of the food—behavior known as purging. Constant binging-and-purging cycles and the use of drugs to induce vomiting or diarrhea can lead to heart failure. Often, though, the weight of a person with bulimia remains normal (Mora-Giral et al., 2004; Couturier & Lock, 2006; Lampard et al., 2011).

Eating disorders represent a growing problem: Estimates show that between 1% and 4% of high school–age and college-age women have either anorexia nervosa or bulimia. As many as 10% of women suffer from bulimia at some point in their lives. Furthermore, an increasing amount of research shows that almost as many men suffer from binge eating as women (Swain, 2006; Park, 2007; Striegel et al., 2011).

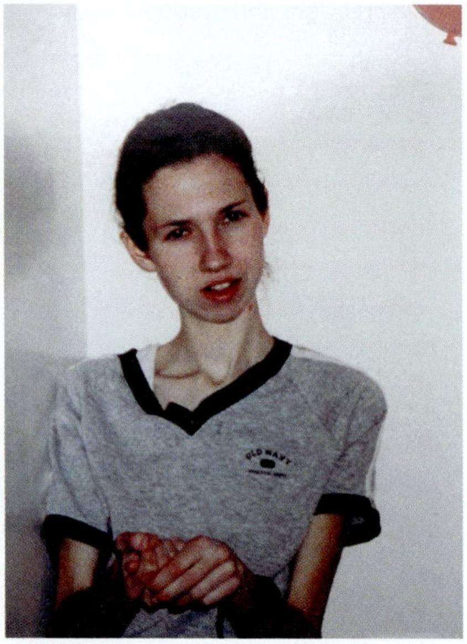

Despite looking skeleton-like to others, people with the eating disorder anorexia nervosa see themselves as overweight.

What are the causes of anorexia nervosa and bulimia? Some researchers suspect a biological cause such as a chemical imbalance in the hypothalamus or pituitary gland, perhaps brought on by genetic factors. Furthermore, brain scans of people with eating disorders show that they process information about food differently from healthy individuals (see *Neuroscience in Your Life;* Polivy & Herman, 2002; Santel et al., 2006; Klump & Culbert, 2007).

Others believe that the cause has roots in society's valuation of slenderness and the parallel notion that obesity is undesirable. These researchers maintain that people with anorexia nervosa and bulimia become preoccupied with their weight and take to heart the cliché that one can never be too thin. This may explain why eating disorders increase as countries become more developed and Westernized and dieting becomes more popular. Finally, some psychologists suggest that the disorders result from overly demanding parents or other family problems (Couturier & Lock, 2006; Kluck, 2008; Cook-Cottone & Smith, 2013).

The complete explanations for anorexia nervosa and bulimia remain elusive. These disorders most likely stem from both biological and social causes, and successful treatment probably encompasses several strategies, including therapy and dietary changes (O'Brien & LeBow, 2007; Wilson, Grilo, & Vitousek, 2007; Cooper & Shafran, 2008).

Neuroscience in Your Life: When Regulation of Eating Behavior Goes Wrong

Research suggests that individuals with eating disorders process information differently. This difference in processing may lead to eating disorders or may be a result of such disordered eating. For example, as seen in these images, those with bulimia show greater connectivity in areas of the brain associated with eating behavior, such as the cerebellum (in red), whereas those who do not have bulimia show greater connectivity in other areas of the brain (in blue) (Amianto et al., 2013).

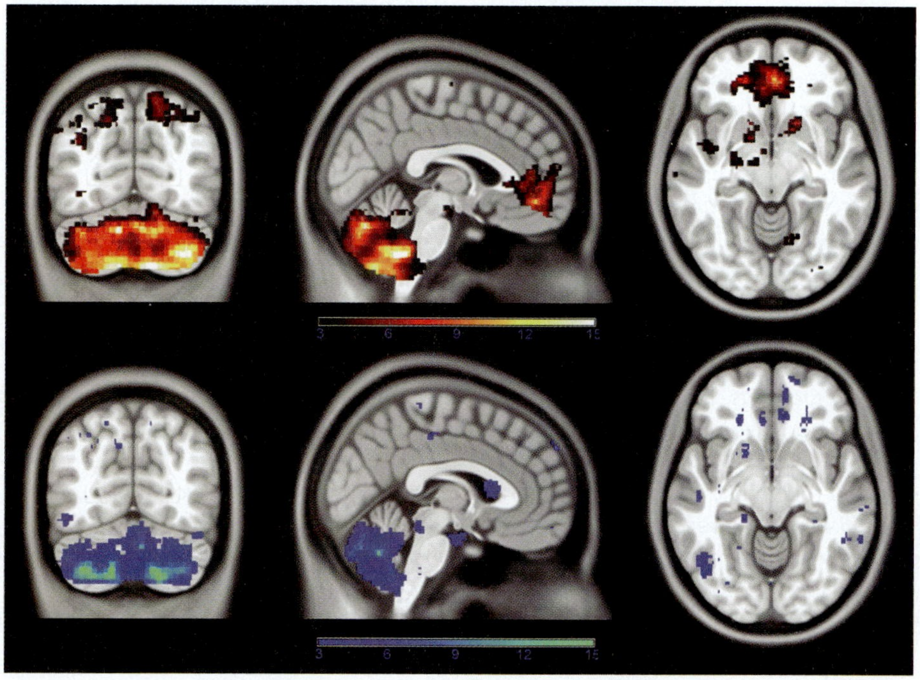

If you or a family member needs advice or help with an eating problem, contact the American Anorexia Bulimia Association at www.aabainc.org or call (212) 575-6200. You can get more information at www.nlm.nih.gov/medlineplus/eating-disorders.html.

BECOMING AN INFORMED CONSUMER of Psychology

Dieting and Losing Weight Successfully

Although 60% of the people in the United States say they want to lose weight, it's a losing battle for most of them. Most people who diet eventually regain the weight they lost, so they try again and get caught in a seemingly endless cycle of weight loss and gain (Parker-Pope, 2003; Cachelin & Regan, 2006).

You should keep several things in mind when trying to lose weight (Heshka et al., 2003; Freedman, 2011):

- *There is no easy route to weight control.* You will have to make permanent changes in your life to lose weight without gaining it back. The most obvious strategy—cutting down on the amount of food you eat—is just the first step toward a lifetime commitment to changing your eating habits.
- *Keep track of what you eat and what you weigh.* Unless you keep careful records, you won't really know how much you are eating and whether any diet is working.
- *Eat "big" foods.* Eat fiber and foods that are bulky and heavy but low in calories, such as grapes and soup. Such foods trick your body into thinking you've eaten more and thus decrease hunger.
- *Cut out television.* One reason for the epidemic of obesity is the number of hours people in the United States spend viewing television. Not only does watching television preclude other activities that burn calories (even walking around the house is helpful), people often gorge on junk food while watching TV (Hu et al., 2003).
- *Exercise.* Exercise at least 30 consecutive minutes three times each week. When you exercise, you use up fat stored in your body as fuel for muscles, which is measured in calories. As you use up this fat, you will probably lose weight. Almost any activity helps burn calories.
- *Decrease the influence of external social stimuli on your eating behavior.* Serve yourself smaller portions of food, and leave the table before you see what is being served for dessert. Don't even buy snack foods such as nachos and potato chips; if they're not readily available in the kitchen cupboard, you're not apt to eat them. Wrap refrigerated foods in aluminum foil so that you cannot see the contents and be tempted every time you open the refrigerator.
- *Avoid fad diets.* No matter how popular they are at a particular time, extreme diets, including liquid diets, usually don't work in the long run and can be dangerous to your health.
- *Avoid taking any of the numerous diet pills advertised on television that promise quick and easy results.* They don't work.
- *Lose weight with others by joining a support group.* Being part of a group that is working to lose weight will encourage you to keep to your diet.
- *Maintain good eating habits.* When you have reached your desired weight, maintain the new habits you learned while dieting to avoid gaining back the weight you have lost.
- *Set reasonable goals.* Know how much weight you want to lose before you start to diet. Don't try to lose too much weight too quickly, or you may doom yourself to failure. Even small changes in behavior—such as walking 15 minutes a day or eating a few less bites at each meal—can prevent weight gain (Kirk et al., 2003; Freedman, 2011).

PsychTech
Wireless monitoring systems that track what dieters eat and how much they exercise help them to increase self-monitoring, one of the keys to effective weight loss.

Sexual Motivation

Anyone who has seen two dogs mating knows that sexual behavior has a biological basis. Their sexual behavior appears to occur naturally without much prompting on the part of others. A number of genetically controlled factors influence the sexual behavior of nonhuman animals. For instance, animal behavior is affected by the presence of certain hormones in the blood. Moreover, female animals are receptive to sexual advances only during certain relatively limited periods of the year.

Human sexual behavior, by comparison, is more complicated, although the underlying biology is not all that different from that of related species. In males, for example, the *testes* begin to secrete **androgens,** male sex hormones, at puberty. (See Figure 2 for the basic anatomy of the male and female **genitals,** or sex organs.) Not only do androgens produce secondary sex characteristics, such as the growth of body

androgens Male sex hormones secreted by the testes.

genitals The male and female sex organs.

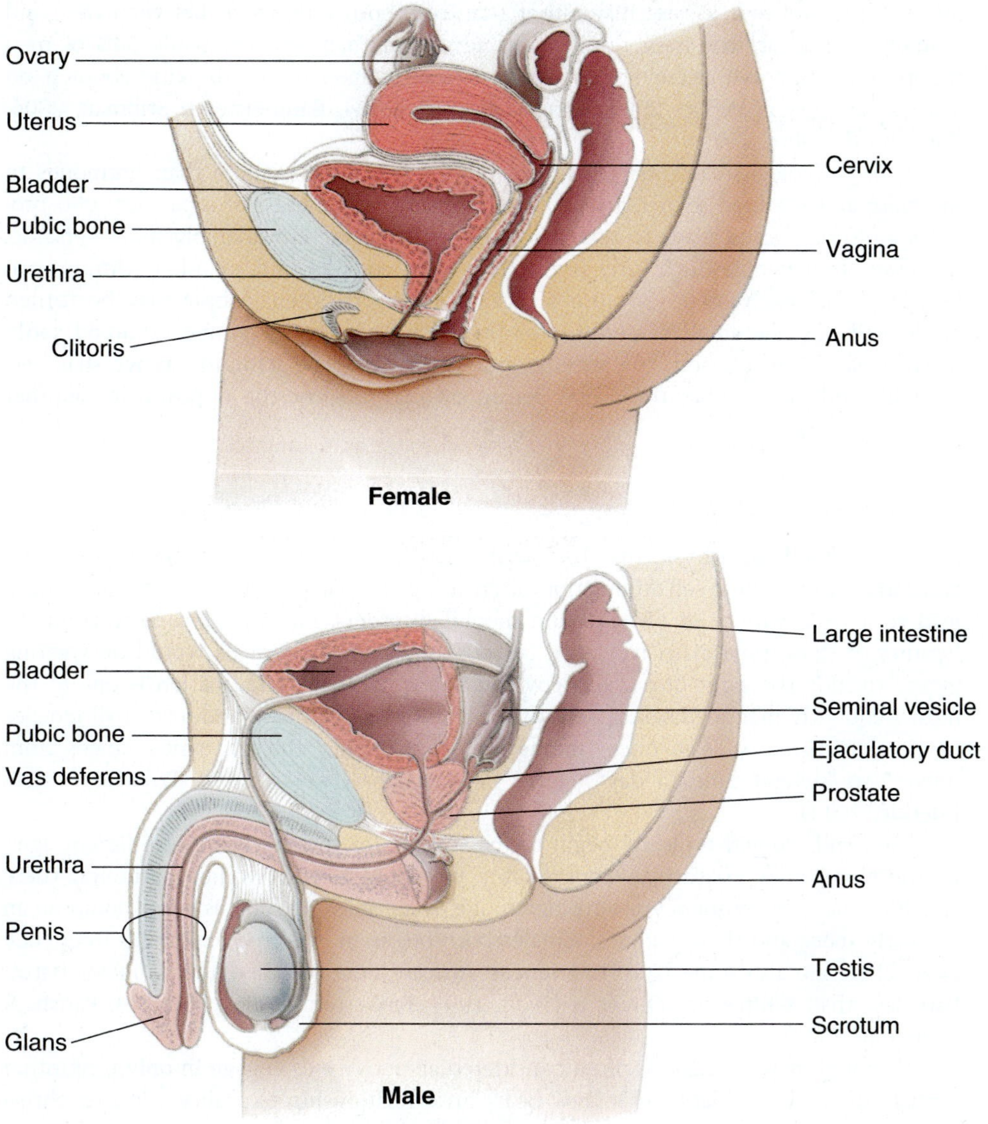

FIGURE 2 Cutaway side views of the female and male sex organs.

hair and a deepening of the voice, they also increase the sex drive. Because the level of androgen production by the testes is fairly constant, men are capable of (and interested in) sexual activities without any regard to biological cycles. Given the proper stimuli leading to arousal, male sexual behavior can occur at any time (Goldstein, 2000).

Women show a different pattern. When they reach maturity at puberty, the two *ovaries* begin to produce **estrogens,** female sex hormones. However, those hormones are not produced consistently; instead, their production follows a cyclical pattern. The greatest output occurs during **ovulation,** when an egg is released from the ovaries, making the chances of fertilization by a sperm cell highest. While in nonhumans the period around ovulation is the only time the female is receptive to sex, people are different. Although there are variations in reported sex drive, women are receptive to sex throughout their cycles (Leiblum & Chivers, 2007).

estrogens Class of female sex hormones.

ovulation The point at which an egg is released from the ovaries.

In addition, some evidence suggests that males have a stronger sex drive than females do, although the difference may be the result of society's discouragement of overt displays of female sexuality rather than of inborn differences between men and women. It is clear that men think about sex more than women: while 54% of men report thinking about sex every day, only 19% of women report thinking about it on a daily basis (Mendelsohn, 2003; Gangestad et al., 2004; Baumeister & Stillman, 2006; Carvalho & Nobre, 2011).

Though biological factors "prime" people for sex, it takes more than hormones to motivate and produce sexual behavior. In animals the presence of a partner who provides arousing stimuli leads to sexual activity. Humans are considerably more versatile; not only other people but nearly any object, sight, smell, sound, or other stimulus can lead to sexual excitement. Because of prior associations, then, people may be turned on sexually by the smell of perfume or the sound of a favorite song hummed softly in their ears. The reaction to a specific, potentially arousing stimulus, as we shall see, is highly individual–what turns one person on may do just the opposite for another (Benson, 2003).

MASTURBATION: SOLITARY SEX

masturbation Sexual self-stimulation.

If you listened to physicians 100 years ago, you would have been told that **masturbation,** sexual self-stimulation often using the hand to rub the genitals, would lead to a wide variety of physical and mental disorders, ranging from hairy palms to insanity. If those physicians had been correct, however, most of us would be wearing gloves to hide the sight of our hair-covered palms because masturbation is one of the most frequently practiced sexual activities. Some 94% of all males and 63% of all females have masturbated at least once; among college students, the frequency ranges from "never" to "several times a day" (Hunt, 1974; Michael et al., 1994; Polonsky, 2006; Buerkle, 2011).

Men and women typically begin to masturbate for the first time at different ages. Furthermore, men masturbate considerably more often than women, although there are differences in frequency according to age. Male masturbation is most common in the early teens and then declines; females both begin and reach a maximum frequency later. There are also some racial differences: African-American men and women masturbate less than whites do (Oliver & Hyde, 1993; Pinkerton et al., 2002; Das, Parish, & Laumann, 2009).

Although masturbation is often considered an activity to engage in only if no other sexual outlets are available, this view bears little relationship to reality. Close to three-fourths of married men (age 20 to 40) report masturbating an average of 24 times a year, and 68% of the married women in the same age group masturbate an average of 10 times a year (Hunt, 1974; Michael et al., 1994; Das, 2007).

Despite the high incidence of masturbation, attitudes toward it still reflect some of the negative views of yesteryear. For instance, one survey found that around 10% of people who masturbated experienced feelings of guilt; 5% of the males and 1% of the females considered their behavior perverted (Arafat & Cotton, 1974). Despite these negative attitudes, however, most experts on sex view masturbation as a healthy and legitimate–and harmless–sexual activity. In addition, masturbation is seen as providing a means of learning about one's own sexuality and a way of discovering changes in one's body such as the emergence of precancerous lumps (Coleman, 2002; Levin, 2007; Herbenick et al., 2009).

HETEROSEXUALITY

heterosexuality Sexual attraction and behavior directed to the other sex.

For heterosexuals, engaging in sexual intercourse often is perceived as achieving one of life's major milestones. However, **heterosexuality,** sexual attraction and behavior directed to the other sex, consists of far more than male-female intercourse. Kissing, petting, caressing, massaging, and other forms of sex play are all components of heterosexual behavior. Still, sex researchers' focus has been on the act of intercourse, especially in terms of its first occurrence and its frequency.

PREMARITAL SEX

Until fairly recently, premarital sexual intercourse, at least for women, was considered one of the major taboos in our society. Traditionally, women have been warned by society that "nice girls don't do it"; men have been told that premarital sex is okay for them, but they should marry virgins. This view that premarital sex is permissible for males but not for females is called the **double standard** (Liang, 2007; Lyons et al., 2011).

double standard The view that premarital sex is permissible for males but not for females.

As recently as the 1970s, the majority of adult Americans believed that premarital sex was always wrong. But there has been a dramatic change in public opinion since then. The percentage of people who believe that premarital sex is "not wrong at all" has increased from just over 25% in the early 1970s to more than 55% in 2012. More than half say that living together before marriage is morally acceptable (Thornton & Young-DeMarco, 2001; Harding & Jencks, 2003; Smith & Son, 2013).

Changes in attitudes toward premarital sex were matched by changes in actual rates of premarital sexual activity. For instance, more than one-half of women between the ages of 15 and 19 have had premarital sexual intercourse. These figures are close to double the number of women in the same age range who reported having intercourse in 1970. Clearly, the trend over the last several decades has been toward more women engaging in premarital sexual activity (Jones, Darroch, & Singh, 2005; Sprecher, Treger, & Sakaluk, 2013).

Males, too, have shown an increase in the incidence of premarital sexual intercourse, although the increase has not been as dramatic as it has been for females—probably because the rates for males were higher to begin with. For instance, the first surveys of premarital intercourse carried out in the 1940s showed an incidence of 84% across males of all ages; recent figures are closer to 95%. Moreover, the average age of males' first sexual experience has been declining steadily. Almost half of males have had sexual intercourse by the age of 18; by the time they reach age 20, 88% have had intercourse. For both men and women, 70% of teens have had intercourse by their 19th birthday (Arena, 1984; Hyde, Mezulis, & Abramson, 2008; Allen Guttmacher Institute, 2011).

MARITAL SEX

To judge by the number of articles about sex in heterosexual marriages, one would think that sexual behavior was the number one standard by which marital bliss is measured. Married couples are often concerned that they are having too little sex, too much sex, or the wrong kind of sex (Harvey, Wenzel, & Sprecher, 2005).

Although there are many different dimensions along which sex in marriage is measured, one is certainly the frequency of sexual intercourse. What is typical? As with most other types of sexual activities, there is no easy answer to the question because there are such wide variations in patterns between individuals. We do know that 43% of married couples have sexual intercourse a few times a month and 36% of couples have it two or three times a week. With increasing age and length of marriage, the frequency of intercourse declines. Still, sex continues into late adulthood with almost half of people reporting that they engage in high-quality sexual activity at least once a month (Michael et al., 1994; Powell, 2006).

Although early research found **extramarital sex** to be widespread, the current reality appears to be otherwise. According to surveys, 85% of married women and more than 75% of married men are faithful to their spouses. Furthermore, the median number of sex partners inside and outside of marriage since the age of 18 was six for men and two for women. Accompanying these numbers is a high, consistent degree of disapproval of extramarital sex, with nine of ten people saying that it is "always" or "almost always" wrong (Daines, 2006; Whisman & Snyder, 2007; DeMaris, 2013).

extramarital sex Sexual activity between a married person and someone who is not his or her spouse.

HOMOSEXUALITY AND BISEXUALITY

homosexuals Persons who are sexually attracted to members of their own sex.

bisexuals Persons who are sexually attracted to people of the same sex and the other sex.

Homosexuals are sexually attracted to members of their own sex, whereas **bisexuals** are sexually attracted to people of the same sex and the other sex. Many male homosexuals prefer the term *gay* and female homosexuals prefer the term *lesbian* because they refer to a broader array of attitudes and lifestyles than the term *homosexual,* which focuses on the sexual act.

The number of people who choose same-sex sexual partners at one time or another is considerable. Estimates suggest that around 20–25% of males and about 15% of females have had at least one gay or lesbian experience during adulthood. The exact number of people who identify themselves as exclusively homosexual has proved difficult to gauge; some estimates are as low as 1.1% and some as high as 10%. Most experts suggest that 5–10% of both men and women are exclusively gay or lesbian during extended periods of their lives (Hunt, 1974; Sells, 1994; Firestein, 1996).

Although people often view homosexuality and heterosexuality as two completely distinct sexual orientations, the issue is not that simple. Pioneering sex researcher Alfred Kinsey acknowledged this when he considered sexual orientation along a scale or continuum with "exclusively homosexual" at one end and "exclusively heterosexual" at the other. In the middle were people who showed both homosexual and heterosexual behavior. Kinsey's approach suggests that sexual orientation is dependent on a person's sexual feelings and behaviors and romantic feelings (Weinberg, Williams, & Pryor, 1991).

DETERMINING THE CAUSES OF SEXUAL ORIENTATION

What determines whether people become homosexual or heterosexual? Although there are a number of theories, none has proved completely satisfactory.

Some explanations for sexual orientation are biological, suggesting that there are genetic causes. Studies of identical twins provide evidence for a genetic cause of sexual orientation. Studies find that when one twin identified himself or herself as homosexual, the occurrence of homosexuality in the other twin was higher than it was in the general population. Such results occur even for twins who have been separated early in life and who therefore are not necessarily raised in similar social environments (Kirk, Bailey, & Martin, 2000; Gooren, 2006; LeVay, 2011).

Hormones also may play a role in determining sexual orientation. For example, research shows that women exposed before birth to DES (diethylstilbestrol–a drug their mothers took to avoid miscarriage) were more likely to be homosexual or bisexual (Meyer-Bahlburg, 1997).

Some evidence suggests that differences in brain structures may be related to sexual orientation. For instance, the structure of the anterior hypothalamus, an area of the brain that governs sexual behavior, differs in male homosexuals and heterosexuals. Similarly, other research shows that, compared with heterosexual men or women, gay men have a larger anterior commissure, which is a bundle of neurons connecting the right and left hemispheres of the brain (LeVay, 1993; Byne, 1996; Witelson et al., 2008).

However, research suggesting that biological causes are at the root of homosexuality is not conclusive because most findings are based on only small samples of individuals. Still, the possibility is real that some inherited or biological factor exists that predisposes people toward homosexuality if certain environmental conditions are met (Veniegas, 2000; Teodorov et al., 2002; Rahman, Kumari, & Wilson, 2003).

Little evidence suggests that sexual orientation is brought about by child-rearing practices or family dynamics. Although proponents of psychoanalytic theories once argued that the nature of the parent-child relationship can produce homosexuality (e.g., Freud, 1922/1959), research evidence does not support such explanations (Isay, 1994; Roughton, 2002).

Another explanation for sexual orientation rests on learning theory (Masters & Johnson, 1979). According to this view, sexual orientation is learned through rewards and punishments in much the same way that we may learn to prefer swimming over tennis. For example, a young adolescent who had an unpleasant heterosexual experience might develop disagreeable associations with the other sex. If the same person had a rewarding, pleasant gay or lesbian experience, homosexuality might be incorporated into his or her sexual fantasies. If such fantasies are used during later sexual activities—such as masturbation—they may be positively reinforced through orgasm, and the association of homosexual behavior and sexual pleasure eventually may cause homosexuality to become the preferred form of sexual behavior.

Although the learning-theory explanation is plausible, several difficulties rule it out as a definitive explanation. Because our society has traditionally held homosexuality in low esteem, one ought to expect that the negative treatment of homosexual behavior would outweigh the rewards attached to it. Furthermore, children growing up with a gay or lesbian parent are statistically unlikely to become homosexual, which thus contradicts the notion that homosexual behavior may be learned from others (Golombok et al., 1995; Victor & Fish, 1995; Tasker, 2005).

Because of the difficulty in finding a consistent explanation for sexual orientation, we can't definitively answer the question of what determines it. It seems unlikely that any single factor orients a person toward homosexuality or heterosexuality. Instead, it seems reasonable to assume that a combination of biological and environmental factors is involved (Bem, 1996; Hyde, Mezulis, & Abramson, 2008).

Although we don't know exactly why people develop a certain sexual orientation, one thing is clear: Despite increasingly positive attitudes toward homosexuality, many gays and lesbians face antigay attitudes and discrimination, and it can take a toll. Lesbians and gays have higher rates of depression and suicide than their straight counterparts. There are even physical health disparities due to prejudice that gays and lesbians may experience. Because of this, the American Psychological Association and other major mental health organizations have endorsed efforts to eliminate discrimination against gays and lesbians (Chakraborty et al., 2011; Ashley, 2013; Lick, Durso, & Johnson, 2013).

Furthermore, attitudes toward homosexuality have changed dramatically in the last two decades, with younger generations in particular becoming more positive. For example, 64% of those under 30 support same-sex marriage. Overall, tolerance for gays and lesbians has grown substantially in the United States (NORC/University of Chicago, 2011).

Study Alert

The determinants of sexual orientation have proven difficult to pinpoint. It is important to know the variety of explanations that have been put forward.

Extensive research has found that bisexuals and homosexuals enjoy the same overall degree of mental and physical health as heterosexuals.

TRANSSEXUALISM

transsexuals People whose sexual identification is with the opposite gender from that they were born with; they feel they are trapped in the body of the other gender.

Transsexuals are people whose sexual identification is with the opposite gender from that they were born with. Transsexuals feel that they are trapped in the body of the other gender. In fundamental ways, transsexualism represents less of a sexual difficulty than a gender issue involving one's sexual identity (Meyerowitz, 2004; Heath, 2006).

Transsexuals sometimes seek sex-change operations in which their existing genitals are surgically removed and the genitals of the desired sex are fashioned. Several steps, including intensive counseling, hormone injections, and living as a member of the desired sex for several years, precede surgery, which is, not surprisingly, highly complicated. The outcome, though, can be quite positive (O'Keefe & Fox, 2003; Stegerwald & Janson, 2003; Lobato, Koff, & Manenti, 2006; Richards, 2011).

Transsexualism is part of a broader category known as transgenderism. The term *transgenderism* encompasses not only transsexuals, but also people who view themselves as a third gender (neither male nor female), transvestites (who dress in the clothes of the other gender), or others who believe that traditional male-female gender classifications inadequately characterize them (Prince, 2005; Hyde, Mezulis, & Abramson, 2008).

Transsexuals are distinct from individuals who are known as *intersex* or by the older term *hermaphrodite*. An intersex person is born with an atypical combination of sexual organs or chromosomal or gene patterns. In some cases, they are born with both male and female sexual organs, or the organs are ambiguous. It is an extremely rare condition found in one in 4,500 births. Intersexism involves a complex mix of physiological and psychological issues (Lehrman, 2007; Diamond, 2009).

The Needs for Achievement, Affiliation, and Power

Although hunger may be one of the more potent primary drives in our day-to-day lives, powerful secondary drives that have no clear biological basis also motivate us. Among the more prominent of these are the needs for achievement, affiliation, and power.

THE NEED FOR ACHIEVEMENT: STRIVING FOR EXCELLENCE

need for achievement A stable, learned characteristic in which a person obtains satisfaction by striving for and achieving challenging goals.

The **need for achievement** is a stable, learned characteristic in which a person obtains satisfaction by striving for and achieving challenging goals (McClelland et al., 1953). People with a high need for achievement seek out situations in which they can compete against some objective standard—such as grades, money, or winning a game—and prove themselves successful.

But people who have a high need for achievement are selective when it comes to picking their challenges: They tend to avoid situations in which success will come too easily (which would be unchallenging) or situations in which success is highly unlikely. Instead, people high in achievement motivation generally choose tasks that are of intermediate difficulty (Speirs-Neumeister & Finch, 2006; Mills, 2011).

Study Alert
A key feature of people with a high need for achievement is that they prefer tasks of *moderate* difficulty.

In contrast, people with low achievement motivation tend to be motivated primarily by a desire to avoid failure. As a result, they seek out easy tasks so they are sure to avoid failure, or they seek out very difficult tasks for which failure has no negative implications because almost anyone would fail at them. People with a high fear of failure will stay away from tasks of intermediate difficulty because they may fail where others have been successful (Martin & Marsh, 2002; Puca, 2005; Morrone & Pintrich, 2006).

A high need for achievement generally produces positive outcomes, at least in a success-oriented culture such as Western society. For instance, people motivated by a high need for achievement are more likely to attend college than their low-achievement counterparts; once they are in college, they tend to receive higher grades in classes that are related to their future careers. Furthermore, high achievement motivation indicates future economic and occupational success (McClelland, 1985; Thrash & Elliot, 2002).

How can we measure a person's need for achievement? The measuring instrument used most frequently is the *Thematic Apperception Test (TAT).* Using the TAT, an examiner shows a series of ambiguous pictures, such as the one in Figure 3. The examiner tells participants to write a story that describes what is happening, who the people are, what led to the situation, what the people are thinking or wanting, and what will happen next. Researchers then use a standard scoring system to determine the amount of achievement imagery in people's stories. For example, someone who writes a story in which the main character strives to beat an opponent, studies in order to do well at some task, or works hard in order to get a promotion shows clear signs of an achievement orientation. The inclusion of such achievement-related imagery in the participants' stories is assumed to indicate an unusually high degree of concern with–and therefore a relatively strong need for–achievement (Tuerlinckx, DeBoeck, & Lens, 2002; Verdon, 2011).

FIGURE 3 This ambiguous picture is similar to those used in the Thematic Apperception Test to determine people's underlying motivation. What do you see? Do you think your response is related to your motivation?

THE NEED FOR AFFILIATION: STRIVING FOR FRIENDSHIP

Few of us choose to lead our lives as hermits. Why?

One main reason is that most people have a **need for affiliation,** an interest in establishing and maintaining relationships with other people. Individuals with a high need for affiliation write TAT stories that emphasize the desire to maintain or reinstate friendships and show concern over being rejected by friends.

need for affiliation An interest in establishing and maintaining relationships with other people.

People who have higher affiliation needs are particularly sensitive to relationships with others. They desire to be with their friends more of the time and alone less often, compared with people who are lower in the need for affiliation. However, gender is a greater determinant of how much time is actually spent with friends: Regardless of their affiliative orientation, female students spend significantly more time with their friends and less time alone than male students do (Cantwell & Andrews, 2002; Johnson, 2004; Semykina & Linz, 2007).

THE NEED FOR POWER: STRIVING FOR IMPACT ON OTHERS

If your fantasies include becoming president of the United States or running Microsoft, your dreams may reflect a high need for power. The **need for power,** a tendency to seek impact, control, or influence over others and to be seen as a powerful individual, is an additional type of motivation (Winter, 2007; Zians, 2007; Pratto et al., 2011).

need for power A tendency to seek impact, control, or influence over others and to be seen as a powerful individual.

As you might expect, people with strong needs for power are more apt to belong to organizations and seek office than are those low in the need for power. They also tend to work in professions in which their power needs may be fulfilled, such as business management and–you may or may not be surprised–teaching (Jenkins, 1994). In addition, they seek to display the trappings of power. Even in college, they are more likely to collect prestigious possessions, such as electronic equipment and sports cars.

Some significant gender differences exist in the display of need for power. Men with high power needs tend to show unusually high levels of aggression, drink heavily, act in a sexually exploitative manner, and participate more frequently in competitive sports–behaviors that collectively represent somewhat extravagant, flamboyant behavior. In contrast, women display their power needs with more restraint;

this is congruent with traditional societal constraints on women's behavior. Women with high power needs are more apt than men to channel those needs in a socially responsible manner, such as by showing concern for others or displaying highly nurturing behavior (Winter, 1995, 2007; Schubert & Koole, 2009; Schultheiss & Schiepe-Tiska, 2013).

From the perspective of . . .

A Human Resources Specialist How might you use characteristics such as need for achievement, need for affiliation, and need for power to select workers for jobs?

RECAP/EVALUATE/RETHINK

RECAP

LO 25-1 What biological and social factors underlie hunger?

- Eating behavior is subject to homeostasis, as most people's weight stays within a relatively stable range. The hypothalamus in the brain is central to the regulation of food intake.
- Social factors, such as mealtimes, cultural food preferences, and other learned habits, also play a role in the regulation of eating by determining when, what, and how much one eats. An oversensitivity to social cues and an insensitivity to internal cues may also be related to obesity. In addition, obesity may be caused by an unusually high weight set point—the weight the body attempts to maintain—and genetic factors.

LO 25-2 What are the varieties of sexual behavior?

- Although biological factors, such as the presence of androgens (male sex hormones) and estrogens and progesterone (female sex hormones), prime people for sex, almost any kind of stimulus can produce sexual arousal depending on a person's prior sexual experience.
- The frequency of masturbation is high, particularly for males. Although attitudes toward masturbation are increasingly liberal, they have traditionally been negative even though no negative consequences have been detected.
- Heterosexuality, or sexual attraction to members of the other sex, is the most common sexual orientation.
- The double standard by which premarital sex is thought to be more permissible for men than for women has declined, particularly among young people. For many people, the double standard has been replaced by endorsement of "permissiveness with affection," the view that premarital intercourse is permissible if it occurs in the context of a loving and committed relationship.
- Homosexuals are sexually attracted to members of their own sex; bisexuals are sexually attracted to people of the same sex and the other sex. No explanation for why people become homosexual has been confirmed; among the possibilities are genetic or biological factors, childhood and family influences, and prior learning experiences and conditioning. However, no relationship exists between sexual orientation and psychological adjustment.

LO 25-3 How are needs relating to achievement, affiliation, and power motivation exhibited?

- Need for achievement refers to the stable, learned characteristic in which a person strives to attain a level of excellence. Need for achievement is usually measured through the Thematic Apperception Test (TAT), a series of pictures about which a person writes a story.
- The need for affiliation is a concern with establishing and maintaining relationships with others, whereas the need for power is a tendency to seek to exert an impact on others.

EVALUATE

1. Match the following terms with their definitions:

1. Hypothalamus	**a.** Leads to refusal of food and starvation
2. Lateral hypothalamic damage	**b.** Responsible for monitoring food intake
3. Ventromedial hypothalamic damage	**c.** Causes extreme overeating

2. The ________ ________ ________ is the specific level of weight the body strives to maintain.

3. __________ is the rate at which the body produces and expends energy.

4. Although the incidence of masturbation among young adults is high, once men and women become involved in intimate relationships, they typically cease masturbating. True or false?

5. The increase in premarital sex in recent years has been greater for women than for men. True or false?

6. Julio is the type of person who constantly strives for excellence. He feels intense satisfaction when he is able to master a new task. Julio most likely has a high need for __________.

7. Debbie's Thematic Apperception Test (TAT) story depicts a young girl who is rejected by one of her peers and seeks to regain her friendship. What major type of motivation is Debbie displaying in her story?

a. Need for achievement
b. Need for motivation
c. Need for affiliation
d. Need for power

RETHINK

1. In what ways do societal expectations, expressed by television shows and commercials, contribute to both obesity and excessive concern about weight loss? How could television contribute to better eating habits and attitudes toward weight? Should it be required to do so?

2. Why do discussions of sexual behavior, which is such a necessary part of human life, have so many negative connotations in Western society?

Answers to Evaluate Questions

1. 1-b, 2-a, 3-c; **2.** weight set point; **3.** Metabolism; **4.** false; **5.** true; **6.** achievement; **7.** c

KEY TERMS

obesity
weight set point
metabolism
anorexia nervosa
bulimia
androgens
genitals
estrogens
progesterone
ovulation
masturbation
heterosexuality
double standard
extramarital sex
homosexuals
bisexuals
transsexuals
need for achievement
need for affiliation
need for power

MODULE 26

Understanding Emotional Experiences

Learning Outcomes

LO 26-1 What are emotions, and how do we experience them?

LO 26-2 What are the functions of emotions?

LO 26-3 What are the explanations for emotions?

LO 26-4 How does nonverbal behavior relate to the expression of emotions?

emotions Feelings that generally have both physiological and cognitive elements and that influence behavior.

Karl Andrews held in his hands the envelope he had been waiting for. It could be the ticket to his future: an offer of admission to his first-choice college. But what was it going to say? He knew it could go either way. His grades were pretty good, and he had been involved in some extracurricular activities, but his SAT scores had not been terrific. He felt so nervous that his hands shook as he opened the thin envelope (not a good sign, he thought). Here it comes. "Dear Mr. Andrews," it read. "The Trustees of the University are pleased to admit you. . . ." That was all he needed to see. With a whoop of excitement, Karl found himself jumping up and down gleefully. A rush of emotion overcame him as it sank in that he had, in fact, been accepted. He was on his way.

At one time or another, all of us have experienced the strong feelings that accompany both very pleasant and very negative experiences. Perhaps we have felt the thrill of getting a sought-after job, the joy of being in love, the sorrow over someone's death, or the anguish of inadvertently hurting someone. Moreover, we experience such reactions on a less intense level throughout our daily lives with such things as the pleasure of a friendship, the enjoyment of a movie, and the embarrassment of breaking a borrowed item.

Despite the varied nature of these feelings, they all represent emotions. Although everyone has an idea of what an emotion is, formally defining the concept has proved to be an elusive task. Here, we'll use a general definition: **Emotions** are feelings that generally have both physiological and cognitive elements and that influence behavior.

Think, for example, about how it feels to be happy. First, we obviously experience a feeling that we can differentiate from other emotions. It is likely that we also experience some identifiable physical changes in our bodies: Perhaps the heart rate increases, or—as in the example of Karl Andrews—we find ourselves "jumping for joy." Finally, the emotion probably encompasses cognitive elements: Our understanding and evaluation of the meaning of what is happening prompts our feelings of happiness.

It is also possible, however, to experience an emotion without the presence of cognitive elements. For instance, we may react with fear to an unusual or novel situation (such as coming into contact with an erratic, unpredictable individual), or we may experience pleasure over sexual excitation without having cognitive awareness or understanding of just what makes the situation exciting.

Some psychologists argue that entirely separate systems govern cognitive responses and emotional responses. A current controversy focuses on whether the emotional response predominates over the cognitive response or vice versa. Some theorists suggest that we first respond to a situation with an emotional reaction and later try to understand it. For example, we may enjoy a complex modern symphony without at first understanding it or knowing why we like it. In contrast, other theorists propose that people first develop cognitions about a situation and then react emotionally. This school of thought suggests that we must think about and understand a stimulus or situation, relating it to what we already know, before we can react on an emotional level (Murphy & Zajonc, 1993; Lazarus, 1995; Oatley, Keltner, & Jenkins, 2006; Martin & Kerns, 2011).

Because proponents of both sides of this debate can cite research to support their viewpoints, the question is far from resolved. Perhaps the sequence varies from situation to situation with emotions predominating in some instances and cognitive processes occurring first in others. Both sides agree that we can experience emotions that involve little or no conscious thought. We may not know why we're afraid of mice because we understand objectively that they represent no danger, but we may still be frightened when we see them. Neuroimaging studies of the brain may help resolve this debate as well as others about the nature of emotions (Barrett & Wager, 2006; Niedenthal, 2007; Karaszewski, 2008).

The Functions of Emotions

Imagine what it would be like if we didn't experience emotion. We would have no depths of despair, no depression, and no remorse, but at the same time we would also have no happiness, joy, or love. Obviously, life would be considerably less satisfying and even dull if we lacked the capacity to sense and express emotion.

But do emotions serve any purpose beyond making life interesting? Indeed they do. Psychologists have identified several important functions that emotions play in our daily lives (Frederickson & Branigan, 2005; Frijda, 2005; Gross, 2006; Siemer, Mauss, & Gross, 2007; Rolls, 2011). Among the most important of those functions are the following:

- *Preparing us for action.* Emotions act as a link between events in our environment and our responses. For example, if you saw an angry dog charging toward you, your emotional reaction (fear) would be associated with physiological arousal of the sympathetic division of the autonomic nervous system, the activation of the "fight-or-flight" response.
- *Shaping our future behavior.* Emotions promote learning that will help us make appropriate responses in the future. For instance, your emotional response to unpleasant events teaches you to avoid similar circumstances in the future.
- *Helping us interact more effectively with others.* We often communicate the emotions we experience through our verbal and nonverbal behaviors, making our emotions obvious to observers. These behaviors can act as a signal to observers, allowing them to understand better what we are experiencing and to help them predict our future behavior.

Determining the Range of Emotions: Labeling Our Feelings

If we were to list the words in the English language that have been used to describe emotions, we would end up with at least 500 examples (Averill, 1975). The list would range from such obvious emotions as *happiness* and *fear* to less common ones, such as *adventurousness* and *pensiveness.*

One challenge for psychologists has been to sort through this list to identify the most important, fundamental emotions. Theorists have hotly contested the issue of cataloging emotions and have come up with different lists, depending on how they define the concept of emotion. In fact, some reject the question entirely, saying that *no* set of emotions should be singled out as most basic and that emotions are best understood by breaking them down into their component parts. Other researchers argue for looking at emotions in terms of a hierarchy, dividing them into positive and negative categories and then organizing them into increasingly narrower subcategories (see Figure 1; Manstead, Frijda, & Fischer, 2003; Dillard & Shen, 2007; Livingstone et al., 2011).

Still, most researchers suggest that a list of basic emotions would include, at a minimum, happiness, anger, fear, sadness, and disgust. Other lists are broader, including emotions such as surprise, contempt, guilt, and joy (Ekman, 1994a; Shweder, 1994; Tracy & Robins, 2004).

One difficulty in defining a basic set of emotions is that substantial differences exist in descriptions of emotions among various cultures. For instance, Germans report

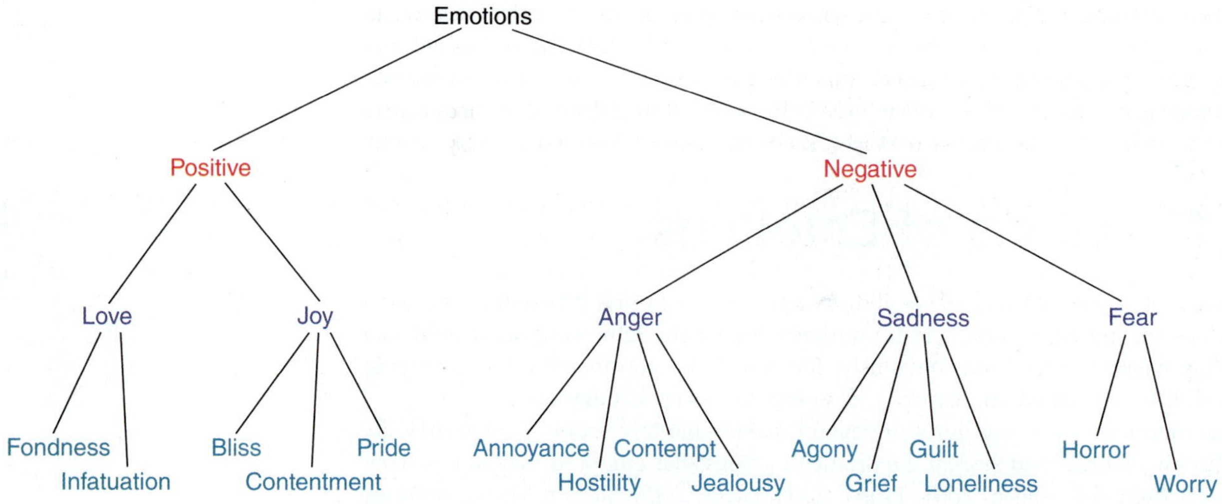

FIGURE 1 One approach to organizing emotions is to use a hierarchy, which divides emotions into increasingly narrow subcategories. (Source: Adapted from Fischer, Shaver, & Carnochan, 1990.)

experiencing *schadenfreude,* a feeling of pleasure over another person's difficulties, and the Japanese experience *hagaii,* a mood of vulnerable heartache colored by frustration. In Tahiti, people experience *musu,* a feeling of reluctance to yield to unreasonable demands made by one's parents.

Finding *schadenfreude, hagaii,* or *musu* in a particular culture doesn't mean that the members of other cultures are incapable of experiencing such emotions, of course. It suggests, though, that fitting a particular emotion into a linguistic category to describe that emotion may make it easier to discuss, contemplate, and perhaps experience (Russell & Sato, 1995; Li, Kuppens, et al., 2006; van Dijk et al., 2011).

The Roots of Emotions

> I've never been so angry before; I feel my heart pounding, and I'm trembling all over. . . . I don't know how I'll get through the performance. I feel like my stomach is filled with butterflies. . . . That was quite a mistake I made! My face must be incredibly red. . . . When I heard the footsteps in the night, I was so frightened that I couldn't catch my breath.

If you examine our language, you will find that there are literally dozens of ways to describe how we feel when we experience an emotion and that the language we use to describe emotions is, for the most part, based on the physical symptoms that are associated with a particular emotional experience (Kobayashi, Schallert, & Ogren, 2003; Manstead & Wagner, 2004; Spackman, Fujiki, & Brinton, 2006).

Consider, for instance, the experience of fear. Pretend that it is late on New Year's Eve. You are walking down a dark road, and you hear a stranger approaching behind you. It is clear that he is not trying to hurry by but is coming directly toward you. You think about what you will do if the stranger attempts to rob you or, worse, hurt you in some way.

While these thoughts are running through your head, something dramatic will be happening to your body. The most likely reactions, which are associated with activation of the autonomic nervous system, include an increase in your rate of breathing, an acceleration of your heart rate, a widening of your pupils (to increase visual sensitivity), and a dryness in your mouth as the functioning of your salivary glands and in fact of your entire digestive system ceases. At the same time, though, your sweat glands probably will increase their activity because increased sweating will help you rid yourself of the excess heat developed by any emergency activity in which you engage.

Of course, all these physiological changes are likely to occur without your awareness. At the same time, though, the emotional experience accompanying them will be obvious to you: You most surely would report being fearful.

Although it is easy to describe the general physical reactions that accompany emotions, defining the specific role that those physiological responses play in the experience of emotions has proved to be a major puzzle for psychologists. As we shall see, some theorists suggest that specific physiological reactions *cause* us to experience a particular emotion. For example, when the heart is pounding and we are breathing deeply, we then experience fear. In contrast, other theorists suggest the opposite sequence–that is, we experience an emotion, and that causes us to have a physiological reaction. In this view, then, as a result of experiencing the emotion of fear, our heart pounds and our breathing deepens.

THE JAMES-LANGE THEORY: DO GUT REACTIONS EQUAL EMOTIONS?

To William James and Carl Lange, who were among the first researchers to explore the nature of emotions, emotional experience is, very simply, a reaction to instinctive bodily events that occur as a response to some situation or event in the environment. This view is summarized in James's statement, "We feel sorry because we cry, angry because we strike, afraid because we tremble" (James, 1890).

James and Lange took the view that the instinctive response of crying at a loss leads us to feel sorrow, that striking out at someone who frustrates us results in our feeling anger, that trembling at a menacing threat causes us to feel fear. They suggested that for every major emotion there is an accompanying physiological or "gut" reaction of internal organs–called a *visceral experience*. It is this specific pattern of visceral response that leads us to label the emotional experience.

In sum, James and Lange proposed that we experience emotions as a result of physiological changes that produce specific sensations. The brain interprets these sensations as specific kinds of emotional experiences (see the first part of Figure 2). This view has come to be called the **James-Lange theory of emotion** (Cobos et al., 2002; Stolorow & Stolorow, 2013).

James-Lange theory of emotion The belief that emotional experience is a reaction to bodily events occurring as a result of an external situation ("I feel sad because I am crying").

The James-Lange theory, however, has some serious drawbacks. For the theory to be valid, visceral changes would have to occur quickly because we experience some emotions–such as fear upon hearing a stranger rapidly approaching on a dark night–almost instantaneously. Yet emotional experiences frequently occur even before there is time for certain physiological changes to be set into motion. Because of the slowness with which some visceral changes take place, it is hard to see how they could be the source of an immediate emotional experience.

The James-Lange theory poses another difficulty: Physiological arousal does not invariably produce emotional experience. For example, a person who is jogging has an increased heartbeat and respiration rate, as well as many of the other physiological changes associated with certain emotions. Yet joggers typically do not think of such changes in terms of emotion. There is not a one-to-one correspondence, then, between visceral changes and emotional experience. Visceral changes by themselves are not always sufficient to produce emotion.

Finally, our internal organs produce a relatively limited range of sensations. Although some types of physiological changes are associated with specific emotional experiences, it is difficult to imagine how each of the myriad emotions that people are capable of experiencing could be the result of a unique visceral change. Many emotions actually are associated with relatively similar sorts of visceral changes, a fact that contradicts the James-Lange theory (Davidson et al., 1994; Cameron, 2002; Rinaman, Banihashemi, & Koehnle, 2011).

THE CANNON-BARD THEORY: PHYSIOLOGICAL REACTIONS AS THE RESULT OF EMOTIONS

In response to the difficulties inherent in the James-Lange theory, Walter Cannon and later Philip Bard suggested an alternative view. In what has come to be known as the

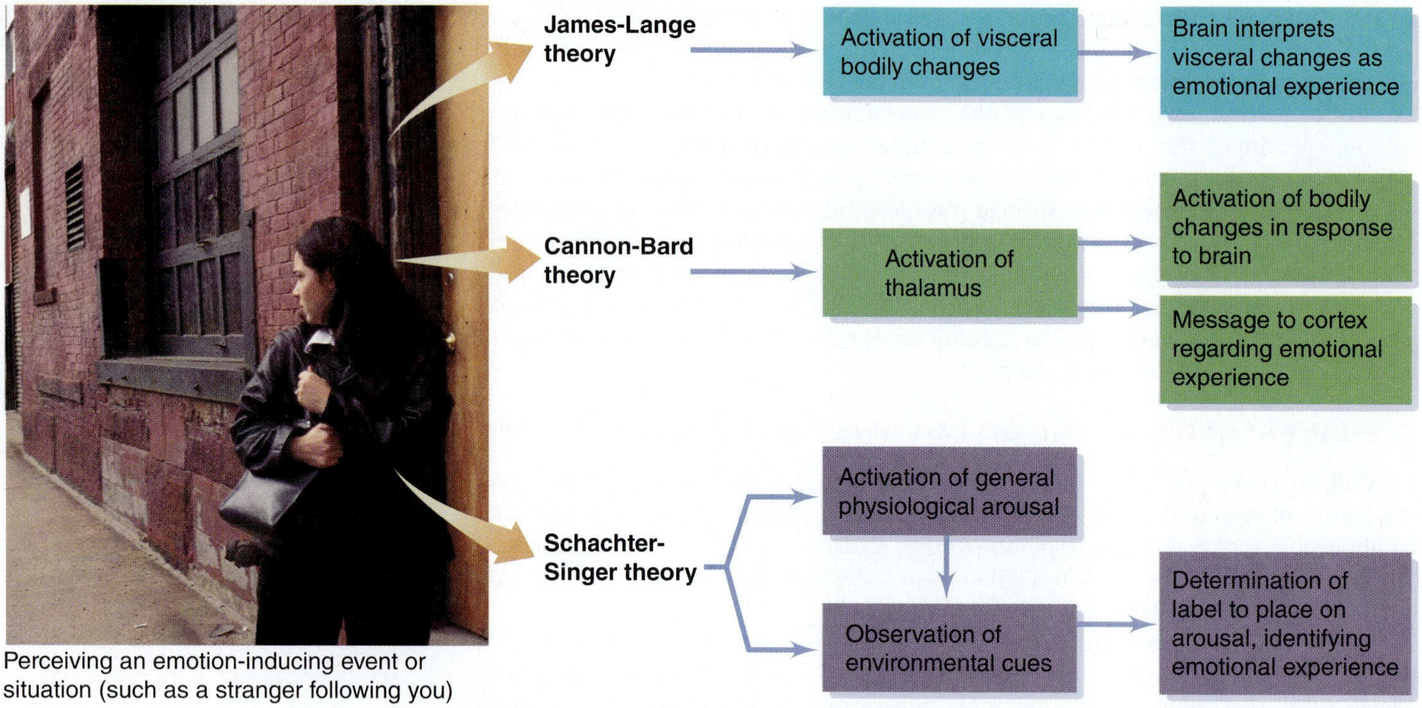

FIGURE 2 A comparison of three models of emotion.

Cannon-Bard theory of emotion The belief that both physiological arousal and emotional experience are produced simultaneously by the same nerve stimulus.

Cannon-Bard theory of emotion, they proposed the model illustrated in the second part of Figure 2 (Cannon, 1929). This theory rejects the view that physiological arousal alone leads to the perception of emotion. Instead, the theory assumes that both physiological arousal *and* the emotional experience are produced simultaneously by the same nerve stimulus, which Cannon and Bard suggested emanates from the *thalamus* in the brain.

The theory states that after we perceive an emotion-producing stimulus, the thalamus is the initial site of the emotional response. Next, the thalamus sends a signal to the autonomic nervous system, thereby producing a visceral response. At the same time, the thalamus also communicates a message to the cerebral cortex regarding the nature of the emotion being experienced. Hence, it is not necessary for different emotions to have unique physiological patterns associated with them—as long as the message sent to the cerebral cortex differs according to the specific emotion.

Study Alert
Use Figure 2 to distinguish the three classic theories of emotion (James-Lange, Cannon-Bard, and Schachter-Singer).

The Cannon-Bard theory seems to have been accurate in rejecting the view that physiological arousal alone accounts for emotions. However, more recent research has led to some important modifications of the theory. For one thing, we now understand that the hypothalamus and the limbic system, not the thalamus, play a major role in emotional experience. In addition, the simultaneous occurrence of the physiological and emotional responses, which is a fundamental assumption of the Cannon-Bard theory, has yet to be demonstrated conclusively. This ambiguity has allowed room for yet another theory of emotions: the Schachter-Singer theory.

THE SCHACHTER-SINGER THEORY: EMOTIONS AS LABELS

Schachter-Singer theory of emotion The belief that emotions are determined jointly by a nonspecific kind of physiological arousal and its interpretation, based on environmental cues.

Suppose that as you are being followed down that dark street on New Year's Eve, you notice a man being followed by another shady figure on the other side of the street. Now assume that instead of reacting with fear, the man begins to laugh and act gleeful. Would the reactions of this other individual be sufficient to lay your fears to rest? Might you, in fact, decide there is nothing to fear and get into the spirit of the evening by beginning to feel happiness and glee yourself?

According to an explanation that focuses on the role of cognition, the **Schachter-Singer theory of emotion,** this might very well happen. This approach to explaining emotions emphasizes that we identify the emotion we are experiencing by observing our environment and comparing ourselves with others (Schachter & Singer, 1962).

Schachter and Singer's classic experiment found evidence for this hypothesis. In the study, participants were told that they would receive an injection of a vitamin. In reality, they were given epinephrine, a drug that causes responses that typically occur during strong emotional reactions, such as an increase in physiological arousal, including higher heart and respiration rates and a reddening of the face. The members of both groups were then placed individually in a situation where a confederate of the experimenter acted in one of two ways. In one condition he acted angry and hostile; in the other condition he behaved as if he were exuberantly happy.

The purpose of the experiment was to determine how the participants would react emotionally to the confederate's behavior. When they were asked to describe their own emotional state at the end of the experiment, the participants exposed to the angry confederate reported that they felt angry, whereas those exposed to the happy confederate reported feeling happy. In sum, the results suggest that participants turned to the environment and the behavior of others for an explanation of the physiological arousal they were experiencing.

The results of the Schachter-Singer experiment, then, supported a cognitive view of emotions in which emotions are determined jointly by a relatively nonspecific kind of physiological arousal *and* the labeling of that arousal on the basis of cues from the environment (refer to the third part of Figure 2). Although later research has found that arousal is more specific than Schachter and Singer believed, they were right in assuming that when the source of physiological arousal is unclear, we may look to our surroundings to determine what we are experiencing.

From the perspective of . . .

An Advertising Executive How might you use Schachter and Singer's findings on the labeling of arousal to create interest in a product?

CONTEMPORARY PERSPECTIVES ON THE NEUROSCIENCE OF EMOTIONS

When Schachter and Singer carried out their groundbreaking experiment in the early 1960s, the ways in which they could evaluate the physiology that accompanies emotion were relatively limited. However, advances in the measurement of the nervous system and other parts of the body have allowed researchers to examine more closely the biological responses involved in individual emotions. As a result, evidence is growing that specific patterns of biological arousal are associated with specific emotions (Vaitl, Schienle, & Stark, 2005; Woodson, 2006; Stifter, Dollar, & Cipriano, 2011).

For instance, researchers have found that different emotions produce activation of different portions of the brain. In one study, participants undergoing positron emission tomography (PET) brain scans were asked to recall events that made them sad, such as deaths and funerals, or events that made them feel happy, such as weddings and births. They also looked at photos of faces that appeared to be happy or sad. The results of the PET scans were clear: Happiness was related to a decrease in activity in certain areas of the cerebral cortex, whereas sadness was associated with increases in activity in particular portions of the cortex (George et al., 1995; Hamann et al., 2002; Prohovnik et al., 2004).

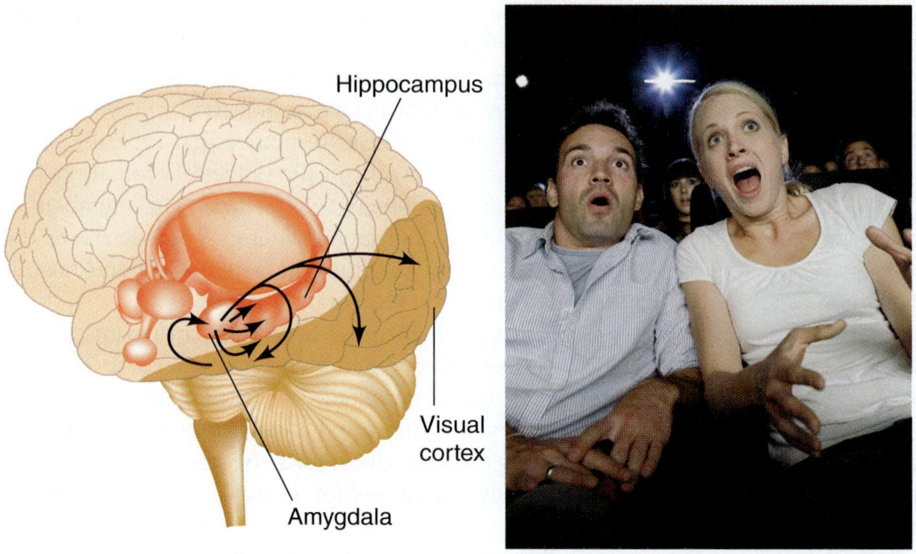

FIGURE 3 Connections from the amygdala allow it to mediate many of the autonomic expressions of emotional states through the hippocampus and visual cortex. (Source: Adapted from Dolan, 2002.)

Study Alert
It is important to understand the basic neuroscience of emotional experience.

In addition, new research shows that the *amygdala*, in the brain's temporal lobe, plays an important role in the experience of emotions. The amygdala provides a link between the perception of an emotion-producing stimulus and the recall of that stimulus later. For example, if we've once been attacked by a vicious pit bull, the amygdala processes that information and leads us to react with fear when we see a pit bull at future times (Berntson et al., 2007; Kensinger, 2007; LaBar, 2007; Pessoa, 2011).

Because neural pathways connect the amygdala, the visual cortex, and the *hippocampus* (which plays an important role in the consolidation of memories), some scientists speculate that emotion-related stimuli can be processed and responded to almost instantaneously (see Figure 3). This immediate response occurs so rapidly that higher-order, more rational thinking, which takes more time, seems not to be involved initially. In a slower but more thoughtful response to emotion-evoking stimuli, emotion-related sensory information is first evaluated and then sent on to the amygdala. It appears that the quicker system offers an immediate response to emotion-evoking stimuli, whereas the slower system helps confirm a threat and prepare a more thoughtful response (Dolan, 2002).

MAKING SENSE OF THE MULTIPLE PERSPECTIVES ON EMOTION

As new approaches to emotion continue to develop, it is reasonable to ask why so many theories of emotion exist and, perhaps more important, which one provides the most complete explanation. Actually, we have only scratched the surface. There are almost as many explanatory theories of emotion as there are individual emotions (e.g., Manstead, Frijda, & Fischer, 2003; Frijda, 2005; Prinz, 2007; Herzberg, 2009).

Why are theories of emotion so plentiful? For one thing, emotions are not a simple phenomenon but are intertwined closely with motivation, cognition, neuroscience, and a host of related branches of psychology. For example, evidence from brain imaging studies shows that even when people come to supposedly rational, nonemotional decisions—such as making moral, philosophical judgments—emotions come into play (Greene et al., 2001).

In short, emotions are such complex phenomena, encompassing both biological and cognitive aspects, that no single theory has been able to explain fully all the facets of emotional experience. Furthermore, contradictory evidence of one sort or another challenges each approach, and therefore no theory has proved invariably accurate in its predictions.

This abundance of perspectives on emotion is not a cause for despair—or unhappiness, fear, or any other negative emotion. It simply reflects the fact that psychology is an evolving, developing science. As we gather more evidence, the specific answers to questions about the nature of emotions will become clearer.

Exploring DIVERSITY

Do People in All Cultures Express Emotion Similarly?

Consider, for a moment, the six photos displayed in Figure 4. Can you identify the emotions being expressed by the person in each of the photos?

If you are a good judge of facial expressions, you will conclude that these expressions display six of the basic emotions: happiness, anger, sadness, surprise, disgust, and fear. Hundreds of studies of nonverbal behavior show that these emotions are consistently distinct and identifiable even by untrained observers (Ekman, 2007).

Interestingly, these six emotions are not unique to members of Western cultures; rather, they constitute the basic emotions expressed universally by members of the human race, regardless of where individuals have been raised and what learning experiences they have had. Psychologist Paul Ekman convincingly demonstrated this point when he studied members of an isolated New Guinea jungle tribe who had had almost no contact with Westerners (Ekman, 1972). The people of the tribe did not speak or understand English, had never seen a movie, and had very limited experience with Caucasians before Ekman's arrival. Yet their nonverbal responses to emotion-evoking stories, as well as their ability to identify basic emotions, were quite similar to those of Westerners.

Being so isolated, the New Guineans could not have learned from Westerners to recognize or produce similar facial expressions. Instead, their similar abilities and manner of responding emotionally appear to have been present innately. Although one could argue that similar experiences in both cultures led the members of each one to learn similar types of nonverbal

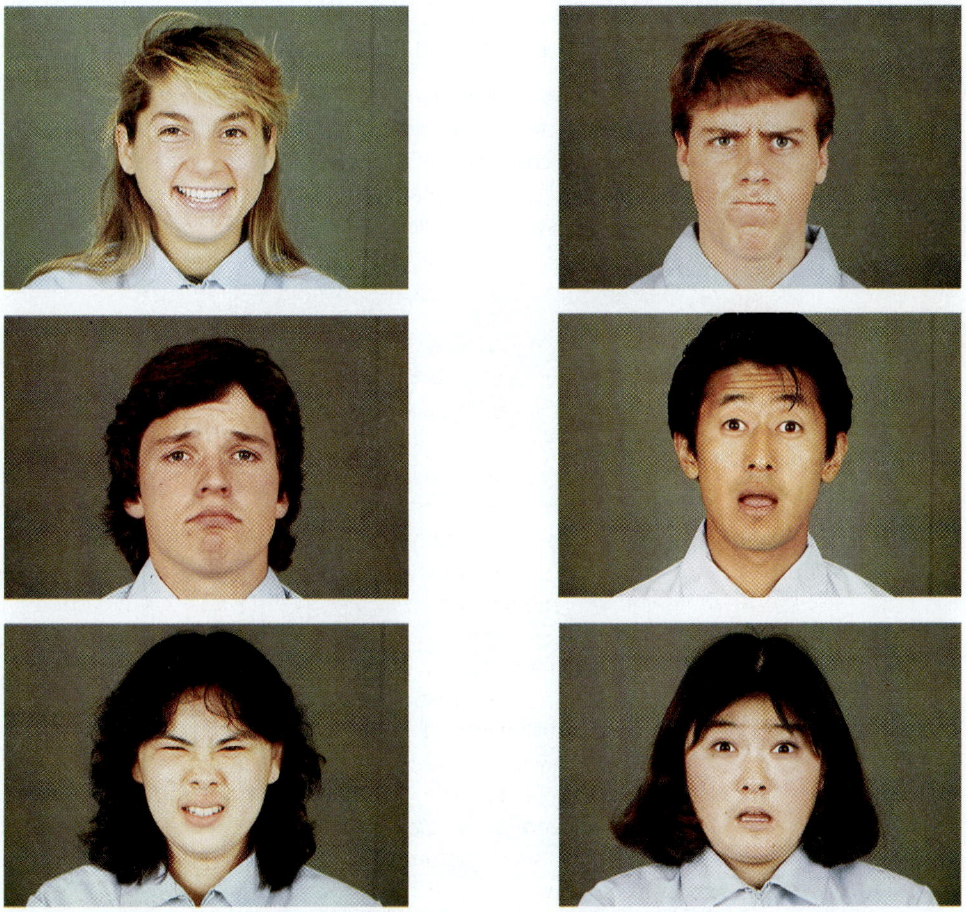

FIGURE 4 These photos demonstrate six of the primary emotions: happiness, anger, sadness, surprise, disgust, and fear.

behavior, this appears unlikely because the two cultures are so very different. The expression of basic emotions, thus, seems to be universal (Ekman, 1994b; Izard, 1994; Matsumoto, 2002).

facial-affect program Activation of a set of nerve impulses that make the face display the appropriate expression.

Why do people across cultures express emotions similarly? A hypothesis known as the **facial-affect program** gives one explanation. The facial-affect program—which is assumed to be universally present at birth—is analogous to a computer program that is turned on when a particular emotion is experienced. When set in motion, the "program" activates a set of nerve impulses that make the face display an appropriate expression. Each primary emotion produces a unique set of muscular movements, forming the kinds of expressions shown in Figure 4. For example, the emotion of happiness is universally displayed by movement of the zygomatic major, a muscle that raises the corners of the mouth and forms what we would call a smile (Ekman, 2003; Kendler et al., 2008; Krumhuber & Scherer, 2011).

facial-feedback hypothesis The hypothesis that facial expressions not only reflect emotional experience but also help determine how people experience and label emotions.

The importance of facial expressions is illustrated by an intriguing notion known as the **facial-feedback hypothesis.** According to this hypothesis, facial expressions not only *reflect* emotional experience, but they also help *determine* how people experience and label emotions. Basically put, "wearing" an emotional expression provides muscular feedback to the brain that helps produce an emotion congruent with that expression (Davis, Senghas, & Ochsner, 2009; Balconi, Bortolotti, & Crivelli, 2013).

For instance, the muscles activated when we smile may send a message to the brain indicating the experience of happiness—even if there is nothing in the environment that would produce that particular emotion. Some theoreticians have gone further by suggesting that facial expressions are *necessary* for an emotion to be experienced (Rinn, 1984, 1991). In this view, if no facial expression is present, the emotion cannot be felt.

Support for this facial-feedback hypothesis comes from a classic experiment carried out by psychologist Paul Ekman and colleagues (Ekman, Levenson, & Friesen, 1983). In the study, professional actors were asked to follow very explicit instructions regarding the movements of muscles in their faces. You might try this example yourself:

- Raise your brows and pull them together.
- Raise your upper eyelids.
- Now stretch your lips horizontally back toward your ears.

After carrying out these directions—which, as you may have guessed, are meant to produce an expression of fear—the actors' heart rates rose and their body temperatures declined, physiological reactions that characterize fear. Overall, facial expressions representing the primary emotions produced physiological effects similar to those accompanying the genuine emotions in other circumstances (Keillor et al., 2002; Soussignan, 2002).

PsychTech

Because human facial expressions of emotions involve using dozens of muscles, it is only recently that researchers, such as Rana el-Kaliouby at M.I.T. Media Lab, have been able to develop software to read them reasonably accurately.

"And just exactly what is that expression intended to convey?"

RECAP/EVALUATE/RETHINK

RECAP

LO 26-1 What are emotions, and how do we experience them?

- Emotions are broadly defined as feelings that may affect behavior and generally have both a physiological component and a cognitive component. Debate continues over whether separate systems govern cognitive and emotional responses and whether one has primacy over the other.

LO 26-2 What are the functions of emotions?

- Emotions prepare us for action, shape future behavior through learning, and help us interact more effectively with others.

LO 26-3 What are the explanations for emotions?

- Several theories explain emotions. The James-Lange theory suggests that emotional experience is a reaction to bodily, or visceral, changes that occur as a response to an environmental event and are interpreted as an emotional response.
- In contrast, the Cannon-Bard theory contends that both physiological arousal and an emotional experience are produced simultaneously by the same nerve stimulus and that the visceral experience does not necessarily differ among differing emotions.
- The Schachter-Singer theory suggests that emotions are determined jointly by a relatively nonspecific physiological arousal and the subsequent labeling of that arousal, using cues from the environment to determine how others are behaving in the same situation.
- The most recent approaches to emotions focus on their biological origins. For instance, it now seems that specific patterns of biological arousal are associated with individual emotions. Furthermore, new scanning techniques have identified the specific parts of the brain that are activated during the experience of particular emotions.

LO 26-4 How does nonverbal behavior relate to the expression of emotions?

- A person's facial expressions can reveal emotions. In fact, members of different cultures understand others' emotional expressions in similar ways. One explanation for this similarity is that an innate facial-affect program activates a set of muscle movements representing the emotion being experienced.
- The facial-feedback hypothesis suggests that facial expressions not only reflect, but also produce, emotional experiences.

EVALUATE

1. Emotions are always accompanied by a cognitive response. True or false?
2. The __________-__________ theory of emotion states that emotions are a response to instinctive bodily events.
3. According to the __________-__________ theory of emotion, both an emotional response and physiological arousal are produced simultaneously by the same nerve stimulus.
4. Your friend—a psychology major—tells you, "I was at a party last night. During the course of the evening, my general level of arousal increased. Since I was at a party where people were enjoying themselves, I assume I must have felt happy." What theory of emotion does your friend subscribe to?
5. What are the six primary emotions that can be identified from facial expressions?

RETHINK

1. If researchers learned how to control emotional responses so that targeted emotions could be caused or prevented, what ethical concerns might arise? Under what circumstances, if any, should such techniques be used?
2. Many people enjoy watching movies, sporting events, and music performances in crowded theaters and arenas more than they like watching them at home alone. Which theory of emotions may help explain this? How?

Answers to Evaluate Questions

1. false; emotions may occur without a cognitive response; **2.** James-Lange; **3.** Cannon-Bard; **4.** Schachter-Singer; **5.** surprise, sadness, happiness, anger, disgust, and fear

KEY TERMS

emotions
James-Lange theory of emotion
Cannon-Bard theory of emotion
Schachter-Singer theory of emotion
facial-affect program
facial-feedback hypothesis

Looking Back

Epilogue

Motivation and emotions are two interrelated aspects of psychology. In these modules, we first considered the topic of motivation, which has spawned a great deal of theory and research examining primary and secondary drives. We then turned to a discussion of emotions, beginning with their functions and proceeding to a review of three major theories that seek to explain what emotions are and how they, and their associated physiological symptoms, emerge in the individual. Finally, we looked at cultural differences in the expression and display of emotions and discussed the facial-affect program, which seems to be innate and to regulate the nonverbal expression of the basic emotions.

Return to the opening prologue of this group of modules, which describes veteran Arthur Boorman and his desire to overcome his disability. Using your knowledge of motivation and emotion, consider the following questions:

1. How could Boorman's determination to walk unassisted again after 15 years be explained by each of the different approaches to motivation?
2. What factors do you think likely played a role in Boorman's becoming so obese?
3. Does Boorman seem to have a high need for achievement? Why or why not?
4. Many people who watch the YouTube video depicting Boorman's transformation become very emotional. Why do you think that is?

VISUAL SUMMARY 8 Motivation and Emotion

MODULE 24 Explaining Motivation

Motivation: The factors that direct and energize the behavior of humans and other organisms

The major approaches to motivation

Instinct People and animals are born with preprogrammed sets of behaviors essential to their survival.

Drive reduction When some basic biological requirement is lacking, a drive is produced.

Arousal People seek an optimal level of stimulation. If the level of stimulation is too high, they act to reduce it; if it is too low, they act to increase it.

Incentive External rewards direct and energize behavior.

Cognitive Thoughts, beliefs, expectations, and goals direct motivation.

Hierarchy of needs Needs form a hierarchy; before higher-order needs are met, lower-order needs must be fulfilled.

MODULE 25 Human Needs and Motivation

Motivation Behind Hunger and Eating

Obesity has reached epidemic proportions

- Factors that affect eating
  - Biological factors
  - Social factors and learned eating behaviors
- Eating disorders
  - Anorexia nervosa
  - Bulimia

Sexual Motivation

- Puberty: Hormone secretion begins
- Men and women differ in hormone production

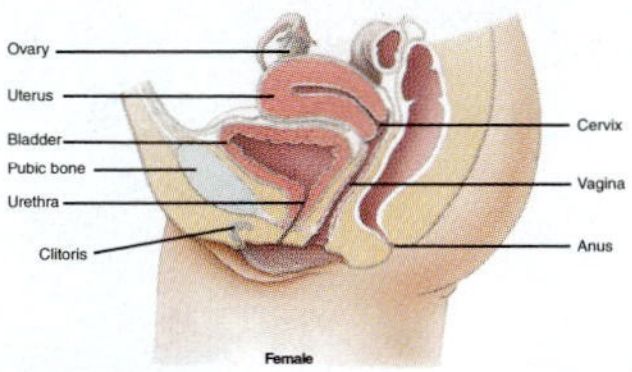

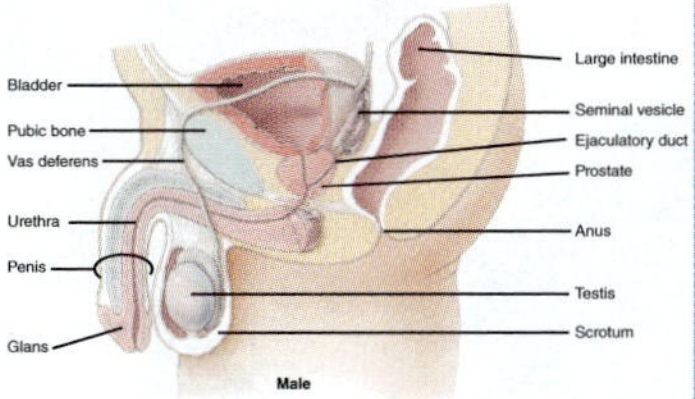

- Masturbation: high incidence
- Heterosexuality: sexual attraction to the other sex
- Premarital sex: decline in double standard
- Homosexuality: sexual attraction to one's own sex
- Bisexuality: sexual attraction to both sexes
- Transsexualism: people who feel they were born with the other gender's body

Needs for Achievement, Affiliation, and Power:

Striving for excellence
Maintaining relationships
Influencing others

MODULE 26 Understanding Emotional Experiences

Functions of Emotions

- Prepare us for action
- Shape our future behavior
- Help us to interact more effectively with others

Theories of Emotions

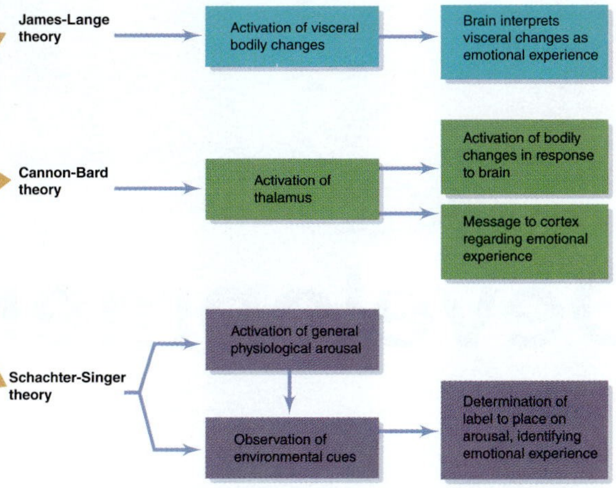

9 Development

Learning Outcomes for Chapter 9

MODULE 27

LO 27-1 How do psychologists study the degree to which development is an interaction of hereditary and environmental factors?

LO 27-2 What is the nature of development before birth?

LO 27-3 What factors affect a child during the mother's pregnancy?

MODULE 28

LO 28-1 What are the major competencies of newborns?

LO 28-2 What are the milestones of physical and social development during childhood?

LO 28-3 How does cognitive development proceed during childhood?

MODULE 29

LO 29-1 What major physical, social, and cognitive transitions characterize adolescence?

MODULE 30

LO 30-1 What are the principal kinds of physical, social, and intellectual changes that occur in early and middle adulthood, and what are their causes?

LO 30-2 How does the reality of late adulthood differ from the stereotypes about that period?

LO 30-3 How can we adjust to death?

Prologue *Life Goes On*

In June of 2013, an elderly man in a hospital in Japan succumbed to complications from pneumonia and passed away. But this was no ordinary elderly man: At 116 years old, Jiroemon Kimura was not only the world's oldest living person, he was also the oldest person who had ever lived whose age could be verified. Kimura attributed his longevity to proper eating habits, preferring light and healthy foods. A former postal worker, Kimura was so elderly that he retired from his career in 1962—enjoying more than 50 years of retirement! By the time he died, his family included 7 children, 14 grandchildren, 25 great-grandchildren, and 14 great-great grandchildren.

Looking Ahead

Although some people dread growing older, others, like Jiroemon Kimura, who was born when Queen Victoria still reigned in Britain, embrace it, understanding that age brings with it the benefits of a lifetime of accumulated memories and wisdom.

Developmental psychology is the branch of psychology that studies the patterns of growth and change that occur throughout life. It deals with issues ranging from new ways of conceiving children, to learning how to raise children most sensibly, to understanding the milestones of life that we all face.

Developmental psychologists study the interaction between the unfolding of biologically predetermined patterns of behavior and a constantly changing, dynamic environment. They ask how our genetic background affects our behavior throughout our lives and whether heredity limits our potential. Similarly, they seek to understand the way in which the environment works with—or against—our genetic capabilities, how the world we live in affects our development, and how we can be encouraged to reach our full potential.

We begin by examining the approaches psychologists use to study development change across the life span. Then we consider the very start of development, beginning with conception and the nine months of life before birth. We look at both genetic and environmental influences on the unborn individual and the way they can affect behavior throughout the remainder of the life cycle.

Next, we examine development that occurs after birth: the enormous and rapid growth that takes place during the early stages of life and the physical, social, and cognitive change throughout infancy, toddlerhood, and middle childhood. We then move on to development from adolescence through adulthood. We end with a discussion of the ways in which people prepare themselves for death.

MODULE 27

Nature and Nurture: The Enduring Developmental Issue

How many bald, six-foot-six, 250-pound volunteer firefighters in New Jersey wear droopy mustaches, aviator-style eyeglasses, and a key ring on the right side of the belt? The answer is two: Gerald Levey and Mark Newman. They are twins who were separated at birth. Each twin did not even know the other existed until they were reunited—in a fire station—by a fellow firefighter who knew Newman and was startled to see his double, Levey, at a firefighters' convention.

The lives of the twins, although separate, took remarkably similar paths. Levey went to college and studied forestry; Newman planned to study forestry in college but instead took a job trimming trees. Both had jobs in supermarkets. One had a job installing sprinkler systems; the other installed fire alarms.

Both men are unmarried and find the same kind of woman—"tall, slender, long hair"—attractive. They share similar hobbies and enjoy hunting, fishing, going to the beach, and watching old John Wayne movies and professional wrestling. Both like Chinese food and drink the same brand of beer. Their mannerisms are also similar—for example, each one throws his head back when he laughs. And, of course, there is one more thing: They share a passion for fighting fires.

Learning Outcomes

LO 27-1 How do psychologists study the degree to which development is an interaction of hereditary and environmental factors?

LO 27-2 What is the nature of development before birth?

LO 27-3 What factors affect a child during the mother's pregnancy?

The similarities we see in twins Gerald Levey and Mark Newman vividly raise one of the fundamental questions posed by **developmental psychology,** the study of the patterns of growth and change that occur throughout life. The question is this: How can we distinguish between the *environmental* causes of behavior (the influence of parents, siblings, family, friends, schooling, nutrition, and all the other experiences to which a child is exposed) and *hereditary* causes (those based on an individual's genetic makeup that influence growth and development throughout life)? This question embodies the **nature-nurture issue.** In this context, nature refers to hereditary factors, and nurture refers to environmental influences.

developmental psychology The branch of psychology that studies the patterns of growth and change that occur throughout life.

nature-nurture issue The issue of the degree to which environment and heredity influence behavior.

Although the question was first posed as a nature-*versus*-nurture issue, developmental psychologists today agree that *both* nature and nurture interact to produce specific developmental patterns and outcomes. Consequently, the question has evolved into this: *How and to what degree* do environment and heredity both produce their effects? No one develops free of environmental influences or without being affected by his or her inherited *genetic makeup.* However, the debate over the comparative influence of the two factors remains active; different approaches and different theories of development emphasize the environment or heredity to a greater or lesser degree (Belsky & Pluess, 2009; Perovic & Radenovic, 2011; Gruber, 2013).

For example, some developmental theories rely on basic psychological principles of learning and stress the role learning plays in producing changes in a developing child's behavior. Such theories emphasize the role of the environment in development. In contrast, other developmental theories emphasize the influence of one's physiological makeup and functioning on development. Such theories stress the role of heredity and

Gerald Levey and Mark Newman.

maturation—the unfolding of biologically predetermined patterns of behavior—in producing developmental change. Maturation can be seen, for instance, in the development of sex characteristics (such as breasts and body hair) that occurs at the start of adolescence.

Furthermore, the work of *behavioral geneticists*, who study the effects of heredity on behavior, and the theories of evolutionary psychologists, who identify behavior patterns that result from our genetic inheritance, have influenced developmental psychologists. Behavioral geneticists are finding increasing evidence that cognitive abilities, personality traits, sexual orientation, and psychological disorders are determined to some extent by genetic factors (Livesley & Jang, 2008; Vernon et al., 2008; Schermer et al., 2011).

Behavioral genetics lies at the heart of the nature–nurture question. Although no one would argue that our behavior is determined *solely* by inherited factors, evidence collected by behavioral geneticists does suggest that our genetic inheritance predisposes us to respond in particular ways to our environment, and even to seek out particular kinds of environments (Davis, Haworth, & Plomin, 2009; Bienvenu, Davydow, & Kendler, 2011; Barnes & Jacobs, 2013).

Despite their differences over theory, developmental psychologists concur on some points. They agree that genetic factors not only provide the potential for specific behaviors or traits to emerge, but also place limitations on the emergence of such behavior or traits. For instance, heredity defines people's general level of intelligence and sets an upper limit that—regardless of the quality of the environment—people cannot exceed. Heredity also places limits on physical abilities; humans simply cannot run at a speed of 60 miles an hour or grow as tall as 10 feet, no matter the quality of their environment (Dodge, 2004; Pinker, 2004).

Figure 1 lists some of the characteristics most affected by heredity. As you consider these items, it is important to keep in mind that these characteristics are not *entirely* determined by heredity, for environmental factors also play a role.

Developmental psychologists also agree that in most instances environmental factors play a critical role in enabling people to reach the potential capabilities that their genetic background makes possible. If Albert Einstein had received no intellectual stimulation as a child and had not been sent to school, it is unlikely that he would have reached his genetic potential. Similarly, a great athlete such as baseball star Derek Jeter would have been unlikely to display much physical skill if he had not been raised in an environment that nurtured his innate talent and gave him the opportunity to train and perfect his natural abilities.

Clearly, the relationship between heredity and environment is complex. Therefore, developmental psychologists typically take an *interactionist* position on the nature–nurture issue by suggesting that a combination of hereditary and environmental factors

Study Alert

The nature–nurture issue is a key question that is pervasive throughout the field of psychology. It explores how and to what degree environment and heredity produce their joint effects.

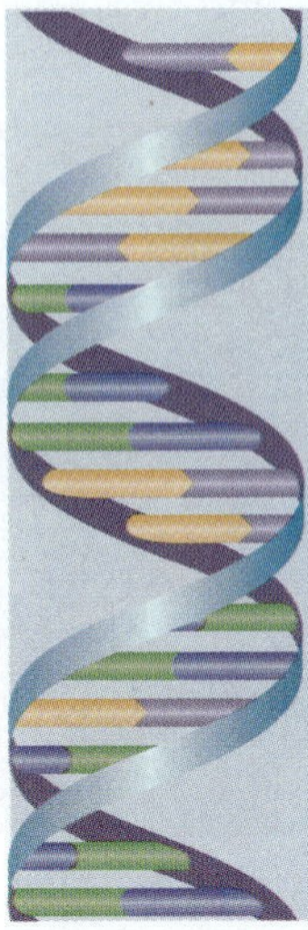

Physical Characteristics	Intellectual Characteristics	Emotional Characteristics and Disorders
Height	Memory	Shyness
Weight	Intelligence	Extraversion
Obesity	Age of language acquisition	Emotionality
Tone of voice	Reading disability	Neuroticism
Blood pressure	Mental retardation	Schizophrenia
Tooth decay		Anxiety
Athletic ability		Alcoholism
Firmness of handshake		
Age of death		
Activity level		

FIGURE 1 Characteristics influenced significantly by genetic factors. Although these characteristics have strong genetic components, they are also affected by environmental factors.

influences development. Developmental psychologists face the challenge of identifying the relative strength of each of these influences on the individual as well as that of identifying the specific changes that occur over the course of development (McGregor & Capone, 2004; Moffitt, Caspi, & Rutter, 2006).

Determining the Relative Influence of Nature and Nurture

Developmental psychologists use several approaches to determine the relative influence of genetic and environmental factors on behavior. In one approach, researchers can experimentally control the genetic makeup of laboratory animals by carefully breeding them for specific traits. For instance, by observing animals with identical genetic backgrounds placed in varied environments, researchers can learn the effects of specific kinds of environmental stimulation. Although researchers must be careful when generalizing the findings of nonhuman research to a human population, findings from animal research provide important information that cannot be obtained for ethical reasons by using human participants.

Human twins serve as another important source of information about the relative effects of genetic and environmental factors. If **identical twins** (those who are genetically identical) display different patterns of development, those differences have to be attributed to variations in the environment in which the twins were raised. The most useful data come from identical twins (such as Gerald Levey and Mark Newman) who are adopted at birth by different sets of adoptive parents and raised apart in differing environments. Studies of nontwin siblings who are raised in totally different environments also shed some light on the issue. Because they have relatively similar genetic backgrounds, siblings who show similarities as adults provide strong evidence for the importance of heredity (Vitaro, Brendgen, & Arseneault, 2009; Sternberg, 2002, 2011).

identical twins Twins who are genetically identical.

Researchers can also take the opposite tack. Instead of concentrating on people with similar genetic backgrounds who are raised in different environments, they may consider people raised in similar environments who have totally dissimilar genetic backgrounds. For example, if they find similar courses of development in two adopted children who have different genetic backgrounds and have been raised in the same family, they have evidence for the importance of environmental influences on development. Moreover, psychologists can carry out research involving animals with dissimilar genetic backgrounds; by experimentally varying the environment in which they are raised, they can determine the influence of environmental factors (independent of heredity) on development (Petrill & Deater-Deckard, 2004; Beam & Turkheimer, 2013).

Developmental Research Techniques

Because of the demands of measuring behavioral change across different ages, developmental researchers use several unique methods. The most frequently used, **cross-sectional research,** compares people of different ages at the same point in time. Cross-sectional studies provide information about differences in development between different age groups (Creasey, 2005; Huijie, 2006).

cross-sectional research A research method that compares people of different ages at the same point in time.

Suppose, for instance, we were interested in the development of intellectual ability in adulthood. To carry out a cross-sectional study, we might compare a sample of 25-, 45-, and 65-year-olds who all take the same IQ test. We then can determine whether average IQ test scores differ in each age group.

Cross-sectional research has limitations, however. For instance, we cannot be sure that the differences in IQ scores we might find in our example are due to age differences alone.

Instead, the scores may reflect differences in the educational attainment of the cohorts represented. A *cohort* is a group of people who grow up at similar times, in similar places, and in similar conditions. In the case of IQ differences, any age differences we find in a cross-sectional study may reflect educational differences among the cohorts studied: People in the older age group may belong to a cohort that was less likely to attend college than were the people in the younger groups.

longitudinal research A research method that investigates behavior as participants get older.

A longitudinal study, the second major research strategy developmental psychologists use, provides one way around this problem. **Longitudinal research** traces the behavior of one or more participants as the participants age. Longitudinal studies assess *change* in behavior over time, whereas cross-sectional studies assess *differences* among groups of people.

For instance, consider how we might investigate intellectual development during adulthood by using a longitudinal research strategy. First, we might give an IQ test to a group of 25-year-olds. We'd then come back to the same people 20 years later and retest them at age 45. Finally, we'd return to them once more when they were 65 years old and test them again.

Study Alert

Be sure to be able to distinguish the two different types of developmental research—cross-sectional (comparing people of different ages at the same time) and longitudinal (studying participants as they age).

By examining changes at several points in time, we can see how individuals develop. Clearly, though, longitudinal research requires a significant expenditure of time as the researcher waits for the participants to get older. In addition, participants who begin a study at an early age may drop out, move away, or even die as the research continues. Moreover, participants who take the same test at several points in time may become "test-wise" and perform better each time they take it because they have become more familiar with the test. Still, longitudinal research is an important technique of developmental researchers.

Prenatal Development: Conception to Birth

Leah and John Howard's joy at learning Leah was pregnant turned to anxiety when Leah's doctor discovered that her brother had died from Duchenne muscular dystrophy (DMD) at age 12. The disease, the doctor explained, was an X-linked inherited disorder. If Leah turned out to be a carrier, there was a 50 percent chance that the baby would inherit the disease if it were male. The doctor advised them to have an ultrasound to determine the baby's sex. It turned out to be a boy.

The Howards faced new options. The doctor could take a chorion villus sampling now or wait a month and perform an amniocentesis. Both carried a very low risk for miscarriage. Leah chose amniocentesis, but the results were inconclusive. The doctor then suggested a fetal muscle biopsy to confirm the presence or lack of the muscle protein dystrophin. No dystrophin signaled DMD. The risk of miscarriage, however, was not inconsiderable.

Four months pregnant at this point and tired of the worries and tears, Leah and John decided to take their chances and look forward to their baby's birth.

The Howards may never know if they made the right choice. But their case shows the difficult choices that parents may encounter due to our increasing understanding of life spent inside a mother's womb.

Yet, our knowledge of the biology of *conception*–when a male's sperm cell penetrates a female's egg cell–and its aftermath makes the start of life no less of a miracle. Let's consider how an individual is created by looking first at the genetic endowment that a child receives at the moment of conception.

THE BASICS OF GENETICS

chromosomes Rod-shaped structures that contain all basic hereditary information.

The one-cell entity established at conception contains 23 pairs of **chromosomes,** rod-shaped structures that contain all basic hereditary information. One member of each pair is from the mother, and the other is from the father.

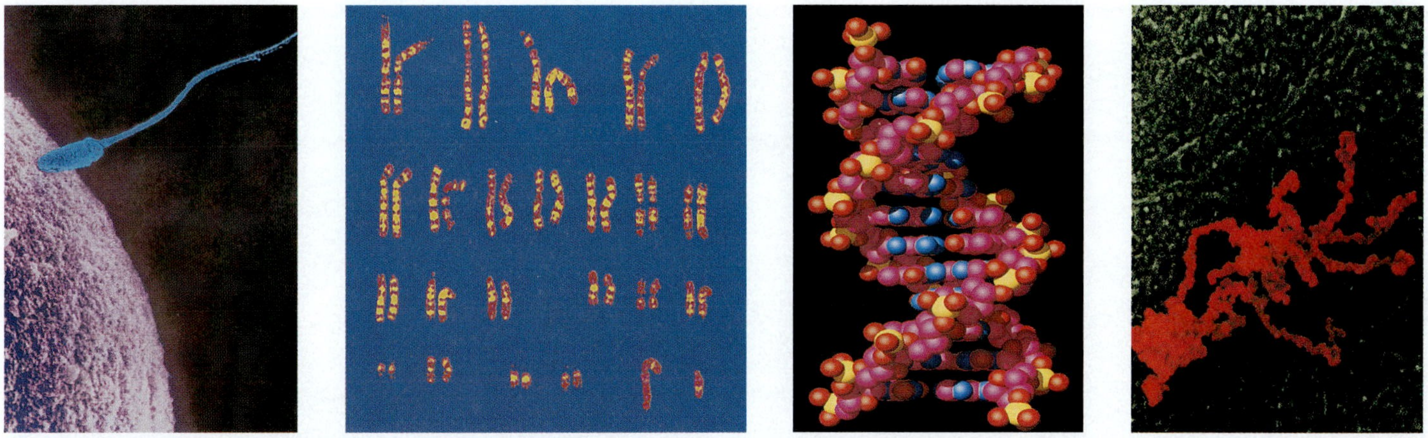

(a) Conception (b) 23 pairs of chromosomes (c) DNA sequence (d) Genes

FIGURE 2 Every individual's characteristics are determined by the individual's specific genetic information. (a) At the moment of conception, (b) humans receive 23 pairs of chromosomes, half from the mother and half from the father. (c) These chromosomes are made up of coils of DNA. (d) Each chromosome contains thousands of genes that "program" the future development of the body.

Each chromosome contains thousands of **genes**–smaller units through which genetic information is transmitted. Either individually or in combination, genes produce each person's particular characteristics. Composed of sequences of *DNA (deoxyribonucleic acid)* molecules, genes are the biological equivalent of "software" that programs the future development of all parts of the body's hardware. Humans have some 25,000 different genes (see Figure 2).

genes The parts of the chromosomes through which genetic information is transmitted.

Some genes control the development of systems common to all members of the human species–the heart, circulatory system, brain, lungs, and so forth; others shape the characteristics that make each human unique, such as facial configuration, height, and eye color. The child's sex is also determined by a particular combination of genes. Specifically, a child inherits an X chromosome from its mother and either an X or a Y chromosome from its father. When it receives an XX combination, it is a female; with an XY combination, it develops as a male. Male development is triggered by a single gene on the Y chromosome; without the presence of that specific gene, the individual will develop as a female.

Study Alert

It's important to understand the basic building blocks of genetics: chromosomes, which contain genes, which in turn are composed of sequences of DNA.

As behavioral geneticists have discovered, genes are also at least partially responsible for a wide variety of personal characteristics, including cognitive abilities, personality traits, and psychological disorders. Of course, few of these characteristics are determined by a single gene. Instead, most traits result from a combination of multiple genes that operate together with environmental influences (Haberstick et al., 2005; Ramus, 2006; Armbruster et al., 2011).

THE HUMAN GENOME PROJECT

Our understanding of genetics took a giant leap forward in 2001, when scientists were able to map the specific location and sequence of every human gene as part of the massive *Human Genome Project*. The accomplishment was one of the most important in the history of biology (International Human Genome Sequencing Consortium, 2003; Grigorenko & Dozier, 2013).

The success of the Human Genome Project started a revolution in health care because scientists can identify the particular genes responsible for genetically caused disorders. It is already leading not only to the identification of risk factors in children, but also to the development of new treatments for physical and psychological disorders.

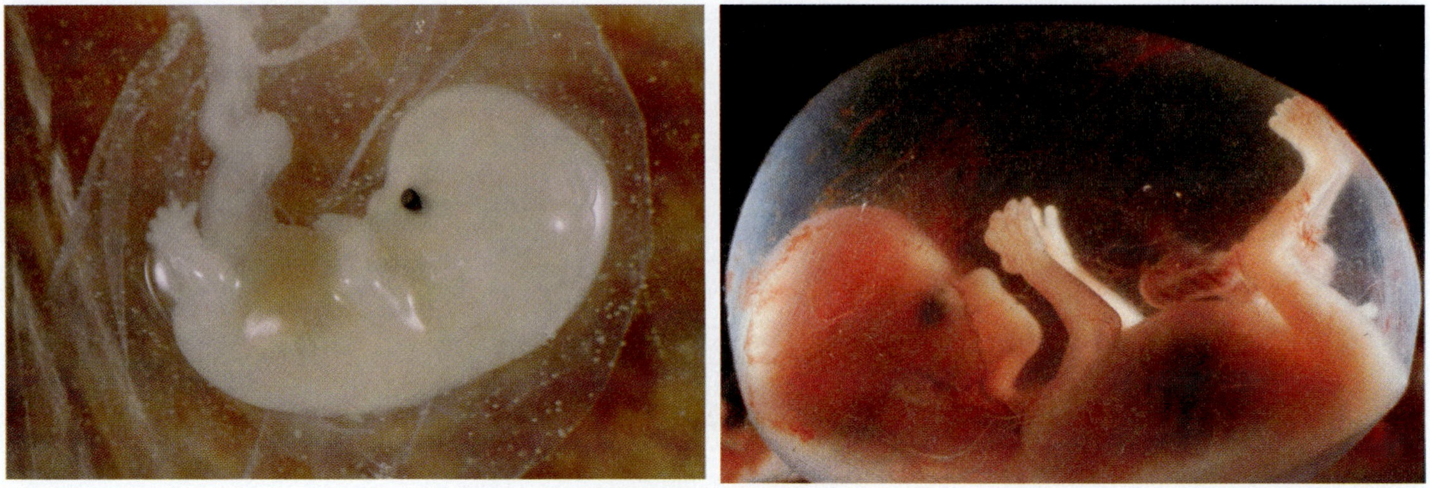

These remarkable photos of live fetuses display the degree of physical development at prenatal ages 4 and 15 weeks.

THE EARLIEST DEVELOPMENT

zygote The new cell formed by the union of an egg and sperm.

When an egg becomes fertilized by the sperm, the resulting one-celled entity, called a **zygote,** immediately begins to develop. The zygote starts out as a microscopic speck. Three days after fertilization, though, the zygote increases to around 32 cells; within a week it has grown to 100–150 cells. These first two weeks are known as the *germinal period.*

embryo A developed zygote that has a heart, a brain, and other organs.

Two weeks after conception, the developing individual enters the *embryonic period,* which lasts from week 2 through week 8; he or she is now called an **embryo.** As an embryo develops through an intricate, preprogrammed process of cell division, it grows 10,000 times larger by 4 weeks of age and attains a length of about one-fifth of an inch. At this point it has developed a rudimentary beating heart, a brain, an intestinal tract, and a number of other organs. Although all these organs are at a primitive stage of development, they are clearly recognizable. Moreover, by week 8, the embryo is about an inch long and has discernible arms, legs, and a face.

fetus A developing individual from 8 weeks after conception until birth.

From week 8 and continuing until birth, the developing individual enters the *fetal period* and is called a **fetus.** At the start of this period, it begins to respond to touch; it bends its fingers when touched on the hand. At 16 to 18 weeks, its movements become strong enough for the mother to sense them. At the same time, hair may begin to grow on its head, and the facial features become similar to those the child will display at birth. The major organs begin functioning, although the fetus could not be kept alive outside the mother. In addition, a lifetime's worth of brain neurons are produced–although it is unclear whether the brain is capable of thinking at this early stage.

age of viability The point at which a fetus can survive if born prematurely.

Within the womb the fetus continues to develop before birth. It begins to grow fatty deposits under the skin, and it gains weight. The fetus reaches the **age of viability,** the point at which it can survive if born prematurely, at about prenatal age 22 weeks. By week 24, a fetus has many of the characteristics it will display as a newborn. In fact, when an infant is born prematurely at this age, it can open and close its eyes; suck; cry; look up, down, and around; and even grasp objects placed in its hands.

At prenatal age 28 weeks, the fetus weighs less than 3 pounds and is about 16 inches long. It may be capable of learning: One study found that the infants of mothers who had repeatedly read aloud *The Cat in the Hat* by Dr. Seuss before the infants' birth preferred the sound of that particular story to other stories after they were born (Spence & DeCasper, 1982; Del Giudice, 2011; Moon, Lagercrantz, & Kuhl, 2013).

Before birth, a fetus passes through several *sensitive periods.* A sensitive period is the time when organisms are particularly susceptible to certain kinds of stimuli. For example, fetuses are especially affected by their mothers' use of drugs during certain sensitive periods before birth. If they are exposed to a particular drug before or after the sensitive period, it may have relatively little impact; if exposure comes during a sensitive period, the impact will be significant (Konig, 2005; Werker & Tees, 2005; Uylings, 2006).

Study Alert

Sensitive (or critical) periods, which can occur before or after birth, are important because they indicate the time that organisms are particularly susceptible to damage that may affect them for the rest of their lives.

From the perspective of . . .

An Educator How would you use your knowledge of sensitive periods in language development to improve students' learning? Would you want to teach children more than one language during this time?

Sensitive periods can also occur after birth. Some language specialists suggest, for instance, that there is a period in which children are particularly receptive to developing language. If children are not exposed to appropriate linguistic stimuli, their language development may be impaired (Sohr-Preston & Scaramella, 2006; Innocenti, 2007).

In the final weeks of pregnancy, the fetus continues to gain weight and grow. At the end of the normal 38 weeks of pregnancy, the fetus typically weighs 7 pounds and is about 20 inches in length. However, the story is different for *preterm infants,* who are born before week 38. Because they have not been able to develop fully, they are at higher risk for illness, future problems, and even death. For infants who have been in the womb for more than 30 weeks, the prospects are relatively good. However, for those born before week 30, the story is often less positive. Such newborns, who may weigh as little as 2 pounds at birth, are in grave danger because they have immature organs; they have less than a 50-50 chance of survival. If they do survive–and it takes extraordinarily heroic (and expensive) medical intervention to assure this–they may later experience significant developmental delays.

GENETIC INFLUENCES ON THE FETUS

The process of fetal growth that we have just described reflects normal development, which occurs in 95–98% of all pregnancies. Some individuals are less fortunate; in the remaining 2–5% of cases, children are born with serious birth defects. A major cause of such defects is faulty genes or chromosomes. Here are some of the more common genetic and chromosomal difficulties.

- *Phenylketonuria (PKU).* A child born with the inherited disease phenylketonuria cannot produce an enzyme that is required for normal development. This deficiency results in an accumulation of poisons that eventually cause profound intellectual disability. The disease is treatable, however, if it is caught early. Most infants today are routinely tested for PKU, and children with the disorder can be placed on a special diet that allows them to develop normally (Ievers-Landis et al., 2005; Christ, Steiner, & Grange, 2006; Widaman, 2009).
- *Sickle-cell anemia.* About 10% of the African-American population has the possibility of passing on sickle-cell anemia, a disease that gets its name from the

abnormally shaped red blood cells it causes. Children with the disease may have episodes of pain, yellowish eyes, stunted growth, and vision problems (Selove, 2007; Wills, 2013).

- *Tay-Sachs disease.* Children born with Tay-Sachs disease, a disorder most often found in Jews of Eastern European ancestry, usually die by age 3 or 4 because of the body's inability to break down fat. If both parents carry the genetic defect that produces the fatal illness, their child has a 1 in 4 chance of being born with the disease (Leib et al., 2005; Weinstein, 2007).
- *Down syndrome.* Down syndrome, one of the causes of intellectual disability, occurs when the zygote receives an extra chromosome at the moment of conception. Down syndrome is often related to the mother's age; mothers over 35 and younger than 18 stand a higher risk than other women of having a child with the syndrome (Roizen & Patterson, 2003; Sherman et al., 2007).

PRENATAL ENVIRONMENTAL INFLUENCES

teratogens Environmental agents such as a drug, chemical, virus, or other factor that produce a birth defect.

Genetic factors are not the only causes of difficulties in fetal development. Environmental influences–the *nurture* part of the nature–nurture equation–also affect the fetus. Some of the more profound consequences are brought about by **teratogens,** environmental agents such as a drug, chemical, virus, or other factor that produce a birth defect. Among the major prenatal environmental influences on the fetus are the following:

- *Mother's nutrition.* What a mother eats during her pregnancy can have important implications for the health of her baby. Seriously undernourished mothers cannot provide adequate nutrition to a growing fetus, and they are likely to give birth to underweight babies. Poorly nourished babies are also more susceptible to disease, and a lack of nourishment may have an adverse impact on their mental development (Najman et al., 2004; Everette, 2008; Nyaradi et al., 2013).
- *Mother's illness.* Even minor illnesses that a mother contracts during the early months of pregnancy can have devastating consequences for a developing fetus. For example, if pregnant women contract rubella (German measles), syphilis, diabetes, or high blood pressure, each disease may produce permanent, lifelong effects on the fetus (Nesheim et al., 2004; Magoni et al., 2005).
- *Mother's emotional state.* A mother's emotional state affects her baby. Mothers who are anxious and tense during the last months of their pregnancies are more apt to have irritable infants who sleep and eat poorly. The reason? The autonomic nervous system of the fetus becomes especially sensitive as a result of chemical changes produced by the mother's emotional state (Hollins, 2007; Kumari & Joshi, 2013).
- *Mother's use of drugs.* Mothers who take illegal, physically addictive drugs such as cocaine run the risk of giving birth to babies who are similarly addicted. Their newborns suffer painful withdrawal symptoms and sometimes show permanent physical and mental impairment. Even legal drugs taken by a pregnant woman (who may not know that she has become pregnant) can have a tragic effect (Ikonomidou et al., 2000; Schechter, Finkelstein, & Koren, 2005; Singer & Richardson, 2011).
- *Alcohol.* Alcohol is extremely dangerous to fetal development. For example, 1 out of every 750 infants is born with *fetal alcohol syndrome* (*FAS*), a condition resulting in below-average intelligence, growth delays, and facial deformities. FAS is now the primary preventable cause of intellectual disability. Even mothers who use small amounts of alcohol during pregnancy place their child at risk. *Fetal alcohol effects* (*FAE*) is a condition in which children display some although not all of the problems of FAS due to their mother's consumption of alcohol during pregnancy (Henderson, Kesmodel, & Gray, 2007; Niccols, 2007; Murthy et al., 2009).

Environmental Factor	Possible Effect on Prenatal Development
Rubella (German measles)	Blindness, deafness, heart abnormalities, stillbirth
Syphilis	Mental retardation, physical deformities, maternal miscarriage
Addictive drugs	Low birth weight, addiction of infant to drug, with possible death after birth from withdrawal
Nicotine	Premature birth, low birth weight and length
Alcohol	Mental retardation, lower-than-average birth weight, small head, limb deformities
Radiation from X-rays	Physical deformities, mental retardation
Inadequate diet	Reduction in growth of brain, smaller-than-average weight and length at birth
Mother's age—younger than 18 at birth of child	Premature birth, increased incidence of Down syndrome
Mother's age—older than 35 at birth of child	Increased incidence of Down syndrome
DES (diethylstilbestrol)	Reproductive difficulties and increased incidence of genital cancer in children of mothers who were given DES during pregnancy to prevent miscarriage
AIDS	Possible spread of AIDS virus to infant; facial deformities; growth failure
Accutane	Mental retardation and physical deformities

FIGURE 3 A variety of environmental factors can play a role in prenatal development.

- *Nicotine use.* Pregnant mothers who smoke put their children at considerable risk. Smoking while pregnant can lead to miscarriage and infant death. For children who do survive, the negative consequences of mother's tobacco use can last a lifetime (Shea & Steiner, 2008; Rogers, 2009; Magee et al., 2013).

Several other environmental factors have an impact on the child before and during birth (see Figure 3). Keep in mind, however, that although we have been discussing the influences of genetics and environment separately, neither factor works alone. Furthermore, despite the emphasis here on some of the ways in which development can go wrong, the vast majority of births occur without difficulty. And in most instances, subsequent development also proceeds normally.

RECAP/EVALUATE/RETHINK

RECAP

LO 27-1 How do psychologists study the degree to which development is an interaction of hereditary and environmental factors?

- Developmental psychology studies growth and change throughout life. One fundamental question is how much developmental change is due to heredity and how much is due to environment–the nature-nurture issue. Heredity seems to define the upper limits of our growth and change, whereas the environment affects the degree to which the upper limits are reached.
- Cross-sectional research compares people of different ages with one another at the same point in time. In contrast, longitudinal research traces the behavior of one or more participants as the participants become older. Finally, sequential research combines the two methods by examining several different age groups at several points in time.

LO 27-2 What is the nature of development before birth?

- At the moment of conception, a male's sperm cell and a female's egg cell unite; each contributes to the new individual's genetic makeup. The union of sperm and egg produces a zygote, which contains 23 pairs of chromosomes; one member of each pair comes from the father and the other comes from the mother.
- Each chromosome contains genes through which genetic information is transmitted. Genes, which are composed of DNA sequences, are the "software" that programs the future development of the body's hardware.
- Genes affect not only physical attributes, but also a wide array of personal characteristics such as cognitive abilities, personality traits, and psychological disorders.
- After two weeks the zygote becomes an embryo. By week 8, the embryo is called a fetus and is responsive to touch and other stimulation. At about week 22 it reaches the age of viability, which means it may survive if born prematurely. A fetus is normally born after 38 weeks of pregnancy; it weighs around 7 pounds and measures about 20 inches.

LO 27-3 What factors can affect a child during the mother's pregnancy?

- Genetic abnormalities produce birth defects such as phenylketonuria (PKU), sickle-cell anemia, Tay-Sachs disease, and Down syndrome.
- Among the environmental influences on fetal growth are the mother's nutrition, illnesses, and drug intake.

EVALUATE

1. Developmental psychologists are interested in the effects of both __________ and __________ on development.
2. Environment and heredity both influence development with genetic potentials generally establishing limits on environmental influences. True or false?
3. By observing genetically similar animals in differing environments, we can increase our understanding of the influences of hereditary and environmental factors in humans. True or false?
4. __________ research studies the same individuals over a period of time, whereas __________ __________ research studies people of different ages at the same time.
5. Match each of the following terms with its definition:

1. Zygote	**a.** Smallest unit through which genetic information is passed
2. Gene	**b.** Fertilized egg
3. Chromosome	**c.** Rod-shaped structure containing genetic information

6. Specific kinds of growth must take place during a __________ period if the embryo is to develop normally.

RETHINK

1. When researchers find similarities in development between very different cultures, what implications might such findings have for the nature-nurture issue?
2. Consider the factors that might determine when a child learns to walk. What kinds of environmental influences might be involved? What kinds of genetic influences might be involved?

Answers to Evaluate Questions

1. heredity (or nature), environment (or nurture); **2.** true; **3.** true; **4.** Longitudinal, cross-sectional; **5.** 1-b, 2-a, 2-c; **6.** sensitive (or critical)

KEY TERMS

developmental psychology
nature-nurture issue
identical twins
cross-sectional research
longitudinal research
chromosomes
genes
zygote
embryo
fetus
age of viability
teratogens

MODULE 28

Infancy and Childhood

> His head was molded into a long melon shape and came to a point at the back. . . . He was covered with a thick greasy white material known as "vernix," which made him slippery to hold and also allowed him to slip easily through the birth canal. In addition to a shock of black hair on his head, his body was covered with dark, fine hair known as "lanugo." His ears, his back, his shoulders, and even his cheeks were furry. . . . His skin was wrinkled and quite loose, ready to scale in creased places such as his feet and hands. . . . His ears were pressed to his head in unusual positions—one ear was matted firmly forward on his cheek. His nose was flattened and pushed to one side by the squeeze as he came through the pelvis. (Brazelton, 1969, p. 3)

What kind of creature is this? Although the description hardly fits that of the adorable babies seen in advertisements for baby food, we are in fact talking about a normal, completely developed child just after the moment of birth. Called a **neonate,** a newborn arrives in the world in a form that hardly meets the standards of beauty against which we typically measure babies. Yet ask any parents: Nothing is more beautiful or exciting than the first glimpse of their newborn.

Learning Outcomes

LO 28-1 What are the major competencies of newborns?

LO 28-2 What are the milestones of physical and social development during childhood?

LO 28-3 How does cognitive development proceed during childhood?

neonate A newborn child.

The Extraordinary Newborn

Several factors cause a neonate's strange appearance. The trip through the mother's birth canal may have squeezed the incompletely formed bones of the skull together and squashed the nose into the head. The skin secretes *vernix,* a white greasy covering, for protection before birth, and the baby may have *lanugo,* a soft fuzz, over the entire body for a similar purpose. The infant's eyelids may be puffy with an accumulation of fluids because of the upside-down position during birth.

reflexes Unlearned, involuntary responses that occur automatically in the presence of certain stimuli.

All these features change during the first 2 weeks of life as the neonate takes on a more familiar appearance. Even more impressive are the capabilities a neonate begins to display from the moment of birth—capabilities that grow at an astounding rate over the ensuing months.

REFLEXES

A neonate is born with a number of **reflexes**—unlearned, involuntary responses that occur automatically in the presence of certain stimuli. Critical for survival, many of those reflexes unfold naturally as part of an infant's ongoing maturation. The *rooting reflex,* for instance, causes neonates to turn their heads toward things that touch their cheeks—such as the mother's nipple or a bottle. Similarly, a *sucking reflex* prompts infants to suck at things that touch their lips. Among other reflexes are a *gag reflex* (to clear the throat), the *startle reflex* (a series of movements in which an infant flings out

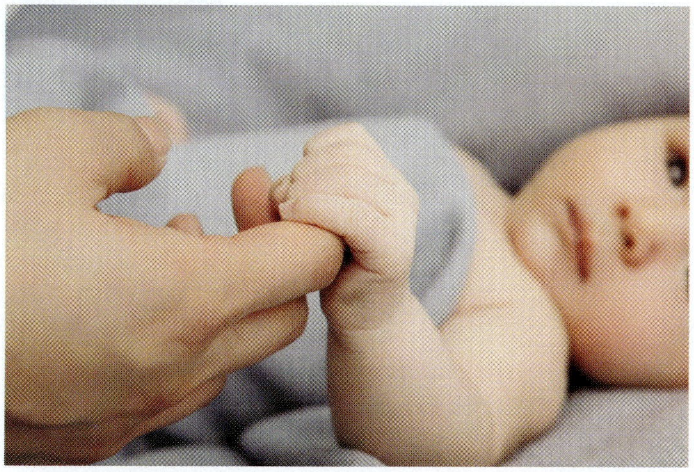

Many of the reflexes that a neonate is born with are critical for survival and unfold naturally as a part of the infant's ongoing maturation. Do you think humans have more or fewer reflexes than other animals?

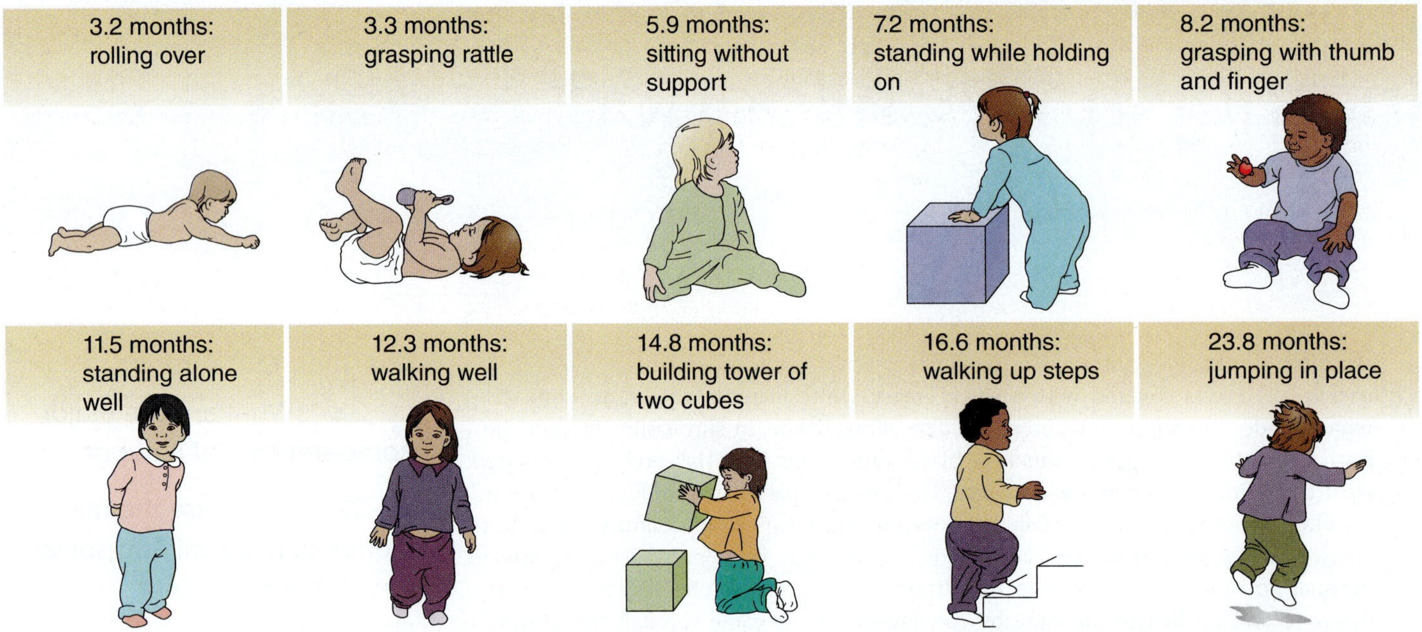

FIGURE 1 Although at birth a neonate can make only jerky, limited voluntary movements, during the first year of life the ability to move independently grows enormously. The ages indicate the time when 50% of children are able to perform each skill. Remember, however, that the time when each skill appears can vary considerably. For example, 25% of children are able to walk well at age 11 months; by 15 months 90% of children are walking well. (Source: Adapted from Frankenburg et al., 1992.)

Study Alert

The basic reflexes—unlearned, involuntary responses—include the rooting reflex, the sucking reflex, the gag reflex, the startle reflex, and the Babinski reflex.

the arms, fans the fingers, and arches the back in response to a sudden noise), and the *Babinski reflex* (a baby's toes fan out when the outer edge of the sole of the foot is stroked).

Infants lose these primitive reflexes after the first few months of life and replace them with more complex and organized behaviors. Although at birth a neonate is capable of only jerky, limited voluntary movements, the ability to move independently grows enormously during the first year of life. The typical baby rolls over by the age of about 3 months, sits without support at about 6 months, stands alone at about 11 months, and walks at just over a year old. Not only does the ability to make large-scale movements improve during this time, but fine-muscle movements also become increasingly sophisticated (see Figure 1).

DEVELOPMENT OF THE SENSES: TAKING IN THE WORLD

When proud parents peer into the eyes of their neonate, is the child able to return their gaze? Although it was thought for some time that newborns can see only a hazy blur, most current findings indicate that neonates' capabilities are far more impressive. Although their eyes have a limited capacity to focus on objects that are not within a 7- to 8-inch distance from the face, neonates can follow objects moving within their field of vision. They also show the beginnings of depth perception as they react by raising their hands when an object appears to be moving rapidly toward the face (Maurer et al., 1999; Craighero et al., 2011).

You might think that it would be hard to figure out just how well neonates can see because their lack of both language and reading ability clearly prevents them from saying what direction the E on a vision chart is facing. However, researchers have devised a number of ingenious methods that rely on the newborn's biological responses and innate reflexes to test perceptual skills.

For instance, infants who see a novel stimulus typically pay close attention to it; as a consequence, their heart rates increase. But if they repeatedly see the same stimulus, their attention to it decreases, as indicated by a return to a slower heart rate. This phenomenon is known as **habituation,** the decrease in the response to a stimulus that occurs after repeated presentations of the same stimulus. By studying habituation, developmental psychologists can tell when a child who is too young to speak can detect and discriminate a stimulus (Grunwald et al., 2003; Hannon & Johnson, 2005; del Rosal, Alonso, & Moreno, 2006).

habituation The decrease in the response to a stimulus that occurs after repeated presentations of the same stimulus.

Researchers have developed many other methods for measuring neonate and infant perception. One technique, for instance, involves babies sucking on a nipple attached to a computer. A change in the rate and vigor with which the babies suck helps researchers infer that babies can perceive variations in stimuli. Other approaches include examining babies' eye movements and observing which way babies move their heads in response to a visual stimulus (Franklin, Pilling, & Davies, 2005; Bulf, Johnson, & Valenza, 2011).

Through the use of such research techniques, we now know that infants' visual perception is remarkably sophisticated from the start of life. At birth, babies prefer patterns with contours and edges over less distinct patterns, indicating that they can respond to the configuration of stimuli. Furthermore, even newborns are aware of size constancy because they are apparently sensitive to the phenomenon by which objects stay the same size even though the image on the retina may change size as the distance between the object and the retina varies (Norcia et al., 2005; Moore, Goodwin, & George, 2007).

In fact, neonates can discriminate facial expressions—and even imitate them. As you can see in Figure 2, newborns can produce a good imitation of an adult's expressions. Even very young infants, then, can respond to the emotions and moods that their caregivers' facial expressions reveal. This capability provides the foundation for social interaction skills in children (Meltzoff, 1996; Grossmann, Striano, & Friederici, 2007; Bahrick, Lickliter, & Castellanos, 2013).

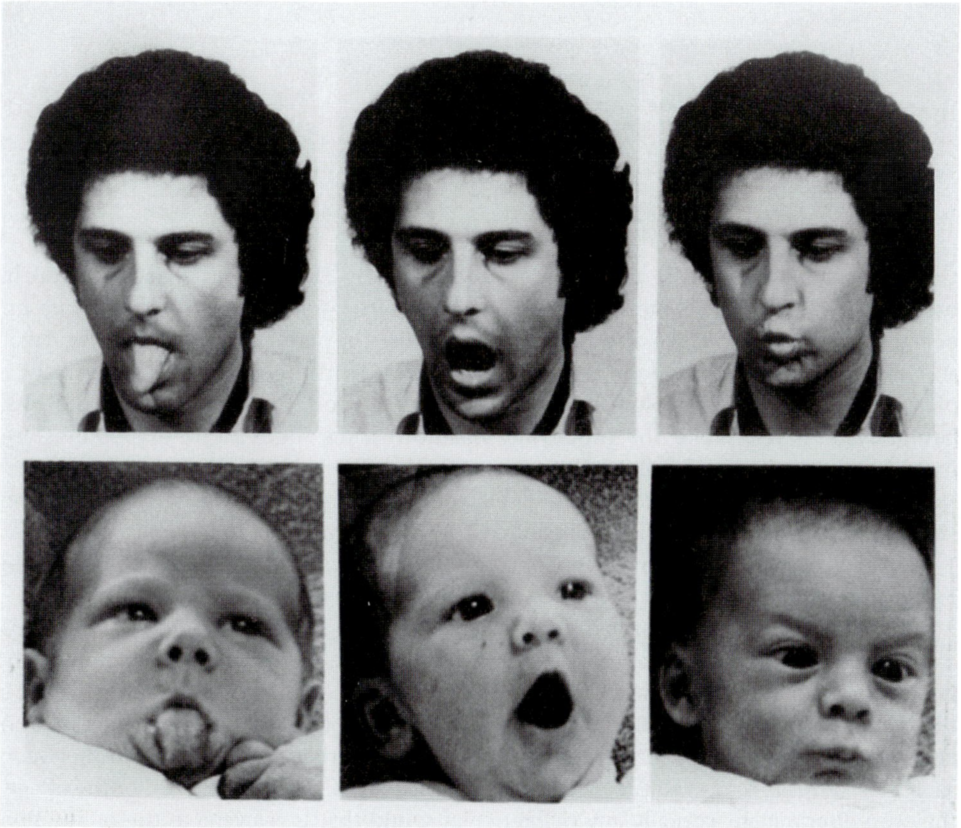

FIGURE 2 This newborn infant is clearly imitating the expressions of the adult model in these amazing photos. How does this ability contribute to social development? (Source: Courtesy of Dr. Tiffany Field.)

Neuroscience in Your Life: Do Infants Recognize Emotion?

To consider how infants process information related to facial expressions, researchers measured cerebral blood flow while they viewed happy and sad faces. When 6- to 7-month-old infants viewed happy faces, they showed greater activity, which tended to persist after the faces disappeared (the difference between the upper and lower lines on each graph). In contrast, when viewing angry faces, they showed greater activity when the face was shown, but this activity quickly disappeared. The results suggest that infants process positive and negative emotions differently. (Source: Adapted from Nakato et al., 2011.)

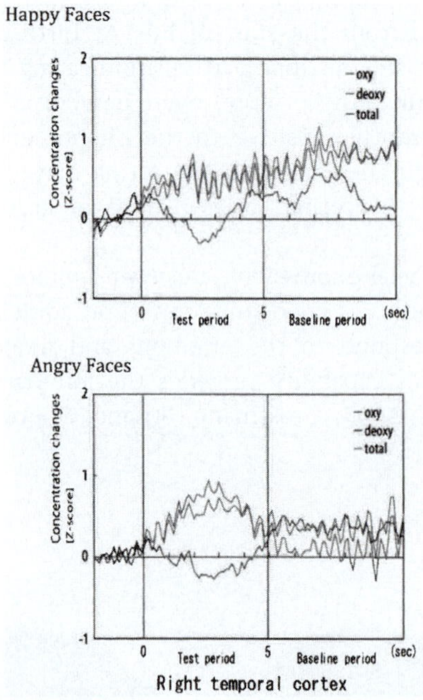

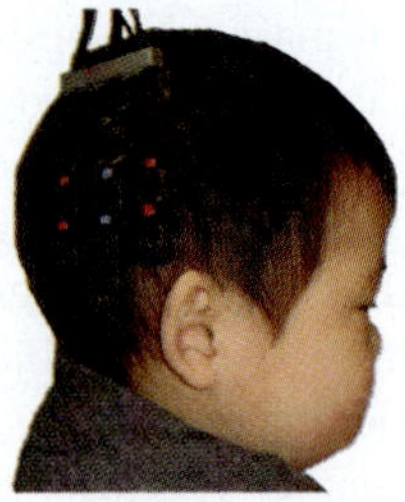

Other visual abilities grow rapidly after birth. By the end of their first month, babies can distinguish some colors from others; after 4 months they can focus on near or far objects. By the age of 4 or 5 months, they are able to recognize two- and three-dimensional objects, and they can perceive the gestalt organizing principles discovered by psychologists who study perception. By the age of 7 months, neural systems related to the processing of information about facial expressions are highly sophisticated and cause babies to respond differently to specific facial expressions (see *Neuroscience in Your Life*). Overall, their perceptual abilities rapidly improve: Sensitivity to visual stimuli, for instance, becomes three to four times greater at 1 year of age than it was at birth (Johnson, 2004; Striano & Vaish, 2006; Leppanen et al., 2007).

In addition to vision, infants display other impressive sensory capabilities. Newborns can distinguish different sounds to the point of being able to recognize their own mothers' voices at the age of 3 days. They can also make the subtle perceptual distinctions that underlie language abilities. For example, at 2 days of age, infants can distinguish between their native tongue and foreign languages, and they can discriminate between such closely related sounds as *ba* and *pa* when they are 4 days old. By 6 months of age, they can discriminate virtually any difference in sound that is relevant to the production of language. Moreover, they can recognize different tastes and smells at a very early age. There even seems to be something of a built-in sweet tooth: Neonates prefer liquids that have been sweetened with sugar over their unsweetened counterparts (Cohen & Cashon, 2003; Rivera-Gaxiola et al., 2005; Purdy et al., 2013).

The Growing Child: Infancy Through Middle Childhood

Three-year-old Lisa Palermo always had Cheerios on her breath. Mindy Crowell, Lisa's day care teacher, thought little of it until she noticed that the classroom Cheerios stash was steadily dwindling.

The Cheerios were stored in a plastic bin in the clothes closet. Keeping an eye on the closet, Mindy soon saw Lisa enter it, manipulate the fastener of the bin, reach in and withdraw a hand laden with Cheerios, and let the bin refasten itself, as it was designed to do. Mindy was amazed: Somehow, Lisa, barely able to navigate a crayon, had learned how to undo the supposedly child-proof fastener–a task that Mindy herself found difficult.

Mindy waited to see what would happen next. What she found was that Lisa was an excellent teacher. In the next few days, Paul, Olivia, and Kelly began to frequent the bin and do exactly what Lisa had done.

At three years old, Lisa asserted her personality, illustrating the tremendous growth that occurs in a variety of domains during the first year of life. Throughout the remainder of childhood, moving from infancy into middle childhood and the start of adolescence around age 11 or 12, children develop physically, socially, and cognitively in extraordinary ways. In the remainder of this module, we'll consider this development.

PHYSICAL DEVELOPMENT

Children's physical growth provides the most obvious sign of development. During the first year of life, children typically triple their birthweight, and their height increases by about half. This rapid growth slows down as the child gets older–think how gigantic adults would be if that rate of growth was constant. From age 3 to the beginning of adolescence at around age 13, growth averages a gain of about 5 pounds and 3 inches a year (see Figure 3).

The physical changes that occur as children develop are not just a matter of increasing growth; the relationship of the size of the various body parts to one another changes dramatically as children age. As you can see in Figure 4, the head of a fetus (and a newborn) is disproportionately large. However, the head soon becomes more proportional in size to the rest of the body as growth occurs mainly in the trunk and legs (Berger, 2011).

DEVELOPMENT OF SOCIAL BEHAVIOR: TAKING ON THE WORLD

As anyone who has seen infants smiling at the sight of their mothers can guess, at the same time that infants grow physically and hone their perceptual abilities, they also develop socially. The nature of a child's early social development provides the foundation for social relationships that will last a lifetime.

Attachment, the positive emotional bond that develops between a child and a particular individual, is the most important form of social development that occurs during infancy. The earliest studies of attachment were carried out by animal ethologist Konrad Lorenz (1966). Lorenz focused on newborn goslings, which under normal circumstances instinctively follow their mother, the first moving object they perceive after birth. Lorenz found that goslings whose eggs were raised

attachment The positive emotional bond that develops between a child and a particular individual.

in an incubator and that viewed him immediately after hatching would follow his every movement as if he were their mother. He labeled this process *imprinting,* behavior that takes place during a critical period and involves attachment to the first moving object that is observed.

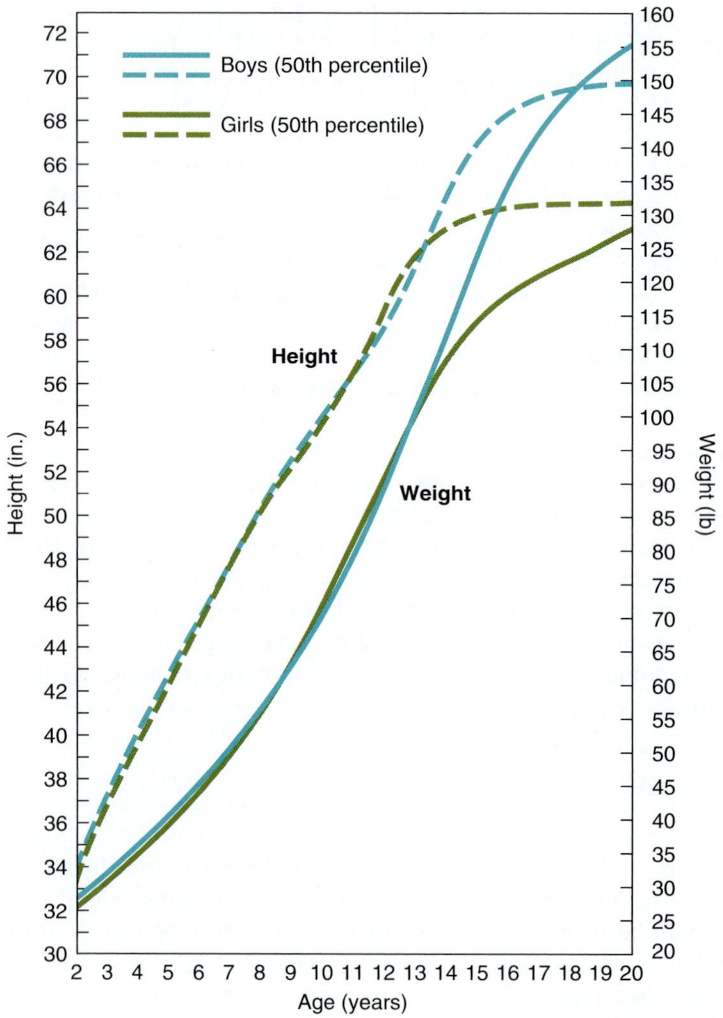

FIGURE 3 The average heights and weights of males and females in the United States from birth through age 20. At what ages are girls typically heavier and taller than boys? (Source: Adapted from National Center for Health Statistics, 2000.)

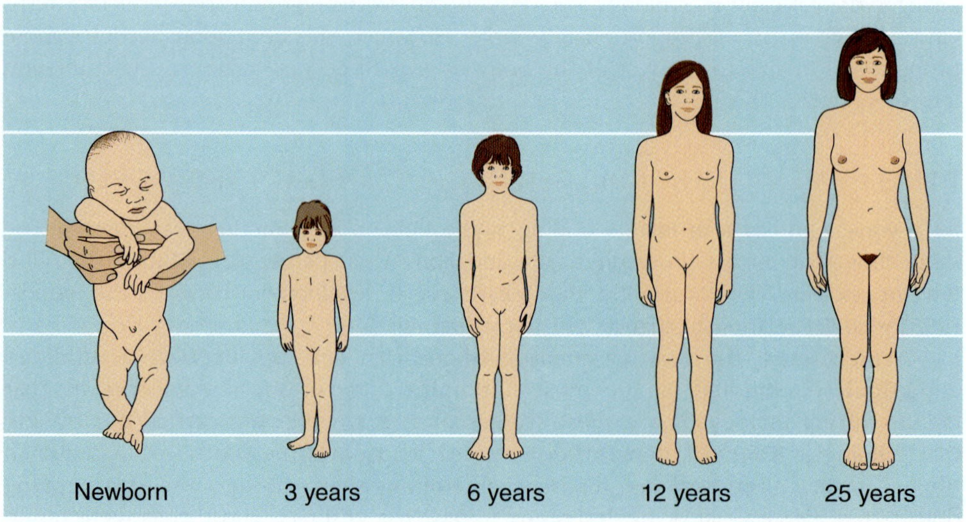

FIGURE 4 As development progresses, the size of the head relative to the rest of the body decreases until the individual reaches adulthood. Why do you think the head starts out so large? (Source: Adapted from Robbins, 1929.)

Our understanding of attachment progressed when psychologist Harry Harlow, in a classic study, gave infant monkeys the choice of cuddling a wire "monkey" that provided milk or a soft, terry-cloth "monkey" that was warm but did not provide milk. Their choice was clear: They spent most of their time clinging to the warm cloth "monkey," although they made occasional forays to the wire monkey to nurse. Obviously, the cloth monkey provided greater comfort to the infants; milk alone was insufficient to create attachment (Harlow & Zimmerman, 1959; Blum, 2002; Levine, 2011; see Figure 5).

Building on this pioneering work with nonhumans, developmental psychologists have suggested that human attachment grows through the responsiveness of infants' caregivers to the signals the babies provide, such as crying, smiling, reaching, and clinging. The more that caregivers respond to the cues that children give off regarding their emotions, the more likely it is that the child will become securely attached to the caregiver. Full attachment eventually develops as a result of the complex series of interactions between caregiver and child. In the course of these interactions, the infant plays as critical and active of a role as the caregiver in the formation of the bond. Infants who respond positively to a caregiver produce more positive behavior on the caregiver's part, which, in turn, produces an even stronger degree of attachment in the child.

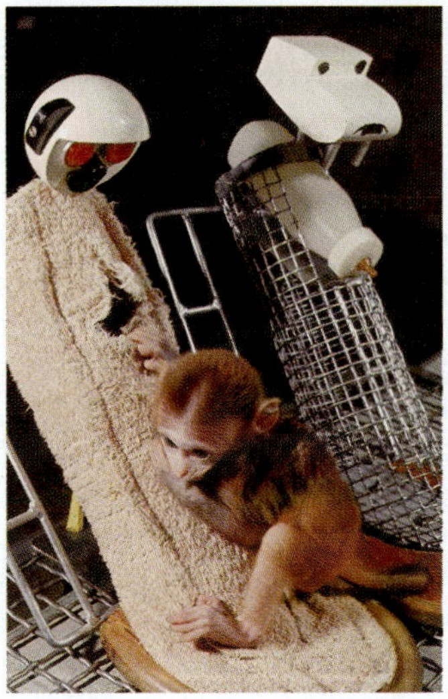

FIGURE 5 Although the wire "mother" dispensed milk to the hungry infant monkey, the infant preferred the soft, terry-cloth "mother." Do you think human babies would react the same way? What does this experiment tell us about attachment? (Source: Harry Harlow Primate Laboratory/University of Wisconsin.)

Study Alert

Attachment—the positive emotional bond that develops between a child and a particular individual—is a key concept in understanding the social development of children.

Assessing Attachment. Developmental psychologists have devised a quick and direct way to measure attachment. Developed by Mary Ainsworth, the *Ainsworth strange situation* consists of a sequence of events involving a child and (typically) his or her mother. Initially, the mother and baby enter an unfamiliar room, and the mother permits the baby to explore while she sits down. An adult stranger then enters the room; after this the mother leaves. The mother returns, and the stranger leaves. The mother once again leaves the baby alone, and the stranger returns. Finally, the stranger leaves, and the mother returns (Ainsworth et al., 1978; Combrink-Graham & McKenna, 2006; Behrens, Parker, & Haltigan, 2011).

Babies' reactions to the experimental situation vary drastically, depending, according to Ainsworth, on their degree of attachment to the mother:

- Securely attached children. Children who are *securely attached* employ the mother as a kind of home base; they explore independently but return to her occasionally. When she leaves, they exhibit distress, and they go to her when she returns.
- Avoidant children. *Avoidant* children do not cry when the mother leaves, and they seem to avoid her when she returns as if indifferent to her.
- Ambivalent children. *Ambivalent* children display anxiety before they are separated and are upset when the mother leaves, but they may show ambivalent reactions to her return, such as seeking close contact but simultaneously hitting and kicking her.
- Disorganized-disoriented children. A fourth reaction is *disorganized-disoriented;* these children show inconsistent and often contradictory behavior.

The nature of attachment between children and their mothers has far-reaching consequences for later development. For example, children who are securely attached to their mothers tend to be more socially and emotionally competent than are their less securely attached peers, and others find them more cooperative, capable, and playful. Furthermore, children who are securely attached at age 1 show fewer psychological difficulties when they grow older compared with avoidant and ambivalent youngsters. As adults, children who are securely attached tend to have more successful romantic relationships. On the other hand, being securely attached at an early age does not guarantee good adjustment later; conversely, children who lack secure attachment do not always have difficulties later in life (Roisman et al., 2005; Hardy, 2007; Redshaw & Martin, 2013).

Applying Psychology in the 21st Century

Distracted Parenting

Between 2007 and 2010, injuries of children under five on playground equipment jumped 17%; in that same time period, injuries of that age group on nursery equipment (such as changing tables) jumped 31% and around swimming pools by 36%. In the years running up to this period, childhood injuries had been on the decline, thanks to improved safety equipment and better awareness of safety issues. So what happened after 2007 to reverse that trend so dramatically (www.cpsc.gov)?

Smartphones happened. Popular use of smartphones rose at the same time childhood injuries did. Parents who are distracted by smartphones probably aren't supervising their children as closely as they may think they are.

It's difficult, however, to establish smartphones as the culprit directly. For one thing, emergency room attendants very rarely ask, much less record, what parents were doing at the moment their child was injured. (Even if they did, few parents would admit that they were sending a text or checking email.) But there are good reasons to suspect these devices as the culprit.

"Young children have a natural risk to hurt themselves if they are not properly watched by an adult," said David Schwebel, an expert in injury prevention. "We know that drivers and pedestrians are distracted and more at risk when they use devices.

It's a fairly small leap to suggest that supervisors [of children] are distracted." Another researcher examined the experiences of families with a 2-year-old child and found that about two-thirds of injuries to their child occurred when parents weren't present or were only listening while doing something else; only 10% happened when children were under close supervision (Worthen, 2012, C1; Morrongiello, Corbett, & Switzer, 2013).

The problem with smartphones, in particular, is that they are a special kind of distraction. When people are engrossed in using a device, they often fail to realize how distracted they are and how much time has gone by. One researcher found that people who have been using a device tend to take longer to refocus their attention elsewhere. It's as if they enter their own reality; they may glance up from the device now and then, but they don't actually "snap out of it" well enough to fully apprehend what they're seeing when they do (Ophir, Nass, & Wagner, 2009; Pea et al., 2012).

Furthermore, it's not just that parents are distracted–it's also that their children know that they're distracted. Realizing that their parents may be physically present but aren't mentally present, children are more likely to behave the way they do when they aren't being supervised at all–and that means taking more risks (Schwebel et al., 2011).

RETHINK

- Why might smartphones and similar devices tend to distract parents to a greater degree and for a longer time than the parents realize?
- What would you tell a friend who recently became a parent about the distractions of smartphones?

The Father's Role. Although early developmental research focused largely on the mother-child relationship, more recent research has highlighted the father's role in parenting–and with good reason: The number of fathers who are primary caregivers for their children has grown significantly, and fathers play an increasingly important role in their children's lives. For example, in almost 13% of families with children, the father is the parent who stays at home to care for preschoolers (Parke, 2004; Day & Lamb, 2004; Halford, 2006).

When fathers interact with their children, their play often differs from mothers' play. Fathers engage in more physical, rough-and-tumble sorts of activities, whereas mothers play more verbal and traditional games, such as peekaboo. Despite such behavioral differences, the nature of attachment between fathers and children compared with that between mothers and children can be similar. In fact, children can form multiple attachments simultaneously (Borisenko, 2007; Pellis & Pellis, 2007; Diener et al., 2008).

Social Relationships with Peers. By the time they are 2 years old, children become less dependent on their parents, more self-reliant, and increasingly prefer to play with friends. Initially, play is relatively independent: Even though they may be sitting side by side, 2-year-olds pay more attention to toys than to one another when playing. Later, however, children actively interact, modify one another's behavior, and exchange roles during play (Lindsey & Colwell, 2003; Colwell & Lindsey, 2005; Whitney & Green, 2011).

Cultural factors also affect children's styles of play. For example, Korean-American children engage in less pretend play than their Anglo-American counterparts (Bai, 2005; Drewes, 2005; Suizzo & Bornstein, 2006).

As children reach school age, their social interactions begin to follow set patterns and become more frequent. They may engage in elaborate games involving teams and rigid rules. This play serves purposes other than mere enjoyment. It allows children to become increasingly competent in their social interactions with others. Through play they learn to take the perspective of other people and to infer others' thoughts and feelings, even when those thoughts and feelings are not directly expressed (Royzman, Cassidy, & Baron, 2003; Yang et al., 2013).

In short, social interaction helps children interpret the meaning of others' behavior and develop the capacity to respond appropriately. Furthermore, children learn physical and emotional self-control: They learn to avoid hitting a playmate who beats them at a game. They learn to be polite and to control their emotional displays and facial expressions (e.g., smiling even when receiving a disappointing gift). Situations that provide children with opportunities for social interaction, then, may enhance their social development (Feldman, 1993; Talukdar & Shastri, 2006; Whitebread et al., 2009).

The Consequences of Child Care Outside the Home. Research on the importance of social interaction is corroborated by work that examines the benefits of child care out of the home, which is an important part of an increasing number of children's lives. For instance, almost 30% of preschool children whose mothers work outside the home spend their days in child-care centers. By the age of 6 months, almost two-thirds of infants are cared for by people other than their mothers for part of the day. Most of these infants begin child care before the age of 4 months and are cared for by people other than their mothers almost 30 hours per week (National Research Council, 2001; NICHD Early Child Care Research Network, 2006; see Figure 6).

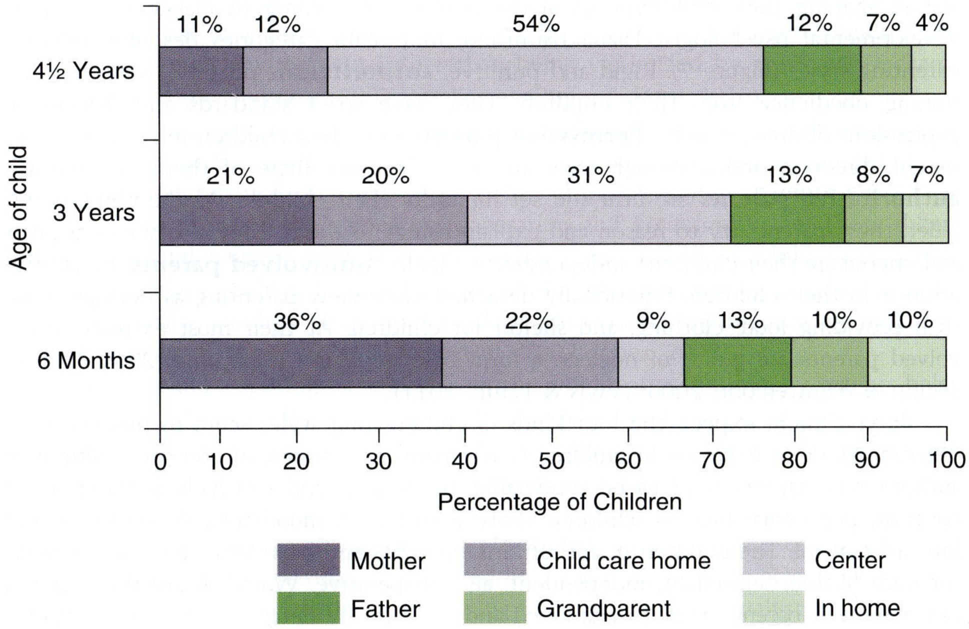

FIGURE 6 According to a study by the National Institute of Child Health and Human Development, children were more likely to spend time in some kind of child care outside the home or family as they got older. (Source: Adapted from NICHD, 2006.)

developed one of the more comprehensive theories of social development. Erikson (1963) viewed the developmental changes that occur throughout life as a series of eight stages of psychosocial development; of these, four occur during childhood. **Psychosocial development** involves changes in our interactions and understanding of one another as well as in our knowledge and understanding of ourselves as members of society.

psychosocial development Development of individuals' interactions and understanding of each other and of their knowledge and understanding of themselves as members of society.

Erikson suggests that passage through each of the stages necessitates the resolution of a crisis or conflict. Accordingly, Erikson represents each stage as a pairing of the most positive and most negative aspects of the crisis of that period. Although each crisis is never resolved entirely–life becomes increasingly complicated as we grow older–it has to be resolved sufficiently to equip us to deal with demands made during the following stage of development.

trust-versus-mistrust stage According to Erikson, the first stage of psychosocial development, occurring from birth to age 1½ years, during which time infants develop feelings of trust or lack of trust.

In the first stage of psychosocial development, the **trust-versus-mistrust stage** (ages birth to 1½ years), infants develop feelings of trust if their physical requirements and psychological needs for attachment are consistently met and their interactions with the world are generally positive. In contrast, inconsistent care and unpleasant interactions with others can lead to mistrust and leave an infant unable to meet the challenges required in the next stage of development.

autonomy-versus-shame-and-doubt stage The period during which, according to Erikson, toddlers (ages 1½ to 3 years) develop independence and autonomy if exploration and freedom are encouraged or shame and self-doubt if they are restricted and overprotected.

In the second stage, the **autonomy-versus-shame-and-doubt stage** (ages 1½ to 3 years), toddlers develop independence and autonomy if exploration and freedom are encouraged, or they experience shame, self-doubt, and unhappiness if they are overly restricted and protected. According to Erikson, the key to the development of autonomy during this period is that the child's caregivers provide the appropriate amount of control. If parents provide too much control, children cannot assert themselves and develop their own sense of control over their environment; if parents provide too little control, the children become overly demanding and controlling.

initiative-versus-guilt stage According to Erikson, the period during which children ages 3 to 6 years experience conflict between independence of action and the sometimes negative results of that action.

Next, children face the crises of the **initiative-versus-guilt stage** (ages 3 to 6). In this stage, children's desire to act independently conflicts with the guilt that comes from the unintended and unexpected consequences of such behavior. Children in this period come to understand that they are persons in their own right, and they begin to make decisions about their behavior. If parents react positively to children's attempts at independence, they will help their children resolve the initiative-versus-guilt crisis positively.

industry-versus-inferiority stage According to Erikson, the last stage of childhood, during which children ages 6 to 12 years may develop positive social interactions with others or may feel inadequate and become less sociable.

The fourth and last stage of childhood is the **industry-versus-inferiority stage** (ages 6 to 12). During this period, increasing competency in all areas, whether social interactions or academic skills, characterizes successful psychosocial development. In contrast, difficulties in this stage lead to feelings of failure and inadequacy.

Erikson's theory suggests that psychosocial development continues throughout life, and he proposes four more crises that are faced after childhood (described in the next module). Although his theory has been criticized on several grounds–such as the imprecision of the concepts he employs and his greater emphasis on male development than female development–it remains influential and is one of the few theories that encompass the entire life span.

Study Alert

Four of Erikson's stages of psychosocial development occur during childhood: trust-versus-mistrust, autonomy-versus-shame-and-doubt, initiative-versus-guilt, and industry-versus-inferiority.

COGNITIVE DEVELOPMENT: CHILDREN'S THINKING ABOUT THE WORLD

Suppose you had two drinking glasses of different shapes–one short and broad and one tall and thin. Now imagine that you filled the short, broad one with soda about halfway and then poured the liquid from that glass into the tall one. The soda would appear to fill about three-quarters of the second glass. If someone asked you whether there was more soda in the second glass than there had been in the first, what would you say?

You might think that such a simple question hardly deserves an answer; of course, there is no difference in the amount of soda in the two glasses. However, most 4-year-olds would be likely to say that there is more soda in the second glass. If you then poured the soda back into the short glass, they would say there is now less soda than there was in the taller glass.

Why are young children confused by this problem? The reason is not immediately obvious. Anyone who has observed preschoolers must be impressed by how far they have progressed from the early stages of development. They speak with ease, know the alphabet, count, play complex games, use computers, tell stories, and communicate ably. Yet despite this seeming sophistication, there are deep gaps in children's understanding of the world. The gaps in children's understanding relate to their level of cognitive development. **Cognitive development** is the process by which children's understanding of the world changes due to their age and experience. In contrast to the theories of physical and social development discussed earlier (such as those of Erikson), theories of cognitive development seek to explain the quantitative and qualitative intellectual advances that occur during development.

cognitive development The process by which a child's understanding of the world changes due to their age and experience.

Piaget's Theory of Cognitive Development. No theory of cognitive development has had more impact than that of Swiss psychologist Jean Piaget. Piaget (1970) suggested that children around the world proceed through a series of four stages in a fixed order. He maintained that these stages differ not only in the *quantity* of information acquired at each stage but in the *quality* of knowledge and understanding as well. Taking an interactionist point of view, he suggested that movement from one stage to the next occurs when a child reaches an appropriate level of maturation *and* is exposed to relevant types of experiences. Piaget assumed that, without having such experiences, children cannot reach their highest level of cognitive growth.

Study Alert
Use Figure 9 to help remember Piaget's stages of cognitive development.

Piaget proposed four stages: the sensorimotor, preoperational, concrete operational, and formal operational (see Figure 8). Let's examine each of them and the approximate ages that they span.

Sensorimotor Stage: Birth to 2 Years. During the **sensorimotor stage,** children base their understanding of the world primarily on touching, sucking, chewing, shaking, and manipulating objects. In the initial part of the stage, children have relatively little competence in representing the environment by using images, language, or other kinds of symbols. Consequently, infants lack what Piaget calls **object permanence,** the awareness that objects—and people—continue to exist even if they are out of sight.

sensorimotor stage According to Piaget, the stage from birth to 2 years, during which a child has little competence in representing the environment by using images, language, or other symbols.

object permanence The awareness that objects—and people—continue to exist even if they are out of sight.

How can we know that children lack object permanence? Although we cannot ask infants, we can observe their reactions when a toy they are playing with is hidden under a blanket. Until the age of about 9 months, children will make no attempt

Cognitive Stage	Approximate Age Range	Major Characteristics
Sensorimotor	Birth–2 years	Development of object permanence, development of motor skills, little or no capacity for symbolic representation
Preoperational	2–7 years	Development of language and symbolic thinking, egocentric thinking
Concrete operational	7–12 years	Development of conservation, mastery of concept of reversibility
Formal operational	12 years–adulthood	Development of logical and abstract thinking

FIGURE 8 According to Piaget, all children pass through four stages of cognitive development.

to locate the hidden toy. However, soon after that age they will begin an active search for the missing object, indicating that they have developed a mental representation of the toy. Object permanence, then, is a critical development during the sensorimotor stage.

Preoperational Stage: 2 to 7 Years. The most important development during the **preoperational stage** is the use of language. Children develop internal representational systems that allow them to describe people, events, and feelings. They even use symbols in play, pretending, for example, that a book pushed across the floor is a car.

preoperational stage According to Piaget, the period from 2 to 7 years of age that is characterized by language development.

Although children use more advanced thinking in this stage than they did in the earlier sensorimotor stage, their thinking is still qualitatively inferior to that of adults. We see this when we observe a preoperational child using **egocentric thought,** a way of thinking in which the child views the world entirely from his or her own perspective. Preoperational children think that everyone shares their perspective and knowledge. Thus, children's stories and explanations to adults can be maddeningly uninformative because they are delivered without any context. For example, a preoperational child may start a story with, "He wouldn't let me go," neglecting to mention who "he" is or where the storyteller wanted to go. We also see egocentric thinking when children at the preoperational stage play hiding games. For instance, 3-year-olds frequently hide with their faces against a wall and covering their eyes–although they are still in plain view. It seems to them that if *they* cannot see, then no one else will be able to see them because they assume that others share their view.

egocentric thought A way of thinking in which a child views the world entirely from his or her own perspective.

In addition, preoperational children have not yet developed the ability to understand the **principle of conservation,** which is the knowledge that quantity is unrelated to the arrangement and physical appearance of objects. Children who understand the principle of conservation have the awareness that important attributes of objects (such as the amount or volume) do not change despite superficial changes. In contrast, children who have not mastered this concept do not know that the overall amount or volume of an object does not change when its shape or configuration changes.

principle of conservation The knowledge that quantity is unrelated to the arrangement and physical appearance of objects.

The question about the two glasses–one short and broad, and the other tall and thin–with which we began our discussion of cognitive development illustrates this point clearly. Children who do not understand the principle of conservation invariably state that the amount of liquid changes as it is poured back and forth between glasses of different sizes. They cannot comprehend that a transformation in appearance does not imply a transformation in amount. Instead, it seems as reasonable to the child that there is a change in quantity as it does to the adult that there is no change.

In a number of other ways, some quite startling, the failure to understand the principle of conservation affects children's responses. Research demonstrates that children during the preoperational period may completely misunderstand principles that are obvious to and unquestioned by adults and that children do not grasp the concept of conservation until the next stage of cognitive development (see Figure 9).

Concrete Operational Stage: 7 to 12 Years. Mastery of the principle of conservation marks the beginning of the **concrete operational stage.** However, children do not fully understand some aspects of conservation–such as conservation of weight and volume–for a number of years.

concrete operational stage According to Piaget, the period from 7 to 12 years of age that is characterized by logical thought and a loss of egocentrism.

Children who have not mastered the principle of conservation assume that the volume of liquid increases when it is poured from a short, wide container to a tall, thin one. What other tasks might a child under age 7 have difficulty comprehending?

During the concrete operational stage, children develop the ability to think in a more logical manner and begin to overcome some of the egocentrism characteristic of the preoperational period. One of the major principles children learn during this stage is reversibility, the idea that some changes can be undone by reversing an earlier action. For example, they can understand that when someone rolls a ball of clay into a long sausage shape, that person can recreate the original ball by reversing the action. Children can even conceptualize this principle in their heads without having to see the action performed before them.

Conservation of ...	Modality	Change in physical appearance	Average age at full mastery
Number	Number of elements in a collection 	Rearranging or dislocating elements 	6–7 years
Substance (mass)	Amount of a malleable substance (e.g., clay or liquid) 	Altering shape 	7–8 years
Length	Length of a line or object 	Altering shape or configuration 	7–8 years
Area	Amount of surface covered by a set of plane figures 	Rearranging the figures 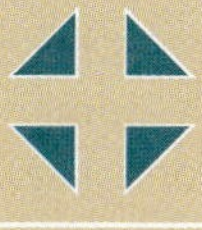	8–9 years
Weight	Weight of an object 	Altering shape 	9–10 years
Volume	Volume of an object (in terms of water displacement) 	Altering shape 	14–15 years

FIGURE 9 These tests are frequently used to assess whether children have learned the principle of conservation across a variety of dimensions. Do you think children in the preoperational stage can be taught to avoid conservation mistakes before the typical age of mastery? (Source: Adapted from Schickedanz et al., 2001.)

Although children make important advances in their logical capabilities during the concrete operational stage, their thinking still displays one major limitation: They are largely bound to the concrete, physical reality of the world. For the most part, they have difficulty understanding questions of an abstract or hypothetical nature.

Formal Operational Stage: 12 Years to Adulthood. The **formal operational stage** produces a new kind of thinking that is abstract, formal, and logical. Thinking is no longer tied to events that individuals observe in the environment but makes use of logical techniques to resolve problems.

formal operational stage According to Piaget, the period from age 12 to adulthood that is characterized by abstract thought.

The way in which children approach the "pendulum problem" devised by Piaget (Piaget & Inhelder, 1958) illustrates the emergence of formal operational thinking. The problem solver is asked to figure out what determines how fast a pendulum swings. Is it the length of the string, the weight of the pendulum, or the force with which the pendulum is pushed? (For the record, the answer is the length of the string.)

Children in the concrete operational stage approach the problem haphazardly without a logical or rational plan of action. For example, they may simultaneously change the length of the string, the weight on the string, and the force with which they push the pendulum. Because they are varying all the factors at once, they cannot tell which factor is the critical one. In contrast, people in the formal operational stage approach the problem systematically. Acting as if they were scientists conducting an experiment, they examine the effects of changes in one variable at a time. This ability to rule out competing possibilities characterizes formal operational thought.

Although formal operational thought emerges during the teenage years, some individuals use this type of thinking only infrequently. Moreover, it appears that many individuals never reach this stage at all; most studies show that only 40–60% of college students and adults fully reach it, with some estimates running as low as 25% of the general population. In addition, in certain cultures–particularly those that are less technically oriented than Western societies–almost no one reaches the formal operational stage (Keating & Clark, 1980; Super, 1980; Genovese, 2006).

Stages Versus Continuous Development: Is Piaget Right? No other theorist has given us as comprehensive a theory of cognitive development as Piaget. Still, many contemporary theorists suggest that a better explanation of how children develop cognitively can be provided by theories that do not involve a stage approach. For instance, children are not always consistent in their performance of tasks that–if Piaget's theory is accurate–ought to be performed equally well at a particular stage (Feldman, 2003, 2004).

Furthermore, some developmental psychologists suggest that cognitive development proceeds in a more continuous fashion than Piaget's stage theory implies. They propose that cognitive development is primarily quantitative rather than qualitative. They argue that although there are differences in when, how, and to what extent a child can use specific cognitive abilities–reflecting quantitative changes–the underlying cognitive processes change relatively little with age (Gelman & Baillargeon, 1983; Case & Okamoto, 1996).

Piaget also underestimated the age at which infants and children can understand specific concepts and principles; in fact, they seem to be more sophisticated in their cognitive abilities than Piaget believed. For instance, some evidence suggests that infants as young as 5 months have rudimentary mathematical skills (Wynn, Bloom, & Chiang, 2002; McCrink & Wynn, 2007; van Marle & Wynn, 2009).

Despite such criticisms, most developmental psychologists agree that although the processes that underlie changes in cognitive abilities may not unfold in the manner Piaget's theory suggests, he has generally provided us with an accurate account of age-related changes in cognitive development. Moreover, his theory has had an enormous influence in education. For example, Piaget suggests that individuals cannot increase their cognitive performance unless both cognitive readiness brought about by maturation and appropriate environmental stimulation are present. This view has inspired the nature and structure of educational curricula and teaching methods. Researchers have also used Piaget's theory and methods to investigate issues surrounding animal cognition, such as whether primates show object permanence (they seem to; Hauser, 2000; Egan, 2005; Cunningham, 2006).

Information-Processing Approaches: Charting Children's Mental Programs. If cognitive development does not proceed as a series of stages as Piaget suggested, what does underlie the enormous growth in children's cognitive abilities that even the most untutored eye can observe? To many developmental psychologists, changes in **information processing,** the way in which people take in, use, and store information, account for cognitive development (Cashon & Cohen, 2004; Munakata, 2006; Casasola, 2011).

information processing The way in which people take in, use, and store information.

According to this approach, quantitative changes occur in children's ability to organize and manipulate information. From this perspective, children become increasingly adept at information processing, much as a computer program may become more sophisticated as a programmer modifies it on the basis of experience. Information-processing approaches consider the kinds of "mental programs" that children invoke when approaching problems.

Several significant changes occur in children's information-processing capabilities. For one thing, speed of processing increases with age as some abilities become more automatic. The speed at which children can scan, recognize, and compare stimuli increases with age. As they grow older, children can pay attention to stimuli longer and discriminate between different stimuli more readily, and they are less easily distracted (Van den Wildenberg & Van der Molen, 2004; Diaz & Bell, 2011).

Memory also improves dramatically with age. Preschoolers can hold only two or three chunks of information in short-term memory, 5-year-olds can hold four, and 7-year-olds can hold five. (Adults are able to keep seven, plus or minus two, chunks in short-term memory.) The size of the chunks also grows with age, as does the sophistication and organization of knowledge stored in memory (see Figure 10). Still, memory capabilities are impressive at a very early age: Even before they can speak, infants can remember for months events in which they actively participated (Bayliss et al., 2005a; Ślusarczyk & Niedźwieńska, 2013).

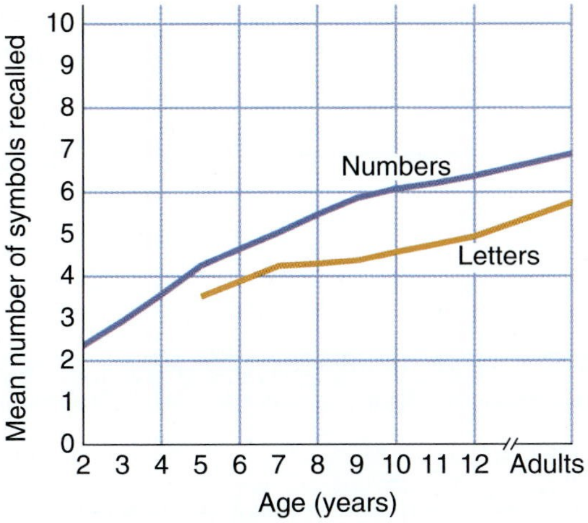

FIGURE 10 Memory span increases with age for both numbers and letters. (Source: Adapted from Dempster, 1981.)

Finally improvement in information processing relates to advances in **metacognition,** an awareness and understanding of one's own cognitive processes. Metacognition involves the planning, monitoring, and revising of cognitive strategies. Younger children, who lack an awareness of their own cognitive processes, often do not realize their incapabilities. Thus, when they misunderstand others, they may fail to recognize their own errors. It is only later, when metacognitive abilities become more sophisticated, that children are able to know when they *don't* understand. Such increasing sophistication reflects a change in children's *theory of mind,* their knowledge and beliefs about the way the mind operates (Matthews & Funke, 2006; Lockl & Schneider, 2007; Sodian, 2011).

metacognition An awareness and understanding of one's own cognitive processes.

PsychTech

A quarter of parents with children between the ages of 0 to 5 report that their children use the Internet.

Vygotsky's View of Cognitive Development: Considering Culture. According to Russian developmental psychologist Lev Vygotsky, the culture in which we are raised significantly affects our cognitive development. In an increasingly influential view, Vygotsky suggests that the focus on individual performance of both Piagetian and information-processing approaches is misplaced. Instead, he holds that we cannot understand cognitive development without taking into account the social aspects of learning (Vygotsky, 1926/1997; Maynard & Martini, 2005; Rieber & Robinson, 2006).

Vygotsky argues that cognitive development occurs as a consequence of social interactions in which children work with others to jointly solve problems. Through such interactions, children's cognitive skills increase, and they gain the ability to function intellectually on their own. More specifically, he suggests that children's cognitive abilities increase when they encounter information that falls within their zone of proximal development. The **zone of proximal development (ZPD)** is the gap between what children already are able to accomplish on their own and what they are not quite ready to do by themselves. When children receive information that falls within the ZPD, they can increase their understanding or master a new task. In contrast, if the information lies outside children's ZPD, they will not be able to master it.

zone of proximal development (ZPD) According to Vygotsky, the gap between what children already are able to accomplish on their own and what they are not quite ready to do by themselves.

In short, cognitive development occurs when parents, teachers, or skilled peers assist a child by presenting information that is both new and within the ZPD. This type of assistance, called *scaffolding,* provides support for learning and problem solving that encourages independence and growth. Vygotsky claims that scaffolding not only promotes the solution of specific problems, but also aids in the development of overall cognitive abilities (Schaller & Crandall, 2004; Coulson & Harvey, 2013).

More than other approaches to cognitive development, Vygotsky's theory considers how an individual's specific cultural and social context affects intellectual growth. The way in which children understand the world grows out of interactions with parents, peers, and other members of a specific culture (John-Steiner & Mahn, 2003; Kozulin et al., 2003).

RECAP/EVALUATE/RETHINK

RECAP

LO 28-1 What are the major competencies of newborns?

- Newborns, or neonates, have reflexes—unlearned, involuntary responses that occur automatically in the presence of certain stimuli.
- Sensory abilities also develop rapidly; infants can distinguish color, depth, sound, tastes, and smells relatively soon after birth.
- After birth, physical development is rapid; children typically triple their birthweight in a year.

LO 28-2 What are the milestones of physical and social development during childhood?

- Attachment—the positive emotional bond between a child and a particular individual—marks social development in infancy. Measured in the laboratory by means of the Ainsworth strange situation, attachment relates to later social and emotional adjustment.
- As children become older, the nature of their social interactions with peers changes. Initially play occurs relatively independently, but it becomes increasingly cooperative.
- The different child-rearing styles include authoritarian, permissive, authoritative, and uninvolved.
- According to Erikson, eight stages of psychosocial development involve people's changing interactions and understanding of themselves and others. During childhood, the four stages are trust-versus-mistrust (birth to 1½ years), autonomy-versus-shame-and-doubt (1½ to 3 years), initiative-versus-guilt (3 to 6 years), and industry-versus-inferiority (6 to 12 years).

LO 28-3 How does cognitive development proceed during childhood?

- Piaget's theory suggests that cognitive development proceeds through four stages in which qualitative changes occur in thinking: the sensorimotor stage (birth to 2 years), the preoperational stage (2 to 7 years), the concrete operational stage (7 to 12 years), and the formal operational stage (12 years to adulthood).
- Information-processing approaches suggest that quantitative changes occur in children's ability to organize and manipulate information about the world, such as significant increases in speed of processing, attention span, and memory. In addition, children advance in metacognition, the awareness and understanding of one's own cognitive processes.
- Vygotsky argued that children's cognitive development occurs as a consequence of social interactions in which children and others work together to solve problems.

EVALUATE

1. Researchers studying newborns use ________, or the decrease in the response to a stimulus that occurs after repeated presentations of the same stimulus, as an indicator of a baby's interest.
2. The emotional bond that develops between a child and its caregiver is known as ________.
3. Match the parenting style with its definition:

1. Permissive	a. Rigid; highly punitive; demanding obedience
2. Authoritative	b. Gives little direction; lax on obedience
3. Authoritarian	c. Firm but fair; tries to explain parental decisions
4. Uninvolved	d. Emotionally detached and unloving

4. Erikson's theory of ________ development involves a series of eight stages, each of which must be resolved for a person to develop optimally.
5. Match the stage of development with the thinking style characteristic of that stage:

1. Egocentric thought	a. Sensorimotor
2. Object permanence	b. Formal operational
3. Abstract reasoning	c. Preoperational
4. Conservation	d. Concrete operational reversibility

6. ________ ________ theories of development suggest that the way in which a child handles information is critical to his or her development.
7. According to Vygotsky, information that is within a child's ________ ________ ________ ________ is most likely to result in cognitive development.

RETHINK

1. Do you think the widespread use of IQ testing in the United States contributes to parents' views that their

children's academic success is due largely to the children's innate intelligence? Why? Would it be possible (or desirable) to change this view?

2. In what ways might the infant's major reflexes–the rooting, sucking, gagging, and Babinski reflexes–have had survival value, from an evolutionary perspective? Does the infant's ability to mimic the facial expressions of adults have a similar value?

Answers to Evaluate Questions

1. habituation; **2.** attachment; **3.** 1-b, 2-c, 3-a, 4-d; **4.** psychosocial; **5.** 1-c, 2-a, 3-b, 4-d; **6.** information-processing; **7.** zone of proximal development

KEY TERMS

neonate
reflexes
habituation
attachment
authoritarian parents
permissive parents
authoritative parents
uninvolved parents
temperament
psychosocial development
trust-versus-mistrust stage
autonomy-versus-shame-and-doubt stage
initiative-versus-guilt stage
industry-versus-inferiority stage
cognitive development
sensorimotor stage
object permanence
preoperational stage
egocentric thought
principle of conservation
concrete operational stage
formal operational stage
information processing
metacognition
zone of proximal development (ZPD)

MODULE 29

Adolescence: Becoming an Adult

Learning Outcome

LO 29-1 What major physical, social, and cognitive transitions characterize adolescence?

Joseph Charles, Age 13: "Being 13 is very hard at school. I have to be bad in order to be considered cool. I sometimes do things that aren't good. I have talked back to my teachers and been disrespectful to them. I do want to be good, but it's just too hard." (Gibbs, 2005, p. 51)

Trevor Kelson, Age 15: "Keep the Hell Out of my Room!" says a sign on Trevor's bedroom wall, just above an unmade bed, a desk littered with dirty T-shirts and candy wrappers, and a floor covered with clothes. Is there a carpet? "Somewhere," he says with a grin. "I think it's gold." (Fields-Meyer, 1995, p. 53)

Lauren Barry, Age 18: "I went to a National Honor Society induction. The parents were just staring at me. I think they couldn't believe someone with pink hair could be smart. I want to be a high-school teacher, but I'm afraid that, based on my appearance, they won't hire me." (Gordon et al., 1999, p. 47)

Although Joseph, Trevor, and Lauren have never met, they share anxieties that are common to adolescence—concerns about friends, parents, appearance, independence, and their futures.

adolescence The developmental stage between childhood and adulthood.

Adolescence, the developmental stage between childhood and adulthood, is a crucial period. It is a time of profound changes and, occasionally, turmoil. Considerable biological change occurs as adolescents attain sexual and physical maturity. At the same time and rivaling these physiological changes, important social, emotional, and cognitive changes occur as adolescents strive for independence and move toward adulthood.

Because many years of schooling precede most people's entry into the workforce in Western societies, the stage of adolescence is fairly long; it begins just before the teenage years and ends just after them. Adolescents are no longer children, yet society doesn't quite consider them adults. They face a period of rapid physical, cognitive, and social change that affects them for the rest of their lives.

Dramatic changes in society also affect adolescents' development. More than half of all children in the United States will spend all or some of their childhood and adolescence in single-parent families. Furthermore, adolescents spend considerably less time with their parents and more with their peers than they did several decades ago. Finally, the ethnic and cultural diversity of adolescents as a group is increasing dramatically. A third of all adolescents today are of non-European descent; by the year 2050 the number of adolescents of Hispanic, African-American, Native-American, and Asian origin collectively will surpass that of whites (National Adolescent Health Information Center, 2003).

Physical Development: The Changing Adolescent

If you think back to the start of your own adolescence, the most dramatic changes you probably remember are physical. A spurt in height, the growth of breasts in girls, deepening voices in boys, the development of body hair, and intense sexual feelings cause curiosity, interest, and sometimes embarrassment for individuals entering adolescence.

The physical changes that occur at the start of adolescence result largely from the secretion of various hormones, and they affect virtually every aspect of an adolescent's life. Not since infancy has development been so dramatic. Weight and height increase rapidly because of a growth spurt that typically begins around age 10 for girls and age 12 for boys. Adolescents may grow as much as 5 inches in one year.

Puberty, the period at which maturation of the sexual organs occurs, begins at about age 11 or 12 for girls, when menstruation starts. However, there are wide variations (see Figure 1). For example, some girls begin to menstruate as early as age 8 or 9 or as late as age 16. Furthermore, in Western cultures, the average age at which adolescents reach sexual maturity has been steadily decreasing over the last century most likely as a result of improved nutrition and medical care. Sexual *attraction* to others begins even before the maturation of the sexual organs at around age 10 (see Figure 1; Tanner, 1990; Finlay, Jones, & Coleman, 2002; Shanahan et al., 2013).

puberty The period at which maturation of the sexual organs occurs, beginning at about age 11 or 12 for girls and 13 or 14 for boys.

For boys, the onset of puberty is marked by their first ejaculation, known as *spermarche*. Spermarche usually occurs around the age of 13 (see Figure 1). At first, relatively few sperm are produced during an ejaculation, but the amount increases significantly within a few years.

The age at which puberty begins has implications for the way adolescents feel about themselves–as well as the way others treat them. Early-maturing boys have a distinct advantage over later-maturing boys. They do better in athletics, are generally more popular with peers, and have more positive self-concepts (Ge et al., 2003; Becker & Luthar, 2007; Mensah et al., 2013).

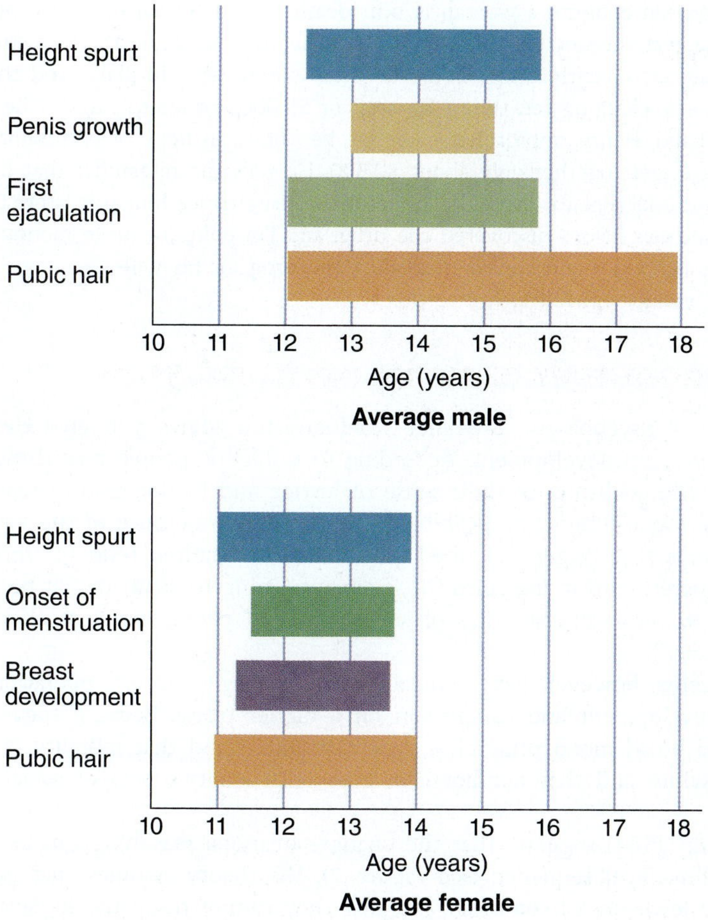

FIGURE 1 The range of ages during which major sexual changes occur during adolescence is shown by the colored bars. (Source: Adapted from Tanner, 1978.)

Although puberty begins around 11 or 12 for girls and 13 or 14 for boys, there are wide variations. What are some of the advantages and disadvantages of early puberty?

The picture differs for girls. Although early-maturing girls are more sought after as dates and have better self-esteem than later-maturing girls, some consequences of early physical maturation may be less positive. For example, early breast development may set them apart from their peers and be a source of ridicule (Olivardia & Pope, 2002; Nadeem & Graham, 2005; Blumenthal et al., 2011).

Late physical maturation may produce certain psychological difficulties for both boys and girls. Boys who are smaller and less coordinated than their more mature peers tend to feel ridiculed and less attractive. Similarly, late-maturing girls are at a disadvantage in middle school and early high school. They hold relatively low social status and may be overlooked in dating (Lanza & Collins, 2002).

Clearly, the rate at which physical changes occur during adolescence can affect the way in which people are viewed by others and the way they view themselves. Just as important as physical changes, however, are the psychological and social changes that unfold during adolescence.

Moral and Cognitive Development: Distinguishing Right from Wrong

In a European country, a woman is near death from a special kind of cancer. The one drug that the doctors think might save her is a medicine that a medical researcher has recently discovered. The drug is expensive to make, and the researcher is charging ten times the cost, or $5,000, for a small dose. The sick woman's husband, Henry, approaches everyone he knows in hope of borrowing money, but he can get together only about $2,500. He tells the researcher that his wife is dying and asks him to lower the price of the drug or let him pay later. The researcher says, "No, I discovered the drug, and I'm going to make money from it." Henry is desperate and considers stealing the drug for his wife.

What would you tell Henry to do?

KOHLBERG'S THEORY OF MORAL DEVELOPMENT

In the view of psychologist Lawrence Kohlberg, the advice you give Henry reflects your level of moral development. According to Kohlberg, people pass through a series of stages in the evolution of their sense of justice and in the kind of reasoning they use to make moral judgments (Kohlberg, 1984). Largely because of the various cognitive limitations that Piaget described, preadolescent children tend to think either in terms of concrete, unvarying rules ("It is always wrong to steal" or "I'll be punished if I steal") or in terms of the rules of society ("Good people don't steal" or "What if everyone stole?").

Adolescents, however, have typically reached Piaget's formal operational stage of cognitive development and can reason on a higher plane. Because they are able to comprehend broad moral principles, they can understand that morality is not always black and white and that conflict can exist between two sets of socially accepted standards.

Kohlberg (1984) suggests that the changes in moral reasoning can be understood best as a three-level sequence (see Figure 2). His theory assumes that people move through the levels in a fixed order and that they cannot reach the highest level until about age 13—primarily because of limitations in cognitive development before that age.

	Sample Moral Reasoning	
Level	In Favor of Stealing the Drug	Against Stealing the Drug
Level 1 Preconventional morality: The main considerations at this level are the avoidance of punishment and the desire for rewards.	"You shouldn't just let your wife die. People will blame you for not doing enough, and they'll blame the scientist for not selling you the drug for less money."	"You can't steal the drug because you'll be arrested and go to jail. Even if you aren't caught, you'll feel guilty and you'll always worry that the police may figure out what you did."
Level 2 Conventional morality: Membership in society becomes important at this level. People behave in ways that will win the approval of others.	"Who will blame you if you steal a life-saving drug? But if you just let your wife die, you won't be able to hold your head up in front of your family or neighbors."	"If you steal the drug, everyone will treat you like a criminal. They will wonder why you couldn't have found some other way to save your wife."
Level 3 Postconventional morality: People accept that there are certain ideals and principles of morality that must govern our actions. At this level, these ideals are more important than any particular society's rules.	"If you simply follow the law, you will violate the underlying principle of saving your wife's life. If you do steal the drug, society will understand your actions and respect them. You can't let an inadequate, outdated law prevent you from doing the right thing."	"You can't change your standards of honesty whenever it suits your needs. Others may not blame you for stealing the drug, but your conscience will blame you for betraying your own moral code."

FIGURE 2 Developmental psychologist Lawrence Kohlberg theorized that people move through a three-level sequence of moral reasoning in a fixed order. However, he contended that few people ever reach the highest level of moral reasoning. (Source: Kohlberg, 1969.)

However, many people never reach the highest level of moral reasoning. In fact, Kohlberg found that only a relatively small percentage of adults rise above the second level of his model (Kohlberg & Ryncarz, 1990; Powers, 2006; Moshman, 2011).

Although Kohlberg's theory has had a substantial influence on our understanding of moral development, the research support is mixed. One difficulty with the theory is that it pertains to moral *judgments,* not moral *behavior.* Knowing right from wrong does not mean that we will always act in accordance with our judgments. In addition, the theory applies primarily to Western society and its moral code; cross-cultural research conducted in cultures with different moral systems suggests that Kohlberg's theory is not necessarily applicable (Nucci, 2002; Barandiaran, Pascual, & Samaniego, 2006; Stey, Lapsley, & McKeever, 2013).

MORAL DEVELOPMENT IN WOMEN

One glaring shortcoming of Kohlberg's research is that he primarily used male participants. Furthermore, psychologist Carol Gilligan (1996) argues that because of men's and women's distinctive socialization experiences, a fundamental difference exists in the way each gender views moral behavior. According to Gilligan, men view morality primarily in terms of broad principles, such as justice and fairness. In contrast, women see it in terms of responsibility toward individuals and willingness to make sacrifices to help a specific individual within the context of a particular relationship. Compassion for individuals is a more salient factor in moral behavior for women than it is for men.

Because Kohlberg's model defines moral behavior largely in terms of abstract principles such as justice, Gilligan finds that it inadequately describes females' moral development. She suggests that women's morality centers on individual well-being and social relationships–a morality of *caring.* In her view, compassionate concern for the welfare of others represents the highest level of morality.

The fact that Gilligan's conception of morality differs greatly from Kohlberg's suggests that gender plays an important role in determining what a person sees as moral. Although the research evidence is not definitive, it seems plausible that their differing

Study Alert

The difference between the Kohlberg and Gilligan approaches to moral development is significant. Kohlberg's theory focuses on stages and Gilligan's rests on gender differences.

conceptions of what constitutes moral behavior may lead men and women to regard the morality of a specific behavior in different ways (Jorgensen, 2006; Sherblom, 2008; Walker & Frimer, 2009).

Social Development: Finding One's Self in a Social World

"Who am I?" "How do I fit into the world?" "What is life all about?"

Questions such as these assume special significance during the teenage years, as adolescents seek to find their place in the broader social world. As we will see, this quest takes adolescents along several routes.

ERIKSON'S THEORY OF PSYCHOSOCIAL DEVELOPMENT: THE SEARCH FOR IDENTITY

Erikson's theory of psychosocial development emphasizes the search for identity during the adolescent years. As noted earlier, psychosocial development encompasses the way people's understanding of themselves, one another, and the world around them changes during the course of development (Erikson, 1963).

The fifth stage of Erikson's theory (summarized, with the other stages, in Figure 3), the **identity-versus-role-confusion stage,** encompasses adolescence. During this stage, a time of major testing, people try to determine what is unique about themselves. They attempt to discover who they are, what their strengths are, and what kinds of roles they are best suited to play for the rest of their lives–in short, their **identity.** A person confused about the most appropriate role to play in life may lack a stable identity, adopt an unacceptable role such as that of a social deviant, or have difficulty maintaining close personal relationships later in life (Updegraff et al., 2004; Vleioras & Bosma, 2005; Goldstein, 2006).

identity-versus-role-confusion stage According to Erikson, a time in adolescence of major testing to determine one's unique qualities.

identity The distinguishing character of the individual: who each of us is, what our roles are, and what we are capable of.

Stage	Approximate Age	Positive Outcomes	Negative Outcomes
1. Trust-vs.-mistrust	Birth–1½ years	Feelings of trust from environmental support	Fear and concern regarding others
2. Autonomy-vs.-shame-and-doubt	1½–3 years	Self-sufficiency if exploration is encouraged	Doubts about self, lack of independence
3. Initiative-vs.-guilt	3–6 years	Discovery of ways to initiate actions	Guilt from actions and thoughts
4. Industry-vs.-inferiority	6–12 years	Development of sense of competence	Feelings of inferiority, no sense of mastery
5. Identity-vs.-role-confusion	Adolescence	Awareness of uniqueness of self, knowledge of role to be followed	Inability to identify appropriate roles in life
6. Intimacy-vs.-isolation	Early adulthood	Development of loving, sexual relationships and close friendships	Fear of relationships with others
7. Generativity-vs.-stagnation	Middle adulthood	Sense of contribution to continuity of life	Trivialization of one's activities
8. Ego-integrity-vs.-despair	Late adulthood	Sense of unity in life's accomplishments	Regret over lost opportunities of life

FIGURE 3 Erikson's stages of psychosocial development. According to Erikson, people proceed through eight stages of psychosocial development across their lives. He suggested that each stage requires the resolution of a crisis or conflict and may produce both positive and negative outcomes.

During the identity-versus-role-confusion period, an adolescent feels pressure to identify what to do with his or her life. Because these pressures come at a time of major physical changes as well as important changes in what society expects of them, adolescents can find the period an especially difficult one. The identity-versus-role-confusion stage has another important characteristic: declining reliance on adults for information with a shift toward using the peer group as a source of social judgments. The peer group becomes increasingly important, enabling adolescents to form close, adult-like relationships and helping them clarify their personal identities. According to Erikson, the identity-versus-role-confusion stage marks a pivotal point in psychosocial development, paving the way for continued growth and the future development of personal relationships.

During early adulthood, people enter the **intimacy-versus-isolation stage.** Spanning the period of early adulthood (from post-adolescence to the early 30s), this stage focuses on developing close relationships with others. Difficulties during this stage result in feelings of loneliness and a fear of such relationships; successful resolution of the crises of this stage results in the possibility of forming relationships that are intimate on a physical, intellectual, and emotional level.

intimacy-versus-isolation stage According to Erikson, a period during early adulthood that focuses on developing close relationships.

generativity-versus-stagnation stage According to Erikson, a period in middle adulthood during which we take stock of our contributions to family and society.

ego-integrity-versus-despair stage According to Erikson, a period from late adulthood until death during which we review life's accomplishments and failures.

Development continues during middle adulthood as people enter the **generativity-versus-stagnation stage.** Generativity is the ability to contribute to one's family, community, work, and society and to assist the development of the younger generation. Success in this stage results in a person's feeling positive about the continuity of life; difficulties in this stage lead a person to feel that his or her activities are trivial or stagnant and have done nothing for upcoming generations. In fact, if a person has not successfully resolved the identity crisis of adolescence, he or she may still be foundering, for example, in identifying an appropriate career.

Finally, the last stage of psychosocial development, the **ego-integrity-versus-despair stage,** spans later adulthood and continues until death. Now a sense of accomplishment signifies success in resolving the difficulties presented by this stage of life; failure to resolve the difficulties results in regret over what might have been achieved but was not.

Notably, Erikson's theory suggests that development does not stop at adolescence but continues throughout adulthood. A substantial amount of research now confirms this view. For instance, a 22-year study by psychologist Susan Whitbourne found considerable support for the fundamentals of Erikson's theory; the study determined that psychosocial development continues through adolescence and adulthood. In sum, adolescence is not an end point but rather a way station on the path of psychosocial development (Whitbourne et al., 1992; McAdams et al., 1997).

Although Erikson's theory provides a broad outline of identity development, critics have pointed out that his approach is anchored in male-oriented concepts of individuality and competitiveness. In an alternative conception, psychologist Carol Gilligan suggests that women may develop identity through the establishment of relationships. In her view, a primary component of women's identity is the construction of caring networks among themselves and others (Gilligan, 2004).

STORMY ADOLESCENCE: MYTH OR REALITY?

Does puberty invariably foreshadow a stormy, rebellious period of adolescence?

At one time, psychologists thought that most children entering adolescence were beginning a period filled with stress and unhappiness. Now, however, research shows that this characterization is largely a myth. The reality is that most young people pass through adolescence without great turmoil in their lives and that they get along with their parents reasonably well (van Wei, Linssen, & Abma, 2000; Granic, Hollenstein, & Dishion, 2003).

Study Alert
The characterization of a stormy adolescence is a myth for most adolescents.

PsychTech

Adolescent use of social media such as Facebook is growing rapidly: Three-quarters of teenagers have a Facebook page, and a quarter of them access their Facebook page continuously throughout the day.

Not that adolescence is completely calm! In most families with adolescents, the amount of arguing and bickering clearly rises. Most young teenagers, as part of their search for identity, experience tension between their attempts to become independent from their parents and their actual dependence on them. They may experiment with a range of behaviors and flirt with a variety of activities that their parents, and even society as a whole, find objectionable. Happily, though, for most families such tensions stabilize during middle adolescence–around age 15 or 16–and eventually decline around age 18 (Smetana, Daddis, & Chuang, 2003; Smetana, 2005).

One reason for the increase in discord during adolescence appears to be the protracted period in which children stay at home with their parents. In prior historical periods–and in some non-Western cultures today–children leave home immediately after puberty and are considered adults. Today, however, sexually mature adolescents may spend as many as 7 or 8 years with their parents. Current social trends even hint at an extension of the conflicts of adolescence beyond the teenage years because a significant number of young adults–known as *boomerang children*–return to live with their parents, typically for economic reasons, after leaving home for some period. Although some parents welcome the return of their children, others are less sympathetic, which opens the way to conflict (Bianchi & Casper, 2000; Lewin, 2003).

Another source of strife with parents lies in the way adolescents think. Adolescence fosters *adolescent egocentrism,* a state of self-absorption in which a teenager views the world from his or her own point of view. Egocentrism leads adolescents to be highly critical of authority figures, unwilling to accept criticism, and quick to fault others. It also makes them believe that they are the center of everyone else's attention, which leads to self-consciousness. Furthermore, they develop *personal fables,* the belief that their experience is unique, exceptional, and shared by no one else. Such personal fables may make adolescents feel invulnerable to the risks that threaten others (Alberts, Elkind, & Ginsberg, 2007; Schwartz, Maynard, & Uzelac, 2008; Boeve-de Pauw, Donche, & Van Petegem, 2011).

Finally, parent-adolescent discord occurs because adolescents are much more apt to engage in risky behavior than later in life. In large part, their riskiness is due to the immaturity of brain systems that regulate impulse control, some of which do not fully develop until people are in their 20s (Steinberg, 2007).

ADOLESCENT SUICIDE

Although the vast majority of teenagers pass through adolescence without major psychological difficulties, some experience unusually severe psychological problems. Sometimes those problems become so extreme that adolescents take their own lives. Suicide is the third leading cause of death for adolescents (after accidents and homicide) in the United States. More teenagers and young adults die from suicide than from cancer, heart disease, AIDS, birth defects, stroke, pneumonia and influenza, and chronic lung disease combined (CDC, 2004b).

These students are kneeling by a friend's tombstone. The rate of suicide among teenagers has risen significantly over the last few decades. Can you think of any reasons for this phenomenon?

A teenager commits suicide every 90 minutes. Furthermore, the reported rate of suicide may actually be understated because medical personnel hesitate to report suicide as a cause of death. Instead, they frequently label a death as an accident in an effort to protect the survivors. Overall, as many as 200 adolescents may attempt suicide for every one who actually takes his or her own life (CDC, 2000; Brausch & Gutierrez, 2009).

Male adolescents are five times more likely to commit suicide than females, although females *attempt* suicide more often than males. The rate of adolescent suicide is significantly greater among whites than among nonwhites. However, the suicide rate of African-American males has increased much more rapidly than that of white males over the last two decades. Native Americans have the highest suicide rate of any ethnic group in the United States, and Asian Americans have the lowest rate (CDC, 2004b; Boden, Fergusson, & Horwood, 2007; Bossarte & Swahn, 2011).

As the rate of suicide has slowly declined, the rates are still higher for adolescents than any other age group except for the elderly. Some psychologists suggest that the sharp rise in stress that teenagers experience–in terms of academic and social pressure, alcoholism, drug abuse, and family difficulties–provokes the most troubled adolescents to take their own lives. However, that is not the whole story, because the suicide rate for other age groups has remained fairly stable in the past few decades. It is unlikely that stress has increased only for adolescents and not for the rest of the population (Lubell et al., 2004; Valois, Zullig, & Hunter, 2013).

Although the question of why adolescent suicide rates are so high remains unanswered, several factors put adolescents at risk. One factor is depression, characterized by unhappiness, extreme fatigue, and–a variable that seems especially important–a profound sense of hopelessness. In other cases, adolescents who commit suicide are perfectionists who are inhibited socially and prone to extreme anxiety when they face any social or academic challenge (see Figure 4; CDC, 2004b; Richardson et al., 2005; Caelian, 2006).

Family background and adjustment difficulties are also related to suicide. A long-standing history of conflicts between parents and children may lead to adolescent behavior problems, such as delinquency, dropping out of school, and aggressive tendencies. In addition, teenage alcoholics and abusers of other drugs have a relatively high rate of suicide (Winstead & Sanchez, 2005; Bagge & Sher, 2008; Hardt et al., 2008).

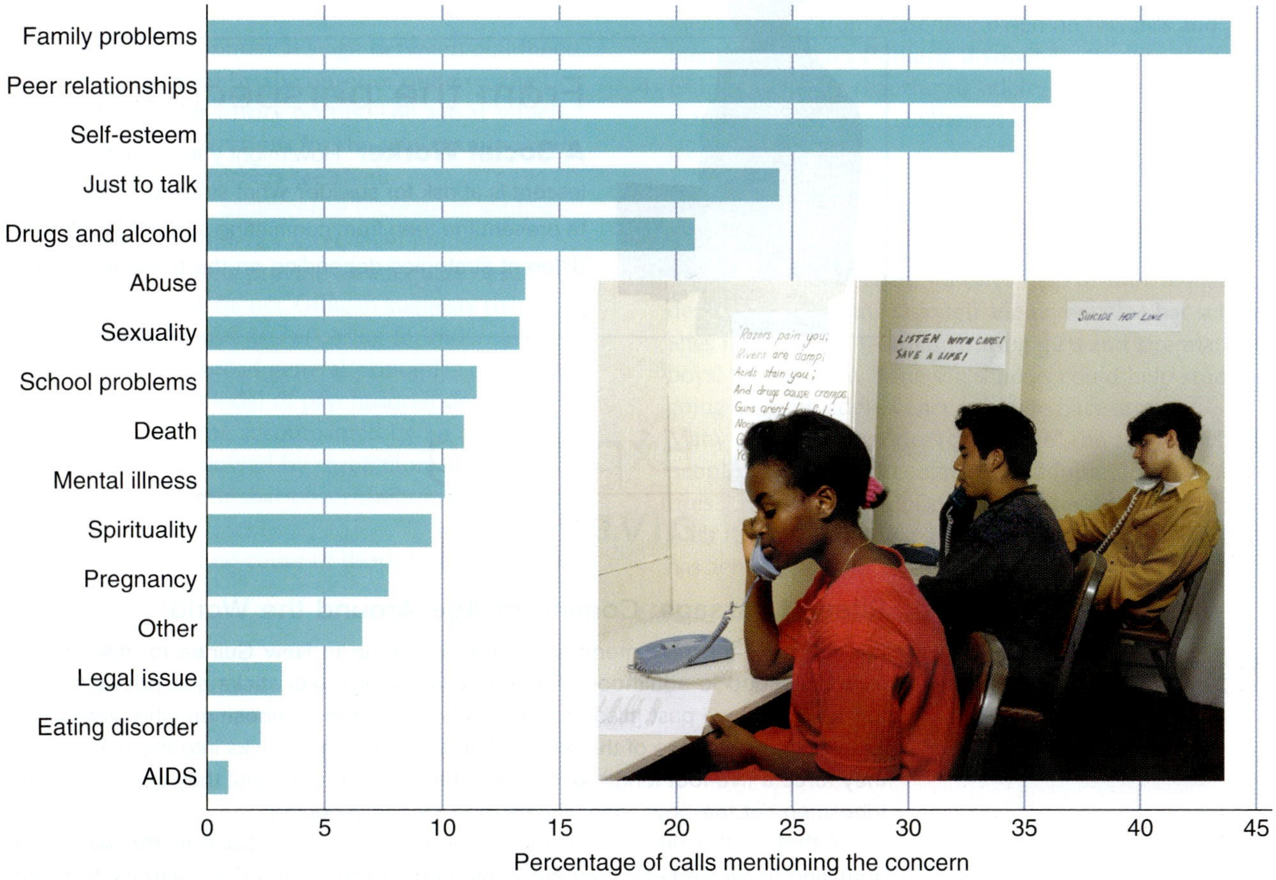

FIGURE 4 According to a review of phone calls to one telephone help line, adolescents who were considering suicide most often mentioned family, peer relationships, and self-esteem problems. (Source: Adapted from Boehm & Campbell, 1995.)

MODULE 30

Adulthood

Learning Outcomes

LO 30-1 What are the principal kinds of physical, social, and intellectual changes that occur in early and middle adulthood, and what are their causes?

LO 30-2 How does the reality of late adulthood differ from the stereotypes about that period?

LO 30-3 How can we adjust to death?

> I thought I got better as I got older. I found out that wasn't the case in a real hurry last year. After going twelve years in professional football and twelve years before that in amateur football without ever having surgery performed on me, the last two seasons of my career I went under the knife three times. It happened very quickly and without warning, and I began to ask myself, "Is this age? Is this what's happening?" Because up until that moment, I'd never realized that I was getting older. (Brian Sipe, quoted in Kotre & Hall, 1990, pp. 257, 259–260)

As a former professional football player, Brian Sipe intensely felt the changes in his body brought about by aging. But the challenges he experienced are part of a normal process that affects all people as they move through adulthood.

Psychologists generally agree that early adulthood begins around age 20 and lasts until about age 40 to 45 when middle adulthood begins and continues until around age 65. Despite the enormous importance of these periods of life in terms of both the accomplishments that occur in them and their overall length (together they span some 44 years), they have been studied less than has any other stage. For one reason, the physical changes that occur during these periods are less apparent and more gradual than those at other times during the life span. In addition, the diverse social changes that arise during this period defy simple categorization.

emerging adulthood The period beginning in the late teenage years and extending into the mid-20s.

The variety of changes that occur in early adulthood have led many developmental psychologists to view the start of the period as a transitional phase called emerging adulthood. **Emerging adulthood** is the period beginning in the late teenage years and extending into the mid-20s. During emerging adulthood, people are no longer adolescents, but they haven't fully taken on the responsibilities of adulthood. Instead, they are still engaged in determining who they are and what their life and career paths should be (Bukobza, 2009; Lamborn & Groh, 2009; Schwartz et al., 2013).

The view that adulthood is preceded by an extended period of emerging adulthood reflects the reality that the economies of industrialized countries have shifted away from manufacturing to an economy that focuses on technology and information and thus requires increases in time spent in educational training. Furthermore, the age at which most people marry and have children has risen significantly (Arnett, 2007, 2011).

There's also an increasing ambivalence about reaching adulthood. When people in their late teens and early 20s are asked if they feel they have reached adulthood, most say "yes and no" (see Figure 1). In short, emerging adulthood is an age of identity exploration in which individuals are more self-focused and uncertain than they will be later in early adulthood (Arnett, 2000, 2006).

As we discuss the changes that occur through emerging adulthood, early adulthood, middle adulthood, and ultimately late adulthood, keep in mind the demarcations between the periods are fuzzy. However, the changes are certainly no less profound than they were in earlier periods of development.

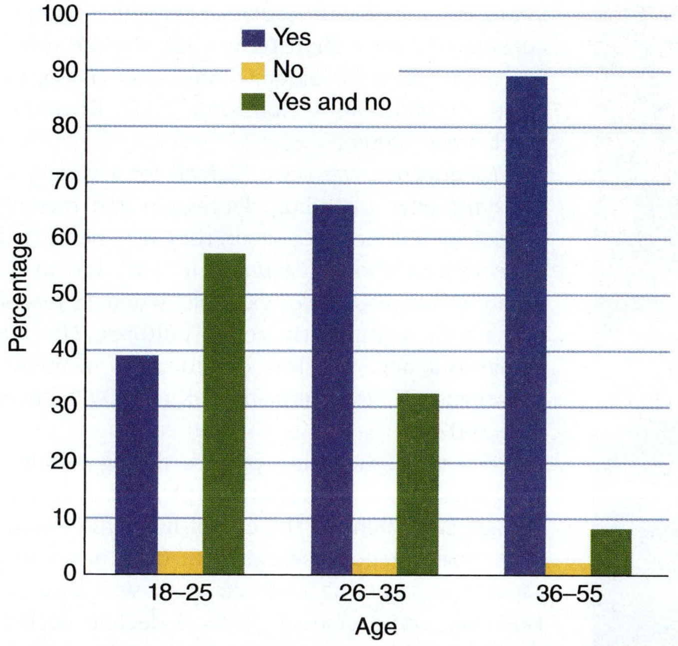

FIGURE 1 Evidence of a period of emerging adulthood is provided by the responses to a questionnaire asking, "Do you feel that you have reached adulthood?" Most people between the ages of 18 and 25 were ambivalent, responding "yes and no." Later, this ambivalence disappeared, with most people 26–35 saying "yes." (Source: Adapted from Arnett, 2006.)

Physical Development: The Peak of Health

For most people, early adulthood marks the peak of physical health. From about 18 to 25 years of age, people's strength is greatest, their reflexes are quickest, and their chances of dying from disease are quite slim. Moreover, reproductive capabilities are at their highest level.

Around age 25, the body becomes slightly less efficient and more susceptible to disease. Overall, however, ill health remains the exception; most people stay remarkably healthy during early adulthood. (Can you think of any machine other than the body that can operate without pause for so long a period?)

During middle adulthood, people gradually become aware of changes in their bodies. They often experience weight gain (although they can avoid such increases through diet and exercise). Furthermore, the sense organs gradually become less sensitive, and reactions to stimuli are slower. But generally, the physical declines that occur during middle adulthood are minor and often unnoticeable (DiGiovanna, 1994). The major biological change that does occur during middle adulthood pertains to reproductive capabilities. On average, during their late 40s or early 50s, women begin **menopause,** during which they stop menstruating and are no longer fertile. Because menopause is accompanied by a significant reduction in the production of estrogen, a female hormone, women sometimes experience symptoms such as hot flashes, sudden sensations of heat. Many symptoms can be treated through *hormone therapy (HT)* in which menopausal women take the hormones estrogen and progesterone.

menopause The period during which women stop menstruating and are no longer fertile.

However, hormone therapy poses several dangers, such as an increase in the risk of breast cancer, blood clots, and coronary heart disease. These uncertainties make the routine use of HT controversial. Currently, the medical consensus seems to be that

Women's reactions to menopause vary significantly across cultures. According to one study, the more a society values old age, the less difficulty its women have during menopause. Why do you think this would be the case?

younger women with severe menopausal symptoms ought to consider HT on a short-term basis. On the other hand, HT is less appropriate for older women after menopause (Lindh-Astrand, Brynhildsen, & Hoffmann, 2007; Rossouw et al., 2007; MacLennan, 2009).

Menopause was once blamed for a variety of psychological symptoms, including depression and memory loss. However, if such difficulties occur, they may be caused by women's expectations about reaching an "old" age in a society that highly values youth. For example, women's reactions to menopause vary significantly across cultures. The more a society values old age, the less difficulty its women have during menopause (Elliot, Berman, & Kim, 2002; Beyene, Gilliss, & Lee, 2007).

For men, the aging process during middle adulthood is somewhat subtler. There are no physiological signals of increasing age equivalent to the end of menstruation in women; that is, no male menopause exists. In fact, men remain fertile and capable of fathering children until well into late adulthood. However, some gradual physical decline occurs. Sperm production decreases, and the frequency of orgasm tends to decline. Once again, though, any psychological difficulties associated with these changes are usually brought about by an aging individual's inability to meet the exaggerated standards of youthfulness and not by the person's physical deterioration.

Social Development: Working at Life

Whereas physical changes during adulthood reflect development of a quantitative nature, social developmental transitions are qualitative and more profound. During this period, people typically launch themselves into careers, marriage, and families.

The entry into early adulthood is usually marked by leaving one's childhood home and entering the world of work. People envision life goals and make career choices. Their lives often center on their careers, which form an important part of their identity (Vaillant & Vaillant, 1990; Levinson, 1990, 1992).

In their early 40s, however, people may begin to question their lives as they enter a period called the *midlife transition*. The idea that life will end at some point can become more influential in their thinking, which leads them to question their past accomplishments (Gould, 1978).

Although some psychologists–and popular opinion–suggest that physical aging and dissatisfaction with one's life mark a so-called "midlife crisis," there is little evidence for such a "crisis." In fact, the passage into middle age is relatively calm for most people. Most 40-year-olds view their lives and accomplishments positively enough to proceed relatively smoothly through midlife, and the 40s and 50s are often a particularly rewarding period. Rather than looking to the future, people concentrate on the present; their involvement with their families, friends, and other social groups takes on new importance. A major developmental thrust of this period is coming to terms with one's circumstances (Whitbourne, 2000, 2010; Dare, 2011).

Finally, during the last stages of adulthood, people become more accepting of others and of their own lives and are less concerned about issues or problems that once bothered them. They come to accept the fact that death is inevitable, and they try to understand their accomplishments in terms of the broader meaning of life.

Although people may begin for the first time to label themselves as "old," many also develop a sense of wisdom and feel freer to enjoy life (Baltes & Kunzmann, 2003; Miner-Rubino, Winter, & Stewart, 2004; Ward-Baker, 2007).

Marriage, Children, and Divorce: Family Ties

In the typical fairy tale, a dashing young man and a beautiful young woman marry, have children, and live happily ever after. However, that scenario does not match the realities of love and marriage in the 21st century. Today, it is just as likely that the man and woman would first live together, then get married and have children, but ultimately get divorced.

The percentage of U.S. households made up of unmarried couples has increased dramatically over the last two decades. At the same time, the average age at which marriage takes place is higher than at any time since the turn of the last century. These changes have been dramatic, and they suggest that the institution of marriage has changed considerably from earlier historical periods.

When people do marry, the probability of divorce is high, especially for younger couples. Even though divorce rates have been declining since they peaked in 1981, about half of all first marriages end in divorce. Before they are 18 years old, two-fifths of children will experience the breakup of their parents' marriages. Moreover, the rise in divorce is not just a U.S. phenomenon: The divorce rate has accelerated over the past several decades in most industrialized countries. In some countries, the increase has been enormous. In South Korea, for example, the divorce rate quadrupled from 11% to 47% in the 12-year period ending in 2002 (Lankov, 2004; Olson & DeFrain, 2005; Park & Raymo, 2013).

Changes in marriage and divorce trends have doubled the number of single-parent households in the United States over the last two decades. Almost 25% of all family households are now headed by one parent compared with 13% in 1970. If present trends continue, almost three-fourths of American children will spend some portion of

Single-parent families have doubled within the past decade, with the mother usually as head of the household. What are some of the challenges facing children in single-parent families?

their lives in a single-parent family before they turn 18. For children in minority households, the numbers are even higher. Almost 60% of all black children and more than a third of all Hispanic children live in homes with only one parent. Furthermore, in most single-parent families, the children live with the mother rather than the father–a phenomenon that is consistent across racial and ethnic groups throughout the industrialized world (U.S. Bureau of the Census, 2000; Sarsour et al., 2011).

What are the economic and emotional consequences for children living in homes with only one parent? Single-parent families are often economically less well off, and this economic disadvantage has an impact on children's opportunities. More than a third of single-mother families with children have incomes below the poverty line. In addition, good child care at an affordable price is often hard to find. Furthermore, for children of divorce, the parents' separation is often a painful experience that may result in obstacles to establishing close relationships later in life. Children may blame themselves for the breakup or feel pressure to take sides (U.S. Bureau of the Census, 2000; Wallerstein et al., 2000; Liu, He, & Wu, 2007).

Most evidence suggests, however, that children from single-parent families are no less well adjusted than those from two-parent families. In fact, children may be more successful growing up in a harmonious single-parent family than in a two-parent family that engages in continuous conflict (Harold et al., 1997; Clarke-Stewart et al., 2000; Kelly, 2000; Olson & DeFrain, 2005).

CHANGING ROLES OF MEN AND WOMEN

One of the major changes in family life in the last two decades has been the evolution of men's and women's roles. More women than ever before act simultaneously as wives, mothers, and wage earners–in contrast to women in traditional marriages in which the husband is the sole wage earner and the wife assumes primary responsibility for care of the home and children.

Almost three-fourths of all women with children under the age of 18 are employed outside the home, and 65% of mothers with children under age 6 are working. In the mid-1960s, only 17% of mothers of 1-year-olds worked full-time; now, more than half are in the labor force (Bureau of Labor Statistics, 2013).

Most married working women are not free of household responsibilities. Even in marriages in which the spouses hold jobs that have similar status and require similar hours, the distribution of household tasks between husbands and wives has not changed substantially. Working wives are still more likely than husbands to feel responsible for traditional homemaking tasks such as cooking and cleaning. In contrast, husbands still view themselves as responsible primarily for household tasks such as repairing broken appliances and doing yardwork (Ganong & Coleman, 1999; Juster, Ono, & Stafford, 2002; Damaske, 2011).

WOMEN'S "SECOND SHIFT"

Working mothers can put in a staggering number of hours. One survey, for instance, found that if we add the number of hours worked on the job and in the home, employed mothers of children under 3 years of age put in an average of 90 hours per week! The additional work women perform is sometimes called the "second shift." National surveys show women who are both employed and mothers put in an extra month of 24-hour days during the course of a year. Researchers see similar patterns in many developing societies throughout the world, with women working at full-time jobs and also having primary responsibilities for child care (Hochschild, 2001; Jacobs & Gerson, 2004; Bureau of Labor Statistics, 2007).

Consequently, rather than careers being a substitute for what women do at home, they are often an addition to the role of homemaker. It is not surprising that some wives feel resentment toward husbands who spend less time on child care and housework than the wives had expected before the birth of their children (Kiecolt, 2003; Gerstel, 2005; Fagan & Press, 2008).

Later Years of Life: Growing Old

> I've always enjoyed doing things in the mountains–hiking or, more recently, active cliff-climbing. The more difficult the climb, the more absorbing it is. The climbs I really remember are the ones I had to work on. Maybe a particular section where it took two or three tries before I found the right combination of moves that got me up easily–and, preferably, elegantly. It's a wonderful exhilaration to get to the top and sit down and perhaps have lunch and look out over the landscape and be so grateful that it's still possible for me to do that sort of thing. (Lyman Spitzer, age 74, quoted in Kotre & Hall, 1990, pp. 358-359)

If you can't quite picture a 74-year-old rock-climbing, some rethinking of your view of late adulthood may be in order. In spite of the societal stereotype of "old age" as a time of inactivity and physical and mental decline, gerontologists, specialists who study aging, are beginning to paint a very different portrait of late adulthood.

By focusing on the period of life that starts at around age 65, gerontologists are making important contributions to clarifying the capabilities of older adults. Their work is demonstrating that significant developmental processes continue even during old age. And as people live longer, the absolute number of people within older adulthood will continue to increase. Consequently, developing an understanding of late adulthood has become a critical priority for psychologists (Moody, 2000; Schaie, 2005b; Jia, Zack, & Thompson, 2011).

PHYSICAL CHANGES IN LATE ADULTHOOD: THE AGING BODY

Napping, eating, walking, conversing. It probably doesn't surprise you that these relatively nonstrenuous activities represent the typical pastimes of late adulthood. But it is striking that these activities are identical to the most common leisure activities reported in a survey of college students (Harper, 1978). Although the students cited more active pursuits–such as sailing and playing basketball–as their favorite activities, in actuality they engaged in such sports relatively infrequently and spent most of their free time napping, eating, walking, and conversing.

Although the leisure activities in which older adults engage may not differ all that much from the ones that younger people pursue, many physical changes are, of course, brought about by the aging process. The most obvious are those of appearance–hair thinning and turning gray, skin wrinkling and folding, and sometimes a slight loss of height as the thickness of the disks between vertebrae in the spine decreases. But subtler changes also occur in the body's biological functioning. For example, sensory capabilities decrease as a result of aging: Vision, hearing, smell, and taste become less sensitive. Reaction time slows, and physical stamina changes (Stenklev & Laukli, 2004; Schieber, 2006; Madden, 2007).

What are the reasons for these physical declines? **Genetic preprogramming theories of aging** suggest that human cells have a built-in time limit to their reproduction. These theories suggest that after a certain time cells stop dividing or become harmful to the body–as if a kind of automatic self-destruct button had been pushed. In contrast, **wear-and-tear theories of aging** suggest that the mechanical functions of the body simply work less efficiently as people age. Waste byproducts of energy production eventually accumulate, and mistakes are made when cells divide. Eventually the body in effect wears out like an old automobile (Ly et al., 2000; Miquel, 2006; Hayflick, 2007).

Evidence supports both the genetic preprogramming and the wear-and-tear views, and it may be that both processes contribute to natural aging. It is clear, however, that physical aging is not a disease but a natural biological process. Many physical functions do not decline with age. For example, sex remains pleasurable well into old age (although the frequency of sexual activity decreases), and some people report that the pleasure they derive from sex increases during late adulthood (Gelfand, 2000; DeLamater & Sill, 2005; Wilkin & Haddock, 2011).

genetic preprogramming theories of aging Theories that suggest that human cells have a built-in time limit to their reproduction and that they are no longer able to divide after a certain time.

wear-and-tear theories of aging Theories that suggest that the mechanical functions of the body simply stop working efficiently.

Study Alert

Two major theories of aging—the genetic preprogramming and the wear-and-tear views—explain some of the physical changes that take place in older adults.

COGNITIVE CHANGES: THINKING ABOUT—AND DURING—LATE ADULTHOOD

At one time, many gerontologists would have agreed with the popular view that older adults are forgetful and confused. Today, however, most research indicates that this assessment is far from an accurate one of older people's capabilities.

One reason for the change in view is that more sophisticated research techniques exist for studying the cognitive changes that occur in late adulthood. For example, if we were to give a group of older adults an IQ test, we might find that the average score was lower than the score achieved by a group of younger people. We might conclude that this signifies a decline in intelligence. Yet, if we looked a little more closely at the specific test, we might find that the conclusion was unwarranted. For instance, many IQ tests include portions based on physical performance (such as arranging a group of blocks) or on speed. In such cases, poorer performance on the IQ test may be due to gradual decreases in reaction time–a physical decline that accompanies late adulthood and has little or nothing to do with older adults' intellectual capabilities.

Other difficulties hamper research into cognitive functioning during late adulthood. For example, older people are often less healthy than younger ones; when only *healthy* older adults are compared to healthy younger adults, intellectual differences are far less evident. Furthermore, the average number of years in school is often lower in older adults (for historical reasons) than in younger ones, and older adults may be less motivated to perform well on intelligence tests than younger people. Finally, traditional IQ tests may be inappropriate measures of intelligence in late adulthood. Older adults sometimes perform better on tests of practical intelligence than younger individuals do (Willis & Schaie, 1994; Dixon & Cohen, 2003; Johnson & Deary, 2011).

Still, some declines in intellectual functioning during late adulthood do occur, although the pattern of age differences is not uniform for different types of cognitive abilities (see Figure 2). In general, skills relating to *fluid intelligence* (which involves information-processing skills such as memory, calculations, and analogy solving) show declines in late adulthood. In contrast, skills relating to *crystallized intelligence* (intelligence based on the accumulation of information, skills, and strategies learned through experience) remain steady and in some cases actually improve (van Hooren, Valentijn, & Bosma, 2007; Kaufman, Johnson, & Liu, 2008; Dixon et al., 2013).

Even when changes in intellectual functioning occur during later adulthood, people often are able to compensate for any decline. They can still learn what they want to learn; it may just take more time. Furthermore, teaching older adults strategies for dealing with new problems can prevent declines in performance (Saczynski, Willis, & Schaie, 2002; Cavallini, Pagnin, & Vecchi, 2003; Peters et al., 2007).

Although there are declines in fluid intelligence in late adulthood, skills relating to crystallized intelligence remain steady and may actually improve.

MEMORY CHANGES IN LATE ADULTHOOD: ARE OLDER ADULTS FORGETFUL?

One of the characteristics most frequently attributed to late adulthood is forgetfulness. How accurate is this assumption?

Most evidence suggests that memory change is not an inevitable part of the aging process. For instance, research shows that older people in cultures in which older adults are held in high esteem, such as mainland China, are less likely to show memory losses than those living in cultures in which the expectation is that memory will decline. Similarly, when older people in Western societies are reminded of the advantages of age (for example, "age brings wisdom"), they tend to do better on tests of memory (Levy, 1996; Hess, Hinson, & Statham, 2004; Dixon, Rust, & Feltmate, 2007).

Even when people show memory declines during late adulthood, their deficits are limited to certain types of memory. For instance, losses tend to be limited to episodic memories that relate to specific experiences in

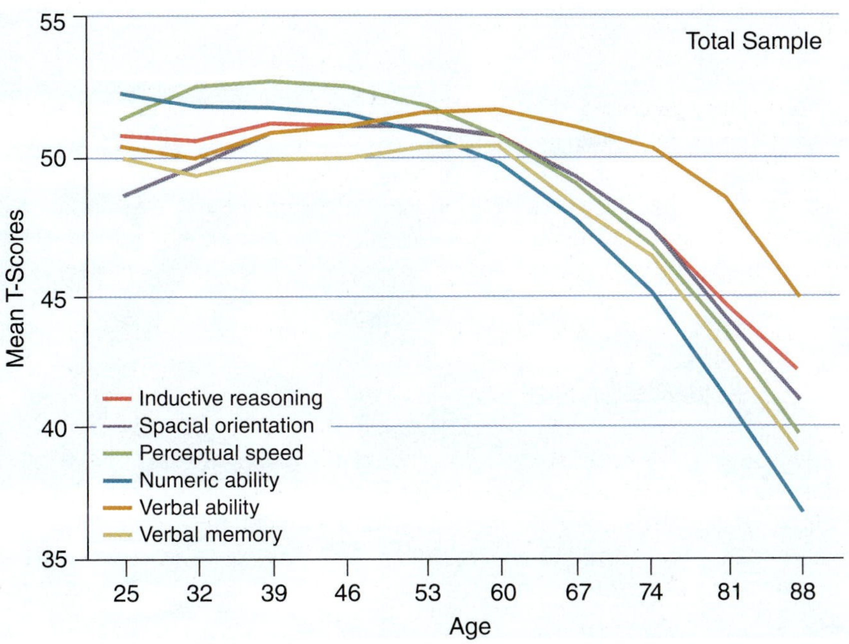

FIGURE 2 Age-related changes in intellectual skills vary according to the specific cognitive ability in question. (Source: Adapted from Schaie, 2005.)

people's lives. Other types of memories, such as semantic memories (that refer to general knowledge and facts) and implicit memories (memories of which we are not consciously aware) are largely unaffected by age (Mitchell & Schmitt, 2006; St. Jacques & Levine, 2007; Blumen, Rajaram, & Henkel, 2013).

Declines in episodic memories can often be traced to changes in older adults' lives. For instance, it is not surprising that a retired person, who may no longer face the same kind of consistent intellectual challenges encountered on the job, may have less practice in using memory or even be less motivated to remember things, which leads to an apparent decline in memory. Even in cases in which long-term memory declines, older adults can profit from training that targets memory skills (Fritsch et al., 2007; West, Bagwell, & Dark-Freudeman, 2007; Morcom & Friston, 2011).

In the past, older adults with severe cases of memory decline accompanied by other cognitive difficulties were said to suffer from *senility*. Now, most gerontologists view senility as an imprecise label that has outlived its usefulness. Instead, gerontologists explain symptoms of mental deterioration using more precise factors.

For example, rather than use senility to describe memory loss in general, gerontologists now recognize **Alzheimer's disease** as a progressive brain disorder that leads to a gradual and irreversible decline in cognitive abilities. More than 5.2 million Americans have the disease, and 1 in 8 people age 65 and older are afflicted. Unless a cure is found, some 14 million people will experience Alzheimer's by 2050 (Rogers, 2007; Alzheimer's Association, 2013).

Alzheimer's disease A progressive brain disorder that leads to a gradual and irreversible decline in cognitive abilities.

Alzheimer's occurs when production of the *beta amyloid precursor protein* goes awry, producing large clumps of cells that trigger inflammation and deterioration of nerve cells. The brain shrinks, neurons die, and several areas of the hippocampus and frontal and temporal lobes deteriorate. So far, there is no effective treatment (Wolfe, 2006; Medeiros et al., 2007; Behrens, Lendon, & Roe, 2009).

Study Alert

It's important to be able to describe the nature of intellectual changes during late adulthood.

In other cases, cognitive declines may be caused by temporary anxiety and depression, which can be treated successfully, or may even be due to overmedication. The danger is that people with such symptoms may be left untreated, thereby continuing their decline (Selkoe, 1997; Sachs-Ericsson et al., 2005; Diniz et al., 2013).

In sum, declines in cognitive functioning in late adulthood are, for the most part, not inevitable. The key to maintaining cognitive skills may lie in intellectual stimulation. Like the rest of us, older adults need a stimulating environment in order to hone and maintain their skills (Bosma et al., 2003; Glisky, 2007; Hertzog et al., 2008).

Maintaining interests and activities one had during middle age can contribute to a more successful late adulthood, according to the activity theory of aging.

THE SOCIAL WORLD OF LATE ADULTHOOD: OLD BUT NOT ALONE

Just as the view that old age predictably means mental decline has proved to be wrong, so has the view that late adulthood inevitably brings loneliness. People in late adulthood most often see themselves as functioning members of society; only a small number of them report that loneliness is a serious problem (Binstock & George, 1996; Jylha, 2004; Berkman, Ertel, & Glymour, 2011).

Certainly, late adulthood brings significant challenges. People who have spent their adult lives working and then enter retirement bring about a major shift in the role they play. Moreover, many people must face the death of their spouse. Especially if the marriage has been a long and good one, the death of a partner means the loss of a companion, confidante, and lover. It can also bring about changes in economic well-being.

disengagement theory of aging The theory that suggests that successful aging is characterized by a gradual withdrawal from the world on physical, psychological, and social levels.

There is no single way to age successfully, and several theories have been developed to describe the process. According to the **disengagement theory of aging,** aging is characterized by a gradual withdrawal from the world. In this view, as people get older, they separate themselves from others on physical, psychological, and social levels. In this view, such disengagement is appropriate and even beneficial. The reason is that disengagement serves the purpose of providing an opportunity for increased reflectiveness and decreased emotional investment in others at a time of life when social relationships will inevitably be ended by death (Adams, 2004; Wrosch, Bauer, & Scheier, 2005).

activity theory of aging The theory that suggests that successful aging is characterized by maintaining the interests and activities of earlier stages of life.

However, only a little research supports the disengagement theory of aging, and alternative theories have been suggested. The major alternative is the activity theory of aging. According to the **activity theory of aging,** people who age most successfully are those who maintain the interests, activities, and level of social interaction they experienced during their earlier periods of adulthood. Activity theory argues that people who are aging effectively show a continuation of the activities in which they participated during the earlier part of their lives (Crosnoe & Elder, 2002; Nimrod & Kleiber, 2007).

Most research supports the activity theory of aging. On the other hand, not all people in late adulthood need a life filled with activities and social interaction to be happy. As in every stage of life, some older adults are just as satisfied leading a relatively inactive, solitary existence. What may be more important is how people view

People in late adulthood usually see themselves as functioning, well-integrated members of society, and many maintain activities in which they participated earlier in life.

the aging process: Evidence shows that positive self-perceptions of aging are associated with increased longevity (Levy et al., 2002; Levy & Myers, 2004).

Regardless of how people age, most engage in a process of **life review** in which they examine and evaluate their lives. Remembering and reconsidering what has occurred in the past, people in late adulthood often come to a better understanding of themselves. They sometimes resolve lingering problems and conflicts and face their lives with greater wisdom and serenity.

life review The process by which people examine and evaluate their lives.

Clearly, people in late adulthood are not just marking time until death. Rather, old age is a time of continued growth and development as important as any other period of life.

From the perspective of . . .

A Health-Care Provider What sorts of recommendations would you make to your older patients about how to deal with aging? How would you handle someone who believed that getting older had only negative consequences?

BECOMING AN INFORMED CONSUMER of Psychology

Adjusting to Death

At some time in our lives, we all face death—certainly our own as well as the deaths of friends, loved ones, and even strangers. Although there is nothing more inevitable in life, death remains a frightening, emotion-laden topic. Certainly, little is more stressful than the

death of a loved one or the contemplation of our own imminent death, and preparing for death is one of our most crucial developmental tasks (Aiken, 2000).

A few generations ago, talk of death was taboo. The topic was never mentioned to dying people, and gerontologists had little to say about it. That changed, however, with the pioneering work of Elisabeth Kübler-Ross (1969), who brought the subject of death into the open with her observation that those facing impending death tend to move through five broad stages:

- *Denial.* In this stage, people resist the idea that they are dying. Even if told that their chances for survival are small, they refuse to admit that they are facing death.
- *Anger.* After moving beyond the denial stage, dying people become angry—angry at people around them who are in good health, angry at medical professionals for being ineffective, angry at God.
- *Bargaining.* Anger leads to bargaining in which the dying try to think of ways to postpone death. They may decide to dedicate their lives to religion if God saves them. They may say, "If only I can live to see my son married, I will accept death then."
- *Depression.* When dying people come to feel that bargaining is no use, they move to the next stage: depression. They realize that their lives really are coming to an end, which leads to what Kübler-Ross calls "preparatory grief" for their own deaths.
- *Acceptance.* In this stage, people accept impending death. Usually they are unemotional and uncommunicative; it is as if they have made peace with themselves and are expecting death with no bitterness.

It is important to keep in mind that not everyone experiences each of these stages in the same way. In fact, Kübler-Ross's stages pertain only to people who are fully aware that they are dying and have the time to evaluate their impending death. Furthermore, vast differences occur in the way individuals react to impending death. The specific cause and duration of dying, as well as the person's sex, age, personality, and the type of support received from family and friends, all have an impact on how people respond to death (Carver & Scheier, 2002; Coyle, 2006).

Few of us enjoy the contemplation of death. Yet awareness of its psychological aspects and consequences can make its inevitable arrival less anxiety producing and perhaps more understandable.

RECAP/EVALUATE/RETHINK

RECAP

LO 30-1 What are the principal kinds of physical, social, and intellectual changes that occur in early and middle adulthood, and what are their causes?

- Early adulthood marks the peak of physical health. Physical changes occur relatively gradually in men and women during adulthood.
- One major physical change occurs at the end of middle adulthood for women: They begin menopause after which they are no longer fertile.
- During middle adulthood, people typically experience a midlife transition in which the notion that life will end becomes more important. In some cases this may lead to a midlife crisis, although the passage into middle age is typically relatively calm.
- As aging continues during middle adulthood, people realize in their 50s that their lives and accomplishments are fairly well set, and they try to come to terms with them.
- Among the important developmental milestones during adulthood are marriage, family changes, and divorce. Another important determinant of adult development is work.

LO 30-2 How does the reality of late adulthood differ from the stereotypes about that period?

- Old age may bring marked physical declines caused by genetic preprogramming or physical wear and tear. Although the activities of people in late adulthood are not all that different from those of younger people, older adults experience declines in reaction time, sensory abilities, and physical stamina.
- Intellectual declines are not an inevitable part of aging. Fluid intelligence does decline with age, and long-term memory abilities are sometimes impaired. In contrast, crystallized intelligence shows slight increases with age, and short-term memory remains at about the same level.
- Although disengagement theory sees successful aging as a process of gradual withdrawal from the physical, psychological, and social worlds, there is little research supporting this view. Instead, activity theory, which suggests that the maintenance of interests and activities from earlier years leads to successful aging, is a more accurate explanation.

LO 30-3 How can we adjust to death?

- According to Kübler-Ross, dying people move through five stages as they face death: denial, anger, bargaining, depression, and acceptance.

EVALUATE

1. Rob recently turned 40 and surveyed his goals and accomplishments to date. Although he has accomplished a lot, he realized that many of his goals will not be met in his lifetime. This stage is called a ________ ________.
2. In households where both partners have similar jobs, the division of labor that generally occurs is the same as in "traditional" households where the husband works and the wife stays at home. True or false?
3. ________ ________ theories suggest that there is a maximum time span in which cells are able to reproduce. This time limit explains the eventual breakdown of the body.
4. Lower IQ test scores during late adulthood do not necessarily mean a decrease in intelligence. True or false?
5. During old age, a person's ________ intelligence continues to increase, whereas ________ intelligence may decline.
6. In Kübler-Ross's ________ stage, people resist the idea of death. In the ________ stage, they attempt to make deals to avoid death, and in the ________ stage, they passively await death.

RETHINK

1. Is the possibility that life may be extended for several decades a mixed blessing? What societal consequences might an extended life span bring about?
2. Does the finding that people in late adulthood require intellectual stimulation have implications for the societies in which older people live? In what way might stereotypes about older individuals contribute to their isolation and lack of intellectual stimulation?

Answers to Evaluate Questions

1. midlife transition; 2. true; 3. Genetic preprogramming; 4. true; 5. crystallized, fluid; 6. denial, bargaining, acceptance

KEY TERMS

emerging adulthood
menopause
genetic preprogramming theories of aging
wear-and-tear theories of aging
Alzheimer's disease
disengagement theory of aging
activity theory of aging
life review

10 Personality

Learning Outcomes for Chapter 10

MODULE 31

LO 31-1 How do psychologists define and use the concept of personality?

LO 31-2 What do the theories of Freud and his successors tell us about the structure and development of personality?

Psychodynamic Approaches to Personality

Freud's Psychoanalytic Theory: Mapping the Unconscious Mind

The Neo-Freudian Psychoanalysts: Building on Freud

MODULE 32

LO 32-1 What are the major aspects of trait, learning, biological and evolutionary, and humanistic approaches to psychology?

Trait, Learning, Biological and Evolutionary, and Humanistic Approaches to Personality

Trait Approaches: Placing Labels on Personality

Applying Psychology in the 21st Century: Fixing What's Inside by Fixing What's Outside?

Learning Approaches: We Are What We've Learned

Biological and Evolutionary Approaches: Are We Born with Personality?

Neuroscience in Your Life: Wired to Be an Extrovert? The Biological Underpinnings of Personality

Humanistic Approaches: The Uniqueness of You

Comparing Approaches to Personality

MODULE 33

LO 33-1 How can we most accurately assess personality?

LO 33-2 What are the major types of personality measures?

Assessing Personality: Determining What Makes Us Distinctive

Exploring Diversity: Should Race and Ethnicity Be Used to Establish Norms?

Self-Report Measures of Personality

Projective Methods

Behavioral Assessment

Becoming an Informed Consumer of Psychology: Assessing Personality Assessments

Prologue *Who Is the Real Lance Armstrong?*

Racing cyclist Lance Armstrong was an idol to many. He had won the prestigious Tour de France road race seven consecutive times—a feat that had been unequaled in his sport. Remarkably, he did all this after having been diagnosed with stage-3 testicular cancer that had spread to his lungs and brain. Despite his poor prognosis, Armstrong defeated the disease and staged an amazing comeback as a professional athlete. Not only that, he founded the Lance Armstrong Foundation to support cancer patients, and he helped to develop other charitable organizations.

But there was a side to Armstrong that most people never saw. His cycling comeback was haunted by allegations of doping—allegations that Armstrong repeatedly and strenuously denied for years. But in the end the evidence caught up with him, and he publicly admitted that he had been doping. He is now facing a $100 million lawsuit for fraud, filed by former teammate Floyd Landis and joined by the U.S government.

Looking Ahead

Who is the real Lance Armstrong? Motivated, hard-working, endlessly persevering sports hero who inspirationally overcomes a dreaded disease? Or someone who takes illegal drugs, lies about it, and cheats his way to victory?

Many people, like Armstrong, have different sides to their personalities, appearing one way to some and quite differently to others. Determining who a person truly is falls to a branch of psychology that seeks to understand the characteristic ways people behave—personality psychology.

Personality is the pattern of enduring characteristics that produce consistency and individuality in a given person. Personality encompasses the behaviors that make each of us unique and that differentiate us from others. Personality also leads us to act consistently in different situations and over extended periods of time.

We will consider a number of approaches to personality. For historical reasons, we begin with psychodynamic theories of personality, which emphasize the importance of the unconscious. Next, we consider approaches that concentrate on identifying the most fundamental personality traits; theories that view personality as a set of learned behaviors; biological and evolutionary perspectives on personality; and approaches, known as humanistic theories, that highlight the uniquely human aspects of personality. We end our discussion by focusing on how personality is measured and how personality tests can be used.

personality The pattern of enduring, distinctive characteristics that produce consistency and individuality in a given person.

MODULE 31

Psychodynamic Approaches to Personality

Learning Outcomes

LO 31-1 How do psychologists define and use the concept of personality?

LO 31-2 What do the theories of Freud and his successors tell us about the structure and development of personality?

The college student was intent on making a good first impression on an attractive woman he had spotted across a crowded room at a party. As he walked toward her, he mulled over a line he had heard in an old movie the night before: "I don't believe we've been properly introduced yet." To his horror, what came out was a bit different. After threading his way through the crowded room, he finally reached the woman and blurted out, "I don't believe we've been properly seduced yet."

Although this student's error may seem to be merely an embarrassing slip of the tongue, according to some personality theorists such a mistake is not an error at all (Motley, 1987). Instead, *psychodynamic personality theorists* might argue that the error illustrates one way in which behavior is triggered by inner forces that are beyond our awareness. These hidden drives, shaped by childhood experiences, play an important role in energizing and directing everyday behavior.

Psychodynamic approaches to personality are based on the idea that personality is primarily unconscious and motivated by inner forces and conflicts about which people have little awareness. The most important pioneer of the psychodynamic approach was Sigmund Freud. A number of Freud's followers, including Carl Jung, Karen Horney, and Alfred Adler, refined Freud's theory and developed their own psychodynamic approaches.

psychodynamic approaches to personality Approaches that assume that personality is primarily unconscious and motivated by inner forces and conflicts about which people have little awareness.

Freud's Psychoanalytic Theory: Mapping the Unconscious Mind

Sigmund Freud, an Austrian physician, developed **psychoanalytic theory** in the early 1900s. According to Freud's theory, conscious experience is only a small part of our psychological makeup and experience. He argued that much of our behavior is motivated by the **unconscious,** a part of the personality that contains the memories, knowledge, beliefs, feelings, urges, drives, and instincts of which the individual is not aware.

psychoanalytic theory Freud's theory that unconscious forces act as determinants of personality.

unconscious A part of the personality that contains the memories, knowledge, beliefs, feelings, urges, drives, and instincts of which the individual is not aware.

Like the unseen mass of a floating iceberg, the contents of the unconscious far surpass in quantity the information in our conscious awareness. Freud maintained that to understand personality, it is necessary to expose what is in the unconscious. But because the unconscious disguises the meaning of the material it holds, the content of the unconscious cannot be observed directly. It is therefore necessary to interpret clues to the unconscious—slips of the tongue, fantasies, and dreams—to understand the unconscious processes that direct behavior. A slip of the tongue such as the one quoted earlier (sometimes termed a *Freudian slip*) may be interpreted as revealing the speaker's unconscious sexual desires.

To Freud, much of our personality is determined by our unconscious. Some of the unconscious is made up of the *preconscious,* which contains material that is not threatening and is easily brought to mind, such as the knowledge that 2 + 2 = 4. But deeper in the unconscious are instinctual drives—the wishes, desires, demands, and needs that are hidden from conscious awareness because of the conflicts and pain they would cause if they were part of our everyday lives. The unconscious provides a "safe haven" for our recollections of threatening events.

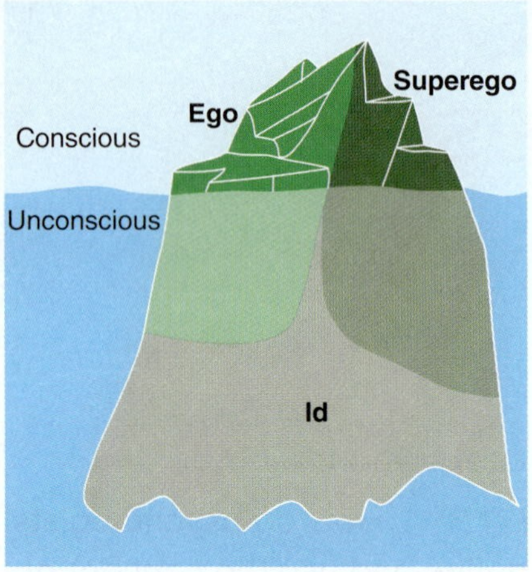

FIGURE 1 In Freud's personality model, there are three major components: the id, the ego, and the superego. As the iceberg analogy shows, only a small portion of personality is conscious. Why do you think that only the ego and superego have conscious components?

STRUCTURING PERSONALITY: ID, EGO, AND SUPEREGO

To describe the structure of personality, Freud developed a comprehensive theory that held that personality consists of three separate but interacting components: the id, the ego, and the superego. Freud suggested that the three structures can be diagrammed to show how they relate to the conscious and the unconscious (see Figure 1).

Although the three components of personality Freud described may appear to be actual physical structures in the nervous system, they are not. Instead, they represent abstract conceptions of a general *model* of personality that describes the interaction of forces that motivate behavior.

If personality consisted only of primitive, instinctual cravings and longings, it would have just one component: the id. The **id** is the raw, unorganized, inborn part of personality. From the time of birth, the id attempts to reduce tension created by primitive drives related to hunger, sex, aggression, and irrational impulses. Those drives are fueled by "psychic energy," which we can think of as a limitless energy source constantly putting pressure on the various parts of the personality.

The id operates according to the *pleasure principle* in which the goal is the immediate reduction of tension and the maximization of satisfaction. However, in most cases, reality prevents the fulfillment of the demands of the pleasure principle: We cannot always eat when we are hungry, and we can discharge our sexual drives only when the time and place are appropriate. To account for this fact of life, Freud suggested a second component of personality, which he called the ego.

The **ego,** which begins to develop soon after birth, strives to balance the desires of the id and the realities of the objective, outside world. In contrast to the pleasure-seeking id, the ego operates according to the *reality principle* in which instinctual energy is restrained to maintain the individual's safety and to help integrate the person into society. In a sense, then, the ego is the "executive" of personality: It makes decisions, controls actions, and allows thinking and problem solving of a higher order than the id's capabilities permit.

The superego is the final personality structure to develop in childhood. According to Freud, the **superego** is the personality structure that harshly judges the morality of our behavior. It represents the rights and wrong of society as taught and modeled

Study Alert
Remember that the three parts of personality in Freud's theory—the id, the ego, and the superego—are abstract conceptions that don't exist as physical structures in the brain.

id The raw, unorganized, inborn part of personality whose sole purpose is to reduce tension created by primitive drives related to hunger, sex, aggression, and irrational impulses.

ego The part of the personality that provides a buffer between the id and the outside world.

superego The personality structure that harshly judges the morality of our behavior.

Freud suggests that the superego, the part of the personality that represents the rights and wrongs of society, develops from direct teaching from parents, teachers, and other significant individuals.

by a person's parents, teachers, and other significant individuals. The superego includes the conscience, which prevents us from behaving in a morally improper way by making us feel guilty if we do wrong. The superego helps us control impulses coming from the id, making our behavior less selfish and more virtuous.

Both the superego and the id are unrealistic in that they do not consider the practical realities imposed by society. The superego, if left to operate without restraint, would create perfectionists unable to make the compromises that life requires. An unrestrained id would create a primitive, pleasure-seeking, thoughtless individual seeking to fulfill every desire without delay. As a result, the ego must mediate between the demands of the superego and the demands of the id.

DEVELOPING PERSONALITY: PSYCHOSEXUAL STAGES

Freud also provided us with a view of how personality develops through a series of five **psychosexual stages** during which children encounter conflicts between the demands of society and their own sexual urges (in which sexuality is more about experiencing pleasure and less about lust). According to Freud, if we are not able to resolve the conflicts that occur at a particular psychosexual stage, we may become locked in that conflict throughout life–something he called fixation. **Fixations** are conflicts or concerns that persist beyond the developmental period in which they first occur. Such conflicts may be due to having needs ignored, such as weaning the child too early or being too strict during toilet training. Alternatively, fixation may occur if children are overindulged during an earlier period, such as when parents are overly attentive to a child or provide lavish rewards during toilet training.

psychosexual stages Developmental periods that children pass through during which they encounter conflicts between the demands of society and their own sexual urges.

fixations Conflicts or concerns that persist beyond the developmental period in which they first occur.

oral stage According to Freud, a stage from birth to age 12 to 18 months, in which an infant's center of pleasure is the mouth.

The sequence Freud proposed is noteworthy because it explains how experiences and difficulties during a particular childhood stage may predict specific characteristics in the adult personality. This theory is also unique in associating each stage with a major biological function, which Freud assumed to be the focus of pleasure in a given period. (See Figure 2 for a summary of the stages.)

In the first psychosexual stage of development, called the **oral stage,** the baby's mouth is the focal point of pleasure. During the first 12 to 18 months of life, children suck, eat, mouth, and bite anything they can put into their mouths. To Freud, this behavior suggested that the mouth is the primary site of a kind of sexual pleasure and that weaning (withdrawing the breast or bottle) represents the main conflict during the oral stage. If infants are either overindulged (perhaps by being fed every time they cry) or frustrated in their search for oral gratification, they may become fixated at this stage. For example, fixation might occur if an infant's oral needs were constantly gratified

Study Alert

The five psychosexual stages of personality development in Freud's theory—oral, anal, phallic, latency, and genital—indicate how personality develops as people age.

Stage	Age	Major Characteristics
Oral	Birth to 12–18 months	Interest in oral gratification from sucking, eating, mouthing, biting
Anal	12–18 months to 3 years	Gratification from expelling and withholding feces; coming to terms with society's controls relating to toilet training
Phallic	3 to 5–6 years	Interest in the genitals, coming to terms with Oedipal conflict leading to identification with same-sex parent
Latency	5–6 years to adolescence	Sexual concerns largely unimportant
Genital	Adolescence to adulthood	Reemergence of sexual interests and establishment of mature sexual relationships

FIGURE 2 Freud's theory of personality development suggests that there are several distinct stages.

In terms of Jung's theory, Harry Potter and Voldemort represent the archetypes, or universally recognizable symbols, of good and evil.

in fairy tales, Mother's Day, and so forth!) Jung also suggested that men possess an unconscious *feminine archetype* that affects how they behave, and women have an unconscious *male archetype* that colors their behavior (Jung, 1961; Bair, 2003; Smetana, 2007).

To Jung, archetypes play an important role in determining our day-to-day reactions, attitudes, and values. For example, Jung might explain the popularity of the Harry Potter books and movies as being due to their use of broad archetypes of good (Harry Potter) and evil (Voldemort).

Although no reliable research evidence confirms the existence of the collective unconscious–and even Jung acknowledged that such evidence would be difficult to produce–Jung's theory has had significant influence in areas beyond psychology. For example, personality types derived from Jung's personality approach form the basis for the Myers-Briggs personality test, which is widely used in business and industry to provide insights into how employees make decisions and perform on the job (Furnham & Crump, 2005; Wilde, 2011; Mills, 2013).

From the perspective of . . .

An Advertising Executive How might you use Jung's concept of archetypes in designing your advertisements? Which of the archetypes would you use?

HORNEY'S NEO-FREUDIAN PERSPECTIVE

Karen Horney (pronounced "HORN-eye") was one of the earliest psychologists to champion women's issues and is sometimes called the first feminist psychologist. Horney suggested that personality develops in the context of social relationships and depends particularly on the relationship between parents and child and how well the child's needs are met. She rejected Freud's suggestion that women have penis envy; she asserted that what women envy most in men is not their anatomy but the independence, success, and freedom women often are denied (Horney, 1937; Smith, 2007; Coolidge et al., 2011).

Horney was also one of the first to stress the importance of cultural factors in the determination of personality. For example, she suggested that society's rigid gender roles for women lead them to experience ambivalence about success because they fear they will make enemies if they are too successful. Her conceptualizations, developed in the 1930s and 1940s, laid the groundwork for many of the central ideas of feminism that emerged decades later (Eckardt, 2005; Jones, 2006).

Karen Horney was one of the earliest proponents of women's issues.

ADLER AND THE OTHER NEO-FREUDIANS

Alfred Adler, another important neo-Freudian psychoanalyst, also considered Freudian theory's emphasis on sexual needs misplaced. Instead, Adler proposed that the primary human motivation is a striving for superiority, not in terms of superiority over others but in a quest for self-improvement and perfection.

Adler used the term *inferiority complex* to describe adults who have not been able to overcome the feelings of inadequacy they developed as children. Early social relationships with parents have an important effect on children's ability to outgrow feelings of personal inferiority. If children have positive experiences, they can orient themselves toward attaining socially useful goals.

Other neo-Freudians included Erik Erikson, whose theory of psychosocial development we discussed in other modules, and Freud's daughter, Anna Freud. Like Adler and Horney, they focused less than Freud on inborn sexual and aggressive drives and more on the social and cultural factors behind personality.

RECAP/EVALUATE/RETHINK

RECAP

LO 31-1 How do psychologists define and use the concept of personality?

- Personality is the pattern of enduring, distinctive characteristics that produce consistency and individuality in a given person.

LO 31-2 What do the theories of Freud and his successors tell us about the structure and development of personality?

- According to psychodynamic approaches to personality, much behavior is caused by parts of personality that are found in the unconscious and of which we are unaware.
- Freud's psychoanalytic theory, one of the psychodynamic approaches, suggests that personality is composed of the id, the ego, and the superego. The id is the unorganized, inborn part of personality whose purpose is to immediately reduce tensions relating to hunger, sex, aggression, and other primitive impulses. The ego restrains instinctual energy to maintain the individual's safety and to help the person be a member of society. The superego represents society's rights and wrongs and includes the conscience.
- Freud's psychoanalytic theory suggests that personality develops through a series of psychosexual stages (oral, anal, phallic, latency, and genital), each of which is associated with a primary biological function.
- Defense mechanisms, according to Freudian theory, are unconscious strategies that people use to reduce anxiety by distorting reality and concealing the true source of the anxiety from themselves.
- Freud's psychoanalytic theory has provoked a number of criticisms, including a lack of supportive scientific data, the theory's inadequacy in making predictions, and its reliance on a highly restricted population. On the other hand, recent neuroscience research has offered some support for the concept of the unconscious.
- Neo-Freudian psychoanalytic theorists built on Freud's work, although they placed greater emphasis on the role of the ego and paid more attention to the role of social factors in determining behavior.

EVALUATE

1. __________ approaches state that behavior is motivated primarily by unconscious forces.

2. Match each section of the personality (according to Freud) with its description:
   1. Ego
   2. Id
   3. Superego

   a. Determines right from wrong on the basis of cultural standards.
   b. Operates according to the "reality principle"; energy is redirected to integrate the person into society.
   c. Seeks to reduce tension brought on by primitive drives.
3. Which of the following represents the proper order of personality development, according to Freud?
   a. Oral, phallic, latency, anal, genital
   b. Anal, oral, phallic, genital, latency
   c. Oral, anal, phallic, latency, genital
   d. Latency, phallic, anal, genital, oral
4. __________ __________ is the term Freud used to describe unconscious strategies used to reduce anxiety by distorting reality and concealing the source of the anxiety from themselves.

RETHINK

1. Can you think of ways in which Freud's theories of unconscious motivations are commonly used in popular culture? How accurately do you think such popular uses of Freudian theories reflect Freud's ideas?
2. What are some examples of archetypes in addition to those mentioned in this module? In what ways are archetypes similar to and different from stereotypes?

Answers to Evaluate Questions

1. Psychodynamic; **2.** 1-b, 2-c, 3-a; **3.** c; **4.** Defense mechanisms

KEY TERMS

personality
psychodynamic approaches to personality
psychoanalytic theory
unconscious
id
ego
superego
psychosexual stages
fixations
oral stage
anal stage
phallic stage
Oedipal conflict
identification
latency period
genital stage
defense mechanisms
repression
neo-Freudian psychoanalysts
collective unconscious
archetypes

MODULE 32

Trait, Learning, Biological and Evolutionary, and Humanistic Approaches to Personality

"Tell me about Nelson," said Johnetta.

"Oh, he's just terrific. He's the friendliest guy I know–goes out of his way to be nice to everyone. He hardly ever gets mad. He's just so even-tempered, no matter what's happening. And he's really smart, too. About the only thing I don't like is that he's always in such a hurry to get things done. He seems to have boundless energy, much more than I have."

"He sounds great to me, especially in comparison to Rico," replied Johnetta. "He is so self-centered and arrogant that it drives me crazy. I sometimes wonder why I ever started going out with him."

Friendly. Even-tempered. Smart. Energetic. Self-centered. Arrogant.

The above exchange is made up of a series of trait characterizations of the speakers' friends. In fact, much of our own understanding of others' behavior is based on the premise that people possess certain traits that are consistent across different situations. For example, we generally assume that if someone is outgoing and sociable in one situation, he or she is outgoing and sociable in other situations (Gilbert et al., 1992; Gilbert, Miller, & Ross, 1998; Mischel, 2004).

Dissatisfaction with the emphasis in psychoanalytic theory on unconscious–and difficult to demonstrate–processes in explaining a person's behavior led to the development of alternative approaches to personality, including a number of trait-based approaches. Other theories reflect established psychological perspectives, such as learning theory, biological and evolutionary approaches, and the humanistic approach.

Learning Outcome

LO 32-1 What are the major aspects of trait, learning, biological and evolutionary, and humanistic approaches to personality?

Trait Approaches: Placing Labels on Personality

If someone asked you to characterize another person, like Johnetta and her friend, you probably would come up with a list of traits. **Traits** are consistent personality characteristics and behaviors displayed in different situations.

Trait theory is the personality approach that seeks to identify the basic traits necessary to describe personality. Trait theorists do not assume that some people have a trait and others do not; rather, they propose that all people possess certain traits, but the degree to which a particular trait applies to a specific person varies and can be quantified. For instance, you may be relatively friendly, whereas I may be relatively unfriendly. But we both have a "friendliness" trait, although your degree of "friendliness" is higher than mine. The major challenge for trait theorists taking this approach has been to identify the specific primary traits necessary to describe personality. As we shall see, different theorists have come up with surprisingly different sets of traits.

traits Consistent personality characteristics and behaviors displayed in different situations.

trait theory A model of personality that seeks to identify the basic traits necessary to describe personality.

Study Alert

All trait theories explain personality in terms of traits (consistent personality characteristics and behaviors), but they differ in terms of which and how many traits are seen as fundamental.

ALLPORT'S TRAIT THEORY: IDENTIFYING BASIC CHARACTERISTICS

When personality psychologist Gordon Allport systematically pored over an unabridged dictionary in the 1930s, he came up with some 18,000 separate terms that could be used to describe personality. Although he was able to pare down the list to a mere 4,500 descriptors after eliminating words with the same meaning, he was left with a problem crucial to all trait approaches: Which of those traits were the most basic?

Allport eventually answered this question by suggesting that there are three fundamental categories of traits: cardinal, central, and secondary (Allport, 1961, 1966). A *cardinal trait* is a single characteristic that directs most of a person's activities. For example, a totally selfless woman may direct all her energy toward humanitarian activities; an intensely power-hungry person may be driven by an all-consuming need for control.

Most people, however, do not develop a single, comprehensive cardinal trait. Instead, they possess a handful of central traits that make up the core of personality. *Central traits,* such as honesty and sociability, are an individual's major characteristics; they usually number from five to ten in any one person. Finally, *secondary traits* are characteristics that affect behavior in fewer situations and are less influential than central or cardinal traits. For instance, a reluctance to eat meat and a love of modern art would be considered secondary traits (Smrtnik-Vitulić & Zupančič, 2011; Kahn et al., 2013).

CATTELL AND EYSENCK: FACTORING OUT PERSONALITY

Later attempts to identify primary personality traits centered on a statistical technique known as factor analysis. *Factor analysis* is a statistical method of identifying patterns among a large number of variables. For example, a personality researcher might ask a large group of people to rate themselves on a number of individual traits. By statistically computing which traits are associated with each other, a researcher can identify the fundamental patterns of traits—called *factors*—that tend to be found together in the same person.

Using factor analysis, personality psychologist Raymond Cattell (1965) suggested that 16 pairs of *traits* represent the basic dimensions of personality. Using that set of traits, he developed the Sixteen Personality Factor Questionnaire, or 16 PF, a personality scale that is still in use today (Cattell, Cattell, & Cattell, 2000; Djapo et al., 2011).

Another trait theorist, psychologist Hans Eysenck (1995), also used factor analysis to identify patterns of traits, but he came to a very different conclusion about the nature of personality. He found that personality could best be described in terms of just three major dimensions: extraversion, neuroticism, and psychoticism. The *extraversion* dimension describes a person's level of sociability, whereas the *neuroticism* dimension encompasses an individual's emotional stability. Finally, *psychoticism* is the degree to which reality is distorted. By evaluating people along these three dimensions, Eysenck was able to predict behavior accurately in a variety of situations. Figure 1 lists specific traits associated with each of the dimensions.

Extraversion
- Sociable
- Lively
- Active
- Assertive
- Sensation-seeking

Neuroticism
- Anxious
- Depressed
- Guilt feelings
- Low self-esteem
- Tense

Psychoticism
- Aggressive
- Cold
- Egocentric
- Impersonal
- Impulsive

FIGURE 1 Eysenck described personality in terms of three major dimensions: extraversion, neuroticism, and psychoticism. Using these dimensions, he could predict people's behavior in many types of situations. (Source: Eysenck, 1990.)

THE BIG FIVE PERSONALITY TRAITS

For the last two decades, the most influential trait approach contends that five traits or factors—called the "Big Five"—lie at the core of personality. Using factor analytic statistical techniques, a host of researchers have identified a similar set of five factors that underlie personality. The five factors, described in Figure 2, are *openness to experience, conscientiousness, extraversion, agreeableness,* and *neuroticism* (emotional stability).

Study Alert

You can remember the "Big Five" set of personality traits by using the acronym OCEAN (*o*penness to experience, *c*onscientiousness, *e*xtraversion, *a*greeableness, and *n*euroticism).

The Big Five Personality Factors and Dimensions of Sample Traits

Openness to experience	**Agreeableness**
Independent—Conforming	Sympathetic—Fault-finding
Imaginative—Practical	Kind—Cold
Preference for variety—Preference for routine	Appreciative—Unfriendly
Conscientiousness	**Neuroticism (Emotional Stability)**
Careful—Careless	Stable—Tense
Disciplined—Impulsive	Calm—Anxious
Organized—Disorganized	Secure—Insecure
Extraversion	
Talkative—Quiet	
Fun-loving—Sober	
Sociable—Retiring	

FIGURE 2 Five broad trait factors, referred to as the "Big Five," are considered to be the core of personality. (Source: Adapted from Pervin, 1990 and McCrae & Costa, 1986.)

The Big Five emerge consistently across a number of domains. For example, factor analyses of major personality inventories, self-report measures made by observers of others' personality traits, and checklists of self-descriptions yield similar factors. In addition, the Big Five emerge consistently in different populations of individuals, including children, college students, older adults, and speakers of different languages. Cross-cultural research conducted in areas ranging from Europe to the Middle East to Africa also has been supportive. Finally, studies of brain functioning show that Big Five personality traits are related to the way the brain processes information (Schmitt, Allik, & McCrae, 2007; Schmitt et al., 2008; Vecchione et al., 2011).

In short, a growing consensus exists that the Big Five represent the best description of personality traits we have today. Still, the debate over the specific number and kinds of traits–and even the usefulness of trait approaches in general–remains a lively one.

EVALUATING TRAIT APPROACHES TO PERSONALITY

Trait approaches have several virtues. They provide a clear, straightforward explanation of people's behavioral consistencies. Furthermore, traits allow us to readily compare one person with another. Because of these advantages, trait approaches to personality have had an important influence on the development of several useful personality measures (Wiggins, 2003; Larsen & Buss, 2006; Cook, 2013).

However, trait approaches also have some drawbacks. For example, we have seen that various trait theories describing personality come to different conclusions about which traits are the most fundamental and descriptive. The difficulty in determining which of the theories is the most accurate has led some personality psychologists to question the validity of trait conceptions of personality in general.

Actually, there is an even more fundamental difficulty with trait approaches. Even if we are able to identify a set of primary traits, we are left with little more than a label or description of personality–rather than an explanation of behavior. If we say that someone who donates money to charity has the trait of generosity, we still do not know *why* that person became generous in the first place or the reasons for displaying generosity in a specific situation. In the view of some critics, then, traits do not provide explanations for behavior; they merely describe it.

Biological and evolutionary approaches to personality seek to explain the consistencies in personality that are found in some families.

assumes that personality traits that led to our ancestors' survival and reproductive success are more likely to be preserved and passed on to subsequent generations (Buss, 2001, 2009, 2011).

The results of research studies conducted on twins who are genetically identical but raised apart illustrate the importance of genetic factors in personality. Personality tests indicate that in major respects, genetically identical twins raised apart are quite similar in personality, despite having been separated at an early age.

Moreover, certain traits are more heavily influenced by heredity than others. For example, *social potency* (the degree to which a person assumes mastery and leadership roles in social situations) and *traditionalism* (the tendency to follow authority) had particularly

Infants are born with particular temperaments—dispositions that are consistent throughout childhood.

strong genetic components, whereas achievement and social closeness had relatively weak genetic components (Tellegen et al., 1988; Bouchard et al., 2004; see Figure 4).

Furthermore, it is increasingly clear that the roots of adult personality emerge early in life. Infants are born with a specific **temperament,** an individual's behavioral style and characteristic way of responding. Temperament encompasses several dimensions, including general activity level and mood. For instance, some individuals are quite active, while others are relatively calm. Similarly, some are relatively easygoing, whereas others are irritable, easily upset, and difficult to soothe. Temperament is quite consistent, with significant stability from infancy well into adolescence (Wachs et al., 2004; Kagan et al., 2007; Evans & Rothbart, 2007, 2009; Hori et al., 2011).

temperament An individual's behavioral style and characteristic way of responding that emerges early in life.

Some researchers contend that specific genes are related to personality. For example, people with a longer dopamine-4 receptor gene are more likely to be thrill-seekers than those without such a gene. These thrill-seekers tend to be extroverted, impulsive, quick-tempered, and always in search of excitement and novel situations. Furthermore, the structure of their brains may reflect their thrill-seeking tendencies (see *Neuroscience in Your Life;* Robins, 2005; Golimbet et al., 2007; Ray et al., 2009).

Does the identification of specific genes linked to personality, coupled with the existence of temperaments from the time of birth, mean that we are destined to have certain types of personalities? Hardly. First, it is unlikely that any single gene is linked to a specific trait. For instance, the dopamine-4 receptor accounts for only around 10% of the variation in novelty seeking between different individuals. The rest of the variation is attributable to other genes and environmental factors (Keltikangas-Järvinen et al., 2004; Lahti et al., 2005; Kandler, Riemann, & Angleitner, 2013).

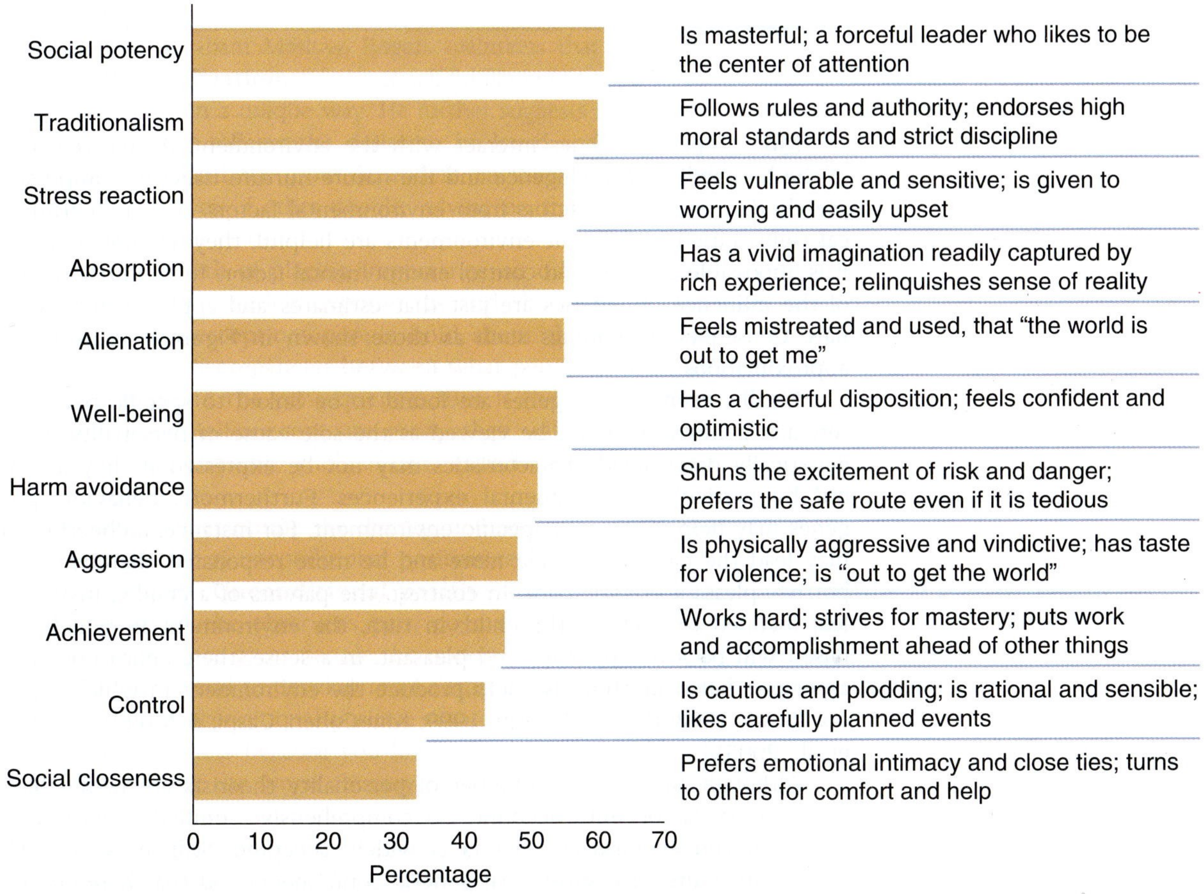

FIGURE 4 The inherited roots of personality. The percentages indicate the degree to which 11 personality characteristics reflect the influence of heredity. (Source: Adapted from Tellegen et al., 1988.)

From the perspective of . . .

A Politician Imagine that you had to vote on a law that would require institutions and organizations to perform race-norming procedures on standardized performance tests. Would you support such a law? Why or why not? In addition to race, should norming procedures take other factors into account? Which ones and why?

Self-Report Measures of Personality

If someone wanted to assess your personality, one possible approach would be to carry out an extensive interview with you to determine the most important events in your childhood, your social relationships, and your successes and failures. Obviously, though, such a technique would take extraordinary time and effort.

self-report measures A method of gathering data about people by asking them questions about their own behavior and traits.

It is also unnecessary. Just as physicians draw only a small sample of your blood to test, psychologists can use self-report measures. In a **self-report measure,** people are asked questions about their own behavior and traits. This sampling of self-report data is then used to infer the presence of particular personality characteristics. For example, a researcher who was interested in assessing a person's orientation to life might administer the questionnaire shown in Figure 1. Although the questionnaire consists of only a few questions, the answers can be used to generalize about personality characteristics. (Try it yourself!)

Minnesota Multiphasic Personality Inventory-2-Restructured Form (MMPI-2-RF) A widely used self-report test that identifies people with psychological difficulties and is employed to predict some everyday behaviors.

One of the best examples of a self-report measure, and one of the most frequently used personality tests, is the **Minnesota Multiphasic Personality Inventory-2-Restructured Form (MMPI-2-RF).** Although the original purpose of this measure was to identify people with specific sorts of psychological difficulties, it has been found to predict a variety of other behaviors. For instance, MMPI-2-RF scores have been shown to be good predictors of whether college students will marry within 10 years of graduating and whether they will get an advanced degree. Police departments use the test to measure whether police officers are likely to use their weapons. Psychologists in Russia administer a modified form of the MMPI-2-RF to their astronauts and Olympic athletes (Butcher, 2005; Sellbom & Ben-Porath, 2006; Sellbom, Fischler, & Ben-Porath, 2007; Butcher, 2011).

The test consists of a series of 338 items to which a person responds "true," "false," or "cannot say." The questions cover a variety of issues ranging from mood ("I feel useless at times") to opinions ("People should try to understand their dreams") to physical and psychological health ("I am bothered by an upset stomach several times a week" and "I have strange and peculiar thoughts").

There are no right or wrong answers. Instead, interpretation of the results rests on the pattern of responses. The test yields scores on 51 separate scales, including several scales meant to measure the validity of the respondent's answers. For example, there is a "lie scale" that indicates when people are falsifying their responses

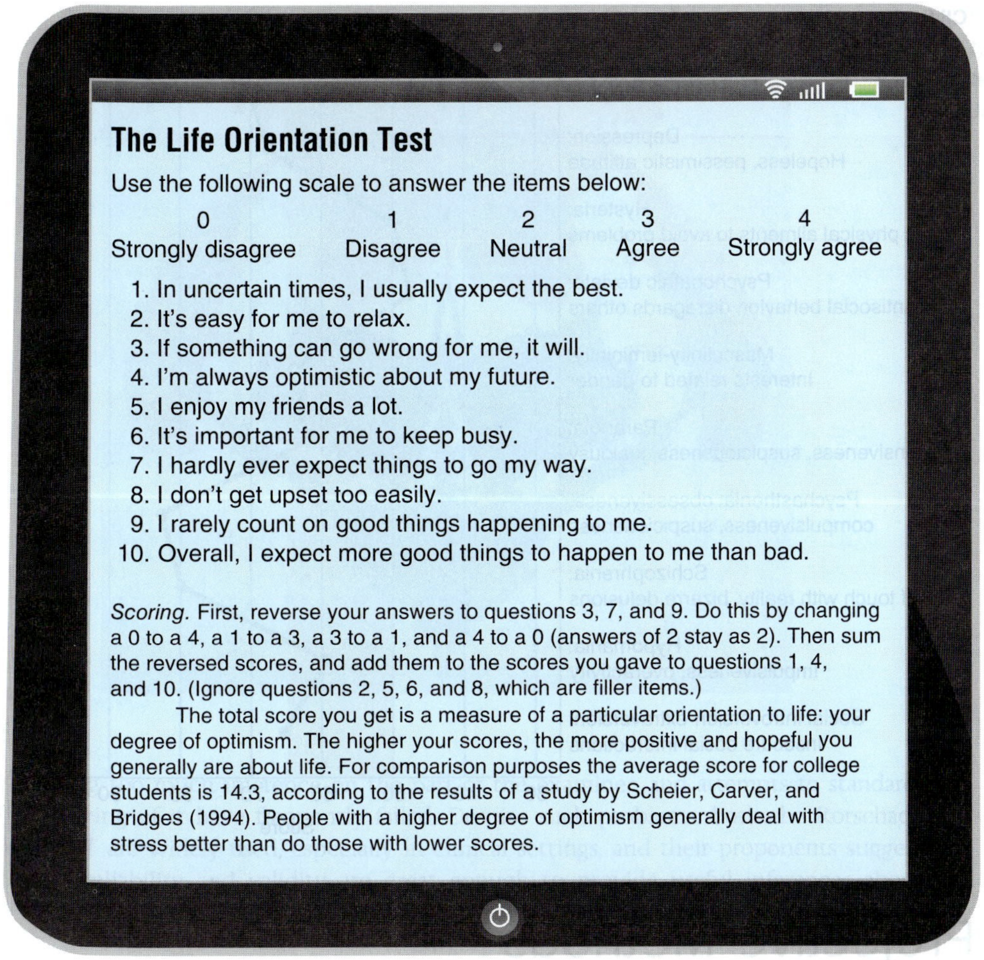

FIGURE 1 The Life Orientation Test. Complete this test by indicating the degree to which you agree with each of the 10 statements using the scale from 0 to 4 for each item. Try to be as accurate as possible. There are no right or wrong answers. (Source: Adapted from Scheier, Carver, & Bridges, 1994.)

in order to present themselves more favorably (through items such as, "I can't remember ever having a bad night's sleep") (Butcher, 2005; Stein & Graham, 2005; Bacchiochi, 2006).

How did the authors of the MMPI-2-RF determine what specific patterns of responses indicate? The procedure they used is typical of personality test construction—a process known as **test standardization.** To create the test, the test authors asked groups of psychiatric patients with a specific diagnosis, such as depression or schizophrenia, to complete a large number of items. They then determined which items best differentiated members of those groups from a comparison group of normal participants and included those specific items in the final version of the test. By systematically carrying out this procedure on groups with different diagnoses, the test authors were able to devise a number of subscales that identified different forms of abnormal behavior (see Figure 2).

test standardization A technique used to validate questions in personality tests by studying the responses of people with known diagnoses.

When the MMPI-2-RF is used for the purpose for which it was devised—identification of personality disorders—it does a good job. However, like other personality tests, it presents an opportunity for abuse. For instance, employers who use it as a screening tool for job applicants may interpret the results improperly by relying too heavily on the results of individual scales instead of taking into account the overall patterns of results, which require skilled interpretation. Furthermore, critics point out that the individual scales overlap, which makes their interpretation difficult. In sum, although the MMPI-2-RF remains the most widely used personality test and has been translated into more than 100 different languages, it must be used with caution (Forbey & Ben-Porath, 2007; Ben-Porath & Archer, 2008; Williams & Butcher, 2011).

Study Alert

In projective tests such as the Rorschach, researchers present an ambiguous stimulus and ask a person to describe or tell a story about it. They then use the responses to make inferences about personality.

Looking Back

Epilogue

We have discussed the different ways in which psychologists have interpreted the development and structure of personality. The perspectives we examined ranged from Freud's analysis of personality based primarily on internal, unconscious factors to the externally based view championed by learning theorists of personality as a learned set of traits and actions. We also noted that there are many ways to interpret personality; by no means does a consensus exist on what the key traits are that are central to personality.

Return to the prologue and consider the case of Lance Armstrong's fall from grace. Use your understanding of personality to consider the following questions.

1. How typical do you think it is for people to have multiple sides to their personality, as Lance Armstrong apparently does?
2. How could you explain Armstrong's heroism and dishonesty from a psychodynamic approach? From a learning approach?
3. How do you think Armstrong might score on a test of the big five personality factors?
4. In what ways does Armstrong's story give support to the humanistic approach? In what ways does it not?

VISUAL SUMMARY 10 Personality

MODULE 31 Psychodynamic Approaches

Freud's Psychoanalytic Theory

- Conscious experience: only part of our psychological experience
- Unconscious: part of the personality of which we are not aware
- Structure of personality
  - Id: Represents the raw, unorganized, inborn part of personality
  - Ego: Strives to balance desires of the id and realities of the outside world
  - Superego: Harshly judges the morality of our behavior

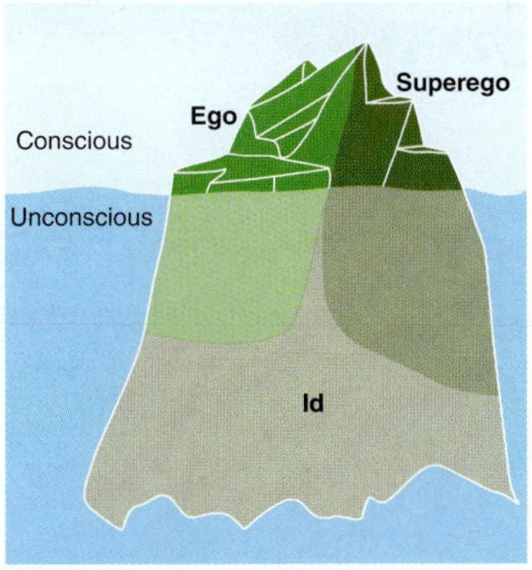

- Psychosexual stages

Stage	Age	Major Characteristics
Oral	Birth to 12–18 months	Interest in oral gratification from sucking, eating, mouthing, biting
Anal	12–18 months to 3 years	Gratification from expelling and withholding feces; coming to terms with society's controls relating to toilet training
Phallic	3 to 5–6 years	Interest in the genitals, coming to terms with Oedipal conflict leading to identification with same-sex parent
Latency	5–6 years to adolescence	Sexual concerns largely unimportant
Genital	Adolescence to adulthood	Reemergence of sexual interests and establishment of mature sexual relationships

- Defense mechanisms: Unconscious strategies people use to reduce anxiety

Neo-Freudian Psychoanalysts: Emphasize the ego more than Freud: Carl Jung, Karen Horney, Alfred Adler

MODULE 32 Trait, Learning, Biological and Evolutionary, and Humanistic Approaches

Trait Approaches: Emphasize consistent personality characteristics and behaviors called traits

- Eysenck: Extraversion, neuroticism, and psychoticism
- The big five personality traits: Openness to experience, conscientiousness, extraversion, agreeableness, neuroticism

Learning Approaches: Emphasize that personality is the sum of learned responses to the external environment

- B. F. Skinner: Personality is a collection of learned behavior patterns and are a result of reinforcement

Learning Approaches *(continued)*

- Social cognitive approaches: Emphasize the influence of cognition as well as observation of others' behavior on personality
- Self-efficacy and self-esteem

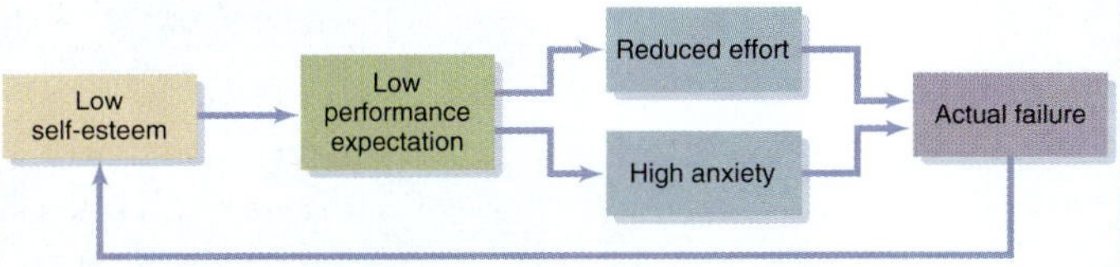

Biological and Evolutionary Approaches: Suggest that important components of personality are inherited, such as temperament

Humanistic Approaches: Emphasize people's inherent goodness and their tendency to move toward higher levels of functioning

- Carl Rogers
  - Self-actualization

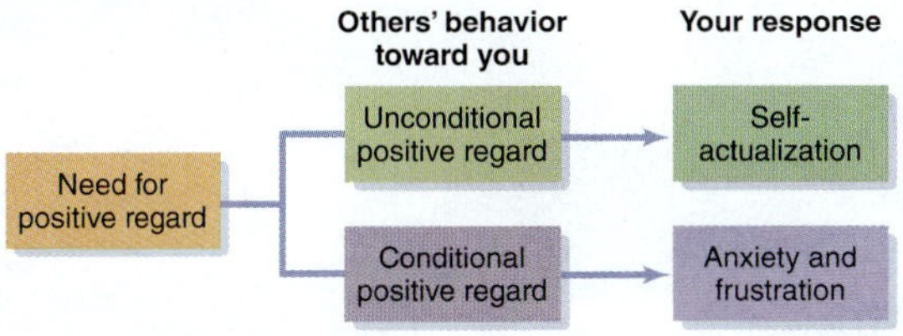

  - Positive regard reflects the desire to be loved and respected

MODULE 33 Assessing Personality

Psychological Tests: Standard measures that assess behavior objectively

- Reliability
- Validity
- Norms

Self-report Measures: A method of gathering data by asking people questions about their own behavior and traits

Projective Methods: People are shown an ambiguous stimulus and asked to describe it or tell a story about it

- Rorschach test
- Thematic Apperception Test (TAT)

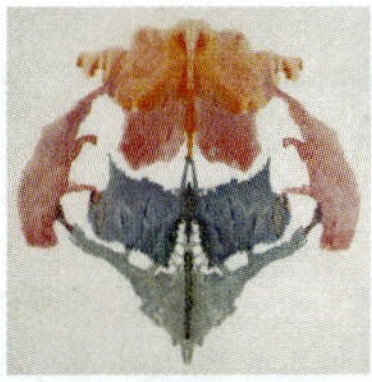

Behavioral Assessment: Measures of a person's behavior designed to describe characteristics indicative of personality

11

Health Psychology: Stress, Coping, and Well-Being

Learning Outcomes for Chapter 11

MODULE 34

LO 34-1 How is health psychology a union between medicine and psychology?

LO 34-2 What is stress, how does it affect us, and how can we best cope with it?

Stress and Coping

Stress: Reacting to Threat and Challenge

The High Cost of Stress

Coping with Stress

Neuroscience in Your Life: Altering Memories of Fear for Those with PTSD

Becoming an Informed Consumer of Psychology: Effective Coping Strategies

MODULE 35

LO 35-1 How do psychological factors affect health-related problems such as coronary heart disease, cancer, and smoking?

Psychological Aspects of Illness and Well-Being

The As, Bs, and Ds of Coronary Heart Disease

Psychological Aspects of Cancer

Smoking

Exploring Diversity: Hucksters of Death: Promoting Smoking Throughout the World

MODULE 36

LO 36-1 How do our interactions with physicians affect our health and compliance with medical treatment?

LO 36-2 How does a sense of well-being develop?

Promoting Health and Wellness

Following Medical Advice

Well-Being and Happiness

Applying Psychology in the 21st Century: Does Money Buy Happiness?

Prologue *Not Catching a Break*

After a long day of classes and a shift at his part-time job, Dennis Hanson was finally able to settle down to his studies. Good thing, too. The midterm test in his English class was tomorrow.

He'd just begun reviewing his notes when his phone rang. He checked the caller. His dad. Anger and exhaustion flooded him. It wasn't fair. He'd visited his father almost every weekend since his stepmother's death. And still his dad called two or three times a day, interrupting him in class, at work, eating heavily into his study time.

In the wake of his irritation, he felt guilt. His dad was alone and grieving, with no one but Dennis to talk to. Sighing, Dennis answered the phone. Twenty minutes later, he returned to his notes. But it was midnight now and he was dead tired. He climbed into bed fully dressed and turned out the light. The stress was getting to him. He couldn't cope with another thing.

Looking Ahead

It's not hard to understand why Dennis Hanson was experiencing stress. For people like him—and that probably includes most of us—the intensity of juggling multiple roles leads to feelings of never having sufficient time and, in some cases, takes a toll on both physical and psychological well-being.

Stress and how we cope with it have long been central topics of interest for psychologists. However, in recent years the focus has broadened as psychology has come to view stress in the broader context of one of psychology's newer subfields: health psychology. **Health psychology** investigates the psychological factors related to wellness and illness, including the prevention, diagnosis, and treatment of medical problems. Health psychologists investigate the effects of psychological factors such as stress on illness. They examine the psychological principles underlying treatments for disease and illness. They also study prevention: how healthier behavior can help people avoid and reduce health problems such as stress and heart disease.

Health psychologists take a decisive stand on the enduring mind–body issue that philosophers, and later psychologists, have debated since the time of the ancient Greeks. In their view, the mind and the body are clearly linked rather than representing two distinct systems (Sternberg, 2000a; Dalal & Misra, 2006).

Health psychologists recognize that good health and the ability to cope with illness are affected by psychological factors such as thoughts, emotions, and the ability to manage stress. They have paid particular attention to the *immune system,* the complex system of organs, glands, and cells that constitute our bodies' natural line of defense in fighting disease.

In fact, health psychologists are among the primary investigators in a growing field called **psychoneuroimmunology,** or **PNI,** the study of the relationship among psychological factors, the immune system, and the brain. PNI has led to discoveries such as the existence of an association between a person's emotional state and the success of the immune system in fighting disease (Kemeny, 2007; Byrne-Davis & Vedhara, 2008; Mathews & Janusek, 2011).

In sum, health psychologists view the mind and the body as two parts of a whole human being that cannot be considered independently. This more recent view marks a sharp departure from earlier thinking. Previously, disease was seen as a purely biological phenomenon, and psychological factors were of little interest to most health-care workers. In the early 20th century, the primary causes of death were short-term infections from which one either rapidly recovered—or died. Now, however, the major causes of death, such as heart disease, cancer, and diabetes, are chronic illnesses that pose significant psychological issues because they often cannot be cured and may linger for years (Rotan & Ospina-Kammerer, 2007; Berecki-Gisolf et al., 2013).

Advances in health psychology have had an impact across a variety of disciplines and professions. For instance, health-care professionals such as physicians and nurses, social workers, dieticians, pharmacists, occupational therapists, and even clergy are increasingly likely to receive training in health psychology.

In the three modules that follow, we discuss the ways in which psychological factors affect health. We first focus on the causes and consequences of stress as well as on the means of coping with it. Next, we explore the psychological aspects of several major health problems, including heart disease, cancer, and ailments resulting from smoking. Finally, we examine the ways in which patient-physician interactions influence our health and offer suggestions for increasing people's compliance with recommendations about behavior that will improve their well-being.

health psychology The branch of psychology that investigates the psychological factors related to wellness and illness, including the prevention, diagnosis, and treatment of medical problems.

psychoneuroimmunology (PNI) The study of the relationship among psychological factors, the immune system, and the brain.

MODULE 34

Stress and Coping

Sheila Gray remembers the worst moment of her life: The day she heard about the mass shootings at Sandy Hook Elementary School in Connecticut. Though Gray lives in Michigan, she immediately jumped in the car and drove to her 7-year-old daughter's school. She brought the girl home. "My heart was pounding. I started crying and I just couldn't stop," Gray says. Then and there, she decided that her daughter, Merilee, would never return to her school. She began homeschooling the girl. Friends could come over, but Gray found she couldn't let Merilee out of her sight. "So much can happen when you walk away from your child," Gray says. "I was terrified by that loss of control."

Learning Outcomes

LO 34-1 How is health psychology a union between medicine and psychology?

LO 34-2 What is stress, how does it affect us, and how can we best cope with it?

Stress: Reacting to Threat and Challenge

Most of us need little introduction to the phenomenon of **stress,** people's response to events that threaten or challenge them. Whether it is a paper or an exam deadline, a family problem, or even the ongoing threat of a terrorist attack, life is full of circumstances and events known as *stressors* that produce threats to our well-being. Even pleasant events–such as planning a party or beginning a sought-after job–can produce stress, although negative events result in greater detrimental consequences than positive ones.

stress A person's response to events that are threatening or challenging.

All of us face stress in our lives. Some health psychologists believe that daily life actually involves a series of repeated sequences of perceiving a threat, considering ways to cope with it, and ultimately adapting to the threat with greater or lesser success. Although adaptation is often minor and occurs without our awareness, adaptation requires a major effort when stress is more severe or long lasting. Ultimately, our attempts to overcome stress may produce biological and psychological responses that result in health problems (Dolbier, Smith, & Steinhardt, 2007; Finan, Zautra, & Wershba, 2011).

Study Alert
Remember the distinction between stressors and stress, which can be tricky: stressors (like an exam) cause stress (the physiological and psychological reaction that comes from the exam).

THE NATURE OF STRESSORS: MY STRESS IS YOUR PLEASURE

Stress is a very personal thing. Although certain kinds of events, such as the death of a loved one or participation in military combat, are universally stressful, other situations may or may not be stressful to a specific person.

Consider, for instance, bungee jumping. Some people would find jumping off a bridge while attached to a slender rubber tether extremely stressful. However, there are individuals who see such an activity as challenging and fun filled. Whether bungee jumping is stressful depends in part, then, on a person's perception of the activity.

For people to consider an event stressful, they must perceive it as threatening or challenging and must lack all the resources to deal with it effectively. Consequently, the same event may at some times be stressful and at other times provoke no stressful reaction at all. A young man experiences stress when he is turned down for a date–if he attributes the refusal to his unattractiveness or unworthiness. But if he attributes it to some factor unrelated to his self-esteem, such as a previous commitment of the woman he asked, the experience of being refused may create no stress at all. Hence, a person's interpretation of events plays an important role in the determination of what is stressful (Folkman & Moskowitz, 2000; Giacobbi Jr., et al., 2004; Friborg et al., 2006).

Even positive events can produce significant stress.

cataclysmic events Strong stressors that occur suddenly and typically affect many people at once (e.g., natural disasters).

personal stressors Major life events, such as the death of a family member, that have immediate negative consequences that generally fade with time.

posttraumatic stress disorder (PTSD) A phenomenon in which victims of major catastrophes or strong personal stressors feel long-lasting effects that may include re-experiencing the event in vivid flashbacks or dreams.

CATEGORIZING STRESSORS

What kinds of events tend to be seen as stressful? There are three general types of stressors: cataclysmic events, personal stressors, and background stressors.

Cataclysmic events are strong stressors that occur suddenly and typically affect many people simultaneously. Disasters such as tornadoes and plane crashes as well as terrorist attacks are examples of cataclysmic events that can affect hundreds or thousands of people simultaneously.

Although it might seem that cataclysmic events would produce potent, lingering stress, in many cases they do not. In fact, cataclysmic events involving natural disasters may produce less stress in the long run than events that initially are not as devastating. One reason is that natural disasters have a clear resolution. Once they are over, people can look to the future knowing that the worst is behind them. Moreover, others who also experienced the disaster share the stress induced by cataclysmic events. Such sharing permits people to offer one another social support and a firsthand understanding of the difficulties others are going through (Yesilyaprak, Kisac, & Sanlier, 2007; Schwarzer & Luszczynska, 2013).

In contrast, terrorist attacks like the one on the World Trade Center in 2001 are cataclysmic events that produce considerable stress. Terrorist attacks are deliberate, and victims (and observers) know that future attacks are likely. Government warnings in the form of heightened terror alerts may further increase the stress (Murphy, Wismar, & Freeman, 2003; Laugharne, Janca, & Widiger, 2007; Watson, Brymer, & Bonanno, 2011).

The second major category of stressor is the personal stressor. **Personal stressors** include major life events such as the death of a parent or spouse, the loss of one's job, a major personal failure, or even something positive such as getting married. Typically, personal stressors produce an immediate major reaction that soon tapers off. For example, stress arising from the death of a loved one tends to be greatest just after the time of death, but people begin to feel less stress and are better able to cope with the loss after the passage of time.

Some victims of major catastrophes and severe personal stressors experience **posttraumatic stress disorder,** or **PTSD,** in which a person has experienced a significantly stressful event that has long-lasting effects that may include re-experiencing the event in vivid flashbacks or dreams. An episode of PTSD may be triggered by an otherwise innocent stimulus, such as the sound of a honking horn, that leads a person to re-experience a past event that produced considerable stress.

Symptoms of posttraumatic stress disorder also include emotional numbing, sleep difficulties, interpersonal problems, alcohol and drug abuse, and in some cases suicide. For instance, the suicide rate for military veterans, many of whom participated in the Iraq and Afghanistan wars, is twice as high as for nonveterans (Pole, 2007; Kaplan et al., 2007; Magruder & Yeager, 2009).

Between 10% to 18% of soldiers returning from Iraq and Afghanistan show symptoms of PTSD. Furthermore, those who have experienced child abuse or rape, rescue workers facing overwhelming situations, and victims of sudden natural disasters or accidents that produce feelings of helplessness and shock may suffer from the same disorder. Even witnessing aggression between two people may trigger PTSD (Friedman, 2006; Marmar, 2009; Horesh et al., 2011).

FIGURE 1 The closer people lived to the site of the World Trade Center terrorist attack, the greater the rate of posttraumatic stress disorder. (Source: Adapted from Susser, Herman, & Aaron, 2002.)

Terrorist attacks produce high incidences of PTSD. For example, 11% of people in New York City had some form of PTSD in the months after the September 11 terrorist attacks. But the responses varied significantly with a resident's proximity to the attacks, as illustrated in Figure 1; the closer someone lived to the World Trade Center, the greater the likelihood of PTSD. Furthermore, for many people, the effects of PTSD were still evident a decade after the attacks (Lee, Isaac, & Janca, 2007; Marshall et al., 2007; Neria, DiGrande, & Adams, 2011).

Background stressors, or more informally, *daily hassles,* are the third major category of stressors. Exemplified by standing in a long line at a bank and getting stuck in a traffic jam, daily hassles are the minor irritations of life that we all face time and time again. Another type of background stressor is a long-term, chronic problem, such as experiencing dissatisfaction with school or a job, being in an unhappy relationship, or living in crowded quarters without privacy (Weinstein et al., 2004; McIntyre, Korn, & Matsuo, 2008; Barke, 2011).

Everyone confronts daily hassles, or background stressors, at some point. At what point do daily hassles become more than mere irritants?

By themselves, daily hassles do not require much coping or even a response on the individual's part, although they certainly produce unpleasant emotions and moods. Yet, daily hassles add up–and ultimately they may take as great of a toll as a single, more stressful incident. In fact, the *number* of daily hassles people face is associated with psychological symptoms and health problems such as flu, sore throat, and backaches.

background stressors ("daily hassles") Everyday annoyances, such as being stuck in traffic, that cause minor irritations and may have long-term ill effects if they continue or are compounded by other stressful events.

The flip side of hassles is *uplifts,* the minor positive events that make us feel good–even if only temporarily. As indicated in Figure 2, uplifts range from relating well to a companion to finding one's surroundings pleasing. What is especially intriguing about uplifts is that they are associated with people's psychological health in just the opposite way that hassles are: The greater the number of uplifts we experience, the fewer the psychological symptoms we report later (Chamberlain & Zika, 1990; Jain, Mills, & Von Känel, 2007; Hurley & Kwon, 2013).

PsychTech

An analysis of the emotional content of words sent in text messages during the hours following the 9/11 terrorist attack showed that, over the course of the day, sadness and anxiety-related words remained steady but anger-related words increased steadily.

The High Cost of Stress

Stress can produce both biological and psychological consequences. Often the most immediate reaction to stress is biological. Exposure to stressors generates a rise in hormone secretions by the adrenal glands, an increase in heart rate and blood pressure, and changes in how well the skin conducts electrical impulses. On a short-term basis, these responses may be adaptive because they produce an "emergency reaction" in which the body prepares to defend itself through activation of the sympathetic nervous system. Those responses may allow more effective coping with the stressful situation (Akil & Morano, 1996; McEwen, 1998).

However, continued exposure to stress results in a decline in the body's overall level of biological functioning because of the constant secretion of stress-related hormones. Over time, stressful reactions can promote deterioration of body tissues such as blood vessels and the heart. Ultimately, we become more susceptible to disease as our ability to fight off infection is lowered (Dean-Borenstein, 2007; Ellins et al., 2008; Miller, Chen, & Parker, 2011).

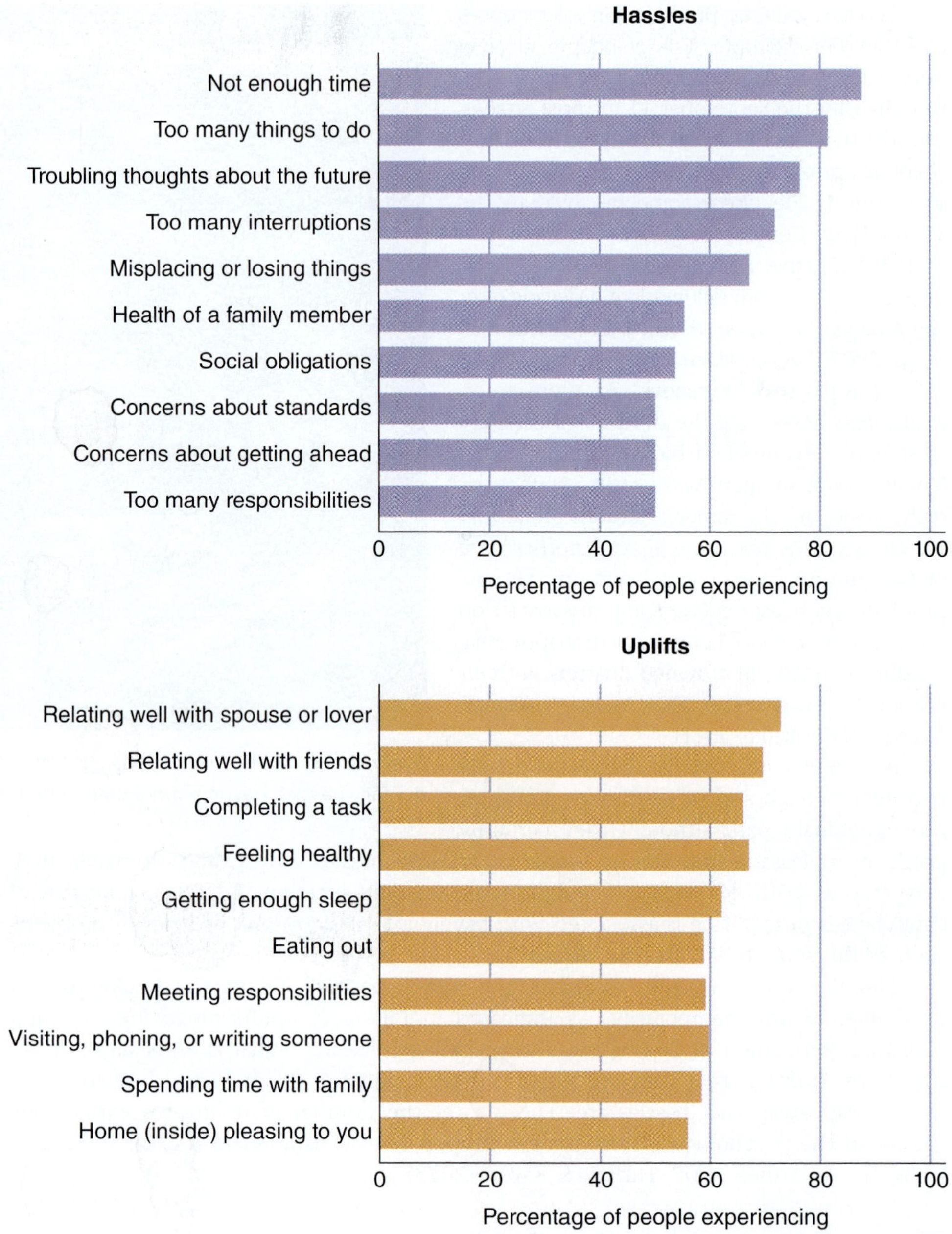

FIGURE 2 The most common everyday hassles and uplifts. How many of these are part of your life, and how do you cope with them? (Source: Adapted from Hassles—Chamberlain & Zika, 1990; Uplifts—Kanner et al., 1981.)

Study Alert

Remember the three categories of stressors—cataclysmic events, personal stressors, and background stressors—and that they produce different levels of stress.

psychophysiological disorders Medical problems influenced by an interaction of psychological, emotional, and physical difficulties.

Furthermore, stress can produce or worsen physical problems. Specifically, **psychophysiological disorders** are medical problems that are influenced by an interaction of psychological, emotional, and physical difficulties. Common psychophysiological disorders include high blood pressure, headaches, backaches, skin rashes, indigestion, fatigue, and constipation. Stress has even been linked to the common cold (Cohen et al., 2003; Andrasik, 2006; Gupta, 2013).

On a psychological level, high levels of stress prevent people from adequately coping with life. Their view of the environment can become clouded (for example, a minor criticism made by a friend is blown out of proportion). Moreover, at the highest levels of stress, emotional responses may be so extreme that people are unable to act at all. People under a lot of stress also become less able to deal with new stressors.

In short, stress affects us in multiple ways. It may increase the risk that we will become ill, it may directly cause illness, it may make us less able to recover from a disease, and it may reduce our ability to cope with future stress. (See Figure 3 to get a measure of your own level of stress.)

How Stressed Are You?

Find out how stressed you are by responding to the following statements in terms of the last month only. Add up the score from each box. The key below will help you get a sense of your stress level.

1. I was convinced that the big things in my life were beyond my control.
   ☐ 0=never, 1=infrequently, 2=sometimes, 3=fairly often, 4=very often
2. I felt that I could at least control the minor irritations in my life.
   ☐ 4=never, 3=infrequently, 2=sometimes, 1=fairly often, 0=very often
3. I became upset at something that I didn't expect to happen.
   ☐ 4=never, 3=infrequently, 2=sometimes, 1=fairly often, 0=very often
4. I felt confident that I could handle my personal problems.
   ☐ 4=never, 3=infrequently, 2=sometimes, 1=fairly often, 0=very often
5. I felt nervous, anxious, and under stress.
   ☐ 0=never, 1=infrequently, 2=sometimes, 3=fairly often, 4=very often
6. I felt myself to be the master of my life.
   ☐ 4=never, 3=infrequently, 2=sometimes, 1=fairly often, 0=very often
7. I realized that I simply couldn't manage or cope with everything I had to do.
   ☐ 0=never, 1=infrequently, 2=sometimes, 3=fairly often, 4=very often
8. I felt that troubles and worries were mounting so high I couldn't get past them.
   ☐ 0=never, 1=infrequently, 2=sometimes, 3=fairly often, 4=very often
9. I felt that, overall, things were heading in the right direction.
   ☐ 4=never, 3=infrequently, 2=sometimes, 1=fairly often, 0=very often
10. I lost my temper because of something that I couldn't control.
   ☐ 0=never, 1=infrequently, 2=sometimes, 3=fairly often, 4=very often

Here's a rough scoring guide:

0–10 low stress
11–20 moderately low stress
21–30 moderately high stress
31–40 high stress

FIGURE 3 To get a sense of the level of stress in your life, complete this questionnaire. (Source: Adapted from Cohen, Kamarck, & Mermelstein, 1983.)

THE GENERAL ADAPTATION SYNDROME MODEL: THE COURSE OF STRESS

The effects of long-term stress are illustrated in a series of stages proposed by Hans Selye (pronounced "sell-yay"), a pioneering stress theorist (Selye, 1976, 1993). This model, the **general adaptation syndrome (GAS),** suggests that the physiological response to stress follows the same set pattern regardless of the cause of stress.

general adaptation syndrome (GAS) A theory developed by Selye that suggests that a person's response to a stressor consists of three stages: alarm and mobilization, resistance, and exhaustion.

As shown in Figure 4, the GAS has three phases. The first stage—*alarm and mobilization*—occurs when people become aware of the presence of a stressor. On a biological level, the sympathetic nervous system becomes energized, which helps a person cope initially with the stressor.

However, if the stressor persists, people move into the second response stage: *resistance*. During this stage, the body is actively fighting the stressor on a biological level. During resistance, people use a variety of means to cope with the stressor—sometimes successfully but at a cost of some degree of physical or psychological well-being. For example, a student who faces the stress of failing several courses might spend long hours studying seeking to cope with the stress.

If resistance is inadequate, people enter the last stage of the GAS: *exhaustion*. During the exhaustion stage, a person's ability to fight the stressor declines to the point where negative consequences of stress appear: physical illness and psychological symptoms in the form of an inability to concentrate, heightened irritability, or, in severe

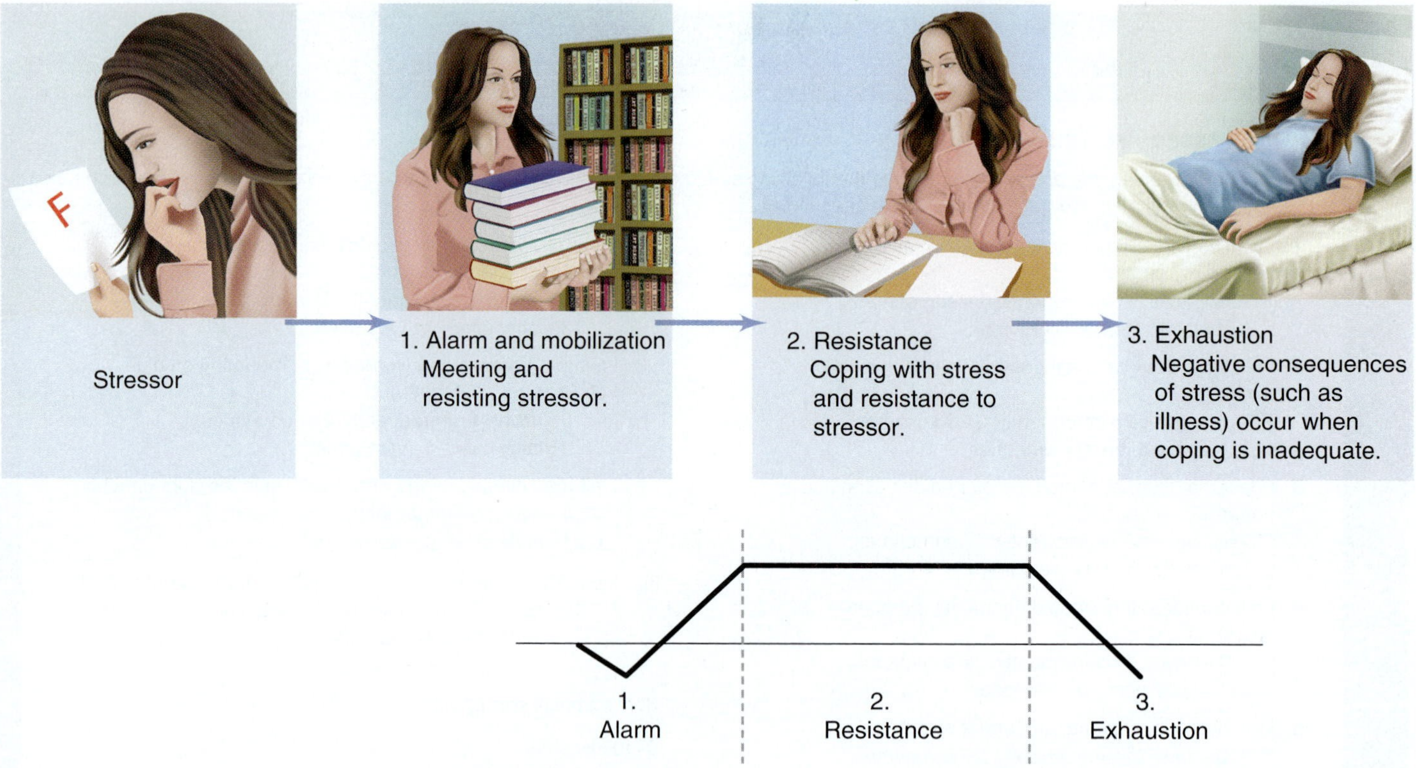

FIGURE 4 According to the general adaptation syndrome (GAS) model there are three major stages to stress responses: alarm and mobilization; resistance; and exhaustion. The graph below the illustration shows the degree of effort expended to cope with stressors at each of the three stages. (Source: Adapted from Selye, 1976.)

cases, disorientation and a loss of touch with reality. In a sense, people wear out, and their physiological resources to fight the stressor are used up.

How do people move out of the third stage after they have entered it? In some cases, exhaustion allows people to escape a stressor. For example, people who become ill from overwork may be excused from their duties for a time, which gives them a temporary respite from their responsibilities. At least for a time, then, the immediate stress is reduced.

Although the GAS has had a substantial impact on our understanding of stress, Selye's theory has not gone unchallenged. For example, the theory suggests that the biological reaction is similar regardless of the stressor, but some health psychologists disagree. They believe that people's biological responses are specific to the way they appraise a stressful event. If a stressor is seen as unpleasant but not unusual, then the biological response may be different than if the stressor is seen as unpleasant, out of the ordinary, and unanticipated. This perspective has led to an increased focus on psychoneuroimmunology (Taylor et al., 2000; Gaab et al., 2005; Irwin, 2008).

Study Alert:
Remember the three stages of the General Adaptation Syndrome with the abbreviation ARE (Alarm and mobilization; Resistance; and Exhaustion)

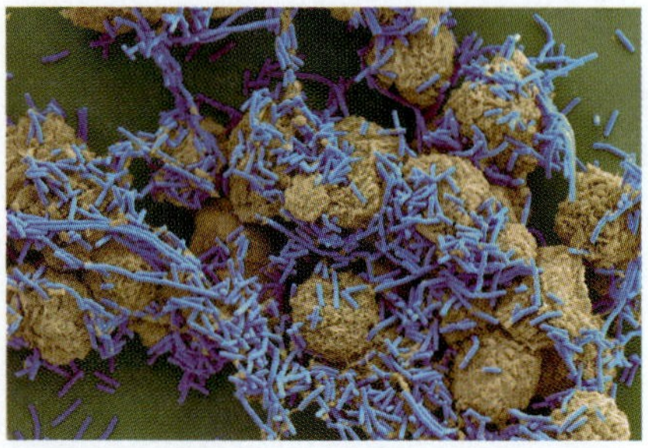

The ability to fight off disease is related to psychological factors. Here a cell from the body's immune system engulfs and destroys disease-producing bacteria.

PSYCHONEUROIMMUNOLOGY AND STRESS

Contemporary health psychologists specializing in PNI have taken a broader approach to stress. Focusing on the outcomes of stress, they have identified three main consequences of it (see Figure 5).

First, stress has direct physiological results, including an increase in blood pressure, an increase in hormonal activity, and an overall decline in the functioning of the immune system. Second, stress leads people to engage in behaviors that are harmful to their health, including increased nicotine, drug, and alcohol use; poor eating habits; and decreased sleep. Third, stress produces some indirect consequences that ultimately

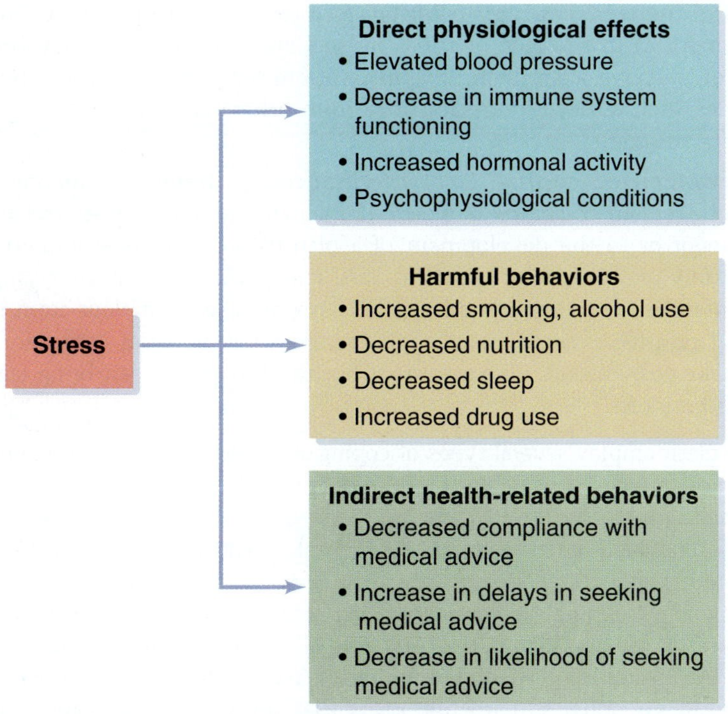

FIGURE 5 Three major types of consequences result from stress: direct physiological effects, harmful behaviors, and indirect health-related behaviors. (Source: Adapted from Baum, 1994.)

result in declines in health. For example, high levels of stress reduce the likelihood a person will seek health care. In addition, stress may result in less compliance with medical advice when it is sought. Both the reductions in seeking medical care and decreased compliance can indirectly lead to declines in health (Broman, 2005; Lindblad, Lindahl, & Theorell, 2006; Stowell, Robles, & Kane, 2013).

Why is stress so damaging to the immune system? One reason is that stress may decrease the ability of the immune system to respond to disease, permitting germs that produce colds to reproduce more easily or allowing cancer cells to spread more rapidly. In normal circumstances, our bodies produce disease-fighting white blood cells called *lymphocytes*. Our bodies can produce them at an extraordinary rate–some 10 million every few seconds. Stress may decrease this level of production.

Another way that stress affects the immune system is by overstimulating it. Rather than fighting invading bacteria, viruses, and other foreign invaders, the immune system may begin to attack the body itself and damage healthy tissue. When that happens, it can lead to disorders such as arthritis and allergic reactions (Segerstrom & Miller, 2004; Dougall & Baum, 2004; Baum, Lorduy, & Jenkins, 2011).

Coping with Stress

Stress is a normal part of life–and not necessarily a completely bad part. For example, without stress, we might not be sufficiently motivated to complete the activities we need to accomplish.

However, it is also clear that too much stress can take a toll on physical and psychological health. How do people deal with stress? Is there a way to reduce its negative effects?

Efforts to control, reduce, or learn to tolerate the threats that lead to stress are known as **coping.** We habitually use certain coping responses to deal with stress. Most of the time, we're not aware of these responses–just as we may be unaware of the minor stressors of life until they build up to harmful levels (Wrzesniewski & Chylinska, 2007; Chao, 2011).

coping The efforts to control, reduce, or learn to tolerate the threats that lead to stress.

We also have other, more direct and potentially more positive ways of coping with stress, which fall into two main categories (Folkman & Moskowitz, 2000, 2004; Baker & Berenbaum, 2007):

- **Emotion-focused coping.** In *emotion-focused coping,* people try to manage their emotions in the face of stress by seeking to change the way they feel about or perceive a problem. Examples of emotion-focused coping include strategies such as accepting sympathy from others and looking at the bright side of a situation.
- **Problem-focused coping.** *Problem-focused coping* attempts to modify the stressful problem or source of stress. Problem-focused strategies lead to changes in behavior or to the development of a plan of action to deal with stress. Starting a study group to improve poor classroom performance is an example of problem-focused coping. In addition, one might take a time-out from stress by creating positive events. For example, taking a day off from caring for a relative with a serious, chronic illness to go a health club or spa can bring significant relief from stress.

People often employ several types of coping strategies simultaneously. Furthermore, they use emotion-focused strategies more frequently when they perceive circumstances as being unchangeable and problem-focused strategies more often in situations they see as relatively modifiable (Stanton et al., 2000; Penley, Tomaka, & Wiebe, 2002).

Some forms of coping are less successful. One of the least effective forms of coping is avoidant coping. In *avoidant coping,* a person may use wishful thinking to reduce stress or use more direct escape routes, such as drug use, alcohol use, and overeating. An example of wishful thinking to avoid a test would be to say to oneself, "Maybe it will snow so hard tomorrow that the test will be canceled." Alternatively, a person might get drunk to avoid a problem. Either way, avoidant coping usually results in a postponement of dealing with a stressful situation, and this often makes the problem even worse (Hutchinson, Baldwin, & Oh, 2006; Glass et al., 2009; Sikkema et al., 2013).

Another way of dealing with stress occurs unconsciously through the use of defense mechanisms. *Defense mechanisms* are unconscious strategies that people use to reduce anxiety by concealing the source from themselves and others. Defense mechanisms permit people to avoid stress by acting as if the stress were not even there. For example, one study examined California college students who lived in dormitories close to a geological fault (Lehman & Taylor, 1988). Those who lived in dorms that were known to be unlikely to withstand an earthquake were significantly *more* likely to doubt experts' predictions of an impending earthquake than were those who lived in safer structures.

Another defense mechanism used to cope with stress is *emotional insulation* in which a person stops experiencing any emotions at all and thereby remains unaffected and unmoved by both positive and negative experiences. The problem with defense mechanisms, of course, is that they merely hide the problem and do not deal with reality.

LEARNED HELPLESSNESS

Have you ever faced an intolerable situation that you just couldn't resolve, and you finally simply gave up and accepted things the way they were? This example illustrates one of the possible consequences of being in an environment in which control over a situation is not possible–a state that produces learned helplessness. **Learned helplessness** occurs when people conclude that unpleasant or aversive stimuli cannot be controlled. They develop a view of the world that becomes so ingrained that they cease trying to remedy the aversive circumstances even if they actually can exert some influence on the situation. For example, students who decide they are simply "no good in math" may not work very hard in math classes because they believe that no matter how hard they try, they'll never succeed. Their learned helplessness virtually ensures that they won't do well in math classes (Seligman, 2007; Aujoulat, Luminet, & Deccache, 2007).

learned helplessness A state in which people conclude that unpleasant or aversive stimuli cannot be controlled–a view of the world that becomes so ingrained that they cease trying to remedy the aversive circumstances even if they actually can exert some influence on the situation.

Victims of learned helplessness have concluded that there is no link between the responses they make and the outcomes that occur. People experience more physical symptoms and depression when they perceive that they have little or no control than they do when they feel a sense of control over a situation (Chou, 2005; Bjornstad, 2006; Figen, 2011).

COPING STYLES: HARDINESS AND RESILIENCE

Most of us characteristically cope with stress by employing a *coping style* that represents our general tendency to deal with stress in a specific way. For example, you may know people who habitually react to even the smallest amount of stress with hysteria and others who calmly confront even the greatest stress in an unflappable manner. These kinds of people clearly have very different coping styles (Taylor, 2003; Kato & Pedersen, 2005).

Hardiness. Among those who cope with stress most successfully are people who are equipped with **hardiness,** a personality trait characterized by a sense of commitment, the perception of problems as challenges, and a sense of control. People with the hardiness trait have a lower rate of stress-related illness (Baumgartner, 2002; Maddi, 2007; Maddi et al., 2011).

hardiness A personality trait characterized by a sense of commitment, the perception of problems as challenges, and a sense of control.

Specifically, the three components of hardiness operate in different ways:

- *Commitment.* People with a strong level of commitment tend to throw themselves into whatever they are doing. They have a sense that their activities are important and meaningful.
- *Challenge.* Hardy people believe that change, rather than stability, is the standard condition of life. To them, the anticipation of change is something positive, rather than change being seen as a threat to their security.
- *Control.* Hardiness is marked by a sense of control—the perception that people can influence the events in their lives.

Hardy individuals approach stress optimistically and take direct action to learn about and deal with stressors; they thereby change stressful events into less threatening ones. As a consequence, hardiness acts as a defense against stress-related illness (Andrew et al., 2008; Bartone et al., 2008; Vogt et al., 2008).

resilience The ability to withstand, overcome, and actually thrive after profound adversity.

Resilience. For those who confront the most profound difficulties, such as the death of a loved one or a permanent injury such as paralysis after an accident, a key ingredient in their psychological recovery is their degree of resilience. **Resilience** is the ability to withstand, overcome, and actually thrive after profound adversity (Bonanno, 2004; Norlander, Von Schedvin, & Archer, 2005; Jackson, 2006).

Resilient people are generally optimistic, good-natured, and have good social skills. They are usually independent, and they have a sense of control over their own destiny—even if fate has dealt them a devastating blow. In short, they work with what they have and make the best of whatever situation they find themselves in (Friborg et al., 2005; Deshields et al., 2006; Sinclair et al., 2013).

Resilience may have its origins in a complex series of biological reactions that occur when people confront devastating situations. These reactions involve the release of the hormone cortisol. Although cortisol is helpful in responding to challenges, too much can produce damage. Other chemicals, however, can moderate the effects of cortisol, and it may be that drugs or therapy can stimulate the production of these moderating chemicals. Furthermore, some people may be genetically predisposed to produce these chemicals, making them more resilient (Cole et al., 2010; Stix, 2011).

"Today, we examined our life style, we evaluated our diet and our exercise program, and we also assessed our behavioral pattern. Then we needed a drink."

social support A mutual network of caring, interested others.

SOCIAL SUPPORT: TURNING TO OTHERS

Our relationships with others also help us cope with stress. Researchers have found that **social support,** the knowledge that we are part of a mutual network of caring, interested others, enables us to experience lower levels of stress and better cope with the stress we do undergo (Martin & Brantley, 2004; Bolger & Amarel, 2007; García-Herrero et al., 2013).

The social and emotional support people provide each other helps in dealing with stress in several ways. For instance, such support demonstrates that a person is an important and valued member of a social network. Similarly, other people can provide information and advice about appropriate ways of dealing with stress (Day & Livingstone, 2003; Lindorff, 2005).

Finally, people who are part of a social support network can provide actual goods and services to help others in stressful situations. For instance, they can supply temporary living quarters to a person whose house has burned down, or they can offer study help to a student who is experiencing stress because of poor academic performance (Natvig, Albrektsen, & Ovarnstrom, 2003; Takizawa, Kondo, & Sakihara, 2007).

Findings that attendance at religious services (as well as spirituality in general) provides health-related benefits also illustrate the importance of social support. For example, healthy people who regularly attend religious services live longer than those who do not attend regularly (Powell, Shahabi, & Thoresen, 2003; Gilbert, 2007; Hayward & Elliott, 2011).

Neuroscience in Your Life: Altering Memories of Fear for Those with PTSD

In recent years, scientists have begun to be able to learn how to intentionally alter how the brain works, including how memories are processed and retained. In fact, it may be possible to help those with disorders such as posttraumatic stress disorder (PTSD) function more effectively. Specifically, some drugs can block memory formation or alter the emotional content associated with those memories by affecting the limbic system, including the amygdala (associated with fear responses) and the hippocampus (associated with the formation of memories). The images below show reduced activation of fear-related areas (in blue) and increased activity in memory-related areas in (orange) when participants were given THC (Δ9-tetrahydrocannabinol) while learning that an image previously associated with fear was no longer something that should be feared. This type of intervention promises to help those with PTSD learn not to overreact to things in their environment that they perceive as threatening (Rabinak et al., 2013).

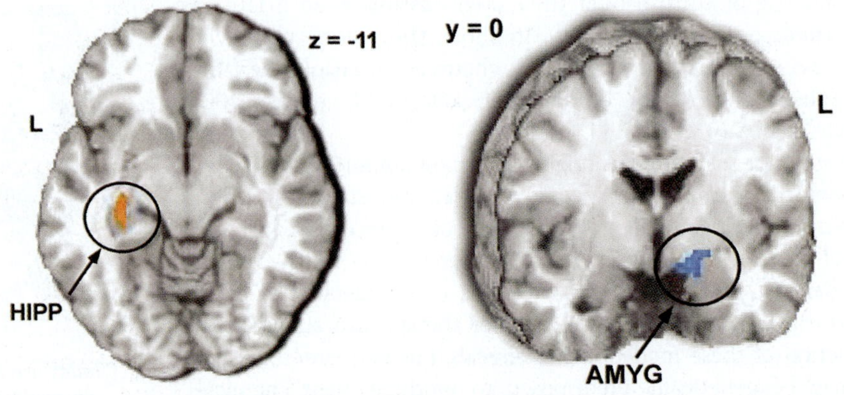

Recent research is also beginning to identify how social support affects brain processing. For instance, one experiment found that activation of the areas of the brain reflecting stress was reduced when social support–simply being able to hold the hand of another person–was available (Coan, Schaefer, & Davidson, 2006).

From the perspective of . . .

A Social Worker How would you help people deal with and avoid stress in their everyday lives? How might you encourage people to create social support networks?

BECOMING AN INFORMED CONSUMER of Psychology

Effective Coping Strategies

How can we deal with the stress in our lives? Although there is no universal solution because effective coping depends on the nature of the stressor and the degree to which it can be controlled, here are some general guidelines (Aspinwall & Taylor, 1997; Folkman & Moskowitz, 2000):

- *Turn a threat into a challenge.* When a stressful situation might be controllable, the best coping strategy is to treat the situation as a challenge and focus on ways to control it. For instance, if you experience stress because your car is always breaking down, you might take a course in auto mechanics and learn to deal directly with the car's problems.
- *Make a threatening situation less threatening.* When a stressful situation seems to be uncontrollable, you need to take a different approach. It is possible to change your appraisal of the situation, view it in a different light, and modify your attitude toward it. Research supports the old truism, "Look for the silver lining in every cloud" (Smith & Lazarus, 2001; Cheng & Cheung, 2005).
- *Change your goals.* If you are faced with an uncontrollable situation, a reasonable strategy is to adopt new goals that are practical in view of the particular situation. For example, a dancer who has been in an automobile accident and has lost full use of her legs may no longer aspire to a career in dance but might modify her goals and try to become a choreographer.
- *Take direct action to alter your physiological reactions to stress.* Changing your physiological reaction to stress can help with coping. For example, biofeedback (in which a person learns to control internal physiological processes through conscious thought) can alter basic physiological reactions to stress and permit the person to reduce blood pressure, heart rate, and other consequences of heightened stress. Exercise can also be effective in reducing stress (Langreth, 2000; Spencer et al., 2003; Hamer, Taylor, & Steptoe, 2006).
- *Alter the situations that are likely to cause stress.* A final strategy for coping with stress is *proactive coping,* anticipating and trying to head off stress *before* it is encountered. For example, if you're expecting to go through a 1-week period in which you must take a number of major tests, you can try to arrange your schedule so you have more time to study (Aspinwall & Taylor, 1997; Bode et al., 2007).

RECAP/EVALUATE/RETHINK

RECAP

LO 34-1 How is health psychology a union between medicine and psychology?

- The field of health psychology considers how psychology can be applied to the prevention, diagnosis, and treatment of medical problems.

LO 34-2 What is stress, how does it affect us, and how can we best cope with it?

- Stress is a response to threatening or challenging environmental conditions. People encounter stressors—the circumstances that produce stress—of both a positive and a negative nature.
- The way an environmental circumstance is interpreted affects whether it will be considered stressful. Still, there are general classes of events that provoke stress: cataclysmic events, personal stressors, and background stressors (daily hassles).
- Stress produces immediate physiological reactions. In the short term those reactions may be adaptive, but in the long term they may have negative consequences, including the development of psychophysiological disorders.
- The consequences of stress can be explained in part by Selye's general adaptation syndrome (GAS), which suggests that there are three stages in stress responses: alarm and mobilization, resistance, and exhaustion.
- Coping with stress can take a number of forms, including the unconscious use of defense mechanisms and the use of emotion-focused or problem-focused coping strategies.
- Stress can be reduced by developing a sense of control over one's circumstances. In some cases, however, people develop a state of learned helplessness.

EVALUATE

1. __________ is defined as a response to challenging or threatening events.

2. Match each portion of the GAS with its definition.

1. Alarm and mobilization	**a.** Ability to adapt to stress diminishes; symptoms appear.
2. Exhaustion	**b.** Activation of sympathetic nervous system.
3. Resistance	**c.** Various strategies are used to cope with a stressor.

3. Stressors that affect a single person and produce an immediate major reaction are known as

- **a.** Personal stressors
- **b.** Psychic stressors
- **c.** Cataclysmic stressors
- **d.** Daily stressors

4. People with the personality characteristic of __________ seem to be better able to successfully combat stressors.

RETHINK

1. Why are cataclysmic stressors less stressful in the long run than other types of stressors? Does the reason relate to the coping phenomenon known as social support? How?

2. Given what you know about coping strategies, how would you train people to avoid stress in their everyday lives? How would you use this information with a group of veterans from the war in Afghanistan suffering from posttraumatic stress disorder?

Answers to Evaluate Questions

1. Stress; **2.** 1-b, 2-a, 3-c; **3.** a; **4.** hardiness

KEY TERMS

health psychology
psychoneuroimmunology (PNI)
stress
cataclysmic events
personal stressors
posttraumatic stress disorder (PTSD)
background stressors ("daily hassles")
psychophysiological disorders
general adaptation syndrome (GAS)
coping
learned helplessness
hardiness
resilience
social support

MODULE 35

Psychological Aspects of Illness and Well-Being

> I feel that it is absolutely necessary to be my own best advocate, and the best place to learn how to do that is in a group of other well-educated patients and their caregivers. We know what life post-diagnosis is like, and we help each other in ways that no docs, nurses, clergy, well-meaning friends and family possibly can. We laugh, we cry, we bitch, and we push and pull each other! We mourn the losses, celebrate small and large victories, and we educate ourselves and others. But most importantly–we embrace each other and our lives. (Anonymous blogpost, 2010.)

Learning Outcome

LO 35-1 How do psychological factors affect health-related problems such as coronary heart disease, cancer, and smoking?

As recently as three decades ago, most psychologists and health-care providers would have scoffed at the notion that a discussion group could improve a cancer patient's chances of survival. Today, however, such methods have gained increasing acceptance.

Growing evidence suggests that psychological factors have a substantial impact both on major health problems that were once seen in purely physiological terms and on our everyday sense of health, well-being, and happiness. We'll consider the psychological components of three major health problems–heart disease, cancer, and smoking–and then consider the nature of people's well-being and happiness.

The As, Bs, and Ds of Coronary Heart Disease

> Tim knew it wasn't going to be his day when he got stuck in traffic behind a slow-moving farm truck. How could the driver dawdle like that? Didn't he have anything of any importance to do? Things didn't get any better when Tim arrived on campus and discovered the library didn't have the books he needed. He could almost feel the tension rising.
>
> "I need that material to finish my paper," he thought to himself.
>
> He knew that meant he wouldn't be able to get his paper done early, and that meant he wouldn't have the time he wanted to revise the paper. He wanted it to be a first-class paper. This time Tim wanted to get a better grade than his roommate, Luis. Although Luis didn't know it, Tim felt they were in competition and that Luis was always trying to better him whether academically or just playing cards.
>
> "In fact," Tim mused to himself, "I feel like I'm in competition with everyone, no matter what I'm doing."

Have you, like Tim, ever seethed impatiently at being caught behind a slow-moving vehicle, felt anger and frustration at not finding material you needed at the library, or experienced a sense of competitiveness with your classmates?

Many of us experience these sorts of feelings at one time or another, but for some people they represent a pervasive, characteristic set of personality traits known as the Type A behavior pattern. The **Type A behavior pattern** is a cluster of behaviors involving hostility, competitiveness, time urgency, and feeling driven. In contrast, the

Type A behavior pattern A cluster of behaviors involving hostility, competitiveness, time urgency, and feeling driven.

Type B behavior pattern A cluster of behaviors characterized by a patient, cooperative, noncompetitive, and nonaggressive manner.

Type B behavior pattern is characterized by a patient, cooperative, noncompetitive, and nonaggressive manner. It's important to keep in mind that Type A and Type B represent the ends of a continuum, and most people fall somewhere in between the two endpoints. Few people are purely a Type A or a Type B.

The importance of the Type A behavior pattern lies in its links to coronary heart disease. Men who display the Type A pattern develop coronary heart disease twice as often and suffer significantly more fatal heart attacks than those classified as having the Type B pattern. Moreover, the Type A pattern predicts who is going to develop heart disease at least as well as–and independently of–any other single factor, including age, blood pressure, smoking habits, and cholesterol levels in the body (Wielgosz & Nolan, 2000; Beresnevaité, Taylor, & Bagby, 2007; Korotkov et al., 2011).

Hostility is the key component of the Type A behavior pattern that is related to heart disease. Although competition, time urgency, and feelings of being driven may produce stress and potentially other health and emotional problems, they aren't linked to coronary heart disease the way that hostility is (Williams, J. E. et al., 2000; Boyle et al., 2005; Ohira et al., 2007).

Why is hostility so toxic? The key reason is that hostility produces excessive physiological arousal in stressful situations. That arousal, in turn, results in increased production of the hormones epinephrine and norepinephrine as well as increases in heart rate and blood pressure. Such an exaggerated physiological response ultimately produces an increased incidence of coronary heart disease (Demaree & Everhart, 2004; Eaker et al., 2004; Myrtek, 2007).

Study Alert
It's important to distinguish among Type A (hostility, competitiveness), Type B (patience, cooperativeness), and Type D (distressed) behaviors.

It's important to keep in mind that not everyone who displays Type A behaviors is destined to have coronary heart disease. For one thing, a firm association between Type A behaviors and coronary heart disease has not been established for women; most findings pertain to males partly because until recently most research was done on men. In addition, other types of negative emotions besides the hostility found in Type A behavior appear to be related to heart attacks. For example, psychologist Johan Denollet has found evidence that what he calls *Type D*–for "distressed"–behavior is linked to coronary heart disease. In this view, insecurity, anxiety, and the negative outlook Type Ds display put them at risk for repeated heart attacks (Schiffer et al., 2005; Spindler et al., 2009; Denollet & Pedersen, 2011).

From the perspective of . . .

A Health-Care Provider What type of advice would you give to your patients about the connections between personality and disease? For example, would you encourage Type A people to become "less Type A" to decrease their risk of heart disease?

Psychological Aspects of Cancer

Hardly any disease is feared more than cancer. Most people think of cancer in terms of lingering pain, and being diagnosed with the disease is typically viewed as receiving a death sentence.

Although a diagnosis of cancer is not as grim as it once was–several kinds of cancer have a high cure rate if detected early enough–cancer remains the second leading cause of death after coronary heart disease. The precise trigger for the disease is not well understood, but the process by which cancer spreads is straightforward. Certain cells in the body become altered and multiply rapidly in an uncontrolled fashion. As those cells grow, they form tumors; if left unchecked, the tumors suck nutrients from healthy cells and body tissue and ultimately destroy the body's ability to function properly.

Although the processes involved in the spread of cancer are basically physiological, some research suggests that the emotional responses of cancer patients to their disease may affect its course. For example, some findings show that a "fighting spirit" leads to better coping. On the other hand, there is little evidence that long-term survival rates are better than for patients with a less positive attitude (Watson et al., 1999; Rom, Miller, & Peluso, 2009; Heitzmann et al., 2011).

Despite conflicting evidence, health psychologists believe that patients' emotions may at least partially determine the course of their disease. In the case of cancer, it is possible that positive emotional responses may help generate specialized "killer" cells that help control the size and spread of cancerous tumors. Conversely, negative emotions may suppress the ability of those cells to fight tumors (Schedlowski & Tewes, 1999; Noy, 2006).

Is a particular personality type linked to cancer? Some researchers suggest that cancer patients are less emotionally reactive, suppress anger, and lack outlets for emotional release. However, the data are too tentative and inconsistent to suggest firm conclusions about a link between personality characteristics and cancer. Certainly no conclusive evidence suggests that people who develop cancer would not have done so if their personality had been of a different sort or if their attitudes had been more positive (Smith, 1988; Zevon & Corn, 1990; Holland & Lewis, 2001).

What is increasingly clear, however, is that certain types of psychological therapy have the potential for improving quality of life and even extending the lives of cancer patients. For example, the results of one study showed that women with breast cancer who received psychological treatment lived at least a year and a half longer and experienced less anxiety and pain than women who did not participate in therapy. Research on patients with other health problems, such as heart disease, also has found that therapy can be both psychologically and medically beneficial (Frasure-Smith, Lesperance, & Talajic, 2000; Butler et al., 2009; Lemogne et al., 2013).

Smoking

Would you walk into a convenience store and buy an item with a label warning you that its use could kill you? Although most people would probably answer no, millions make such a purchase everyday: a pack of cigarettes. Furthermore, they do this despite clear, well-publicized evidence that smoking is linked to cancer, heart attacks, strokes, bronchitis, emphysema, and a host of other serious illnesses. Smoking is the leading preventable cause of death in the United States; one in five U.S. deaths is caused by smoking. Worldwide, more than 5 million people die each year from the effects of smoking (Danaei et al., 2005).

WHY PEOPLE SMOKE

Why do people smoke despite all the evidence showing that it is bad for their health? It is not that they are somehow unaware of the link between smoking and disease; surveys show that most *smokers* agree with the statement, "Cigarette smoking frequently causes disease and death." And almost three-quarters of the 45 million smokers in the United States say they would like to quit. Still, each day, almost 4,000 persons younger than 18 years of age smoke their first cigarette, and each day about 1,000 persons under the age of 18 become new daily cigarette smokers (Wetter et al., 1998; Price, 2008; CDC, 2013).

Genetics seems to determine, in part, whether people will become smokers, how much they will smoke, and how easily they can quit. Genetics also influences how susceptible people are to the harmful effects of smoking. For instance, there is an

Although smoking is prohibited in an increasing number of places, it remains a substantial social problem.

almost 50% higher rate of lung cancer in African-American smokers than in white smokers. This difference may be due to genetically produced variations in the efficiency with which enzymes are able to reduce the effects of the cancer-causing chemicals in tobacco smoke (Pomerlau, 1995; Li et al., 2003; Li et al., 2008).

However, although genetics plays a role in smoking, situational factors are the primary cause of the habit. Smoking at first may be seen as "cool" or sophisticated, as a rebellious act, or as facilitating calm performance in stressful situations. Greater exposure to smoking in media such as film also leads to a higher risk of becoming an established smoker. In addition, smoking a cigarette is sometimes viewed as a "rite of passage" for adolescents undertaken at the urging of friends and viewed as a sign of growing up (Sargent et al., 2007; Wills et al., 2008; Heatherton & Sargent, 2009).

Ultimately, smoking becomes a habit. And it's an easy habit to pick up: Smoking even a single cigarette leads to a smoker finding that *not* smoking requires an effort or involves discomfort. Subsequently, people begin to label themselves smokers, and smoking becomes part of how they view themselves. Moreover, they become dependent physiologically because nicotine, a primary ingredient of tobacco, is highly addictive. A complex relationship develops among smoking, nicotine levels, and a smoker's emotions in which a certain nicotine level becomes associated with a positive emotional state. As a result, people smoke in an effort to regulate *both* emotional states and nicotine levels in the blood (Kassel et al., 2007; Ursprung, Sanouri, & DiFranza, 2009; Dennis, 2011).

The newest trend in smoking is the use of *electronic cigarettes*, or *e-cigarettes*, which are battery-powered cigarette-shaped devices that deliver nicotine that is vaporized to form a mist. They simulate the experience of smoking tobacco. Although less harmful than traditional cigarettes, their health effects are unclear. Still, their use is growing: 10% of high school students tried an e-cigarette in 2012, double the number of the previous year, and the numbers continue to increase. The jury is out on whether e-cigarettes will provide a safer alternative to traditional cigarettes or whether their increasing use will ultimately give rise to a new health threat (Gray, 2013; Tavernise, 2013).

QUITTING SMOKING

Because smoking has both psychological and biological components, few habits are as difficult to break. Long-term successful treatment typically occurs in just 15% of those who try to stop smoking; once smoking becomes a habit, it is as hard to stop as an addiction to cocaine or heroin. In fact, some of the biochemical reactions to nicotine are similar to those to cocaine, amphetamines, and morphine. Furthermore, changes in brain chemistry brought about by smoking may make smokers more resistant to antismoking messages (Vanasse, Niyonsenga, & Courteau, 2004; Foulds et al., 2006; Dani & Montague, 2007).

Many people try to quit smoking but fail. The average smoker tries to quit 8 to 10 times before being successful, and even then many relapse. Even long-time quitters can fall off the wagon: About 10% relapse after more than a year of avoiding cigarettes (Grady & Altman, 2008).

Among the most effective tools for ending the smoking habit are drugs that replace the nicotine found in cigarettes. Whether in the form of gum, patches, nasal sprays, or inhalers, these products provide a dose of nicotine that reduces dependence on cigarettes. Another approach is exemplified by the drugs Zyban and Chantix; rather than replacing nicotine, they reduce the pleasure from smoking and suppress withdrawal symptoms that smokers experience when they try to stop (Shiffman, 2007; Brody, 2008; Dohnke, Weiss-Gerlach, & Spies, 2011).

Behavioral strategies, which view smoking as a learned habit and concentrate on changing the smoking response, can also be effective. Initial "cure" rates of 60% have been reported, and 1 year after treatment more than half of those who quit have not resumed smoking. Individual or group counseling also increases the rate

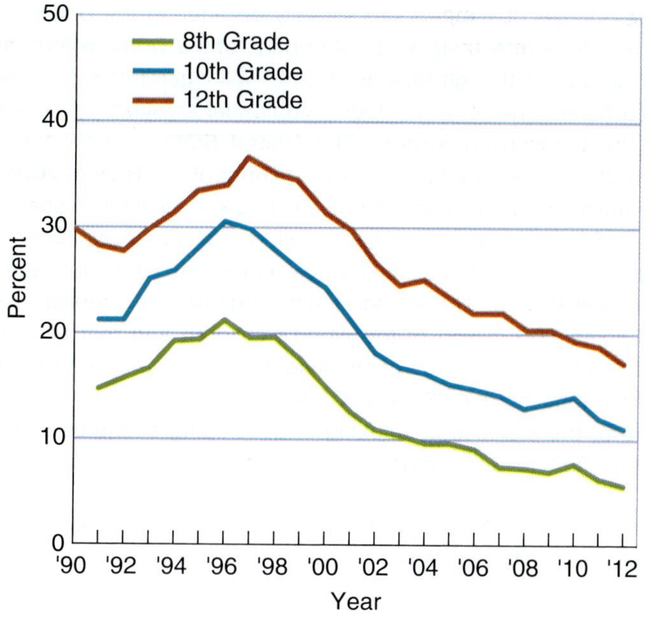

FIGURE 1 Although smoking among teenagers is lower than it was 20 years ago, a significant number still report smoking regularly. What factors might account for the continued high use of tobacco by teenagers despite the increase in antismoking advertising? (Source: Adapted from Johnston et al., 2013.)

of success in breaking the habit. The best treatment seems to be a combination of nicotine replacement and counseling. What doesn't work? Going it alone: Only 5% of smokers who quit cold-turkey on their own are successful (Rock, 1999; Woodruff, Conway, & Edwards, 2007).

In the long term, the most effective means of reducing smoking may be changes in societal norms and attitudes toward the habit. For instance, many cities and towns have made smoking in public places illegal; legislation based on strong popular sentiment that bans smoking in places such as college classrooms and buildings is being passed with increasing frequency. In addition, smokers are more likely to quit when their friends are quitting, so the social support of others quitting is helpful (Christakis & Fowler, 2008; McDermott et al., 2013).

The long-term effect of the barrage of information regarding the negative consequences of smoking on people's health has been substantial; overall, smoking has declined over the last 2 decades, particularly among males. Still, more than one-fourth of students enrolled in high school are active smokers by the time they graduate, and there is evidence that the decline in smoking is leveling off. Among these students, around 10% become active smokers as early as the 8th grade (see Figure 1; Fichtenberg & Glantz, 2006; Johnston et al., 2013).

Exploring DIVERSITY

Hucksters of Death: Promoting Smoking Throughout the World

A Jeep decorated with the Camel logo pulls up to a high school in Buenos Aires. A woman begins handing out free cigarettes to 15- and 16-year-olds during their lunch recess. At a video arcade in Taipei, free American cigarettes are strewn atop each game. At a disco filled with high school students, free packs of Salems are on each table (Ecenbarger, 1993, p. 50).

12 Psychological Disorders

Learning Outcomes for Chapter 12

MODULE 37

LO 37-1 How can we distinguish normal from abnormal behavior?

LO 37-2 What are the major perspectives on psychological disorders used by mental health professionals?

LO 37-3 What are the major categories of psychological disorders?

Normal Versus Abnormal: Making the Distinction

Defining Abnormality

Perspectives on Abnormality: From Superstition to Science

Classifying Abnormal Behavior: The ABCs of DSM

MODULE 38

LO 38-1 What are the major psychological disorders?

The Major Psychological Disorders

Anxiety Disorders

Obsessive-Compulsive Disorder

Somatic Symptom Disorders

Dissociative Disorders

Mood Disorders

Schizophrenia

Neuroscience in Your Life: Brain Changes with Schizophrenia

Personality Disorders

Disorders That Impact Childhood

Other Disorders

Applying Psychology in the 21st Century: Internet Addiction

MODULE 39

LO 39-1 How prevalent are psychological disorders?

LO 39-2 What indicators signal a need for the help of a mental health practitioner?

Psychological Disorders in Perspective

The Social and Cultural Context of Psychological Disorders

Exploring Diversity: DSM and Culture—and the Culture of DSM

Becoming an Informed Consumer of Psychology: Deciding When You Need Help

Prologue *Coping with Schizophrenia*

It was in the wee hours of the morning that Chris Coles first heard the voice. He was not alarmed. The voice was calm, even soothing. It directed him to go to the beach cove immediately and apologize to his friend for planning to date the man's girlfriend.

Though he had never thought about deceiving his friend in such a way, Coles followed the instructions. The beach was deserted when he arrived, and he put the whole episode down to a sort of half dream between waking and sleeping. But he continued to hear voices, and he began having visions, as well. Sometimes, he spotted an incandescent, golden Buddha in the dunes near his beach house. Other times, he saw dolphins and whales swim right onto the sand.

He began to think he could work magic—control nature. "Delusions of grandeur," Coles, now 47, calls the feelings that made him believe he could direct the waves and the dolphins and the whales (Begley, 2013).

Looking Ahead

Chris Coles was losing his grip on reality. It turned out that he was suffering from schizophrenia, one of the more severe psychological disorders. Although drug treatments eventually stilled the voices that ran through his head, his experience raises many questions. What caused his disorder? Were genetic factors involved, or were stressors in his life primarily responsible? Were there signs that family and friends should have noticed earlier? Could his schizophrenia have been prevented? And, more generally, how do we distinguish normal from abnormal behavior, and how can Chris' behavior be categorized and classified in such a way as to pinpoint the specific nature of his problem?

We address the issues raised by Coles' case in this chapter. We begin by discussing the difference between normal and abnormal behavior, which can be surprisingly indistinct. We then turn to a consideration of the most significant kinds of psychological disorders. Finally, we'll consider ways of evaluating behavior—one's own and that of others—to determine whether seeking help from a mental health professional is warranted.

MODULE 37

Normal Versus Abnormal: Making the Distinction

> Universally that person's acumen is esteemed very little perceptive concerning whatsoever matters are being held as most profitable by mortals with sapience endowed to be studied who is ignorant of that which the most in doctrine erudite and certainly by reason of that in them high mind's ornament deserving of veneration constantly maintain when by general consent they affirm that other circumstances being equal by no exterior splendour is the prosperity of a nation . . .

It would be easy to conclude that these words are the musings of a madman. To most people, the passage does not seem to make any sense at all. But literary scholars would disagree. Actually, this passage is from James Joyce's classic *Ulysses*, hailed as one of the major works of 20th-century literature (Joyce, 1934).

As this example illustrates, casually examining a person's writing is insufficient to determine the degree to which that person is "normal." But even when we consider more extensive samples of a person's behavior, we will find that there may be only a fine line between behavior that is considered normal and behavior that is considered abnormal.

Learning Outcomes

LO 37-1 How can we distinguish normal from abnormal behavior?

LO 37-2 What are the major perspectives on psychological disorders used by mental health professionals?

LO 37-3 What are the major categories of psychological disorders?

Defining Abnormality

Because of the difficulty in distinguishing normal from abnormal behavior, psychologists have struggled to devise a precise, scientific definition of "abnormal behavior." For instance, consider the following definitions, each of which has advantages and disadvantages:

- *Abnormality as deviation from the average.* According to this definition, behaviors that are rare or unusual in a society or culture are considered abnormal. It is basically a statistical definition: If most people carry out a behavior, it is normal; if only a few people do it, it is considered abnormal.

  The difficulty with this definition is that some statistically rare behaviors are not abnormal. If most people prefer to have cornflakes for breakfast but you prefer raisin bran, this deviation from the average hardly makes your behavior abnormal. Similarly, such a concept of abnormality would unreasonably label a person who has an unusually high IQ as abnormal simply because a high IQ is statistically rare. In short, a definition of abnormality that rests on deviation from the average is insufficient.
- *Abnormality as deviation from the ideal.* An alternative definition of abnormality considers behavior in relation to some kind of ideal or morally appropriate standard toward which most people are striving.

  This sort of definition considers behavior abnormal if it is different from what society considers ideal behavior or some moral standard. However, society has few ideals on which people universally agree. (For example, it would be hard to find agreement on whether the New Testament, the Koran, the Talmud, or the Book of Mormon provides the most appropriate ideal behavior.) Furthermore, standards that do arise change over time and vary across cultures. Thus, the deviation-from-the-ideal approach is also inadequate.
- *Abnormality as a sense of personal discomfort.* A more useful definition concentrates on the psychological consequences of the behavior for the individual. In this

Study Alert

Remember the different definitions of abnormality (deviation from the average, deviation from the ideal, a sense of personal discomfort, inability to function effectively, and abnormality as a legal concept).

Andrea Yates, who initially was found sane by a jury despite having drowned her five children in a bathtub, was later found innocent due to insanity.

approach, behavior is considered abnormal if it produces a sense of personal distress, anxiety, or guilt in an individual–or if it is harmful to others in some way.

Even a definition that relies on personal discomfort has drawbacks, though, because in some especially severe forms of mental disturbance, people report feeling wonderful even though their behavior seems bizarre to others. In such cases, a personal state of well-being exists, yet most people would consider the behavior abnormal. For example, most of us would think that a woman who says she is hearing uplifting messages from Martians would be displaying abnormal behavior even though she may say that the messages make her feel happy.

- *Abnormality as the inability to function effectively.* Most people are able to feed themselves, hold a job, get along with others, and in general live as productive members of society. Yet there are those who are unable to adjust to the demands of society or function effectively.

  According to this view of abnormality, people who are unable to function effectively and to adapt to the demands of society are considered abnormal. For example, an unemployed, homeless woman living on the street may be considered unable to function effectively. Therefore, her behavior can be viewed as abnormal even if she has chosen to live this way. Her inability to adapt to the requirements of society is what makes her "abnormal," according to this approach.
- *Abnormality as a legal concept.* According to the jury that first heard her case, Andrea Yates, a woman who drowned her five children in a bathtub, was sane. She was sentenced to life in prison for her act.

  Although you might question this view (and a later appeals jury overturned the conviction), the initial verdict reflected the way in which the law defines abnormal behavior. To the judicial system, the distinction between normal and abnormal behavior rests on the definition of insanity, which is a legal but not a psychological term. The definition of insanity varies from one jurisdiction to another. In some states, insanity simply means that defendants cannot understand the difference between right and wrong at the time they commit a criminal act. Other states consider whether defendants are substantially incapable of understanding the criminality of their behavior or unable to control themselves. And in some jurisdictions, pleas of insanity are not allowed at all (Frost & Bonnie, 2001; Sokolove, 2003; Ferguson & Ogloff, 2011; Reisner, Piel, & Makey, 2013).

abnormal behavior Behavior that causes people to experience distress and prevents them from functioning in their daily lives.

Clearly, none of the previous definitions is broad enough to cover all instances of **abnormal behavior.** Consequently, the distinction between normal and abnormal behavior often remains ambiguous even to trained professionals. Furthermore, to a large extent, cultural expectations for "normal" behavior in a particular society influence the understanding of "abnormal behavior" (Scheff, 1998; Sanderson, 2007). Given the difficulties in precisely defining the construct, psychologists typically use a broad definition of abnormal behavior. Specifically, abnormal behavior is behavior that causes people to experience distress and prevents them from functioning in their daily lives (Nolen-Hoeksema, 2007).

From the perspective of . . .

An Employer Imagine that you learned about a well-paid employee who was arrested for shoplifting a sweater that costs $25. Would you fire the employee if you thought the behavior was caused by a psychological disorder?

Because this definition is imprecise, it's best to view abnormal behavior and normal behavior as marking two ends of a continuum rather than as an absolute, precise condition. Behavior should be evaluated in terms of gradations that range from fully normal functioning to extremely abnormal behavior. Behavior typically falls somewhere between those extremes.

Perspectives on Abnormality: From Superstition to Science

Throughout much of human history, people linked abnormal behavior to superstition and witchcraft. Individuals who displayed abnormal behavior were accused of being possessed by the devil or some sort of demonic god. Authorities felt justified in "treating" abnormal behavior by attempting to drive out the source of the problem. This typically involved whipping, immersion in hot water, starvation, or other forms of torture in which the cure was often worse than the affliction (Berrios, 1996).

Contemporary approaches take a more enlightened view. Today, six major perspectives are used to understand psychological disorders. These perspectives suggest not only different causes of abnormal behavior but different treatment approaches as well. Furthermore, some perspectives are more applicable to specific disorders than are others.

MEDICAL PERSPECTIVE

When people display the symptoms of tuberculosis, medical professionals can generally find tubercular bacteria in their body tissue. Similarly, the **medical perspective** suggests that when an individual displays symptoms of abnormal behavior, the fundamental cause will be found through a physical examination of the individual, which may reveal a hormonal imbalance, a chemical deficiency, or a brain injury. Indeed, when we speak of mental "illness," "symptoms" of abnormal behavior, and mental "hospitals," we are using terminology associated with the medical perspective.

medical perspective The perspective that suggests that when an individual displays symptoms of abnormal behavior, the root cause will be found in a physical examination of the individual, which may reveal a hormonal imbalance, a chemical deficiency, or a brain injury.

Because many abnormal behaviors have been linked to biological causes, the medical perspective provides at least part of the explanation for abnormal behavior. Yet serious criticisms have been leveled against it. For one thing, many types of abnormal behavior have no apparent biological cause. In addition, some critics have argued that the use of the term *mental illness* implies that people who display abnormal behavior have no responsibility for or control over their actions (Laing & Szasz, 2004; Szasz, 2006; Yang & Tsai, 2013).

Still, recent advances in our understanding of the biological bases of behavior underscore the importance of considering physiological factors in abnormal behavior. For instance, some of the more severe forms of psychological disturbance, such as major depression and schizophrenia, are influenced by genetic factors and malfunctions in neurotransmitter signals (Iversen & Iversen, 2007; Howes & Kapur, 2009; Li et al., 2011).

PSYCHOANALYTIC PERSPECTIVE

Whereas the medical perspective suggests that biological causes are at the root of abnormal behavior, the **psychoanalytic perspective** holds that abnormal behavior stems from childhood conflicts over opposing wishes regarding sex and aggression. According to Freud, children pass through a series of stages in which sexual and aggressive impulses take different forms and produce conflicts that require resolution. If these childhood conflicts are not dealt with successfully, they remain unresolved in the unconscious and eventually bring about abnormal behavior during adulthood.

psychoanalytic perspective The perspective that suggests that abnormal behavior stems from childhood conflicts over opposing wishes regarding sex and aggression.

To uncover the roots of people's disordered behavior, the psychoanalytic perspective scrutinizes their early life history. However there is no sure way to link what happens to people during childhood to abnormal behavior that they display as adults. Consequently, we can never be sure that specific childhood experiences can be linked to specific adult abnormal behaviors.

In addition, psychoanalytic theory paints a picture of people as having relatively little control over their behavior because much of it is guided by unconscious impulses. In the eyes of some critics, this perspective suggests that people have little responsibility for their own behavior.

On the other hand, the contributions of psychoanalytic theory have been significant. More than any other approach to abnormal behavior, this perspective highlights the fact that people can have a rich, involved inner life and that prior experiences can have a profound effect on current psychological functioning (Elliott, 2002; Bornstein, 2003; Rangell, 2007).

BEHAVIORAL PERSPECTIVE

behavioral perspective The perspective that looks at the rewards and punishments in the environment that determine abnormal behavior.

Both the medical and psychoanalytic perspectives look at abnormal behaviors as *symptoms* of an underlying problem. In contrast, the **behavioral perspective** looks at the rewards and punishments in the environment that determine abnormal behavior. It views the disordered behavior itself as the problem. Using the basic principles of learning, behavioral theorists see both normal and abnormal behaviors as responses to various stimuli–responses that have been learned through past experience and are guided in the present by stimuli in the individual's environment. To explain why abnormal behavior occurs, we must analyze how an individual has learned it and observe the circumstances in which it is displayed.

The emphasis on observable behavior represents both the greatest strength and the greatest weakness of the behavioral approach to abnormal behavior. This perspective provides the most precise and objective approach for examining behavioral symptoms of specific disorders, such as attention-deficit hyperactivity disorder (ADHD), which we discuss in a later module. At the same time, though, critics charge that the perspective ignores the rich inner world of thoughts, attitudes, and emotions that may contribute to abnormal behavior.

COGNITIVE PERSPECTIVE

The medical, psychoanalytic, and behavioral perspectives view people's behavior as the result of factors largely beyond their control. To many critics of these views, however, people's thoughts cannot be ignored.

cognitive perspective The perspective that suggests that people's thoughts and beliefs are a central component of abnormal behavior.

In response to such concerns, some psychologists employ a **cognitive perspective.** Rather than considering only external behavior, as in traditional behavioral approaches, the cognitive approach assumes that *cognitions* (people's thoughts and beliefs) are central to a person's abnormal behavior. A primary goal of treatment using the cognitive perspective is to explicitly teach new, more adaptive ways of thinking.

For instance, suppose that you develop the erroneous belief that "doing well on this exam is crucial to my entire future" whenever you take an exam. Through therapy, you might learn to hold the more realistic and less anxiety-producing thought, "my entire future is not dependent on this one exam." By changing cognitions in this way, psychologists working within a cognitive framework help people free themselves from thoughts and behaviors that are potentially maladaptive (Clark, 2004; Everly & Lating, 2007).

The cognitive perspective is not without critics. For example, it is possible that maladaptive cognitions are the symptoms or consequences of disorders rather than their cause. Furthermore, there are circumstances in which negative beliefs may not be irrational at all but simply reflect accurately the unpleasant circumstances in people's lives. Still, cognitive theorists would argue that one can find a more adaptive way of framing beliefs even in the most negative circumstances.

HUMANISTIC PERSPECTIVE

humanistic perspective The perspective that emphasizes the responsibility people have for their own behavior, even when such behavior is abnormal.

Psychologists who subscribe to the **humanistic perspective** emphasize the responsibility people have for their own behavior even when their behavior is considered abnormal. The humanistic perspective–growing out of the work of Carl Rogers and

Abraham Maslow–concentrates on what is uniquely human–that is, it views people as basically rational, oriented toward a social world, and motivated to seek self-actualization (Rogers, 1995).

Humanistic approaches focus on the relationship of the individual to society; it considers the ways in which people view themselves in relation to others and see their place in the world. The humanistic perspective views people as having an awareness of life and of themselves that leads them to search for meaning and self-worth. Rather than assuming that individuals require a "cure," the humanistic perspective suggests that they can, by and large, set their own limits of what is acceptable behavior. As long as they are not hurting others and do not feel personal distress, people should be free to choose the behaviors in which they engage.

Although the humanistic perspective has been criticized for its reliance on unscientific, unverifiable information and its vague, almost philosophical formulations, it offers a distinctive view of abnormal behavior. It stresses the unique aspects of being human and provides a number of important suggestions for helping those with psychological problems.

SOCIOCULTURAL PERSPECTIVE

The **sociocultural perspective** assumes that people's behavior–both normal and abnormal–is shaped by the society and culture in which they live. According to this view, societal and cultural factors such as poverty and prejudice may be at the root of abnormal behavior. Specifically, the kinds of stresses and conflicts people experience in their daily lives can promote and maintain abnormal behavior.

sociocultural perspective The perspective that people's behavior–both normal and abnormal–is shaped by the society and culture in which they live.

This perspective is supported by research showing that some kinds of abnormal behavior are far more prevalent among certain social classes than they are in others. For instance, diagnoses of schizophrenia tend to be higher among members of lower socioeconomic groups than among members of more affluent groups. Proportionally more African-American individuals are hospitalized involuntarily for psychological disorders than are whites. Furthermore, poor economic times seem to be linked to general declines in psychological functioning, and social problems such as homelessness are associated with psychological disorders (Nasir & Hand, 2006; Greenberg & Rosenheck, 2008; Padgett, Stanhope, & Henwood, 2011).

Perspectives on Psychological Disorders

Perspective	Description	Possible Application of Perspective to Chris' Case
Medical	Assumes that physiological causes are at the root of psychological disorders	Examine Chris for medical problems, such as brain tumor, chemical imbalance in the brain, or disease
Psychoanalytic	Argues that psychological disorders stem from childhood conflicts	Seek out information about Chris' past, considering possible childhood conflicts
Behavioral	Assumes that abnormal behaviors are learned responses	Concentrate on rewards and punishments for Chris' behavior, and identify environmental stimuli that reinforce his behavior
Cognitive	Assumes that cognitions (people's thoughts and beliefs) are central to psychological disorders	Focus on Chris' perceptions of self and his environment
Humanistic	Emphasizes people's responsibility for their own behavior and the need to self-actualize	Consider Chris' behavior in terms of his choices and efforts to reach his potential
Sociocultural	Assumes that behavior is shaped by family, society, and culture	Focus on how societal demands contributed to Chris' disorder

FIGURE 1 In considering the case of Chris Coles, discussed in the prologue, we can employ each of the different perspectives on abnormal behavior. Note, however, that because of the nature of his psychological disorder, some of the perspectives are more applicable than others.

Study Alert
Use Figure 1 to review the six major perspectives on abnormality and consider how they relate to the major perspectives on the field of psychology.

On the other hand, alternative explanations abound for the association between abnormal behavior and social factors. For example, people from lower socioeconomic levels may be less likely than those from higher levels to seek help, gradually reaching a point where their symptoms become severe and warrant a serious diagnosis. Furthermore, sociocultural explanations provide relatively little specific guidance for the treatment of individuals showing mental disturbance because the focus is on broader societal factors (Paniagua, 2000).

Figure 1 summarizes the main perspectives on psychological disorders. In addition, it applies each of them to the case of Chris Coles, discussed in the chapter prologue.

Classifying Abnormal Behavior: The ABCs of DSM

Crazy. Whacked. Mental. Loony. Insane. Neurotic. Psycho. Strange. Demented. Odd. Possessed.

Society has long placed labels on people who display abnormal behavior. Unfortunately, most of the time these labels have reflected intolerance and have been used with little thought as to what each label signifies.

Providing appropriate and specific names and classifications for abnormal behavior has presented a major challenge to psychologists. It is not hard to understand why, given the difficulties discussed earlier in simply distinguishing normal from abnormal behavior. Yet psychologists and other careproviders need to classify abnormal behavior in order to diagnose it and ultimately treat it.

DSM-5: DETERMINING DIAGNOSTIC DISTINCTIONS

Over the years, mental health professionals have developed many classification systems that vary in terms of their utility and the degree to which they have been accepted. However, one standard system, devised by the American Psychiatric Association, has emerged in the United States. Most professionals today use this classification system, known as the ***Diagnostic and Statistical Manual of Mental Disorders,* Fifth Edition *(DSM-5),*** to diagnose and classify abnormal behavior (American Psychiatric Association, 2013).

Diagnostic and Statistical Manual of Mental Disorders,* Fifth Edition, *(DSM-5) A system, devised by the American Psychiatric Association, used by most professionals to diagnose and classify abnormal behavior.

The DSM-5, most recently revised in 2013, attempts to provide comprehensive and relatively precise definitions for more than 200 disorders. By following the criteria presented in the DSM-5 classification system, diagnosticians use clients' reported symptoms to identify the specific problem an individual is experiencing. (Figure 2 provides a brief outline of the major diagnostic categories; American Psychiatric Association, 2013.)

The manual takes an *atheoretical* approach to identifying psychological disorders, though some practitioners have argued that this diagnostic approach is too heavily based on a medical model. The authors of the newest update of DSM suggest that the manual should be viewed as the "DSM-5.0." The "5.0" name emphasizes that the DSM-5 is a work in progress, subject to revision based on users' feedback. (The next revision will be called DSM-5.1.)

Among the major changes to DSM-5 are the following (Kupfer, Kuhl, & Regier, 2013; Wakefield, 2013):

- **A lifespan development focus.** Disorders have been arranged in terms of what age they are likely to first appear. In addition, the DSM-5 is more specific about how the same disorder may change over the course of a person's lifetime.
- **Childhood and late-life conditions have been renamed.** Along with removing the outdated term "mental retardation" in favor of *intellectual disability,* the DSM-5 renames childhood conditions as *neurodevelopmental disorders,* and "dementia and amnestic disorders" as *neurocognitive disorders.*

Categories of Disorders	Examples
Anxiety (problems in which anxiety impedes daily functioning)	Generalized anxiety disorder, panic disorder, phobic disorder
Somatic symptom and related disorders (psychological difficulties displayed through physical problems)	Illness anxiety disorder, conversion disorder
Dissociative (the splitting apart of crucial parts of personality that are usually integrated)	Dissociative identity disorder (multiple personality), dissociative amnesia, dissociative fugue
Mood (emotions of depression or euphoria that are so strong they intrude on everyday living)	Major depressive disorders, bipolar disorder
Schizophrenia spectrum and other psychotic disorders (declines in functioning, thought and language disturbances, perception disorders, emotional disturbances, and withdrawal from others)	Delusional disorder
Personality (problems that create little personal distress but that lead to an inability to function as a normal member of society)	Antisocial (sociopathic) personality disorder, narcissistic personality disorder
Sexual (problems related to sexual arousal from unusual objects or problems related to functioning)	Paraphilic disorders, sexual dysfunction
Substance-related (problems related to drug dependence and abuse)	Alcohol, cocaine, hallucinogens, marijuana
Neurocognitive disorders	Alzheimer's

FIGURE 2 This list of disorders represents the major categories from the DSM-5. It is only a partial list of the scores of disorders included in the diagnostic manual. (Source: Adapted from DSM-5, 2013.)

- **Autism disorder has been reclassified.** Different forms of autism are now grouped together and called *Autism Spectrum Disorder (ASD)*, which focuses on the degree of severity of autism.
- **Sexually based disorders have been reconceptualized and renamed.** "Gender identity disorder" has been reclassified as *gender dysphoria*. This distinction makes it clear that having a gender identity that is in conflict with one's biological sex does not imply a psychological disorder. Additionally, "paraphilia" has been renamed *paraphilic disorders*, emphasizing the presence of some atypical sexual interests that do not necessarily indicate a psychological disorder.
- **Criteria for some disorders have been made less restrictive.** In particular, the conditions that need to be met for an adult attention-deficit hyperactivity disorder (ADHD) diagnosis are broader–meaning that more people are likely to be classified with adult ADHD. Additionally, bereaved clients are no longer diagnosed with depression if symptoms arose within a few months of the death of a loved one.
- **The "five axes model" is eliminated.** In the previous version of DSM, disorders were categorized along one of five axes (Axis I, Clinical Disorders; Axis II, Personality Disorders and Mental Retardation; Axis III, General Medical Conditions; Axis IV, Psychosocial and Environmental Problems; and Axis V, Global Assessment of Functioning). These axes have been eliminated from the new version of DSM-5.

In many other respects, the DSM remains unchanged in the newest revision. Like its predecessors, DSM-5 is primarily descriptive and avoids suggesting an underlying cause for an individual's behavior and problems. For instance, the term *neurotic*–a label that is commonly used by people in their everyday descriptions of abnormal behavior—is not listed as a DSM-5 category. Because the term *neurosis* refers to problems associated with a specific cause based in Freud's theory of personality, it is not included in DSM-5.

DSM-5 has the advantage, then, of providing a descriptive system that does not specify the cause of or reason for a problem. Rather, it paints a picture of the behavior that is being displayed. Why should this approach be important? For one thing, it allows communication between mental health professionals of diverse backgrounds and theoretical approaches. In addition, precise classification enables researchers to explore the causes of a problem. Without reliable descriptions of abnormal behavior, researchers would be hard pressed to find ways to investigate the disorder. Finally, DSM-5 provides a kind of conceptual shorthand through which professionals can describe the behaviors that tend to occur together in an individual (First, Frances, & Pincus, 2002; Gordon & Heimberg, 2011).

CONNING THE CLASSIFIERS: THE SHORTCOMINGS OF DSM

When clinical psychologist David Rosenhan and eight colleagues sought admission to separate mental hospitals across the United States in the 1970s, each stated that he or she was hearing voices—"unclear voices" that said "empty," "hollow," and "thud"—and each was immediately admitted to the hospital. However, the truth was that they actually were conducting a study, and none of them was really hearing voices. Aside from these misrepresentations, *everything* else they did and said represented their true behavior, including the responses they gave during extensive admission interviews and their answers to the battery of tests they were asked to complete. In fact, as soon as they were admitted, they said they no longer heard any voices. In short, each of the pseudo-patients acted in a "normal" way (Rosenhan, 1973).

We might assume that Rosenhan and his colleagues would have been quickly discovered as the impostors they were, but this was not the case. Instead, each of them was diagnosed as severely abnormal on the basis of observed behavior. Mental health professionals labeled most as suffering from schizophrenia and kept them in the hospital 3–52 days, with the average stay of 19 days. Even when they were discharged, most of the "patients" left with the label *schizophrenia—in remission,* implying that the abnormal behavior had only temporarily subsided and could recur at any time. Most disturbing, no one on the hospital staff identified any of the pseudo-patients as impostors—although some of the actual patients figured out the ruse.

THE STIGMA OF LABELING

The results of Rosenhan's classic study illustrate that placing labels on individuals powerfully influences the way mental health workers perceive and interpret their actions. It also points out that determining who is psychologically disordered is not always a clear-cut or accurate process.

Gender dysphoria (in which one's gender identity is in conflict with one's biological sex) provides a modern illustration of the dilemma between the pros of a formal diagnosis and the cons of patient labeling. For example, most medical insurance providers require a formal, specific diagnosis in order to provide healthcare coverage for procedures such as a sex change operation. Many individuals who experience a conflict between their gender identity and their biological sex object theoretically to the idea that their desire to be the other sex should be labeled a "disorder." Yet without a formal diagnosis, those same individuals may be forced to pay out-of-pocket for what is an expensive medical procedure.

This diagnosis-based system of insurance coverage often creates a Catch-22 for mental health-care professionals: They must decide between potentially stigmatizing their clients by providing a formal diagnosis, implying some type of disorder, or leaving patients undiagnosed and potentially without the financial support necessary to receive important procedures that will significantly improve a client's quality of life (Kamens, 2011; Kleinplatz, Moser, & Lev, 2013).

Critics of the DSM argue that labeling an individual as abnormal provides a dehumanizing, lifelong stigma. (Think, for example, of political contenders whose candidacies have been terminated by the disclosure that they received treatment for severe psychological disorders.) Furthermore, after an initial diagnosis has been made, mental health professionals, who may concentrate on the initial diagnostic category, could overlook other diagnostic possibilities (McNally, 2011; Szasz, 2011; Frances, 2013).

Although the DSM-5 was developed to provide more accurate and consistent diagnoses of psychological disorders, it isn't always successful. For instance, critics charge that it relies too much on the medical perspective. Because it was drawn up by psychiatrists—who are physicians—some condemn it for viewing psychological disorders primarily in terms of the symptoms of an underlying physiological disorder. Moreover, critics suggest that DSM-5 compartmentalizes people into inflexible, all-or-none categories rather than considering the degree to which a person displays psychologically disordered behavior (Samuel & Widiger, 2006; Frances, 2013).

Still, despite the drawbacks inherent in any labeling system, the DSM-5 has had an important influence on the way in which mental health professionals view psychological disorders. It has increased both the reliability and the validity of diagnostic categorization. In addition, it offers a logical way to organize examination of the major types of mental disturbance.

Study Alert

It is important to understand the advantages and weaknesses of the DSM classification system.

RECAP/EVALUATE/RETHINK

RECAP

LO 37-1 How can we distinguish normal from abnormal behavior?

- Definitions of abnormality include deviation from the average, deviation from the ideal, a sense of personal discomfort, the inability to function effectively, and legal conceptions.
- Although no single definition is adequate, abnormal behavior can be considered to be behavior that causes people to experience distress and prevents them from functioning in their daily lives. Most psychologists believe that abnormal and normal behavior should be considered in terms of a continuum.

LO 37-2 What are the major perspectives on psychological disorders used by mental health professionals?

- The medical perspective views abnormality as a symptom of an underlying disease.
- Psychoanalytic perspectives suggest that abnormal behavior stems from childhood conflicts in the unconscious.
- Behavioral approaches focus on the rewards and punishments in the environment that determine abnormal behavior.
- The cognitive approach suggests that abnormal behavior is the result of faulty cognitions (thoughts and beliefs). In this view, abnormal behavior can be remedied by changing one's flawed thoughts and beliefs.
- Humanistic approaches emphasize the responsibility people have for their own behavior even when such behavior is seen as abnormal.
- Sociocultural approaches view abnormal behavior in terms of difficulties arising from family and other social relationships.

LO 37-3 What are the major categories of psychological disorders?

- The most widely used system for classifying psychological disorders is DSM-5—*Diagnostic and Statistical Manual of Mental Disorders,* Fifth Edition.

EVALUATE

1. One problem in defining abnormal behavior is that
   a. Statistically rare behavior may not be abnormal.
   b. Not all abnormalities are accompanied by feelings of discomfort.
   c. Cultural standards are too general to use as a measuring tool.
   d. All of the above.
2. If abnormality is defined as behavior that causes personal discomfort or harms others, which of the following people is most likely to need treatment?
   a. An executive is afraid to accept a promotion because it would require moving from his ground-floor office to the top floor of a tall office building.
   b. A woman decides to quit her job and chooses to live on the street in order to live a "simpler life."
   c. A man believes that friendly spacemen visit his house every Thursday.
   d. A photographer lives with 19 cats in a small apartment, lovingly caring for them.
3. Virginia's mother thinks that her daughter's behavior is clearly abnormal because, despite being offered admission to medical school, Virginia decides to become a waitress. What approach is Virginia's mother using to define abnormal behavior?

4. Which of the following is a strong argument against the medical perspective on abnormality?
  a. Physiological abnormalities are almost always impossible to identify.
  b. There is no conclusive way to link past experience and behavior.
  c. The medical perspective rests too heavily on the effects of nutrition.
  d. Assigning behavior to a physical problem takes responsibility away from the individual for changing his or her behavior.

5. Cheryl is painfully shy. According to the behavioral perspective, the best way to deal with her "abnormal" behavior is to
  a. Treat the underlying physical problem.
  b. Use the principles of learning theory to modify her shy behavior.
  c. Express a great deal of caring.
  d. Uncover her negative past experiences through hypnosis.

RETHINK

1. Do you agree or disagree that DSM should be updated every several years? Why? What makes abnormal behavior so variable?

2. Imagine that an acquaintance of yours was recently arrested for shoplifting a $15 necktie. Write an explanation for this behavior from *each* perspective on abnormality: the medical perspective, the psychoanalytic perspective, the behavioral perspective, the cognitive perspective, the humanistic perspective, and the sociocultural perspective.

Answers to Evaluate Questions

1. d; **2.** a; **3.** deviation from the ideal; **4.** d; **5.** b

KEY TERMS

abnormal behavior
medical perspective
psychoanalytic perspective
behavioral perspective
cognitive perspective
humanistic perspective
sociocultural perspective
Diagnostic and Statistical Manual of Mental Disorders,* Fifth Edition *(DSM-5)

MODULE 38

The Major Psychological Disorders

Learning Outcome

LO 38-1 What are the major psychological disorders?

Sally's first panic attack was a surprise. Visiting her parents after college, she suddenly felt dizzy, broke into a cold sweat, and began hyperventilating. Her father clocked her pulse at 180 and rushed her to the hospital, where all symptoms vanished. She laughed it off and returned to her apartment.

But the panic attacks continued. At the gym, at work, in restaurants and movie theaters, Sally was never safe from them. Not just frightening, they were downright embarrassing. She quit her job to work at home. She avoided crowds and turned down dinners, parties, and movies. The only way to escape humiliation was to wall herself inside her apartment with a blanket and a pillow.

Sally suffered from panic disorder, one of the specific psychological disorders we'll consider in this module. Keep in mind that although we'll be discussing these disorders objectively, each represents a very human set of difficulties that influence and in some cases considerably disrupt people's lives.

Anxiety Disorders

All of us at one time or another experience *anxiety,* a feeling of apprehension or tension, in reaction to stressful situations. There is nothing "wrong" with such anxiety. It is a normal reaction to stress that often helps rather than hinders our daily functioning. Without some anxiety, for instance, most of us probably would not have much motivation to study hard, undergo physical exams, or spend long hours at our jobs.

But some people experience anxiety in situations in which there is no apparent reason or cause for such distress. **Anxiety disorders** occur when anxiety arises without external justification and begins to affect people's daily functioning. We'll discuss three major types of anxiety disorders: phobic disorder, panic disorder, and generalized anxiety disorder.

anxiety disorder The occurrence of anxiety without an obvious external cause that affects daily functioning.

PHOBIC DISORDER

Forty-five-year-old Donna is terrified of electricity. She's unable to change a light bulb for fear of getting electrocuted. The thought of static electricity on clothing sends her into a panic. She can't even open a refrigerator door without being terrified a short-circuit will send electricity through her body. And thunderstorms? Forget it: she is beside herself with fear of getting electrocuted by lightning (Kluger, 2001).

Donna suffers from a **specific phobia,** an intense, irrational fear of a specific object or situation. For example, claustrophobia is a fear of enclosed places, acrophobia is a fear of high places, xenophobia is a fear of strangers, social phobia is the fear of being judged or embarrassed by others, and—as in Donna's case—electrophobia is a fear of electricity.

specific phobia Intense, irrational fear of specific objects or situations.

The objective danger posed by an anxiety-producing stimulus (which can be just about anything, as you can see in Figure 1) is typically small or nonexistent. However, to someone suffering from the phobia, the danger is great, and a full-blown panic attack

Phobic Disorder	Description	Example
Agoraphobia	Fear of places, such as unfamiliar or crowded spaces, where help might not be available in case of emergency	Person becomes housebound because any place other than the person's home arouses extreme anxiety symptoms. 
Specific phobias	Fear of specific objects, places, or situations	
Animal type	Specific animals or insects 	Person has extreme fear of dogs, cats, or spiders.
Natural environment type	Events or situations in the natural environment	Person has extreme fear of storms, heights, or water.
Situational type	Public transportation, tunnels, bridges, elevators, flying, driving	Person becomes extremely claustrophobic in elevators. 
Blood injection-injury type	Blood, injury, injections 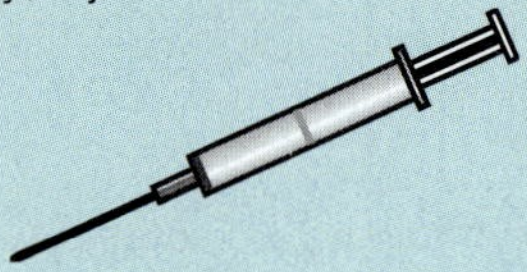	Person panics when viewing a child's scraped knee.
Social phobia	Fear of being judged or embarrassed by others	Person avoids all social situations and becomes a recluse for fear of encountering others' judgment.

FIGURE 1 Phobic disorders differ from generalized anxiety and panic disorders because a specific stimulus can be identified. Listed here are a number of types of phobias and their triggers. (Source: Adapted from Nolen-Hoeksema, 2007.)

may follow exposure to the stimulus. Phobic disorders differ from generalized anxiety disorders and panic disorders in that there is a specific, identifiable stimulus that sets off the anxiety reaction.

Phobias may have only a minor impact on people's lives if those who suffer from them can avoid the stimuli that trigger fear. For example, a fear of heights may have little impact on people's everyday lives (although it may prevent them from living in a high floor in an apartment)–unless they are firefighters or window-washers. On the other hand, a *social phobia,* or a fear of strangers, presents a more serious problem. In one extreme case, a Washington woman left her home just three times in 30 years–once to visit her family, once for an operation, and once to purchase ice cream for a dying companion (Kimbrel, 2007; Wong, Sarver, & Beidel, 2011; Stopa et al., 2013).

PANIC DISORDER

panic disorder Anxiety disorder that takes the form of panic attacks lasting from a few seconds to several hours.

In another type of anxiety disorder, **panic disorder,** *panic attacks* occur that last from a few seconds to several hours. Panic disorders do not have any identifiable triggers (unlike phobias, which are triggered by specific objects or situations). Instead, during an attack such as those Sally experienced in the case described earlier, anxiety suddenly–and often without warning–rises to a peak, and an individual feels a sense of impending, unavoidable doom. Although the physical symptoms differ from person to person, they may include heart palpitations, shortness of breath, unusual amounts of sweating, faintness and dizziness, gastric sensations, and sometimes a sense of imminent death. After such an attack, it is no wonder that people tend to feel exhausted (Rachman & deSilva, 2004; Laederach-Hofmann & Messerli-Buergy, 2007; Montgomery, 2011).

Panic attacks seemingly come out of nowhere and are unconnected to any specific stimulus. Because they don't know what triggers their feelings of panic, victims of panic attacks may become fearful of going places. In fact, some people with panic disorder develop a complication called *agoraphobia,* the fear of being in a situation in which escape is difficult and in which help for a possible panic attack would not be available. In extreme cases, people with agoraphobia never leave their homes (Herrán, Carrera, & Sierra-Biddle, 2006; Wittchen et al., 2008; McTeague et al., 2011).

In addition to the physical symptoms, panic disorder affects how the brain processes information. For instance, people with panic disorder have reduced reactions in the anterior cingulate cortex to stimuli (such as viewing a fearful face) that normally produce a strong reaction in those without the disorder. It may be that recurring high levels of emotional arousal that patients with panic disorder experience desensitizes them to emotional stimuli (Pillay et al., 2007; Maddock et al., 2013).

Acrophobia, the fear of heights, is not an uncommon phobia. What sort of behavior-modification approaches might be used to deal with acrophobia?

GENERALIZED ANXIETY DISORDER

People with **generalized anxiety disorder** experience long-term, persistent anxiety and uncontrollable worry. Sometimes their concerns are about identifiable issues involving family, money, work, or health. In other cases, though, people with the disorder feel that something dreadful is about to happen but can't identify the reason and thus experience "free-floating" anxiety.

generalized anxiety disorder The experience of long-term, persistent anxiety and worry.

Because of persistent anxiety, people with generalized anxiety disorder cannot concentrate or set their worry and fears aside; their lives become centered on their worry. Furthermore, their anxiety is often accompanied by physiological symptoms, such as muscle tension, headaches, dizziness, heart palpitations, or insomnia (Starcevic et al., 2007). Figure 2 shows the most common symptoms of generalized anxiety disorder.

Obsessive-Compulsive Disorder

In **obsessive-compulsive disorder (OCD),** people are plagued by unwanted thoughts, called obsessions, or feel that they must carry out behaviors, termed compulsions, which they feel driven to perform.

obsessive-compulsive disorder (OCD) A disorder characterized by obsessions or compulsions.

An **obsession** is a persistent, unwanted thought or idea that keeps recurring. For example, a student may be unable to stop thinking that she has neglected to put her name on a test and may think about it constantly for the 2 weeks it takes to get the paper back. A man may go on vacation and wonder the whole time whether he locked his house. A woman may hear the same tune running through her head over and over. In each case, the thought or idea is unwanted and difficult to put out of mind. Of course, many people suffer from mild obsessions from time to time, but usually such thoughts persist only for a short period. For people with serious obsessions, however, the thoughts persist for days or months and may consist of bizarre, troubling images (Lee et al., 2005; Rassin & Muris, 2007; Wenzel, 2011).

obsession A persistent, unwanted thought or idea that keeps recurring.

As part of an obsessive-compulsive disorder, people may also experience **compulsions,** irresistible urges to repeatedly carry out some act that seems strange and unreasonable even to them. Whatever the compulsive behavior is, people experience extreme anxiety if they cannot carry it out even if it is something they want to stop. The acts may be relatively trivial, such as repeatedly checking the stove to make sure all the burners are turned off, or more unusual, such as washing one's hands so much that they bleed (Frost & Steketee, 2002; Clark, 2007; Moretz & McKay, 2009).

compulsion An irresistible urge to repeatedly carry out some act that seems strange and unreasonable.

FIGURE 2 Frequency of symptoms in cases of generalized anxiety disorder. (Source: Adapted from Beck & Emery, 1985.)

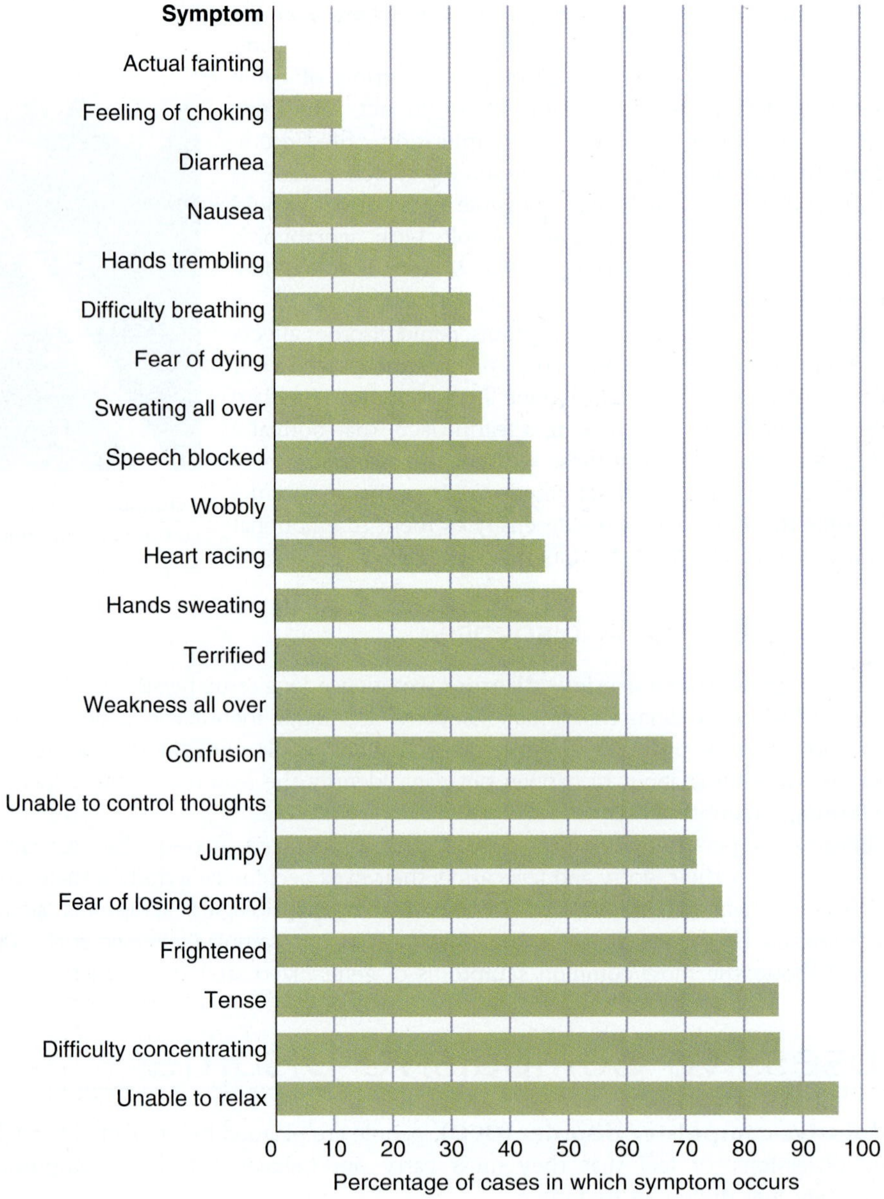

For example, consider this passage from the autobiography of a person with obsessive-compulsive disorder:

> I thought my parents would die if I didn't do everything in exactly the right way. When I took my glasses off at night I'd have to place them on the dresser at a particular angle. Sometimes I'd turn on the light and get out of bed seven times until I felt comfortable with the angle. If the angle wasn't right, I felt that my parents would die. The feeling ate up my insides.
>
> If I didn't grab the molding on the wall just the right way as I entered or exited my room; if I didn't hang a shirt in the closet perfectly; if I didn't read a paragraph a certain way; if my hands and nails weren't perfectly clean, I thought my incorrect behavior would kill my parents. (Summers, 2000.)

Although carrying out compulsive rituals may lead to some immediate reduction of anxiety, in the long run the anxiety returns. In fact, people with severe cases lead lives filled with unrelenting tension (Penzel, 2000; Dittrich, Johansen, & Fineberg, 2011; Kalanthroff et al., 2013).

PsychTech

Although some people seem to use the Internet compulsively, psychologists have yet to agree on whether it represents a true psychological disorder.

THE CAUSES OF ANXIETY DISORDERS AND OBSESSIVE-COMPULSIVE DISORDER

We've considered several of the major types of anxiety disorders and obsessive-compulsive disorder, but there are many other related disorders. The variety of anxiety disorders means that no single explanation fits all cases. Genetic factors clearly are part of the picture. For example, if one member of a pair of identical twins has panic disorder, there is a 30% chance that the other twin will have it also. Furthermore, a person's characteristic level of anxiety is related to a specific gene involved in the production of the neurotransmitter serotonin. This is consistent with findings indicating that certain chemical deficiencies in the brain appear to produce some kinds of anxiety disorder (Holmes et al., 2003; Beidel & Turner, 2007; Chamberlain et al., 2008).

"Spin your partner round and round, then spin your partner round again, spin her round six more times, now touch the light switch near the door."

Some researchers believe that an overactive autonomic nervous system may be at the root of panic attacks. Specifically, they suggest that poor regulation of the brain's locus ceruleus may lead to panic attacks, which cause the limbic system to become overstimulated. In turn, the overstimulated limbic system produces chronic anxiety, which ultimately leads the locus ceruleus to generate still more panic attacks (Balaban, 2002; Davies et al., 2008; Dresler et al., 2013).

There are also biological causes at work in OCD. For example, researchers have found differences in the brains of those with the disorder compared to those without it (Christian et al., 2008).

Psychologists who employ the behavioral perspective have taken a different approach that emphasizes environmental factors. They consider anxiety to be a learned response to stress. For instance, suppose a dog bites a young girl. When the girl next sees a dog, she is frightened and runs away–a behavior that relieves her anxiety and thereby reinforces her avoidance behavior. After repeated encounters with dogs in which she is reinforced for her avoidance behavior, she may develop a full-fledged phobia regarding dogs.

Finally, the cognitive perspective suggests that anxiety disorders grow out of inappropriate and inaccurate thoughts and beliefs about circumstances in a person's world. For example, people with anxiety disorders may view a friendly puppy as a ferocious and savage pit bull, or they may see an air disaster looming every moment they are in the vicinity of an airplane. According to the cognitive perspective, people's maladaptive thoughts about the world are at the root of an anxiety disorder (Frost & Steketee, 2002; Wang & Clark, 2002; Ouimet, Gawronski, & Dozois, 2009).

Somatic Symptom Disorders

Somatic symptom disorders are psychological difficulties that take on a physical (somatic) form but for which there is no medical cause. Even though an individual with a somatic symptom disorder reports physical symptoms, no biological cause exists, or if there is a medical problem, the person's reaction is greatly exaggerated.

One type of somatic symptom disorder is **illness anxiety disorder** in which people have a constant fear of illness and a preoccupation with their health. These individuals believe that everyday aches and pains are symptoms of a dread disease. The "symptoms" are not faked; rather, they are misinterpreted as evidence of some serious illness–often in the face of inarguable medical evidence to the contrary (Abramowitz, Olatunji, & Deacon, 2007; Olatunji, 2008; Weck et al., 2011).

Another somatic symptom disorder is conversion disorder. Unlike illness anxiety disorder, in which there is no physical problem, **conversion disorders** involve an actual physical disturbance, such as the inability to see or hear or to move an arm or

somatic symptom disorders Psychological difficulties that take on a physical (somatic) form, but for which there is no medical cause.

illness anxiety disorder A disorder in which people have a constant fear of illness and a preoccupation with their health.

conversion disorder A major somatic symptom disorder that involves an actual physical disturbance, such as the inability to use a sensory organ or the complete or partial inability to move an arm or leg.

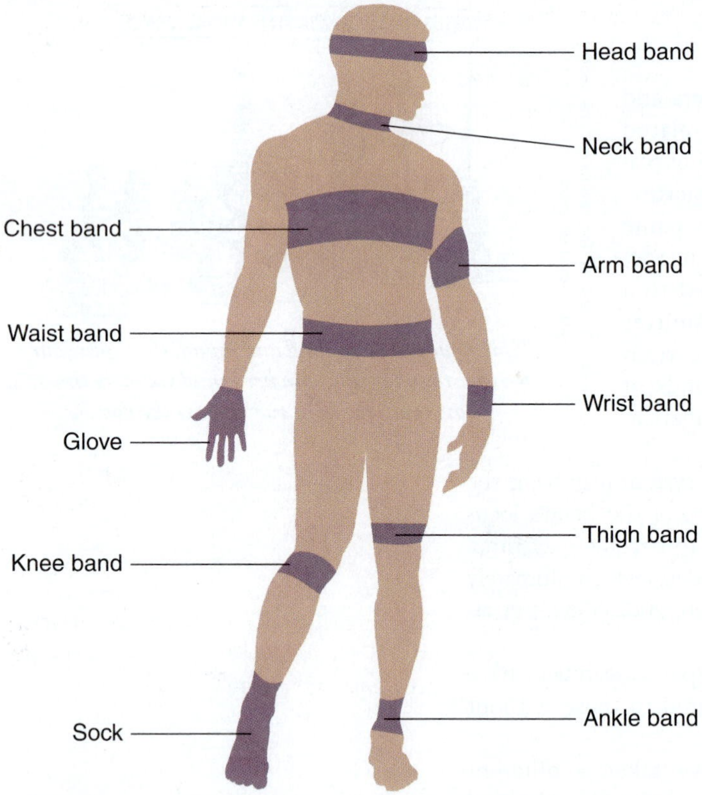

FIGURE 3 Conversion disorders sometimes produce numbness in specific and isolated areas of the body (indicated by the shaded areas in the figure). For instance, in glove anesthesia, the area of the body covered by a glove feels numb. However, the condition is biologically implausible because of the nerves involved, which suggests that the problem results from a psychological disorder rather than from actual nerve damage.

leg. The *cause* of such a physical disturbance is purely psychological; there is no biological reason for the problem. Some of Freud's classic cases involved conversion disorders. For instance, one of Freud's patients suddenly became unable to use her arm without any apparent physiological cause. Later, just as abruptly, the problem disappeared.

Conversion disorders often begin suddenly. Previously normal people wake up one day blind or deaf, or they experience numbness that is restricted to a certain part of the body. A hand, for example, may become entirely numb, while an area above the wrist, controlled by the same nerves, remains sensitive to touch–something that is physiologically implausible. Mental health professionals refer to such a condition as "glove anesthesia" because the numb area is the part of the hand covered by a glove and not a region related to pathways of the nervous system (see Figure 3).

Surprisingly, people who experience conversion disorders frequently remain unconcerned about symptoms that most of us would expect to be highly anxiety producing. For instance, a person in good health who wakes up blind may react in a bland, matter-of-fact way. Considering how most of us would feel if we woke up unable to see, this unemotional reaction (called *la belle indifférence,* a French phrase meaning "a beautiful indifference") hardly seems appropriate (Brasic, 2002).

Dissociative Disorders

dissociative disorders Psychological dysfunctions characterized by the separation of different facets of a person's personality that are normally integrated.

dissociative identity disorder (DID) A disorder in which a person displays characteristics of two or more distinct personalities.

The classic movie *The Three Faces of Eve* (about a woman with three wildly different personalities) and the book *Sybil* (about a girl who allegedly had 16 personalities) represent a highly dramatic, rare, and controversial class of disorders: dissociative disorders. **Dissociative disorders** are characterized by the separation (or dissociation) of different facets of a person's personality that are normally integrated and work together. By dissociating key parts of who they are, people are able to keep disturbing memories or perceptions from reaching conscious awareness and thereby reduce their anxiety (Maldonado & Spiegel, 2003; Houghtalen & Talbot, 2007).

Several dissociative disorders exist, although all of them are rare. A person with a **dissociative identity disorder (DID)** (once called *multiple personality disorder*) displays characteristics of two or more distinct personalities, identities, or personality fragments. Individual personalities often have a unique set of likes and dislikes and their own reactions to situations. Some people with multiple personalities even carry several pairs of glasses because their vision changes with each personality. Moreover, each individual personality can be well adjusted when considered on its own (Ellason & Ross, 2004; Stickley & Nickeas, 2006; Howell, 2011).

The diagnosis of dissociative identity disorder is controversial. It was rarely diagnosed before 1980, when it was added as a category in the third edition of DSM for the first time. At that point, the number of cases increased significantly. Some clinicians suggest the increase was due to more precise identification of the disorder, while others suggest the increase was due to an overreadiness to use the classification. In addition, widespread publicity about cases of DID may have influenced patients to report symptoms of more common personality disorders in ways that made it more likely they would receive a diagnosis of DID. There are also significant cross-cultural differences in the incidence of DID (Kihlstrom, 2005a; Xiao et al., 2006).

Dissociative amnesia is another dissociative disorder in which a significant, selective memory loss occurs. Dissociative amnesia is unlike simple amnesia, which involves an actual loss of information from memory and typically results from a physiological cause. In contrast, in cases of dissociative amnesia, the "forgotten" material is still present in memory–it simply cannot be recalled. The term *repressed memories* is sometimes used to describe the lost memories of people with dissociative amnesia.

dissociative amnesia A disorder in which a significant, selective memory loss occurs.

In the most severe form of dissociative amnesia, individuals cannot recall their names, are unable to recognize parents and other relatives, and do not know their addresses. In other respects, though, they may appear quite normal. Apart from an inability to remember certain facts about themselves, they may be able to recall skills and abilities that they developed earlier. For instance, even though a chef may not remember where he grew up and received training, he may still be able to prepare gourmet meals.

In some cases of dissociative amnesia, the memory loss is profound. For example, in one dramatic case, Raymond Power Jr., an attorney, husband, father of two, and Boy Scout leader, left home to go to work one morning. Two days later he was homeless, living a new life a thousand miles away, and had no memory of who he was or how he got there. He was found 6 months later but still had no recollection of his previous life, including any knowledge of his wife of 30 years or even that he had children (Foderaro, 2006; Dell, 2013).

Dissociative fugue is a form of amnesia in which a person leaves home suddenly and assumes a new identiy. In this unusual and rare state, people take sudden, impulsive trips and adopt a new identity. After a period of time–days, months, or sometimes even years–they suddenly realize that they are in a strange place and completely forget the time they have spent wandering. Their last memories are those from the time just before they entered the fugue state (Hennig-Fast et al., 2008).

dissociative fugue A form of amnesia in which a person leaves home suddenly and assumes a new identity.

The common thread among dissociative disorders is that they allow people to escape from some anxiety-producing situation. Either the person produces a new personality to deal with stress, or the individual forgets or leaves behind the situation that caused the stress as he or she journeys to some new–and perhaps less anxiety-ridden–environment (Putnam, 2000; R. J. Brown, 2006).

Mood Disorders

> From the time I woke up in the morning until the time I went to bed at night, I was unbearably miserable and seemingly incapable of any kind of joy or enthusiasm. Everything–every thought, word, movement–was an effort. Everything that once was sparkling now was flat. I seemed to myself to be dull, boring, inadequate, thick brained, unlit, unresponsive, chill skinned, bloodless, and sparrow drab. I doubted, completely, my ability to do anything well. It seemed as though my mind had slowed down and burned out to the point of being virtually useless. (Jamison, 1995.)

We all experience mood swings. Sometimes we are happy, perhaps even euphoric; at other times we feel upset, saddened, or depressed. Such changes in mood are a normal part of everyday life. In some people, however, moods are so pronounced and lingering–like the feelings described above by writer (and psychiatrist) Kay Jamison–that they interfere with the ability to function effectively. **Mood disorders** are disturbances in emotional experience that are strong enough to intrude on everyday living. In extreme cases, a mood may become life threatening; in other cases, it may cause the person to lose touch with reality.

mood disorder A disturbance in emotional experience that is strong enough to intrude on everyday living.

MAJOR DEPRESSIVE DISORDER

President Abraham Lincoln. Queen Victoria. Newscaster Mike Wallace.

The common link among these people? Each suffered from periodic attacks of **major depressive disorder,** a severe form of depression that interferes with concentration, decision making, and sociability. Major depression is one of the more common forms of

major depressive disorder A severe form of depression that interferes with concentration, decision making, and sociability.

mood disorders. Some 15 million people in the United States suffer from major depression, and at any one time, 6-10% of the U.S. population is clinically depressed. Almost one in five people in the United States experiences major depression at some point in life, and 15% of college students have received a diagnosis of depression. The cost of depression is more than $34 billion a year in lost productivity (Scelfo, 2007; Simon et al., 2008; Edoka, Petrou, & Ramchandani, 2011).

Women are twice as likely to experience major depression as men, with one-fourth of all females apt to encounter it at some point during their lives. Furthermore, although no one is sure why, the rate of depression is going up throughout the world. Results of in-depth interviews conducted in the United States, Puerto Rico, Taiwan, Lebanon, Canada, Italy, Germany, and France indicate that the incidence of depression has increased significantly over previous rates in every area. In fact, in some countries, the likelihood that individuals will have major depression at some point in their lives is three times higher than it was for earlier generations. In addition, people are developing major depression at increasingly younger ages (Kendler et al., 2006a; Staley, Sanacora, & Tagman, 2006; Sado et al., 2011).

Study Alert

Major depression differs from the normal depression that occasionally occurs during most people's lives; major depression is more intense, lasts longer, and may have no clear trigger.

When psychologists speak of major depression, they do not mean the sadness that comes from experiencing one of life's disappointments that we all have experienced. Some depression is normal after the breakup of a long-term relationship, the death of a loved one, or the loss of a job. It is normal even after less serious problems, such as doing badly on a test or having a romantic partner forget one's birthday.

People who suffer from major depression experience similar feelings, but the severity tends to be considerably greater. They may feel useless, worthless, and lonely, and they may think the future is hopeless and no one can help them. They may lose their appetite and have no energy. Moreover, they may experience such feelings for months or even years. They may cry uncontrollably, have sleep disturbances, and be at risk for suicide. The depth and duration of such behavior are the hallmarks of major depression. (Figure 4 provides a self-assessment of depression.)

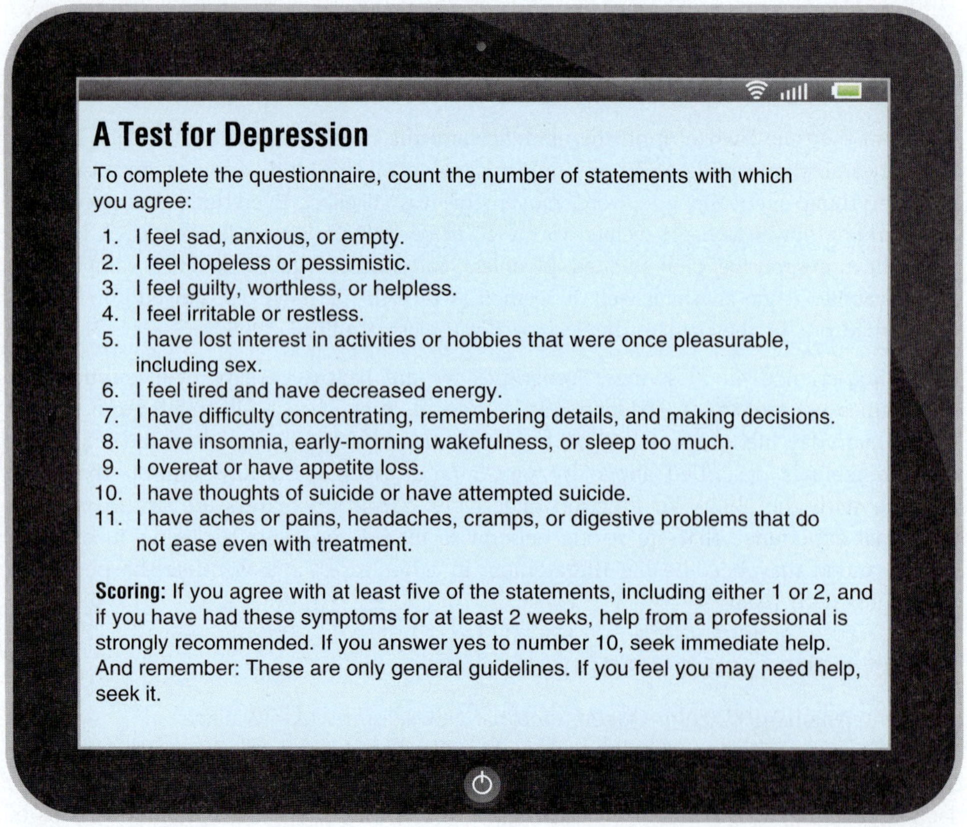

FIGURE 4 This test is based on the list of signs and symptoms of depression found on the National Institute of Mental Health website at http://www.nimh.nih.gov/health/publications/depression/what-are-the-signs-and-symptoms-of-depression.shtml

MANIA AND BIPOLAR DISORDER

While depression leads to the depths of despair, mania leads to emotional heights. **Mania** is an extended state of intense, wild elation. People experiencing mania feel intense happiness, power, invulnerability, and energy. Believing they will succeed at anything they attempt, they may become involved in wild schemes. Consider, for example, the following description of an individual who experienced a manic episode:

mania An extended state of intense, wild elation.

> Mr. O'Reilly took a leave of absence from his civil service job. He purchased a large number of cuckoo clocks and then an expensive car, which he planned to use as a mobile showroom for his wares, anticipating that he would make a great deal of money. He proceeded to "tear around town" buying and selling clocks and other merchandise, and when he was not out, he was continuously on the phone making "deals." . . . He was $3,000 in debt and had driven his family to exhaustion with his excessive activity and talkativeness. He said, however, that he felt "on top of the world." (Spitzer et al., 1983.)

Some people sequentially experience periods of mania and depression. This alternation of mania and depression is called **bipolar disorder** (a condition previously known as manic-depressive disorder). The swings between highs and lows may occur a few days apart or may alternate over a period of years. In addition, in bipolar disorder, periods of depression are usually longer than periods of mania.

bipolar disorder A disorder in which a person alternates between periods of euphoric feelings of mania and periods of depression.

Ironically, some of society's most creative individuals may have suffered from bipolar disorder. The imagination, drive, excitement, and energy that they display during manic stages allow them to make unusually creative contributions. For instance, historical analysis of the composer Robert Schumann's music shows that he was most prolific during periods of mania. In contrast, his output dropped off drastically during periods of depression (see Figure 5). On the other hand, the high output associated with mania does not necessarily lead to higher quality: Some of Schumann's greatest works were created outside his periods of mania (Szegedy Maszak, 2003; Kyaga et al., 2013).

Although creativity may be generated by mania, persons who experience this disorder often show a recklessness that produces emotional and sometimes physical self-injury. They may alienate people with their talkativeness, inflated self-esteem, and indifference to the needs of others.

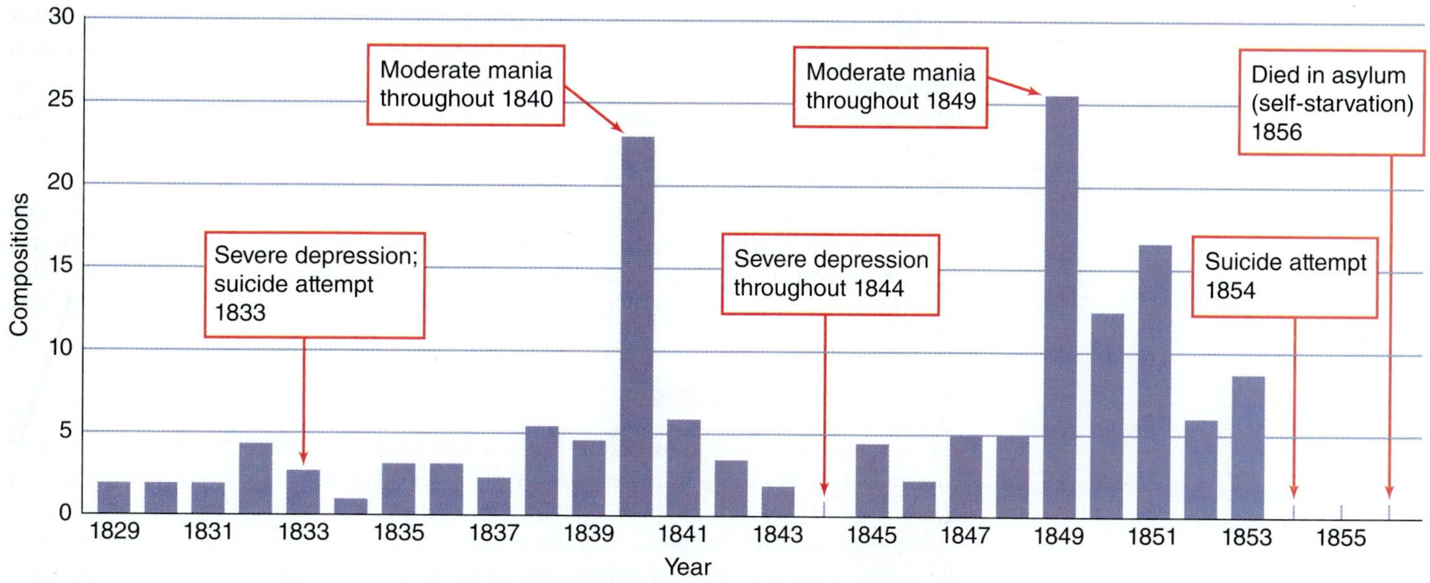

FIGURE 5 The number of pieces written by composer Robert Schumann in a given year is related to his periods of depression and mania (Slater & Meyer, 1959; reprinted in Jamison, 1993). Why do you think mania might be associated with creative productivity in some people?

CAUSES OF MOOD DISORDERS

Because they represent a major mental health problem, mood disorders—and, in particular, depression—have received a good deal of study. Several approaches have been used to explain the disorders.

Genetic and biological factors. Some mood disorders clearly have genetic and biological roots. In fact, most evidence suggests that bipolar disorders are caused primarily by biological factors. For instance, bipolar disorder (and some forms of major depression) clearly runs in some families, pointing to a genetic cause. Furthermore, researchers have found that several neurotransmitters play a role in depression. For example, alterations in the functioning of serotonin and norepinephrine in the brain are related to the disorder.

Finally, research on neuroimaging suggests that a brain structure called area 25 is related to depression: When area 25 is smaller than normal, it is associated with a higher risk of depression. Furthermore, the right anterior insula, a region of the brain related to self-awareness and interpersonal experience, also appears to be related to depression (Popa et al., 2008; Insel, 2010; Cisler et al., 2013).

Psychological causes. Other explanations for depression have also included a focus on psychological causes. For instance, proponents of psychoanalytic approaches see depression as the result of feelings of loss (real or potential) or of anger directed at oneself. One psychoanalytic approach, for instance, suggests that depression is produced by the loss or threatened loss of a parent early in life (Vanheule et al., 2006).

Environmental factors. Behavioral theories of depression argue that the stresses of life produce a reduction in positive reinforcers. As a result, people begin to withdraw, which only reduces positive reinforcers further. In addition, people receive attention for their depressive behavior, which further reinforces the depression (Lewinsohn & Essau, 2002; Lewinsohn et al., 2003; Domschke, 2013).

Cognitive and emotional factors. Some explanations for mood disorders attribute them to cognitive factors. For example, psychologist Martin Seligman suggests that depression is largely a response to learned helplessness. *Learned helplessness* is a learned expectation that events in one's life are uncontrollable and that one cannot escape from the situation. As a consequence, people simply give up fighting aversive events and submit to them, which thereby produces depression. Other theorists go a step further and suggest that depression results from hopelessness, a combination of learned helplessness and an expectation that negative outcomes in one's life are inevitable (Kwon & Laurenceau, 2002; Bjornstad, 2006; Li, B., 2011).

Clinical psychologist Aaron Beck has proposed that faulty cognitions underlie people's depressed feelings. Specifically, his cognitive theory of depression suggests that depressed individuals typically view themselves as life's losers and blame themselves whenever anything goes wrong. By focusing on the negative side of situations, they feel inept and unable to act constructively to change their environment. In sum, their negative cognitions lead to feelings of depression (Newman et al., 2002).

Brain imaging studies suggest that people with depression experience a general blunting of emotional reactions. For example, one study found that the brains of people with depression showed significantly less activation when they viewed photos of human faces displaying strong emotions than did those without the disorder (Gotlib et al., 2004).

DEPRESSION IN WOMEN

The various theories of depression have not provided a complete answer to an elusive question that has dogged researchers: Why does depression occur in approximately twice as many women as men—a pattern that is similar across a variety of cultures?

One explanation suggests that the stress women experience may be greater than the stress men experience at certain points in their lives—such as when a woman must simultaneously earn a living and be the primary caregiver for her children. In addition, women have a higher risk for physical and sexual abuse, typically earn lower wages than men, report greater unhappiness with their marriages, and generally experience chronic negative circumstances. Furthermore, women and men may respond to stress with different coping mechanisms. For instance, men may abuse drugs, while women respond with depression (Nolen-Hoeksema, 2007; Hyde, Mezulis, & Abramson, 2008; Komarovskaya et al., 2011).

Biological factors may also explain some women's depression. For example, the rate of female depression begins to rise during puberty, so some psychologists believe that hormones make women more vulnerable to the disorder. In addition, 25–50% of women who take oral contraceptives report symptoms of depression, and depression that occurs after the birth of a child is linked to hormonal changes. Finally, structural differences in men's and women's brains may be related to gender differences in depression (Holden, 2005; Graham, Bancroft, & Doll, 2007; Solomon & Herman, 2009; Silverstein et al., 2013).

Ultimately, it is clear that researchers have discovered no definitive solutions to the puzzle of depression, and there are many alternative explanations. Most likely, a complex interaction of several factors causes mood disorders.

Schizophrenia

> Things that relate, the town of Antelope, Oregon, Jonestown, Charlie Manson, the Hillside Strangler, the Zodiac Killer, Watergate, King's trial in L.A., and many more. In the last 7 years alone, over 23 Star Wars scientists committed suicide for no apparent reason. The AIDS cover-up, the conference in South America in 87 had over 1,000 doctors claim that insects can transmit it. To be able to read one's thoughts and place thoughts in one's mind without the person knowing it's being done. Realization is a reality of bioelectromagnetic control, which is thought transfer and emotional control, recording individual brainwave frequencies of thought, sensation, and emotions. (Nolen-Hoeksema, 2007.)

This excerpt illustrates the efforts of a person with schizophrenia, one of the more severe forms of mental disturbance, to communicate. People with schizophrenia account for by far the largest percentage of those hospitalized for psychological disorders. They are also in many respects the least likely to recover from their difficulties.

schizophrenia A class of disorders in which severe distortion of reality occurs.

Schizophrenia refers to a class of disorders in which severe distortion of reality occurs. Thinking, perception, and emotion may deteriorate; the individual may withdraw from social interaction; and the person may display bizarre behavior. The symptoms displayed by persons with schizophrenia may vary considerably over time Nonetheless, a number of characteristics reliably distinguish schizophrenia from other disorders. They include the following:

- *Decline from a previous level of functioning.* An individual can no longer carry out activities he or she was once able to do.
- *Disturbances of thought and speech.* People with schizophrenia use logic and language in a peculiar way. Their thinking often does not make sense, and their logic is frequently faulty, which is referred to as a *formal thought disorder.* They also do not follow conventional linguistic rules (Penn et al., 1997). Consider, for example, the following response to the question "Why do you think people believe in God?"

  > Uh, let's, I don't know why, let's see, balloon travel. He holds it up for you, the balloon. He don't let you fall out, your little legs sticking down through the clouds. He's down to the smokestack, looking through the smoke trying to get the balloon gassed up you know. Way they're flying on top that way, legs sticking out. I don't know, looking down on the ground, heck, that'd make you so dizzy you just stay and sleep you know, hold down and sleep there. I used to be sleep outdoors, you know, sleep outdoors instead of going home. (Chapman & Chapman, 1973, p. 3.)

FIGURE 6 This unusual art was created by an individual suffering from a severe psychological disorder.

As this selection illustrates, although the basic grammatical structure may be intact, the substance of thinking characteristic of schizophrenia is often illogical, garbled, and lacking in meaningful content (Holden, 2003; Heinrichs, 2005).

- *Delusions.* People with schizophrenia often have delusions, firmly held, unshakable beliefs with no basis in reality. Among the common delusions people with schizophrenia experience are the beliefs that they are being controlled by someone else, they are being persecuted by others, and their thoughts are being broadcast so that others know what they are thinking (Coltheart, Langdon, & McKay, 2007; Startup, Bucci, & Langdon, 2009).
- *Hallucinations and perceptual disorders.* People with schizophrenia do not perceive the world as most other people do. They also may have *hallucinations,* the experience of perceiving things that do not actually exist. Furthermore, they may see, hear, or smell things differently from others (see Figure 6); they do not even have a sense of their bodies in the way that others do and have difficulty determining where their bodies stop and the rest of the world begins (Botvinick, 2004; Thomas et al., 2007; Bauer et al., 2011).
- *Inappropriate emotional displays.* People with schizophrenia sometimes show a lack of emotion in which even the most dramatic events produce little or no emotional response. Alternately, they may display emotion that is inappropriate to a situation. For example, a person with schizophrenia may laugh uproariously at a funeral or react with anger when being helped by someone.
- *Withdrawal.* People with schizophrenia tend to have little interest in others. They tend not to socialize or hold real conversations with others, although they may talk at another person. In the most extreme cases, they do not even acknowledge the presence of other people and appear to be in their own isolated world.

Usually, the onset of schizophrenia occurs in early adulthood, and the symptoms follow one of two primary courses. In *process schizophrenia,* the symptoms develop slowly and subtly. There may be a gradual withdrawal from the world, excessive daydreaming, and a blunting of emotion until eventually the disorder reaches the point where others cannot overlook it. In other cases, known as *reactive schizophrenia,* the onset of symptoms is sudden and conspicuous. The treatment outlook for reactive schizophrenia is relatively favorable, but process schizophrenia has proved more difficult to treat.

DSM-5 classifies the symptoms of schizophrenia into two types. Positive-symptom schizophrenia is indicated by the presence of disordered behavior such as hallucinations, delusions, and emotional extremes. In contrast, negative-symptom schizophrenia shows an absence or loss of normal functioning, such as social withdrawal or blunted emotions (Levine & Rabinowitz, 2007; Tandon et al., 2013).

The distinction between positive and negative symptoms of schizophrenia is important because it suggests that two different kinds of causes might trigger schizophrenia. Furthermore, it has implications for predicting treatment outcomes.

SOLVING THE PUZZLE OF SCHIZOPHRENIA: BIOLOGICAL CAUSES

Although schizophrenic behavior clearly departs radically from normal behavior, its causes are less apparent. It does appear, however, that schizophrenia has both biological and environmental origins (Sawa & Snyder, 2002).

Let's first consider the evidence pointing to a biological cause. Because schizophrenia is more common in some families than in others, genetic factors seem

Risk of Developing Schizophrenia, Based on Genetic Relatedness to a Person with Schizophrenia		
Relationship	**Genetic Relatedness, %**	**Risk of Developing Schizophrenia, %**
Identical twin	100	48
Child of two schizophrenic parents	100	46
Fraternal twin	50	17
Offspring of one schizophrenic parent	50	17
Sibling	50	9
Nephew or niece	25	4
Spouse	0	2
Unrelated person	0	1

FIGURE 7 The closer the genetic links between two people, the greater the likelihood that if one experiences schizophrenia, so will the other sometime during his or her lifetime. However, genetics is not the full story; if it were, the risk of identical twins having schizophrenia would be 100% and not the 48% shown in this figure. (Source: Adapted from Gottesman, 1991.)

to be involved in producing at least a susceptibility to or readiness for developing schizophrenia. For example, the closer the genetic link between a person with schizophrenia and another individual, the greater the likelihood that the other person will experience the disorder (see Figure 7; Brzustowicz et al., 2000; Plomin & McGuffin, 2003; Gottesman & Hanson, 2005).

However, if genetics alone were responsible for schizophrenia, the chance of both of two identical twins having schizophrenia would be 100% instead of just under 50% because identical twins have the same genetic makeup. Moreover, attempts to find a link between schizophrenia and a particular gene have been only partly successful. Apparently, genetic factors alone do not produce schizophrenia (Franzek & Beckmann, 1996; Lenzenweger & Dworkin, 1998).

According to one hypothesis, the brains of people with schizophrenia may have a biochemical imbalance. For example, the *dopamine hypothesis* suggests that schizophrenia occurs when there is excess activity in the areas of the brain that use dopamine as a neurotransmitter. This hypothesis came to light after the discovery that drugs that block dopamine action in brain pathways can be highly effective in reducing the symptoms of schizophrenia. Other research suggests that glutamate, another neurotransmitter, may be a major contributor to the disorder (Stone, Morrison, & Pilowsky, 2007; Howes & Kapur, 2009; Kendler & Schaffner, 2011).

Another biological explanation is that there may be structural abnormalities in the brains of people with schizophrenia. Such brain abnormalities may be caused by exposure to a virus during prenatal development.

Support for such a view comes from research showing abnormalities in the neural circuits of the cortex and limbic systems. Furthermore, differences exist in the way the brain functions (see *Neuroscience in Your Life;* Bartzokis et al., 2003; Reichenberg & Harvey, 2007; Reichenberg et al., 2009).

Further evidence for the importance of biological factors shows that when people with schizophrenia hear voices during hallucinations, the parts of the brain responsible for hearing and language processing become active. When they have visual hallucinations, the parts of the brain involved in movement and color are active. At the same time, people with schizophrenia often have unusually low activity in the brain's frontal lobes–the parts of the brain involved with emotional regulation, insight, and the evaluation of sensory stimuli (Stern & Silbersweig, 2001).

Neuroscience in Your Life: Brain Changes with Schizophrenia

Changes in the brain have been found in people with schizophrenia. In an MRI reconstruction of the brain of a person with schizophrenia (a), the hippocampi (yellow) are shrunken, and the ventricles (gray) are enlarged and fluid-filled. In contrast, an MRI reconstruction of the brain of a person without the disorder (b) is structurally different with larger hippocampi and smaller ventricles. (Source: N.C. Andreasen, University of Iowa.)

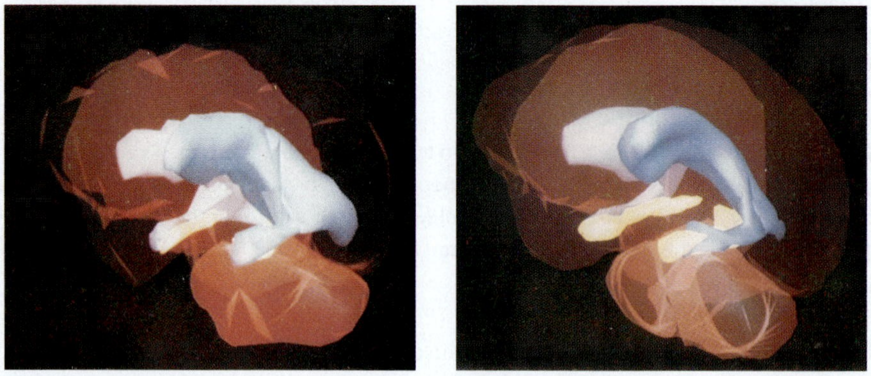

(a) (b)

SITUATIONAL CAUSES OF SCHIZOPHRENIA

Although biological factors provide important pieces of the puzzle of schizophrenia, we still need to consider past and current experiences of people who develop the disturbance. For instance, psychoanalytic explanations suggest that schizophrenia occurs when people experience regression to earlier experiences and stages of life. Specifically, Freud believed that people with schizophrenia lack egos that are strong enough to cope with their unacceptable impulses. They regress to the oral stage–a time when the id and ego are not yet separated. Therefore, individuals with schizophrenia essentially lack an ego and act out impulses without concern for reality.

However, little evidence supports psychoanalytic explanations. More plausible theories suggest that the emotional and communication patterns of the families of people with schizophrenia are to blame for the disorder. For instance, some researchers suggest that schizophrenia is related to a family interaction style known as expressed emotion. *Expressed emotion* is an interaction style characterized by high levels of criticism, hostility, and emotional intrusiveness within a family. Other researchers suggest that faulty communication patterns lie at the heart of schizophrenia (Lobban, Barrowclough, & Jones, 2006; Nader et al., 2013).

Psychologists who take a cognitive perspective on schizophrenia suggest that the problems in thinking that people with the disorder experience point to a cognitive cause. Some suggest that schizophrenia results from *overattention* to stimuli in the environment. Rather than being able to screen out unimportant or inconsequential stimuli and focus on the most important things in the environment, people with schizophrenia may be excessively receptive to virtually everything in their environment. As a consequence, their information-processing capabilities become overloaded and eventually break down. Other cognitive experts argue that schizophrenia results from *underattention* to certain stimuli. According to this explanation, people with schizophrenia fail to focus sufficiently on important stimuli and pay attention to other, less important information in their surroundings (Cadenhead & Braff, 1995).

Although it is plausible that overattention and underattention are related to different forms of schizophrenia, these phenomena do not explain the origins of such information-processing disorders. Consequently, cognitive approaches–like other environmental explanations–do not provide a full explanation of the disorder.

THE MULTIPLE CAUSES OF SCHIZOPHRENIA

Most scientists now believe that schizophrenia is caused by both biological and situational factors. Specifically, the *predisposition model of schizophrenia* suggests that individuals may inherit a predisposition or an inborn sensitivity to develop schizophrenia. This genetic predisposition makes them particularly vulnerable to stressful factors in the environment, such as social rejection or dysfunctional family communication patterns. The stressors may vary, but if they are strong enough and are coupled with a genetic predisposition, they result in the appearance of schizophrenia. Furthermore, a strong genetic predisposition may lead to the onset of schizophrenia even when the environmental stressors are relatively weak. On the other hand, someone with a genetic predisposition to develop schizophrenia may avoid developing the disorder if that person experiences relatively few life stressors.

Study Alert
Remember that the multiple causes of schizophrenia include biological and environmental factors.

In short, the models used today associate schizophrenia with several kinds of biological and situational factors. It is increasingly clear, then, that no single factor but a combination of interrelated variables produces schizophrenia (Meltzer, 2000; McDonald & Murray, 2004; Opler et al., 2008).

Personality Disorders

> I had always wanted lots of things; as a child I can remember wanting a bullet that a friend of mine had brought in to show the class. I took it and put it into my school bag and when my friend noticed it was missing, I was the one who stayed after school with him and searched the room, and I was the one who sat with him and bitched about the other kids and how one of them took his bullet. I even went home with him to help him break the news to his uncle, who had brought it home from the war for him.
>
> But that was petty compared with the stuff I did later. I wanted a Ph.D. very badly, but I didn't want to work very hard–just enough to get by. I never did the experiments I reported; hell, I was smart enough to make up the results. I knew enough about statistics to make anything look plausible. I got my master's degree without even spending one hour in a laboratory. I mean, the professors believed anything. I'd stay out all night drinking and being with my friends, and the next day I'd get in just before them and tell 'em I'd been in the lab all night. They'd actually feel sorry for me. (Duke & Nowicki, 1979.)

This excerpt provides a graphic first-person account of a person with a personality disorder. A **personality disorder** is characterized by a set of inflexible, maladaptive behavior patterns that keep a person from functioning appropriately in society.

personality disorder A disorder characterized by a set of inflexible, maladaptive behavior patterns that keep a person from functioning appropriately in society.

Personality disorders differ from the other disorders we have discussed because those affected by them often have little sense of personal distress associated with the psychological maladjustment. In fact, people with personality disorders frequently lead seemingly normal lives. However, just below the surface lies a set of inflexible, maladaptive personality traits that do not permit them to function effectively as members of society (Davis & Millon, 1999; Clarkin & Lenzenweger, 2004; Friedman, Oltmanns, & Turkheimer, 2007).

The best-known type of personality disorder, illustrated by the case above, is the **antisocial personality disorder** (sometimes referred to as a sociopathic personality). Individuals with this disturbance show no regard for the moral and ethical rules of society or the rights of others. Although they can appear quite intelligent and likable (at least at first), upon closer examination they turn out to be manipulative and deceptive.

antisocial personality disorder A disorder in which individuals show no regard for the moral and ethical rules of society or the rights of others.

Study Alert

Unlike most psychological disorders, personality disorders produce little or no personal distress.

Moreover, they lack any guilt or anxiety about their wrongdoing. When those with antisocial personality disorder behave in a way that injures someone else, they understand intellectually that they have caused harm but feel no remorse (Goodwin & Hamilton, 2003; Hilarski, 2007; Bateman, 2011).

People with antisocial personality disorder are often impulsive and lack the ability to withstand frustration. They can be extremely manipulative. They also may have excellent social skills; they can be charming, engaging, and highly persuasive. Some of the best con artists have antisocial personalities.

What causes such an unusual constellation of problem behaviors? A variety of factors have been suggested ranging from an inability to experience emotions appropriately to problems in family relationships. For example, in many cases of antisocial behavior, the individual has come from a home in which a parent has died or left or one in which there is a lack of affection, a lack of consistency in discipline, or outright rejection. Other explanations concentrate on sociocultural factors because an unusually high proportion of people with antisocial personalities come from lower socioeconomic groups. Still, no one has been able to pinpoint the specific causes of antisocial personalities, and it is likely that some combination of factors is responsible (Rosenstein & Horowitz, 1996; Costa & Widiger, 2002; Chen et al., 2011).

borderline personality disorder
A disorder characterized by problems regulating emotions and thoughts, displaying impulsive and reckless behavior, and having unstable relationships with others.

People with **borderline personality disorder** have problems regulating emotions and thoughts, display impulsive and reckless behavior, and have unstable relationships with others. They also have difficulty in developing a secure sense of who they are. As a consequence, they tend to rely on relationships with others to define their identity. The problem with this strategy is that rejections are devastating. Furthermore, people with this disorder distrust others and have difficulty controlling their anger. Their emotional volatility leads to impulsive and self-destructive behavior.

Individuals with borderline personality disorder often feel empty and alone, and they have difficulty cooperating with others. They may form intense, sudden, one-sided relationships in which they demand the attention of another person and then feel angry when they don't receive it. One reason for this behavior is that they may have a background in which others discounted or criticized their emotional reactions, and they may not have learned to regulate their emotions effectively (King-Casas et al., 2008; Hopwood et al., 2009; Samuel et al., 2013).

narcissistic personality disorder
A personality disturbance characterized by an exaggerated sense of self-importance.

The narcissistic personality disorder is another type of personality disorder. The **narcissistic personality disorder** is characterized by an exaggerated sense of self-importance. Those with the disorder expect special treatment from others while at the same time disregarding others' feelings. In some ways, in fact, the main attribute of the narcissistic personality is an inability to experience empathy for other people.

There are several other categories of personality disorder that range in severity from individuals who may simply be regarded by others as eccentric, obnoxious, or difficult to people who act in a manner that is criminal and dangerous to others. Although they are not out of touch with reality like people with schizophrenia, people with personality disorders lead lives that put them on the fringes of society (Millon, Davis, & Millon, 2000; Trull & Widiger, 2003).

From the perspective of . . .

A Social Worker Because people with personality disorders often appear from the outside to function well in society, should you try to address their problems?

Disorders That Impact Childhood

We typically view childhood as a time of innocence and relative freedom from stress. In reality, though, almost 20% of children and 40% of adolescents experience significant emotional or behavioral disorders (Romano et al., 2001; Broidy, Nagin, & Tremblay, 2003; Nolen-Hoeksema, 2007).

For example, although major depression is more prevalent in adults, around 2.5% of children and more than 8% of adolescents suffer from the disorder. In fact, by the time they reach age 20, between 15% and 20% of children and adolescents will experience an episode of major depression (Garber & Horowitz, 2002).

Children do not always display depression the same way adults do. Rather than showing profound sadness or hopelessness, childhood depression may produce the expression of exaggerated fears, clinginess, or avoidance of everyday activities. In older children, the symptoms may be sulking, school problems, and even acts of delinquency (Koplewicz, 2002; Seroczynski, Jacquez, & Cole, 2003).

A considerably more common childhood disorder is **attention-deficit hyperactivity disorder,** or **ADHD,** a disorder marked by inattention, impulsiveness, a low tolerance for frustration, and generally a great deal of inappropriate activity. Although all children show such behavior some of the time, it is so common in children diagnosed with ADHD that it interferes with their everyday functioning (Barkley, 2005; Smith, Barkley, & Shapiro, 2006; Barkley, Knouse, & Murphy, 2011).

attention-deficit hyperactivity disorder (ADHD) A disorder marked by inattention, impulsiveness, a low tolerance for frustration, and a great deal of inappropriate activity.

ADHD is surprisingly widespread with estimates ranging between 3% and 5% of the school-age population—or some 3.5 million children under the age of 18 in the United States. Children diagnosed with the disorder are often exhausting to parents and teachers, and even their peers find them difficult to deal with.

The cause of ADHD is not known, although most experts feel that it is produced by dysfunctions in the nervous system. For example, one theory suggests that unusually low levels of arousal in the central nervous system cause ADHD. To compensate, children with ADHD seek out stimulation to increase arousal. Still, such theories are speculative. Furthermore, because many children occasionally show behaviors characteristic of ADHD, it often is misdiagnosed or in some cases overdiagnosed. Only the frequency and persistence of the symptoms of ADHD allow for a correct diagnosis, which only a trained professional can do (Barkley, 2000; Sciutto & Eisenberg, 2007; Ketisch & Jones, 2013).

autism spectrum disorder A severe developmental disability that impairs one's ability to communicate and relate to others.

Autism spectrum disorder, a severe developmental disability that impairs one's ability to communicate and relate to others, is another disorder that usually appears in the first 3 years and typically continues throughout life. Children with autism have difficulties in both verbal and nonverbal communication, and they may avoid social contact. About 1 in 88 children are now thought to have the disorder, and its prevalence has risen significantly in the last decade. Whether the increase is the result of an actual rise in the incidence of autism or is due to better reporting is a question of intense debate among researchers (Rice, 2009; Neal, Matson, & Belva, 2013).

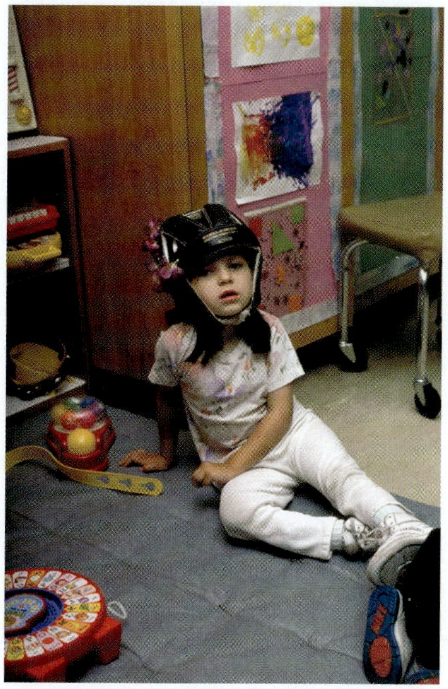

In the most severe cases of autism spectrum disorder, children display self-injurious behavior and must wear protective head gear.

Other Disorders

It's important to keep in mind that the various forms of psychological disorders described in DSM-5 cover much more ground than we have been able to discuss in this module. Some relate to topics considered in other chapters. For example, *psychoactive substance use disorder* relates to problems that arise from the use and abuse of drugs. Furthermore, *alcohol use disorders* are among the most serious and widespread problems. Both psychoactive substance use disorder and alcohol use disorder co-occur with many other psychological disorders, such as mood disorders, trauma- and stressor-related disorders, and schizophrenia, which complicate treatment considerably (Salgado, Quinlan, & Zlotnick, 2007).

Applying Psychology in the 21st Century

Internet Addiction

If someone challenged you to go for a week without plugging into the Internet, how easy would it be?

Many people feel an almost constant need to check their Twitter or Instagram accounts, e-mail, or Facebook feeds. For some people, though, the behavior borders on an addictive behavior, in which real-world tasks and activities get pushed aside by the need to compulsively check what's going on in their virtual world. In fact, some psychologists believe that such behavior represents a new disorder: Internet addiction disorder.

The disorder has been given many names by different researchers studying it: iPhone addiction, Facebook addiction, and Facebook depression, among others. Researchers considered including what has been called *Internet addiction disorder* in DSM-5, but they ultimately decided to omit it, believing that the phenomenon has yet to be sufficiently delineated. But new research is beginning to suggest that the problem is real (Dokoupil, 2012).

The picture that is emerging of Internet addiction is one of depression and anxiety, obsessive and compulsive behaviors, attention deficits, and in some cases, occasional breaks with reality. One of the common signs of Internet addiction is a compulsion to check messages or social networks—checking them first thing in the morning, while driving, at work, during social events, and even taking a device to bed. Some people who appear to be addicted commonly spend more time online than they expect to or even realize, to the detriment of other activities and obligations. Many report feeling a sense of guilt and anxiety about the costs of their Internet compulsion, but they also feel anxious if they don't check in online—a fear that they might be missing something. And while they might cultivate a large network of social media friends, the obligation they feel to maintain an active online presence often leaves them feeling drained and disconnected from life (Carr, 2011; Rosen, 2012).

Moreover, some researchers are finding that online life creates a sort of alternative reality for people, one filled with opportunities for attention and validation. The technology also enables people to develop alternate personalities, whereby they can express radically different traits and behaviors online than they do in real life (Aboujaoude, 2008).

While the scope of the disorder and its specific symptoms and complications are still unresolved, the reality and seriousness of Internet addiction disorder are no longer easy to dismiss.

RETHINK

- What are some features of online activity that might make it particularly addictive?
- If heavy Internet use leaves people feeling anxious, guilty, and empty, why would they keep coming back to it?

Another widespread problem is *eating disorders.* They include such disorders as *anorexia nervosa* and *bulimia,* which we considered in the chapter on motivation and emotion, as well as *binge-eating disorder,* characterized by binge eating without behaviors designed to prevent weight gain. Finally, *sexual disorders,* in which one's sexual activity is unsatisfactory, are another important class of problems. They include *sexual desire disorders, sexual arousal disorders,* and *paraphilic disorders,* atypical sexual activities that may include nonhuman objects or nonconsenting partners.

Another important class of disorders is *neurocognitive disorders,* some of which we touched on previously. These are problems that have a purely biological basis, such as Alzheimer's disease and some types of developmental disability. Remember, there are other disorders that we have not mentioned at all, and each of the classes we have discussed can be divided into several subcategories (Kopelman & Fleminger, 2002; Pratt et al., 2003; Reijonen et al., 2003; also see *Applying Psychology in the 21st Century*).

RECAP/EVALUATE/RETHINK

RECAP

LO 38-1 What are the major psychological disorders?

- Anxiety disorders are present when a person experiences so much anxiety that it affects daily functioning. Specific types of anxiety disorders include phobic disorder, panic disorder, and generalized anxiety disorder. Also related is obsessive-compulsive disorder.
- Somatic symptom disorders are psychological difficulties that take on a physical (somatic) form but for which there is no medical cause. Examples are illness anxiety disorder and conversion disorders.
- Dissociative disorders are marked by the separation, or dissociation, of different facets of a person's personality that are usually integrated. Major kinds of dissociative disorders include dissociative identity disorder, dissociative amnesia, and dissociative fugue.
- Mood disorders are characterized by emotional states of depression or euphoria so strong that they intrude on everyday living. They include major depression and bipolar disorder.
- Schizophrenia is one of the more severe forms of mental illness. Symptoms of schizophrenia include declines in functioning, thought and language disturbances, perceptual disorders, emotional disturbance, and withdrawal from others.
- Strong evidence links schizophrenia to genetic, biochemical, and environmental factors. According to the predisposition model, an interaction among various factors produces the disorder.
- People with personality disorders experience little or no personal distress, but they do suffer from an inability to function as normal members of society. These disorders include antisocial personality disorder, borderline personality disorder, and narcissistic personality disorder.
- Childhood disorders include major depression, attention-deficit hyperactivity disorder (ADHD), and autism spectrum disorder.

EVALUATE

1. Kathy is terrified of elevators. She could be suffering from a(n)
   a. Obsessive-compulsive disorder
   b. Phobic disorder
   c. Panic disorder
   d. Generalized anxiety disorder

2. Carmen described an incident in which her anxiety suddenly rose to a peak, and she felt a sense of impending doom. Carmen experienced a(n) ________ ________.

3. Troubling thoughts that persist for weeks or months are known as
   a. Obsessions
   b. Compulsions
   c. Rituals
   d. Panic attacks

4. An overpowering urge to carry out a strange ritual is called a(n) ________.

5. The separation of the personality, which provides escape from stressful situations, is the key factor in ________ disorders.

6. States of extreme euphoria and energy paired with severe depression characterize ________ disorder.

7. ________ schizophrenia is characterized by symptoms that are sudden and of easily identifiable onset; ________ schizophrenia develops gradually over a person's life span.

8. The ________ ________ states that schizophrenia may be caused by an excess of certain neurotransmitters in the brain.

RETHINK

1. What cultural factors might contribute to the rate of anxiety disorders found in a culture? How might the experience of anxiety differ among people of different cultures?

2. Personality disorders are often not apparent to others, and many people with these problems seem to live basically normal lives and are not a threat to others. Because these people can function well in society, why should they be considered psychologically disordered?

Answers to Evaluate Questions

1. b; **2.** panic attack; **3.** a; **4.** compulsion; **5.** dissociative; **6.** bipolar; **7.** Reactive, process; **8.** dopamine hypothesis

KEY TERMS

anxiety disorder
phobias
panic disorder
generalized anxiety disorder
obsessive-compulsive disorder (OCD)
obsession
compulsion
somatic symptom disorder
illness anxiety disorder
conversion disorder
dissociative disorders
dissociative identity disorder (DID)
dissociative amnesia
dissociative fugue
mood disorder
major depressive disorder
mania
bipolar disorder
schizophrenia
personality disorder
antisocial personality disorder
borderline personality disorder
narcissistic personality disorder
attention-deficit hyperactivity disorder (ADHD)
autism spectrum disorder

MODULE 39

Psychological Disorders in Perspective

Learning Outcomes

LO 39-1 How prevalent are psychological disorders?

LO 39-2 What indicators signal a need for the help of a mental health practitioner?

How common are the kinds of psychological disorders we've been discussing? Here's one answer: One out of two people in the United States is likely to suffer at some point in their lives from a psychological disorder.

That's the conclusion drawn from a massive study on the prevalence of psychological disorders. In that study, researchers conducted face-to-face interviews with more than 8,000 men and women between the ages of 15 and 54. The sample was designed to be representative of the population of the United States. According to results of the study, 48% of those interviewed had experienced a disorder at some point in their lives. In addition, 30% experienced a disorder in any particular year. Furthermore, many people experience comorbidity. *Cormorbidity* is the appearance of multiple simultaneous psychological disorders in the same person (Welkowitz et al., 2000; Merikangas et al., 2007; Kessler & Wang, 2008).

The most common disorder reported in the study was depression. Some 17% of those surveyed reported at least one major episode. Ten percent had suffered from depression during the current year. The next most common disorder was alcohol dependence, which occurred at a lifetime incidence rate of 14%. In addition, 7% of those interviewed had experienced alcohol dependence in the last year. Other frequently occurring psychological disorders were drug dependence, disorders involving panic (such as an overwhelming fear of talking to strangers and terror of heights), and posttraumatic stress disorder.

Study Alert

Remember that the incidence of various psychological disorders in the general population is surprisingly high, particularly in terms of depression and alcohol dependence.

Although some researchers think the estimates of severe disorders may be too high (Narrow et al., 2002), the national findings are consistent with studies of college students and their psychological difficulties. For example, in one study of the problems of students who visited a college counseling center, more than 40% of students reported being depressed (see Figure 1). These figures include only students who sought help from the counseling center and not those who did not seek treatment. Consequently, the figures are not representative of the entire college population (Benton et al., 2003).

From the perspective of . . .

A College Counselor What indicators might be most important in determining whether a college student is experiencing a psychological disorder?

The significant level of psychological disorders is a problem not only in the United States; according to the World Health Organization, mental health difficulties are also a global concern. Throughout the world, psychological disorders are widespread. Furthermore, there are economic disparities in treatment; more affluent people with mild disorders receive more and better treatment than poor people who have more severe disorders. In fact, psychological disorders make up 14% of

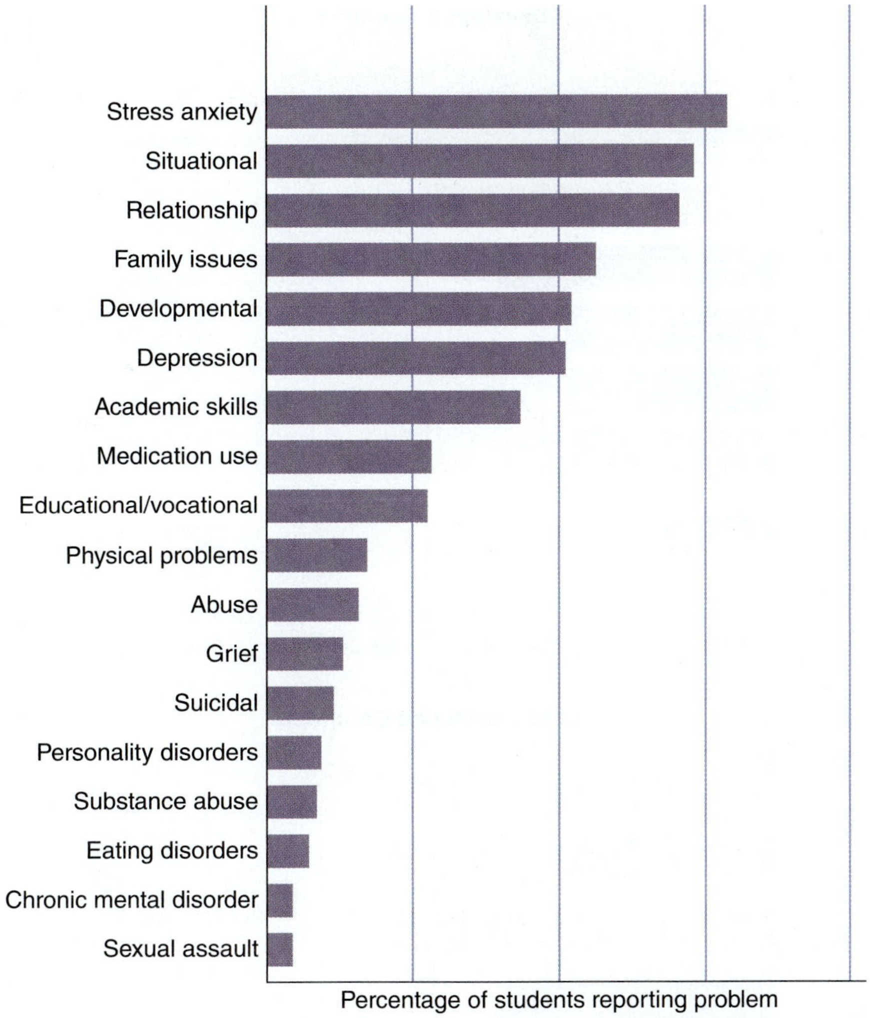

FIGURE 1 The problems reported by students visiting a college counseling center. Would you have predicted this pattern of psychological difficulties? (Source: Adapted from Benton et al., 2003.)

global illness, and 90% of people in developing countries receive no care at all for their disorders (see Figure 2; WHO World Mental Health Survey Consortium, 2004; Jacob et al., 2007; Wang et al., 2007).

Also, keep in mind that the incidence of specific disorders varies significantly in other cultures. For instance, cross-cultural surveys show that the incidence of major depression varies significantly from one culture to another. The probability of having at least one episode of depression is only 1.5% in Taiwan and 2.9% in Korea compared with 11.6% in New Zealand and 16.4% in France. Such notable differences underscore the importance of considering the cultural context of psychological disorders (Weissman et al., 1997; Tseng, 2003).

The Social and Cultural Context of Psychological Disorders

In considering the nature of the psychological disorders described in DSM-5, it's important to keep in mind that the disorders that were included in the manual are a reflection of Western culture at the start of the 21st century. The classification system provides a snapshot of how its authors viewed mental disorder when it was published. In fact, the development of the most recent version of the DSM was a source of great debate, which in part reflects issues that divide society.

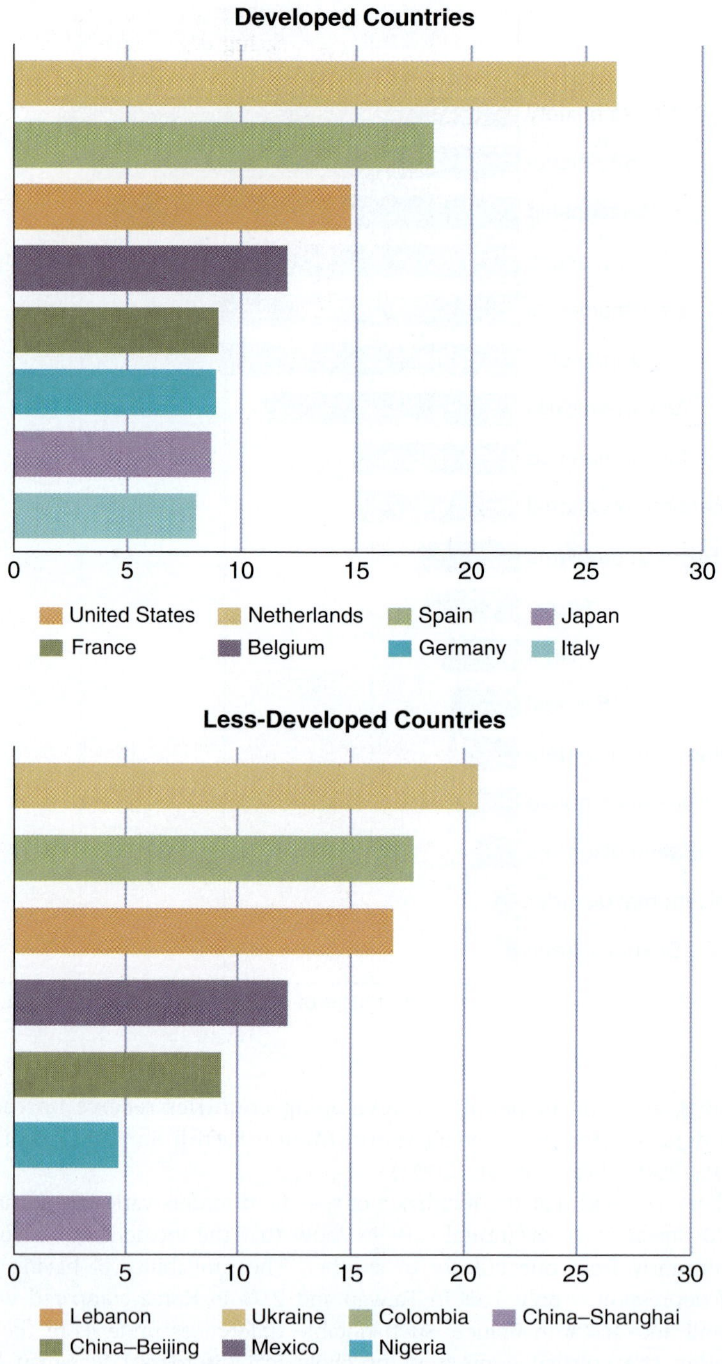

FIGURE 2 According to a global survey conducted by the World Health Organization, the prevalence of psychological disorders is widespread. These figures show the percentage of people who have experienced any psychological disorder within the prior 12-month period. (Source: Adapted from WHO World Mental Health Survey Consortium, 2004.)

Study Alert

It is important to understand that the DSM is a living document that presents a view of disorders that reflects the culture and historical context of its authors.

One specific, newly classified disorder that has been added to DSM-5 that has caused controversy is known as disruptive mood dysregulation disorder. This particular diagnosis is characterized by temperamental outbursts grossly out of proportion to the situation, both verbally and physically, in children between the ages of 6 and 18. Some practitioners argue these symptoms simply define a child having a temper tantrum rather than a disorder (Dobbs, 2012; Marchand & Phillips McEnany, 2012; Frances, 2013).

Similarly, someone who overeats 12 times in three months can be considered to be suffering from the new classification of binge eating disorder, which seems to some critics to be overly inclusive. Finally, hoarding behavior is now placed in its own category of psychological disorder. Some critics suggest this change is more a reflection of the rise of reality shows focusing on hoarding rather than reflecting a distinct category of psychological disturbance (Hudson et al., 2012).

Such controversies underline the fact that our understanding of abnormal behavior reflects the society and culture in which we live. Future revisions of DSM may include a different catalog of disorders. Even now, other cultures might include a list of disorders that are very different from the list that appears in the current DSM, as we discuss next.

Exploring DIVERSITY

DSM and Culture—and the Culture of DSM

In most people's estimation, a person who hears voices of the recently deceased is probably a victim of a psychological disturbance. Yet some Plains Indians routinely hear the voices of the dead calling to them from the afterlife.

This is only one example of the role of culture in labeling behavior as "abnormal." In fact, among all the major adult disorders included in the DSM categorization, a minority are found across all cultures of the world. Most others are prevalent primarily in North America and Western Europe (Kleinman, 1996; Cohen, Slomkowski, & Robins, 1999; López & Guarnaccia, 2000).

For instance, take anorexia nervosa, the disorder in which people become obsessed with their weight and sometimes stop eating, ultimately starving to death in the process. This disorder occurs most frequently in cultures that hold the societal standard that slender female bodies are the most desirable. In most of the world, where such a standard does not exist, anorexia nervosa is rare. Furthermore, the disorder may appear in specific ways in a particular culture. For instance, in Hong Kong, symptoms of one form of anorexia relate to complaints of bloated stomachs, rather than fears of becoming fat (Watters, 2010).

Similarly, dissociative identity (multiple personality) disorder makes sense as a problem only in societies in which a sense of self is fairly concrete. In India, the self is based more on external factors that are relatively independent of the person. There, when an individual displays symptoms of what people in a Western society would call dissociative identity disorder, Indians assume that that person is possessed either by demons (which they view as a malady) or by gods (which does not require treatment).

Furthermore, even though disorders such as schizophrenia are found throughout the world, cultural factors influence the specific symptoms of the disorder. Hence, catatonic schizophrenia in which unmoving patients appear to be frozen in the same position (sometimes for days), is rare in North America and Western Europe. In contrast, in India, 80% of those with schizophrenia are catatonic.

Other cultures have disorders that do not appear in the West. For example, in Malaysia, a behavior called *amok* is characterized by a wild outburst in which a usually quiet and withdrawn person kills or severely injures another. *Koro* is a condition found in Southeast Asian males who develop an intense panic that the penis is about to withdraw into the abdomen. Some West African men develop a disorder when they first attend college that they call "brain fag"; it includes feelings of heaviness or heat in the head as well as depression and anxiety. Finally, *ataque de nervios* is a disorder found most often among Latinos from the Caribbean. It is characterized by trembling, crying, uncontrollable screams, and incidents of verbal or physical aggression (Cohen et al., 1999; López & Guarnaccia, 2000; Adams & Dzokoto, 2007).

Explanations for psychological disorders also differ among cultures. For example, in China, psychological disorders are commonly viewed as a weakness of the heart, a concept that derives from thousands of years of traditional Chinese medicine. Many terms used to describe emotions and symptoms of psychological disorders make direct reference to the heart—but the association isn't simply a metaphorical one. Chinese people are more likely than people in Western cultures to express their emotional anguish in terms of physical symptoms such as heart pain, "heart panic," or "heart vexed." They may also see their emotional pain as merely a side effect of some underlying physical cause or even focus more on the effects that their symptoms are having on their relationships with friends and family members (Miller, 2006; Lee, Kleinman, & Kleinman, 2007; Watters, 2010).

In sum, we should not assume that the DSM provides the final word on psychological disorders. The disorders it includes are very much a creation and function of Western cultures at a particular moment in time, and its categories should not be seen as universally applicable (Tseng, 2003).

BECOMING AN INFORMED CONSUMER of Psychology

Deciding When You Need Help

After you've considered the range and variety of psychological disturbances that can afflict people, you may begin to feel that you suffer from one (or more) of the problems we have discussed. In fact, this perception has a name: *medical student's disease*. Although in this case it might more aptly be labeled "psychology student's disease," the basic symptoms are the same: feeling that you suffer from the same sorts of problems you are studying.

Most often, of course, your concerns will be unwarranted. As we have discussed, the differences between normal and abnormal behavior are often so fuzzy that it is easy to jump to the conclusion that you might have the same symptoms that are involved in serious forms of mental disturbance.

Before coming to such a conclusion, though, keep in mind that from time to time we all experience a wide range of emotions, and it is not unusual to feel deeply unhappy, fantasize about bizarre situations, or feel anxiety about life's circumstances. It is the persistence, depth, and consistency of such behavior that set normal reactions apart from abnormal ones. If you have not previously had serious doubts about the normality of your behavior, it is unlikely that reading about others' psychological disorders will prompt you to re-evaluate your earlier conclusion.

On the other hand, many people do have problems that merit concern, and in such cases, it is important to consider the possibility that professional help is warranted. The following list of symptoms can serve as a guideline to help you determine whether outside intervention might be useful (Engler & Goleman, 1992):

- Long-term feelings of distress that interfere with your sense of well-being, competence, and ability to function effectively in daily activities
- Occasions in which you experience overwhelmingly high stress accompanied by feelings of inability to cope with the situation
- Prolonged depression or feelings of hopelessness, especially when they do not have any clear cause (such as the death of someone close)
- Withdrawal from other people
- Thoughts of inflicting harm on oneself or suicide
- A chronic physical problem for which no physical cause can be determined
- A fear or phobia that prevents you from engaging in everyday activities
- Feelings that other people are out to get you or are talking about and plotting against you
- Inability to interact effectively with others, preventing the development of friendships and loving relationships

This list offers a rough set of guidelines for determining when the normal problems of everyday living have escalated beyond your ability to deal with them by yourself. In such situations, the *least* reasonable approach would be to pore over the psychological disorders we have discussed in an attempt at self-diagnosis. A more reasonable strategy is to consider seeking professional help.

RECAP/EVALUATE/RETHINK

RECAP

LO 39-1 How prevalent are psychological disorders?

- About half the people in the United States are likely to experience a psychological disorder at some point in their lives; 30% experience a disorder in any specific year.

LO 39-2 What indicators signal a need for the help of a mental health practitioner?

- The signals that indicate a need for professional help include long-term feelings of psychological distress, feelings of inability to cope with stress, withdrawal from other people, thoughts of inflicting harm on oneself or suicide, prolonged feelings of hopelessness, chronic physical problems with no apparent causes, phobias and compulsions, paranoia, and an inability to interact with others.

EVALUATE

1. The latest version of DSM is considered to be the definitive guide to defining psychological disorders. True or false?

2. Match the disorder with the culture in which it is most common:

1. amok	**a.** India
2. anorexia nervosa	**b.** Malaysia
3. brain fag	**c.** United States
4. catatonic schizophrenia	**d.** West Africa

RETHINK

1. Why is inclusion in the DSM-5 of disorders such as hoarding behavior so controversial and political? What disadvantages does inclusion bring? Does inclusion bring any benefits?

2. What societal changes would have to occur for psychological disorders to be regarded as the equivalent of appendicitis or another treatable physical disorder? Do you think a person who has been treated for a psychological disorder could become president of the United States? Should such a person become president?

Answers to Evaluate Questions

1. false; the development of the latest version of DSM was a source of great controversy, in part reflecting issues that divide society; **2.** 1-b, 2-c, 3-d, 4-a

Looking Back

Epilogue

We've discussed some of the many types of psychological disorders to which people are prone, noted the difficulty psychologists and physicians have in clearly differentiating normal from abnormal behavior, and looked at some of the approaches mental health professionals have taken to explain and treat psychological disorders. We considered today's most commonly used classification scheme, categorized in the DSM-5, and examined some of the more prevalent forms of psychological disorders. To gain a perspective on the topic of psychological disorders, we discussed the surprisingly broad incidence of psychological disorders in U.S. society and the cultural nature of such disorders.

Turn back to the prologue that described the case of Chris Coles. Using the knowledge you've gained about psychological disorders, consider the following questions.

1. Coles was diagnosed as suffering from schizophrenia. What elements of his behavior seem to fit the description of this disorder?
2. How might each of the perspectives on psychological disorders address the causes of his symptoms?
3. Which perspective provides the most useful explanation for Coles' case, in your opinion, and why?
4. What advantages might there be in using multiple perspectives to address Coles' case?

VISUAL SUMMARY 12 Psychological Disorders

MODULE 37 Normal Versus Abnormal: Making the Distinction

Defining Abnormality

- Deviation from the average
- Deviation from the ideal
- Sense of personal discomfort
- Inability to function effectively
- Legal concept

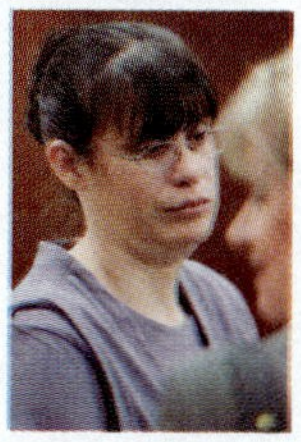

Perspectives on Abnormality

Perspectives on Psychological Disorders

Perspective	Description	Possible Application of Perspective to Chris' Case
Medical	Assumes that physiological causes are at the root of psychological disorders	Examine Chris for medical problems, such as brain tumor, chemical imbalance in the brain, or disease
Psychoanalytic	Argues that psychological disorders stem from childhood confl icts	Seek out information about Chris' past, considering possible childhood conflicts
Behavioral	Assumes that abnormal behaviors are learned responses	Concentrate on rewards and punishments for Chris' behavior, and identify environmental stimuli that reinforce his behavior
Cognitive	Assumes that cognitions (people's thoughts and beliefs) are central to psychological disorders	Focus on Chris' perceptions of self and his environment
Humanistic	Emphasizes people's responsibility for their own behavior and the need to self-actualize	Consider Chris' behavior in terms of his choices and efforts to reach his potential
Sociocultural	Assumes that behavior is shaped by family, society, and culture	Focus on how societal demands contributed to Chris' disorder

Classifying Abnormal Behavior: DSM-5 attempts to provide comprehensive and relatively precise definitions for more than 200 disorders

MODULE 38 Major Psychological Disorders

Anxiety Disorders: Anxiety without external justification

- Phobic disorder
- Panic disorder

- Generalized anxiety disorder
- Causes of anxiety disorders

Obsessive-compulsive Disorder

Somatic Symptom Disorders: Psychological difficulties that take on a physical form with no medical cause

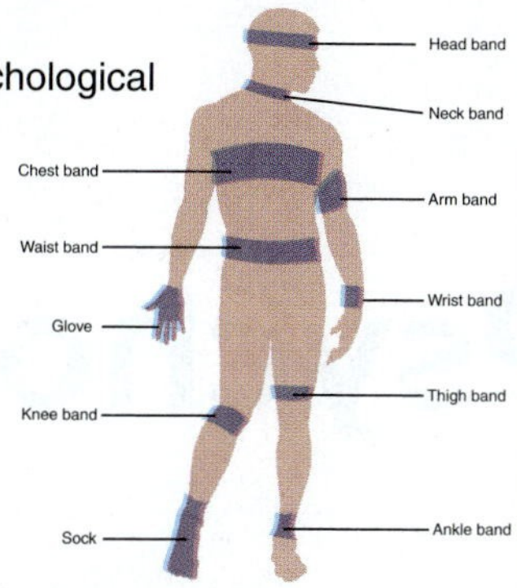

Dissociative Disorders: Separation of different facets of a person's personality that normally work together

Mood Disorders: Disturbances in emotional experience

- Major depressive disorder
- Mania and bipolar disorder
- Causes of mood disorders
  - Genetics
  - Psychological: feelings of loss or anger
  - Behavioral: stress
  - Cognitive: learned helplessness and no hope

Schizophrenia Spectrum: A class of disorders in which distortion of reality occurs

- Decline from a previous level of functioning
- Disturbances of thought and language
- Delusions
- Hallucinations and perceptual disorders
- Emotional disturbances

Personality Disorders: A set of inflexible, maladaptive behavior patterns

- Antisocial personality disorder
- Borderline personality disorder
- Narcissistic personality disorder

Childhood Disorders: Start during childhood or adolescence

- Attention-deficit hyperactivity disorder
- Autism spectrum disorder

MODULE 39 Psychological Disorders in Perspective

Social and Cultural Context: Our understanding of abnormal behavior reflects the society and culture in which we live

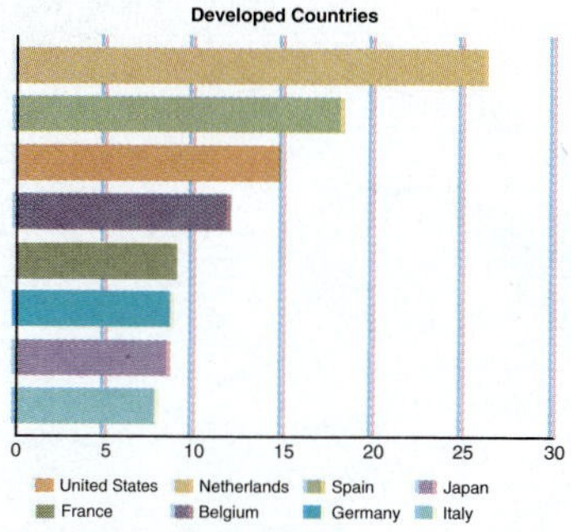

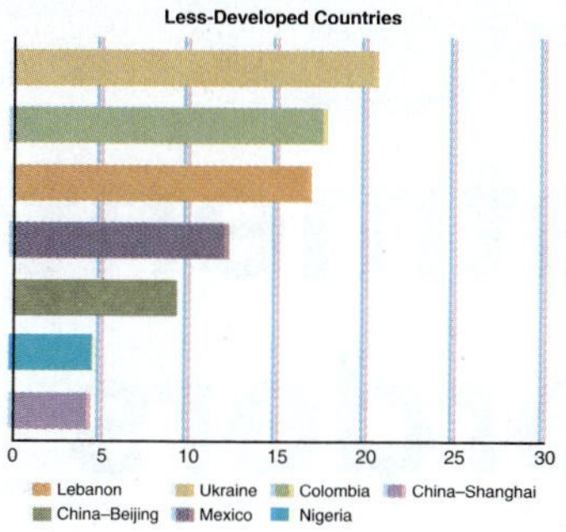

13 Treatment of Psychological Disorders

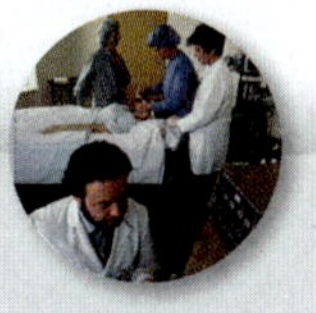

Learning Outcomes for Chapter 13

MODULE 40

LO 40-1 What are the goals of psychologically based and biologically based treatment approaches?

LO 40-2 What are the psychodynamic, behavioral, and cognitive approaches to treatment?

Psychotherapy: Psychodynamic, Behavioral, and Cognitive Approaches to Treatment

Psychodynamic Approaches to Therapy

Behavioral Approaches to Therapy

Cognitive Approaches to Therapy

Neuroscience in Your Life: How Cognitive Behavioral Therapy Changes Your Brain

MODULE 41

LO 41-1 What are the humanistic approaches to treatment?

LO 41-2 What is interpersonal therapy?

LO 41-3 How does group therapy differ from individual types of therapy?

LO 41-4 How effective is psychotherapy, and which kind of psychotherapy works best in a given situation?

Psychotherapy: Humanistic, Interpersonal, and Group Approaches to Treatment

Humanistic Therapy

Interpersonal Therapy

Applying Psychology in the 21st Century: High-Tech Therapy

Group Therapies

Evaluating Psychotherapy: Does Therapy Work?

Exploring Diversity: Racial and Ethnic Factors in Treatment: Should Therapists Be Color Blind?

MODULE 42

LO 42-1 How are drug, electroconvulsive, and psychosurgical techniques used today in the treatment of psychological disorders?

Biomedical Therapy: Biological Approaches to Treatment

Drug Therapy

Electroconvulsive Therapy (ECT)

Psychosurgery

Biomedical Therapies in Perspective

Community Psychology: Focus on Prevention

Becoming an Informed Consumer of Psychology: Choosing the Right Therapist

Prologue *Moving in the Right Direction*

Marisol Rodriguez had seen several therapists for help with her social anxiety. Some of them were more helpful than others; still, Marisol wasn't seeing the kind of improvement she had hoped for. But she believed it was just a matter of finding the right match. "The therapist I'm seeing now has me write down what I was thinking in situations where I had to interact with others, like in group discussions in class. She's helping me to see how negative my self-talk is, like when I would go over and over in my mind every little social mistake I made and just beat myself up because of them. That helped. I was just making it worse, you know? So I do whatever I have to do to stop it, even if that means getting up and forcing myself to do something distracting. When those negative thoughts come, I just tell myself 'Stop,' and I go do something else.

"You know what? It seems to be working!" said Marisol. "I'm actually beginning to feel more relaxed in social situations."

Looking Ahead

The kind of therapy that Marisol Rodriguez was receiving is one of the dozens of methods that therapists use to assist people suffering from psychological pain. Although treatment can range from one-meeting informal counseling sessions to long-term drug therapy, all the approaches have a common objective: the relief of psychological disorders with the ultimate aim of enabling individuals to achieve richer, more meaningful, and more fulfilling lives.

Despite their diversity, approaches to treating psychological disorders fall into two main categories: psychologically based and biologically based therapies. Psychologically based therapy, or **psychotherapy,** is treatment in which a trained professional—a therapist—uses psychological techniques to help someone overcome psychological difficulties and disorders, resolve problems in living, or bring about personal growth. In psychotherapy, the goal is to produce psychological change in a person (called a "client" or "patient") through discussions and interactions with the therapist. In contrast, **biomedical therapy** relies on drugs and medical procedures to improve psychological functioning.

As we describe the various approaches to therapy, keep in mind that although the distinctions may seem clear cut, the classifications and procedures overlap a good deal. In fact, many therapists today take an *eclectic approach* to therapy, which means they use a variety of methods with an individual patient. Assuming that both psychological and biological processes often produce psychological disorders, eclectic therapists may draw from several perspectives simultaneously to address both the psychological and the biological aspects of a person's problems.

psychotherapy Treatment in which a trained professional—a therapist—uses psychological techniques to help a person overcome psychological difficulties and disorders, resolve problems in living, or bring about personal growth.

biomedical therapy Therapy that relies on drugs and other medical procedures to improve psychological functioning.

MODULE 40

Psychotherapy: Psychodynamic, Behavioral, and Cognitive Approaches to Treatment

Learning Outcomes

LO 40-1 What are the goals of psychologically based and biologically based treatment approaches?

LO 40-2 What are the psychodynamic, behavioral, and cognitive approaches to treatment?

There are about 400 varieties of psychotherapy. Although the methods are diverse, all psychological approaches have a common perspective: They seek to solve psychological problems by modifying people's behavior and helping them obtain a better understanding of themselves and their past, present, and future.

In light of the variety of psychological approaches, it is not surprising that the people who provide therapy vary considerably in educational background and training (see Figure 1). Many have doctoral degrees in psychology, having attended graduate school, learned clinical and research techniques, and held an internship in a facility that treats people with psychological disorders. But therapy is also provided by people in fields allied with psychology, such as psychiatrists (who have a medical degree with a specialization in psychological disorders) and social workers (with a master's degree and who have specialized in psychological disorders).

The nature of the problem a person is experiencing often makes one type of therapist more appropriate than others, as Marisol Rodriguez in the chapter prologue realized. For example, a person who is suffering from a severe disturbance and who has lost touch with reality may typically require some sort of biologically based drug

Getting Help from the Right Person

Clinical Psychologists
Psychologists with a Ph.D. or Psy.D. with about five years of training and who have also completed a postgraduate internship. They specialize in assessment and treatment of psychological difficulties, providing psychotherapy and, in some U.S. states, can prescribe drugs.

Counseling Psychologists
Psychologists with a Ph.D. or Ed.D. who typically treat day-to-day adjustment problems, often in a university mental health clinic.

Psychiatrists
M.D.s with postgraduate training in psychological disorders. Because they can prescribe medication, they often treat the most severe disorders.

Psychoanalysts
Either M.D.s or psychologists who specialize in psychoanalysis, the treatment technique first developed by Freud.

Licensed Professional Counselors or Clinical Mental Health Counselors
Professionals with a master's degree who provide therapy to individuals, couples, and families and who hold a national or state certification.

Clinical or Psychiatric Social Workers
Professionals with a master's degree and specialized training who may provide therapy, usually regarding common family and personal problems.

FIGURE 1 A variety of professionals provide therapy and counseling. Each could be expected to give helpful advice and direction. However, the nature of the problem a person is experiencing may make one or another therapy more appropriate.

therapy. In that case, a psychiatrist—who is a physician—would be the professional of choice. In contrast, those suffering from milder disorders, such as difficulty adjusting to the death of a family member, have a broader choice that might include other types of professionals listed in Figure 1.

Regardless of their specific training, all psychotherapists employ one of four major approaches to therapy that we'll consider next: psychodynamic, behavioral, cognitive, and humanistic treatments. These approaches are based on the models of personality and psychological disorders developed by psychologists.

Psychodynamic Approaches to Therapy

psychodynamic therapy Therapy that seeks to bring unresolved past conflicts and unacceptable impulses from the unconscious into the conscious, where patients may deal with the problems more effectively.

Psychodynamic therapy seeks to bring unresolved past conflicts and unacceptable impulses from the unconscious into the conscious, where patients may deal with the problems more effectively. Psychodynamic approaches are based on Freud's psychoanalytic approach to personality, which holds that individuals employ *defense mechanisms*, psychological strategies to protect themselves from unacceptable unconscious impulses.

The most common defense mechanism is *repression*, which pushes threatening and unpleasant thoughts and impulses back into the unconscious. However, because people cannot completely bury their unacceptable thoughts and impulses, anxiety associated with them can produce abnormal behavior. How do we rid ourselves of the anxiety produced by unconscious, unwanted thoughts and impulses? To Freud, the answer was to confront the conflicts and impulses by bringing them out of the unconscious part of the mind and into the conscious part. Freud assumed that this technique would reduce anxiety stemming from past conflicts and that the patient could then participate in his or her daily life more effectively.

A psychodynamic therapist, then, faces the challenge of finding a way to assist patients' attempts to explore and understand the unconscious. The technique that has evolved has a number of components, but basically it consists of guiding patients to consider and discuss their past experiences in explicit detail from the time of their first memories. This process assumes that patients will eventually stumble upon long-hidden crises, traumas, and conflicts that are producing anxiety in their adult lives. They will then be able to "work through"—understand and rectify—those difficulties.

PSYCHOANALYSIS: FREUD'S THERAPY

psychoanalysis Freud's psychotherapy in which the goal is to release hidden thoughts and feelings from the unconscious part of our minds in order to reduce their power in controlling behavior.

Freudian psychodynamic therapy, called **psychoanalysis,** tends to be a lengthy and expensive affair. Psychoanalysis is Freud's psychotherapy in which the goal is to release hidden thoughts and feelings from the unconscious part of our mind in order to reduce their power in controlling behavior.

Study Alert
To better understand how psychodynamic therapy works, review Freud's psychoanalytic theory discussed in the chapter on personality.

In psychoanalysis, patients may meet with a therapist with considerable frequency, sometimes as much as 50 minutes a day, 4 to 5 days a week, for several years. In their sessions, they often use a technique developed by Freud called *free association*. Psychoanalysts using this technique tell patients to say aloud whatever comes to mind, regardless of its apparent irrelevance or senselessness, and the analysts attempt to recognize and label the connections between what a patient says and the patient's unconscious. Therapists also use *dream interpretation*, examining dreams to find clues to unconscious conflicts and problems. Moving beyond the surface description of a dream (called the *manifest content*), therapists seek its underlying meaning (the *latent content*), which thereby reveals the true unconscious meaning of the dream (Bodin, 2006; Blum, 2011; Hill et al., 2013).

The processes of free association and dream interpretation do not always move forward easily. The same unconscious forces that initially produced repression may keep past difficulties out of the conscious mind, which produces resistance. *Resistance* is an inability or unwillingness to discuss or reveal particular memories, thoughts, or motivations. Patients can express resistance in many ways. For instance, they may be discussing a childhood memory and suddenly forget what they were saying, or they may abruptly change the subject completely. It is the therapist's job to pick up instances of resistance and interpret their meaning as well as to ensure that patients return to the subject–which is likely to hold difficult or painful memories for the patients.

Because of the close, almost intimate interaction between patient and psychoanalyst, the relationship between the two often becomes emotionally charged and takes on a complexity unlike most other relationships. Patients may eventually think of the analyst as a symbol of a significant other in their past, perhaps a parent or a lover, and apply some of their feelings for that person to the analyst–a phenomenon known as transference. **Transference** is the transfer of feelings to a psychoanalyst of love or anger that had been originally directed to a patient's parents or other authority figures (Evans, 2007; Steiner, 2008; Høglend et al., 2011).

The close and intense relationship between therapist and patient may become highly complex.

transference The transfer of feelings to a psychoanalyst of love or anger that had been originally directed to a patient's parents or other authority figures.

A therapist can use transference to help a patient recreate past relationships that were psychologically difficult. For instance, if a patient undergoing transference views her therapist as a symbol of her father–with whom she had a difficult relationship–the patient and therapist may "redo" an earlier interaction, this time including more positive aspects. Through this process, the patient may resolve conflicts regarding her real father–something that is beginning to happen in the following therapy session:

Sandy: My father . . . never took any interest in any of us. . . . It was my mother–rest her soul–who loved us, not our father. He worked her to death. Lord, I miss her. . . . I must sound angry at my father. Don't you think I have a right to be angry?
Therapist: Do you think you have a right to be angry?
Sandy: Of course, I do! Why are you questioning me? You don't believe me, do you?
Therapist: You want me to believe you.
Sandy: I don't care whether you believe me or not. . . . I know what you're thinking–you think I'm crazy–you must be laughing at me–I'll probably be a case in your next book! You're just sitting there–smirking–making me feel like a bad person–thinking I'm wrong for being mad, that I have no right to be mad.
Therapist: Just like your father.
Sandy: Yes, you're just like my father.–Oh my God! Just now–I–I–thought I was talking to him. (Sue, Sue, & Sue, 1990, pp. 514–515)

CONTEMPORARY PSYCHODYNAMIC APPROACHES

Few people have the time, money, or patience to participate in years of traditional psychoanalysis. Moreover, no conclusive evidence shows that psychoanalysis, as originally conceived by Freud in the 19th century, works better than other, more recent forms of psychodynamic therapy.

Today, psychodynamic therapy tends to be of shorter duration, usually lasting no longer than 3 months or 20 sessions. The therapist takes a more active role than Freud would have liked by actively controlling the course of therapy and prodding and advising the patient with considerable directness. Finally, contemporary psychodynamic therapists put less emphasis on a patient's past history and childhood and concentrate instead on an individual's current relationships and specific complaints (Charman, 2004; Wolitzky, 2006; Brafman, 2011).

"And when did you first realize you weren't like other precipitation?"

EVALUATING PSYCHODYNAMIC THERAPY

Even with its current modifications, psychodynamic therapy has its critics. In its longer versions, it can be time consuming and expensive, especially in comparison with other forms of psychotherapy, such as behavioral and cognitive approaches. Furthermore, less articulate patients may not do as well as more articulate ones.

Ultimately, the most important concern about psychodynamic treatment is whether it actually works, and there is no simple answer to this question. Psychodynamic treatment techniques have been controversial since Freud introduced them. Part of the problem is the difficulty in establishing whether patients have improved after psychodynamic therapy. Determining effectiveness depends on reports from the therapist or the patients themselves–reports that are obviously open to bias and subjective interpretation.

Furthermore, critics have questioned the entire theoretical basis of psychodynamic theory; they maintain that constructs such as the unconscious have not been scientifically confirmed. Despite the criticism, though, the psychodynamic treatment approach has remained viable. For some people, it provides solutions to difficult psychological issues, provides effective treatment for psychological disturbance, and also permits the potential development of an unusual degree of insight into one's life (Bond, 2006; Anestis, Anestis, & Lilienfeld, 2011; Thase, 2013).

Behavioral Approaches to Therapy

Perhaps, when you were a child, your parents rewarded you with an ice cream cone when you were especially good . . . or sent you to your room if you misbehaved. Sound principles back up such a child-rearing strategy: Good behavior is maintained by reinforcement, and unwanted behavior can be eliminated by punishment.

behavioral treatment approaches
Treatment approaches that make use of the basic processes of learning, such as reinforcement and extinction, to reduce or eliminate maladaptive behavior.

These principles represent the basic underpinnings of behavioral treatment approaches. **Behavioral treatment approaches** build on the basic processes of learning, such as reinforcement and extinction, to reduce or eliminate maladaptive behavior. These approaches use this fundamental assumption: Both abnormal behavior and normal behavior are *learned*. People who act abnormally either have failed to learn the skills they need to cope with the problems of everyday living or have acquired faulty skills and patterns that are being maintained through some form of reinforcement. To modify abnormal behavior, then, proponents of behavioral approaches propose that people must learn new behavior to replace the faulty skills they have developed and unlearn their maladaptive behavior patterns (Krijn et al., 2004; Norton & Price, 2007; Kowalik et al., 2011).

Behavioral approaches to treatment would seek to modify the behavior of this couple rather than to focus on the underlying causes of the behavior.

Behavioral psychologists do not need to delve into people's pasts or their psyches. Rather than viewing abnormal behavior as a symptom of an underlying problem, they consider the abnormal behavior as the problem in need of modification. The goal of therapy is to change people's behavior to allow them to function more effectively. In this view, then, there is no problem other than the maladaptive behavior itself; if you can change that behavior, treatment is successful.

CLASSICAL CONDITIONING TREATMENTS

Suppose you bite into your favorite candy bar and find that not only is it infested with ants, but you've also swallowed a bunch of them. You immediately become sick to your stomach and throw up. Your long-term reaction? You never eat that kind of candy bar again, and it may be months before you eat any type of candy. You have learned through the basic process of classical conditioning to avoid candy so that you will not get sick and throw up.

Aversive Conditioning. This simple example illustrates how a person can be classically conditioned to modify behavior. Behavior therapists use this principle when they employ **aversive conditioning,** a form of therapy that reduces the frequency of undesired behavior by pairing an aversive, unpleasant stimulus with undesired behavior. For example, behavior therapists might use aversive conditioning by pairing alcohol with a drug that causes severe nausea and vomiting. After the two have been paired a few times, the person associates the alcohol alone with vomiting and finds alcohol less appealing.

aversive conditioning A form of therapy that reduces the frequency of undesired behavior by pairing an aversive, unpleasant stimulus with undesired behavior.

Aversion therapy works reasonably well in inhibiting substance-abuse problems such as alcoholism and with certain kinds of sexual disorders. Critics, however, question its long-term effectiveness. Also, important ethical concerns surround aversion techniques that employ such potent stimuli as electric shock, which therapists use only in the most extreme cases, such as patient self-mutilation. Clearly, though, aversion therapy offers an important procedure for eliminating maladaptive responses for some period of time—a respite that provides, even if only temporarily, an opportunity to encourage more adaptive behavior patterns (Delgado, Labouliere, & Phelps, 2006; Pautassi et al., 2011).

Systematic Desensitization. Another treatment that grew out of the classical conditioning is systematic desensitization. **Systematic desensitization** is a behavioral technique in which exposure to an anxiety-producing stimulus is paired with deep relaxation to extinguish the response of anxiety. The idea is to learn to associate relaxation with a stimulus that previously produced anxiety (Choy, Fyer, & Lipsitz, 2007; Dowling, Jackson, & Thomas, 2008; Triscari et al., 2011).

systematic desensitization A behavioral technique based on classical conditioning in which exposure to an anxiety-producing stimulus is paired with deep relaxation to extinguish the response of anxiety.

Suppose, for instance, you were extremely afraid of flying. The very thought of being in an airplane would make you begin to sweat and shake, and you couldn't get yourself near enough to an airport to know how you'd react if you actually had to fly somewhere. Using systematic desensitization to treat your problem, you would first be trained in relaxation techniques by a behavior therapist and learn to relax your body fully—a highly pleasant state, as you might imagine (see Figure 2).

To achieve a state of relaxation, follow these steps once or twice a day.

Step 1. Choose a word or phrase that you can repeat to achieve calm. This might be a yoga mantra (*Om* or *Om Mani Padme Hum*, for instance), a word like *Peace* or *Shalom*, or any word or phrase that sounds soft and resonant to you (such as *Peace to my heart*).

Step 2. Find a quiet and comfortable place and sit down.

Step 3. Close your eyes and try to see and feel the darkness.

Step 4. Relax your muscles one by one, starting from your toes and moving slowly up to your scalp.

Step 5. Keep your breathing steady and natural, neither deep nor shallow, and repeat your word or phrase continuously.

Step 6. Do not monitor yourself, but become passive and accepting. If outside thoughts arrive, dismiss them lightly with a smile and return to your repeated word or phrase.

Step 7. Keep this up for 15 minutes. Do not set an alarm; just open your eyes when you feel it is right. If you fall asleep, that is fine.

Step 8. When you have finished, sit quietly, eyes closed, for a minute or two, then stand up.

FIGURE 2 Following these basic steps will help you achieve a sense of calmness by employing the relaxation response. (Source: Adapted from Bensen.)

The next step would involve constructing a *hierarchy of fears*–a list in order of increasing severity of the things you associate with your fears. For instance, your hierarchy might resemble this one:

1. Watching a plane fly overhead
2. Going to an airport
3. Buying a ticket
4. Stepping into the plane
5. Seeing the plane door close
6. Having the plane taxi down the runway
7. Taking off
8. Being in the air

From the perspective of . . .

A Child-Care Provider How might you use systematic desensitization to help children overcome their fears?

Study Alert

To help remember the concept of hierarchy of fears, think of something that you are afraid of and construct your own hierarchy of fears.

Once you had developed this hierarchy and learned relaxation techniques, you would learn to associate the two sets of responses. To do this, your therapist might ask you to put yourself into a relaxed state and then imagine yourself in the first situation identified in your hierarchy. Once you could consider that first step while remaining relaxed, you would move on to the next situation. Eventually you would move up the hierarchy in gradual stages until you could imagine yourself being in the air without experiencing anxiety. Ultimately, you would be asked to make a visit to an airport and later to take a flight.

flooding A behavioral treatment for anxiety in which people are suddenly confronted with a stimulus that they fear.

Flooding Treatments. Although systematic desensitization has proven to be a successful treatment, today it is often replaced with a less-complicated form of therapy called flooding. **Flooding** is a behavioral treatment for anxiety in which people are suddenly confronted with a stimulus that they fear. However, unlike systematic desensitization, relaxation training is not included. The goal behind flooding is to allow the maladaptive response of anxiety or avoidance to become extinct (Havermans et al., 2007; Hofmann, 2007; Bush, 2008).

For example, a patient who has a deep fear of germs may be made to soil her hands in dirt and to keep them dirty for hours. For a person with a fear of germs, initially this is a highly anxiety-producing situation. After a few hours, however, the anxiety will decline, leading to extinction of the anxiety.

Flooding has proved to be an effective treatment for a number of problems, including phobias, anxiety disorders, and even impotence and fear of sexual contact. Through this technique, people can learn to enjoy the things they once feared (Franklin, March, & Garcia, 2007; Powers & Emmelkamp, 2008; Tuerk et al., 2011).

OPERANT CONDITIONING TECHNIQUES

Some behavioral approaches make use of the operant conditioning principles that we discussed in the chapter on learning. These approaches are based on the notion that we should reward people for carrying out desirable behavior and extinguish undesirable behavior by either ignoring it or punishing it.

One example of the systematic application of operant conditioning principles is the *token system,* which rewards a person for desired behavior with a token such as a poker chip or some kind of play money that can later be exchanged for an actual reward, such as real money or for the purchase of food. It is most frequently employed in institutional settings for individuals with relatively serious problems and sometimes with children as a classroom management technique. The system resembles what parents do when they give children money for being well behaved–money that the children can later exchange for something they want. The desired behavior may range from simple things such as keeping one's room neat to personal grooming and interacting with other people. In institutions, patients can exchange tokens for some object or activity, such as snacks, new clothes, or, in extreme cases, sleeping in one's own bed rather than in a sleeping bag on the floor.

A "Fearless Peer" who models appropriate and effective behavior can help children overcome their fears.

Contingency contracting, a variant of the token system, has proved quite effective in producing behavior modification. In *contingency contracting,* the therapist and client (or teacher and student or parent and child) write a written agreement, known as a contract. The contract states a series of behavioral goals the client hopes to achieve. It also specifies the positive consequences for the client if the client reaches goals–usually an explicit reward such as money or additional privileges. Contracts frequently state negative consequences if the client does not meet the goals. For example, clients who are trying to quit smoking might write out a check to a cause they have no interest in supporting (for instance, the National Rifle Association if they are strong supporters of gun control). If the client smokes on a given day, the therapist will mail the check.

Behavior therapists also use *observational learning,* the process in which the behavior of other people is copied, to systematically teach people new skills and ways of handling their fears and anxieties. For example, observational learning occurs when therapists teach basic social skills, such as maintaining eye contact during conversation and acting assertively. Similarly, children with dog phobias have been able to overcome their fears by watching another child–called the "Fearless Peer"–repeatedly walk up to a dog, touch it, pet it, and finally play with it. Observational learning, then, can play an effective role in resolving some kinds of behavior difficulties, especially if the person being observed receives a reward for his or her behavior (Bandura, Grusec, & Menlove, 1967; Egliston & Rapee, 2007; Helsen, Goubert, & Vlaeyen, 2013).

EVALUATING BEHAVIOR THERAPY

Behavior therapy works especially well for eliminating anxiety disorders, treating phobias and compulsions, establishing control over impulses, and learning complex social skills to replace maladaptive behavior. More than any of the other therapeutic techniques, it provides methods that nonprofessionals can use to change their own behavior. Moreover, it is efficient because it focuses on solving carefully defined problems (Richard & Lauterbach, 2006; Barlow, 2007).

Critics of behavior therapy believe that because it emphasizes changing external behavior, people do not necessarily gain insight into thoughts and expectations that may be fostering their maladaptive behavior. On the other hand, neuroscientific evidence shows that behavioral treatments can produce actual changes in brain functioning, which suggests that behavioral treatments can produce changes beyond external behavior.

For example, one experiment looked at the neurological reactions of patients with borderline personality disorder who participated in a 12-week behavioral therapy program. Compared with a control group composed of people who did not have the disorder, the patients showed significant changes in their reactions to highly arousing emotion-evoking stimuli. Following therapy, the patients' neurological functioning was more similar to those without the disorder than it was prior to therapy (Schnell & Herpertz, 2007).

Cognitive Approaches to Therapy

If you assumed that illogical thoughts and beliefs lie at the heart of psychological disorders, wouldn't the most direct treatment route be to teach people new, more adaptive modes of thinking? The answer is yes, according to psychologists who take a cognitive approach to treatment.

cognitive treatment approaches Treatment approaches that teach people to think in more adaptive ways by changing their dysfunctional cognitions about the world and themselves.

cognitive-behavioral approach A treatment approach that incorporates basic principles of learning to change the way people think.

Cognitive treatment approaches teach people to think in more adaptive ways by changing their dysfunctional cognitions about the world and themselves. In contrast to behavior therapists, who primarily focus on modifying external behavior, cognitive therapists focus on changing the way people think. Because they often use basic principles of learning, the methods they employ are sometimes referred to as the **cognitive-behavioral approach** (Beck & Rector, 2005; Friedberg, 2006; Kalodner, 2011).

Although cognitive treatment approaches take many forms, they all share the assumption that anxiety, depression, and negative emotions develop from maladaptive thinking. Accordingly, cognitive treatments seek to change the thought patterns that lead to getting "stuck" in dysfunctional ways of thinking. Therapists systematically teach clients to challenge their assumptions and adopt new approaches to old problems.

Cognitive therapy is relatively short term and usually lasts a maximum of 20 sessions. Therapy tends to be highly structured and focused on concrete problems. Therapists often begin by teaching the theory behind the approach and then continue to take an active role throughout the course of therapy by acting as a combination of teacher, coach, and partner.

rational-emotive behavior therapy A form of therapy that attempts to restructure a person's belief system into a more realistic, rational, and logical set of views by challenging dysfunctional beliefs that maintain irrational behavior.

One good example of cognitive treatment, **rational-emotive behavior therapy,** attempts to restructure a person's belief system into a more realistic, rational, and logical set of views. According to psychologist Albert Ellis (2002, 2004), many people lead unhappy lives and suffer from psychological disorders because they harbor irrational, unrealistic ideas such as these:

- We need the love or approval of virtually every significant other person for everything we do.
- We should be thoroughly competent, adequate, and successful in all possible respects in order to consider ourselves worthwhile.
- It is horrible when things don't turn out the way we want them to.

Such irrational beliefs trigger negative emotions, which in turn support the irrational beliefs and lead to a self-defeating cycle. Ellis calls it the A-B-C model in which negative activating conditions (A) lead to the activation of an irrational belief system (B), which in turn leads to emotional consequences (C). For example, if a person experiences the breakup of a close relationship (A) and holds the irrational belief (B) that "I'll never be loved again," this triggers negative emotions (C) that in turn feed back into support of the irrational belief (see Figure 3).

The goal of rational-emotive therapy is to help clients eliminate maladaptive thoughts and beliefs and adopt more effective thinking. To accomplish this goal, therapists take an active, directive role during therapy and openly challenge patterns of thought that appear to be dysfunctional. Consider this example:

> Martha: The basic problem is that I'm worried about my family. I'm worried about money. And I never seem to be able to relax.
>
> Therapist: Why are you worried about your family? . . . What's to be concerned about? They have certain demands which you don't want to adhere to.
>
> Martha: I was brought up to think that I mustn't be selfish.
>
> Therapist: Oh, we'll have to knock that out of your head!
>
> Martha: My mother feels that I shouldn't have left home—that my place is with them. There are nagging doubts about what I should—

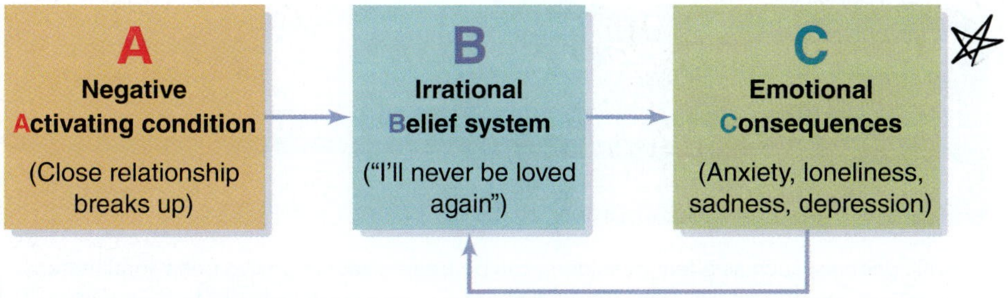

FIGURE 3 In the A-B-C model of rational-emotive behavior therapy, negative activating conditions (A) lead to the activation of an irrational belief system (B), which leads to emotional consequences (C). Those emotional consequences then feed back and support the belief system. At what steps in the model could change occur as a result of rational-emotive behavior therapy?

Therapist: Why are there doubts? Why should you?

Martha: I think it's a feeling I was brought up with that you always have to give of yourself. If you think of yourself, you're wrong.

Therapist: That's a belief. Why do you have to keep believing that—at your age? You believed a lot of superstitions when you were younger. Why do you have to retain them? Your parents indoctrinated you with this nonsense, because that's their belief. . . . Who needs that philosophy? All it's gotten you, so far, is guilt. (Ellis, 1974, pp. 223–286)

By poking holes in Martha's reasoning, the therapist is attempting to help her adopt a more realistic view of herself and her circumstances (Ellis, 2002; Dryden & David, 2008).

Another influential form of therapy that builds on a cognitive perspective is that of Aaron Beck (Beck, 1995, 2004). Like rational-emotive behavior therapy, Beck's cognitive behavior therapy aims to change people's illogical thoughts about themselves and the world.

However, cognitive behavior therapy is considerably less confrontational and challenging than rational-emotive behavior therapy. Instead of the therapist actively arguing with clients about their dysfunctional cognitions, cognitive behavior therapists more often play the role of teacher. Therapists urge clients to obtain information on their own that will lead them to discard their inaccurate thinking through a process of cognitive appraisal. In *cognitive appraisal,* clients are asked to evaluate situations, themselves, and others in terms of their memories, values, beliefs, thoughts, and expectations. During the course of treatment, therapists help clients discover ways of thinking more appropriately about themselves and others (Beck, Freeman, & Davis, 2004; Moorey, 2007; Leaper, Brown, & Ayres, 2013; also see *Neuroscience in Your Life*).

EVALUATING COGNITIVE APPROACHES TO THERAPY

Cognitive approaches to therapy have proved successful in dealing with a broad range of disorders, including anxiety disorders, depression, substance abuse, and eating disorders. Furthermore, the willingness of cognitive therapists to incorporate additional treatment approaches (e.g., combining cognitive and behavioral techniques in cognitive behavior therapy) has made this approach a particularly effective form of treatment (Mitte, 2005; Ishikawa et al., 2007; Bhar et al., 2008).

At the same time, critics have pointed out that the focus on helping people to think more rationally ignores the fact that life is in reality sometimes irrational. Changing one's assumptions to make them more reasonable and logical thus may not always be helpful—even assuming it is possible to bring about true cognitive change. Still, the success of cognitive approaches has made it one of the most frequently employed therapies (Beck & Rector, 2005; Fresco, 2013).

PsychTech

Psychologist David Mohr found that an Internet-based treatment for depression in which patients logged into a website and also received e-mail and telephone support was effective in reducing depressive episodes.

Neuroscience in Your Life: How Cognitive Behavioral Therapy Changes Your Brain

Specific phobias, such as a fear of spiders, can be treated with cognitive behavioral therapy (CBT) to help change how the brain responds when seeing fearful stimuli. As seen in these images, when people with a specific phobia of spiders see images of spiders (a) they respond differently than people without the phobia. Following CBT, however, they do not report feeling the fear, and their brains react like control participants without the disorder (b). These results clearly show the power of psychological therapy in making changes in how the brain responds. (Wright et al., 2013)

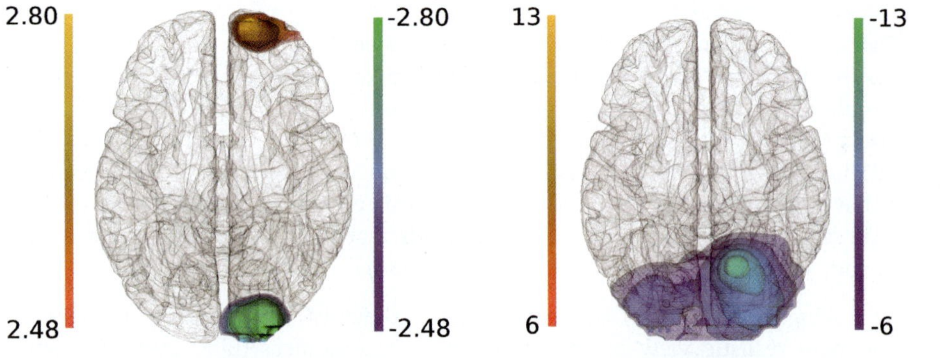

(a) (b)

RECAP/EVALUATE/RETHINK

RECAP

LO 40-1 What are the goals of psychologically based and biologically based treatment approaches?

- Psychotherapy (psychologically based therapy) and biomedical therapy (biologically based therapy) share the goal of resolving psychological problems by modifying people's thoughts, feelings, expectations, evaluations, and ultimately behavior.

LO 40-2 What are the psychodynamic, behavioral, and cognitive approaches to treatment?

- Psychoanalytic approaches seek to bring unresolved past conflicts and unacceptable impulses from the unconscious into the conscious, where patients may deal with the problems more effectively. To do this, therapists use techniques such as free association and dream interpretation.
- Behavioral approaches to treatment view abnormal behavior as the problem rather than viewing that behavior as a symptom of some underlying cause. To bring about a "cure," this view suggests that the outward behavior must be changed by using methods such as aversive conditioning, systematic desensitization, observational learning, token systems, and contingency contracting.
- Cognitive approaches to treatment consider that the goal of therapy is to help a person restructure his or her faulty belief system into a more realistic, rational, and logical view of the world. Two examples of cognitive treatments are the rational-emotive behavior therapy and cognitive behavior therapy.

EVALUATE

1. Match the following mental health practitioners with the appropriate description.

1. Psychiatrist	**a.** PhD specializing in the treatment of psychological disorders
2. Clinical psychologist	**b.** Professional specializing in Freudian therapy techniques
3. Counseling psychologist	**c.** MD trained in abnormal behavior
4. Psychoanalyst	**d.** PhD specializing in the adjustment of day-to-day problems

2. According to Freud, people use __________ __________ as a means of preventing unwanted impulses from intruding on conscious thought.
3. In dream interpretation, a psychoanalyst must learn to distinguish between the __________ content of a dream, which is what appears on the surface, and the __________ content, its underlying meaning.
4. Which of the following treatments deals with phobias by gradual exposure to the item producing the fear?
   - **a.** Systematic desensitization
   - **b.** Partial reinforcement
   - **c.** Behavioral self-management
   - **d.** Aversion therapy

RETHINK

1. In what ways are psychoanalysis and cognitive therapy similar, and how do they differ?
2. How might you examine the reliability of dream interpretation?

Answers to Evaluate Questions

1. 1-c, 2-a, 3-d, 4-b; **2.** defense mechanisms; **3.** manifest, latent; **4.** a

KEY TERMS

psychotherapy
biomedical therapy
psychodynamic therapy
psychoanalysis
transference
behavioral treatment approaches
aversive conditioning
systematic desensitization
flooding
cognitive treatment approaches
cognitive-behavioral approach
rational-emotive behavior therapy

Applying Psychology in the 21st Century

High-Tech Therapy

Advances in digital technologies have made profound social changes across many domains. And the practice of psychotherapy has also been affected, in ways that are beneficial as well as in ways that are problematic.

For one thing, the Web puts a great deal of information at people's fingertips, including information on the diagnosis and treatment of mental disorders. This can certainly be a good thing if it helps people to recognize that they need treatment and explore the approaches to treatment that are available, helping them find a therapist that they will like and trust. On the other hand, people who need the assistance of a professional therapist might avoid getting help if they mistakenly believe they have found sufficient self-help information online (Ellis et al., 2013).

Smartphone apps have the potential to be a real boon to therapy, given the strong tendency for users to keep their phones handy at all times. Patients can use apps to keep real-time journals of their thoughts, behaviors, moods, social interactions, anxieties–whatever their therapist directs them to record. Rather than rely on their memories to give retrospective accounts during a therapy session, patients can log events as they happen to provide a more thorough and objective account. Specialized apps can be used to prod patients to record their thoughts, feelings, and behaviors at random times throughout their day, documenting slices of the patient's day-to-day experiences.

Smartphones can be used to give information, as well as to collect it. For example, some therapies require "homework" to be done between therapy sessions. Patients can rely on apps to prod them to keep up with these tasks–or if they need regular structure and guidance to get through their day, they can use an app for that, too. Videoconferencing, group blogging, and online support groups are just a few new channels for delivering therapy that digital technologies have made possible (Barak & Grohol, 2011).

But technology can present problems, too. It can enable certain counterproductive behaviors that undermine the therapeutic process. For example, a patient with social anxiety who needs to practice real-life social interactions might avoid them by using social networking as a social outlet instead. Or patients who need to learn impulse control, or to compartmentalize their work stress, or to tolerate being alone, might have difficulty achieving such goals if they are not willing to unplug from their devices.

Finally, the ability patients have to cyber-stalk their therapists produces a new set of challenges. Most therapists believe they need to maintain a certain distance from patients in order to maintain authority and trust. Patients who indulge their curiosity might find it easy to dig up their therapist's published papers, letters to the editor, family photos, college blogs, and other information that has the potential to upset the patient or undermine the therapist's authority. Therapists need to be vigilant about their online presence for these reasons (Friedman, 2012).

One of the newest forms of therapy is delivered via mobile phone applications.

Digital technology is a double-edged sword; for some patients, it can be an invaluable therapeutic tool; for others, it can be a roadblock. Both patients and therapists need to be mindful of how they are using technology and whether it is helping or hurting.

RETHINK

- How seriously should therapists and patients take the potential pitfalls of digital technology?
- Do you think digital devices have more potential to be helpful or harmful?

than traditional psychodynamic approaches and typically lasts only 12–16 weeks. During those sessions, therapists make concrete suggestions on improving relations with others and offer recommendations and advice.

Because interpersonal therapy is short and structured, researchers have been able to demonstrate its effectiveness more readily than longer-term types of therapy. Evaluations of the approach have shown that interpersonal therapy is especially effective in dealing with depression, anxiety, addictions, and eating disorders (Grigoriadis & Ravitz, 2007; Miller et al., 2008; Bohn et al., 2013).

Group Therapies

Although most treatment takes place between a single individual and a therapist, some forms of therapy involve groups of people seeking treatment. In **group therapy,** several unrelated people meet with a therapist to discuss some aspect of their psychological functioning.

"So, would anyone in the group care to respond to what Clifford has just shared with us?"

People typically discuss with the group their problems, which often center on a common difficulty, such as alcoholism or a lack of social skills. The other members of the group provide emotional support and dispense advice on ways they have coped effectively with similar problems (Scaturo, 2004; Rigby & Waite, 2007; Schachter, 2011).

Groups vary greatly in terms of the particular model they employ; there are psychoanalytic groups, humanistic groups, and groups corresponding to the other therapeutic approaches. Furthermore, groups also differ with regard to the degree of guidance the therapist provides. In some, the therapist is quite directive; in others, the members of the group set their own agenda and determine how the group will proceed (Beck & Lewis, 2000; Stockton, Morran, & Krieger, 2004).

Because several people are treated simultaneously in group therapy, it is a much more economical means of treatment than individual psychotherapy. On the other hand, critics argue that group settings lack the individual attention inherent in one-to-one therapy and that especially shy and withdrawn individuals may not receive the attention they need in a group setting.

group therapy Therapy in which people meet in a group with a therapist to discuss problems.

FAMILY THERAPY

One specialized form of group therapy is family therapy. As the name implies, **family therapy** involves two or more family members, one (or more) of whose problems led to treatment. But rather than focusing simply on the members of the family who present the initial problem, family therapists consider the family as a unit to which each member contributes. By meeting with the entire family simultaneously, family therapists try to understand how the family members interact with one another (Cooklin, 2000; Strong & Tomm, 2007; Bischoff et al., 2011).

family therapy An approach that focuses on the family and its dynamics.

Family therapists view the family as a "system" and assume that individuals in the family cannot improve without understanding the conflicts found in interactions among family members. Thus, the therapist expects each member to contribute to the resolution of the problem being addressed.

Many family therapists believe that family members fall into rigid roles or set patterns of behavior with one person acting as the scapegoat, another as a bully, and so forth. In their view, that system of roles perpetuates family disturbances. One goal of this type of therapy, then, is to get the family members to adopt new, more constructive roles and patterns of behavior (Sprenkle & Moon, 1996; Minuchin, 1999; Sori, 2006).

In group therapy, people with psychological difficulties meet with a therapist to discuss their problems.

SELF-HELP THERAPY

In many cases, group therapy does not involve a professional therapist. Instead, people with similar problems get together to discuss their shared feelings and experiences. For example, people who have recently experienced the death of a spouse might meet in a *bereavement support group,* or college students may get together to discuss their adjustment to college.

One of the best-known self-help groups is Alcoholics Anonymous (AA), designed to help members deal with alcohol-related problems. AA prescribes 12 steps that alcoholics must pass through on their road to recovery. Alcoholics begin with an admission that they are alcoholics and powerless over alcohol and move through additional steps in the process of recovery by attending frequent AA meetings. Proponents of AA believe that no one is fully cured of alcoholism and that members should permanently think of themselves as recovering alcoholics (Greenfield & Tonigan, 2013).

Alcoholics Anonymous does not work for everyone. For one thing, there is a strong spiritual component and emphasis on the need for a higher power that does not appeal to some people. More important, some critics say that AA's requirement of total abstinence from alcohol may not be the most effective or realistic approach (Kelly, 2012).

Still, AA provides more treatment for alcoholics than any other therapy. Furthermore, research studies show that AA and other 12-step programs (such as Narcotics Anonymous) can be as successful in treating alcohol and other substance-abuse problems as traditional types of therapy (Galanter, 2007; Gossop, Stewart, & Marsden, 2008; Pagano et al., 2013).

Evaluating Psychotherapy: Does Therapy Work?

Your best friend, Ben, comes to you because he just hasn't been feeling right about things lately. He's upset because he and his girlfriend aren't getting along, but his difficulties go beyond that. He can't concentrate on his studies, has a lot of trouble getting to sleep, and—this is what really bothers him—has begun to think that people are ganging up on him, talking about him behind his back. It seems that no one really cares about or understands him or makes any effort to see why he's become so miserable.

Ben knows that he ought to get *some* kind of help, but he is not sure where to turn. He is fairly skeptical of psychologists and thinks that a lot of what they say is just mumbo-jumbo, but he's willing to put his doubts aside and try anything to feel better. He also knows there are many different types of therapy, and he doesn't have a clue about which would be best for him. He turns to you for advice because he knows you are taking a psychology course. He asks, "Which kind of therapy works best?"

IS THERAPY EFFECTIVE?

Study Alert
Pay special attention to the discussion of (1) whether therapy is effective in general and (2) what specific types of therapy are effective, because it is a key issue for therapists.

This question requires a complex response. In fact, identifying the single most appropriate form of treatment is a controversial and still unresolved task for psychologists specializing in psychological disorders. In fact, even before considering whether one form of therapy works better than another, we need to determine whether therapy in any form effectively alleviates psychological disturbances.

Until the 1950s, most people simply assumed that therapy was effective. But in 1952 psychologist Hans Eysenck published an influential study challenging that assumption. He claimed that people who received psychodynamic treatment and related therapies were no better off at the end of treatment than were people who were placed on a waiting list for treatment but never received it. Eysenck concluded that people would go into **spontaneous remission,** recovery without formal treatment, if they were simply left alone—certainly a cheaper and simpler process.

spontaneous remission Recovery without formal treatment.

Although other psychologists quickly challenged Eysenck's conclusions, his review stimulated a continuing stream of better controlled, more carefully crafted studies on the effectiveness of psychotherapy. Today most psychologists agree: Therapy does work. Several comprehensive reviews indicate that therapy brings about greater improvement than no treatment at all, with the rate of spontaneous remission being fairly low. In most cases, then, the symptoms of abnormal behavior do not go away by themselves if left untreated–although the issue continues to be hotly debated (Westen, Novotny, & Thompson-Brenner, 2004; Lutz et al., 2006; Gaudiano & Miller, 2013).

WHICH KIND OF THERAPY WORKS BEST?

Most psychologists feel confident that psychotherapeutic treatment *in general* is more effective than no treatment at all. However, the question of whether any specific *kind* of treatment is superior to any other has not been answered definitively (Nathan, Stuart, & Dolan, 2000; Westen, Novotny, & Thompson-Brenner, 2004; Abboud, 2005).

For instance, one classic study comparing the effectiveness of various approaches found that although success rates vary somewhat by treatment form, most treatments show fairly equal success rates. As Figure 1 indicates, the rates ranged from about 70–85% greater success for treated compared with untreated individuals. Behavioral and cognitive approaches tended to be slightly more successful, but that result may have been due to differences in the severity of the cases treated (Smith, Glass, & Miller, 1980; Orwin & Condray, 1984).

Other research, which relies on *meta-analysis* in which data from a large number of studies are statistically combined, yields similar general conclusions. Furthermore, a large survey of 186,000 individuals found that respondents felt they had benefited substantially from psychotherapy. However, there was little difference in "consumer satisfaction" on the basis of the specific type of treatment they had received (Seligman, 1995; Cuijpers et al., 2008; Dakin & Areán, 2013).

In short, converging evidence allows us to draw several conclusions about the effectiveness of psychotherapy:

- *For most people, psychotherapy is effective.* This conclusion holds over different lengths of treatment, specific kinds of psychological disorders, and various types of treatment. Thus, the question, "Does psychotherapy work?" appears to have been answered convincingly: It does (Westen, Novotny, & Thompson-Brenner, 2004; Payne & Marcus, 2008; Gaudiano & Miller, 2013).
- *On the other hand, psychotherapy doesn't work for everyone.* As many as 10% of people treated show no improvement or actually deteriorated (Boisvert & Faust, 2003; Pretzer & Beck, 2005; Coffman et al., 2007; Lilienfeld, 2007).
- *No single form of therapy works best for every problem, and certain specific types of treatment are better, although not invariably, for specific types of problems.* For example, cognitive therapy works especially well for panic disorders, and flooding therapy relieves specific phobias effectively. However, there are exceptions to

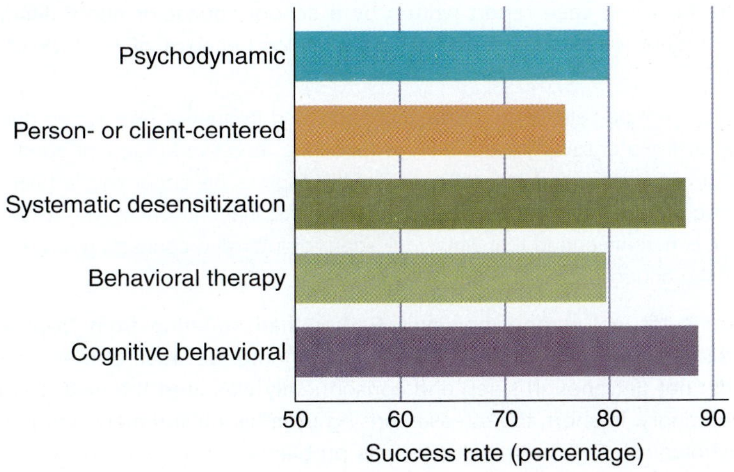

FIGURE 1 Estimates of the effectiveness of different types of treatment, in comparison to control groups of untreated people. The percentile score shows how much more effective a specific type of treatment is for the average patient rather than is no treatment. For example, people given psychodynamic treatment score, on average, more positively on outcome measures than about three-quarters of untreated people. (Source: Adapted from Smith, Glass, & Miller, 1980.)

these generalizations, and often the differences in success rates for different types of treatment are not substantial (Miller & Magruder, 1999; Westen et al., 2004).

- *Most therapies share several basic similar elements.* Despite the fact that the specific methods used in different therapies are very different from one another, there are several common themes that lead them to be effective. These elements include the opportunity for a client to develop a positive relationship with a therapist, an explanation or interpretation of a client's symptoms, and confrontation of negative emotions. The fact that these common elements exist in most therapies makes it difficult to compare one treatment against another (Norcross, 2002; Norcross, Beutler, & Levant, 2006).

Consequently, there is no single, definitive answer to the broad question, "Which therapy works best?" because of the complexity in sorting out the various factors that enter into successful therapy. Recently, however, clinicians and researchers have reframed the question by focusing on evidence-based psychotherapy practice. *Evidence-based psychotherapy practice* seeks to use research findings to determine the best practices for treating a specific disorder. To determine best practices, researchers use clinical interviews, client self-reports of improvement in quality of life, reductions in symptoms, observations of behavior, and other outcomes to compare different therapies. By using objective research findings, clinicians are increasingly able to determine the most effective treatment for a specific disorder (American Psychological Association Presidential Task Force, 2006; Kazdin, 2008; Gaudiano & Miller, 2013).

PsychTech
Internet-based therapy, in which clients and therapists consult online using teleconferencing software but do not meet in person, is still in the experimental stages, but is being viewed as a way to increase access to treatment for more people.

Because no single type of psychotherapy is invariably effective for every individual, some therapists use an eclectic approach to therapy. In an *eclectic approach to therapy*, therapists use a variety of techniques, thus integrating several perspectives, to treat a person's problems. By employing more than one approach, therapists can choose the appropriate mix of evidence-based treatments to match the individual's specific needs. Furthermore, therapists with certain personal characteristics may work better with particular individuals and types of treatments, and—as we consider next—even racial and ethnic factors may be related to the success of treatment (Cheston, 2000; Chambless et al., 2006; Hays, 2008).

Exploring DIVERSITY

Racial and Ethnic Factors in Treatment: Should Therapists Be Color Blind?

Consider the following case report written by a school counselor about Jimmy Jones, a 12-year-old student who was referred to a counselor because of his lack of interest in schoolwork:

> Jimmy does not pay attention, daydreams often, and frequently falls asleep during class. There is a strong possibility that Jimmy is harboring repressed rage that needs to be ventilated and dealt with. His inability to directly express his anger had led him to adopt passive-aggressive means of expressing hostility, i.e., inattentiveness, daydreaming, falling asleep. It is recommended that Jimmy be seen for intensive counseling to discover the basis of the anger. (Sue & Sue, 1990)

The counselor was wrong, however. Rather than suffering from "repressed rage," Jimmy lived in a poverty stricken and disorganized home. Because of overcrowding at his house, he did not get enough sleep and consequently was tired the next day. Frequently, he was also hungry. In short, the stresses arising from his environment and not any deep-seated psychological disturbances caused his problems.

This incident underscores the importance of taking people's environmental and cultural backgrounds into account during treatment for psychological disorders. In particular, members of racial and ethnic minority groups, especially those who are also poor, may behave in ways that help them deal with a society that discriminates against them. As a consequence, behavior that may signal psychological disorder in middle-class and upper-class whites may simply be adaptive in people from other racial and socioeconomic groups. For instance, characteristically suspicious and distrustful people may be displaying a survival strategy to protect themselves from psychological and physical injury rather than suffering from a psychological disturbance (Paniagua, 2000; Tseng, 2003; Pottick et al., 2007).

From the perspective of . . .

A Social Worker How might the types of therapies you employ vary depending on a client's cultural and socioeconomic background?

In fact, therapists must question some basic assumptions of psychotherapy when dealing with racial, ethnic, and cultural minority group members. For example, compared with the dominant culture, Asian and Latino cultures typically place much greater emphasis on the group, family, and society. When an Asian or Latino faces a critical decision, the family helps make it—a cultural practice suggesting that family members should also play a role in psychological treatment. Similarly, the traditional Chinese recommendation for dealing with depression or anxiety is to urge people who experience such problems to avoid thinking about whatever is upsetting them. Consider how this advice contrasts with treatment approaches that emphasize the value of insight (Ponterotto, Gretchen, & Chauhan, 2001; McCarthy, 2005; Leitner, 2007).

Clearly, therapists *cannot* be "color blind." Instead, they must take into account the racial, ethnic, cultural, and social class backgrounds of their clients in determining the nature of a psychological disorder and the course of treatment (Pedersen et al., 2002; Hays, 2008; Moodley, Gielen, & Wu, 2013).

Therapists' interpretation of their clients' behavior is influenced by racial, ethnic, cultural, and social class backgrounds of the clients.

RECAP/EVALUATE/RETHINK

RECAP

LO 41-1 What are humanistic approaches to treatment?

- Humanistic therapy is based on the premise that people have control of their behavior, that they can make choices about their lives, and that it is up to them to solve their own problems. Humanistic therapies, which take a nondirective approach, include person-centered therapy.

LO 41-2 What is interpersonal therapy?

- Interpersonal therapy focuses on interpersonal relationships and strives for immediate improvement during short-term therapy.

LO 41-3 How does group therapy differ from individual types of therapy?

- In group therapy, several unrelated people meet with a therapist to discuss some aspect of their psychological functioning and often center on a common problem.

LO 41-4 How effective is psychotherapy, and which kind of psychotherapy works best in a given situation?

- Most research suggests that, in general, therapy is more effective than no therapy, although how much more effective is not known.
- The more difficult question of which therapy works best is harder to answer, but it is clear particular kinds of therapy are more appropriate for some problems than for others.
- Because no single type of psychotherapy is invariably effective, eclectic approaches in which a therapist uses a variety of techniques and thus integrates several perspectives are sometimes used.

EVALUATE

1. Match each of the following treatment strategies with the statement you might expect to hear from a therapist using that strategy.

   1. Group therapy
   2. Unconditional positive regard
   3. Behavioral therapy
   4. Nondirective counseling

   a. "In other words, you don't get along with your mother because she hates your girlfriend, is that right?"
   b. "I want you all to take turns talking about why you decided to come and what you hope to gain from therapy."
   c. "I can understand why you wanted to wreck your friend's car after she hurt your feelings. Now tell me more about the accident."
   d. "That's not appropriate behavior. Let's work on replacing it with something else."

2. __________ therapies assume that people should take responsibility for their lives and the decisions they make.
3. One of the major criticisms of humanistic therapies is that
   a. They are too imprecise and unstructured.
   b. They treat only the symptom of the problem.
   c. The therapist dominates the patient-therapist interaction.
   d. They work well only on clients of lower socioeconomic status.
4. In a controversial study, Eysenck found that some people go into __________ __________, or recovery without treatment, if they are simply left alone instead of treated.

RETHINK

1. How can people be successfully treated in group therapy when individuals with the "same" problem are so different? What advantages might group therapy offer over individual therapy?
2. List some examples of behavior that might be considered abnormal among members of one cultural or economic group and normal by members of a different cultural or economic group. Suppose that most therapies had been developed by psychologists from minority culture groups and lower socioeconomic status; how might they differ from current therapies?

Answers to Evaluate Questions

1. 1-b, 2-c, 3-d, 4-a; **2.** Humanistic; **3.** a; **4.** spontaneous remission

KEY TERMS

humanistic therapy
person-centered therapy
interpersonal therapy (IPT)
group therapy
family therapy
spontaneous remission

MODULE 42

Biomedical Therapy: Biological Approaches to Treatment

If you get a kidney infection, your doctor gives you an antibiotic; with luck your kidney should be as good as new about a week later. If your appendix becomes inflamed, a surgeon removes it and your body functions normally once more. Could a comparable approach that focuses on the body's physiology be effective for psychological disturbances?

According to biological approaches to treatment, the answer is yes. Therapists routinely use biomedical therapies that rely on drugs and medical procedures to improve psychological functioning. This approach suggests that rather than focusing on a patient's psychological conflicts, past traumas, or environmental factors that may produce abnormal behavior, focusing treatment directly on brain chemistry and other neurological factors may be most appropriate. To do this, therapists can provide treatment with drugs, electric shock, or surgery.

Learning Outcome

LO 42-1 How are drug, electroconvulsive, and psychosurgical techniques used today in the treatment of psychological disorders?

Drug Therapy

Drug therapy, the control of psychological disorders through drugs, works by altering the operation of neurotransmitters and neurons in the brain. Some drugs operate by inhibiting neurotransmitters or receptor neurons, which reduces activity at particular synapses, the sites where nerve impulses travel from one neuron to another. Other drugs do just the opposite: They increase the activity of certain neurotransmitters or neurons, which allows particular neurons to fire more frequently (see Figure 1).

drug therapy Control of psychological disorders through the use of drugs.

ANTIPSYCHOTIC DRUGS

Probably no greater change has occurred in mental hospitals than the successful introduction in the mid-1950s of **antipsychotic drugs**–drugs used to reduce severe symptoms of disturbance, such as loss of touch with reality and agitation. Previously, the typical mental hospital wasn't very different from the stereotypical 19th-century insane asylum; it gave mainly custodial care to screaming, moaning, clawing patients who displayed bizarre behaviors. However, in just a matter of days after hospital staff members administered antipsychotic drugs, the wards became considerably calmer environments in which professionals could do more than just try to get patients through the day without causing serious harm to themselves or others.

antipsychotic drugs Drugs that temporarily reduce psychotic symptoms such as agitation, hallucinations, and delusions.

This dramatic change came about through the introduction of the drug *chlorpromazine.* Along with other similar drugs, chlorpromazine rapidly became the most popular and successful treatment for schizophrenia. Today, drug therapy is typically the preferred treatment for most cases of severely abnormal behavior and is used for most patients hospitalized with psychological disorders. The newest generation of antipsychotics, referred to as *atypical antipsychotics,* have fewer side effects; they include *risperidone, olanzapine,* and *paliperidone* (Lublin, Eberhard, & Levander, 2005; Savas, Yumru, & Kaya, 2007; Nasrallah et al., 2008).

How do antipsychotic drugs work? Most block dopamine receptors at the brain's synapses, the space between pairs of neurons that communicate via chemical messengers. Atypical antipsychotics affect both serotonin and dopamine levels in certain parts of

Drug Treatments

Class of Drug	Effects of Drug	Primary Action of Drug	Examples
Antipsychotic Drugs	Reduction in loss of touch with reality, agitation	Block dopamine receptors	Antipsychotic: chlorpromazine (Thorazine), clozapine (Clozaril), haloperidol (Haldol) Atypical antipsychotic: risperidone, olanzapine
Antidepressant Drugs			
Tricyclic antidepressants	Reduction in depression	Permit rise in neurotransmitters such as norepinepherine	Trazodone (Desyrel), amitriptyline (Elavil), desipramine (Norpamin)
MAO inhibitors	Reduction in depression	Prevent MAO from breaking down neurotransmitters	Phenelzine (Nardil), tranylcypromine (Parnate)
Selective serotonin reuptake inhibitors (SSRIs)	Reduction in depression	Inhibit reuptake of serotonin	Fluoxetine (Prozac), Luvox, Paxil, Celexa, Zoloft, nefazodone (Serzone)
Mood Stabilizers			
Lithium	Mood stabilization	Can alter transmission of impulses within neurons	Lithium (Lithonate), Depakote, Tegretol
Antianxiety Drugs	Reduction in anxiety	Increase activity of neurotransmitter GABA	Benzodiazepines (Valium, Xanax)

FIGURE 1 The major classes of drugs used to treat psychological disorders have different effects on the brain and nervous system.

the brain, such as those related to planning and goal-directed activity (Sawa & Snyder, 2002; Advokat, 2005; Mizrahi et al., 2011).

Despite the effectiveness of antipsychotic drugs, they do not produce a "cure" in the same way that, say, penicillin cures an infection. Most of the time, the symptoms reappear when the drug is withdrawn. Furthermore, such drugs can have long-term side effects, such as dryness of the mouth and throat, dizziness, and sometimes tremors and loss of muscle control, which may continue after drug treatments are stopped (Voruganti et al., 2007).

ANTIDEPRESSANT DRUGS

antidepressant drugs Medications that improve a severely depressed patient's mood and feeling of well-being.

As their name suggests, **antidepressant drugs** are a class of medications used in cases of severe depression to improve a patient's mood and feeling of well-being. They are also sometimes used for other disorders, such as anxiety disorders and bulimia (Walsh et al., 2006; Hedges et al., 2007).

Most antidepressant drugs work by changing the concentration of specific neurotransmitters in the brain. For example, *tricyclic drugs* increase the availability of norepinephrine at the synapses of neurons, whereas *MAO inhibitors* prevent the enzyme monoamine oxidase (MAO) from breaking down neurotransmitters. Newer antidepressants–such as Lexapro–are *selective serotonin reuptake inhibitors (SSRIs)*. SSRIs target the neurotransmitter serotonin and permit it to linger at the synapse. Some antidepressants produce a combination of effects. For instance, nefazodone (Serzone) blocks serotonin at some receptor sites but not others, while bupropion (Wellbutrin and Zyban) affects the norepinephrine and dopamine systems (see Figure 2; Lucki & O'Leary, 2004; Robinson, 2007; Dhillon, Yang, & Curran, 2008).

Finally, there are some newer drugs on the horizon. For instance, scientists have found that the anesthetic ketamine blocks the neural receptor NMDA, which affects the neurotransmitter glutamate. Glutamate plays an important role in mood regulation

Study Alert

To help organize your study of different drugs used in therapy, review Figure 1, which classifies them according to the categories of antipsychotic, atypical antipsychotic, antidepressant, mood-stabilizing, and antianxiety drugs.

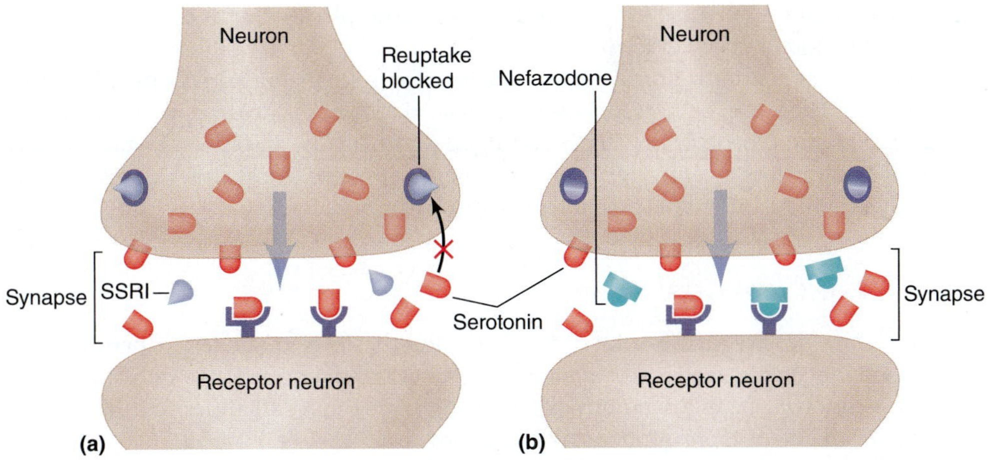

FIGURE 2 In (a), selective serotonin reuptake inhibitors (SSRIs) reduce depression by permitting the neurotransmitter serotonin to remain in the synapse. In (b), a newer antidepressant, nefazodone (Serzone), operates more selectively to block serotonin at some sites but not others, which helps to reduce the side effects of the drug. (Source: Adapted from Mischoulon, 2000.)

and the ability to experience pleasure, and researchers believe that ketamine blockers may prove to be useful in the treatment of depression (Skolnick, Popik, & Trullas, 2009; Schwartzmant & Alexander, 2011).

The overall success rates of antidepressant drugs are good: Antidepressants can produce lasting, long-term recovery from depression. In many cases, even after patients stop taking the drugs, their depression does not return. On the other hand, antidepressant drugs may produce side effects such as drowsiness and faintness, and there is evidence that SSRI antidepressants can increase the risk of suicide in children and adolescents (Gibbons et al., 2007; Leckman & King, 2007; Olfson & Marcus, 2008).

Consumers spend billions of dollars each year on antidepressant drugs. Ten percent of Americans now take an antidepressant, and for women in their 40s and 50s, the figure is 25%. In particular, the antidepressant *fluoxetine,* sold under the trade name *Prozac,* has been highlighted on magazine covers and has been the topic of best-selling books (Rabin, 2013).

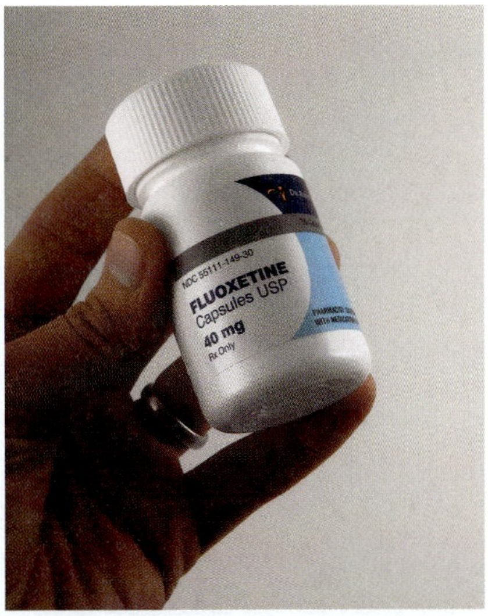

The drug fluoxetine, commonly known as Prozac, is a widely prescribed antidepressant.

Does Prozac deserve its acclaim? In some respects, yes. It is effective and has relatively few side effects. Furthermore, many people who do not respond to other types of antidepressants do well on Prozac. On the other hand, 20–30% of users report experiencing nausea and diarrhea, and a smaller number report sexual dysfunctions (Kramer, 1993; Brambilla et al., 2005; Fenter, 2006).

Another substance that has received a great deal of publicity is *St. John's wort,* an herb that some have called a "natural" antidepressant. Although it is widely used in Europe for the treatment of depression, the U.S. Food and Drug Administration considers it a dietary supplement, and therefore the substance is available here without a prescription.

Despite the popularity of St. John's wort, definitive clinical tests have found that the herb is ineffective in the treatment of depression. However, because some research shows that the herb successfully reduces certain psychological symptoms, some proponents argue that using it is reasonable. In any case, people should not use St. John's wort to medicate themselves without consulting a mental health-care professional (Shelton et al., 2002; Thachil, Mohan, & Bhugra, 2007; Rapaport et al., 2011).

MOOD STABILIZERS

Mood stabilizers are used to treat mood disorders characterized by intense mood swings, especially manic episodes in bipolar disorder. For example, the drug *lithium,* a form of mineral salts, has been used very successfully in patients with bipolar disorders. Although no one knows definitely why, lithium and other mood stabilizers such as divalproex sodium (*Depakote*) and carbamazepine (*Tegretol*) effectively reduce manic episodes. However, they do not effectively treat depressive phases of bipolar disorder,

mood stabilizers Drugs used to treat mood disorders characterized by intense mood swings, especially manic episodes in bipolar disorder.

so antidepressants are usually prescribed during those phases (Smith et al., 2007; Salvi et al., 2008; Inoue et al., 2011).

Lithium and similar drugs have a quality that sets them apart from other drug treatments: They can be a *preventive* treatment that blocks future episodes of manic depression. Often, people who have had episodes of bipolar disorder can take a daily dose of lithium to prevent a recurrence of their symptoms. Most other drugs are useful only when symptoms of psychological disturbance occur.

ANTIANXIETY DRUGS

antianxiety drugs Drugs that reduce the level of anxiety a person experiences essentially by reducing excitability and increasing feelings of well-being.

As the name implies, **antianxiety drugs** reduce the level of anxiety a person experiences and increase feelings of well-being. They are prescribed not only to reduce general tension in people who are experiencing temporary difficulties, but also to aid in the treatment of more serious anxiety disorders (Zito, 1993).

Antianxiety drugs such as alprazolam and Valium are among the medications physicians most frequently prescribe. In fact, more than half of all U.S. families have someone who has taken such a drug at one time or another.

Although the popularity of antianxiety drugs suggests that they hold few risks, they can produce a number of potentially serious side effects. For instance, they can cause fatigue, and long-term use can lead to dependence. Moreover, when taken in combination with alcohol, some antianxiety drugs can be lethal. But a more important issue concerns their use to suppress anxiety. Almost every therapeutic approach to psychological disturbance views continuing anxiety as a signal of some other sort of problem. Thus, drugs that mask anxiety may simply be hiding other difficulties. Consequently, rather than confronting their underlying problems, people may be hiding from them through the use of antianxiety drugs.

Electroconvulsive Therapy (ECT)

electroconvulsive therapy (ECT) A procedure used in the treatment of severe depression in which an electric current of 70–150 volts is briefly administered to a patient's head.

First introduced in the 1930s, **electroconvulsive therapy (ECT)** is a procedure used in the treatment of severe depression. In the procedure, an electric current of 70–150 volts is briefly administered to a patient's head, which causes a loss of consciousness and often causes seizures. Typically, health-care professionals sedate patients and give them muscle relaxants before administering the current; such preparations help reduce the intensity of muscle contractions produced during ECT. The typical patient receives about 10 ECT treatments in the course of a month, but some patients continue with maintenance treatments for months afterward (Greenberg & Kellner, 2005; Stevens & Harper, 2007).

ECT is a controversial technique. Apart from the obvious distastefulness of a treatment that evokes images of electrocution, side effects occur frequently. For instance, after treatment patients often experience disorientation, confusion, and sometimes memory loss that may remain for months. Furthermore, ECT often does not produce long-term improvement; one study found that without follow-up medication, depression returned in most patients who had undergone ECT treatments. Finally, even when ECT does work, we do not know why, and some critics believe it may cause permanent brain damage (Gardner & O'Connor, 2008; Kato, 2009; Weiner & Falcone, 2011).

In light of the drawbacks to ECT, why do therapists use it at all? Basically, they use it because in many severe cases of depression, it offers the only quickly effective treatment. For instance, it may prevent depressed, suicidal individuals from committing suicide, and it can act more quickly than antidepressive medications.

The use of ECT has risen in the last decade with more than 100,000 people undergoing it each year. Still, ECT tends to be used only when other treatments have proved ineffective, and researchers continue to search for alternative treatments (Eranti & McLoughlin, 2003; Pandya, Pozuelo, & Malone, 2007; Tokutsu et al., 2013).

One new and promising alternative to ECT is **transcranial magnetic stimulation (TMS).** TMS creates a precise magnetic pulse in a specific area of the brain. By activating particular neurons, TMS has been effective in relieving the symptoms of major depression in a number of controlled experiments. However, the therapy can produce side effects, such as seizures and convulsions, and it is still considered experimental (Leo & Latif, 2007; Kim, Pesiridou, & O'Reardon, 2009; Bentwich et al., 2011).

transcranial magnetic stimulation (TMS) A depression treatment in which a precise magnetic pulse is directed to a specific area of the brain.

Psychosurgery

If ECT strikes you as a questionable procedure, the use of **psychosurgery**–brain surgery in which the object is to reduce symptoms of mental disorder–probably appears even more dubious. A technique used only rarely today, psychosurgery was introduced as a "treatment of last resort" in the 1930s.

psychosurgery Brain surgery once used to reduce the symptoms of mental disorder but rarely used today.

The initial form of psychosurgery, a *prefrontal lobotomy,* consisted of surgically destroying or removing parts of a patient's frontal lobes, which surgeons thought controlled emotionality. In the 1930s and 1940s, surgeons performed the procedure on thousands of patients often with little precision. For example, in one common technique, a surgeon literally would jab an ice pick under a patient's eyeball and swivel it back and forth (Ogren & Sandlund, 2007; Phillips, 2013).

Psychosurgery sometimes did improve a patient's behavior–but not without drastic side effects. Along with remission of the symptoms of the mental disorder, patients sometimes experienced personality changes and became bland, colorless, and unemotional. In other cases, patients became aggressive and unable to control their impulses. In the worst cases, treatment resulted in the patient's death.

With the introduction of effective drug treatments–and the obvious ethical questions regarding the appropriateness of forever altering someone's personality–psychosurgery became nearly obsolete. However, it is still used in very rare cases when all other procedures have failed and the patient's behavior presents a high risk to the patient and others. For example, surgeons sometimes use a more precise form of psychosurgery called a *cingulotomy* in rare cases of obsessive-compulsive disorder in which they destroy tissue in the *anterior cingulate* area of the brain. In another technique, *gamma knife surgery,* beams of radiation are used to destroy areas of the brain related to obsessive-compulsive disorder (Shah et al., 2008; Carey, 2009c; Lopes et al., 2009; Wilkinson, 2009).

Occasionally, dying patients with severe, uncontrollable pain also receive psychosurgery. Still, even these cases raise important ethical issues, and psychosurgery remains a highly controversial treatment (Mashour, Walker, & Martuza, 2005; Steele et al., 2007).

From the perspective of . . .

A Politician How would you go about regulating the use of electroconvulsive therapy and psychosurgery?

Biomedical Therapies in Perspective

In some respects, no greater revolution has occurred in the field of mental health than biological approaches to treatment. As previously violent, uncontrollable patients have been calmed by the use of drugs, mental hospitals have been able to concentrate more on actually helping patients and less on custodial functions. Similarly, patients whose lives have been disrupted by depression or bipolar episodes have been able to function normally, and other forms of drug therapy have also shown remarkable results.

Furthermore, new forms of biomedical therapy are promising. For example, the newest treatment possibility–which remains experimental at this point–is gene therapy. Specific genes may be introduced to particular regions of the brain. These genes then have the potential to reverse or even prevent biochemical events that give rise to psychological disorders (Sapolsky, 2003; Lymberis et al., 2004; Tuszynski, 2007).

Study Alert

Remember that biomedical treatments have both benefits and drawbacks.

Despite their current usefulness and future promise, biomedical therapies do not represent a complete cure for psychological disorders. For one thing, critics charge that biomedical therapies merely provide relief of the symptoms of mental disorder, because in most cases, as soon as the drugs are withdrawn, symptoms return. Consequently, biomedical treatment may not solve the underlying problems that led a patient to therapy in the first place.

Second, critics of biomedical therapies note that drugs may produce side effects that range from minor to serious physical reactions. In the worst case, biomedical therapies may lead to the development of new symptoms of abnormal behavior. Finally, an overreliance on biomedical therapies may lead therapists to overlook alternative forms of treatment, such as psychotherapy, that may be helpful.

Still, biomedical therapies–sometimes alone and more often in conjunction with psychotherapy–have permitted millions of people to function more effectively. Furthermore, although biomedical therapy and psychotherapy appear distinct, research shows that biomedical therapies ultimately may not be as different from talk therapies as one might imagine, at least in terms of their consequences.

Specifically, measures of brain functioning as a result of drug therapy compared with psychotherapy show little difference in outcomes. For example, one study compared the reactions of patients with major depression who received either an antidepressant drug or psychotherapy. After 6 weeks of either therapy, activity in the portion of the brain related to the disorder–the basal ganglia–had changed in similar ways, and that area appeared to function more normally. Although such research is not definitive, it does suggest that at least for some disorders, psychotherapy may be just as effective as biomedical interventions–and vice versa. Research also makes it clear that no single treatment is effective universally and that each type of treatment has both advantages and disadvantages (Pinquart, Duberstein, & Lyness, 2006; Greenberg & Goldman, 2009; Gaudiano & Miller, 2013).

"The drug has, however, proved more effective than traditional psychoanalysis."

Community Psychology: Focus on Prevention

community psychology A branch of psychology that focuses on the prevention and minimization of psychological disorders in the community.

Each of the treatments we have reviewed has a common element: It is a "restorative" treatment aimed at alleviating psychological difficulties that already exist. However, an approach known as **community psychology** has a different aim: to prevent or minimize the incidence of psychological disorders.

Community psychology came of age in the 1960s, when mental health professionals developed plans for a nationwide network of community mental health centers. The hope was that those centers would provide low-cost mental health services, including short-term therapy and community educational programs. In another development, the population of mental hospitals has plunged as drug treatments made physical restraint of patients unnecessary.

The community psychology movement encouraged **deinstitutionalization,** the transfer of mental patients out of institutions and into the community (see Figure 3). Proponents of deinstitutionalization wanted to ensure not only that deinstitutionalized patients received proper treatment, but also that their civil rights were maintained (Wolff, 2002; St. Dennis et al., 2006; Henckes, 2011).

Unfortunately, the promise of deinstitutionalization has not been met largely because insufficient resources are provided to deinstitutionalized patients. What started as a worthy attempt to move people out of mental institutions and into the community ended, in many cases, with former patients being dumped into the community without any real support. Many became homeless–between 15% and 35% of all homeless adults are thought to have a major psychological disorder–and some became involved in illegal acts caused by their disorders. In short, many people who need treatment do not get it, and in some cases care for people with psychological disorders has simply shifted from one type of treatment site to another. In fact, for many people, the only form of mental health treatment comes in emergency rooms of hospitals, with little or no follow-up care (Dumont & Dumont, 2008; Price, 2009; Searight, 2013).

On the other hand, the community psychology movement has had some positive outcomes. Its emphasis on prevention has led to new approaches to psychological disorders. Furthermore, telephone "hot lines" are now common. At any time of the day or night, people experiencing acute stress can call a trained, sympathetic listener who can provide immediate–although obviously limited–treatment (Reese, Conoley, & Brossart, 2002; Paukert, Stagner, & Hope, 2004; Cauce, 2007).

College and high school crisis centers are another innovation that grew out of the community psychology movement. Modeled after suicide prevention hot-line centers, crisis centers give callers an opportunity to discuss life crises with a sympathetic listener, who is often a volunteer.

While deinstitutionalization has had many successes, it has also contributed to the release of mental patients into the community with little or no support. As a result, many have become homeless.

deinstitutionalization The transfer of mental patients from institutions to the community.

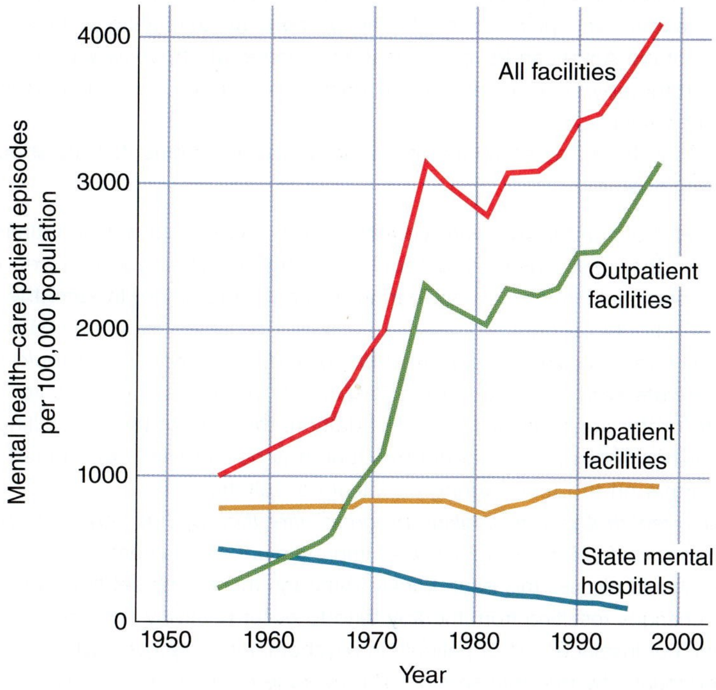

FIGURE 3 As deinstitutionalization has become prevalent over the years, the number of patients being treated in state mental hospitals declined significantly, while the number of outpatient facilities increased. (Source: Adapted from Doyle, 2002.)

Looking Back

Epilogue

We have examined how psychological professionals treat people with psychological disorders. We have considered a range of approaches that include both psychologically based and biologically based therapies. Clearly, the field has made substantial progress in recent years both in treating the symptoms of mental disorders and in understanding their underlying causes.

Before we leave the topic of treatment of psychological disorders, turn back to the prologue in which Marisol Rodriguez discusses seeking therapy for her social anxiety. On the basis of your understanding of the treatment of psychological disorders, consider the following questions:

1. What approach to therapy does Marisol Rodriguez seem to be describing?
2. Was Marisol right to assume that if one therapist wasn't helping her much, she should try another? Why or why not?
3. How might a practitioner of person-centered therapy approach Marisol's problem? How might a family therapist?

VISUAL SUMMARY 13 Treatment of Psychological Disorders

MODULE 40 Psychotherapy: Psychodynamic, Behavioral, and Cognitive Approaches

Psychodynamic Therapy

- Psychoanalysis
  - Free association: say aloud whatever comes to mind
  - Dream interpretation: looking for clues to unconscious conflicts and problems in dreams
  - Frequent sessions for a long time
- Contemporary psychodynamic approaches
  - Sessions are of shorter duration
  - Therapist takes more active role: focus is more in the present

Behavioral Treatment Approaches: Help modify behavior rather than find underlying causes

- Classical conditioning treatments
  - Aversive conditioning
  - Systematic desensitization
  - Flooding
- Operant conditioning techniques
  - Token system
  - Contingency contracting
  - Observational learning

Cognitive Approaches: Teach people to think in adaptive ways

- Rational-emotive behavior therapy

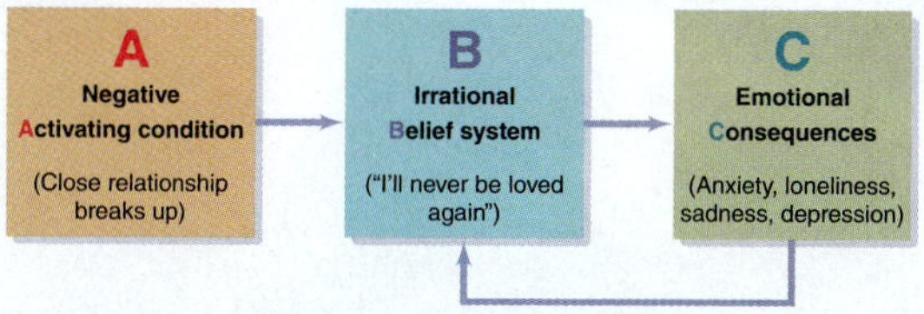

MODULE 41 Psychotherapy: Humanistic, Interpersonal, and Group Approaches

Humanistic Therapy: Focuses on self-responsibility in treatment techniques

- Person-centered therapy: helps people to reach their potential for self-actualization using unconditional positive regard

Interpersonal Therapy: Focuses on interpersonal relationships and improvement through short-term therapy

Group Therapy: Several people meet with a therapist to discuss psychological functioning

- Family therapy
- Self-help therapy

Does Psychotherapy Work?

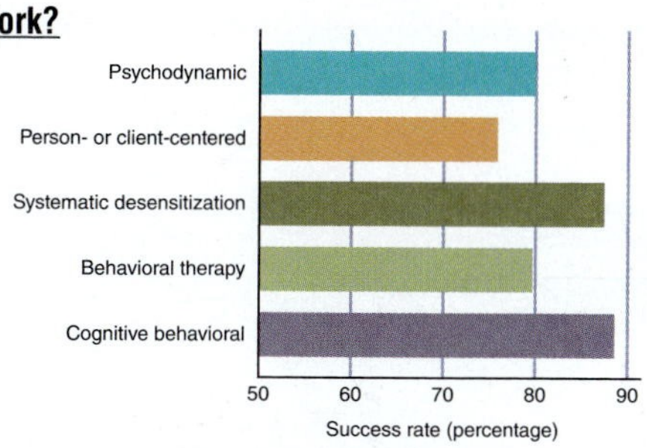

- More effective than no treatment for most people
- Certain types of therapy work better for particular problems
- Most therapy approaches share basic elements

MODULE 42 Biomedical Therapy: Biological Approaches to Treatment

Drug Therapy: Controlling psychological disorders with drugs

Drug Treatments

Class of Drug	Effects of Drug	Primary Action of Drug	Examples
Antipsychotic Drugs, Atypical Antipsychotic Drugs	Reduction in loss of touch with reality, agitation	Block dopamine receptors	Antipsychotic: chlorpromazine (Thorazine), clozapine (Clozaril), haloperidol (Haldol) Atypical antipsychotic: risperidone, olanzapine
Antidepressant Drugs			
Tricyclic antidepressants	Reduction in depression	Permit rise in neurotransmitters such as norepinepherine	Trazodone (Desyrel), amitriptyline (Elavil), desipramine (Norpamin)
MAO inhibitors	Reduction in depression	Prevent MAO from breaking down neurotransmitters	Phenelzine (Nardil), tranylcypromine (Parnate)
Selective serotonin reuptake inhibitors (SSRIs)	Reduction in depression	Inhibit reuptake of serotonin	Fluoxetine (Prozac), Luvox, Paxil, Celexa, Zoloft, nefazodone (Serzone)
Mood Stabilizers			
Lithium	Mood stabilization	Can alter transmission of impulses within neurons	Lithium (Lithonate), Depakote, Tegretol
Antianxiety Drugs	Reduction in anxiety	Increase activity of neurotransmitter GABA	Benzodiazepines (Valium, Xanax)

Electroconvulsive Therapy: Used as the only quickly effective treatment for severe depression

Psychosurgery: Brain surgery to reduce symptoms of mental disorders

Community Psychology: Prevention of the incidence of psychological disorders

- Deinstitutionalization: transfer of mental patients into the community where they may not receive necessary treatment

14 Social Psychology

Learning Outcomes for Chapter 14

MODULE 43

LO 43-1 What are attitudes, and how are they formed, maintained, and changed?

LO 43-2 How do people form impressions of what others are like and the causes of their behavior?

LO 43-3 What are the biases that influence the ways in which people view others' behavior?

Attitudes and Social Cognition

Persuasion: Changing Attitudes

Social Cognition: Understanding Others

Exploring Diversity: Attribution Biases in a Cultural Context: How Fundamental Is the Fundamental Attribution Error?

MODULE 44

LO 44-1 What are the major sources and tactics of social influence?

Social Influence and Groups

Conformity: Following What Others Do

Compliance: Submitting to Direct Social Pressure

Obedience: Following Direct Orders

MODULE 45

LO 45-1 How do stereotypes, prejudice, and discrimination differ?

LO 45-2 How can we reduce prejudice and discrimination?

Prejudice and Discrimination

Applying Psychology in the 21st Century: Decreasing the Damage of Negative Stereotypes

The Foundations of Prejudice

Neuroscience in Your Life: The Prejudiced Brain

Measuring Prejudice and Discrimination: The Implicit Association Test

Reducing the Consequences of Prejudice and Discrimination

MODULE 46

LO 46-1 Why are we attracted to certain people, and what progression do social relationships follow?

LO 46-2 What factors underlie aggression and prosocial behavior?

Positive and Negative Social Behavior

Liking and Loving: Interpersonal Attraction and the Development of Relationships

Aggression and Prosocial Behavior: Hurting and Helping Others

Helping Others: The Brighter Side of Human Nature

Becoming an Informed Consumer of Psychology: Dealing Effectively with Anger

Prologue *I'm Not a Racist*

In April 2014, Donald Sterling, owner of the Los Angeles Clippers basketball team, made what he later called a "mistake." During a phone call with his girlfriend, Sterling objected to an online photo of her with ex-player Magic Johnson. "It bothers me a lot that you want to broadcast that you're associating with black people," Sterling told her, urging her "not to bring them to my games." When the conversation, which she had secretly recorded, became public, Sterling was banned for life from the NBA.

In a subsequent interview, Sterling appealed to the NBA and the general public, insisting that he was not racist.

Looking Ahead

Should we accept Donald Sterling's apology and agree that he just made a mistake? Was his apology sincere and his remorse genuine, or did his comments reflect deep-seated racial prejudice? Can he reform, as he has said he wants to do, or are his attitudes and opinions unlikely to change? More broadly, can individuals change in fundamental ways, and are there actions we can take to help people get along better and live in harmony?

We can fully answer these questions only by taking into account findings from the field of social psychology, the branch of psychology that focuses on the aspects of human behavior that unite—and separate—us from one another. **Social psychology** is the scientific study of how people's thoughts, feelings, and actions are affected by others. Social psychologists consider the kinds and causes of the individual's behavior in social situations. They examine how the nature of situations in which we find ourselves influences our behavior in important ways.

The broad scope of social psychology is conveyed by the kinds of questions social psychologists ask, such as: How can we convince people to change their attitudes or adopt new ideas and values? In what ways do we come to understand what others are like? How are we influenced by what others do and think? Why do some people display so much violence, aggression, and cruelty toward others that people throughout the world live in fear of annihilation at their hands? And why, in comparison, do some people place their own lives at risk to help others? In exploring these and other questions, we also discuss strategies for confronting and solving a variety of problems and issues that all of us face—ranging from achieving a better understanding of persuasive tactics to forming more accurate impressions of others.

We begin with a look at how our attitudes shape our behavior and how we form judgments about others. We'll discuss how we are influenced by others, and we will consider prejudice and discrimination by focusing on their roots and the ways we can reduce them. After examining what social psychologists have learned about the ways people form friendships and relationships, we'll conclude with a look at the determinants of aggression and helping—two opposing sides of human behavior.

social psychology The scientific study of how people's thoughts, feelings, and actions are affected by others.

MODULE 43

Attitudes and Social Cognition

What do Rachael Ray and Tom Brady have in common? Both have appeared in advertisements designed to mold or change our attitudes. Such commercials are part of the barrage of messages we receive each day from sources as varied as politicians, sales staff in stores, and celebrities—all of which are meant to influence us.

Persuasion: Changing Attitudes

Attitudes are one of the central concepts of social psychology. **Attitudes** are evaluations of people, objects, ideas, and behavior. We have all sorts of attitudes, ranging from those about others ("I think the President is great"), to attitudes about behavior ("I hate it when people are late for appointments"), to attitudes toward more abstract concepts ("I support affirmative action") (Hegarty & Massey, 2007; Simon & Hoyt, 2008).

Persuasion involves changing attitudes. The ease with which attitudes can be changed depends on a number of factors, including:

- *Message source.* The characteristics of a person who delivers a persuasive message, known as an *attitude communicator,* have a major impact on the effectiveness of that message. Communicators who are physically and socially attractive produce greater attitude change than those who are less attractive. Moreover, the communicator's expertise and trustworthiness are related to the impact of a message—except in situations in which the audience believes the communicator has an ulterior motive (Ariyanto, Hornsey, & Gallois, 2006; McClure, Sutton, & Sibley, 2007; Messner, Reinhard, & Sporer, 2008).
- *Characteristics of the message.* It is not just *who* delivers a message but what the message is like that affects attitudes. Generally, two-sided messages—which include both the communicator's position and the one he or she is arguing against—are more effective than one-sided messages, given the assumption that the arguments for the other side can be effectively refuted and the audience is knowledgeable about the topic. In addition, fear-producing messages ("If you don't practice safer sex, you'll get AIDS") are generally effective when they provide the audience with a means for reducing the fear. However, if the fear that is aroused is too strong, messages may evoke people's defense mechanisms and be ignored (Perloff, 2003; Keer et al., 2013).
- *Characteristics of the target.* Once a communicator has delivered a message, characteristics of the *target* of the message may determine whether the message will be accepted. For example, intelligent people are more resistant to persuasion than those who are less intelligent. Gender differences in persuasibility also seem to exist. In public settings, women are somewhat more easily persuaded than men, particularly when they have less knowledge about the message's topic. However, they are as likely as men to change their private attitudes. In fact, the magnitude of the differences in resistance to persuasion between men and women is not large (Wood, 2000; Guadagno & Cialdini, 2002).

Learning Outcomes

LO 43-1 What are attitudes, and how are they formed, maintained, and changed?

LO 43-2 How do people form impressions of what others are like and the causes of their behavior?

LO 43-3 What are the biases that influence the ways in which people view others' behavior?

attitudes Evaluations of people, objects, ideas, and behavior.

Do celebrities such as Patriot quarterback Tom Brady influence attitudes? Advertisers certainly believe this is true, investing millions of dollars in endorsement fees.

these quick impressions are surprisingly accurate and typically match those of people who make judgments based on longer samples of behavior (Pavitt, 2007; Holleran, Mehl, & Levitt, 2009; Pretsch et al., 2013).

Of course, as we gain more experience with people and see them exhibiting behavior in a variety of situations, our impressions of them become more complex. However, because our knowledge of others usually has gaps, we still tend to fit individuals into personality schemas that represent particular "types" of people. For instance, we may hold a "gregarious person" schema made up of the traits of friendliness, aggressiveness, and openness. The presence of just one or two of those traits may be sufficient to make us assign a person to a particular schema.

However, our schemas are susceptible to error. For example, mood affects how we perceive others. Happy people form more favorable impressions and make more positive judgments than people who are in a bad mood (Forgas & Laham, 2005; Human & Biesanz, 2011).

Even when schemas are not entirely accurate, they serve an important function: They allow us to develop expectations about how others will behave. Those expectations permit us to plan our interactions with others more easily and serve to simplify a complex social world.

ATTRIBUTION PROCESSES: UNDERSTANDING THE CAUSES OF BEHAVIOR

> When Barbara Washington, a new employee at the Ablex Computer Company, completed a major staffing project 2 weeks early, her boss, Yolanda, was delighted. At the next staff meeting, she announced how pleased she was with Barbara and explained that *this* was an example of the kind of performance she was looking for in her staff. The other staff members looked on resentfully, trying to figure out why Barbara had worked night and day to finish the project not just on time but 2 weeks early. She must be an awfully compulsive person, they decided.

At one time or another, most of us have puzzled over the reasons behind someone's behavior. Perhaps it was in a situation similar to the one above, or it may have been in more formal circumstances, such as being a judge on a student judiciary board in a cheating case. **Attribution theory** considers how we decide, on the basis of samples of a person's behavior, what the specific causes of that behavior are. Unlike impression formation, which focuses on how people develop an overall impression of others' personality traits, attribution theory asks the "why" question: Why is someone acting in a particular way?

attribution theory The theory that considers how we decide, on the basis of samples of a person's behavior, what the specific causes of that behavior are.

In seeking an explanation for behavior, we must answer one central question: Is the cause situational or dispositional? **Situational causes** are causes of behavior that are external to a person. For instance, someone who knocks over a quart of milk and then cleans it up probably does the cleaning not because he or she is necessarily a neat person but because the *situation* requires it. In contrast, a person who spends hours shining the kitchen floor probably does so because he or she is an unusually neat person. Hence, the behavior has a dispositional cause. **Dispositional causes** are causes of behavior brought about by a person's traits or personality characteristics.

situational causes (of behavior) Causes of behavior that are external to a person.

dispositional causes (of behavior) Perceived causes of behavior brought about by a person's traits or personality characteristics.

In our example involving Barbara Washington, her fellow employees attributed her behavior to her disposition rather than to the situation. But from a logical standpoint, it is equally plausible that something about the situation caused the behavior. If asked, Barbara might attribute her accomplishment to situational factors and explain that she had so much other work to do she just had to get the project out of the way, or the project was not all that difficult and was easy to complete ahead of schedule. To her, then, the reason for her behavior might not be dispositional at all; it could be situational.

Study Alert
The central question in making an attribution is whether the cause of behavior is due to situational or dispositional factors.

ATTRIBUTION BIASES: TO ERR IS HUMAN

If we always processed information in the rational manner that attribution theory suggests, the world might run a lot more smoothly. Unfortunately, although attribution theory generally makes accurate predictions, people do not always process information about others as logically as the theory seems to suggest. In fact, research reveals consistent biases in the ways people make attributions. Typical biases include the following:

- *The halo effect.* Harry is intelligent, kind, and loving. Is he also conscientious? If you were to guess, your most likely response probably would be yes. Your guess reflects the **halo effect,** a phenomenon in which an initial understanding that a person has positive traits is used to infer other uniformly positive characteristics. The opposite would also hold true. Learning that Harry was unsociable and argumentative would probably lead you to assume that he was lazy as well. However, few people have either uniformly positive or uniformly negative traits, so the halo effect leads to misperceptions of others (Goffin, Jelley, & Wagner, 2003; Dennis, 2007; Park, Park, & Dubinsky, 2011).
- *Assumed-similarity bias.* How similar to you–in terms of attitudes, opinions, likes, and dislikes–are your friends and acquaintances? Most people believe that their friends and acquaintances are fairly similar to themselves. But this feeling goes beyond just people we know to a general tendency–known as the **assumed-similarity bias**–to think of people as being similar to oneself even when meeting them for the first time. Given the range of people in the world, this assumption often reduces the accuracy of our judgments (Lemay, Clark, & Feeney, 2007; Lemay & Clark, 2008).
- *The self-serving bias.* When their teams win, coaches usually feel that the success is due to their coaching. But when their teams lose, coaches may think it's due to their players' poor skills. Similarly, if you get an A on a test, you may think it's due to your hard work, but if you get a poor grade, it's due to the professor's inadequacies. The reason is the **self-serving bias,** the tendency to attribute success to personal factors (skill, ability, or effort) and attribute failure to factors outside oneself (Krusemark, Campbell, & Clementz, 2008; Shepperd, Malone, & Sweeny, 2008).
- *The fundamental attribution error.* One of the more common attribution biases is the **fundamental attribution error,** which is the tendency to overattribute others' behavior to dispositional causes and the corresponding failure to recognize the importance of situational causes. The fundamental attribution error is prevalent in Western cultures. We tend to exaggerate the importance of personality characteristics (dispositional causes) in producing others' behavior and minimize the influence of the environment (situational factors). For example, we are more likely to jump to the conclusion that someone who is often late to work is too lazy to take an earlier bus (a dispositional cause) than to assume that the lateness is due to situational factors, such as the bus always running behind schedule.

halo effect A phenomenon in which an initial understanding that a person has positive traits is used to infer other uniformly positive characteristics.

assumed-similarity bias The tendency to think of people as being similar to oneself even when meeting them for the first time.

self-serving bias The tendency to attribute personal success to personal factors (skill, ability, or effort) and to attribute failure to factors outside oneself.

fundamental attribution error A tendency to overattribute others' behavior to dispositional causes and minimize the importance of situational causes.

The assumed-similarity bias leads us to believe that others hold similar attitudes, opinions, and likes and dislikes.

Rorschach test A test that involves showing a series of symmetrical visual stimuli to people who then are asked what the figures represent to them. (Module 33)

Schachter-Singer theory of emotion The belief that emotions are determined jointly by a nonspecific kind of physiological arousal and its interpretation, based on environmental cues. (Module 26)

schedules of reinforcement Different patterns of frequency and timing of reinforcement following desired behavior. (Module 16)

schemas Organized bodies of information stored in memory that bias the way new information is interpreted, stored, and recalled. (Module 19)

schemas Sets of cognitions about people and social experiences. (Module 43)

schizophrenia A class of disorders in which severe distortion of reality occurs. (Module 38)

scientific method The approach through which psychologists systematically acquire knowledge and understanding about behavior and other phenomena of interest. (Module 3)

self-actualization A state of self-fulfillment in which people realize their highest potential in their own unique way. (Modules 24, 32)

self-efficacy The belief that we can master a situation and produce positive outcomes. (Module 32)

self-esteem The component of personality that encompasses our positive and negative self-evaluations. (Module 32)

self-report measures A method of gathering data about people by asking them questions about their own behavior and traits. (Module 33)

self-serving bias The tendency to attribute personal success to personal factors (skill, ability, or effort) and to attribute failure to factors outside oneself. (Module 43)

semantic memory Memory for general knowledge and facts about the world, as well as memory for the rules of logic that are used to deduce other facts. (Module 18)

semantic networks Mental representations of clusters of interconnected information. (Module 18)

semantics The meaning of words and sentences. (Module 22)

semicircular canals Three tube-like structures of the inner ear containing fluid that sloshes through them when the head moves, signaling rotational or angular movement to the brain. (Module 10)

sensation The activation of the sense organs by a source of physical energy. (Module 8)

sensorimotor stage According to Piaget, the stage from birth to 2 years, during which a child has little competence in representing the environment by using images, language, or other symbols. (Module 28)

sensory (afferent) neurons Neurons that transmit information from the perimeter of the body to the nervous system and brain. (Module 6)

sensory area The site in the brain of the tissue that corresponds to each of the senses, with the degree of sensitivity related to the amount of tissue. (Module 7)

sensory memory The initial, momentary storage of information, lasting only an instant. (Module 18)

shaping The process of teaching a complex behavior by rewarding closer and closer approximations of the desired behavior. (Module 16)

short-term memory Memory that holds information for 15 to 25 seconds. (Module 18)

significant outcome Meaningful results that make it possible for researchers to feel confident that they have confirmed their hypotheses. (Module 3)

situational causes (of behavior) Causes of behavior that are external to a person. (Module 43)

skin senses The senses of touch, pressure, temperature, and pain. (Module 10)

social cognition The cognitive processes by which people understand and make sense of others and themselves. (Module 43)

social cognitive approaches to personality Theories that emphasize the influence of a person's cognitions—thoughts, feelings, expectations, and values—as well as observation of others' behavior, in determining personality. (Module 32)

social influence The process by which social groups and individuals exert pressure on an individual, either deliberately or unintentionally. (Module 44)

social neuroscience The subfield of social psychology that seeks to identify the neurological basis of social behavior. (Module 45)

social psychology The scientific study of how people's thoughts, feelings, and actions are affected by others. (Module 43)

social support A mutual network of caring, interested others. (Module 34)

social supporter A group member whose dissenting views make non-conformity to the group easier. (Module 44)

sociocultural perspective The perspective that assumes that people's behavior—both normal and abnormal—is shaped by the kind of family group, society, and culture in which they live. (Module 37)

somatic division The part of the peripheral nervous system that specializes in the control of voluntary movements and the communication of information to and from the sense organs. (Module 6)

somatic symptom disorders Psychological difficulties that take on a physical (somatic) form, but for which there is no medical cause. (Module 38)

sound The movement of air molecules brought about by a source of vibration. (Module 10)

specific phobia Intense, irrational fears of specific objects or situations. (Module 38)

spinal cord A bundle of neurons that leaves the brain and runs down the length of the back and is the main means for transmitting messages between the brain and the body. (Module 6)

spontaneous recovery The reemergence of an extinguished conditioned response after a period of rest and with no further conditioning. (Module 15)

spontaneous remission Recovery without formal treatment. (Module 41)

stage 1 sleep The state of transition between wakefulness and sleep, characterized by relatively rapid, low-amplitude brain waves. (Module 12)

stage 2 sleep A sleep deeper than that of stage 1, characterized by a slower, more regular wave pattern, along with momentary interruptions of "sleep spindles." (Module 12)

stage 3 sleep A sleep characterized by slow brain waves, with greater peaks and valleys in the wave pattern than in stage 2 sleep. (Module 12)

stage 4 sleep The deepest stage of sleep, during which we are least responsive to outside stimulation. (Module 12)

status The social standing of someone in a group. (Module 44)

stereotype A set of generalized beliefs and expectations about a particular group and its members. (Module 45)

stimulants Drugs that have an arousal effect on the central nervous system, causing a rise in heart rate, blood pressure, and muscular tension. (Module 14)

stimulus Energy that produces a response in a sense organ. (Module 8)

stimulus discrimination The process that occurs if two stimuli are sufficiently distinct from one another that one evokes a conditioned response but the other does not; the ability to differentiate between stimuli. (Module 15)

stimulus generalization A process in which, after a stimulus has been conditioned to produce a particular response, stimuli that are similar to the original stimulus produce the same response. (Module 15)

stress A person's response to events that are threatening or challenging. (Module 34)

structuralism Wundt's approach, which focuses on uncovering the fundamental mental components of consciousness, thinking, and other kinds of mental states and activities. (Module 2)

subjective well-being People's sense of their happiness and satisfaction with their lives. (Module 36)

superego The personality structure that harshly judges the morality of our behavior. (Module 31)

survey research Research in which people chosen to represent a larger population are asked a series of questions about their behavior, thoughts, or attitudes. (Module 3)

sympathetic division The part of the autonomic division of the nervous system that acts to prepare the body for action in stressful situations, engaging all the organism's resources to respond to a threat. (Module 6)

synapse The space between two neurons where the axon of a sending neuron communicates with the dendrites of a receiving neuron by using chemical messages. (Module 5)

syntax Ways in which words and phrases can be combined to form sentences. (Module 22)

systematic desensitization A behavioral technique based on classical conditioning in which exposure to an anxiety-producing stimulus is paired with deep relaxation to extinguish the response of anxiety. (Module 40)

telegraphic speech Sentences in which only essential words are used. (Module 22)

temperament A basic, inborn characteristic way of responding and behavioral style. (Module 28)

temperament An individual's behavioral style and characteristic way of responding that emerges early in life. (Module 32)

teratogens Environmental agents such as a drug, chemical, virus, or other factor that produce a birth defect. (Module 27)

terminal buttons Small bulges at the end of axons that send messages to other neurons. (Module 5)

test standardization A technique used to validate questions in personality tests by studying the responses of people with known diagnoses. (Module 33)

thalamus The part of the brain located in the middle of the central core that acts primarily to relay information about the senses. (Module 7)

Thematic Apperception Test (TAT) A test consisting of a series of pictures about which a person is asked to write a story. (Module 33)

theories Broad explanations and predictions concerning phenomena of interest. (Module 3)

theory of multiple intelligences Gardner's intelligence theory that proposes that there are eight distinct spheres of intelligence. (Module 23)

thinking Brain activity in which people mentally manipulate information, including words, visual images, sounds, or other data. (Module 21)

tip-of-the-tongue phenomenon The inability to recall information that one realizes one knows–a result of the difficulty of retrieving information from long-term memory. (Module 19)

top-down processing Perception that is guided by higher-level knowledge, experience, expectations, and motivations. (Module 11)

traits Consistent personality characteristics and behaviors displayed in different situations. (Module 32)

trait theory A model of personality that seeks to identify the basic traits necessary to describe personality. (Module 32)

transcranial magnetic stimulation (TMS) A depression treatment in which a precise magnetic pulse is directed to a specific area of the brain. (Module 42)

transference The transfer of feelings to a psychoanalyst of love or anger that had been originally directed to a patient's parents or other authority figures. (Module 40)

transsexuals People whose sexual identification is with the opposite gender from that they were born with; they feel they are trapped in the body of the other gender. (Module 25)

treatment The manipulation implemented by the experimenter. (Module 3)

trichromatic theory of color vision The theory that there are three kinds of cones in the retina, each of which responds primarily to a specific range of wavelengths. (Module 9)

trust-versus-mistrust stage According to Erikson, the first stage of psychosocial development, occurring from birth to age 1½ years, during which time infants develop feelings of trust or lack of trust. (Module 28)

Type A behavior pattern A cluster of behaviors involving hostility, competitiveness, time urgency, and feeling driven. (Module 35)

Type B behavior pattern A cluster of behaviors characterized by a patient, cooperative, noncompetitive, and nonaggressive manner. (Module 35)

unconditional positive regard An attitude of acceptance and respect on the part of an observer, no matter what a person says or does. (Module 32)

unconditioned response (UCR) A response that is natural and needs no training (e.g., salivation at the smell of food). (Module 15)

unconditioned stimulus (UCS) A stimulus that naturally brings about a particular response without having been learned. (Module 15)

unconscious A part of the personality that contains the memories, knowledge, beliefs, feelings, urges, drives, and instincts of which the individual is not aware. (Module 31)

unconscious wish fulfillment theory Sigmund Freud's theory that dreams represent unconscious wishes that dreamers desire to see fulfilled. (Module 12)

uninvolved parents Parents who show little interest in their children and are emotionally detached. (Module 28)

validity The property by which tests actually measure what they are supposed to measure. (Module 23)

variable-interval schedule A schedule by which the time between reinforcements varies around some average rather than being fixed. (Module 16)

variable-ratio schedule A schedule by which reinforcement occurs after a varying number of responses rather than after a fixed number. (Module 16)

variables Behaviors, events, or other characteristics that can change, or vary, in some way. (Module 3)

visual illusions Physical stimuli that consistently produce errors in perception. (Module 11)

wear-and-tear theories of aging Theories that suggest that the mechanical functions of the body simply stop working efficiently. (Module 30)

Weber's law A basic law of psychophysics stating that a just noticeable difference is a constant proportion to the intensity of an initial stimulus (rather than a constant amount). (Module 8)

weight set point The particular level of weight that the body strives to maintain. (Module 25)

working memory A memory system that holds information temporarily while actively manipulating and rehearsing that information. (Module 18)

zone of proximal development (ZPD) According to Vygotsky, the gap between what children already are able to accomplish on their own and what they are not quite ready to do by themselves. (Module 28)

zygote The new cell formed by the union of an egg and sperm. (Module 27)

References

60 Minutes. (2010, December 19). CBS News Transcripts. Retrieved June 21, 2011 from LexisNexis Academic.

AAA Foundation for Traffic Safety. (2008). Cell phones and driving: Research update. Retrieved from www.aaafoundation.org/pdf/CellPhonesandDrivingReport.pdf

AAA Foundation for Traffic Safety. (2009). Distracted Driving the Top Reason that 35 Percent of Drivers Feel Less Safe Than Five Years Ago, According to the AAA Foundation. Retrieved from www.aaafoundation.org/pdf/2009TSCIndexPR.pdf

Aartsen, M. J., Martin, M., & Zimprich, D. (2002). Gender differences in level and change in cognitive functioning: Results from the longitudinal aging study Amsterdam. *Gerontology, 50*, 35–38.

AAUW. *See* American Association of University Women.

Aazh, H., & Moore, B. C. J. (2007). Dead regions in the cochlea at 4 kHz in elderly adults: Relation to absolute threshold, steepness of audiogram, and pure-tone average. *Journal of the American Academy of Audiology, 18*, 97–106.

Abboud, L. (2005, July 27). The next phase in psychiatry. *The Wall Street Journal*, pp. D1, D5.

Abelman, R. (2007). Fighting the war on indecency: Mediating TV, Internet, and video-game usage among achieving and underachieving gifted children. *Roeper Review, 29*, 100–112.

Aboujaoude, E. (2008). *Compulsive acts: A psychiatrist's tales of ritual and obsession.* Berkeley, CA: University of California Press.

Abraham, A., Thybusch, K., Pieritz, K., & Hermann, C. (2013). Gender differences in creative thinking: Behavioral and fmri findings. *Brain Imaging and Behavior*. Retrieved from http://link.springer.com/article/10.1007-2Fs11682-013-9241-4

Abraham, P. F., & Calabrese, J. R. (2007). Review of: Lithium treatment of mood disorders: A practical guide (6th rev. ed.). *Bipolar Disorders, 9*, 548.

Abramowitz, J. S., Olatunji, B. O., & Deacon, B. J. (2007). Health anxiety, hypochondriasis, and the anxiety disorders. *Behavior Therapy, 38*, 86–94.

Accardi, M., & Milling, L. (2009, August). The effectiveness of hypnosis for reducing procedure-related pain in children and adolescents: A comprehensive methodological review. *Journal of Behavioral Medicine, 32*, 328–339.

Ackard, D. M., & Neumark-Sztainer, D. (2002). Date violence and date rape among adolescents: Associations with disordered eating behaviors and psychological health. *Child Abuse and Neglect, 26*, 455–473.

Ackerman, P. L. (2011). Intelligence and expertise. In R. J. Sternberg & S. Kaufman (Eds.), *The Cambridge handbook of intelligence.* New York: Cambridge University Press.

Adams-Byers, J., Squilkr, S., & Moon, S. M. (2004). Gifted students' perceptions of the academic and social/emotional effects of homogeneous and heterogeneous grouping. *Gifted Child Quarterly, 48*, 7–20.

Adams, G., & Dzokoto, V. A. (2007). Genital-shrinking panic in Ghana: A cultural psychological analysis. *Culture & Psychology, 13*, 83–104.

Adams, K. B. (2004). Changing investment in activities and interests in elders' lives: Theory and measurement. *International Journal of Aging and Human Development, 58*, 87–108.

Adams, M., Bell, L. A., & Griffin, P. (2007). *Teaching for diversity and social justice (2nd Ed.).* New York: Routledge/Taylor & Francis Group.

Addus, A. A., Chen, D., & Khan, A. S. (2007). Academic performance and advisement of university students: A case study. *College Student Journal, 41*, 316–326.

Adler, J. (1984, April 23). The fight to conquer fear. *Newsweek*, pp. 66–72.

Adler, M. (2013). Hunger and longing: A developmental regulation model for exploring core relational needs. In S. P. Gantt & B. Badenoch (Eds.), *The interpersonal neurobiology of group psychotherapy and group process.* London: Karnac Books.

Adolph, K. E., & Berger, S. E. (2011). Physical and motor development. In M. H. Bornstein & M. E. Lamb (Eds.), *Cognitive development: An advanced textbook.* New York: Psychology Press.

Advokat, C. (2005). Differential effects of clozapine versus other antipsychotics on clinical outcome and dopamine release in the brain. *Essential Psychopharmacology, 6*, 73–90.

Aftanas, L., & Golosheykin, S. (2005). Impact of regular meditation practice on EEG activity at rest and during evoked negative emotions. *International Journal of Neuroscience, 115*, 893–909.

Aguilar, J., Prato, F., Bravo, C., & Rivas, E. (2009). A multi-agent system for the management of abnormal situations in an artificially gas-lifted well. *Applied Artificial Intelligence, 23*, 406–426.

Aiello, R. J. (2006). Hypermasculinity and psychosocial development as predictors of potential date-rape perpetration on campus. *Dissertation Abstracts International: Section B: The Sciences and Engineering, 67*(2-B), 1178.

Aikawa, A., & Fujii, T. (2011). Using the Implicit Association Test (IAT) to measure implicit shyness. *Japanese Journal Of Psychology, 82*, 41–48.

Aiken, L. (2000). *Dying, death, and bereavement* (4th ed.). Mahwah, NJ: Erlbaum.

Aiken, L. R. (1996). *Assessment of intellectual functioning* (2nd ed.). New York: Plenum.

Aiken, L. R. (1997). *Psychological testing and assessment* (9th ed.). Needham Heights, MA: Allyn & Bacon.

Ainsworth, M. D. S., Blehar, M. C., Waters, E., & Wall, S. (1978). *Patterns of attachment: A psychological study of the strange situation.* Hillsdale, NJ: Erlbaum.

Ajzen, I. (2002). Residual effects of past on later behavior: Habituation and reasoned action perspectives. *Personality and Social Psychology Review, 6*, 107–122.

Akil, H., & Morano, M. I. (1996). The biology of stress: From periphery to brain. In S. J. Watson (Ed.), *Biology of schizophrenia and affective disease.* Washington, DC: American Psychiatric Press.

Akirav, I., Raizel, H., & Maroun, M. (2006). Enhancement of conditioned fear extinction by infusion of the GABA-sub(A) agonist muscimol into the rat prefrontal cortex and amygdala. *European Journal of Neuroscience, 23*, 758–764.

Aknin, L. B., Barrington-Leigh, C. P., Dunn, E. W., Helliwell, J. F., Burns, J., Biswas-Diener, R., & Norton, M. I. (2013). Prosocial spending and well-being: Cross-cultural evidence for a psychological universal. *Journal of Personality and Social Psychology.* Retrieved from http://www.hbs.edu/faculty/Publication%20Files/11-038.pdf

Aknin, L. B., Dunn, E. W., & Norton, M. I. (2012). Happiness runs in a circular motion: Evidence for a positive feedback loop between prosocial spending and happiness. *Journal of Happiness Studies, 13*, 347–355.

Aknin, L. B., Hamlin, J., & Dunn, E. W. (2012). Giving leads to happiness in young children. *Plos ONE, 7*, 88–93.

Alberts, A., Elkind, D., & Ginsberg, S. (2007). The personal fable and risk-taking in early adolescence. *Journal of Youth and Adolescence, 36*, 71–76.

Aleksander, I. (2013, June 23). Molly: Pure, but not so simple. *The New York Times*, p. ST1.

Alexandersen, P., Karsdal, M. A., & Christiansen, C. (2009). Long-term prevention with hormone-replacement therapy after the menopause: Which women should be targeted? *Women's Health, 5*, 637–647.

Alho, K., Vorobyev, V. A., Medvedev, S. V., Pakhomov, S. V., Starchenko, M. G., Terganiemi, M., & Näätänen, R. (2006). Selective attention to human voice enhances brain activity bilaterally in the superior temporal sulcus. *Brain Research, 1075*, 142–150.

Allen, M. (2011). Theory-led confirmation bias and experimental persona. *Research in Science & Technological Education, 29*, 107–127.

Alloy, L. B., Jacobson, N. S., & Acocella, J. (1999). *Abnormal psychology* (8th ed.). New York: McGraw-Hill.

Allport, G. W. (1961). *Pattern and growth in personality.* New York: Holt, Rinehart and Winston.

Allport, G. W. (1966). Traits revisited. *American Psychologist, 21*, 1–10.

Allport, G. W., & Postman, L. J. (1958). The basic psychology of rumor. In E. D. Maccoby,

T. M. Newcomb, & E. L. Hartley (Eds.), *Readings in social psychology* (3rd ed.). New York: Holt, Rinehart and Winston.

Allwood, M. A. (2007). The relations of violence exposure, trauma symptoms and aggressive cognitions to youth violent behavior. *Dissertation Abstracts International: Section B: The Sciences and Engineering, 67,* 5387.

Aloia, M. S., Smith, K., & Arnedt, J. T. (2007). Brief behavioral therapies reduce early positive airway pressure discontinuation rates in sleep apnea syndrome: Preliminary findings. *Behavioral Sleep Medicine, 5,* 89–104.

Alon, I., & Brett, J. M. (2007). Perceptions of time and their impact on negotiations in the Arabic-speaking Islamic world. *Negotiation Journal, 23,* 55–73.

Alonso, A., Alonso, S., & Piper, W. (2003). Group psychotherapy. In G. Stricker, T. A. Widiger, et al. (Eds.), *Handbook of psychology: Clinical psychology* (Vol. 8). New York: Wiley.

Altman, N. (1996). The accommodation of diversity in psychoanalysis. In R. P. Foster, M. Moskowitz, & R. A. Javier (Eds.), *Reaching across boundaries of culture and class: Widening the scope of psychotherapy.* Northvale, NJ: Jason Aronson.

Alzheimer's Association. (2013). *2013 Alzheimer's Disease: Facts and Figures.* Chicago, IL: Alzheimer's Association.

Amato, L., Davoili, M., Perucci, C. A., Ferri, M., Faggiano, F., & Mattick R. P. (2005). An overview of systematic reviews of the effectiveness of opiate maintenance therapies: Available evidence to inform clinical practice and research. *Journal of Substance Abuse Treatment, 28,* 321–329.

American Association of Mental Retardation (AAMR). (2002). *Mental retardation: Definition, classification, and systems of supports* (10th ed.). Washington, DC: AAMR.

American Association of University Women (AAUW). (1992). *How schools shortchange women: The A.A.U.W. Report.* Washington, DC: AAUW Educational Foundation. American Association of University Women.

American Association of University Women (AAUW). (2001). *Hostile hallways: Bullying, teasing, and sexual harassment in school.* Washington, DC: American Association of University Women.

American College Health Association. (2006). *Acquaintance and date rape: What everyone should know.* Baltimore, MD: American College Health Association.

American Psychiatric Association. (2013). *Diagnostic and Statistical Manual of Mental Disorders, Fifth Edition (DSM-5).* Washington, DC: Author.

American Psychological Association (APA). (1993, January/February). Subgroup norming and the Civil Rights Act. *Psychological Science Agenda, 5,* 6.

American Psychological Association (APA). (2000). Psychology careers for the twenty-first century. Washington, DC: American Psychological Association.

American Psychological Association (APA). (2002, August 21). *APA ethics code, 2002.* Washington, DC: American Psychological Association.

American Psychological Association (APA). (2007). *Where psychologists work.* Washington, DC: American Psychological Association.

American Psychological Association Presidential Task Force on Evidence-Based Practice. (2006). *Evidence-based practice in psychology, 61,* 271–285.

American Psychological Association Task Force on Intelligence. (1996). *Intelligence: Knowns and unknowns.* Washington, DC: American Psychological Association.

Amianto, F., D'Agata, F., Lavagnino, L., Caroppo, P., Abbate-Daga, G., Righi, D., Scarone, S., Bergui, M., Mortara, P., Fassino, S. (2013). Intrinsic connectivity networks within cerebellum and beyond in eating disorders. *The Cerebellum, 12*(5), 623–631.

Amid, P. K., & Chen, D. C. (2011). Surgical treatment of chronic groin and testicular pain after laparoscopic and open preperitoneal inguinal hernia repair. *Journal of the American College of Surgeons, 213,* 531–536.

Amodio, D. M., & Ratner, K. G. (2011). A memory systems model of implicit social cognition. *Current Directions In Psychological Science, 20,* 143–148.

Amos, A., Wiltshire, S., & Haw, S. (2006). Ambivalence and uncertainty: Experiences of and attitudes towards addiction and smoking cessation in the mid-to-late teens. *Health Education Research, 21,* 181–191.

Anastasi, A., & Urbina, S. (1997). *Psychological testing* (7th ed.). Englewood Cliffs, NJ: Prentice Hall.

Anderson, B. F. (1980). *The complete thinker: A handbook of techniques for creative and critical problem solving.* Englewood Cliffs, NJ: Prentice Hall.

Anderson, C. A., Shibuya, A., Ihori, N., Swing, E. L., Bushman, B. J., Sakamoto, A., Rothstein, H. R., & Saleem, M. (2010). Violent video game effects on aggression, empathy, and prosocial behavior in eastern and western countries: a meta-analytic review. *Psychological Bulletin, 136,* 151–173.

Anderson, C., & Carnagey, N. (2009). Causal effects of violent sports video games on aggression: Is it competitiveness or violent content? *Journal of Experimental Social Psychology, 45,* 731–739.

Anderson, C., & Home, J. A. (2006). Sleepiness enhances distraction during monotonous task. *Sleep: Journal of Sleep and Sleep Disorders Research, 29,* 573–576.

Anderson, C., Carnagey, N. L., Flanagan, M., Benjamin, A. J., Jr., Eubanks, J., & Valentine, J. C. (2004). Violent video games: Specific effects of violent content on aggressive thoughts and behavior. In M. P. Zanna (Ed.), *Advances in experimental social psychology* (Vol. 36). San Diego, CA: Elsevier Academic Press.

Anderson, J. (1988). Cognitive styles and multicultural populations. *Journal of Teacher Education, 39,* 2–9.

Anderson, J. A., & Adams, M. (1992). Acknowledging the learning styles of diverse student populations: Implications for instructional design. *New Directions for Teaching and Learning, 49,* 19–33.

Anderson, J. R. (1981). Interference: The relationship between response latency and response accuracy. *Journal of Experimental Psychology: Human Learning and Memory, 7,* 311–325.

Anderson, K. B., Cooper, H., & Okamura, L. (1997). Individual differences and attitudes toward rape: A meta-analytic review. *Personality and Social Psychology Bulletin, 23,* 295–315.

Andrasik, F. (2006). Psychophysiological disorders: Headache as a case in point. In F. Andrasik, *Comprehensive handbook of personality and psychopathology, Vol. 2: Adult psycho-pathology.* Hoboken, NJ: John Wiley & Sons.

Andrasik, F. (2007). What does the evidence show? Efficacy of behavioural treatments for recurrent headaches in adults. *Neurological Science, 28, Supplement,* S70–S77.

Andreasen, N. C. (2005). *Research advances in genetics and genomics: Implications for psychiatry.* Washington, DC: American Psychiatric Publishing.

Andrew, M., McCanlies, E., Burchfiel, C., Charles, L., Hartley, T., Fekedulegn, D., et al. (2008). Hardiness and psychological distress in a cohort of police officers. *International Journal of Emergency Mental Health, 10,* 137–148.

Andrews, F. M., & Withey, S. B. (1976). *Social indicators of well-being: Americans' perceptions of life quality.* New York: Plenum.

Anestis, M. D., Anestis, J. C., & Lilienfeld, S. O. (2011). When it comes to evaluating psychodynamic therapy, the devil is in the details. *American Psychologist, 66,* 149–151.

Angel, L. A., Polzella, D. J., & Elvers, G. C. (2010). Background music and cognitive performance. *Perceptual and Motor Skills, 110,* 1059–1064.

Angier, N., & Chang, K. (2005, January 24). Gray matter and the sexes: Still a scientific gray area. *The New York Times,* pp. A1, A15.

Angoff, W. H. (1988). The nature-nurture debate, aptitudes, and group differences. *American Psychologist, 43,* 713–720.

Anker, A. E., & Feeley, T. (2011). Are nonparticipants in prosocial behavior merely innocent bystanders? *Health Communication, 26,* 13–24.

Ansaldo, A. I., Arguin, M., & Roch Locours, L. A. (2002). The contribution of the right cerebral hemisphere to the recovery from aphasia: A single longitudinal case study. *Brain Languages, 82,* 206–222.

Antonini, A., & Barone, P. (2008, December). Dopamine agonist-based strategies in the treatment of Parkinson's disease. *Neurological Sciences, 29,* S371–SS374.

Antony, M. M., Brown, T. A., & Barlow, D. H. (1992). Current perspectives on panic and panic disorder. *Current Directions in Psychological Science, 1,* 79–82.

Apanovich, A. M., McCarthy, D., & Salovey, P. (2003). Using message framing to motivate HIV testing among low-income, ethnic minority women. *Health Psychology, 22,* 88–94.

Aponte, J. F., & Wohl, J. (2000). *Psychological intervention and cultural diversity.* Needham Heights, MA: Allyn & Bacon.

Arafat, I., & Cotton, W. L. (1974). Masturbation practices of males and females. *Journal of Sex Research, 10,* 293–307.

Arbuthnott, A., & Sharpe, D. (2009). The effect of physician-patient collaboration on patient adherence in non-psychiatric medicine. *Patient Education and Counseling, 77,* 60–67.

Arcelus, J., Mitchell, A. J., Wales, J., & Nielsen, S. (2011). Mortality rates in patients with anorexia nervosa and other eating disorders: A meta-analysis of 36 studies. *Archives of General Psychiatry, 68,* 724–731.

Archer, J., & Lloyd, B. B. (2002). *Sex and gender* (2nd ed.). New York: Cambridge University Press.

Arena, J. M. (1984, April). A look at the opposite sex. *Newsweek on Campus,* p. 21.

Ariely, D., & Norton, M. I. (2009). Conceptual consumption. *Annual Review of Psychology, 60,* 475–499.

Arimoto, M., Shiomi, T., Sasanabe, R., Inagawa, S., Ueda, H., & Inafuku, S. (2011). A sheet-type device for home-monitoring sleep apneas in children. *Sleep and Biological Rhythms, 9,* 103–111.

Ariyanto, A., Hornsey, M. J., & Gallois, C. (2006). Group-directed criticism in Indonesia: Role of message source and audience. *Asian Journal of Social Psychology, 9,* 96–102.

Armbruster, D., Mueller, A., Strobel, A., Lesch, K., Kirschbaum, C., & Brocke, B. (2011). Variation in genes involved in dopamine clearance influence the startle response in older adults. *Journal of Neural Transmission, 118,* 1281–1292.

Arnett, J. (2008). The neglected 95%: Why American psychology needs to become less American. *American Psychologist, 63,* 602–614.

Arnett, J. (2011). Emerging adulthood(s): The cultural psychology of a new life stage. In L. Jensen (Ed.), *Bridging cultural and developmental approaches to psychology: New syntheses in theory, research, and policy.* New York: Oxford University Press.

Arnett, J. J. (2000). Emerging adulthood. *American Psychologist, 55,* 469–480.

Arnett, J. J. (2001). Conceptions of the transition to adulthood: Perspectives from adolescence through midlife. *Journal of Adult Development, 8*(2), pp. 133–144.

Arnett, J. J. (2006). *Emerging adulthood: The winding road from the late teens through the twenties.* New York: Oxford University Press.

Arnett, J. J. (2007). Afterword: Aging out of care—Toward realizing the possibilities of emerging adulthood. *New Directions for Youth Development, 113,* 151–161.

Aronson, J., & Dee, T. (2012). Stereotype threat in the real world. In M. Inzlicht & T. Schmader (Eds.), *Stereotype threat: Theory, process, and application.* New York: Oxford University Press.

Aronson, J., & Steele, Claude M. (2005). Stereotypes and the fragility of academic competence, motivation, and self-concept. In A. J. Elliot & C. S. Dweck (Eds.), *Handbook of competence and motivation.* New York, NY: Guilford Publications.

Arshamian, A., Iannilli, E., Gerber, J. C., Willander, J., Persson, J., Seo, H., & . . . Larsson, M. (2013). The functional neuroanatomy of odor evoked auto-biographical memories cued by odors and words. *Neuropsychologia, 51,* 123–131.

Artistico, D., Pinto, A., Douek, J., Black, J., & Pezzuti, L. (2013). The value of removing daily obstacles via everyday problem-solving theory: Developing an applied novel procedure to increase self-efficacy for exercise. *Frontiers In Psychology, 4,* Retrieved from http://www.ncbi.nlm.nih.gov/pubmed/23372560

Asch, S. E. (1951). Effects of group pressure upon the modification and distortion of judgments. In H. Guetzkow (Ed.), *Groups, leadership, and men.* Pittsburgh: Carnegie Press.

Aschcraft, M. H. (1994). *Human memory and cognition* (2nd ed.). New York: Harper-Collins.

Aschheim, K. (2011). Toward human therapeutic cloning. *Nature Biotechnology, 29,* 986–989.

Ashley, K. B. (2013). The science on sexual orientation: A review of the recent literature. *Journal of Gay & Lesbian Mental Health, 17,* 175–182.

Aspinwall, L. G., & Taylor, S. E. (1997). A stitch in time: Self-regulation and proactive coping. *Psychological Bulletin, 121,* 417–436.

Associated Press. (2009, May 21). AP-mtvU: College students and depression. Retrieved from http://surveys.ap.org/data/Edison/APMTV%20Topline%20marginals.pdf

Association for the Advancement of Artificial Intelligence. (2009). AAAI Presidential Panel on Long-Term AI Futures: 2008–2009 Study. Retrieved from http://research.microsoft.com/en-us/um/people/horvitz/AAAI_Presidential_Panel_2008-2009.htm

Astbury-Ward, E. (2002). From Kama Sutra to dot.com: The history, myths and management of premature ejaculation. *Sexual and Relationship Therapy, 17,* 367–380.

Astin, A. W., Korn, W. S., & Berz, E. R. (2004). *The American freshman: National norms for fall 2004.* Los Angeles, CA: Higher Education Research Institute, UCLA.

Atkinson, H. (Ed.). (1997, January 21). Understanding your diagnosis. *HealthNews,* p. 3.

Atkinson, H. G. (2003, August). Are you a "good" patient? *HealthNews,* p. 5.

Atkinson, R. C., & Shiffrin, R. M. (1968). Human memory: A proposed system and its control processes. In K. W. Spence & J. T. Spence (Eds.), *The psychology of learning and motivation: Advances in research and theory* (Vol. 2). New York: Academic Press.

Atkinson, R. C., & Shiffrin, R. M. (1971). The control of short-term memory. *Scientific American, 225,* pp. 82–90.

Auer, J. A., Goodship, A., Arnoczky, S., Pearce, S., Price, J., Claes, L., von Rechenberg, B., Hofmann-Amtenbrinck, M., Schneider, E., Muller-Terpitz, R., Thiele, F., Rippe, K. P., & Grainger, D. W. (2007). Refining animal models in fracture research: seeking consensus for changing the agenda in optimising both animal welfare and scientific validity for appropriate biomedical use. *BMC Musculoskeletal Disorders, 8,* 72.

Aujoulat, I., Luminet, O., & Deccache, A. (2007). The perspective of patients on their experience of powerlessness. *Quality Health Research, 17,* 772–785.

Aussilloux, C., & Bagdadli, A. (2006). Handicap mental et société: Soigner, éduquer, intégrer. Mental handicap and society. *Neuropsychiatrie de l'Enfance et de l'Adolescence, 54,* 336–340.

Auyeung, B., Baron-Cohen, S., Ashwin, E., Taylor, K., Hines, M., Hackett, G., et al. (2009). Fetal testosterone predicts sexually differentiated childhood behavior in girls and in boys. *Psychological Science, 20,* 144–148.

Averill, J. R. (1975). A semantic atlas of emotional concepts. *Catalog of Selected Documents in Psychology, 5,* 330.

Avery, D., McKay, P., & Wilson, D. (2008). What are the odds? How demographic similarity affects the prevalence of perceived employment discrimination. *Journal of Applied Psychology, 93,* 235–249.

Azevedo, R. T., Macaluso, E., Avenanti, A., Santangelo, V., Cazzato, V., Aglioti, S. M. (2013). Their pain is not our pain: Brain and autonomic correlates of empathic resonance with the pain of same and different race individuals. *Human Brain Mapping, 34*(12), 3168–3181.

Baars, B., & Seth, A. K. (2009). Consciousness: Theories and models. In W. Banks (Ed.). *Encyclopedia of consciousness.* New York: Elsevier.

Babson, K., Feldner, M., Trainor, C., & Smith, R. (2009, September). An experimental investigation of the effects of acute sleep deprivation on panic-relevant biological challenge responding. *Behavior Therapy, 40,* 239–250.

Bacchiochi, J. R. (2006). Development and validation of the Malingering Discriminant Function Index (M-DFI) for the Minnesota Multiphasic Personality Inventory-2 (MMPI-2). *Dissertation Abstracts International: Section B: The Sciences and Engineering, 66*(10-B), 5673.

Baddeley, A. (2001). Is working memory still working? *American Psychologist, 56,* 851–864.

Baddeley, A. D., Allen, R. J., & Hitch, G. J. (2011). Binding in visual working memory: The role of the episodic buffer. *Neuropsychologia, 49,* 1393–1400.

Baddeley, A., & Wilson, B. (1985). Phonological coding and short-term memory in patients without speech. *Journal of Memory and Language, 24,* 490–502.

Baddeley, A., Chincotta, D., & Adlam, A. (2001). Working memory and the control of action: Evidence from task switching. *Journal of Experimental Psychology: General, 130,* 641–657.

Badke, M. B., Sherman, J., Boyne, P., Page, S., & Dunning, K. (2011). Tongue-based biofeedback for balance in stroke: results of an 8-week pilot study. *Archives of Physical and Medical Rehabilitation, 92,* 1364–1370.

Bagge, C., & Sher, K. (2008). Adolescent alcohol involvement and suicide attempts: Toward the development of a conceptual framework. *Clinical Psychology Review, 28,* 1283–1296.

Bagnall, D. (2010). The use of spinal cord stimulation and intrathecal drug delivery in the treatment of low back-related pain. *Physical Medicine & Rehabilitation Clinics of North America, 21,* 851–858.

Bahrick, H. P., Hall, L. K., & Berger, S. A. (1996). Accuracy and distortion in memory for high school grades. *Psychological Science, 7,* 265–269.

Bahrick, L. E., Lickliter, R., & Castellanos, I. (2013). The development of face perception in infancy: Intersensory interference and unimodal visual facilitation. *Developmental Psychology, 49,* 1919–1930.

Bai, L. (2005). Children at play: A childhood beyond the Confucian shadow. *Childhood: A Global Journal of Child Research, 12,* 9–32.

Bailey, K., West, R., & Anderson, C. A. (2011). The association between chronic exposure to video game violence and affective picture processing: an ERP study. *Cognitive, Affective, and Behavioral Neuroscience, 11,* 259–76.

Bains, O. S. (2006). Insomnia: Difficulty falling and staying asleep. In N. F. Watson & B. V. Bradley (Eds.), *Clinician's guide to sleep disorders.* Philadelphia: Taylor & Francis.

Bair, D. (2003). *Jung: A biography.* New York: Little, Brown, and Company.

Baker, J., & Berenbaum, H. (2007). Emotional approach and problem-focused coping: A comparison of potentially adaptive strategies. *Cognition and Emotion, 21,* 95–118.

Baker, S. (2011). *Final Jeopardy: Man vs. machine and the quest to know everything.* New York: Houghton Mifflin Harcourt.

Baker, S. C., & Serdikoff, S. L. (2013). Addressing the role of animal research in psychology. In D. S. Dunn, R. R. Gurung, K. Z. Naufel, & J. H. Wilson (Eds.), *Controversy in the psychology classroom: Using hot topics to foster critical thinking.* Washington, DC: American Psychological Association.

Baker, S. E., Johnson, P. J., & Slater, D. (2007). Learned food aversion with and without an odour cue for protecting untreated baits from wild mammal foraging [Special issue: Conservation, enrichment, and animal behavior]. *Applied Animal Behaviour Science, 102,* 410–428.

Balaban, C. D. (2002). Neural substrates linking balance control and anxiety [Special issue: The

Pittsburgh special issue]. *Physiology and Behavior, 77,* 469–475.

Balaban, C. D., McBurney, D. H., & Affeltranger, M. A. (2005). Three distinct categories of time course of pain produced by oral capsaicin. *The Journal of Pain, 6,* 315–322.

Balconi, M., Bortolotti, A., & Crivelli, D. (2013). Self-report measures, facial feedback, and personality differences (BEES) in cooperative vs. noncooperative situations: Contribution of the mimic system to the sense of empathy. *International Journal of Psychology, 48,* 631-640.

Ball, D. (2004). Genetic approaches to alcohol dependence. *British Journal of Psychiatry, 185,* 449–451.

Baltes, P. B., & Kunzmann, U. (2003). Wisdom. *Psychologist, 16,* 131–133.

Bandura, A. (1977). *Social learning theory.* Englewood Cliffs, NJ: Prentice Hall.

Bandura, A. (1986). *Social foundations of thought and action: A social cognitive theory.* Englewood Cliffs, NJ: Prentice Hall.

Bandura, A. (1994). Social cognitive theory of mass communication. In J. Bryant & D. Zillmann (Eds.), *Media effects: Advances in theory and research: LEA's communication series.* Hillsdale, NJ: Erlbaum.

Bandura, A. (1999). Social cognitive theory of personality. In D. Cervone & Y. Shod (Eds.), *The coherence of personality.* New York: Guilford.

Bandura, A. (2000). Self-efficacy: The foundation of agency. In W. J. Perrig & A. Grob (Eds.), *Control of human behavior, mental processes, and consciousness: Essays in honor of the 60th birthday of August Flammer.* Mahwah, NJ: Erlbaum.

Bandura, A. (2004). Swimming against the mainstream: The early years from chilly tributary to transformative mainstream. *Behavior Research and Therapy, 42,* 613–630.

Bandura, A. (2009). Social cognitive theory goes global. *The Psychologist, 22,* 504–506.

Bandura, A., & Locke, E. A. (2003). Negative self-efficacy and goal effects revisited. *Journal of Applied Psychology, 88,* 87–99.

Bandura, A., Grusec, J. E., & Menlove, F. L. (1967). Vicarious extinction of avoidance behavior. *Journal of Personality and Social Psychology, 5,* 16–23.

Bandura, A., Ross, D., & Ross, S. (1963a). Imitation of film-mediated aggressive models. *Journal of Abnormal and Social Psychology, 66,* 3–11.

Bandura, A., Ross, D., & Ross, S. (1963b). Vicarious reinforcement and imitative learning. *Journal of Abnormal and Social Psychology, 67,* 601–607.

Banich, T., & Heller, W. (1998). Evolving perspectives on lateralization of function. *Current Directions in Psychological Science, 7,* 1–2.

Banks, J. A. (2006). Improving race relations in schools: From theory and research to practice. *Journal of Social Issues, 62,* 607–614.

Bannon, L. (2000, February 14). Why boys and girls get different toys. *The Wall Street Journal,* pp. B1, B4.

Baraas, R. C., Foster, D. H., & Amano, K. (2006). Anomalous trichromats' judgments of surface color in natural scenes under different daylights. *Neuroscience, 23,* 629–635.

Barak, A., & Grohol, J. M. (2011). Current and future trends in Internet-supported mental health interventions. *Journal of Technology in Human Services, 29,* 155–196.

Barandiaran, A. A., Pascual, A. C., & Samaniego, C. M. (2006). A criticism of the Kohlberg theory: The moral development in adults and educative implications. *Revista de Psicologia General y Aplicada, 59,* 165–182.

Barash, D. P., & Lipton, J. E. (2011). *Payback: Why we retaliate, redirect aggression, and take revenge.* New York: Oxford University Press.

Barke, D. B. (2011). Self-selection for stressful experiences. *Stress and Health: Journal of the International Society for the Investigation of Stress, 27,* 194–205.

Barker, J., & Jones, M. (2008, June). The effects of hypnosis on self-efficacy, affect, and soccer performance: A case study. *Journal of Clinical Sport Psychology, 2,* 127–147.

Barkley, R. (2000). *Taking charge of ADHD* (rev. ed.). New York: Guilford Press.

Barkley, R. (2005). *ADHD and the nature of self-control.* New York: Guildford.

Barkley, R. A., Knouse, L. E., & Murphy, K. R. (2011). Correspondence and disparity in the self- and other ratings of current and childhood ADHD symptoms and impairment in adults with ADHD. *Psychological Assessment, 23,* 437–446.

Barlow, D. H. (2007). *Clinical handbook of psychological disorders: A step-by-step treatment manual* (4th ed.). New York: Guilford Press.

Barmeyer, C. I. (2004). Learning styles and their impact on cross-cultural training: An international comparison in France, Germany and Quebec. *International Journal of Intercultural Relations, 28,* 577–594.

Barnes, J. C., & Jacobs, B. A. (2013). Genetic risk for violent behavior and environmental exposure to disadvantage and violent crime: The case for gene–environment interaction. *Journal of Interpersonal Violence, 28,* 92–120.

Barnes, T., & Eardley, I. (2007). Premature ejaculation: The scope of the problem. *Journal of Sex & Marital Therapy, 33,* 151–170.

Barnes, V. A., Davis, H. C., Murzynowski, J., & Treiber, F. A. (2004). Impact of meditation on resting and ambulatory blood pressure and heart rate in youth. *Medicine, 66,* 909–914.

Barnett, J. E., Wise, E. H., & Johnson-Greene, D. (2007). Informed consent: Too much of a good thing or not enough? *Professional Psychology: Research and Practice, 38,* 179–186.

Barnett, K. (2013). *The spark: A mother's story of nurturing, genius, and autism.* New York: Random House.

Barnett, R. C. (2004). Woman and work: Where are we, where did we come from, and where are we going? [Preface]. *Journal of Social Issues, 60,* 667–674.

Barnett, S. M., Rindermann, H., Williams, W. M., & Ceci, S. J. (2011). Society and intelligence. In R. J. Sternberg & S. Kaufman (Eds.), *The Cambridge handbook of intelligence.* New York: Cambridge University Press.

Baron, R. S. (2005). So right it's wrong: Groupthink and the ubiquitous nature of polarized group decision making. In M. P. Zanna (Ed.), *Advances in experimental social psychology* (Vol. 37). San Diego, CA: Elsevier Academic Press.

Barr, V., Rando, R., Krylowicz, B., and Reetz, D. (2010). The Association for University and College Counseling Center Directors annual survey. The Association for University and College Counseling Center Directors. Retrieved September 6, 2011 from http://aucccd.org/img/pdfs/aucccd_directors_survey_monograph_2010.pdf

Barrada, J., Abad, F., & Olea, J. (2011). Varying the valuating function and the presentable bank in computerized adaptive testing. *The Spanish Journal of Psychology, 14,* 500–508.

Barresi, J. (2007). Consciousness and intentionality. *Journal of Consciousness Studies, 14, Special issue: Concepts of Consciousness: Integrating an Emerging Science,* 77–93.

Barrett, D. (2001). *The committee of sleep: How artists, scientists, and athletes use dreams for creative problem-solving–and how you can too.* Norwalk, CT: Crown House Publishing Limited.

Barrett, L. (2011). *Beyond the brain: How body and environment shape animal and human minds.* Princeton, NJ: Princeton University Press.

Barrett, L. F., & Salovey, P. (Eds.). (2002). *The wisdom in feeling: Psychological processes in emotional intelligence.* New York: Guilford Press.

Barrett, L. F., & Wager, T. D. (2006). The structure of emotion: Evidence from neuroimaging studies. *Current Directions in Psychological Science, 15,* 79–83.

Barron, F. (1990). *Creativity and psychological health: Origins of personal vitality and creative freedom.* Buffalo, NY: Creative Education Foundation.

Barron, G., & Yechiam, E. (2002). Private e-mail requests and the diffusion of responsibility. *Computers in Human Behavior, 18,* 507–520.

Barson, J. R., Morganstern, I., & Leibowitz, S. F. (2011). Similarities in hypothalamic and mesocorticolimbic circuits regulating the overconsumption of food and alcohol. *Physiology & Behavior, 104,* 128–137.

Bartecchi, C. E., MacKenzie, T. D., & Schrier, R. W. (1995, May). The global tobacco epidemic. *Scientific American,* pp. 44–51.

Bartholow, B. D., Bushman, B. J., & Sestir, M. A. (2005). Chronic violent video game exposure and desensitization to violence: Behavioral and event-related brain potential data. *Journal of Experimental Social Psychology, 42,* 532–539.

Bartlett, F. (1932). *Remembering: A study in experimental and social psychology.* Cambridge, England: Cambridge University Press.

Bartlett, M. Y., & DeSteno, D. (2006). Gratitude and prosocial behavior: Helping when it costs you. *Psychological Science, 17,* 319–325.

Bartocci, G. (2004). Transcendence techniques and psychobiological mechanisms underlying religious experience. *Mental Health, Religion and Culture, 7,* 171–181.

Bartolomeo, J., Cruz, C., Messer, L., Dodd, J., Herndon, J., & Warrick, P. (2009, June 29). Chastity Bono's sex change: Becoming Chaz. *People,* p. 54.

Bartone, P., Roland, R., Picano, J., & Williams, T. (2008). Psychological hardiness predicts success in U.S. Army Special Forces candidates. *International Journal of Selection and Assessment, 16,* 78–81.

Bartoshuk, L. (2000, July/August). The bitter with the sweet. *APS Observer, 11,* 33.

Bartoshuk, L., & Lucchina, L. (1997, January 13). Are you a supertaster? *U.S. News & World Report,* pp. 58–59.

Bartzokis, G., Nuechterlein, K. H., Lu, P. H., Gitlin, M., Rogers, S., & Mintz, J. (2003). Dysregulated brain development in adult men with schizophrenia: A magnetic resonance imaging study. *Biological Psychiatry, 53,* 412–421.

Baruss, I. (2003). *Alterations of consciousness: An empirical analysis for social scientists.* Washington, DC: American Psychological Association.

Basak, C., Boot, W., Voss, M., & Kramer, A. (2008). Can training in a real-time strategy video game attenuate cognitive decline in older adults? *Psychology and Aging, 23,* 765–777.

Bassotti, G., Villanacci, V., Fisogni, S., Rossi, E., Baronio, P., Clerici, C., et al. (2007). Enteric glial cells and their role in gastrointestinal motor abnormalities: Introducing the neuro-gliopathies. *World Journal of Gastroenterology, 14,* 4035–4041.

Bassotti, G., & Villanacci, V. (2011). Can 'functional' constipation be considered as a form of enteric neuro-gliopathy? *Glia, 59,* 345–350.

Bateman, A. W. (2011). Commentary on 'Minding the difficult patient': Mentalizing and the use of formulation in patients with borderline personality disorder comorbid with antisocial personality disorder. *Personality and Mental Health, 5,* 85–90.

Bates, E. (2005). Plasticity, localization, and language development. In S. T. Parker & J. Langer (Eds.), *Biology and knowledge revisited: From neurogenesis to psychogenesis.* Mahwah, NJ: Lawrence Erlbaum Associates.

Bates, P. E., Cuvo, T., Miner, C. A., & Korabek, C. A. (2001). Simulated and community-based instruction involving persons with mild and moderate mental retardation. *Research in Developmental Disabilities, 22,* 95–115.

Bates, R. (2002). Liking and similarity as predictors of multi-source ratings. *Personnel Review, 31,* 540–552.

Batson, C. (2011). *Altruism in humans.* New York: Oxford University Press.

Batson, C. D., & Powell, A. A. (2003). Altruism and prosocial behavior. In T. Millon & M. J. Lerner (Eds.), *Handbook of psychology: Personality and social psychology* (Vol. 5). New York: Wiley.

Bauer, J. J., Schwab, J. R., & McAdams, D. P. (2011). Self-actualizing: Where ego development finally feels good? *The Humanistic Psychologist, 39,* 121–136.

Bauer, P. (2008). Toward a neuro-developmental account of the development of declarative memory. *Developmental Psychobiology, 50,* 19–31.

Bauer, S. M., Schanda, H., Karakula, H., Olajossy-Hilkesberger, L., Rudaleviciene, P., Okribelashvili, N., & . . . Stompe, T. (2011). Culture and the prevalence of hallucinations in schizophrenia. *Comprehensive Psychiatry, 52,* 319–325.

Baum, A. (1994). Behavioral, biological, and environmental interactions in disease processes. In S. Blumenthal, K. Matthews, & S. Weiss (Eds.), *New research frontiers in behavioral medicine: Proceedings of the National Conference.* Washington, DC: NIH Publications.

Baum, A., Lorduy, K., & Jenkins, F. J. (2011). The molecular biology of stress: Cellular defense, immune response, and aging. In R. J. Contrada & A. Baum (Eds.), *The handbook of stress science: Biology, psychology, and health.* New York: Springer Publishing Co.

Bauman, S., & Kopp, T. G. (2006). Integrating a humanistic approach in outpatient sex offender groups. *Journal for Specialists in Group Work, 31,* 247–261.

Baumeister, R. F., & Stillman, T. (2006). Erotic plasticity: Nature, culture, gender, and sexuality. In R. D. McAnulty & M. M. Burnette (Eds.), *Sex and sexuality, Vol 1: Sexuality today: Trends and controversies.* Westport, CT: Praeger Publishers/Greenwood Publishing.

Baumeister, R. F., Twenge, J. M., & Nuss, C. K. (2002). Effects of social exclusion on cognitive processes: Anticipated aloneness reduces intelligent thought. *Journal of Personality and Social Psychology, 83,* 817–827.

Baumgartner, F. (2002). The effect of hardiness in the choice of coping strategies in stressful situations. *Studia Psychologica, 44,* 69–75.

Baumrind, D. (2005). Patterns of parental authority and adolescent autonomy. *New Directions for Child and Adolescent Development, 108,* 61–69.

Baumrucker, S., Mingle, P., Harrington, D., Stolick, M., Carter, G. T., & Oertli, K. A. (2011). Medical marijuana and organ transplantation: Drug of abuse, or medical necessity? *American Journal of Hospice & Palliative Medicine, 28,* 130–134.

Bazalakova, M. H., Wright, J., Schneble, E. J., McDonald, M. P., Heilman, C. J., Levey, A. I., & Blakely, R. D. (2007). Deficits in acetylcholine homeostasis, receptors and behaviors in choline transporter heterozygous mice. *Genes, Brain & Behavior, 6,* 411–424.

Bayliss, D. M., Jarrold, C., Baddeley, A. D., & Gunn, D. M. (2005a). The relationship between short-term memory and working memory: Complex span made simple? *Memory,* 13, 414–421.

Beam, C. R., & Turkheimer, E. (2013). Phenotype–environment correlations in longitudinal twin models. *Development and Psychopathology, 25,* 7–16.

Beardslee, W., Wright, E., Gladstone, T., & Forbes, P. (2007). Long-term effects from a randomized trial of two public health preventive interventions for parental depression. *Journal of Family Psychology, 21,* 703–713.

Bearman, C. R., Ball, L. J., & Ormerod, T. C. (2007). The structure and function of spontaneous analogising in domain-based problem solving. *Thinking & Reasoning, 13,* 273–294.

Beatty, J. (2000). *The human brain: Essentials of behavioral neuroscience.* Thousand Oaks, CA: Sage.

Bechara, A., Damasio, A. R., Damasio, H., & Anderson, S. (1994). Insensitivity to future consequences following damage to human prefrontal cortex. *Cognition, 50,* 7–15.

Beck, A. P., & Lewis, C. M. (Eds.). (2000). *The process of group psychotherapy: Systems for analyzing change.* Washington, DC: American Psychological Association.

Beck, A. T. (1995). Cognitive therapy: Past, present, and future. In M. J. Mahoney (Ed.), *Cognitive and constructive psychotherapies: Theory, research, and practice.* New York: Springer.

Beck, A. T. (2004). Cognitive therapy, behavior therapy, psychoanalysis, and pharmacotherapy: A cognitive continuum. In A. Freeman, M. J. Mahoney, P. Devito, & D. Martin (Eds.), *Cognition and Psychotherapy* (2nd ed.). New York: Springer Publishing Co.

Beck, A. T., & Emery, G., with Greenberg, R. L. (1985). *Anxiety disorders and phobias: A cognitive perspective.* New York: Basic Books.

Beck, A. T., & Rector, N. A. (2005). Cognitive approaches to schizophrenia: Theory and therapy. *Annual Review of Clinical Psychology, 1,* 577–606.

Beck, A. T., Freeman, A., & Davis, D. D. (2004). *Cognitive therapy of personality disorders* (2nd ed.). New York: Guilford Press.

Beck, H. P., Levinson, S., & Irons, G. (2009). Finding little Albert: A journey to John B. Watson's infant laboratory. *American Psychologist, 64,* 605–614.

Becker, B. E., & Luthar, S. S. (2007). Peer-perceived admiration and social preference: Contextual correlates of positive peer regard among suburban and urban adolescents. *Journal of Research on Adolescence, 17,* 117–144.

Becker, T. (2003). Is emotional intelligence a viable concept? *Academy of Management Review, 28,* 192–195.

Bedard, W. W., & Persinger, M. A. (1995). Prednisolone blocks extreme intermale social aggression in seizure-induced, brain-damaged rats: Implications for the amygdaloid central nucleus, corticotrophin-releasing factor, and electrical seizures. *Psychological Reports, 77,* 3–9.

Beersma, D. G. M., & Gordijn, M. C. M. (2007). Circadian control of the sleep-wake cycle. *Physiology & Behavior, 90.*

Begeny, J. C., & Martens, B. K. (2007). Inclusionary education in Italy: A literature review and call for more empirical research. *Remedial and Special Education, 28,* 80–94.

Begg, D., & Langley, J. (2001). Changes in risky driving behavior from age 21 to 26 years. *Journal of Safety Research, 32,* 491–499.

Beghetto, R. A., & Kaufman, J. C. (Eds.). (2010). *Nurturing creativity in the classroom.* New York: Cambridge University Press.

Begley, S. (2002, September 13). The memory of September 11 is seared in your mind; but is it really true? *The Wall Street Journal,* p. B1.

Begley, S. (2005, April 29). Evolution psychology may not help explain our behavior after all. *The Wall Street Journal,* p. D1.

Begley, S. (2009, February 16). Will the BlackBerry sink the presidency? *Newsweek,* p. 37.

Begley, S. (2010, August 2). What's really human? The trouble with student guinea pigs. *Newsweek,* p. 30.

Begley, S. (2013, June 5). *The schizophrenic mind.* Retrieved from http://www.sharonlbegley.com/the-schizophrenic-mind

Behrendt, R. (2011). *Neuroanatomy of social behaviour: An evolutionary and psychoanalytic perspective.* London England: Karnac Books.

Behrens, K. Y., Parker, A. C., & Haltigan, J. D. (2011). Maternal sensitivity assessed during the Strange Situation Procedure predicts child's attachment quality and reunion behaviors. *Infant Behavior & Development, 34,* 378–381.

Behrens, M., Lendon, C., & Roe, C. (2009). A common biological mechanism in cancer and Alzheimer's disease? *Current Alzheimer Research, 6,* 196–204.

Beidel, D. C., & Turner, S. M. (2007). Etiology of social anxiety disorder. In D. C. Beidel & S. M. Turner (Eds.), *Shy children, phobic adults: Nature and treatment of social anxiety disorders* (2nd ed.). Washington, DC: American Psychological Association.

Belar, C. (2008, April). Clinical health psychology: A health care specialty in professional psychology. *Professional Psychology: Research and Practice, 39,* 229–233.

Belasen, A. T., & Fortunato, M. V. (2013). Situational motivation: Challenge the binary. In M. A. Paludi (Ed.), *Psychology for business success, Vol 1: Juggling, balancing, and integrating work and family roles and responsibilities, Vol 2: Institutional equity and compliance, Vol 3: Managing, leading, and developing employees, Vol 4: Implementing best practices in human resources.* Santa Barbara, CA: Praeger/ABC-CLIO.

Bellezza, E. S. (2000). Mnemonic devices. In A. E. Kazdin (Ed.), *Encyclopedia of psychology* (Vol. 5). Washington, DC: American Psychological Association.

Belov, D. I., & Armstrong, R. D. (2009). Direct and inverse problems of item pool design for computerized adaptive testing. *Educational and Psychological Measurement, 69,* 533–547.

Belsky, J., & Pluess, M. (2009). The nature (and nurture?) of plasticity in early human development. *Perspectives on Psychological Science, 4,* 345–351.

Bem, D. J. (1996). Exotic becomes erotic: A developmental theory of sexual orientation. *Psychological Review, 103,* 320–335.

Bem, D. J., & Honorton, C. (1994). Does psi exist? Replicable evidence for an anomalous process of information transfer. *Psychological Bulletin, 115,* 4–18.

Bem, S. L. (1998). *An unconventional family.* New Haven, CT: Yale University Press.

Ben-Porath, Y., & Archer, R. (2008). The MMPI-2 and MMPI-A. *Personality assessment.* New York: Routledge/Taylor & Francis Group.

Benac, N., & Tompson, T. (2009, May 21). AP poll: Most students stressed, some depressed. Retrieved from http://www.denverpost.com/popular/ci_12418610

Benca, R. M. (2005). Diagnosis and treatment of chronic insomnia: a review. *Psychiatric Services,* 56: 332–343.

Benderly, B. L. (2004). Looking beyond the SAT. *American Psychological Society, 17,* 12–18.

Benet-Martinez, V., Lee, F., & Leu, J. (2006). Biculturalism and cognitive complexity: Expertise in cultural representations. *Journal of Cross-Cultural Psychology, 37,* 386–407.

Benham, G., Woody, E. Z., & Wilson, K. S. (2006). Expect the unexpected: Ability, attitude, and responsiveness to hypnosis. *Journal of Personality and Social Psychology, 91,* 342–350.

Benjamin, L. T., Jr. (1985, February). Defining aggression: An exercise for classroom discussion. *Teaching of Psychology, 12*(1), 40–42.

Benson, E. (2003, April). The science of sexual arousal. *Monitor on Psychology,* pp. 50–56.

Benson, H., Kornhaber, A., Kornhaber, C., LeChanu, M. N., et al. (1994). Increases in positive psychological characteristics with a new relaxation-response curriculum in high school students. *Journal of Research and Development in Education, 27,* 226–231.

Benson, Herbert. (1975). Benson-Henry Institute for Mind Body Medicine, Massachusetts General Hospital. http://relaxationresponse.org/steps/

Benton, S. A., Robertson, J. M., Tseng, W., Newton, F. B., & Benton, S. L. (2003) "Changes in counceling center client problems across 13 years". *Professional Psychology: Research and Practice 34*(1) 66–72.

Bentwich, J., Dobronevsky, E., Aichenbaum, S., Shorer, R., Peretz, R., Khaigrekht, M., & . . . Rabey, J. M. (2011). Beneficial effect of repetitive transcranial magnetic stimulation combined with cognitive training for the treatment of Alzheimer's disease: A proof of concept study. *Journal of Neural Transmission, 118,* 463–471.

Beran, M. J., Smith, J., & Perdue, B. M. (2013). Language-trained chimpanzees (Pan troglodytes) name what they have seen but look first at what they have not seen. *Psychological Science, 24,* 660–666.

Berecki-Gisolf, J., McKenzie, S. J., Dobson, A. J., McFarlane, A., & McLaughlin, D. (2013). A history of comorbid depression and anxiety predicts new onset of heart disease. *Journal of Behavioral Medicine, 36,* 347–353.

Beresnevaité, M., Taylor, G. J., & Bagby, R. M. (2007). Assessing alexithymia and type A behavior in coronary heart disease patients: A multimethod approach. *Psychotherapy and Psychosomatics, 76,* 186–192.

Bergman, S. M., Fearrington, M. E., Davenport, S. W., & Bergman, J. Z. (2011). Millennials, narcissism, and social networking: What narcissists do on social networking sites and why. *Personality and Individual Differences, 50,* 706–711.

Berk, L. E. (2005). Why parenting matters. In S. Olfman (Ed.), *Childhood lost: How American culture is failing our kids.* Westport, CT: Praeger Publishers/Greenwood Publishing Group.

Berkman, L. F., Ertel, K. A., & Glymour, M. M. (2011). Aging and social intervention: Life course perspectives. In R. H. Binstock & L. K. George (Eds.), *Handbook of aging and the social sciences (7th ed.).* San Diego, CA: Elsevier Academic Press.

Berkowitz, L. (2001). On the formation and regulation of anger and aggression: A cognitive-neoassociationistic analysis. In W. G. Parrott (Ed.), *Emotions in social psychology: Essential readings.* New York: Psychology Press.

Berliner, L., & Elliott, D. M. (2002). Sexual abuse of children. In J. E. B. Myers, L. Berliner, et al. (Eds.), *The APSAC handbook on child maltreatment* (2nd ed.). Thousand Oaks, CA: Sage.

Bernal, G., Trimble, J. E., Burlew, A. K., & Leong, F. T. (Eds.). (2002). *Handbook of racial and ethnic minority psychology.* Thousand Oaks, CA: Sage.

Bernard, L. L. (1924). *Instinct: A study in social psychology.* New York: Holt.

Bernstein, D. M., Loftus, G. R., & Meltzoff, A. N. (2005). Object identification in preschool children and adults. *Developmental Science, 8,* 151–161.

Bernstein, D., & Loftus, E. (2009a). How to tell if a particular memory is true or false. *Perspectives on Psychological Science, 4,* 370–374.

Bernstein, D., & Loftus, E. (2009b). The consequences of false memories for food preferences and choices. *Perspectives on Psychological Science, 4,* 135–139.

Bernstein, E. (2011, April 19). Friendly fight: A smarter way to say 'I'm angry.' *Wall Street Journal,* pp. D1, D4.

Berntsen, D., & Rubin, D. C. (2004). Cultural life scripts structure recall from autobiographical memory. *Memory and Cognition, 32,* 427–442.

Berntsen, D., & Thomsen, D. K. (2005). Personal memories for remote historical events: Accuracy and clarity of flashbulb memories related to World War II. *Journal of Experimental Psychology: General, 134,* 242–257.

Berntson, G. G., Bechara, A., Damasio, H., Tranel, D., & Cacioppo, J. T. (2007). Amygdala contribution to selective dimensions of emotion. *Social Cognitive and Affective Neuroscience, 2,* 123–129.

Berridge, K. C. (2004). Motivation concepts in behavioral neuroscience. *Physiology and Behavior, 81,* 179–209.

Berrios, G. E. (1996). *The history of mental symptoms: Descriptive psychopathology since the 19th century.* Cambridge: Cambridge University Press.

Bertakis, K. (2009). The influence of gender on the doctor-patient interaction. *Patient Education and Counseling, 76,* 356–360.

Bertakis, K., Franks, P., & Epstein, R. (2009). Patient-centered communication in primary care: Physician and patient gender and gender concordance. *Journal of Women's Health, 18,* 539–545.

Berthoud, H. R. (2002). Multiple neural systems controlling food intake and body weight. *Neuroscience and Biobehavioral Reviews, 26,* 393–428.

Betz, N. (2007). Career self-efficacy: Exemplary recent research and emerging directions. *Journal of Career Assessment, 15,* 403–422.

Beyene, Y., Gilliss, C., & Lee, K. (2007). "I take the good with the bad, and I moisturize": Defying middle age in the new millennium. *Menopause, 14,* 734–741.

Bhar, S., Gelfand, L., Schmid, S., Gallop, R., DeRubeis, R., Hollon, S., et al. (2008). Sequence of improvement in depressive symptoms across cognitive therapy and pharmacotherapy. *Journal of Affective Disorders, 110,* 161–166.

Bialystok, E. (2011). Reshaping the mind: The benefits of bilingualism. *Canadian Journal of Experimental Psychology, 65,* 229–235.

Bialystok, E., & Craik, F. I. M. (2011). Cognitive and linguistic processing in the bilingual mind. *Current Directions in Psychological Science, 19,* 19–23.

Bialystok, E., & Martin, M. M. (2004). Attention and inhibition in bilingual children: Evidence from the dimensional change card sort task. *Developmental Science, 7,* 325–339.

Bialystok, E., Barac, R., Blaye, A., & Poulin-Dubois, D. (2010). Word mapping and executive functioning in young monolingual and bilingual children. *Journal of Cognition and Development, 11,* 485–508.

Bialystok, E., Fergus, F. I. M., Green, D. W., & Gollan, T. H. (2009). Bilingual minds. *Psychological Science in the Public Interest, 10,* 89–129.

Bialystok, E., Luk, G., Peets, K. F., & Yang, S. (2010). Receptive vocabulary differences in monolingual and bilingual children. *Bilingualism: Language and Cognition, 13,* 525–531.

Bianchi, S. M., & Casper, L. M. (2000). American families. *Population Bulletin, 55*(4).

Bienvenu, O. J., Davydow, D. S., & Kendler, K. S. (2011). Psychiatric 'diseases' versus behavioral disorders and degree of genetic influence. *Psychological Medicine: A Journal of Research in Psychiatry and the Allied Sciences, 41,* 33–40.

Billiard, M. (2008). Narcolepsy: Current treatment options and future approaches. *Neuropsychiatric Disease and Treatment, 4,* 557–566.

Bindemann, M., Burton, A., Leuthold, H., & Schweinberger, S. (2008, July). Brain potential correlates of face recognition: Geometric distortions and the N250r brain response to stimulus repetitions. *Psychophysiology, 45,* 535–544.

Binet, A., & Simon, T. (1916). *The development of intelligence in children (The Binet-Simon Scale).* Baltimore: Williams & Wilkins.

Bingenheimer, J. B., Brennan, R. T., & Earls, E. J. (2005, May 27). Firearm violence exposure and serious violent behavior. *Science, 308,* 1323–1327.

Binstock, R., & George, L. K. (Eds.). (1996). *Handbook of aging and the social sciences* (4th ed.). San Diego, CA: Academic Press.

Birren, J. E. (Ed.). (1996). *Encyclopedia of gerontology: Age, aging and the aged.* San Diego, CA: Academic Press.

Bischoff, R. J., Springer, P. R., Felix, D. S., & Hollist, C. S. (2011). Finding the heart of medical family therapy: A content analysis of medical family therapy casebook articles. *Families, Systems, & Health, 29,* 184–196.

Bitterman, M. E. (2006). Classical conditioning since Pavlov. *Review of General Psychology, 10,* 365–376.

Bittles, A. H., Bower, C., & Hussain, R. (2007). The four ages of Down syndrome. *European Journal of Public Health, 17,* 121–225.

Bizley, J., Walker, K., Silverman, B., King, A., & Schnupp, J. (2009, February). Interdependent encoding of pitch, timbre, and spatial location in auditory cortex. *Journal of Neuroscience, 29,* 2064–2075.

Bjornstad, R. (2006). Learned helplessness, discouraged workers, and multiple unemployment equilibria. *The Journal of Socio-Economics, 35,* 458–475.

Black, A. L., & McCafferty, D. (1998, July 3–5). The age of contentment. *USA Weekend,* 4–6.

Black, B. M., & Weisz, A. N. (2004). Dating violence: A qualitative analysis of Mexican American youths' views. *Journal of Ethnic and Cultural Diversity in Social Work, 13,* 69–90.

Black, P. (2006). Thrust to wholeness: The nature of self-protection. *Review of General Psychology, 10,* 191–209.

Blair, C. A., Thompson, L. F., & Wuensch, K. L. (2005). Electronic helping behavior: The virtual presence of others makes a difference. *Basic and Applied Social Psychology, 27,* 171–178.

Blakeslee, S. (1991, August 7). Levels of caffeine in various foods. *The New York Times.*

Blakeslee, S. (1992, August 11). Finding a new messenger for the brain's signals to the body. *The New York Times,* p. C3.

Blakeslee, S. (1992, September 29). Radical brain surgery, the earlier the better, offers epileptics hope. *The New York Times*

Blass, T. (1996). Attribution of responsibility and trust in the Milgram obedience experiment. *Journal of Applied Social Psychology, 26,* 1529–1535.

Blass, T. (2004). *The man who shocked the world: The life and legacy of Stanley Milgram.* New York: Basic Books.

Blass, T. (2009). From New Haven to Santa Clara: A historical perspective on the Milgram obedience experiments. *American Psychologist, 64,* 37–45.

Blatter, K., & Cajochen, C. (2007). Circadian rhythms in cognitive performance: Methodological constraints, protocols, theoretical underpinnings. *Physiology & Behavior, 90,* 196–208.

Blechner, M. J. (2013). New ways of conceptualizing and working with dreams. *Contemporary Psychoanalysis, 49,* 259–275.

Blixen, C. E., Singh, A., & Xu, M. (2006). What women want: Understanding obesity and preferences for primary care weight reduction interventions among African-American and Caucasian women. *Journal of the National Medical Association, 98,* 1160–1170.

Bloom, Floyd, et al. (1975). Brain, Mind and Behavior. *Educational Broadcasting Corp.*

Bloom, P. N., McBride, C. M., & Pollak, K. I. (2006). Recruiting teen smokers in shopping malls to a smoking-cessation program using the foot-in-the-door technique. *Journal of Applied Social Psychology, 36,* 1129–1144.

Blum, D. (2002). *Love at goon park: Harry Harlow and the science of affection.* Cambridge, MA: Perseus.

Blum, H. P. (2011). To what extent do you privilege dream interpretation in relation to other forms of mental representations? *The International Journal of Psychoanalysis, 92,* 275–277.

Blumen, H. M., Rajaram, S., & Henkel, L. (2013). The applied value of collaborative memory research in aging: Considerations for broadening the scope. *Journal of Applied Research in Memory and Cognition, 2,* 133–135.

Blumenthal, H., Leen-Feldner, E. W., Babson, K. A., Gahr, J. L., Trainor, C. D., & Frala, J. L. (2011). Elevated social anxiety among early maturing girls. *Developmental Psychology, 47,* 1133–1140.

Boahen, K. (2005, May). Neuromorphic microchips. *Scientific American,* pp. 56–64.

Boake, C. (2008, April). Clinical neuropsychology. *Professional Psychology: Research and Practice, 39,* 234–239.

Board of Educational Affairs. (2002). *2002 APA task force report on undergraduate student competencies.* Washington, DC: American Psychological Association.

Bode, C., de Ridder, D. T., Kuijer, R. G., & Bensing, J. M. (2007). Effects of an intervention promoting proactive coping competencies in middle and late adulthood. *Gerontologist, 47,* 42–51.

Boden, J. M., Fergusson, D. M., & Horwood, L. J. (2007). Anxiety disorders and suicidal behaviours in adolescence and young adulthood: Findings from a longitudinal study. *Psychological Medicine, 37,* 431–440.

Bodin, G. (2006). Review of harvesting free association. *Psychoanalytic Quarterly, 75,* 629–632.

Boehm, K. E., & Campbell, N. B. (1995). Suicide: A review of calls to an adolescent peer listening phone service. *Child Psychiatry and Human Development, 26,* 61–66.

Boeve-de Pauw, J., Donche, V., & Van Petegem, P. (2011). Adolescents' environmental worldview and personality: An explorative study. *Journal of Environmental Psychology, 31,* 109–117.

Bogart, R. K., McDaniel, R. J., Dunn, W. J., Hunter, C., Peterson, A. L., & Write, E. E. (2007). Efficacy of group cognitive behavior therapy for the treatment of masticatory myo-fascial pain. *Military Medicine, 172,* 169–174.

Bohart, A. C. (2006). Understanding person-centered therapy: A review of Paul Wilkins' person-centered therapy in focus. *Person-Centered and Experiential Psychotherapies, 5,* 138–143.

Bohn, A., & Berntsen, D. (2007). Pleasantness bias in flashbulb memories: Positive and negative flashbulb memories of the fall of the Berlin Wall among East and West Germans. *Memory and Cognition, 35,* 565–577.

Bohn, C., Aderka, I. M., Schreiber, F., Stangier, U., & Hofmann, S. G. (2013). Sudden gains in cognitive therapy and interpersonal therapy for social anxiety disorder. *Journal of Consulting and Clinical Psychology, 81,* 177–182.

Boisvert, C. M., & Faust, D. (2003). Leading researchers' consensus on psychotherapy research findings: Implications for the teaching and conduct of psychotherapy. *Professional Psychology: Research and Practice, 34,* 508–513.

Boles, D. B. (2005). A large-sample study of sex differences in functional cerebral lateralization. *Journal of Clinical and Experimental Neuropsychology, 27,* 759–768.

Bolger, N., & Amarel, D. (2007). Effects of social support visibility on adjustment to stress: Experimental evidence. *Journal of Personality and Social Psychology, 92,* 458–475.

Boller, F. (2004). Rational basis of rehabilitation following cerebral lesions: A review of the concept of cerebral plasticity. *Functional Neurology: New Trends in Adaptive and Behavioral Disorders, 19,* 65–72.

Bonanno, G. A. (2004). Loss, trauma, and human resilience: Have we underestimated the human capacity to thrive after extremely aversive events? *American Psychologist, 59,* 20–28.

Bond, J. T., Thompson, C., Galinsky, E., & Prottas, D. (2003). *Highlights of the 2002 national survey of the changing workforce (No. 3).* New York: Families and Work Institute.

Bond, M. (2006). Psychodynamic psychotherapy in the treatment of mood disorders. *Current Opinion in Psychiatry, 19,* 40–43.

Bonezzi, A., Brendl, C., & De Angelis, M. (2011). Stuck in the middle: The psychophysics of goal pursuit. *Psychological Science, 22,* 607–612.

Bonham, V. L., Warshauer-Baker, E., & Collins, F. S. (2005). Race and ethnicity in the genome era: The complexity of the constructs. *American Psychologist, 60,* 9–15.

Bonnardel, V. (2006). Color naming and categorization in inherited color vision deficiencies. *Visual Neuroscience, 23,* 637–643.

Borbely, A. (1988). *Secrets of sleep* (p. 43, graph). New York: Basic Books.

Bordnick, P. S., Elkins, R. L., Orr, T. E., Walters, P., & Thyer, B. A. (2004). Evaluating the relative effectiveness of three aversion therapies designed to reduce craving among cocaine abusers. *Behavioral Interventions, 19,* 1–24.

Borisenko, J. (2007). Fatherhood as a personality development factor in men. *The Spanish Journal of Psychology, 10,* 82–90.

Bornstein, R. F. (2003). Psychodynamic models of personality. In T. Millon & M. J. Lerner (Eds.), *Handbook of psychology: Personality and social psychology* (Vol. 5). New York: Wiley.

Boroditsky, L. (2010, July 24–25). Lost in translation. *Wall Street Journal,* p. W3.

Bosma, H., van Boxtel, M. P. J., Ponds, R. W. H. M., Houx, P. J. H., & Jolles, J. (2003). Education and age-related cognitive decline: The contribution of mental workload. *Educational Gerontology, 29,* 165–173.

Bossarte, R. M., & Swahn, M. H. (2011). The associations between early alcohol use and suicide attempts among adolescents with a history of major depression. *Addictive Behaviors, 36.*

Bosse, T., Gerritsen, C., & Treur, J. (2011). Combining rational and biological factors in virtual agent decision making. *Applied Intelligence, 34,* 87–101.

Botvinick, M. (2004, August 6). Probing the neural basis of body ownership. *Science, 305,* 782–783.

Bouchard, C., & Bray, G. A. (Eds.). (1996). *Regulation of body weight: Biological and behavioral mechanisms.* New York: Wiley.

Bouchard, T. J., Jr. (2004). Genetic influence on human psychological traits: A survey. *Current Directions in Psychological Science, 13,* 148–151.

Bouchard, T. J., Jr., Segal, N. L., Tellegen, A., McGue, M., Keyes, M., & Krueger, R. (2004). Genetic influence on social attitudes: Another challenge to psychology from behavior genetics. In L. F. DiLalla (Ed.), *Behavior genetics principles: Perspectives in development, personality, and psychopathology.* Washington, DC: American Psychological Association.

Bourne, L. E., & Dominowski, R. L. (1979). *Cognitive processes.* Upper Saddle River, NJ: Pearson Education.

Bourne, L. E., Dominowski, R. L., Loftus, E. F., & Healy, A. F. (1986). *Cognitive processes* (2nd ed.). Englewood Cliffs, NJ: Prentice Hall.

Bouton, M. E., Todd, T. P., Vurbic, D., & Winterbauer, N. E. (2011). Renewal after the extinction of free operant behavior. *Learning & Behavior, 39,* 57–67.

Bower, G. H., Thompson, S. S., & Tulving, E. (1994). Reducing retroactive interference: An interference analysis. *Journal of Experimental Psychology Learning, Memory, and Cognition, 20,* 51-66.

Bower, J. M., & Parsons, L. M. (2003, August). Rethinking the "lesser brain." *Scientific American,* pp. 51-57.

Boxer, P., Huesmann, L., Bushman, B., O'Brien, M., & Moceri, D. (2009). The role of violent media preference in cumulative developmental risk for violence and general aggression. *Journal of Youth and Adolescence, 38,* 417-428.

Boyce, W. T., & Ellis, B. J. (2005). Biological sensitivity to context: An evolutionary-developmental theory of the origins and functions of stress reactivity. *Development and Psychopathology, 17,* 271-301.

Boyd-Wilson, B. M., McClure, J., & Walkey, E. H. (2004). Are well-being and illusory perceptions linked? The answer may be yes, but. . . . *Australian Journal of Psychology, 56,* 1-9.

Boyle, G. J., Goldman, R., Svoboda, J. S., & Fernandez, E. (2002). Male circumcision: Pain, trauma and psychosexual sequelae. *Journal of Health Psychology, 7,* 329-343.

Boyle, S. H., Williams, R. B., Mark, D. B., Brummett, B. H., Siegler, I. C., & Barefoot, J. C. (2005). Hostility, age, and mortality in a sample of cardiac patients. *American Journal of Cardiology, 96,* 64-72.

Bozarth, J. D., Zimring, F. M., & Tausch, R. (2002). Client-centered therapy: The evolution of a revolution. In D. J. Cain (Ed.), *Humanistic psychotherapies: Handbook of research and practice.* Washington, DC: American Psychological Association.

Bradley, R. J., Moulin, C. A., & Kvavilashvili, L. (2013). Involuntary autobiographical memories. *The Psychologist, 26,* 190-193.

Brafman, A. H. (2011). *Fostering independence: Helping and caring in psychodynamic therapies.* London: Karnac Books.

Brambilla, P., Cipriani, A., Hotopf, M., & Barbui, C. (2005). Side-effect profile of fluoxetine in comparison with other SSRIs, tricyclic and newer antidepressants: A meta-analysis of clinical trial data. *Pharmacopsychiatry, 38,* 69-77.

Brandon, M., & Saffran, J. R. (2011). Apparent motion enhances visual rhythm discrimination in infancy. *Attention, Perception, & Psychophysics, 73,* 1016-1020.

Brang, D., Rouw, R., Ramachandran, V. S., & Coulson, S. (2011). Similarly shaped letters evoke similar colors in grapheme-color synesthesia. *Neuropsychologia, 49,* 1355-1358.

Brant, A. M., Munakata, Y., Boomsma, D. I., DeFries, J. C., Haworth, C. A., Keller, M. C., & . . . Hewitt, J. K. (2013). The nature and nurture of high IQ: An extended sensitive period for intellectual development. *Psychological Science, 24,* 1487-1495.

Brasic, J. R. (2002). Conversion disorder in childhood. *German Journal of Psychiatry, 5,* 54-61.

Braun, A. R., Balkin, T. J., Wesensten, N. J., Gwadry, F., Carson, R. E., Varga, M., et al. (1998). Dissociated pattern of activity in visual cortices and their projections during human rapid eye movement sleep. *Science, 279,* pp. 91-95.

Brausch, A. M., & Gutierrez, P. M. (2009). Differences in non-suicidal self-injury and suicide attempts in adolescents. *Journal of Youth and Adolescence, 21,* 46-51.

Brazelton, T. B. (1969). *Infants and mothers: Differences in development.* New York: Dell.

Breland, K., & Breland, M. (1966). *Animal behavior.* New York: Macmillan.

Brennan, P. (2011). Pheromones: Fact or fantasy? *Ethology, 117,* 265-266.

Brennen, T., Vikan, A., & Dybdahl, R. (2007). Are tip-of-the-tongue states universal? Evidence from the speakers of an unwritten language. *Memory, 15,* 167-176.

Breslin, C. W., & Safer, M. A. (2011). Effects of event valence on long-term memory for two baseball championship games. *Psychological Science, 20,* 1-5.

Breslin, M. M. (2004, June 27). Boy, interrupted. *Chicago Tribune,* p. 12.

Brewer, M. B., & Hewstone, M. (Eds.). (2003). *Social cognition.* Malden, MA: Blackwell Publishers.

Bright, P., Buckman, J., & Fradera, A. (2006). Retrograde amnesia in patients with hippocampal, medial temporal, temporal lobe, or frontal pathology. *Learning & Memory, 13,* 545-557.

Brock, T. C., & Green, M. C. (Eds.). (2005). *Persuasion: Psychological insights and perspectives* (2nd ed.). Thousand Oaks, CA: Sage Publications.

Bröder, A., & Schiffer, S. (2006). Stimulus format and working memory in fast and frugal strategy selection. *Journal of Behavioral Decision Making, 19,* 361-380.

Brody, J. (2008, May 20). Trying to break nicotine's grip. *The New York Times,* p. E9.

Broeders, R., van den Bos, K., Müller, P. A., & Ham, J. (2011). Should I save or should I not kill? How people solve moral dilemmas depends on which rule is most accessible. *Journal of Experimental Social Psychology, 47,* 923-934.

Broidy, L. M., Nagin, D. S., & Tremblay, R. E. (2003). Developmental trajectories of childhood disruptive behaviors and adolescent delinquency: A six-site, cross-national study. *Developmental Psychology, 39,* 222-245.

Broman, C. L. (2005). Stress, race and substance use in college. *College Student Journal, 39,* 340-352.

Bronson, P., & Merryman, A. (2009). *NurtureShock.* New York: Twelve.

Brooker, R. J., Widmaier, E. P., Graham, L., & Stiling, P. (2008). *Biology.* New York: McGraw-Hill.

Brown, D. L. (2008, July 16). The impassive bystander. Someone is hurt, in need of compassion. Is it human instinct to do nothing? *Washington Post,* C4.

Brown, E. (2001, September 17). The World Health Organization takes on big tobacco (but don't hold your breath): Anti-smoking advocates are mounting a global campaign: It's going to be a long, hard fight. *Forbes,* pp. 37-41.

Brown, L. S., & Pope, K. S. (1996). *Recovered memories of abuse: Assessment, therapy, forensics.* Washington, DC: American Psychological Association.

Brown, P. K., & Wald, G. (1964). Visual pigments in single rod and cones of the human retina. *Science, 144,* 45-52.

Brown, R. (1958). How shall a thing be called? *Psychological Review, 65,* 14-21.

Brown, R. J. (2006). Different types of "dissociation" have different psychological mechanisms. *Journal of Trauma Dissociation, 6,* 7-28.

Brown, R., & Robertson, E. (2007). Off-line processing: Reciprocal interactions between declarative and procedural memories. *The Journal of Neuroscience, 27*(39), 10468-10475.

Brown, S., & Martinez, M. J. (2007). Activation of premotor vocal areas during musical discrimination. *Brain and Cognition, 63,* 9-69.

Brown, S., Martinez, M. J., & Parsons, L. M. (2006). Music and language side by side in the brain: A PET study of the generation of melodies and sentences. *European Journal of Neuroscience, 23,* 2791-2803.

Bruce, V., Green, P. R., & Georgeson, M. (1997). *Visual perception: Physiology, psychology and ecology* (3rd ed.). Mahwah, NJ: Erlbaum.

Bruggeman, H., Yonas, A., & Konczak, J. (2007). The processing of linear perspective and binocular information for action and perception. *Neuropsychologia, 45,* 1420-1426.

Brunet, A., Orr, S. P., Tremblay, J., Robertson, K., Nader, K., & Pitman, R. K. (2007). Effect of post-retrieval propranolol on psychophysiologic responding during subsequent script-driven traumatic imagery in post-traumatic stress disorder. *Journal of Psychiatric Research, 22,* 301-315.

Bryant, R. M., Coker, A. D., Durodoye, B. A., McCollum, V. J., Pack-Brown, S. P., Constantine, M. G., & O'Bryant, B. J. (2005). Having our say: African American women, diversity, and counseling. *Journal of Counseling and Development, 83,* 313-319.

Brydon, L., Edwards, S., Mohamed-Ali, V., & Steptoe, A. (2004). Socioeconomic status and stress-induced increases in interleukin-6. *Brain, Behavior, and Immunity, 18,* 281-290.

Brzustowicz, L. M., Hodgkinson, K. A., Chow, E. W. C., Honer, W. G., & Bassett, A. S. (2000, April 28). Location of major susceptibility locus for familial schizophrenia on chromosome 1q21-q22. *Science, 288,* 678-682.

Bub, K. L., Buckhalt, J. A., & El-Sheikh, M. (2011). Children's sleep and cognitive performance: A cross-domain analysis of change over time. *Developmental Psychology.*

Buchanan, T. W., & Adolphs, R. (2004). The neuroanatomy of emotional memory in humans. In D. Reisberg & P. Hertel (Eds.), *Memory and emotion.* London: Oxford University Press.

Buchanan, T., & Selmon, N. (2008). Race and gender differences in self-efficacy: Assessing the role of gender role attitudes and family background. *Sex Roles, 58,* 822-836.

Buchert, R., Thomasius, R., Wilke, F., Petersen, K., Nebeling, B., Obrocki, J., Schulze, O., Schmidt, U., & Clausen, M. (2004). A voxel-based PET investigation of the long-term effects of "ecstasy" consumption on brain serotonin transporters. *American Journal of Psychiatry, 161,* 1181-1189.

Buehner, M., Krumm, S., & Ziegler, M. (2006). Cognitive abilities and their interplay: Reasoning, crystallized intelligence, working memory components, and sustained attention. *Journal of Individual Differences, 27,* 57-72.

Buerkle, C. (2011). Masters of their domain: Seinfeld and the discipline of mediated men's sexual economy. In E. Watson & M. E. Shaw (Eds.), *Performing American masculinities: The 21st-century man in popular culture.* Bloomington, IN: Indiana University Press.

Bukobza, G. (2009). Relations between rebelliousness, risk-taking behavior, and identity status during emerging adulthood. *Identity, 9,* 159-177.

Bulf, H., Johnson, S. P., & Valenza, E. (2011). Visual statistical learning in the newborn infant. *Cognition, 121,* 127-132.

Bulik, C. M., Tozzi, F., Anderson, C., Mazzeo, S. E., Aggen, S., & Sullivan, P. E. (2003). The relation between eating disorders and components of perfectionism. *American Journal of Psychiatry, 160,* 366-368.

Bunge, S. A., & Wallis, J. D. (2008). *Neuroscience of rule-guided behavior.* New York: Oxford University Press.

Bunting, M. (2006). Proactive interference and item similarity in working memory. *Journal of Experimental Psychology: Learning, Memory, and Cognition, 32,* 183–196.

Burbach, M. E., Matkin, G. S., & Fritz, S. M. (2004). Teaching critical thinking in an introductory leadership course utilizing active learning strategies: A confirmatory study. *College Student Journal, 38,* 482–493.

Burchinal, M. R., Roberts, J. E., & Riggins, R., Jr. (2000). Relating quality of center-based child care to early cognitive and language development longitudinally. *Child Development, 71,* 338–357.

Bureau of Labor Statistics. (2007). *American time use survey.* Washington, DC: Bureau of Labor Statistics.

Bureau of Labor Statistics. (2013, April 26). Employment characteristics of families–2012. Washington, DC: Bureau of Labor Statistics.

Burger, J. M. (2009). Replicating Milgram: Would people still obey today? *American Psychologist, 64,* 1–11.

Burger, J. M., & Caldwell, D. F. (2003). The effects of monetary incentives and labeling on the foot-in-the-door effect: Evidence for a self-perception process. *Basic and Applied Social Psychology, 25,* 235–241.

Burger, J. M., Reed, M., & DeCesare, K. (1999). The effects of initial request size on compliance: More about the that's-not-all technique. *Basic and Applied Social Psychology, 21,* 243–249.

Burgoon, J. K., & Bacue, A. E. (2003). Nonverbal communication skills. In J. O. Greene & B. R. Burleson (Eds.), *Handbook of communication and social interaction skills.* Mahwah, NJ: Lawrence Erlbaum.

Burgoon, J. K., Bonito, J. A., Ramirez, A. J. R., Dunbar, N. E., Kam, K., & Fischer, J. (2002). Testing the interactivity principle: Effects of mediation, propinquity, and verbal and nonverbal modalities in interpersonal interaction [Special Issue: Research on the relationship between verbal and nonverbal communication: Emerging integrations]. *Journal of Communication, 52,* 657–677.

Burke, C., & McDaniel, J. (2001). *A special kind of hero.* Lincoln, NE: Doubleday.

Burns, J. W., Quartana, P. J., & Bruehl, S. (2007). Anger management style moderates effects of emotion suppression during initial stress on pain and cardiovascular responses during subsequent pain-induction. *Annals of Behavioral Medicine, 34,* 154–165.

Burns, N. R., Bryan, J., & Nettelbeck, T. (2006). Ginkgo biloba: No robust effect on cognitive abilities or mood in healthy young or older adults. *Human Psychopharmacology: Clinical and Experimental, 21,* 27–37.

Burton, L., Bensimon, E., Allimant, J., Kinsman, R., Levin, A., Kovacs, L., & . . . Bahrami, J. (2013). Relationship of prosody perception to personality and aggression. *Current Psychology: A Journal for Diverse Perspectives on Diverse Psychological Issues, 32,* 275–280.

Busey, T. A., & Loftus, G. R. (2007). Cognitive science and the law. *Trends in Cognitive Science, 11,* 111–117.

Bush, J. (2008). Viability of virtual reality exposure therapy as a treatment alternative. *Computers in Human Behavior, 24,* 1032–1040.

Bushman, B. J., & Anderson, C. (2001). Media violence and the American public: Scientific facts versus media misinformation. *American Psychologist, 56,* 477–489.

Bushman, B. J., Wang, M. C., & Anderson, C. (2005). Is the curve relating temperature to aggression linear or curvilinear? Assaults and temperature in Minneapolis reexamined. *Journal of Personality and Social Psychology, 89,* 62–66.

Buss, A. H. (2011). *Pathways to individuality: Evolution and development of personality traits.* Washington, DC: American Psychological Association.

Buss, D. (2003). *Evolutionary psychology.* Boston: Allyn & Bacon.

Buss, D. (2009). How can evolutionary psychology successfully explain personality and individual differences? *Perspectives on Psychological Science, 4,* 359–366.

Buss, D. M. (2001). Human nature and culture: An evolutionary psychological perspective. *Journal of Personality, 69,* 955–978.

Buss, D. M. (2003a). *The evolution of desire: Strategies of human mating.* New York: Basic Books.

Buss, D. M. (2004). Sex differences in human mate preferences: Evolutionary hypotheses tested in 37 cultures. In H. T. Reis & C. E. Rusbult (Eds.), *Close relationships: Key readings.* Philadelphia: Taylor & Francis.

Buss, D. M., Abbott, M., & Angleitner, A. (1990). International preferences in selecting mates: A study of 37 cultures. *Journal of Cross-Cultural Psychology, 21,* 5–47.

Buss, D. M., Larsen, R. J., Westen, D., & Semmelroth, J. (1992). Sex differences in jealousy: Evolution, physiology, and psychology. *Psychological Science, 3,* 251–255.

Butcher, J. N. (2005). *A beginner's guide to the MMPI-2* (2nd ed.). Washington, DC: American Psychological Association.

Butcher, J. N. (2011). *A beginner's guide to the MMPI-2* (3rd ed.). Washington, DC US: American Psychological Association.

Butler, A. C., Chapman, J. E., Forman, E. M., & Beck, A. T. (2006). The empirical status of cognitive-behavioral therapy: A review of meta-analyses. *Clinical Psychology Review, 26,* 17–31.

Butler, L. D., Koopman, C., Neri, E., Giese-Davis, J., Palesh, O., Thorne-Yocam, K. A., et al. (2009). Effects of supportive-expressive group therapy on pain in women with metastatic breast cancer. *Health Psychology, 28,* 579–587.

Butler, L. T., & Berry, D. C. (2004). Understanding the relationship between repetition priming and mere exposure. *British Journal of Psychology, 95,* 467–487.

Buysse, D. J., Germain, A., Moul, D. E., Franzen, P. L., Brar, L. K., Fletcher, M. E., et al. (2011). Efficacy of brief behavioral treatment for chronic insomnia in older adults. *Archives of Internal Medicine, 171,* 887–895.

Buzi, R., Weinman, M., & Smith, P. (2007). The relationship between adolescent depression and a history of sexual abuse. *Adolescence, 42*(168), 679–688.

Byne, W. (1996). Biology and homosexuality: Implications of neuroendocrinological and neuroanatomical studies. In R. P. Cabaj & T. S. Stein (Eds.), *Textbook of homosexuality and mental health.* Washington, DC: American Psychiatric Press.

Byrne-Davis, L., & Vedhara, K. (2008). Psycho-neuroimmunology. *Social and Personality Psychology Compass, 2,* 751–764.

Byrne, B. M., & Watkins, D. (2003). The issue of measurement invariance revisited. *Journal of Cross-Cultural Psychology, 34,* 155–175.

Cabioglu, M., Ergene, N., & Tan, Ü. (2007, May). Smoking cessation after acupuncture treatment. *International Journal of Neuroscience, 117,* 571–578.

Cachelin, F. M., & Regan, P. C. (2006). Prevalence and correlates of chronic dieting in a multiethnic U.S. community sample. *Eating and Weight Disorders, 11,* 91–99.

Cacioppo, J. T., & Decety, J. (2009). What are the brain mechanisms on which psychological processes are based? *Perspectives on Psychological Science, 4,* 10–18.

Cacioppo, J. T., Berntson, G. G., & Crites, S. L., Jr. (1996). Social neuroscience: Principles of psychophysiological arousal and response. In E. T. Higgins & A. W. Kruglanski (Eds.), *Social psychology: Handbook of basic principles.* New York: Guilford.

Cacioppo, J. T., Visser, P. S., & Pickett, C. L. (2005). *Social neuroscience: People thinking about thinking people.* Cambridge, MA: MIT Press.

Cadenhead, K., & Braff, D. L. (1995). Neurophysiology of schizophrenia: Attention, information processing, and inhibitory processes in schizophrenia. In J. A. Den Boer, H. G. M. Westenberg, & H. M. van Praag (Eds.), *Advances in the neurobiology of schizophrenia.* Oxford, England: John Wiley & Sons.

Caelian, C. F. (2006). The role of perfectionism and stress in the suicidal behaviour of depressed adolescents. *Dissertation Abstracts International: Section B: The Sciences and Engineering, 66*(12-B), 6915.

Cai, D. J., Mednick, S. A., Harrison, E. M., Kanady, J. C., & Mednick, S. C. (2009). REM, not incubation, improves creativity by priming associative networks. *PNAS Proceedings of the National Academy of Sciences of the United States of America, 106,* 10130–10134.

Cai, D., Shuman, T., Gorman, M., Sage, J., & Anagnostaras, S. (2009). Sleep selectively enhances hippocampus-dependent memory in mice. *Behavioral Neuroscience, 123,* 713–719.

Cain, D. J. (Ed.). (2002). *Humanistic psychotherapies: Handbook of research and practice.* Washington, DC: American Psychological Association.

Cameron, O. G. (2002). *Visceral sensory neuroscience: Interoception.* London: Oxford University Press.

Campbell, R. (2008). The psychological impact of rape victims. *American Psychologist, 63,* 702–717.

Campbell, T. S., & Ditto, B. (2002). Exaggeration of blood pressure-related hypoalgesia and reduction of blood pressure with low frequency transcutaneous electrical nerve stimulation. *Psychophysiology, 39,* 473–481.

Campos, R. C. (2011). 'It might be what I am': Looking at the use of Rorschach in psychological assessment. *Journal of Projective Psychology & Mental Health, 18,* 28–38.

Canadian Journal of Experimental Psychology/Revue canadienne de psychologie expérimentale, 65, 229–235.

Cannon, W. B. (1929). Organization for physiological homeostatics. *Physiological Review, 9,* 280–289.

Cantwell, R. H., & Andrews, B. (2002). Cognitive and psychological factors underlying secondary school students' feelings towards group work. *Educational Psychology, 22,* 75–91.

Capaldi, E. D. (Ed.). (1996). *Why we eat what we eat: The psychology of eating.* Washington, DC: American Psychological Association.

Caplan, D., Waters, G., & Dede, G. (2007). A study of syntactic processing in aphasia I: Behavioral (psycholinguistic) aspects. *Brain and Language, 101,* 103–150.

Carbon, C., & Ditye, T. (2011). Sustained effects of adaptation on the perception of familiar faces. *Journal of Experimental Psychology: Human Perception and Performance, 37,* 615-625.

Cardemil, E. V., Pinedo, T. M., & Miller, I. W. (2005). Developing a culturally appropriate depression prevention program: The family coping skills program. *Cultural Diversity and Ethnic Minority Psychology, 11,* 99-112.

Carels, R. A., Young, K. M., Koball, A., Gumble, A., Darby, L. A., Oehlhof, M., & . . . Hinman, N. (2011). Transforming your life: An environmental modification approach to weight loss. *Journal of Health Psychology, 16,* 430-438.

Carey, B. (2008, May 29). Monkeys think, moving artificial arm as own. *The New York Times,* p. A1.

Carey, B. (2009a, April 6). So you just want to forget? Science is working on an eraser. *The New York Times,* p. A1.

Carey, B. (2009b, July 28). In battle, hunches prove to be valuable assets. *The New York Times,* p. A1.

Carey, B. (2009c, November 27). Surgery for mental ills offers hope and risk. *The New York Times,* p. A1.

Carey, B. (2011, August, 7). Learning to cope with a mind's taunting voices. *The New York Times,* A1.

Carhart-Harris, R. (2007). Speed > Ecstasy > Ritalin: The science of amphetamines. *Journal of Psychopharmacology, 21,* 225.

Carnagey, N., Anderson, C. A., & Bushman, B. J. (2007). The effect of video game violence on physiological desensitization to real-life violence. *Journal of Experimental Social Psychology, 43,* 489-496.

Carnagey, N., Anderson, C., & Bartholow, B. (2007). Media violence and social neuroscience: New questions and new opportunities. *Current Directions in Psychological Science, 16,* 178-182.

Carney, R. N., & Levin, J. R. (1998). Coming to terms with the keyword method in introductory psychology: A "neuromnemonic" example. *Teaching of Psychology, 25,* 132-135.

Carney, R. N., & Levin, J. R. (2003). Promoting higher-order learning benefits by building lower-order mnemonic connections. *Applied Cognitive Psychology, 17,* 563-575.

Carpenter, S. (2002, April). What can resolve the paradox of mental health disparities? *APA Monitor, 33,* 18.

Carr, A. (2002). *Avoiding risky sex in adolescence.* New York: Blackwell.

Carr, N. (2011). *The shallows: What the Internet is doing to our brains.* New York: W. W. Norton & Co.

Carr, P., & Steele, C. (2009). Stereotype threat and inflexible perseverance in problem solving. *Journal of Experimental Social Psychology, 45,* 853-859.

Carrillo, M., Ricci, L., Coppersmith, G., & Melloni, R. (2009, August). The effect of increased serotonergic neurotransmission on aggression: A critical meta-analytical review of preclinical studies. *Psychopharmacology, 205,* 349-368.

Carter, R. T. (2003). Becoming racially and culturally competent: The racial-cultural counseling laboratory. *Journal of Multicultural Counseling and Development, 31,* 20-30.

Cartwright, R. (2006). A neuroscientist looks at how the brain makes up our minds. *PsycCRITIQUES, 51,* 35-41.

Cartwright, R., Agargum, M. Y., & Kirkby, J. (2006). Relation of dreams to waking concerns. *Psychiatry Research, 141,* 261-270.

Caruso, E. (2008). Use of experienced retrieval ease in self and social judgments. *Journal of Experimental Social Psychology, 44,* 148-155.

Carvalho, E. M., Pereira, S. R. C., Pires, R. G. W., Ferraz, V. P., Romano-Silva, M. A., Oliveira-Silva, I. F., & Ribeiro, A. M. (2006). Thiamine deficiency decreases glutamate uptake in the prefrontal cortex and impairs spatial memory performance in a water maze test. *Pharmacology, Biochemistry and Behavior, 83,* 481-489.

Carvalho, J., & Nobre, P. (2011). Biopsychosocial determinants of men's sexual desire: Testing an integrative model. *Journal of Sexual Medicine, 8,* 754-763.

Carver, C., & Scheier, M. (2002). Coping processes and adjustment to chronic illness. In A. Christensen & M. Antoni (Eds.), *Chronic physical disorders: Behavioral medicine's perspective.* Malden: Blackwell Publishers.

Cary, P. (2007). A brief history of the concept of free will: Issues that are and are not germane to legal reasoning. *Behavioral Sciences & the Law, 25, Special issue: Free will,* 165-181.

Casad, B. J. (2007). Gender stereotype violation among job applicants: An examination of theory and measurement. *Dissertation Abstracts International: Section B: The Sciences and Engineering, 67(7-B),* 4154.

Casasanto, D. (2008). Who's afraid of the big bad whorf? Crosslinguistic differences in temporal language and thought. *Language Learning, 58,* 63-79.

Casasola, M. (2011). Infant spatial categorization from an information processing approach. In L. M. Oakes, C. H. Cashon, M. Casasola, & D. H. Rakison (Eds.), *Infant perception and cognition: Recent advances, emerging theories, and future directions.* New York: Oxford University Press.

Case, R., & Okamoto, Y. (1996). The role of central conceptual structures in the development of children's thought. *Monographs of the Society for Research in Child Development, 61,* v-265.

Casey, S. D., Cooper-Brown, L. J., & Wacher, D. P. (2006). The use of descriptive analysis to identify and manipulate schedules of reinforcement in the treatment of food refusal. *Journal of Behavioral Education, 15,* 41-52.

Cashon, C. H., & Cohen, L. B. (2004). Beyond U-shaped development in infants' processing of faces: An information-processing account. *Journal of Cognition and Development, 5,* 59-80.

Cassells, J. V. S. (2007). The virtuous roles of truth and justice in integral dialogue: Research, theory, and model practice of the evolution of collective consciousness. *Dissertation Abstracts International Section A: Humanities and Social Sciences, 67*(10-A), 4005.

Catalano, S. M. (2006, September). Criminal victimization, 2005. *Bureau of Justice Statistics Bulletin.* Washington, DC: Bureau of Justice Statistics.

Cattell, R. B., Cattell, A. K., & Catell, H. E. P. (1993). *Sixteen personality factor questionnaire (16PF)* (5th ed.). San Antonio, TX: Harcourt Brace.

Cattell, R. B., Cattell, A. K., & Cattell, H. E. P. (2000). *The sixteen personality factor™ (16PF®) questionnaire.* Champaign, IL: Institute for Personality and Ability Testing.

Cauce, A. M. (2007). Bringing community psychology home: The leadership, community and values initiative. *American Journal of Community Psychology, 39,* 1-11.

Cavallini, E., Pagnin, A., & Vecchi, T. (2003). Aging and everyday memory: The beneficial effect of memory training. *Archives of Gerontology & Geriatrics, 37,* 241-257.

Cavenett, T., & Nixon, R. D. V. (2006). The effect of arousal on memory for emotionally-relevant information: A study of sky divers. *Behaviour Research and Therapy, 44,* 1461-1469.

CDC. (2013). Adult cigarette smoking in the United States: Current estimate. Retrieved from http://www.cdc.gov/tobacco/data_statistics/fact_sheets/adult_data/cig_smoking/

Centers for Disease Control and Prevention. (2008). *STD surveillance tables.* Atlanta: Centers for Disease Control and Prevention.

Centers for Disease Control and Prevention (CDC). (2000). *Suicide prevention fact sheet.* Atlanta: National Center for Injury Prevention and Control.

Centers for Disease Control and Prevention (CDC). (2004a). *Chlamydia–CDC fact sheet.* Washington, DC.

Centers for Disease Control and Prevention (CDC). (2004b, June 11). Suicide and attempted suicide. *MMWR, 53,* 471.

Centers for Disease Control. (2013, February). *HIV in the United States: At a glance.* Washington, DC: National Center for HIV/AIDS, Viral Hepatitis, STD, and TB Prevention.

Center for Science in the Public Interest. (2007). *Caffeine Content of Food & Drugs.* Washington, DC: Center for Science in the Public Interest.

Centola, D. (2011, December 2). An experimental study of homophily in the adoption of health behavior. *Science, 334,* 1269-1272.

Chakraborty, A., McManus, S., Brugha, T. S., Bebbington, P., & King, M. (2011). Mental health of the non-heterosexual population of England. *The British Journal of Psychiatry, 198,* 143-148.

Chamberlain, K., & Zika, S. (1990). The minor events approach to stress: Support for the use of daily hassles. *British Journal of Psychology, 81,* 469-481.

Chamberlain, S. R., Menzies, L., Hampshire, A., Suckling, J., Fineberg, N. A., del Campo, N., et al. (2008, July 18). Orbitofrontal dysfunction in patients with obsessive-compulsive disorder and their unaffected relatives. *Science, 321,* 421-422.

Chambless, D. L., Crits-Christoph, P., Wampold, B. E., Norcross, J. C., Lambert, M. J., Bohart, A. C., et al. (2006). What should be validated? In J. C. Norcross, L. E. Beutler, & R. E Levant (Eds.). *Evidence-based practices in mental health: Debate and dialogue on the fundamental questions.* Washington, DC: American Psychological Association.

Chandler, D. R. (2011). Proactively addressing the shortage of Blacks in psychology: Highlighting the school psychology subfield. *Journal of Black Psychology, 37,* 99-127.

Chandra, P. (2007). Review of Language, mind, and brain: Some psychological and neurological constraints on theories of grammar. *Cognitive Systems Research, 8,* 53-56.

Chandran, S., & Menon, G. (2004). When a day means more than a year: Effects of temporal framing on judgments of health risk. *Journal of Consumer Research, 31,* 375-389.

Chang, J., & Sue, S. (2005). Culturally sensitive research: Where have we gone wrong and what do we need to do now? In M. G. Constantine, *Strategies for building multicultural competence in mental health and educational settings.* Hoboken, NJ: John Wiley & Sons.

Chang, L., & Geary, D. C. (2007). The future of psychology: Evolutionary approach to scientific psychology [Special issue: Evolutionary psychology]. *Acta Psychologica Sinica, 39,* 381–382.

Chang, S. W., & Ansley, T. N. (2003). A comparative study of item exposure control methods in computerized adaptive testing. *Journal of Educational Measurement, 40,* 71–103.

Chao, R. (2011). Managing stress and maintaining well-being: Social support, problem-focused coping, and avoidant coping. *Journal of Counseling & Development, 89,* 338–348.

Chapman, J. (2006). Anxiety and defective decision making: An elaboration of the group-think model. *Management Decision, 44,* 1391–1404.

Chapman, L. J., & Chapman, J. P. (1973). *Disordered thought in schizophrenia.* New York: Appleton-Century-Crofts.

Charlton, S. (2009, January). Driving while conversing: Cell phones that distract and passengers who react. *Accident Analysis & Prevention, 41,* 160–173.

Charman, D. P. (2004). *Core processes in brief psychodynamic psychotherapy: Advancing effective practice.* Mahwah, NJ: Lawrence Erlbaum Associates.

Chavez, P. R., Nelson, D. E., Naimi, T. S., & Brewer, R. D. (2011). Impact of a new gender-specific definition for binge drinking on prevalence estimates for women. *American Journal of Preventive Medicine, 40,* 468–471.

Cheakalos, C., & Heyn, E. (1998, November 2). Mercy mission. *People Weekly,* pp. 149–150.

Chechile, R. A. (2003). Review of 'Elements of Psychophysical Theory.' *Journal of Mathematical Psychology, 47,* 385.

Chen, A., Zhou, Y., & Gong, H. (2004). Firing rates and dynamic correlated activities of ganglion cells both contribute to retinal information processing. *Brain Research, 1017,* 13–20.

Chen, C., & Stevenson, H. W. (1995). Motivation and mathematics achievement: A comparative study of Asian-American, Caucasian-American, and East Asian high school students. *Child Development, 66,* 1215–1234.

Chen, Z., Fu, L., Peng, Y., Cai, R., & Zhou, S. (2011). The relationship among childhood abuse, parenting styles, and antisocial personality disorder tendency. *Chinese Journal of Clinical Psychology, 19,* 212–214.

Cheney, C. D. (1996). Medical non adherence: A behavior analysis. In J. R. Cautela & W. Ishaq (Eds.), *Contemporary issues in behavior therapy: Improving the human condition: Applied Clinical Psychology.* New York: Plenum Press.

Cheng, C., & Cheung, M. L. (2005). Cognitive processes underlying coping flexibility: Differentiation and integration. *Journal of Personality, 73,* 859–886.

Cheng, S., & Kwan, K. (2008). Attachment dimensions and contingencies of self-worth: The moderating role of culture. *Personality and Individual Differences, 45,* 509–514.

Cheston, S. E. (2000). A new paradigm for teaching counseling theory and practice. *Counselor Education & Supervision, 39,* 254–269.

Chin, J. (2013). Eastern and Western learning styles: The paradox of Asian learners. *Psyccritiques, 58,* 102–111.

Chiodo, D., Wolfe, D., Crooks, C., Hughes, R., & Jaffe, P. (2009). Impact of sexual harassment victimization by peers on subsequent adolescent victimization and adjustment: A longitudinal study. *Journal of Adolescent Health, 45,* 246–252.

Cho, A. (2000, June 16). What's shakin' in the ear? *Science, 288,* 1954–1955.

Cho, S., Holyoak, K. J., & Cannon, T. D. (2007). Analogical reasoning in working memory: Resources shared among relational integration, interference resolution, and maintenance. *Memory & Cognition, 35,* 1445–1455.

Choi, H., Kensinger, E. A., & Rajaram, S. (2013). Emotional content enhances true but not false memory for categorized stimuli. *Memory & Cognition, 41,* 403–415.

Chomsky, N. (1968). *Language and mind.* New York: Harcourt Brace Jovanovich.

Chomsky, N. (1978). On the biological basis of language capacities. In G. A. Miller & E. Lennenberg (Eds.), *Psychology and biology of language and thought.* New York: Academic Press.

Chomsky, N. (1991). Linguistics and cognitive science: Problems and mysteries. In A. Kasher (Ed.), *The Chomskyan turn.* Cambridge, MA: Blackwell.

Chou, K. (2005). Everyday competence and depressive symptoms: Social support and sense of control as mediators or moderators? *Aging and Mental Health, 9,* 177–183.

Choy, Y., Fyer, A. J., & Lipsitz, J. D. (2007). Treatment of specific phobia in adults. *Clinical Psychology Review, 27,* 266–286.

Christ, S. E., Steiner, R. D., & Grange, D. K. (2006). Inhibitory control in children with phenylketonuria. *Developmental Neuropsychology, 30,* 845–864.

Christakis, A., & Fowler, J. (2007). The spread of obesity in a large social network over 32 years. *The New England Journal of Medicine, 357,* 370–379.

Christakis, N. A., & Fowler, J. H. (2008). The collective dynamics of smoking in a large social network. *The New England Journal of Medicine, 358,* 2249–2258.

Christensen, A. J., & Johnson, J. A. (2002). Patient adherence with medical treatment regimens: An interactive approach. *Current Directions in Psychological Science, 11,* 94–101.

Christian, C. J., Lencz, T., Robinson, D. G., Burdick, K. E., Ashtari, M., Malhotra, A. K., et al. (2008). Gray matter structural alterations in obsessive-compulsive disorder: Relationship to neuropsychological functions. *Neuroimaging, 164,* 123–131.

Chronicle, E. P., MacGregor, J. N., & Ormerod, T. C. (2004). What makes an insight problem? The roles of heuristics, goal conception, and solution recoding in knowledge-lean problems. *Journal of Experimental Psychology: Learning, Memory, and Cognition, 30,* 14–27.

Chrysikou, E. G. (2006). When a shoe becomes a hammer: Problem solving as goal-derived, ad hoc categorization. *Dissertation Abstracts International: Section B: The Sciences and Engineering, 67*(1-B), 569.

Cialdini, R. B. (2006). *Influence: The psychology of persuasion.* New York: Collins.

Cialdini, R. B., & Sagarin, B. J. (2005). Principles of interpersonal influence. In T. C. Brock & M. C. Green (Eds.), *Persuasion: Psychological insights and perspectives* (2nd ed.). Thousand Oaks, CA: Sage Publications.

Cialdini, R. B., Schaller, M., Houlihan, D., Arps, K., Fultz, J., & Beaman, A. L. (1975). Reciprocal concessions procedure for inducing compliance: The door-in-the-face technique. *Journal of Personality and Social Psychology, 31,* 206–215.

Cisler, J. M., James, G. A., Tripathi, S., Mletzko, T., Heim, C., Hu, X. P., Mayberg, H. S., Nemeroff, C. B., & Kilts, C. D. (2013). Differential functional connectivity within an emotion regulation neural network among individuals resilient and susceptible to the depressogenic effects of early life stress. *Psychological Medicine, 43,* 507–518.

Clark, D. A. (2004). *Cognitive-behavioral therapy for OCD.* New York: Guilford.

Clark, D. A. (2007). Obsessions and compulsions. In N. Kazantzis & L. L'Abate (Eds.), *Handbook of homework assignments in psychotherapy: Research, practice, prevention.* New York: Springer Science + Business Media.

Clark, L., Bechara, A., Damasio, H., Sahakian, B., Robbins, T., & Aitken, M. (2008). Differential effects of insular and ventromedial prefrontal cortex lesions on risky decision-making. *Brain: A Journal of Neurology, 131,* 1311–1322.

Clarke-Stewart, K. A., Vandell, D. L., McCartney, K., Owen, M. T., & Booth, C. (2000). Effects of parental separation and divorce on very young children. *Journal of Family Psychology, 14,* 304–326.

Clarkin, J. F., & Lenzenweger, M. F. (Eds.). (2004). *Major theories of personality disorders* (2nd ed.). New York: Guilford.

Clay, D. L. (2000). Commentary: Rethinking our interventions in pediatric chronic pain and treatment research. *Journal of Pediatric Psychology, 25,* 53–55.

Clayton, K., & Lundberg-Love, P. (2009). Caffeine: Pharmacology and effects of the world's most popular drug. *The Praeger international collection on addictions, Vol 2: Psychobiological profiles.* Santa Barbara, CA: Praeger/ABC-CLIO.

Cleary, A. M. (2006). Relating familiarity-based recognition and the tip-of-the-tongue phenomenon: Detecting a word's recency in the absence of access to the word. *Memory & Cognition, 34,* 804–816.

Clément-Guillotin, C., & Fontayne, P. (2011). Situational malleability of gender schema: The case of the competitive sport context. *Sex Roles, 64,* 426–439.

Clements, A. M., Rimrodt, S. L., & Abel, J. R. (2006). Sex differences in cerebral laterality of language and visuospatial processing. *Brain, 8,* 150–158.

Clements, M. (1994, August 7). Making love, how old, how often. *Parade,* p. 18.

Clemons, T. L. (2006). Underachieving gifted students: A social cognitive model. *Dissertation Abstracts International Section A: Humanities and Social Sciences, 66*(9-A), 3208.

Cloud, J. (2009, January 19). Minds on the Edge. *Time,* pp. 40–46.

Cloud, J. (2009, June 22). Staying sane may be easier than you think. *Time,* p. 72.

Coan, J. A., Schaefer, H. S., & Davidson, R. J. (2006). Lending a hand: Social regulation of the neural response to threat. *Psychological Science, 17*(12), 1032–1039.

Coats, E. J., & Feldman, R. S. (1996). Gender differences in nonverbal correlates of social status. *Personality and Social Psychology Bulletin, 22,* 1014–1022.

Cobos, P., Sanchez, M., Garcia, C., Vera, M. N., & Vila, J. (2002). Revisiting the James versus Cannon debate on emotion: Startle and autonomic modulation in patients with spinal cord injuries. *Biological Psychology, 61,* 251–269.

Coderre, T. J. (2011). Complex regional pain syndrome: What's in a name? *The Journal of Pain, 12,* 2–12.

Coffman, S. J., Martell, C. R., Dimidjian, S., Gallop, R., & Holon, S. D. (2007). Extreme non-response in cognitive therapy: Can behavioral activation succeed where cognitive therapy fails? *Journal of Consulting Clinical Psychology, 75,* 531–545.

Cohen, B. H. (2002). *Explaining psychological statistics* (2nd ed.). New York: Wiley.

Cohen, G. L., Garcia, J., Apfel, N., & Master, A. (2006). Reducing the racial achievement gap: A social-psychological intervention. *Science, 313,* 1307–1310.

Cohen, J. (2003). Things I have learned (so far). In A. E. Kazdin (Ed.), *Methodological issues and strategies in clinical research* (3rd ed.). Washington, DC: American Psychological Association.

Cohen, L., & Cashon, C. (2003). Infant perception and cognition. In R. Lerner & M. Easterbrooks (Eds.), *Handbook of psychology: Developmental psychology* (Vol. 6). New York: Wiley.

Cohen, P. (2009). Medical marijuana: The conflict between scientific evidence and political ideology. Part one of two. *Journal of Pain & Palliative Care Pharmacotherapy, 23,* 4–25.

Cohen, P., Slomkowski, C., & Robins, L. N. (Eds.). (1999). *Historical and geographical influences on psychopathology.* Mahwah, NJ: Erlbaum.

Cohen, S., Doyle, W. J., Turner, R., Alper, C. M., & Skoner, D. P. (2003). Sociability and susceptibility to the common cold. *Psychological Science, 14,* 389–395.

Cohen, S., Hamrick, N., & Rodriguez, M. (2002). Reactivity and vulnerability to stress-associated risk for upper respiratory illness. *Psychosomatic Medicine, 64,* 302–310.

Cohen, S., Kamarck, T., & Mermelstein, R. (1983). A global measure of perceived stress. *Journal of Health and Social Behavior, 24,* 385–396.

Cole, S. W., Arevalo, J. M., Takahashi, R., Sloan, E. K., Lutgendorf, S. L., Sood, A. K., Sheridan, J. F., & Seeman, T. E. (2010). Computational identification of Gene-Social Environment interaction at the human IL6 locus. *Proceedings of the National Academy of Sciences of the USA, 107,* 5681–5686.

Coleman, E. (2002). Masturbation as a means of achieving sexual health. *Journal of Psychology and Human Sexuality, 14,* 5–16.

Coles, R., & Stokes, G. (1985). *Sex and the American teenager.* New York: Harper & Row.

Colland, V. T., Van Essen-Zandvliet, L. E. M., Lans, C., Denteneer, A., Westers, P., & Brackel, H. J. L. (2004). Poor adherence to self-medication instructions in children with asthma and their parents. *Patient Education and Counseling, 55,* 416–421.

Collinger, J. L., Wodlinger, B., Downey, J. E., Wang, W., Tyler-Kabara, E. C., Weber, D. J., McMorland, A. J., Velliste, M., Boninger, M. L., & Schwartz, A. B. (2013). High-performance neuroprosthetic control by an individual with tetraplegia. *Lancet, 381,* 557–64.

Collins, A. M., & Loftus, E. E. (1975). A spreading-activation theory of semantic processing. *Psychological Review, 82,* 407–428.

Collins, A. M., & Quillian, M. R. (1969). Retrieval times from semantic memory. *Journal of Verbal Learning and Verbal Behavior, 8,* 240–247.

Colom, R., Haier, R. J., Head, K., Alvarez-Linera, J., Quiroga, M. A., Shih, P. C., et al. (2009). Gray matter correlates of fluid, crystallized, and spatial intelligence: Testing the P-FIT model. *Intelligence, 37,* 124–135.

Colom, R., Jung, R. E., & Haier, R. J. (2006). Finding the g-factor in brain structure using the method of correlated vectors. *Intelligence, 34,* 561–570.

Coltheart, M., Langdon, R., & McKay, R. (2007). Schizophrenia and monothematic delusions. *Schizophrenia Bulletin, 33,* 642–647.

Coltraine, S., & Messineo, M. (2000). The perpetuation of subtle prejudice: Race and gender imagery in 1990s television advertising. *Sex Roles, 42,* 363–389.

Colwell, M. J., & Lindsey, E. W. (2005). Preschool children's pretend and physical play and sex of play partner: Connections to peer competence. *Sex Roles, 52,* 497–509.

Combrink-Graham, L., & McKenna, S. B. (2006). Families with children with disrupted attachments. In L. Combrink-Graham (Ed.), *Children in family contexts: Perspectives on treatment.* New York: Guilford Press.

Compagni, A., & Manderscheid, R. W. (2006). A neuroscientist-consumer alliance to transform mental health care. *Journal of Behavioral Health Services & Research, 33,* 265–274.

Concept analysis. *Journal of Advanced Nursing, 52,* 651–657.

Conduit, R., Crewther, S. G., & Coleman, G. (2004). Spontaneous eyelid movements (ELMS) during sleep are related to dream recall on awakening. *Journal of Sleep Research, 13,* 137–144.

Conger, R. D., Wallace, L. E., Sun, Y., Simons, R. L., McLoyd, V. C., & Brody, G. H. (2002). Economic pressure in African American families: A replication and extension of the family stress model. *Developmental Psychology, 38,* 179–193.

Conger, R., & Donnellan, M. (2007). An interactionist perspective on the socioeconomic context of human development. *Annual Review of Psychology, 58,* 175–199.

Conner, M., Povey, R., Sparks, P., James, R., & Shepherd, R. (2003). Moderating role of attitudinal ambivalence within the theory of planned behaviour. *British Journal of Social Psychology, 42,* 75–94.

Connolly, A. C. (2007). Concepts and their features: Can cognitive science make good on the promises of concept empiricism? *Dissertation Abstracts International: Section B: The Sciences and Engineering, 67*(7-B), 4125.

Conte, H. R., Plutchik, R., & Draguns, J. G. (2004). The measurement of ego defenses in clinical research. In U. Hentschel, G. Smith, J. G. Draguns, & W. Ehlers (Eds.), *Defense mechanisms: Theoretical, research and clinical perspectives.* Oxford, England: Elsevier Science Ltd.

Conway, M. A. (Ed.). (2002). *Levels of processing 30 years on special issue of memory.* Hove, UK: Psychology Press.

Cook-Cottone, C., & Smith, A. (2013). Eating disorders. In C. A. Noggle & R. S. Dean (Eds.), *The neuropsychology of psychopathology.* New York: Springer Publishing Co.

Cook, M. (2013). *Levels of personality* (3rd ed.). New York: Cambridge University Press.

Cooklin, A. (2000). Therapy, the family and others. In H. Maxwell (Ed.), *Clinical psychotherapy for health professionals.* Philadelphia: Whurr Publishers.

Coolidge, F. L., Segal, D. L., Estey, A. J., & Neuzil, P. J. (2011). Preliminary psychometric properties of a measure of Karen Horney's Tridimensional Theory in children and adolescents. *Journal of Clinical Psychology, 67,* 383–390.

Cooper, H., & Patall, E. (2009, June). The relative benefits of meta-analysis conducted with individual participant data versus aggregated data. *Psychological Methods, 14,* 165–176.

Cooper, J. (2007). *Cognitive dissonance: Fifty years of a classic theory.* Thousand Oaks, CA: Sage Publications.

Cooper, J., & Strayer, D. (2008). Effects of simulator practice and real world experience on cell-phone-related driver distraction. *Human Factors, 50,* 893–902.

Cooper, J., Mirabile, R., & Scher, S. J. (2005). Actions and attitudes: The theory of cognitive dissonance. In T. C. Brock & M. C. Green (Eds.), *Persuasion: Psychological insights and perspectives* (2nd ed.). Thousand Oaks, CA: Sage Publications.

Cooper, M. (2007). Humanizing psychotherapy. *Journal of Contemporary Psychotherapy, 37,* 11–16.

Cooper, M. (2010, September 4). Vermont turns out for its dairies as they take stock and dig out. *The New York Times,* A10.

Cooper, M., & McLeod, J. (2011). Person-centered therapy: A pluralistic perspective. *Person-Centered and Experiential Psychotherapies, 10,* 210–223.

Cooper, Z., & Shafran, R. (2008). Cognitive behaviour therapy for eating disorders. *Behavioural and Cognitive Psychotherapy, 36,* 713–722.

Cope, D. (2001). *Virtual music.* Cambridge, MA: MIT.

Cope, D. (2003). Computer analysis of musical allusions. *Computer Music Journal, 27,* 11–28.

Copeland, J. B., & Proudfoot, D. (2007). Artificial intelligence: History, foundations, and philosophical issues. In P. Thagard (Ed.), *Philosophy of psychology and cognitive science.* Amsterdam, Netherlands: North Holland/Elsevier.

Coplan, R., Reichel, M., & Rowan, K. (2009). Exploring the associations between maternal personality, child temperament, and parenting: A focus on emotions. *Personality and Individual Differences, 46,* 241–246.

Copolov, D. L., Seal, M. L., Maruff, P., Ulusoy, R., Wong, M. T. H., et al. (2003). Cortical activation associated with the human experience of auditory hallucinations and perception of human speech in schizophrenia: A PET correlation study. *Psychiatry Research: Neuroimaging, 123,* 139–152.

Cordnoldi, C., De Beni, R., & Helstrup, T. (2007). Memory sensitivity in auto-biographical memory. In S. Magnussen & T. Helstrup (Eds.), *Everyday memory.* New York: Psychology Press.

Coren, S. (1992). The moon illusion: A different view through the legs. *Perceptual and Motor Skills, 75,* 827–831.

Coren, S. (2004). Sensation and perception. In I. B. Weiner (Ed.), *Handbook of Psychology* (Vol. 1). Hoboken, NJ: John Wiley & Sons.

Coren, S., & Ward, L. M. (1989). *Sensation and perception* (3rd ed.). San Diego, CA: Harcourt Brace Jovanovich.

Cornelius, M. D., Taylor, P. M., Geva, D., & Day, N. L. (1995). Prenatal tobacco and marijuana use among adolescents: Effects on offspring gestational age, growth, and morphology. *Pediatrics, 95,* 57–68.

Cornell, C. B. (2006). A graduated scale for determining mental age. *Dissertation Abstracts International: Section B: The Sciences and Engineering, 66*(9-B), 5121.

Cornier, M. (2011). Is your brain to blame for weight regain? *Physiology & Behavior, 104,* 608–612.

Corsello, A. (2005). The wronged man. In *The best American magazine writing, 2005.* New York: Columbia University Press.

Cosmides, L., & Tooby, J. (2004). Social exchange: The evolutionary design of a neurocognitive system. In M. S. Gazzaniga (Ed.), *Cognitive neurosciences* (3rd ed.). Cambridge, MA: MIT.

Costa, P. T., Jr., & Widiger, T. A. (Eds.). (2002). *Personality disorders and the Five-Factor Model of personality* (2nd ed.). Washington, DC: American Psychological Association.

Costa, R., & Figueiredo, B. (2011). Infant's psychophysiological profile and temperament at 3 and 12 months. *Infant Behavior & Development, 34,* 270–279.

Cottencin, O., Rolland, B., & Karila, L. (2013). New designer drugs (synthetic cannabinoids and synthetic cathinones): review of literature. *Current Pharmaceutical Design.* Retrieved from http://www.ncbi.nlm.nih.gov/pubmed/24001292

Cotton, P. (1993, July 7). Psychiatrists set to approve DSM-IV. *Journal of the American Medical Association, 270,* 13–15.

Coulson, D., & Harvey, M. (2013). Scaffolding student reflection for experience-based learning: A framework. *Teaching in Higher Education, 18,* 401–413.

Council of National Psychological Associations for the Advancement of Ethnic Minority Interests (CNPAAEMI). (2000, January). *Guidelines for research in ethnic minority communities.* Washington, DC: American Psychological Association.

Couturier, J., & Lock, J. (2006). Eating-disorders: Anorexia nervosa, bulimia nervosa, and binge eating disorder. In T. G. Plante (Ed.), *Mental disorders of the new millennium: Biology and function* (Vol 3). Westport, CT: Praeger Publishers/Greenwood Publishing.

Coventry, K. R., Venn, S. F., Smith, G. D., & Morley, A. M. (2003). Spatial problem solving and functional relations. *European Journal of Cognitive Psychology, 15,* 71–99.

Cowley, G. (2000, January 31). Alzheimer's: Unlocking the mystery. *Time,* pp. 46–54.

Cowley, G. (2003, February 24). Our bodies, our fears. *Newsweek,* pp. 43–44.

Cox, J. (2003, May 6). How far would you go to save your life? *Denver Post,* p. F1.

Cox, R., Baker, S. E., Macdonald, D. W., & Berdoy, M. (2004). Protecting egg prey from carrion crows: The potential of aversive conditioning. *Applied Animal Behaviour Science, 87,* 325–342.

Coyle, N. (2006). The hard work of living in the face of death. *Journal of Pain and Symptom Management, 32,* 266–274.

Coyle, T. R. (2006). Test-retest changes on scholastic aptitude tests are not related to g. *Intelligence, 34,* 15–27.

Craighero, L., Leo, I., Umilta, C., & Simion, F. (2011). Newborns' preference for goal-directed actions. *Cognition, 120,* 26–32.

Craik, F. I. M. (1990). Levels of processing. In M. E. Eysenck (Ed.), *The Blackwell dictionary of cognitive psychology.* London: Blackwell.

Craik, F., & Lockhart, R. (2008). Levels of processing and Zinchenko's approach to memory research. *Journal of Russian & East European Psychology, 46,* 52–60.

Cramer, P. (2007). Longitudinal study of defense mechanisms: Late childhood to late adolescence. *Journal of Personality, 75,* 1–23.

Crawford, M., & Unger, R. (2004). *Women and gender: A feminist psychology* (4th ed.). New York: McGraw-Hill.

Creasey, G. L. (2005). *Research methods in lifespan development* (6th ed.). Boston: Allyn & Bacon.

Creel, S. C., & Bregman, M. R. (2011). How talker identity relates to language processing. *Language and Linguistics Compass, 5,* 190–204.

Creswell, J., & Landon, T. (2009, January 25). The talented Mr. Madoff. *The New York Times,* p. 1.

Crews, F. (1996). The verdict on Freud. *Psychological Science, 7,* 63–68.

Criswell, H., Ming, Z., Kelm, M., & Breese, G. (2008, August). Brain regional differences in the effect of ethanol on GABA release from presynaptic terminals. *Journal of Pharmacology and Experimental Therapeutics, 326,* 596–603.

Critelli, J., & Bivona, J. (2008). Women's erotic rape fantasies: An evaluation of theory and research. *Journal of Sex Research, 45,* 57–70.

Crits-Christoph, P. (1992). The efficacy of brief dynamic psychotherapy: A meta-analysis. *American Journal of Psychiatry, 149,* 151–158.

Crombag, H. S., & Robinson, R. E. (2004). Drugs, environment, brain, and behavior. *Current Directions in Psychological Science, 13,* 107–111.

Cropley, A. (2006). In praise of convergent thinking. *Creativity Research Journal, 18,* 391–404.

Crosnoe, R., & Elder, G. H., Jr. (2002). Successful adaptation in the later years: A life course approach to aging. *Social Psychology Quarterly, 65,* 309–328.

Cross, C. P., & Campbell, A. (2011). Women's aggression. *Aggression and Violent Behavior, 16,* 390–398.

Crowne, K. (2013). Cultural exposure, emotional intelligence, and cultural intelligence: An exploratory study. *International Journal of Cross-Cultural Management, 13*(1), 5–22.

Crum, A. J., & Langer, E. J. (2007). Mind-set matters: Exercise and the placebo effect. *Psychological Science, 18,* 165–171.

Cruz, A., & Green, B. G. (2000). Thermal stimulation of taste. *Nature, 403,* 889–892.

Cuddy, A. J. C., Fiske, S. T., & Glick, P. (2004). When professionals become mothers, warmth doesn't cut the ice. *Journal of Social Issues, 60,* 701–718.

Cuijpers, P., van Straten, A., Andersson, G., & van Oppen, P. (2008). Psychotherapy for depression in adults: A meta-analysis of comparative outcome studies. *Journal of Consulting and Clinical Psychology, 76,* 909–922.

Culhane-Pera, K. A., Borkan, J. M., & Patten, S. (2007). Culture and ethnicity. In O. J. Z. Sahler & J. E. Carr (Eds.), *The behavioral sciences and health care* (2nd rev. and updated ed.). Ashland, OH: Hogrefe & Huber Publishers.

Cullinane, C. A., Chu, D. Z. J., & Mamelak, A. N. (2002). Current surgical options in the control of cancer pain. *Cancer Practice, 10,* s21–s26.

Cummings, A., Ceponiene, R., & Koyama, A. (2006). Auditory semantic networks for words and natural sounds. *Brain Research, 1115,* 92–107.

Cunningham, P. (2006). Early years teachers and the influence of Piaget: Evidence from oral history. *Early Years An International Journal of Research and Development, 26,* 5–16.

Cwikel, J., Behar, L., & Rabson-Hare, J. (2000). A comparison of a vote count and a meta-analysis review of intervention research with adult cancer patients. *Research on Social Work Practice, 10,* 139–158.

Cynkar, A. (2007). The changing gender composition of psychology. *Monitor on Psychology, 38,* 46–48.

Czopp, A. M., & Monteith, M. J. (2006). Thinking well of African Americans: Measuring complimentary stereotypes and negative prejudice. *Basic and Applied Social Psychology, 28,* 233–250.

D'Arcy, R. C. N., Bolster, R. B., & Ryner, L. (2007). A site directed fMRI approach for evaluating functional status in the anterolateral temporal lobes. *Neuroscience Research, 57,* 120–128.

Daftary, F., & Meri, J. W. (2002). *Culture and memory in medieval Islam.* London: I. B. Tauris.

Dai, D. Y., & Wang, X. (2007). The role of need for cognition and reader beliefs in text comprehension and interest development. *Contemporary Educational Psychology, 32,* 332–347.

Daines, B. (2006). Violations of agreed and implicit sexual and emotional boundaries in couple relationships–some thoughts arising from Levine's 'A clinical perspective on couple infidelity'. *Sexual and Relationship Therapy, 21,* 45–53.

Dakin, E. K., & Areán, P. (2013). Patient perspectives on the benefits of psychotherapy for late-life depression. *The American Journal of Geriatric Psychiatry, 21,* 155–163.

Dalal, A. K., & Misra, G. (2006). Psychology of health and well-being: Some emerging perspectives [Special issue: Psychology of health and well-being]. *Psychological Studies, 51,* 91–104.

Dale, A. (2006). Quality issues with survey research. *International Journal of Social Research Methodology: Theory & Practice, 9, Special issue: Quality in Social Research,* 143–158.

Dale, J. W., & von Schantz, M. (2007). *From genes to genomes: Concepts and applications of DNA technology.* New York: John Wiley & Sons.

Damasio, A. (2003, May 15). Mental self: The person within. *Nature, 423, 227.*

Damaske, S. (2011). A "major career woman"?: How women develop early expectations about work. *Gender & Society, 25,* 409–430.

Danaei, G., Vender Hoorn, S., Lopez, A. D., Murray, C. J. L., & Ezzati, M. (2005). Causes of cancer in the world: Comparative risk assessment of nine behavioural and environmental risk factors. Comparative Risk Assessment collaborating group (Cancers). *Lancet, 366,* 1784–1793.

Dani, J. A., & Montague, P. (2007). Disrupting addiction through the loss of drug-associated internal states. *Nature Neuroscience, 10,* 403–404.

Danner, D., Hagemann, D., Schankin, A., Hager, M., & Funke, J. (2011). Beyond IQ: A latent state-trait analysis of general intelligence, dynamic decision making, and implicit learning. *Intelligence, 39,* 323–334.

Dare, J. S. (2011). Transitions in midlife women's lives: Contemporary experiences. *Health Care for Women International, 32,* 111–133.

Darley, J. M., & Latané, B. (1968). Bystanders' intervention in emergencies: Diffusion of responsibility. *Journal of Personality and Social Psychology, 8,* 377–383.

Das, A. (2007). Masturbation in the United States. *Journal of Sex & Marital Therapy, 33,* 301–317.

Das, A., Parish, W., & Laumann, E. (2009). Masturbation in urban China. *Archives of Sexual Behavior, 38,* 108–120.

Davern, M. (2013). Nonresponse rates are a problematic indicator of nonresponse bias in survey research. *Health Services Research, 48,* 905–912.

Davidson, R. J., Gray, J. A., LeDoux, J. E., Levenson, R. W., Pankseep, J., & Ekman, P. (1994). Is there emotion-specific physiology? In P. Ekman & R. J. Davidson (Eds.), *The nature of emotion.* New York: Oxford University Press.

Davies, S., Jackson, P., Lewis, G., Hood, S., Nutt, D., & Potokar, J. (2008). Is the association of hypertension and panic disorder explained by clustering of autonomic panic symptoms in hypertensive patients? *Journal of Affective Disorders, 111,* 344–350.

Davis, J., Senghas, A., & Ochsner, K. (2009). How does facial feedback modulate emotional experience? *Journal of Research in Personality, 43,* 822–829.

Davis, K., Christodoulou, J., Seider, S., & Gardner, H. (2011). The theory of multiple intelligences. In R. J. Sternberg & S. Kaufman (Eds.), *The Cambridge handbook of intelligence.* New York: Cambridge University Press.

Davis, L. J. (2009, June 15). Sotomayor and the New Haven firefighters case: More myths than facts. *The Washington Times,* p. A04.

Davis, O., Haworth, C., & Plomin, R. (2009, January). Learning abilities and disabilities: Generalist genes in early adolescence. *Cognitive Neuropsychiatry, 14,* 312–331.

Davis, R. D., & Millon, T. (1999). Models of personality and its disorders. In T. Millon, P. H. Blaney, & R. D. Davis (Eds.), *Oxford textbook of psychopathology.* New York: Oxford University Press.

Davis, S. R. (2007). The nose knows best. *PsycCRITIQUES, 52,* 22–31.

Day, A. L., & Livingstone, H. A. (2003). Gender differences in perceptions of stressors and utilization of social support among university students. *Canadian Journal of Behavioural Science, 35,* 73–83.

Day, R. D., & Lamb, M. E. (2004). *Conceptualizing and measuring father involvement.* Mahwah, NJ: Lawrence Erlbaum Associates.

De Beni, R., Pazzaglia, F., & Gardini, S. (2007). The generation and maintenance of visual mental images: Evidence from image type and aging. *Brain and Cognition, 63,* 271–278.

De Dreu, C. W., Greer, L. L., Van Kleef, G. A., Shalvi, S., & Handgraaf, M. J. (2011). Oxytocin promotes human ethnocentrism. *PNAS Proceedings of the National Academy of Sciences of the United States of America, 108,* 1262–1266.

de Gelder, B. (2000). More to seeing than meets the eye. *Science, 289,* 1148–1149.

Dean-Borenstein, M. T. (2007). The long-term psychosocial effects of trauma on survivors of human-caused extreme stress situations. *Dissertation Abstracts International: Section B: The Sciences and Engineering, 67*(11-B), 6733.

Dean, C., & Dresbach, T. (2006). Neuroligins and neurexins: Linking cell adhesion, synapse formation and cognitive function. *International Journal of Psychiatry in Clinical Practice, 10 (Suppl.),* 5–11.

DeAngelis, D., & Monahan, J. (2008). Professional credentials and professional regulations: Social work professional development. In B. W. White, K. M. Sowers, & C. N. Dulmus (Eds.), *Comprehensive handbook of social work and social welfare, Vol. 1: The profession of social work.* Hoboken, NJ: John Wiley & Sons.

Dearing, E., McCartney, K., & Taylor, B. (2009). Does higher quality early child care promote low-income children's math and reading achievement in middle childhood? *Child Development, 80,* 1329–1349.

Deater-Deckard, K., Ivy, L., & Smith, J. (2005). Resilience in gene-environment transactions. In S. Goldstein & R. B. Brooks (Eds.), *Handbook of resilience in children.* New York: Kluwer Academic/Plenum Publishers.

Deci, E. L., & Ryan, R. M. (2008). Facilitating optimal motivation and psychological well-being across life's domains. *Canadian Psychology/Psychologie Canadienne, 49,* 14–23.

Dediu, D., & Ladd, D. R. (2007). From the Cover: Linguistic tone is related to the population frequency of the adaptive haplogroups of two brain size genes, ASPM and microcephalin. *Proceedings of the National Academy of Sciences, 104,* 10944–10949.

DeGaton, J. F., Weed, S., & Jensen, L. (1996). Understanding gender differences in adolescent sexuality. *Adolescence, 31,* 217–231.

deGroot, A. (1978). *Thought and choice in chess.* Paris: Mouton de Gruyter.

deGroot, A. D. (1966). Perception and memory versus thought: Some old ideas and recent findings. In B. Kleinmuntz (Ed.), *Problem solving: Research, method, and theory.* New York: Wiley.

Del Giudice, M. (2011). Alone in the dark? Modeling the conditions for visual experience in human fetuses. *Developmental Psychobiology, 53,* 214–219.

del Rosal, E., Alonso, L., & Moreno, R. (2006). Simulation of habituation to simple and multiple stimuli. *Behavioural Processes, 73,* 272–277.

Delacollette, N., Dumont, M., Sarlet, M., & Dardenne, B. (2013). Benevolent sexism, men's advantages and the prescription of warmth to women. *Sex Roles, 68,* 296–310.

DeLamater, J. D., & Sill, M. (2005). Sexual desire in later life. *Journal of Sex Research, 42,* 138–149.

Delcourt, M. A. B., Cornell, D. G., & Goldberg, M. D. (2007). Cognitive and affective learning outcomes of gifted elementary school students. *The Gifted Child Quarterly, 51,* 359–382.

Delgado, M. R., Labouliere, C. D., & Phelps, E. A. (2006). Fear of losing money? Aversive conditioning with secondary reinforcers [Special issue: Genetic, comparative and cognitive studies of social behavior]. *Social Cognitive and Affective Neuroscience, 1,* 250–259.

Dell, P. F. (2013). Three dimensions of dissociative amnesia. *Journal of Trauma & Dissociation, 14,* 25–39.

DeLoache, J., & LoBue, V. (2009). The narrow fellow in the grass: Human infants associate snakes and fear. *Developmental Science, 12,* 201–207.

Demaree, H. A., & Everhart, D. E. (2004). Healthy high-hostiles: Reduced para-sympathetic activity and decreased sympathovagal flexibility during negative emotional processing. *Personality and Individual Differences, 36,* 457–469.

DeMaris, A. (2013). Burning the candle at both ends: Extramarital sex as a precursor of marital disruption. *Journal of Family Issues, 34,* 1474–1499.

Dement, W. C., & Wolpert, E. A. (1958). The relation of eye movements, body mobility, and external stimuli to dream content. *Journal of Experimental Psychology, 55,* 543–553.

Dempster, F. N. (1981). Memory span: Sources for individual and developmental differences. *Psychological Bulletin, 89,* 63–100.

Dender, A., & Stagnitti, K. (2011). Development of the Indigenous Child-Initiated Pretend Play Assessment: Selection of play materials and administration. *Australian Occupational Therapy Journal, 58,* 34–42.

Denmark, G. L., & Fernandez, L. C. (1993). Historical development of the psychology of women. In F. L. Denmark & M. A. Paludi (Eds.), *A handbook of issues and theories.* Westport, CT: Greenwood Press.

Dennis, I. (2007). Halo effects in grading student projects. *Journal of Applied Psychology, 92,* 1169–1176.

Dennis, S. (2011). Smoking causes creative responses: On state antismoking policy and resilient habits. *Critical Public Health, 21,* 25–35.

Dennis, T. A., Cole, P. M., Zahn-Waxler, C., & Mizuta, I. (2002). Self in context: Autonomy and relatedness in Japanese and U.S. mother-preschooler dyads. *Child Development, 73,* 1803–1817.

Denollet, J. (2005). DS14: Standard assessment of negative affectivity, social inhibition, and Type D personality. *Psychosomatic Medicine, 67,* 89–97.

Denollet, J., & Pedersen, S. S. (2011). Type D personality in patients with cardiovascular disorders. In R. Allan & J. Fisher (Eds.), *Heart and mind: The practice of cardiac psychology (2nd ed.)* (pp. 219–247). Washington, DC US: American Psychological Association.

Deouell, L. Y., Parnes, A., & Pickard, N. (2006). Spatial location is accurately tracked by human auditory sensory memory: Evidence from the mismatch negativity. *European Journal of Neuroscience, 24,* 1488–1494.

Deregowski, J. B. (1973). Illusion and culture. In R. L. Gregory & G. H. Combrich (Eds.), *Illusion in nature and art.* New York: Scribner.

Deroy, O., & Spence, C. (2013). Are we all born synaesthetic? Examining the neonatal synaesthesia hypothesis. *Neuroscience and Biobehavioral Reviews, 37,* 1240–1253.

Des Jarlais, D. C., Sloboda, A., Friedman, S. R., Tempakski, B., McKnight, C., & Braine, N. (2006). Diffusion of the *D.A.R.E* and Syringe Exchange Programs. *American Journal of Public Health, 96,* 1354–1357.

Deshields, T., Tibbs, T., Fan, M. Y., & Taylor, M. (2006). Differences in patterns of depression after treatment for breast cancer [Electronic article published August 12, 2005]. *Psycho-Oncology, 15*(5), 398–406.

Desimone, R. (1992, October 9). The physiology of memory: Recordings of things past. *Science, 258,* 245–255.

Dessing, J. C., Peper, C. E., Bullock, D., & Beek, P. J. (2005). How position, velocity, and temporal information combine in the prospective control of catching: Data and model. *Journal of Cognitive Neuroscience, 17,* 668–686.

DeSteno, D., Bartlett, M. Y., Braverman, J., & Salovey, P. (2002). Sex differences in jealousy: Evolutionary mechanism or artifact of measurement? *Journal of Personality and Social Psychology, 83,* 1103–1116.

Detoledo-Morrell, L., Stoub, T. R., & Wang, C. (2007). Hippocampal atrophy and disconnection in incipient and mild Alzheimer's disease. *Progressive Brain Research, 163C,* 741–823.

Detterman, D. K. (2011). A challenge to Watson. *Intelligence, 39*(2-3), 77–78.

Detterman, D. K., Gabriel, L. T., & Ruthsatz, J. M. (2000). Intelligence and mental retardation. In R. J. Sternberg et al. (Eds.), *Handbook of intelligence.* New York: Cambridge University Press.

Devonport, J. J., & Lane, A. M. (2006). Relationships between self-efficacy, coping and student retention. *Social Behavior and Personality, 34,* 127–138.

Devos, T. (2011). The role of race in American politics: Lessons learned from the 2008 presidential election. In G. S. Parks & M. W. Hughey (Eds.), *The Obamas and a (post) racial America?* New York: Oxford University Press.

Dey, E. L., Astin, A. W., Korn, W. S., & Berz, E. R. (2004). *The American freshman: National norms for fall, 1990.* Los Angeles: Higher Education Research Institute, Graduate School of Education, UCLA.

Dhillon, S., Yang, L., & Curran, M. (2008). Spotlight on bupropion in major depressive disorder. *CNS Drugs, 22,* 613–617.

Di Fabio, A., & Palazzeschi, L. (2009). An in-depth look at scholastic success: Fluid intelligence, personality traits or emotional intelligence? *Personality and Individual Differences, 46*, 581–585.

Di Forti, M., Lappin, J., & Murray, R. (2007, March). Risk factors for schizophrenia–All roads lead to dopamine. *European Neuropsychopharmacology, 17*, S101–SS107.

Di Paola, M., Luders, E., Rubino, I. A., Siracusano, A., Manfredi, G., Girardi, P., Martinotti, G., Thompson, P. M., Chou, Y. Y., Toga, A. W., Caltagirone, C., Spalletta, G. (2013). The structure of the corpus callosum in obsessive compulsive disorder. *European Psychiatry, 28*(8), 499–506.

Diamond, M. (2009). Human intersexuality: Difference or disorder? *Archives of Sexual Behavior, 38*, 172.

Dias, A. M., & van Deusen, A. (2011). A new neurofeedback protocol for depression. *Spanish Journal of Psychology, 14*, 374–384.

Diaz, A., & Bell, M. (2011). Information processing efficiency and regulation at five months. *Infant Behavior & Development, 34*, 239–247.

Díaz, E., & De la Casa, L. G. (2011). Extinction, spontaneous recovery and renewal of flavor preferences based on taste–taste learning. *Learning and Motivation, 42*, 64–75.

DiCano, P., & Everitt, B. J. (2002). Reinstatement and spontaneous recovery of cocaine-seeking following extinction and different durations of withdrawal. *Behavioural Pharmacology, 13*, 397–406.

Dickens, W. T., & Flynn, J. R. (2001). Heritability estimates versus large environmental effects: The IQ paradox resolved. *Psychological Review, 108*, 291–310.

Dickerson, S. S., Kemeny, M. E., Aziz, N., Kim, K. H., & Fahey, J. L. (2004). Immunological effects of induced shame and guilt. *Psychosomatic Medicine, 66*, 124–131.

Dickinson, D. L., & Oxoby, R. J. (2011). Cognitive dissonance, pessimism, and behavioral spillover effects. *Journal of Economic Psychology, 32*, 295–306.

Dickinson, M. D., & Hiscock, M. (2011). The Flynn effect in neuropsychological assessment. *Applied Neuropsychology, 18*, 136–142.

Diemand-Yauman, D., Oppenheimer, D. M., & Vaughan, E. B. (2011). Fortune favors the bold (and the italicized): Effects of disfluency on educational outcomes. *Cognition, 118*, 114–118.

Diener, E., & Biswas-Diener, R. (2002). Will money increase subjective well-being? *Social Indicators Research, 57*, 119–169.

Diener, E., & Clifton, D. (2002). Life satisfaction and religiosity in broad probability samples. *Psychological Inquiry, 13*, 206–209.

Diener, E., & Seligman, M. E. P. (2002). Very happy people. *Psychological Science, 18*, 81–84.

Diener, E., & Seligman, M. E. P. (2004). Beyond money: Toward an economy of well-being. *Psychological Science in the Public Interest, 5*, 1–31.

Diener, E., Lucas, R. E., & Oishi, S. (2002). Subjective well-being: The science of happiness and life satisfaction. In C. R. Snyder & S. J. Lopez (Eds.), *Handbook of positive psychology*. London: Oxford University Press.

Diener, E., Lucas, R. E., & Scollon, C. N. (2006). Beyond the hedonic treadmill: Revising the adaptation theory of well-being. *American Psychologist, 61*, 305–314.

Diener, M., Isabella, R., Behunin, M., & Wong, M. (2008). Attachment to mothers and fathers during middle childhood: Associations with child gender, grade, and competence. *Social Development, 17*, 84–101.

DiGiovanna, A. G. (1994). *Human aging: Biological perspectives*. New York: McGraw-Hill.

Dijksterhuis, A., Chartrand, T. L., & Aarts, H. (2007). Effects of Priming and Perception on Social Behavior and Goal Pursuit. *Frontiers of Social Psychology, 17*, 33–40.

Dill, K. E. (Ed.). (2013). *The Oxford handbook of media psychology*. New York: Oxford University Press.

Dill, K., & Thill, K. (2007). Video game characters and the socialization of gender roles: Young people's perceptions mirror sexist media depictions. *Sex Roles, 57*, 851–864.

Dillard, J. P., & Shen, L. (2004). On the nature of reactance and its role in persuasive health communication. *Communication Monographs, 72*, 144–168.

Dillard, J. P., & Shen, L. (2007). Self-report measures of discrete emotions. In R. A. Reynolds, R. Woods, & J. D. Baker (Eds.), *Handbook of research on electronic surveys and measurements*. Hershey, PA: Idea Group Reference/IGI Global, 2007.

DiLorenzo, P. M., & Yougentob, S. L. (2003). Olfaction and taste. In M. Gallagher & R. J. Nelson (Eds.), *Handbook of psychology: Biological psychology* (Vol 3). New York: Wiley.

Dingfelder, S. (2011). Reflecting on narcissism. *Monitor on Psychology, 42*, 64–68.

Diniz, B. S., Butters, M. A., Albert, S. M., Dew, M., & Reynolds, C. (2013). Late-life depression and risk of vascular dementia and Alzheimer's disease: Systematic review and meta-analysis of community-based cohort studies. *The British Journal of Psychiatry, 202*, 329–335.

Dirie, W. (2011). *Desert Flower*. NY: William Morrow.

Dittrich, W. H., Johansen, T., & Fineberg, N. A. (2011). Cognitive Assessment Instrument of Obsessions and Compulsions (CAIOV-13)–A new 13-item scale for evaluating functional impairment associated with OCD. *Psychiatry Research, 187*, 283–290.

Dixon, R. A., & Cohen, A. L. (2003). Cognitive development in adulthood. In R. M. Lerner, M. A. Easterbrooks, et al. (Eds.), *Handbook of psychology: Developmental psychology* (Vol. 6). New York: Wiley.

Dixon, R. A., McFall, G., Whitehead, B. P., & Dolcos, S. (2013). Cognitive development in adulthood and aging. In R. M. Lerner, M. Easterbrooks, J. Mistry, & I. B. Weiner (Eds.), *Handbook of psychology, Vol. 6: Developmental psychology (2nd ed.)*. Hoboken, NJ: John Wiley & Sons Inc.

Dixon, R. A., Rust, T. B., & Feltmate, S. E. (2007). Memory and aging: Selected research directions and application issues. *Canadian Psychology Psychologie Canadienne, 48*, 67–76.

Djamba, Y. K. (2013). Sexual practices in Africa. In A. K. Baumle (Ed.), *International handbook on the demography of sexuality*. New York: Springer Science + Business Media.

Djapo, N., Kolenovic-Djapo, J., Djokic, R., & Fako, I. (2011). Relationship between Cattell's 16PF and fluid and crystallized intelligence. *Personality and Individual Differences, 51*, 63–67.

Do, V. T. (2006). Asian American men and the media: The relationship between ethnic identity, self-esteem, and the endorsement of stereotypes. *Dissertation Abstracts International: Section B: The Sciences and Engineering, 67*(6-B), 3446.

Dobbins, A. C., Jeo, R. M., Fiser, J., & Allman, J. M. (1998, July 24). Distance modulation of neural activity in the visual cortex. *Science, 281*, 552–555.

Dobbs, D. (2012). The new temper tantrum disorder. Posted Friday, Dec. 7, 2012 in *Slate*. Retrieved from http://www.slate.com/articles/double_x/doublex/2012/12/disruptive_mood_dysregulation_disorder_in_dsm_5_criticism_of_a_new_diagnosis.html

Dodds, P. S., et al. (2011). Science. *American Association for the Advancement of Science* (AAAS).

Dodge, K. A. (2004). The nature-nurture debate and public policy [Special issue: 50th anniversary issue, part 2: The maturing of the human development sciences–Appraising past, present, and prospective agendas]. *Merrill-Palmer Quarterly: Journal of Developmental Psychology, 50*, 418–427.

Dohnke, B., Weiss-Gerlach, E., & Spies, C. D. (2011). Social influences on the motivation to quit smoking: Main and moderating effects of social norms. *Addictive Behaviors, 36*, 286–293.

Doi, T. (1990). The cultural assumptions of psychoanalysis. In J. W. Stigler, R. A. Shweder, & G. Herdt (Eds.), *Cultural psychology: Essays on comparative human development*. New York: Cambridge University Press.

Dokoupil, T. (2012, July 16). Is the onslaught making us crazy? *Newsweek*, 24–30.

Dolan, P., & White, M. P. (2007). How can measures of subjective well-being be used to inform public policy? *Perspectives on Psychological Science, 2*, 71–85.

Dolan, R. J. (2002, November 8). Emotion, cognition, and behavior. *Science, 298*, 1191–1194.

Dolbier, C. L., Smith, S. E., & Steinhardt, M. A. (2007). Relationships of protective factors to stress and symptoms of illness. *American Journal of Health Behavior, 31*, 423–433.

Dolinski, D. (2011). A rock or a hard place: The foot-in-the-face technique for inducing compliance without pressure. *Journal of Applied Social Psychology, 41*, 1514–1537.

Dollinger, S. J. (2003). Need for uniqueness, need for cognition and creativity. *Journal of Creative Behavior, 37*, 99–116.

Domhoff, G. W. (1996). *Finding meaning in dreams: A quantitative approach*. New York: Plenum Press.

Domhoff, G. W. (2011). The neural substrate for dreaming: Is it a subsystem of the default network? *Consciousness and Cognition, 20*, 1163–1174.

Domschke, K. (2013). Clinical and molecular genetics of psychotic depression. *Schizophrenia Bulletin, 39*, 766–775.

Donahoe, J. W. (2003). Selectionism. In K. A. Lattal & P. N. Chase (Eds.), *Behavior theory and philosophy*. New York: Kluwer Academic/Plenum Publishers.

Donahoe, J. W., & Vegas, R. (2004). Pavlovian Conditioning: The CSUR Relation. *Journal of Experimental Psychology: Animal Behavior Processes, 30*, 17–33.

Dornhoff, G. W., & Schneider, A. (1998). New rationales and methods for quantitative dream research outside the laboratory. *Sleep 21*(4) 1814.

Dortch, S. (1996, October). Our aching heads. *American Demographics*, 44–52.

Doty, R. L., Green, P. A., Ram, C., & Yankell, S. L. (1982). Communication of gender from human breath odors: Relationship to perceived intensity and pleasantness. *Hormones and Behavior, 16*, 13–22.

Dougall, A. L., & Baum, A. (2004). Psychoneuroimmunology and trauma. In P. P. Schnurr & B. L. Green (Eds.), *Trauma and health: Physical health consequences of exposure to extreme stress*. Washington, DC: American Psychological Association.

Douglas Brown, R., Goldstein, E., & Bjorklund, D. F. (2000). The history and zeitgeist of the repressed-false-memory debate: Scientific and sociological perspectives on suggestibility and childhood memory. In D. F. Bjorklund (Ed.), *False-memory creation in children and adults: Theory, research, and implications.* Mahwah, NJ: Lawrence Erlbaum.

Douglas, O., Burton, K. S., & Reese-Durham, N. (2008). The effects of the multiple intelligence teaching strategy on the academic achievement of eighth grade math students. *Journal of Instructional Psychology, 35,* 182–187.

Dovidio, J. F., & Gaertner, S. L. (2006). A multilevel perspective on prejudice: Crossing disciplinary boundaries. In P. A. M. Van Lange (Ed.), *Bridging social psychology: Benefits of transdisci-plinary approaches.* Mahwah, NJ: Lawrence Erlbaum Associates.

Dovidio, J. F., Gaertner, S. L., & Kawakami, K. (2003). Intergroup contact: The past, present, and the future. *Group Processes and Intergroup Relations, 6,* 5–20.

Dovidio, J. F., Gaertner, S. L., & Pearson, A. R. (2005). On the nature of prejudice: The psychological foundations of hate. In R. J. Sternberg (Ed.), *Psychology of hate.* Washington, DC: American Psychological Association.

Dovidio, J. F., Piliavin, J. A., Schroeder, D. A., & Penner, L. A. (2006). *The social psychology of prosocial behavior.* Mahwah, NJ: Lawrence Erlbaum Associates.

Dowling, N., Jackson, A., & Thomas, S. (2008). Behavioral interventions in the treatment of pathological gambling: A review of activity scheduling and desensitization. *International Journal of Behavioral Consultation and Therapy, 4,* 172–187.

Doyle, R. (2002, December). Deinstitutionalization. *Scientific American,* 38.

Dresler, T., Guhn, A., Tupak, S. V., Ehlis, A., Herrmann, M. J., Fallgatter, A. J., & . . . Domschke, K. (2013). Revise the revised? New dimensions of the neuroanatomical hypothesis of panic disorder. *Journal of Neural Transmission, 120,* 3–29.

Drewes, A. A. (2005). Play in selected cultures: Diversity and universality. In E. Gil & A. A. Drewes (Eds.), *Cultural issues in play therapy.* New York: Guilford Press.

Drews, F., Pasupathi, M., & Strayer, D. (2008, December). Passenger and cell phone conversations in simulated driving. *Journal of Experimental Psychology: Applied, 14,* 392–400.

Drob, S. (2005). The mystical symbol: Some comments on Ankor, Giegerich, Scholem, and Jung. *Journal of Jungian Theory & Practice, 7,* 25–29.

Dryden, W., & David, D. (2008). Rational emotive behavior therapy: Current status. *Journal of Cognitive Psychotherapy,* 22, 195–209.

Dudai, Y. (2011). The Engram revisited: On the elusive permanence of memory. In S. Nalbantian, P. M. Matthews, & J. L. McClelland (Eds.), *The memory process: Neuroscientific and humanistic perspectives.* Cambridge, MA: MIT Press.

Duffy, M., Gillig, S. E., Tureen, R. M., & Ybarra, M. A. (2002). A critical look at the DSM-IV. *Journal of Individual Psychology, 58,* 363–373.

Dugger, C. W. (1996, December 28). Tug of taboos: African genital rite vs. U.S. law. *The New York Times,* pp. 1, 9.

Dugger, C. W. (2013, July 22). Genital Cutting Found in Decline in Many Nations. *The New York Times,* p. A1.

Duke, M., & Nowicki, S., Jr. (1979). *Abnormal psychology: Perspectives on being different.* Monterey, CA: Brooks/Cole.

Dumont, M., & Dumont, D. (2008). Deinstitutionalization in the United States and Italy: A historical survey. *International Journal of Mental Health, 37,* 61–70.

Duncan, D. E. (2012, April 3). A little device that's trying to read your thoughts. *The New York Times,* p. D2.

Duncker, K. (1945). On problem solving. *Psychological Monographs, 58* (5, whole no. 270).

Dunlop, W. L., Beatty, D. J., & Beauchamp, M. R. (2011). Examining the influence of other-efficacy and self-efficacy on personal performance. *Journal of Sport & Exercise Psychology, 33,* 586–593.

Dunn, E., & Norton, M. (2012, July 8). Don't indulge. Be happy. *The New York Times Sunday Review,* p. 1.

Durán, M., Moya, M., & Megías, J. L. (2011). It's his right, it's her duty: Benevolent sexism and the justification of traditional sexual roles. *Journal of Sex Research, 48,* 470–478.

Durante, K. M., Li, N. P., & Haselton, M. G. (2008). Changes in women's choice of dress across the ovulatory cycle: Naturalistic and laboratory task-based evidence. *Personality and Social Psychology Bulletin, 34,* 1451–1460.

Durik, A. M., Hyde, J. S., & Marks, A. C. (2006). Ethnicity and gender stereotypes of emotion. *Sex Roles, 54,* 429–445.

Eagly, A. H., Beall, A., & Sternberg, R. S. (Eds.). (2004). *The psychology of gender* (2nd ed.). New York: Guilford Press.

Eagly, A., & Chaiken, S. (1998). Attitude structure and function. In D. T. Gilbert & S. T. Fiske (Eds.), *Handbook of social psychology* (Vol. 1, 4th ed.). New York: McGraw-Hill.

Eagly, A. H., & Wood, W. (2013). The nature-nurture debates: 25 years of challenges in understanding the psychology of gender. *Perspectives on Psychological Science, 8,* 340–357.

Eaker, E. D., Sullivan, L. M., Kelly-Hayes, M., D'Agostino, R. B., Sr., & Benjamin, E. J. (2004). Anger and hostility predict the development of atrial fibrillation in men in the Framingham Offspring Study. *Circulation, 109,* 1267–1271.

Ebbinghaus, H. (1885/1913). *Memory: A contribution to experimental psychology* (H. A. Roger & C. E. Bussenius, Trans.). New York: Columbia University Press.

Eberhardt, J. L., Goff, P. A., Purdie, V. J., & Davies, P. G. (2004). Seeming black: Race, crime, and visual processing. *Journal of Personality and Social Psychology, 87,* 876–893.

Eberling, J., Jagust, W., Christine, C., Starr, P., Larson, P., Bankiewicz, K., et al. (2008, May). Results from a phase I safety trial of hAADC gene therapy for Parkinson disease. *Neurology, 70*(21), 1980–1983.

Ebstein, R. P., Benjamin, J., & Belmaker, R. H. (2003). Behavioral genetics, genomics, and personality. In R. Plomin & J. C. DeFries (Eds.), *Behavioral genetics in the postgenomic era.* Washington, DC: American Psychological Association.

Ebster, C., & Neumayr, B. (2008). Applying the door-in-the-face compliance technique to retailing. *The International Review of Retail, Distribution and Consumer Research, 18,* 121–128.

Ecenbarger, W. (1993, April 1). America's new merchants of death. *The Reader's Digest,* p. 50.

Eckardt, M. H. (2005). Karen Horney: A portrait: The 120th anniversary, Karen Horney, September 16, 1885. *American Journal of Psychoanalysis, 65,* 95–101.

Edoka, I. P., Petrou, S., & Ramchandani, P. G. (2011). Healthcare costs of paternal depression in the postnatal period. *Journal of Affective Disorders, 133,* 356–360.

Edwards, R. R., & Fillingim, R. B. (2007). Self-reported pain sensitivity: Lack of correlation with pain threshold and tolerance. *European Journal of Pain, 11,* 594–598.

Efklides, A., & Moraitou, D. (2013). *A positive psychology perspective on quality of life.* New York: Springer Science + Business Media.

Egan, K. (2005). Students' development in theory and practice: The doubtful role of research. *Harvard Educational Review, 75,* 25–41.

Egliston, K., & Rapee, R. (2007). Inhibition of fear acquisition in toddlers following positive modelling by their mothers. *Behaviour Research and Therapy, 45,* 1871–1882.

Ehrenfeld, T. (2011). Reflections on mirror neurons. *Association for Psychological Science, 24,* 11–13.

Einarsson, C., & Granstroem, K. (2002). Gender-biased interaction in the classroom: The influence of gender and age in the relationship between teacher and pupil. *Scandinavian Journal of Educational Research, 46,* 117–127.

Eisch, A., Cameron, H., Encinas, J., Meltzer, L., Ming, G., & Overstreet-Wadiche, L. (2008, November). Adult neurogenesis, mental health, and mental illness: Hope or hype? *Journal of Neuroscience, 28*(46), 1785–1791.

Eizenberg, M. M., & Zaslavsky, O. (2004). Students' verification strategies for combinatorial problems. *Mathematical Thinking and Learning, 6,* 15–36.

Ekman, P. (1972). Universals and cultural differences in facial expressions of emotion. In J. Cole (Ed.), *Darwin and facial expression: A century of research in review.* New York: Academic Press.

Ekman, P. (1994a). All emotions are basic. In P. Ekman & R. J. Davidson (Eds.), *The nature of emotion: Fundamental questions.* New York: Oxford University Press.

Ekman, P. (1994b). Strong evidence for universals in facial expressions: A reply to Russell's mistaken critique. *Psychological Bulletin, 115,* 268–287.

Ekman, P. (2003). *Emotions revealed: Recognizing faces and feelings to improve communication and emotional life.* New York: Times Books.

Ekman, P. (2007). *Emotions revealed* (2nd ed.). NY: Holt.

Ekman, P., & O'Sullivan, M. (1991). Facial expression: Methods, means, and moues. In R. S. Feldman & B. Rimé (Eds.), *Fundamentals of nonverbal behavior.* Cambridge, England: Cambridge University Press.

Ekman, P., Levenson, R. W., & Friesen, W. V. (1983, September 16). Autonomic nervous system activity distinguishes among emotions. *Science, 223,* 1208–1210.

Ekroll, V., & Scherzer, T. R. (2009). Apparent visual motion of the observer's own limbs. *Perception, 38,* 778–780.

El-Mallakh, R. S., & Abraham, H. D. (2007). MDMA (Ecstasy). *Annals of Clinical Psychiatry, 19,* 45–52.

Elen, M., D'Heer, E., Geuens, M., & Vermeir, I. (2013). The influence of mood on attitude-behavior consistency. *Journal of Business Research, 66,* 917–923.

Elfhag, K., Tynelius, P., & Rasmussen, F. (2007). Sugar-sweetened and artificially sweetened soft drinks in association to restrained, external and emotional eating. *Physiology & Behavior, 91,* 191–195.

Elgot, J. (2012). Hit-and-Run Killer of Chinese Toddler Wang Yue Jailed for Three Years for Foshan Van Accident (VIDEO). *The Huffington Post UK*. Retrieved from http://www.huffingtonpost.co.uk/2012/09/06/chinese-toddler-hit-run-foshan-van-jailed_n_1860228.html

Elkins, D. (2009). Why humanistic psychology lost its power and influence in American psychology: Implications for advancing humanistic psychology. *Journal of Humanistic Psychology, 49*, 267–291.

Elkins, G., Marcus, J., Bates, J., Hasan, R. M., & Cook, T. (2006). Intensive hypnotherapy for smoking cessation: a prospective study. *International Journal of Clinical Experimental Hypnosis, 54*, 303–315.

Ellason, J. W., & Ross, C. A. (2004). SCL-90-R norms for dissociative identity disorder. *Journal of Trauma and Dissociation, 5*, 85–91.

Ellins, E., Halcox, J., Donald, A., Field, B., Brydon, L., Deanfield, J., et al. (2008). Arterial stiffness and inflammatory response to psychophysiological stress. *Brain, Behavior, and Immunity, 22*, 941–948.

Elliott, A. (2002). *Psychoanalytic theory: An introduction* (2nd ed.). Durham, NC: Duke University Press.

Elliott, J., Berman, H., & Kim, S. (2002). Critical ethnography of Korean Canadian women's menopause experience. *Health Care for Women International, 23*, 377–388.

Ellis, A. (1974). *Growth through reason*. Hollywood, CA: Wilshire Books.

Ellis, A. (2000). *How to control your anger before it controls you*. New York: Citadel.

Ellis, A. (2002). *Overcoming resistance: A rational emotive behavior therapy integrated approach* (2nd ed.). New York: Springer.

Ellis, A. (2004). Expanding the ABCs of rational emotive behavior therapy. In A. Freeman, M. J. Mahoney, P. Devito, & D. Martin (Eds.), *Cognition and psychotherapy* (2nd ed.). New York: Springer Publishing Co.

Ellis, L. A., Collin, P., Hurley, P. J., Davenport, T. A., Burns, J. M., & Hickie, I. B. (2013). Young men's attitudes and behaviour in relation to mental health and technology: Implications for the development of online mental health services. *BMC Psychiatry*. Retrieved from http://www.biomedcentral.com/1471-244X/13/119

Elua, I., Laws, K. R., & Kvavilashvili, L. (2012). From mind-pops to hallucinations? A study of involuntary semantic memories in schizophrenia. *Psychiatry Research, 196*, 165–170.

Emberson, L. L., Lupyan, G., Goldstein, M. H., & Spivey, M. J. (2010). Overheard cell-phone conversations: When less speech is more distracting. *Psychological Science, 21*, 1383–1388.

Emick, J., & Welsh, M. (2005). Association between formal operational thought and executive function as measured by the Tower of Hanoi-Revised. *Learning and Individual Differences, 15*, 177–188.

Emmett, J., & McGee, D. (2013). Extrinsic motivation for large-scale assessments: A case study of a student achievement program at one urban high school. *The High School Journal, Vol 96*, 116–137.

Endres, T., & Fendt, M. (2007). Conditioned behavioral responses to a context paired with the predator odor trimethylthiazoline. *Behavioral Neuroscience, 121*, 594–601.

Engen, T. (1987). Remembering odors and their names. *American Scientist, 75*, 497–503.

Engler, J., & Goleman, D. (1992). *The consumer's guide to psychotherapy*. New York: Simon & Schuster.

Epstein, R. (1996). *Cognition, creativity, and behavior: Selected essays*. Westport, CT: Praeger/Greenwood.

Eranti, S. V., & McLoughlin, D. M. (2003). Electroconvulsive therapy: State of the art. *British Journal of Psychiatry, 182*, 8–9.

Erb, J., Henry, M. J., Eisner, F., & Obleser, J. (2013). The brain dynamics of rapid perceptual adaptation to adverse listening conditions. *The Journal of Neuroscience, 33*, 10688–10697.

Erickson, R. (2008, February). A study of the science of taste: On the origins and influence of the core ideas. *Behavioral and Brain Sciences, 31*, 59–75.

Erikson, E. H. (1963). *Childhood and society*. New York: Norton.

Ervik, S., Abdelnoor, M., & Heier, M. S. (2006). Health-related quality of life in narcolepsy. *Acta Neurologica Scandinavica, 114*, 198–204.

Etchegary, H. (2004). Psychological aspects of predictive genetic-test decision: What do we know so far? *Analyses of Social Issues and Public Policy, 4*, 13–31.

Etienne, J. (2013). Thoughts on how to regulate behaviours: An overview of the current debate. *British Journal of Guidance & Counselling, 41*, 36–45.

Etzrodt, C. M. (2013). Ethical considerations of therapeutic hypnosis and children. *American Journal of Clinical Hypnosis, 55*, 370–377.

Evans, A. M. (2007). Transference in the nurse patient relationship. *Journal of Psychiatric and Mental Health Nursing, 14*, 189–195.

Evans, D. E., & Rothbart, M. K. (2007). Developing a model for adult temperament. *Journal of Research in Personality, 41*, 868–888.

Evans, D., & Rothbart, M. (2009). A two-factor model of temperament. *Personality and Individual Differences, 47*, 565–570.

Evans, J. B. T. (2004). Informal reasoning: Theory and method. *Canadian Journal of Experimental Psychology, 58*, 69–74.

Evans, J. B. T., & Feeney, A. (2004). The role of prior belief in reasoning. In J. P. Leighton (Ed.), *Nature of reasoning*. New York: Cambridge University Press.

Evcik, D., Kavuncu, V., Cakir, T., Subasi, V., & Yaman, M. (2007). Laser therapy in the treatment of carpal tunnel syndrome: A randomized controlled trial. *Photomedical Laser Surgery, 25*, 34–39.

Everette, M. (2008). Gestational weight and dietary intake during pregnancy: Perspectives of African American women. *Maternal & Child Health Journal, 12*, 718–724.

Everly, G. S., Jr., & Lating, J. M. (2007). Psychotherapy: A cognitive perspective. In A. Monat, R. S. Lazarus, & G. Reevy (Eds.), *The Praeger handbook on stress and coping* (Vol. 2). Westport, CT: Praeger Publishers/Greenwood Publishing.

Eysenck, H. J. (1990). Biological dimensions of personality. In L. A. Pervin (Ed.), *Handbook of personality: Theory and research*. New York: Guilford Press.

Eysenck, H. J. (1995). *Eysenck on extraversion*. New York: Wiley.

Fagan, J. F., & Holland, C. R. (2002). Equal opportunity and racial differences in IQ. *Intelligence, 30*, 361–387.

Fagan, J. F., & Holland, C. R. (2007). Racial equality in intelligence: Predictions from a theory of intelligence as processing. *Intelligence, 35*, 319–334.

Fagan, J. F., & Holland, C. R. (2009). Culture-fair prediction of academic achievement. *Intelligence, 37*, 62–67.

Fagan, J., & Press, J. (2008). Father influences on employed mothers' work-family balance. *Journal of Family Issues, 29*, 1136–1160.

Fairfield, H. (2012, February 4). Clues to a troubling gap. *New York Times*, S1.

Falck-Ytter, T., & Gredebäck, G. (2006). Infants predict other people's action goals. *Nature Neuroscience, 9*, 878–879.

Fallon, A. (2006). Informed consent in the practice of group psychotherapy. *International Journal of Group Psycho-therapy, 56*, 431–453.

Fallon, B. A., & Feinstein, S. (2001). Hypochondriasis. In K. A. Phillips (Ed.), *Somatoform and factitious disorders*. Washington, DC: American Psychiatric Association.

Fanselow, M. S., & Poulos, A. M. (2005). The neuroscience of mammalian associative learning. *Annual Review of Psychology, 56*, 207–234.

Farrell, E. F. (2005, July 15). To test or not to test? *The Chronicle of Higher Education*, pp. A39–A40.

Fearing, V. G., & Clark, J. (Eds.). (2000). *Individuals in context: A practical guide to client-centered practice*. Chicago: Slack Publishing.

Fedeli, A., Braconi, S., Economidou, D., Cannella, N., Kallupi, M., Guerrini, R., et al. (2009). The paraventricular nucleus of the hypothalamus is a neuroanatomical substrate for the inhibition of palatable food intake by neuropeptide S. *European Journal of Neuroscience, 30*, 1594–1602.

Fee, E., Brown, T. M., Lazarus, J., & Theerman, P. (2002). Exploring acupuncture: Ancient ideas, modern techniques. *American Journal of Public Health, 92*, 1592.

Feinberg, A. W. (2002, April). Homocysteine may raise Alzheimer's risk: A physician's perspective. *HealthNews*, p. 4.

Feingold, A. (1994). Gender differences in personality: A meta-analysis. *Psychological Bulletin*, 116, 429–456.

Feldhusen, J. F. (2006). The role of the knowledge base in creative thinking. In J. C. Kaufman & J. Baer (Eds.), *Creativity and reason in cognitive development*. New York: Cambridge University Press.

Feldman, D. H. (2003). Cognitive development in childhood. In R. M. Lerner, M. A. Easterbrooks, et al. (Eds.), *Handbook of psychology: Developmental psychology* (Vol. 6). New York: Wiley.

Feldman, D. H. (2004). Piaget's stages: The unfinished symphony of cognitive development. *New Ideas in Psychology, 22*, 175–231.

Feldman, R. S. (2010). *P.O.W.E.R. Learning: Strategies for Success in College and Life* (5th ed). New York: McGraw-Hill.

Feldman, R. S. (2013a). *P.O.W.E.R. Learning: Foundations of student success*. New York: McGraw-Hill.

Feldman, R. S. (2013b). *Psychology and Your Life*. New York: McGraw-Hill, 233.

Feldman, R. S. (Ed.). (1993). *Applications of nonverbal behavioral theories and research*. Hillsdale, NJ: Erlbaum.

Feng, B., Bell, R. A., Jerant, A. F., & Kravitz, R. L. (2011). What do doctors say when prescribing medications?: An examination of medical recommendations from a communication perspective. *Health Communication, 26*, 286–296.

Fenter, V. L. (2006). Concerns about Prozac and direct-to-consumer advertising of prescription drugs. *International Journal of Risk & Safety in Medicine, 18*, 1–7.

Feret, A., Steinweg, S., Griffin, H. C., & Glover, S. (2007). Macular degeneration: types, causes, and possible interventions. *Geriatric Nursing, 28*, 387–392.

Ferguson, C. J. (2010). Blazing angels or resident evil? Can violent video games be a force for good? *Review of General Psychology, 14,* 68–81.

Ferguson, C. J. (2011). Video games and youth violence: A prospective analysis in adolescents. *Journal of Youth and Adolescence, 40,* 377–391.

Ferguson, M., & Ogloff, J. P. (2011). Criminal responsibility evaluations: Role of psychologists in assessment. *Psychiatry, Psychology and Law, 18,* 79–94.

Fernandez, A. M., Vera-Villarroel, P., & Sierra, J. C. (2007). Distress in response to emotional and sexual infidelity: Evidence of evolved gender differences in Spanish students. *Journal of Psychology: Interdisciplinary and Applied, 141,* 17–24.

Feshbach, S., & Tangney, J. (2008, September). Television viewing and aggression: Some alternative perspectives. *Perspectives on Psychological Science, 3,* 387–389.

Festinger, D., Marlowe, D., Croft, J., Dugosh, K., Arabia, P., & Benasutti, K. (2009). Monetary incentives improve recall of research consent information: It pays to remember. *Experimental and Clinical Psychopharmacology, 17,* 99–104.

Festinger, L. (1957). *A theory of cognitive dissonance.* Stanford, CA: Stanford University Press.

Festinger, L., & Carlsmith, J. M. (1959). Cognitive consequences of forced compliance. *Journal of Abnormal and Social Psychology, 58,* 203–210.

Fichtenberg, C. M., & Glantz, S. A. (2006). Association of the California tobacco control program with declines in cigarette consumption and mortality from heart disease. In K. E. Warner (Ed.), *Tobacco control policy.* San Francisco, CA: Jossey-Bass.

Fields-Meyer, T. (1995, September 25). Having their say. *People,* pp. 50–60.

Fields, C. (2011). From "Oh, OK" to "Ah, yes" to "Aha!": Hyper-systemizing and the rewards of insight. *Personality and Individual Differences, 50,* 1159–1167.

Fields, R. D. (2004, April). The other half of the brain. *Scientific American,* pp. 55–61.

Figen, A. (2011). The relationship between test anxiety and learned helplessness. *Social Behavior and Personality, 39,* 101–112.

Finan, P. H., Zautra, A. J., & Wershba, R. (2011). The dynamics of emotion in adaptation to stress. In R. J. Contrada & A. Baum (Eds.), *The handbook of stress science: Biology, psychology, and health.* New York: Springer Publishing Co.

Fine, R., & Fine, L. (2003). *Basic chess endings.* New York: Random House.

Fingelkurts, A., Fingelkurts, A. A., & Kallio, S. (2007). Hypnosis induces a changed composition of brain oscillations in EEG: A case study. *Contemporary Hypnosis, 24,* 3–18.

Fink, B., Manning, J. T., & Williams, J. H. G. (2007). The 2nd to 4th digit ratio and developmental psychopathology in school-aged children. *Personality and Individual Differences, 42,* 369–379.

Fink, G. (Ed.). (2000). *Encyclopedia of stress.* New York: Academic Press.

Finkelhor, D. (2002). *Sexual abuse in the United States.* Durham, NH: University of New Hampshire.

Finkelhor, D., & Jones, L. M. (2004, January). Explanations for the decline in child sexual abuse cases. *Juvenile Justice Bulletin.* Washington, DC: Office of Juvenile Justice and Delinquency Prevention.

Finkelhor, D., Ormrod, R., & Turner, H. (2005). The victimization of children and youth: A comprehensive, national survey. *Child Maltreatment: Journal of the American Professional Society on the Abuse of Children, 10,* 5–25.

Finkelstein, M. (2009). Intrinsic vs. extrinsic motivational orientations and the volunteer process. *Personality and Individual Differences, 46,* 653–658.

Finkler, K. (2004). Traditional healers in Mexico: The effectiveness of spiritual practices. In U. P. Gielen, J. M. Fish, & J. G. Draguns (Eds.), *Handbook of culture, therapy, and healing.* Mahwah, NJ: Lawrence Erlbaum Associates.

Finlay, F. O., Jones, R., & Coleman, J. (2002). Is puberty getting earlier? The views of doctors and teachers. *Child: Care, Health and Development, 28,* 205–209.

Finley, C. L., & Cowley, B. J. (2005). The effects of a consistent sleep schedule on time taken to achieve sleep. *Clinical Case Studies, 4,* 304–311.

Finn, A. (2011). Jungian analytical theory. In D. Capuzzi & D. R. Gross (Eds.), *Counseling and psychotherapy (5th ed.).* Alexandria, VA: American Counseling Association.

Firestein, B. A. (Ed.). (1996). *Bisexuality: The psychology and politics of an invisible minority.* Thousand Oaks, CA: Sage.

First, M. B., Frances, A., & Pincus, H. A. (2002). *DSM-IV-TR handbook of differential diagnosis.* Arlington, VA: American Psychiatric Publishing.

Fischer, K. W., Shaver, P. R., & Carnochan, P. (1990). How emotions develop and how they organize development. *Cognition and Emotion, 4,* 81–127.

Fischer, P., Krueger, J. I., Greitemeyer, T., Vogrincic, C., Kastenmüller, A., Frey, D., & . . . Kainbacher, M. (2011). The bystander-effect: A meta-analytic review on bystander intervention in dangerous and non-dangerous emergencies. *Psychological Bulletin, 137,* 517–537.

Fishbach, A., Dhar, R., & Zhang, Y. (2006). Subgoals as substitutes or complements: The role of goal accessibility. *Journal of Personality and Social Psychology, 91,* 232–242.

Fisher, C. B. (2003). *Decoding the ethics code: A practical guide for psychologists.* Thousand Oaks, CA: Sage.

Fisher, C. B., Hoagwood, K., Boyce, C., Duster, T., Frank, D. A., Grisso, T., et al. (2002). Research ethics for mental health science involving ethnic minority children and youths. *American Psychologist, 57,* 1024–1040.

Fisher, G. G., & Barnes-Farrell, J. L. (2013). Use of archival data in occupational health psychology research. In R. R. Sinclair, M. Wang, & L. E. Tetrick (Eds.), *Research methods in occupational health psychology: Measurement, design, and data analysis.* New York: Routledge/Taylor & Francis Group.

Fisk, J. E., & Sharp, C. (2002). Syllogistic reasoning and cognitive aging. *Quarterly Journal of Experimental Psychology: Human Experimental Psychology, 55A,* 1273–1293.

Fisk, J. E., Bury, A. S., & Holden, R. (2006). Reasoning about complex probabilistic concepts in childhood. *Scandinavian Journal of Psychology, 47,* 497–504.

Fitzgerald, H., Mann, T., Cabrera, N., & Wong, M. M. (2003). Diversity in caregiving contexts. In R. M. Lerner, M. A. Easterbrooks, et al. (Eds.), *Handbook of psychology: Developmental psychology* (Vol. 6). New York: Wiley.

Fitzgerald, P., & Daskalakis, Z. (2008, January). The use of repetitive transcranial magnetic stimulation and vagal nerve stimulation in the treatment of depression. *Current Opinion in Psychiatry, 21,* 25–29.

Flam, F. (1991, June 14). Queasy riders. *Science, 252,* 1488.

Flavell, S. W., Cowan, C. W., Kim, T., Greer, P. L., Lin, Y., Paradis, S., et al. (2006, February 17). Activity-dependent regulation of MEF2 transcription factors suppresses excitatory synapse number. *Science, 311,* 1008–1010.

Fleck, J. I., Green, D. L., Payne, L., Stevenson, J. L., Bowden, E. M., Jung-Beeman, M., et al. (2008). The transliminal brain at rest: Baseline EEG, unusual experiences, and access to unconscious mental activity. *Cortex, 44,* 1353–1363.

Fleming, J. (2000). Affirmative action and standardized test scores. *Journal of Negro Education, 69,* 27–37.

Flynn, J. R. (2007). *What is intelligence? Beyond the Flynn effect.* New York: Cambridge University Press.

Flynn, J. R. (2012). *Are we getting smarter? Rising IQ in the twenty-first century.* New York: Cambridge University Press.

Flynn, J., Shaughnessy, M. F., & Fulgham, S. W. (2012). An interview with Jim Flynn about the Flynn effect. *North American Journal of Psychology, 14,* 25–38.

Foderaro, L. W. (2006, February 16). Westchester lawyer, his memory lost, is found in Chicago shelter after 6 months. *The New York Times,* p. B3.

Fogarty, J. S., & Young, G. A., Jr. (2000). Patient-physician communication. *Journal of the American Medical Association, 289,* 92.

Folk, C., & Remington, R. (2008, January). Bottom-up priming of top-down attentional control settings. *Visual Cognition, 16,* 215–231.

Folkman, S., & Moskowitz, J. T. (2000). Stress, positive emotion, and coping. *Current Directions in Psychological Science, 9,* 115–118.

Folkman, S., & Moskowitz, J. T. (2004). Coping: Pitfalls and promise. *Annual Review of Psychology, 55,* 745–774.

Follett, K., & Hess, T. M. (2002). Aging, cognitive complexity, and the fundamental attribution error. *Journal of Gerontology: Series B: Psychological Sciences and Social Sciences, 57B,* P312–P323.

Forbes, G. B., Jung, J., & Haas, K. B. (2006). Benevolent sexism and cosmetic use: A replication with three college samples and one adult sample. *Journal of Social Psychology, 146,* 635–640.

Forbey, J., & Ben-Porath, Y. (2007). Computerized adaptive personality testing: A review and illustration with the MMPI-2 computerized adaptive version. *Psychological Assessment, 19,* 14–24.

Ford, C. S., & Beach, F. A. (1951). *Patterns of sexual behavior.* New York: Harper.

Forer, B. (1949). The fallacy of personal validation: A classroom demonstration of gullibility. *Journal of Abnormal and Social Psychology, 44,* 118–123.

Forgas, J. P., & Laham, S. M. (2005). The interaction between affect and motivation in social judgments and behavior. In J. P. Forgas, K. P. Williams, & S. M. Laham (Eds.), *Social motivation: Conscious and unconscious processes.* New York: Cambridge University Press.

Forlenza, M. J., & Baum, M. J. (2004). Psychoneuroimmunology. In T. J. Boll, R. G. Frank, A. Baum, & J. L. Wallander (Eds.). *Handbook of clinical health psychology, Vol. 3: Models and perspectives in health psychology.* Washington, DC: American Psychological Association 81–114.

Foster, K. M. (2005). Introduction: John Uzo Ogbu (1939–2003): How do you ensure the fair consideration of a complex ancestor? Multiple approaches to assessing the work and legacy of John Uzo Ogbu. *International Journal of Qualitative Studies in Education, 18,* 559–564.

Foster, K., & Stiffman, A. (2009). Child welfare workers' adoption of decision support technology. *Journal of Technology in Human Services, 27,* 106–126.

Foulds, J., Gandhi, K. K., Steinberg, M. B., Richardson, D. L., Williams, J. M., Burke, M. V., et al. (2006). Factors associated with quitting smoking at a tobacco dependence treatment clinic. *American Journal of Health Behavior, 30,* 400–412.

Fountas, K. N., & Smith, J. R. (2007). Historical evolution of stereotactic amygdalotomy for the management of severe aggression. *Journal of Neurosurgery, 106,* 716–713.

Fournier, J., Deremaux, S., & Bernier, M. (2008). Content, characteristics and function of mental images. *Psychology of Sport and Exercise, 9,* 734–748.

Fowler, J., & Christakis, N. (2009). Dynamic spread of happiness in a large social network: Longitudinal analysis over 20 years in the Framingham Heart Study. *British Medical Journal, 338,* 1–13.

Fox, C. R. (2006). The availability heuristic in the classroom: How soliciting more criticism can boost your course ratings. *Judgment and Decision Making, 1,* 86–90.

Fox, S., & Spector, P. E. (2000). Relations of emotional intelligence, practical intelligence, general intelligence, and trait affectivity with interview outcomes: It's not all just "G." *Journal of Organizational Behavior, 21,* 203–220.

Frances, A. (2013). *Saving Normal: An Insider's Revolt Against Out-of-Control Psychiatric Diagnosis, DSM-5, Big Pharma, and the Medicalization of Ordinary Life.* New York: Morrow.

Frank, S., Goldwater, S., & Keller, F. (2013). Adding sentence types to a model of syntactic category acquisition. *Topics in Cognitive Science, 5,* 495–521.

Frankenberg, W. K., et al. (1992). *Denver II training manual.* Denver, CO: Denver Developmental Materials.

Franklin, A., Pilling, M., & Davies, I. (2005). The nature of infant color categorization: Evidence from eye movements on a target decision task. *Journal of Experimental Child Psychology, 91,* 227–248.

Franklin, M. E., March, J. S., & Garcia, A. (2007). Treating obsessive-compulsive disorder in children and adolescents. In C. Purdon, M. M. Antony, & L. J. Summerfeldt (Eds.), *Psychological treatment of obsessive-compulsive disorder: Fundamentals and beyond.* Washington, DC: American Psychological Association.

Franklin, T. B., & Mansuy, I. M. (2011). The involvement of epigenetic defects in mental retardation. *Neurobiology of Learning and Memory, 96,* 61–67.

Franko, D. L., & Roehrig, J. P. (2011). African American body images. In T. F. Cash & L. Smolak (Eds.), *Body image: A handbook of science, practice, and prevention (2nd ed.).* New York: Guilford Press.

Franko, D., & Striegel-Moore, R. (2002). The role of body dissatisfaction as a risk factor for depression in adolescent girls: Are the differences black and white? *Journal of Psychosomatic Research, 53,* 975–983.

Franks, D. D., & Smith, T. S. (Eds.). (1999). *Mind, brain, and society: Toward a neuro-sociology of emotion.* Stamford, CT: JAI Press.

Franzek, E., & Beckmann, H. (1996). Gene-environment interaction in schizophrenia: Season-of-birth effect reveals etiologically different subgroups. *Psychopathology, 29,* 14–26.

Frasure-Smith, N., Lesperance, F., & Talajic, M. (2000). The prognostic importance of depression, anxiety, anger, and social support following myocardial infarction: Opportunities for improving survival. In P. M. McCabe, N. Schneiderman, T. M. Field, & A. R. Wellens (Eds.), *Stress, coping, and cardiovascular disease.* Mahwah, NJ: Erlbaum.

Frawley, T. (2008). Gender schema and prejudicial recall: How children misremember, fabricate, and distort gendered picture book information. *Journal of Research in Childhood Education, 22,* 291–303.

Fredrickson, B. L., & Branigan, C. (2005). Positive emotions broaden the scope of attention and thought-action repertoires. *Cognition and Emotion, 19,* 313–332.

Freedberg, D. (2011). Memory in art: History and the neuroscience of response. In S. Nalbantian, P. M. Matthews, & J. L. McClelland (Eds.), *The memory process: Neuroscientific and humanistic perspectives.* Cambridge, MA: MIT Press.

Freedman, D. S. (1995). The importance of body fat distribution in early life. *American Journal of the Medical Sciences, 310,* S72–S76.

Freedman, J. L., & Fraser, S. C. (1966). Compliance without pressure: The foot-in-the-door technique. *Journal of Personality and Social Psychology, 4,* 195–202.

Freeman, J. (2013). The long-term effects of families and educational provision on gifted children. *Educational and Child Psychology, 30*(2), 7–17.

Freeman, J. E. (2006). Psychology of race and ethnicity. In W. Buskit & S. F. Davis (Eds.), *Handbook of the teaching of psychology.* Malden, MA: Blackwell Publishing.

French, S., Coleman, B., & DiLorenzo, M. (2013). Linking racial identity, ethnic identity, and racial-ethnic socialization: A tale of three race-ethnicities. *Identity: An International Journal of Theory and Research, 13,* 1–45.

Frensch, P. A., & Rünger, D. (2003). Implicit learning. *Current Directions in Psychological Science, 12,* 13–18.

Fresco, D. M. (2013). Tending the garden and harvesting the fruits of behavior therapy. *Behavior Therapy, 44,* 177–179.

Freud, S. (1900). *Group psychology and the analysis of the ego.* London: Hogarth.

Friborg, O., Barlaug, D., Martinussen, M., Rosenvinge, J. H., & Hjemdal, O. (2005). Resilience in relation to personality and intelligence. *International Journal of Methods in Psychiatric Research, 14,* 29–42.

Friborg, O., Hjemdal, O., & Rosenvinge, J. H. (2006). Resilience as a moderator of pain and stress. *Journal of Psychosomatic Research, 61,* 213–219.

Friedberg, R. D. (2006). A cognitive-behavioral approach to family therapy. *Journal of Contemporary Psychotherapy, 36,* 159–165.

Friedman, J. N. W., Oltmanns, T. F., & Turkheimer, E. (2007). Interpersonal perception and personality disorders: Utilization of a thin slice approach. *Journal of Research in Personality, 41,* 667–688.

Friedman, M. J. (2006). Posttraumatic stress disorder among military returnees from Afghanistan and Iraq. *American Journal of Psychiatry, 163,* 586–593.

Friedman, R. (2012, October 9). Recalibrating therapy for our wired world. *The New York Times,* D-6.

Frijda, N. H. (2005). Emotion experience. *Cognition and Emotion, 19,* 473–497.

Frincke, J. L., & Pate, W. E., II. (2004, March). *Yesterday, today, and tomorrow. Careers in Psychology 2004, what students need to know.* Paper presented at the Annual Convention of the Southeastern Psychological Association, Atlanta, GA.

Frings, L., Wagner, K., Unterrainer, J., Spreer, J., Halsband, U., & Schulze-Bonhage, A. (2006). Gender-related differences in lateralization of hippocampal activation and cognitive strategy. *Neuroreport, 17,* 417–421.

Fritsch, T., McClendon, M. J., Smyth, K. A., Lerner, A. J., Friedland, R. P., & Larsen, J. D. (2007). Cognitive functioning in healthy aging: The role of reserve and lifestyle factors early in life. *Gerontologist, 47,* 307–322.

Frosch, A. (2011). The effect of frequency and duration on psychoanalytic outcome: A moment in time. *Psychoanalytic Review, 98,* 11–38.

Frost, L. E., & Bonnie, R. J. (Eds.). (2001). *The evolution of mental health law.* Washington, DC: American Psychological Association.

Frost, R. O., & Steketee, G. (Eds.). (2002). *Cognitive approaches to obsessions and compulsions: Theory, assessment, and treatment.* New York: Pergamon Press.

Fuhrman, O., McCormick, K., Chen, E., Jiang, H., Shu, D., Mao, S., & Boroditsky, L. (2011). How linguistic and cultural forces shape conceptions of time: English and Mandarin time in 3D. *Cognitive Science: A Multidisciplinary Journal, 7,* 1305–1328.

Fuller, A. (2006). Hypnosis and ideomotor compliance in the treatment of smoking tobacco and cannabis. *Australian Journal of Clinical Hypnotherapy and Hypnosis, 27,* 14–18.

Furnham, A., & Crump, J. (2005). Personality traits, types, and disorders: An examination of the relationship between three self-report measures. *European Journal of Personality, 19,* 167–184.

Furnham, A., & Swami, V. (2007). Perception of female buttocks and breast size in profile. *Social Behavior and Personality, 35,* 1–8.

Furumoto, L., & Scarborough, E. (2002). Placing women in the history of psychology: The first American women psychologists. In W. E. Pickren (Ed.), *Evolving perspectives on the history of psychology.* Washington, DC: American Psychological Association.

Fusari, A., & Ballesteros, S. (2008, August). Identification of odors of edible and nonedible stimuli as affected by age and gender. *Behavior Research Methods, 40,* 752–759.

Gaab, J., Rohleder, N., Nater, U. M., & Ehlert, U. (2005). Psychological determinants of the cortisol stress response: The role of anticipatory cognitive appraisal. *Psychoneuroendocrinology, 30,* 599–610.

Gadbois, S. A., & Sturgeon, R. D. (2011). Academic self-handicapping: Relationships with learning specific and general self-perceptions and academic performance over time. *British Journal of Educational Psychology, 81,* 207–222.

Gaffney, K. F., & Henry, L. L. (2007). Identifying risk factors for postpartum tobacco use. *Journal of Nursing Scholarship, 39,* 126–132.

Gafner, G. (2013). Review of Subliminal: How your unconscious mind rules your behavior. *American Journal of Clinical Hypnosis, 56,* 192–193.

Gagnon, G. H. (1977). *Human sexualities.* Glenview, IL: Scott, Foresman.

Galanter, E. (1962). Contemporary psychophysics. In R. Brown, E. Galanter, E. Hess, & G. Maroler (Eds.), *New directions in psychology.* New York: Holt.

Galanter, M. (2007). Spirituality and recovery in 12-step programs: An empirical model. *Journal of Substance Abuse Treatment, 33,* 265–272.

Galatzer-Levy, R. M., & Cohler, B. J. (1997). *Essential psychoanalysis: A contemporary introduction.* New York: Basic Books.

Galef, D. (2001, April 27). The information you provide is anonymous, but what was your name again? *The Chronicle of Higher Education, 47,* p. B5.

Gallese, V., Gernsbacher, M. A., Heyes, C., Hickok, G., & Iacoboni, M. (2011). Mirror neuron forum. *Perspectives on Psychological Science, 6,* 369-407.

Gallup News Service. (1998). *Adults who find that premarital sex is not wrong.* Washington, DC: Gallup News Service.

Gallup Poll. (2001, June 8). *Americans' belief in psychic and paranormal phenomena is up over last decade.* Washington, DC: The Gallup Organization.

Galván, V., Vessal, R., & Golley, M. (2013). The effects of cell phone conversations on the attention and memory of bystanders. *PLoS ONE 8,* 58-59.

Gami, A. S., Howard, D. E., Olson, E. J., & Somers, V. K. (2005). Day-night pattern of sudden death in obstructive sleep apnea. *New England Journal of Medicine, 353,* 1206-1214.

Gangestad, S. W., Simpson, J. A., Cousins, A. J., Garver-Apgar, C. E., & Christensen, P. N. (2004). Women's preferences for male behavioral displays change across the menstrual cycle. *Psychological Science, 15,* 203-207.

Ganong, L. H., & Coleman, M. (1999). *Changing families, changing responsibilities: Family obligations following divorce and remarriage.* Mahwah, NJ: Erlbaum.

Garb, H. N., Wood, J. M., Lilenfeld, S. O., & Nezworski, M. T. (2005). Roots of the Rorschach controversy. *Clinical Psychology Review, 25,* 97-118.

Garber, J., & Horowitz, J. L. (2002). Depression in children. In I. H. Gotlib & C. L. Hammen (Eds.), *Handbook of depression.* New York: Guilford Press.

Garber, J., Clarke, G., Weersing, V., Beardslee, W., Brent, D., Gladstone, T., et al. (2009). Prevention of depression in at-risk adolescents: A randomized controlled trial. *Journal of the American Medical Association, 301,* 2215-2224.

Garcia-Andrade, C., Wall, T. L., & Ehlers, C. L. (1997). The firewater myth and response to alcohol in Mission Indians. *Journal of Psychiatry, 154,* 983-988.

García-Herrero, S., Mariscal, M. A., Gutiérrez, J. M., & Ritzel, D. O. (2013). Using Bayesian networks to analyze occupational stress caused by work demands: Preventing stress through social support. *Accident Analysis and Prevention, 57,* 114-123.

Garcia-Palacios, A., Hoffman, H., & Carlin, A. (2002). Virtual reality in the treatment of spider phobia: A controlled study. *Behavior Research & Therapy, 40,* 983-993.

Garcia, J. (1990). Learning without memory. *Journal of Cognitive Neuroscience, 2,* 287-305.

Garcia, J. (2003). Psychology is not an enclave. In R. J. Sternberg (Ed.), *Psychologists defying the crowd: Stories of those who battled the establishment and won.* Washington, DC: American Psychological Association.

Garcia, J., & Cohen, G. L. (2013). A social psychological approach to educational intervention. In E. Shafir (Ed.), *The behavioral foundations of public policy.* Princeton, NJ: Princeton University Press.

Garcia, S. M., Weaver, K., Moskowitz, G. B., & Darley, J. M. (2002). Crowded minds: The implicit bystander effect. *Journal of Personality and Social Psychology, 83,* 843-853.

Gardini, S., Cornoldi, C., De Beni, R., & Venneri, A. (2009). Cognitive and neuronal processes involved in sequential generation of general and specific mental images. *Psychological Research/Psychologische Forschung, 73,* 633-643.

Gardner, B., & O'Connor, D. (2008). A review of the cognitive effects of electroconvulsive therapy in older adults. *The Journal of ECT, 24,* 68-80.

Gardner, E. P., & Kandel, E. R. (2000). Touch. In E. R. Kandel, J. H. Schwartz, & T. M. Jessell (Eds.), *Principles of neural science* (4th ed.). New York: McGraw-Hill.

Gardner, F., & Moore, Z. (2008). Understanding clinical anger and violence: The anger avoidance model. *Behavior Modification, 32,* 897-912.

Gardner, H. (1975). *The shattered mind: The person after brain damage.* New York: Knopf.

Gardner, H. (1999). *Intelligence reframed: Multiple intelligences for the 21st century.* New York: Basic Books.

Gardner, H. (2000). The giftedness matrix: A developmental perspective. In R. C. Friedman & B. M. Shore (Eds.), *Talents unfolding: Cognition and development.* Washington, DC: American Psychological Association.

Gardner, H. (2005). Scientific psychology: Should we bury it or praise it? In R. J. Sternberg (Ed.), *Unity in psychology: Possibility or pipe dream?* Washington, DC: American Psychological Association.

Gardner, H. (2006). *Multiple Intelligences: New Horizons in theory and practice.* New York: Basic Books.

Garlow, S. J., Purselle, D. C., & Heninger, M. (2007). Cocaine and alcohol use preceding suicide in African American and White adolescents. *Journal of Psychiatric Research, 41,* 530-536.

Garn, C. L., Allen, M. D., Larsen, J. D., & Cortex, A. (2009). An fMRI study of sex differences in brain activation during object naming. *Journal Devoted to the Study of the Nervous System and Behavior, 45,* 610-618.

Garrigan, P., & Kellman, P. (2008, February). Perceptual learning depends on perceptual constancy. *PNAS Proceedings of the National Academy of Sciences of the United States of America, 105,* 2248-2253.

Garwick, G. B. (2007). Intelligence-related terms in mental retardation, learning disability, and gifted/talented professional usage, 1983-2001: The 1992 mental retardation redefinition as natural experiment. *Dissertation Abstracts International Section A: Humanities and Social Sciences, 67*(9-A), 3296.

Garwood, C. L., & Potts, L. A. (2007). Emerging pharmacotherapies for smoking cessation. *American Journal of Health Systems Pharmacology, 64,* 1693-1698.

Garza-Guerrero, C. (2000). Idealization and mourning in love relationships: Normal and pathological spectra. *Psychoanalytic Quarterly, 69,* 121-150.

Gass, C. S., Luis, C. A., Meyers, T. L., & Kuljis, R. O. (2000). Familial Creutzfeldt-Jakob disease: A neuropsychological case study. *Archives of Clinical Neuropsychology, 15,* 165-175.

Gatchel, R. J., & Weisberg, J. N. (2000). *Personality characteristics of patients with pain.* Washington, DC: APA Books.

Gatchel, R. J., & Oordt, M. S. (2003). Obesity. In R. J. Gatchel & M. S. Oordt (Eds.), *Clinical health psychology and primary care: Practical advice and clinical guidance for successful collaboration.* Washington, DC: American Psychological Association.

Gates, G., & Newport, F. (2012, October 18). Special report: 3.4% of U.S. adults identify as LGBT. Retrieved from http://www.gallup.com/poll/158066/special-reportadults-identify-lgbt.aspx

Gathercole, S. E., & Baddeley, A. D. (1993). *Working memory and language processing.* Hillsdale, NJ: Erlbaum.

Gaudiano, B. A., & Miller, I. W. (2013). The evidence-based practice of psychotherapy. *Clinical Psychology Review, 33,* 813-824.

Gazzaniga, M. S. (1998, July). The split brain revisited. *Scientific American,* pp. 50-55.

Gazzaniga, M. S., Ivry, R. B., & Mangun, G. R. (2002). *Cognitive neuroscience: The biology of the mind* (2nd ed.). New York: W. W. Norton.

Ge, X., Kim, I. J., Brody, G. H., Conger, R. D., Simons, R. L., Gibbons, E. X., et al. (2003). It's about timing and change: Pubertal transition effects on symptoms of major depression among African American youths. *Developmental Psychology, 39,* 430-439.

Gelbard-Sagiv, H., Mukamel, R., Harel, M., Malach, R., & Fried, I. (March 2008). Internally generated reactivation of single neurons in human hippocampus during free recall. *Science, 322,* 96-101.

Gelfand, M. M. (2000). Sexuality among older women. *Journal of Women's Health and Gender Based Medicine, 9*(Suppl. 1), S15-S20.

Geller, E. S. (2011). Psychological science and safety: Large-scale success at preventing occupational injuries and fatalities. *Psychological Science, 20,* 109-114.

Gelman, R., & Baillargeon, R. (1983). A review of some Piagetian concepts. In J. H. Flavell & E. M. Markman (Eds.), *Handbook of child psychology, Vol. 3: Cognitive development* (4th ed.). New York: Wiley.

Gelman, R., & Kit-Fong Au, T. (Eds.). (1996). *Perceptual and cognitive development.* New York: Academic Press.

Gelstein, S., Yeshurun, Y., Rozenkrantz, L., Shusha, S., Frumin, I., Roth, Y., & Sobel, N. (2011, January 14). Human tears contain a chemosignal. *Science, 331,* 226-230.

Gennaro, R. J. (2004). *Higher-order theories of consciousness: An anthology.* Amsterdam, Netherlands: John Benjamins.

Genovese, J. E. C. (2006). Piaget, pedagogy, and evolutionary psychology. *Evolutionary Psychology, 4,* 2127-2137.

Gentile, B., Grabe, S., Dolan-Pascoe, B., Twenge, J., Wells, B., & Maitino, A. (2009). Gender differences in domain-specific self-esteem: A meta-analysis. *Review of General Psychology, 13,* 34-45.

Gentner, D., Goldin, S., & Goldin-Meadow, S. (Eds.). (2003). *Language in mind: Advances in the study of language and cognition.* Cambridge, MA: MIT.

Genzlinger, N. (2013, July 1). If hackers inherit the earth. *The New York Times,* C1.

George, M. S., Wassermann, E. M., Williams, W. A., Callahan, A., Ketter, T. A., Baser, P., et al. (1995). Daily repetitive transcranial magnetic stimulations (rTMS) improves mood in depression. *Neuroreport: An International Journal for the Rapid Communication of Research in Neuroscience, 6,* 1853-1856.

George, T. P. (1999). Design, measurement, and analysis in developmental research. In M. Bornstein & M. Lamb (Eds.), *Developmental psychology.* Mahwah, NJ: Erlbaum.

Georgiou, G. A., Bleakley, C., Hayward, J., Russo, R., Dutton, K., Eltiti, S., et al. (2005). Focusing on fear: Attentional disengagement from emotional faces. *Visual Cognition, 12,* 145-158.

Gerdes, A., Uhl, G., & Alpers, G. (2009). Spiders are special: Fear and disgust evoked by pictures of arthropods. *Evolution and Human Behavior, 30,* 66-73.

Gershkoff-Stowe, L., Connell, B., & Smith, L. (2006). Priming overgeneralizations in two- and four-year-old children. *Journal of Child Language, 33,* 461–486.

Gershoff, E. T. (2013). Spanking and child development: We know enough now to stop hitting our children. *Child Development Perspectives, 7,* 133–137.

Gerstel, N. (2005, April 8). In search of time. *Science, 308,* 204–205.

Getner, D., & Holyoak, K. J. (1997, January). Reasoning and learning by analogy. *American Psychologist, 52,* 32–34.

Geyer, T., Gokce, A., & Müller, H. J. (2011). Reinforcement of inhibitory positional priming by spatial working memory contents. *Acta Psychologica, 137,* 235–242.

Ghavami, N., & Peplau, L. (2013). An intersectional analysis of gender and ethnic stereotypes: Testing three hypotheses. *Psychology of Women Quarterly, 37,* 113–127.

Giacobbi, P. R., Jr., Lynn, T. K., Wetherington, J. M., Jenkins, J., Bodendorf, M., & Langley, B. (2004). Stress and coping during the transition to university for first-year female athletes. *Sports Psychologist, 18,* 1–20.

Giacomini, M., Baylis, F., & Robert, J. (2007). Banking on it: Public policy and the ethics of stem cell research and development. *Social Sciences Medicine, 22,* 88–84.

Giannopoulos, V. L., & Vella-Brodrick, D. A. (2011). Effects of positive interventions and orientations to happiness on subjective well-being. *The Journal of Positive Psychology, 6,* 95–105.

Gibb, K., Tunbridge, D., Chua, A., & Frederickson, N. (2007). Pathways to inclusion: Moving from special school to mainstream. *Educational Psychology in Practice, 23,* 109–127.

Gibbons, R. D., Brown, C. H., Hur, K., Marcus, S. M., Bhamik, D. K., Erkens, J. A., et al. (2007). Early evidence on the effects of regulators' suicidal warnings on SSRI prescriptions and suicide in children and adolescents. *American Journal of Psychiatry, 164,* 1356–1363.

Gibbs, N. (2005, August 8). Being 13. *Time,* pp. 41–55.

Gibbs, W. W. (2002, August). From mouth to mind. *Scientific American,* p. 26.

Gibson, S. (2013). Milgram's obedience experiments: A rhetorical analysis. *British Journal of Social Psychology, 52,* 290–309.

Giedd, J., Stockman, M., Weddle, C.,Liverpool, M., Alexander-Bloch, A., Wallace, G., Lee, N., Lalonde, F., & Lenroot, R. (2010). Anatomic magnetic resonance imaging of the developing child and adolescent brain and effects of genetic variation. *Neuropsychology Review, 20,* 349–361.

Gigerenzer, G. (2007). *Gut feelings: The intelligence of the unconscious.* Penguin Group: New York.

Gilbert, D. T., McNulty, S. E., Guiliano, T. A., & Benson, J. E. (1992). Blurry words and fuzzy deeds: The attribution of obscure behavior. *Journal of Personality and Social Psychology, 62,* 18–25.

Gilbert, D. T., Miller, A. G., & Ross, L. (1998). Speeding with Ned: A personal view of the correspondence bias. In J. M. Darley & J. Cooper (Eds.), *Attribution and social interaction: The legacy of Edward E. Jones.* Washington, DC: American Psychological Association.

Gilbert, P. D. (2007). Spirituality and mental health: A very preliminary overview. *Current Opinions in Psychiatry, 20,* 594–598.

Gilboa, A., Winocur, G., & Rosenbaum, R. S. (2006). Hippocampal contributions to recollection in retrograde and anterograde amnesia. *Hippocampus, 16,* 966–980.

Gilchrist, A., Cowan, N., & Naveh-Benjamin, M. (2009). Investigating the childhood development of working memory using sentences: New evidence for the growth of chunk capacity. *Journal of Experimental Child Psychology, 104,* 252–265.

Gilestro, G. F., Tononi, G., & Cirelli, C. (2009, April 3). Widespread changes in synaptic markers as a function of sleep and wakefulness in *Drosophila. Science, 324,* 109–112.

Gillam, B., Palmisano, S. A., & Govan, D. G. (2011). Depth interval estimates from motion parallax and binocular disparity beyond interaction space. *Perception, 40,* 39–49.

Gilligan, C. (1996). The centrality of relationships in psychological development: A puzzle, some evidence, and a theory. In G. G. Noam & K. W. Fischer (Eds.), *Development and vulnerability in close relationships.* Hillsdale, NJ: Erlbaum.

Gilligan, C. (2004). Recovering psyche: Reflections on life-history and history. *Annual of Psychoanalysis, 32,* 131–147.

Gizer, I. R., Ehlers, C. L., Vieten, C., Seaton-Smith, K. L., Feiler, H. S., Lee, J. V., & . . . Wilhelmsen, K. C. (2011). Linkage scan of alcohol dependence in the UCSF Family Alcoholism Study. *Drug and Alcohol Dependence, 113,* 125–132.

Gladwell, M. (2004, September 20). Annals of psychology: Personality, plus how corporations figure out who you are. *The New Yorker,* 42–45.

Gladwin, T. (1964). Culture and logical process. In N. Goodenough (Ed.), *Explorations in cultural anthropology: Essays in honor of George Peter Murdoch.* New York: McGraw-Hill.

Glass, K., Flory, K., Hankin, B., Kloos, B., & Turecki, G. (2009). Are coping strategies, social support, and hope associated with psychological distress among Hurricane Katrina survivors? *Journal of Social and Clinical Psychology, 28,* 779–795.

Glick, P., Lameiras, M., Fiske, S. T., Eckes, T., Masser, B., Volpato, C., et al. (2004). Bad but bold: Ambivalent attitudes toward men predict gender inequality in 16 nations. *Journal of Personality and Social Psychology, 86,* 713–728.

Glickler, J. (2006). Advancing in advancement: A self-efficacy study of development practitioners in higher education. *Dissertation Abstracts International: Section B: The Sciences and Engineering, 67*(2-B), 1190.

Glicksohn, J., & Nahari, G. (2007). Interacting personality traits? Smoking as a test case. *European Journal of Personality, 21,* 225–234.

Glisky, E. L. (2007). Changes in cognitive function in human aging. In D. R. Riddle (Ed.), *Brain aging: Models, methods, and mechanisms.* Boca Raton, FL: CRC Press.

Goffin, R. D., Jelley, R. B., & Wagner, S. H. (2003). Is halo helpful? Effects of inducing halo on performance rating accuracy. *Social Behavior and Personality, 31,* 625–636.

Gold, P. E., Cahill, L., & Wenk, G. L. (2002). Ginkgo biloba: A cognitive enhancer? *Psychological Science in the Public Interest, 3,* 2–7.

Golden, R. N., Gaynes, B. N., Ekstsrom, R. D., Hamer, R. M., Jacobsen, F. M., Suppes, T., et al. (2005). The efficacy of light therapy in the treatment of mood disorders: A review and meta-analysis of the evidence. *The American Journal of Psychiatry, 162,* 656–662.

Golden, W. L. (2006). Hypnotherapy for anxiety, phobias and psychophysiological disorders. In R. A. Chapman (Ed.), *The clinical use of hypnosis in cognitive behavior therapy: A practitioner's casebook.* New York: Springer Publishing.

Golder, S. A., & Macy, M. W. (2011, September 30). Diurnal and seasonal mood vary with work, sleep, and day length across diverse cultures. *Science, 333,* 1878–1881.

Goldey, K. L., & van Anders, S. M. (2011). Sexy thoughts: Effects of sexual cognitions on testosterone, cortisol, and arousal in women. *Hormones and Behavior, 59,* 754–764.

Goldfried, M. R., & Pachankis, J. E. (2007). On the next generation of process research. *Clinical Psychology Review, 27,* 760–768.

Goldstein, I. (2000). Female sexual arousal disorder: New insights. *International Journal of Impotence Research, 12*(Suppl. 4), S152–S157.

Goldstein, S. N. (2006). The exploration of spirituality and identity status in adolescence. *Dissertation Abstracts International: Section B: The Sciences and Engineering, 67*(6-B), 3481.

Goldstone, R. L., & Kersten, A. (2003). Concepts and categorization. In A. E. Healy & R. W. Proctor (Eds.), *Handbook of psychology: Experimental psychology* (Vol. 4). New York: Wiley.

Goleman, D. (1988, January 21). Doctor and patient; physicians may bungle key part of treatment: The medical interview. *The New York Times,* p. B16.

Goleman, D. (1993, July 21). "Expert" babies found to teach others. *The New York Times,* p. C10.

Golimbet, V. E., Alfimova, M. V., Gritsenko, I. K., & Ebstein, R. P. (2007). Relationship between dopamine system genes and extraversion and novelty seeking. *Neuroscience Behavior and Physiology, 37,* 601–606.

Golombok, S., Cook, R., Bish, A., & Murray, C. (1995). Families created by the new reproductive technologies: Quality of parenting and social and emotional development of the children. *Child Development, 66,* 285–298.

Gontier, N. (2008). Genes, brains, and language: An epistemological examination of how genes can underlie human cognitive behavior. *Review of General Psychology, 12,* 170–180.

Gontkovsky, S. T. (2005). Neurobiological bases and neuropsychological correlates of aggression and violence. In J. P. Morgan (Ed.), *Psychology of aggression.* Hauppauge, NY: Nova Science Publishers.

Goode, E. (1999, April 13). If things taste bad, "phantoms" may be at work. *The New York Times,* pp. D1–D2.

Goode, E. (2003, January 28). Even in the age of Prozac, some still prefer the couch. *The New York Times,* Section F, p. 1.

Goodman, G., & Quas, J. (2008). Repeated interviews and children's memory: It's more than just how many. *Current Directions in Psychological Science, 17,* 386–390.

Goodwin, R. D., & Hamilton, S. P. (2003). Lifetime comorbidity of antisocial personality disorder and anxiety disorders among adults in the community. *Psychiatry Research, 117,* 159–166.

Goodwin, R., Costa, P., & Adonu, J. (2004). Social support and its consequences: 'Positive' and 'deficiency' values and their implications for support and self-esteem. *British Journal of Social Psychology, 43,* 465–474.

Gooren, L. (2006). The biology of human psychosexual differentiation. *Hormones and Behavior, 50,* 589–601.

Gopie, N., Craik, F. M., & Hasher, L. (2011). A double dissociation of implicit and explicit memory in younger and older adults. *Psychological Science, 22,* 634–640.

Gordon, D., & Heimberg, R. G. (2011). Reliability and validity of DSM-IV generalized anxiety disorder features. *Journal of Anxiety Disorders, 25*, 813–821.

Gordon, E. F. (2001). *Mockingbird years: A life in and out of therapy*. New York: Basic Books.

Gorin, A. A., Powers, T. A., Koestner, R., Wing, R. R., & Raynor, H. A. (2013). Autonomy support, self-regulation, and weight loss. *Health Psychology*, Retrieved from *http://www.ncbi.nlm.nih.gov/pubmed/23730718*

Gossop, M., Stewart, D., & Marsden, J. (2008). Attendance at Narcotics Anonymous and Alcoholics Anonymous meetings, frequency of attendance and substance use outcomes after residential treatment for drug dependence: A 5-year follow-up study. *Addiction, 103*, 119–125.

Gotlib, I. H., Krasnoperova, E., Yue, D. N., & Joorman, J. (2004). Attentional biases for negative interpersonal stimuli in clinical depression. *Journal of Abnormal Psychology, 113*, 127–135.

Gottesman, I. I. (1991). *Schizophrenia genesis: The origins of madness*. New York: Freeman.

Gottesman, I. I., & Hanson, D. R. (2005). Human development: Biological and genetic processes. *Annual Review of Psychology, 56*, 263–286.

Gottlieb, D. A. (2006). Effects of partial reinforcement and time between reinforced trials on terminal response rate in pigeon autoshaping. *Behavioural Processes, 72*, 6–13.

Gotts, S. J., Jo, H., Wallace, G. L., Saad, Z. S., Cox, R. W., & Martin, A. (2013). Two distinct forms of functional lateralization in the human brain. *PNAS Proceedings of the National Academy of Sciences of the United States of America, 110*, E3435–E3444.

Gould, E., Reeves, A. J., Graziano, M. S. A., & Gross, C. G. (1999, October 15). Neurogenesis in the neocortex of adult primates. *Science*, 548–552.

Gould, R. L. (1978). *Transformations*. New York: Simon & Schuster.

Govindarajan, A., Kelleher, R. J., & Tonegawa, S. (2006). A clustered plasticity model of long-term memory engrams. *Nature Reviews Neuroscience, 7*, 575–583.

Gowaty, P. A. (2003). Power asymmetries between the sexes, mate preferences, and components of fitness. In C. B. Travis (Ed.), *Evolution, gender, and rape*. Cambridge, MA: MIT.

Gradinaru, V., Mogri, M., Thompson, K. R., Henderson, J. M., & Deisseroth, K. (2009). Optical deconstruction of Parkinsonian neural circuitry. *Science, 324*, 354–359.

Grady, D., & Altman, L. K. (2008, December 29). Lessons for other smokers in Obama's efforts to quit. *The New York Times*, p. A12.

Graham, C. A., Bancroft, J., & Doll, H. A. (2007). Does oral contraceptive-induced reduction in free testosterone adversely affect the sexuality or mood of women? *Psychoneuroendocrinology, 32*, 246–255.

Graham, S. (1992). Most of the subjects were white and middle class. *American Psychologist 47*(5), 629–639.

Grahek, N. (2007). *Feeling pain and being in pain* (2nd ed.). Cambridge, MA: MIT Press.

Granic, I., Hollenstein, T., & Dishion, T. (2003). Longitudinal analysis of flexibility and reorganization in early adolescence: A dynamic systems study of family interactions. *Developmental Psychology, 39*, 606–617.

Grann, J. D. (2007). Confidence in knowledge past: An empirical basis for a differential decay theory of very long-term memory monitoring. *Dissertation Abstracts International Section A: Humanities and Social Sciences, 67*, 2462.

Grant, A. (2008). Does intrinsic motivation fuel the prosocial fire? Motivational synergy in predicting persistence, performance, and productivity. *Journal of Applied Psychology, 93*, 48–58.

Grant, D. M., & Wingate, L. R. (2011). Cognitive-behavioral therapy. In C. Silverstein (Ed.), *The initial psychotherapy interview: A gay man seeks treatment*. Amsterdam Netherlands: Elsevier.

Gray, E. (2013, September 30). This is not a cigarette. *Time*, 38–46.

Gray, G. C. (2006). The regulation of corporate violations: Punishment, compliance, and the blurring of responsibility. *British Journal of Criminology, 46*, 875–892.

Gray, J. R., Chabris, C. F., & Braver, T. S. (2003, February 18). Neural mechanisms of general fluid intelligence. *Nature: Neurosciences*. Retrieved from http://www.nature.com/cgitaf/DynaPage.taf?file=/neuro/journal/vaop/ncurrent/abs/nn1014.html

Graziano, W. G., Habashi, M. M., Sheese, B. E., & Tobin, R. M. (2007). Agreeableness, empathy, and helping: A person situation perspective. *Journal of Personality and Social Psychology, 93*, 583–599.

Green, B. G., & George, P. (2004). Thermal taste predicts higher responsiveness to chemical taste and flavor. *Chemical Senses, 29*, 617–628.

Green, J. S., Henderson, F. R., & Collinge, M. D. (2003). *Prevention and control of wildlife damage: Coyotes*. Lincoln: University of Nebraska, Institute of Agriculture and Natural Resources. Retrieved from http://wildlifedamage.unl.edu/handbook/handbook/carnivor/ca_c51.pdf

Green, J., Lynn, S., & Montgomery, G. (2008, January). Gender-related differences in hypnosis-based treatments for smoking: A follow-up meta-analysis. *American Journal of Clinical Hypnosis, 50*, 259–271.

Green, M. C., & Dill, K. E. (2013). Engaging with stories and characters: Learning, persuasion, and transportation into narrative worlds. In K. E. Dill (Ed.), *The Oxford handbook of media psychology*. New York: Oxford University Press.

Greenberg, G., & Rosenheck, R. (2008). Jail incarceration, homelessness, and mental health: A national study. *Psychiatric Services, 59*, 170–177.

Greenberg, R. M., & Kellner, C. H. (2005). Electroconvulsive therapy: A selected review. *The American Journal of Geriatric Psychiatry, 13*, 268–281.

Greenberg, R., & Goldman, E. (2009). Antidepressants, psychotherapy or their combination: Weighing options for depression treatments. *Journal of Contemporary Psychotherapy, 39*, 83–91.

Greene, J. D., & Paxton, J. M. (2009). Patterns of neural activity associated with honest and dishonest moral decisions. *PNAS Proceedings of the National Academy of Sciences of the United States of America, 106*(30), 12506–12511.

Greene, J. D., Sommerville, R. B., Nystrom, L. E., Darley, J. M., & Cohen, J. D. (2001, September 14). An fMRI investigation of emotional engagement in moral judgment. *Science, 293*, 2105–2108.

Greenfield, B. L., & Tonigan, J. S. (2013). The general Alcoholics Anonymous tools of recovery: The adoption of 12-step practices and beliefs. *Psychology of Addictive Behaviors, 27*, 553–561.

Greenfield, P. M. (1997). You can't take it with you: Why ability assessments don't cross cultures. *American Psychologist, 52*, 1115–1124.

Greenfield, S. (2002). Mind, brain and consciousness. *British Journal of Psychiatry, 181*, 91–93.

Greenspan, S. (2006). Functional concepts in mental retardation: Finding the natural essence of an artificial category. *Exceptionality, 14*, 205–224.

Greenwald, A. G., Draine, S. C., & Abrams, R. L. (1996, September 20). Three cognitive markers of unconscious semantic activation. *Science, 272*, 1699–1702.

Greenwald, A. G., Nosek, B. A., & Banaji, M. R. (2003). Understanding and using the Implicit Association Test: 1. An improved scoring algorithm. *Journal of Personality and Social Psychology 85*, 197–216.

Greenwald, A. G., Nosek, B. A., & Sririam, N. (2006). Consequential validity of the implicit association test: Comment on Blanton and Jaccard. *American Psychologist, 61*, 56–61.

Greenwald, A., Poehlman, T., Uhlmann, E., & Banaji, M. (2009). Understanding and using the Implicit Association Test: III. Meta-analysis of predictive validity. *Journal of Personality and Social Psychology, 97*, 17–41.

Greer, R. D., Dudek-Singer, J., & Gautreaux, G. (2006). Observational learning. *International Journal of Psychology, 41*, 486–499.

Grefkes, C., & Fink, G. R. (2011). Reorganization of cerebral networks after stroke: New insights from neuroimaging with connectivity approaches. *Brain, 134*, 1264–1276.

Gregg, J. P., Lit, L., Baron, C. A., Hertz-Picciotto, I., Walker, W., Davis, R. A., et al. (2007). Gene expression changes in children with autism. *Genomics, 12*, 88–97.

Gregory, R. L. (1978). *The psychology of seeing* (3rd ed.). New York: McGraw-Hill.

Gregory, R. L. (2008). Emmert's Law and the moon illusion. *Spatial Vision, 21*, 407–720.

Gregory, S. (1856). *Facts for young women*. Boston.

Gregory, S. S. (1994, March 21). At risk of mutilation. *Time*, pp. 45–46.

Grenfell-Essam, R., Ward, G., & Tan, L. (2013). The role of rehearsal on the output order of immediate free recall of short and long lists. *Journal of Experimental Psychology: Learning, Memory, and Cognition, 39*, 317–347.

Grigorenko, E. (2009). Speaking genes or genes for speaking? Deciphering the genetics of speech and language. *Journal of Child Psychology and Psychiatry, 50*, 116–125.

Grigorenko, E. L., & Dozier, M. (2013). Introduction to the special section on genomics. *Child Development, 84*, 6–16.

Grigoriadis, S., & Ravitz, P. (2007). An approach to interpersonal psychotherapy for postpartum depression: Focusing on interpersonal changes. *Canadian Family Physician, 53*, 1469–1475.

Grimes, T., & Bergen, L. (2008, April). The epistemological argument against a causal relationship between media violence and sociopathic behavior among psychologically well viewers. *American Behavioral Scientist, 51*, 1137–1154.

Grimm, J. W. (2011). Craving. In M. C. Olmstead (Ed.), *Animal models of drug addiction*. Totowa, NJ: Humana Press.

Grindstaff, J. S., & Fisher, L. A. (2006). Sport psychology consultants' experience of using hypnosis in their practice: An exploratory investigation. *The Sport Psychologist, 20*, 368–386.

Gronholm, P., Rinne, J. O., Vorobyev, V., & Laine, M. (2005). Naming of newly learned objects: A PET activation study. *Brain Research and Cognitive Brain Research, 14*, 22–28.

Gross, D. M. (2006). *The secret history of emotion: From Aristotle's rhetoric to modern brain science.* Chicago: University of Chicago Press.

Grossberg, S. (2013). Adaptive Resonance Theory: How a brain learns to consciously attend, learn, and recognize a changing world. *Neural Networks, 47,* 88–94.

Grossmann, T., Striano, T., & Friederici, A. D. (2007). Developmental changes in infants' processing of happy and angry facial expressions: A neurobehavioral study. *Brain and Cognition, 64,* 30–41.

Groves, R. M., Singer, E., Lepkowski, J. M., Heeringa, S. G., & Alwin, D. F. In S. J. House, F. T. Juster, R. L. Kahn, H. Schuman, & E. Singer. (2004). *A telescope on society: Survey research and social science at the University of Michigan and beyond.* Ann Arbor, MI: University of Michigan Press.

Gruber, T. R. (2013). Nature, nurture, and knowledge acquisition. *International Journal of Human-Computer Studies, 71,* 191–194.

Grünert, U., Jusuf, P. R., Lee, S. S., & Nguyen, D. (2011). Bipolar input to melanopsin containing ganglion cells in primate retina. *Visual Neuroscience, 28,* 39–50.

Grunwald, T., Boutros, N. N., Pezer, N., von Oertzen, J., Fernandez, G., Schaller, C., & Elger, C. E. (2003). Neuronal substrates of sensory gating within the human brain. *Biological Psychiatry, 15,* 511–519.

Guadagno, R. E., & Cialdini, R. B. (2002). Online persuasion: An examination of gender differences in computer-mediated interpersonal influence [Special issue: Groups and Internet]. *Group Dynamics, 6,* 38–51.

Guastella, A., Mitchell, P., & Dadds, M. (2008, January). Oxytocin increases gaze to the eye region of human faces. *Biological Psychiatry, 63,* 3–5.

Guéguen, N., Marchand, M., Pascual, A., & Lourel, M. (2008). Foot-in-the-door technique using a courtship request: A field experiment. *Psychological Reports, 103,* 529–534.

Guerrero, L., La Valley, A., & Farinelli, L. (2008, October). The experience and expression of anger, guilt, and sadness in marriage: An equity theory explanation. *Journal of Social and Personal Relationships, 25,* 699–724.

Guiard, B. P., Chenu, F., Mansari, M., & Blier, P. (2011). Characterization of the electrophysiological properties of triple reuptake inhibitors on monoaminergic neurons. *International Journal of Neuropsychopharmacology, 14,* 211–223.

Guida, A. A., Tardieu, H. H., Le Bohec, O. O., & Nicolas, S. S. (2013). Are schemas sufficient to interpret the personalization effect? Only if long-term working memory backs up. *European Review of Applied Psychology/Revue Européenne De Psychologie Appliquée, 63,* 99–107.

Guilleminault, C., Kirisoglu, C., Bao, G., Arias, V., Chan, A., & Li, K. K. (2005). Adult chronic sleepwalking and its treatment based on polysomnography. *Brain, 128* (Pt. 5), 1062–1069.

Guldemond, H., Bosker, R., Kuyper, H., & van der Werf, G. (2007). Do highly gifted students really have problems? [Special issue: Current research on giftedness: International perspectives]. *Educational Research and Evaluation, 13,* 555–568.

Gupta, M. A. (2013). Review of somatic symptoms in post-traumatic stress disorder. *International Review of Psychiatry, 25,* 86–99.

Gurin, P. (2006). Informing theory from practice and applied research. *Journal of Social Issues, 62,* 621–628.

Guthrie, R. V. (1998). *Even the rat was white: A historical view of psychology* (2nd ed.). Needham Heights, MA: Allyn & Bacon.

Gutierrez, P. M., Muehlenkamp, J. L., Konick, L. C., & Osman, A. (2005). What role does race play in adolescent suicidal ideation? *Archives of Suicide Research, 9,* 177–192.

Gwynn, M. I., & Spanos, N. P. (1996). Hypnotic responsiveness, nonhypnotic suggestibility, and responsiveness to social influence. In R. G. Kunzendorf, N. P. Spahos, & B. Wallace (Eds.), *Hypnosis and imagination.* Amityville, NY: Baywood.

Haberstick, B. C., Schmitz, S., Young, S. E., & Hewitt, J. K. (2005). Contributions of genes and environments to stability and change in externalizing and internalizing problems during elementary and middle school. *Behavior Genetics, 35,* 381–396.

Hackam, D. G. (2007). Translating animal research into clinical benefit. *British Medical Journal, 334,* 163–1644.

Hadjistavropoulos, T., Craig, K. D., & Fuchs-Lacelle, S. (2004). *Social influences and the communication of pain.* Mahwah, NJ: Lawrence Erlbaum Associates.

Hagelskamp, C., Hughes, D., Yoshikawa, H., & Chaudry, A. (2011). Negotiating motherhood and work: A typology of role identity associations among low-income, urban women. *Community, Work & Family, 14,* 335–366.

Haier, R. J. (2003). Brain imaging studies of intelligence: Individual differences and neurobiology. In R. J. Sternberg & J. Lautrey (Eds.), *Models of intelligence: International perspectives.* Washington, DC: American Psychological Association.

Haier, R. J. (2011). Biological basis of intelligence. In R. J. Sternberg & S. Kaufman (Eds.), *The Cambridge handbook of intelligence.* New York: Cambridge University Press.

Haier, R. J., Colom, R., Schroeder, D. H., Condon, C. A., Tang, C., Eaves, E., et al. (2009). Gray matter and intelligence factors: Is there a neuro-g? *Intelligence, 37,* 136–144.

Haley, W. E., Clair, J. M., & Saulsberry, K. (1992). Family caregiver satisfaction with medical care of their demented relatives. *Gerontologist, 32,* 219–226.

Halford, S. (2006). Collapsing the boundaries? Fatherhood, organization and home-working. *Gender, Work & Organization, 13,* 383–402.

Halkitis, P. (2009). *Methamphetamine addiction: Biological foundations, psychological factors, and social consequences.* Washington, DC: American Psychological Association.

Hall, G. C. N. (1996). *Theory-based assessment, treatment, and prevention of sexual aggression.* New York: Oxford University Press.

Hall, P. J., Chong, C., McNaughton, N., & Corr, P. J. (2011). An economic perspective on the reinforcement sensitivity theory of personality. *Personality and Individual Differences, 51,* 242–247.

Hall, R. E. (2002). *The Bell Curve*: Implications for the performance of black/white athletes. *Social Science Journal, 39,* 113–118.

Halle, M. (2009, August 4). Can drilling electrodes into your brain help you lose weight? *Daily Mail* (London).

Hallschmid, M., Benedict, C., Born, J., Fehm, H., & Kern, W. (2004). Manipulating central nervous mechanisms of food intake and body weight regulation by intranasal administration of neuropeptides in man. *Physiology and Behavior, 83,* 55–64.

Halpern, D. F. (2000). *Sex differences in cognitive abilities* (3rd ed.). Mahwah, NJ: Erlbaum.

Halpern, D. F. (2010, December, 3). How neuromythologies support sex role stereotypes. *Science, 330,* 1320–1322.

Halpern, D., & Riggio, H. (2002). *Thinking critically about critical thinking.* Mahwah, NJ: Erlbaum.

Halpert, J. (2003, April 28). What do patients want? *Newsweek,* pp. 63–64.

Hamani, Y., Sciaki-Tamir, Y., Deri-Hasid, R., Miller-Pogrund, T., Milwidsky, A., & Haimov-Kochman, R. (2007). Misconceptions about oral contraception pills among adolescents and physicians. *Human Reproduction, 22,* 3078–3083.

Hamann, S. B., Ely, T. D., Hoffman, J. M., & Kilts, C. D. (2002). Ecstasy and agony: Activation of human amygdala in positive and negative emotion. *Psychological Science, 13,* 135–141.

Hambleton, R. K. (2006). Psychometric models, test designs and item types for the next generation of educational and psychological tests. In D. Bartram & R. K. Hambleton (Eds.), *Computer-based testing and the Internet: Issues and advances.* New York: John Wiley & Sons.

Hambleton, R. K., & Zenisky, A. L. (2013). Reporting test scores in more meaningful ways: A research-based approach to score report design. In K. F. Geisinger, B. A. Bracken, J. F. Carlson, J. C. Hansen, N. R. Kuncel, S. P. Reise, & M. C. Rodriguez (Eds.), *APA handbook of testing and assessment in psychology, Vol. 3: Testing and assessment in school psychology and education.* Washington, DC: American Psychological Association.

Hamer, D. H., Hu, S., Magnuson, V. L., Hu, N., & Pattatucci, A. M. L. (1993, July 16). A linkage between DNA markers on the X chromosome and male sexual orientation. *Science, 261,* 321–327.

Hamer, M., Taylor, A., & Steptoe, A. (2006). The effect of acute aerobic exercise on stress related blood pressure responses: A systematic review and meta-analysis. *Bi Psychology, 71,* 183–190.

Hamilton, A. (2009, July 11). Can gaming slow mental decline in the elderly? *Time.* Retrieved from http://www.time.com/time/health/article/0,8599,1909852,00.html

Hamilton, A. C., & Martin, R. C. (2007). Semantic short-term memory deficits and resolution of interference: A case for inhibition? In D. S. Gorfein & C. M. Macleod (Eds.), *Inhibition in cognition.* Washington, DC: American Psychological Association.

Hamilton, L. K., Joppé, S. E., Cochard, L. M., & Fernandes, K. L. (2013). Aging and neurogenesis in the adult forebrain: What we have learned and where we should go from here. *European Journal of Neuroscience, 37,* 1978–1986.

Hammond, C., & Gold, M. (2008). Caffeine dependence, withdrawal, overdose and treatment: A review. *Directions in Psychiatry, 28,* 177–190.

Hammond, D. C. (2007, April). Review of the efficacy of clinical hypnosis with headaches and migraines [Special issue: Evidence-based practice clinical hypnosis–part 1]. *International Journal of Clinical and Experimental Hypnosis 55,* 207–219.

Haney, C., & Zimbardo, P. (2009). Persistent dispositionalism in interactionist clothing: Fundamental attribution error in explaining prison abuse. *Personality and Social Psychology Bulletin, 35,* 807–814.

Hangya, B., Tihanyi, B. T., Entz, L., Fabo, D., Erőss, L., Wittner, L., & . . . Ulbert, I. (2011). Complex propagation patterns characterize human cortical activity during slow-wave sleep. *The Journal of Neuroscience, 31,* 8770–8779.

Hannon, E. E., & Johnson, S. P. (2005). Infants use meter to categorize rhythms and melodies: Implications for musical structure learning. *Cognitive Psychology, 50,* 354–377.

Harden, R., Oaklander, A., Burton, A. W., Perez, R. M., Richardson, K., Swan, M., & . . . Bruehl, S. (2013). Complex regional pain syndrome: Practical diagnostic and treatment guidelines, 4th edition. *Pain Medicine, 14,* 180–229.

Harding, D. J., & Jencks, C. (2003). Changing attitudes toward premarital sex: Cohort, period, and aging effects. *The Public Opinion Quarterly, 67,* 211–226.

Hardison, D. M. (2006). Review of phonetics and phonology in language comprehension and production: Differences and similarities. *Studies in Second Language Acquisition, 28,* 138–140.

Hardt, J., Sidor, A., Nickel, R., Kappis, B., Petrak, P., & Egle, U. (2008). Childhood adversities and suicide attempts: A retrospective study. *Journal of Family Violence, 23,* 713–718.

Hardt, O., Nader, K., & Nadel, L. (2013). Decay happens: The role of active forgetting in memory. *Trends in Cognitive Sciences, 17,* 111–120.

Hardy, L. T. (2007). Attachment theory and reactive attachment disorder: theoretical perspectives and treatment implications. *Journal of Child and Adolescent Psychiatric Nursing, 20,* 27–39.

Harlow, H. F., & Zimmerman, R. R. (1959). Affectional responses in the infant monkey. *Science, 130,* 421–432.

Harlow, J. M. (1869). Recovery from the passage of an iron bar through the head. *Massachusetts Medical Society Publication, 2,* 329–347.

Harmon-Jones, E., & Winkielman, P. (2007). *Social neuroscience: Integrating biological and psychological explanations of social behavior.* New York, NY: Guilford Press.

Harold, G. T., Fincham, F. D., Osborne, L. N., & Conger, R. D. (1997). Mom and dad are at it again: Adolescent perceptions of marital conflict and adolescent psychological distress. *Developmental Psychology, 33,* 333–350.

Harper, T. (1978, November 15). It's not true about people 65 or over. *Green Bay Press-Gazette* (Wisconsin), p. D-1.

Hart, B., & Risley, T. R. (1997). Use of language by three-year-old children. Courtesy of Drs. Betty Hart and Todd Risley, University of Kansas.

Hartmann, E. (1967). *The biology of dreaming.* Springfield, IL: Charles C. Thomas Publisher.

Hartung, C. M., & Widiger, T. A. (1998). Gender differences in the diagnosis of mental disorders: Conclusions and controversies of the DSM-IV. *Psychological Bulletin, 123,* 260–278.

Harvard Mental Health Letter (HMHL). (1994, March). Brief psychodynamic therapy–Part I. *Harvard Mental Health Letter,* p. 10.

Harvey, J. H., Wenzel, A., & Sprecher, S. (Eds.). (2004). *The handbook of sexuality in close relationships.* Mahwah, NJ: Lawrence Erlbaum Associates.

Haselton, M. G., & Gildersleeve, K. (2011). Can men detect ovulation? *Current Directions in Psychological Science, 20,* 87–92.

Haslam, A., O'Brien, A., Jetten, J., Penna, S., & Vormedal, K. (2005). Taking the strain: Social identity, social support, and the experience of stress. *British Journal of Social Psychology, 44,* 355–370.

Hasnain, N. N., Ansari, S., & Sethi, S. (2011). Life satisfaction and self esteem in married and unmarried working women. *Journal of the Indian Academy of Applied Psychology, 37,* 316–319.

Hassold, T. J., & Patterson, D. (1999). *Down syndrome: A promising future, together.* New York, NY: Wiley-Liss.

Hassouneh, D., Alcala-Moss, A., & McNeff, E. (2011). Practical strategies for promoting full inclusion of individuals with disabilities in community-based participatory intervention research. *Research in Nursing & Health, 34,* 253–265.

Hastings, R. P., & Oakford, S. (2003). Student teachers' attitudes towards the inclusion of children with special needs. *Educational Psychology, 23,* 87–94.

Hauke, C. (2006). The unconscious: Personal and collective. In R. K. Papadopoulos (Ed.), *The handbook of Jungian psychology: Theory, practice and applications.* New York: Routledge.

Hauser, M. D. (2000). The sound and the fury: Primate vocalizations as reflections of emotion and thought. In N. L. Wallin & B. Merker (Eds.), *The origins of music.* Cambridge, MA: MIT.

Hauser, M. D., Chomsky, N., & Fitch, W. T. (2002, November, 22). The faculty for language: What is it, who has it, and how did it evolve? *Science, 298,* 1569–1579.

Hausmann, R., Tyson, L. D., Bekhouche, Y., & Zahidi, S. (2012). *The Global Gender Gap Report 2012.* Geneva: World Economic Forum.

Hausmann, R., Tyson, L. D., & Zahidi, S. (2009). *The Global Gender Gap Report, 2009.* Geneva, Switzerland: World Economic Forum.

Havermans, R. C., Mulkens, S., Nederkoorn, C., & Jansen, A. (2007). The efficacy of cue exposure with response prevention in extinguishing drug and alcohol cue reactivity. *Behavioral Interventions, 22,* 121–135.

Haviland-Jones, J. M., & Wilson, P. J. (2008). A 'nose' for emotion: Emotional information and challenges in odors and semiochemicals. In M. Lewis, J. M. Haviland-Jones, & L. G. Barrett (Eds.), *Handbook of emotions* (3rd ed.). New York: Guilford Press.

Haviland-Jones, J., & Chen, D. (1999, April 17). *Human olfactory perception.* Paper presented at the Association for Chemoreception Sciences, Sarasota, Florida.

Hawkes, Christopher H., & Doty, R. L. (2009). *The neurology of olfaction.* Cambridge, UK: Cambridge University Press.

Hayflick, L. (2007). Biological aging is no longer an unsolved problem. *Annals of the New York Academy of Sciences, 1100,* 1–13.

Haynes, P., Nixon, J. C., & West, J. F. (1990). Time perception and consumer behaviour: Some cross-cultural implications. *International Journal of Consumer Studies, 14,* 14–27.

Hays, P. A. (2008). *Addressing cultural complexities in practice: Assessment, diagnosis, and therapy* (2nd ed.). Washington, DC: American Psychological Association.

Hayward, R., & Elliott, M. (2011). Subjective and objective fit in religious congregations: Implications for well-being. *Group Processes & Intergroup Relations, 14,* 127–139.

Health Pages. (2003, March 13). Just what the doctor ordered. Retrieved from http://www.thehealthpages.com/articles/ar-drord.html

Heath, R. A. (2006). *The Praeger handbook of transsexuality: Changing gender to match mindset.* Westport, CT: Praeger Publishers/ Greenwood Publishing.

Heatherton, T., & Sargent, J. (2009). Does watching smoking in movies promote teenage smoking? *Current Directions in Psychological Science, 18,* 63–67.

Hecht, J. M. (2007). *The happiness myth: Why what we think is right is wrong. A history of what really makes us happy.* New York: HarperSanFrancisco/HarperCollins.

Hedgepeth, E. (2005). Different lenses, different vision. *School Administrator, 62,* 36–39.

Hedges, D. W., Brown, B. L., Shwalk, D. A., Godfrey, K., & Larcher, A. M. (2007). The efficacy of selective serotonin reuptake inhibitors in adult social anxiety disorder: A meta-analysis of double-blind, placebo-controlled trials. *Journal of Psychopharmacology, 21,* 102–111.

Hegarty, P. (2007). From genius inverts to gendered intelligence: Lewis Terman and the power of the norm [Special issue: Power matters: Knowledge politics in the history of psychology]. *History of Psychology, 10,* 132–155.

Hegarty, P., & Massey, S. (2007). Anti-homosexual prejudice . . . as opposed to what? Queer theory and the social psychology of anti-homosexual attitudes. *Journal of Homosexuality, 52,* 47–71.

Heilman, K. M. (2005). *Creativity and the brain.* New York: Psychology Press.

Heinrichs, R. W. (2005). The primacy of cognition in schizophrenia. *American Psychologist, 60,* 229–242.

Heitzmann, C. A., Merluzzi, T. V., Jean-Pierre, P., Roscoe, J. A., Kirsh, K. L., & Passik, S. D. (2011). Assessing self-efficacy for coping with cancer: Development and psychometric analysis of the brief version of the Cancer Behavior Inventory (CBI-B). *Psycho-Oncology, 20,* 302–312.

Heller, S. (2005). *Freud A to Z.* New York: Wiley.

Helms, J. E. (1992). Why is there no study of cultural equivalence in standardized cognitive ability testing? *American Psychologist, 47,* 1083–1101.

Helmuth, L. (2000, August 25). Synapses shout to overcome distance. *Science, 289,* 1273.

Helsen, K., Goubert, L., & Vlaeyen, J. S. (2013). Observational learning and pain-related fear: Exploring contingency learning in an experimental study using colored warm water immersions. *The Journal of Pain, 14,* 676–688.

Henckes, N. (2011). Reforming psychiatric institutions in the mid-twentieth century: A framework for analysis. *History of Psychiatry, 22,* 164–181.

Henderlong, J., & Lepper, M. R. (2002). The effects of praise on children's intrinsic motivation: A review and synthesis. *Psychological Bulletin, 128,* 774–795.

Henderson, J., Kesmodel, U., & Gray, R. (2007). Systematic review of the fetal effects of prenatal binge-drinking. *Journal of Epidemiology and Community Health, 61,* 1069–1073.

Henderson, N. D. (1982). Correlations in IQ for pairs of people with varying degrees of genetic relatedness and shared environment. *Annual Review of Psychology, 33,* 219–243.

Hennig-Fast, K., Meister, F., Frodl, T., Beraldi, A., Padberg, F., Engel, R., et al. (2008). The case of persistent retrograde amnesia following a dissociative fugue: Neuropsychological and neurofunctional underpinnings of loss of autobiographical memory and self-awareness. *Neuropsychologia, 46*(12), 2993–3005.

Henningsen, D. D., Henningsen, M. L., & Eden, J. (2006). Examining the symptoms of group-think and retrospective sensemaking. *Small Group Research, 37,* 36–64.

Henrich, J., Heine, S., and Norenzayan, A. (2010). The weirdest people in the world? *Behavioral and Brain Sciences, 33,* 61–83.
Henry, D., McClellen, D., Rosenthal, L., Dedrick, D., & Gosdin, M. (2008, February). Is sleep really for sissies? Understanding the role of work in insomnia in the US. *Social Science & Medicine, 66,* 715–726.
Herbenick, D., Reece, M., Sanders, S., Dodge, B., Ghassemi, A., & Fortenberry, J. (2009). Prevalence and characteristics of vibrator use by women in the United States: Results from a nationally representative study. *Journal of Sexual Medicine, 6,* 1857–1866.
Herbert, W. (2011). *On second thought: Outsmarting your mind's hard-wired habits.* New York: Broadway.
Herrán, A., Carrera, M., & Sierra-Biddle, D. (2006). Panic disorder and the onset of agoraphobia. *Psychiatry and Clinical Neurosciences, 60,* 395–396.
Herrnstein, R. J., & Murray, D. (1994). *The bell curve.* New York: Free Press.
Hertlein, K. M., Weeks, G. R., & Gambescia, N. (2007). The treatment of hypoactive sexual desire disorder: An intersystem approach. In L. VandeCreek, F. L. Peterson, Jr., & J. W. Bley (Eds.), *Innovations in clinical practice: Focus on sexual health.* Sarasota, FL: Professional Resource Press/Professional Resource Exchange.
Hertzog, C., Kramer, A., Wilson, R., & Lindenberger, U. (2008). Enrichment effects on adult cognitive development: Can the functional capacity of older adults be preserved and enhanced? *Psychological Science in the Public Interest, 9,* 1–65.
Herzberg, L. (2009). Direction, causation, and appraisal theories of emotion. *Philosophical Psychology, 22,* 167–186.
Heshka, S., Anderson, J. W., Atkinson, R. L., Greenway, F. L., Hill, J. O., Phinney, S. D., et al. (2003). Weight loss with self-help compared with a structured commercial program: A randomized trial. *Journal of the American Medical Association, 289,* 1792–1798.
Hess, M. J., Houg, S., & Tammaro, E. (2007). The experience of four individuals with paraplegia enrolled in an outpatient interdisciplinary sexuality program. *Sexuality and Disability, 25,* 189–195.
Hess, T. M., Hinson, J. T., & Statham, J. A. (2004). Explicit and implicit stereotype activation effects on memory: Do age and awareness moderate the impact of priming? *Psychology and Aging, 19,* 495–505.
Heward, W. L., & Orlansky, M. D. (1988). *Exceptional children* (3rd ed.). Columbus, OH: Merrill.
Hewitt, B., & Egan, H. W. (2009, February 23). Flight 1549: The right stuff. *People, 71,* pp. 10–14.
Hiby, E. F., Rooney, N. J., & Bradshaw, J. W. S. (2004). Dog training methods: Their use, effectiveness and interaction with behaviour and welfare. *Animal Welfare, 13,* 63–69.
Hilarski, C. (2007). Antisocial personality disorder. In B. A. Thyer & J. S. Wodarski (Eds.), *Social work in mental health: An evidence-based approach.* Hoboken, NJ: John Wiley & Sons.
Hilgard, E. (1992). Disassociation and theories of hypnosis. In E. Fromm & M. E. Nash (Eds.), *Contemporary hypnosis research.* New York: Guilford.
Hill, B. D., Foster, J. D., Elliott, E. M., Shelton, J., McCain, J., & Gouvier, W. (2013). Need for cognition is related to higher general intelligence, fluid intelligence, and crystallized intelligence, but not working memory. *Journal of Research in Personality, 47,* 22–25.
Hill, C. E., Gelso, C. J., Gerstenblith, J., Chui, H., Pudasaini, S., Burgard, J., & . . . Huang, T. (2013). The dreamscape of psychodynamic psychotherapy: Dreams, dreamers, dream work, consequences, and case studies. *Dreaming, 23,* 1–45.
Hill, J. O., Catenacci, V., & Wyatt, H. R. (2005). Obesity: Overview of an epidemic. *Psychiatric Clinics of North America, 28,* 1–23.
Hillix, W. A. (2007). The past, present, and possible futures of animal language research. In D. A. Washburn, *Primate perspectives on behavior and cognition.* Washington, DC: American Psychological Association.
Hilton, R. C., Rengasamy, M., Mansoor, B., He, J., Mayes, T., Emslie, G. J., & . . . Brent, D. A. (2013). Impact of treatments for depression on comorbid anxiety, attentional, and behavioral symptoms in adolescents with selective serotonin reuptake inhibitor–resistant depression. *Journal of the American Academy of Child & Adolescent Psychiatry, 52,* 482–492.
Hines, M. (2004). *Brain gender.* New York: Oxford University Press.
Hines, M., & Alexander, G. (2008). Monkeys, girls, boys and toys: A confirmation letter regarding sex differences in toy preferences: Striking parallels between monkeys and humans. *Hormones and Behavior, 54,* 478–479.
Hines, M., Golombok, S., Rust, J., Johnston, K. J., Golding, J., & Avon Longitudinal Study of Parents and Children Study Team. (2002). Testosterone during pregnancy and gender role behavior of preschool children: A longitudinal, population study. *Child Development, 73,* 1678–1687.
Hinterberger, T., Schöner, J., & Halsband, U. (2011). Analysis of electrophysiological state patterns and changes during hypnosis induction. *International Journal of Clinical and Experimental Hypnosis, 59,* 165–179.
Hirschler, B. (2007, May 1). Doctors test gene therapy to treat blindness. *Reuters,* p. 9.
Hirsh, I. J., & Watson, C. S. (1996). Auditory psychophysics and perception. *Annual Review of Psychology, 47,* 461–484.
Ho, S. M. Y., Saltel, P., Machavoine, J., Rapoport-Hubschman, N., & Spiegel, D. (2004). Cross-cultural aspects of cancer care. In National Institutes of Health and Stanford University School of Medicine, *Cancer, culture, and communication.* New York: Kluwer Academic/ Plenum Publishers.
Hobfoll, S. E., Hall, B. J., & Canetti-Nisim, D. (2007). Refining our understanding of traumatic growth in the face of terrorism: Moving from meaning cognitions to doing what is meaningful. *Applied Psychology: An International Review, 56,* 345–366.
Hobson, J. A. (2005). In bed with Mark Solms? What a nightmare! A reply to Domhoff (2005). *Dreaming, 15,* 21–29.
Hobson, J. A. (2007). States of conciseness: Normal and abnormal variation. In P. D. Zelazo, M. Moscovitch, & E. Thompson (Eds.), *The Cambridge Handbook of Consciousness.* London: Cambridge University Press.
Hobson, J. A. *Sleep.* (1989). New York: W. H. Freeman.
Hobson, K. (2011, March 28). How can you help the medicine go down? *The Wall Street Journal,* R10.
Hochschild, A. (2001, February). A generation without public passion. *Atlantic Monthly,* pp. 33–42.
Hock, H. S., & Ploeger, A. (2006). Linking dynamical perceptual decisions at different levels of description in motion pattern formation: Psychophysics. *Perception & Psychophysics, 68,* 505–514.
Hoff, E. (2003). Language development in childhood. In R. M. Lerner et al. (Eds.), *Handbook of psychology: Developmental psychology* (Vol. 6). New York: Wiley.
Hoff, E. (2008). *Language development.* New York: Wadsworth.
Hoffer, T. B., Selfa, L., Welch, V., Jr., Williams, K., Hess, M., Friedman, J., et al. (2005, March 8). *Doctorate recipients from United States universities: Summary report 2003.* Chicago: NORC at the University of Chicago.
Hofmann, S. G. (2007). Enhancing exposure-based therapy from a translational research perspective. *Behaviour Research and Therapy, 45,* 1987–2001.
Hofmann, W., Gschwendner, T., Castelli, L., & Schmitt, M. (2008). Implicit and explicit attitudes and interracial interaction: The moderating role of situationally available control resources. *Group Processes & Intergroup Relations, 11,* 69–87.
Hogan, J., Davies, S., & Hogan, R. (2007). Generalizing personality-based validity evidence. In S. M. McPhail (Ed.), *Alternative validation strategies: Developing new and leveraging existing validity evidence.* Hoboken, NJ: John Wiley & Sons.
Hoge, C. W., & Castro, C. A. (2006, September 2). Post-traumatic stress disorder in UK and US forces deployed to Iraq. *Lancet, 368,* 837.
Hogg, M. A. (2006). Social identity theory. In P. J. Burke (Ed.), *Contemporary social psychological theories.* Palo Alto, CA: Stanford University Press.
Hogg, M. A., & Hains, S. C. (2001). Intergroup relations and group solidarity: Effects of group identification and social beliefs on depersonalized attraction. In M. A. Hogg & D. Abrams (Eds.), *Intergroup relations: Essential readings.* New York: Psychology Press.
Høglend, P. P., Dahl, H. S., Hersoug, A. G., Lorentzen, S. S., & Perry, J. C. (2011). Long-term effects of transference interpretation in dynamic psychotherapy of personality disorders. *European Psychiatry, 26,* 419–424.
Holden, C. (2003, January 17). Deconstructing schizophrenia. *Science, 299,* 333–335.
Holden, C. (2007, June 29). Embryonic stem cells. Stem cell science advances as politics stall. *Science, 316,* 1825.
Holden, L. M. (2005). Complex adaptive systems: concept analysis. *Journal of Advanced Nursing, 52,* 651–657.
Holland, J. C., & Lewis, S. (2001). *The human side of cancer: Living with hope, coping with uncertainty.* New York: Quill.
Holleran, S., Mehl, M., & Levitt, S. (2009). Eavesdropping on social life: The accuracy of stranger ratings of daily behavior from thin slices of natural conversations. *Journal of Research in Personality, 43,* 660–672.
Hollingworth, H. L. (1943/1990). *Leta Stetter Hollingworth: A biography.* Boston: Anker.
Hollins, K. (2007). Consequences of antenatal mental health problems for child health and development. *Current Opinions on Obstetric Gynecology, 19,* 568–573.
Hollis, K. L. (1997, September). Contemporary research on Pavlovian conditioning: A "new" functional analysis. *American Psychologist, 52,* 956–965.
Holloway, L. (2000, December 16). Chief of New York City schools plans to revamp bilingual study. *The New York Times,* p. A1.

Holmes, A., Yang, R. J., Lesch, K. P., Crawley, J. N., & Murphy, D. L. (2003). Mice lacking the Serotonin Transporter Exhibit 5-HT-sub(1A) receptor-mediated abnormalities in tests for anxiety-like behavior. *Neuropsychopharmacology, 28,* 2077–2088.

Holowka, S., & Pettito, L. A. (2002, August 30). Left hemisphere cerebral specialization for babies while babbling. *Science, 297,* 1515.

Holt, M., & Jahn, R. (2004, March, 26). Synaptic vesicles in the fast lane. *Science, 303,* 1986–1987.

Holtyn, A. F., & Lattal, K. A. (2013). Briefly delayed reinforcement effects on variable "ratio and yoked" interval schedule performance. *Journal of the Experimental Analysis of Behavior, 100,* 198–210.

Holtz, J. (2011). *Applied clinical neuropsychology: An introduction.* NY: Springer Publishing Co.

Holy, T. E., Dulac, C., & Meister, M. (2000, September 1). Responses of vomeronasal neurons to natural stimuli. *Science, 289,* 1569–1572.

Hongchun, W., & Ming, L. (2006). About the research on suggestibility and false memory. *Psychological Science (China), 29,* 905–908.

Hoobler, J. M., Lemmon, G., & Wayne, S. J. (2011). Women's underrepresentation in upper management: New insights on a persistent problem. *Organizational Dynamics, 40,* 151–156.

Hopkins, W., & Cantalupo, C. (2008, June). Theoretical speculations on the evolutionary origins of hemispheric specialization. *Current Directions in Psychological Science, 17,* 233–237.

Hopwood, C., Newman, D., Donnellan, M., Markowitz, J., Grilo, C., Sanislow, C., et al. (2009). The stability of personality traits in individuals with borderline personality disorder. *Journal of Abnormal Psychology, 118,* 806–815.

Horesh, D., Solomon, Z. Z., Zerach, G. G., & Ein-Dor, T. T. (2011). Delayed-onset PTSD among war veterans: The role of life events throughout the life cycle. *Social Psychiatry and Psychiatric Epidemiology, 46,* 863–870.

Hori, H., Teraishi, T., Sasayama, D., Matsuo, J., Kawamoto, Y., Kinoshita, Y., & Kunugi, H. (2011). Relationships between season of birth, schizotypy, temperament, character and neurocognition in a non-clinical population. *Psychiatry Research, 189,* 388–397.

Horiguchi, H., Winawer, J., Dougherty, R. F., & Wandell, B. A. (2013). Human trichromacy revisted. *Proceedings of the National Academy of Sciences, 110,* 199–106.

Horn, J. L. (2002). Selections of evidence, misleading assumptions, and oversimplifications: The political message of *The Bell Curve.* In J. M. Fish (Ed.), *Race and intelligence: Separating science from myth.* Mahwah, NJ: Erlbaum.

Horney, K. (1937). *Neurotic personality of our times.* New York: Norton.

Horton, C. L. (2011). Recall and recognition of dreams and waking events: A diary paradigm. *International Journal of Dream Research, 4,* 8–16.

Horton, K. D., Wilson, D. E., Vonk, J., Kirby, S. L., & Nielsen, T. (2005). Measuring automatic retrieval: A comparison of implicit memory, process dissociation, and speeded response procedures. *Acta Psychologica, 119,* 235–263.

Houghtalen, R. P., & Talbot, N. (2007). Dissociative disorders and cognitive disorders. In O. J. Z. Sahler & J. E. Carr (Eds.), *The behavioral sciences and health care* (2nd rev. and updated ed.). Ashland, OH: Hogrefe & Huber Publishers, 2007.

Howe, C. J. (2002). The countering of overgeneralization. *Journal of Child Language, 29,* 875–895.

Howe, M. L. (2011). The adaptive nature of memory and its illusions. *Psychological Science, 20,* 312–315.

Howell, E. F. (2011). *Understanding and treating dissociative identity disorder: A relational approach.* New York: Routledge/Taylor & Francis Group.

Howes, O., & Kapur, S. (2009). The dopamine hypothesis of schizophrenia: Version III–The final common pathway. *Schizophrenia Bulletin, 35,* 549–562.

Howitt, D., & Cramer, D. (2000). *First steps in research and statistics: A practical workbook for psychology students.* Philadelphia: Psychology Press.

Hsu, B., Kling, A., Kessler, C., Knapke, K., Diefenbach, P., & Elias, J. (1994). Gender differences in sexual fantasy and behavior in a college population: A ten-year replication. *Journal of Sex and Marital Therapy, 20,* 103–118.

Hu, E. B., Li, T. Y., Colditz, G. A., Willett, W. C., & Manson, J. E. (2003). Television watching and other sedentary behaviors in relation to risk of obesity and type 2 diabetes mellitus in women. *Journal of the American Medical Association, 289,* 1785–1791.

Hubbard, K., O'Neill, A., & Cheakalos, C. (1999, April 12). Out of control. *People,* pp. 52–72.

Hubel, D. H., & Wiesel, T. N. (2004). *Brain and visual perception: The story of a 25-year collaboration.* New York: Oxford University Press.

Huber, F., Beckmann, S. C., & Herrmann, A. (2004). Means-end analysis: Does the affective state influence information processing style? *Psychology and Marketing, 21,* 715–737.

Hudson, J. I., Coit, C. E., Lalonde, J. K., & Pope, H. G. (2012). By how much will the proposed new DSM-5 criteria increase the prevalence of binge eating disorder? *International Journal of Easting Disorders, 45,* 139–141.

Hudson, W. (1960). Pictorial depth perception in subcultural groups in Africa. *Journal of Social Psychology, 52,* 183–208.

Hudspeth, A. J. (2000). Hearing. In E. R. Kandel, J. H. Schwartz, & T. M. Jessell (Eds.), *Principles of neural science* (4th ed.). New York: McGraw-Hill.

Huerta, M., Cortina, L. M., & Pang, J. S. (2006). Sex and power in the academy: Modeling sexual harassment in the lives of college women. *Personality and Social Psychology Bulletin, 32,* 616–628.

Huesmann, L., Dubow, E. F., & Boxer, P. (2011). The transmission of aggressiveness across generations: Biological, contextual, and social learning processes. In P. R. Shaver & M. Mikulincer (Eds.), *Human aggression and violence: Causes, manifestations, and consequences.* Washington, DC: American Psychological Association.

Hugdahl, K., Thomsen, T., & Ersland, L. (2006). Sex differences in visuo-spatial processing: An fMRI study of mental rotation. *Neuropsychologia, 44,* 1575–1583.

Hugenberg, K., & Sacco, D. (2008). Social categorization and stereotyping: How social categorization biases person perception and face memory. *Social and Personality Psychology Compass, 2,* 1052–1072.

Huijie, T. (2006). The measurement and assessment of mental health: A longitudinal and cross-sectional research on undergraduates, adults and patients. *Psychological Science (China), 29,* 419–422.

Hull, C. L. (1943). *Principles of behavior.* New York: Appleton-Century-Crofts.

Human, L. J., & Biesanz, J. C. (2011). Through the looking glass clearly: Accuracy and assumed similarity in well-adjusted individuals' first impressions. *Journal of Personality and Social Psychology, 100,* 349–364.

Hummer, T. A., & McClintock, M. K. (2009). Putative human pheromone androstadienone attunes the mind specifically to emotional information, *Hormones and Behavior, 55,* 548–559.

Humphrey, N., Curran, A., & Morris, E. (2007). Emotional intelligence and education: A critical review. *Educational Psychology, 27,* 235–254.

Humphreys, K. L., & Lee, S. S. (2011). Risk taking and sensitivity to punishment in children with ADHD, ODD, ADHD+ODD, and controls. *Journal of Psychopathology and Behavioral Assessment, 33,* 299–307.

Hunt, E. (1994). Problem solving. In R. J. Sternberg (Ed.), *Thinking and problem solving: Handbook of perception and cognition* (2nd ed.). San Diego, CA: Academic Press.

Hunt, J. S., Seifert, A. L., & Armenta, B. E. (2006). Stereotypes and prejudice as dynamic constructs: Reminders about the nature of inter-group bias from the hurricane Katrina relief efforts. *Analyses of Social Issues and Public Policy (ASAP), 6,* 237–253.

Hunt, M. (1974). *Sexual behaviors in the 1970s.* New York: Dell.

Huoviala, P., & Rantala, M. J. (2013). Putative human pheromone, androstadienone, increases cooperation between men. PLOSONE, retrived from http://www.plosone.org/article/info%3Adoi%2F10.1371%2Fjournal.pone.0062499

Hurley, D. B., & Kwon, P. (2013). Savoring helps most when you have little: Interaction between savoring the moment and uplifts on positive affect and satisfaction with life. *Journal of Happiness Studies, 14,* 1261–1271.

Huston, A. C., Donnerstein, E., Fairchild, H. H., Feshback, N. D., Katz, P., Murray, J. P., et al. (1992). *Big world, small screen: The role of television in American society.* Omaha, NE: University of Nebraska Press.

Huston, J. P., Silva, M., Komorowski, M., Schulz, D., & Topic, B. (2013). Animal models of extinction-induced depression: Loss of reward and its consequences. *Neuroscience and Biobehavioral Reviews.* Retrieved from http://www.ncbi.nlm.nih.gov/pubmed/23466533

Hutchinson, S. L., Baldwin, C. K., & Oh, S-S. (2006). Adolescent coping: Exploring adolescents' leisure-based responses to stress. *Leisure Sciences, 28,* 115–131.

Hyde, J. S. (2005). The gender similarities hypothesis. *American Psychologist, 50,* 581–592.

Hyde, J. S., & Mertz, J. E. (2009). Gender, culture, and mathematics performance. *Proceedings of the National Academy of Sciences of the United States of America, 106,* 8801–8807.

Hyde, J. S., Lindberg, S. M., Linn, M. C., Ellis, A. B., & Williams, C. C. (2008). Gender similarities characterize math performance. *Science, 321,* 494–495

Hyde, J., Mezulis, A. H., & Abramson, L. Y. (2008). The ABCs of depression: Integrating affective, biological, and cognitive models to explain the emergence of the gender difference in depression. *Psychological Review, 115,* 291–313.

Hyde, K., Peretz, I., & Zatorre, R. (2008, February). Evidence for the role of the right auditory cortex in fine pitch resolution. *Neuropsychologia, 46,* 632–639.

Hyman, B. T. (2011). Amyloid-dependent and amyloid-independent stages of Alzheimer disease. *Archives of Neurology, 68,* 1662–1664.

Hyman, R. (1994). Anomaly or artifact? Comments on Bem and Honorton. *Psychological Bulletin, 115,* 19–24.

Hyman, S. E. (2003, September). Diagnosing disorders. *Scientific American,* pp. 96–103.

Iacoboni, M. (2009, January). Imitation, empathy, and mirror neurons. *Annual Review of Psychology, 60,* 653–670.

Iaria, G., Palermo, L., Committeri, G., & Barton, J. (2009). Age differences in the formation and use of cognitive maps. *Behavioural Brain Research, 196,* 187–191.

IBM. (2012). Citi and IBM enter exploratory agreement on use of Watson technologies. Retrieved from www-03.ibm.com/press/us/en/pressrelease/37029.wss

IBM. (2013, May). *IBM Watson engagement advisor.* Somers, NY: IBM Corporation Software Group.

Ievers-Landis, C. E., Hoff, A. L., Brez, C., Cancilliere, M. K., McConnell, J., & Kerr, D. (2005). Situational analysis of dietary challenges of the treatment regimen for children and adolescents with phenylketonuria and their primary caregivers. *Journal of Developmental and Behavioral Pediatrics, 26,* 186–193.

Iglesias, A. (2005). Awake-alert hypnosis in the treatment of panic disorder: A case report. *American Journal of Clinical Hypnosis, 47,* 249–257.

Igo, S. E. (2006). Review of A telescope on society: Survey research and social science at the University of Michigan and beyond. *Journal of the History of the Behavioral Sciences, 42,* 95–96.

Ikonomidou, C., Bittigau, P., Ishimaru, M. J., Wozniak, D. F., Koch, C., Genz, K., et al. (2000, February 11). Ethanol-induced apoptotic neurodegeneration and fetal alcohol syndrome. *Science, 287,* 1056–1060.

Ilies, R., Arvey, R. D., & Bouchard, T. J., Jr. (2006). Darwinism, behavioral genetics, and organizational behavior: A review and agenda for future research [Special issue: Darwinian perspectives on behavior in organizations]. *Journal of Organizational Behavior, 27,* 96–141.

Imamura, M., & Nakamizo, S. (2006). An empirical test of formal equivalence between Emmert's Law and the size-distance invariance hypothesis. *The Spanish Journal of Psychology, 9*(2), 295–299.

Innocenti, G. M. (2007). Subcortical regulation of cortical development: Some effects of early, selective deprivations. *Progressive Brain Research, 164,* 23–37.

Inoue, T., Abekawa, T., Nakagawa, S., Suzuki, K., Tanaka, T., Kitaichi, Y., & . . . Koyama, T. (2011). Long-term naturalistic follow-up of lithium augmentation: Relevance to bipolarity. *Journal of Affective Disorders, 129,* 64–67.

Insel, T. R. (2010, April). Faulty circuits. *Science,* pp. 44–51.

Interlandi, J. (2008, March 3). What addicts need. *Newsweek,* p. 31–16.

International Human Genome Sequencing Consortium. (2003). *International Consortium completes Human Genome Project.* Bethesda, MD: National Human Genome Research Institute.

Inzlicht, M., & Schmader, T. (Eds.). (2012). *Stereotype threat: Theory, process, and application.* New York: Oxford University Press.

Irwin, M. (2008). Human psychoneuroimmunology: 20 years of discovery. *Brain, Behavior, and Immunity,* 22, 129–139.

Irwin, R. R. (2006). Spiritual development in adulthood: Key concepts and models. In C. Hoare (Ed.), *Handbook of adult development and learning.* New York: Oxford University Press.

Isacson, O., & Kordower, J. (2008). Future of cell and gene therapies for Parkinson's disease. *Annals of Neurology, 64,* S122–SS138.

Isay, R. A. (1994). *Being homosexual: Gay men and their development.* Lanham, MD: Jason Aronson.

Isbell, L. M., & Tyler, J. M. (2003). Teaching students about in-group favoritism and the minimal groups paradigm. *Teaching of Psychology, 30,* 127–130.

Ishikawa, S., Okajima, I., Matsuoka, H., & Sakano, Y. (2007). Cognitive behavioural therapy for anxiety disorders in children and adolescents: A meta-analysis. *Child and Adolescent Mental Health, 12,* 164–172.

Iversen, S., & Iversen, L. (2007). Dopamine: 50 years in perspective. *Trends in Neurosciences, 30,* 188–193.

Iverson, L. (2000). *The science of marijuana.* Oxford, England: Oxford University Press.

Iverson, P., Kuhl, P. K., Reiko, A. Y., Diesch, E., Tohkura, Y., Ketterman, A., et al. (2003). A perceptual interference account of acquisition difficulties for non-native phonemes. *Cognition, 87,* B47–B57.

Ivtzan, I., Gardner, H. E., Bernard, I., Sekhon, M., & Hart, R. (2013). Wellbeing through self-fulfilment: Examining developmental aspects of self-actualization. *The Humanistic Psychologist, 41,* 119–132.

Iwai, Y., Honda, S., Ozeki, H., Hashimoto, M., & Hirase, H. (2011). A simple head-mountable LED device for chronic stimulation of optogenetic molecules in freely moving mice. *Neuroscience Research, 70,* 124–127.

Izard, C. E. (1994). Innate and universal facial expressions: Evidence from developmental and cross-cultural research. *Psychological Bulletin, 115,* 288–299.

Izard, C. E., & Abe, J. A. (2004). Developmental changes in facial expressions of emotions in the strange situation during the second year of life. *Emotion, 4,* 251–265.

Jackson, J. D. (2006). Trauma, attachment, and coping: Pathways to resilience. *Dissertation Abstracts International: Section B: The Sciences and Engineering, 67*(1-B), 547.

Jackson, M. L., Gunzelmann, G., Whitney, P., Hinson, J. M., Belenky, G., Rabat, A., & Van Dongen, H. A. (2013). Deconstructing and reconstructing cognitive performance in sleep deprivation. *Sleep Medicine Reviews, 17,* 215–225.

Jacob, B. C. (2011). Testosterone replacement therapy in males with erectile dysfunction. *Journal of Pharmacy Practice, 24,* 298–306.

Jacob, K. S., Kumar, P. S., Gayathri, K., Abraham, S., & Prince, M. J. (2007). *The diagnosis of dementia in the community* [Special issue: Focus on psychogeriatrics in the developing world]. *International Psychogeriatrics, 19,* 669–678.

Jacobs, E. G., Kroenke, C., Lin, J., Epel, E. S., Kenna, H. A., Blackburn, E. H., & Rasgon, N. L. (2013). Accelerated cell aging in female APOE-4 carriers: Implications for hormone therapy use. *Plos ONE, 8,* 103–111.

Jacobs, J. A., & Gerson, K. (2004). *The time divide: Work, family, and gender inequality.* Cambridge, MA: Harvard University Press.

Jacobs, M., Roesch, S., Wonderlich, S., Crosby, R., Thornton, L., Wilfley, D., et al. (2009). Anorexia nervosa trios: Behavioral profiles of individuals with anorexia nervosa and their parents. *Psychological Medicine, 39,* 451–461.

Jacobson, S. W., Stanton, M. E., Dodge, N. C., Pienaar, M., Fuller, D. S., Molteno, C. D., & . . . Jacobson, J. L. (2011). Impaired delay and trace eyeblink conditioning in school-age children with fetal alcohol syndrome. *Alcoholism: Clinical and Experimental Research, 35,* 250–264.

Jacoby, L. L., & Wahlheim, C. N. (2013). On the importance of looking back: The role of recursive remindings in recency judgments and cued recall. *Memory & Cognition, 41,* 625–637.

Jacoby, L. L., Bishara, A. J., Hessels, S., & Hughes, A. (2007). Probabilistic retroactive interference: The role of accessibility bias in interference effects. *Journal of Experimental Psychology: General, 136,* 200–216.

Jaffé, A., Prasad, S. A., & Larcher, V. (2006). Gene therapy for children with cystic fibrosis–Who has the right to choose? *Journal of Medical Ethics, 32,* 361–364.

Jain, S., Mills, P. J., & Von Känel, R. (2007). Effects of perceived stress and uplifts on inflammation and coagulability. *Psychophysiology, 44,* 154–160.

James, H. S., Jr. (2005). Why did you do that? An economic examination of the effect of extrinsic compensation on intrinsic motivation and performance. *Journal of Economic Psychology, 26,* 549–566.

James, M. H., Charnley, J. L., Flynn, J. R., Smith, D. W., & Dayas, C. V. (2011). Propensity to 'relapse' following exposure to cocaine cues is associated with the recruitment of specific thalamic and epithalamic nuclei. *Neuroscience, 125,* 88–96.

James, W. (1890). *The principles of psychology.* New York: Holt.

Jamieson, G. A. (2007). *Hypnosis and conscious states: The cognitive neuroscience perspective.* New York: Oxford University Press.

Jamison, K. R. (1995a). *An unquiet mind: A memoir of moods and madness.* New York: Knopf.

Janes, A. C., Frederick, B. deB., Merlo-Pich, E., Renshaw, P. F., Evins, A. E., Fava, M., et al. (2009). Brain fMRI reactivity to smoking-related images before and during extended smoking abstinence. *Experimental and Clinical Psychopharmacology, 17*(6), 365–373.

Jang, H., Reeve, J., Ryan, R. M., & Kim, A. (2009, August). Can self-determination theory explain what underlies the productive, satisfying learning experiences of collectivistically oriented Korean students? *Journal of Educational Psychology, 101,* pp. 644–661.

Jang, S. J., You, S. H., & Ahn, S. H. (2007). Neurorehabilitation-induced cortical reorganization in brain injury: A 14-month longitudinal follow-up study. *NeuroRehabilitation, 22,* 117–122.

Janis, I. L. (1997). Groupthink. In R. P. Vecchio (Ed.), *Leadership: Understanding the dynamics of power and influence in organizations.* Notre Dame, IN: University of Notre Dame Press.

Jannini, E. A., McMahon, C. G., & Waldinger, M. D. (2013). *Premature ejaculation: From etiology to diagnosis and treatment.* New York: Springer-Verlag Publishing.

Jarlais, D. C. D., Arasteh, K., & Perlis, T. (2007). The transition from injection to non-injection drug use: Long-term outcomes among heroin and cocaine users in New York City. *Addiction, 102,* 778–785.

Jarrold, C., & Tam, H. (2011). Rehearsal and the development of working memory. In P. Barrouillet & V. Gaillard (Eds.), *Cognitive development and working memory: A dialogue between neo-Piagetian theories and cognitive approaches.* New York: Psychology Press.

Jayson, S. (2008, August 18). More than 50% of college students felt suicidal. *USA Today*, p. 10B.
Jefferson, D. J. (2005, August 8). America's most wanted drug. *Newsweek, 146*, 40-48.
Jenkins, A. M., Albee, G. W., Paster, V. S., Sue, S., Baker, D. B., Comas-Diaz, L., et al. (2003). Ethnic minorities. In D. K. Freedheim (Ed.), *Handbook of psychology: History of psychology* (Vol. 1). Hoboken, NJ: John Wiley & Sons.
Jenkins, S. R. (1994). Need for power and women's careers over 14 years: Structural power, job satisfaction, and motive change. *Journal of Personality and Social Psychology, 66*, 155-165.
Jennings, D. J., Alonso, E., Mondragón, E., Franssen, M., & Bonardi, C. (2013). The effect of stimulus distribution form on the acquisition and rate of conditioned responding: Implications for theory. *Journal of Experimental Psychology: Animal Behavior Processes, 39*, 233-248.
Jensen, A. R. (2002). Galton's legacy to research on intelligence. *Journal of Biosocial Science, 34*, 145-172.
Jequier, E. (2002). Pathways to obesity. *International Journal of Obesity and Related Metabolic Disorders, 26*, S12-S17.
Jetten, J., Hornsey, M. J., & Adarves-Yorno, I. (2006). When group members admit to being conformist: The role of relative intragroup status in conformity self-reports. *Personality and Social Psychology Bulletin, 32*, 162-173.
Jha, A. (2006, February 3). Pill could make painful memories a thing of past: Common drug may help to fight post traumatic stress. *The Guardian* (London), p. 15.
Jia, H., Zack, M. M., & Thompson, W. W. (2011). State Quality-Adjusted Life Expectancy for U.S. Adults from 1993 to 2008. *Quality of Life Research: An International Journal of Quality of Life Aspects of Treatment, Care & Rehabilitation, 20*, 853-863.
Joe, G. W., Flynn, P. M., & Broome, K. M. (2007). Patterns of drug use and expectations in methadone patients. *Addictive Behaviors, 32*, 1640-1656.
John-Steiner, V., & Mahn, H. (2003). Sociocultural contexts for teaching and learning. In W. M. Reynolds & G. E. Miller (Eds.), *Handbook of psychology: Educational psychology* (Vol. 7). New York: Wiley.
Johnsdotter, S., & Essén, B. (2005). It is only a tradition: Making sense of Swedish Somalis' narratives of female circumcision and avoiding submission to hegemonic political discourse. *Critical Social Policy, 25*, 577-589.
Johnson-Laird, P. N. (2006). *How we reason*. Oxford, England: Oxford University Press.
Johnson, A. (2011, March 22). As little girls and boys grow, they think alike. *Wall Street Journal*, p. D-1.
Johnson, G. (1997, July 29). To test a powerful computer, play an ancient game. *The New York Times*, p. C3.
Johnson, G. B. (2000). *The Living World* (p. 600), Boston: McGraw-Hill.
Johnson, H. D. (2004). Gender, grade and relationship differences in emotional closeness within adolescent friendships. *Adolescence, 39*, 243-255.
Johnson, J. G., Cohen, P., Smailes, E. M., Kasen, S., & Brook, J. S. (2002, March 29). Television viewing and aggressive behavior during adolescence and adulthood. *Science, 295*, 2468-2471.
Johnson, S. P. (2004). Development of perceptual completion in infancy. *Psychological Science, 15*, 769-775.
Johnson, S. S., Driskell, M., Johnson, J. L., Prochaska, J. M., Zwick, W., & Prochaska, J. O. (2006). Efficacy of a Transtheoretical Model-Based Expert System For Antihypertensive Adherence. *Disease Management, 9*, 291-301.
Johnson, W., & Deary, I. J. (2011). Placing inspection time, reaction time, and perceptual speed in the broader context of cognitive ability: The VPR model in the Lothian Birth Cohort 1936. *Intelligence, 39*, 405-417.
Johnston, L. D., O'Malley, P. M., Bachman, J. G., & Schulenberg, J. E. (2012). *Monitoring the Future Study*. An Arbor, MI: University of Michigan News Service. Retrieved from http://www.monitoringthefuture.org
Johnston, L. D., O'Malley, P. M., & Bachman, J. G. (2003). *Monitoring the future: National results on adolescent drug use: Overview of key findings, 2002*. Bethesda MD: National Institute on Drug Abuse.
Johnston, L. D., O'Malley, P. M., Bachman, J. G., & Schulenberg, J. E. (2007). *Monitoring the future national results on adolescent drug use: Overview of key findings, 2006* (NIH Publication No. 07-6202). Bethesda, MD: National Institute on Drug Abuse.
Johnston, L. D., O'Malley, P. M., Bachman, J. G., & Schulenberg, J. E. (2009). *Monitoring the future national results on adolescent drug use; overview of key findings, 2008* (NIH Publication No. 09-7401). Bethesda, MD: National Institute on Drug Abuse.
Johnston, L. D., O'Malley, P. M., Bachman, J. G., & Schulenberg, J. E. (2009). *Monitoring the future national survey results on drug use: 1975-2008. Volume I: Secondary school students* (NIH Publication No. 09-7402). Bethesda, MD: National Institute on Drug Abuse.
Johnston, L. D., O'Malley, P. M., Bachman, J. G., & Schulenberg, J. E. (2013). *Monitoring the Future–National results on drug use: 2012 overview, key findings on adolescent drug use*. Ann Arbor, MI: Institute for Social Research, The University of Michigan.
Johnston, M. V. (2004). Clinical disorders of brain plasticity. *Brain and Development, 26*, 73-80.
Jones, A. L. (2006). The contemporary psychoanalyst: Karen Horney's theory applied in today's culture. *PsycCRITIQUES, 51*, 127-134.
Jones, D. (2010). A WEIRD view of human nature skews psychologists' studies. *Science, 328*, 1627.
Jones, J. E., & Corp, E. S. (2003). Effect of naltrexone on food intake and body weight in Syrian hamsters depends on metabolic status. *Physiology and Behavior, 78*, 67-72.
Jones, J. M. (2007). Exposure to chronic community violence: Resilience in African American children. *Journal of Black Psychology, 33*, 125-149.
Jones, K., Callen, F., Blagrove, M., & Parrott, A. (2008). Sleep, energy and self rated cognition across 7 nights following recreational ecstasy/MDMA use. *Sleep and Hypnosis, 10*, 2-38.
Jones, N., Corrigan, P. W., James, D., Parker, J., & Larson, N. (2013). Peer support, self-determination, and treatment engagement: A qualitative investigation. *Psychiatric Rehabilitation Journal, 36*, 209-214.
Jones, R. K., Darroch, J. E., & Singh, S. (2005). Religious differentials in the sexual and reproductive behaviors of young women in the United States. *Journal of Adolescent Health, 36*, 279-288.
Jorgensen, G. (2006). Kohlberg and Gilligan: Duet or duel? *Journal of Moral Education, 35*, 179-196.
Jovanović, D., Stanojević, P., & Stanojević, D. (2011). Motives for, and attitudes about, driving-related anger and aggressive driving. *Social Behavior and Personality, 39*, 755-764.
Joyce, J. (1934). *Ulysses*. New York: Random House.
Julien, R. M. (2001). *A primer of drug action* (9th ed.). New York: Freeman.
Jung, C. G. (1961). *Freud and psychoanalysis*. New York: Pantheon.
Jung, J. (2002). *Psychology of alcohol and other drugs: A research perspective*. Thousand Oaks, CA: Sage.
Juster, E. T., Ono, H., & Stafford, E. (2002). *Report on housework and division of labor*. Ann Arbor, MI: Institute for Social Research.
Justman, S. (2011). From medicine to psychotherapy: The placebo effect. *History of the Human Sciences, 24*, 95-107.
Jylha, M. (2004). Old age and loneliness: Cross-sectional and longitudinal analyses in the Tampere longitudinal study on aging. *Canadian Journal on Aging/La Revue Canadienne du Vieillissement, 23*, 157-168.
Kadosh, R., Henik, A., & Walsh, V. (2009, May). Synaesthesia: Learned or lost? *Developmental Science, 12*, 484-491.
Kagan, J., Snidman, N., Kahn, V., & Towsley, S. (2007). The preservation of two infant temperaments into adolescence. *Monographs of the Society for Research in Child Development, 72*, 1-75.
Kahn, R. E., Frick, P. J., Youngstrom, E. A., Kogos Youngstrom, J., Feeny, N. C., & Findling, R. L. (2013). Distinguishing primary and secondary variants of callous-unemotional traits among adolescents in a clinic-referred sample. *Psychological Assessment, 25*, 966-978.
Kahneman, D., Diener, E., & Schwarz, N. (1998). *Well-being: The foundations of hedonic psychology*. New York: Russell Sage Foundation.
Kaiser Family Foundation. (2010). *Generation M2: Media in the lives of 8-to-18 year olds*. Menlo Park, CA: Kaiser Family Foundation.
Kalanthroff, E., Anholt, G. E., Keren, R., & Henik, A. (2013). What should I (not) do? Control over irrelevant tasks in obsessive-compulsive disorder patients. *Clinical Neuropsychiatry: Journal of Treatment Evaluation, 10*, Suppl. 1, 61-64.
Kalb, C. (2001, February 26). DARE checks into rehab. *Newsweek*, pp. 56.
Kalb, C. (2003, May 19). Taking a new look at pain. *Newsweek*, pp. 51-52.
Kaller, C. P., Unterrainer, J. M., Rahm, B., & Halsband, U. (2004). The impact of problem structure on planning: Insights from the Tower of London task. *Cognitive Brain Research, 20*, 462-472.
Kallio, S., & Revonsuo, A. (2003). Hypnotic phenomena and altered states of consciousness: A multilevel framework of description and explanation. *Contemporary Hypnosis, 20*, 111-164.
Kalodner, C. R. (2011). Cognitive-behavioral theories. In D. Capuzzi & D. R. Gross (Eds.), *Counseling and psychotherapy* (5th ed.). Alexandria, VA: American Counseling Association.
Kamens, S. R. (2011). On the proposed sexual and gender identity diagnoses for DSM-5: History and controversies. *The Humanistic Psychologist, 39*, 37-59.
Kaminski, P., Chapman, B. P., Haynes, S. D., & Own, L. (2005). Body image, eating behaviors, and attitudes toward exercise among gay and straight men. *Eating Behaviors, 6, 179-187*.
Kandel, E. R., Schwartz, J. H., & Jessell, T. M. (Eds.). (2000). *Principles of neural science* (4th ed.). New York: McGraw-Hill.
Kandler, C., Riemann, R., & Angleitner, A. (2013). Patterns and sources of continuity and change of energetic and temporal aspects of temperament in adulthood: A longitudinal twin study of self- and peer reports. *Developmental Psychology, 49*, 1739-1753.

Kane, M. J., & Engle, R. W. (2002). The role of prefrontal cortex in working-memory capacity, executive attention, and general fluid intelligence: An individual-differences perspective. *Psychonomic Bulletin and Review, 9,* 637–671.

Kanner, A. D., Coyne, J. C., Schaefer, C., & Lazarus, R. S. (1981). Comparison of two modes of stress measurement: Daily hassles and uplifts versus major life events. *Journal of Behavioral Medicine, 4,* 14.

Kanoski, S. E., Hayes, M. R., Greenwald, H. S., Fortin, S. M., Gianessi, C. A., Gilbert, J. R., & Grill, H. J. (2011). Hippocampal leptin signaling reduces food intake and modulates food-related memory processing. *Neuropsychopharmacology, 36,* 1859–1870.

Kantrowitz, B., & Underwood, A. (2007, June 25). The teen drinking dilemma. *Newsweek,* pp. 36–37.

Kao, D. (2011). Message sidedness in advertising: The moderating roles of need for cognition and time pressure in persuasion. *Scandinavian Journal of Psychology, 52,* 329–340.

Kaplan, H. S. (1974). *The new sex therapy.* New York: Brunner-Mazel.

Kaplan, J. R., & Manuck, S. B. (1989). The effect of propranolol on behavioral interactions among adult male cynomolgus monkeys *(Macacafas-cicularis)* housed in disrupted social groupings. *Psychosomatic Medicine, 51,* 449–462.

Kaplan, M. (2013). Sharkbot: The machine that taught itself to be all but invincible at poker. *New York Times Magazine,* 44–47; 58–59.

Kaplan, M. S., Huguer, N., McFarland, B. H., & Newsom, J. T. (2007). Suicide among male veterans: A prospective population-based study. *Journal of Epidemiological Community Health, 61,* 619–624.

Kaplan, R. M., & Saccuzzo, D. P. (2001). *Psychological testing: Principles, applications, and issues* (5th ed.). Belmont, CA: Wadsworth/Thomson Learning.

Kara, P., & Boyd, J. (2009, April). A micro-architecture for binocular disparity and ocular dominance in visual cortex. *Nature,* 458(7238), 627–631.

Karama, S., Ad-Dab'bagh, Y., Haier, R. J., Deary, I. J., Lyttelton, O. C., Lepage, C., et al. (2009). Positive association between cognitive ability and cortical thickness in a representative US sample of healthy 6 to 18 year-olds. *Brain Development Cooperative Group; Intelligence, 37,* 145–155.

Karaszewski, B. (2008). Sub-neocortical brain: A mechanical tool for creative generation? *Trends in Cognitive Sciences, 12,* 171–172.

Karlson, C. W., Gallagher, M. W., Olson, C. A., & Hamilton, N. A. (2013). Insomnia symptoms and well-being: Longitudinal follow-up. *Health Psychology, 32,* 311–319.

Kasof, J. (2009, May). Cultural variation in seasonal depression: Cross-national differences in winter versus summer patterns of seasonal affective disorder. *Journal of Affective Disorders, 115,* 79–86.

Kassam, K. S., Gilbert, D. T., Swencionis, J. K., & Wilson, T. D. (2009). Misconceptions of memory: The Scooter Libby effect. *Psychological Science, 20,* 551–552.

Kassel, J. D., Evatt, D. P., Greenstein, J. E., Wardle, M. C., Yates, M. C., & Veilleux, J. C. (2007). The acute effects of nicotine on positive and negative affect in adolescent smokers. *Journal of Abnormal Psychology, 116,* 543–553.

Kassin, S. M. (2005). On the psychology of confessions: Does innocence put innocents at risk? *American Psychologist, 60,* 215–228.

Kaštelan, A., Franciškovic, A., Tanja, M., & Moro, L. (2007). Psychotic symptoms in combat-related post-traumatic stress disorder. *Military Medicine, 172,* 273–277.

Kato, K., & Pedersen, N. L. (2005). Personality and coping: A study of twins reared apart and twins reared together. *Behavior Genetics, 35,* 147–158.

Kato, N. (2009). Neurophysiological mechanisms of electroconvulsive therapy for depression. *Neuroscience Research, 64,* 3–11.

Kato, R., Yokoi, H., Arieta, A. H., Yu, W., & Arai, T. (2009). Mutual adaptation among man and machine by using f-MRI analysis. *Robotics and Autonomous Systems,* 161–166.

Katsiyannis, A., Zhang, D., & Woodruff, N. (2005). Transition supports to students with mental retardation: An examination of data from the national longitudinal transition study 2. *Education and Training in Developmental Disabilities, 40,* 109–116.

Katz, L., Fotti, S., & Postl, L. (2009). Cognitive-behavioral therapy and dialectical behavior therapy: Adaptations required to treat adolescents. *Psychiatric Clinics of North America, 32,* 95–109.

Katz, M. (2001). The implications of revising Freud's empiricism for drive theory. *Psychoanalysis and Contemporary Thought, 24,* 253–272.

Kaufman, A., Johnson, C., & Liu, X. (2008). A CHC theory-based analysis of age differences on cognitive abilities and academic skills at ages 22 to 90 years. *Journal of Psychoeducational Assessment, 26,* 350–381.

Kaufman, J. C., & Baer, J. (2006). *Creativity and reason in cognitive development.* New York: Cambridge University Press.

Kaufman, J. C., & Plucker, J. A. (2011). Intelligence and creativity. In R. J. Sternberg & S. Kaufman (Eds.), *The Cambridge handbook of intelligence.* New York: Cambridge University Press.

Kaufman, J. C., Kaufman, S., & Plucker, J. A. (2013). Contemporary theories of intelligence. In D. Reisberg (Ed.), *The Oxford handbook of cognitive psychology.* New York: Oxford University Press.

Kawasaki, C., Nugent, J. K., Miyashita, H., Miyahara, H., & Brazelton, T. B. (1994). The cultural organization of infants' sleep [Special issue: Environments of birth and infancy]. *Children's Environment, 11,* 135–141.

Kawashima, H., Izaki, Y., & Grace, A. A. (2006). Cooperativity between hippocampal-pre-frontal short-term plasticity through associative long-term potentiation. *Brain Research, 1109,* 37–44.

Kazar, D. B. (2006). Forensic psychology: Did we leave anything out? *PsycCRITIQUES, 51,* 88–97.

Kazdin, A. (2008). Evidence-based treatment and practice: New opportunities to bridge clinical research and practice, enhance the knowledge base, and improve patient care. *American Psychologist, 63,* 146–159.

Keating, D. P., & Clark, L. V. (1980). Development of physical and social reasoning in adolescence. *Developmental Psychology, 16,* 23–30.

Keehn, J. D. (1996). *Master builders of modern psychology: From Freud to Skinner.* New York: New York University Press.

Keer, M., van den Putte, B., Neijens, P., & de Wit, J. (2013). The influence of affective and cognitive arguments on message judgement and attitude change: The moderating effects of meta-bases and structural bases. *Psychology & Health, 28,* 895–908.

Keillor, J. M., Barrett, A. M., Crucian, G. P., Kortenkamp, S., & Heilman, K. M. (2002). Emotional experience and perception in the absence of facial feedback. *Journal of the International Neuropsychological Society, 8,* 130–135.

Keller, J. (2007). Stereotype threat in classroom settings: The interactive effect of domain identification, task difficulty and stereotype threat on female students' math performance. *British Journal of Educational Psychology, 77,* 323–338.

Kelley, H. (1950). The warm-cold variable in first impressions of persons. *Journal of Personality and Social Psychology, 18,* 431–439.

Kelly, D., & Tangney, B. (2006). Adapting to intelligence profile in an adaptive educational system. *Interacting with Computers, 18,* pp. 385–409.

Kelly, J. B. (2000). Children's adjustment in conflicted marriage and divorce: A decade review of research. *Journal of the American Academy of Child & Adolescent Psychiatry, 39,* 963–973.

Kelly, T. (2012, May 7). Arthur Boorman, disabled veteran, walks again after discovering yoga. *Huffington Post. http://www.huffingtonpost.com/2012/05/04/arthur-boorman-veteran-walks-again-yoga n 1478847.html.* Downloaded November 6, 2013.

Keltikangas-Järvinen, L., Räikkönen, K., Ekelund, J., & Peltonen, L. (2004). Nature and nurture in novelty seeking. *Molecular Psychiatry, 9,* 308–311.

Kemeny, M. E. (2007). Psychoneuroimmunology. In H. S. Friedman & R. C. Silver (Eds.), *Foundations of health psychology.* New York: Oxford University Press.

Kempermann, G. (2011). Seven principles in the regulation of adult neurogenesis. *European Journal of Neuroscience, 33,* 1018–1024.

Kempermann, G., & Gage, F. H. (1999, May). New nerve cells for the adult brain. *Scientific American,* pp. 48–53.

Kemps, E., & Tiggemann, M. (2007). Reducing the vividness and emotional impact of distressing autobiographical memories: The importance of modality-specific interference. *Memory, 15,* 412–422.

Kendler, K. S., & Schaffner, K. F. (2011). The dopamine hypothesis of schizophrenia: An historical and philosophical analysis. *Philosophy, Psychiatry, & Psychology, 18,* 41–63.

Kendler, K. S., Gatz, M., & Gardner, C. O. (2006). Personality and major depression. *Archives of General Psychiatry, 63,* 1113–1120.

Kendler, K. S., Gatz, M., & Gardner, C. O. (2006a). Personality and major depression. *Archives of General Psychiatry, 63,* 1113–1120.

Kendler, K., Halberstadt, L., Butera, F., Myers, J., Bouchard, T., & Ekman, P. (2008). The similarity of facial expressions in response to emotion-inducing films in reared-apart twins. *Psychological Medicine, 38*(10), 1475–1483.

Kennedy, C. E., Moore, P. J., Peterson, R. A., Katzman, M. A., Vermani, M., & Charmak, W. D. (2011). What makes people anxious about pain? How personality and perception combine to determine pain anxiety responses in clinical and non-clinical populations. *Anxiety, Stress & Coping: An International Journal, 24,* 179–200.

Kennedy, D. O., & Haskell, C. F. (2011). Cerebral blood flow and behavioural effects of caffeine in habitual and non-habitual consumers of caffeine: A near infrared spectroscopy study. *Biological Psychology, 86,* 296–305.

Kennedy, J. E. (2004). A proposal and challenge for proponents and skeptics of psi. *Journal of Parapsychology, 68,* 157–167.

Kennedy, P. (2011, September 18). The cyborg in us all. *New York Times Magazine*, pp. 24–31.

Kennison, S. M., & Bowers, J. (2011). Illustrating brain lateralisation in a naturalistic observation of cell-phone use. *Psychology Learning & Teaching, 10*, 46–51.

Kensinger, E. (2007). Negative emotion enhances memory accuracy: Behavioral and neuro-imaging evidence. *Current Directions in Psychological Science, 16*, 213–218.

Kensinger, E. A., & Schacter, D. L. (2006). Neural processes underlying memory attribution on a reality-monitoring task. *Cerebral Cortex, 16*, 1126–1133.

Kenway, L., & Wilson, M. A. (2001). Temporally structured replay of awake hippocampal ensemble activity during rapid eye movement sleep. *Neuron, 29*, 145–156.

Kesebir, P., & Diener, E. (2008). In pursuit of happiness: Empirical answers to philosophical questions. *Perspectives on Psychological Science, 3*, 117–125.

Kess, J. F., & Miyamoto, T. (1994). *Japanese psycholinguistics*. Amsterdam, Netherlands: John Benjamins.

Kessler, R. C., & Wang, P. S. (2008). The descriptive epidemiology of commonly occurring mental disorders in the United States. *Annual Review of Public Health, 29*, 115–129.

Ketisch, T., & Jones, R. A. (2013). Review of 'ADHD diagnosis & management'. *American Journal of Family Therapy, 41*, 272–274.

Key, W. B. (2003). Subliminal sexuality: The fountainhead for America's obsession. In T. Reichert & J. Lambaiase (Eds.), *Sex in advertising: Perspectives on the erotic appeal. LEA's communication series*. Mahwah, NJ: Lawrence Erlbaum.

Khalil, E. L. (2011). The mirror neuron paradox: How far is understanding from mimicking? *Journal of Economic Behavior & Organization, 77*, 86–96.

Khazaal, Y., Chatton, A., Claeys, F., Ribordy, F., Zullino, D., & Cabanac, M. (2008). Antipsychotic drug and body weight set-point. *Physiology & Behavior, 95*, 157–160.

Kidd, E., & Lum, J. (2008). Sex differences in past tense overregularization. *Developmental Science, 11*, 882–889.

Kiecolt, J. K. (2003). Satisfaction with work and family life: No evidence of a cultural reversal. *Journal of Marriage and Family, 65*, 23–35.

Kiefer, A. K. (2006). The effects of stereotypes on performance attributions: How gender-math stereotypes lead women to internalize failure. *Dissertation Abstracts International: Section B: The Sciences and Engineering, 66*(9-B), 5140.

Kihlstrom, J. F. (2005a). Dissociative disorders. *Annual Review of Clinical Psychology, 1*, 227–253.

Kihlstrom, J. F. (2005b). Is hypnosis an altered state of consciousness or what? Comment. *Contemporary Hypnosis, 22*, 34–38.

Kihlstrom, J. F., Schacter, D. L., Cork, R. C., Hurt, C. A., & Behr, S. E. (1990). Implicit and explicit memory following surgical anesthesia. *Psychological Science, 1*, 303–306.

Killingsworth, M. A., & Gilbert, D. T. (2010, November 12). A Wandering Mind Is an Unhappy Mind. *Science, 330*, 932.

Kim-Cohen, J., Caspi, A., & Moffitt, T. E. (2003). Prior juvenile diagnoses in adults with mental disorder: Developmental follow-back of a prospective-longitudinal cohort. *Archives of General Psychiatry, 60*, 709–717.

Kim-Cohen, J., Moffitt, T. E., Taylor, A., Pawlby, S. J., & Caspi, A. (2005). Maternal depression and children's antisocial behavior: Nature and nurture effects. *Archives of General Psychiatry, 62*, 173–181.

Kim, D. R., Pesiridou, A., & O'Reardon, J. P. (2009). Transcranial magnetic stimulation in the treatment of psychiatric disorders. *Current Psychiatry Reports, 11*, 447–52.

Kim, H., Clark, D., & Dionne, R. (2009, July). Genetic contributions to clinical pain and analgesia: Avoiding pitfalls in genetic research. *The Journal of Pain, 10*, 663–693.

Kim, K. H., Relkin, N. R., Lee, K. M., & Hirsch, J. (1997, July 10). Distinct cortical areas associated with native and second languages. *Nature, 388*, 171–174.

Kim, N. (2008). The moon illusion and the size-distance paradox. In Cummins-Sebree, S., Riley, M. A., & Shockley, K. (Eds.). *Studies in perception and action IX: Fourteenth International Conference on Perception and Action*. Mahwah, NJ: Lawrence Erlbaum Associates.

Kim, S. E., Kim, J. W., & Kim, J. J. (2007). The neural mechanism of imagining facial affective expression. *Brain Research, 1145*, 128–137.

Kimbrel, N. A. (2007). A model of the development and maintenance of generalized social phobia. *Clinical Psychological Review, 8*, 69–75.

King-Casas, B., Sharp, C., Lomax-Bream, L., Lohrenz, T., Fonagy, P., & Montague, P. R. (2008, August, 8). The rupture and repair of cooperation in borderline personality disorder. *Science, 321*, 806–810.

Kinsey, A. C., Pomeroy, W. B., & Martin, C. E. (1948). *Sexual behavior in the human male*. Philadelphia: Saunders.

Kinsey, A. C., Pomeroy, W. B., Martin, C. E., & Gebhard, P. H. (1953). *Sexual behavior in the human female*. Philadelphia: Saunders.

Kirby, D. (1977). The methods and methodological problems of sex research. In J. S. DeLora & C. A. B. Warren (Eds.), *Understanding sexual interaction*. Boston: Houghton Mifflin.

Kirk, E. P., Jacobsen, D. J., Gibson, C., Hill, J. O., & Donnelly, J. E. (2003). Time course for changes in aerobic capacity and body composition in overweight men and women in response to long-term exercise: The Midwest exercise trial (MET). *International Journal of Obesity, 27*, 912–919.

Kirk, K. M., Bailey, J. M., & Martin, N. G. (2000). Etiology of male sexual orientation in an Australian twin sample. *Psychology, Evolution & Gender, 2*, 301–311.

Kirsch, I., & Braffman, W. (2001). Imaginative suggestibility and hypnotizability. *Current Directions in Psychological Science, 10*, 57–61.

Kirsch, I., Lynn, S. J., Vigorito, M., & Miller, R. R. (2004). The role of cognition in classical and operant conditioning. *Journal of Clinical Psychology, 60*, 369–392.

Kirschenbaum, H. (2004). Carl Rogers's life and work: An assessment on the 100th anniversary of his birth. *Journal of Counseling and Development, 82*, 116–124.

Kish, S., Fitzmaurice, P., Boileau, I., Schmunk, G., Ang, L., Furukawa, Y., et al. (2009). Brain serotonin transporter in human methamphetamine users. *Psychopharmacology, 202*, 649–661.

Kiss, A. (2004). Does gender have an influence on the patient-physician communication? *Journal of Men's Health and Gender, 1*, 77–82.

Klapp, S. T., & Jagacinski, R. J. (2011). Gestalt principles in the control of motor action. *Psychological Bulletin, 137*, 443–462.

Klein, K. M., Apple, K. J., & Kahn, A. S. (2011). Attributions of blame and responsibility in sexual harassment: Reexamining a psychological model. *Law and Human Behavior, 35*, 92–103.

Kleinman, A. (1996). How is culture important for DSM-IV? In J. E Mezzich, A. Kleinman, H. Fabrega, Jr., & D. L. Parron (Eds.), *Culture and psychiatric diagnosis: A DSM-IV perspective*. Washington, DC: American Psychiatric Press.

Kleinplatz, P. J., Moser, C., & Lev, A. (2013). Sex and gender identity disorders. In G. Stricker, T. A. Widiger, & I. B. Weiner (Eds.), *Handbook of psychology, Vol. 8: Clinical psychology* (2nd ed.). Hoboken, NJ: John Wiley & Sons Inc.

Kling, K. C., Ryff, C. D., & Love, G. (2003). Exploring the influence of personality on depressive symptoms and self-esteem across a significant life transition. *Journal of Personality and Social Psychology, 85*, 922–932.

Klötz, F., Garle, M., & Granath, F. (2006). Criminality among individuals testing positive for the presence of anabolic androgenic steroids. *Archives of General Psychiatry, 63*, 1274–1279.

Kluck, A. (2008). Family factors in the development of disordered eating: Integrating dynamic and behavioral explanations. *Eating Behaviors, 9*, 471–483.

Kluger, J. (2001, April 2). Fear not! *Time*, pp. 51–62.

Kluger, J. (2006, December 4). Why we worry about the things we shouldn't and ignore the things we should. *Time*, pp. 64–71.

Kluger, J. (2013, July 29). The power of the bilingual brain. *Time*, 42–47.

Klump, K., & Culbert, K. (2007). Molecular genetic studies of eating disorders: Current status and future directions. *Current Directions in Psychological Science, 16*, 37–41.

Knight, S. C., & Meyer, R. G. (2007). Forensic hypnosis. In A. M. Goldstein (Ed.), *Forensic psychology: Emerging topics and expanding roles*. Hoboken, NJ: John Wiley & Sons.

Knoblich, G., & Sebanz, N. (2006). The social nature of perception and action. *Current Directions in Psychological Science, 15*, 99–111.

Kobayashi, F., Schallert, D. L., & Ogren, H. A. (2003). Japanese and American folk vocabularies for emotions. *Journal of Social Psychology, 143*, 451–478.

Koçak, O., Özpolat, A., Atbaşoğlu, C., & Çiçek, M. (2011). Cognitive control of a simple mental image in patients with obsessive-compulsive disorder. *Brain and Cognition, 76*, 390–399.

Koch, C., & Greenfield, S. (2007, October). How does consciousness happen? *Scientific American*, pp. 76–83.

Koch, J. (2003). Gender issues in the classroom. In W. M. Reynolds & G. E. Miller (Eds.), *Handbook of psychology: Educational psychology* (Vol. 7). New York: Wiley.

Koelkebeck, K., Hirao, K., Kawada, R., Miyata, J., Saze, T., Ubukata S., . . . Murai, T. (2011). Transcultural differences in brain activation patterns during theory of mind (ToM) task performance in Japanese and Caucasian participants. *Social Neuroscience, 6*(5–6), 615–626.

Kogstad, R. E., Ekeland, T. J., & Hummelvoll, J. K. (2011). In defence of a humanistic approach to mental health care: Recovery processes investigated with the help of clients' narratives on turning points and processes of gradual change. *Journal of Psychiatric and Mental Health Nursing, 18*, 479–486.

Kohlberg, L. (1984). *The psychology of moral development: Essays on moral development* (Vol. 2). San Francisco: Harper & Row.

Kohlberg, L., & Ryncarz, R. A. (1990). Beyond justice reasoning: Moral development and consideration of a seventh stage. In C. N. Alexander & E. J. Langer (Eds.), *Higher stages of human development: Perspectives on adult growth*. New York: Oxford University Press.

Kohlberg, L. (1969). Stage and sequence: The cognitive-developmental approach to socialization. In D. Goslin (Ed.), *Handbook of Socialization Theory and Research* (381–382). Chicago: Rand McNally.

Kohler, C. G., Turner, T., Stolar, N. M., Bilker, W. B., Brensinger, C. M., Gur, R. E., et al. (2004). Differences in facial expressions of four universal emotions. *Psychiatry Research, 128,* 235–244.

Köhler, W. (1927). *The mentality of apes*. London: Routledge & Kegan Paul.

Kojima, M., & Kangawa, K. (2008). Structure and function of ghrelin. *Results & Problems in Cell Differentiation, 46,* 89–115.

Kolata, G. (2002, December 2). With no answers on risks, steroid users still say "yes." *The New York Times*, p. 1A.

Kolb, B., Gibb, R., & Robinson, T. E. (2003). Brain plasticity and behavior. *Current Directions in Psychological Science, 12,* 1–5.

Komarovskaya, I., Loper, A., Warren, J., & Jackson, S. (2011). Exploring gender differences in trauma exposure and the emergence of symptoms of PTSD among incarcerated men and women. *Journal of Forensic Psychiatry & Psychology, 22,* 395–410.

Konig, R. (2005). Introduction: Plasticity, learning, and cognition. In R. Konig., P. Heil., E. Budinger, & H. Scheich (Eds.), *The auditory cortex: A synthesis of human and animal research*. Mahwah, NJ: Lawrence Erlbaum Associates.

Koocher, G. P., Norcross, J. C., & Hill, S. S. (2005). *Psychologists' desk reference* (2nd ed.). New York: Oxford University Press.

Kopelman, M. D., & Fleminger, S. (2002). Experience and perspectives on the classification of organic mental disorders. *Psychopathology, 35,* 76–81.

Koper, R. J., & Jaasma, M. A. (2001). Interpersonal style: Are human social orientations guided by generalized interpersonal needs? *Communications Reports, 14,* 117–129.

Koplewicz, H. (2002). *More than moody: Recognizing and treating adolescent depression*. New York: Putnam.

Korcha, R. A., Polcin, D. L., Bond, J. C., Lapp, W. M., & Galloway, G. (2011). Substance use and motivation: A longitudinal perspective. *The American Journal of Drug and Alcohol Abuse, 37,* 48–53.

Korecka, J. A., Verhaagen, J., & Hol, E. M. (2007). Cell-replacement and gene-therapy strategies for Parkinson's and Alzheimer's disease. *Regenerative Medicine, 2,* 425–426.

Korotkov, D., Perunovic, M., Claybourn, M., Fraser, I., Houlihan, M., Macdonald, M., & Korotkov, K. (2011). The Type B behavior pattern as a moderating variable of the relationship between stressor chronicity and health behavior. *Journal of Health Psychology, 16,* 397–409.

Kosambi, D. D. (1967). The Vedic "Five Tribes." *American Oriental Society, 14,* 5–12.

Kosfeld, M., Heinrich, M., Zak, P. J., Fischbacher, U., & Fehr, E. (2005, June 2). Oxytocin increases trust in humans. *Nature, 435,* 673–676.

Koslowski, B. (2013). Scientific reasoning: Explanation, confirmation bias, and scientific practice. In G. J. Feist & M. E. Gorman (Eds.), *Handbook of the psychology of science*. New York: Springer Publishing Co.

Koss, M. P. (1993). Rape: Scope, impact, interventions, and public policy responses. *American Psychologist, 48,* 1062–1069.

Koss, M. P. (2011). Hidden, unacknowledged, acquaintance, and date rape: Looking back, looking forward. *Psychology of Women Quarterly, 35,* 348–354.

Kosslyn, S. M. (2005). Mental images and the brain. *Cognitive Neuropsychology, 22,* 333–347.

Kosslyn, S. M., Cacioppo, J. T., Davidson, R. J., Hugdahl, K., Lovallo, W. R., Spiegel, D., et al. (2002). Bridging psychology and biology. *American Psychologist, 57,* 341–351.

Kosslyn, S. M., & Miller, G. W. (2013). *Top brain, bottom brain: Surprising insights into how you think*. New York: Simon & Schuster.

Kotre, J., & Hall, E. (1990). *Seasons of life*. Boston: Little, Brown.

Kounios, J., Fleck, J. I., Green, D. L., Payne, L., Stevenson, J. L., Bowden, E. M., et al. (2008). The origins of insight in resting-state brain activity. *Neuropsychologia, 46,* 281–291.

Kovacs, A. M., & Mehler, J. (2009, July 31). Flexible learning of multiple speech structures in bilingual infants. *Science, 325,* 611–612.

Kovelman, I., Baker, S. A., & Petitto, L. A. (2008). Bilingual and monolingual brains compared: A functional magnetic resonance imaging investigation of synatictic processing and a possible "neural signature" of bilingualism. *Journal of Cognitive Neuroscience, 20*(1), 153–169.

Kovelman, I., Shalinsky, M. H., Berens, M. S., & Petitto, L. A. (2008). Shining new light on the brain's "bilingual signature": A functional Near Infrared Spectroscopy investigation of semantic processing. *Neuroimage, 39,* 1457–1471.

Kowalik, J., Weller, J., Venter, J., & Drachman, D. (2011). Cognitive behavioral therapy for the treatment of pediatric posttraumatic stress disorder: A review and meta-analysis. *Journal of Behavior Therapy and Experimental Psychiatry, 42,* 405–413.

Kowert, P. A. (2002). *Groupthink or deadlock: When do leaders learn from their advisors? SUNY Series on the presidency*. Albany: State University of New York Press.

Kozaric-Kovacic, D., & Borovecki, A. (2005). Prevalence of psychotic comorbidity in combat-related post-traumatic stress disorder. *Military Medicine, 170,* 223–226.

Kozulin, A., Gindis, B., Ageyev, V. S., & Miller, S. M. (2003). *Vygotsky's educational theory in cultural context*. New York: Cambridge University Press.

Kramer, P. (1993). *Listening to Prozac*. New York: Viking.

Kreher, D., Holcomb, P., Goff, D., & Kuperberg, G. (2008). Neural evidence for faster and further automatic spreading activation in schizophrenic thought disorder. *Schizophrenia Bulletin, 34,* 473–482.

Kreppner, J., Rutter, M., Marvin, R., O'Connor, T., & Sonuga-Barke, E. (2011). Assessing the concept of the 'insecure-other' category in the Cassidy-Marvin scheme: Changes between 4 and 6 years in the English and Romanian adoptee study. *Social Development, 20,* 1–16.

Kreuger, A. (2007). Are we having fun yet? Categorizing and evaluating changes in time allocation. *Brookings Papers on Economic Activity*, (Vol. 2), 38, 193–218.

Krijn, M., Emmelkamp, P. M. G., Olafsson, R. P., & Biemond, R. (2004). Virtual reality exposure therapy of anxiety disorders: A review. *Clinical Psychology Review, 24,* 259–281.

Krishman, S., Cairns, R., & Howard, R. (2009). Cannabinoids for the treatment of dementia. *Cochrane Database of Systematic Reviews*. Retrieved from http://www.ncbi.nlm.nih.gov/pubmed/19370677

Krueger, K., & Dayan, P. (2009). Flexible shaping: How learning in small steps helps. *Cognition, 110,* 380–394.

Krueger, R. G., Hicks, B. M., & McGue, M. (2001). Altruism and antisocial behavior: Independent tendencies, unique personality correlates, distinct etiologies. *Psychological Science, 12,* 397–402.

Krumhuber, E. G., & Scherer, K. R. (2011). Affect bursts: Dynamic patterns of facial expression. *Emotion, 11,* 825–841.

Krusemark, E., Campbell, W., & Clementz, B. (2008). Attributions, deception, and event related potentials: An investigation of the self-serving bias. *Psychophysiology, 45,* 511–515.

Ku, L., St. Louis, M., Farshy, C., Aral, S., Turner, C. F., Lindberg, L. D., et al. (2002). Risk behaviors, medical care, and chlamydial infection among young men in the United States. *American Journal of Public Health, 92,* 1140–1143.

Kübler-Ross, E. (1969). *On death and dying*. New York: Macmillan.

Kubovy, M., Epstein, W., & Gepshtein, S. (2003). Foundations of visual perception. In A. F. Healy & R. W. Proctor (Eds.), *Handbook of psychology: Experimental psychology* (Vol. 4). New York: Wiley.

Kumar, S., Ruchi, R., James, S. R., & Chidiac, E. J. (2011). Gene therapy for chronic neuropathic pain: How does it work and where do we stand today? *Pain Medicine, 12,* 808–822.

Kumari, S., & Joshi, S. (2013). Neonatal outcomes in women with depression during pregnancy. *Journal of Projective Psychology & Mental Health, 20,* 141–145.

Kuncel, N. R., & Beatty, A. S. (2013). Thinking at work: Intelligence, critical thinking, job knowledge, and reasoning. In K. F. Geisinger, B. A. Bracken, J. F. Carlson, J. C. Hansen, N. R. Kuncel, S. P. Reise, & M. C. Rodriguez (Eds.), *APA handbook of testing and assessment in psychology, Vol. 1: Test theory and testing and assessment in industrial and organizational psychology*. Washington, DC: American Psychological Association.

Kuo, L. J. (2007). Effects of bilingualism on development of facets of phonological competence (China). *Dissertation Abstracts International Section A: Humanities and Social Sciences, 67*(11-A), 4095.

Kupfer, D. J., Kuhl, E. A., & Regier, D. A. (2013). DSM-5–The future arrived. *JAMA: Journal of the American Medical Association, 309,* 1691–1692.

Kuppens, P., Ceulemans, E., Timmerman, M. E., Diener, E., & Kim-Prieto, C. (2006). Universal intracultural and intercultural dimensions of the recalled frequency of emotional experience. *Journal of Cross Cultural Psychology, 37,* 491–515.

Kurdziel, L., Duclos, K., & Spencer, R. M. C. (2013). Sleep spindles in midday naps enhance learning in preschool children. *PNAS Early Edition*, 1–6.

Kuriyama, K., Stickgold, R., & Walker, M. P. (2004). Sleep-dependent learning and motor-skill complexity. *Learning and Memory, 11,* 705–713.

Kuther, T. L. (2003). *Your career in psychology: Psychology and the law*. New York: Wadsworth.

Kwang, T., Crockett, E. E., Sanchez, D. T., & Swann, W. B., Jr. (2013). Men seek social standing, women seek companionship: Sex differences in deriving self-worth from relationships. *Psychological Science, 24,* 1142–1150.

Kwate, N. O. A. (2001). Intelligence or misorientation? Eurocentrism in the WISC-III. *Journal of Black Psychology, 27,* 221–239.

Kwon, K., Bingham, G., Lewsader, J., Jeon, H., & Elicker, J. (2013). Structured task versus free play: The influence of social context on parenting quality, toddlers' engagement with parents and play behaviors, and parent-toddler language use. *Child & Youth Care Forum, 42,* 207–224.

Kwon, P., & Laurenceau, J. P. (2002). A longitudinal study of the hopelessness theory of depression: Testing the diathesis- stress model within a differential reactivity and exposure framework [Special issue: Reprioritizing the role of science in a realistic version of the scientist- practitioner model]. *Journal of Clinical Psychology, 50,* 1305–1321.

Kyaga, S., Landén, M., Boman, M., Hultman, C. M., Långström, N., & Lichtenstein, P. (2013). Mental illness, suicide and creativity: 40-year prospective total population study. *Journal of Psychiatric Research, 47,* 83–90.

Laas, I. (2006). Self-actualization and society: A new application for an old theory. *Journal of Humanistic Psychology, 46,* 77–91.

LaBar, K. (2007). Beyond fear: Emotional memory mechanisms in the human brain. *Current Directions in Psychological Science, 16,* 173–177.

Lacerda, F., von Hofsten, C., & Heimann, M. (2001). *Emerging cognitive abilities in early infancy.* Mahwah, NJ: Lawrence Erlbaum Associates.

Lacey, M. (2002, January 6). In Kenyan family, ritual for girls still divides. *The New York Times,* p. 6.

Laederach-Hofmann, K., & Messerli-Buergy, N. (2007). Chest pain, angina pectoris, panic disorder, and Syndrome X. In J. Jordan, B. Barde, & A. M. Zeiher (Eds.), *Contributions toward evidence-based psychocardiology: A systematic review of the literature.* Washington, DC: American Psychological Association.

LaFrance, M., & Harris, J. L. (2004). Gender and verbal and nonverbal communication. In M. A. Paludi (Ed.), *Praeger guide to the psychology of gender.* Westport, CT: Praeger Publishers/ Greenwood Publishing Group.

Lagacé-Séguin, D. G., & d'Entremont, M. L. (2006). The role of child negative affect in the relations between parenting styles and play. *Early Child Development and Care, 176,* 461–477.

Lahti, J., Räikkönen, K., Ekelund, J., Peltonen, L., Raitakari, O. T., & Keltikangas-Järvinen, L. (2005). Novelty seeking: Interaction between parental alcohol use and dopamine D4 receptor gene exon III polymorphism over 17 years. *Psychiatric Genetics, 15,* 133–139.

Laing, R. D., & Szasz, T. (2004). "Knowing what ain't so." *Psychoanalytic Review, 91,* 331–346.

Lal, S. (2002). Giving children security: Mamie Phipps Clark and the racialization of child psychology. *American Psychologist, 57,* 20–28.

Lalasz, C. B., & Weigel, D. J. (2011). Understanding the relationship between gender and extradyadic relations: The mediating role of sensation seeking on intentions to engage in sexual infidelity. *Personality and Individual Differences, 50,* 1079–1083.

LaLumiere, R. T., & Kalivas, P. W. (2013). Motivational systems: Rewards and incentive value. In R. J. Nelson, S. Y. Mizumori, & I. B. Weiner (Eds.), *Handbook of psychology, Vol. 3: Behavioral neuroscience* (2nd ed.). New York: John Wiley & Sons Ltd.

Lamal, P. A. (1979). College students' common beliefs about psychology. *Teaching of Psychology, 6,* 155–158.

Lamb, M. E., & Garretson, M. E. (2003). The effects of interviewer gender and child gender on the informativeness of alleged child sexual abuse victims in forensic interviews. *Law and Human Behavior, 27,* 157–171.

Lamborn, S. D., & Groh, K. (2009). A four-part model of autonomy during emerging adulthood: Associations with adjustment. *International Journal of Behavioral Development, 33,* 393–401.

Lampard, A. M., Byrne, S. M., McLean, N., & Fursland, A. (2011). An evaluation of the enhanced cognitive-behavioural model of bulimia nervosa. *Behaviour Research and Therapy, 49,* 529–535.

Lanciano, T., Curci, A., Mastandrea, S., & Sartori, G. (2013). Do automatic mental associations detect a flashbulb memory? *Memory, 21,* 482–493.

Landro, L. (2010, May 11). New ways to treat pain. *Wall Street Journal,* p. D1–D2.

Landro, L. (2011, April 26). 'Use only as direct' isn't easy. *Wall Street Journal,* p. D1–D2.

Landry, S. H., Zucker, T. A., Taylor, H. B., Swank, P. R., Williams, J. M., Assel, M., & . . . Klein, A. (2013). Enhancing Early Child Care Quality and Learning for Toddlers at Risk: The Responsive Early Childhood Program. *Developmental Psychology,* Retrieved from http://www.ncbi.nlm.nih.gov/pubmed/23772822

Lane, K. A., Banaji, M. R., Nosek, B. A., & Greenwald, A. G. (Eds.). (2007). Understanding and using the implicit association test: IV: What we know (so far) about the method. In B. Wittenbrink & N. Schwarz (Eds.), *Implicit measures of attitudes.* New York: Guilford Press.

Lane, S. D., Cherek, D. R., & Tcheremissine, O. V. (2007). Response perseveration and adaptation in heavy marijuana-smoking adolescents. *Addictive Behaviors, 32,* 977–990.

Lang, A. J., Sorrell, J. T., & Rodgers, C. S. (2006). Anxiety sensitivity as a predictor of labor pain. *European Journal of Pain, 10,* 263–270.

Lang, P. J., & Bradley, M. M. (2013). Appetitive and defensive motivation: Goal-directed or goal-determined? *Emotion Review, 5,* 230–234.

Langan-Fox, J., & Grant, S. (2006). The Thematic Apperception Test: Toward a standard measure of the big three motives. *Journal of Personality Assessment, 87,* 277–291.

Langdridge, D., & Butt, T. (2004). The fundamental attribution error: A phenomenological critique. *British Journal of Social Psychology, 43,* 357–369.

Langlois, F., Langlois, M., Carpentier, A. C., Brown, C., Lemieux, S., & Hivert, M. (2011). Ghrelin levels are associated with hunger as measured by the Three-Factor Eating Questionnaire in healthy young adults. *Physiology & Behavior, 104,* 373–377.

Langreth, R. (2000, May 1). Every little bit helps: How even moderate exercise can have a big impact on your health. *The Wall Street Journal,* p. R5.

Lankov, A. (2004). The dawn of modern Korea: Changes for better or worse. *The Korea Times,* p. A1.

Lanza, S. T., & Collins, L. M. (2002). Pubertal timing and the onset of substance use in females during early adolescence. *Prevention Science, 3,* 69–82.

LaPointe, L. L. (2013). *Paul Broca and the origins of language in the brain.* San Diego, CA: Plural Publishing.

Laqueur, T. W. (2003). *Solitary sex: A cultural history of masturbation.* New York: Zone.

Larsen, R. J., & Buss, D. M. (2006). *Personality psychology: Domains of knowledge about human nature with PowerWeb* (2nd ed.). New York: McGraw-Hill.

Lascaratos, G., Ji, D., & Wood, J. P. (2007). Visible light affects mitochondrial function and induces neuronal death in retinal cell cultures. *Vision Research, 47,* 1191–1201.

Latané, B., & Darley, J. M. (1970). *The unresponsive bystander: Why doesn't he help?* New York: Appleton-Century-Crofts.

Laugharne, J., Janca, A., & Widiger, T. (2007). Posttraumatic stress disorder and terrorism: 5 years after 9/11. *Current Opinion in Psychiatry, 20,* 36–41.

Laumann, E. O., Paik, A., & Rosen, R. C. (1999, February 10). Sexual dysfunction in the United States: Prevalence and predictors. *Journal of the American Medical Association, 281,* 537–544.

Lavazza, A., & Manzotti, R. (2013). An externalist approach to creativity: Discovery versus recombination. *Mind & Society, 12,* 61–72

Laven, A. (2008). Freshmen college student mental health and their resource usage. *Dissertation Abstracts International Section A: Humanities and Social Sciences, 69,* 136.

Lavenex, P., & Lavenex, P. (2009). Spatial memory and the monkey hippocampus: Not all space is created equal. *Hippocampus, 19,* 8–19.

Lawrence, J., Ashford, K., & Dent, Paul. (2006). Gender differences in coping strategies of undergraduate students and their impact on self-esteem and attainment. *Active Learning in Higher Education, 7,* 273–281.

Lazarus, A. A. (1997). *Brief but comprehensive psychotherapy: The multimodal way.* New York: Springer.

Lazarus, R. S. (1995). Emotions express a social relationship, but it is an individual mind that creates them. *Psychological Inquiry, 6,* 253–265.

Le Maner-Idrissi, G., & Renault, L. (2006). Développement du 'schéma de genre': Une asymétrie entre filles et garçons? Are there sex differences in the acquisition of a gender schema? *Enfance, 58,* 251–265.

Leahey, T., Kumar, R., Weinberg, B., & Wing, R. (2012). Teammates and social influence affect weight loss outcomes in a team-based weight loss competition. *Obesity, 20,* 1413–1418.

Leaper, C., & Ayres, M. (2007). A meta-analytic review of gender variations in adults' language use: Talkativeness, affiliative speech, and assertive speech. *Personality and Social Psychology Review, 11,* 328–363.

Leaper, C., & Friedman, C. K. (2007). The socialization of gender. In J. E. Grusec & P. D. Hastings (Eds.), *Handbook of socialization: Theory and research.* New York: Guilford Press.

Leaper, C., Brown, C., & Ayres, M. M. (2013). Adolescent girls' cognitive appraisals of coping responses to sexual harassment. *Psychology in the Schools, 50,* 969–986.

Leary, C., Kelley, M., Morrow, J., & Mikulka, P. (2008). Parental use of physical punishment as related to family environment, psychological well-being, and personality in undergraduates. *Journal of Family Violence, 23,* 1–7.

Leckman, J. F., & King, R. A. (2007). A developmental perspective on the controversy surrounding the use of SSRIs to treat pediatric depression. *American Journal of Psychiatry, 164,* 1304–1306.

Leclair-Visonneau, L., Oudiette, D., Gaymard, B., Leu-Semenescu, S., & Arnulf, I. (2011). 'Do the eyes scan dream images during rapid eye movement sleep? Evidence from the rapid eye movement sleep behaviour disorder model': Corrigendum. *Brain: A Journal of Neurology, 134*, 88-97.

Lee-Chai, A. Y., & Bargh, J. A. (Eds.). (2001). *The use and abuse of power: Multiple perspectives on the causes of corruption.* Philadelphia, PA: Psychology Press.

Lee-Chiong, T. L. (2006). *Sleep: A comprehensive handbook.* New York: Wiley-Liss.

Lee, A. Y., & Aaker, J. L. (2004). Bringing the frame into focus: The influence of regulatory fit on processing fluency and persuasion. *Journal of Personality and Social Psychology, 86*, 205-218.

Lee, A., Isaac, M., & Janca, A. (2007). Posttraumatic stress disorder and terrorism. In A. Monat, R. S. Lazarus, & G. Reevy (Eds.), *The Praeger handbook on stress and coping* (Vol. 1). Westport, CT: Praeger Publishers/Greenwood Publishing Group.

Lee, D., Kleinman, J., & Kleinman, A. (2007). Rethinking depression: An ethnographic study of the experiences of depression among Chinese. *Harvard Review of Psychiatry, 15*, 1-8.

Lee, E., & Troop-Gordon, W. (2011). Peer processes and gender role development: Changes in gender atypicality related to negative peer treatment and children's friendships. *Sex Roles, 64*, 90-102.

Lee, F. H., & Raja, S. N. (2011). Complementary and alternative medicine in chronic pain. *Pain, 152*, 28-30.

Lee, H. J., & Kwon, S. M. (2003). Two different types of obsession: Autogenous obsessions and reactive obsessions. *Behaviour Research & Therapy, 41*, 11-29.

Lee, H. J., Kwon, S. M., Kwon, J. S., & Telch, M. J. (2005). Testing the autogenous reactive model of obsessions. *Depress Anxiety, 21*, 118-129.

Leeman, R. F., Fischler, C., & Rozin, P. (2011). Medical doctors' attitudes and beliefs about diet and health are more like those of their lay countrymen (France, Germany, Italy, UK and USA) than those of doctors in other countries. *Appetite, 56*, 558-563.

Lefaucheur, I., Wendling, S., Pommier, M., & Bellivier, E. (2007). The value of navigation-guided rTMS for the treatment of depression: An illustrative case. *Neurophysiologic Clinics, 37*, 265-271.

Lehrer, J. (2012, April 13). When memory commits an injustice. *Wall Street Journal*, p. C18.

Lehman, D. R., & Taylor, S. E. (1988). Date with an earthquake: Coping with a probable, unpredictable disaster. *Personality and Social Psychology Bulletin, 13*, 546-555.

Lehrman, S. (2007). Going beyond X and Y. *Scientific American*, pp. 40-41.

Leib, J. R., Gollust, S. E., Hull, S. C., & Wilfond, B. S. (2005). Carrier screening panels for Ashkenazi Jews: Is more better? *Genetic Medicine, 7*, 185-190.

Leibel, R. L., Rosenbaum, M., & Hirsch, J. (1995, March 9). Changes in energy expenditure resulting from altered body. *New England Journal of Medicine, 332*, 621-628.

Leiblum, S. R., & Chivers, M. L. (2007). Normal and persistent genital arousal in women: New perspectives. *Journal of Sex & Marital Therapy, 33*, 357-373.

Leigh, J. H., Zinkhan, G. M., & Swaminathan, V. (2006). Dimensional relationships of recall and recognition measures with selected cognitive and affective aspects of print ads. *Journal of Advertising, 35*, 105-122.

Leiter, S., & Leiter, W. M. (2003). *Affirmative action in antidiscrimination law and policy: An overview and synthesis. SUNY series in American constitutionalism.* Albany: State University of New York Press.

Leitner, L. M. (2007). Diversity issues, postmodernism, and psychodynamic therapy. *PsycCRITIQUES, 52*, no pagination specified.

Lemay, E. P., Jr., Clark, M. S., & Feeney, B. C. (2007). Projection of responsiveness to needs and the construction of satisfying communal relationships. *Journal of Personality and Social Psychology, 92*, 834-853.

Lemay, E., & Clark, M. (2008). How the head liberates the heart: Projection of communal responsiveness guides relationship promotion. *Journal of Personality and Social Psychology, 94*, 647-671.

Lemogne, C., Consoli, S. M., Geoffroy-Perez, B., Coeuret-Pellicer, M., Nabi, H., Melchior, M., & . . . Cordier, S. (2013). Personality and the risk of cancer: A 16-year follow-up study of the GAZEL cohort. *Psychosomatic Medicine, 75*, 262-271.

Lenhart, A. (2009, January 14). *Adults and social network websites.* Washington, DC: Pew Internet & American Life Project.

Lenzenweger, M. F., & Dworkin, R. H. (Eds.). (1998). *The origins and development of schizophrenia: Advances in experimental psychopathology.* Washington, DC: American Psychological Association.

Leo, R. J., & Latif, T. (2007). Repetitive transcranial magnetic stimulation (rTMS) in experimentally induced and chronic neuropathic pain: A review. *The Journal of Pain, 8*, 453-459.

Leonard, E. (2009, May 18). Kirstie Alley: I've let myself go. *People*, p. 50.

Lepage, J. F., & Theoret, H. (2007). The mirror neuron system: grasping others' actions from birth? *Developmental Science, 10*, 513-523.

Leppänen, J. M., Moulson, M. C., Vogel-Farley, V. K., & Nelson, C. A. (2007). An ERP study of emotional face processing in the adult and infant brain. *Child Development, 78*, 232-245.

Lepper, M. R., Corpus, J. H., & Iyengar, S. S. (2005). Intrinsic and extrinsic motivational orientations in the classroom: Age differences and academic correlates. *Journal of Educational Psychology, 97*, 184-196.

Leung, E. K. S. (2002). Behind the high achievement of East Asian students [Special issue: Achievements in mathematics and science in an international context]. *Education Research and Evaluation, 8*, 87-108.

Leuthardt, E. C., Gaona, C., Sharma, M., Szrama, N., Roland, J., Freudenberg, Z., Solis, J., Breshears, J., & Schalk, G. (2011). Using the electrocorticographic speech network to control a brain-computer interface in humans. *Journal of Neural Engineering, 8*, 332-339.

Leuthardt, E. C., Roland, J., Breshears, J., Bandt, S. K., & Shimony, J. S. (2013). Listening to the brain: new techniques in intraoperative brain mapping. *Neurosurgery, 60*, 64-69.

LeVay, S. (1993). *The sexual brain.* Cambridge, MA: MIT.

LeVay, S. (2011). *Gay, straight, and the reason why: The science of sexual orientation.* New York: Oxford University Press.

Levi, A., Chan, K. K., & Pence, D. (2006). Real men do not read labels: The effects of masculinity and involvement on college students' food decisions. *Journal of American College Health, 55*, 91-98.

Levin, B. E. (2006). Metabolic sensing neurons and the control of energy homeostasis. *Physiology & Behavior, 89*, 486-489.

Levin, R. J. (2007). Sexual activity, health and well-being–the beneficial roles of coitus and masturbation. *Sexual and Relationship Therapy, 22*, 135-148.

Levin, R., & Nielsen, T. (2009, April). Nightmares, bad dreams, and emotion dysregulation: A review and new neurocognitive model of dreaming. *Current Directions in Psychological Science, 18*, 84-88.

Levine, J. M., & Moreland, R. L. (2006). Small groups: An overview. In J. M. Levine & R. L. Moreland (Eds.), *Small groups.* New York: Psychology Press.

Levine, L. E., & Munsch, J. (2011). *Child development: An active learning approach.* Thousand Oaks, CA: Sage Publications, Inc.

Levine, S. Z. (2011). Elaboration on the association between IQ and parental SES with subsequent crime. *Personality and Individual Differences, 50*, 1233-1237.

Levine, S. Z., & Rabinowitz, J. (2007). Revisiting the 5 dimensions of the Positive and Negative Syndrome Scale. *Journal of Clinical Psychopharmacology, 27*, 431-436.

Levinson, D. (1992). *The seasons of a woman's life.* New York: Knopf.

Levinson, D. J. (1990). A theory of life structure development in adulthood. In C. N. Alexander & E. J. Langer (Eds.), *Higher stages of human development: Perspectives on adult growth.* New York: Oxford University Press.

Levy, B. (1996). Improving memory in old age through implicit self-stereotyping. *Journal of Personality and Social Psychology, 71*, 1092-1107.

Levy, B. R., & Myers, L. M. (2004). Preventive health behaviors influenced by self-perceptions of aging. *Preventive Medicine: An International Journal Devoted to Practice and Theory, 39*, 625-629.

Levy, B. R., Slade, M. D., Kunkel, S. R., & Kasl, S. V. (2002). Longevity increased by positive self-perceptions of aging. *Journal of Personality & Social Psychology, 83*, 261-270.

Lewin, T. (2003, December 22). For more people in their 20s and 30s, going home is easier because they never left. *The New York Times*, p. A27.

Lewinsohn, P. M., & Essau, C. A. (2002). Depression in adolescents. In I. H. Gotlib & C. L. Hammen (Eds.), *Handbook of depression.* New York: Guilford Press.

Lewinsohn, P. M., Petit, J. W., Joiner, T. E., Jr., & Seeley, J. R. (2003). The symptomatic expression of major depressive disorder in adolescents and young adults. *Journal of Abnormal Psychology, 112*, 244-252.

Lewis, C., & Lamb, M. (2011). The role of parent-child relationships in child development. In M. E. Lamb & M. H. Bornstein (Eds.), *Social and personality development: An advanced textbook.* New York: Psychology Press.

Li, B., Piriz, J., Mirrione, M., Chung, C., Proulx, C. D., Schulz, D., & . . . Malinow, R. (2011). Synaptic potentiation onto habenula neurons in learned helplessness model of depression. *Nature, 470*, 535-539.

Li, J. (2005). Mind or virtue: Western and Chinese beliefs about learning. *Current Directions in Psychological Science, 14*, 190-194.

Li, J., Wang, L., & Fischer, K. W. (2004). The organization of Chinese shame concepts. *Cognition and Emotion, 18*, 767-797.

Li, J., Zhou, G., Ji, W., Feng, G., Zhao, Q., Liu, J., & . . . Shi, Y. (2011). Common variants in the BCL9 gene conferring risk of schizophrenia. *Archives of General Psychiatry, 68*, 232-240.

Li, M. D., Cheng, R., Ma, J. Z., & Swan, G. E. (2003). A meta-analysis of estimated genetic and environmental effects on smoking behavior in male and female adult twins. *Addiction, 98,* 23-31.

Li, M. D., Lou, X., Chen, G., Ma, J. Z., & Elston, R. C. (2008). Gene-gene interactions among CHRNA4, CHRNB2, BDNF, and NTRK2 in nicotine dependence. *Biological Psychiatry, 64,* 951-957.

Li, T. K., Volkow, N. D., & Balu, R. D. (2007). The biological bases of nicotine and alcohol co-addiction. *Biological Psychiatry, 61,* 1-3.

Li, X., Wang, M., Poliakoff, E., & Luo, Y. (2007). Attention to threat in high and low trait-anxious individuals: A study using extremely threatening pictorial cues. *Perceptual and Motor Skills, 104,* 1097-1106.

Liang, K. A. (2007). Acculturation, ambivalent sexism, and attitudes toward women who engage in premarital sex among Chinese American young adults. *Dissertation Abstracts International: Section B: The Sciences and Engineering,* 67(10-B), 6065.

Libedinsky, C., & Livingstone, M. (2011). Role of prefrontal cortex in conscious visual perception. *The Journal of Neuroscience, 31,* 64-69.

Liben, L. S., & Bigler, R. S. (2002). The development course of gender differentiations: Conceptualizing, measuring, and evaluation constructs and pathways. *Monographs of the Society for Research in Child Development, 67,* 148-167.

Lick, D. J., Durso, L. E., & Johnson, K. L. (2013). Minority stress and physical health among sexual minorities. *Perspectives on Psychological Science, 8,* 521-548.

Lickiesh, M. (1921, June 6). Visual illusions in the arts. *Scientific American Monthly, 3(6).*

Licis, A. K., Desruisseau, D. M., Yamada, K. A., Duntley, S. P., & Gurnett, C. A. (2011). Novel genetic findings in an extended family pedigree with sleepwalking. *Neurology, 76,* 49-52.

Lidz, J., & Gleitman, L. R. (2004). Argument structure and the child's contribution to language learning. *Trends in Cognitive Sciences, 8,* 157-161.

Lieberman, M. D. (2007). Social cognitive neuroscience: A review of core processes. *Annual Review of Psychology, 58,* 259-289.

Lieberman, M. D., Hariri, A., Jarcho, J. M., Eisenberger, N. I., & Bookheimer, S. Y. (2005). An fMRI investigation of race-related amygdala activity in African-American and Caucasian-American individuals. *Nature Neuroscience, 8,* 720-722.

Liedl, A., Müller, J., Morina, N., Karl, A., Denke, C., & Knaevelsrud, C. (2011). Physical activity within a CBT intervention improves coping with pain in traumatized refugees: results of a randomized controlled design. *Pain Medicine, 12,* 138-145.

Lien, Y. W., Chu, R. L., Jen, C. H., & Wu, C. H. (2006). Do Chinese commit neither fundamental attribution error nor ultimate attribution error? *Chinese Journal of Psychology, 48,* 163-181.

Lilienfeld, S. O. (2007). Psychological treatments that cause harm. *Perspectives on Psychological Science, 2,* 53-58.

Lilienfeld, S. O., Lynn, S. J., & Lohr, J. M. (2003). Dissociative identity disorder: Multiple personalities, multiple controversies. In S. O. Lilienfeld & S. J. Lynn (Eds.), *Science and pseudoscience in clinical psychology.* New York: Guilford Press.

Lilienfeld, S. O. (2012). Further sources of our field's embattled public reputation. *American Psychologist,* 808-809.

Lin, C. H., & Lin, H. M. (2007). What price do you ask for the 'extra one'? A social value orientation perspective. *Social Behavior and Personality, 35,* 9-18.

Lin, Y. Y., Chen, W. T., Liao, K. K., Yeh, T. C., Wu, Z. Z., & Ho, L. T. (2005). Hemispheric balance in coding speech and non-speech sounds in Chinese participants. *Neuroreport, 16,* 469-473.

Lin, Y., Li, K., Sung, W., Ko, H., Tzeng, O. L., Hung, D. L., & Juan, C. (2011). The relationship between development of attention and learning in children: A cognitive neuroscience approach. *Bulletin of Educational Psychology, 42,* 517-542.

Lindblad, F., Lindahl, M., & Theorell, T. (2006). Physiological stress reactions in 6th and 9th graders during test performance. *Stress and Health: Journal of the International Society for the Investigation of Stress, 22,* 189-195.

Lindemann, O., & Bekkering, H. (2009). Object manipulation and motion perception: Evidence of an influence of action planning on visual processing. *Journal of Experimental Psychology: Human Perception and Performance, 35,* 1062-1071.

Lindh-Astrand, L., Brynhildsen, J., & Hoffmann, M. (2007). Attitudes towards the menopause and hormone therapy over the turn of the century. *Maturitas, 56,* 12-20.

Lindley, L. D. (2006). The paradox of self-efficacy: Research with diverse populations. *Journal of Career Assessment, 14,* 143-160.

Lindorff, M. (2005). Determinants of received social support: Who gives what to managers? *Journal of Social and Personal Relationships, 22,* 323-337.

Lindsay, P. H., & Norman, D. A. (1977). *Human information processing* (2nd ed.). New York: Academic Press.

Lindsay, P., Maynard, I., & Thomas, O. (2005). Effects of hypnosis on flow states and cycling performance. *Sport Psychologist, 19,* 164-177.

Lindsey, E., & Colwell, M. (2003). Preschoolers' emotional competence: Links to pretend and physical play. *Child Study Journal, 33,* 39-52.

Linley, P. (2013). Human strengths and well-being: Finding the best within us at the intersection of eudaimonic philosophy, humanistic psychology, and positive psychology. In A. S. Waterman (Ed.), *The best within us: Positive psychology perspectives on eudaimonia.* Washington, DC: American Psychological Association.

Lippa, R. A. (2005). *Gender, nature, and nurture* (2nd ed.). Mahwah, NJ: Erlbaum.

Lips, H. M. (2003). *A new psychology of women: Gender, culture, and ethnicity.* New York: McGraw-Hill.

Liszkowski, U., Schäfer, M., Carpenter, M., & Tomasello, M. (2009). Prelinguistic infants, but not chimpanzees, communicate about absent entities. *Psychological Science, 20,* 654-660.

Litowitz, B. E. (2007). Unconscious fantasy: A once and future concept. *Journal of the American Psychoanalytic Association, 55,* 199-228.

Little, A., Burt, D. M., & Perrett, D. I. (2006). What is good is beautiful: Face preference reflects desired personality. *Personality and Individual Differences, 41,* 1107-1118.

Little, K., Ramssen, E., Welchko, R., Volberg, V., Roland, C., & Cassin, B. (2009). Decreased brain dopamine cell numbers in human cocaine users. *Psychiatry Research, 168,* 173-180.

Liu, C., Tardif, T., Wu, H., Monk, C. S., Luo, Y. J., & Mai, X. (2013). The representation of category typicality in the frontal cortex and its cross-linguistic variations. *Brain and Language, 127*(3), 415-427.

Liu, H., Liu, M., Wang, Y., Wang, X., Qiu, Y., Long, J., & Zhang, S. (2011). Association of 5-HTT gene polymorphisms with migraine: A systematic review and meta-analysis. *Journal of the Neurological Sciences, 305,* 57-66.

Liu, J. H., & Mills, D. (2006). Modern racism and neoliberal globalization: The discourses of plausible deniability and their multiple functions. *Journal of Community & Applied Social Psychology, 16,* 83-99.

Liu, L., He, S-Z., & Wu, Y. (2007). An analysis of the characteristics of single parent families with different structures and their children. *Chinese Journal of Clinical Psychology, 15,* 68-70.

Livesley, W., & Jang, K. (2008). The behavioral genetics of personality disorder. *Annual Review of Clinical Psychology, 4,* 247-274.

Livingstone, A. G., Spears, R., Manstead, A. R., Bruder, M., & Shepherd, L. (2011). We feel, therefore we are: Emotion as a basis for self-categorization and social action. *Emotion, 11,* 754-767.

Lobato, M. I., Koff, W. J., & Manenti, C. (2006). Follow-up of sex reassignment surgery in transsexuals: A Brazilian cohort. *Archives of Sexual Behavior, 35,* 711-715.

Lobban, F., Barrowclough, C., & Jones, S. (2006). Does expressed emotion need to be understood within a more systemic framework? An examination of discrepancies in appraisals between patients diagnosed with schizophrenia and their relatives. *Social Psychiatry and Psychiatric Epidemiology, 41,* 50-55.

Lobo, I., & Harris, R. (2008, July). $GABA_a$ receptors and alcohol. *Pharmacology, Biochemistry and Behavior, 90,* 90-94.

Locicero, A., & Sinclair, S. (2008, March). Terrorism and terrorist leaders: Insights from developmental and ecological psychology. *Studies in Conflict & Terrorism, 31,* 227-250.

Lockl, K., & Schneider, W. (2007). Knowledge about the mind: Links between theory of mind and later metamemory. *Child Development, 78,* 148-167.

Lofholm, N. (2003, May 6). Climber's kin share relief: Ralston saw 4 options, they say; death wasn't one of them. *Denver Post,* p. A1.

Loftus, E. F. (1993). Psychologists in the eyewitness world. *American Psychologist, 48,* 550-552.

Loftus, E. F., & Bernstein, D. M. (2005). Rich false memories: The royal road to success. In A. F. Healy (Ed.), *Experimental cognitive psychology and its applications.* Washington, DC: American Psychological Association.

Loftus, E. F., & Palmer, J. C. (1974). Reconstruction of automobile destruction: An example of the interface between language and memory. *Journal of Verbal Learning and Verbal Behavior, 13,* 585-589.

Loitfelder, M. M., Fazekas, F. F., Petrovic, K. K., Fuchs, S. S., Ropele, S. S., Wallner-Blazek, M. M., & . . . Enzinger, C. C. (2011). Reorganization in cognitive networks with progression of multiple sclerosis: Insights from fMRI. *Neurology, 76,* 526-533.

London, B. (2013, October 16). From a child bride who was circumcised at five to woman of the year: Extraordinary story of Somali supermodel who starred in James Bond film. Mail Online. Retrieved from http://www.dailymail.co.uk/femail/article-2461477/Waris-Dirie-fights-female-circumcision-receives-Woman-Year-Campaigning-award.html

Lopes, A. C., Greenberg, B. D., Noren, G., Canteras, M. M., Busatto, G. F. de Mathis, et al. (2009). Treatment of resistant obsessive-compulsive disorder with ventral capsular/ventral striatal gamma capsulotomy: A pilot prospective study. *The Journal of Neuropsychiatry and Clinical Neurosciences, 21,* 381–392.

López, S. R., & Guarnaccia, P. J. (2005). Cultural dimensions of psychopathology: The social world's impact on mental illness. In J. E. Maddux & B. A. Winstead (Eds.), *Foundations for a contemporary understanding.* Mahwah, NJ: Lawrence Erlbaum Associates.

López, S. R., & Guarnaccia, P. J. J. (2000). Cultural psychopathology: Uncovering the social world of mental illness. *Annual Review of Psychology, 51,* 571–598.

Lorenz, K. (1966). *On aggression.* New York: Harcourt Brace Jovanovich.

Lorenz, K. (1974). *Civilized man's eight deadly sins.* New York: Harcourt Brace Jovanovich.

Lothane, Z. (2005). Jung, A biography. *Journal of the American Psychoanalytic Association, 53,* 317–324.

Love, Dylan (2013, October 21). IBM's Watson supercomputer is becoming the best cancer doctor in the world. Retrieved from www.businessinsider.com/ibm-watson-cancer-2013-10

Loving, T., Crockett, E., & Paxson, A. (2009). Passionate love and relationship thinkers: Experimental evidence for acute cortisol elevations in women. *Psychoneuroendocrinology, 34,* 939–946.

Lowe, P., Humphreys, C., & Williams, S. J. (2007). Night terrors: Women's experiences of (not) sleeping where there is domestic violence. *Violence against Women, 13,* 549–561.

Lowery, D., Fillingim, R. B., & Wright, R. A. (2003). Sex differences and incentive effects on perceptual and cardiovascular responses to cold pressor pain. *Psychosomatic Medicine, 65,* 284–291.

Lu, J., Sherman, D., Devor, M., & Saper, C. B. (2006). A putative flip-flop switch for control of REM sleep. *Nature, 441,* 589–594.

Lubell, K. M., Swahn, M. H., Crosby, A. E., & Kegler, S. R. (2004). Methods of suicide among persons aged 10–19 years–United States, 1992–2001. *MMWR, 53,* 471–473. Retrieved from http://www.cdc.gov/ mmwr/PDF/wk/mm5322.pdf

Lubinski, D., & Benbow, C. P. (2006). Study of mathematically precocious youth after 35 years: Uncovering antecedents for the development of math-science expertise. *Perspectives on Psychological Science, 1,* 316–345.

Lublin, H., Eberhard, J., & Levander, S. (2005). Current therapy issues and unmet clinical needs in the treatment of schizophrenia: A review of the new generation antipsychotics. *International Clinical Psychopharmacology, 20,* 183–198.

Lucas, W. (2008). Parents' perceptions of the Drug Abuse Resistance Education program (DARE). *Journal of Child & Adolescent Substance Abuse, 17,* 99–114.

Luchins, A. S. (1946). Classroom experiments on mental set. *American Journal of Psychology, 59,* 295–298.

Lucki, I., & O'Leary, O. E. (2004). Distinguishing roles for norepinephrine and serotonin in the behavioral effects of antidepressant drugs. *Journal of Clinical Psychiatry, 65,* 11–24.

Luders, E., Narr, K. L., Thompson, P. M., & Toga, A. W. (2009). Neuroanatomical correlates of intelligence. *Intelligence, 37,* 156–163.

Luders, E., Narr, K. L., Zaidel, E., Thompson, P. M., & Toga, A. W. (2006). Gender effects on callosal thickness in scaled and unscaled space. *Neuroreport, 17,* 1103–1106.

Lun, V. M., & Bond, M. H. (2006). Achieving relationship harmony in groups and its consequence for group performance. *Asian Journal of Social Psychology, 9,* 195–202.

Luo, S., & Zhang, G. (2009). What leads to romantic attraction: Similarity, reciprocity, security, or beauty? Evidence from a speed-dating study. *Journal of Personality, 77,* 933–964.

Luria, A. R. (1968). *The mind of a mnemonist.* Cambridge, MA: Basic Books.

Lurie, K., Robinson, A., & Pecsenye, M. (2005). *Cracking the GRE 2006.* New York: Random House.

Lutz, C. K., & Novak, M. A. (2005). Environmental enrichment for nonhuman primates: theory and application. *ILAR Journal, 46,* 178–191.

Lutz, W., Lambert, M. J., Harmon, S. C., Tschitsaz, A., Schurch, E., & Stulz, N. (2006). The probability of treatment success, failure and duration–What can be learned from empirical data to support decision making in clinical practice? *Clinical Psychology & Psychotherapy, 13,* 223–232.

Ly, D. H., Lockhart, D. J., Lerner, R. A., & Schultz, P. G. (2000, March 31). Mitotic misregulation and human aging. *Science, 287,* 2486–2492.

Lykken, D. T. (1995). *The antisocial personalities.* Mahwah, NJ: Erlbaum.

Lymberis, S. C., Parhar, P. K., Katsoulakis, E., & Formenti, S. C. (2004). Pharmacogenomics and breast cancer. *Pharmacogenomics, 5,* 31–55.

Lynch, T. R., Trost, W. T., Salsman, N., & Linehan, M. M. (2007). Dialectical behavior therapy for borderline personality disorder. *Annual Review of Clinical Psychology, 3,* 181–205.

Lyness, K. S., & Heilman, M. E. (2006). When fit is fundamental: performance evaluations and promotions of upper-level female and male managers. *Journal of Applied Psychology, 91,* 777–785.

Lynn, R. (2009). What has caused the Flynn effect? Secular increases in the Development Quotients of infants. *Intelligence, 37,* 16–24.

Lynn, S. J., Fassler, O., & Knox, J. (2005). Hypnosis and the altered state debate: Something more or nothing more? Comment. *Contemporary Hypnosis, 22,* 39–45.

Lynn, S. J., Kirsch, I., Barabasz, A., Cardena, E., & Patterson, D. (2000). Hypnosis as an empirically supported clinical intervention: The state of the evidence and a look to the future. *International Journal of Clinical and Experimental Hypnosis, 48,* 239–259.

Lynn, S. J., Lock, T., Loftus, E. F., Krackow, E., & Lilienfeld, S. O. (2003). The remembrance of things past: Problematic memory recovery techniques in psychotherapy. In S. O. Lilienfeld, S. J. Lynn, & J. M. Lohr (Eds.), *Science and pseudoscience in clinical psychology.* New York: Guilford Press.

Lyons, H., Giordano, P. C., Manning, W. D., & Longmore, M. A. (2011). Identity, peer relationships, and adolescent girls' sexual behavior: An exploration of the contemporary double standard. *Journal of Sex Research, 48,* 437–449.

Ma, Y., Wang, C., & Han, S. (2011). Neural responses to perceived pain in others predict real-life monetary donations in different socioeconomic contexts. *NeuroImage, 57,* 1273–1280.

Macaluso, E., & Driver, J. (2005). Multisensory spatial interactions: a window onto functional integration in the human brain. *Trends in Neurosciences, 28, Issue 5,* 264–271.

Macaluso, E., Frith, C. D., & Driver, J. (2000, August 18). Modulation of human visual cortex by crossmodal spatial attention. *Science, 289,* 1206–1208.

MacDonald, D. J. (2011). Germline mutations in cancer susceptibility genes: an overview for nurses. *Seminars in Oncology Nursing, 27,* 21–33.

Macduff, I. (2006). Your pace or mine? Culture, time and negotiation. *Negotiation Journal, 22,* 31–45.

Mack, J. (2003). *The museum of the mind.* London: British Museum Publications.

Mackay, J., & Eriksen, M. (2002). *The tobacco atlas.* Geneva, Switzerland: World Health Organization.

MacLean, L., Edwards, N., Garrard, M., Sims-Jones, N., Clinton, K., & Ashley, L. (2009, March). Obesity, stigma and public health planning. *Health Promotion International, 24,* 88–93.

MacLennan, A. (2009). Evidence-based review of therapies at the menopause. *International Journal of Evidence-Based Healthcare, 7,* 112–123.

Macmillan, M. (1996). *Freud evaluated: The completed arc.* Cambridge, MA: MIT.

MacNeilage, P. F., Rogers, L. J., & Vallortigara, G. (2009, July). Origins of the left & right brain. *Scientific American,* pp. 60–67.

MacPherson, K. (2002, March 17). Unfilled pink-collar jobs threaten service cuts. *Pittsburgh Post-Gazette,* p. 7.

Madden, D. J. (2007). Aging and visual attention. *Current Directions in Psychological Science, 16,* 70–74.

Madden, G. J., Dube, W. V., Hackenberg, T. D., Hanley, G. P., & Lattal, K. A. (2013). *APA handbook of behavior analysis, Vol. 1: Methods and principles.* Washington, DC: American Psychological Association.

Maddi, S. R. (2007). The story of hardiness: Twenty years of theorizing, research, and practice. In A. Monat, R. S. Lazarus, & G. Reevy (Eds.), *The Praeger handbook on stress and coping* (Vol. 2). Westport, CT: Praeger Publishers/Greenwood Publishing.

Maddi, S. R., Khoshaba, D. M., Harvey, R. H., Fazel, M., & Resurreccion, N. (2011). The personality construct of hardiness, V: Relationships with the construction of existential meaning in life. *Journal of Humanistic Psychology, 51,* 369–388.

Maddock, R. J., Buonocore, M. H., Miller, A. R., Yoon, J. H., Soosman, S. K., & Unruh, A. M. (2013). Abnormal activity-dependent brain lactate and glutamate + glutamine responses in panic disorder. *Biological Psychiatry, 73,* 1111–1119.

Mader, S. S. (2000). *Biology* (6th ed.). Boston: McGraw-Hill.

Madon, S., Willard, J., & Guyll, M. (2006). Self-fulfilling prophecy effects of mothers' beliefs on children's alcohol use: Accumulation, dissipation, and stability over time. *Journal of Personality and Social Psychology, 90,* 911–926.

Magee, S. R., Bublitz, M. H., Orazine, C., Brush, B., Salisbury, A., Niaura, R., & Stroud, L. R. (2013). The relationship between maternal-fetal attachment and cigarette smoking over pregnancy. *Maternal and Child Health Journal.* Retrieved from http://www.ncbi.nlm.nih.gov/pubmed/23892790

Magida, A. J. (2006). *Opening the doors of wonder: Reflections on religious rites of passage.* Berkeley, CA: University of California Press.

Magis, D., & Schoenen, J. (2011). Treatment of migraine: update on new therapies. *Current Opinions in Neurology, 24,* 203–210.

Magley, V. J. (2002). Coping with sexual harassment: Reconceptualizing women's resistance. *Journal of Personality and Social Psychology, 83,* 930–946.

Magoni, M., Bassani, L., Okong, P., Kituuka, P., Germinario, E. P., Giuliano, M., et al. (2005). Mode of infant feeding and HIV infection in children in a program for prevention of mother-to-child transmission in Uganda. *AIDS, 19,* 433–437.

Magoon, M., & Critchfield, T. (2008). Concurrent schedules of positive and negative reinforcement: Differential-impact and differential-outcomes hypotheses. *Journal of the Experimental Analysis of Behavior, 90,* 1–22.

Magruder, K., & Yeager, D. (2009). The prevalence of PTSD across war eras and the effect of deployment on PTSD: A systematic review and meta-analysis. *Psychiatric Annals, 39,* 778–788.

Maguire, E. A., Kumaran, D., Hassabis, D., & Kopelman, M. D. (2010). Autobiographical memory in semantic dementia: A longitudinal fMRI study. *Neuropsychologia, 48,* 123–136.

Maguire, E. A., Woollett, K., & Spiers, H. J. (2006). London taxi drivers and bus drivers: A structural MRI and neuropsychological analysis. *Hippocampus, 16,* 1091–1101.

Mahmood, M., & Black, J. (2005). Narcolepsycataplexy: How does recent understanding help in evaluation and treatment. *Current Treatment Options in Neurology, 7,* 363–371.

Maier, S. F., & Watkins, L. R. (2000). Learned helplessness. In A. E. Kazdin (Ed.), *Encyclopedia of psychology* (Vol. 4). Washington, DC: American Psychological Association.

Majdandzic, M., & van den Boom, D. C. (2007). Multimethod longitudinal assessment of temperament in early childhood. *Journal of Personality, 75,* 121–167.

Majeres, R. L. (2007). Sex differences in phonological coding: Alphabet transformation speed. *Intelligence, 35,* 335–346.

Major, J. T., Johnson, W., & Bouchard, T. r. (2011). The dependability of the general factor of intelligence: Why small, single-factor models do not adequately represent g. *Intelligence, 39,* 418–433.

Majorano, M., & D'Odorico, L. (2011). The transition into ambient language: A longitudinal study of babbling and first word production of Italian children. *First Language, 31,* 47–66.

Malamuth, N. M., Linz, D., Heavey, C. L., & Barnes, G. (1995). Using the confluence model of sexual aggression to predict men's conflict with women: A 10-year follow-up study. *Journal of Personality and Social Psychology, 69,* 353–369.

Maldonado, J. R., & Spiegel, D. (2003). Dissociative disorders. In R. E. Hales & S. C. Yudofsky (Eds.), *The American Psychiatric Publishing textbook of clinical psychiatry* (4th ed.). Washington, DC: American Psychiatric Publishing.

Malloy, L. C., Brubacher, S. P., & Lamb, M. E. (2011). Expected consequences of disclosure revealed in investigative interviews with suspected victims of child sexual abuse. *Applied Developmental Science, 15,* 8–19.

Malouff, J. M., & Rooke, S. E. (2013). Expert-recommended warnings for medical marijuana. *Substance Abuse, 34,* 92–93.

Malpas, P. (2008, April). Predictive genetic testing of children for adult-onset diseases and psychological harm. *Journal of Medical Ethics, 34,* 275–278.

Mamassis, G., & Doganis, G. (2004). The effects of a mental training program on juniors pre-competitive anxiety, self-confidence, and tennis performance. *Journal of Applied Sport Psychology, 16,* 118–137.

Mancinelli, R., Binetti, R., & Ceccanti, M. (2007). Woman, alcohol and environment: Emerging risks for health. *Neuroscience & Biobehavioral Reviews, 31,* 246–253.

Mandler, G. (2007). Involuntary memories: Variations on the unexpected. In J. H. Mace (Ed.), *Involuntary memory* (pp. 208–223). Malden, MA: Blackwell Publishing.

Manly, J. J. (2005). Advantages and disadvantages of separate norms for African Americans. *Clinical Neuropsychologist, 19,* 270–275.

Manly, J. J. (2006). Deconstructing race and ethnicity: Implications for measurement of health outcomes [Special issue: Measurement in a multi-ethnic society]. *Medical Care, 44,* S10–S16.

Manly, J., & Echemendia, R. (2007). Race-specific norms: Using the model of hypertension to understand issues of race, culture, and education in neuropsychology. *Archives of Clinical Neuropsychology, 22,* 319–325.

Mann, K., Ackermann, K., Croissant, B., Mundle, G., Nakovics, H., & Diehl, A. (2005). Neuroimaging of gender differences in alcohol dependence: are women more vulnerable? *Alcoholism: Clinical & Experimental Research, 29,* 896–901.

Mann, R. E., & Hollin, C. R. (2007). Sexual offenders' explanations for their offending. *Journal of Sexual Aggression, 13,* 3–9.

Manni, R., & Terzaghi, M. (2013). Dreaming and enacting dreams in nonrapid eye movement and rapid eye movement parasomnia: A step toward a unifying view within distinct patterns? *Sleep Medicine, 14,* 387–388.

Manning, M. A., & Hoyme, E. H. (2007). Fetal alcohol spectrum disorders: A practical clinical approach to diagnosis. *Neuroscience & Biobehavioral Reviews, 31,* 230–238.

Manning, S. Y. (2005). Dialectical behavior therapy of severe and chronic problems. In L. VandeCreek (Ed.), *Innovations in clinical practice: Focus on adults.* Sarasota, FL: Professional Resource Press/Professional Resource Exchange.

Manor, J. K., & Gailliot, M. T. (2007). Altruism and egoism: Prosocial motivations for helping depend on relationship context. *European Journal of Social Psychology,* Retrieve from http://onlinelibrary.wiley.com/doi/10.1002/ejsp.364/abstract

Manstead, A. S. R., & Wagner, H. L. (2004). *Experience emotion.* Cambridge, England: Cambridge University Press.

Manstead, A. S. R., Frijda, N., & Fischer, A. H. (Eds.). (2003). *Feelings and emotions: The Amsterdam Symposium.* Cambridge, England: Cambridge University Press.

Marcaurelle, R., Bélanger, C., & Marchand, A. (2005). Marital predictors of symptom severity in panic disorder with agoraphobia. *Journal of Anxiety Disorders, 19,* 211–232.

Marchand, S., & Phillips, G. E. (2012). Hoarding's place in the DSM-5: Another symptom, or a newly listed disorder? *Issues in Mental Health Nursing, 33,* 591–597.

Marcus-Newhall, A., Pedersen, W. C., & Carlson, M. (2000). Displaced aggression is alive and well: A meta-analytic review. *Journal of Personality and Social Psychology, 78,* 670–689.

Margraf, J., Meyer, A., & Lavallee, K. (2013). Well-being from the knife? Psychological effects of aesthetic surgery. *Clinical Psychological Science, 1*(3), 239–252.

Markoff, J. (2009, July 25). Scientists worry machines may outsmart man. *The New York Times,* p. A1.

Marks, I. M. (2004). The Nobel prize award in physiology to Ivan Petrovich Pavlov-1904. *Australian and New Zealand Journal of Psychiatry, 38,* 674–677.

Markus, H. R. (2007). Sociocultural psychology: The dynamic interdependence among self systems and social systems. In S. Kitayama & D. Cohen (Eds.), *Handbook of cultural psychology.* New York: Guilford Press.

Markus, H. R., & Kitayama, S. (2003). Models of agency: Sociocultural diversity in the construction of action. In V. Murphy-Berman & J. J. Berman (Eds.), *Cross-cultural differences in perspectives on the self.* Lincoln, NE: University of Nebraska Press.

Markus, K. A., & Borsboom, D. (2013). *Frontiers of test validity theory: Measurement, causation, and meaning.* New York: Routledge/Taylor & Francis Group.

Marmar, C. (2009). Mental health impact of Afghanistan and Iraq deployment: Meeting the challenge of a new generation of veterans. *Depression and Anxiety, 26,* 493–497.

Maroda, K. J. (2004). A relational perspective on women and power. *Psychoanalytic Psychology, 21,* 428–435.

Marsh, B. (2008, February 24). A growing cloud over the planet. *The New York Times,* p. WK4.

Marsh, H. W., Hau, K. T., & Sung, R. Y. T. (2007). Childhood obesity, gender, actual-ideal body image discrepancies, and physical self-concept in Hong Kong children: Cultural differences in the value of moderation. *Developmental Psychology, 43,* 647–662.

Marsh, R., Steinglass, J. E., Gerber, A. J., Graziano O'Leary, A., Wang, Z., Murphy, D., Walsh, T., & Peterson, B. S. (2009). Defficient activity in the neural systems that mediate self-regulatory control in bulimia nervosa. *Archives of General Psychiatry, 66,* 51–63.

Marshall, J. R. (2011). Ultimate causes and the evolution of altruism. *Behavioral Ecology and Sociobiology, 65,* 503–512.

Marshall, K., Laing, D. G., & Jinks, A. L. (2006). The capacity of humans to identify components in complex odor-taste mixtures. *Chemical Senses, 31,* 539–545.

Marshall, L., & Born, J. (2007, October). The contribution of sleep to hippocampus-dependent memory consolidation. *Trends in Cognitive Sciences, 11*(10), 442–450.

Marshall, M. K. (2007). The critical factors of coaching practice leading to successful coaching outcomes. *Dissertation Abstracts International: Section B: The Sciences and Engineering, 67*(7-B), 4092.

Marshall, R. D., Bryant, R. A., & Amsel, L. (2007). The psychology of ongoing threat: Relative risk appraisal, the September 11 attacks, and terrorism-related fears. *American Psychologist, 62,* 304–316.

Marshall, R. D., Bryant, R. A., Amsel, L., Suh, E. J., Cook, J. M., & Neria, Y. (2007). The psychology of ongoing threat: Relative risk appraisal, the September 11 attacks and terrorism-related fears. *American Psychologist, 62,* 304–316.

Marszalek, J. (2007). Computerized adaptive testing and the experience of flow in examinees. *Dissertation Abstracts International Section A: Humanities and Social Sciences, 67*(7-A), 2465.

Martelle, S., Hanley, C., & Yoshino K. (2003, January 28). "Sopranos" scenario in slaying? *Los Angeles Times*, p. B1.
Martin, A. J., & Marsh, H. W. (2002). Fear of failure: Friend or foe? *Australian Psychologist, 38*, 31–38.
Martin, E. A., & Kerns, J. G. (2011). The influence of positive mood on different aspects of cognitive control. *Cognition and Emotion, 25*, 265–279.
Martin, L., & Pullum, G. K. (1991). *The great Eskimo vocabulary hoax*. Chicago: University of Chicago Press.
Martin, P. D., & Brantley, P. J. (2004). Stress, coping, and social support in health and behavior. In J. M. Raczynski & L. C. Leviton (Eds.), *Handbook of clinical health psychology, Vol. 2: Disorders of behavior and health*. Washington, DC: American Psychological Association.
Martindale, C. (1981). *Cognition and consciousness*. Homewood, IL: Dorsey.
Mascia, K., & Servis, R. (2009, August 24). Mail carriers to the rescue. *People*, p. 108–110.
Mashour, G. A., Walker, E. E., & Martuza, R. L. (2005). Psychosurgery: Past, present, and future. *Brain Research Reviews, 48*, 409–419.
Masi, S., Asselain, N., Robelin, L., Bourgeois, A., Hano, C., Dousseau, G., & . . . Krief, S. (2013). Response to bitter substances in primates: Roles of diet tendency and weaning age. *Cognitive, Affective & Behavioral Neuroscience*. Retrieved from http://www.ncbi.nlm.nih.gov/pubmed/23712664
Maslow, A. H. (1970). *Motivation and personality*. New York: Harper & Row.
Maslow, A. H. (1987). *Motivation and personality* (3rd ed.). New York: Harper & Row.
Mason, M. (1995). *The making of Victorian sexuality*. New York: Oxford University Press.
Mast, F. W., & Kosslyn, S. M. (2002). Visual mental images can be ambiguous: Insights from individual differences in spatial transformation abilities. *Cognition, 86, 57–70.*
Masters, W. H., & Johnson, V. E. (1966). *Human sexual response*. Boston: Little, Brown.
Masters, W. H., & Johnson, V. E. (1979). *Homosexuality in perspective*. Boston: Little, Brown.
Masters, W., & Johnson, V. (1994). *Hetero-sexuality*. New York: Harper Collins.
Masuda, M. (2003). Meta-analyses of love scales: Do various love scales measure the same psychological constructs? *Japanese Psychological Research, 45*, 25–37.
Mataix-Cols, D., & Bartres-Faz, D. (2002). Is the use of the wooden and computerized versions of the Tower of Hanoi Puzzle equivalent? *Applied Neuropsychology, 9*, 117–120.
Matchock, R. L., & Mordkoff, J. T. (2009). Chronotype and time-of-day influences on the alerting, orienting, and executive components of attention. *Experimental Brain Research, 192*, 189–198.
Mathews, H. L., & Janusek, L. (2011). Epigenetics and psychoneuroimmunology: Mechanisms and models. *Brain, Behavior, and Immunity, 25*, 25–39.
Matlin, M. W. (1996). *The psychology of women* (3rd ed.). Orlando, FL: Harcourt Brace College Publishers.
Maton, K. I., Kohout, J. L., Wicherski, M., Leary, G. E., & Vinokurov, A. (2006). Minority students of color and the psychology graduate pipeline. *American Psychologist, 61*, 117–131.
Matsumoto, D. (2002). Methodological requirements to test a possible in-group advantage in judging emotions across cultures: Comment on Elfenbein and Ambady (2002) and evidence. *Psychological Bulletin, 128*, 236–242.
Matsumoto, D., & Willingham, B. (2009). Spontaneous facial expressions of emotion of congenitally and noncongenitally blind individuals. *Journal of Personality and Social Psychology, 96*, 1–10.
Matthews, G., & Funke, G. J. (2006). Worry and information-processing. In G. C. L. Davey & A. Wells (Eds.), *Worry and its psychological disorders: Theory, assessment and treatment*. Hoboken, NJ: Wiley Publishing.
Mattys, S. L., Seymour, F. F., Attwood, A. S., & Munafò, M. R. (2013). Effects of acute anxiety induction on speech perception: Are anxious listeners distracted listeners? *Psychological Science, 24*, 1606–1608.
Maurer, D., Lewis, T. L., Brent, H. P., & Levin, A. V. (1999, October 1). Rapid improvement in the acuity of infants after visual input. *Science, 286*, 108–110.
Maxson, S. C. (2013). Behavioral genetics. In R. J. Nelson, S. Y. Mizumori, & I. B. Weiner (Eds.), *Handbook of psychology, Vol. 3: Behavioral neuroscience (2nd ed.)*. New York: John Wiley & Sons Ltd.
Mayer, J. D., Salovey, P., & Caruso, D. R. (2004). Emotional intelligence: Theory, findings, and implications. *Psychological Inquiry, 15*, 197–215.
Mayer, J. D., Salovey, P., & Caruso, D. R. (2008). Emotional intelligence: New ability or eclectic traits? *American Psychologist, 63*, 503–517.
Mayer, R. E. (2013). Problem solving. In D. Reisberg (Ed.), *The Oxford handbook of cognitive psychology*. New York: Oxford University Press.
Maynard, A. E., & Martini, M. I. (2005). *Learning in cultural context: Family, peers, and school*. New York: Kluwer Academic/Plenum Publishers.
Mazard, A., Laou, L., Joliot, M., & Mellet, E. (2005). Neural impact of the semantic content of visual mental images and visual percepts. *Brain Research and Cognitive Brain Research, 24*, 423–435.
McAdams, D. P., Diamond, A., de St. Aubin, E., & Mansfield, E. (1997). Stories of commitment: The psychosocial construction of generative lives. *Journal of Personality and Social Psychology, 72*, 678–694.
McCabe, C., & Rolls, E. T. (2007). Umami: A delicious flavor formed by convergence of taste and olfactory pathways in the human brain. *European Journal of Neuroscience, 25*, 1855–1864.
McCabe, M. (2009). Anorgasmia in women. *Journal of Family Psychotherapy, 20*, 177–197.
McCarthy, J. (2005). Individualism and collectivism: What do they have to do with counseling? *Journal of Multicultural Counseling and Development, 33*, 108–117.
McCarthy, R. J., & Skowronski, J. J. (2011). You're getting warmer: Level of construal affects the impact of central traits on impression formation. *Journal of Experimental Social Psychology, 47*, 1304–1307.
McCaul, K. D., Johnson, R. J., & Rothman, A. J. (2002). The effects of framing and action instructions on whether older adults obtain flu shots. *Health Psychology, 21*, 624–628.
McCauley, R. N., & Henrich, J. (2006). Susceptibility to the Müller-Lyer illusion, theory-neutral observation, and the diachronic penetrability of the visual input. *Philosophical Psychology, 19*, 79–101.
McClelland, D. C. (1985). How motives, skills, and values determine what people do. *American Psychologist, 40*, 812–825.
McClelland, D. C. (1993). Intelligence is not the best predictor of job performance. *Current Directions in Psychological Research, 2*, 5–8.
McClelland, D. C., Atkinson, J. W., Clark, R. A., & Lowell, E. L. (1953). *The achievement motive*. New York: Appleton-Century-Crofts.
McClintock, B. (1983). *A Feeling for the Organism*. New York: W.H. Freeman and Company.
McClure, J., Sutton, R. M., & Sibley, C. G. (2007). Listening to reporters or engineers? How instance-based messages about building design affect earthquake fatalism. *Journal of Applied Social Sciences, 37*, 1956–1973.
McCrae, R. R., & Costa, P. T., Jr. (1986). A five-factor theory of personality. In L. A. Pervin & O. P. John (Eds.), *Handbook of personality: Theory and research* (2nd ed.). New York: Guilford.
McCrae, R. R., Kurtz, J. E., Yamagata, S., & Terracciano, A. (2011). Internal consistency, retest reliability, and their implications for personality scale validity. *Personality and Social Psychology Review, 15*, 28–50.
McCrae, R. R., Terracciano A., & 78 Members of the Personality Profiles of Cultures Project. (2005). Universal features of personality traits from the observer's perspective: Data from 50 cultures. *Journal of Personality and Social Psychology, 88*, 547–561.
McCrink, K., & Wynn, K. (2007). Ratio abstraction by 6-month-old infants. *Psychological Science, 18*, 740–745.
McDaniel, M. A., Maier, S. F., & Einstein, G. O. (2002). "Brain specific" nutrients: A memory cure? *Psychological Science in the Public Interest, 3*, 12–18.
McDermott, M. S., Beard, E., Brose, L. S., West, R., & McEwen, A. (2013). Factors associated with differences in quit rates between 'specialist' and 'community' stop-smoking practitioners in the English stop-smoking services. *Nicotine & Tobacco Research, 15*, 1239–1247.
McDonald, C., & Murray, R. M. (2004). Can structural magnetic resonance imaging provide an alternative phenotype for genetic studies of schizophrenia? In M. S. Keshavan, J. L. Kennedy, & R. M. Murray (Eds.), *Neurodevelopment and schizophrenia*. New York: Cambridge University Press.
McDonald, H. E., & Hirt, E. R. (1997). When expectancy meets desire: Motivational effects in reconstructive memory. *Journal of Personality and Social Psychology, 72*, 5–23.
McDougall, W. (1908). *Introduction to social psychology*. London: Methuen.
McDowell, D. M., & Spitz, H. I. (1999). *Substance abuse*. New York: Brunner/Mazel.
McElreath, R., Wallin, A., & Fasolo, B. (2013). The evolutionary rationality of social learning. In R. Hertwig & U. Hoffrage (Eds.), *Simple heuristics in a social world*. New York: Oxford University Press.
McEwen, B. S. (1998, January 15). Protective and damaging effects of stress mediators [Review article]. *New England Journal of Medicine, 338*, 171–179.
McGaugh, J. L. (2003). *Memory and emotion: The making of lasting memories*. New York: Columbia University Press.
McGilvray, J. (Ed.). (2004). *The Cambridge companion to Chomsky*. Oxford, England: Cambridge University Press.
McGinn, D. (2003, June 9). Testing, testing: The new job search. *Time*, pp. 36–38.

McGregor, K. K., & Capone, N. C. (2004). Genetic and environmental interactions in determining the early lexicon: Evidence from a set of tri-zygotic quadruplets. *Journal of Child Language, 31,* 311–337.

McIntyre, K., Korn, J., & Matsuo, H. (2008). Sweating the small stuff: How different types of hassles result in the experience of stress. *Stress and Health: Journal of the International Society for the Investigation of Stress, 24,* 383–392.

McKinley, J. C. Jr. (2013, September 12). Overdoses of 'Molly' led to Electric Zoo deaths. *The New York Times.* Retrieved from http://artsbeat.blogs.nytimes.com/2013/09/12/overdoses-of-molly-led-to-electric-zoo-deaths/

McKinley, M. J., Cairns, M. J., Denton, D. A., Egan, G., Mathai, M. L., Uschakov, A., et al. (2004). Physiological and pathophysiological influences on thirst. *Physiology and Behavior, 81,* 795–803.

McMurtray, A. M., Licht, E., Yeo, T., Krisztal, E., Saul, R. E., & Mendez, M. F. (2007). Positron emission tomography facilitates diagnosis of early-onset Alzheimer's disease. *European Neurology, 59,* 31–37.

McNally, R. J. (2011). *What is mental illness?* Cambridge, MA: Harvard University Press.

McNamara, P. (2004). *An evolutionary psychology of sleep and dreams.* Westport, CT: Praeger Publishers/Greenwood Publishing Group.

McNamara, T. P. (2013). Semantic memory and priming. In A. F. Healy, R. W. Proctor, & I. B. Weiner (Eds.), *Handbook of psychology, Vol. 4: Experimental psychology (2nd ed.).* Hoboken, NJ: John Wiley & Sons Inc.

McTeague, L. M., Lang, P. J., Laplante, M., & Bradley, M. M. (2011). Aversive imagery in panic disorder: Agoraphobia severity, comorbidity, and defensive physiology. *Biological Psychiatry, 70,* 415–424.

Mead, M. (1949). *Male and female.* New York: Morrow.

Mealey, L. (2000). *Sex differences: Developmental and evolutionary strategies.* San Diego, CA: Academic Press.

Medeiros, R., Prediger, R. D. S., Passos, G. F., Pandolfo, P., et al. (2007). Connecting TNF-Î± signaling pathways to iNOS expression in a mouse model of Alzheimer's disease: Relevance for the behavioral and synaptic deficits induced by amyloid Î² protein. *Journal of Neuroscience, 27,* 5394–5404.

Medicine of the National Academies. (2009). *Preventing mental, emotional, and behavioral disorders among young people: Progress and possibilities.* Washington, DC: National Academies Press.

Meeter, M., & Murre, J. M. J. (2004). Consolidation of long-term memory: Evidence and alternatives. *Psychological Bulletin, 130,* 843–857.

Megill, J. (2013). Emotion, cognition and artificial intelligence. *Minds and Machines.* Retrieved from http://link.springer.com/article/10.1007%2Fs11023-013-9320-8

Mehl-Madrona, L. E. (2004). Hypnosis to facilitate uncomplicated birth. *American Journal of Clinical Hypnosis, 46,* 299–312.

Mehl, M. R., Vazire, S., Ramirez-Esparza, N., Slatcher, R. B., & Pennebaker, J. W. (2007, July 6). Are women really more talkative than men? *Science, 317,* 82.

Meinlschmidt, G., & Heim, C. (2007). Sensitivity to intranasal oxytocin in adult men with early parental separation. *Biological Psychiatry, 61,* 1109–1111.

Mel, B. W. (2002, March 8). What the synapse tells the neuron. *Science, 295,* 1845–1846.

Mel'nikov, K. S. (1993, October-December). On some aspects of the mechanistic approach to the study of processes of forgetting. *Vestnik Moskovskogo Universiteta Seriya 14 Psikhologiya,* pp. 64–67.

Meltzer, H. Y. (2000). Genetics and etiology of schizophrenia and bipolar disorder. *Biological Psychiatry, 47,* 171–173.

Meltzoff, A. N. (1996). The human infant as imitative generalist: A 20-year progress report on infant imitation with implications for comparative psychology. In C. M. Heyes & B. G. Galef, Jr. (Eds.), *Social learning in animals: The roots of culture.* San Diego, CA: Academic Press.

Melzack, R., & Katz, J. (2001). The McGill Pain Questionnaire: Appraisal and current status. In D. Turk & R. Melzack (Eds.), *Handbook of pain assessment* (2nd ed.). New York: Guilford Press.

Melzack, R., & Katz, J. (2004). *The gate control theory: Reaching for the brain.* Mahwah, NJ: Lawrence Erlbaum Associates.

Mendelsohn, J. (2003, November 7–9). What we know about sex. *USA Weekend,* pp. 6–9.

Mensah, F. K., Bayer, J. K., Wake, M., Carlin, J. B., Allen, N. B., & Patton, G. C. (2013). Early puberty and childhood social and behavioral adjustment. *Journal of Adolescent Health, 53,* 118–124.

Mental Health Information Center, U.S. Department of Health and Human Services. (2002, December). Deinstitutionalization. *Scientific American,* p. 38.

Mercadillo, R. E., Díaz, J., Pasaye, E. H., & Barrios, F. A. (2011). Perception of suffering and compassion experience: Brain gender disparities. *Brain and Cognition, 76,* 5–14.

Merikangas, K. R., Ames, M., Cui, L., Stang, P. E., Ustun, T. B., VonKorff, M., et al. (2007). The impact of comorbidity of mental and physical conditions on role disability in the US adult household population. *Archives of General Psychiatry, 64,* 1180–1188.

Mesoudi, A. (2011). Evolutionary psychology meets cultural psychology. *Journal of Evolutionary Psychology, 9,* 83–87.

Messer, S. B., & McWilliams, N. (2003). The impact of Sigmund Freud and *The Interpretation of Dreams.* In R. J. Sternberg (Ed.), *The anatomy of impact: What makes the great works of psychology great.* Washington, DC: American Psychological Association.

Messner, M., Reinhard, M., & Sporer, S. (2008). Compliance through direct persuasive appeals: The moderating role of communicator's attractiveness in interpersonal persuasion. *Social Influence, 3,* 67–83.

Meston, C. M. (2003). Validation of the female sexual function index (FSFI) in women with female orgasmic disorder and in women with hypoactive sexual desire disorder. *Journal of Sex and Marital Therapy, 29,* 39–46.

Meyer-Bahlburg, H. (1997). The role of prenatal estrogens in sexual orientation. In L. Ellis & L. Ebertz (Eds.), *Sexual orientation: Toward biological understanding.* Westport, CT: Praeger.

Meyer, I., & Ladewig, J. (2008). The relationship between number of training sessions per week and learning in dogs. *Applied Animal Behaviour Science, 111,* 311–320.

Meyerowitz, J. (2004). *How sex changed: A history of transsexuality in the United States.* Cambridge, MA: Harvard University Press.

Michaels, D., et al. (2009). 2009 Doctorate: Employment Survey. *American Psychological Association,* table 3.

Michael, R. T., Gagnon, J. H., Laumann, E. O., & Kolata, G. (1994). *Sex in America: A definitive survey.* Boston: Little, Brown.

Michalski, D., Kohout, J., Wicherski, M. & Hart, B., (2009). *2009: Doctorate Employment Survey.* APA Center for Workforce Studies, American Psychological Association.

Micheau, J., & Marighetto, A. (2011). Acetylcholine and memory: A long, complex and chaotic but still living relationship. *Behavioural Brain Research, 221,* 424–429.

Midanik, L. T., Tam, T. W., & Weisner, C. (2007). Concurrent and simultaneous drug and alcohol use: Results of the 2000 national alcohol survey. *Drug and Alcohol Dependence, 90,* 72–80.

Middlebrooks, J. C., Furukawa, S., Stecker, G. C., & Mickey, B. J. (2005). Distributed representation of sound-source location in the auditory cortex. In R. König, P. Heil, E. Budinger, & H. Scheich (Eds.), *Auditory cortex: A synthesis of human and animal research.* Mahwah, NJ: Lawrence Erlbaum Associates.

Miesenbock, G. (2008, October). Lighting up the brain. *Scientific American,* pp. 52–59.

Mifflin, L. (1998, January 14). Study finds a decline in TV network violence. *The New York Times,* p. A14.

Mignon, A., & Mollaret, P. (2002). Applying the affordance conception of traits: A person perception study. *Personality and Social Psychology Bulletin, 28,* 1327–1334.

Miguez, G., Witnauer, J. E., & Miller, R. R. (2011). The role of contextual associations in producing the partial reinforcement acquisition deficit. *Journal of Experimental Psychology: Animal Behavior Processes, 37,* 88–97.

Mika, V. S., Wood, P. R., Weiss, B. D., & Trevino, L. (2007). Ask Me 3: Improving communication in a Hispanic pediatric outpatient practice. *American Journal of Behavioral Health, 31,* S115–S121.

Miles, P., Schaufeli, W. B., & van den Bos, K. (2011). When weak groups are strong: How low cohesion groups allow individuals to act according to their personal absence tolerance norms. *Social Justice Research, 24,* 207–230.

Miletic, M. P. (2002). The introduction of a feminine psychology to psychoanalysis: Karen Horney's legacy [Special issue: Interpersonal psychoanalysis and feminism]. *Contemporary Psychoanalysis, 38,* 287–299.

Milgram, S. (1965). *Obedience* [film]. New York University Film Library and Pennsylvania State University, PCR.

Milgram, S. (2005). *Obedience to authority.* Pinter & Martin: New York.

Miller-Jones, D. (1991). Informal reasoning in inner-city children. In J. F. Voss & D. N. Perkins (Eds.), *Informal reasoning and education.* Hillsdale, NJ: Lawrence Erlbaum.

Miller-Perrin, C., Perrin, R., & Kocur, J. (2009). Parental physical and psychological aggression: Psychological symptoms in young adults. *Child Abuse & Neglect, 33,* 1–11.

Miller, C., & Williams, A. (2011). Ethical guidelines in research. In J. C. Thomas & M. Hersen (Eds.), *Understanding research in clinical and counseling psychology (2nd ed.).* New York: Routledge/Taylor & Francis Group.

Miller, G. (2006). A spoonful of medicine–and a steady diet of normalcy. *Science, 311,* 464–465.

Miller, G. (2008, May 9). The roots of morality. *Science, 320,* 734–737.

Miller, G. A. (1956). The magical number seven, plus or minus two: Some limits on our capacity for processing information. *Psychology Review, 63,* 81–97.

Miller, G. E., Chen, E., & Parker, K. J. (2011). Psychological stress in childhood and susceptibility to the chronic diseases of aging: Moving toward a model of behavioral and biological mechanisms. *Psychological Bulletin, 137*, 959–997.

Miller, G. F., & Penke, L. (2007). The evolution of human intelligence and the coefficient of additive genetic variance in human brain size. *Intelligence, 35*, 97–114.

Miller, J. A., & Leffard, S. A. (2007). Behavioral assessment. In S. R. Smith & L. Handler (Eds.), *The clinical assessment of children and adolescents: A practitioner's handbook*. Mahwah, NJ: Lawrence Erlbaum Associates.

Miller, J. G. (1984). Culture and the development of everyday social explanation. *Journal of Personality and Social Psychology, 46*, 961–978.

Miller, L. A., McIntire, S. A., & Lovler, R. L. (2011). *Foundations of psychological testing: A practical problem (3rd ed.)*. Thousand Oaks, CA: Sage Publications, Inc.

Miller, L. A., Taber, K. H., Gabbard, G. O., & Hurley, R. A. (2005). Neural underpinnings of fear and its modulation: Implications for anxiety disorders. *The Journal of Neuropsychiatry and Clinical Neurosciences, 17*, 1–6.

Miller, L., Gur, M., Shanok, A., & Weissman, M. (2008). Interpersonal psychotherapy with pregnant adolescents: Two pilot studies. *Journal of Child Psychology and Psychiatry, 49*, 733–742.

Miller, M. N., & Pumariega, A. J. (2001). Culture and eating disorders: A historical and cross-cultural review. *Psychiatry: Interpersonal and Biological Processes, 64*, 93–110.

Miller, N. E., & Magruder, K. M. (Eds.). (1999). *Cost-effectiveness of psychotherapy: A guide for practitioners, researchers, and policymakers*. New York: Oxford University Press.

Miller, W. R., & Thoresen, C. E. (2003). Spirituality, religion, and health: An emerging research field. *American Psychologist, 58*, 24–35.

Millon, T., Davis, R., & Millon, C. (2000). *Personality disorders in modern life*. New York: Wiley.

Mills, J. (2013). Jung's metaphysics. *International Journal of Jungian Studies, 5*, 19–43.

Mills, M. J. (2011). Associations among achievement measures and their collective prediction of work involvement. *Personality and Individual Differences, 50*, 360–364.

Milner, B. (1966). Amnesia following operation on temporal lobes. In C. W. M. Whitty & P. Zangwill (Eds.), *Amnesia*. London: Butterworth.

Milner, B. (2005). The medial temporal-lobe amnesic syndrome. *Psychiatric Clinics of North America, 28*, 599–611.

Milton, J., & Wiseman, R. (1999). Does psi exist? Lack of replication of an anomalous process of information transfer. *Psychological Bulletin, 125*, 387–391.

Miner-Rubino, K., & Cortina, L. M. (2007). Beyond targets: Consequences of vicarious exposure to misogyny at work. *Journal of Applied Psychology, 92*, 1254–1269.

Miner-Rubino, K., Winter, D. G., & Stewart, A. J. (2004). Gender, social class, and the subjective experience of aging: Self-perceived personality change from early adulthood to late midlife. *Personality and Social Psychology Bulletin, 30*, 1599–1610.

Miner, J., & Clarke-Stewart, K. (2008). Trajectories of externalizing behavior from age 2 to age 9: Relations with gender, temperament, ethnicity, parenting, and rater. *Developmental Psychology, 44*, 771–786.

Minnesota Multiphasic Personality Inventory-2. (1989). Regents of the University of Minnesota.

Mintz, A., & Brule, D. (2009). Methodological issues in studying suicide terrorism. *Political Psychology, 30*, 361–367.

Minuchin, S. (1999). Retelling, reimagining, and re-searching: A continuing conversation. *Journal of Marital and Family Therapy, 25*, 9–14.

Miquel, J. (2006). Integración de teorías del envejecimiento (parte I). Integration of theories of ageing. *Revista Espanola de Geriatria y Gerontologia, 41*, 55–63.

Mischel, W. (2004). Toward an integrative science of the person. *Annual Review of Psychology, 55*, 1–22.

Mischel, W. (2009). From Personality and Assessment (1968) to Personality Science, 2009. *Journal of Research in Personality, 43*, 282–290.

Mischel, W., & Shoda, Y. (2008). Toward a unified theory of personality: Integrating dispositions and processing dynamics within the cognitive-affective processing system. In O. P. Oliver, R. W. Robins, & L. A. Pervin (Eds.), *Handbook of personality psychology: Theory and research* (3rd ed.). New York: Guilford Press.

Mischoulon, D. (2000, June). Anti-depressants: Choices and controversy. *HealthNews*, p. 4.

Miserando, M. (1991). Memory and the seven dwarfs. *Teaching of Psychology, 18*, 169–171.

Mitchell, D. B., & Schmitt, F. A. (2006). Short- and long-term implicit memory in aging and Alzheimer's disease. *Neuropsychological Development and Cognition, B, Aging and Neuropsychological Cognition, 13*, 611–635.

Mitte, K. (2005). Meta-analysis of cognitive-behavioral treatments for generalized anxiety disorder: A comparison with pharmacotherapy. *Psychological Bulletin, 131*, 785–795.

Mizrahi, R., Agid, O., Borlido, C., Suridjan, I., Rusjan, P., Houle, S., & . . . Kapur, S. (2011). Effects of antipsychotics on D3 receptors: A clinical PET study in first episode antipsychotic naive patients with schizophrenia using [^{11}C]-(+)-PHNO. *Schizophrenia Research, 131*, 63–68.

MLA. (2010). MLA Language Map; all languages other than English combined. Retrieved from http://www.mla.org/census_map&source=county (based on 2000 U.S. Census Bureau figures).

Moayedi, M., & Davis, K. D. (2013). Theories of pain: From specificity to gate control. *Journal of Neurophysiology, 109*, 5–12.

Mobasher, B., & Tuzhilin, A. (2009). Preface to the special issue on data mining for personalization. *User Modeling and User-Adapted Interaction, 19*, 1–3.

Moffitt, T. E., & Caspi, A. (2007). Evidence from behavioral genetics for environmental contributions to antisocial conduct. In J. E. Grusec & P. D. Hastings (Eds.), *Handbook of socialization: Theory and research*. New York: Guilford Press.

Moffitt, T. E., Caspi, A., & Rutter, M. (2006). Measured gene-environment interactions in psychopathology: Concepts, research strategies, and implications for research, intervention, and public understanding of genetics. *Perspectives on Psychological Science, 1*, 5–27.

Mograss, M., Guillem, F., Brazzini-Poisson, V., & Godbout, R. (2009, May). The effects of total sleep deprivation on recognition memory processes: A study of event-related potential. *Neurobiology of Learning and Memory, 91*, 343–352.

Mohan, A., Sharma, R., & Bijlani, R. L. (2011). Effect of meditation on stress-induced changes in cognitive functions. *The Journal of Alternative and Complementary Medicine, 17*, 207–212.

Mohapel, P., Leanza, G., Kokaia, M., & Lindvall, O. (2005). Forebrain acetylcholine regulates adult hippocampal neurogenesis and learning. *Neurobiology of Aging, 26*, 939–946.

Moher, C., Gould, D., Hegg, E., & Mahoney, A. (2008). Non-generalized and generalized conditioned reinforcers: Establishment and validation. *Behavioral Interventions, 23*, 13–38.

Mohr, D. C., Cuijpers, P., & Lehman, K. (2011). Supportive accountability: A model for providing human support to enhance adherence to eHealth interventions. *Journal of Medical Internet Research, 13*, 136–146.

Mokdad, A. H., Brewer, R. D., & Naimi, T. (2007). Binge drinking is a problem that cannot be ignored. *Preventive Medicine: An International Journal Devoted to Practice and Theory, 44*, 303–304.

Møller, A. R. (2011). Anatomy and physiology of the auditory system. In A. R. Møller, B. Langguth, . . . T. Kleinjung (Eds.), *Textbook of tinnitus*. New York: Springer Science + Business Media.

Monk, T. H., Buysse, D. J., Billy, B. D., Fletcher, M. E., Kennedy, K. S., Schlarb, J. E., & Beach, S. R. (2011). Circadian type and bed-timing regularity in 654 retired seniors: correlations with subjective sleep measures. *Sleep, 34*, 235–239.

Monnier, J., Resnick, H. S., Kilpatrick, D. G., & Seals, B. (2002). The relationship between distress and resource loss following rape. *Violence and Victims, 17*, 85–92.

Monteleone, P., Martiadis, V., & Maj, M. (2011). Circadian rhythms and treatment implications in depression. *Progress in Neuro-Psychopharmacology & Biological Psychiatry, 35*, 1569–1574.

Montgomery, K. J., Isenberg, N., & Haxby, J. V. (2007). Communicative hand gestures and object-directed hand movements activated the mirror neuron system. *Social, Cognitive and Affective Neuroscience, 2*, 114–122.

Montgomery, K. L. (2011). Living with panic, worry, and fear: Anxiety disorders. In C. Franklin & R. Fong (Eds.), *The church leader's counseling resource book: A guide to mental health and social problems*. New York: Oxford University Press.

Montgomery, S. A., Nil, R., Dürr-Pal, N., Loft, H., & Boulenger, J. P. (2005). A 24-week randomized, double-blind, placebo-controlled study of escitalopram for the prevention of generalized social anxiety disorder. *Journal of Clinical Psychiatry, 66*, 1270–1278.

Montoya, R., & Insko, C. (2008). Toward a more complete understanding of the reciprocity of liking effect. *European Journal of Social Psychology, 38*, 477–498.

Moodley, R., Gielen, U. P., & Wu, R. (2013). *Handbook of counseling and psychotherapy in an international context*. New York: Routledge/Taylor & Francis Group.

Moody, H. R. (2000). *Aging: Concepts and controversies*. Thousand Oaks, CA: Sage.

Moon, C., Lagercrantz, H., & Kuhl, P. (2013). Language experienced in utero affects vowel perception after birth: A two-country study. *Acta Paediatrica, 102*, 156–160.

Moore, D. G., Goodwin, J. E., & George, R. (2007). Infants perceive human point-light displays as solid forms. *Cognition, 104*, 377–396.

Moore, M. M. (2002). Behavioral observation. In M. W. Wiederman & B. E. Whitley (Eds.), *Handbook for conducting research on human sexuality*. Mahwah, NJ: Lawrence Erlbaum.

Moorey, S. (2007). Cognitive therapy. In W. Dryden (Ed.), *Dryden's handbook of individual therapy* (5th ed.). Thousand Oaks, CA: Sage Publications.

Mora-Giral, M., Raich-Escursell, R. M., Segues, C. V., Torras-Claras, A. J., & Huon, G. (2004). Bulimia symptoms and risk factors in university students. *Eating and Weight Disorders, 9*, 163-169.

Morad, Y., Barkana, Y., Zadok, D., Hartstein, M., Pras, E., & Bar-Dayan, Y. (2009, July). Ocular parameters as an objective tool for the assessment of truck drivers fatigue. *Accident Analysis and Prevention, 41*, 856-860.

Moran, A. (2009). Cognitive psychology in sport: Progress and prospects. *Psychology of Sport and Exercise, 10*, 420-426.

Morcom, A. M., & Friston, K. J. (2011, September 1). Decoding episodic memory in ageing: A Bayesian analysis of activity patterns predicting memory. *NeuroimageI, 33*, 88-91.

Moretz, M., & McKay, D. (2009). The role of perfectionism in obsessive-compulsive symptoms: 'Not just right' experiences and checking compulsions. *Journal of Anxiety Disorders, 23*, 640-644.

Morgan, A. A., Marsiske, M., & Whitfield, K. E. (2008). Characterizing and explaining differences in cognitive test performance between African American and European American older adults. *Experimental Aging Research, 34*, 80-100.

Morone, N. E., & Greco, C. M. (2007). Mind-body interventions for chronic pain in older adults: A structured review. *Pain Medicine, 8*, 359-375.

Morrone, A. S., & Pintrich, P. R. (2006). Achievement motivation. In G. G. Bear & K. M. Minke (Eds.), *Children's needs III: Development, prevention, and intervention.* Washington, DC: National Association of School Psychologists.

Morrongiello, B. A., Corbett, M., & Switzer, J. (2013). Understanding and preventing pediatric unintentional injury: An evidence-based model outlining factors that influence children's risk taking. In J. Assailly (Ed.), *Psychology of risk-taking.* Hauppauge, NY: Nova Science Publishers.

Morrow, J., & Wolf, R. (1991, May). Wired for a miracle. *Health*, pp. 64-84.

Moscoso, S. C., Chaves, S. S., & Argilaga, M. T. A. (2013). Reporting a program evaluation: Needs, program plan, intervention, and decisions. *International Journal of Clinical and Health Psychology, 13*, 58-66.

Mosher, C. J., & Akins, S. (2007). *Drugs and drug policy: The control of consciousness alteration.* Thousand Oaks, CA: Sage Publications.

Moshman, D. (2011). *Adolescent rationality and development: Cognition, morality, and identity (3rd ed.).* New York: Psychology Press.

Moskowitz, G. B. (2004). *Social cognition: Understanding self and others.* New York: Guilford Press.

Motley, M. T. (1987, February). What I meant to say. *Psychology Today*, pp. 25-28.

Muammar, O. M. (2007). An integration of two competing models to explain practical intelligence. *Dissertation Abstracts International: Section B: The Sciences and Engineering, 67(7-B)*, 4128.

Mueller, C. E. (2009). Protective factors as barriers to depression in gifted and nongifted adolescents. *Gifted Child Quarterly, 53*, 3-14.

Mullen, B., & Rice, D. R. (2003). Ethnophaulisms and exclusion: The behavioral consequences of cognitive representation of ethnic immigrant groups. *Personality and Social Psychology Bulletin, 29*, 1056-1067.

Munakata, Y. (2006). Information processing approaches to development. In D. Kuhn, R. S. Siegler, W. Damon, & R. M. Lerner, *Handbook of child psychology: Vol 2, Cognition, perception, and language* (6th ed.). Hoboken, NJ: John Wiley & Sons.

Mungan, E., Peynircioğlu, Z. F., & Halpern, A. R. (2011). Levels-of-processing effects on 'remember' responses in recognition for familiar and unfamiliar tunes. *The American Journal of Psychology, 124*, 37-48.

Munger, D. (2009, April 20). Super-recognizers: people with an amazing ability to recognize faces. Retrieved from http://scienceblogs.com/cognitivedaily/2009/04/super-recognizers_people_with.php

Munroe, R. L., Hulefeld, R., Rodgers, J. M., Tomeo, D. L., & Yamazaki, S. K. (2000). Aggression among children in four cultures. *Cross-Cultural Research: The Journal of Comparative Social Science, 34*, 3-25.

Murayama, K., & Kitagami, S. (2013). Consolidation Power of Extrinsic Rewards: Reward Cues Enhance Long-Term Memory for Irrelevant Past Events. *Journal of Experimental Psychology: General.* Retrieved from http://www.ncbi.nlm.nih.gov/pubmed/23421444

Murphy, D., et al. (2008, November). How the serotonin story is being rewritten by new gene-based discoveries principally related to SLC6A4, the serotonin transporter gene, which functions to influence all cellular serotonin systems. *Neuropharmacology, 55*, 932-960.

Murphy, G. J., Glickfield, L. L., Balsen, Z., & Isaacson, J. S. (2004). Sensory neuron signaling to the brain: Properties of transmitter release from olfactory nerve terminals. *Journal of Neuroscience, 24*, 3023-3030.

Murphy, G. L. (2005). The study of concepts inside and outside the laboratory: Medin versus Medin. In W. Ahn, R. L. Goldstone, B. C. Love, A. B. Markman, & P. Wolff (Eds.), *Categorization inside and outside the laboratory: Essays in honor of Douglas L. Medin.* Washington, DC: American Psychological Association.

Murphy, R. T., Wismar, K., & Freeman, K. (2003). Stress symptoms among African-American college students after the September 11, 2001 terrorist attacks. *Journal of Nervous and Mental Disease, 191*, 108-114.

Murphy, S. T., & Zajonc, R. B. (1993). Affect, cognition, and awareness: Affective priming with optimal and suboptimal stimulus exposures. *Journal of Personality and Social Psychology, 64*, 723-739.

Murphy, S., et al. (1998). Interference under the influence. *Personality and Social Psychology Bulletin, 24*, 517-528.

Murray, B. (June 2002). Good news for bachelor's grads. *Monitor on Psychology*, pp. 30-32.

Murray, R., Lappin, J., & Di Forti, M. (2008, August). Schizophrenia: From developmental deviance to dopamine dysregulation. *European Neuropsychopharmacology, 18*, S129-SS134.

Murray, S. L., Holmes, J. G., & Griffin, D. W. (2004). The benefits of positive illusions: Idealization and the construction of satisfaction in close relationships. In H. T. Reis & C. E. Rusbult (Eds.), *Close relationships: Key readings.* Philadelphia, PA: Taylor & Francis.

Murthy, P., Kudlur, S., George, S., & Mathew, G. (2009). A clinical overview of fetal alcohol syndrome. *Addictive Disorders & Their Treatment, 8*, 1-12.

Myers, D. G. (2000). The funds, friends, and faith of happy people. *American Psychologist, 55*, 56-67.

Myers, L. L. (2007). Anorexia nervosa, bulimia nervosa, and binge eating disorder. In B. A. Thyer & J. S. Wodarski (Eds.), *Social work in mental health: An evidence-based approach.* Hoboken, NJ: John Wiley & Sons.

Myerson, J., Adams, D. R., Hale, S., & Jenkins, L. (2003). Analysis of group differences in processing speed: Brinley plots, Q-Q plots, and other conspiracies. *Psychonomic Bulletin and Review, 10*, 224-237.

Myrtek, M. (2007). Type A behavior and hostility as independent risk factors for coronary heart disease. In J. Jordan, B. Barde, & A. M. Zeiher (Eds.), *Contributions toward evidence-based psychocardiology: A systematic review of the literature.* Washington, DC: American Psychological Association.

Mytinger, C. (2001). *Headhunting in the Solomon Islands: Around the Coral Sea.* Santa Barbara, CA: Narrative Press.

Nadeem, E., & Graham, S. (2005). Early puberty, peer victimization, and internalizing symptoms in ethnic minority adolescents. *Journal of Early Adolescence, 25*, 197-222.

Nader, E. G., Kleinman, A., Gomes, B., Bruscagin, C., Santos, B., Nicoletti, M., & Caetano, S. C. (2013). Negative expressed emotion best discriminates families with bipolar disorder children. *Journal of Affective Disorders, 148*, 418-423.

Nagai, Y., Goldstein, L. H., Fenwick, P. B. C., & Trimble, M. R. (2004). Clinical efficacy of galvanic skin response biofeedback training in reducing seizures in adult epilepsy: A preliminary randomized controlled study. *Epilepsy and Behavior, 5*, 216-223.

Nagda, B. A., Tropp, L. R., & Paluck, E. L. (2006). Looking back as we look ahead: Integrating research, theory, and practice on intergroup relations. *Journal of Social Research, 62*, 439-451.

Naglieri, J. A., LeBuffe, P. A., & Ross, K. M. (2013). Measuring resilience in children: From theory to practice. In S. Goldstein & R. B. Brooks (Eds.), *Handbook of resilience in children (2nd ed.).* New York: Springer Science + Business Media.

Nagy, T. F. (2011). Informed consent. In T. F. Nagy (Ed.), *Essential ethics for psychologists: A primer for understanding and mastering core issues.* Washington, DC: American Psychological Association.

Naik, G. (2004, December 29). New obesity boom in Arab countries has old ancestry. *The Wall Street Journal*, p. A1.

Naik, G. (2009, February 3). Parents agonize over treatment in the womb. *Wall Street Journal*, p. D1.

Najman, J. M., Aird, R., Bor, W., O'Callaghan, M., Williams, G. M., & Shuttlewood, G. J. (2004). The generational transmission of socioeconomic inequalities in child cognitive development and emotional health. *Social Science and Medicine, 58*, 1147-1158.

Nakamura, Y. (2004). Isolation of p53-target genes and their functional analysis. *Cancer Science, 95*, 7-11.

Nakamura, Y., Goto, T. K., Tokumori, K., Yoshiura, T., Kobayashi, K., Nakamura, Y., & . . . Yoshiura, K. (2011). Localization of brain activation by umami taste in humans. *Brain Research, 1390*, 156-163.

Nakato, E., Otsuka, Y., Kanazawa, S., Yamaguchi, M. K., & Kakigi, R. (2011). Distinct differences in the pattern of hemodynamic response to happy and angry facial expressions in infants–A near-infrared spectroscopic study. *NeuroImage, 54*, 1600-1606.

Nalbantian, S. (2011). Autobiographical memory in modernist literature and neuroscience. In S. Nalbantian, P. M. Matthews, & J. L. McClelland (Eds.), *The memory process: Neuroscientific and humanistic perspectives*. Cambridge, MA: MIT Press.

Nargeot, R., & Simmers, J. (2011). Neural mechanisms of operant conditioning and learning-induced behavioral plasticity in Aplysia. *Cellular and Molecular Life Sciences, 68,* 803–816.

Narrow, W. E., Rae, D. S., Robins, L. N., & Regier, D. A. (2002). Revised prevalence estimates of mental disorders in the United States: Using a clinical significance criterion to reconcile 2 surveys' estimates. *Archives of General Psychiatry, 59,* 115–123.

Nasir, N. S., & Hand, V. (2006). From the court to the classroom: Opportunities for engagement, learning, and identity in basketball and classroom mathematics. *Journal of the Learning Sciences, 17,* 143–179.

Nasrallah, H., Black, D., Goldberg, J., Muzina, D., & Pariser, S. (2008). Issues associated with the use of atypical antipsychotic medications. *Annals of Clinical Psychiatry, 20,* S24–S29.

Nathan, P. E., Stuart, S. P., & Dolan, S. L. (2000). Research on psychotherapy efficacy and effectiveness: Between Scylla and Charybdis? *Psychological Bulletin, 126,* 964–981.

National Adolescent Health Information Center. (2003). *Fact Sheet on Demographics: Adolescents.* San Francisco: University of California, San Francisco.

National Association for the Education of Young Children. (2005). *Position statements of the NAEYC.* Retrieved from http://www.naeyc.org/about/positions.asp#where.

National Center for Health Statistics. (2000). *Health United States, 2000 with adolescent health chartbook.* National Center for Health Statistics, Hyattsville, MD.

National Depression Screening Day. (2003, March 26). Questionnaire on website. Retrieved from http: //www.mentalhealthscreening.org/dep/depsample.htm#sampletest

National Institute of Child Health and Human Development (NICHD) Early Child Care Research Network. (1999). Child care and mother-child interaction in the first 3 years of life. *Psychology, 35,* 1399–1413.

National Institute of Child Health and Human Development (NICHD) Early Child Care Research Network. (2000). The relation of child care to cognitive and language development. *Child Development, 71,* 960–980.

National Institute of Child Health and Human Development (NICHD) Early Child Care Research Network. (2001). Child-care and family predictors of preschool attachment and stability from infancy. *Development Psychology, 37,* 847–862.

National Institute of Child Health and Human Development (NICHD) Early Child Care Research Network. (2002). Child-care structure–process–outcome: Direct and indirect effects of child-care quality on young children's development. *Psychological Science, 13,* 199–206.

National Institute of Child Health and Human Development (NICHD) Early Child Care Research Network. (2006). Child-care effect sizes for the NICHD study of early child care and youth development. *American Psychologist, 61,* 99–116.

National Institute on Drug Abuse. (2000). *Monitoring the future study.* Bethesda, MD: National Institutes of Health.

National Prevention Information Network. (2011). *STDs today.* Retrieved from http://www.cdcnpin.org/scripts/std/std.asp

National Research Council. (2001). *Eager to learn: Educating our preschoolers.* Washington, DC: National Academy Press.

Natvig, G. K., Albrektsen, G., & Ovarnstrom, U. (2003). Methods of teaching and class participation in relation to perceived social support and stress: Modifiable factors for improving health and well-being among students. *Educational Psychology, 23,* 261–274.

Naveh-Benjamin, M., Guez, J., & Sorek, S. (2007). The effects of divided attention on encoding processes in memory: Mapping the locus of interference. *Canadian Journal of Experimental Psychology, 61,* 1–12.

Naveh-Benjamin, M., Craik, F. I. M., Gavrilescu, D., & Anderson, N. D. (2000). Asymmetry between encoding and retrieval processes: Evidence from divided attention and a calibration analysis. *Memory & Cognition, 28,* 965–967.

Neal, D., Matson, J. L., & Belva, B. C. (2013). An examination of the reliability of a new observation measure for Autism spectrum disorders: The autism spectrum disorder observation for children. *Research in Autism Spectrum Disorders, 7,* 29–34.

Neher, A. (2006). Evolutionary psychology: Its programs, prospects, and pitfalls. *American Journal of Psychology, 119,* 517–566.

Neitz, J., Neitz, M., & Kainz, P. M. (1996, November 1). Visual pigment gene structure and the severity of color vision defects. *Science, 274,* 801–804.

Nelson, D. L., Kitto, K., Galea, D., McEvoy, C. L., & Bruza, P. D. (2013). How activation, entanglement, and searching a semantic network contribute to event memory. *Memory & Cognition, 41,* 797–819.

Nelson, P. D. (2007). The globalization of psychology: What does it mean? *The Educator, 5,* 1–4.

Nelson, T. D. (2013). The neurobiology of stereotyping and prejudice. In D. D. Franks & J. H. Turner (Eds.), *Handbook of neurosociology.* New York: Springer Science + Business Media.

Nelson, W. M., III, & Finch, A. J., Jr. (2000). Managing anger in youth: A cognitive-behavioral intervention approach. In P. C. Kendall (Ed.), *Child & adolescent therapy: Cognitive-behavioral procedures* (2nd ed.). New York: Guilford Press.

Neria, Y., DiGrande, L., & Adams, G. G. (2011). Postraumatic stress disorder following the September 11, 2011, terrorist attacks. *American Psychologist, 66,* 429–446.

Neron, S., & Stephenson, R. (2007). Effectiveness of hypnotherapy with cancer patients' trajectory: Emesis, acute pain, and analgesia and anxiolysis in procedures. *International Journal of Clinical Experimental Hypnosis, 55,* 336–354.

Nesdale, D., Maass, A., & Durkin, K. (2005). Group norms, threat, and children's racial prejudice. *Child Development, 76,* 652–663.

Nesheim, S., Henderson, S., Lindsay, M., Zuberi, J., Grimes, V., Buehler, J., et al. (2004). *Prenatal HIV testing and antiretroviral prophylaxis at an urban hospital–Atlanta, Georgia, 1997–2000.* Atlanta, GA: Centers for Disease Control.

Nestler, E. J., & Malenka, R. C. (2004, March). The addicted brain. *Scientific American,* 78–83.

Nestoriuc, Y., & Martin, A. (2007, March). Efficacy of biofeedback for migraine: A meta-analysis. *Pain, 128,* 111–127.

Nestoriuc, Y., Martin, A., Rief, W., & Andrasik, F. (2008, September). Biofeedback treatment for headache disorders: A comprehensive efficacy review. *Applied Psychophysiology and Biofeedback, 33,* 125–140.

Neumark-Sztainer, D. (2009, March). Preventing obesity and eating disorders in adolescents: What can health care providers do? *Journal of Adolescent Health, 44,* 206–213.

Newby-Clark, I. R., & Ross, M. (2003). Conceiving the past and future. *Personality and Social Psychology Bulletin, 29,* 807–818.

Newell, A., & Simon, H. (1972). *Human problem solving.* Englewood Cliffs, NJ: Prentice Hall.

Newman, C. F., Leahy, R. L., Beck, A. T., Reilly-Harrington, N. A., & Gyulai, L. (2002). *Bipolar disorder: A cognitive therapy approach.* Washington, DC: American Psychological Association.

Newman, M., & Bakay, R. (2008, April). Therapeutic potentials of human embryonic stem cells in Parkinson's disease. *Neurotherapeutics, 5,* 237–251.

Newman, S. D., Willoughby, G., & Pruce, B. (2011). The effect of problem structure on problem-solving: An fmri study of word versus number problems. *Brain Research, 30,* 88–96.

Newport, F., & Carroll, J. (2002, November 27). Battle of the bulge: Majority of Americans want to lose weight. *Gallup News Service,* pp. 1–9.

Niccols, A. (2007). Fetal alcohol syndrome and the developing socio-emotional brain. *Brain Cognition, 65,* 135–142.

Nichols, S. (2011, March 18). Experimental philosophy and the problem of free will. *Science, 331,* 1401–1403.

Nicholson, I. A. M. (2003). *Inventing personality: Gordon Allport and the science of selfhood.* Washington, DC: American Psychological Association.

Nickerson, R. S., & Adams, M. J. (1979). *Cognitive Psychology, 11,* 297.

Niedenthal, P. M. (2007, May 18). Embodying emotion. *Science, 316,* 1002–1005.

Nielsen, C., Staud, R., & Price, D. (2009, March). Individual differences in pain sensitivity: Measurement, causation, and consequences. *The Journal of Pain, 10,* 231–237.

Nielson, T. A., Stenstrom, P., & Levin, R. (2006). Nightmare frequency as a function of age, gender, and September 11, 2001: Findings from an internet questionnaire. *Dreaming, 16,* 145–158.

Nigg, J. T., & Goldsmith, H. H. (1994). Genetics of personality disorders: Perspectives from personality and psychopathology research. *Psychological Bulletin, 115,* 346–380.

Nijboer, T. C. W., te Pas, S. F., & van der Smagt, M. J. (2011). Detecting gradual visual changes in colour and brightness agnosia: A double dissociation. *NeuroReport: For Rapid Communication of Neuroscience Research, 22,* 175–180.

Nimrod, G., & Kleiber, D. A. (2007). Reconsidering change and continuity in later life: Toward an innovation theory of successful aging. *International Journal of Human Development, 65,* 1–22.

Nisbet, E. K., Zelenski, J. M., & Murphy, S. A. (2011). Happiness is in our nature: Exploring nature relatedness as a contributor to subjective well-being. *Journal of Happiness Studies, 12,* 303–322.

Nisbett, R. (2003). *The geography of thought.* New York: Free Press.

Nisbett, R. E. (2007, December 9). All brains are the same color. *The New York Times,* p. E11.

Nisbett, R. E. (2009, February). All brains are the same color. *Association for Psychological Science Observer, 22*(3), 20–21.

Nishida, M., Pearsall, J., Buckner, R., & Walker, M. (2009, May). REM sleep, prefrontal theta, and the consolidation of human emotional memory. *Cerebral Cortex, 19,* 1158–1166.

Nishimoto, S., Vu, A. T., Naselaris, T., Benjamini, Y., Yu, B., & Gallant, J. L. (2011). Reconstructing visual experiences from brain activity evoked by natural movies. *Current Biology, 10,* 22–29.

Nishimura, T., Kawamura, S., & Sakurai, S. (2011). Autonomous motivation and meta-cognitive strategies as predictors of academic performance: Does intrinsic motivation predict academic performance? *Japanese Journal of Educational Psychology, 59,* 77–87.

Nishino, S. (2007, June). Clinical and neurobiological aspects of narcolepsy. *Sleep Medicine, 8,* 373–399.

Nissle, S., & Bschor, T. (2002). Winning the jackpot and depression: Money cannot buy happiness. *International Journal of Psychiatry in Clinical Practice, 6,* 183–186.

Nittrouer, S., & Lowenstein, J. H. (2007). Children's weighting strategies for word-final stop voicing are not explained by auditory sensitivities. *Journal of Speech, Language, and Hearing Research, 50,* 58–73.

Niu, W., & Brass, J. (2011). Intelligence in worldwide perspective. In R. J. Sternberg & S. Kaufman (Eds.), *The Cambridge handbook of intelligence.* New York: Cambridge University Press.

Noble, H. B. (1999, March 12). New from the smoking wars: Success. *The New York Times,* pp. D1–D2.

Nolen-Hoeksema, S. (2007). *Abnormal psychology* (4th ed.). New York: McGraw-Hill.

Norcia, A. M., Pei, F., Bonneh, Y., Hou, C., Sampath, V., & Petter, M. W. (2005). Development of sensitivity to texture and contour information in the human infant. *Journal of Cognitive Neuroscience, 17,* 569–579.

Norcross, J. C. (2002). Empirically supported therapy relationships. In J. C. Norcross (Ed.), *Psychotherapy relationships that work: Therapist contributions and responsiveness to patients.* New York: Oxford University Press.

Norcross, J. C., Beutler, L. E., & Levant, R. F. (2006). *Evidence-based practices in mental health: Debate and dialogue on the fundamental questions.* Washington, DC: American Psychological Association.

Norlander, T., Von Schedvin, H., & Archer, T. (2005). Thriving as a function of affective personality: Relation to personality factors, coping strategies and stress. *Anxiety, Stress & Coping: An International Journal, 18,* 105–116.

Norton, D., Heath, D., & Ventura, D. (2013). Finding creativity in an artificial artist. *The Journal of Creative Behavior, 47,* 106–124.

Norton, P. J., & Price, E. C. (2007). A meta-analytic review of adult cognitive-behavioral treatment outcome across the anxiety disorders. *Journal of Nervous and Mental Disease, 195,* 521–531.

Noy, V. M. (2006). A psychoneuroimmunology program for Hispanic women with stage I–H breast cancer. *Dissertation Abstracts International: Section B: The Sciences and Engineering, 66*(11-B), 6287.

Noyes, R., Jr., Stuart, S. P., Langbehn, D. R., Happel, R. L., Longley, S. L., Muller, B. A., et al. (2003). Test of an interpersonal model of hypochondriasis. *Psychosomatic Medicine, 65,* 292–300.

Nucci, L. P. (2002). The development of moral reasoning. In U. Goswami (Ed.), *Blackwell handbook of childhood cognitive development. Blackwell Handbooks of developmental psychology.* Malden, MA: Blackwell.

Nunes, A., & Kramer, A. F. (2009). Experience-based mitigation of age-related performance declines: Evidence from air traffic control. *Journal of Experimental Psychology: Applied, 15,* 12–24.

Nurnberger, J. I., Jr., & Bierut, L. J. (2007, April). Seeking the connections: Alcoholism and our genes. *Scientific American,* pp. 46–53.

Nussbaum, A. D., & Steele, C. M. (2007). Situational disengagement and persistence in the face of adversity. *Journal of Experimental Social Psychology, 43,* 127–134.

Nyaradi, A., Li, J., Hickling, S., Foster, J., & Oddy, W. H. (2013). The role of nutrition in children's neurocognitive development, from pregnancy through childhood. *Frontiers In Human Neuroscience.* Retrieved from http://www.ncbi.nlm.nih.gov/pubmed/23532379

Nyberg, L., & Tulving, E. (1996). Classifying human long-term memory: Evidence from converging dissociations. *European Journal of Cognitive Psychology, 8,* 163–183.

O'Brien, W. H., & Young, K. M. (2013). Assessment of psychopathology: Behavioral approaches. In J. R. Graham, J. A. Naglieri, & I. B. Weiner (Eds.), *Handbook of psychology, Vol. 10: Assessment psychology (2nd ed.).* Hoboken, NJ: John Wiley & Sons Inc.

O'Brien, K. M., & LeBow, M. D. (2007). Reducing maladaptive weight management practices: Developing a psychoeducational intervention program. *Eating Behaviors, 8,* 195–210.

O'Donohue, W. (Ed.). (1997). *Sexual harassment: Theory, research, and treatment.* Boston: Allyn & Bacon.

O'Grady, W. D., & Dobrovolsky, M. (Eds.). (1996). *Contemporary linguistic analysis: An introduction* (3rd ed.). Toronto: Copp Clark Pitman.

O'Keefe, T., & Fox, K. (Eds.). (2003). *Finding the real me: True tales of sex and gender diversity.* San Francisco: Jossey-Bass.

O'Leary-Kelly, A., Bowes-Sperry, L., Bates, C., & Lean, E. (2009). Sexual harassment at work: A decade (plus) of progress. *Journal of Management, 35,* 503–536.

Oatley, K., Keltner, D., & Jenkins, J. M. (2006). *Understanding emotions.* Oxford, England: Blackwell.

Occhionero, M. (2004). Mental processes and the brain during dreams. *Dreaming, 14,* 54–64.

Odeku, K., Rembe, S., & Anwo, J. (2009). Female genital mutilation: A human rights perspective. *Journal of Psychology in Africa, 19,* 55–62.

Oehman, A., & Mineka, S. (2003). The malicious serpent: Snakes as a prototypical stimulus for an evolved module of fear. *Current Directions in Psychological Science, 12,* 5–9.

Offer, D., Kaiz, M., Howard, K. I., & Bennett, E. S. (2000). The altering of reported experiences. *Journal of the American Academy of Child & Adolescent Psychiatry, 39, 735–742.*

Ogbu, J. (1992). Understanding cultural diversity and learning. *Educational Researcher, 21,* 5–14.

Ogbu, J. U. (2003). *Black American students in an affluent suburb: A study of academic disengagement.* New Jersey: Lawrence Erlbaum.

Ogletree, S. M., Martinez, C. N., & Turner, T. R. (2004). Pokémon: Exploring the role of gender. *Sex Roles, 50,* 851–859.

Ogren, K., & Sandlund, M. (2007). Lobotomy at a state mental hospital in Sweden. A survey of patients operated on during the period 1947–1958. *Nordic Journal of Psychiatry, 61,* 355–362.

Ohara, K. (2007). The n-3 polyunsaturated fatty acid/dopamine hypothesis of schizophrenia. *Progress in Neuro-Psychopharmacology & Biological Psychiatry, 31,* 469–474.

Ohira, T., Hozawa, A., Iribarren, C., Daviglus, M. L., Matthews, K. A., Gross, M. D., et al. (2007). Longitudinal association of serum carotenoids and tocopherols with hostility: The CARDIA study. *American Journal of Epidemiology, 18,* 235–241.

Ojha, H., & Pramanick, M. (2009). Effects of age on intensity and priority of life needs. *Journal of the Indian Academy of Applied Psychology, 35,* 131–136.

Olatunji, B. (2008). New directions in research on health anxiety and hypochondriasis: Commentary on a timely special series. *Journal of Cognitive Psychotherapy, 22,* 183–190.

Olds, M. E., & Fobes, J. L. (1981). The central basis of motivation: Intracranial self-stimulation studies. *Annual Review of Psychology, 32,* 123–129.

Olfson, M., & Marcus, S. (2008). A case-control study of antidepressants and attempted suicide during early phase treatment of major depressive episodes. *Journal of Clinical Psychiatry, 69,* 425–432.

Olivardia, R., & Pope, H. (2002). Body image disturbance in childhood and adolescence. In D. Castle & K. Phillips (Eds.), *Disorders of body image.* Petersfield, England: Wrightson Biomedical Publishing.

Oliver, M. B., & Hyde, J. S. (1993). Gender differences in sexuality: A meta-analysis. *Psychological Bulletin, 114,* 29–51.

Olson, D. H., & DeFrain, J. (2005). *Marriages and families: Intimacy, diversity, and strengths with PowerWeb.* New York: McGraw-Hill.

Olson, T. R., Perry, J., Janzen, J. I., Petraglia, J., & Presniak, M. D. (2011). Addressing and interpreting defense mechanisms in psychotherapy: General considerations. *Psychiatry: Interpersonal and Biological Processes, 74,* 142–165.

Oosterhof, N. N., & Todorov, A. (2008). The functional basis of face evaluation. *Proceedings of the National Academy of Sciences of the United States of America, 105,* 11087–11092.

Ophir, E., Nass, C., & Wagner, A. D. (2009). Cognitive control in media multitaskers. *PNAS Proceedings of the National Academy of Sciences of the United States of America, 106,* 15583–15587.

Ophir, E., Nass, C., & Wagner, A. D. (2009). Cognitive control in media multitaskers. *PNAS Proceedings of the National Academy of Sciences of the United States of America, 106,* 15583–15587.

Opler, M., Perrin, M., Kleinhaus, K., & Malaspina, D. (2008). Factors in the etiology of schizophrenia: Genes, parental age, and environment. *Primary Psychiatry, 15,* 37–45.

Oppenheimer, D. M. (2004). Spontaneous discounting of availability in frequency judgment tasks. *Psychological Science, 15,* 100–105.

OpportunityNYC.org. (2009). *About Opportunity NYC family rewards.* Retrieved from http://opportunitynyc.org/about

Ornat, S. L., & Gallo, P. (2004). Acquisition, learning, or development of language? Skinner's "Verbal behavior" revisited. *Spanish Journal of Psychology, 7,* 161–170.

Orwin, R. G., & Condray, D. S. (1984). Smith and Glass' psychotherapy conclusions need further probing: On Landman and Dawes' re-analysis. *American Psychologist, 39,* 71–72.

Oskamp, S. (Ed.). (2000). *Reducing prejudice and discrimination.* Mahwah, NJ: Erlbaum.
Otake, K., Shimai, S., & Tanaka-Matsumi, J. (2006). Happy people become happier through kindness: A counting kindnesses intervention. *Journal of Happiness Studies, 7,* 361–375.
Ouimet, A., Gawronski, B., & Dozois, D. (2009). Cognitive vulnerability to anxiety: A review and an integrative model. *Clinical Psychology Review, 29,* 459–470.
Oveis, C., Gruber, J., Keltner, D., Stamper, J., & Boyce, W. (2009). Smile intensity and warm touch as thin slices of child and family affective style. *Emotion, 9,* 544–548.
Oviedo-Joekes, E., et al. (2009). Diacetylmorphine versus methadone for the treatment of opioid addiction. *The New England Journal of Medicine, 361,* 777–786.
Owens, D. (2009, May 12). Park Street hit-and-run victim Angel Arce Torres dies. *The Hartford Courant.*
Oz, M. (2012, September 17). Goal power. *Time,* 46.
Packer, D. (2009). Avoiding groupthink: Whereas weakly identified members remain silent, strongly identified members dissent about collective problems. *Psychological Science, 20,* 546–548.
Padgett, D. K., Stanhope, V., & Henwood, B. F. (2011). Housing-first services for homeless adults with co-occurring disorders: An evidence-based practice. In M. Roberts-DeGennaro & S. J. Fogel (Eds.), *Using evidence to inform practice for community and organizational change.* Chicago: Lyceum Books.
Pagano, M. E., White, W. L., Kelly, J. F., Stout, R. L., & Tonigan, J. S. (2013). The 10-year course of Alcoholics Anonymous participation and long-term outcomes: A follow-up study of outpatient subjects in Project MATCH. *Substance Abuse, 34,* 51–59.
Pager, D., & Shepherd, H. (2008). The sociology of discrimination: Racial discrimination in employment, housing, credit, and consumer markets. *Annual Review of Sociology, 34,* 181–209.
Pagonis, T. A., Angelopoulos, N., & Koukoulis, G. N. (2006). Psychiatric side effects induced by supraphysiological doses of combinations of anabolic steroids correlate to the severity of abuse. *European Psychiatry, 21,* 551–562.
Pagoto, S. L., Kozak, A. T., & Spates, C. R. (2006). Systematic desensitization for an older woman with a severe specific phobia: An application of evidenced-based practice. *Clinical Gerontologist, 30,* 89–98.
Pahlke, E., Hyde, J., & Mertz, J. E. (2013). The effects of single-sex compared with coeducational schooling on mathematics and science achievement: Data from Korea. *Journal of Educational Psychology, 105,* 444–452.
Palladino, J. J., & Carducci, B. J. (1984). Students' knowledge of sleep and dreams. *Teaching of Psychology, 11*(3), 189–191.
Pallanti, S., & Bernardi, S. (2009, July). Neurobiology of repeated transcranial magnetic stimulation in the treatment of anxiety: A critical review. *International Clinical Psychopharmacology, 24,* 163–173.
Pandya, M., Pozuelo, L., & Malone, D. (2007). Electroconvulsive therapy: What the internist needs to know. *Cleveland Clinic Journal of Medicine, 74,* 679–685.
Paniagua, F. A. (2000). *Diagnosis in a multicultural context: A casebook for mental health professionals.* Thousand Oaks, CA: Sage.
Paquier, P. F., & Mariën, P. (2005). A synthesis of the role of the cerebellum in cognition. *Aphasiology, 19,* 3–19.
Parish, C. L., & Arenas, E. (2007). Stem-cell-based strategies for the treatment of Parkinson's disease. *Neurodegenerative Disease, 4,* 339–347.
Park, A. (2008, December 22). The happiness effect: How emotions and even behaviors can spread like an epidemic. *Time,* p. 40.
Park, A. (2011, March 7). Healing the hurt. *Time,* 64–71.
Park, D. C. (2007). Eating disorders: A call to arms. *American Psychologist, 62,* 158.
Park, H., & Antonioni, D. (2007). Personality, reciprocity, and strength of conflict resolution strategy. *Journal of Research in Personality, 41,* 110–125.
Park, H., & Raymo, J. M. (2013). Divorce in Korea: Trends and educational differentials. *Journal of Marriage and Family, 75,* 110–126.
Park, J., Park, K., & Dubinsky, A. J. (2011). Impact of retailer image on private brand attitude: Halo effect and summary construct. *Australian Journal Of Psychology, 63,* 173-183.
Parke, B. N. (2003). *Discovering programs for talent development.* Thousand Oaks, CA: Corwin Press.
Parke, R. D. (2004). Development in the family. *Annual Review of Psychology, 55,* 365–399.
Parker-Pope, T. (2003, April 22). The diet that works. *The Wall Street Journal,* pp. R1, R5.
Parker, E. S., Cahill, L., & McGaugh, J. L. (2006). A case of unusual autobiographical remembering. *Neurocase, 12,* 35–49.
Parra, A., & Argibay, J. C. (2007). Comparing psychics and non-psychics through a 'token-object' forced-choice ESP test. *Journal of the Society for Psychical Research, 71,* 80–90.
Pascual-Leone, A., Nguyet, D., Coehn, L. G., Brasil-Neto, J. P., Cammarota, A., & Hallett, M. (1995). Modulation of muscle responses evoked by transcranial magnetic stimulation during the acquisition of new fine motor skills. *Journal of Neurophysiology, 74,* 1037–1045.
Pascual, A., & Guéguen, N. (2005). Foot-in-the-door and door-in-the-face: A comparative meta-analytic study. *Psychological Reports, 96,* 122–128.
Pascual, A., & Guéguen, N. (2006). Door-in-the-face technique and monetary solicitation: An evaluation in a field setting. *Perceptual and Motor Skills, 103,* 974–978.
Passos, V. L., Berger, M. P. F., & Tan, F. E. (2007). Test design optimization in CAT early stage with the nominal response model. *Applied Psychological Measurement, 31,* 213–232.
Pastalkova, E., Serrano, P., Pinkhasova, D., Wallace, E., Fenton, A., & Sacktor, T. (2006). Storage of Spatial Information by the Maintenance Mechanism of LTP. *Science, 313,* 1141–1144.
Pasterski, V., Geffner, M., Brain, C., Hindmarsh, P., Brook, C., & Hines, M. (2005). Prenatal hormones and postnatal socialization by parents as determinants of male-typical toy play in girls with congenital adrenal hyperplasia. *Child Development, 76,* 264–278.
Paterson, H. M., Kemp, R. I., & Ng, J. R. (2011). Combating co-witness contamination: Attempting to decrease the negative effects of discussion on eyewitness memory. *Applied Cognitive Psychology, 25,* 43–52.
Patterson, T. G., & Joseph, S. (2013). Unconditional positive self-regard. In M. E. Bernard (Ed.), *The strength of self-acceptance: Theory, practice and research.* New York: Springer Science + Business Media.
Patterson, T. G., & Joseph, S. (2013). Unconditional positive self-regard. In M. E. Bernard (Ed.), *The strength of self-acceptance: Theory, practice and research.* New York: Springer Science + Business Media.
Pauk, W., & Owens, R. (2007). *How to study in college.* Florence, KY: Cengage Press.
Paukert, A., Stagner, B., & Hope, K. (2004). The assessment of active listening skills in helpline volunteers. *Stress, Trauma, and Crisis: An International Journal, 7,* 61–76.
Paul, A. M. (2004). *Cult of personality: How personality tests are leading us to miseducate our children, mismanage our companies and misunderstand ourselves.* New York: Free Press.
Paulmann, S., Jessen, S., & Kotz, S. A. (2009). Investigating the multimodal nature of human communication: Insights from ERPs. *Journal of Psychophysiology, 23,* 63–76.
Paulozzi, L. J. (2006). Opioid analgesic involvement in drug abuse deaths in American metropolitan areas. *American Journal of Public Health, 96,* 1755–1757.
Pautassi, R., Myers, M., Spear, L., Molina, J., & Spear, N. E. (2011). Ethanol induces second-order aversive conditioning in adolescent and adult rats. *Alcohol, 45,* 45–55.
Pavitt, C. (2007). Impression formation. In B. B. Whaley & W. Samter (Eds.), *Explaining communication: Contemporary theories and exemplars.* Mahwah, NJ: Lawrence Erlbaum Associates.
Pavot, W., & Diener, E. (2013). Happiness experienced: The science of subjective well-being. In S. A. David, I. Boniwell, & A. Conley Ayers (Eds.), *The Oxford handbook of happiness.* New York: Oxford University Press.
Payne, D. G. (1986). Hyperamnesia for pictures and words: Testing the recall level hypothesis. *Journal of Experimental Psychology: Learning, Memory, and Cognition, 12,* 16–29.
Payne, K., & Marcus, D. (2008). The efficacy of group psychotherapy for older adult clients: A meta-analysis. *Group Dynamics: Theory, Research, and Practice, 12,* 268–278.
Pea, R., Nass, C., Meheula, L., Rance, M., Kumar, A., Bamford, H., & . . . Zhou, M. (2012). Media use, face-to-face communication, media multitasking, and social well-being among 8- to 12-year-old girls. *Developmental Psychology, 48,* 327–336.
Pearce, J. M. S. (2007). Synaesthesia. *European Neurology, 57,* 120–124.
Pearce, R. R., & Lin, Z. (2007). Chinese American post-secondary achievement and attainment: A cultural and structural analysis. *Educational Review, 59,* 19–36.
Pearlstein, T., & Steiner, M. (2008). Premenstrual dysphoric disorder: Burden of illness and treatment update. *Journal of Psychiatry & Neuroscience, 33,* 291–301.
Pearson, A. R., Dovidio, J. F., & Pratto, E. (2007). Racial prejudice, intergroup hate, and blatant and subtle bias of whites toward blacks in legal decision making in the United States. *International Journal of Psychology & Psychological Therapy, 7,* 125–134.
Pearson, J., & Clifford, C. W. G. (2005). When your brain decides what you see: Grouping across monocular, binocular, and stimulus rivalry. *Psychological Science, 16,* 516–519.
Pedersen, P. B., Draguns, J. G., Lonner, W. J., & Trimble, J. E. (Eds.). (2002). *Counseling across cultures* (5th ed.). Thousand Oaks, CA: Sage.

Pedraza, O., & Mungas, D. (2008). Measurement in cross-cultural neuropsychology. *Neuropsychology Review, 18,* 184–193.

Peiro, J. M., & Lunt, I. (2002). The context for a European framework for psychologists' training. *European Psychologist, 7,* 169–179.

Pell, M. D., Monetta, L., Paulmann, S., & Kotz, S. A. (2009). Recognizing emotions in a foreign language. *Journal of Nonverbal Behavior, 33,* 107–120.

Pellegrini, S., Muzio, R. N., Mustaca, A. E., & Papini, M. R. (2004). Successive negative contrast after partial reinforcement in the consummatory behavior of rats. *Learning and Motivation, 35,* 303–321.

Pelli, D. G., Burns, C. W., & Farell, B. (2006). Feature detection and letter identification. *Vision Research, 46,* 4646–4674.

Pellis, S. M., & Pellis, V. C. (2007). Rough-and-tumble play and the development of the social brain. *Current Directions in Psychological Science, 16,* 95–97.

Pelphrey, K., & Shultz, S. (2013). Brain mechanisms for social perception: Moving toward an understanding of autism. In K. L. Johnson & M. Shiffrar (Eds.), *People watching: Social, perceptual, and neurophysiological studies of body perception.* New York: Oxford University Press.

Pempek, T., Yermolayeva, Y., & Calvert, S. (2009). College students' social networking experiences on Facebook. *Journal of Applied Developmental Psychology, 30,* 227–238.

Pendyam, S., Bravo-Rivera, C., Burgos-Robles, A., Sotres-Bayon, F., Quirk, G. J., & Nair, S. S. (2013). Fear signaling in the prelimbic-amygdala circuit: A computational modeling and recording study. *Journal of Neurophysiology, 110,* 844–861.

Penley, J. A., Tomaka, J., & Wiebe, J. S. (2002). The association of coping to physical and psychological health outcomes: A meta-analytic review. *Journal of Behavioral Medicine, 25,* 551–603.

Penn, D. L., Corrigan, P. W., Bentall, R. P., Racenstein, J. M., & Newman, L. (1997). Social cognition in schizophrenia. *Psychological Bulletin, 121,* 114–132.

Penney, J. B., Jr. (2000). Neurochemistry. In B. S. Fogel, et al. (Eds.), *Synopsis of neuropsychiatry.* New York: Lippincott Williams & Wilkins.

Penza, K. M., Heim, C., & Nemeroff, C. B. (2006). Trauma and depression. In C. L. Keyes & S. H. Goodman (Eds.), *Women and depression: A handbook for the social, behavioral, and biomedical sciences.* New York: Cambridge University Press.

Penzel, F. (2000). *Obsessive-compulsive disorders: A complete guide to getting well and staying well.* New York: Oxford University Press.

People Weekly. (2003, June 23). Kid Doc: He's no brain surgeon–yet. But Sho Yano, 12, is about to start med school. *People Weekly,* 125.

Pérez-Leroux, A. T., Pirvulescu, M., & Roberge, Y. (2011). Topicalization and object omission in child language. *First Language, 31,* 280–299.

Perham, N., & Sykora, M. (2012). Disliked music can be better for performance than liked music. *Applied Cognitive Psychology, 26,* 550–555.

Perloff, R. M. (2003). *The dynamics of persuasion: Communication and attitudes in the 21st century* (2nd ed.). Mahwah, NJ: Erlbaum.

Perovic, S., & Radenovic, L. (2011). Fine-tuning nativism: The 'nurtured nature' and innate cognitive structures. *Phenomenology and the Cognitive Sciences, 10,* 399–417.

Perovic, S., & Radenovic, L. (2011). Fine-tuning nativism: The 'nurtured nature' and innate cognitive structures. *Phenomenology and the Cognitive Sciences, 10,* 399–417.

Perry, B. (2008, May 19). 'I don't know how to forget.' *People,* p. 143.

Perry, G. (2013). *Behind the shock machine.* New York: New Press.

Perry, J., Presniak, M. D., & Olson, T. R. (2013). Defense mechanisms in schizotypal, borderline, antisocial, and narcissistic personality disorders. *Psychiatry: Interpersonal and Biological Processes, 76,* 32–52.

Pert, C. B. (2002). The wisdom of the receptors: Neuropeptides, the emotions, and body-mind. *Advances in Mind-Body Medicine, 18,* 30–35.

Pervin, L. A. (1990). *Handbook of personality: Theory and research.* New York: Guilford Press.

Pervin, L. A. (2003). *The science of personality* (2nd ed.). London: Oxford University Press.

Pesmen, C. (2006). Health and wealth techniques to help keep chronic pain from taking over. *Money Builder, 35,* 48.

Pessoa, L. (2011). Reprint of: Emotion and cognition and the amygdala: From "what is it?" to "what's to be done?". *Neuropsychologia, 49,* 681–694.

Peterfi, Z., McGinty, D., Sarai, E., & Szymusiak, R. (2010). Growth hormone-releasing hormone activates sleep regulatory neurons of the rat preoptic hypothalamus. *American Journal of Physiology: Regulatory, Integrative and Comparative Physiology, 298,* R147–R156.

Peters, E., Hess, T. M., Västfjäll, D., & Auman, C. (2007). Adult age differences in dual information processes. *Perspectives on Psychological Science, 2,* 1–23.

Peters, J., Suchan, B., Koster, O., & Daum, I. (2007). Domain-specific retrieval of source information in the medial temporal lobe. *European Journal of Neuroscience, 26,* 1333–1343.

Petersen, A. (2011, August 23). A sleep battle of the sexes. *Wall Street Journal,* pp. D1, D4.

Peterson, C. (2000). The future of optimism. *American Psychologist, 55,* 44–55.

Peterson, F. L., Jr., & Fuerst, D. E. (2007). Assessment and treatment of erection dysfunction. In L. VandeCreek, F. L. Peterson, Jr., & J. W. Bley (Eds.), *Innovations in clinical practice: Focus on sexual health.* Sarasota, FL: Professional Resource Press/Professional Resource Exchange.

Peterson, L. R., & Peterson, M. J. (1959). Short-term retention of individual items. *Journal of Experimental Psychology, 58,* 193–198.

Petersson, K. M., Silva, C., Castro-Caldas, A., Ingvar, M., & Reis, A. (2007). Literacy: A cultural influence on functional left-right differences in the inferior parietal cortex. *European Journal of Neuroscience, 26,* 791–799.

Petrill, S. A. (2005). Introduction to this special issue: Genes, environment, and the development of reading skills. *Scientific Studies of Reading, 9,* 189–196.

Petrill, S. A., & Deater-Deckard, K. (2004). The heritability of general cognitive ability: A within-family adoption design. *Intelligence, 32,* 403–409.

Pettigrew, T. F. (2004). Justice deferred: A half century after *Brown v. Board of Education. American Psychologist, 59,* 521–529.

Pettigrew, T. F., & Tropp, L. R. (2006). A meta-analytic test of intergroup contact theory. *Journal of Personality and Social Psychology, 90,* 751–783.

Pettito, L. A. (1993). On the ontogenetic requirements for early language acquisition. In B. de Boysson-Bardies, S. de Schonen, P. W. Jusczyk, P. McNeilage, & J. Morton (Eds.), *Developmental neurocognition: Speech and face processing in the first year of life. NATO ASI series D: Behavioural and social sciences* (Vol. 69). Dordrecht, Netherlands: Kluwer Academic.

Petty, R. E., Cacioppo, J. T., Strathman, A. J., & Priester, J. R. (2005). To think or not to think: Exploring two routes to persuasion. In T. C. Brock & M. C. Green (Eds.), *Persuasion: Psychological insights and perspectives* (2nd ed.). Thousand Oaks, CA: Sage Publications.

Pew Research Center. (2013). The global divide on homosexuality. Pew Research Center. Retrieved from http://www.pewglobal.org/files/2013/06/Pew-Global-Attitudes-Homosexuality-Report-FINAL-JUNE-4-2013.pdf

Phelps, R. P. (2005). *Defending standardized testing.* Mahwah, NJ: Lawrence Erlbaum Associates.

Philip, P., Sagaspe, P., Moore, N., Taillard, J., Charles, A., Guilleminault, C., et al. (2005). Fatigue, sleep restriction and driving performance. *Accident Analysis and Prevention, 37,* 473–478.

Phillips, M. (2013, December 12). The Lobotomy Files. *Wall Street Journal,* p. A1.

Phinney, J. S. (2003). Ethnic identity and acculturation. In K. M. Chun, O. Balls, & P. Organista (Eds.), *Acculturation: Advances in theory, measurement, and applied research.* Washington, DC: American Psychological Association.

Pi-Sunyer, X. (2003). A clinical view of the obesity problem. *Science, 299,* 859–860.

Piaget, J. (1970). Piaget's theory. In P. H. Mussen (Ed.), *Carmichael's manual of child psychology* (3rd ed., Vol. I). New York: Wiley.

Piaget, J., & Inhelder, B. (1958). *The growth of logical thinking from childhood to adolescence* (A. Parsons & S. Seagrin, Trans.). New York: Basic Books.

Picchioni, D., Goeltzenleucher, B., Green, D. N., Convento, M. J., Crittenden, R., Hallgren, M., et al. (2002). Nightmares as a coping mechanism for stress. *Dreaming: Journal of the Association for the Study of Dreams, 12,* 155–169.

Pickel, K. (2009). The weapon focus effect on memory for female versus male perpetrators. *Memory, 17,* 664–678.

Pickering, G. J., & Gordon, R. (2006). Perception of mouthfeel sensations elicited by red wine are associated with sensitivity to 6-N-propylthiouracil. *Journal of Sensory Studies, 21,* 249–265.

Piechowski, M. M. (2003). From William James to Maslow and Dabrowski: Excitability of character and self-actualization. In D. Ambrose, L. M. Cohen, et al. (Eds.), *Creative intelligence: Toward theoretic integration: Perspectives on creativity.* Cresskill, NJ: Hampton Press.

Pietarinen, A.-V. (2006). The evolution of semantics and language-games for meaning. *Interaction Studies: Social Behaviour and Communication in Biological and Artificial Systems, 7,* 79–104.

Pillay, S. S., Gruber, S. A., Rogowska, J., Simpson, N., & Yurgelun-Todd, D. A. (2006). fMRI of fearful facial affect recognition in panic disorder: the cingulate gyrus-amygdala connection. *Journal of Affective Disorders, 94,* 173–181.

Pillay, S. S., Rogowska, J., Gruber, S. A., Simpson, N., & Yurgelun-Todd, D. A. (2007). Recognition of happy facial affect in panic disorder: an fMRI study. *Journal of Anxiety Disorders, 21,* 381–393.

Pilotti, M., Chodorow, M., & Shono, Y. (2009). The benefits and costs of prior exposure: A large-scale study of interference effects in stimulus identification. *American Journal of Psychology, 122,* 191–208.

Pina, A., Gannon, T., & Saunders, B. (2009). An overview of the literature on sexual harassment: Perpetrator, theory, and treatment issues. *Aggression and Violent Behavior, 14,* 126–138.

Pincus, T., & Morley, S. (2001). Cognitive processing bias in chronic pain: A review and integration. *Psychological Bulletin, 127,* 599–617.

Pinker, S. (1994). *The language instinct.* New York: William Morrow.

Pinker, S. (2004). Clarifying the logical problem of language acquisition. *Journal of Child Language, 31,* 949–953.

Pinker, S., & Jackendoff, R. (2005). The faculty of language: What's special about it? *Cognition, 96,* 201–236.

Pinkerton, S. D., Bogart, L. M., Cecil, H., & Abramson, P. R. (2002). Factors associated with masturbation in a collegiate sample. *Journal of Psychology and Human Sexuality, 14,* 103–121.

Pinquart, M., Duberstein, P. R., & Lyness J. M. (2006). Treatments for later-life depressive conditions: A meta-analytic comparison of pharmacotherapy and psychotherapy. *American Journal of Psychiatry, 163,* 1493–1501.

Pisarik, C. T., Rowell, P., & Currie, L. K. (2013). Work-related daydreams: A qualitative content analysis. *Journal of Career Development, 40,* 87–106.

Pitman, R. K., & Delahanty, D. L. (2005). Conceptually driven pharmacologic approaches to acute trauma. *CNS Spectrums, 10,* 99–106.

Platek, S., & Kemp, S. (2009, February). Is family special to the brain? An event-related fMRI study of familiar, familial, and self-face recognition. *Neuropsychologia, 47,* 849–858.

Plomin, R. (2003). 50 years of DNA: What it has meant to psychological science. *American Psychological Society, 16,* 7–8.

Plomin, R. (2005). Finding genes in child psychology and psychiatry: When are we going to be there? *Journal of Child Psychology and Psychiatry, 46,* 1030–1038.

Plomin, R. (2009). The nature of nurture. In K. McCartney & R. A. Weinberg (Eds.), *Experience and development: A festschrift in honor of Sandra Wood Scarr.* New York: Psychology Press.

Plomin, R., & Caspi, R. (1999). Behavioral genetics and personality. In L. A. Pervin & O. P. John (Eds.), *Handbook of personality: Theory and research.* (2nd ed.). New York: Guilford.

Plomin, R., & Davis, O. (2009, January). The future of genetics in psychology and psychiatry: Microarrays, genome-wide association, and non-coding RNA. *Journal of Child Psychology and Psychiatry, 50,* 63–71.

Plomin, R., & McGuffin, P. (2003). Psychopathology in the postgenomic era. *Annual Review of Psychology, 54,* 205–228.

Pluess, M., & Belsky, J. (2009). Differential susceptibility to rearing experience: The case of childcare. *Journal of Child Psychology and Psychiatry, 50,* 396–404.

Pogarksy, G., & Piquero, A. R. (2003). Can punishment encourage offending? Investigating the 'resetting' effect. *Journal of Research in Crime and Delinquency, 40,* 95–120.

Pole, N. (2007).The psychophysiology of post-traumatic stress disorder: A meta-analysis. *Psychological Bulletin, 133,* 34–45.

Polivy, J., & Herman, C. P. (2002). Causes of eating disorders. *Annual Review of Psychology, 53,* 187–213.

Polivy, J., Herman, C. P., & Boivin, M. (2005). Eating disorders. In J. E. Maddux & B. A. Winstead (Eds.), *Psychopathology: Foundations for a contemporary understanding.* Mahwah, NJ: Lawrence Erlbaum Associates.

Polonsky, D. C. (2006). Review of the big book of masturbation: From angst to zeal. *Journal of Sex & Marital Therapy, 32,* 75–78.

Pomerlau, O. F. (1995). Individual differences in sensitivity to nicotine: Implications of genetic research on nicotine dependence [Special issue: Genetic, environmental, and situational factors mediating the effects of nicotine]. *Behavior Genetics, 25,* 161–177.

Ponterotto, J. G., Gretchen, D., & Chauhan, R. V. (2001). Cultural identity and multicultural assessment: Quantitative and qualitative tools for the clinician. In L. A. Suzuki & J. G. Ponterotto (Eds.), *Handbook of multicultural assessment: Clinical, psychological, and educational applications* (2nd ed.). San Francisco: Jossey-Bass/Pfeiffer.

Ponterotto, J. G., Utsey, S. O., & Pedersen, P. B. (2006). *Preventing prejudice: A guide for counselors, educators, and parents.* Thousand Oaks, CA: Sage Publications.

Poo, C., & Isaacson, J. S. (2007). An early critical period for long-term plasticity and structural modification of sensory synapses in olfactory cortex. *Journal of Neuroscience, 27,* 7553–7558.

Pool, E., Rehme, A. K., Fink, G. R., Eickhoff, S. B., & Grefkes, C. (2013). Network dynamics engaged in the modulation of motor behavior in healthy subjects. *Neuroimage, 88,* 68–76.

Popa, D., Léna, C., Alexandre, C., & Adrien, J. (2008). Lasting syndrome of depression produced by reduction in serotonin uptake during postnatal development: Evidence from sleep, stress, and behavior. *The Journal of Neuroscience, 28,* 88–97.

Popp, D., Donovan, R. A., & Crawford, M. (2003). Gender, race, and speech style stereotypes. *Sex Roles, 48,* 317–325.

Porkka-Heiskanen, T. (2013). Sleep homeostasis. *Current Opinion in Neurobiology, 23,* 799–805.

Porkka-Heiskanen, T., & Kalinchuk, A. V. (2011). Adenosine, energy metabolism and sleep homeostasis. *Sleep Medicine Reviews, 15,* 123–135.

Porte, H. S., & Hobson, J. A. (1996). Physical motion in dreams: One measure of three theories. *Journal of Abnormal Psychology, 105,* 329–335.

Posner, M. I., & DiGirolamo, G. J. (2000). Cognitive neuroscience: Origins and promise. *Psychological Bulletin, 126,* 873–889.

Post, J. M. (2011). Crimes of obedience: 'Groupthink' at Abu Ghraib. *International Journal of Group Psychotherapy, 61,* 49–66.

Post, J., Ali, F., Henderson, S., Shanfield, S., Victoroff, J., & Weine, S. (2009, Spring). The psychology of suicide terrorism. *Psychiatry: Interpersonal and Biological Processes, 72,* 13–31.

Pottick, K. J., Kirk, S. A., Hsieh, D. K., & Tian, X. (2007). Judging mental disorder in youths: Effects of client, clinician, and contextual differences. *Journal of Consulting Clinical Psychology, 75,* 1–8.

Poulin-Dubois, D., Blaye, A., Coutya, J., & Bialystok, E. (2011). The effects of bilingualism on toddlers' executive functioning. *Journal of Experimental Child Psychology, 108,* 567–579.

Powell, L. H., Shahabi, L., & Thoresen, C. E. (2003). Religion and spirituality: Linkages to physical health. *American Psychology, 58,* 36–52.

Powell, L. H. (2006). Review of marital and sexual lifestyles in the United States: Attitudes, behaviors, and relationships in social context. *Family Relations, 55,* 149.

Powell, L., Richmond, V. P., & Williams, G. C. (2011). Social networking and political campaigns: Perceptions of candidates as interpersonal constructs. *North American Journal of Psychology, 13,* 331–342.

Powell, R. A. (2011). Research notes: Little Albert, lost or found: Further difficulties with the Douglas Merritte hypothesis. *History of Psychology, 14,* 106–107.

Powers, K. D. (2006). An analysis of Kohlbergian moral development in relationship to biblical factors of morality in seminary students (Lawrence Kohlberg). *Dissertation Abstracts International: Section B: The Sciences and Engineering, 67*(6-B), 3485.

Powers, M., & Emmelkamp, P. (2008). Virtual reality exposure therapy for anxiety disorders: A meta-analysis. *Journal of Anxiety Disorders, 22,* 561–569.

Praisner, C. L. (2003). Attitudes of elementary school principals toward the inclusion of students with disabilities. *Exceptional Children, 69,* 135–145.

Prasad, B. (2006). Recent advances in artificial intelligence [Special issue: Recent advances in AI]. *Journal of Experimental & Theoretical Artificial Intelligence, 18,* 433–434.

Pratkanis, A. R. (2007). Social influence analysis: An index of tactics. In A. R. Pratkanis (Ed.), *The science of social influence: Advances and future progress.* New York: Psychology Press.

Pratkanis, A. R., Epley, N., & Savitsky, K. (2007). Issue 12: Is subliminal persuasion a myth? In J. A. Nier, *Taking sides: Clashing views in social psychology* (2nd ed.). New York: McGraw-Hill.

Pratt, H. D., Phillips, E. L., Greydanus, D. E., & Patel, D. R. (2003). Eating disorders in the adolescent population: Future directions [Special issue: Eating disorders in adolescents]. *Journal of Adolescent Research, 18,* 297–317.

Pratto, F., Lee, I., Tan, J. Y., & Pitpitan, E. Y. (2011). Power basis theory: A psychoecological approach to power. In D. Dunning (Ed.), *Social motivation.* New York: Psychology Press.

Pretsch, J., Heckmann, N., Flunger, B., & Schmitt, M. (2013). Agree or Disagree?: Influences on Consensus in Personality Judgments. *European Journal of Psychological Assessment.* Retrieved from http://psycnet.apa.org/psycinfo/2013-30588-001/

Pretzer, J. L., & Beck, A. T. (2005). A cognitive theory of personality disorders. In M. F. Lenzenweger & J. F. Clarkin (Eds.), *Major theories of personality disorder* (2nd ed.). New York: Guilford Press.

Price, D. D. (2000, June 9). Psychological and neural mechanisms of the affective dimension of pain. *Science, 288,* 1769–1772.

Price, J. (2013). Meet the real Jill Price. http://www.jillprice.com/. Downloaded October 15, 2013.

Price, M. (2008, September). Against doctors' orders. *Monitor on Psychology,* pp. 34–36.

Priester, J. R., & Petty, R. E. (2011). The pot-holed path to happiness, possibly paved with money: A research dialogue. *Journal of Consumer Psychology, 21,* 113–114.

Prince, C. V. (2005). Homosexuality, transvestism and transsexuality: Reflections on their etymology and differentiation. *International Journal of Transgenderism, 8,* 15–18.

Prinz, J. J. (2007). Emotion: Competing theories and philosophical issues. In P. Thagard (Ed.), *Philosophy of psychology and cognitive science.* Amsterdam, Netherlands: North Holland/Elsevier.

Prislin, R., Brewer, M., & Wilson, D. J. (2002). Changing majority and minority positions within a group versus an aggregate. *Personality and Social Psychology Bulletin, 28,* 640–647.

Proffitt, D. R. (2006). Distance perception. *Current Directions in Psychological Science, 15,* 131–139.

Prohovnik, I., Skudlarski, P., Fulbright, R. K., Gore, J. C., & Wexler, B. E. (2004). Functional MRI changes before and after onset of reported emotions. *Psychiatry Research: Neuroimaging, 132,* 239–250.

Proudfoot, D. (2009). Meaning and mind: Wittgenstein's relevance for the 'does language shape thought?' debate. *New Ideas in Psychology, 27,* 163–183.

Proyer, R. T., Gander, F., Wellenzohn, S., & Ruch, W. (2013). What good are character strengths beyond subjective well-being? The contribution of the good character on self-reported health-oriented behavior, physical fitness, and the subjective health status. *The Journal of Positive Psychology, 8,* 222–232.

Puca, R. M. (2005). The influence of the achievement motive on probability estimates in pre- and post-decisional action phases. *Journal of Research in Personality, 39,* 245–262.

Puhl, R., & Latner, J. (2007). Stigma, obesity, and the health of the nation's children. *Psychological Bulletin, 133,* 557–580.

Purdy, S. C., Sharma, M. M., Munro, K. J., & Morgan, C. A. (2013). Stimulus level effects on speech-evoked obligatory cortical auditory evoked potentials in infants with normal hearing. *Clinical Neurophysiology, 124,* 474–480.

Putnam, E. W. (2000). Dissociative disorders. In A. J. Sameroff & M. Lewis (Eds.), *Handbook of developmental psychopathology* (2nd ed.). Dordrecht, Netherlands: Kluwer Academic Publishers.

Qu, C., Zhang, A., & Chen, Q. (2013). Monetary effects on fear conditioning. *Psychological Reports, 112,* 353–364.

Quartana, P. J., & Burns, J. W. (2007). Painful consequences of anger suppression. *Emotion, 7,* 400–414.

Quas, J. A., Malloy, L. C., & Melinder, A. (2007). Developmental differences in the effects of repeated interviews and interviewer bias on young children's event memory and false reports. *Developmental Psychology, 43,* 823–837.

Quenot, J. P., Boichot, C., Petit, A., Falcon-Eicher, S., d'Athis, P., Bonnet, C., et al. (2005). Usefulness of MRI in the follow-up of patients with repaired aortic coarctation and bicuspid aortic valve. *International Journal of Cardiology, 103,* 312–316.

Quinn, D. M., Kahng, S. K., & Crocker, J. (2004). Discreditable: Stigma effects of revealing a mental illness history on test performance. *Personality and Social Psychology Bulletin, 30,* 803–815.

Quinn, T. C., & Overbaugh, J. (2005, June 10). HIV/AIDS in women: An expanding epidemic. *Science, 308,* 1582–1583.

Quintana, S. M., Aboud, F. E., & Chao, R. K. (2006). Race, ethnicity, and culture in child development: Contemporary research and future directions. *Child Development, 77,* 1129–1141.

Quiroga, R. (2012). Concept cells: The building blocks of declarative memory functions. *Nature Reviews Neuroscience, 13,* 587–597.

Quiroga, R., Fried, I., & Koch, C. (2013, February). Brain cells for grandmother. *Scientific American,* 31–35.

Quoidbach, J., Dunn, E. W., Petrides, K. V., & Mikolajczak, M. (2010). Money giveth, money taketh away: The dual effect of wealth on happiness. *Psychological Science, 21,* 759–763.

Rabin, J. (2004). Quantification of color vision with cone contrast sensitivity. *Visual Neuroscience, 21,* 483–485.

Rabin, R. C. (2013, August 13). A glut of antidepressants. *The New York Times,* p. D4.

Rachlin, H. (2012). Making IBM's computer, Watson, human. *The Behavior Analyst, 35,* 1–16.

Rachman, S. (1990). Learned resourcefulness in the performance of hazardous tasks. In M. Rosenbaum (Ed.), *Learned resourcefulness: On coping skills, self-control, and adaptive behavior.* New York: Springer.

Rachman, S., & deSilva, P. (2004). *Panic disorders: The facts.* Oxford, England: Oxford University Press.

Rado, J., Dowd, S., & Janicak, P. (2008). The emerging role of transcranial magnetic stimulation (TMS) for treatment of psychiatric disorders. *Directions in Psychiatry, 28,* 315–332.

Raffaele, P. (2006, November). Speaking Bonobo. *Smithsonian Magazine.*

Ragins, B., & Winkel, D. E. (2011). Gender, emotion and power in work relationships. *Human Resource Management Review, 21,* 377–393.

Rahman, Q., Kumari, V., & Wilson, G. D. (2003). Sexual orientation-related differences in pre-pulse inhibition of the human startle response. *Behavioral Neuroscience, 117,* 1096–1102.

Rajagopal, S. (2006). The placebo effect. *Psychiatric Bulletin, 30,* 185–188.

Rajecki, D. W., & Borden, V. M. H. (2011). Psychology degrees: Employment, wage, and career trajectory consequences. *Perspectives on Psychological Science, 6,* 321–335.

Ramachandra, V. (2009, February). On whether mirror neurons play a significant role in processing affective prosody. *Perceptual and Motor Skills, 108,* 30–36.

Ramachandran, V. S., & Hubbard, E. M. (2006, August 17). Hearing colors, tasting shapes. Scientific American, *16,* 76–83.

Ramachandran, V. S. (2004). *A brief tour of human consciousness: From impostor poodles to purple numbers.* New York: Pi Press.

Ramachandran, V. S., & Hubbard, E. M. (2001). Synesthesia–a window into perception, thought and language. *Journal of Consciousness Studies, 8,* 3–34.

Ramos, R. A., Ferguson, C. J., Frailing, K., & Romero-Ramirez, M. (2013). Comfortably numb or just yet another movie? Media violence exposure does not reduce viewer empathy for victims of real violence among primarily Hispanic viewers. *Psychology of Popular Media Culture, 2,* 2–10.

Ramos, R. T. (2006). Antidepressants and dizziness. *Journal of Psychopharmacology, 20,* 708–713.

Rampon, C., Jiang, C. H., Dong, H., Tang, Y., Lockhart, D. J., Schultaz, P. G., et al. (2000). Effects of environmental enrichment on gene expression in the brain. *Proceedings of the National Academy of Sciences, 97,* 12880–12884.

Ramus, F. (2006). Genes, brain, and cognition: A roadmap for the cognitive scientist. *Cognition, 101,* 247–269.

Randall, D. K. (2012, August 4–5). Decoding the science of sleep. *Wall Street Journal,* pp. C1–C2.

Randolph-Seng, B., & Nielsen, M. E. (2009). Opening the doors of perception: Priming altered states of consciousness outside of conscious awareness. *Archivfür Religionspsychologie/ Archive for the Psychology of Religions, 31,* 237–260.

Rangell, L. (2007). *The road to unity in psychoanalytic theory.* Lanham, MD: Jason Aronson.

Rapaport, M., Nierenberg, A. A., Howland, R., Dording, C., Schettler, P. J., & Mischoulon, D. (2011). The treatment of minor depression with St. John's wort or citalopram: Failure to show benefit over placebo. *Journal of Psychiatric Research, 45,* 931–941.

Rapport, R. L. (2005). *Nerve endings: The discovery of the synapse.* New York: W. W. Norton.

Raskin, N. J., & Rogers, C. R. (1989). Person-centered therapy. In R. J. Corsini & D. Wedding (Eds.), *Current psychotherapies* (4th ed.). Itasca, IL: F. E. Peacock.

Rassin, E. (2008). Individual differences in the susceptibility to confirmation bias. *Netherlands Journal of Psychology, 64,* 87–93.

Rassin, E., & Muris, P. (2007). Abnormal and normal obsessions: A reconsideration. *Behaviour Research and Therapy, 45,* 1065–1070.

Rattan, A., Savani, K., Naidu, N. V. R., & Dweck, C. S. (2012). Can everyone become highly intelligent? Cultural differences in and societal consequences of beliefs about the universal potential for intelligence. *Journal of Personality and Social Psychology, 103,* 787–803.

Ray, L. A., & Hutchison, K. E. (2007). Effects of naltrexone on alcohol sensitivity and genetic moderators of medication response: a double-blind placebo-controlled study. *Archives of General Psychiatry, 64,* 1069–1077.

Ray, L., Bryan, A., MacKillop, J., McGeary, J., Hesterberg, K., & Hutchison, K. (2009). The dopamine D4 receptor gene exon III polymorphism, problematic alcohol use and novelty seeking: Direct and mediated genetic effects. *Addiction Biology, 14,* 238–244.

Ray, R., et al. (2008). Neuroimaging, genetics and the treatment of nicotine addiction. *Behavioural Brain Research, 193,* 159–169.

Raz, A. (2007). Suggestibility and hypnotizability: Mind the gap. *American Journal of Clinical Hypnosis, 49,* 205–210.

Raznahan, A., Lee, Y., Stidd, R., Long, R., Greenstein, D., Clasen, L., Addington, A., Gogtay, N., Rapoport, J., & Giedd, J. (2010). Longitudinally mapping the influence of sex and androgen signaling on the dynamics of human cortical maturation in adolescence. *Proceedings of the National Academy of Sciences, 107,* 16988–16993.

Redding, G. M. (2002). A test of size-scaling and relative-size hypotheses for the moon illusion. *Perception and Psychophysics, 64,* 1281–1289.

Redding, G. M., & Hawley, E. (1993). Length illusion in fractional MüllerLyer stimuli: An object-perception approach. *Perception, 22,* 819–828.

Reddy, S. (2013, March 19). People who taste too much. *Wall Street Journal,* p. D1.

Reddy, S. (2013, September 3). A field guide to the perfect nap. *Wall Street Journal,* pp. D1–D2.

Redish, A. D. (2004). Addiction as a computational process gone awry. *Science, 306,* 1944–1947.

Redshaw, M., & Martin, C. (2013). Babies, 'bonding' and ideas about parental 'attachment'. *Journal of Reproductive and Infant Psychology, 31,* 219–221.

Reece, M., Herbenick, D., Sanders, S., Dodge, B., Ghassemi, A., & Fortenberry, J. (2009, July). Prevalence and character-istics of vibrator use by men in the United States. *Journal of Sexual Medicine, 6,* 1867–1874.

Reed, P. (2007). Response rate and sensitivity to the molar feedback function relating response and reinforcement rate on VI+ schedules of reinforcement. *Journal of Experimental Psychology: Animal Behavior Processes, 33,* 428–439.

Reed, P., & Morgan, T. (2008). Effect on subsequent fixed-interval schedule performance of prior exposure to ratio and interval schedules of reinforcement. *Learning & Behavior, 36,* 82–91.

Reed, S. K. (1996). *Cognition: Theory and applications* (4th ed.). Pacific Grove, CA: Brooks/Cole.

Rees, P., & Seaton, N. (2011). Psychologists' response to crises: International perspectives. *School Psychology International, 32,* 73–94.

Reese, R. J., Conoley, C. W., & Brossart, D. F. (2002). Effectiveness of telephone counseling: A field-based investigation. *Journal of Counseling Psychology, 49,* 233–242.

Regan, P. C. (2006). Love. In R. D. McAnulty & M. M. Burnette (Eds.), *Sex and sexuality, Vol 2: Sexual function and dysfunction.* Westport, CT: Praeger Publishers/Greenwood Publishing.

Reichenberg, A., & Harvey, P. D. (2007). Neuropsychological impairments in schizophrenia: Integration of performance-based and brain imaging findings. *Psychological Bulletin, 133,* 212–223.

Reichenberg, A., Harvey, P., Bowie, C., Mojtabai, R., Rabinowitz, J., Heaton, R., et al. (2009). Neuropsychological function and dysfunction in schizophrenia and psychotic affective disorders. *Schizophrenia Bulletin, 35,* 1022–1029.

Reid, J. R., MacLeod, J., & Robertson, J. R. (2010). Cannabis and the lung. *Journal of the Royal College of Physicians, 40, 328 –334.*

Reif, A., & Lesch, K. P. (2003). Toward a molecular architecture of personality. *Behavioural Brain Research, 139,* 1–20.

Reijonen, J. H., Pratt, H. D., Patel, D. R., & Greydanus, D. E. (2003). Eating disorders in the adolescent population: An overview [Special issue: Eating disorders in adolescents]. *Journal of Adolescent Research, 18,* 209–222.

Reilly, T., & Waterhouse, J. (2007). Altered sleep-wake cycles and food intake: The Ramadan model. *Physiology & Behavior, 90,* 219–228.

Reiner, R. (2008, March). Integrating a portable biofeedback device into clinical practice for patients with anxiety disorders: Results of a pilot study. *Applied Psychophysiology and Biofeedback, 33,* 55–61.

Reisberg, D. (1997). *Cognition: Exploring the science of the mind.* New York: Norton.

Reisberg, D. (2009). *Cognition: Exploring the science of the mind.* New York: Norton.

Reisberg, D. (2013). Mental images. In D. Reisberg (Ed.), *The Oxford handbook of cognitive psychology.* New York: Oxford University Press.

Reisner, A. D., Piel, J., & Makey, M. r. (2013). Competency to stand trial and defendants who lack insight into their mental illness. *Journal of the American Academy of Psychiatry and the Law, 41,* 85–91.

Rende, R. (2007). Thinking inside and outside the (black) box: Behavioral genetics and human development. *Human Development, 49,* 343–346.

Renshaw, D. C. (2006). Male and female circumcision today. *The Family Journal, 14,* 283–285.

Repp, B. H., & Knoblich, G. (2007). Action can affect auditory perception. *Psychological Science, 18,* 6–7.

Rescorla, R. A. (1988). Pavlovian conditioning: It's not what you think it is. *American Psychologist, 43,* 151–160.

Reynolds, C. R., & Ramsay, M. C. (2003). Bias in psychological assessment: An empirical review and recommendations. In J. R. Graham & J. A. Naglieri (Eds.), *Handbook of psychology: Assessment psychology* (Vol. 10). New York: Wiley.

Reynolds, R. I., & Takooshian, H. (1988, January). Where were you August 8, 1985? *Bulletin of the Psychonomic Society, 26,* 23–25.

Rice, C. (2009, December 18). Prevalence of Autism Spectrum Disorders–Autism and Developmental Disabilities Monitoring Network, United States, 2006. *MMWR,* 58(SS10), 1–20.

Rice, E., Milburn, N. G., & Monro, W. (2011). Social networking technology, social network composition, and reductions in substance use among homeless adolescents. *Prevention Science, 12,* 80–88.

Rice, M. L., Tomblin, J. B., Hoffman, L., Richman, W. A., & Marquis, J. (2004). Grammatical tense deficits in children with SLI and nonspecific language impairment: Relationships with non-verbal IQ over time. *Journal of Speech, Language, and Hearing Research, 47,* 816–834.

Rich, E. L., & Shapiro, M. L. (2007). Prelimbic/infralimbic inactivation impairs memory for multiple task switches, but not flexible selection of familiar tasks. *Journal of Neuroscience, 27,* 4747–4755.

Richard, D. C. S., & Lauterbach, D. (Eds.). (2006). *Handbook of exposure therapies.* New York: Academic Press.

Richards, C. (2011). Transsexualism and existentialism. *Existential Analysis, 22*(2), 272–279.

Richards, R. (2006). Frank Barron and the study of creativity: A voice that lives on. *Journal of Humanistic Psychology, 46,* 352–370.

Richardson, A. S., Bergen, H. A., Martin, G., Roeger, L., & Allison, S. (2005). Perceived academic performance as an indicator of risk of attempted suicide in young adolescents. *Archives of Suicide Research, 9,* 163–176.

Richardson, B. (2002, September 30). Light-bulb moments. *The Wall Street Journal,* p. R7.

Richardson, D., & Hammock, G. S. (2011). Is it aggression?: Perceptions of and motivations for passive and psychological aggression. In J. P. Forgas, A. W. Kruglanski, & K. D. Williams (Eds.), *The psychology of social conflict and aggression.* New York: Psychology Press.

Richgels, D. J. (2004). Paying attention to language. *Reading Research Quarterly, 39,* 470–477.

Rieber, R. W., & Robinson, D. K. (2006). Review of the essential Vygotsky. *Journal of the History of the Behavioral Sciences, 42,* 178–180.

Riedel, G., Platt, B., & Micheau, J. (2003). Glutamate receptor function in learning and memory. *Behavioural Brain Research, 140,* 1–47.

Rigby, L., & Waite, S. (2007). Group therapy for self-esteem: Using creative approaches and metaphor as clinical tools. *Behavioural and Cognitive Psychotherapy, 35,* 361–364.

Riley, A., Valdez, C., Barrueco, S., Mills, C., Beardslee, W., Sandler, I., et al. (2008). Development of a family-based program to reduce risk and promote resilience among families affected by maternal depression: Theoretical basis and program description. *Clinical Child and Family Psychology Review, 11,* 12–29.

Rinaman, L., Banihashemi, L., & Koehnle, T. J. (2011). Early life experience shapes the functional organization of stress-responsive visceral circuits. *Physiology & Behavior, 104,* 632–640.

Riniolo, T. C., Koledin, M., Drakulic, G. M., & Payne, R. A. (2003). An archival study of eyewitness memory of the Titanic's final plunge. *Journal of General Psychology, 130,* 89–95.

Rinn, W. E. (1984). The neuropsychology of facial expression: A review of neurological and psychological mechanisms for producing facial expressions. *Psychological Bulletin, 95,* 52–77.

Rinn, W. E. (1991). Neuropsychology of facial expression. In R. S. Feldman & B. Rimé (Eds.), *Fundamentals of non-verbal behavior.* Cambridge, England: Cambridge University Press.

Riolo, E. (2007). Ricordare, ripetere e rielaborare: Un lascito di Freud alia psicoanalisi futura. Remembering, repeating, and working through: Freud's legacy to the psychoanalysis of the future. *Rivista di Psicoanalisi, 53,* 439–446.

Ripley, A. (2005, March 7). Who says a woman can't be Einstein? *Time,* 51–60.

Ritter, S. M., Strick, M., Bos, M. W., Van Baaren, R. B., & Dijksterhuis, A. P. (2012). Good morning creativity: Task reactivation during sleep enhances beneficial effect of sleep on creative performance. *Journal of Sleep Research, 21,* 643–647.

Rivera-Gaxiola, M., Klarman, L., Garcia-Sierra, A., & Kuhl, P. K. (2005). Neural patterns to speech and vocabulary growth in American infants. *Neuroreport: For Rapid Communication of Neuroscience Research, 16,* 495–498.

Rivis, A., & Sheeran, P. (2013). Automatic risk behavior: Direct effects of binge drinker stereotypes on drinking behavior. *Health Psychology, 32,* 571–580.

Rizzi, T. S., & Posthuma, D. (2013). Genes and intelligence. In D. Reisberg (Ed.), *The Oxford handbook of cognitive psychology.* New York: Oxford University Press.

Robbins, B. (2008). What is the good life? Positive psychology and the renaissance of humanistic psychology. *The Humanistic Psychologist, 36,* 96–112.

Robbins, W. J. (1929). *Growth.* New Haven, CT: Yale University Press.

Robert, S. (2006). Deictic space in Wolof: Discourse, syntax and the importance of absence. In M. Hickman & S. Robert (Eds.), *Space in languages: Linguistic systems and cognitive categories.* Amsterdam, Netherlands: John Benjamins.

Roberts, M. E., Moore, S. D., & Beckham, J. C. (2007). Post-traumatic stress disorder and substance use disorders. In M. Al'bsi (Ed.), *Stress and addiction: Biological and psychological mechanisms.* San Diego, CA: Elsevier Academic Press.

Robins, C. J., & Rosenthal, M. (2011). Dialectical behavior therapy. In J. D. Herbert & E. M. Forman (Eds.), *Acceptance and mindfulness in cognitive behavior therapy: Understanding and applying the new therapies.* Hoboken, NJ: John Wiley & Sons Inc.

Robins, R. W. (2005, October 7). The nature of personality: Genes, culture, and national character. *Science, 310,* 62–63.

Robinson, D. N. (2007). Theoretical psychology: What is it and who needs it? *Theory & Psychology, 17,* 187–198.

Robinson, N. M. (2003). Two wrongs do not make a right: Sacrificing the needs of gifted students does not solve society's unsolved problems. *Journal for the Education of the Gifted, 26,* 251–273.

Robson, H., Grube, M., Lambon Ralph, M. A., Griffiths, T. D., & Sage, K. (2013). Fundamental deficits of auditory perception in Wernicke's aphasia. *Cortex: A Journal Devoted to the Study of the Nervous System and Behavior, 49,* 1808–1822.

Rock, A. (1999, January). Quitting time for smokers. *Money,* pp. 139–141.

Roediger, H. L., III, & McCabe, D. P. (2007). Evaluating experimental research: Critical issues. In R. J. Sternberg, H. L. Roediger, III, & D. F. Halpern (Eds.), *Critical thinking in psychology*. New York: Cambridge University Press.

Roets, A., & Van Hiel, A. (2011). An integrative process approach on judgment and decision making: The impact of arousal, affect, motivation, and cognitive ability. *The Psychological Record, 61*, 497–520.

Roffman, R. A. (2013). Legalization of marijuana: Unraveling quandaries for the addiction professional. *Frontiers in Psychiatry, 4*, 88–93.

Rogalsky, C., Love, T., Driscoll, D., Anderson, S. W., & Hickok, G. (2011). Are mirror neurons the basis of speech perception? Evidence from five cases with damage to the purported human mirror system. *Neurocase, 17*, 178–187.

Rogers, C. (1980). *A way of being*. Boston: Houghton Mifflin.

Rogers, C. R. (1951). *Client-centered therapy*. Boston: Houghton-Mifflin.

Rogers, C. R. (1971). A theory of personality. In S. Maddi (Ed.), *Perspectives on personality*. Boston: Little, Brown.

Rogers, C. R. (1995). *A way of being*. Boston: Houghton Mifflin.

Rogers, J. M. (2009). Tobacco and pregnancy: Overview of exposures and effects. *Birth Defects Res. C. Embryo Today, 84*, 152–160.

Rogers, P. (2002, August 2). Too much, too soon. *People*, pp. 79–82.

Rogers, P., & Eftimiades, M. (1995, July 24). Bearing witness. *People Weekly*, pp. 42–43.

Rogers, S. (2007). The underlying mechanisms of semantic memory loss in Alzheimer's disease and semantic dementia. *Dissertation Abstracts International: Section B: The Sciences and Engineering, 67*(10-B), 5591.

Rohan, K. J., Roecklein, K. A., & Tierney Lindsey, K. (2007). A randomized controlled trial of cognitive-behavioral therapy, light therapy, and their combination for seasonal affective disorder. *Journal of Consulting and Clinical Psychology, 75*, 489–500.

Roid, G., Nellis, L., & McLellan, M. (2003). Assessment with the Leiter International Performance Scale–Revised and the S-BIT. In R. S. McCallum & R. Steve (Eds.), *Handbook of nonverbal assessment*. New York: Kluwer Academic/Plenum Publishers.

Roisman, G. I., Collins, W. A., Sroufe, L. A., & Egeland, B. (2005). Predictors of young adults' representations of and behavior in their current romantic relationship: Prospective tests of the prototype hypothesis. *Attachment and Human Development, 7*, 105–121.

Roizen, N. J., & Patterson, D. (2003). Down's syndrome. *Lancet, 361*, 1281–1289.

Rollman, G. B. (2004). *Ethnocultural variations in the experience of pain*. Mahwah, NJ: Lawrence Erlbaum Associates.

Rolls, E. T. (2011). Functions of human emotional memory: The brain and emotion. In S. Nalbantian, P. M. Matthews, & J. L. McClelland (Eds.), *The memory process: Neuroscientific and humanistic perspectives*. Cambridge, MA: MIT Press.

Rom, S. A., Miller, L., & Peluso, J. (2009). Playing the game: Psychological factors in surviving cancer. *International Journal of Emergency Mental Health, 11*, 25–36.

Romano, E., Tremblay, R. E., Vitaro, E., Zoccolillo, M., & Pagani, L. (2001). Prevalence of psychiatric diagnoses and the role of perceived impairment: Findings from an adolescent community sample. *Journal of Child Psychology and Psychiatry and Allied Disciplines, 42*, 451–461.

Roncero, C. C., Daigre, C. C., Gonzalvo, B. B., Valero, S. S., Castells, X. X., Grau-López, L. L., & . . . Casas, M. M. (2013). Risk factors for cocaine-induced psychosis in cocaine-dependent patients. *European Psychiatry, 28*, 141–146.

Rooke, S. E., & Hine, D. W. (2011). A dual process account of adolescent and adult binge drinking. *Addictive Behaviors, 36*, 341–346.

Rorschach, H. (1924). *Psychodiagnosis: A diagnostic test based on perception*. New York: Grune & Stratton.

Rosch, E., & Mervis, C. B. (1975). Family resemblances: Studies in the internal structure of categories. *Cognitive Psychology, 7*, 573–605.

Rose, N., & Blackmore, S. (2002). Horses for courses: Tests of a psychic claimant. *Journal of the Society for Psychical Research, 66*, 29–40.

Rosen, J. (2005, August 28). The future v. Roberts. *The New York Times Magazine*, pp. 24–29, 44, 50–51.

Rosen, L. D. (2012). *iDisorder: Understanding our obsession with technology and overcoming its hold on us*. New York: Palgrave Macmillan.

Rosenberg, L., & Park, S. (2002). Verbal and spatial functions across the menstrual cycle in healthy young women. *Psychoneuroendocrinology, 27*, 834–841.

Rosenbloom, T., & Wolf, Y. (2002). Sensation seeking and detection of risky road signals: A developmental perspective. *Accident Analysis and Prevention, 34*, 569–580.

Rosenhan, D. L. (1973). On being sane in insane places. *Science, 179*, 250–258.

Rosenman, R. H., Grand, R. J., Jenkins, C. D., Friedman, M., Straus, R., & Wurm, M. (1994). Coronary heart disease in the Western Collaborative Group Study: Final follow-up experience of 8½ years. In A. Steptoe & J. Wardle (Eds.), *Psychosocial processes and health: A reader*. New York: Cambridge University Press.

Rosenstein, D. S., & Horowitz, H. A. (1996). Adolescent attachment and psychopathology. *Journal of Consulting and Clinical Psychology, 64*, 244–253.

Rosenthal, A. M. (2008). *Thirty-eight witnesses: The Kitty Genovese case*. Hoboken, NJ: Melville House Publishing.

Rosenthal, N. F. (2003). *The emotional revolution: How the new science of feeling can transform your life*. New York: Citadel.

Rosenthal, R. (2002). Covert communication in classrooms, clinics, courtrooms and cubicles. *American Psychologist, 57*, 838–849.

Rosenthal, R. (2003). Covert communication in laboratories, classrooms, and the truly real world. *Current Directions in Psychological Science, 12*, 151–154.

Rosner, H. (2001, April 30). The science of O. *New York Magazine*, pp. 25–31.

Ross, H. E. (2000). Sensation and perception. In D. S. Gupta, et al. (Eds.), *Psychology for psychiatrists*. London: Whurr Publishers.

Ross, H. E., & Plug, C. (2002). *The mystery of the moon illusion: Exploring size perception*. Oxford: University Press.

Ross, J. (2006). Sleep on a problem . . . It works like a dream. *The Psychologist, 19*, 738–740.

Ross, K. (Ed.). (2012). *The handbook of gender, sex and media*. Malden, MA: Wiley & Sons.

Ross, L. A., Molholm, S., Blanco, D., Gomez-Ramirez, M., Saint-Amour, D., & Foxe, J. J. (2011). The development of multisensory speech perception continues into the late childhood years. *European Journal of Neuroscience, 33*, 2329–2337.

Ross, P. E. (2004, April). Draining the language out of color. *Scientific American*, pp. 46–51.

Rossato, M., Pagano, C., & Vettor, R. (2008). The cannabinoid system and male reproductive functions. *Journal of Neuroendocrinology, 20*, 90–93.

Rossell, S. L., Bullmore, E. T., Williams, S. C. R., & David, A. S. (2002). Sex differences in functional brain activation during a lexical visual field task. *Brain and Language, 80*, 97–105.

Rossouw, J. E., Prentice, R. L., Manson, J. E., Wu, L., Barad, D., Barnabei, V. M., et al. (2007). Postmenopausal hormone therapy and risk of cardiovascular disease by age and years since menopause. *Journal of the American Medical Association, 297*, 1465–1477.

Rotan, L. W., & Ospina-Kammerer, V. (2007). *Mindbody medicine: Foundations and practical applications*. New York: Routledge/Taylor & Francis Group.

Roter, D. L., Hall, J. A., & Aoki, Y. (2002). Physician gender effects in medical communication: A meta-analytic review. *Journal of the American Medical Association, 288*, 756–764.

Rothblum, E. D. (1990). Women and weight: Fad and fiction. *Journal of Psychology, 124*, 5–24.

Rouder, J. N., Morey, R. D., & Province, J. M. (2013). A Bayes factor meta-analysis of recent extrasensory perception experiments: Comment on Storm, Tressoldi, and Di Risio (2010). *Psychological Bulletin, 139*, 241–247.

Roughton, R. E. (2002). Rethinking homosexuality: What it teaches us about psychoanalysis. *Journal of the American Psychoanalytic Association, 50*, 733–763.

Routtenberg, A., & Lindy, J. (1965). Effects of the availability of rewarding septal and hypothalamic stimulation on bar pressing for food under conditions of deprivation. *Journal of Comparative and Physiological Psychology, 60*, 158–161.

Rowe, J. B., Toni, I., Josephs, O., Frackowiak, R. S. J., & Passingham, R. E. (2000, June 2). The pre-frontal cortex: Response selection or maintenance within working memory? *Science, 288*, 1656–1660.

Royzman, E. B., Cassidy, K. W., & Baron, J. (2003). "I know, you know": Epistemic egocentrism in children and adults. *Review of General Psychology, 7*, 38–65.

Rozin, P., Kabnick, K., Pete, E., Fischler, C., & Shields, C. (2003). The ecology of eating: Smaller portion sizes in France than in the United States help explain the French paradox. *Psychological Science, 14*, 450–454.

Rubichi, S., Ricci, F., Padovani, R., & Scaglietti, L. (2005). Hypnotic susceptibility, baseline attentional functioning, and the Stroop task. *Consciousness and Cognition: An International Journal, 14*, 296–303.

Rubin, B. D., & Katz, L. C. (1999). Optical imaging of odorant representations in the mammalian olfactory bulb. *Neuron 23*, 499–511.

Rubin, D. C. (1985, September). The subtle deceiver: Recalling our past. *Psychology Today*, pp. 39–46.

Rubin, D. C., Schrauf, R. W., Gulgoz, S., & Naka, M. (2007). Cross-cultural variability of component processes in autobiographical remembering: Japan, Turkey, and the USA. *Memory, 15*, 536–547.

Rudner, M., & Rönnberg, J. (2008). The role of the episodic buffer in working memory for language processing. *Cognitive Processing, 9,* 19–28.

Rule, N. O., Ambady, N., & Hallett, K. C. (2009). Female sexual orientation is perceived accurately, rapidly, and automatically from the face and its features. *Journal of Experimental Social Psychology, 45,* 1245–1251.

Rulison, K. L., & Loken, E. (2009). I've fallen and I can't get up: Can high-ability students recover from early mistakes in CAT? *Applied Psychological Measurement, 33,* 83–101.

Runco, M. A. (2006). Introduction to the special issue: Divergent thinking. *Creativity Research Journal, 18,* 249–250.

Rusche, B. (2003). The 3Rs and animal welfare–conflict or the way forward? *ALTEX, 20, (Suppl. 1),* 63–76.

Ruscher, J. B., Fiske, S. T., & Schnake, S. B. (2000). The motivated tactician's juggling act: Compatible vs. incompatible impression goals. *British Journal of Social Psychology, 39,* 241–256.

Rushton, J. P., & Jensen, A. R. (2006). The totality of available evidence shows the race IQ gap still remains. *Psychological Science, 17,* 921–922.

Russell, J. A., & Sato, K. (1995). Comparing emotion words between languages. *Journal of Cross Cultural Psychology, 26,* 384–391.

Russell, R., Duchaine, B., & Nakayama, K. (2009). Super-recognizers: People with extraordinary face recognition ability. *Psychonomic Bulletin & Review, 16,* 252–257.

Russo, N. (1981). Women in psychology. In L. T. Benjamin, Jr. & K. D. Lowman (Eds.), *Activities handbook for the teaching of psychology.* Washington, DC: American Psychological Association.

Rustin, M. (2006). Infant observation research: What have we learned so far? *Infant Observation, 9,* 35–52.

Rutherford, B., Rose, S., Sneed, J., & Roose, S. (2009, April). Study design affects participant expectations: A survey. *Journal of Clinical Psychopharmacology, 29,* 179–181.

Rutter, M. (2002). Nature, nurture, and development: From evangelism through science toward policy and practice. *Child Development, 73,* 1–21.

Rutter, M. (2006). *Genes and behavior: Nature-nurture interplay explained.* Malden, MA: Blackwell Publishing.

Ryan, R. M., & Deci, E. L. (2011). A self-determination theory perspective on social, institutional, cultural, and economic supports for autonomy and their importance for well-being. In V. I. Chirkov, R. M. Ryan, & K. M. Sheldon (Eds.), *Human autonomy in cross-cultural context: Perspectives on the psychology of agency, freedom, and well-being.* New York: Springer Science + Business Media.

Rychlak, J. (1997). *In defense of human consciousness.* Washington, DC: American Psychological Association.

Rydell, R., McConnell, A., & Mackie, D. (2008). Consequences of discrepant explicit and implicit attitudes: Cognitive dissonance and increased information processing. *Journal of Experimental Social Psychology, 44,* 1526–1532.

Rymer, R. (1994). *Genie: A scientific tragedy.* New York: Penguin.

Saarni, C. (1999). *Developing emotional competence.* New York: Guilford.

Sachs-Ericsson, N., Joiner, T., Plant, E. A., & Blazer, D. G. (2005). The influence of depression on cognitive decline in community-dwelling elderly persons. *American Journal of Geriatric Psychiatry, 13,* 402–408.

Sackeim, H. A., Haskett, R. F., Mulsant, B. H., Thase, M. E., Mann, J. J., Pettinati, H. M., et al. (2001). Continuation pharmaco-therapy in the prevention of relapse following electroconvulsive therapy: A randomized controlled trial. *Journal of the American Medical Association, 285,* 1299–1307.

Sacks, O. (2003, July 28). The mind's eye. *The New Yorker,* pp. 48–59.

Saczynski, J., Willis, S., & Schaie, K. (2002). Strategy use in reasoning training with older adults. *Aging, Neuropsychology, & Cognition, 9,* 48–60.

Sadeghi-Nejad, H., & Watson, R. (2008). Premature ejaculation: Current medical treatment and new directions. *Journal of Sexual Medicine, 5,* 1037–1050.

Sadker, M., & Sadker, D. (1994). *Failing at fairness: How America's schools cheat girls.* New York: Scribners.

Sado, M., Yamauchi, K., Kawakami, N., Ono, Y., Furukawa, T. A., Tsuchiya, M., & . . . Kashima, H. (2011). Cost of depression among adults in Japan in 2005. *Psychiatry and Clinical Neurosciences, 65,* 442–450.

Saggino, A., Perfetti, B., & Spitoni, G. (2006). Fluid intelligence and executive functions: New perspectives. In L. V. Wesley (Ed.), *Intelligence: New research.* Hauppauge, NY: Nova Science Publishers.

Sahin, N. T., Pinker, S., & Halgren, E. (2006). Abstract grammatical processing of nouns and verbs in Broca's area: Evidence from fMRI. *Cortex, 42,* 540–562.

Sakai, K. L. (2005, November 4). Language acquisition and brain development. *Science, 310,* 815–817.

Salgado, D. M., Quinlin, K. J., & Zlotnick, C. (2007). The relationship of lifetime polysubstance dependence to trauma exposure, symptomatology, and psychosocial functioning in incarcerated women with comorbid PTSD and substance use disorder. *Journal of Trauma Dissociation, 8,* 9–26.

Sallquist, J., Eisenberg, N., Spinrad, T. L., Eggum, N. D., & Gaertner, B. (2009). Assessment of preschoolers' positive empathy: Concurrent and longitudinal relations with positive emotion, social competence, and sympathy. *The Journal of Positive Psychology, 4,* 223–233.

Salmela-Aro, K., & Nurmi, J.-E. (2007). Self-esteem during university studies predicts career characteristics 10 years later. *Journal of Vocational Behavior, 70,* 463–477.

Salsman, N. L. (2006). Interpersonal change as an outcome of Time-Limited Interpersonal Therapy. *Dissertation Abstracts International: Section B: The Sciences and Engineering, 66*(9-B), 5103.

Salvi, V., Fagiolini, A., Swartz, H., Maina, G., & Frank, E. (2008). The use of antidepressants in bipolar disorder. *Journal of Clinical Psychiatry,* 69, 1307–1318.

Samantaray, S. K., Srivastava, M., & Mishra, P. K. (2002). Fostering self concept and self actualization as bases for empowering women in national development: A challenge for the new millennium. *Social Science International, 18,* 58–63.

Samoilov, V., & Zayas, V. (2007). Ivan Petrovich Pavlov (1849–1936). *Journal of the History of the Neurosciences, 16,* 74–89.

Sampson, S., & Moore, L. (2008). Is there a glass ceiling for women in development? *Nonprofit Management and Leadership, 18,* 321–339.

Samuel, D. B., & Widiger, T. A. (2006). Differentiating normal and abnormal personality from the perspective of the DSM. In S. Strack (Ed.), *Differentiating normal and abnormal personality* (2nd ed.). New York: Springer Publishing.

Samuel, D. B., Carroll, K. M., Rounsaville, B. J., & Ball, S. A. (2013). Personality disorders as maladaptive, extreme variants of normal personality: Borderline personality disorder and neuroticism in a substance using sample. *Journal of Personality Disorders, 27,* 625–635.

Sanders, C., Sadoski, M., van Walsum, K., Bramson, R., Wiprud, R., & Fossum, T. (2008). Learning basic surgical skills with mental imagery: Using the simulation centre in the mind. *Medical Education, 42,* 607–612.

Sanderson, M. (2007). Assessment of manic symptoms in different cultures. *British Journal of Psychiatry, 190,* 178.

Sandomir, R. (2007, July 17). W. W. E.'s testing is examined after Bennoit murder-suicide. *The New York Times,* p. S3.

Sandoval, J., Frisby, C. L., Geisinger, K. F., Scheuneman, J. D., & Grenier, J. R. (Eds.). (1998). *Test interpretation and diversity: Achieving equity in assessment.* Washington, DC: American Psychological Association.

Sandoval, T. C., Gollan, T. H., Ferreira, V. S., & Salmon, D. P. (2010). What causes the bilingual disadvantage in verbal fluency? The dual-task analogy. *Bilingualism: Language and Cognition, 13,* 231–252.

Saneyoshi, A., Niimi, R., Suetsugu, T., Kaminaga, T., & Yokosawa, K. (2011). Iconic memory and parietofrontal network: fMRI study using temporal integration. *Neuroreport: For Rapid Communication of Neuroscience Research, 22,* 515–519.

Santel, S., Baving, L., Krauel, K., Munte, T. F., & Rotte, M. (2006, October 9). Hunger and satiety in anorexia nervosa: fMRI during cognitive processing of food pictures. *Brain Research, 1114,* 138–148.

Santelli, J., Carter, M., Orr, M., & Dittus, P. (2009, April). Trends in sexual risk behaviors, by nonsexual risk behavior involvement, U.S. high school students, 1991–2007. *Journal of Adolescent Health, 44,* 372–379.

Santtila, P., Wager, I., Witting, K., Harlaar, N., Jern, P., Johansson, A., et al. (2008). Discrepancies between sexual desire and sexual activity: Gender differences and associations with relationship satisfaction. *Journal of Sex & Marital Therapy, 34,* 31–44.

Saper, C. B. (2013). The neurobiology of sleep. *CONTINUUM: Lifelong Learning In Neurology, 19,* 19–31.

Saper, C. B., Lu, J., Chou, T. C., & Gooley, J. (2005). The hypothalamic integrator for circadian rhythms. *Trends in Neuroscience, 28,* 152–157.

Sapolsky, R. M. (2003). Gene therapy for psychiatric disorders. *American Journal of Psychiatry, 160, 208–220.*

Sargent, J. D., Stoolmiller, M., Worth, K. A., Cal, C. S., Wills, T. A., Gibbons, F. X., et al. (2007). Exposure to smoking depictions in movies: Its association with established adolescent smoking. *Archives of Pediatric Adolescent Medicine, 161,* 849–856.

Sarmiento, I. (2011). Rape stereotypes and labeling: Awareness of victimization and trauma. *Psychological Reports, 108,* 141–148.

Sarsour, K., Sheridan, M., Jutte, D., Nuru-Jeter, A., Hinshaw, S., & Boyce, W. (2011). Family socioeconomic status and child executive functions: The roles of language, home environment, and single parenthood. *Journal of the International Neuropsychological Society, 17,* 120–132.

Shaikholeslami, R., & Khayyer, M. (2006). Intrinsic motivation, extrinsic motivation, and learning English as a foreign language. *Psychological Reports, 99,* 813–818.

Shanahan, L., Copeland, W. E., Worthman, C. M., Erkanli, A., Angold, A., & Costello, E. (2013). Sex-differentiated changes in C-reactive protein from ages 9 to 21: The contributions of BMI and physical/ sexual maturation. *Psychoneuroendocrinology, 38,* 2209–2217.

Shankar, G., & Simmons, A. (2009, January). Understanding ethics guidelines using an internet-based expert system. *Journal of Medical Ethics, 35,* 65–68.

Shapiro, L. R. (2006). Remembering September 11th: The role of retention interval and rehearsal on flashbulb and event memory. *Memory, 14,* 129–147.

Sharma, H. S., Sjoquist, P. O., & Ali, S. F. (2007). Drugs of abuse-induced hyperthermia, blood-brain barrier dysfunction and neurotoxicity: neuroprotective effects of a new antioxidant compound h-290/51. *Current Pharmaceutical Design, 13,* 1903–1923.

Sharpe, Lindsey. (2013, November 1). U.S. obesity rate climbing in 2013. *Gallup Poll.*

Shaver, P., Schwartz, J., Kirson, D., & O'Connor, C. (1987, June). Emotion knowledge: Further exploration of a prototype approach. *Journal of Personality and Social Psychology, 52*(6) 1067.

Shea, A., & Steiner, M. (2008). Cigarette smoking during pregnancy. *Nicotine & Tobacco Research, 10,* 267–278.

Shehata-Dieler, W., Ehrmann-Mueller, D., Wermke, P., Voit, V., Cebulla, M., & Wermke, K. (2013). Pre-speech diagnosis in hearing-impaired infants: How auditory experience affects early vocal development. *Speech, Language and Hearing, 16,* 99–106.

Shellenbarger, S. (2012, August 22). Are you a hero or a bystander? *The Wall Street Journal,* D1.

Shellenbarger, S. (2012, May 29). At work, do headphones really help? *The Wall Street Journal,* D1.

Shellenbarger, S. (2012, September 26). The peak time for everything. *Wall Street Journal,* p. D1, D3.

Shelton, R. C., Keller, M. B., Gelenberg, A., Dunner, D. L., Hirschfeld, R. M. A., Thase, M. E., et al. (2002). The effectiveness of St. John's wort in major depression: A multi-center, randomized placebo-controlled trial. *Journal of the American Medical Association, 285,* 1978–1986.

Shepard, R. N., & Metzler, J. (1971). Mental rotation of three-dimensional objects. *Science, 171(3972),* 701–703.

Shepperd, J., Malone, W., & Sweeny, K. (2008). Exploring causes of the self-serving bias. *Social and Personality Psychology Compass, 2,* 895–908.

Sherblom, S. (2008). The legacy of the 'care challenge': Re-envisioning the outcome of the justice-care debate. *Journal of Moral Education, 37,* 81–98.

Sherman, S. L., Allen, E. G., Bean, L. H., & Freeman, S. B. (2007). Epidemiology of Down syndrome [Special issue: Down syndrome]. *Mental Retardation and Developmental Disabilities Research Reviews, 13,* 221–227.

Shier, D., Butler, J., & Lewis, R. (2000). *Hole's essentials of human anatomy and physiology* (7th ed.). Boston: McGraw-Hill.

Shiffman, S. (2007). Use of more nicotine lozenges leads to better success in quitting smoking. *Addiction, 102,* 809–814.

Shimono, K., & Wade, N. J. (2002). Monocular alignment in different depth planes. *Vision Research, 42,* 1127–1135.

Shin, Hyon B., and Robert A. Kominski. 2010. *Language Use in the United States: 2007.* American Community Survey Reports, ACS-12. U.S. Census Bureau, Washington, DC.

Shmuel, A., Chaimow, D., Raddatz, G., Ugurbil, K., & Yacoub, E. (2010). Mechanisms underlying decoding at 7 T: Ocular dominance columns, broad structures, and macroscopic blood vessels in V1 convey information on the stimulated eye. *NeuroImage, 49,* 1957–1964.

Shnabel, N., Purdie-Vaughns, V., Cook, J. E., Garcia, J., & Cohen, G. L. (2013). Demystifying values-affirmation interventions: Writing about social belonging is a key to buffering against identity threat. *Personality and Social Psychology Bulletin, 39,* 663–676.

Shoda, Y., & Mischel, W. (2006). Applying meta-theory to achieve generalisability and precision in personality science. *Applied Psychology: An International Review, 55,* 439–452.

Shors, T. J. (2009, March). Saving new brain cells. *Scientific American,* pp. 47–54.

Shugart, H. A. (2011). Shifting the balance: The contemporary narrative of obesity. *Health Communication, 26,* 37-47.

Shulman, J. L., & Horne, S. G. (2006). Guilty or not? A path model of women's sexual force fantasies. *Journal of Sex Research, 43,* 368–377.

Shultz, S. K., Scherman, A., & Marshall, L. J. (2000). Evaluation of a university-based date rape prevention program: Effect on attitudes and behavior related to rape. *Journal of College Student Development, 41,* 193–201.

Shurkin, J. N. (1992). *Terman's kids: The groundbreaking study of how the gifted grow up.* Boston: Little, Brown.

Shweder, R. A. (1994). You're not sick, you're just in love: Emotion as an interpretive system. In P. Ekman & R. J. Davidson (Eds.), *The nature of emotion: Fundamental questions.* New York: Oxford.

Sidman, M. (2006). The distinction between positive and negative reinforcement: Some additional considerations. *Behavior Analyst, 29,* 135–139.

Siegel, J. M. (2003, November). Why we sleep. *Scientific American,* pp. 92–97.

Siegel, R. K. (1989). *Intoxication: Life in pursuit of artificial paradise.* New York: E. P. Dutton.

Siemer, M., Mauss I., & Gross, J. J. (2007). Same situation–different emotions: How appraisals shape our emotions. *Emotion, 7,* 592–600.

Sifrit, K. J. (2006). The effects of aging and cognitive decrements on simulated driving performance. *Dissertation abstracts international: Section B: The sciences and engineering, 67,* 2863.

Sikkema, K. J., Ranby, K. W., Meade, C. S., Hansen, N. B., Wilson, P. A., & Kochman, A. (2013). Reductions in traumatic stress following a coping intervention were mediated by decreases in avoidant coping for people living with HIV/AIDS and childhood sexual abuse. *Journal of Consulting and Clinical Psychology, 81,* 274–283.

Silva, A. J. (2011). Molecular genetic approaches to memory consolidation. In S. Nalbantian, P. M. Matthews, & J. L. McClelland (Eds.), *The memory process: Neuroscientific and humanistic perspectives.* Cambridge, MA: MIT Press.

Silva, M. T. A., Gonçalves, E. L., & Garcia-Mijares, M. (2007). Neural events in the reinforcement contingency. *Behavior Analyst, 30,* 17–30.

Silverman, C. (2012). *Understanding autism: Parents, doctors, and the history of a disorder.* Princeton, NJ: Princeton University Press.

Silverman, K., Roll, J., & Higgins, S. (2008). Introduction to the special issue on the behavior analysis and treatment of drug addiction. *Journal of Applied Behavior Analysis, 41,* 471–480.

Silverstein, B. B., Edwards, T. T., Gamma, A. A., Ajdacic-Gross, V. V., Rossler, W. W., & Angst, J. J. (2013). The role played by depression associated with somatic symptomatology in accounting for the gender difference in the prevalence of depression. *Social Psychiatry and Psychiatric Epidemiology, 48,* 257–263.

Silverstein, M. L. (2007). Rorschach test findings at the beginning of treatment and 2 years later, with a 30-year follow-up. *Journal of Personality Assessment, 88,* 131–143.

Simcock, G., & Hayne, H. (2002). Breaking the barrier? Children fail to translate their pre-verbal memories into language. *Psychological Science, 13,* 225–231.

Simon, G., Ludman, E., Unützer, J., Operskalski, B., & Bauer, M. (2008). Severity of mood symptoms and work productivity in people treated for bipolar disorder. *Bipolar Disorders, 10,* 718–725.

Simon, S., & Hoyt, C. (2008). Exploring the gender gap in support for a woman for president. *Analyses of Social Issues and Public Policy (ASAP), 8,* 157–181.

Simons, D. L., Boye, S. L., Hauswirth, W. W., & Wu, S. M. (2011). Gene therapy prevents photoreceptor death and preserves retinal function in a Bardet-Biedl syndrome mouse model. *PNAS Proceedings of the National Academy of Sciences of the United States of America, 108,* 6276–6281.

Simonton, D. K. (2000). Archival research. In A. E. Kazdin (Ed.), *Encyclopedia of psychology* (Vol. 1). Washington, DC: American Psychological Association.

Simonton, D. K. (2009). Varieties of (scientific) creativity: A hierarchical model of domain-specific disposition, development, and achievement. *Perspectives on Psychological Science, 4,* 441–452.

Sinclair, R. R., Waitsman, M. C., Oliver, C. M., & Deese, M. (2013). Personality and psychological resilience in military personnel. In R. R. Sinclair & T. W. Britt (Eds.), *Building psychological resilience in military personnel: Theory and practice.* Washington, DC: American Psychological Association.

Singer, J. L. (2006). Why imagery, personal memories, and daydreams matter. In J. L. Singer (Ed.), *Imagery in psychotherapy.* Washington, DC: American Psychological Association.

Singer, L. T., & Richardson, G. A. (2011). Introduction to "understanding developmental consequences of prenatal drug exposure: Biological and environmental effects and their interactions". *Neurotoxicology and Teratology, 33,* 5–8.

Singh, S., Wulf, D., Samara, R., & Cuca, Y. P. (2000). Gender differences in the timing of first intercourse: Data from 14 countries. *International Family Planning Perspectives, 26,* 21–28, 43.

Sininger, Y. S., & Cone-Wesson, B. (2004, September 10). Asymmetric cochlear processing mimics hemispheric specialization. *Science, 305,* 1581.

Sininger, Y. S., & Cone-Wesson, B. (2006). Lateral asymmetry in the ABR of neonates: evidence and mechanisms. *Hearing Research, 212,* 203–211.

Sio, U. N., Monaghan, P., & Ormerod, T. (2013). Sleep on it, but only if it is difficult: Effects of sleep on problem solving. *Memory & Cognition, 41,* 159–166.

Skinner, B. F. (1957). *Verbal behavior.* New York: Appleton-Century-Crofts.

Skinner, B. F. (1975). The steep and thorny road to a science of behavior. *American Psychologist, 30,* 42–49.
Skipp, C., & Campo-Flores, A. (2007, September 3). Taking on Tourette's. *Newsweek,* p. 53.
Skolnick, P., Popik, P., & Trullas, R. (2009). Glutamate-based antidepressants: 20 years on. *Trends in Pharmacological Science, 30,* 563–569.
Slater, E., & Meyer, A. (1959). Contributions to a pathography of the musicians: Robert Schumann. *Confinia Psychiatrica.* Reprinted in K. R. Jamison, *Touched with fire: Manic-depressive illness and the artistic temperament.* New York: Free Press.
Sloan, E. P., et al. (1993). The nuts and bolts of behavioral therapy for insomnia. *Journal of Psychosomatic Research, 37* (Suppl.), 19–37.
Slocombe, K. E., Waller, B. M., & Liebal, K. (2011). The language void: The need for multimodality in primate communication research. *Animal Behaviour, 81,* 919–924.
Ślusarczyk, E., & Niedźwieńska, A. (2013). A naturalistic study of prospective memory in preschoolers: The role of task interruption and motivation. *Cognitive Development, 28,* 179–192.
Smart, R. G. (2007). Review of introduction to addictive behaviours. *Addiction, 102,* 831.
Smetana, J. B. (2007). Strategies for understanding archetypes and the collective unconscious of an organization. *Dissertation Abstracts International Section A: Humanities and Social Sciences, 67* (12-A), 4714.
Smetana, J. G. (2005). Adolescent-parent conflict: Resistance and subversion as developmental process. In L. Nucci (Ed.), *Conflict, contradiction, and contrarian elements in moral development and education.* Mahwah, NJ: Lawrence Erlbaum Associates.
Smetana, J., Daddis, C., & Chuang, S. (2003). "Clean your room!" A longitudinal investigation of adolescent-parent conflict and conflict resolution in middle-class African American families. *Journal of Adolescent Research, 18,* 631–650.
Smith, B. H., Barkley, R. A., & Shapiro, C. J. (2006). Attention-Deficit/Hyperactivity Disorder. In E. J. Mash & R. A. Barkley (Eds.), *Treatment of childhood disorders* (3rd ed.). New York: Guilford Press.
Smith, C. (2006). Symposium V–Sleep and learning: New developments [Special issue: Methods and learning in functional MRI]. *Brain and Cognition, 60,* 331–332.
Smith, C. A., & Lazarus, R. S. (2001). Appraisal components, core relational themes, and the emotions. In W. G. Parrott (Ed.), *Emotions in social psychology: Essential readings* (pp. 94–114). Philadelphia: Psychology Press.
Smith, C. D., Chebrolu, J., Wekstein, D. R., Schmitt, F. A., & Markesbery, W. R. (2007). Age and gender effects on human brain anatomy: a voxel-based morphometric study in healthy elderly. *Neurobiology of Aging, 28,* 1057–1087.
Smith, D. E., Springer, C. M., & Barrett, S. (2011). Physical discipline and socioemotional adjustment among Jamaican adolescents. *Journal of Family Violence, 26,* 51–61.
Smith, E. (1988, May). Fighting cancerous feelings. *Psychology Today,* pp. 22–23.
Smith, E. R., & Semin, G. R. (2007). Situated social cognition. *Current Directions in Psychological Science, 16,* 132–135.
Smith, E. S., Geissler, S. A., Schallert, T., & Lee, H. J. (2013). The role of central amygdala dopamine in disengagement behavior. *Behavioral Neuroscience, 127,* 164–174.
Smith, L., Cornelius, V., Warnock, A., Bell, A., & Young, A. (2007). Effectiveness of mood stabilizers and antipsychotics in the maintenance phase of bipolar disorder: A systematic review of randomized controlled trials. *Bipolar Disorders, 9,* 394–412.
Smith, M. B. (2003). Moral foundations in research with human participants. In A. E. Kazdin (Ed.), *Methodological issues & strategies in clinical research* (3rd ed.). Washington, DC: American Psychological Association.
Smith, M. L., Glass, G. V., & Miller, T. I. (1980). *The benefits of psychotherapy.* Baltimore: The Johns Hopkins University Press.
Smith, R. A., & Weber, A. L. (2005). Applying social psychology in everyday life. In F. W. Schneider, J. A. Gruman, & L. M. Coutts (Eds.), *Applied social psychology: Understanding and addressing social and practical.* Thousand Oaks, CA: Sage Publications.
Smith, T. W., & Son, J. (2013). *Trends in public attitudes about sexual morality.* Chicago: NORC at the University of Chicago.
Smith, W. B. (2007). Karen Horney and psychotherapy in the 21st century. *Clinical Social Work Journal, 35,* 57–66.
Smolowe, J. (2008, June 23). Medical miracle surgery for an unborn child. *People,* p. 96.
Smrtnik-Vitulić, H., & Zupančič, M. (2011). Personality traits as a predictor of academic achievement in adolescents. *Educational Studies, 37,* 127–140.
Snyder, D. J., Fast, K., & Bartoshuk, L. M. (2004). Valid comparisons of suprathreshold sensations. *Journal of Consciousness Studies, 11,* 96–112.
Snyder, J., Cramer, A., & Afrank, J. (2005). The contributions of ineffective discipline and parental hostile attributions of child misbehavior to the development of conduct problems at home and school. *Developmental Psychology, 41,* 30–41.
Snyder, M. (2002). Applications of Carl Rogers' theory and practice to couple and family therapy: A response to Harlene Anderson and David Bott. *Journal of Family Therapy, 24,* 317–325.
Snyder, M. D., & Dwyer, P. C. (2013). Altruism and prosocial behavior. In H. Tennen, J. Suls, & I. B. Weiner (Eds.). *Handbook of psychology, Vol. 5: Personality and social psychology (2nd ed.).* Hoboken, NJ: John Wiley & Sons.
Sobel, K., Gerrie, M., Poole, B., & Kane, M. (2007, October). Individual differences in working memory capacity and visual search: The roles of top-down and bottom-up processing. *Psychonomic Bulletin & Review, 14,* 840–845.
Society for Personality Assessment. (2005). The status of Rorschach in clinical and forensic practice: An official statement by the board of trustees of the Society for Personality Assessment. *Journal of Personality Assessment, 85,* 219–237.
Sodian, B. (2011). Theory of mind in infancy. *Child Development Perspectives, 5,* 39–43.
Sohr-Preston, S. L., & Scaramella, L. V. (2006). Implications of timing of maternal depressive symptoms for early cognitive and language development. *Clinical Child and Family Psychology Review, 9,* 65–83.
Sokolove, M. (2003, November 16). Should John Hinckley go free? *The New York Times Magazine,* pp. 52–54, 92.
Soler, J., Pascual, J., Tiana, T., Cebrià, A., Barrachina, J., Campins, M., et al. (2009). Dialectical behaviour therapy skills training compared to standard group therapy in borderline personality disorder: A 3-month randomised controlled clinical trial. *Behaviour Research and Therapy, 47,* 353–358.
Solesio-Jofre, E., Lorenzo-López, L., Gutiérrez, R., López-Frutos, J., Ruiz-Vargas, J., & Maestú, F. (2011). Age effects on retroactive interference during working memory maintenance. *Biological Psychology, 88,* 72–82.
Solomon, M., & Herman, J. (2009). Sex differences in psychopathology: Of gonads, adrenals and mental illness. *Physiology & Behavior, 97,* 250–258.
Somers, T. J., Moseley, G., Keefe, F. J., & Kothadia, S. M. (2011). Neuroimaging of pain: A psychosocial perspective. In R. A. Cohen & L. H. Sweet (Eds.), *Brain imaging in behavioral medicine and clinical neuroscience.* New York: Springer Science + Business Media.
Sommer, R., & Sommer, B. (2001). *A practical guide to behavioral research: Tools and techniques* (5th ed.). New York: Oxford University Press.
Soorya, L. V., Carpenter, L., & Romanczyk, R. G. (2011). Applied behavior analysis. In E. Hollander, A. Kolevzon, & J. T. Coyle (Eds.), *Textbook of autism spectrum disorders.* Arlington, VA: American Psychiatric Publishing, Inc.
Sori, C. E. (Ed.). (2006). *Engaging children in family therapy: Creative approaches to integrating theory and research in clinical practice.* New York: Routledge/Taylor & Francis Group.
Soussignan, R. (2002). Duchenne smile, emotional experience, and automatic reactivity: A test of the facial feedback hypothesis. *Emotion, 2,* 52–74.
South, S. C., Reichborn-Kjennerud, T., Eaton, N. R., & Krueger, R. F. (2013). Genetics of personality. In H. Tennen, J. Suls, & I. B. Weiner (Eds.), *Handbook of psychology, Vol. 5: Personality and social psychology (2nd ed.).* Hoboken, NJ: John Wiley & Sons Inc.
South, S., & Krueger, R. (2008). An interactionist perspective on genetic and environmental contributions to personality. *Social and Personality Psychology Compass, 2,* 929–948.
Spackman, M. P., Fujiki, M., & Brinton, B. (2006). Understanding emotions in context: The effects of language impairment on children's ability to infer emotional reactions. *International Journal of Language & Communication Disorders, 41,* 173–188.
Spangler, W. D. (1992). Validity of questionnaire and TAT measures of need for achievement: Two meta-analyses. *Psychological Bulletin, 112,* 140–154.
Spanos, N. P., Barber, T. X., & Lang, G. (2005). Cognition and self-control: Cognitive control of painful sensory input. *Integrative Physiological & Behavioral Science, 40,* 119–128.
Sparks, S. D. (2007, October 2). Foundation: Gifted poor students given short shrift. *Education Daily, 40,* 3.
Sparrow, B., Liu, J., & Wegner, D. M. (2011, August 5). Google effects on memory: cognitive consequences of having information at our fingertips. *Science, 333,* 776–778.
Spaulding, S. (2013). Mirror neurons and social cognition. *Mind & Language, 28,* 233–257.
Spearman, C. (1927). *The abilities of man.* London: Macmillan.
Speirs-Neumeister, K. L., & Finch, H. (2006). Perfectionism in high-ability students: Relational precursors and influences on achievement motivation. *Gifted Child Quarterly, 50,* 238–251.
Spence-Cochran, K., & Pearl, C. (2006). Moving toward full inclusion. In P. Wehman (Ed.), *Life beyond the classroom: Transition strategies for young people with disabilities* (4th ed.). Baltimore: Paul H. Brookes Publishing.

Spence, M. J., & DeCasper, A. J. (1982, March). *Human fetuses perceive maternal speech.* Paper presented at the meeting of the International Conference on Infant Studies, Austin, TX.

Spencer-Rodgers, J., Peng, K., Wang, L., & Hou, Y. (2004). Dialectical self-esteem and East-West differences in psychological well-being. *Personality and Social Psychology Bulletin, 30,* 1416–1432.

Spencer, S. J., Fein, S., Zanna, M. P., & Olson, J. M. (Eds.). (2003). *Motivated social perception: The Ontario Symposium* (Vol. 9). Mahwah, NJ: Erlbaum.

Sperling, G. (1960). The information available in brief visual presentation. *Psychological Monographs, 74,* pp. 29.

Sperry, R. (1982). Some effects of disconnecting the cerebral hemispheres. *Science, 217,* 1223–1226.

Spielberger, C. D. (2006). Cross-cultural assessment of emotional states and personality traits. *European Psychologist, 11,* 297–303.

Spiers, H. J., & Maguire, E. A. (2007). Decoding human brain activity during real-world experiences. *Trends in Cognitive Science, 11,* 356–365.

Spindler, H., Kruse, C., Zwisler, A., & Pedersen, S. (2009). Increased anxiety and depression in Danish cardiac patients with a type D personality: Cross-validation of the Type D Scale (DS14). *International Journal of Behavioral Medicine, 16,* 98–107.

Spinella, M., & Lester, D. (2006). Can money buy happiness? *Psychological Reports, 99,* 992.

Spitz, H. H. (1987). Problem-solving processes in special populations. In J. G. Borkowski & J. D. Day (Eds.), *Cognition in special children: Comparative approaches to retardation, learning disabilities, and giftedness.* Norwood, NJ: Ablex.

Spitzer, R. L., Skodol, A. E., Gibbon, M., & Williams, J. B. W. (1983). *Psychopathology: A case book.* New York: McGraw-Hill.

Sprecher, S., & Hatfield, E. (1996). Premarital sexual standards among U.S. college students: Comparison with Russian and Japanese students. *Archives of Sexual Behavior, 25,* 261–288.

Sprecher, S., & Regan, P. C. (2002). Liking some things (in some people) more than others: Partner preferences in romantic relationships and friendships. *Journal of Social and Personal Relationships, 19,* 436–481.

Sprecher, S., Treger, S., & Sakaluk, J. K. (2013). Premarital sexual standards and sociosexuality: Gender, ethnicity, and cohort differences. *Archives of Sexual Behavior.* Retrieved from http://link.springer.com/article/10.1007%2Fs10508-013-0145-6

Sprenger, M. (2007). *Memory 101 for educators.* Thousand Oaks, CA: Corwin Press.

Sprenkle, D. H., & Moon, S. M. (Eds.). (1996). *Research methods in family therapy.* New York: Guilford Press.

Springen, K. (2004, August 9). Anxiety: Sweet and elusive sleep. *Newsweek,* p. 21.

Spunt, R. P., Satpute, A. B., & Lieberman, M. D. (2011). Identifying the what, why, and how of an observed action: An fMRI study of mentalizing and mechanizing during action observation. *Journal of Cognitive Neuroscience, 23,* 63–74.

Squire, L. R., Clark, R. E., & Bayley, P. J. (2004). Medial temporal lobe function and memory. In M. S. Gazzaniga (Ed.), *Cognitive neurosciences* (3rd ed.). Cambridge, MA: MIT.

St. Dennis, C., Hendryx, M., Henriksen, A. L., Setter, S. M., & Singer, B. (2006). Postdischarge treatment costs following closure of a state geropsychiatric ward: Comparison of 2 levels of community care. *Primary Care Companion Journal of Clinical Psychiatry, 8,* 279–284.

St. Jacques, P. L., & Levine, B. (2007). Ageing and autobiographical memory for emotional and neutral events. *Memory, 15,* 129–144.

Staats, S., Wallace, H., Anderson, T., Gresley, J., Hupp, J. M., & Weiss, E. (2009). The hero concept: Self, family, and friends who are brave, honest, and hopeful. *Psychological Reports, 104,* 820–832.

Stainton, T., & Clare, I. C. H. (2012). Human rights and intellectual disabilities: An emergent theoretical paradigm? *Journal of Intellectual Disability Research, 56,* 1011–1013.

Staley, J. K., Sanacora, G., & Tamagnan, G. (2006). Sex differences in diencephalon serotonin transporter availability in major depression. *Biological Psychiatry, 59,* 40–47.

Stam, K., Verbakel, E., & Graaf, P. M. (2013). Do values matter? The impact of work ethic and traditional gender role values on female labour market supply. *Social Indicators Research.* Retrieved from http://link.springer.com/article/10.1007%2Fs11205-013-0287-x

Stangier, U., Schramm, E., Heidenreich, T., Berger, M., & Clark, D. M. (2011). Cognitive therapy vs interpersonal psychotherapy in social anxiety disorder: A randomized controlled trial. *Archives of General Psychiatry, 68,* 692–700.

Stankov, L. (2003). Complexity in human intelligence. In R. J. Sternberg, J. Lautrey, et al. (Eds.), *Models of intelligence: International perspectives.* Washington, DC: American Psychological Association.

Stanojevic, S., Mitic, K., & Vujic, V. (2007). Exposure to acute physical and psychological stress alters the response of rat macrophages to corticosterone, neuropeptide Y and beta-endorphin. *International Journal on the Biology of Stress, 10,* 65–73.

Stanton, A. L., Danoff-Burg, S., Cameron, C. L., Bishop, M., Collins, C. A., Kirk, S. B., et al. (2000). Emotionally expressive coping predicts psychological and physical adjustment to breast cancer. *Journal of Consulting and Clinical Psychology, 68,* 875–882.

Stapel, D. A., & Semin, G. R. (2007). The magic spell of language: Linguistic categories and their perceptual consequences. *Journal of Personality and Social Psychology, 93,* 23–33.

Starcevic, V., Berle, D., Milicevic, D., Hannan, A., Pamplugh, C., & Eslick, G. D. (2007). Pathological worry, anxiety disorders and the impact of co-occurrence with depressive and other anxiety disorders. *Journal of Anxiety Disorders, 21,* 1016–1027.

Startup, M., Bucci, S., & Langdon, R. (2009). Delusions of reference: A new theoretical model. *Cognitive Neuropsychiatry, 14,* 110–126.

Staub, A. (2011). Word recognition and syntactic attachment in reading: Evidence for a staged architecture. *Journal of Experimental Psychology: General, 140,* 407–433.

Steblay, N., Dysart, J., Fulero, S., & Lindsay, R. C. L. (2003). Eyewitness accuracy rates in police showup and lineup presentations: A meta-analytic comparison. *Law & Human Behavior, 27,* 523–540.

Steele, C. M. (1997). A threat in the air: How stereotypes shape intellectual identity and performance. *American Psychologist, 52,* 613–629.

Steele, C. M., & Josephs, R. A. (1990). Alcohol myopia: Its prized and dangerous effects. *American Psychologist, 45,* 921–933.

Steele, C. M., Spencer, S. J., & Aronson, J. (2002). Contending with group image. The psychology of stereotype and social identity threat. In M. P. Zanna (Ed.), *Advances in experimental social psychology* (Vol. 34). San Diego: Academic Press.

Steele, J. D., Christmas, D., Eljamel, M. S., & Matthews, K. (2007). Anterior cingulotomy for major depression: clinical outcome and relationship to lesion characteristics. *Biological Psychiatry, 12,* 127–134.

Stegerwald, F., & Janson, G. R. (2003). Conversion therapy: Ethical considerations in family counseling. *Family Journal–Counseling and Therapy for Couples and Families, 11,* 55–59.

Steiger, A. (2007). Neurochemical regulation of sleep. *Journal of Psychiatric Research, 41,* 537–552.

Stein, L. A. R., & Graham, J. R. (2005). Ability of substance abusers to escape detection on the Minnesota Multiphasic Personality Inventory-Adolescent (MMPI-A) in a juvenile correctional facility. *Assessment, 12,* 28–39.

Steinberg, L. (2007). Risk taking in adolescence: New perspectives from brain and behavioral science. *Current Directions in Psychological Science, 16,* 55–59.

Steiner, J. (2008). Transference to the analyst as an excluded observer. *The International Journal of Psychoanalysis, 89,* 39–54.

Steinfeld, C., Ellison, N., & Lampe, C. (2008). Social capital, self-esteem, and use of online social network sites: A longitudinal analysis. *Journal of Applied Developmental Psychology, 29,* 434–445.

Stemler, S. E., & Sternberg, R. J. (2006). Using situational judgment tests to measure practical intelligence. In J. A. Weekley & R. E. Ployhart (Eds.), *Situational judgment tests: Theory, measurement, and application.* Mahwah, NJ: Lawrence Erlbaum Associates.

Stemler, S. E., Sternberg, R. J., Grigorenko, E. L., Jarvin, L., & Sharpes, K. (2009). Using the theory of successful intelligence as a framework for developing assessments in AP physics. *Contemporary Educational Psychology, 34,* 195–209.

Stenbacka, L., & Vanni, S. (2007). fMRI of peripheral visual field representation. *Clinical Neurophysiology, 108,* 1303–1314.

Stenklev, N. C., & Laukli, E. (2004). Cortical cognitive potentials in elderly persons. *Journal of the American Academy of Audiology, 15,* 401–413.

Stephenson, R. H., & Banet-Weiser, S. (2007). Super-sized kids: Obesity, children, moral panic, and the media. In J. A. Bryant (ed.), *The children's television community.* Mahwah, NJ: Lawrence Erlbaum Associates.

Stern, E., & Silbersweig, D. A. (2001). Advances in functional neuroimaging methodology for the study of brain systems underlying human neuropsychological function and dysfunction. In D. A. Silbersweig & E. Stern (Eds.), *Neuropsychology and functional neuroimaging: Convergence, advances and new directions.* Amsterdam, Netherlands: Swets and Zeitlinger.

Stern, R. M., & Koch, K. L. (1996). Motion sickness and differential susceptibility. *Current Directions in Psychological Science, 5,* 115–120.

Sternberg, R. J. (1998). *Successful intelligence: How practical and creative intelligence determine success in life.* New York: Plume.

Sternberg, R. J. (2000a). Intelligence and wisdom. In R. J. Sternberg et al. (Eds.), *Handbook of intelligence.* New York: Cambridge University Press.

Sternberg, R. J. (2000b). The Holey Grail of general intelligence. *Science, 289,* 399–401.
Sternberg, R. J. (2002). Individual differences in cognitive development. In U. Goswami (Ed.), *Blackwell handbook of childhood cognitive development. Blackwell handbooks of developmental psychology.* Malden, MA: Blackwell.
Sternberg, R. J. (2004). A triangular theory of love. In H. T. Reis & C. E. Rusbult (Eds.), *Close relationships: Key readings.* Philadelphia, PA: Taylor & Francis.
Sternberg, R. J. (2005). Culture and measurement. *Measurement: Interdisciplinary Research and Perspectives, 3,* 108–113.
Sternberg, R. J. (2006). A duplex theory of love. In R. J. Sternberg (Ed.), *The new psychology of love.* New Haven, CT: Yale University Press.
Sternberg, R. J. (2007). Who are the bright children? The cultural context of being and acting intelligent. *Educational Researcher, 36,* 148–155.
Sternberg, R. J. (2011a). Individual differences in cognitive development. In U. Goswami (Ed.), *The Wiley-Blackwell handbook of childhood cognitive development (2nd ed.).* NY: Wiley-Blackwell.
Sternberg, R. J. (2011b, September 27). Classroom Styles. *Inside Higher Education.* Retrieved from http://www.insidehighered.com/views/2011/09/27/essay_on_different_teaching_and_learning_styles
Sternberg, R. J. (2013). What is cognitive education? *Journal of Cognitive Education and Psychology, 12*(1), 45–58.
Sternberg, R. J., & Beall, A. E. (1991). How can we know what love is? An epistemological analysis. In G. J. O. Fletcher & F. D. Fincham (Eds.), *Cognition in close relationships.* Hillsdale, NJ: Erlbaum.
Sternberg, R. J., & Hedlund, J. (2002). Practical intelligence, "g," and work psychology. *Human Performance, 15,* 143–160.
Sternberg, R. J., & Jarvin, L. (2003). Alfred Binet's contributions as a paradigm for impact in psychology. In R. J. Sternberg (Ed.), *The anatomy of impact: What makes the great works of psychology great.* Washington, DC: American Psychological Association.
Sternberg, R. J., & O'Hara, L. A. (2000). Intelligence and creativity. In R. Sternberg et al. (Eds.), *Handbook of intelligence.* New York: Cambridge University Press.
Sternberg, R. J., Grigorenko, E. L., & Kidd, K. K. (2005). Intelligence, race, and genetics. *American Psychologist, 60,* 46–59.
Sternberg, R. J., Hojjat, M., & Barnes, M. L. (2001). Empirical aspects of a theory of love as a story. *European Journal of Personality, 15,* 1–20.
Sternberg, R. J., Jarvin, L., & Grigorenko, E. L. (2011). *Explorations in giftedness.* New York: Cambridge University Press.
Sternberg, R. J., Kaufman, J. C., & Pretz, J. E. (2004). A propulsion model of creative leadership [Special issue: Creativity in the workplace]. *Creativity and Innovation Management, 13,* 145–153.
Sternberg, R. J., & Pretz, J. E. (2005). *Cognition and intelligence: Identifying the mechanisms of the mind.* New York: Cambridge University Press.
Sternson, S. M., Betley, J., & Cao, Z. (2013). Neural circuits and motivational processes for hunger. *Current Opinion in Neurobiology, 23,* 353–360.
Stettler, N., Stallings, V. A., Troxel, A. B., Zhao, J. Z., Schinnar, R., Nelson, S. E., et al. (2005). Weight gain in the first week of life and overweight in adulthood. *Circulation, 111,* 1897–1903.
Stevens, C. F. (1979, September). The neuron. *Scientific American,* p. 56.
Stevens, C., Lauinger, B., & Neville, H. (2009). Differences in the neural mechanisms of selective attention in children from different socio-economic backgrounds: An event-related brain potential study. *Developmental Science, 12,* 634–646.
Stevens, G., & Gardner, S. (1982). *The women of psychology: Pioneers and innovators* (Vol. 1). Cambridge, MA: Schenkman.
Stevens, M. C., Skudlarski, P., Pearlson, G. D., & Calhoun, V. D. (2009). Age-related cognitive gains are mediated by the effects of white matter development on brain network integration. *Neuroimage, 48,* 738–746.
Stevens, M. J., & Gielen, U. P. (Eds.). (2007). *Toward a global psychology: Theory, research, intervention, and pedagogy.* Mahwah, NJ: Lawrence Erlbaum.
Stevens, P., & Harper, D. J. (2007). Professional accounts of electroconvulsive therapy: A discourse analysis. *Social Science & Medicine, 64,* 1475–1486.
Stevens, S. S., & Pashler, H. E. (2002). *Steven's handbook of experimental psychology: Learning, motivation, and emotion.* New York: Wiley.
Stevenson, H. W., Lee, S., & Mu, X. (2000). Successful achievement in mathematics: China and the United States. In C. F. M. van Lieshout & P. G. Heymans (Eds.), *Developing talent across the life span.* New York: Psychology Press.
Stey, P. C., Lapsley, D., & McKeever, M. O. (2013). Moral judgement in adolescents: Age differences in applying and justifying three principles of harm. *European Journal of Developmental Psychology, 10,* 206–220.
Stickgold, R., & Wehrwein, P. (2009, April 27). Sleep now, remember later. *Newsweek,* pp. 56–57.
Stickgold, R., Hobson, J. A., Fosse, R., & Fosse, M. (2001, November 2). Sleep, learning, and dreams: Off-line memory reprocessing. *Science, 294,* 1052–1057.
Stickley, T., & Nickeas, R. (2006). Becoming one person: Living with dissociative identity disorder. *Journal of Psychiatric and Mental Health Nursing, 13,* 180–187.
Stifter, C. A., Dollar, J. M., & Cipriano, E. A. (2011). Temperament and emotion regulation: The role of autonomic nervous system reactivity. *Developmental Psychobiology, 53,* 266–279.
Stix, G. (2008, November). Jacking into the brain. *Scientific American,* pp. 56–61.
Stix, G. (2011, March). The neuroscience of true grit. *Scientific American,* 29–33.
Stockdale, M. S., & Sagrestano, L. M. (2011). Resources for targets of sexual harassment. In M. A. Paludi, C. R. Paludi, & E. R. DeSouza (Eds.), *Praeger handbook on understanding and preventing workplace discrimination (Vols 1 & 2).* Santa Barbara, CA: Praeger/ABC-CLIO.
Stocks, E., Lishner, D., & Decker, S. (2009). Altruism or psychological escape: Why does empathy promote prosocial behavior? *European Journal of Social Psychology, 39,* 649–665.
Stockton, R., Morran, D. K., & Krieger, K. (2004). An overview of current research and best practices for training beginning group leaders. In J. L. DeLucia-Waack, D. A. Gerrity, C. R. Kalodner, & M. T. Riva (Eds.), *Handbook of group counseling and psychotherapy.* Thousand Oaks, CA: Sage Publications.
Stolorow, R. D., & Stolorow, B. A. (2013). Blues and emotional trauma. *Clinical Social Work Journal, 41,* 5–10.
Stone, J. (2002). Battling doubt by avoiding practice: The effects of stereotype threat on self-handicapping in white athletes. *Personality and Social Psychology Bulletin, 28,* 1667–1678.
Stone, J., Morrison, P., & Pilowsky, L. (2007). Glutamate and dopamine dysregulation in schizophrenia–A synthesis and selective review. *Journal of Psychopharmacology, 21,* 440–452.
Stopa, L., Denton, R., Wingfield, M., & Taylor, K. (2013). The fear of others: A qualitative analysis of interpersonal threat in social phobia and paranoia. *Behavioural and Cognitive Psychotherapy, 41,* 188–209.
Storm, B. C. (2011). The benefit of forgetting in thinking and remembering. *Science, 20,* 291–295.
Storm, L., & Ertel, S. (2001). Does psi exist? Comments on Milton and Wiseman's (1999) meta-analysis of Ganzfeld's research. *Psychological Bulletin, 127,* 424–433.
Stouffer, E. M., & White, N. M. (2006). Neural circuits mediating latent learning and conditioning for salt in the rat. *Neurobiology of Learning and Memory, 86,* 91–99.
Stowell, J. R., Robles, T. F., & Kane, H. S. (2013). Psychoneuroimmunology: Mechanisms, individual differences, and interventions. In A. M. Nezu, C. Nezu, P. A. Geller, & I. B. Weiner (Eds.), *Handbook of psychology, Vol. 9: Health psychology (2nd ed.).* Hoboken, NJ: John Wiley & Sons Inc.
Strange, D., Clifasefi, S., & Garry, M. (2007). False memories. In M. Garry & H. Hayne (Eds.), *Do justice and let the sky fall: Elizabeth Loftus and her contributions to science, law, and academic freedom.* Mahwah, NJ: Lawrence Erlbaum Associates.
Strathern, A., & Stewart, P. J. (2003). *Landscape, memory and history: Anthropological perspectives.* London: Pluto Press.
Strayer, D. L., & Drews, F. A. (2007). Cell-phone-induced driver distraction. *Current Directions in Psychological Science, 16,* 128–131.
Strayer, D. L., Drews, F. A., Crouch, D. J., & Johnston, W. A. (2005). Why do cell phone conversations interfere with driving? In W. R. Walker & D. Herrmann (Eds.), *Cognitive technology: Transforming thought and society.* Jefferson, NC: McFarland & Company.
Striano, T., & Vaish, A. (2006). Seven- to 9-month-old infants use facial expressions to interpret others' actions. *British Journal of Developmental Psychology, 24,* 753–760.
Striegel-Moore, R., & Bulik, C. M. (2007). Risk factors for eating disorders. *American Psychologist, 62,* 181–198.
Striegel, R. H., Bedrosian, R., Wang, C., & Schwartz, S. (2011). Why men should be included in research on binge eating: Results from a comparison of psychosocial impairment in men and women. *International Journal of Eating Disorder.* Retrieved from http://onlinelibrary.wiley.com/doi/10.1002/eat.20962/full
Stroink, M. (2007). Processes and preconditions underlying terrorism in second-generation immigrants. *Peace and Conflict: Journal of Peace Psychology, 13,* 293–312.
Strong, T., & Tomm, K. (2007). Family therapy as re-coordinating and moving on together. *Journal of Systemic Therapies, 26,* 42–54.
Subrahmanyam, K., Reich, S., Waechter, N., & Espinoza, G. (2008). Online and offline social networks: Use of social networking sites by emerging adults. *Journal of Applied Developmental Psychology, 29,* 420–433.

Sue, D. W., & Sue, D. (1990). *Counseling the culturally different: Theory and practice* (2nd ed.). Oxford, England: John Wiley & Sons.

Sue, D. W., Sue, D., & Sue, S. (1990). *Understanding abnormal behavior* (3rd ed.). Boston: Houghton-Mifflin.

Suh, E. M. (2002). Culture, identity consistency, and subjective well-being. *Journal of Personality & Social Psychology, 83,* 1378–1391.

Suhail, K., & Chaudhry, H. R. (2004). Predictors of subjective well-being in an Eastern Muslim culture. *Journal of Social and Clinical Psychology, 23,* 359–376.

Suizzo, M.-A., & Bornstein, M. H. (2006). French and European American child-mother play: Culture and gender considerations. *International Journal of Behavioral Development, 30,* 498–508.

Sullivan, B., & Thompson, H. (2013). *The plateau effect: Getting from stuck to success.* New York: The Penguin Group.

Sullivan, E. L., Smith, S. M., & Grove, K. L. (2011). Perinatal exposure to high-fat diet programs energy balance, metabolism and behavior in adulthood. *Neuroendocrinology, 93,* 1–8.

Sullivan, J., Riccio, C., & Reynolds, C. (2008, September). Variations in students' school- and teacher-related attitudes across gender, ethnicity, and age. *Journal of Instructional Psychology, 35,* 296–305.

Summers, M. (2000). *Everything in its place.* New York: Putnam.

Sunder, J. M., Borren, I., & Tambs, K. (2008). The Flynn effect is partly caused by changing fertility patterns. *Intelligence, 36,* 183–191.

Super, C. M. (1980). Cognitive development: Looking across at growing up. In C. M. Super & S. Harakness (Eds.), *New directions for child development: Anthropological perspectives on child development.* San Francisco: Jossey-Bass.

Surette, R. (2002). Self-reported copycat crime among a population of serious and violent juvenile offenders. *Crime & Delinquency, 48,* 46–69.

Susser, E. S., Herman, D. B., & Aaron, B. (2002, August). Combating the terror of terrorism. *Scientific American,* pp. 70–77.

Sutin, A. R., & Robins, R. W. (2007). Phenomenology of autobiographical memories: The Memory Experiences Questionnaire. *Memory, 15,* 390–411.

Suzuki, L. A., Short, E. L., & Lee, C. S. (2011). Racial and ethnic group differences in intelligence in the United States: Multicultural perspectives. In R. J. Sternberg & S. Kaufman (Eds.), *The Cambridge handbook of intelligence.* New York: Cambridge University Press.

Svarstad, B. (1976). Physician-patient communication and patient conformity with medical advice. In D. Mechanic (Ed.), *The growth of bureaucratic medicine.* New York: Wiley.

Svartdal, F. (2003). Extinction after partial reinforcement: Predicted vs. judged persistence. *Scandinavian Journal of Psychology, 44,* 55–64.

Swain, P. I. (2006). *New developments in eating disorders research.* Hauppauge, NY: Nova Science Publishers.

Swain, R. A., Kerr, A. L., & Thompson, R. F. (2011). The cerebellum: A neural system for the study of reinforcement learning. *Frontiers in Behavioral Neuroscience, 18,* 89–96.

Swales, M. A., & Heard, H. L. (2007). The therapy relationship in dialectical behaviour therapy. In P. Gilbert & R. L. Leahy (Eds.), *The therapeutic relationship in the cognitive behavioral psycho-therapies.* New York: Routledge/Taylor & Francis.

Swann, W. B., Jr., Chang-Schneider, C., & Larsen McClarty, K. (2007). Do people's self-views matter? Self-concept and self-esteem in everyday life. *American Psychologist, 62,* 84–94.

Swanson, H. L., Harris, K. R., & Graham, S. (Eds.). (2003). *Handbook of learning disabilities.* New York: Guilford Press.

Swets, J. A., & Bjork, R. A. (1990). Enhancing human performance: An evaluation of "new age" techniques considered by the U.S. Army. *Psychological Science, 1,* 85–96.

Swing, E., & Anderson, C. (2007). The unintended negative consequences of exposure to violent video games. *International Journal of Cognitive Technology, 12,* 3–13.

Szasz, T. (2006). The pretense of psychology as science: The myth of mental illness in statu nascendi. *Current Psychology: Developmental, Learning, Personality, Social, 25,* 42–49.

Szasz, T. S. (1994). *Cruel compassion: Psychiatric control of society's unwanted.* New York: Wiley.

Szasz, T. S. (2011). *The myth of mental illness: Foundations of a theory of personal conduct.* New York: HarperCollins.

Szegedy Maszak, M. (2003, January 13). The sound of unsound minds. *U.S. News & World Report,* pp. 45–46.

Tadmor, C. T. (2007). Biculturalism: The plus side of leaving home? The effects of second-culture exposure on integrative complexity and its consequences for overseas performance. *Dissertation Abstracts International Section A: Humanities and Social Sciences, 67*(8-A), 3068.

Taggi, F., Crenca, A., Cedri, C., Giustini, M., Dosi, G., & Marturano, P. (2007). Road safety and the tsunami of cell phones. *Ann Ig, 19,* 269–274.

Tajfel, H., & Turner, J. C. (2004). The social identity theory of intergroup behavior. In J. T. Jost & J. Sidanius (Eds.), *Political psychology: Key readings.* New York: Psychology Press.

Takahashi, M., Nakata, A., Haratani, T., Ogawa, Y., & Arito, H. (2004). Post-lunch nap as a worksite intervention to promote alertness on the job. *Ergonomics, 47,* 1003–1013.

Taki, Y., Thyreau, B., Kinomura, S., Sato, K., Goto, R., Wu, K., & . . . Fukuda, H. (2013). A longitudinal study of age and gender related annual rate of volume changes in regional gray matter in healthy adults. *Human Brain Mapping, 34,* 2292–2301.

Takizawa, T., Kondo, T., & Sakihara, S. (2007). Stress buffering effects of social support on depressive symptoms in middle age: Reciprocity and community mental health: Corrigendum. *Psychiatry and Clinical Neurosciences, 61,* 336–337.

Tal-Or, N., & Papirman, Y. (2007). The fundamental attribution error in attributing fictional figures' characteristics to the actors. *Media Psychology, 9,* 331–345.

Talarico, J. (2009). Freshman flashbulbs: Memories of unique and first-time events in starting college. *Memory, 17,* 256–265.

Talarico, J., & Rubin, D. (2007). Flashbulb memories are special after all; in phenomenology, not accuracy. *Applied Cognitive Psychology, 21,* 557–578.

Talmi, D., Anderson, A., Riggs, L., Caplan, J., & Moscovitch, M. (2008). Immediate memory consequences of the effect of emotion on attention to pictures. *Learning & Memory, 15, 172–182.*

Talukdar, S., & Shastri, J. (2006). Contributory and adverse factors in social development of young children. *Psychological Studies, 51,* 294–303.

Tamini, B., Bojhd, F., & Yazdani, S. (2011). Love types, psychological well-being and self-concept. *Journal of the Indian Academy of Applied Psychology, 37,* 169–178.

Tan, G., Rintala, D. H., Jensen, M. P., Richards, J. S., Holmes, S. A., Parachuri, R., Lashgari-Saegh, S., & Price, L. R. (2011). Efficacy of cranial electrotherapy stimulation for neuropathic pain following spinal cord injury: a multi-site randomized controlled trial with a secondary 6-month open-label phase. *Journal of Spinal Cord Medicine, 34,* 285–296.

Tan, L., & Ward, G. (2008). Rehearsal in immediate serial recall. *Psychonomic Bulletin & Review, 15,* 535–542.

Tan, L., Chan, A., Kay, P., Khong, P., Yip, L., & Luke, K. (2008). Language affects patterns of brain activation associated with perceptual decision. *PNAS Proceedings of the National Academy of Sciences of the United States of America, 105(10),* 4004–4009.

Tandon, R., Gaebel, W., Barch, D. M., Bustillo, J., Gur, R. E., Heckers, S., & . . . Carpenter, W. (2013). Definition and description of schizophrenia in the dsm-5. *Schizophrenia Research.* Retrieved from http://ccpweb.wustl.edu/pdfs/2013_defdes.pdf

Tanner, J. M. (1978). *Education and physical growth* (2nd ed.). New York: International Universities Press.

Tanner, J. M. (1990). *Foetus into man: Physical growth from conception to maturity* (rev. ed.). Cambridge, MA: Harvard University Press.

Tasker, F. (2005). Lesbian mothers, gay fathers, and their children: A review. *Journal of Developmental and Behavioral Pediatrics, 26,* 224–240.

Tavernise, S. (2013, September 6). Rise is seen in students who use e-cigarettes. *The New York Times,* p. A11.

Taylor, F., & Bryant, R. A. (2007). The tendency to suppress, inhibiting thoughts, and dream rebound. *Behaviour Research and Therapy, 45,* 163–168.

Taylor, S. (2003). Anxiety sensitivity and its implications for understanding and treating PTSD. *Journal of Cognitive Psychotherapy, 17,* 179–186.

Taylor, S. E. (1995). Quandary at the crossroads: Paternalism versus advocacy surrounding end-of-treatment decisions. *American Journal of Hospital Palliatory Care, 12,* 43–46.

Taylor, S. E., Kemeny, M. E., Reed, G. M., Bower, J. E., & Gruenewald, T. L. (2000). Psychological resources, positive illusions, and health. *American Psychologist, 55,* 99–109.

Teague, R. (2013). The American view of Freud's couch. *Psyccritiques, 58,* 12–21.

Teff, K. L., Petrova, M., & Havel, P. J. (2007). 48-h Glucose infusion in humans: Effect on hormonal responses, hunger and food intake. *Physiology & Behavior, 90,* 733–743.

Tellegen, A., Lykken, D. T., Bouchard, T. J., Jr., Wilcox, K. J., Segal, N. L., & Rich, S. (1988). Personality similarity in twins reared apart and together. *Journal of Personality and Social Psychology, 54,* 1031–1039.

Templer, D. I., & Arkawa, H. (2006). Association of race and color with mean IQ across nations. *Psychological Reports, 99,* 191–196.

Tenenbaum, H. R., & Leaper, C. (2002). Are parents' gender schemas related to their children's gender-related cognitions? A meta-analysis. *Developmental Psychology, 38,* 615–630.

Tenenbaum, H. R., & Ruck, M. D. (2007). Are teachers' expectations different for racial minority than for European American students? A meta-analysis. *Journal of Educational Psychology, 99,* 253–273.

Teodorov, E., Salzgerber, S. A., Felicio, L. F., Varolli, F. M. F., & Bernardi, M. M. (2002). Effects of perinatal picrotoxin and sexual experience on heterosexual and homosexual behavior in male rats. *Neurotoxicology and Teratology, 24,* 235–245.

Terry, W. S. (2003). *Learning and memory: Basic principles, processes, and procedures* (2nd ed.). Boston: Allyn & Bacon.

Thachil, A. F., Mohan, R., & Bhugra, D. (2007). The evidence base of complementary and alternative therapies in depression. *Journal of Affective Disorders, 97,* 23–35.

Thanos, P. K., Robison, L. S., Robinson, J. K., Michaelides, M., Wang, G., & Volkow, N. D. (2013). Obese rats with deficient leptin signaling exhibit heightened sensitivity to olfactory food cues. *Synapse, 67,* 171–178.

Tharp, R. G. (1989). Psychocultural variables and constants: Effects on teaching and learning in schools [Special issue: Children and their development: Knowledge base, research agenda, and social policy application]. *American Psychologist, 44,* 349–359.

Thase, M. E. (2013). Comparative effectiveness of psychodynamic psychotherapy and cognitive-behavioral therapy: It's about time, and what's next? *The American Journal of Psychiatry, 170,* 953–956.

Thatcher, D. L., & Clark, D. B. (2006). Adolescent alcohol abuse and dependence: Development, diagnosis, treatment and outcomes. *Current Psychiatry Reviews, 2,* 159–177.

The New York Times. (1993, November 15). No. 2 pencil fades as graduate exam moves to computer. *The New York Times,* p. B9.

The Toronto Star. (2011, August 10). 'A bright light trapped in a dark room'; Student's death draws attention to wait for treatment of disorder. *The Toronto Star,* p. GT1.

Thomas, P., Mathur, P., Gottesman, I. I., Nagpal, R., Nimgaonkar, V. L., & Deshpande, S. N. (2007). Correlates of hallucinations in schizophrenia: A cross-cultural evaluation. *Schizophrenia Research, 92,* 41–49.

Thorkildsen, T. A. (2006). An empirical exploration of language and thought. *PsycCRITIQUES, 51,* no pagination specified.

Thorndike, E. L. (1932). *The fundamentals of learning.* New York: Teachers College.

Thornhill, R., Gangestad, S. W., Miller, R., Scheyd, G., McCollough, J. K., & Franklin, M. (2003). Major histocompatibility complex genes, symmetry, and body scent attractiveness in men and women. *Behavioral Ecology, 14,* 668–678.

Thornton, A., & McAuliffe, K. (2006, July 14). Teaching in wild meerkats. *Science, 313,* 227–229.

Thornton, A., & Young-DeMarco, L. (2001). Four decades of trends in attitudes toward family issues in the United States: The 1960s through the 1990s. *Journal of Marriage and the Family, 63,* 1009–1017.

Thorpe, K. (2009). *The future costs of obesity: National and state estimates of the impact of obesity on direct health care expenses.* Washington, DC: United Health Foundation.

Thrash, T. M., & Elliot, A. J. (2002). Implicit and self-attributed achievement motives: Concordance and predictive validity. *Journal of Personality, 70,* 729–755.

Thurman, S. M., & Lu, H. (2013). Physical and biological constraints govern perceived animacy of scrambled human forms. *Psychological Science, 24,* 1133–1141.

Time. (1966, July 22). Less pain, more gain. *Time.*

Tippin, J., Sparks, J., & Rizzo, M. (2009, August). Visual vigilance in drivers with obstructive sleep apnea. *Journal of Psychosomatic Research, 67,* 143–151.

Tirri, K., & Nokelainen, P. (2008). Identification of multiple intelligences with the Multiple Intelligence Profiling Questionnaire III [Special issue: High-ability assessment]. *Psychology Science, 50,* 206–221.

Todorov, A. (Ed.), Fiske, S. (Ed.), & Prentice, D. (Ed.). (2011). *Social neuroscience: Toward understanding the underpinnings of the social mind.* New York: Oxford University Press.

Todorov, A., & Duchaine, B. (2008). Reading trustworthiness in faces without recognizing faces. *Cognitive Neuropsychology, 25,* 1–16.

Toft, A., Tome, M., Barnett, S. C., & Riddell, J. S. (2013). A comparative study of glial and non neural cell properties for transplant mediated repair of the injured spinal cord. *Glia, 61,* 513–528.

Tokutsu, Y., Umene-Nakano, W., Shinkai, T., Yoshimura, R., Okamoto, T., Katsuki, A., & . . . Nakamura, J. (2013). Follow-up study on electroconvulsive therapy in treatment-resistant depressed patients after remission: A chart review. *Clinical Psychopharmacology and Neuroscience, 11,* 34–38.

Tolman, E. C., & Honzik, C. H. (1930). Introduction and removal of reward and maze performance in rats. *University of California Publications in Psychology, 4,* 257–275.

Tommasi, L. (2009). Mechanisms and functions of brain and behavioural asymmetries. *Philosophical Transactions of the Royal Society B, 364,* 855–859.

Tonidandel, S., Quinones, M. A., & Adams, A. A. (2002). Computer-adaptive testing: The impact of test characteristics on perceived performance and test takers' reactions. *Journal of Applied Psychology, 87,* 320–332.

Tononi, G., & Koch, C. (2008). The neural correlates of consciousness: An update. In A Kingstone & M. B. Miller (Eds.), *The year in cognitive neuroscience.* Malden, MA: Blackwell Publishing.

Toole, L. M., DeLeon, I. G., Kahng, S., Ruffin, G. E., Pletcher, C. A., & Bowman, L. G. (2004). Re-evaluation of constant versus varied punishers using empirically derived consequences. *Research in Developmental Disabilities, 25,* 577–586.

Toth, J. P., & Daniels, K. A. (2002). Effects of prior experience on judgments of normative word frequency: Automatic bias and correction. *Journal of Memory and Language, 46,* 845–874.

Touhara, K. (2007). Molecular biology of peptide pheromone production and reception in mice. *Advanced Genetics, 59,* 147–171.

Tracy, J. L., & Robins, R. W. (2004). Show your pride: Evidence for a discrete emotion expression. *Psychological Science, 15,* 194–197.

Tramontana, J. (2011). *Sports hypnosis in practice: Scripts, strategies and case examples.* Norwalk, CT: Crown House Publishing Limited.

Tranter, L. J., & Koutstaal, W. (2008). Age and flexible thinking: An experimental demonstration of the beneficial effects of increased cognitively stimulating activity on fluid intelligence in healthy older adults. *Neuropsychology and Cognition, 15,* 184–207.

Travis, F. (2006). From I to I: Concepts of self on a object-referral/self-referral continuum. In A. P. Prescott (Ed.), *The concept of self in psychology.* Hauppauge, NY: Nova Science Publishers.

Travis, F., et al. (2009, February). Effects of transcendental meditation practice on brain functioning and stress reactivity in college students. *International Journal of Psychopathy, 71,* 170–176.

Tremblay, A. (2004). Dietary fat and body weight set point. *Nutrition Review, 62*(7, Pt 2), S75–S77.

Triesch, J., Jasso, H., & Deák, G. O. (2007). Emergence of mirror neurons in a model of gaze following. *Adaptive Behavior, 15,* 149–165.

Triscari, M., Faraci, P., D'Angelo, V., Urso, V., & Catalisano, D. (2011). Two treatments for fear of flying compared: Cognitive behavioral therapy combined with systematic desensitization or eye movement desensitization and reprocessing (EMDR). *Aviation Psychology and Applied Human Factors, 1,* 9–14.

Tropp, L. R., & Bianchi, R. A. (2006). Valuing diversity and interest in intergroup contact. *Journal of Social Issues, 62,* 533–551.

Tropp, L. R., & Pettigrew, T. F. (2005). Differential relationships between intergroup contact and affective and cognitive dimensions of prejudice. *Personality and Social Psychology Bulletin, 31,* 1145–1158.

Troyer, A. K., Hafliger, A., & Cadieux, M. J. (2006). Name and face learning in older adults: Effects of level of processing, self-generation, and intention to learn. *Journals of Gerontology: Series B: Psychological Sciences and Social Sciences, 61,* P67–P74.

Trudel, G. (2002). Sexuality and marital life: Results of a survey. *Journal of Sex and Marital Therapy, 28,* 229–249.

Trujillo-Pisanty, I., Hernandez, G., Moreau-Debord, I., Cossette, M. P., Conover, K., Cheer, J. F., & Shizgal, P. (2011). Cannabinoid receptor blockade reduces the opportunity cost at which rats maintain operant performance for rewarding brain stimulation. *Journal of Neuroscience, 31,* 5426–5430.

Trull, T. J., & Widiger, T. A. (2003). Personality disorders. In G. Stricker, T. A. Widiger, et al. (Eds.), *Handbook of psychology: Clinical psychology* (Vol. 8). New York: Wiley.

Tsai, A., Yang, M., Lan, C., & Chen, C. (2008). Evaluation of effect of cognitive intervention programs for the community-dwelling elderly with subjective memory complaints. *International Journal of Geriatric Psychiatry, 23,* 1172–1174.

Tsaousis, I., Nikolaou, I., & Serdaris, N. (2007). Do the core self-evaluations moderate the relationship between subjective well-being and physical and psychological health? *Personality and Individual Differences, 42,* 1441–1452.

Tseng, W. S. (2003). *Clinician's guide to cultural psychiatry.* San Diego, CA: Elsevier Publishing.

Tsenkova, V., Boylan, J., & Ryff, C. (2013). Stress eating and health. Findings from MIDUS, a national study of US adults. *Appetite, 69,* 151–155.

Tsukasaki, T., & Ishii, K. (2004). Linguistic-cultural relativity of cognition: Rethinking the Sapir-Whorf hypothesis. *Japanese Psychological Review, 47,* 173–186.

Tsunoda, T. (1985). *The Japanese brain: Uniqueness and universality.* Tokyo: Taishukan Publishing.

Tucker Blackwell, V. G. (2006). Factors which influence the academic motivation and disengagement of adolescent, African American males within a social-historical and psychological context. *Dissertation Abstracts International, 67,* 1654A.

Tucker, C. M., & Herman, K. C. (2002). Using culturally sensitive theories and research to meet the academic needs of low-income African American children. *American Psychologist, 57,* 762–773.

Tuerk, P. W., Yoder, M., Grubaugh, A., Myrick, H., Hamner, M., & Acierno, R. (2011). Prolonged exposure therapy for combat-related posttraumatic stress disorder: An examination of treatment effectiveness for veterans of the wars in Afghanistan and Iraq. *Journal of Anxiety Disorders, 25,* 397–403.

Tuerlinckx, F., De Boeck, P., & Lens, W. (2002). Measuring needs with the Thematic Apperception Test: A psychometric study. *Journal of Personality and Social Psychology, 82,* 448–461.

Tugay, N., et al. (2007). Effectiveness of transcutaneous electrical nerve stimulation and interferential current in primary dysmenorrhea. *Pain Medicine, 8,* 295–300.

Tulving, E. (2000). Concepts of memory. In E. Tulving, F. I. M. Craik, et al. (Eds.), *The Oxford handbook of memory.* New York: Oxford University Press.

Tulving, E. (2002). Episodic memory and common sense: How far apart? In A. Baddeley & J. P. Aggleton (Eds.), *Episodic memory: New directions in research.* London: Oxford University Press.

Tulving, E., & Psotka, J. (1971). Retroactive inhibition in free recall: Inaccessibility of information available in the memory store. *Journal of Experimental Psychology, 87,* 1–8.

Tulving, E., & Thompson, D. M. (1983). Encoding specificity and retrieval processes in episodic memory. *Psychological Review, 80,* 352–373.

Tunstall, B. J., Verendeev, A., & Kearns, D. N. (2013). Outcome specificity in deepened extinction may limit treatment feasibility: Co-presentation of a food cue interferes with extinction of cue-elicited cocaine seeking. *Drug and Alcohol Dependence,* Retrieved from http://www.ncbi.nlm.nih.gov/pubmed/24071568

Turk, D. C. (1994). Perspectives on chronic pain: The role of psychological factors. *Current Directions in Psychological Science, 3,* 45–49.

Turkel, R. A. (2002). From victim to heroine: Children's stories revisited. *Journal of the American Academy of Psychoanalysis, 30,* 71–81.

Turkewitz, G. (1993). The origins of differential hemispheric strategies for information processing in the relationships between voice and face perception. In B. de Boysson-Bardies, S. de Schonen, P. W. Jusczyk, P. McNeilage, & J. Morton (Eds.), *Developmental neurocognition: Speech and face processing in the first year of life. NATO ASI series D: Behavioural and social sciences* (Vol. 69). Dordrecht, Netherlands: Kluwer Academic.

Turnbull, O., & Solms, M. (2007). Awareness, desire, and false beliefs: Freud in the light of modern neuropsychology. *Cortex, 43,* 1083–1090.

Turner, M. E., Pratkanis, A. R., & Struckman, C. K. (2007). Groupthink as social identity maintenance. In C. K. Struckman (Ed.), *The science of social influence: Advances and future progress.* New York: Psychology Press.

Turner, M., Tamborini, R., Limon, M., & Zuckerman-Hyman, C. (2007). The moderators and mediators of door-in-the-face requests: Is it a negotiation or a helping experience? *Communication Monographs, 74,* 333–356.

Turner, W. J. (1995). Homosexuality, Type 1: An Xq28 phenomenon. *Archives of Sexual Behavior, 24,* 109–134.

Tuszynski, M. H. (2007). Nerve growth factor gene therapy in Alzheimer's disease. *Alzheimer's Disease and Associated Disorders, 21,* 179–189.

Tutwiler, S., Lin, M., & Chang, C. (2013). The use of a gesture-based system for teaching multiple intelligences: A pilot study. *British Journal of Educational Technology, 44,* E133–E138.

Tversky, A., & Kahneman, D. (1987). Rational choice and the framing of decisions. In R. Hogarth & M. Reder (Eds.), *Rational choice: The contrast between economics and psychology.* Chicago: University of Chicago Press.

Twenge, J., & Foster, J. (2010). Birth cohort increases in narcissistic personality traits among american college students, 1982–2009. *Social Psychological and Personality Science, 1,* 99–106.

Twenge, J. M. (2013). Does online social media lead to social connection or social disconnection? *Journal of College and Character,* 14, 11–20.

Twenge, J. M., & Kasser, T. (2013). Generational changes in materialism and work centrality, 1976–2007: Associations with temporal changes in societal insecurity and materialistic role-modeling. *Personality and Social Psychology Bulletin. Retrieved from* http://psp.sagepub.com/content/early/2013/05/01/0146167213484586

Twenge, J. M., Campbell, W. K., & Gentile, B. (2013). Changes in pronoun use in American books and the rise of individualism, 1960–2008. *Journal of Cross-Cultural Psychology,* 44, 406–415.

Twenge, J., Abebe, E., and Campbell, W. (2010). Fitting in or standing out: trends in American parents' choices for children's names, 1880–2007. *Social Psychological and Personality Science, 1,* 19–25.

Tydgat, I., & Grainger, J. (2009). Serial position effects in the identification of letters, digits, and symbols. *Journal of Experimental Psychology: Human Perception and Performance, 35,* 480–498.

U.S. Bureau of Labor Statistics. (2012). *Women's weekly earnings as a percentage of men's earnings.* Washington, DC: U.S. Bureau of Labor Statistics.

U.S. Bureau of Labor Statistics. (2013). *Women's weekly earnings as a percentage of men's earnings.* Washington, DC: U.S. Bureau of Labor Statistics.

U.S. Bureau of Labor Statistics. (2009). *Women's weekly earnings as a percentage of men's earnings.* Washington, DC: U.S. Bureau of Labor Statistics.

U.S. Bureau of the Census. (2000). *Census 2000.* Retrieved from American Fact Finder http://factfinder.census.gov/servlet/ BasicFactsServlet

U.S. Senate Select Committee on Intelligence. (2004, July 9). *Report of the U.S. intelligence community's prewar intelligence assessments on Iraq.* Retrieved from http://www.gpoaccess.gov/serialset/creports/iraq.html

Ubell, E. (1993, January 10). Could you use more sleep? *Parade,* pp. 16–18.

Ullman, S. E., & Townsend, S. M. (2007). Barriers to working with sexual assault survivors: A qualitative study of rape crisis center workers. *Violence Against Women, 13,* 412–443.

Umphress, E. E., Smith-Crowe, K., & Brief, A. P. (2007). When birds of a feather flock together and when they do not: Status composition, social dominance orientation, and organizational attractiveness. *Journal of Applied Psychology, 92,* 396–409.

UNAIDS. (December, 2007). *07 AIDS epidemic update.* Geneva, Switzerland: United Nations Programme on HIV/AIDS.

Ünal-Karagüven, M. (2009). Psychological impact of an economic crisis: A Conservation of Resources approach. *International Journal of Stress Management, 16,* 177–194.

Underwood, A. (2005, October 3). The good heart. *Newsweek,* p. 49.

University of Chicago. (2009). MSTP recent PhD theses. Retrieved from http://pritzker.uchicago.edu/jointdegrees/mstp/theses.shtml

Unsworth, N., & Engle, R. W. (2005). Individual differences in working memory capacity and learning: Evidence from the serial reaction time task. *Memory and Cognition, 33,* 213–220.

Updegraff, K. A., Helms, H. M., McHale, S. M., Crouter, A. C., Thayer, S. M., & Sales, L. H. (2004). Who's the boss? Patterns of perceived control in adolescents' friendships. *Journal of Youth & Adolescence, 33,* 403–420.

Ursprung, W. W., Sanouri, A., & DiFranza, J. R. (2009). The loss of autonomy over smoking in relation to lifetime cigarette consumption. *Addictive Behaviors, 22,* 12–19.

Uttl, B., Graf, P., & Cosentino, S. (2003). Implicit memory for new associations: Types of conceptual representations. In J. S. Bowers & C. J. Marsolek (Eds.), *Rethinking implicit memory.* London: Oxford University Press.

Uylings, H. B. M. (2006). Development of the human cortex and the concept of 'critical' or 'sensitive' periods. *Language Learning, 56,* 59–90.

Vaillant, G. E., & Vaillant, C. O. (1990). Natural history of male psychological health: XII. A 46-year study of predictors of successful aging at age 65. *American Journal of Psychiatry, 147,* 31–37.

Vaitl, D., Schienle, A., & Stark, R. (2005). Neurobiology of fear and disgust. *International Journal of Psychophysiology, 57,* 1–4.

Valencia, R. R., & Suzuki, L. A. (2003). *Intelligence testing and minority students: Foundations, performance factors, and assessment issues.* Thousand Oaks, CA: Sage.

Valenzuela, S., Park, N., & Kee, K. F. (2009). Is there social capital in a social network site? Facebook use and college students' life satisfaction, trust, and participation. *Journal of Computer-Mediated Communications, 14,* 875–901.

Valois, R. F., Zullig, K. J., & Hunter, A. A. (2013). Association between adolescent suicide ideation, suicide attempts and emotional self-efficacy. *Journal of Child and Family Studies.* Retrieved from http://link.springer.com/article/10.1007%2Fs10826-013-9829-8

Valsecchi, M., Caziot, B., Backus, B. T., & Gegenfurtner, K. R. (2013). The role of binocular disparity in rapid scene and pattern recognition. *I-Perception, 4*(2), 254–262.

Valsiner, J., Diriwächter, R., & Sauck, C. (2005). Diversity in unity: Standard questions and nonstandard interpretations. In *Science and medicine in dialogue: Thinking through particulars and universals.* Westport, CT: Praeger Publishers/Greenwood Publishing Group.

Van Beekum, S. (2005). The therapist as a new object. *Transactional Analysis Journal, 35,* 187–191.

Van Belle, V., Pelckmans, K., Suykens, J. A. K., & Van Huffel, S. (2011). Learning transformation models for ranking and survival analysis. *Journal of Machine Learning Research, 12,* 819–862.

Van De Graaff, K. (2000). *Human anatomy* (5th ed.). Boston: McGraw-Hill.

Van den Wildenberg, W. P. M., & Van der Molen, M. W. (2004). Developmental trends in simple and selective inhibition of compatible and incompatible responses. *Journal of Experimental Child Psychology, 87,* 201–220.

van der Helm, P. A. (2006). Review of perceptual dynamics: Theoretical foundations and philosophical implications of gestalt psychology. *Philosophical Psychology, 19,* 274–279.

van der Leij, M. J. (2011, December 2). Experimenting with buddies. *Science, 334,* 1220–1221.

Van der Zee, E. A., Platt, B. B., & Riedel, G. G. (2011). Acetylcholine: Future research and perspectives. *Behavioural Brain Research, 221,* 583–586.

van Dijk, W. W., Ouwerkerk, J. W., Wesseling, Y. M., & van Koningsbruggen, G. M. (2011). Towards understanding pleasure at the misfortunes of others: The impact of self-evaluation threat on schadenfreude. *Cognition and Emotion, 25,* 360–368.

van Hooren, S. A. H., Valentijn, A. M., & Bosma, H. (2007). Cognitive functioning in healthy older adults aged 64–81: A cohort study into the effects of age, sex, and education. *Aging, Neuropsychology, and Cognition, 14,* 40–54.

van Marle, K., & Wynn, K. (2009). Infants' auditory enumeration: Evidence for analog magnitudes in the small number range. *Cognition, 111,* 302–316.

van Nieuwenhuijzen, M. M., Vriens, A. A., Scheepmaker, M. M., Smit, M. M., & Porton, E. E. (2011). The development of a diagnostic instrument to measure social information processing in children with mild to borderline intellectual disabilities. *Research in Developmental Disabilities, 32,* 358–370.

van Oort, R., & Kessels, R. (2009). Executive dysfunction in Korsakoff's syndrome: Time to revise the DSM criteria for alcohol-induced persisting amnestic disorder? *International Journal of Psychiatry in Clinical Practice, 13,* 78–81.

Van Overwalle, F., & Siebler, F. (2005). A connectionist model of attitude formation and change. *Personality and Social Psychology Review, 9,* 231–274.

van Soelen, I. C., Brouwer, R. M., van Leeuwen, M., Kahn, R. S., Pol, H., & Boomsma, D. I. (2011). Heritability of verbal and performance intelligence in a pediatric longitudinal sample. *Twin Research and Human Genetics, 14,* 119–128.

van Wei, E., Linssen, H., & Abma, R. (2000). The parental bond and the well-being of adolescents and young adults. *Journal of Youth & Adolescence, 29,* 307–318.

van Wesel, F., Boeije, H., & Hoijtink, H. (2013). Use of hypotheses for analysis of variance models: Challenging the current practice. *Quality & Quantity: International Journal of Methodology, 47,* 137–150.

Vanasse, A., Niyonsenga, T., & Courteau, J. (2004). Smoking cessation within the context of family medicine: Which smokers take action? *Preventive Medicine: An International Journal Devoted to Practice and Theory, 38,* 330–337.

Vandell, D. L., Burchinal, M. R., Belsky, J., Owen, M. T., Friedman, S. L., Clarke-Stewart, et al. (2005). *Early child care and children's development in the primary grades: Follow-up results from the NICHD Study of Early Child Care.* Paper presented at the biennial meeting of the Society for Research in Child Development, Atlanta, GA.

Vandervert, L. R., Schimpf, P. H., & Liu, H. (2007). How working memory and the cerebellum collaborate to produce creativity and innovation. *Creativity Research Journal, 19,* 1–18.

Vandierendonck, A., & Szmalec, A. (Eds.). (2011). *Spatial working memory.* New York: Psychology Press.

Vanheule, S., Desmet, M., Rosseel, Y., & Meganck, R. (2006). Core transference themes in depression. *Journal of Affective Disorders, 91,* 71–75.

Vansteenkiste, M., Simons, J., Lens, W., Soenens, B., & Matos, L. (2005). Examining the motivational impact of intrinsic versus extrinsic goal framing and autonomy-supportive versus internally controlling communication style on early adolescents' academic achievement. *Child Development, 76,* 483–501.

Varma, S. (2007). A computational model of Tower of Hanoi problem solving. *Dissertation Abstracts International: Section B: The Sciences and Engineering, 67*(8-B), 4736.

Vassalli, A., & Dijk, D. (2009). Sleep function: Current questions and new approaches. *European Journal of Neuroscience, 29,* 1830–1841.

Vecchione, M., Schoen, H., Castro, J., Cieciuch, J., Pavlopoulos, V., & Caprara, G. (2011). Personality correlates of party preference: The Big Five in five big European countries. *Personality and Individual Differences, 51,* 737–742.

Vedantam, S. (2005, January 23). See no bias. *Washington Post,* p. W12.

Vega, C. P. (2006). The effects of therapeutic components on at-risk middle school children's grades and attendance: An archival study of an after-school prevention program. *Dissertation Abstracts International: Section B: The Sciences and Engineering, 66,* 4504.

Velentzas, K., Heinen, T., & Schack, T. (2011). Routine integration strategies and their effects on volleyball serve performance and players' movement mental representation. *Journal of Applied Sport Psychology, 23,* 209–222.

Vellacott, J. (2007). Resilience: A psychoanalytic exploration. *British Journal of Psychotherapy, 23,* 163–170.

Velliste, M., Perel, S., Spalding, M., Whitford, S., & Schwartz, A. (2008). Cortical control of a prosthetic arm for self-feeding. *Nature, 453,* 1098–1101.

Veltman, M. W. M., & Browne, K. D. (2001). Three decades of child maltreatment research: Implications for the school years. *Trauma Violence and Abuse, 2,* 215–239.

Veniegas, R. C. (2000). Biological research on women's sexual orientations: Evaluating the scientific evidence. *Journal of Social Issues, 56,* 267–282.

Verdejo, A., Toribio, I., & Orozco, C. (2005). Neuropsychological functioning in methadone maintenance patients versus abstinent heroin abusers. *Drug and Alcohol Dependence, 78,* 283–288.

Verdon, B. (2011). The case of thematic tests adapted to older adults: On the importance of differentiating latent and manifest contents in projective tests. *Rorschachiana, 32,* 46–71.

Verfaellie, M., & Keane, M. M. (2002). Impaired and preserved memory processes in amnesia. In L. R. Squire & D. L. Schacter (Eds.), *Neuropsychology of memory* (3rd ed.). New York: Guilford Press.

Verhaeghen, P., Aikman, S. N., & Van Gulick, A. E. (2011). Prime and prejudice: Co-occurrence in the culture as a source of automatic stereotype priming. *British Journal of Social Psychology, 50,* 501–518.

Verleger, R., Schuknecht, S., Jaskowski, P., & Wagner, U. (2008). Changes in processing of masked stimuli across early- and late-night sleep: A study on behavior and brain potentials. *Brain and Cognition, 68,* 180–192.

Vernon, P., Villani, V., Vickers, L., & Harris, J. (2008, January). A behavioral genetic investigation of the Dark Triad and the Big 5. *Personality and Individual Differences, 44,* 445–452.

Verona, E., & Sullivan, E. (2008). Emotional catharsis and aggression revisited: Heart rate reduction following aggressive responding. *Emotion, 8,* 331–340.

Vesely, A. K., Saklofske, D. H., & Leschied, A. W. (2013). Teachers–The vital resource: The contribution of emotional intelligence to teacher efficacy and well-being. *Canadian Journal of School Psychology, 28,* 71–89.

Vicari, S., Pontillo, M., & Armando, M. (2013). Neurodevelopmental and psychiatric issues in Down's syndrome: Assessment and intervention. *Psychiatric Genetics, 23,* 95–107.

Victor, S. B., & Fish, M. C. (1995). Lesbian mothers and the children: A review for school psychologists. *School Psychology Review, 24,* 456–479.

Vieira, E. M., & Freire, J. C. (2006). Alteridade e psicologia humanista: Uma leitura ética da abordagem centrada na pessoa. Alterity and humanistic psychology: An ethical reading of the person-centered approach. *Estudos de Psicologia, 23,* 425–432.

Villarosa, L. (2002, December 3). To prevent sexual abuse, abusers step forward. *The New York Times,* p. B1.

Villemure, C., Slotnick, B. M., & Bushnell, M. C. (2003). Effects of odors on pain perception: Deciphering the roles of emotion and attention. *Pain, 106,* 101–108.

Vincus, A. A., Ringwalt, C., Harris, M. S., & Shamblen, S. R. (2010). A short-term, quasi-experimental evaluation of D.A.R.E.'s revised elementary school curriculum. *Journal of Drug Education, 40,* 37–49.

Virginia Tech Transportation Institute. (2009). New data from VTTI provides insight into cell phone use and driving distraction. Retrieved from http://www.vtti.vt.edu/ PDF/7-22-09-VTTI-Press Release Cell _phones and Driver_ Distraction.pdf

Viskontas, I. V., Quiroga, R. Q., & Fried, I. (2009, December 1). Human medial temporal lobe neurons respond preferentially to personally relevant images. *Proceedings of the National Academy of Science of the United States of America (PNAS), 106,* 21329–21334.

Vitak, J., Zube, P., Smock, A., Carr, C. T., Ellison, N., & Lampe, C. (2011). It's complicated: Facebook users' political participation in the 2008 election. *Cyberpsychology, Behavior, and Social Networking, 14,* 107–114.

Vitaro, F., Brendgen, M., & Arseneault, L. (2009). Methods and measures: The discordant MZ-twin method: One step closer to the holy grail of causality. *International Journal of Behavioral Development, 33,* 376–382.

Vitello, P. (2006, June 12). A ring tone meant to fall on deaf ears. *The New York Times,* A1.

Vitiello, A. L., Bonello, R. P., & Pollard, H. P. (2007). The effectiveness of ENAR® for the treatment of chronic neck pain in Australian adults: A preliminary single-blind, randomised controlled trial. *Chiropractic Osteopathology, 9,* 9.

Vlassova, A., & Pearson, J. (2013). Look before you leap: Sensory memory improves decision making. *Psychological Science, 24,* 1635–1643.

Vleioras, G., & Bosma, H. A. (2005). Are identity styles important for psychological well-being? *Journal of Adolescence, 28,* 397–409.

Vogt, D., Rizvi, S., Shipherd, J., & Resick, P. (2008). Longitudinal investigation of reciprocal relationship between stress reactions and hardiness. *Personality and Social Psychology Bulletin, 34,* 61–73.

Volterra, V., Caselli, M. C., Capirci, O., Tonucci, F., & Vicari, S. (2003). Early linguistic abilities of Italian children with Williams syndrome [Special issue: Williams syndrome]. *Developmental Neuropsychology, 23,* 33–58.

Vonasch, A. J., & Baumeister, R. F. (2013). Implications of free will beliefs for basic theory and societal benefit: Critique and implications for social psychology. *British Journal of Social Psychology, 52,* 219–227.

Voruganti, L. P., Awad, A. G., Parker, B., Forrest, C., Usmani, Y., Fernando, M. L. D., et al. (2007). Cognition, functioning and quality of life in schizophrenia treatment: Results of a one-year randomized controlled trial of olanzapine and quetiapine. *Schizophrenia Research, 96,* 146–155.

Voss, J., & Paller, K. (2008). Brain substrates of implicit and explicit memory: The importance of concurrently acquired neural signals of both memory types. *Neuropsychologia, 46*(13), 3021–3029.

Vrieze, S. I., McGue, M., Miller, M. B., Hicks, B. M., & Iacono, W. G. (2013). Three mutually informative ways to understand the genetic relationships among behavioral disinhibition, alcohol use, drug use, nicotine use/dependence, and their co-occurrence: Twin biometry, GCTA, and genome-wide scoring. *Behavior Genetics, 43,* 97–107.

Vygotsky, L. S. (1926/1997). *Educational psychology.* Delray Beach, FL: St. Lucie Press.

Wachs, T. D., Pollitt, E., Cueto, S., & Jacoby, E. (2004). Structure and cross-contextual stability of neonatal temperament. *Infant Behavior and Development, 27,* 382–396.

Waddell, J., & Shors, T. J. (2008). Neurogenesis, learning and associative strength. *European Journal of Neurosciences, 27,* 3020–3028.

Wadden, T. A., Crerand, C. E., & Brock, J. (2005). Behavioral treatment of obesity. *Psychiatric Clinics of North America, 28,* 151–170.

Wade, K. A., Sharman, S. J., & Garry, M. (2007). False claims about false memory research. *Consciousness and Cognition: An International Journal, 16,* 18–28.

Wagemans, J., Elder, J. H., Kubovy, M., Palmer, S. E., Peterson, M. A., Singh, M., & von der Heydt, R. (2012). A century of Gestalt psychology in visual perception: I. Perceptual grouping and figure-ground organization. *Psychological Bulletin, 138,* 1172–1217.

Wager, T. D. (2005). The neural bases of placebo effects in pain. *Current Directions in Psychological Science, 14,* 175–180.

Wagner, A. W., Rizvi, S. L., & Hamed, M. S. (2007). Applications of dialectical behavior therapy to the treatment of complex trauma-related problems: When one case formulation does not fit all. *Journal of Trauma Stress, 20,* 391–400.

Wagner, H. J., et al. (2004). A strategy for treatment of Epstein Barr virus-positive Hodgkin's disease by targeting interleukin 12 to the tumor environment using tumor antigen-specific T cells. *Cancer Gene Therapy, 2,* 81–91.

Wagner, R. K. (2002). Smart people doing dumb things: The case of managerial incompetence. In R. J. Sternberg (Ed.), *Why smart people can be so stupid.* New Haven, CT: Yale University Press.

Wagner, R. K. (2011). Practical intelligence. In R. J. Sternberg & S. Kaufman (Eds.), *The Cambridge handbook of intelligence.* New York: Cambridge University Press.

Wagner, U., Gais, S., Haider, H., Verleger, R., & Born, J. (2004). Sleep inspires insight. *Nature, 427,* 352–355.

Wagstaff, G. (2009, January). Is there a future for investigative hypnosis? *Journal of Investigative Psychology and Offender Profiling, 6,* 43–57.

Wagstaff, G. F., Wheatcroft, J. M., & Jones, A. (2011). Are high hypnotizables especially vulnerable to false memory effects? A sociocognitive perspective. *International Journal of Clinical and Experimental Hypnosis, 59,* 310–326.

Wain, H. J., Grammer, G. G., & Stasinos, J. (2006). Psychiatric intervention for medical and surgical patients following traumatic injuries. In E. C. Ritchie, P. J. Watson, & M. J. Friedman (Eds.), *Interventions following mass violence and disasters: Strategies for mental health practice.* New York: Guilford Press.

Wakefield, J. C. (2013). DSM-5: An overview of changes and controversies. *Clinical Social Work Journal, 41,* 139–154.

Walker, L. J., & Frimer, J. A. (2007). Moral personality of brave and caring exemplars. *Journal of Personality and Social Psychology, 93,* 845–860.

Walker, L. J., Frimer, J. A., & Dunlop, W. L. (2010). Varieties of moral personality: Beyond the banality of heroism. *Journal of Personality, 78,* 907–942.

Walker, L., & Frimer, J. (2009). The song remains the same: Rebuttal to Sherblom's re-envisioning of the legacy of the care challenge. *Journal of Moral Education, 38,* 53–68.

Walker, M. P., & van der Helm, E. (2009). Overnight therapy? The role of sleep in emotional brain processing. *Psychological Bulletin, 135,* 731–748.

Walker, W. (2008, May). Introducing hypnosis for pain management to your practice. *Australian Journal of Clinical & Experimental Hypnosis, 36,* 23–29.

Walker, W. R., Skowronski, J. J., & Thompson, C. P. (2003). Consolidation of long-term memory: Evidence and alternatives. *Review of General Psychology, 7,* 203–210.

Wallace, L. S., Chisolm, D. J., Abdel-Rasoul, M., & DeVoe, J. E. (2013). Survey mode matters: Adults' self-reported statistical confidence, ability to obtain health information, and perceptions of patient-health-care provider communication. *Journal of Health Psychology, 18,* 1036–1045.

Wallen, K., & Lloyd, E. A. (2011). Female sexual arousal: genital anatomy and orgasm in intercourse. *Hormonal Behavior, 59,* 780–792.

Waller, B., Cray, J., & Burrows, A. (2008, June). Selection for universal facial emotion. *Emotion, 8,* 435–439.

Wallerstein, J. S., Lewis, J., Blakeslee, S., & Lewis, J. (2000). *The unexpected legacy of divorce.* New York: Hyperion.

Walsh, B. T., Kaplan, A. S., Attia, E., Olmstead, M., Parides, M., Carter, J. C., et al. (2006). Fluoxetine after weight restoration in anorexia nervosa: A randomized controlled trial. *JAMA: Journal of the American Medical Association, 295,* 2605–2612.

Walsh, R., & Shapiro, S. L. (2006). The meeting of meditative disciplines and western psychology. *American Psychologist, 61,* 227–239.

Walton, G. M., & Cohen, G. L. (2011, March 18). A brief social-belonging intervention improves academic and health outcomes of minority students. *Science, 331,* 1447–1451.

Wang, A., & Clark, D. A. (2002). Haunting thoughts: The problem of obsessive mental intrusions [Special issue: Intrusions in cognitive behavioral therapy]. *Journal of Cognitive Psychotherapy, 16,* 193–208.

Wang, F. F., Kameda, M. M., Yasuhara, T. T., Tajiri, N. N., Kikuchi, Y. Y., Liang, H. B., & . . . Date, I. I. (2011). Gdnf-pretreatment enhances the survival of neural stem cells following transplantation in a rat model of Parkinson's disease. *Neuroscience Research, 18,* 202–211.

Wang, M. T., & Kenny, S. (2013). Longitudinal links between fathers' and mothers' harsh verbal discipline and adolescents' conduct problems and depressive symptoms. *Child Development.* Retrieved from http://onlinelibrary.wiley.com/doi/10.1111/cdev.12143/abstract

Wang, O. (2003). Infantile amnesia reconsidered: A cross-cultural analysis. *Memory, 11,* 65–80.

Wang, P. S., Aguilar-Gaxiola, S., Alonso, J., Angermeyer, M. C., Borges, G., Bromet, E. J., et al. (2007, September 8). Use of mental health services for anxiety, mood, and substance disorders in 17 countries in the WHO world mental health surveys. *Lancet, 370,* 841–850.

Wang, Q. (2004). The emergence of cultural self-constructs: Autobiographical memory and self-description in European American and Chinese children. *Developmental Psychology, 40,* 3–15.

Wang, Q., & Conway, M. A. (2006). Autobiographical memory, self, and culture. In L-G. Nilsson & N. Ohta, *Memory and society: Psychological perspectives.* New York: Psychology Press.

Wang, S. (2011, May 10). The tricky chemistry of attraction. *The Wall Street Journal,* D-1.

Wang, V. O., & Sue, S. (2005). In the eye of the storm: Race and genomics in research and practice. *American Psychologist, 60,* 37–45.

Wang, X., Lu, T., Snider, R. K., & Liang, L. (2005). Sustained firing in auditory cortex evoked by preferred stimuli. *Nature, 435,* 341–346.

Ward-Baker, P. D. (2007). The remarkable oldest old: A new vision of aging. *Dissertation Abstracts International Section A: Humanities and Social Sciences, 67*(8-A), 3115.

Ward, A., Wallaert, M., & Schwartz, B. (2011). Who likes evolution? Dissociation of human evolution versus evolutionary psychology. *The Journal of Social, Evolutionary, and Cultural Psychology, 5,* 122–130.

Ward, L. M. (2004). Wading through the stereotypes: Positive and negative associations between media use and Black adolescents' conceptions of self. *Developmental Psychology, 40,* 284–294.

Ward, L. M. (2011). The thalamic dynamic core theory of conscious experience. *Consciousness and Cognition: An International Journal, 20,* 464–486.

Ward, W. C., Kogan, N., & Pankove, E. (1972). Incentive effects in children's creativity. *Child Development, 43,* 669–677.

Warden, C. A., Wu, W. Y., & Tsai, D. (2006). Online shopping interface components: Relative importance as peripheral and central cues. *CyberPsychology & Behavior, 9,* 285–296.

Wark, B., Lundstrom, B., & Fairhall, A. (2007, August). Sensory adaptation. *Current Opinion in Neurobiology, 17,* 423–429.

Wasserman, E. A., & Miller, R. R. (1997). What's elementary about associative learning? *Annual Review of Psychology, 48,* 573–607.
Watkins, C. (2007). *Date rape.* Farmington Hills, MI: Greenhaven Press.
Watson, J. B. (1924). *Behaviorism.* New York: Norton.
Watson, J. C., Goldman, R. N., & Greenberg, L. S. (2011). Humanistic and experiential theories of psychotherapy. In J. C. Norcross, G. R. VandenBos, & D. K. Freedheim (Eds.), *History of psychotherapy: Continuity and change (2nd ed.).* Washington, DC: American Psychological Association.
Watson, M., Haviland, J. S., Greer, S., Davidson, J., & Bliss, J. M. (1999). Influence of psychological response on survival in breast cancer: A population-based cohort study. *Lancet, 354,* 1331–1336.
Watson, P. J., Brymer, M. J., & Bonanno, G. A. (2011). Postdisaster psychological intervention since 9/11. *American Psychologist, 66,* 482–494.
Watters, E. (2010, January 10). The Americanization of mental illness. *The New York Times,* p. C2.
Waxman, S. (2009). Learning from infants' first verbs. *Monographs of the Society for Research in Child Development, 74,* 127–132.
Wechsler, H., Kuo, M., Lee, H., & Dowdall, G. W. (2000). *Environmental correlates of underage alcohol use and related problems of college students.* Cambridge, MA: Harvard School of Public Health.
Wechsler, H., Lee, J. E., Nelson, T. F., & Kuo, M. (2002). Underage college students' drinking behavior, access to alcohol, and the influence of deterrence policies. *Journal of American College Health, 50,* 223–236.
Weck, F., Bleichhardt, G., Witthöft, M., & Hiller, W. (2011). Explicit and implicit anxiety: Differences between patients with hypochondriasis, patients with anxiety disorders, and healthy controls. *Cognitive Therapy and Research, 35,* 317–325.
Weeks, M., & Lupfer, M. B. (2004). Complicating race: The relationship between prejudice, race, and social class categorizations. *Personality and Social Psychology Bulletin, 30,* 972–984.
Wegener, D. T., Petty, R. E., Smoak, N. D., & Fabrigar, L. R. (2004). Multiple routes to resisting attitude change. In E. S. Knowles & J. A. Linn (Eds.), *Resistance and persuasion.* Mahwah, NJ: Lawrence Erlbaum Associates.
Wehrle, R., Kaufmann, C., Wetter, T. C., Holsboer, F., Auer, D. P., Pollmacher, T., & Czisch, M. (2007). Functional microstates within human REM sleep: First evidence from fMRI of a thalamocortical network specific for phasic REM periods. *European Journal of Neuroscience, 25,* 863–871.
Wehrum, S., Klucken, T., Kagerer, S., Walter, B., Hermann, A., Vaitl, D., & Stark, R. (2013). Gender commonalities and differences in the neural processing of visual sexual stimuli. *Journal of Sexual Medicine, 10,* 1328–1342.
Weinberg, M. S., Williams, C. J., & Pryor, D. W. (1991, February 27). Personal communication. Indiana University, Bloomington.
Weiner, B. A., & Wettstein, R. (1993). *Legal issues in mental health care.* New York: Plenum Press.
Weiner, I. B. (2004a). Monitoring psychotherapy with performance-based measures of personality functioning. *Journal of Personality Assessment, 83,* 323–331.
Weiner, I. B. (2004b). Rorschach Inkblot method. In M. E. Maruish (Ed.), *Use of psychological testing for treatment planning and outcomes assessment, Vol. 3: Instruments for adults* (3rd ed.). Mahwah, NJ: Lawrence Erlbaum Associates.
Weiner, R. D., & Falcone, G. (2011). Electroconvulsive therapy: How effective is it? *Journal of the American Psychiatric Nurses Association, 17,* 217–218.
Weinstein, L. (2007). Selected genetic disorders affecting Ashkenazi Jewish families. *Family & Community Health, 30,* 50–62.
Weinstein, M., Glei, D. A., Yamazaki, A., & Ming-Cheng, C. (2004). The role of intergenerational relations in the association between life stressors and depressive symptoms. *Research on Aging, 26,* 511–530.
Weiss, A., Bates, T., & Luciano, M. (2008). Happiness is a personal(ity) thing: The genetics of personality and well-being in a representative sample. *Psychological Science, 19,* 205–210.
Weiss, W. M., & Weiss, M. R. (2003). Attraction- and entrapment-based commitment among competitive female gymnasts. *Journal of Sport & Exercise Psychology, 25,* 229–247.
Weissman, M. M., Bland, R. C., Canino, G. J., Faravelli, C., Greenwald, S., Hwu, H. G., et al. (1997, July 24–31). Cross-national epidemiology of major depression and bipolar disorder. *Journal of the American Medical Association, 276,* 293–299.
Weissman, M., Markowitz, J., & Klerman, G. L. (2007). *Clinician's quick guide to interpersonal psychotherapy.* New York: Oxford University Press.
Welkowitz, L. A., Struening, E. L., Pittman, J., Guardino, M., & Welkowitz, J. (2000). Obsessive-compulsive disorder and comorbid anxiety problems in a national anxiety screening sample. *Journal of Anxiety Disorders, 14,* 471–482.
Wells, G. L., Olson, E. A., & Charman, S. D. (2002). The confidence of eyewitnesses in their identifications from lineups. *Current Directions in Psychological Science, 11,* 151–154.
Wells, R., Phillips, R. S., & McCarthy, E. P. (2011). Patterns of mind-body therapies in adults with common neurological conditions. *Neuroepidemiology, 36,* 46–51.
Wen, M., Butler, L. T., & Koutstaal, W. (2013). Improving insight and noninsight problem solving with brief interventions. *British Journal of Psychology, 104,* 97–118.
Wenar, C. (1994). *Developmental psychopathology: From infancy through adolescence* (3rd ed.). New York: McGraw-Hill.
Wensley, D., & King, M. (2008, June). Scientific responsibility for the dissemination and interpretation of genetic research: Lessons from the 'warrior gene' controversy. *Journal of Medical Ethics, 34,* 507–509.
Wenzel, A. (2011). Obsessions and compulsions. In A. Wenzel & S. Stuart (Eds.), *Anxiety in childbearing women: Diagnosis and treatment.* Washington, DC: American Psychological Association.
Wenzel, A., Zetocha, K., & Ferraro, R. F. (2007). Depth of processing and recall of threat material in fearful and nonfearful individuals. *Anxiety, Stress & Coping: An International Journal, 20,* 223–237.
Werhane, P. H., Pincus Hartman, L., Archer, C., Englehardt, E. E., & Pritchard, M. S. (2013). *Obstacles to ethical decision-making: Mental models, Milgram and the problem of obedience.* New York: Cambridge University Press.
Werker, J. F., & Tees, R. C. (2005). Speech perception as a window for understanding plasticity and commitment in language systems of the brain. *Developmental Psychobiology, 46,* 233–234.
Werner, J. S., Pinna, B., & Spillmann, L. (2007, March). Illusory color and the brain. *Scientific American,* 90–96.
Wertheimer, M. (1923). Untersuchungen zur Lehre von der Gestalt, II. *Psychol. Forsch., 5,* 301–350. In R. Beardsley & M. Wertheimer (Eds.) (1958), *Readings in perception.* New York: Van Nostrand.
West, D. S., Harvey-Berino, J., & Raczynski, J. M. (2004). Behavioral aspects of obesity, dietary intake, and chronic disease. In J. M. Raczynski & L. C. Leviton (Eds.), *Handbook of clinical health psychology: Vol. 2. Disorders of behavior and health.* Washington, DC: American Psychological Association.
West, J. R., & Blake, C. A. (2005). Fetal alcohol syndrome: An assessment of the field. *Experimental Biological Medicine, 6,* 354–356.
West, R. L., Bagwell, D. K., & Dark-Freudeman, A. (2007). Self-efficacy and memory aging: The impact of a memory intervention based on self-efficacy. *Neuropsychological Development and Cognition, B, Aging and Neuropsychological Cognition, 14,* 1–28.
West, S. L., & O'Neal, K. K. (2004). Project D.A.R.E. outcome effectiveness revisited. *American Journal of Public Health, 94,* 1027–1029.
Westen, D., Novotny, C. M., & Thompson-Brenner, H. (2004). The empirical status of empirically supported psychotherapies: Assumptions, findings, and reporting in controlled clinical trials. *Psychological Bulletin, 130,* 631–663.
Wester, A. J., van Herten, J. C., Egger, J. M., & Kessels, R. C. (2013). Applicability of the Rivermead Behavioural Memory Test-Third Edition (RBMT-3) in Korsakoff's syndrome and chronic alcoholics. *Neuropsychiatric Disease and Treatment, 9,* 202–212.
Westerberg, H., Brehmer, Y., D'Hondt, N., Söderman, D., & Bäckman, L. (2008, April). *Computerized training of working memory: A controlled, randomized trial.* Paper presented at the 2008 annual meeting of the Cognitive Neuroscience Society.
Westerhausen, R., Moosmann, M., Alho, K., Medvedev, S., Hämäläinen, H., & Hugdahl, K. (2009, January). Top-down and bottom-up interaction: Manipulating the dichotic listening ear advantage. *Brain Research, 1250,* 183–189.
Westerterp, K. R. (2006). Perception, passive overfeeding and energy metabolism. *Physiology & Behavior, 89,* 62–65.
Westmarland, N., & Alderson, S. (2013). The health, mental health, and well-being benefits of rape crisis counseling. *Journal of Interpersonal Violence, 28,* 3265–3282.
Wetter, D. W., Fiore, M. C., Gritz, E. R., Lando, H. A., Stitzer, M. L., Hasselblad, V., et al. (1998). The Agency for Health Care Policy and Research. Smoking cessation clinical practice guideline: Findings and implications for psychologists. *American Psychologist, 53,* 657–669.
Whaley, B. B. (Ed.). (2000). *Explaining illness: Research, theory, and strategies.* Mahwah, NJ: Erlbaum.
Whisman, M., & Snyder, D. (2007). Sexual infidelity in a national survey of American women: Differences in prevalence and correlates as a function of method of assessment. *Journal of Family Psychology, 21,* 14–154.
Whitbourne, S. (2010). *The search for fulfillment.* New York: Ballantine.

Whitbourne, S. K. (2000). The normal aging process. In S. K. Whitbourne & S. Krauss (Eds.), *Psychopathology in later adulthood.* New York: Wiley.

Whitbourne, S. K., & Wills, K. (1993). Psychological issues in institutional care of the aged. In S. B. Goldsmith (Ed.), *Long-term care.* Gaithersburg, MD: Aspen Press.

Whitbourne, S. K., Zuschlag, M. K., Elliot, L. B., & Waterman, A. S. (1992). Psychosocial development in adulthood: A 22-year sequential study. *Journal of Personality and Social Psychology, 63,* 260–271.

White, K. (2013). Remembering and forgetting. In G. J. Madden, W. V. Dube, T. D. Hackenberg, G. P. Hanley, & K. A. Lattal (Eds.), *APA handbook of behavior analysis, Vol. 1: Methods and principles.* Washington, DC: American Psychological Association.

White, L. (2007). Linguistic theory, universal grammar, and second language acquisition. In B. Van Patten & J. Williams (Eds.), *Theories in second language acquisition: An introduction.* Mahwah, NJ: Lawrence Erlbaum Associates.

Whitebread, D., Coltman, P., Jameson, H., & Lander, R. (2009). Play, cognition and self-regulation: What exactly are children learning when they learn through play? *Educational and Child Psychology, 26,* 40–52.

Whitehouse, W. G., Orne, E. C., Dinges, D. F., Bates, B. L., Nadon, R., & Orne, M. T. (2005). The cognitive interview: Does it successfully avoid the dangers of forensic hypnosis? *American Journal of Psychology, 118,* 213–234.

Whitfield, J. B., Zhu, G., Madden, P. A., Neale, M. C., Heath, A. C., & Martin, N. G. (2004). The genetics of alcohol intake and of alcohol dependence. *Alcoholism: Clinical and Experimental Research, 28,* 1153–1160.

Whitney, P. G., & Green, J. A. (2011). Changes in infants' affect related to the onset of independent locomotion. *Infant Behavior & Development, 34,* 459–466.

WHO World Mental Health Survey Consortium. (2004). Prevalence, severity, and unmet need for treatment of mental disorders in the World Health Organization World Mental Health Surveys. *Journal of the American Medical Association, 291,* 2581–2590.

Whorf, B. L. (1956). *Language, thought, and reality.* New York: Wiley.

Wickelgren, E. A. (2004). Perspective distortion of trajectory forms and perceptual constancy in visual event identification. *Perception and Psychophysics, 66,* 629–641.

Widaman, K. (2009). Phenylketonuria in children and mothers: Genes, environments, behavior. *Current Directions in Psychological Science, 18,* 48–52.

Widiger, T. A., & Clark, L. A. (2000). Toward *DSM-V* and the classification of psychopathology. *Psychological Bulletin, 126,* 946–963.

Widmeyer, W. N., & Loy, J. W. (1988). When you're hot, you're hot! Warm-cold effects in first impressions of persons and teaching effectiveness. *Journal of Educational Psychology, 80,* 118–121.

Wiederman, M. W. (2011). Body image and sexual functioning. In T. F. Cash & L. Smolak (Eds.), *Body image: A handbook of science, practice, and prevention (2nd ed.).* New York: Guilford Press.

Wiehe, V. R., & Richards, A. L. (1995). *Intimate betrayal: Understanding and responding to the trauma of acquaintance rape.* Thousand Oaks, CA: Sage Publications.

Wielgosz, A. T., & Nolan, R. P. (2000). Biobehavioral factors in the context of ischemic cardiovascular disease. *Journal of Psychosomatic Research, 48,* 339–345.

Wieth, M., & Zacks, R. (2011). Time of day effects on problem solving: When the non-optimal is optimal. *Thinking & Reasoning, 17,* 387–401.

Wiggins, J. S. (2003). *Paradigms of personality assessment.* New York: Guilford Press.

Wildavsky, B. (2000, September 4). A blow to bilingual education. *U.S. News & World Report,* 22–28.

Wilde, D. J. (2011). *Jung's personality theory quantified.* New York: Springer-Verlag Publishing.

Wiley, C., & Sisson, M. (2006, November). *Ethics, accuracy, and assumption: The use of Facebook by students and employers.* Paper presented at the Southwestern Ohio Council for Higher Education Special Topics Forum, Dayton, OH.

Wilgoren, J. (1999, October 22). Quality day care, early, is tied to achievements as an adult. *The New York Times,* p. A16.

Wilkin, L., & Haddock, B. (2011). Functional fitness of older adults. *Activities, Adaptation & Aging, 35,* 197–209.

Wilkinson, H. A. (2009). Cingulotomy. *Journal of Neurosurgery, 110,* 607–611.

Wilkinson, L., & Olliver-Gray, Y. (2006). The significance of silence: Differences in meaning, learning styles, and teaching strategies in cross-cultural settings [Special issue: Child language]. *Psychologia: An International Journal of Psychology in the Orient, 49,* 74–88.

Willander, J., & Larsson, M. (2006). Smell your way back to childhood: Autobiographical odor memory. *Psychonomic Bulletin & Review, 13,* 240–244.

Willems, R. M., & Hagoort, P. (2007). Neural evidence for the interplay between language, gesture, and action: a review. *Brain Language, 101,* 278–289.

Williams, C. L., & Butcher, J. N. (2011). The nuts and bolts: Administering, scoring, and augmenting MMPI-A assessments. In C. L. Williams & J. N. Butcher (Eds.), *A beginner's guide to the MMPI–A.* Washington, DC: American Psychological Association.

Williams, J. E., & Bennett, S. M. (1975). The definition of sex stereotypes via the Adjective Check List. *Sex Roles, 1,* 327–337.

Williams, J. E., & Best, D. L. (1990). *Measuring sex stereotypes: A multinational study.* Newbury Park, CA: Sage.

Williams, J. E., Paton, C. C., Siegler, I. C., Eigenbrodt, M. L., Nieto, F. J., & Tyroler, H. A. (2000). Anger proneness predicts coronary heart disease risk: Prospective analysis from the Atherosclerosis Risk in Communities (ARIC) Study. *Circulation, 101,* 2034–2039.

Williams, J. W., Mulrow, C. D., Chiquette, E., Noel, P. H., Aguilar, C., & Cornell, J. (2000). A systematic review of newer pharmacotherapies for depression in adults: Evidence report summary. *Annals of Internal Medicine, 132,* 743–756.

Williamson, P., McLeskey, J., & Hoppey, D. (2006). Educating students with mental retardation in general education classrooms. *Exceptional Children, 72,* 347–361.

Willis, G. (2008, June). Intraocular microinjections repair experimental Parkinson's disease. *Brain Research, 1217,* 119–131.

Willis, G. L. (2005). The therapeutic effects of dopamine replacement therapy and its psychiatric side effects are mediated by pineal function. *Behavioural Brain Research, 160,* 148–160.

Willis, J., & Todorov, A. (2006). First impressions: Making up your mind after a 100-ms exposure to a face. *Psychological Science, 17,* 592–598.

Willis, S. L., & Schaie, K. W. (1994). In C. B. Fisher & R. M. Lerner (Eds.), *Applied developmental psychology.* New York: McGraw-Hill.

Willness, C. R., Steel, P., & Lee, K. (2007). A meta-analysis of the antecedents and consequences of workplace sexual harassment. *Personnel Psychology, 60,* 127–162.

Wills, K. E. (2013). Sickle cell disease. In I. Baron & C. Rey-Casserly (Eds.), *Pediatric neuropsychology: Medical advances and lifespan outcomes.* New York, NY: Oxford University Press.

Wills, T., Sargent, J., Stoolmiller, M., Gibbons, F., & Gerrard, M. (2008). Movie smoking exposure and smoking onset: A longitudinal study of mediation processes in a representative sample of U.S. adolescents. *Psychology of Addictive Behaviors, 22,* 269–277.

Willyard, C. (2011). Men: A growing minority? Women earning doctoral degrees in psychology outnumber men three to one. What does this mean for the future of the field? *GradPsych, p. 40.* Retrieved from http://www.apa.org/gradpsych/2011/01/cover-men.aspx

Wilson, T. D. (2006, September 1). The power of social psychological interventions. *Science, 313,* 1251–1252.

Wilson, T. G., Grilo, C. M., & Vitousek, K. M. (2007). Psychological treatment of eating disorders [Special issue: Eating disorders]. *American Psychologist, 62,* 199–216.

Winerip, M. (1993, November 15). A new approach in testing. *The New York Times* B9.

Winerman, L. (2005, June). ACTing up. *Monitor on Psychology,* pp. 44–45.

Winik, L. W. (2006, October 1). The true cost of depression. *Parade,* p. 7.

Winner, E. (2003). Creativity and talent. In M. H. Bornstein & L. Davidson (Eds.), *Well-being: Positive development across the life course.* Mahwah, NJ: Lawrence Erlbaum.

Winsler, A., Madigan, A. L., & Aquilino, S. A. (2005). Correspondence between maternal and paternal parenting styles in early childhood. *Early Childhood Research Quarterly, 20,* 1–12.

Winson, J. (1990, November). The meaning of dreams. *Scientific American,* pp. 86–96.

Winstead, B. A., & Sanchez, A. (2005). Gender and psychopathology. In J. E. Maddux & B. A. Winstead (Eds.), *Psychopathology: Foundations for a contemporary understanding.* Mahwah, NJ: Lawrence Erlbaum Associates.

Winter, D. G. (1988). The power motive in women–and men. *Journal of Personality and Social Psychology, 54,* 510–519.

Winter, D. G. (2007). The role of motivation, responsibility, and integrative complexity in crisis escalation: Comparative studies of war and peace crises. *Journal of Personality and Social Psychology, 92,* 920–937.

Winters, B. D., & Bussey, T. J. (2005). Glutamate receptors in perirhinal cortex mediate encoding, retrieval, and consolidation of object recognition memory. *Journal of Neuroscience, 25,* 4243–4251.

Wiseman, R., & Greening, E. (2002). The mind machine: A mass participation experiment into the possible existence of extra-sensory perception. *British Journal of Psychology, 93,* 487–499.

Witelson, S., Kigar, D., Scamvougeras, A., Kideckel, D., Buck, B., Stanchev, P., et al. (2008). Corpus callosum anatomy in right-handed homosexual and heterosexual men. *Archives of Sexual Behavior, 37,* 857–863.

Witt, C. M., Jena, S., & Brinkhaus, B. (2006). Acupuncture for patients with chronic neck pain. *Pain, 125,* 98–106.

Wittchen, H., Nocon, A., Beesdo, K., Pine, D., Hofler, M., Lieb, R., et al. (2008). Agoraphobia and panic. *Psychotherapy and Psychosomatics, 77,* 147–157.

Wittenbrink, B., & Schwarz, N. (Eds.). (2007). *Implicit measures of attitudes.* New York: Guilford Press.

Wixted, J. T., & Carpenter, S. K. (2007). The Wickelgren Power Law and the Ebbinghaus Savings Function. *Psychological Science, 18,* 133–134.

Wolf, A. J., Guyer, M. J., & Sharpe, L. (2010). Repressed memories in a controversial conviction. *Journal of the American Academy of Psychiatry Law, 38,* 607–609.

Wolfe, D. A. (1999). *Child abuse: Implications for child development and psychopathology.* Thousand Oaks, CA: Sage.

Wolfe, M. S. (2006, May). Shutting down Alzheimer's. *Scientific American,* 73–79.

Wolff, N. (2002). Risk, response, and mental health policy: Learning from the experience of the United Kingdom. *Journal of Health Politic and Policy Law, 27,* 801–802.

Wolitzky, D. L. (2006). Psychodynamic theories. In J. C. Thomas, D. L. Segal, & M. Hersen (Eds.), *Comprehensive handbook of personality and psychopathology, Vol. 1: Personality and everyday functioning.* Hoboken, NJ: John Wiley & Sons.

Woller, K., Buboltz, W., & Loveland, J. (2007). Psychological reactance: Examination across age, ethnicity, and gender. *American Journal of Psychology, 120,* 15–24.

Wolman, D. (2012, March 15). The split brain: A tale of two halves. *Nature, 483,* 260–263.

Wong, N., Sarver, D. E., & Beidel, D. C. (2011). Quality of life impairments among adults with social phobia: The impact of subtype. *Journal of Anxiety Disorders, 14,* 88–95.

Wood, E., Desmarais, S., & Gugula, S. (2002). The impact of parenting experience on gender stereotyped toy play of children. *Sex Roles, 47,* 39–49.

Wood, J. M., Nezworski, M. T., Lilienfeld, S. O., & Garb, H. N. (2003). *What's wrong with the Rorschach? Science confronts the controversial inkblot test.* New York: Wiley.

Wood, J. V., Perunovic, W. Q. E., & Lee, J. W. (2009). Positive self-statements: Power for some, peril for others. *Psychological Science, 20,* 860–866.

Wood, W. (2000). Attitude change: Persuasion and social influence. *Annual Review of Psychology, 51,* 539–570.

Wood, W., & Eagly, A. H. (2002). A cross-cultural analysis of the behavior of women and men: Implications for the origins of sex differences. *Psychological Bulletin, 128,* 699–727.

Woodruff, S. I., Conway, T. L., & Edwards, C. C. (2007). Sociodemographic and smoking-related psychosocial predictors of smoking behavior change among high school smokers. *Addictive Behaviors, 33,* 354–358.

Woods, S. C., & Seeley, R. J. (2002). Hunger and energy homeostasis. In H. Pashler & R. Gallistel (Eds.). *Steven's handbook of experimental psychology* (3rd ed.), *Vol. 3: Learning, motivation, and emotion.* New York: Wiley.

Woods, S. C., Schwartz, M. W., Baskin, D. G., & Seeley, R. J. (2000). Food intake and the regulation of body weight. *Annual Review of Psychology, 51,* 255–277.

Woodson, S. R. J. (2006). Relationships between sleepiness and emotion experience: An experimental investigation of the role of subjective sleepiness in the generation of positive and negative emotions. *Dissertation Abstracts International: Section B: The Sciences and Engineering,* 67(5-B), 2849.

Woollett, K., & Maguire, E. (2009). Navigational expertise may compromise anterograde associative memory. *Neuropsychologia, 47,* 1088–1095.

Worthen, B. (2012, September 29). The perils of texting while parenting. *The Wall Street Journal Review,* C1.

Worthen, J. B., & Hunt, R. (2011). *Mnemonology: Mnemonics for the 21st century.* New York: Psychology Press.

Wren, A. M., & Bloom, S. R. (2007). Gut hormones and appetite control. *Gastroenterology, 132,* 2116–2130.

Wright, B., Alderson-Day, B., Prendergast, G., Kennedy, J., Bennett, S., Docherty, M., Whitton, C., Manea, L., Gouws, A., Tomlinson, H., & Green, G. (2013). Neural correlation of successful cognitive behaviour therapy for spider phobia: A agnetoencephalography study. *Psychiatry Research: Neuroimaging, 214*(3), 444–451.

Wright, K. (2002, September). Times of our lives. *Scientific American,* pp. 59–65.

Wrosch, C., Bauer, I., & Scheier, M. (2005, December). Regret and quality of life across the adult life span: The influence of disengagement and available future goals. *Psychology and Aging, 20,* 657–670.

Wrzesniewski, K., & Chylinska, J. (2007). Assessment of coping styles and strategies with school-related stress. *School Psychology International, 28,* 179–194.

Wu, L.-T., Schlenger, W. E., & Galvin, D. M. (2006). Concurrent use of methamphetamine, MDMA, LSD, ketamine, GHB, and flunitrazepam among American youths. *Drug and Alcohol Dependence, 84,* 102–113.

Wu, Y. (2013). An empirical study of narrative imagery in implicit and explicit contexts. *Computers in Human Behavior, 29,* 1580–1589.

Wuethrich, B. (2001, March 16). Does alcohol damage female brains more? *Science, 291,* 2077–2079.

Wurtz, R. H., & Kandel, E. R. (2000). Central visual pathways. In E. R. Kandel, J. H. Schwartz, & T. M. Jessell (Eds.), *Principles of neural science* (4th ed.). New York: McGraw-Hill.

Wynn, K., Bloom, P., & Chiang, W. C. (2002). Enumeration of collective entities by 5-month-old infants. *Cognition, 83,* B55-B62.

Wyra, M., Lawson, M. J., & Hungi, N. (2007). The mnemonic keyword method: The effects of bidirectional retrieval training and of ability to image on foreign language vocabulary recall. *Learning and Instruction, 17,* 360–371.

Xiao, Z., Yan, H., Wang, Z., Zou, Z., Xu, Y., Chen, J., et al. (2006). Trauma and dissociation in China. *American Journal of Psychiatry, 163,* 1388–1391.

Yamada, R., & Itsukushima, Y. (2013). The schema provokes a disparity of false recollection between actions and objects in an everyday scene. *Scandinavian Journal of Psychology, 54,* 276–282.

Yamawaki, N., Darby, R., & Queiroz, A. (2007). The moderating role of ambivalent sexism: The influence of power status on perception of rape victim and rapist. *Journal of Social Psychology, 147,* 41–56.

Yang, A. C., & Tsai, S. (2013). Is mental illness complex? From behavior to brain. *Progress In Neuro-Psychopharmacology & Biological Psychiatry, 45,* 253-257.

Yang, D., Bushnell, E. W., Buchanan, D. W., & Sobel, D. M. (2013). Infants' use of contextual cues in the generalization of effective actions from imitation. *Journal of Experimental Child Psychology, 116,* 510–531.

Yang, J., Hou, C., Ma, N., Liu, J., Zhang, Y., Zhou, J., et al. (2007). Enriched environment treatment restores impaired hippocampal synaptic plasticity and cognitive deficits induced by prenatal chronic stress. *Neurobiology of Learning and Memory, 87,* 257–263.

Yao, S.-Q., Zhour, Y.-H., & Jiang, L. (2006). The intelligence scale for Chinese adults: Item analysis, reliability and validity. *Chinese Journal of Clinical Psychology, 14,* 441–445.

Yao, Y., Kelly, M., Sajikumar, S., Serrano, P., Tian, D., Bergold, P., et al. (2008). PKMζ maintains late long-term potentiation by n-ethylmaleimide-sensitive factor/gluR2-dependent trafficking of postsynaptic AMPA receptors. *Journal of Neuroscience, 28,* 7820–7827.

Yapko, M. D. (2006). Utilizing hypnosis in addressing ruminative depression-related insomnia. In M. D. Yapko (Ed.), *Hypnosis and treating depression: Applications in clinical practice.* New York: Routledge/Taylor & Francis Group.

Yardley, L., & Moss-Morris, R. (2009, January). Current issues and new directions in psychology and health: Increasing the quantity and quality of health psychology research. *Psychology & Health, 24,* 1–4.

Yeomans, M. R., Tepper, B. J., & Ritezschel, J. (2007). Human hedonic responses to sweetness: Role of taste genetics and anatomy. *Physiology & Behavior, 91,* 264–273.

Yesilyaprak, B., Kisac, I., & Sanlier, N. (2007). Stress symptoms and nutritional status among survivors of the Marmara region earthquakes in Turkey. *Journal of Loss & Trauma, 12,* 1–8.

Yim, D., & Rudoy, J. (2013). Implicit statistical learning and language skills in bilingual children. *Journal of Speech, Language, and Hearing Research, 56,* 310–322.

Yoo, H., & Castro, K. S. (2011). Does nativity status matter in the relationship between perceived racism and academic performance of Asian American college students? *Journal of College Student Development, 52,* 234–245.

Yoo, H., & Pituc, S. T. (2013). Assessments of perceived racial stereotypes, discrimination, and racism. In K. F. Geisinger, B. A. Bracken, J. F. Carlson, J. C. Hansen, N. R. Kuncel, S. P. Reise, & M. C. Rodriguez (Eds.), *APA handbook of testing and assessment in psychology, Vol. 2: Testing and assessment in clinical and counseling psychology.* Washington, DC: American Psychological Association.

Yordanova, J., Kolev, V., Verleger, R., Bataghva, Z., Born, J., & Wagner, U. (2008). Shifting from implicit to explicit knowledge: Different roles of early- and late-night sleep. *Learning & Memory, 15,* 508–515.

Yost, M. R., & Zurbiggen, E. L. (2006). Gender differences in the enactment of sociosexuality: An examination of implicit social motives, sexual fantasies, coercive sexual attitudes, and aggressive sexual behavior. *Journal of Sex Research, 43,* 163–173.

Zacks, J. (2008). Neuroimaging studies of mental rotation: A meta-analysis and review. *Journal of Cognitive Neuroscience, 20,* 1–19.

Zaitsu, W. (2007). The effect of fear on eyewitness' retrieval in recognition memory. *Japanese Journal of Psychology, 77,* 504–511.

Zajonc, R. B. (2001). Mere exposure: A gateway to the subliminal. *Current Directions in Psychological Science, 10,* 224–228.

Zaragoza, M. S., Belli, R. F., & Payment, K. E. (2007). Misinformation effects and the suggestibility of eyewitness memory. In M. Garry & H. Hayne (Eds.), *Do justice and let the sky fall: Elizabeth Loftus and her contributions to science, law, and academic freedom.* Mahwah, NJ: Lawrence Erlbaum Associates.

Zaslow, J. (2003, May 1). Going on after the unthinkable: A rape victim shares her story. *The Wall Street Journal,* p. A2.

Zebrowitz-McArthur, L. (1988). Person perception in cross-cultural perspective. In M. H. Bond (Ed.), *The cross-cultural challenge to social psychology.* Newbury Park, CA: Sage.

Zebrowitz, L. A., & Montepare, J. M. (2005, June 10). Appearance DOES matter. *Science, 308,* 1565–1566.

Zeigler, D. W., et al. (2005). The neurocognitive effects of alcohol on adolescents and college students. *Preventive Medicine: An International Journal Devoted to Practice and Theory, 40,* 23–32.

Zeng, L., Proctor, R. W., & Salvendy, G. (2011). Can traditional divergent thinking tests be trusted in measuring and predicting real-world creativity? *Creativity Research Journal, 23,* 24–37.

Zepf, S., & Zepf, F. D. (2011). 'You are requested to close an eye': Freud's seduction theory and theory of the Oedipus complex revisited. *Psychoanalytic Review, 98,* 287–323.

Zevon, M., & Corn, B. (1990). Paper presented at the annual meeting of the American Psychological Association, Boston, MA.

Zhang, F., Chen, Y., Heiman, M., & Dimarchi, R. (2005). Leptin: Structure, function and biology. *Vitamins and Hormones: Advances in Research and Applications, 71,* 345–372.

Zhang, W., Bansback, N., & Anis, A. H. (2011). Measuring and valuing productivity loss due to poor health: A critical review. *Social Science & Medicine, 72,* 185–192.

Zhou, Z., & Buck, L. B. (2006, March 10). Combinatorial effects of odorant mixes in olfactory cortex. *Science,* 1477–1481.

Zhou, Z., Liu, Q., & Davis, R. L. (2005). Complex regulation of spiral ganglion neuron firing patterns by neurotrophin-3. *Journal of Neuroscience, 25,* 7558–7566.

Zians, J. (2007). A comparison of trait anger and depression on several variables: Attribution style, dominance, submissiveness, need for power, efficacy and dependency. *Dissertation Abstracts International: Section B: The Sciences and Engineering, 67*(7-B), 4124.

Zigler, E., Bennett-Gates, D., Hodapp, R., & Henrich, C. (2002). Assessing personality traits of individuals with mental retardation. *American Journal on Mental Retardation, 107,* 181–193.

Zilbergeld, B., & Ellison, C. R. (1980). Desire discrepancies and arousal problems in sex therapy. In S. R. Leiblum & L. A. Pervin (Eds.), *Principles and practices of sex therapy.* New York: Guilford.

Zimbardo, P. (2007). *The Lucifer effect: Understanding how good people turn evil.* New York: Random House.

Zimbardo, P. G. (1973). On the ethics of intervention in human psychological research: With special reference to the Stanford Prison Experiment. *Cognition, 2,* 243–256.

Zimbardo, P. G. (2004). Does psychology make a significant difference in our lives? *American Psychologist, 59,* 339–351.

Zimbardo, P. G., Maslach, C., & Haney, C. (2000). Reflections on the Stanford Prison Experiment: Genesis, transformations, consequences. In T. Blass (Ed.), *Obedience to authority: Current perspectives on the Milgram Paradigm.* Mahwah, NJ: Lawrence Erlbaum Associates.

Zimmerman, U. S., Blomeyer, D., & Laucht, M. (2007). How gene-stress-behavior interactions can promote adolescent alcohol use: The roles of predrinking allostatic load and childhood behavior disorders [Special issue: Adolescents, drug abuse and mental disorders]. *Pharmacology, Biochemistry and Behavior, 86,* 246–262.

Zito, J. M. (1993). *Psychotherapeutic drug manual* (3rd ed., rev.). New York: Wiley.

Zolotor, A., Theodore, A., Chang, J., Berkoff, M., & Runyan, D. (2008). Speak softly–and forget the stick: Corporal punishment and child physical abuse. *American Journal of Preventive Medicine, 35,* 364–369.

Zuckerman, M. (1978, February). The search for high sensation. *Psychology Today,* pp. 30–46.

Zuckerman, M., & Kuhlman, D. M. (2000). Personality and risk-taking: Common biosocial factors [Special issue: Personality processes and problem behavior]. *Journal of Personality, 68,* 999–1029.

Zuger, A. (2005, November 10). Doctors learn how to say what no one wants to hear. *The New York Times,* p. S1.

Zvyagintsev, M., Clemens, B., Chechko, N., Mathiak, K. A., Sack, A. T., & Mathiak, K. (2013). Brain networks underlying mental imagery of auditory and visual information. *European Journal of Neuroscience, 37,* 1421–1434.

Credits

Text and Line Art Credits

Chapter 1

No credits

Chapter 2

Page 52: Kent Van De Graff, *Human Anatomy–Updated Fifth Edition*, New York: McGraw-Hill Education. Copyright © 2000 McGraw-Hill Education. All rights reserved. Used with permission. Page 55a: Sylvia Mader, *Human Biology, 6e*. New York: McGraw-Hill Education. Copyright © 2000 McGraw-Hill Education. All rights reserved. Used with permission. Page 55b: George Johnson and Thomas Emmel, *The Living World, 2e*. New York: McGraw-Hill Education. Copyright © 2000 McGraw-Hill Education. All rights reserved. Used with permission. Page 61, 63: Michael Passer and Ronald Smith, *Psychology: Frontiers and Applications*. New York: McGraw-Hill Education. Copyright © 2001 McGraw-Hill Education. All rights reserved. Used with permission. Page 65: Robert Brooker, Eric Widmaier, Linda Graham and Peter Stiling, *Biology*. New York: McGraw-Hill Education. Copyright © 2008 McGraw-Hill Education. All rights reserved. Used with permission. Page 70: Rod Seeley, Trent Stephens and Philip Tate, *Anatomy & Physiology, 5e*. New York: McGraw-Hill Education. Copyright © 2000 McGraw-Hill Education. All rights reserved. Used with permission. Page 73: Allen Schneider and Barry Tarshis, *Elements of Psychobiology*. New York: McGraw-Hill Education. Copyright © 1995 McGraw-Hill Education. All rights reserved. Used with permission. Page 81: Robert Brooker, Eric Widmaier, Linda Graham and Peter Stiling, *Biology*. New York: McGraw-Hill Education. Copyright © 2008 McGraw-Hill Education. All rights reserved. Used with permission.

Chapter 3

Page 94: Camille Wortman, Elizabeth Loftus and Charles Weaver, III, *Psychology, 5e*. New York: McGraw-Hill Education. Copyright © 1999 McGraw-Hill Education. All rights reserved. Used with permission. Page 97: David Shier, Jackie Butler and Ricki Lewis, *Hole's Essentials of Human Anatomy and Physiology, 7e*. New York: McGraw-Hill Education. Copyright © 2000 McGraw-Hill Education. All rights reserved. Used with permission. Page 99: Sylvia Mader, *Human Biology, 6e*. New York: McGraw-Hill Education. Copyright © 2000 McGraw-Hill Education. All rights reserved. Used with permission. Page 104: Robert Brooker, Eric Widmaier, Linda Graham and Peter Stiling, *Biology*. New York: McGraw-Hill Education. Copyright © 2008 McGraw-Hill Education. All rights reserved. Used with permission. Page 105 (top): Rod Seeley, Trent Stephens and Philip Tate, *Anatomy & Physiology, 5e*. New York: McGraw-Hill Education. Copyright © 2000 McGraw-Hill Education. All rights reserved. Used with permission.

Chapter 4

Page 135: Ernest Hartmann, *The Biology of Dreaming*. Springfield, IL: Charles C. Thomas. Copyright © 1967 Charles C. Thomas. All rights reserved. Used with permission. Page 154 (bottom): Sylvia Mader, *Human Biology, 6e*. New York: McGraw-Hill Education. Copyright © 2000 McGraw-Hill Education. All rights reserved. Used with permission.

Chapter 5

No credits

Chapter 6

Page 214: Kent Van De Graff, *Human Anatomy–Updated Fifth Edition*, New York: McGraw-Hill Education. Copyright © 2000 McGraw-Hill Education. All rights reserved. Used with permission.

Chapter 7

No Credits

Chapter 8

No credits

Chapter 9

No credits

Chapter 10

Page 410: Richard P. Halgin and Susan Krauss Whitbource, *Abnormal Psychology: The Human Experience of Psychological Disorders*. New York: McGraw-Hill Education. Copyright © 1993 McGraw-Hill Education. All rights reserved. Used with permission.

Chapter 11

Page 420: From E.S. Susser, D.B. Herman and B. Aaron, "Combating the Terror of Terrorism" *Scientific American*, August 2002, p. 74. © Cleo Vilett. All rights reserved. Used by permission. Page 424: Hans Selye, *The Stress of Life*. New York: McGraw-Hill Education. Copyright © 1978 McGraw-Hill Education. All rights reserved. Used with permission.

Chapter 12

No credits

Chapter 13

no credits

Chapter 14

Page 525: J.T. Cacioppo, G.G. Bernsten and S.L. Crites, Jr. "Social Neuroscience: Principles of Psychosociological Arousal and Response" *Social Psychology: Handbook of Basic Principles*, E. Tory Higgins and Arie W; Kruglanski, ed., p. 120. New York: Guilford Publications, Inc. Copyright © 1996 Guilford Publications, Inc. All rights reserved. Used with permission.

Photo Credits

Frontmatter: p. xxxvi: © Comstock/PunchStock RF; p. xxxviii: © Stockbyte/Getty RF; p. xxxix: © Photodisc/PunchStock RF; p. xl: © Digital Vision/Getty RF; p. xli: © Fuse/Getty RF; p. xlii: © Stockbyte/Getty RF; p. xlv: © Stockbyte/PunchStock RF; xlix: © Rubbergall/PunchStock RF

Chapter 1

Opener: © Blend Images/Ariel Skelley/Getty Images RF; CO1.2: © Don Hammond/DesignPics RF; CO1.3: © Bettmann/Corbis; CO1.4: © Peter Byron/Photo Researchers; CO1.5: © Douglas Faulkner/Science Source; Looking Ahead p. 4: © Blend Images/Ariel Skelley/Getty Images RF; p. 7 (top): © Spencer Grant/Science Source; p. 7 (middle): © chris Ryan/age fotostock RF; p. 7 (bottom): © Don Hammond/DesignPics RF; p. 10: © Blend Images/Getty Images RF; p. 14: © Bettmann/Corbis; p. 15: © Photo by Paul Thompson/FPG/Getty Images; p. 16 Descartes: © SPL/Science Source; p. 16 Locke: © Bettmann/Corbis; p. 16 James: © Photo by Paul Thompson/FPG/Getty Images; p. 16 Pavlov: © Bettmann/

Corbis; p. 16 Calkins: © Wellesley College Archives, Photographed by Notman; p. 17 Watson: © Underwood & Underwood/Corbis; p. 17 Maslow: © Bettmann/Corbis; p. 17 Piaget: © Bettmann/Corbis; p. 17 Loftus: © Elizabeth Loftus; p. 17 Cognitive: © David Sanger/The Image Bank/Getty Images; p. 17 Behavioral: © Blend Images RF; p. 17 Humanistic: © White Packer/The Image Bank/Getty Images; p. 18 (top): © Bettmann Corbis; p. 18 (bottom): © Tetra Images/Getty Images RF; p. 20: © ANWAR AMRO/AFP/Getty Images; p. 21 Cognitive: © David Sanger/The Image Bank/Getty Images; p. 21 Behavioral: © Blend Images RF; p. 21 Humanistic: © White Packer/The Image Bank/ Getty Images; p. 23: Attribution: modified from Shinji Nishimoto, An T. Vu, Thomas Naselaris, Yuval Benjamini, Bin Yu & Jack L. Gallant (2011). "Reconstructing dynamic visual experiences from brain activity evoked by natural movies" in *Current Biology.*; p. 24: © Sam Edwards/ Fotostock RF; p. 29: © Robert I. M. Campbell/ National Geographic Image Collection; p. 30: © Jack Hollingsworth/Getty Images RF; p. 32: © Peter Byron/Photo Researchers; p. 33: © J. Wilson/Woodfin Camp; p. 36 (top): © Bill Aron/ PhotoEdit; 36 (bottom): © Marc Steinmetz/ VISUM/Image Works; p. 41: © Thomas Pflaum/ Visum/The Image Works; Exp Div. p. 41: © PunchStock/Digital Vision RF; p. 43: © Douglas Faulkner/Science Source; Inf Consumer p. 44: © Jim Arbogast Getty Images RF; Looking Back p. 46: © Blend Images/Ariel Skelley/Getty Images RF; Vs Sum 2.1 p. 47: © Blend Images RF; Vs Sum 2.2 p. 47: © David Sanger/The Image Bank/Getty Images; Vs Sum 2.3 p. 47: © White Packer/The Image Bank/Getty Images; Vs Sum 4.1 p. 47: © Thomas Pflaum/Visum/The Image Works; Vs Sum 4.2 p. 47: © Douglas Faulkner/ Science Source

Chapter 2

Opener: © Zero Creatives/Getty Images RF; CO2.1 © David McCarthy/Science Source; CO2.2 © Passieka/SPL/Science Source; CO2.3 © Martin Rotker/Science Source; Looking Ahead p. 50: © Zero Creatives/Getty Images RF; p. 52: © David McCarthy/Science Source; p. 57: © Theo Wargo/Getty Images; p. 58: © Tetra Images/Getty Images RF; p. 63: © Rubberball/Getty Images RF; p. 66: © Corey Sipkin/NY Daily News Archive via Getty Images; p. 68: © Martin Rotker/Science Source; p. 69a: © SPL/Science Source; p. 69b: © Volker Steger/Peter Arnold/Getty Images; p. 69c: © Roger Ressmeyer/Corbis; p. 69d: © Garo/Phanie/Science Source; p. 71: © Photo by Paul E. Alers/NASA via Getty Images; p. 75: © Natural History Museum London/SPL/ Science Source; p. 77: © Sandra Preissler, Friedrich Schiller University, Jena, Germany; p. 79: © Caia Images/Glow Images RF; Exp Div p. 79: © Punchstock/Digital Vision RF; Inf Consumer p. 81: © Jim Arbogast Getty Images RF; Looking Back p. 84: © Zero Creatives/ Getty Images RF; Vs Sum 5.1 p. 85: © David McCarthy/Science Source

Chapter 3

Opener: © Darryl Leniuk/Taxi/Getty Images; CO3.1: © Digital Vision/Getty RF; CO3.2: © iStockphoto; CO3.3: © Digital Vision/Getty RF; Looking Ahead p. 88: © Darryl Leniuk/Taxi/Getty Images; p. 91: © Digital Vision/Getty RF; p. 92 (top): © Rubberball/PunchStock RF; p. 92 (bottom): © iStockphoto; p. 95 (left & right): © Biophoto Associates/Science Source; p. 100 (bottom): © Rubberball/PunchStock RF; p. 100 a&b: © Ralph C. Eagle Jr./Science Source; p. 107 (top): © Warner Bros/Album/Newscom; p. 107 (bottom): © Prof. P. Motta/Dept. of Anatomy/ University "La Sapienza", Rome/SPL/Science Source; p. 108: © Omikron/Science Source; p. 111 (top): © Liu Yang/Redlink/Corbis RF; p. 111 (bottom): © Robert Daly/age fotostock RF; Inf Consumer p. 112: © Jim Arbogast Getty Images RF; p. 111: From S.N. Tomson, et al., "Neural networks of colored sequence synethesia" in *Journal of Neuroscience*, 2013, Vol 33(35), pp. 14098-14106 fig 6a and 6c p. 14104. Reprinted by permission of Society for Neuroscience; p. 119: © Corbis RF; p. 120 (top): © Paul Souders/The Image Bank/Getty Images; p. 120 (bottom): © Sam Edwards/age fotostock RF; p. 122: © Hill Street Studios/Blend Images LLC RF; p. 123: © John G. Ross/Science Source; Exp Div p. 124: © PunchStock/Digital Vision RF; Looking Back p. 128: © Darryl Leniuk/Taxi/Getty Images; Vs Sum 8.1 p. 129: © iStockphoto; Vs Sum 10.1 p. 129: © Liu Yang/Redlink/Corbis RF

Chapter 4

Opener: © chrisgramly/Getty Images RF; CO4.1: © Ted Spagna/Science Source; CO4.2: © liquidlibrary/PictureQuest RF; CO4.3: © Exactostock/SuperStock RF; Looking Ahead p. 132: © chrisgramly/Getty Images RF; p. 135 (All): © Ted Spagna/Science Source; p. 136: © Blend Images/Getty Images RF; p. 137: © K. Mishima; p. 139: © J. Luke/PhotoLink/ Getty RF; p. 141: © Don Smith/Alamy; p. 142: © B. Boissonnet/BSIP/Corbis; p. 143: © Andreas Schlegel/fsto/Corbis RF; Inf Cosumer p. 144: © Jim Arbogast Getty Images RF; p. 147: © AP Images/Midland Daily News/Erin Painter; p. 149 (top): © liquidlibrary/PictureQuest RF; p. 149 (bottom): © Dex Image/Getty Images RF; p. 150: © MIXA/Getty Images RF; Exp Div p. 151: © PunchStock/Digital Vision RF; p. 153: © Suzanne Opton; p. 159 (left): © Exactostock/ SuperStock RF; p. 159 (right): © Jim Arbogast/ Getty RF; p. 161: © Andrew Brookes/Corbis; Inf Consumer p. 163: © Jim Arbogast Getty Images RF; p. 164: © Uppercut RF/Getty Images RF; Looking Back p. 166: © chrisgramly/Getty Images RF; Vs Sum 12.1 p. 167: © Don Smith/ Alamy; Vs Sum 13.1 p. 167: © AP Images/ Midland Daily News/Erin Painter; Vs Sum 13.2 p. 167: © liquidlibrary/PictureQuest RF

Chapter 5

Opener: © Blend Images/Getty Images/RF; CO5.1: © Scott T. Baxter/Getty RF; CO5.3: © Ty Milford/Getty Images RF; Looking Ahead p. 170: © Blend Images/Getty Images/RF; p. 172: © Sovfoto/UIG via Getty Images; p. 175: © Image Source/Getty Images RF; p. 176: © Scott T. Baxter/Getty RF; p. 180: © Nina Leen/Time & Life Pictures/Getty Images; p. 183 (TL): © Ryan McVay/Getty RF; p. 183 (TR): © Stockbyte/ Corbis RF; p. 183 (BL): © BananaStock/ PunchStock RF; p. 183 (BR): © Amy Etra/ PhotoEdit; p. 186: © Blend Images/Getty Images RF; p. 188 (top): © Dr. Marian Breland Bailey; p. 188 (left): © McGraw-Hill Education./Jill Braaten, photographer; p. 188 (right): © Robin Nelson/ Photo Edit; Inf Consumer p. 189: © Jim Arbogast Getty Images RF; p. 194 (top): © Albert Bandura; p. 194 (bottom): © Ty Milford/Getty Images RF; p. 195: © Mikael Heimann; p. 196 (top & bottom): © Sam Edwards/Fotostock RF; p. 196 (bottom): From Meltzoff, A.N. (1988). Imitation of Televised Models by Infants. *Child Development*, 59, 1221-1229. Photo Courtesy of A.N. Meltzhoff & M. Hanak; p. 197: © UNIMEDIA IMAGES/Twentieth Century/ Unimedia International/Twentieth/Newscom; Exp Div p. 197: © PunchStock/Digital Vision RF; p. 198: © Graham Bell/Corbis RF; Looking Back p. 200: © Blend Images/Getty Images/RF; Vs Sum 16.1 p. 201: © Ryan McVay/Getty RF; Vs Sum 16.2 p. 201: © Stockbyte/Corbis RF; Vs Sum 16.3 p. 201: © BananaStock/PunchStock RF; Vs Sum 16.4 p. 201: © Amy Etra/PhotoEdit; Vs Sum 16.5 p. 201: © Dr. Marian Breland Bailey; Vs Sum 17.1 p. 201: © Ty Milford/Getty Images RF

Chapter 6

Opener: © Davan Images/The Image Bank/Getty Images; CO6.1: © Brand X Pictures RF; CO6.2: © PRNewsFoto/Walt Disney Studios Home Entertainment/AP Photos; Looking Ahead p. 204: © Davan Images/The Image Bank/Getty Images; p. 207: © Brand X Pictures RF; p. 213: © McGraw-Hill Education; p. 215: © Indre V. Viskontas; p. 217: © PRNewsFoto/Walt Disney Studios Home Entertainment/AP Photos; p. 220 (top): © Image Source/Getty Images RF; p. 220 (mid): © Digital Vision/SuperStock RF; p. 220 (bottom): © Blend Images/SuperStock RF; p. 222: © Stockdisc/Getty Images RF; p. 224: © Matt Stone/AFP/Getty Images; Exp Div p. 225: © PunchStock/Digital Vision RF; p. 225: © Albert Moldvay/National Geographic/Getty Images; p. 231: © Rubberball/Getty Images RF; Inf Consumer p. 232: © Jim Arbogast Getty Images RF; Looking Back p. 234: © Davan Images/The Image Bank/Getty Images; Vs Sum 19.1 p. 235: © Digital Vision/SuperStock RF

Chapter 7

Opener: © Hero Images/Getty Images RF; CO7.2: © Hoby Finn/Getty RF; CO7.3 © Anna Clopet/ Corbis; CO7.4 © Harold Holt/Hulton Archive/ Getty Images; Looking Ahead p. 238: © Hero Images/Getty Images RF; p. 240 (left): © Kevin C. Cox/Getty Images; p. 240 (right): © Dex Image/ Getty Images RF; p. 241: © Twila Tardif; p. 246 (left): © Hoby Finn/Getty RF; p. 246 (right): © Stockbyte/PunchStock RF; p. 248a-c: © Superstock; p. 249 © Jose Luis Pelaez Inc/

Blend Images LLC RF; p. 252 (top): © Roberto Otero/Black Star; p. 252 (bottom): © Kali Nine LLC/Getty Images RF; Inf Consumer p. 253: © Jim Arbogast Getty Images RF; p. 256: Courtesy, Dr. Laura Ann Petitto, 1991. Photo by Robert LaMarche; p. 258: © AP Images; p. 259: © Rubberball/Getty Images RF; p. 260: © Anna Clopet/Corbis; Exp Div p. 263: © PunchStock/ Digital Vision RF; p. 266: © David Hiser/ Photographers Aspen; p. 266 © Paul Souders/ Corbis; p. 267 Yehudi: © Harold Holt/Hulton Archive/Getty Images Images; p. 267 Babe: © Bettmann/Corbis; p. 267 McClintock: © Science Source; p. 267 Eliot: © Bettmann/Corbis; p. 267 Trukese: © David Hiser/Photographers Aspen; p. 267 Sullivan: © Bettmann/Corbis; p. 267 Woolf: © George C. Beresford/Getty Images; p. 267 Redwoods: © Corbis RF; p. 270: © Roger Viollet/The Image Works; p. 272: © Lewis J. Merrim/Science Source; p. 274 © Dex Image/Getty Images RF; Exp Div p. 278: © PunchStock/Digital Vision RF; p. 280 © Flying Colours Ltd/Getty Images RF; Looking Back p. 282 © Hero Images/Getty Images RF; Vs Sum 22.1 p. 283: © Anna Clopet/Corbis

Chapter 8

Opener: © Terry Vine/Blend Images/Getty Images RF; CO8.2: © LCPL Casey N. Thurston, USMC/DoD Media; CO8.3: © Ed Quinn/Corbis; CO8.4: © Image Source/Getty RF; Looking Ahead p. 286: © Terry Vine/Blend Images/ Getty Images RF; p. 287: © George Pimentel/ WireImage/Getty Images; p. 291: © Blend Images/Getty Images RF; p. 293 mother: © Digital Vision/PunchStock RF; p. 293 rollercoaster: © Digital Vision RF; p. 293 student: © BananaStock/JupiterImages RF; p. 293 runner: © LCPL Casey N. Thurston, USMC/ DoD Media; p. 293 food: © Corbis RF; p. 298: © Andy Richter/Aurora Photos/Corbis; p. 298: © Rick Wilking/Reuters/Corbis; p. 300: © Ed Quinn/Corbis; p. 301 (top): From A. Abraham, et al., "Gender differences in creative thinking" in *Brain Imaging and Behavior*, (2013) DOI 10.1007/s11682-013-9241-4, fig 3. Reprinted by permission of Springer Verlag; p. 301 (bottom): © Jim Arbogast Getty Images RF; p. 307: © Rachel Epstein/The Image Works; p. 309: © Science Source; p. 310: © Dex Image/ Getty Images RF; p. 316: © Eric Fowke/ PhotoEdit; p. 317: © Image Source/Getty Images RF; p. 318: © Image Source/Getty Images RF; Exp Div p. 319: © PunchStock/ Digital Vision RF; p. 319 (all): © 1988 Matsumoto Photos; © 1988 Matsumoto Photos; Looking Back p. 322: © Terry Vine/Blend Images/Getty Images RF; Vs sum 24.1 p. 323 mother: © Digital Vision/PunchStock RF; Vs Sum 24.2 p. 323 Rollercoaster: © Digital Vision RF; Vs Sum 24.3 p. 323 student: © BananaStock/JupiterImages RF; Vs Sum 24.4 p. 323 runner: © LCPL Casey N. Thurston, USMC/DoD Media RF; Vs Sum 24.5 p. 323 food: © Corbis RF; Vs Sum 25.1 p. 323 © Andy Richter/Aurora Photos/Corbis; Vs Sum 26.1 p. 323 © Eric Fowke/PhotoEdit

Chapter 9

Opener: © Blend Images/Getty Images/RF; CO9.2: © SPL/Photo Researchers; CO9.3: © Tony Freeman/Photo Edit; CO9.4: © Purestock/ PunchStock RF; CO9.5: © Deborah Davis/ PhotoEdit; Looking Ahead p. 326: © Blend Images/Getty Images/RF; p. 327: © Thomas Wanstall/The Image Works; p. 331a: © D.W. Fawcett/Science Source; p. 331b: © L. Willatt, East Anglian Regional Genetics Service/SPL/ Science Source; p. 331c: © Kenneth Eward/ Science Source; p. 331d: © Biophoto Associates/ Science Source/Science Source; p. 332 (left): © SPL/Photo Researchers; p. 332 (right): © Petit Format/Science Source/Science Source; p. 333: © Blend Images/Getty Images RF; p. 337: © Emma Kim/Cultura/Getty RF; p. 339 (all): From: A.N. Meltzoff & M.K. Moore, 'Imitation of facial and manual gestures by human neonates.' *Science*, 1977, 198, 75–78. Copyright © 1977 Andrew Meltzoff; p. 340: © Reprinted by permission of Emi Nakato; p. 343: © Photo by Nina Leen/Time Life Pictures/Getty Images; p. 344: © Radius/SuperStock RF; p. 347: © SW Productions/Getty RF; p. 349: © Farrell Grehan/ Corbis; p. 350: © Tony Freeman/Photo Edit; p. 358: © Purestock/PunchStock RF; p. 359: © Steven Puetzer/Getty Images; p. 360: © Joe Erikson/Science Source; p. 362: © Photodisc/ SuperStock RF; p. 363: © Mary Kate Denny/ PhotoEdit; p. 364: © Sam Edwards/Fotostock RF; Exp Div p. 364: © PunchStock/Digital Vision/RF; p. 368: © image100/Corbis RF; p. 369: © Robert Houser/UpperCut Images/Getty; p. 372: © Deborah Davis/PhotoEdit; p. 374: © AP Images/Gary Malerba; p 375 (top): © LWA/Dann Tardif/Getty Images RF; p. 375 (bottom): © Tetra Images/Getty Images RF; Inf Consumer p. 375: © Jim Arbogast/Getty Images RF; Looking Back p. 378: © Blend Images/Getty Images/RF; Vs Sum 27.1 p. 379: © D.W. Fawcett/Science Source; Vs Sum 27.2 p. 379: © SPL/Photo Researchers; Vs Sum 28.1 p. 379: © Emma Kim/ Cultura/Getty RF; Vs Sum 28.2 p. 379: © Photo by Nina Leen/Time Life Pictures/Getty Images; Vs Sum 28.3 p. 379: © Farrell Grehan/Corbis; Vs Sum 29.1 p. 379: © Steven Puetzer/Getty Images; Vs Sum 29.2 p. 379: © Joe Erikson/ Science Source; Vs Sum 30.1 p. 379: © image100/Corbis RF; Vs Sum 30.2 p. 379: © AP Images/Gary Malerba

Chapter 10

Opener: © Greg Hindsdale/Corbis; CO10.2: © Margaret Miller/Science Source; CO10.3: © BananaStock/PunchStock RF; CO10.4: © Spencer Grant/Science Source; Looking Ahead p. 382: © Greg Hindsdale/Corbis; p. 384: © Corbis Premium/Alamy RF; p. 385: © Bettmann/Corbis; p. 386: © Margaret Miller/Science Source; p. 388: © Steve Hix/age fotostock RF; p. 390 (top): © 2011 Warner Bros. Ent. Harry Potter publishing rights © J.K.R. Harry Potter characters, names and related indicia are trademarks of and © Warner Bros. Ent. All rights reserved./Courtesy Everett Collection; p. 390 (bottom): © Image Source/Getty Images RF; p. 391: © Bettmann/ Corbis; p. 396: © image100/Corbis RF; p. 397: © McGraw-Hill Education/Lars A. Niki, photographer; p. 399: © Blend Images/Getty Images RF; p. 400 (top): © BananaStock/ PunchStock RF; p. 400 (bottom): © Brand X Pictures/PunchStock RF; p. 402: From M. Aghajani, et al., *Cognective, Affective & Behavioral Neuroscience*, DOI 10.3758/s13415-013-0224-0, Fig D1. Reprinted by permission of Springer Verlag.; Exp Div p. 411: © PunchStock/Digital Vision RF; p. 408: © Exactostock/SuperStock RF; p. 411: © Spencer Grant/Science Source; Inf Consumer p. 412: © Jim Arbogast Getty Images RF; Looking Back p. 414: © Greg Hindsdale/ Corbis; Vs Sum 31.1 p. 415: © Bettmann/Corbis; Vs Sum 32.1 p. 415: © BananaStock/PunchStock RF; Vs Sum 33.1 p. 416: © Spencer Grant/ Science Source

Chapter 11

Opener: © Alja E+/Getty Images RF; CO11.2: © Ariel Skelley/Blend Images/Corbis; CO11.3: © Reza/Webistan/Corbis; CO11.4: © Jose Luis Pelaez/Corbis; Looking Ahead p. 418: © Alja E+/ Getty Images RF; p. 419: © Ariel Skelley/Blend Images/Corbis; p. 421: © Corbis RF; p. 424: © Science Source; p. 429: © Sam Edwards/ Fotostock RF; p. 428: From C.A. Rabinak, et al., *Neurobiology of Learning and Memory*, (2013) Fig 2 and fig 3 on pp. 5 and 7. Reprinted by permission of Elsevier; Inf Consumer p. 429: © Jim Arbogast Getty Images RF; p. 432: © Rubberball/Getty Images RF; p. 434: © McGraw-Hill Education/Jack Holtel, photographer; Exp Div p. 434: © PunchStock/ Digital Vision RF; p. 436: © Reza/Webistan/ Corbis; p. 439: © Jose Luis Pelaez/Corbis; p. 440: © Tetra Images/Getty Images RF; p. 442: © Buena Vista Images/Getty Images RF; Looking Back p. 444: © Alja E+/Getty Images RF; Vs Sum 35.1 p. 445: © Reza/Webistan/Corbis; Vs Sum 36.1 p. 445: © Jose Luis Pelaez/Corbis

Chapter 12

Opener: © Lorand Geiner/Vetta/Getty Images RF; CO2.2: © AP Images/Brett Coomer, Pool; CO2.3: © Welcome Images/ScienceSource; CO2.4: © McGraw-Hill Education./Gary He, photographer; Looking Ahead p. 448: © Lorand Geiner/Vetta/Getty Images RF; p. 450 (top): © AP Images/Brett Coomer, Pool; p. 450 (bottom): © San Edwards/age fotostock RF; p. 455: © Editorial Image, LLC/Alamy; p. 461: © Owen Franken/Corbis; p. 470: © Welcome Images/ScienceSource; p. 472: Courtesy Nancy Andreasen, University of Iowa Hospitals & Clinics; p. 474: © Sam Edwards/Fotostock RF; p. 475: © Tony Freeman/PhotoEdit; p. 476: © Peter Cade/The Image Bank/Getty Images; p. 478: © Chris Ryan/age fotostock RF; Exp Div p. 481: © PunchStock/Digital Vision RF; Inf Consumer p. 482: © Jim Arbogast Getty Images RF; Looking Back p. 484: © Lorand Geiner/Vetta/ Getty Images RF; Vs Sum 37.1 p. 485: © AP Images/Brett Coomer, Pool; Vs Sum 37.2 p. 485: © Editorial Image, LLC/Alamy; Vs Sum 38.1 p. 485: © Owen Franken/Corbis

Chapter 13

Opener: © urbancow/Getty Images RF; CO13.2: © Bruce Ayres/Getty; CO13.3: © Jon Bradley/Getty; CO13.4: © Will & Deni McIntyre/Science Source; Looking Ahead p. 494: © urbancow/Getty Images RF; p. 491: © Getty RF; p. 492: © Jonathan Nourok/PhotoEdit; p. 493: © Bill Aron/PhotoEdit; p. 494: © Rubberball/Getty Images RF; p. 495: © Michael Newman/PhotoEdit; p. 498: © Professor Barry Wright, Hull York Medical School and Andre Gouws and Ben Aldersen-Day from the York Neuroimaging Centre.; p. 500: © Don Hammond/Design Pics/Corbis RF; p. 502: Courtesy of the National Center for PTSD. www.ptsd.va.gov; p. 503: © Jon Bradley/Getty; Exp Div p. 506: © PunchStock/Digital Vision RF; p. 507 (left): © Sam Edwards/Fotostock RF; p. 507 (right): © Image Source/Alamy RF; p. 511: © McGraw-Hill Education./Jill Braaten, photographer; p. 513: © Exactostock/SuperStock RF; p. 515: © McGraw-Hill Education./Gary He, photographer; Inf Consumer p. 516: © Jim Arbogast Getty Images RF; Looking Back p. 518: © urbancow/Getty Images RF; Vs Sum 41.1 p. 519: © Jon Bradley/Getty; Vs Sum 42.1 p. 519: © McGraw-Hill Education./Gary He, photographer

Chapter 14

Opener: © Hero Images/Corbis RF; CO14.1: © Paul Barton/Corbis; CO14.2: © Francisco Cruz/SuperStock; CO14.3: © Barbara Burnes/Science Source; CO14.4: © Somos Photography/Veer RF; Looking Ahead p. 522: © Hero Images/Corbis RF; p. 523: © AP Images/Elise Amendola; p. 524: © Amos Morgan/Getty Images RF; p. 529: © Paul Barton/Corbis; Exp Div p. 530: © PunchStock/Digital Vision RF; p. 534: © Jim Sugar/Corbis; p. 536: © Francisco Cruz/SuperStock; p. 537 (left & right): From the film OBEDIENCE © 1968 by Stanley Milgram, © renewed 1993 by Alexandra Milgram. Permission granted by Alexandra Milgram.; p. 538: © Blend Images/Getty Images RF; p. 541: © Stretch Photography/Getty Images RF; p. 542: © Barbara Burnes/Science Source; p. 543: Lieberman, M.D., et al. (2005) "An fMRI investigation of race-related amygdala activity in African-American and Caucasian-American individuals" in *Nature Neuroscience*, 8(6), 72-722. Reprinted by permission from Macmillan Publishers Ltd.; p. 545: © Corbis RF; p. 551: © Somos Photography/Veer RF; p. 552: © Corbis RF; p. 553: © Reuters NewMedia Inc./Corbis; Inf Consumer p. 554: © Jim Arbogast Getty Images RF; Looking Back p. 556: © Hero Images/Corbis RF; Vs Sum 44.1 p. 557: © Jim Sugar/Corbis; Vs Sum 44.2 p. 557: From the film OBEDIENCE © 1968 by Stanley Milgram, © renewed 1993 by Alexandra Milgram. Permission granted by Alexandra Milgram.; Vs Sum 45.1 p. 557: © Barbara Burnes/Science Source

Name Index

Note: Page numbers followed by *f* indicate figures.

C

D

E

F

G

H

I

J

K

N

Q

R

S

T

U

X

Y

Z

Subject Index

Note: Page numbers followed by *f* indicate figures.

D

E

F

N

O

P

Q

R

S

T

U

V

W

X

Z

MODULE 21

Thinking and Reasoning

Learning Outcomes

LO 21-1 What is thinking?

LO 21-2 What processes underlie reasoning and decision making?

LO 21-3 How do people approach and solve problems?

LO 21-4 What are the major obstacles to problem solving?

What are you thinking about at this moment?

The mere ability to pose such a question underscores the distinctive nature of the human ability to think. No other species contemplates, analyzes, recollects, or plans the way humans do. Understanding what thinking is, however, goes beyond knowing that we think. Philosophers, for example, have argued for generations about the meaning of thinking, with some placing it at the core of human beings' understanding of their own existence.

Psychologists define **thinking** as brain activity in which we mentally manipulate information, including words, visual images, sounds, or other data. Thinking transforms information into new and different forms, allowing us to answer questions, make decisions, solve problems, or make plans.

thinking Brain activity in which people mentally manipulate information, including words, visual images, sounds, or other data.

Although a clear sense of what specifically occurs when we think remains elusive, our understanding of the nature of the fundamental elements involved in thinking is growing. We begin by considering our use of mental images and concepts, the building blocks of thought.

Mental Images: Examining the Mind's Eye

Think of your best friend.

Chances are that you "see" some kind of visual image when asked to think of her or him, or any other person or object for that matter. To some cognitive psychologists, such mental images constitute a major part of thinking.

Mental images are representations in the mind of an object or event. They are not just visual representations; our ability to "hear" a tune in our heads also relies on a mental image. In fact, every sensory modality may produce corresponding mental images (De Beni, Pazzaglia, & Gardini, 2007; Gardini et al., 2009; Koçak et al., 2011).

mental images Representations in the mind of an object or event.

Research has found that our mental images have many of the properties of the actual stimuli they represent. For example, it takes the mind longer to scan mental images of large objects than small ones, just as the eye takes longer to scan an actual large object than an actual small one. Similarly, we are able to manipulate and rotate mental images of objects, just as we are able to manipulate and rotate them in the real world (Mast & Kosslyn, 2002; Zacks, 2008; Reisberg, 2013; see Figure 1).

Some experts see the production of mental images as a way to improve various skills. For instance, many athletes use mental imagery in their training. Basketball players may try to produce vivid and detailed images of the court, the basket, the ball, and the noisy crowd. They may visualize themselves taking a foul shot, watching the ball, and hearing the swish as it goes through the net. And it works: The use of mental imagery can lead to improved performance in sports (Fournier, Deremaux, & Bernier, 2008; Moran, 2009; Velentzas, Heinen, & Schack, 2011).

PsychTech
Researcher Adam Wilson has developed a method of tweeting by thinking. The process involves being outfitted with electrodes that react to changes in brain activity. It's slow going, though: the fastest tweeters are able to create tweets at only 8 characters per minute.

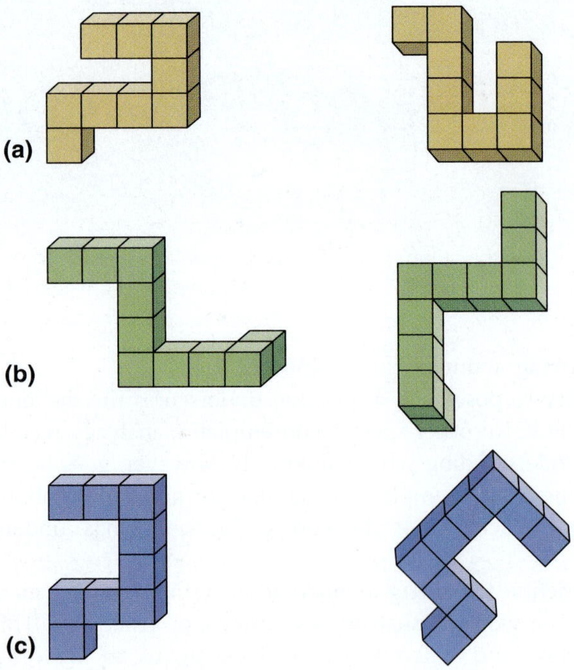

FIGURE 1 Try to mentally rotate one of each pair of patterns to see if it is the same as the other member of that pair. It's likely that the more you have to mentally rotate a pattern, the longer it will take to decide if the patterns match one another. Does this mean that it will take you longer to visualize a map of the world than a map of the United States? Why or why not? (Source: Adapted from Shepard & Metzler, 1971.)

Athletes use mental imagery to focus on a task, a process they call "getting in the zone." What other occupations might require the use of strong mental imagery?

concept A mental grouping of similar objects, events, or people.

From the perspective of . . .

A Human Resources Specialist How might you use the research on mental imagery to improve employees' performance?

Concepts: Categorizing the World

If someone asks you what is in your kitchen cabinet, you might answer with a detailed list of items (a jar of peanut butter, three boxes of macaroni and cheese, six unmatched dinner plates, and so forth). More likely, though, you would respond by naming some broader categories, such as "food" and "dishes."

Using such categories reflects the operation of concepts. **Concepts** are mental groupings of similar objects, events, or people. Concepts enable us to organize complex phenomena into cognitive categories that are easier to understand and remember (Murphy, 2005; Connolly, 2007; Kreppner et al., 2011).

Concepts help us classify newly encountered objects on the basis of our past experience. For example, we can surmise that someone tapping a handheld screen is probably using some kind of computer or PDA, even if we have never encountered that specific model before. Ultimately, concepts influence behavior. We would assume, for instance, that it might be appropriate to pet an animal after determining that it is a dog, whereas we would behave differently after classifying the animal as a wolf. (Also see *Neuroscience in Your Life*.)

When cognitive psychologists first studied concepts, they focused on those that were clearly defined by a unique set of properties or features. For example, an equilateral

Neuroscience in Your Life: How Culture Influences How We Categorize the World

The way we categorize our world is heavily influenced by the culture in which we develop. For example, when English-speaking and Mandarin Chinese-speaking individuals are asked if certain things belong in a category, they will place them in the same one. For example, if they are asked if ducks and penguins are both birds, they will process the information similarly as seen in the fMRI images (A). However, when they are asked if those same items are typical or atypical of that category, different patterns of brain activity are seen in images (B). Only English speakers, however, show different processing between typical and atypical images within categories, suggesting that while overall we use similar areas for categorization across cultures, the way we distinguish between those in a category may be different (Liu et al., 2013).

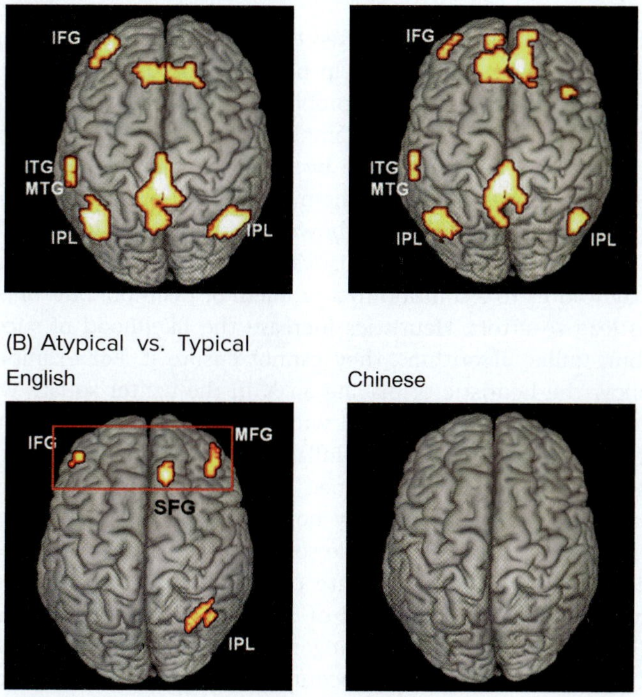

triangle is a closed shape that has three sides of equal length. If an object has these characteristics, it is an equilateral triangle; if it does not, it is not an equilateral triangle.

Other concepts–often those with the most relevance to our everyday lives–are more ambiguous and difficult to define. For instance, broader concepts such as "table" and "bird" have a set of general, relatively loose characteristic features, rather than unique, clearly defined properties that distinguish an example of the concept from a nonexample. When we consider these more ambiguous concepts, we usually think in terms of examples called **prototypes.** Prototypes are typical, highly representative examples of a concept that correspond to our mental image or best example of the concept. For instance, although a robin and an ostrich are both examples of birds, the robin is an example that comes to most people's minds far more readily. Consequently, robin is a prototype of the concept "bird." Similarly, when we think of the concept of a table, we're likely to think of a coffee table before we think of a drafting table, making a coffee table closer to our prototype of a table.

prototypes Typical, highly representative examples of a concept.

Relatively high agreement exists among people in a particular culture about which examples of a concept are prototypes as well as which examples are not. For instance, most people in Western cultures consider cars and trucks good examples of vehicles, whereas elevators and wheelbarrows are not considered very good examples. Consequently, cars and trucks are prototypes of the concept of a vehicle.

Concepts enable us to think about and understand more readily the complex world in which we live. For example, the suppositions we make about the reasons for other people's behavior are based on the ways in which we classify behavior. Hence, our conclusion about a person who washes her hands 20 times a day could vary, depending on whether we place her behavior within the conceptual framework of a health-care worker or a mental patient. Similarly, physicians make diagnoses by drawing on concepts and prototypes of symptoms that they learned about in medical school. Finally, concepts and prototypes facilitate our efforts to draw suitable conclusions through the cognitive process we turn to next: reasoning.

Algorithms and Heuristics

algorithm A rule that, if applied appropriately, guarantees a solution to a problem.

When faced with making a decision, we often turn to various kinds of cognitive shortcuts, known as algorithms and heuristics, to help us. An **algorithm** is a rule that, if applied appropriately, guarantees a solution to a problem. We can use an algorithm even if we cannot understand why it works. For example, you may know that you can find the length of the third side of a right triangle by using the formula $a^2 + b^2 = c^2$, although you may not have the foggiest notion of the mathematical principles behind the formula.

heuristic A thinking strategy that may lead us to a solution to a problem or decision, but–unlike algorithms–may sometimes lead to errors.

For many problems and decisions, however, no algorithm is available. In those instances, we may be able to use heuristics to help us. A **heuristic** is a thinking strategy that may lead us to a solution to a problem or decision, but–unlike algorithms–may sometimes lead to errors. Heuristics increase the likelihood of success in coming to a solution, but, unlike algorithms, they cannot ensure it. For example, when I play tic-tac-toe, I follow the heuristic of placing an X in the center square when I start the game. This tactic doesn't guarantee that I will win, but experience has taught me that it will increase my chances of success. Similarly, some students follow the heuristic of preparing for a test by ignoring the assigned textbook reading and only studying their lecture notes–a strategy that may or may not pay off.

Study Alert

Remember that algorithms are rules that *always* provide a solution, whereas heuristics are shortcuts that *may* provide a solution.

Although heuristics often help people solve problems and make decisions, certain kinds of heuristics may lead to inaccurate conclusions. For example, the *availability heuristic* involves judging the likelihood of an event occurring on the basis of how easy it is to think of examples. According to this heuristic, we assume that events we remember easily are likely to have occurred more frequently in the past–and are more likely to occur in the future–than events that are harder to remember.

For instance, the availability heuristic makes us more afraid of dying in a plane crash than in an auto accident, despite statistics clearly showing that airplane travel is much safer than auto travel. Similarly, although 10 times as many people die from falling out of bed than from lightning strikes, we're more afraid of being hit by lightning. The reason is that plane crashes and lightning strikes receive far more publicity, and they are therefore more easily remembered (Oppenheimer, 2004; Fox, 2006; Kluger, 2006; Caruso, 2008).

We also make use of a *familiarity heuristic*, in which familiar items are seen as superior to those that are unfamiliar. For example, suppose each time you went to a supermarket you had to ponder every type of yogurt to decide which you wanted–as well as every other item on your grocery list. Instead, you see the brand of yogurt you usually buy and settle for it. Usually it's a good rule of thumb because it saves a lot of time.

On the other hand, it's not so good if you are an emergency room physician susceptible to the familiarity heuristic. If you simply settle on the first, most obvious diagnosis for a patient presenting particular symptoms (the ones that are most familiar to you), you may miss making a more accurate diagnosis (Herbert, 2011).

Algorithms and heuristics may be characteristic of human thinking, but scientists are now programming computers to mimic human thinking and problem solving. In fact, they are making significant inroads with computers in terms of the ability to solve problems and carry out some forms of intellectual activities. According to experts who study *artificial intelligence,* the field that examines how to use technology to imitate the outcome of human thinking, problem solving, and creative activities, computers can show rudiments of humanlike thinking because of their knowledge of where to look—and where not to look—for an answer to a problem. They suggest that the capacity of computer programs (such as those that play chess) to evaluate potential moves and to ignore unimportant possibilities gives them thinking ability (Prasad, 2006; Copeland & Proudfoot, 2007; Megill, 2013).

Solving Problems

According to an old legend, a group of Vietnamese monks guard three towers on which sit 64 golden rings. The monks believe that if they succeed in moving the rings from the first tower to the third according to a series of rigid rules, the world as we know it will come to an end. (Should you prefer that the world remain in its present state, there's no need for immediate concern: The puzzle is so complex that it will take the monks about a trillion years to solve it.)

In the Tower of Hanoi puzzle, a simpler version of the task facing the monks, three disks are placed on three posts in the order shown in Figure 2. The goal of the puzzle is to move all three disks to the third post, arranged in the same order, by using as few moves as possible. There are two restrictions: Only one disk can be moved at a time, and no disk can ever cover a smaller one during a move.

Why are cognitive psychologists interested in the Tower of Hanoi problem? Because the way people go about solving such puzzles helps illuminate how people solve complex, real-life problems. Psychologists have found that problem solving typically involves the three steps illustrated in Figure 3: preparing to create solutions, producing solutions, and evaluating the solutions that have been generated.

Study Alert

Use the three steps of problem solving to organize your studying: Preparation, Production, and Judgment (PPJ).

PREPARATION: UNDERSTANDING AND DIAGNOSING PROBLEMS

When approaching a problem like the Tower of Hanoi, most people begin by trying to understand the problem thoroughly. If the problem is a novel one, they probably will pay particular attention to any restrictions placed on coming up with a solution—such as the rule for moving only one disk at a time in the Tower of Hanoi problem. If, by contrast, the problem is a familiar one, they are apt to spend considerably less time in this preparation stage.

Problems vary from well defined to ill defined. In a *well-defined problem*—such as a mathematical equation or the solution to a jigsaw puzzle—both the nature of the problem itself and the information needed to solve it are available and clear. Thus, we can

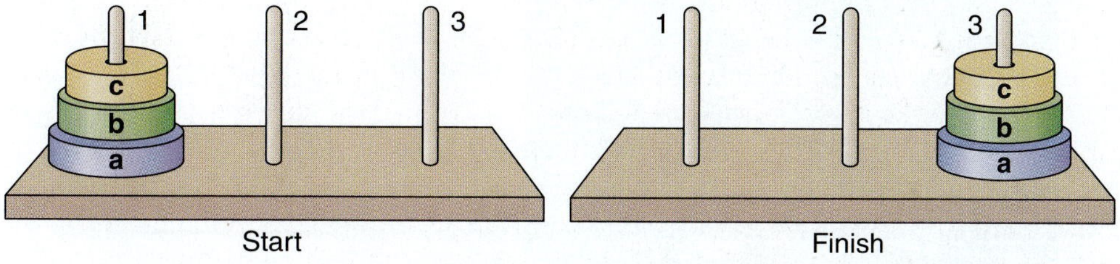

FIGURE 2 The goal of the Tower of Hanoi puzzle is to move all three disks from the first post to the third and still preserve the original order of the disks, using the fewest number of moves possible while following the rules that only one disk at a time can be moved and no disk can cover a smaller one during a move. Try it yourself before you look at the solution, which is listed according to the sequence of moves.

(Solution: Move C to 3, B to 2, C to 2, A to 3, C to 1, B to 3, and C to 3.)

FIGURE 3 Steps in problem solving.

FIGURE 4 The three major categories of problems: (a) arrangement, (b) inducing structure, and (c) transformation. Solutions appear in Figure 5. (Source: Adapted from Bourne et al., 1986.)

a. Arrangement problems

1. Anagrams: Rearrange the letters in each set to make an English word:

2. Two strings hang from a ceiling but are too far apart to allow a person to hold one and walk to the other. On the floor are a book of matches, a screwdriver, and a few pieces of cotton. How could the strings be tied together?

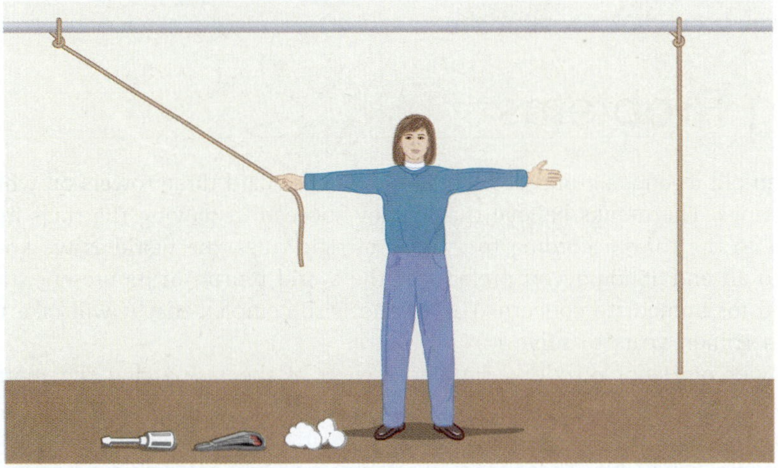

b. Problems of inducing structure

1. What number comes next in the series?

   1 4 2 4 3 4 4 4 5 4 6 4

2. Complete these analogies:

   baseball is to bat as tennis is to __________

   merchant is to sell as customer is to __________

c. Transformation problems

1. Water jars: A person has three jars with the following capacities:

Jar A:
28 ounces

Jar B:
7 ounces

Jar C:
5 ounces

   How can the person measure exactly 11 ounces of water?

2. Ten coins are arranged in the following way. By moving only *two* of the coins, make two rows that each contains six coins.

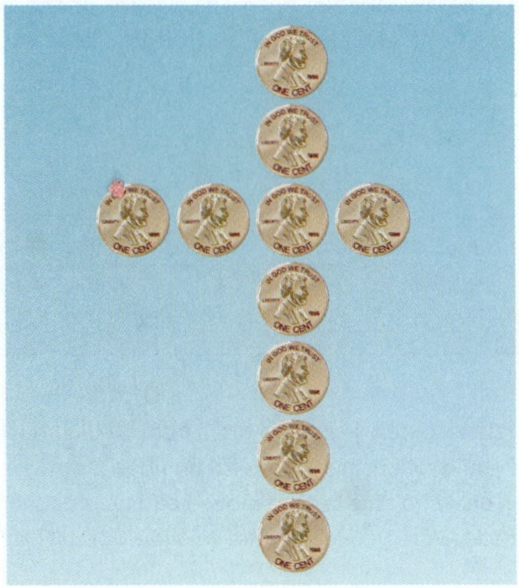